THE NEW
INTERNATIONAL

Webster's
Pocket
Dictionary
OF THE ENGLISH LANGUAGE

════════ ◆◆◆ ════════

TRIDENT
PRESS
INTERNATIONAL

Pulished by
Trident Press International
2002 Edition.

Cover Design Copyright © Trident Press International
Copyright © 2002 Trident Press International

ISBN 1-888777-48-6
ISBN 1-58279-421-9

a, A *n.* first letter of the English alphabet —*indefinite article,* used before a word beginning with a consonant: *a house, a car;* —*adj.* per, for each: *twice a month;* first in order: *grade A quality, section A*

aard·vark *n.* a large burrowing African mammal that feeds on ants and temites; an ant bear

aard·wolf *n.* an African mammal of the hyena family that feeds on termites and larvae

a·ba´ *n.* a sleeveless Arab robe

a·back´ *adv.* pressed backward; to the rear; catching a headwind so as to force a sailing vessel backward —**taken aback** caught by surprise, disconcerted; caught by a wind change which reverses the sails

ab´a·cus *n.* an ancient device from the Orient for performing mathematical calculations by the use of rows of beads on rods

a·baft´ *adv.* toward the stern of a ship; back —*prep.* further back than

ab·a·lo´ne *n.* an edible shellfish lined with mother-of-pearl that is used for buttons, beads, inlay, etc.

a·ban´don *n.* spontaneity, unrestrained enthusiasm or emotion —*vt.* to give up completely, to forsake or desert; to give in completely to emotion —**a·ban´don·ment** *n.*

a·ban´doned *adj.* left behind, forsaken; unrestrained; lacking modesty or moderation; shameless —**a·ban´don·er** *n.*

a·base´ *vt.* to humble; to degrade; to dishonor

a·base´ment *n.* humiliation, shame

a·bash´ *vt.* to disconcert or make confused; to embarrass —**a·bash´ed·ly** *adv.*

a·bash´ment *n.* confusion, disorientation, embarrassment

a·bate´ *vi., vt.* to lessen; to reduce in amount, force, etc. —**a·bat´a·ble** *adj.* —**a·bat´er** *n.*

a·bate´ment *n.* a lessening or alleviation, mitigation; in law, the conclusion of a suit —**a·bat´or** *n.*

ab´a·tis *n.* a defensive barricade of felled or bent trees

a·bat·jour´ *n.* a device for deflecting sunlight; a skylight

ab´at·toir *n.* a slaughterhouse

ab·ax´i·al *adj.* facing away from the axis

ab´ba·cy *n.* the office or jurisdiction of an abbot

ab´bess *n.* the director of a nunnery

ab´bey *n.* a monastery or nunnery

ab´bot *n.* the director of a monestary

ab´bot·cy, ab´bot·ship *n.* the office and trappings of an abbot

ab·bre´vi·ate *vt.* to abridge or shorten

ab·bre´vi·a´tion *n.* a shortened form; a contraction of a word or phrase

ABC´s *n.* the basics; rudimentary elements; beginning knowledge

ab´di·cate *vi., vt.* to formally renounce, as a right or responsibility; to give up claim, as to a throne —**ab´di·ca´tion** *n.* —**ab´di·ca·tor** *n.*

ab·do´men *n.* the part of the human body comprising the lower portion of the trunk, from the diaphragm to the pelvic girdle

ab·dom´i·nal *adj.* pertaining to the abdomen —**ab·dom´i·nal·ly** *adv.*

ab·du´cent *adj.* of a muscle that pulls away from the median axis of the body

ab·duct´ *vt.* to kidnap; to carry away by force

ab·duc´tion *n.* a kidnapping; the abducting of a person by force or deceit

ab·duc´tor *n.* a muscle that pulls away from the median axis of the body

a·beam´ *adj., adv.* at right angles to the keel of a ship

a·be·ce·dar´i·an *adj.* primary, rudimentry —*n.* a beginning student, one learning the alphabet

a·bed´ *adj.* in bed

ab·er´rance, ab·er´ran·cy *n.* deviation from the right or usual course —**ab·er´rant·ly** *adv.*

ab·er´rant *adj.* straying from what is right; abnormal —*n.* a strange or abnormal person —**ab·er´rant·ly** *adv.*

ab·er·ra´tion *n.* an abnormality; a deviation from the customary course or condition; delusion, derangement —**ab·er·ra´tion·al** *adj.*

a·bet´ *vt.* assist; to support; to encourage, especially in wrongdoing —**a·bet´ment** *n.*

a·bet´tor, a·bet´ter *n.* one who assists; an accessory or collaborator

a·bey´ance *n.* temporary state of suspension; a hiatus

a·bey´ant *adj.* in a dormant state, inactive.

ab·hor´ *vt.* to loathe; to look upon with repugnance

ab·hor´rence *n.* a hatred or loathing; a strong aversion.

ab·hor´rent *adj.* detestable; causing a feeling of disgust —**ab·hor·rent·ly** *adv.*

a·bid´ance *n.* continuance

a·bide´ *vi.* to dwell; to stay in a place; to remain unchanging —*vt.* to wait for; to endure: *the luggage will abide rough handling*; to submit to: *we will abide by your decision*; to accept the consquences of

a·bid´ing *adj.* continuing, steadfast —**a·bid·ing·ly** *adv.*

a·bil´i·ty *n.* power, faculty; competence; endowed with the necessary skill

a·bi·o·gen´e·sis *n.* the theory that life may be created from inorganic matter —**a·bi·o·ge·net´ic** *adj.* — **a·bi·o·ge·net´i·cal·ly** *adv.*

a·bi·og´e·nist *n.* one who believes in the spontaneous generation of life

a·bi·ot´ic *adj.* of inorganic matter, such as light or heat; not organic; not living

ab·ject´, ab´ject *adj.* wretched, degrading; disheartening, beyond all hope; without self esteem —**ab·ject´ly** *adv.* —**ab·ject´ness** *n.*

ab·jec´tion *n.* a wretched, degrading condition.

ab·jure´ *vt.* to renounce under oath; to recant or retract, as an unpopular belief; to abstain from, as a practice: *to abjure traditional ceremony* —**ab·ju·ra´tion** *n.* —**ab·jur´a·to·ry** *adj.* —**ab·jur´er** *n.*

ab·la´tion *n.* the process of wearing away; erosion; the surgical excision of body tissue; disintegration of the nose cone of a space vehicle as it reenters the atmosphere —**ab·late** *vt., vi.*

ab´la·tive *adj.* in grammar, expressing separation or removal from source, as *freedom from fear*

a·blaze´ *adj., adv.* on fire; aroused to passion or excitement; fervent

a´ble *adj.* possessing adequate ability; capable; qualified; one legally allowed, as by qualification or competence —**a´bly** *adv.*

a´ble-bod´ied *adj.* sound of body; physically capable

a·bloom´ *adj.* in bloom; flowering.

ab´lu·ent *adj.* used for cleaning —*n.* a cleansing agent

ab·lu´tion *n.* the act of washing, especially of the body; a bath; a ceremonial washing of the priest's hands or of the chalice during a religious ceremony

a´bly *adv.* in a competent manner; proficiently

ab´ne·gate *vt.* to give up, as a privilege or desire —**ab´ne·ga·tor** *n.*

ab·ne·ga´tion *n.* rejection or renunciation of a belief or desire; self-denial; disavowal

ab·nor´mal *adj.* unnatural; differing from the normal or average; not according to rule; curious, irregular, or odd

ab·nor·mal´i·ty *n.* an aberration; an oddity or anomaly; a malformation, a peculiarity

ab·nor´mal·ly *adv.* to an unusual degree; exceedingly; exceptionally.

ab·nor´mi·ty *n.* a monstrosity or perversion.

a·board´ *adv.* into or on a conveyance, as a passenger or baggage; in agreement, as to support for a common cause —**all aboard** a warning to passengers to board, or that the vehicle, usually a train, is about to depart

a·bode´ *n.* a dwelling; a place of habitation or residence

a·bol´ish *vt.* to put an end to; to invalidate —**a·bol´ish·er** *n.* —**a·bol´ish·ment** *n.*

ab·o·li´tion *n.* the act of terminating or eliminating, as the abolition of slavery in the U.S.

ab·o·li´tion·ist *n.* one who wishes to abolish, especially those who supported the abolition of slavery in the U.S.

a·bom´i·na·ble *adj.* hateful; horrible; that which is frightening or offensive —**a·bom´in·a·bly** *adv.*

a·bom·i·na´tion *n.* extreme disgust or abhorrence; any action, custom, practice, or thing which arouses feelings of disgust

ab´o·rig´i·nal *adj.* native or indigenous; primitive; pertaining to aborigines —*n.* a native inhabitant; an aborigine

ab·o·rig´i·ne *n.* a native or earliest known inhabitant of a region

ab´o·rig´i·nes *pl. n.* first inhabitants; the flora and fauna of an area

a·bort´ *vi.* to bring forth young before the full term of development; to terminate prematurely, as a task or mission —*vt.* to cause to bring to an early, unsuccessful conclusion

a·bor´tion *n.* a miscarriage, usually intentional; any failure to evolve normally or as planned; the product of such failure, a monstrosity; a failed attempt —**a·bor´tion·ist** *n.*

a·bor´tive *adj.* useless; vain or futile; fruitless

a·bound´ *vi.* to be plentiful; available in abundance

a·bout´ *adv.* almost or approximately: *in about an hour,* around or in another direction: *turn about, wander about* or *look about* —*prep.* in or around an area: *somewhere about the office;* particular to or associated with: *she has an air about her;* approximating or near: *departing about noon, a group of about thirty;* in regard to: *a book about money management*

a·bout´-face *n.* in a military drill, a turn to the rear; any reversal of opinion or direction, especially one that is abrupt

a·bove *adv.* over; overhead; higher in rank —*adj.* foregoing or preceding: *the above paragraph* —*n.* that which is before or overhead —*prep.* rising over or higher: *the moon above the lake, boxes stacked above one another* —**above all** having precedence over everything else; the most important consideration

a·bove´board *adj., adv.* candid, forthright; in the open without anything concealed

a·brade´ *vt.* to scrape or wear away by friction

a·bra´sion *n.* the act or result of a wearing away, as of stone by the force of the elements; an injury resulting from passing contact with a rough surface

a·bra´sive *adj.* wearing; capable of eroding; disagreeable or offensive, as *his abrasive manner* —*n.* a material which abrades, as sandpaper or emery —**a·bra´sive·ly** *adv.*

—a·bra′sive·ness *n.*

a·breast′ *adv.* side by side

a·bridge′ *vt.* to shorten; to condense, as a book or article, by reducing the material to fewer words; to lessen or deprive, as of civil rights

a·bridg′ment *n.* that which has been shortened; an abstract

a·broad′ *adv.* away from one's usual place; in a foreign land; widely circulated

ab′ro·gate′ *vt.* to repeal or annul, esp. legally; to abolish —ab′ro·ga′ tion *n.* —ab′ro·ga·tor *n.*

a·brupt′ *adj.* happening suddenly or unexpectedly —ab·rupt′ly *adv.* — ab·rupt′ness *n.*

ab′scess *n.* a collection of pus in a body cavity

ab·scis′sa *n.* in a graph, the distance of a reference point from the Y-axis, parallel to the X-axis

ab·scis′sion *n.* the act of cutting off; severance or removal; in public speaking, an abrupt pause for dramatic effect

ab·scond′ *vi.* to leave quickly and secretly, esp. to avoid legal action

ab′sence *n.* a deficiency or inadequacy; the condition of being away; lack or want

ab′sent *adj.* not present; lacking or nonexistent; inattentive —ab·sent′ *vt.* to keep oneself away —ab′ sent·ness *n.* —ab′sent·ly *adv.*

ab·sen·tee′ *n.* one who is missing, as from school or work —*adj.* referring to one not presently in residence: *an absentee landlord*; describing an action taken by one who is absent: *an absentee vote*

ab′sen·tee′ism *n.* the state of being absent; a measure of the frequency of absence from work, school, etc.

ab′sent–mind′ed *adj.* preoccupied, and thus unmindful of immediate demands; forgetful —ab′sent· mind′ed·ly *adv.* —ab′sent·mind′ ed·ness *n.*

ab′sinthe *n.* wormwood; an anise flavored liqueur

ab′so·lute *adj.* complete; perfect; without restriction or reservation; pure and unadulterated; not related to or dependent on any arbitrary standard —*n.* that which is perfect —ab′so·lute′ly *adv.* —ab· so·lute′ness *n.*

absolute zero *n.* 459.6° F. below zero; the temperature at which a substance would be wholly deprived of heat

ab′so·lu·tion *n.* exoneration; vindication; forgiveness; in some churches, the ceremonial remission of sin

ab′so·lut·ism *n.* despotism; a principle that grants a ruler unlimited powers —ab′so·lut·ist *adj., n.* —ab·so·lu·tis′tic *adj.*

ab·solve′ *vt.* to acquit of guilt or complicity; to free from an obligation; to pardon or remit from sin and its attendant punishment — ab·solv′a·ble *adj.* —ab·solv′er *n.*

ab·sorb′ *vt.* to swallow up or engross completely; to assimilate; to engage or occupy entirely —ab·sorb′ a·ble *adj.* —ab·sorb·a·bil′i·ty *n.* — ab·sorb′er *n.*

ab·sor′bent *adj.* absorbing or disposed to absorb —*n.* a substance that absorbs —ab·sorb′en·cy *n.*

ab·sorb′ing *adj.* stimulating or enticing, as *an absorbing story* — ab·sorb′ing·ly *adv.*

ab·sorp′tion *n.* the process of absorbing or being absorbed; concentration or preoccupation of the mind —ab·sorp′tive *adj.* —ab· sorp′tive·ness, ab·sorp·tiv′i·ty *n.*

ab·stain′ *vi.* to forbear; to avoid or shun voluntarily

ab·ste′mi·ous *adj.* avoiding excess; temperate —ab·ste′mi·ous·ly *adv.*

ab·sten·tion *n.* temperance; foregoing —ab·sten′tious *adj.*

ab′sti·nence *n.* the practice of

avoiding something, such as for intoxicating drink —**ab´sti·nent** adj. —**ab´sti·nent·ly** adv.

ab´stract adj. expressing a quality apart from the absolute or concrete; theoretical; difficult to understand; impersonal; of a style of art —n. an abridgment; a summary or essence; a non–specific idea or term —**ab·stract´** vt. to take from; to condense or summarize; to form a general notion of: *the abstract concept of equal rights* —adj. general; theoretical; considered apart from the specific or practical —**ab·stract´er** n. —**ab·strac´tion·al** adj. —**ab·strac´tion·ism** n.

abstract art a school of art that makes use of designs based on the relationship of elements rather than on the representation of objects

ab·stract´ed adj. disassociated or apart; obscure or puzzling; preoccupied —**ab·stract´ed·ly** adv.

ab·strac´tion n. preoccupation or absorption; a theory or ideal —**ab·strac´tive** adj.

ab·struse´ adj. difficult to comprehend —**ab·struse´ly** adv. —**ab·struse´ness** n.

ab·surd´ adj. irrational; preposterous; ridiculous —**ab·surd´ly** adv.

ab·surd´i·ty n. that which is preposterous or ridiculous

a·bun´dance n. a quantity in excess of need; plenty

a·bun´dant adj. plentiful; bountiful; more than enough —**a·bun´dant·ly** adv.

a·buse´ n. improper use; misapplication; vicious or cruel treatment —vt. to use incorrectly; to harm by improper use: *abuse a privilege*; to injure by mistreating: *abuse an animal* —**a·bus´er** n.

a·bu´sive adj. characterized by abuse; serving to abuse as *abusive*

language —**a·bu´sive·ly** adv. —**a·bu´sive·ness** n.

a·but´ vi. to touch or join; to border; to form a line of contact, with *on, upon,* or *against* —vt. to border on

a·but´ment n. a supporting element of a structure such as a bridge or wall; a buttress

a·bys´mal adj. bottomless; extreme: *abysmal despair* —**a·bys´mal·ly** adv.

a·byss´ n. a bottomless gulf; a chasm; a tremendous depth

ac·a·deme´, ac´a·deme n. a place of learning; an academy; a scholarly environment

ac´a·dem´ia n. the academic world; institutions of learning collectively

ac´a·dem´ic adj. scholarly; of traditional learning rather than vocational; theoretical or hypothetical rather than practical —n. a student or scholar; a member of a learned society —**ac·a·dem´i·cal** n. —**ac·a·dem´i·cal·ly** adv.

a·cad´e·my n. a preparatory school; a society of scholars devoted to the advancement of art or science

a cap·pel´la adj. vocal music without instrumental accompaniment

ac·cede´ vi. to come into an office; to give assent or agree to —**ac·ced´ence** n.

ac·cel´er·ate vi. to move more rapidly; to hurry —vt. to increase the speed of; to hasten the natural course of: *to accelerate growth with plant food*

ac·cel´er·a´tion n. a hastening of progress; the rate of increase in the speed of a body

ac·cel´er·a´tor n. a device that controls speed by regulating the flow of fuel, power, etc.; that which increases speed, flow, etc.

ac´cent n. voice stress on a syllable in the pronunciation of a word; a mark (´)to indicate vocal stress; a manner of speaking which differs from place to place or from one language to another —*vt.* to stress; to speak or produce with an accent

ac·cen´tu·ate *vt.* to stress; to emphasize —**ac·cen´tu·a·tion** *n.*

ac·cept´ *vt.* to receive or take what is offered; to agree to or approve; to embrace as true, such as a belief; to take in as a member —**ac·cept´ance** *n.*

ac·cept´a·ble *adj.* satisfactory; worthy of being accepted; without need for further modification or negotiation, although not entirely pleasing: *an acceptable level of error* —**ac·cept´a·bil´i·ty** *n.* —**ac·cept´a·bly** *adv.*

ac·cept´ed *adj.* generally recognized or believed

ac´cess *n.* an approach or passage; permission to approach or enter; a means of obtaining —*vt.* to gain the use of, as a computer program or data

ac·ces´si·ble *adj.* easily approached or reached; easily influenced; allowing access; attainable —**ac·ces´si·bil´i·ty** *n.*

ac·ces´so·ry, ac·ces´sa·ry *adj.* extra or added; aiding, contributing; supplemental —*n.* an accomplice or abettor; something added as an incidental item of apparel —**ac·ces´so·rize** *vt.*

ac´ci·dent *n.* an unexpected occurrence, often unpleasant; a misadventure; an unintentional act

ac·ci·den´tal *adj.* happening by chance; fortuitous; incidental to the character of a thing —**ac·ci·den´tal·ly** *adv.*

ac·claim´ *vt.* to applaud; to receive with approval; to approve by proclamation —*vi.* to applaud or shout approval —*n.* enthusiastic applause

ac´cla·ma´tion *n.* applause; general approval

ac·cli·mate, ac·cli·ma·tize´ *vi., vt.*

to grow accustomed to a new environment or circumstance

ac·clam´a·to·ry *adj.* expressing joy and adulation

ac·cliv´i·ty *n.* an upward slope, opposite of *declivity*

ac´co·lade´ *n.* any honor or award; words of praise

ac·com´mo·date´ *vi.* to become adjusted, as to a disability —*vt.* to supply food or lodging; to adapt; to be suitable for: *the room will accommodate four persons* —**ac·com´mo·dat·ing·ly** *adv.* —**ac·com´mo·da·tive** *adj.*

ac·com´mo·da´tion *n.* an adaptation; a reconciliation; a convenience; board or lodging; assistance; a willingness to provice assistance —**ac·com·mo·da´tion·al** *adj.*

ac·com´pa·nist *n.* one who plays a musical instrument or vocalizes to enhance the performance or presentation of another —**ac·com´pa·ni·ment** *n.*

ac·com´pa·ny *vt.* to go with; to escort; to play an instrument or sing with another; to supplement: *wine accompanied the meal*; to occur at the same time: *a cold accompanied by fever*

ac·com´plice *n.* an associate in crime; a knowing confederate

ac·com´plish *vt.* to perform; to fulfill, as an obligation; to complete

ac·com´plished *adj.* completed; fulfilled; proficient or expert: *an accomplished musician*; refined or cultivated

ac·com´plish·ment *n.* something completed; a worthly attainment

ac·cord´ *n.* harmony or agreement; spontaneous desire —*vi.* to be in agreement; to harmonize —*vt.* to grant; to bring into harmony —**of one´s own accord** freely done, without urging —**according to** as per direction or plan; as reported

ac·cord´ance *n.* conformity; accord;

harmony

ac·cord´ing·ly *adv.* consequently; as a result

ac·cost´ *vt.* to confront; to approach and greet first

ac·count´ *n.* a computation; a report or statement; a record of financial or commercial transactions —*vi.* to provide a reason; to explain; to be responsible —*vt.* to impute —**give a good account** to do well —**on account** on credit —**on no account** under no circumstance — **take into account** bear in mind

ac·count´a·ble *adj.* having liability; responsible; capable of being explained —**ac·count·a·bil´i·ty** *n.* — **ac·count´a·bly** *adv.*

ac·count´an·cy *n.* the office and duties of an accountant

ac·count´ant *n.* one experienced in the keeping of accounts; one whose business is to record or audit the financial records of an institution —**public accountant** an accountant whose services are available to the public for a fee —**certified public accountant** in the U.S., a public accountant who has been certified by a state examining body

ac·count´ing *n.* a settlement; a statement of the financial condition and transactions of an organization; the principals or profession of recording the financial transactions of an organization

ac·cred´it *vt.* to certify; to send with credentials

ac·cre´tion *n.* a growth; growth by accumulation or addition, as of sediment deposited along the course of a river or on a seashore

ac·cru´al *n.* an increase or accumulation; something that increases

ac·crue´ *vi.* to increase; be added to, as interest

ac·cu´mu·late *vt.* to amass or pile up; to gather —*vi.* to increase

—**ac·cu´mu·la·ble** *adj.* —**ac·cu´mu·la·tor** *n.*

ac·cu´mu·la´tion *n.* a collection; growth or increase

ac·cu´mu·la·tive *adj.* tending to increase —**ac·cu´mu·la·tive·ly** *adv.* —**ac·cu´mu·la·tive·ness** *n.*

ac´cu·ra·cy *n.* a measure of the degree of precision; correctness; exactness

ac´cu·rate *adj.* very exact; precise; capable of providing precise measurement; within established limits —**ac´cu·rate·ly** *adv.* —**ac´cu·rate·ness** *n.*

ac·curs´ed, ac·curst´ *adj.* under a curse; deserving a curse —**ac·curs´ed·ly** *adv.*

ac·cu·sa´tion, ac·cu´sal *n.* the act of charging with a crime; arraignment

ac·cuse´ *vi.* to verbalize charges —*vt.* to bring a charge against —**ac·cus´er** *n.* —**ac·cus´ing·ly** *adv.*

ac·cused´ *n.* a person or persons charged with the commission of a crime

ac·cus´tom *vt.* to make or become familiar through use; to adapt to

ac·cus´tomed *adj.* habitual or usual; customary; characteristic

ace *n.* a single spot, as on a playing card or die; a person who excels, an expert; in tennis, a point won on the serve —*vt.* to score an ace

ac´er·bate *vt.* to make harsh or bitter; to intensify; to annoy

a·cer´bic, a·cerb´ *adj.* sour tasting; harsh, as in manner or language —**a·cer´bi·ty** *n.*

ac´e·tate´ *n.* a salt or ester of acetic acid; a type of fiber used in the making of textiles

a·ce´tic *adj.* sour; having the sour properties of vinegar; pertaining to or containing acetic acid or vinegar —**a·ce´ti·fy** *vi., vt.*

acetic acid *n.* a colorless sour acid which is the chief component of vinegar

ac´e·tone *n.* a colorless, flammable liquid ketone used as a solvent

a·cet´y·lene *n.* a colorless, flammable gas used as a fuel in welding

a·ce´tyl·sal·i·cyl´ic acid *n.* aspirin

ache *vi.* to hurt; to suffer throbbing pain; to suffer absence or loss: *to ache for a loved one*; to feel sympathy for —*n.* a dull protracted pain —**ach´i·ness** *n.* —**ach´ing·ly** *adv.* —**ach·y** *adj.*

a·chieve´ *vi.* to reach an objective —*vt.* to accomplish; to complete successfully —**a·chiev´a·ble** *adj.* —**a·chiev´er** *n.*

a·chieve´ment *n.* the act of accomplishing; a notable act; a distinguished accomplishment

ac´id *adj.* sour and sharp to the taste; caustic or sarcastic, as of humor —*n.* a sour substance

a·cid´ic *adj.* having the properties of acid

a·cid´i·fy *vi.* to turn acid —*vt.* to transform into an acid —**a·cid´i·fi·ca´tion** *n.* —**a·cid´i·fi´er** *n.*

a·cid´i·ty *n.* sourness and tartness; degree of acid strength

acid test a test of quality, veracity, etc.; a severe test

ac·knowl´edge *vt.* to admit or confess; to certify as valid; to show appreciation; to confirm receipt of —**ac·knowl´edge·a·ble** *adj.*

ac·knowl´edge·ment, ac·knowl´edg·ment *n.* a confession; a recognition of responsibility; something said or done in response or appreciation; confirmation of receipt

ac´me *n.* the highest point; zenith

ac´ne *n.* a skin affliction, mainly in adolescents

a´corn *n.* the fruit of the oak tree

a·cous´tic, a·cous´ti·cal *adj.* pertaining to sound or the sense of hearing —**a·cous´ti·cal·ly** *adv.* —**ac·ous·ti´cian** *n.*

a·cous´tics *pl. n.* the scientific study of sound; the degree to which sound quality is maintained in a particular place

ac·quaint´ *vt.* to make one aware of; to inform; to introduce —**be ac·quainted with** familiar, but not well known

ac·quaint´ance *n.* familiarity; knowledge; an associate; one who is known to another —**ac·quaint´ance·ship** *n.*

ac´qui·esce´ *vi.* to agree or comply without enthusiasm; to submit to or accept as inevitable —**ac´qui·es´cence** *n.* —**ac´qui·es´cent** *adj.* —**ac·qui·es´cent·ly, ac·qui·esc´ing·ly** *adv.*

ac·quire´ *vt.* to obtain or gain, esp. through personal effort —**ac·quir´a·ble** *adj.* —**ac·quir´er** *n.*

ac´qui·si´tion *n.* a thing gained, an appropriation

ac·quis´i·tive *adj.* prone to acquire, as property —**ac·quis´i·tive·ly** *adv.* —**ac·quis´i·tive·ness** *n.* —**ac·quis´i·tor** *n.*

ac·quit´ *vt.* to pronounce innocent; to discharge a trust; to behave or act: *he acquitted himself well*

ac·quit´tal *n.* a discharge of duty; in law, a finding of not guilty as charged or of being set free by judgment of a court

ac·quit´tance *n.* a settlement of liability; a receipt or proof of such settlement

a´cre *n.* a land measure equal to 4,840 square yards

a´cre·age *n.* property; a number of acres comprising a single piece of property

ac´rid *adj.* sharp in taste or smell; pungent —**a·crid´i·ty** *n.* —**ac´rid·ly** *adv.* —**ac´rid·ness** *n.*

ac·ri·mo´ni·ous *adj.* sarcastic; caustic; acerbic

ac´ri·mo·ny *n.* sharp or bitter speech or temperament

ac´ro·bat *n.* an athlete skilled in gymnastics; a trapeze artist; a tumbler —**ac´ro·bat´ic** *adj.*

ac´ro·bat´ics *n.* gymnastics

ac´ro·nym *n.* a word formed from the initial letters or syllables of a group of words which make up the name of an organization, title, etc. as NASA for National Aeronautics and Space Administration

ac·ro·pho˝bi·a *n.* a unnatural fear of heights —**ac´ro·phobe** *n.* —**ac·ro·pho˝bic** *adj.*

a·cross´ *adv.* from one side to the other; on the opposite side —*prep.* on or at the other side; from one side to the other; upon or in contact with: *I came across the papers yesterday*

a·cros´tic *n.* a written message whose initial letters form a word or another message

a·cryl´ic *adj.* of acrylic acid or any of the products made from it —*n.* a class of transparent resins; a substance obtained from an acrylic resin, as a paint, fiber, etc.

act *vi.* to behave oneself; to perform a function or produce an effect: *the acid will act on the metal* —*vt.* to play a part on the stage; to behave in a proper manner: *act like a gentleman*; to pretend to be something out of the ordinary: *don't act like a fool* —**act as** to serve in a temporary capacity —**act on** follow an order or advice —**act up** to be troublesome —**get into the act** join in an activity —**put on an act** to pretend

act´ing *adj.* standing in for another, as *acting manager*; operating —*n.* a performance on the stage; an affectation

ac´tion *n.* putting forth or exerting energy; decisiveness: *a man of action*: the result of activity; a manner of movement: *the up and down action of a piston*; parts that move

in a mechanism; a thing done; a law suit —**ac´tions** *pl. n.* one's behavior or conduct

ac´tion·a·ble *adj.* in law, forming the basis for a lawsuit or for prosecution —**ac´tion·a·bly** *adv.*

ac´ti·vate *vt.* to make active; to purify sewage by means of aeration —**ac´ti·va´tion** *n.* —**ac´ti·va·tor** *n.*

ac´tive *adj.* energetic, lively; busy; operative, as *an active volcano*; taking part, as *an active member*; —**ac´tive·ly** *adv.* —**ac´tive·ness** *n.*

ac·tiv´i·ty *n.* lively movement; a planned or specific undertaking or pursuit; a transaction

ac´tiv·ism *n.* involvement in social issues —**ac´tiv·ist** *n.*

ac´tu·al *adj.* existing in fact —*n.* a thing of substance; real —**ac´tu·al´i·ty** *n.*

ac´tu·al·ise (*Brit.*), **ac´tu·al·ize** (*US*) *vt.* to make real; to portray realistically —**ac´tu·al·i·sa·tion**, **ac´tu·al·i·za·tion** *n.*

ac´tu·al·ly *adv.* truly, as a matter of fact

ac´tu·ar·y *n.* a statistician who calculates risk for investors or insurers —**ac·tu·ar´i·al** *adj.*

ac´tu·ate *vt.* to impel, to put in motion; to cause to act —**ac´tu·a·tion** *n.* —**ac´tu·a·tor** *n.*

a·cu·i·ty *n.* insight; discernment, especially of reasoning or of perception

a·cu˝men *n.* quickness of understanding and acting; sharpness of intellect; soundnes of judgment

ac·u·punc·ture *n.* an Oriental treatment for pain or illness in which fine needles are inserted through the skin at points determined to be beneficial according to the condition being treated —**ac´u·punc·tur·ist** *n.*

a·cute´ *adj.* pointed, sharp; keen of mind; serious, critical, as an acute illness or disease; sharp or

9

intense, as pain —**a·cute´ly** *adv.*
—**a·cute´ness** *n.*

acute angle *n.* an angle of less than 90°

ad *n.* an advertisement

ad´age *n.* a proverb or maxim

ad´a·mant *adj.* unyielding; resolute in belief —**ad´a·mant·ly** *adv.*

a·dapt´ *vi.* to grow adjusted to, as an environment —*vt.* to make suitable by adjusting or altering; to accommodate by changing oneself —**a·dapt´a·ble** *adj.* —**a·dapt·a·bil´i·ty** *n.*

ad·ap·ta´tion *n.* that which has been modified for a specific use; the process of modification

a·dapt´er, a·dap´tor *n.* a device for modifying an apparatus for a different or additional use; a connecting device that joins units whose connections are otherwise incompatible

a·dap´tive *adj.* capable of being modified —**a·dap´tive**·ly *adv.*

add *vi.* to produce an increase; to perform an addition; —*vt.* to increase in importance or size; to total a column of numbers; to speak or write more —**add up** to total; to seem reasonable or believable —**add´a·ble, add´i·ble** *adj.*

ad´dend *n., pl.* **ad·den´da** in mathematics, a number which is to be added to an existing number, called the *augend*

ad·den´dum *n.* an addition; a thing to be added, usually at the end, such as an appendix

ad´dict *n.* one given to an obsession, as illegal drugs or alcohol —**ad·dict´** *vt.* to devote oneself to: *addicted to the latest fashions, addicted to work;* to be dependent on: *addicted to drugs*

ad·dic´tion *n.* psychological or physiological dependence on anything; a compulsion

ad·dict´ed *adj.* predisposed to a

practice or substance

ad·dic´tive *adj.* habit-forming

ad·di´tion *n.* the process of finding the sum of two or more numbers; something added, as a room to a house; an increase —**ad·di´tion·al** *adj., n.* —**ad·di´tion·al·ly** *adv.*

ad´di·tive *n.* an ingredient added to alter the flavor, performance, cost, etc. of a product —*adj.* tending to increase

ad´dle *vi.* to become disconnected or confused, as in speech —*vt.* to cause to become confused or disjointed; to muddle: *his thinking is addled by strong drink* —*adj.* confused, incoherent

ad´dle·brained´ *adj.* confused; flustered; also **ad´dle·pat´ed**

ad·dress´ *vt.* to speak or write to; to direct to specifically: *address a letter;* to direct attention or energy: *we'll address this problem now —n.* a formal speech; one's place of abode or work; the bearing or manner of a person; a specific location, as of a block of data, in a computer —**ad·dress´er** *n.*

ad·dress´a·ble *adj.* approachable; able to locate and use, as a block of data in computer memory.

ad·dress·ee´ *n.* one who is addressed

ad·duce´ *vt.* to cite as an example or proof —**ad·duc´i·ble** *adj.*

ad·duct´ *vt.* to pull toward the median axis of the body —**ad·duc´tion** *n.*

ad·duc´tor *n.* of a muscle that pulls toward the median axis of the body

ad´e·noid *n.* a glandular tissue behind the nose at the upper part of the throat —*adj.* glandular

a·dept´ *adj.* extremely skilled; proficient —**ad´ept** *n.* a person who is highly skilled; an expert —**a·dept´ly** *adv.* —**a·dept´ness** *n.*

ad´e·quate *adj.* barely satisfactory or sufficient; enough or suitable for immediate need —**ad´e·qua·cy** *n.*

—ad´e·quate·ly   adv.   —ad´e·quate·ness n.

ad·here´ vi. to stick fast; to follow closely: *adhere to the rules*; to follow faithfully or devotedly —ad·her´ence n. —ad·her´ent n.

ad·he´sion n. the act of sticking; the condition of being stuck; a close attachment

ad·he´sive adj. tending to stick; gummed —n. a substance which causes adhesion —ad·he´sive·ness n.

adhesive tape material coated with an adhesive, used for securing bandages, binding wounds, etc.

ad hoc´ relating to a particular thing

ad hoc committee a committee formed for a particular purpose

ad in´fi·ni´tum to infinity; forever; unlimited

ad´i·pose adj. pertaining to fat — ad·i·pose´ness, ad·i·pos´i·ty n.

ad·ja´cence ad·ja´cen·cy n. the state of being near or neighboring

ad·ja´cent adj. near or joining; connected; neighboring —ad·ja´cent·ly adv.

ad´jec·ti´val, ad´jec·ti·val adj. like or performing the function of an adjective —ad´jec·ti·val·ly adv.

ad´jec·tive n. in grammar, a word that modifies a noun, as by color, size, location, etc.; a clause or phrase used as an adjective —adj. pertaining to or functioning as an adjective

ad·join´ vt. to be in close proximity; to touch; to unite —vi. to lie close by; to be in contact

ad·journ´ vi., vt. to end, as a meeting; to postpone proceedings; to move to another place: *adjourn to the living room*—ad·journ´ment n.

ad·judge´ vt. to order by law; to decide judicially

ad·ju´di·cate vi. to perform the function of a judge —vt. to decide judicially —ad·ju´di·ca´tion n.

—ad·ju´di·ca·tive adj. —ad·ju´di·ca·tor n. —ad·ju´di·ca·to·ry adj.

ad´junct adj. supplementary; additional —n. something added, as a peripheral device; a person assigned to another as a subordinate; a nonessential quality —ad·junc´tive adj. —ad´junc´tive·ly adv.

ad·jure´ vt. to charge under oath; to appeal intently —ad´ju·ra´tion n. —ad·jur´a·to·ry adj. —ad·jur´er, ad·ju´ror n.

ad·just´ vi. to adapt or conform as to a new environment; —vt. to arrange or regulate so as to fit, match, or produce a desired result; to settle differences or arrive at an amount: *to adjust an insurance claim* —ad·just´a·ble n. — ad·just´er, ad·just´or n.

ad·just´ment n. the process or result of adjusting; the amount of settlement on a claim, as *an insurance adjustment*; an allowance in settlement of a claim, as for wear on a tire that is warranted against damage

ad´ju·tant n. an assistant, usu. one who publishes or carries out the directives of a superior

ad lib´ adj. created spontaneously: *ad lib remarks* —adv. spontaneously: *to compose ad lib* —vi., vt. to improvise —n.

ad·min´is·ter vi. to carry out the duties of a manager; to be of assistance —vt. to manage; to dispense, as a penalty; to conduct the taking of an oath, test, etc.; to provide assistance —ad·min´is·tra·ble adj. —ad·min´is·trant

ad·min´is·trate vt. to administer

ad·min´is·tra´tion n. the act of administering; the power or party in office and which runs the government; the term of the party in power; settlement of the estate of a deceased person by an executor or

11

trustee —ad·min´is·tra´tive adj.
—ad·min´is·tra·tive·ly adv. —ad·
min´is·tra´tor n.

ad´mi·ra·ble adj. deserving admiration; commendable —ad´mi·ra·bly
adv.

ad·mi·ral·ty n. the office and jurisdiction of an admiral; the branch
of the juiciary that is responsible
for maritime affairs

ad·mi·ra´tion n. wonder and appreciation of that which is rare, beautiful, etc.; something that engen-
ders wonder, appreciation, approval, etc.

ad·mire´ vt. to regard with wonder
and appreciation; to esteem; to respect —vi. to feel or express admiration —ad·mir´er n. —ad´mi·ra·
bly adv. —ad·mir´ing·ly adv.

ad·mis´si·ble adj. worthy of admission or consideration; allowable —
ad·mis´si·bil´i·ty n. —ad·mis´si·
bly adv.

ad·mis´sion n. the act of admitting
the price paid for entrance; the
right to enter; the confession of a
deed or fault

ad·mit´ vt. to allow to enter; to be
the means to enter: this pass will
admit you; to allow inclusion or
membership, as to a club or professional society; to accede to or
acknowledge, as an error in reasoning or in wrongdoing —vi. to
afford entrance

ad·mit´tance n. right or permission
to enter; the act of admitting; admission or entrance

ad·mit´ted adj. accepted as valid;
confessed; acclaimed; acknowledged

ad·mit´ted·ly adv. confessedly

ad·mix´ture n. a combination; a
blending of ingredients; the additional ingredient which is combined to form an admixture

ad·mon´ish vt. to counsel against
error; to offer a mild rebuke; to

instruct with authority —ad·mon´
ish·ing·ly adv. —ad·mon´ish·
ment n.

ad·mo·ni´tion n. a mild rebuke; a
warning —ad·mon´i·to´ry adj.

a·do´ n. activity, often overdone or
unnecessary; bustle; commotion

a·do´be adj. made from sun-dried
brick —n. a sun-dried brick; a
building made from such bricks;
the earth or clay of which such
building blocks are made

ad·o·les´cence n. the period of
growth from childhood to maturity

ad·o·les´cent adj. characteristic of
youth; youthful; lacking maturity,
often used pejoratively —n. a
youth

a·dopt´ vt. to take in and raise as
one's own; to take up and follow,
as a change in method or policy; to
enact, as a law or ordinance —
a·dopt´a·ble adj. —a·dopt´er n. —
a·dop´tion n. —a·dop´tive adj.

a·dor´a·ble adj. delightful; en-
chanting —a·dor´a·ble·ness n. —
a·dor´a·bly adv.

ad´o·ra´tion n. worship or reverence;
deep affection, esteem, and dedication

a·dore´ vi., vt. to cherish with unwavering affection; to be especially
fond of —a·dor´er n. —a·dor´ing·
ly adv.

a·dorn´ vt. to decorate or embellish
with ornaments; to beautify —
a·dorn´er n. —a·dorn´ment n.

ad·re´nal adj. near the kidneys; of
the adrenal glands —n. an adrenal
gland

adrenal gland either of two small
endocrine glands located above the
kidneys

ad·ren´al·in, ad·ren´al·ine n. a
stimulant secreted by the adrenal
glands

a·drift´ adj., adv. wandering; lacking
direction or purpose

a·droit´ adj. clever or resourceful,

especially intellectually; expert — **a·droit´ly** *adv.* —**a·droit´ness** *n.*

ad·sorb´ *vt.* to retain a gas or liquid on the surface, as contrasted with *absorb* —**ad·sorb´ent** *adj.* —**ad·sorp´tion** *n.* —**ad·sorp´tive** *adj.*

ad·u·la´tion *n.* base flattery; extravagant praise —**ad´u·late** *vt.* —**ad´u·la·to·ry** *adj.*

a·dult´ *adj.* fully developed; full-grown; mature in manners and attitude; of or for a mature person: *adult education* —*n.* a fully grown person or animal; one who has attained legal majority

a·dul´ter·ant *n.* a substance that tends to contaminate

a·dul´ter·ate´ *adj.* impure; contaminated —*vt.* to make impure by adding an undesirable substance; to lessen the value of by adding inferior ingredients —**a·dul´ter·a´tion** *n.* —**a·dul´ter·a·tor** *n.*

a·dul´ter·ous *adj.* characterized by or relating to adultery —**a·dul´ter·ous·ly** *adv.*

a·dul´ter·y *n.* sexual unfaithfulness by one who is married —**a·dul´ter·er** *n.*

ad va·lo·rem in proportion to the value, as *an ad valorem tax*

ad·vance´ *adj.* before due: *an advance payment*; before the rest: *an advance party* —*n.* progress; an improvement; a prepayment or loan of money not yet due or earned —*vi.* to make progress or move forward; to rise in rank or value, etc. —*vt.* to put or move forward; to offer or promote, as a suggestion; to pay or loan money before it is due

ad·vanced´ *adj.* at the front or ahead: *an advanced student*; late in the progression of events: *the advanced stage of a project*

ad·vance·ment *n.* furtherance or promotion: *the advancement of science*

ad·van´tage *n.* a circumstance favorable to success; superiority; a gain or benefit —*vt.* to benefit; to be of service to —**take advantage of** put to good use; to exploit

ad·van·ta´geous *adj.* providing advantage; beneficial —**ad´van·ta´geous·ly** *adv.* —**ad´van·ta´geous·ness** *n.*

ad´vent *n.* a coming, as of an important event

ad·ven´ture *n.* an exciting undertaking, often involving hazard; a speculative commercial venture —*vi.* to venture; to take risks —*vt.* to place at risk —**ad·ven´tur·er** *n.*

ad·ven´ture·some *adj.* inclined to take part in risky or hazardous activities —**ad·ven´ture·some·ly** *adv.* —**ad·ven´ture·some·ness** *n.*

ad·ven´tur·ous *adj.* inclined to take risks; characterized by risk; hazardous —**ad·ven´tur·ous·ly** *adv.* —**ad·ven·tur·ous·ness** *n.*

ad´verb´ *n.* word that qualifies a verb, adjective, or other adverb, as to define time, place, manner, degree, etc. —**ad·verb´i·al** *adj.*

ad´ver·sar´y *n.* an opponent; one who is openly antagonistic —**ad´ver·sar´i·al** *adj.*

ad´verse, ad·verse´ *adj.* acting against, as *adverse commentary*; unpropitious or unfavorable, as *adverse weather*; moving in opposition: *an adverse current* —**ad·verse´ly** *adv.* —**ad·verse´ness** *n.*

ad·ver´si·ty *n.* a state of hardship; difficult circumstances; misfortune

ad´ver·tise´ *vi.* to proclaim publicly, as to create awareness of a product or business; to publicly request something such as living quarters or employment —*vt.* to give public notice of; to proclaim the quality or advantage of so as to sell —**ad´ver·tis·er** *n.*

ad·ver·tise´ment *n.* public notice in a periodical or the broadcast media to sell a product, announce an event, etc.

ad·ver·tis·ing *n.* any method of publicizing a product, event, etc.; the business of publicizing

ad·vice´ *n.* counsel or guidance

ad·vis·a·ble *adj.* deserving of recommendation; opportune —**ad·vis´ a·bil´i·ty, ad·vis´a·ble·ness** *n.* — **ad·vis´a·bly** *adv.*

ad·vise´ *vi.* to offer advice —*vt.* to give advice; to recommend to; to notify or inform of —**ad·vis´er, ad·vi·sor** *n.*

ad·vised´ *adj.* deliberately considered; prudent; informed —**ad·vise´ ment** *n.*

ad·vis´ed·ly *adv.* with forethought; carefully; prudently

ad·vi·so·ry *adj.* having power to advise; offered as advice —*n.* a recommendation; an information bulletin, as *a weather advisory*

ad·vo·ca·cy *n.* the act of pleading a cause; support for a cause

ad·vo·cate *n.* one who pleads for another; one who argues a cause; a supporter; a lawyer —*vt.* to support or defend; to promote a cause or point of view; to argue in favor of —**ad´vo·ca·tor** *n.* —**ad·voc´a· to·ry** *adj.*

adze, adz *n.* a hand tool similar to an axe with the blade at right angles to its handle, used for trimming and dressing lumber, etc.

ae´gis *n.* in Greek mythology, the shield of Zeus; protective power; sponsorship or patronage

aer´ate *vt.* to oxygenate; to charge with gas; to purify by exposure to air, as for drinking water —**aer· a´tion** *n.* —**aer´a·tor** *n.*

aer´i·al *adj.* of or like air; performed in the air or by an aircraft, as *aerial photography*; living and growing in the air; insubstantial or spiritual —*n.* (*Brit.*) a device used for the transmission or reception

of radio or television signals

aer´i·al·ist *n.* an aerial acrobat; a tightrope walker or trapeze artist

aer·ie *n.* the nest of a predatory bird, as the eagle; any dwelling at a high elevation

aer´o·dy·nam´ics *n.* the study of bodies moving in the air, esp. of the force of the atmosphere on objects in motion —**aer´o·dy·nam´ i·cist** *n.*

aer´o·nau´tics *pl. n.* the science of aviation; the study of the design and operation of aircraft —**aer´o· naut** *n.* —**aer·o·nau´tic, aer·o· nau´ti·cal** *adj.* —**aer·o·nau´ti·cal· ly** *adv.*

aer´o·plane (*Brit.*) *n.* a fixed–wing aircraft

aer´o·sol *adj.* pertaining to a substance under pressure that is dispensed as a fine spray —*n.* a suspension of fine particles; a substance contained under pressure with an inert gas propellent which produces a fine spray when released

aerosol bomb *n.* container holding liquid under pressure to be released as spray or foam

aer´o·space *adj.* of the Earth's atmosphere and near outer space; of the science and technology of aeronautics and space flight —*n.*

aerospace industry the sector of commerce concerned with the design and manufacture of equipment for use in space

aes´thete *n.* a connoisseur of beauty, culture, fine art, etc.; one overly devoted to refinement and pretentious in appreciation of art and culture

aes·thet´ic, aes·thet´i·cal *adj.* appreciating the artistic or beautiful; characterized by fine taste —**aes· thet´i·cal·ly** *adv.*

aes·thet´ics *n.* the philosophical consideration or study of the expression of beauty and art, and the feelings they evoke —**aes·the·ti´cian** *n.* —**aes·thet´i·cism** *n.*

a·far´ *adv.* remotely; from a distance

af·fa·ble *adj.* pleasant; friendly; courteous of manner; amiable — **af´fa·bil´i·ty** *n.* —**af´fa·bly** *adv.*

af·fair´ *n.* a thing done or to be done; a bit of business; a social gathering; a minor dispute; a small matter; a vague or indefinite thing; a romantic liaison

af·fect´ *vt.* to influence; to change; to arouse emotion; be partial to; to make a pretense of; to infect, as a disease —*n.* an emotion, as distinguished from thought or action

af·fec·ta´tion *n.* a calculated or elaborate pretense; an artificial manner

af·fect´ed *adj.* acted upon, as by a drug or disease; influenced emotionally; simulated so as to impress others; speaking or acting in an unnatural or insincere manner

af·fec´tion *n.* good or kind feelings for another; a fondness for anything; love —**af·fec´tion·al** *adj.* — **af·fec´tion·al·ly** *adv.*

af·fec´tion·ate *adj.* expressing fondness or love; loving —**af·fec´tion·ate·ly** *adv.*

af·fi·da´vit *n.* a written statement made under oath and notarized

af·fil´i·ate *vt.* to take in as a member; to join or associate with —*vi.* to become allied or associated —*n.* a person or organization allied with another as a member, partner, etc. —**af·fil´i·a´tion** *n.*

af·fin´i·ty *n.* any natural attraction; a close relationship; a platonic or spiritual attraction existing between persons; the force by which chemical elements are attracted to form compounds; in biology, a resemblance that suggests common origin

af·firm´ *vt.* to declare or claim to be true; to ratify or confirm, as a legal judgment, a statute, etc. —*vi.* in law, to make a formal declaration not under oath —**af·firm´a·bly** *adv.* —**af·firm´a·ble** *adj.* —**af´fir·ma´tion** *n.*

af·firm´a·tive *adj.* positive, supportive —*n.* a word expressing confirmation or agreement —**af·firm´a·tive·ly** *adv.*

affirmative action a program of practical measures for correcting past discrimination, as in education or employment

af·fix´ *vt.* to attach or fasten, as a label; to add, as the signature on a letter; to attribute, as responsibility or blame —**af´fix** *n.* something added

af·fla´tus *n.* articulation of divine knowledge; any creative impulse

af·flict´ *vt.* to oppress; to rack with pain; to cause distress —**af·flict´er** *n.* —**af·flic´tive** *adj.* —**af·flic´tive·ly** *adv.*

af·flic´tion *n.* a state of pain or distress; that which causes suffering; a misfortune; a calamity

af·flu·ence *n.* wealth; abundance; a rich supply

af·flu·ent *adj.* wealthy; prosperous; generously supplied; abounding — *n.* a wealthy person; a stream or river that flows into another —**af´flu·ent·ly** *adv.*

af·ford´ *vt.* to be able to pay or meet expenses; to undergo without inconvenience: *we can afford the time off now;* to confer on or grant: *it affords them pleasure* —**af·ford·a·bil´i·ty** *n.* —**af·ford´a·ble** *adj.* —**af·ford´a·bly** *adv.*

af·front´ *n.* an intentional insult or indignity —*vt.* to insult flagrantly; treat with arrogance

a·fi·cio·na´do *n.* an enthusiastic fan, as of a sport

a·field´ *adv.* to the field or off the usual path: said, often disapprovingly, of ideas or endeavors which are thought to have gone astray

a·fire´ *adj., adv.* on fire: often figuratively, of one who exhibits great enthusiasm for an idea or task

a·float´ *adj., adv.* resting on the surface of a liquid; drifting with no fixed plan; the state of an organization: *they will have a difficult time remaining afloat*

a·foot´ *adj., adv.* on foot; walking; on the move or progressing: *something is afoot*

a·fore´men·tioned *adj.* stated earlier; referred to previously

a·fore´said *adj.* said before

a·fore´thought *adj.* premeditated; considered earlier

a·foul´ *adj., adv.* entangled —**run afoul of** get into difficulty with

a·fraid´ *adj.* filled with fear or apprehension: *afraid of the dark*; anxious about something: *afraid to show emotion*; regretful: *I'm afraid there's been a mistake*

a·fresh´ *adv.* once again; anew

aft *adj.* of the stern of a vessel —*adv.* toward the rear; astern

af´ter *adj.* subsequent; succeeding in time or place —*adv.* at a later time —*prep.* farther back, or later than: *salad was served after the soup*; in succession: *it happens time after time*; in pursuit of: *searching after knowledge*; concerning: *to inquire after someone* —*conj.* following the time that: *after dinner, we took a walk*

aft´er·burn´er *n.* a device in a jet engine that ignites unburned gas and increases thrust

af´ter·ef·fect *n.* a symptom which follows the initial effects of a medicine, an ailment, etc.

af´ter·glow *n.* the glow which remains after a light source has disappeared, as in the sky after sunset; an agreeable or pleasant feeling retained after an enjoyable experience

af´ter·hours´ *adj.* following the normal business day; of an establishment that remains open past the legal closing time, as a club or tavern

af´ter·im·age *n.* the impression which remains after stimulus is removed

af´ter·life *n.* life after death

af´ter·math *n.* the consequence or result of an action

af´ter·noon *n.* the part of the day between noon and sunset

af´ter·shock *n.* tremors that follow in the wake of an earthquake

af´ter·taste *n.* a taste remaining in the mouth after eating a particular food

af´ter·thought *n.* a notion occurring after a decision or action

af´ter·ward, af´ter·wards *adv.* subsequently; in the time succeeding an event

a·gain´ *adv.* one more; at another time; repeated; furthermore: *again, the poor roads may delay us*

a·gainst´ *prep.* in contact and pressing upon; in comparison to; in opposition to

a·gape´ *adj., adv.* open-mouthed; anything left open, as a door

a´gar *n.* a gelatinous substance obtained from seaweed employed as a culture medium and as a food product

ag´ate *n.* a variegated quartz; a child's marble; in printing, 5½ point type

age *n.* a distinct stage of life; a time in history; the condition of being old —*vi.* to ripen or mature —*vt.* to cause to grow old —**of age** old enough to be legally responsible

a´ged *adj.* advanced in years; characteristic of old age —*n.* elderly persons collectively —**aged´** *adj.* at the age of; brought to a desired state by time, as *an aged steak*

—**ag′ed·ly** *adv.* —**ag′ed·ness** *n.*

age′ism *n.* discrimination based on age; undue preoccupation with age

age′less *adj.* seeming not to change with the passage of time; not limited by time; eternal —**age′less·ly** *adv.* —**age′less·ness** *n.*

a′gen·cy *n.* an active force; the means by which something is done; the business of acting for others; the office of an agent; a division of a governmental department

a·gen′da *n., pl.* **a·gen′da** or **a·gen′dum** a catalogue of aims or goals; a schedule of duties, programs, or events to be discussed or carried out, especially of a business meeting

a′gent *n.* person or thing that serves to change; one who acts for another; an authorized representative

ag·glom′er·ate′ *adj.* densely clustered; gathered into a mass —*n.* things thrown together without discrimination; fused volcanic rock —*vi., vt.* to form into a mass —**ag·glom·er·a′tion** *n.* —**ag·glom′er·a·tive** *adj.*

ag·glu′ti·nate *adj.* joined together, as by adhesion —*vi., vt.* to join, as with glue; to form a new word or term by combining two words; to mass together, as cells, by adhesion —**ag·glu′ti·nant** *adj.*

ag·glu·ti·na′tion *n.* a mass formed by adhesion; a combination of word elements which form a new word —**ag·glu′ti·na·tive** *adj.*

ag·gran′dize *vt.* to make great or greater; to make to seem greater; to exalt —**ag·gran′dize·ment** *n.* —**ag·gran′diz·er** *n.*

ag′gra·vate′ *vt.* to make worse; to make more burdensome; to exasperate or annoy —**ag′gra·va′tion** *n.* —**ag′gra·va·tor** *n.*

ag′gre·gate′ *adj.* gathered together; forming a dense cluster; a mixture

of mineral fragments existing naturally, as *aggregate rock* —*n.* a collection; an entire amount; a mixture of mineral fragments, as stones used in making concrete —*vt.* to bring together or collect into a mass; to total or amount to —**ag′gre·gate·ly** *adv.* —**ag′gre·ga′tion** *n.*

ag·gres′sion *n.* an unprovoked act of hostility; the instinct to act in a forceful manner; assertiveness

ag·gres′sive *adj.* characterized by or disposed to hostile or belligerent action; bold and assertive, as *an aggressive salesman* —**ag·gres′sive·ly** *adv.* —**ag·gres′sive·ness** *n.* —**ag·gres′sor** *n.*

ag·grieve′ *vt.* to cause sorrow; to distress

a·ghast′ *adj.* horrified; astonished

ag′ile *adj.* exhibiting physical quickness and dexterity; mentally alert —**ag′ile·ly** *adv.* —**ag′ile·ness**, **a·gil′i·ty** *n.*

ag′i·tate′ *vi.* to stir public interest in by incessant discussion or debate —*vt.* to stir up, attempt to excite; to perturb or trouble; to shake or move sharply and irregularly —**ag′i·tat·ed·ly** *adv.* —**ag′i·ta′tion** *n.* —**ag′i·ta′tor** *n.*

a·glow′ *adj., adv.* glowing

ag·nos′tic *adj.* claiming the inability to prove the existence of God, an afterlife, the mysteries of the universe, etc.; skeptical —*n.* one who embraces the theory of agnosticism; a doubter or questioner

ag·nos′ti·cism *n.* the doctrine that man does not have any valid knowledge; the theory that origins must remain unknown; the belief that the existence of God cannot be proved

a·gog′ *adj., adv.* excited; agitated; in a state of impatient curiosity

a·gon′ic *adj.* forming no angle — **agonic line** an imaginary line

17

along the surface of the earth where magnetic north and true north coincide

ag·o·nize *vi.* to sustain extreme distress; to struggle over —*vt.* to subject to torture; to cause torment, as *an agonizing decision* —**ag´o·niz·ing** *adj.* —**ag´o·niz·ing·ly** *adv.*

ag´o·ny *n.* suffering caused by extreme physical or mental pain; an intense emotion; a violent effort

ag·o·ra·pho´bi·a *n.* the fear of open spaces

a·grar´i·an *adj.* pertaining to the distribution of lands; relating to or furthering agricultural interests — *n.* an advocate for the equitable distribution of farm land or farm income

a·gree´ *vi.* to be of like mind; to consent; to correspond, be equal; to come to terms on, as of a contract —*vt.* to acknowledge

a·gree´a·ble *adj.* pleasurable to the senses; amiable; in accord with —**a·gree·a·bil´i·ty**,   **a·gree´a·bl·ness** *n.* —**a·gree´a·bly** *adj.*

a·greed´ *adj.* brought into harmony; resolved by consent

a·gree´ment *n.* an understanding between two or more parties; a contract

ag´ri·bus´i·ness *n.* non-farm activities or enterprises associated with agriculture, such as the processing, packaging, and distribution of food, or the manufacturing of farm machinery

ag´ri·cul´ture *n.* the science or business that deals with the cultivation of the land, the breeding and raising of livestock, etc. —**ag·ri·cul´tur·al** *adj.* —**ag·ri·cul´tur·al·ly** *adv.*

ag·ri·cul´tur·al·ist, **ag·ri·cul´tur·ist** *n.* one who makes a study of or engages in the business of agriculture

a·gron´o·my, **ag·ro·nom´ics** *n.* the application of scientific principles to the raising of field crops — **ag·ro·nom´ic**, **ag·ro·nom´i·cal** *adj.* —**a·gron´o·mist** *n.*

a·ground´ *adj., adv.* on the shore; stranded —**run aground** of a vessel which touches land in shallow water

a´gue *n.* chills and fever

ah *interj.* an exclamation of surprise, success, gratification, etc.

a·ha´ *interj.* an exclamation of triumph, derision, etc.

a·head´ *adv.* in advance; at the front; early or before due: *arrived ahead of time* —**get ahead** to improve one's lot financially or socially

a·hem´ *interj.* a sound made in the throat to gain attention

aid *n.* the act or effect of providing assistance; one who assists —*vi., vt.* to provide assistance to

aide *n.* a confidential assistant, usually to a person of high rank in the military, business, politics, etc.

AIDS *Acquired Immune Deficiency Syndrome n.* a viral disease that attacks the body´s immune system

ail *vi.* be in poor health; to feel pain or distress —*vt.* to affect with pain or distress —**ail´ing** *adj.*

ail´ment *n.* a slight illness of body or mind

aim *vi.* to have a purpose: *aim to improve*; to point, as a firearm —*vt.* to point at or act against a person, object, etc.: *aim your remarks at the audience* —*n.* the act of aiming; an intention

aim´less *adj.* without purpose —**aim´less·ly** *adv.* —**aim´less·ness** *n.*

air *n.* the atmosphere that surrounds the earth; a light breeze; a tune or melody; a characteristic appearance or manner; an affectation —*vt.* to ventilate or expose to the air; to announce abroad: *give air to one's feelings* —**up in the air** undecided

air bag a safety device designed to protect the occupants of an automobile from being thrown forward in the event of a collision

air´borne´ *adj.* carried by air; in the air, flying

air´ brake´ *n.* a brake controlled by compressed air

air cham´ber *n.* a compartment filled with air such as in a hydraulic system in which air is compressed and expanded to regulate the flow of a fluid

air´ con·di´tion·ing *n.* the process by which the temperature and humidity of inside air can be regulated —**air´·con·di´tioned** *adj.* —**air con·di´tion·er** *n.*

air´craft´ *n.* flying machine

aircraft carrier a ship for carrying airplanes which take off from and land on its deck

air´drop *n.* personnel or supplies delivered by parachute from an aircraft —*vt.* to discharge personnel or supplies by parachute from an aircraft

air ex·press´ *n.* shipment by air, usually of small packages for overnight delivery

air´frame´ *n.* the structural framework of an aircraft, excluding the engine

air´freight´ *n.* freight shipped by air

air gun *n.* a weapon or tool that operates on compressed air

air´hole, air´ hole *n.* a hole made by air under pressure or by which air is allowed to escape; a breathing hole in ice covering a body of water

air´ing *n.* exposure to air, as to freshen or dry; a stroll outdoors; a public debate; a broadcast on radio or television

air´lift´ *n.* the movement of supplies by air —*vt.*, *vi.*

air line *n.* a tube, hose, pipe, etc. for supplying air, as for an internal combustion engine or a deep–sea diver

air´line *n.* an organization operating aircraft for the transport of passengers and cargo; the routes over which aircraft travel

air´lock *n.* an intermediate chamber with carefully controlled air pressure which provides a link between a vessel and it's surrounding environment, as on a submarine or spacecraft

air´mail´ *n.* mail carried by airplane —*vt.*

air´plane´ (*US*) *n.* a fixed–wing aircraft

air pocket *n.* a vertical current of air which can cause aircraft passing through it to rise or fall suddenly

air´port´ *n.* a base for aircraft

air pres´sure *n.* pressure of the atmosphere

air pump *n.* a device for compressing, moving, or removing air

air´speed *n.* the speed of an aircraft measured in relation to the surrounding air rather than to the ground

air´space´ *n.* thearea above a nation's territory and that is subject to its jurisdiction

air´strip *n.* an airport; a stretch of straight, level ground used by aircraft to take off and land

air´tight *adj.* not allowing movement of air in or out; completely closed, with no weakness: *an airtight alibi*

air´waves *n. pl.* the medium through which radio and television signals travel

air´worthy *adj.* of an aircraft which is in proper condition for flight

air´y *adj.* open to the atmosphere; breezy; porous

aisle *n.* a narrow passageway between sections of seats, rows of people, etc.

a·jar′ *adj., adv.* partly open, as a door

a·kin′ *adj., adv.* related by blood; similar in some fashion

à la after the manner of

al′a·bas′ter *n.* a variety of whitish gypsum used for carved statuary, vases, etc. —*adj.* smooth and white, like alabaster

à la carte according to the bill of fare; items, usually food, that are priced and selected individually

a·lac′ri·ty *n.* willingness; readiness; prompt and lively —**a·lac′ri·tous** *adj.*

à la mode′ according to the fashion; in food service, usually denoting a dish served with ice cream as *pie à la mode*

a·larm′ *n.* a warning of danger; a device or sound which alerts or warns; a sudden fright or apprehension —*vt.* to warn of danger; to frighten

a·larm′ing *adj.* causing fright or apprehension —**a·larm′ing·ly** *adv.*

a·larm′ist *n.* one easily alarmed; one who attempts to excite others without just cause

a·las′ *interj.* an expression of disappointment or sorrow

al′ba·core *n.* a tunny; a long-finned salt water food fish of the tuna family

al′ba·tross′ *n.* sea bird of the South Seas; a symbol of hardship or affliction

al·be′it *conj.* although; even though; notwithstanding

al·bi′no *n.* a person, animal, or plant lacking natural pigmentation

al′bum *n.* a blank book for holding a collection of photographs, autographs, stamps, etc.; a sound recording containing multiple selections

al·bu′men *n.* any of a number of proteins as found in eggs, milk, etc. —**al·bu′mi·nous** *adj.*

al′che·my *n.* an ancient art dedicated to unlocking the mysteries of universal healing, eternal youth, and the changing of base metals into gold

al′co·hol *n.* a clear liquid used as a solvent or intoxicant; the intoxicant contained in beer, wine and distilled liquor; any beverage containing alcohol

al·co·hol′ic *adj.* containing alcohol; caused by alcohol or alcoholism — *n.* one suffering from alcoholism

al′co·hol·ism *n.* a condition marked by the habitual and excessive consumption of alcoholic beverages

al′cove *n.* a recess connected to a large room; a secluded retreat

ale *n.* a type of beer

ale′house *n.* a place where beer is sold for consumption on premises

a·lert′ *adj.* ready for action; bright; lively —*n.* a warning signal; an attitude of preparedness —*vt.* to prepare for action; to warn of an impending threat —**on the alert** prepared; watchful —**a·lert′ly** *adv.* —**a·lert′ness** *n.*

al·fres′co, al fres′co *adj.* occuring out of doors, as *dining alfresco*, a picnic —*adv.* in the open air

al′gae *pl. n., sing.* **al′ga** any of a number of simple organisms that live and grow in water

al′ge·bra *n.* a mathematical system that uses highly formalized rules of procedure and symbols to represent numbers —**al·ge·bra′ic, al·ge·bra′i·cal** *adj.* —**al·ge·bra′i·cal·ly** *adv.*

al′go·rithm *n.* a systematic method of problem solving; a set of computer instructions that has a specific beginning and end

a′li·as *n.* an assumed name

al′i·bi *n.* a defensive plea by one accused that establishes whereabouts at the time of a crime; any excuse

a·li·en *adj.* foreign; owing allegiance to another country; strange or unfamiliar; inconsistent or contrary: *conduct alien to his character* —*n.* a person who is not a citizen of the country in which he resides; a person of another country; a stranger

al·ien·a·ble *adj.* that can be legally transferred, as property

al·ien·ate *vt.* to antagonize or estrange; to transfer property or title to another

al·ien·a·tion *n.* a feeling of not belonging; indifference

a·light *adj., adv.* lighted, as a fire — *vi.* to get off or dismount; to descend and land or perch, as a bird from flight

a·lign *vt.* to bring or arrange into a line; to adjust, as *to align the wheels of a car*; to identify with a cause: *aligned with the conservationists* —*vi.* to come into line — **a·lign·ment** *n.*

a·like *adj.* matching in some way; equivalent —*adv.* in like manner

al·i·ment *n.* food, nourishment; something that provides nourishment —**al·i·men·tal** *adj.* —**al·i·men·tal·ly** *adv.*

al·i·men·ta·ry *adj.* pertaining to food or nutrition; supplying nutrition — **al·i·men·ta·tion** *n.*

alimentary canal the path traveled by food through the body

al·i·mo·ny *n.* an allowance for living expenses paid by one party to the other of a dissolved marriage

a·line *vi.* to come into line —*vt.* to arrange or bring into line; to come or bring into agreement with — **a·line·ment** *n.*

a·live *adj.* functioning; alert; in existence; animated —**alive with** abounding: *a campus alive with students*

al·ka·li *n.* a soluble substance that neutralizes acids —**al·ka·line** *adj.*

—**al·ka·lin·i·ty** *n.*

al·ka·loid *n.* an alkaline substance in plants, etc.

all *adj.* entire; greatest possible: *in all respects*; primarily; *the giraffe is all neck and legs* —*n.* entirety: *he gave his all* —*pron.* everyone or each one; everything —*adv.* entirely; exclusively: *it's all about the economy*; for each; *the score is tied at one all* —**above all** most important —**after all** nevertheless —**all but** almost: *the job is all but finished* —**all in** tired —**all in all** all together; all things considered — **all out** without constraint: *an all out effort* —**at all** under any condition; in any way

al·lay *vt.* to calm; to reduce in intensity, alleviate

al·le·ga·tion *n.* an assertion made without proof

al·lege *vt.* to attest; to assert, especially without proof; to plead in support or denial of a claim —**al·lege·a·ble** *adj.* —**al·lege·er** *n.*

al·leg·ed *adj.* purported or asserted, but not proven —**al·leg·ed·ly** *adv.*

al·le·giance *n.* loyalty, as to a cause; an obligation of loyalty, as to a government or private organization

al·le·gor·ic, al·le·gor·i·cal *adj.* pertaining to or consisting of allegory —**al·le·gor·i·cal·ly** *adv.*

al·le·go·ry *n.* literature or art that uses people, animals, etc. as symbolic representations of abstract concepts; the symbols employed in such literature; any symbolic representation: *the owl is an allegory for wisdom*

al·ler·gen *n.* any substance capable of producing an allergic reaction

al·ler·gic *adj.* caused by an allergy; susceptible to, as an allergen; having an aversion: *he seems allergic to hard work*

al·ler·gist *n.* a physician who specializes in the diagnosis and treatement of allergies

al′ler·gy *n.* unusual sensitivity to certain substances, such as dust or pollen

al·le′vi·ate′ *vt.* to relieve or make easier to bear; to lessen **—al·le′vi·a′tion** *n.* **—al·le′vi·a′tor** *n.*

al·le′vi·a′tive, al·le′vi·a·to·ry *adj.* tending to relieve, as in severity

al′ley *n.* a narrow street or passageway, esp. between or behind buildings **—al′ley·way** *n.*

al·li′ance *n.* a formal agreement, as between countries or persons; a union, as by treaty, blood, or marriage

al·lied′ *adj.* closely related; associated or affiliated, as by treaty or relationship

al′li·ga′tor *n.* an American or Chinese reptile, similar to the crocodile with a shorter, wider snout

al·lit′er·a′tion *n.* a series of words beginning with the same consonant sound: "Peter Piper picked a peck…" **—al·lit′er·a·te** *vi., vt.* **—al·lit′er·a·tive** *adj.* **—al·lit′er·a·tive·ly** *adv.*

al′lo·cate *vt.* to allot or assign a share; to designate for a particular purpose

al′lo·ca′tion *n.* a thing or amount set aside

al·lot′ *vt.* to apportion to; to distribute by lot **—al·lot′ment** *n.*

all′-out′ *adj.* wholehearted, concentrated

al·low′ *vt.* permit to have, happen, do, etc.; to acknowledge as true; to provide for: *allow extra money for incidentals* **—allow for** consider a condition: *allow for his inexperience* **—al·low′a·ble** *adj.*

al·low′ance *n.* that which is allowed; a fixed amount available or budgeted for a particular purpose: *an allowance for expenses*; a discount: *a trade-in allowance*; a variance to be reckoned due to circumstances: *make an allowance for traffic*

al′loy *n.* a mixture of metals; anything that that lessens value or purity **—vt.** to combine metals to make an alloy; to make metal less pure by mixing

all′-time′ *adj.* unparalleled to the present

al·lude′ *vi.* to refer to casually or indirectly

al·lure′ *vt.* to tempt; to attract **—vi.** to be subtly attractive or seductive **—n.** appeal; the ability to attract; a quality that attracts **—al·lur′er** *n.*

al·lur′ing *adj.* appealing; attractive; seductive **—al·lur′ing·ly** *adv.* **—al·lur′ing·ness** *n.*

al·lu′sion *n.* a casual or indirect reference **—al·lu′sive** *adj.* **—al·lu′sive·ness** *n.*

al·lu′vi·um *n.* soil deposited gradually by a moving body of water **— al·lu′vi·al** *adj.*

al′ly *n.* a person or group unified with another for a common purpose **—vt.** to unite for a purpose **— vi.** to enter into an alliance; to become united or associated

al′ma·nac *n.* a yearly calendar or book containing information about the weather and tides, astronomical information, etc.

al′mond *adj.* of the taste, color, etc. of an almond **—n.** the edible kernel of the fruit of the almond tree or the tree itself

al′most, al·most′ *adj., adv.* close to; very nearly

alms *n., sing. & pl.* a donation made to a poor person

a·lone′ *adj., adv.* unaccompanied; detached; excluding all others; *he alone knows why*; unique, without equal

a·long′ *adv.* tracing the length of; progressing beside or in the company of; advanced in distance or time: *well along the way* **—prep**

following the path of: *along the road* —**all along** the entire time; from the beginning —**get along** to persevere in spite of adversity; to live in harmony

a·loof´ *adj.* distant; in a reserved manner —*adv.* apart, but nearby —**a·loof´ly** *adv.* —**a·loof´ness** *n.*

a·loud´ *adv.* audibly; out loud

al´pha·bet´ *n.* the symbols of a written language

al´pha·bet´ic, al´pha·bet´i·cal *adj.* of a written language; arranged in the order of the alphabet —**al·pha·bet·i·za´tion** *n.* —**al´pha·bet·ize** *vt.*

al·pha·nu·mer´ic *adj.* comprised of both letters and numbers

al·read´y *adv.* by this time or a time referred to

al´tar *n.* a place for sacred offerings; the front of a church or focus of any place of worship

al´ter *vt.* to modify; to adjust the fit of a garment; to castrate or spay —*vi.* to undergo change, as in appearance or manner —**al´ter·a·ble** *adj.* —**al·ter·a´tion** *n.*

al´ter·cate´ *vi.* to quarrel; to argue bitterly —**al´ter·ca´tion** *n.*

al´ter·nate *adj.* every other; following by turns —*vt.* to arrange or use in turn —*vi* to occur by turns; to take turns —*n.* a temporary substitute —**al´ter·nate·ly** *adv.* —**al´ter·nate·ness** *n.*

al´ter·na´tion *n.* a changing back and forth from one condition or state to another

al·ter´na·tive *adj.* providing a choice —*n.* a choice between two things; one of the options available; something that must be decided: *what is the alternative?* —**al·ter´na·tive·ly** *adv.*

al·though´ *conj.* even though

al·tim´e·ter *n.* an instrument for measuring altitude

al´ti·tude´ *n.* the height or elevation

from a reference point, as above ground or sea level; in astronomy, the angle of a celestial body in relation to the horizon —**al·ti·tu´di·nal** *adj.*

al´to´ *n.* the musical range between tenor and mezzo–soprano

al´to·geth´er *adv.* in all; all things being considered

al´tru·ism *n.* unselfish regard for the welfare of others —**al´tru·ist** *n.* —**al·tru·is´tic** *adj.* —**al·tru·is´ti·cal·ly** *adv.*

a·lum´na *n., pl.* **a·lum´nae** a female who has attended or graduated from a school

a·lum´nus *n., pl.* **a·lum´ni** a person, esp. a male, who has attended or graduated from a school

al´ways *adv.* for all time; every time

A.M., amplitude modulation a means of radio broadcasting

a·mal´gam *n.* a combination of mercury and another metal; any mixture or combination

a·mal´ga·mate *vt.* to combine with mercury; to unite or integrate: *amalgated industries* —*vi.* to become combined; to mix with another metal —**a·mal´ga·ma·tive** *adj.* —**a·mal´ga·ma·tor** *n.*

a·man´u·en´sis *n., pl.* **a·man´u·en´ses** one employed to copy manuscripts or to take dictation; a secretary

a·mass´ *vt.* to accumulate for oneself, as wealth —**a·mass´a·ble** *adj.* —**a·mass´er** *n.* —**a·mass´ment** *n.*

am´a·teur *adj.* of that done or performed by one lacking professional skill or standing —*n.* one who engages in an activity for pleasure only, rather than for profit; one who lacks the skill of a professional —**am´a·teur·ism** *n.*

am·a·teur´ish *adj.* lacking the skill of a professional —**am·a·teur´ish·ly** *adv.* —**am·a·teur´ish·ness** *n.*

a·maze´ *vt.* to fill with wonder or

surprise; to astonish —**a·maz´ed·
ly** *adv.* —**a·maz´ed·ness, a·maze´
ment** *n.*

am·bas´sa·dor *n.* the highest ranking diplomat in an embassy —**am·
bas·sa·do´ri·al** *adj.* —**am·bas´sa·
dor·ship** *n.*

am´bi·ance, am´bi·ence *n.* the
character of a place; atmosphere

am´bi·dex´trous *adj.* able to use
both hands equally well; skillful,
dexterous —**am·bi·dex·ter´i·ty,
am´bi·dex´trous** *n.* —**am´bi·dex´
trous·ly** *adv.*

am´bi·ent *adj.* encompassing; of the
surrounding area

am·big´u·ous *adj.* not clear; vague;
open to misinterpretation; possible
to be understood in more than one
way —**am´bi·gu´i·ty** *n.*

am·bi´tion *n.* a firm aspiration to
attain a particular goal; a desired
goal; passion or energy, as for
work or play

am·bi´tious *adj.* marked by aspiration; desirous; eager; difficult: *an
ambitious agenda* —**am·bi´tious·ly**
adv. —**am·bi´tious·ness** *n.*

am·biv´a·lent *adj.* uncertain, especially as related to contradictory
emotions; unsure how to proceed
—**am·biv´a·lence** *n.* —**am·biv´a·
len·cy** *adj.* —**am·biv´a·lent·ly** *adv.*

am´bu·lance *n.* a vehicle for transporting the sick or injured

am´bu·lant *adj.* moving about

am´bu·late *vi.* to walk or move from
place to place —**am·bu·la´tion** *n.*
—**am´bu·la·tive** *adj.*

am´bu·la·to´ry *adj.* able to walk;
able to move about

am´bus·cade´ *n.* an ambush; a hiding place —*vt.* to attack suddenly
from hiding —**am´bus·cad·er** *n.*

am´bush *n.* a surprise attack from
hiding; those hiding in wait; a deception or trap —*vt.* to lie in wait
for; to attack from hiding

a·mel´io·rate´ *vi., vt.* to make or

become better; to improve —**a·mel´
io·rant** *n.* —**a·me·lio·ra´tion** *n.* —
a·mel´io·ra·tive *adj.*

a·men´a·ble *adj.* agreeable; responsive, as to advice or authority;
open to criticism —**a·me·na·bil´
i·ty, a·me´na·ble·ness** *n.* —**a·me´
na·bly** *adv.*

a·mend´ *vt.* to improve; to change or
correct; to free or fault or error —
vi. to improve one's behavior —
a·mend´a·ble *adj.* —**a·mend´a·ble·
ness** *n.* —**a·mend´er** *n.*

a·mend´a·to·ry *adj.* serving to correct or improve

a·mend´ment *n.* a correction; a
removal of fault or error; an addition to a document which alters or
adds to it

a·mends´ *pl. n.* compensation for a
wrong; an apology

a·men´i·ty *n.* a pleasant quality;
something that makes one more
comfortable

A·mer·i·ca´na *n.* things typically
American; papers, antiques, etc.
associated with American history
and customs

A·mer´i·can·ism *n.* a manner of
speech, custom, etc. peculiar to
the people of the United States; a
fondness for or loyalty to the U.S.
and its institutions

am´e·thyst *n.* bluish–violet type of
quartz; a bluish–violet color

a´mi·a·ble *adj.* friendly; good–natured —**a·mi·a·bil´i·ty, a´mi·a·ble·
ness** *n.*

am´i·ca·ble *adj.* agreeable; of a congenial manner; —**am·i·ca·bil´i·ty,
am´i·ca·ble·ness** *n.* —**am´i·ca·bly**
adv.

a·mid´, a·midst´ *prep.* among; in the
middle of

a·mi´no ac´id organic acid containing the amino group NH_2, part
of the protein molecule

a·miss´ *adj.* out of order; improper,
faulty —*adv.* wrongly; in an

improper fashion —**take amiss** to be offended

am·i·ty *n.* friendly relations; good will

am·me·ter *n.* an instrument for measuring the strength of an electric current

am·mu·ni·tion *n.* any projectile fired from a weapon; an explosive used as a weapon; information used to attack or defend

am·ne·si·a *n.* loss of memory due to shock or injury —**am·ne·si·ac** *n.,* *adj.* —**am·ne·sic, am·nes·tic** *adj.*

am·nes·ty *n.* an official pardon, esp. for a political offender —*vt.* to grant a pardon to

am·ni·on *n.* the membranous sac surrounding a fetus

a·moe·ba *n.* a one celled protozoan, characterized by indefinite shape and reproduction by splitting — **a·moe·bic** *adj.*

a·mong·, a·mongst· *prep.* in the midst of; included within an array

a·mor·al *adj.* without recognition or concern of ethical distinction; lacking a sense of right or wrong —**a·mor·al·i·ty** *n.* —**a·mor·al·ly** *adv.*

am·o·rous *adj.* loving; passionate; suggesting desire: *an amorous gaze*; connected with love: *an amorous letter* —**am·o·rous·ly** *adv.* — **am·o·rous·ness** *n.*

a·mor·phous *adj.* lacking definite form or shape; unorganized — **a·mor·phism, a·mor·phous·ness** *n.* —**a·mor·phous·ly** *adv.*

am·or·tise (*Brit.*), **am·or·tize** (US) *vt.* to discharge a debt by regular payments —**am·or·tis·a·ble, am·or·tiz·a·ble** *adj.* —**am·or·ti·sa·tion, am·or·ti·za·tion** *n.* —**am·or·tise·ment, am·or·tize·ment** *n.*

a·mount· *n.* a total; a quantity; the entire value or effect —*vi.* to add up to; be equal to: *the lack of response amounts to rejection*

am·per·age, am·per·age *n.* the strength of an electrical current

am·pere *n.* standard unit for measuring the strength of an electric current

am·per·sand *n.* a symbol (&) representing the word *and*

am·phet·a·mine *n.* a stimulant used as a medication for colds, depression, etc.

am·phib·i·an *n.* an animal that functions equally well in water or on land; a craft able to navigate on land or water; an airplane designed to take off from either land or water

am·phib·i·ous *adj.* living or operating in water and on land —**am·phib·i·ous·ly** *adv.* —**am·phib·i·ous·ness** *n.*

am·phi·the·a·ter *n.* a round building or room with tiers of seats rising from a central open stage or arena

am·ple *adj.* large in capacity, size, etc.; more than enough; sufficient to meet ones needs —**am·ple·ness** *n.* —**am·ply** *adv.*

am·pli·fi·er *n.* an electronic device that strengthens electrical impulses

am·pli·fy *vt.* to increase or expand —**am·pli·fi·ca·tion** *n.*

am·pli·tude· *n.* extent, largeness, fullness

am·pul, am·pule *n.* a vial of medication, often for injection

am·pu·tate· *vt.* to cut off, usually by surgery —**am·pu·ta·tion** *n.* —**am·pu·tee·** *n.*

a·muck· *adj.* in a frenzy; crazed — *adv.* in a barbarous manner

am·u·let *n.* a magical charm or talisman

a·muse· *vt.* to occupy pleasantly, to entertain; to induce a smile or laughter —**a·mus·a·ble** *adj.* — **a·mus·er** *n.*

a·mus·ing *adj.* entertaining; causing

laughter —a·mus´ing·ly adv. —
a·mus´ing·ness n.

a·muse´ment n. a diversion; that
which brings pleasure; a feeling of
enjoyment brought on by a diversion

amusement park a recreational area
featuring rides, refreshments,
shows, etc.

an adj., indef. art. each or any; an
article before words beginning with
a vowel sound

a·nach´ro·nism n. the representation of something existing or occurring out of it proper order;
something placed out of its appropriate time —a·nach·ro·nis´tic,
a·nach´ro·nous adj.

an·aer´obe n. a microorganism that
flourishes in the absence of oxygen
—an·aer·o´bic adj. —an·aer·o´bic·
al·ly adv.

an·aes·the´si·a (Brit.) n. a loss of
sensation caused by disease; a
loss of sensitivity to pain produced
by an anaesthetic

an·aes·the·si·ol·o·gy (Brit.) n. the
study of anaesthesia and its effects
—an·aes·the·si·ol´o·gist (Brit.) n.

an·aes·thet´ic (Brit.) adj. pertaining
to anaesthesia; producing anaesthesia: making insensitive to pain
—n. an agent that produces a loss
of feeling —an·aes·thet´i·cal·ly
adv.

an·aes´the·tise (Brit.) vt. to render
insensitive to pain, as by administering an anaesthetic —an·aes·
the·ti´za·tion n.

an·aes´the·tist (Brit.) n. one who
administers anaesthetics

an´a·gram´ n. a word or phrase
made by rearranging the letters of
another word or phrase —an·a·
gram·mat´ic, an·a·gram·mat´i·cal
adj. —an·a·gram·mat´i·cal·ly adv.

an·al·ge´si·a n. a deadening of pain
without loss of consciousness

an·al·ge´sic n. a medication that

relieves pain — adj. causing anal-
gesia

an´a·log (US) adj. of data represented by a continuous variable,
such as for a slide rule, sound
level, etc. —an·a·log´ic, an·a·log´i·
cal adj. —an·a·log´i·cal·ly adv.

analog device (US) a mechanism
which represents physical relationships, as a thermometer or
analog computer

an´a·logue (Brit.) adj. of data represented by a continuous variable,
such as for a slide rule, sound
level, etc.

analogue device (Brit.) a mechanism
which represents physical relationships, as a thermometer or
analogue computer

a·nal´o·gous adj. similar in certain
ways —a·nal´o·gous·ly adv. —
a·nal´o·gous·ness n.

a·nal´o·gy n. a partial similarity; a
comparison based on some similarity between two things —
a·nal´o·gist n.

a·nal´y·sis n. the division of a thing
into parts for examination

an´a·lyst n. one skilled in careful
examination or study, as a systems analyst; a psychoanalyst

an´a·lyt´ic, an·a·lyt´i·cal adj. pertaining to analysis; separating into
basic parts; expert in analysis, as
an analytical mind; psychoanalitic
—an·a·lyt´i·cal·ly adv.

an·a·lyt´ics n. the branch of logic
concerned with analysis

an´a·lyse (Brit.), an´a·lyze (US) vt. to
break down into parts for detailed
study; to make a chemical or
mathematical analysis; to psycho-
analyze —an·a·ly·sa´tion, an·a·ly·
za´tion n.

an·a·phy·lac´tic adj. pertaining to a
severe reaction to a usually harmless substance introduced into the
body for the second time —an·a·
phy·lac´ti·cal·ly adv.

an·a·phy·lax´is *n.* abnormal sensitivity to a substance, such as a drug or sting; anaphylactic shock

anaphylactic shock a severe allergic reaction caused by the second exposure to usually harmless substance

an·ar´chic, an·ar´chi·cal *adj.* endorsing or promoting anarchy; lacking order —**an·ar´chi·cal·ly** *adv.*

an´arch·y *n.* the absence of government or governmental authority —**an´ar·chism** *n.* —**an´arch·ist** *n.* —**an·ar·chis´tic** *adj.*

a·nath´e·ma *n.* an ecclesiastical ban, as of a person or book for heresy; a denunciation or condemnation; a person so condemned; anything greatly disliked

a·nat´o·mist *n.* a specialist in or student of anatomy

a·nat´o·mise (*Brit.*), **a·nat´o·mize** (*US*) *vt.* to dissect for study; to study and analyze in great detail —**a·nat·o·mi·sa´tion, a·nat·o·mi·za´tion** *n.*

a·nat´o·my *n.* the scientific study of the structure of an animal or plant; the physical structure of an organism; dissection of a plant or animal for study; any detailed study or analysis —**an·a·tom´ic, an·a·tom´i·cal** *adj.* —**an·a·tom´i·cal·ly** *adv.*

an´ces·tor *n.* a forefather; one from whom a person is descended; anything considered as a forerunner of a later form —**an·ces´tral** *adj.* —**an·ces´tral·ly** *adv.* —**an´ces·try** *n.*

an´chor *n.* a heavy device that can be lowered in the water to hold a ship or boat in place by its weight or by hooks that grip the bottom; any device that secures something in place —*vt.* to hold in place with an anchor; to fix firmly —*vi.* to lie at anchor, as of a ship; to be or become fixed in place

an´chor·age *n.* a place where ships lie at anchor; a fee charged for anchoring

an´cho·rite *n.* a religious recluse —**an·cho·rit´ic** *adj.*

an´chor·per´son *n.* the primary reporter for a newscast

an´cient *adj.* very old; antiquated —*n.* one who lived in the distant past; a very old person —**an´cient·ly** *adv.* —**an´cient·ness** *n.*

an´cil·lar·y *adj.* secondary; auxiliary

and *conj.* as well as; added to; to: *try and do better*

and´i·ron *n.* a metal support for wood in a fireplace

an·drog´y·nous *adj.* bearing both male and female characteristics; unisex: of a style that is not distinctly male or female, as in dress or appearance —**an·drog´y·nous·ly** *adv.* —**an·drog´y·ny** *n.*

an´droid *n.* an automaton that resembles a human

an´ec·dot·al *adj.* characterized by or consisting of anecdotes —**an´ec·dot·al·ly** *adv.*

an´ec·dote *n.* a short amusing story —**an·ec·dot´ic, an·ec·dot´i·cal** *adj.* —**an·ec·dot´i·cal·ly** *adv.*

a·ne´mi·a *n.* a deficiency of red blood corpuscles or hemoglobin in the blood

a·ne´mic *adj.* pertaining to or afflicted with anemia; listless; lacking vitality —**a·ne´mi·cal·ly** *adv.*

an·e·mom´e·ter *n.* a device for measuring the force of wind

an·er·oid *adj.* not using fluid, as *an aneroid barometer*

an´es·the·si·a (*US*) *n.* a loss of sensation caused by disease; a loss of sensitivity to pain produced by an anesthetic

an´es·the·si·ol´o·gy (*US*) *n.* the study of anesthesia and its effects —**an·es·the·si·ol´o·gist** (*US*) *n.*

an´es·thet´ic (*US*) *adj.* pertaining to

anesthesia; producing anesthesia: making insensitive to pain —*n.* an agent that produces a loss of feeling —**an´es·thet´i·cal·ly** (*US*) *adv.*

an·es´the·tist (*US*) *n.* one who administers anesthetics

an·es´the·tize (*US*) *vt.* to render insensitive to pain, as by administering an anesthetic —(*US*) **an·es·the·ti´za·tion** *n.*

an´eu·rysm, an´eu·rism *n.* swelling in an artery at a point weakened by disease or injury

a·new´ *adv.* again; freshly

an´gel *n.* a supernatural being; a guiding influence; a financial backer

an´ger *n.* strong displeasure or hostility; ire; wrath —*vt.* to make irate; to provoke —*vi.* to become angry

an·gi´na pec´to·ris a heart condition marked by severe pains in the chest

an´gle *n.* an ulterior motive; stratagem; point of view; fishing tackle; a figure made by the intersection of two lines or planes —*vi.* to attempt to obtain by cunning; to fish with a hook and line —**an´gu·lar** *adj.* — **an·gu·lar´i·ty** *n.*

an´gler *n.* a fisherman; one who schemes to achieve an end

an´gli·cise (Brit.), **an´gli·cize** (US) *vi.* to become more like the English — *vt.* to appropriate an English trait or style

an´gling *n.* the skill of fishing with special hooked lures

An·glo´phile *n.* a devotee of England and its institutions

an·gos·tu´ra bark the bark of a South American tree used as a tonic or flavoring

Angostura® bitters a bitter flavoring, used primarily in beverages and desserts

an´gry *adj.* feeling or showing displeasure; threatening: *angry skies*; indicating anger: *an angry letter*

—**an´gri·ly** *adv.* —**an´gri·ness** *n.*

angst *n.* a feeling of trepidation or apprehension

ang´strom, ang´strom u´nit a factor for the measure of wavelength; a hundred millionth of a centimeter

an´guish *n.* severe misery, as from grief or pain —*vi.* be distressed —*vt.* to cause distress —**an´guished** *adj.*

an´gu·lar *adj.* of or like an angle; bony, gaunt; lacking grace: *angular gestures* —**an´gu·lar·ly** *adv.* — **an´gu·lar·ness** *n.*

an·hy´drous *adj.* of a chemical compound which contains no water

an·i·mad·ver´sion *n.* severe criticism or condemnation

an·i·mad·vert´ *vi.* to comment, especially adversely or critically; to censure

an´i·mal *n.* a living creature distinguished from plants mainly by a need for complex organic nutrients and the inability to perform photosynthesis; the creatures of the earth, separate from man; a brutal human —*adj.* pertaining to animals; like an animal

an´i·mate *adj.* living; lively —*vt.* bring to life or make lifelike; to stimulate, inspire

an´i·mated *adj.* spirited; lively; vivacious —**an´i·mat·ed·ly** *adv.*

an´i·ma´tion *n.* the process of imparting life, spirit, interest, etc.; the condition of being alive; the process and technique of preparing animated cartoon drawings — **an´i·ma·tor** *n.*

an´i·mism *n.* the belief in a personal spirit or soul; the belief that inanimate objects possess a spirit or soul —**an´i·mist** *n.* —**an´i·mis´tic** *adj.*

an·i·mos´i·ty *n.* a strong feeling of hostility; hatred

an´i·mus *n.* animosity; an animating energy or purpose

an·ise *n.* a plant bearing aromatic seeds used for flavoring and medicine

an·i·seed *n.* anise seed; the seed of the anise plant valued for its flavor and aroma

an·kle *n.* the joint connecting the foot and the leg

an·nals *pl. n.* a chronological historical record; any historical account; a periodical that reports discoveries, etc. —**an·nal·ist** *n.* —**an·nal·is·tic** *adj.*

an·neal *vt.* to heat and then cool slowly in order to make less brittle, as glass or metal; to strengthen by trial, as of determination

an·ne·lid *adj.* pertaining to any of a group of segmented invertebrates, as earthworms, leeches, etc. —*n.*

an·nex *n.* something added, as to a building; an auxiliary building — **an·nex** *vt.* to add on; to incorporate into, as territory —**an·nex·a·tion** *n.*

an·ni·hi·late *vt.* to destroy entirely; to defeat utterly —**an·ni·hi·la·bil·i·ty** *n.* —**an·ni·hi·la·ble** *adj.* — **an·ni·hi·la·tor** *n.*

an·ni·hi·la·tion *n.* total destruction or elimination

an·ni·ver·sa·ry *n.* a date or celebration occurring at the same time each year; the celebration of a past event; the date of the event

an·no·tate *vt.* to provide a commentary, such as explanatory notes of a literary work —**an·no·ta·tion** *n.* —**an·no·ta·tor** *n.* —**an·no·ta·tive** *adj.*

an·nounce *vt.* to proclaim publicly; to make known; to give notice of the approach or appearance of; a radio or television speaker who delivers periodic messages, provides commentary, etc. —**an·nounce·ment** *n.* —**an·nounc·er** *n.*

an·noy *vt.* to bother; to irritate by some action —*vi.* to be annoying

—**an·noy·ance** *n.* —**an·noy·ing** *adj.* —**an·noy·ing·ly** *adv.*

an·nu·al *adj.* yearly; occuring once a year or every year —*n.* a publication that comes out once a year; a plant that lives only one season — **an·nu·al·ize** *vt.* —**an·nu·al·ly** *adv.*

an·nu·i·ty *n.* an annual allowance; the right to receive or the duty to pay an annual stipend; the periodic payment of money as an investment for future return

an·nul *vt.* to make or declare invalid, as of a law or a marriage; to revoke or cancel —**an·nul·la·ble** *adj.* —**an·nul·ment** *n.*

an·nu·lar *adj.* formed like a ring; marked by rings —**an·nu·lar·i·ty** *n.* —**an·nu·late, an·nu·lat·ed** *adj.* —**an·nu·la·tion** *n.*

an·nun·ci·ate *vt.* to announce —**an·nun·ci·a·tor** *n.*

an·nun·ci·a·tion *n.* a proclamation; the act of proclaiming or announcing

an·o·dyne *adj.* soothing; having power to soothe or eliminate pain —*n.* a medication that eases pain; anything that soothes or comforts

a·noint *vt.* to sprinkle or rub with oil or ointment; to consecrate — **a·noint·er** *n.* —**a·noint·ment** *n.*

a·nom·a·ly *n.* a deviation from the norm; a peculiarity; one who is peculiar or difficult to categorize — **a·nom·a·lis·tic, a·nom·a·lis·ti·cal, a·nom·a·lous** *adj.* —**a·nom·a·lis·ti·cal·ly** *adv.*

an·o·mic *adj.* socially unstable or disorganized —*n.* one who is alienated from normal society

an·o·mie, an·o·my *n.* concern that the values of society have no personal relevance; a condition of society characterized by ineffectual norms or moral standards; individual disorientation that results in antisocial conduct

a·non·y·mous *adj.* of a work lacking

the name of the donor or author; lacking distinctive characteristics —**an·o·nym´i·ty, a·non´y·mous· ness** n. —**a·non´y·mous·ly** adv.

an·oth´er adj., pron. one other; different, though similar in some aspect, as another person, another car, another place

an´ser·ine adj. of or like a goose; foolish or silly

an´swer n. any response to a question, inquiry, or request; an action in kind: retaliation; the solution to a problem —vi. to respond or reply; to prove sufficient to: answer a need; to be accountable: answer for your actions; to correspond: he answers to your description —vt. to speak, write, or act in response; to be sufficient; to correspond —**an´ swer·er** n.

an´swer·a·ble adj. accountable; capable of being responded to — **an´swer·a·bil´i·ty, an´swer·a·ble· ness** n. —**an´swer·a·bly** adv.

answering machine a device that responds to incoming telephone calls and records messages from the caller

ant n. a small communal insect

ant·ac´id adj. correcting acidity —n. an alkali; a remedy for acidity in the stomach

an·tag´o·nism n. animosity; mutual hostility or opposition

an·tag´o·nist n. an adversary; one who or that which opposes, as of a muscle or chemical —**an·tag·o· nis´tic** adj. —**an·tag·o·nis´ti·cal· ly** adv.

an·tag´o·nize´ vt. to oppose or struggle against; to counteract

ant´ bear n. an aardvark

an´te n. the initial stake in a hand of poker; a prize or reward; an inducement to participate —vt. to contribute to the initial stake before a poker hand is dealt; to pay one's share —vi. to pay up

ante up to pay as promised or obligated

ant´eat·er n. any of the mammals or birds that feed mainly on ants

an´te·ce´dent adj. going before, preceding —n. anything that logically precedes; in grammar, a noun or pronoun to which a relative pronoun refers —**an·te·cede´** vt., vi. —**an·te·ce´dence, an·te· ce´den·cy** n. —**an´te·ce´dent·ly** adv.

an´te·cham·ber n. a room which serves mainly as an entranceway to other rooms

an´te·date vt. to backdate; to occur earlier than

an·te·di·lu´vi·an adj. before the Biblical flood; antiquated —n. anything that lived before the Biblical flood; anything very old

an´te·lope´ n. a graceful quadruped allied to the deer

an´te·me·rid´i·an adj. before noon

an·ten´na n., pl. **an·ten´nae, an·ten´ nas** sense organs on the head of an insect, crab, etc.; a device used for the transmission or reception of radio or television signals

an·te·pe´nult n. the third syllable from the end of a word

an·te·pe·nul´ti·mate adj. the third from the end of anything

an·te´ri·or adj. toward or at the front; earlier in time

an´te·room n. a waiting room; an antechamber

an´them n. a hymn; a piece of joyous or triumphal music, often set to words from sacred writing —**na· tional anthem** the official song of a nation or a people

an´ther n. part of the stamen in a flower that holds pollen

an·thol´o·gise (Brit.), **an·thol´o·gize** (US) vi. to compile or publish an anthology —vt. to include in an anthology —**an·thol´o·gis·er, an· thol´o·gist, an·thol´o·giz·er** n.

an·thol´o·gy *n.* a collection of literary selections, as poems, novellas, etc.; an assortment or catalog, as of propositions or comments —**an·tho·log´i·cal** *adj.*

an·tho·zo´an *n.* a class of marine creatures that includes the corals and sea anemones —**an·tho·zo´an, an·tho·zo´ic** *adj.*

an´thra·cite´ *n.* a hard coal that burns with a little flame and gives off substantial heat

an´thrax *n.* an infectious disease of man and some animals

an´thro·poid *adj.* similar to a human being; pertaining to man, apes and monkeys —*n.* any of the larger apes —**an´thro·poid´al** *adj.*

an´thro·pol´o·gy *n.* the scientific study of the customs, culture, etc. of man through the ages —**an·thro·po·log´ic, an·thro·po·log´i·cal** *adj.* —**an·thro·po·log´i·cal·ly** *adv.* —**an·thro·pol´o·gist** *n.*

an·thro·po·mor´phic *adj.* having human form or characteristics — **an·thro·po·mor´phi·cal·ly** *adv.*

an·thro·po·mor´phism *n.* characterizing a spiritual being, natural phenomena, etc. as having human attributes

an·thro·po·mor´phise (*Brit.*), **an·thro·po·mor´phize** (*US*) to attribute human characteristics to —*vt., vi.* to attribute human qualities to things that are not human

an´ti- *prefix* against or opposed to

an´ti·bi·ot´ic *adj.* preventing the growth of bacteria —*n.* a substance that destroys bacteria and other microorganisms —**an´ti·bi·ot´i·cal·ly** *adv.*

an´ti·bod´y *n.* a protein produced in the body to neutralize harmful matter

an´tic *adj.* bizarre; incongruous —*n.* a caper or prank; a ridiculous act

an·tic´i·pate´ *vt.* to expect; to foresee; to be prepared for; to act so as

to forestall; to take or make use of too hastily, as profits not yet available —*vi.* to consider prematurely —**an·tic´i·pa´tion** *n.* —**an·tic´i·pa·tive** *adj.* —**an·tic´i·pa·to·ry** *adj.*

an´ti·cli´max *n.* a reduction in impressiveness or effectiveness; a decline in contrast to a previous rise —**an´ti·cli·mac´tic** *adj.* —**an´ti·cli·mac´ti·cal·ly** *adv.*

an·ti·cli´nal, an·ti·clin´ic *adj.* downward inclination on both sides from a median line, as an upward arch of rock stratum

an´ti·cline *n.* a rock stratum forming an upward bend

an´ti·dote´ *n.* a substance used to counteract or neutralize a poison —**an·ti·dot´al** *adj.* —**an·ti·dot´al·ly** *adv.*

an´ti·freeze *n.* a liquid cooling agent with a low freezing point, used in automobile radiators to prevent freezing

an´ti·gen, an´ti·gene´ *n.* a substance that stimulates the development of antibodies when introduced into an organism —**an·ti·gen´ic** *adj.* —**an·ti·gen´i·cal·ly** *adv.*

an´ti·he·ro *n.* an unlikely champion; one who does not possess the usual qualities attributed to a hero —**an´ti·he·ro´ic** *adj.*

an´ti·his´ta·mine´ *n.* any of a number of synthetic drugs used to treat cold syptoms and some allergies by preventing or reducing the action of histamine —**an´ti·his´ta·min´ic** *adj.*

an·ti·log´a·rithm *n.* the number that results from a base raised to a power by a logarithm

an·ti·ma·cas´sar *n.* a covering used to protect the backs and arms of chairs

an·ti·mag·net´ic *adj.* resistant to or protected from the influence of a magnetic field

an·ti·mat´ter *n.* particles composed of negative protons and positive electrons, the opposite of that in ordinary matter

an´ti·mo·ny *n.* a metallic element used primarily in alloys and pigments

an·ti·neu·tri´no *n.* the antiparticle of the neutrino, lacking electic charge

an·ti·neu´tron *n.* the antiparticle of the neutron, lacking electric charge

an·ti·par´ti·cle *n.* a subatomic particle with charge and magnetic property opposite to its corresponding particle

an·ti·pas´to *n.* an appetizer of delicacies, as smoked or salted fish and meat, cheese, fresh or pickled vegetables, etc.

an·tip´a·thy *n.* a strong or deep-seated aversion or dislike — **an·tip·a·thet´ic, an·tip·a·thet´i·cal** *adj.* —**an·tip·a·thet´i·cal·ly** *adv.*

an´ti·phon *n.* a verse chanted in response, often a group response to a leader; an arrangement of passages for alternate chanting or singing —**an·tiph´o·nal, an´ti·phon´ic, an´ti·phon´i·cal** *adj.* — **an´tiph·o·nal·ly** *adv.*

an´ti·pode *n.* an exact opposite

an·tip´o·des *pl. n.* the people or place on the opposite side of the globe; anything at the opposite extreme

an·ti·py·ret´ic *adj.* preventive or palliative for fever —*n.* a medicine to relieve fever

an·ti·quar´i·an *adj.* of antiquity or the collection of antiquities —*n.* a collector or dealer in antiquities — **an·ti·quar´i·an·ism** *n.*

an´ti·quate *vt.* to make old or obsolete; to make appear old —**an·ti·qua´tion** *n.*

an´ti·quat·ed *adj.* old–fashioned; out of date; no longer useful

an·tique´ *adj.* old; made in an earlier time; in the syle of an ancient time, esp. of ancient Greece or Rome —*n.* a relic; an object valued because of its age; the style of an ancient time —*vt.* to finish so as to resemble an antique —**an·tique´ly** *adv.* —**an·tique´ness** *n.*

an·tiq´ui·ty *n.* ancient history; an ancient relic

an·ti·sep´sis *n.* the prevention of infection by preventing the growth of or destroying harmful bacteria

an´ti·sep´tic *adj.* pertaining to antisepsis; thoroughly clean; capable of destroying harmful bacteria — *n.* a substance that destroys disease–causing microorganisms — **an´ti·sep´ti·cal·ly** *adv.*

an·ti·so´cial *adj.* adverse to social contact or society; opposed to social order; disruptive —**an·ti·so´cial·ly** *adv.*

an·tith´e·sis *n., pl.* **an·tith´e·ses** contrasting thoughts or expressions; the direct opposite: *joy is the antithesis of sorrow*

an·ti·thet´ic, an·ti·thet´i·cal *adj.* being in opposition or antagonistic —**an·ti·thet´i·cal·ly** *adv.*

an´ti·tox´in *n.* an antibody that acts against a disease; a preparation used in treating a disease —**an·ti·tox´ic** *adj.*

an·ti·trust´ *adj.* opposition to practices that are in restraint of trade: pertaining to the regulation of trusts, monopolies, etc.

an·ti·ven´in *n.* antitoxin which protects against snake bite or venom

an´to·nym *n.* a word opposite in meaning to another word —**an·to·nym´ic, an·ton´y·mous** *adj.*

an´trum *n., pl.* **an´tra** a cavity, esp. in a bone; a sinus cavity

a´nus *n.* the opening at the lower end of the alimentary canal

an´vil *n.* a heavy iron or steel block which forms a base for hammering metals, etc.; a fixed base which is struck to create an effect, as the lower contact of a telegraph key

anx·i·e·ty *n.* a feeling of uneasiness or worry; a cause for such feelings; extreme eagerness; a mental state marked by tension or dread

anx´ious *adj.* apprehensive regarding some uncertainty; impatient for the fulfillment of a desire — **anx´ious·ness** *n.* —**anx´ious·ly** *adv.*

an´y *adj.* one or some, without preference as to which —*pron.* one or more out of several —*adv.* at all: *feeling any better,*

an´y·bod·y *pron.* any person —*n.* a person of importance

an´y·how *adv.* in any way whatever; in any case

an´y·more *adv.* at this time: *it's not done anymore*

an´y·one *pron.* any person

an´y·thing *adv.* at all; in any way: *is cricket anything like baseball?* —*n., pron.* a thing of any kind

an´y·way *adv.* in any event; nevertheless

an´y·where *adv.* in any place

a·or´ta *n.* the large artery from the left ventricle of the heart that carries blood to all of the body except the lungs

a·part´ *adj.* separated; disassociated —*adv.* separately; independently —**apart from** with the exception of

a·part´heid *n.* the policy of racial discrimination in South Africa

a·part´ment (*US*) *n.* a room or rooms serving as living quarters

ap·a·thy *n.* a lack of emotion; unconcern; lacking interest —**ap´a·thet´ic, ap´a·thet´i·cal** *adj.* —**ap·a·thet´i·cal·ly** *adv.*

ape *n.* a large tailless primate, as a chimpanzee or gorilla; one who imitates; one who is rude or clumsy —*vt.* to imitate or mimic — **ape´like** *adj.* —**go ape** show great

emotion, as anger or pleasure

a·per·ri·tif´ *n.* a beverage, often wine, served before a meal

ap´er·ture´ *n.* an opening; a hole or slit —**ap´er·tur·al** *adj.* —**ap´er·tured** *adj.*

a´pex *n.* a climax; the highest point

a·pha´sia *n.* loss of the ability to speak or understand language — **a·pha´si·ac, a·pha´sic** *adj., n.*

a·phe´li·on *n.* the point in an orbit farthest from the sun

aph´o·rism *n.* a wise saying; an adage —**aph´o·rist** *n.* —**aph·o·ris´tic, aph·o·ris´ti·cal** *adj.* —**aph·o·ris´ti·cal·ly** *adv.*

aph·ro·dis´i·ac *adj.* intensifying sexual desire —*n.* a food, beverage, etc. which is reputed to intensify sexual desire

a·pi´an *adj.* pertaining to bees

a´pi·ar´y *n.* a place where bees are kept —**a·pi·ar´i·an** *adj.* —**a´pi·a·rist** *n.*

a·piece *adv.* for each; to each

a·plomb *n.* self-confidence; assurance

a·poc´a·lypse´ *n.* the symbolic destruction of evil; a prophetic revelation; total or near total destruction —**a·poc·a·lyp´tic, a·poc·a·lyp´ti·cal** *adj.* —**a·poc·a·lyp´ti·cal·ly** *adv.*

a·poc´ry·pha *pl. n.* writings of questionable authenticity

a·poc´ry·phal *adj.* not genuine; of dubious origin; fictitious —**a·poc´ry·phal·ly** *adv.*

ap´o·gee *n.* in the orbit of a satellite, the point farthest from the earth — **ap·o·ge´al, ap·o·ge´an** *adj.*

a·po·lit´i·cal *adj.* lacking interest in politics; of no importance politically —**a·po·lit´i·cal·ly** *adv.*

a·pol´o·gist *n.* one speaking in defense of a person or cause

a·pol´o·gy *n.* a formal argument or defense; an expression of regret —**a·pol·o·get´ic, a·pol·o·get´i·cal**

adj. —a·pol´o·get´i·cal·ly *adv.* — a·pol´o·gise, a·pol´o·gize *vi.*

ap·o·plec´tic *n.* one subject to attacks of apoplexy —ap·o·plec´tic, ap·o·plec´ti·cal *adj.* exhibiting the symptoms of apoplexy —ap·o·plec´ti·cal·ly *adv.*

a·pos´ta·sy *n.* abandonment of one's political or religious beliefs, principles, etc.

a·pos´tate *n.* one guilty of apostasy —*adj.*

a·pos´ta·tize *vi.* to abandon one's political or religious beliefs, principles, etc.

a·pos´tle *n.* one of the twelve sent by Christ to preach the gospel; a missionary; any devoted advocate — a·pos´tle·ship *n.*

a·pos´to·late *n.* the office, duties, etc. of an apostle

ap·os·tol´ic, ap·os·tol´i·cal *adj.* pertaining to an apostle; in accordance with the practice of the apostles; of the line of succession from the Apostles; papal —ap·os·tol´i·cism, a·pos·to·lic´i·ty *n.*

a·pos´tro·phe´ *n.* a mark (') used to show omission of a letter, to form a possessive, or to form some plurals —ap·os·troph´ic *adj.* —a·pos´tro·phize *vi., vt.*

a·poth´e·car·y *n.* one who prepares prescription medicine —**apothecaries' measure** the system of liquid measure used in preparing prescription medicine —**apothecaries' weight** the system of weights used in preparing prescription medicine

ap´o·thegm *n.* a terse saying; a maxim —ap·o·theg·mat´ic, ap·o·theg·mat´i·cal *adj.* —ap·o·theg·mat´i·cal·ly

a·poth´e·o·sis *n.* the exaltation of a person to divine honors; deification —a·po·the´o·size *vt.*

ap·pal´, ap·pall´ *vt.* to horrify or frighten; to stun —ap·pal´ling,

ap·pall´ing *adj.* —ap·pal´ling·ly, ap·pall´ing·ly *adv.*

ap´pa·ra´tus *n.* a machine or equipment designed for a particular use

ap·par´el *n.* clothing

ap·par´ent *adj.* evident, visible; seeming to be, possible —ap·par´ent·ly *adv.* —ap·par´ent·ness *n.*

ap·pa·ri´tion *n.* a strange or unusual manifestation —ap·pa·ri´tion·al *adj.*

ap·peal´ *vi.* to request aid or comfort; to be looked on favorably: *good food appeals to me*; to plead the rehearing of a case —*vt.* request a hearing in a higher court —*n.* a request for aid or support; a favorable quality; a petition to a higher power —ap·peal·a·bil´i·ty *n.* —ap·peal´a·ble *adj.* —ap·peal´er *n.* —ap·peal´ing·ly *adv.*

ap·pear´ *vi.* to come into view; to seem to be; to be published or issued, as a book; to present oneself in a court of law

ap·pear´ance *n.* that which appears; a semblance; one's demeanor or countenance; publication; attendance, as in court, before an audience, etc.

ap·pease´ *vt.* to calm or soothe, as by granting concessions; to satisfy or please —ap·pease´ment *n.* —ap·peas´a·ble *adj.* —ap·peas´er *n.*

ap·pel´lant *adj.* regarding appeals —*n.* one who appeals

ap´pel·la´tion *n.* a name, title, or designation that identifies a person or thing —ap·pel´la·tive *adj., n.* —ap·pel´la·tive·ly *adv.*

ap·pend´ *vt.* to add; to attach, as an addendum or supplement

ap·pen´dage *n.* a subordinate addition; a subsidiary part —ap·pen´di·cal *n.* —ap·pen·dic´u·lar *adj.*

ap·pend´ant *adj.* attached; allied in a subordinate position

ap·pen·dec´to·my *n.* removal of the appendix

ap·pen´di·ci´tis *n.* inflammation of the vermiform appendix

ap·pen´dix *n., pl.* **ap·pen´dix·es** *or* **ap·pen´di·ces** an addition, such as supplementary material at the end of a book; an outgrowth, such as the vermiform appendix

ap´per·tain´ *vi.* be relevant; to relate to

ap´pe·tite´ *n.* a desire for food or drink; any compelling desire or longing

ap´pe·tiz´er *n.* a small amount of food or drink served before a meal to whet the appetite; a sample that stimulates the desire for more

ap´pe·tiz´ing *adj.* stimulating the appetite; tantalizingly attractive

ap·plaud´ *vi., vt.* to express approval, esp. by clapping the hands; to commend or praise —**ap·plaud´a·ble** *adj.* —**ap·plaud´a·bly, ap·plaud´ing·ly** *adv.* —**ap·plaud´er** *n.*

ap·plause´ *n.* approval shown by clapping of hands

ap´ple *n.* the fruit of the apple tree; the apple tree; various exotic fruits or trees bearing little or no resemblance to the apple —**apple of his or her eye** one who is cherished

ap´ple·jack *n.* brandy distilled from apple cider

ap´ple·sauce *n.* a dish of cooked, spiced and puréed apples; slang for that which is nonsense or not believed

ap·pli´ance *n.* a device, usually mechanical or electircal, designed for a special purpose

ap´pli·ca·ble *adj.* pertinent; appropriate —**ap·pli·ca·bil´i·ty, ap´pli·ca·ble·ness** *n.* —**ap´pli·ca·bly** *adv.*

ap´pli·cant *n.* a candidate, as for a job opening

ap´pli·ca´tion *n.* something applied, as a medication; a formal request, as for employment or admission; the act of putting into effect, as of an ordinance, plan, etc.; close and consistent attention

ap´pli·ca·to·ry *adj.* that can be used; practical

ap´pli·ca·tor *n.* a device for applying a substance to a surface

ap·plied´ *adj.* put into practice; of something practical in contrast to merely theoretical

ap·pli·qué´ *n.* an ornament or embellishment —*vt.* to decorate by applying, as ornaments of one material to the surface of another

ap·ply´ *vi.* to request: *apply for a loan, apply for admission;* to be relevant —*vt.* to put or spread on; to use; to devote to a particular use

ap·point´ *vt.* to name or select

ap·point·ee´ *n.* one selected for a position

ap·point´ment *n.* a scheduled meeting; a position for which one is selected

ap·por´tion *vt.* to distribute in shares —**ap·por´tion·er** *n.* —**ap·por´tion·ment** *n.*

ap·pose´ *vt.* to arrange side by side or opposite —**ap·pos´i·tive** *adj.* —**ap·pos´i·tive·ly** *adv.*

ap´po·site *adj.* pertinent; fit for the purpose

ap·po·si´tion *n.* in immediate connection —**ap·po·si´tion·al** *adj.* —**ap·po·si´tion·al·ly** *adv.*

ap·praise´ *vt.* to set a value for; to estimate the worth of —**ap·prais´al** *n.* —**ap·prais´er** *n.*

ap·pre´ci·a·ble *adj.* sufficient to be noticed; apparent; discernible —**ap·pre´ci·a·bly** *adv.*

ap·pre´ci·ate *vt.* to show gratitude; to recognize and understand, as the opinion of another; to increase in value

ap·pre´ci·a´tion *n.* awareness and recognition, such as for a favor from another, the value or beauty of a thing, etc.; the amount of an increase in value

ap·pre·ci·a·tive *adj.* able to or showing appreciation —**ap·pre´cia·tive·ly** *adv.* —**ap·pre´cia·tive·ness** *n.*

ap´pre·hend´ *vt.* to capture; grasp mentally; await with dread —*vi.* to comprehend —**ap´pre·hen´sion** *n.*

ap·pre·hen´si·ble *adj.* capable of being understood —**ap·pre·hen·si·bil´i·ty** *n.* —**ap·pre·hen´si·bly** *adv.*

ap·pre·hen´sive *adj.* troubled or uneasy, especially about something pending; possessing awareness or understanding —**ap·pre·hen´sive·ly** *adv.* —**ap·pre·hen´sive·ness** *n.*

ap·pren´tice *n.* one learning a trade under the charge of a craftsman; any beginner or learner —*vt.* to accept as an apprentice —**ap·pren´tice·ship** *n.*

ap·prise´, ap·prize´ *vt.* to notify or inform

ap·proach´ *vi.* to draw near —*vt.* to come near; to be similar to; to start or restart: *approach a new job* —*n.* a means of access; a way of doing something —**ap·proach·a·bil´i·ty** *n.* —**ap·proach´a·ble** *adj.*

ap´pro·ba´tion *n.* approval; high regard —**ap´pro·ba·tive, ap·pro´ba·to·ry** *adj.*

ap·pro´pri·ate´ *adj.* suitable or proper under the circumstances —*vt.* to take, often in an improper manner; set apart for a particular use: *monies appropriated to fund the school budget* —**ap·pro´pri·ate·ly** *adv.* —**ap·pro´pri·ate·ness** *n.* —**ap·pro´pri·a·tive** *adj.* —**ap·pro´pri·a´tion** *n.*

ap·prov´al *n.* consent; official sanction; favorably opinion —**on approval** of merchandise that may be examined or tested without obligation to buy

ap·prove´ *vi.* to express approval —*vt.* to give consent; to view favorably —**ap·prov´a·ble** *adj.*

—**ap·prov´ing·ly** *adv.*

ap·prox´i·mate *adj.* near in position or exactness —*vt.* to come near in position or kind —**ap·prox´i·mate·ly** *adv.* —**ap·prox·i·ma´tion** *n.*

ap·pur´te·nance´ *n.* an adjunct or accessory —**ap·pur´te·nant** *adj.*

a´pron *n.* a covering to protect a person's clothes; a covering to protect or adorn furniture; an overlapping piece to shield parts of a machine; the part of a theater stage in front of the curtain

ap´ro·pos´ *adj.* appropriate —*adv.* with respect to, regarding

apse *n.* an extended portion of a building, especially a semicircular, domed recess at the altar of a church

apt *adj.* appropriate; likely, probable; competent, talented —**apt´ly** *adv.* —**apt´ness** *n.*

ap´ti·tude *n.* a natural gift; quickness of understanding

aq´ua *adj.* light blue–green —*n.* a blue–green color

aq´ua·cul´ture *n.* cultivation of plants in water; commercial cultivation of fish

a·quar´i·um *n.* a tank for water plants or animals; a building where sea life is kept for public exhibition

aq´ua·tint *n.* a type of etching in which tints or washes may be produced; the copper plate so produced; the print produced from such a plate

aq´ua vi´tae *n.* alcohol; distilled spirits, as whiskey, rum, etc.

aq´ue·duct´ *n.* a conduit for carrying water

a´que·ous *adj.* watery; formed by or containing water

aq´ui·line *adj.* like an eagle, or its beak; curved or hooked like an eagle's beak

ar·a·besque´ *n.* an intricate scroll-work design, often found in

Arabian or moorish architecture; a ballet position in which the dancer extends one arm forward, and the other arm and leg backward

Ar´a·bic *adj.* pertaining to the language and culture of Arabia —*n.* any of the dialects of the language of the Middle East

Arabic numerals the figures 0, 1, 2, 3, 4, 5, 6, 7, 8, 9

ar´a·ble *adj.* of land capable of being plowed or cultivated —*n.* land suitable for cultivation —**ar·a·bil´i·ty** *n.*

a·rach´nid *n.* member of a class of arthropods, such as a spider, mite or scorpion

Ar´a·ma´ic *n.* of a group of Semitic languages, including that which was spoken in Palestine at the time of Christ

ar´bi·ter *n.* one qualified to judge a dispute

ar´bi·trar·y *adj.* based on opinion or chance; discretionary; capricious; autocratic —**ar·bi·trar´i·ly** *adv.* —**ar´bi·trar·i·ness** *n.*

ar´bi·trate *vi.*, *vt.* to settle a dispute by submitting to the judgment of a third party —**ar´bi·tra·ble, ar´bi·tra·tive** *adj.*

ar´bi·tra´tion *n.* the referral of disputes to a disinterested party for settlement

ar´bi·tra´tor *n.* a judge; one chosen to settle disputes between parties

ar´bor *n.* a place shaded by low trees or vines

ar·bo´re·al *adj.* pertaining to trees; situated among trees —**ar·bo´re·al·ly** *adv.*

ar·bo·res´cent *adj.* treelike in structure; branching —**ar·bo·res´cence** *n.*

ar·bo·re´tum *n.* a botanical garden exhibiting trees

ar´bor·vi´tae *n.* a type of evergreen shrub or tree

arc *n.* a part of a curve

ar·cade´ *n.* a covered passageway, often with shops along the sides

ar·cane´ *adj.* secret; mysterious

arch *adj.* most distinguished; crafty —*n.* a curved structure, often supporting the wall above it —*vi.* to be curved like an arch —*vt.* to form into a curve

ar´chae·ol´o·gy (*Brit.*) *n.* the recovery and study of the places and artifacts of past cultures —**ar·chae·o·log´ic, ar·chae·o·log´i·cal** *adj.* —**ar·chae·ol´o·gist** *n.*

ar·cha´ic *adj.* ancient; old–fashioned

arch´an·gel *n.* an angel of highest rank

ar´cha·ism *n.* an obsolete expression; an antiquated style or usage —**ar´cha·ist** *n.* —**ar·cha·is´tic** *adj.*

arch´bish´op *n.* a church official who supervises bishops

arch·bish´op·ric *n.* the office of an archbishop

arch·dea´con *n.* a church official who oversees the temporal affairs of a diocese —**arch·dea´con·ate** *n.* —**arch·dea´con·ry** *n.* —**arch·dea´con·ship** *n.*

arch´di´o·cese *n.* the jurisdiction of an archbishop

arch·en´e·my *n.* a chief adversary

ar´che·ol´o·gy (*US*) *n.* var. of *archaeology* —**ar·che·o·log´ic, ar·che·o·log´i·cal** *adj.* —**ar·che·ol´o·gist** *n.*

arch´er *n.* one who shoots with a bow and arrow

ar´cher·y *n.* the art of shooting with bow and arrow

ar´che·type *n.* a standard pattern; model —**ar´che·typ·al, ar·che·typ´ic, ar·che·typ´i·cal** *adj.* —**ar·che·typ´i·cal·ly** *adv.*

arch´fiend´ *n.* a principal demon

ar´chi·pel´a·go *n.* a sea with many small islands; a chain of islands

ar´chi·tect´ *n.* one who designs and supervises the building of large structures; one who contrives or arranges: *the chief architect of peace* —**ar·chi·tec´tur·al** *adj.* — **ar·chi·tec´tur·al·ly** *adv.* —**ar´chi·tec´ture** *n.*

ar´chive, ar´chives *n.* a place where records are collected and stored — **ar·chi´val** *adj.*

ar´chi·vist *n.* one who maintains an archive

arch´way *n.* the passage under an arch

arc lamp, arc light a device that creates a high intensity light by means of an electric arc between two electrodes

arc´tic *adj.* of the polar regions

ar´dent *adj.* passionate; intensely enthusiastic; zealous —**ar´dent·cy** *n.* —**ar´dent·ly** *adv.*

ar´dor *n.* passion; enthusiasm

ar´du·ous *adj.* laborious; strenuous —**ar´du·ous·ly** *adv.* —**ar´du·ous·ness** *n.*

a´re·a *n.* a section of land; the extent or scope of anything

area code (*US*) a three digit prefix to a telephone number that identifies the locality to which a call is being placed

a´re·a·way´ *n.* an open space in or around a building; a passageway

a·re´na *n.* an area where sporting events are staged, usually surrounded by seating; any sphere of conflict

ar´gent *adj.* like silver; gray-white — *n.* silver; that which has a silvery quality or color

ar´gen·tine *adj.* silvery —*n.* a silver-white metal of tin and zinc

ar´gil *n.* white clay or potter's earth

ar´gon *n.* an inert gas used in the manufacture of light bulbs

ar´got *n.* the words and phrases peculiar to any group, trade, etc., generally not understood by those outside the group

ar´gue *vi.* to debate or dispute —*vt.* to attempt to prove by reason or evidence —**ar´gu·a·ble** *adj.* —**ar´gu·a·bly** *adv.* —**ar´gu·er** *n.*

ar´gu·ment *n.* a reason offered as proof or confirmation; the art of reasoning; a discussion, debate, or quarrel; —**ar·gu·men·ta´tion** *n.*

ar·gu·men´ta·tive *adj.* disposed to argue, often unnecessarily; characterized by argument, as *an argumentative meeting;* moot or open to question, as *an argumentative view* —**ar·gu·men´ta·tive·ly** *adv.* —**ar·gu·men´ta·tive·ness** *n.*

ar´gyle, ar´gyll *n.* a design of solid blocks or diamonds overlaid with a contrasting design, from the tartan of the clan Campbell of Argyll; socks or stockings made in such a design

a´ri·a *n.* a melody; an elegant solo, as in an opera or oratorio

ar´id *adj.* dry, parched; desolate, barren; dull, uninteresting —**a·rid´i·ty, ar´id·ness** *n.*

a·rise´ *vi.* to rise, as from sitting or lying down; to ascend upward; to originate or emanate from something

ar·is·toc´ra·cy *n.* government by a privileged minority; nobility; the upper class

a·ris´to·crat´ *n.* a member of the aristocracy —**a·ris·to·crat´ic, a·ris·to·crat´i·cal** *adj.* —**a·ris·to·crat´i·cal·ly** *adv.*

a·rith´me·tic´ *n.* the art of calculating by numbers —**ar·ith·met´ic, ar·ith·met´i·cal** *adj.* —**ar·ith·met´i·cal·ly** *adv.*

arithmetic mean the sum of a group of values divided by the number of values in the group

arithmetic progression a sequence of values which, after the first, differ from the previous value by a constant quantity

ark *n.* the ship of Noah; a flat–bottomed boat or scow

ark of the covenant the chest

containing the sacred tablets of the Hebrews

arm *n.* an upper limb of the human body; the part of a garment that covers the arm; the part of a chair that supports the arm; anything the looks like or functions like the human arm; a weapon —*vi.* to prepare for a conflict —*vt.* to provide with weapons; to provide anything needed for an encounter: *armed with information* —**an arm and a leg** an extremely high price —**arm's length** sufficiently distant to preclude intimacy or conspiracy

ar·ma´da *n.* a fleet of warships

Ar´ma·ged´don *n.* any final, decisive battle

ar´ma·ment *n.* all of the weapons and military equipment contained in an arsenal, military installation, airplane, seagoing vessel, etc.; all of the forces equipped for battle in a given area or situation; the act of equipping for war

ar´ma·ture *n.* a piece of soft iron connecting the poles of a magnet; in a motor, the wrapped core which revolves through the magnetic field; arms or armor; protective devises for defense, as an animal's shell or a plant's thorns

arm´chair *n.* a chair with sides to support the arms

ar´mis´tice *n.* a truce; a temporary cessation of hostilities

ar·moire´ a large cabinet or cupboard, originally for storing arms, now often used for dinnerware or clothing

ar´mor *n.* any protective covering; the armored vehicles of war —*vt.* to don armor

ar´mored *adj.* protected by armor; a military unit equipped with armored vehicles

ar´mor·er *n.* a manufacturer of arms; the custodian of small arms in a military unit

ar´mor·y *n.* place where arms are manufactured or stored

ar´my *n.* body of soldiers trained for war; a large number of anything

a·ro´ma *n.* a smell; an agreeable odor; a subtle, distinctive quality —**ar´o·mat´ic, ar´o·mat´i·cal** *adj.* —**ar·o·mat´i·cal·ly** *adv.*

a·round´ *adv.* so as to surround or encompass; in the opposite direction; from place to place; in proximity —*prep.* encircling; on the other side of; in proximity —**to come around** to recover consciousness; to be persuaded

a·rouse´ *vt.* to awaken; to stir up, excite —**a·rous´al** *n.*

ar·peg´gi·o *n.* the sounding of the notes of a chord in rapid succession

ar·raign´ *vt.* to accuse; summon to face charges in court —**ar·raign´ment** *n.*

ar·range´ *vt.* to put in a defined order; come to terms; to adapt or orchestrate a musical composition —**ar·rang´er** *n.*

ar·range´ment *n.* that which has been arranged; the fashion in which something is ordered; a musical adaptation or orchestration

ar´rant *adj.* notoriously wicked —**ar´rant·ly** *adv.*

ar·ray´ *n.* an orderly display; fine garments; an impressive gathering —*vt.* to gather in order; to adorn

ar·rear´, ar·rears´ *n.* being behind, as in work or a debt; that which is behind —**in arrears** behind in making payment on a debt —**ar·rear´age** *n.*

ar·rest´ *n.* capture —*vt.* to slow or stop, to capture and detain; to attract or engage, as the attention —**ar·rest´er, ar·res´tor** *n.*

ar·rest´ing *adj.* attracting attention; noteworthy —**ar·rest´ing·ly** *adv.*

ar·rive´ *vi.* to reach a destination; to attain success —**ar·riv´al** *n.*

ar´ro·gant *adj.* overbearing; insolent; marked by excessive pride or vanity —**ar´ro·gance** *n.* —**ar´ro·gant·ly** *adv.*

ar´row *n.* a pointed shaft shot from a bow; a drawing in the shape of an arrow to show direction, etc.

ar´row·root *n.* a nutritious starch obtained from a tropical American plant, used in food preparation; the plant from which the starch is obtained

ar·roy´o *n.* a steep–sided dry gulch; a stream which flows in such a gulch

ar´se·nal *n.* a place where arms and munitions are made or stored

ar´son *n.* the setting of fire to a structure with criminal intent — **ar´son·ist** *n.*

art *n.* skill; any craft requiring skill; creative work —**arts** *pl. n.* the humanities

ar·te´ri·al *adj.* pertaining to the vessels that carry blood from the heart; corresponding to an artery, as in a course which has a complex of secondary paths: *an arterial highway*

ar´ter·y *n.* a vessel that carries blood from the heart; any main channel of communication or transportation

art´ful *adj.* crafty or cunning; ingenious or resourceful, esp. in deception —**art´ful·ly** *adv.* —**art´ful·ness** *n.*

ar·thri´tis *n.* painful inflammation of a joint —**ar·thrit´ic** *adj.* —**ar·thrit´i·cal·ly** *adv.*

ar´thro·pod *n.* any of a large group of invertebrates characterized by segmented limbs and bodies, including insects, spiders, crabs, etc. —**ar·throp´o·dous, ar·throp´o·dal** *adj.*

ar´ti·choke´ *n.* an edible plant resembling the thistle

ar´ti·cle *n.* a written piece; a clause in a document; a separate item

ar·tic´u·lar *adj.* pertaining to the joints —**ar·tic´u·lar·ly** *adv.*

ar·tic´u·late *adj.* clearly spoken —*vi.* to speak clearly; to be jointed —*vt.* to speak clearly; to form with joints —**ar·tic´u·late·ly** *adv.* —**ar·tic´u·late·ness, ar·tic´u·la·cy** *n.* —**ar·tic´u·la´tion** *n.*

ar´ti·fact´ *n.* an article fashioned by humans, especially a relic

ar´ti·fice *n.* a clever scheme

ar·ti·fi´cial *adj.* not natural; imitation; affected —**ar·ti·fi·ci·al´i·ty** *n.* —**ar·ti·fi´cial·ly** *adv.* —**ar·ti·fi´cial·ness** *n.*

ar·til´ler·y *n.* ordnance, cannon; the branch of military using ordnance

ar´ti·san *n.* a craftsman; one working at a skilled trade

art´ist *n.* one who is skilled, particularly one with a sense of style —**ar´tist·ry** *n.*

ar·tiste´ *n.* a skillful performer, as a dancer or singer

ar·tis´tic, ar·tis´ti·cal *adj.* pertaining to arts; aesthetically pleasing; experienced in and receptive to art —**ar·tis´ti·cal·ly** *adv.*

art´less *adj.* without deception; natural; innocent; rough; unskilled; lacking taste —**art´less·ly** *adv.* —**art´less·ness** *n.*

art´y *adj.* affected; ostentatious — **art´i·ness** *n.*

as *adv.* equally—*this car is as fast as the other one*; for example—*to quote, as a verse;* conj. equal to—*such a plan as this cannot fail;* at the same time; in proportion—*the light grows brighter as he draws near;* in the manner that—*do as you are told;* because—*as it was raining, we drove slowly*

as·cend´ *vi.* to move upward; to slope upward; to move from a lower to a higher place, position, etc. —*vt.* to move upward on or along; to succeed, as to a throne

—**as·cend´a·ble, as·cend´i·ble** *adj.* —**as·cend´er** *n.* —**as·cen´sion** *n.* —**as·cent´** *n.*

as·cend´ant, as·cend´ent *adj.* rising; commanding —*n.* a position of prominence or dominance —**as· cend´an·cy, as·cend´en·cy** *n.*

as·cer·tain´ *vt.* to make certain —**as· cer·tain´a·ble** *adj.* —**as·cer·tain´a· bly** *adv.* —**as·cer·tain´ment** *n.*

as·cet´ic *adj.* austere; *n.* one who leads a life of austerity and self-denial —**as·cet´i·cal·ly** *adv.* —**as· cet´i·cism** *n.*

as·cribe´ *vt.* to impute; to attribute as coming from or caused by

a·scor´bic ac´id *n.* vitamin C, a protection against scurvy, found in citrus fruits and some vegetables

as´cot *n.* a type of scarf worn in place of a necktie

a·sex´u·al *adj.* having no distinct sexual organs —**a·sex·u·al´i·ty** *n.* —**a·sex´u·al·ly** *adv.*

ash *n.* the pale, powdery residue left from burning; a tree cultivated for its tough, elastic wood

a·shamed´ *adj.* a feeling of shame engendered by a failing or gaffe; impeded by fear of embarrassment —**a·sham´ed·ly** *adj.*

ash´en *adj.* pale in color, like ashes; pertaining to the wood of the ash tree

a·shore´ *adv.* on the shore; aground

ash´y *adj.* like ashes; ash colored; covered with ashes

a·side´ *adv.* to one side; apart

as´i·nine *adj.* like an ass; stupid or silly —**as´i·nine·ly** *adv.* —**as·i·nin´ i·ty** *n.*

ask *vi.* to make inquiries —*vt.* to question; to inquire about; to make a request; to state a price

a·skance´, a·skant´ *adv.* with suspicion or disapproval; with a sideways glance

a·skew´ *adj., adv.* out of line; to one side

a·slant´ *adj.* slanting; tilted —*adv.* in a slanting position —*prep.* across at an angle

a·sleep´ *adj.* dormant; sleeping; dead —*adv.* into a state of rest

a·so´cial *adj.* avoiding social contact; self-centered

asp *n.* the European viper

as·par´a·gus *n.* a plant with tender, edible shoots

as´pect *n.* the appearance of a thing; consideration from a particular viewpoint

as·per´i·ty *n.* roughness or harshness

as·perse´ *vt.* to accuse falsely; to slander —**as·per´sion** *n.*

as´phalt´ *n.* a tarlike material used for paving, etc. —**as·phal´tic** *adj.* —**as·phal´tum** *n.*

as·phyx´i·ate *vt.* to suffocate —**as· phyx´i·a´tion** *n.*

as´pic *n.* a gelatin garnish or mold

as´pir·ant *adj.* aspiring —*n.* one who tries; a candidate

as´pi·ra´tion *n.* extreme desire; a thing desired

as·pire´ *vi.* to long for or seek after something

as´pi·rin *n.* acetylsalicylic acid, taken as a remedy for headache, fever, etc.

ass *n.* a beast of burden; a stubborn or foolish person

as·sail´ *vt.* to attack violently; to set on with vigor —**as·sail´a·ble** *adj.* —**as·sail´a·ble·ness** *n.* —**as·sail´ant as·sail´er** *n.*

as·sas´si·nate *vt.* to murder; to attack by slander, inuendo, etc. —**as·sas´sin, as·sas·si·na´tor** *n.* —**as·sas·si·na´tion** *n.*

as·sault´ *n.* a vicious attack —*vi., vt.* to make an attack upon —**as·sault´er** *n.*

as·say´ *n.* a testing —*vt.* to test or analyze

as·sem´blage *n.* a gathering

as·sem´ble *vi., vt.* to gather together;

to fit parts or put together —**as·sem´bly** n.

assembly line workers and machines arranged so as to permit the efficient fabrication of products on a large scale

as·sent´ n. agreement; consent —vi. to agree —**as·sent´er, as·sen·tor** n. —**as·sent´ing·ly** adv. —**as·sen´tive** adj. —**as·sen´tive·ness** n.

as·sert´ vt. to declare; to state with conviction —**as·sert´a·ble, as·sert´i·ble** adj. —**as·sert´er, as·ser´tor** n. —**as·ser´tion** n.

as·ser´tive adj. authoritative; insistent —**as·ser´tive·ly** adv. —**as·ser´tive·ness** n.

as·sess´ vt. to set a value for; to impose an amount, as a fine, tax, etc.; to evaluate, as a situation —**as·sess´a·ble** adj. —**as·sess´ment** n. —**as·ses´sor** n.

as´set n. property that has a market value; anything useful or appealing

as·sev´er·ate vt. to declare emphatically

as·sid´u·ous adj. painstaking; diligent —**as·sid´u·ous·ly** adv. —**as·sid´u·ous·ness** n.

as·sign´ vt. to disignate; to appoint; to ascribe —**as·sign´a·ble** adj. —**as·sign·ee´** n. —**as·sign´er, as·sign´or** n. —**as·sign´ment** n.

as·sig·na´tion n. an appointment; a secret or illicit meeting

as·sim´i·late vi. to be absorbed; to become like —vt. to absorb and digest; adapt or conform —**as·sim´i·la´tion** n. —**as·sim´i·la·tive, as·sim´i·la·to·ry** adj.

as·sist´ n. the act of helping —vi. to aid —vt. to help; to work as a helper —**as·sis´tance** n. —**as·sis´tant** n.

as·so´ci·ate adj. joined with others; linked —n. a co-worker; a thing linked in some way —vt. to bring into relationship; to unite, as in friendship; to connect in the mind: associate poetry with romance —vi. to join or be in company with —**as·so´ci·a´tion** n.

as´so·nance n. resemblance in sound; an approximation

as·sort´ vi. to fall into like groups —vt. to classify; to divide into like groups

as·sor´ted adj. consisting of variety; diverse; sorted or classified

as·sort´ment n. a collection or accumulation

as·suage´ vt. to alleviate; to calm; to satisfy

as·sume´ vt. to undertake; to take for granted —**as·sum´a·ble** adj. —**as·sum´a·bly** adv.

as·sump´tion n. act of assuming; supposition —**as·sump´tive** adj.

as·sur´ance n. confidence; conviction; a positive or encouraging statement

as·sure´ vt. to convey confidence; to offer a guarantee —**as·sur´ance** n.

as·sured´ adj. undoubted; sure; confident —**as·sur´ed·ly** adv. —**as·sur´ed·ness** n.

as´ter·isk n. a star–like character (*) used to mark references

asth´ma n. a chronic illness that affects respiration

asth·mat´ic, n. one suffering from asthma —**asth·mat´ic, asth·mat´i·cal** adj. affected with asthma —**asth·mat´i·cal·ly** adv.

a·stig´ma·tism' n. a visual defect causing distorted or blurred vision —**as·tig·mat´ic** adj.

a·stir´ adj., adv. moving about

as·ton´ish vt. to stun, amaze —**as·ton´ish·ing** adj. —**as·ton´ish·ing·ly** adv.

as·ton´ish·ment n. surprise; amazement; a thing which causes such surprise

a·stound´ vt. to overcome with amazement —**as·tound´ing** adj. —**as·tound´ing·ly** adv.

as´tral *adj.* of the stars

a·stray´ *adj., adv.* off the correct path; straying into error or evil

a·stride´ *adj., adv.* with one leg on each side —*prep.* with one leg on each side of

as·trin´gent *adj.* stern; severe; disposed to drawing together organic tissue —**as·trin´gen·cy** *n.* —**as·trin´gent·ly** *adv.*

as´tro·dome *n.* an enclosed field for sporting events, etc.; a transparent structure in some aircraft for making celestial observations

as´tro·labe *n.* an old navigational instrument used to obtain the altitude of planets and stars

as·trol´o·gy *n.* the belief that the stars can influence human affairs —**as·trol´o·ger** *n.* —**as·tro·log´ic, as·tro·log´i·cal** *adj.* —**as·tro·log´i·cal·ly** *adv.*

as´tro·naut´ *n.* a space traveler

as·tro·nau´tics *pl. n.* the science of space travel

as·tro·nom´ic, as·tro·nom´i·cal *adj.* pertaining to astronomy; extremely numerous —**as·tro·nom´i·cal·ly** *adv.*

as·tron´o·my *n.* the study of stars, planets, etc. —**as·tron´o·mer** *n.*

as´tro·phys´ics *n.* the study of the physical properties of stars, planets, etc. —**as·tro·phys´i·cal** *adj.* —**as·tro·phys´i·cist** *n.*

as·tute´ *adj.* exhibiting a keen mind; shrewd —**as·tute´ly** *adv.* —**as·tute´ness** *n.*

a·sun´der *adj.* disconnected —*adv.* in pieces

a·sy´lum *n.* sanctuary; home for the sick

a·sym´me·try *n.* lack of proportion

a·sym·met´ric, a·sym·met´ri·cal *adj.* disproportionate —**a·sym·met´ri·cal·ly** *adv.*

at *prep.* in the exact location; on or near; toward; in the condition of: *two people at odds*

at´a·vism *n.* retrogression to an earlier state —**at´a·vist** *n.* —**at·a·vis´tic** *adj.* —**at·a·vis´ti·cal·ly** *adj.*

a·tax´i·a *n.* failure to control muscular movement —**a·tax´ic** *adj., n.*

at´el·ier *n.* an artists studio

a´the·ism *n.* denial that gods exist —**a´the·ist** *n.* —**a·the·is´tic, a·the·is´ti·cal** *adj.* —**a·the·is´ti·cal·ly** *adv.*

ath´lete *n.* one trained in an endeavor requiring physical ability —**ath·let´ic** *adj.* —**ath·let´i·cal·ly** *adv.*

ath´let´ics *pl. n.* sporting contests, gymnastics, etc. collectively

a·thwart´ *adv.* from side to side —*prep.* across the path of; in opposition to

a·tilt´ *adj., adv.* tilted up; in lively conflict

at´las *n.* a book of maps

at´mos·phere´ *n.* the air surrounding the earth; the general feeling or mood of an environment; decor —**at·mos·pher´ic, at·mos·pher´i·cal** *adj.* —**at·mos·pher´i·cal·ly** *adv.*

at·mos·pher´ics *n.* broadcast interference caused by disturbance in the atmosphere

a´toll *n.* a coral island and its reef, enclosing a lagoon

at´om *n.* a tiny particle; smallest combinable particle of an element —**a·tom´ic, a·tom´i·cal** *adj.* —**a·tom´i·cal·ly** *adv.*

atomic clock a precise instrument for the measurement of time

atomic energy energy liberated by the fission or fusion of atoms

atomic number the number of protons, etc. in an element which serves to identify the element

atomic weight the weight of an atom of an element relative to that of an atom of carbon

at´om·ize´ *vt.* to separate into atoms; to make liquid into a fine spray —**at´om·iz·er** *n.*

a·to·nal´i·ty n. a lack of tonal quality —**a·ton´al**, **a·ton´al·ist**, **a·ton·al·is´tic** adj. —**a·ton´al·ly** adv. —**a·ton´al·ism** n.

a·tone´ vi. to make amends —**a·ton´a·ble**, **a·tone´a·ble** adj. —**a·ton´er** n.

a·tone´ment n. reparation for wrong or injury

a·top´ adj., adv. on or at the top

a´tri·um n. an entrance hall; an open area in the center of a building; one of the upper chambers of the human heart

a·tro´cious adj. cruel, wicked; offensive, tasteless —**a·tro´cious·ly** adv. —**a·tro´cious·ness** n. —**a·troc´i·ty** n.

at´ro·phy n. a wasting away, especially of muscles or other body tissue —vi. to waste away —vt. to cause to waste away —**a·troph´ic** adj.

at·tach´ vi. to adhere —vt. to fasten on; to take by legal means —**at·tach´a·ble** adj. —**at·tach´ment** n.

at·ta·ché n. a person assigned to a diplomatic mission

attaché case n. a briefcase; a flat case with hinged lid for carrying business papers

at·tack´ n. any hostile action —vt. to strike out against; to assault; to take up vigorously —**at·tack´er** n.

at·tain´ vi. to arrive —vt. to reach or gain; to achieve or accomplish —**at·tain·a·bil´i·ty** n. —**at·tain´a·ble** adj. —**at·tain´ment** n.

at·tain´der n. the loss of all civil rights when a person is sentenced for a serious crime

at·tar n. a fragrant oil extracted from flower petals

at·tempt´ n. a try —vt. to try; to make an effort —**at·tempt´a·bil·i·ty** n. —**at·tempt´a·ble** adj. —**at·tempt´er** n.

at·tend´ vi. to heed; to give care —vt. to minister to; to accompany; to be present at

at·tend´ance n. one's presence at a particular place and time; the record of one's presence over a period of time, as in school; collectively, those who attend

at·tend´ant adj. present; waiting upon; following, as a consequence —n. one who waits upon; a servant; an accompaniment, as the result of action

at·ten´tion n. concentration; alertness; observation, notice; attentiveness

at·ten´tive adj. considerate, thoughtful —**at·ten´tive·ly** adv. —**at·ten´tive·ness** n.

at·ten´u·ate vt., vi. to make or become thin or fine; to reduce or become lessened in value, strength, quantity, severity, etc. —**at·ten´u·a·ble** adj. —**at·ten·u·a´tion** n.

at·test´ vt. to testify; to certify under oath

at´tic n. an area or room directly beneath the roof and above the last full floor of a building

at·tire´ n. clothing —vt. to dress

at´ti·tude´ n. the posture or bearing of a person; the position of a thing in relation to a plane surface; a state of mind; a disposition

at·tor´ney (US) n. a lawyer

at·tract´ vt. to draw or be drawn towards; to entice —**at·tract´a·ble** adj. —**at·tract´a·ble·ness**, **at·tract·a·bil´i·ty** n. —**at·tract´er**, **at·trac´tor** n. —**at·trac´tion** n.

at·tract´ive adj. possessing the power to entice, especially by charm or beauty —**at·tract´ive·ly** adv. —**at·tract´ive·ness** n.

at´tri·bute´ n. a quality or characteristic —**at·tri´bute** vt. to impute as belonging —**at·trib´ut·a·ble** adj. —**at·tri·bu´tion** n.

at·tri´tion n. a wearing away; loss of personnel by resignation, retirement, etc.

at·tune´ *vt.* to adjust; to bring into conformity with

a·typ´i·c, a·typ´i·cal *adj.* not characteristic; inconsistent with the normal or usual pattern —**a·typ´i·cal·ly** *adv.*

au´burn *adj., n.* a reddish–brown color

auc´tion *n.* a sale conducted by bidding —*vt.* to dispose of at such a sale —**auc·tion·eer´** *n.*

au cou·rant´ *adj.* up to date; fashionable

au·da´cious *adj.* bold, daring; shameless —**au·da´cious·ly** *adv.* —**au·da´cious·ness, au·dac´i·ty** *n.*

au´di·ble *adj.* within the range of hearing; able to be heard —**au·di·bil´i·ty, au´di·ble·ness** *n.* —**au´di·bly** *adv.*

au´di·ence *n.* a formal interview; all who attend a show, concert, speech, etc.

au´di·o *adj.* pertaining to audible sound waves —*n.* that part of a device or occurrence concerned with sound

audio frequency a frequency of sound waves within the range of normal human hearing, about 20 to 20,000 cycles per second

au´di·o·phile´ *n.* person interested in high–fidelity sound equipment

au´di·o·vis´u·al *adj.* embracing both sound and sight —*n.* material that incorporates both sound and sight

au´dit *n.* a verification of financial accounts —*vt.* to carefully examine so as to confirm the validity of; to attend a college course as a listener only

au·di´tion *n.* a tryout, as of an actor or dancer for a part —*vi.* a tryout to show one's competence when applying for a job —*vt.* to try out, as for a job

au´dit·or *n.* one who examines the accounts of a business and certifies as to their accuracy; one who attends a college class, but does not participate for credit

au´di·to´ri·um *n.* a room or building for large gatherings

au´di·to·ry *adj.* pertaining to the sense of hearing

au´ger *n.* a boring tool

aug·ment´ *vi., vt.* to increase; to supplement —**aug·ment´a·ble** *adj.* —**aug·men·ta´tion** *n.* —**aug·men´tive, aug·men´ta·tive** *adj.*

au grat´in *adj.* cooked with cheese or bread crumbs

au´gur *vi., vt.* to predict from signs or omens; to be an omen

au´gu·ry *n.* the art of divination; an omen

au·gust´ *adj.* inspiring reverence; imposing —**au·gust´ly** *adv.* —**au·gust´ness** *n.*

au na·tu·rel´ *adj.* ungarnished, as food prepared without sauce; nude

aunt *n.* the sister of one's parent or the wife of one's uncle; an affectionate designation for an older female not related by blood or marriage

au´ra *n.* an invisible field or quality surrounding a person or object; a gentle breeze

au´ral *adj.* pertaining to the sense of hearing

au´re·ate *adj.* the color of gold

au´ri·cle *n.* one of the two atriums of the heart; the outer ear

au·ric´u·lar *adj.* pertaining to the sense of hearing

au·rif´er·ous *adj.* containing gold

au·ro´ra *n.* the dawn; a luminous display seen in the polar night sky

aus´cul·tate *vt.* to examine by listening, especially with a stethoscope —**aus·cul·ta´tion** *n.* —**aus´cul·ta·tive, aus·cul´ta·to·ry** *adj.*

aus´pice *n.* an omen, usually favorable; patronage

aus·pi´cious *adj.* favorable; fortunate —**aus·pi´cious·ly** *adv.* —**aus·pi´cious·ness** *n.*

aus·tere´ *adj.* of a stern demeanor; plain in decor —**aus·ter´i·ty** *n.*

au·then´tic *adj.* genuine; official —**au·then´ti·cal·ly** *adv.* —**au´then·tic´i·ty** *n.*

au·then´ti·cate´ *vt.* to verify; to prove genuine —**au·then´ti·ca´tion** *n.* —**au·then´ti·ca´tor** *n.*

au´thor *n.* one who creates or originates —**au´thor·ship** *n.*

au·thor·i·tar´i·an *adj.* autocratic; strict —*n.* an advocate of authority over individual rights

au·thor´i·ta·tive *adj.* with authority —**au·thor´i·ta·tive·ly** *adv.* —**au·thor´i·ta·tive·ness** *n.*

au·thor´i·ty *n.* the power to command or act; one invested with such power

au´thor·ise´ (*Brit.*), **au´thor·ize´** (*US*) *vt.* to give approval; to permit —**au·tho·ri·sa´tion, au·tho·ri·za´tion** *n.* —**au´thor·ised, au´thor·ized** *adj.*

au´to·bi·og´ra·phy *n.* the story of a person's life written by that person —**au´to·bi´o·graph´ic, au´to·bi´o·graph´i·cal** *adj.* —**au´to·bi´o·graph´i·cal·ly** *adv.*

au·toc´ra·cy *n.* absolute rule by a single person; a dictatorship; the rule of a dictator; a state governed by an absolute ruler

au´to·crat´ *n.* an absolute ruler —**au·to·crat´ic, au·to·crat´i·cal** *adj.* —**au·to·crat´i·cal·ly** *adv.*

au´to·graph´ *n.* a signature —*vt.* to write one's signature; to sign

au´to·mate *vt.* to operate by or adapt for automation

au´to·mat´ic, au·to·mat´i·cal *adj.* involuntary; self-operating —**au·to·mat´i·cal·ly** *adv.*

au´to·ma´tion *n.* machinery, devices, etc. that once programmed, operate with minimal human intervention

au·tom´a·ton *n.* a robot; a machine controlled by a computer or a concealed mechanism; a person whose actions appear mechanical

au´to·mo·bile (*US*) *n.* a passenger vehicle; a car

au·to·nom´ic, au·to·nom´i·cal *adj.* involuntary; acting without conscious control —**au·to·nom´i·cal·ly** *adv.*

autonomic nervous system that part of the nervous system which controls involuntary actions of the body, as heartbeat, flow of blood, glands, digestion, etc.

au·ton´o·mous *adj.* independent; acting without the supervision or control of another, as *an autonomous nation* —**au·ton´o·mous·ly** *adv.*

au·ton´o·my *n.* self government; the functioning of a group or part of an organization independent of its parent

au´to·pi´lot *n.* a device that can be set to maintain an aircraft's course and attitude

au´top·sy *n.* the medical examination of a dead body

au´tumn *n.* the season between summer and winter; fall —**au·tum´nal** *adj.* —**au·tum´nal·ly** *adv.*

aux·il´ia·ry *adj.* helping; supplementary —*n.* a supplemental person or thing

a·vail´ *vi.* to assist or aid —*vt.* to be of value —*n.* benefit: *pleaded to no avail*

a·vail´a·ble *adj.* at one's disposal; obtainable —**a·vail´a·bil´i·ty, a·vail´a·ble´ness** *n.* —**a·vail´a·bly** *adv.*

av´a·lanche´ *n.* a mass of snow, earth, etc. falling from a height; anything that comes in an abnormal quantity

a·vant–garde´ *adj.* reflecting the most recent trends, as *avant–garde paintings* —*n.* those persons, as artists or writers, who promote, mirror, or employ the most recent or unconventional techniques

av·a·rice *n.* greed; a passion for wealth —**av·a·ri´cious** *adj.* —**av·a·ri´cious·ly** *adv.* —**av·a·ri´cious·ness** *n.*

av´a·tar *n.* in Hindu legend, the incarnation of a god; any physical phenomenon

a·venge´ *vt.* to exact punishment for a wrong or on behalf of another —**a·veng´er** *n.*

av´e·nue *n.* a wide street; an approach bordered with greenery or statuary; a means of access, as, through an intermediary, etc.

a·ver´ *vt.* to declare to be true

av´er·age *adj.* of a median value; not exceptional: *an average student* — *n.* the value of several elements divided by the number of elements, as, the total cost of three items divided by three yields the average cost of the items —*vi.* to buy or sell so as to increase the average price; *vt.* to find or fix an average value —**av´er·age·ly** *adv.* —**av´er·age·ness** *n.*

a·verse´ *adj.* opposed; reluctant —**a·verse´ly** *adv.* —**a·verse´ness** *n.*

a·ver´sion *n.* a dislike; a profound distaste; that which is distasteful —**a·ver´sive** *adj.*

a·vert´ *vt.* to turn away; to ward off, prevent —**a·vert´ed·ly** *adv.* —**a·vert´a·ble, a·vert´i·ble** *adj.*

a´vi·ar´y *n.* a place for keeping birds

a´vi·a´tion *n.* the development and operation of aircraft —**a´vi·a·tor** *n.*

av´id *adj.* eager; extremely fervent or enthusiastic —**av´id·ly** *adv.* —**av´id·ness** *n.*

av·o·ca´tion *n.* a hobby; a sideline —**av·o·ca´tion·al** *adj.* —**av·o·ca´tion·al·ly** *adv.*

a·void´ *vt.* to evade, shun; to keep from happening —**a·void´a·ble** *adj.* —**a·void´a·bly** *adv.* —**a·void´ance** *n.* —**a·void´er** *n.*

av´oir·du·pois´ *n.* the common system of weights of the United States in which 16 ounces equal a pound

a·vow´ *vt.* to declare openly; to confess —**a·vow´a·ble** *adj.* —**a·vow´a·bly** *adv.* —**a·vow´er** *n.*

a·vow´al *n.* acknowledgment; open admission

a·vowed´ *adj.* readily acknowledged; openly declared —**a·vow´ed·ly** *adv.* —**a·vow´ed·ness** *n.*

a·vun´cu·lar *adj.* pertaining to an uncle

a·wait´ *vt.* to watch for; to be ready for

a·wake´ *adj.* not sleeping; alert —*vi.* to wake; to become aware —*vt.* to arouse; to make aware

a·wak´en *vi., vt.* to awake

a·wak´en·ing *adj.* stimulating; exciting —*n.* a rekindling of interest

a·ward´ *n.* a judgment; a prize —*vt.* to grant by judgement

a·ware´ *adj.* familiar with; conscious —**a·ware´ness** *n.*

a·wash´ *adj., adv.* at or near water level; overflowing with water; inundated with anything, as *awash in job applications*

a·way´ *adj.* at a distance —*adv.* distant; to the side; diligently: *he's working away*; from one's keeping or possession; immediately: *fire away* —*interj.* begone

awe *n.* a feeling of wonder and fear —*vt.* to fill with wonder

awe´some *adj.* overwhelming; enkindling awe

awe´strick·en, awe´struck *adj.* stunned; impressed by awe

aw´ful *adj.* inspiring fear; dreadful; formidable

aw´ful·ly *adv.* in a dreadful manner; exceedingly, as *awfully bright*

a·while´ *adv.* for a time, usually short-lived

awk´ward *adj.* clumsy; inconvenient; embarrassing —**awk´ward·ly** *adv.* —**awk´ward·ness** *n.*

awl *n.* a pointed tool for making small holes

awn *n.* a bristlelike part of some grasses

awn˘ing *n.* a structural projection to ward off sun and rain

awry˘ *adj., adv.* not straight

ax, axe *n.* a tool for chopping wood

ax˘i·al *adj.* along an axis

ax˘i·ol˘o·gy *n.* the study of values or the nature of value

ax˘i·om *n.* an adage —**ax˘i·o·mat˘ic** **ax˘i·o·mat˘i·cal** *adj.* —**ax˘i·o·mat˘ i·cal·ly** *adv.*

ax˘is *n., pl.* **ax˘es** a line around which an object rotates

ax˘le *n.* a shaft on which a wheel is mounted

az˘i·muth *n.* the arc of the horizon between the meridian of the observation point and a star sighting

a·zo˘ic *adj.* referring to the time on earth before the appearance of life

az˘ure *adj.* sky-blue —*n.*

b, B *n.* second letter of the English alphabet; not of the first order; second-rate, as *a B-movie*

bab˘ble *n.* a rippling sound, as *a babbling brook* —*vi.* make incoherent noises; to prattle foolishly —*vt.* to disclose carelessly —**bab˘bler** *n.*

babe *n.* an infant; one lacking in experience or knowledge

ba˘bel *n.* a bedlam of speech or sounds

ba˘by *adj.* childish; small —*n.* an infant; the youngest or smallest of a group; one who acts like a small child —*vt.* to handle gingerly, as something very delicate —**ba˘by· ish** *adj.*

baby doll a short, sheer woman's nightgown

baby food puréed food for an infant

baby grand a small grand piano

baby's-breath a plant having small white or pink flowers

ba˘by·sit˘ *vi., vt.* to care for children

—**ba˘by-sit·ter** *n.*

bac˘ca·lau˘re·ate *n.* a bachelor of arts, science, etc. degree

bac·cha·nal˘ *adj.* a drunken revelry —*n.* a reveler; a riotous feast — **bac·cha·na˘lia** *n.* —**bac·cha·na˘ lian** *adj.*

back *adj.* in the rear; isolated: *the back woods*; of an earlier period: *back payments* —*adv.* toward the rear; to a bygone place or condition —*n.* the posterior or hindmost part; the body from the neck to the base of the spine; the far side, away from the subject: *the back of the shelf*; the part of an object away from that which is normally used: *the back of a knife*; the part of a book where the leaves are joined and the cover is affixed —*vi.* to move backward —*vt.* to cause to move backward; to support or assist

back˘bit˘er *vt.* one who speaks ill of another

back˘bone *n.* the spinal column; the main support: *the workers are the backbone of the organization*; courage; spunk

back burner of lower priority, as *to place the project on a back burner*

back˘drop *n.* that which forms a background, as the curtain at the back of a stage

back˘er *n.* a supporter; one who provides financial help or encouragement; an apologist

back˘fire *n.* a line of fire deliberately set to halt the advance of a forest fire; premature explosion in an internal-combustion engine; a backward explosion in a gun —*vi.* to set a backfire; to give evidence of a backfire, as an explosive sound of an automobile exhaust; to achieve a result opposite to that anticipated

back˘gam˘mon *n.* a board game for two players, often involving wagers

back´ground n. that which is in the rear; that part of a picture, scene, etc. which is behind the main object, often serving to enhance; secondary; peripheral; one's past experience; sound which accompanies or serves to enhance a performance; a description of the events leading up to an event

back´hand adj. not straightforward or sincere —adv. with a backhand stroke —n. a movement made with the hand turned backward, as a tennis stroke

back´hand·ed adj. with the hand turned backward; insincere; ironic; turned in a direction opposite to the normal

back´ing n. financial or verbal support; a group of supporters; the act of moving backward; material added for additional strength

back´lash´ n. a sharp recoil; a reaction

back´log´ n. a reserve; orders to be filled or processed

back´-ped·al vi. to retreat from an earlier position, as of an opinion

back seat n. a seat in the rear of a theater, vehicle, etc.; a position of secondary importance

back´side n. the back part of a thing; the posterior or rump of a person or animal

back´slap vi. friendliness that is too effusive, often insincere —vt. to be overly friendly —**back´slap·per** n.

back´slide vi. to return to old ways, usually after eschewing them

back´spin n. reverse rotation, as of a ball; the rebounded effect or results of an action

back´stage´ adj. situated off-stage so as to escape notice —adv. in any of the parts of a theater behind or to the side of the stage —n. the parts of the theater to the rear or sides of the stage, as wings, dressing rooms, etc.

back´stairs´ n. stairs at the back of a dwelling, usually for the use of servants —adj. underhanded; indirect

back´stop n. a screen on a playing field to confine the game projectile such as a ball or puck —vi. to sustain or reinforce, as the opinions of another

back´stretch n. the part of a racecourse farthest from the spectators

back talk n. an insolent or argumentative response

back´track vi. to retrace one's steps; to retreat from an earlier statement or opinion

back´up n. support; an accumulation: something held in readiness for contingencies

back´ward adj. reversed; bashful; retarded in growth or development —adv. in the direction of the back; toward time past; in reverse order —**back´wards** adv. —**back´ward·ness** n.

back´wa·ter n. a place judged to be backward or undeveloped

back´woods adj. undeveloped; culturally deprived —n. a sparsely settled area; an area which is not culturally advanced

ba´con n. cured meat from the back or side of a hog

bac·te´ri·a n. pl., sing. **bac·te´ri·um** a division of microorganisms that cause various diseases, fermentation, etc. —**bac·te´ri·al** adj. —**bac·te·ri·ol´o·gist** n. —**bac·te·ri·ol´o·gy** n.

bac·te´ri·cide n. a substance which destroys bacteria —**bac·te´ri·cid·al** adj.

bad adj. not satisfactory; unacceptable; evil; naughty: a bad boy; unlucky, as a bad break; offensive: a bad attitude; incorrect: we received bad information; detrimental, as a bad habit or illness; unfortunate; improper: she chose a *bad time to leave;* concerned, as, *to feel bad about* —**not bad, not half bad, not so bad** rather good, usually after low expectation —*n.* that which is bad; collectively, those who are bad

badge *n.* a symbol to show authority, rank, etc.

badg'er *n.* a burrowing mammal — *vt.* to tease or pester

bad'i·nage *n.* playful banter

bad'ly *adv.* incorrectly; offensively; detrimentally; severely or with intense desire, as *they need food badly*

baf'fle *vt.* to perplex, confuse or confound; to obstruct or impede — **baf'fle·ment** *n.* —**baf'fler** *n.* —**baf'fling** *adj.*

bag *n.* a sack, purse, suitcase, etc.; the amount a bag contains —*vi.* to bulge or hang loosely —*vt.* to place in a bag; to attain, as a prize or game in hunting —**in the bag** almost certain —**left holding the bag** left to be charged with responsibility or blame —**bag and baggage** completely; with all of one's possessions —**bag'ger** *n.*

bag'a·telle' *n.* a trifle

ba'gel *n.* a hard roll shaped like a doughnut

bag'gage *n.* luggage for traveling; a lascivious woman; a useless idea or practice

bag'gy *adj.* loose; ill-fitting

bag'man *n.* a person who collects or distributes illegal money, as bribes or wagers

ba·guet', ba·guette' *n.* a crystal cut to a narrow, rectangular shape

bail *n.* security to insure one's appearance in court —*vt.* to free one who has given security; to remove water from a boat —**bail·ee'** *n.* — **bail'ment** *n.* —**bail'or** *n.*

bail'iff *n.* an officer of the court responsible for custody of prisoners, serving processes, etc.

bail'i·wick *n.* the office of a bailiff; one's special place or sphere of influence, knowledge, etc.

bail out jump from an airplane with a parachute; to post bond; sell off a bad investment; to distance oneself from an unpleasant situation

bails'man *n.* one who posts bail for a fee

bait *n.* any enticement —*vt.* to lure or entice; to tease or provoke

bake *vi.* to become firm and dry by exposure to heat, as food baked in an oven or soil dried by the sun — *vt.* to cook with dry heat, as in an oven; to harden with heat, as pottery or soil

bak'er *n.* one skilled in the preparation of pastries, breads, etc.; one who makes and sells baked products —**baker's dozen** thirteen, from an old custom of giving extra to avoid the penalties for short count or measure

bak'er·y *n.* a place for making baked goods; a shop where baked goods are sold

baking powder a mixture of baking soda and an acid salt used as a leavening agent

baking soda (*US*) sodium bicarbonate; a white crystalline compound used in cooking, cleaning, as an antacid, etc.

bak'sheesh, bak'shish *n.* In certain Middle Eastern countries, a gratuity; a bribe

bal·a·lai'ka *n.* a three-stringed musical instrument of Russian origin

bal'ance *n.* a device for weighing; an amount owed; a state of equilibrium; the amount left after deducting that which has been or is to be used; a state of harmony, as in arrangement or design —*vi.* to be equal —*vt.* to compare; to compensate; to reconcile, as financial records

balance of payments the difference

in the value of payments and receipts for trade between nations

balance of power a comparison of the relative strength of nations or of a group of nations

balance of trade a comparison of the value of imports and exports of a country

balance sheet a statement of the financial condition of a business on a specific date

bal´co·ny n. a platform outside an upper window; an upper level of seats in a theater

bald adj. without hair or natural covering; unadorned —**bald´head·ed** adj. —**bald´ness** n.

bal´der·dash n. nonsense; meaningless words

bald´faced adj. audacious, brazen; obvious, as a baldfaced lie

bale n. a large bundle tied or wrapped for ease in handling —vt. to tie or wrap —**bal´er** n.

ba·leen´ n. whalebone

bale´ful adj. noxious; harmful

balk vi. stop and refuse to proceed or take part

balk´y adj. prone to stop suddenly; reluctant to participate

ball n. a spherical object; any of a number of games that require a round object for throwing, hitting, etc.; a formal dance —**on the ball** qualified; alert

bal´lad n. a sentimental song; a song or poem that tells a story —**bal·lad·eer´** n. —**bal´lad·ry** n.

bal·lis´tics n. the study of the motion of projectiles —**bal·lis´tic** adj. —**bal·lis´ti·cal·ly** adv.

bal·loon´ n. a bag inflated with gas so as to float in the air; a small inflated bag used as a toy or decoration; a large final payment on an installment loan —**bal·loon´ist** n.

bal´lot n. a paper for recording a vote; a vote cast; a list of those running for office

ball´point pen´ a pen that distributes ink by means of a ball bearing point

ball´room n. a large room used for parties and dancing

bal´ly·hoo n. boisterous patter; any overblown promotion

balm n. an ointment for healing or soothing; anything soothing

balm´y adj. aromatic; having a healing or soothing effect; silly; slightly mad; very foolish —**balm´i·ly** adv. —**balm´i·ness** n.

ba·lo´ney, bo·lo´gna n. a large, mild sausage; idle or nonsensical talk

bal´sa n. a tree of tropical America; the very light wood from the balsa tree used in the construction of models and rafts

bal´sam n. the fragrant oleoresin obtained from various trees; a tree which exudes balsam; an aromatic ointment; any soothing or healing agent

bal´us·ter n. one of the small pillars which support a hand rail

bal´us·trade n. a hand rail and its supporting balusters

bam·boo´ n. a tall hollow–stemmed grass

bam·boo´zle vi. to practice trickery or deception —vt. to mislead or deceive —**bam·boo´zle·ment** n. —**bam·boo´zler** n.

ban n. any prohibition, as of a motion picture, book, etc. in a community; an ecclesiastical sentence of excommunication or interdiction —vt. to forbid or prohibit; to impose an ecclesiastical ban

ba´nal adj. commonplace; trite —**ba·nal´i·ty** n. —**ba·nal´ly** adv.

band n. a flat strip of material used to bind, connect, reinforce, etc.; a broad stripe, contrasting to its surroundings in color, texture, etc.; a range of frequencies within set limits, as a broadcast band; a group of persons associated for a common purpose —*vi.* to associate —*vt.* to encircle or join with a strip of material; to unite

band´age *n.* material used to bind a wound —*vt.* to bind or cover with a bandage

ban·dan´a, ban·dan´na *n.* a large, brightly colored handkerchief

ban´dit *n.* a robber, thief; anyone who steals or defrauds

band´lead·er, band´mas·ter *n.* the leader of a group of musicians

ban·do·leer´, ban·do·lier´ a broad belt with loops for holding rifle or shotgun cartidges

band saw a motor driven saw the blade of which consists of a toothed, endless belt

band shell (*US*) a bandstand for outdoor concerts

band´stand *n.* an outdoor platform, often of temporary construction, which serves as a stage for musicians or other entertainers

band´wag·on *n.* a decorated wagon which carries a band in a parade —**climb (or jump) on the bandwagon** change openly to an apparently winning position or candidate

ban´dy *adj.* curved or bowed —*vt.* to exchange quips; to pass along

ban´dy·leg´ged *adj.* bowlegged

bane *n.* a cause of distress or destruction; a deadly poison

bang *n.* a sudden loud noise; a show of enthusiasm —*vt.* to beat or strike loudly —*vi.* to make a loud noise; to strike noisily

ban´ish *vt.* to exile; to dismiss or drive away, as *to banish worries* —**ban´ish·ment** *n.*

ban·is·ter, ban´nis·ter *n.* a handrail along a staircase; a baluster

ban´jo *n.* a stringed instrument with a long narrow neck and circular sound box

bank *n.* a mound or heap; the edge of an inland body of water; the

sloping of a road, an airplane, etc. at a curve or turn; an institution where money is deposited, borrowed, etc.; a supply of anything held in reserve; like elements stored together: *a food bank* —*vi.* to incline an airplane; to do business with a bank —*vt.* to form a lateral slope; to cause to rebound at an angle, as in billiards; to deposit in a bank; to furnish financial backing —**bank a fire** to cover a fire so as to make it last longer by burning low —**bank on** to have complete faith in —**bank´a·ble** *adj.*

bank account an account held with a bank for the purpose of writing checks, accumulating funds, etc.; the funds available to the holder of such an account

bank book a book in which the transactions affecting a bank account are recorded

bank´er *n.* the owner or manager of a bank; a bank executive; the person who holds the stakes in a game of chance

bank note a promissary note issued by a bank

bank´roll (*US*) *n.* the money which one possesses —*vt.* to back financially —**bank´roll·er** *n.*

bank´rupt *adj.* insolvent; unable to pay one´s debts; wanting of anything, as *morally bankrupt* —*n.* a person or company unable to honor its debts —*vt.* to cause to become bankrupt

ban´ner *n.* a flag; a cloth displaying a greeting, advertisement, etc.; a large newspaper headline

ban´quet *n.* a feast; a formal dinner

ban·quette´ *n.* a bench for seating along a wall, as in a restaurant

ban´shee *n.* in Gaelic folklore, a spirit whose wailing predicts death

ban´tam *n.* a small domestic fowl

ban´tam·weight *n.* a boxer who weighs from 113 to 118 pounds

ban´ter *n.* light–hearted jesting —*vi.* to exchange good–natured jibes — *vt.* to tease good–naturedly —**ban´ter·ing·ly** *adv.*

bap´tism *n.* purification rite of the Christian Church; any initiatory rite or experience —**bap´tis´mal** *adj.* —**bap´tis´mal·ly** *adj.*

bap´tise (*Brit.*), **bap´tize** (*US*) *vt.* to consecrate or dedicate to a special purpose by a ceremony

bar[1] *n.* an oblong piece of rigid material; anything that blocks access; the legal profession or system; a stripe, as to denote rank; a division in a musical score —*vt.* to close off, as with a bar; to prevent or exclude

bar[2] *n.* (*Brit.*) a room in a public house or club where drink is sold

bar[3] *n.* (*US*) an establishment where beverages or food are sold

barb *n.* a sharp spine on the shaft of an arrow, fish–hook, etc.; a sharp retort

bar·bar´i·an *adj.* uncivilized —*n.* an uncivilized or uncultured person —**bar·bar´i·an·ism** *n.* —**bar·bar´ic** *adj.* —**bar·bar´i·cal·ly** *adv.*

bar´bar·ism *n.* a savage state, brutality

bar·bar´i·ty *n.* brutal or crude conduct; vulgarity

bar´ba·rous *adj.* lacking in culture; crude; brutal —**bar´ba·rous·ly** *adv.* —**bar´ba·rous·ness** *n.*

bar´be·cue´ *n.* an outdoor celebration featuring food cooked over an open fire; the manner of cooking food over an open fire, often with a basting of well–seasoned sauce; any food cooked over an open fire —*vt.* to roast meat over a charcoal fire; to cook, usually meat, basted with a tangy sauce

barbed *adj.* having pointed ends; sharp or piercing, as *a barbed retort*

barbed wire a fencing wire with

sharp pointed pieces at regular intervals

bar´ber *n.* one who trims the hair, beard, etc. —*vt.* to trim the hair or beard

bard *n.* a poet

bare *adj.* lacking clothing or covering; stark, plain; meager —*vt.* to uncover, expose —**bare´ness** *n.*

bare´back *adj.* riding an animal without a saddle —*adv.* without a saddle

bare´faced *adj.* with nothing concealed; impudent; obvious, as *a barefaced lie* —**bare´fac·ed·ly** *adv.* —**bare´fac·ed·ness** *n.*

bare´hand´ed *adj.* with nothing in the hands; without benefit of a tool or weapon other than the hands

bare´ly *adv.* only just; scarcely

bar´gain *n.* an understanding; a good price —*vi.* to negotiate

barge *n.* a boat that carries freight on inland waters —*vi.* to act clumsily

bar´i·tone´ *n.* the musical range between bass and tenor

bark *n.* the covering of a woody plant; the sound made by a dog — *vt.* to strip the covering from a tree; to make or imitate the sound of a dog

bar´keep *n.* one who operates an establishment where alcoholic beverages are dispensed; a bartender

bark´er *n.* a person whose continuous patter is intended to attract patrons into an establishment

barn *n.* a farm building used for storing livestock, feed, etc.

bar´na·cle *n.* a type of crustacean that clings to submerged surfaces

barn´storm *vi.* to tour rural areas, usually for politicking, staging shows, etc. —**barn´storm·er** *n.*

ba·rom´e·ter *n.* an instrument that measures atmospheric pressure; anything that predicts change, esp. of statistical data **—bar·o·met´ric, bar·o·met´ri·cal** *adj.* **—bar·o·met´ri·cal** *adv.* **—ba·rom´e·try** *n.*

bar´on *n.* in British peerage, the rank above a baronet and below a viscount; one having great power in industry or finance

bar´on·age, bar´o·ny *n.* the sphere of influence of a baron

ba·roque´ *adj.* characteristic of the ornate style in art and architecture popular in 16th and 17th century Europe; pertaining to anything from that period, as *baroque music* **—***n.* the baroque form; anything characteristic of the baroque style

bar´racks *pl. n.* buildings for housing soldiers, workers, etc.

bar·ra·cu´da *n.* a large, voracious fish found in tropical seas

bar·rage´ *n.* heavy artillery fire; anything overwhelming: *a barrage of accusations*

barred *adj.* blocked or decorated with bars; banned; not allowed

bar´rel *n.* a large cylindrical storage container; any cylinder, as *the barrel of a gun* **—over a barrel** at the mercy of another

bar´ren *adj.* incapable of reproducing; unproductive; desolate **—bar´ren·ly** *adv.* **—bar´ren·ness** *n.*

bar·rette´ (*US*) *n.* a small appliance for keeping hair in place

bar·ri·cade´ *n.* a barrier or blockade **—***vt.* to create a barrier

bar´ri·er *n.* an obstruction

bar´ris·ter *n.* an attorney

bar´tend´er *n.* one who mixes and serves beverages at a tavern

bar´ter *n.* the exchange of goods or services **—***vi., vt.* to trade

ba´sal *adj.* fundamental; a standard of reference

ba·salt´ *n.* a dark volcanic rock

base *adj.* humble; cowardly; corrupt **—***n.* a foundation; a starting place **—***vt.* to form or place on a foundation; to establish a basis for **— base´ly** *adv.* **—base´ness** *n.*

base´born *adj.* illegitimate; born of lower class parents; common

base´less *adj.* with no foundation in fact; groundless; gratuitous **— base´less·ness** *n.*

base´line *n.* anything specified as a main point of reference

base´ment *n.* a foundation or floor below the main floor of a building

bash *n.* a shattering blow **—***vt.* to strike with a heavy blow

bash´ful *adj.* timid; shy **—bash´ful·ly** *adv.* **—bash´ful·ness** *n.*

ba´sic *adj.* fundamental; forming the foundation for that which follows **—ba´si·cal·ly** *adv.*

ba´sil *n.* an aromatic plant of the mint family; the leaves of the plant, used to flavor food

ba·sil´i·ca *n.* an ancient Roman building with a long central nave and side aisles divided by columns; a church built after the style of the Roman basilica

ba´sin *n.* a wide, shallow container for wash water; an area drained by a body of water

ba´sis *n.* a fundament principle; an essential quality or ingredient

bask *vi.* to relax in warmth; to revel in the glow of a pleasant situation: *to bask in the glory of ones deeds*

bas´ket *n.* a container made of woven material

bas-re·lief´ *n.* a type of sculpture in which the subject is raised only slightly from the background

bass *adj.* of the lowest musical range, as *a bass guitar* **—***n.* the lowest voice in music; a musical instrument in the lower range **— bass´ist** *n.*

bass *n.* any of a number of species of food and game fish

bas·si·net´ *n.* a small basket which can hold a baby; a container for baby clothes, diapers, etc.

bas·soon *n.* a double–reed bass wind instrument —**bas·soon·ist** *n.*

bass·wood *n.* the linden tree; the wood of the linden tree

bas·tard *adj.* born out of wedlock; unusual or irregular so as not to be usable; not the real thing or of inferior quality —*n.* an illegitimate child; any hybrid plant or animal; anything which deviates from the usual in size, quality, etc. —**bas·tard·ize** *vt.* —**bas·tard·i·za·tion** *n.* —**bas·tard·ly** *adv.* —**bas·tard·y** *n.*

baste *vt.* to sew with temporary stitches; to moisten food with drippings or other liquid while cooking —**bast·er** *n.*

bas·ti·on *n.* a strongly defended position

bat *n.* a cudgel; in some games, a stick for striking a ball; a nocturnal flying mammal —*vi.* in certain games, to take a turn at bat —*vt.* to strike with a bat

batch *n.* a quantity processed at one time, as *a batch of cookies*; a number of things collectively

bate *vi.* to diminish —*vt.* to lessen the intensity of; to take away

bath *n.* the act of cleansing the body by immersing in water or other liquid; liquid for bathing; a room or building set aside for bathing; a resort where natural springs, etc. are claimed to have healing power —**take a bath** to suffer a loss

bathe *vi.* to wash; to take a bath; to go into water; to be covered as with liquid —*vt.* to immerse in liquid; to wash; to cover, as though with liquid: *trees bathed in moonlight* —**bath·er** *n.*

bath·robe (*US*) *n.* a loose, casual garment, usually closed at the front with a belt

ba·tik, **bat·tik** *n.* a process for dying fabric in which portions are protected with melted wax, then the wax removed and the process repeated through a series of colors to obtain a complex, multicolored design; the fabric so dyed

ba·tiste *n.* a fine, sheer fabric of cotton, silk or rayon

bat·on *n.* a short staff borne as weapon or emblem of office

bat·tal·ion *n.* any large group united in a common cause

bat·ten *n.* a narrow strip of wood placed in the sail of a ship to keep it flat or to secure the tarpaulin cover of a hatchway; in the theater, a wood or metal strip used to stiffen a muslin flat or to hold a strip of lights —*vt.* to strengthen or secure with battens

bat·ter *n.* a mixture used to make or coat baked or fried food —*vt.* to subject to repeated blows; to damage by beating or with use

bat·ter·y *n.* a number of things used together: *a battery of tests*; the illegal touching of a person; a device for storing an electrical charge

bat·ting *n.* a material used for stuffing pillows, comforters, etc.

bat·ty *adj.* a little crazy; odd

bau·ble *n.* a worthless trinket

bawd *n.* the operator of a brothel

bawd·y *adj.* racy; indecent; vulgar —**bawd·i·ly** *adv.* —**bawd·i·ness** *n.* —**bawd·ry** *n.*

bawl *n.* a loud outcry —*vi.* to sob noisily; to bellow or call out loudly —**bawl out** to berate

bay *adj.* reddish–brown —*n.* a reddish–brown horse; a wide inlet of the **sea** or a lake; a compartment or space used for storage as in a warehouse; the laurel, especially *Laurus nobilis* which provides the bay leaf for seasoning food; the cry of a dog, as in pursuit of game —*vi.* to cry out as a hound in pursuit —**at bay** cornered; held off: *keeping one's creditors at bay*

bay·ou *n.* a marshy inlet; a creek flowing through a delta

bay window an arrangement of windows that extends beyond the wall of a building

ba·zaar´ *n.* a market or fair for selling a variety of goods

beach *n.* a sandy shore; a place for sunbathing, swimming, etc. —*vi.*, *vt.* to strand a boat on land or on the bottom in shallow water

bea´con *n.* a warning signal, as a flag, fire, lamp, etc.

bead *n.* a small decorative ornament strung with others and worn around the neck or arm, or attached to a garment; a drop of liquid; the front sight of a rifle —*vi.* to gather in drops —*vt.* to decorate with beads —**draw a bead** take careful aim

beak *n.* a bird's bill; anything that is like a beak

beak´er *n.* a container with a lip formed for pouring

beam *n.* a large piece of wood or metal used for building; part of a balance; a shaft of light —*vi.*, *vt.* to shine, radiate

bean *n.* the edible seed of any leguminous plant; the plant that bears the seeds; the head —*vt.* to hit on the head, as by something thrown

bear *vi.* to suffer a burden; to be productive; to have reference to — *vt.* to possess; to endure, as trouble or hardship; to produce offspring; to assume, as a responsibility —**bear down** to exert pressure —**bear in mind** remain conscious of —**bear out** or **bear witness** to confirm or support —**bear up** to maintain strength or attitude —**bear´a·ble** *adj.* —**bear´a·bly** *adv.* —**bear´er** *n.*

bear *n.* a large wild animal with shaggy hair; an ill–tempered person; one who expects a decline in stock prices

beard *n.* facial hair —*vt.* to take hold or pull the beard of; to defy boldly —**beard´ed** *adj.*

bear´ing *n.* mode of conduct; a part in a machine which is in contact with a moving part; a compass heading; relevance or significance: *this has little bearing on the matter*

bear´ish *adj.* rough; surly; inclined to sell stock in anticipation of a decline in prices —**bear´ish·ly** *adv.* —**bear´ish·ness** *n.*

beast *n.* any animal, other than a human; animal qualities in a person; one who is savage or brutal —**beast´li·ness** *n.* —**beast´ly** *adj.*

beat *adj.* exhausted —*n.* a blow; a repeated fluctuation, as of sound or the heart; area covered by a policeman, watchman, etc. —*vi.* to strike repeatedly or with force; to sound by striking; to pulsate —*vt.* to strike repeatedly; to shape by hammering; to mix by stirring forcefully; to best another —**beat´er** *n.*

be·a·tif´ic *adj.* making happy; showing pleasure —**be·a·tif´i·cal·ly** *adv.*

be·at´i·fi·ca´tion *n.* a condition of blessedness —**be·at´i·fy** *vt.*

be·at´i·tude´ *n.* perfect happiness

beau *n.* an escort; a sweetheart

beau·ti´cian *n.* one skilled in the arts of hairdressing, manicure, cosmetics, etc.

beau´ti·ful *adj.* pleasing to the senses

beau´ti·fy *vt.* to make beautiful — **beau´ti·fi·ca´tion** *n.* —**beau´ti·fi·er** *n.*

beau´ty *n.* anything that by its quality pleases the senses —**beau´te·ous** *adj.* —**beau´te·ous·ly** *adv.* — **beau´te·ous·ness** *n.*

beaux–arts´ *n.* fine arts

bea´ver *n.* a large aquatic rodent or its fur; a high hat, formerly made from beaver fur

be´bop *n.* a type of improvisational jazz

be·calm *vt.* to induce tranquility; to cease from moving for lack of wind, as of a sailing ship

be·cause´ *conj.* for the reason that

beck´on *vi., vt.* to summon —*n.* a summoning gesture

be·cloud´ *vt.* to obscure, as an issue, by presenting irrelevant or misleading information

be·come´ *vi.* to come to be; to change into —*vt.* to suit

be·com´ing *adj.* attractive; suitable —**be·com´ing·ly** *adv.*

bed *n.* a piece of furniture, matting, place, etc. on which one sleeps or rests; a base or foundation; a specially prepared area, as *a flower bed* or *road bed* —**marriage bed** lying down together for the purpose of procreation

be·daz´zle *vt.* to blind; to impress or bewilder with brilliance

bed´ding *n.* linens for a bed; litter for an animal's bed; anything that forms a foundation

be·deck´ *vt.* to adorn; to decorate

be·dev´il *vt.* to harass or torment; to bewitch —**be·dev´il·ment** *n.*

bed´lam *n.* a place or condition of great confusion

bed´pan *n.* a vessel used in bed by a sick person for urination, etc.

be·drag´gle *vi., vt.* to soil or soak

bed´rid·den *adj.* confined to bed

bed´rock *n.* solid rock beneath the surface material

bed´room *n.* a room for sleeping

bedroom community a residential area populated mostly by those who work outside the community

bed´sore *n.* an ulcer on the body caused by long confinement to bed

bed´spread *n.* a bed covering

bed´spring *n.* the springs which support the mattress of a bed

bed´stead *n.* the framework which supports springs, mattress, etc.

bed´time *n.* the time for going to bed —*adj.*

bee *n.* one of a family of insects which produce honey and are valuable for pollinating certain crops; a social gathering, usually in a rural area: *a quilting bee*

bee´bread *n.* a substance stored by bees for food

beech *n.* a tree with smooth, ash-gray bark which grows in temperate regions and produces an edible nut; the wood of the beech

beef *n.* an adult ox, cow, steer, etc. or its flesh; muscle; a complaint

beef´y *adj.* large or muscular —**beef´i·ness** *n.*

bee´hive *n.* a nesting place for a colony of honey bees; a busy place

bee´line *n.* the shortest distance from one place to another —**make a beeline for** to rush directly and quickly to

beer *n.* an alcoholic beverage fermented from malts and hops; a beverage made from one of a variety of roots, as sassafras or ginger

bees´wax *n.* a substance secreted by honey bees, used to make the cells of a honeycomb

beet *n.* a fleshy root commonly used as a vegetable and in the production of sugar

be·fall´ *vi.* to come about; to occur —*vt.* to happen to

be·fore´ *adj.* preceding in time or place —*conj.* sooner than; rather than —*prep.* ahead of; in front of; in advance of

be·foul´ *vt.* to contaminate or pollute —**be·foul´er** *n.* —**be·foul´ment** *n.*

be·friend´ *vt.* to accept as a friend; to assist

be·fud´dle *vt.* to confuse

beg *vi., vt.* to ask for alms; to plead

beg´gar *n.* one who lives by begging; one who is impoverished —*vt.* to seem inadequate: *his answer beggars the question*; to impoverish

beg´gar·ly *adj.* like a beggar; pov-

erty–stricken; squalid —**beg´gar·li·
ness** *adv.*

be·gin´ *vi., vt.* to start; to come into
being

be·gin´ner *n.* a novice; one starting,
as of school or to learn a sport

be·gin´ning *n.* onset; a starting time
or place; the first part

be·grudge´ *vt.* to envy another's
pleasure; to give reluctantly —
be·grudg´ing·ly *adv.*

be·guile´ *vt.* to deceive by trickery; to
defraud; to charm or delight —**be·
guile´ment** *n.* —**be·guil´er** *n.* —**be·
guil´ing·ly** *adv.*

be·have´ *vi., vt.* to conduct oneself
well —**be·hav´ior** (*US*), **be·hav´
iour** (*Brit.*) *n.* —**be·hav´ior·al,** be·
hav´iour·al *adj.*

be·he´moth *n.* a huge beast

be·hest´ *n.* a decree or mandate; a
command

be·hind´ *adv.* toward the rear; past
in place or time; in arrears —*prep.*
at the back or far side of; following
after; not in the open or revealed

be·hold´ *vt.* to view

beige *adj.* of the light brownish–gray
color of natural wool —*n.* the color
of natural wool; a fabric of undyed,
unbleached wool

be´ing *n.* anything that exists; conscious existence; the essential
nature of a thing

be·la´bor *vt.* to denounce at length;
to needlessly prolong an argument

be·lat´ed *adj.* past the proper time
—**be·lat´ed·ly** *adv.* —**be·lat´ed·
ness** *n.*

belch *vi.* to expel gas through the
mouth; to expel violently

be·lea´guer *vt.* to harrass or annoy;
to besiege

bel´fry *n.* a bell tower

be·lie´ *vt.* to misrepresent; to prove
false

be·lief´ *n.* faith; trust; an expectation

be·lieve´ *vi.* to have trust or faith —
vt. to accept as true; to expect

—**be·liev·a·bil´i·ty** *n.* —**be·liev´a·
ble** *adj.* —**be·liev´a·bly** *adv.* —
be·liev´er *n.*

be·lit´tle *vt.* to disparage

bell *n.* a hollow, metallic instrument
which emits a tone when struck;
anything shaped like a bell; the
flared end of a wind instrument
which provides amplification and
resonance

bel·la·don´na *n.* deadly nightshade;
a perennial herb which yields a
number of poisonous alkaloids

bell´boy *n.* a hotel porter

belle *n.* a pretty female

bel´li·cose´ *adj.* hostile; of an aggressive nature —**bel´li·cose·ly**
adv. —**bel´li·cose·ness** *n.* —**bel·li·
cos´i·ty** *n.*

bel·lig´er·ent *adj.* warlike; at war —
n. one engaged in war —**bel·lig´er·
ence, bel·lig´er·en·cy** *n.*; **bel·lig´
er·ent·ly** *adv.*

bel´low *vi., vt.* to cry out loudly —*n.*
a loud cry

bel´lows *pl. n.* a device for producing
a stream of air, as for feeding a fire
or playing a pipe organ

bel´ly *n.* the abdomen; the stomach
and organs associated with it, as
the intestines; any protrusion
similar to the stomach

bel´ly·ache *n.* a pain in the stomach;
vi. to complain

bel´ly·but·ton *n.* the navel

belly dance a dance characterized
by gyrations of the hips and abdomen

belly flop a dive in which the stomach lands flat against the water

bel´ly·ful *n.* all that one can hold; all
that one can endure

belly laugh boisterous laughter

be·long´ *vi.* to be part of

be·long´ings *pl. n.* all that one owns

be·lov´ed *adj.* cherished —*n.* one
who is loved

be·low´ *adv.* in a lower place —*prep.*
farther down; inferior level, as of

rank, value, etc.

belt *n.* an article of clothing worn around the waist; a moveable band connecting two or more wheels in a machine; a moving line which transports parts or people from one place to another; a distinctive geographic zone: *the Bible belt, the wheat belt*; a blow; a shot of whiskey —*vt.* to encircle or secure with a belt; to strike —**below the belt** in boxing, an illegal punch, hence, any unfair act

belt´way (*US*) *n.* a roadway around a city

be·moan´ *vi., vt.* to express sorrow; mourn

be·muse´ *vt.* to absorb or preoccupy —**be·mus´ed·ly** *adv.* —**be·muse´ ment** *n.*

bench *n.* a long hard seat; a work table; the office of a judge; judges collectively

bench mark, bench´mark *n.* a surveyor´s marker used as a reference point; any standard for measuring quality, performance, etc.

bend *vi.* to turn; to yield, as from pressure; bow —*vt.* to curve or turn, incline; to subdue —*n.* a curved part —**bend´a·ble** *adj.*

be·neath´ *adj., adv.* below; in a lower position —*prep.* below or under; subordinate; unbefitting: *it is beneath her dignity*

ben´e·dick´, ben´e·dict´ *n.* a man recently married

ben´e·dic´tion *n.* an invocation of blessing —**ben·e·dic´tive, ben·e· dic´to·ry** *adj.*

ben´e·fac´tion *n.* the act of giving help; the help given —**ben´e·fac´ tor** *n.*

be·nef´i·cence *n.* active goodness; a charitable act —**be·nef´i·cent** *adj.* —**be·nef´i·cent·ly** *adv.*

ben´e·fi´cial *adj.* advantageous; profitable —**ben·e·fi´cial·ly** *adv.*

ben´e·fi´ci·ar·y *n.* one who holds or receives a benefit or inheritance

ben´e·fit *n.* a thing that helps; an activity to benefit a cause; payments received for retirement, illness, unemployment, etc. —*vi.* to help —*vt.* to aid

be·nev´o·lence *n.* a bent to do good; a charitable act —**be·nev´o·lent** *adj.* —**be·nev´o·lent·ly** *adv.*

be·nign´ *adj.* kindly; medically harmless —**be·nig·ni·ty** *n.* —**be· nign´ly** *adv.*

be·nig´nant *adj.* favorably inclined; agreeable —**be·nig´nan·cy** —**be· nig´nant·ly** *adv.*

bent *adj.* curved or warped; deformed; resolved: *bent on going* — *n.* a tendency; an inclination; an innate talent: *a bent for decorating*

be·numb *vt.* to daze or stun, as by shocking news; to deaden or paralyze, as with an anesthetic

be·queath´ *vt.* to pass on, especially by will —**be·queath´al** *n.*

be·quest´ *n.* a thing passed on

be·rate´ *vt.* to reprimand or scold severely

be·reave´ *vt.* to deprive of, especially by death —**be·reave´ment** *n.*

be·ret´ *n.* a flat soft cap, usually of cloth

ber´ry *n.* a small juicy fruit

ber·serk´ *adj., adv.* violent, rampaging; out of control —*n.* a berserker

ber·serk´er *n.* an early Norse warrior notable for viciousness and **sav**agery

berth *n.* a sleeping place; a position in a ship´s crew; room for ships to clear at sea; space to anchor

be·seech´ *vt.* to ask earnestly; to implore; to beg —**be·seech´er** *n.* — **be·seech´ing·ly** *adv.*

be·set´ *adj.* troubled; beleaguered — *vt.* to plague or torment; to embellish or decorate

be·side´ *prep.* adjacent to; alongside

be·sides´ *adv.* furthermore; else; in

addition —*prep.*

be·siege´ *vt.* to lay siege to; to overwhelm, as with information —**be·sieg´er** *n.*

be·smirch´ *vt.* to defame; bring dishonor upon

best *adj.* finest; of premium quality —*adv.* to the highest degree —*vt.* to defeat

bes´tial *adj.* of or like a beast; savage; brutal —**bes·ti·al´i·ty** *n.* —**bes´tial·ize** *vt.*

be·stir´ *vt.* to stir to action

be·stow´ *vt.* to give or endow —**be·stow´al** *n.*

best´sell´er *n.* that which is outselling all others of its type, as a book, record, etc.; often, that which is selling extremely well —**best´-sell´ing** *adj.*

bet *vi., vt.* to wager —*n.* the act of wagering; the stake in a wager —**bet´tor, bet·ter** *n.*

be·ta·tron´ *n.* an electron accelerator

be·tray´ *vt.* to be disloyal or unfaithful; to lead astray —**be·tray´al** *n.* —**be·tray´er** *n.*

be·troth´ *vt.* to commit oneself to marry; to promise in marriage, as a daughter —**be·troth´al** *n.*

be·throthed´ *adj.* engaged to be married —*n.* the person to whom one is engaged; bound to a pledge of marriage

bet´ter *adj.* more appropriate or suitable; improved, such as for health; recovering —*adv.* in a more suitable fashion —*n.* one in authority or a superior position —*vt.* to improve upon or refine; to outdo —**bet´ter·ment** *n.*

be·tween´ *adv.* in an intermediate position —*prep.* in or of that which separates or connects two things: *between friends, between light and dark, between events*

bev´el *adj.* biased; sloping —*n.* a sloping surface; an angle of more or less than 90°; a tool for measuring and marking angles —*vi.* to slant —*vt.* to cut at an angle

bev´er·age *n.* a liquid for drinking

bev´y *n.* a group

be·wail´ *vt.* to lament

be·ware´ *vi., vt.* to be on one's guard

be·wil´der *vt.* to confuse or confound, as by something mysterious or unexplainable; to astonish or shock —**be·wil´der·ed·ly, be·wil´der·ing·ly** *adv.* —**be·wil´der·ed·ness, be·wil´der·ment** *n.*

be·witch´ *vt.* to enchant or charm; to captivate —**be·witch´ing** *adj.* —**be·witch´ing·ly** *adv.*

be·yond´ *adv.* farther away —*prep.* farther than; greater than; surpassing

bi·an´nu·al *adj.* occurring twice each year —**bi·an´nu·al·ly** *adv.*

bi´as *n.* prejudice; partiality —*vt.* to influence

Bible *n.* the Scriptures

bible *n.* any book or writing recognized as sanctioned or approved —**bib´li·cal** *adj.* —**bib´li·cal·ly** *adv.*

bib·li·og´ra·phy *n.* a list of information sources for a given subject —**bib·li·og´ra·pher** *n.* —**bib´li·o·graph´ic, bib´li·o·graph´i·cal** *adj.*

bib´li·o·phile *n.* a collector of books

bi·cam´er·al *adj.* having two legislative bodies

bicarbonate of soda (*Brit.*) sodium bicarbonate; a white crystalline compound used in cooking, cleaning, as an antacid, etc.

bi·cen·ten´ni·al *adj.* occurring once in two hundred years —*n.* a two hundred year anniversary —**bi·cen·ten´a·ry** *adj., n.*

bi´ceps *n.* a muscle having two points of connection

bick´er *n.* a petty quarrel —*vi.* to quarrel

bi·cus´pid *n.* an adult tooth with a two-pointed crown —**bi·cus´pi·date** *adj.*

bi·cy·cle *n.* a two-wheeled vehicle propelled by the rider —*vi.*, *vt.* to propel a bicycle —**bi´cy·cler, bi´cy·clist** *n.*

bid *n.* an amount offered; an attempt —*vt.* to request or order; to make an offer; to declare openly —**bid´der** *n.*

bid´dy *n.* a hen; a person considered a gossip

bi·en´ni·al *adj.* lasting two years; occurring every two years —*n.* a plant that lives two years —**bi·en´ni·al·ly** *adv.* —**bi·en´ni·um** *n.*

bi´fo·cals *pl. n.* eyeglasses with part of the lens for near vision and part for distant vision

bi´fur·cate *vi.*, *vt.* to split into two parts —**bi´fur·cate, bi·fur·cat·ed** *adj.* forked; having two branches —**bi´fur·cat·ly** *adv.* —**bi·fur·ca´tion** *n.*

big *adj.* large in size, quantity, force, etc.; important; massive; substantial; generous —**big´ness** *n.*

big´a·mist *n.* one is who married to two or more persons at one time —**big´a·mous** *adj.* —**big´a·mous·ly** *adv.* —**big´a·my** *n.*

big´heart·ed *adj.* generous —**big´heart·ed·ly** *adv.* —**big´heart·ed·ness** *n.*

big´ot *n.* an intolerant person —**big´ot·ed** *adj.* —**big´ot·ry** *n.*

bi´jou *n.* an ornament or bauble; a piece of jewelry; a trinket

bike *n.* a bicycle; a motorcycle —**bik´er** *n.*

bi·ki´ni *n.* a brief bathing suit

bi·lat´er·al *adj.* reciprocal; involving or affecting two parties —**bi·lat´er·al·ly** *adv.*

bile *n.* a digestive fluid secreted in the liver; bitterness, hostility

bi·lin´gual *adj.* capable of conversing in two languages —**bi·lin´gual·ism** *n.* —**bi·lin´gual·ly** *adv.*

bil´ious *adj.* of bile or an ailment of the liver; ill-tempered —**bil´ious·ly**

adv. —**bil´ious·ness** *n.*

bilk *vt.* to cheat or swindle; to defraud —**bilk´er** *n.*

bill *n.* an invoice; (*US*) paper money; a draft of a law; the bony structure of a bird's jaw: a beak —*vt.* to make or tender an invoice —**bill´a·ble** *adj.*

bill´board *n.* a large outdoor signboard

bil´lion (US) *n.* one thousand million

bill of fare a restaurant menu

bill of lading a document listing the particulars relating to goods being shipped

bill of sale a document attesting to the transfer of property

bil´low *n.* a large wave; any surging mass —*vi.*, *vt.* to surge or swell —**bil´low·i·ness** *n.* —**bil´low·y** *adj.*

bi·month·ly *adj.*, *adv.* once every two months; of that occurring every two months, as *a bimonthly report* —*n.* a publication issued every two months

bin *n.* a receptacle for storing coal, corn, etc.

bi´na·ry *adj.* comprised of two parts; of a numbering system in base two

binary star a double star

binary system a numbering system in base two

bind —*vt.* to make fast; to fasten together; to obligate —*vi.* to tie; to be obligatory —*n.* a difficult situation

bind´er *n.* one who binds, especially books; something that holds together; a temporary agreement that remains in effect until execution of a final contract

bind´ing *adj.* obligatory, required —*n.* something used to hold together, as a strap, bandage, book cover, etc.

bi·no´mi·al *adj.* of a two part equation —*n.* a mathematical equation

bi´o·as·tro·nau´tics *n.* the study of living things in a weightless environment

bi·o·chem·is·try *n.* biological or physiological chemistry

bi·o·de·grad·a·ble *adj.* readily decomposed through bacterial action —**bi·o·de·grad·a·bil·i·ty, bi·o·deg·ra·da·tion** *n.* —**bi·o·de·grade** *vt.*

bi·o·e·col·o·gy *n.* the study of the interrelationship of animals and plants to their environment

bi·og·ra·phy *n.* the story of a person's life —**bi·og·ra·pher** *n.* —**bi·o·graph·ic, bi·o·graph·i·cal** *adj.*

biological clock the natural cycles in the life of an organism

biological warfare the use of microorganisms as a weapon of war

bi·ol·o·gy *n.* the science that deals with life forms —**bi·ol·o·gist** *n.* —**bi·o·log·ic, bi·o·log·i·cal** *adj.* —**bi·o·log·i·cal·ly** *adv.*

bi·op·sy *n.* the removal of tissue from the body for laboratory analysis

bi·o·sphere *n.* the living creatures of earth; the area in which earth's creatures exist

bi·o·tin *n.* a B vitamin

bi·par·ti·san *adj.* consisting of two political parties —**bi·par·ti·san·ism** *n.* —**bi·par·ti·san·ship** *n.*

bi·par·tite *adj.* having two parts or sections

bi·ped *n.* an animal with two feet

bi·po·lar *adj.* having two poles; of opposing doctrines, characteristics, etc.

birch·bark *n.* the outer covering of the birch tree; a canoe made from the bark of the birch tree —*adj.* resembling the outer covering of the birch tree, especially the white birch

birch beer a beverage flavored with oil of birch

bird *n.* a warm-blooded, feathered animal with wings

bird of prey any of a variety of birds that catch and eat other animals

birth *n.* the act of coming into life; background or lineage

birth·mark *n.* an impression on the skin that is evident at birth; a blemish

birth·right *n.* the rights that come to one by virtue of being born into a family, country, etc.

birth·stone *n.* a gem associated with a particular birth month

bisect *vt.* to divide into two parts —**bi·sec·tion** *n.* —**bi·sec·tion·al** *adj.* —**bi·sec·tor** *n.*

bi·sex·u·al *adj.* of both sexes; having both male and female organs

bish·op *n.* a ranking member of the clergy; a chess piece

bish·op·ric *n.* the office of a bishop

bisque *n.* a thick, creamed soup

bit *n.* a small scrap or quantity; a boring tool; a minor part in a play; the mouthpiece of a bridle

bitch *n.* a female dog —*vi.* to complain

bite *n.* the act of taking by the teeth; the amount taken; hurt or damage made by teeth; a stinging —*vi.* to grip; to hurt, as from a sting; to have a sharp taste; to take bait —*vt.* to seize with the teeth; to sting

bit·ter *adj.* having an acrid taste; cruel, harsh; resentful —**bit·ter·ly** *adv.* —**bit·ter·ness** *n.*

bit·ters *n.* a flavoring, medication or tonic made from bitter herbs

bit·ter·sweet *adj.* of a flavor that is both bitter and sweet; pleasure accompanied by sadness, as of memories that are both pleasant and painful

bi·week·ly *adj., adv.* occurring once every two weeks

bi·year·ly *adj., adv.* occurring once every two years

bi·zarre *adj.* extremely unusual or unexpected —**bi·zarre·ly** *adv.* —**bi·zarre·ness** *n.*

blab *vi., vt.* to chatter, jabber; to reveal or tattle —**blab·ber** *n., vi.*

black *adj.* of the Afro–American peoples or their culture —*n.* technically, the absence of color; the opposite of white; an Afro–American —**black´en** *vi., vt.* —**black´en·er** *n.* —**black´ish** *adj.*

black-and-blue *adj.* bruised

black and white committed to writing; of a reproduction that is not in full color; of that expressed clearly or precisely

black art sorcery or witchcraft

black´ball´ *vt.* to vote against, as a nominee for membership; to ostracize

black´board´ *n.* a surface for drawing or writing with chalk

black eye discoloration around the eye following a blow; a disgrace or blemish; a blemish on one's reputation

black´guard *n.* a villain, scoundrel

black´-heart´ed *adj.* wicked, sinister —**black´-heart´ed·ly** *adv.* —**black´-heart´ed·ness** *n.*

black hole a collapsed star with a gravitational field so strong that no light or matter can escape it

black light infrared or ultraviolet light used for special effects, night vision, etc.

black´list *n.* a list of those to be excluded, as from working, trading, etc. —*vt.* to deliberately exclude

black magic sorcery, witchcraft

black´mail´ *n.* extortion —*vt.* to extort payment by threat of disclosure

black mar´ket *n.* illegal trade in goods or currency —**black´-mar´ket** *adj.* —**black´-mar´ket·eer**, **black´-mar´ket·er** *n.*

black´-mar´ket *vt.* to trade on the black market

black´out´ *n.* the extinguishing of all lights; a loss of electricity to an area; a temporary loss of consciousness or memory

black sheep a family or group member who is considered different, usually less reputable or successful

black´smith *n.* one who works in iron

black tie of a mode of dress that includes a black bow tie, tuxedo, etc.; formal; of an affair that requires formal dress

black´top (*US*) *n.* a material such as asphalt used to surface roads; a road so surfaced —*vt.* to surface a road with asphalt

bladder *n.* a pouch in animals to hold gas or liquid; anything resembling such a pouch

blade *n.* a plant leaf, such as grass; any broad, flat surface, as of an oar or certain bones; the cutting part of an instrument, as a knife or scissors

blame *n.* condemnation, denunciation; accountability for a wrong —*vt.* to charge with responsibility for a wrong; to condemn or rebuke —**blam´a·ble** *adj.* —**blam´a·bly** *adv.* —**blame´ful** *adj.* —**blame´ful·ly** *adv.* —**blame´ful·ness** *n.*

blame´less *adj.* innocent; irreproachable; free of blame —**blame´less·ly** *adv.* —**blame´less·ness** *n.*

blanch *vi.* to whiten —*vt.* to make white; to bleach; to immerse food briefly in boiling water prior to skinning, freezing, etc.

bland *adj.* soothing, mild; insipid, dull

blan´dish *vt.* to persuade by guile or flattery —**blan´dish·er** *n.* —**blan´dish·ment** *n.*

blank *adj.* empty, vacant, unadorned; not filled out, as of a form —*n.* a void; emptiness; a form or questionnaire —**draw a blank** unable to remember or accomplish something **blank´ly** *adv.* —**blank´ness** *n.*

blan´ket *adj.* of that encompassing a

number of elements, as *blanket insurance coverage* —*n.* a bed covering; anything that covers like a blanket: *a blanket of flowers* —*vt.* to cover; to canvass: *blanket the area with pollsters*

blank verse poetry that does not rhyme

blare *n.* a harsh noise —*vi., vt.* to sound loudly

blar´ney *n.* flattering speech

bla·sé´ *adj.* indifferent, unconcerned; bored

blas´pheme´ *vt.* to speak or act in an irreverent manner —*vi.* to utter blasphemy —**blas´phem·er** *n.*

blas´phe·my *n.* a profane or irreverent act or expression, esp. toward something considered sacred —**blas´phe·mous** *adj.* —**blas´phe·mous·ly** *adv.*

blast *n.* sudden rush of air; a harsh sound; an explosion —*vi.* to make a harsh sound; to set off an explosive —*vt.* to explode; to denounce

blast furnace a furnace for separating impurities from metallic ore

bla´tant *adj.* offensively noisy; obvious, conspicuous —**bla´tan·cy** *n.* —**bla´tant·ly** *adv.*

blaze *n.* a burst of flame or light —*vi.* to burn brightly; to shine brightly

bla´zer *n.* a sports jacket

bleach *n.* a substance used to whiten —*vi.* to grow white —*vt.* to remove color; to make white —**bleach´er** *n.*

bleach´ers *pl. n.* the least expensive seating, often long benches, especially at sporting events

bleak *adj.* desolate; dreary; gloomy

blear´y *adj.* blurred or indistinct —**blear´i·ly** *adv.* —**blear´i·ness** *n.*

bleat *n.* the characteristic cry of an animal —*vi., vt.*

bleed *vi.* to lose vital fluid, as blood from a person or sap from a tree; to run together, as paints or dye; to be printed off the edge of a page —*vt.* to draw fluid or gas from; to print off the edge of a page; to impoverish

blem´ish *n.* a flaw or defect —*vt.* to deface

blend *n.* a mixture —*vi., vt.* to mix; to combine so as to make a gradual transition, as of colors

bless *vt.* to consecrate; to favor —**bless´ed·ness** *n.*

bless´ed *adj.* consecrated; blissful; rewarded —**bless´ed·ly** *adv.*

bless´ing *n.* an invocation; grace before a meal; divine sanction; good fortune

blight *n.* a plant disease; anything that damages —*vt.* to destroy

blimp *n.* an airship

blind *adj.* sightless; unseen —*n.* anything that obscures or conceals —*vt.* to deprive of sight; to dazzle —**blind´er** *n.* —**blind´ly** *adv.* —**blind´ness** *n.*

blind´fold *n.* anything that restricts sight or comprehension —*vt.* to cover the eyes of; to mislead

blind´ing *adj.* with great speed; faster than the eye can follow —**blind´ing·ly** *adv.*

blind spot an area where vision or visual reception is restricted; a prejudice that distorts ones perception or thinking

blink *vi., vt.* to close and open the eyelids quickly; to flash on and off, as a light

blink´er *n.* a flashing light, as on a vehicle or a stationary mounting; (*US*) an automobile turn signal

blintz, blintze *n.* a thin pancake rolled around a filling

bliss *n.* great happiness; ecstasy, rapture —**bliss´ful** *adj.* —**bliss´ful·ly** *adv.* —**bliss´ful·ness** *n.*

blis´ter *n.* a bulging sac of matter on the skin; anything similar to a skin blister; a transparent covering for merchandise attached to a cardboard backing —*vi., vt.* to form a blister —**blis´ter·y** *adj.*

blithe *adj.* gay; lighthearted; vivacious —**blithe´ly** *adv.* —**blithe´ ness** *n.* —**blithe´some** *adj.*

bliz´zard *n.* a violent snowstorm

bloat *vi., vt.* to swell

blob *n.* a clump of indefinite shape; a large person

bloc *n.* a political alliance

block *n.* a large chunk of material; a system of pulleys; a related or contiguous group; a barrier —*vt.* to hinder or restrict; to form a rough plan —**block´age** *n.*

block·ade´ *n.* a barrier —*vt.* to set up a barrier —**block·ad´er** *n.*

block´bust·er *adj.* of that which is extravagant, as a movie, book, etc. —*n.* an extravagant or ostentatious work; an investor or real estate agent who creates the impression of a change in the ethnic makeup of a neighborhood so as to buy property at reduced prices

block´head *n.* a stupid person; **block´head·ed** *adj.*; **block´head· ed·ness** *n.*

block letter a plain alphanumeric character, without serifs or any embellishment

blond *adj.* of fair skin, hair, etc.; of a light wood finish

blonde *n.* a blond female

blood *n.* a vital body fluid; heritage; kinship —**new blood** a new member or members

blood bank a reserve of liquid or dried human blood

blood bath a massacre; wholesale replacement of a company's executives

blood brother a male sibling; one bound by an oath or ceremony

blood count clinical analysis of the contents of a quantity of blood

blood´curd·ling *adj.* frightening; ghastly

blood´ed *adj.* pedigreed; of known stock

blood´hound *n.* a breed of dog used in tracking; a person who is relentless in pursuit

blood´less *adj.* lacking blood; without bloodshed, peacful; lacking feeling, indifferent —**blood´less·ly** *adv.* —**blood´less·ness** *n.*

blood´let·ting *n.* bloodshed; figuratively, the replacement of a number of employees in a company or division

blood money payment for performance of that which is illegal or unethical; financial gain from the suffering of others

blood pressure a measure of the force of blood coursing through the arteries

blood relation, blood relative one related by birth

blood´shed *n.* carnage; slaughter

blood´stained *adj.* soiled by blood; guilty of shedding the blood of another

blood´suck·er *n.* a leech; one who takes as much as possible from another; a parasite —**blood´suck· ing** *adj.*

blood´thirst·y *adj.* barbarous; inclined to murder; of a ruthless nature —**blood´thirst·i·ly** *adv.* — **blood´thirst·i·ness** *n.*

blood vessel any of the arteries, veins or capillaries which carry blood throughout the body

blood´y *adj.* of the shedding of blood; bleeding or containing blood; bloodstained; murderous — **blood´i·ly** *adv.* —**blood´i·ness** *n.*

bloom *n.* a flower; a healthy glow — *vi.* to flower; to glow

bloop´er *n.* a mistake; a silly blunder

blos´som *n.* a flower —*vi.* to flower; to develop

blot *n.* a flaw; dishonor; a spot or stain —*vt.* to stain; to dishonor; to get rid of —**blot´ter** *n.*

blotch *n.* a stain or blemish —*vt.* to blemish

blotch´y *adj.* marked by discoloration; covered with blemishes — **blotch´i·ness** *n.*

blouse *n.* a loose shirt

blow *n.* a sharp rap; a setback; a blast of air; a windstorm —*vi.* to move air, as by the wind or the lungs; to be carried by moving air; to be stormy —*vt.* to expel air; to propel by moving air; to waste money; to fail; to leave —**blow up** to explode; to form by blowing, as a balloon; to enlarge a photograph

blow´out *n.* the bursting of a tire; a large party or celebration

blow´torch *n.* a tool that produces a flame for softening metal, removing paint, etc.

blow·up *n.* an explosion; an enlarged photograph

blub´ber *n.* whale fat; excess fat on humans —*vi.* to weep —**blub´ber·y** *adj.*

bludg´eon *n.* a heavy club —*vt.* to strike with a club; to bully

blue *adj.* bluish in color; despondent —*n.* anything the color or near the color of the clear sky —*vt.* to make blue in color

blue baby a child born with a heart or respiratory defect

blue´bell *n.* any of a variety of plants with blue bell-shaped flowers

blue blood, blue´blood *n.* one descended from aristocracy; high society, upper class —**blue´-blood·ed** *adj.*

blue chip, blue´chip *adj.* designating of a group of companies whose stocks are characterized by stability of price and earnings; of anything that is preceived as stable — **blue´-chip** *adj.*

blue collar a label applied to industrial workers

blue´grass *adj.* of a type of southern mountain music —*n.*

blue jeans, blue·jeans *n.* a type of trouser made from blue denim

blue laws any of the state laws or local ordinances that prohibit the transaction of business on Sunday

blue´nose *n.* one who attempts to impose his or her moral code on others

blue–pen´cil *vt.* to edit or correct

blue´print *n.* an architect or engineer´s drawing; any detailed plan of action

blue ribbon first prize in a judged competition

blue–sky´ *adj.* of no intrinsic value; a wish or dream

blue streak of anything fast, lively or animated

bluff *adj.* exhibiting an abrupt manner —*n.* a steep bank; an act of deception —*vt.* to mislead by feigning; to deceive

blun´der *n.* a foolish mistake —*vi.* to make a foolish error; to move clumsily —**blun´der·er** *n.* —**blun´der·ing·ly** *adv.*

blunt *adj.* not sharp; plain–spoken, curt; slow-witted, dull —*vt.* to dull; to reduce the effectiveness of — **blunt´ly** *adv.* —**blunt´ness** *n.*

blur *n.* anything indistinct —*vt., vi.* to make or become indistinct — **blur´ry** *adj.*

blurb *n.* a brief commercial or announcement; a brief comment or extract from a review on a book cover or jacket

blurt *vt.* to say without thinking

blush *n.* a sudden reddening of the face; a reddish color —*vi., vt.* to become red or reddish —**blush´er** *n.* —**blush´ing·ly** *adv.*

blus´ter *n.* arrogant speech, often empty threats —*vi.* to blow in violent gusts; to act in an arrogant, bullying manner —**blus´ter·ing·ly** *adv.* —**blus´ter·ous, blus´ter·y** *adj.*

bo´a *n.* a large snake; a long scarf made of soft material, as of fur or feathers

boar *n.* a mature male pig

board *n.* a thin plank; any of various flat panels fashioned for a special purpose; meals provided for pay; a group that controls or regulates — *vt.* to supply with meals; to get on a vessel —*vi.* to take meals at a boarding house

board´er *n.* a lodger; a paying guest who is provided room and meals

board foot a measure of lumber that equals one square foot, one inch thick

boarding house an establishment that provides rooms and meals for paying guests

boarding school a school that provides a residence and meals for the students

board´walk *n.* a wooden walkway built along a beach

boast *vi., vt.* to brag —*n.* pretension —**boast´er** *n.* —**boast´ful** *adj.* — **boast´ful·ly, boast´ing·ly** *adv.*

boat *n.* any vessel that plies the inland seas —**boat´er** *n.* — **boat´ing** *adj., n.*

bob´bin *n.* a spool for thread or yarn

bobby pin (*US*) a metal hair pin

bob´sled *n.* a long sled with two sets of runners and a steering mechanism

bock beer a dark German beer

bod´ice *n.* the upper part of a woman´s dress

bod´i·ly *adj.* physical; of the body — *adv.* totally, entirely

bod´y *n.* physical structure; the main part of anything; a person; a group considered as a unit; characteristic density

body politic society; those who are united under a government

bog *n.* a small swamp or marsh

bo´gus *adj.* of doubtful authenticity

bo·he´mi·an *n.* one who is unconventional, as an artist, writer, etc.

boil *vi.* to bubble from heat; to cook in a boiling liquid; to churn; to seethe with rage —*vt.* to heat to the boiling point; to process in a boiling liquid

boil´er *n.* a tank for heating water to produce steam; a tank for heating and storing water

boiling point the temperature at which a liquid boils; conditions under which one is inclined to lose control

bois´ter·ous *adj.* noisy; rowdy — **bois´ter·ous·ly** *adv.* —**bois´ter· ous·ness** *n.*

bold *adj.* daring; forceful; impudent —**bold´ly** *adv.* —**bold´ness** *n.*

bold´-faced, bold´faced *adj.* impudent; brazen

bo·le´ro *n.* a Spanish dance; a short jacket

bol´lix *vt.* to bungle; to mismanage

bol´ster *n.* a long pillow —*vt.* to prop up; to reinforce —**bol´ster·er** *n.*

bolt *n.* a bar for securing an entrance; a threaded fastener; a roll of cloth; a sudden start —*vi.* to spring suddenly; to break away — *vt.* to secure with a bar or lock; to fasten with a bolt; to eat hurriedly; to break away, as from a group

bomb *n.* a casing filled with an explosive, compressed gas, etc.; a failure —*vi.* to fail utterly —*vt.* to attack with bombs

bom·bas´tic *adj.* high–sounding but meaningless —**bom´bast´** *n.* — **bom·bas´ti·cal·ly** *adv.*

bomb´shell *n.* a bomb; any sudden shock or surprise; a rude awakening

bo´na fide *adj.* genuine; sincere; in good faith

bo·nan´za *n.* a rich source of ore; any profitable venture

bon´bon *n.* a small candy

bond *n.* a formal obligation; a thing that binds —*vt.* to place or hold under bond; to place in a bonded warehouse; to tie or join together —**bond´a·ble** *adj.* —**bond´er** *n.*

bond´age *n.* servitude, enslavement

bond´ed *adj.* secured by a bond; in a bonded warehouse; bound by fetters

bonds´man *n.* one who furnishes a bond for another for a fee

bone *n.* hard tissue forming the parts of a skeleton —*vt.* to remove bones from

bon´er *n.* a silly mistake; a blooper

bon´fire´ *n.* a large outdoor fire

bon´net *n.* a females hat

bo´nus *n.* an extra payment, especially an incentive; any extra benefit

bon´y *adj.* of a bone or bones; skinny, emaciated; with many bones, as of a food fish —**bon´i·ness** *n.*

boob *n.* one who is foolish; an oaf — **boo´by** *n.*

booby trap a device designed to be set off by an unsuspecting victim

book *n.* a set of pages bound together with a protective cover; a division of a lengthly literary work; a body of information about a particular subject

book´case *n.* a freestanding set of shelves for holding books, artifacts, etc.

book´end *n.* a device to keep a row of books in place

book´ie *n.* a bookmaker: one who takes bets, as on horse races or athletic contests

book´ish *adj.* scholarly; given to studying —**book´ish·ly** *adv.* — **book´ish·ness** *n.*

book´keep·ing *n.* the recording of the financial transactions of an organization —**book´keep·er** *n.*

book´let *n.* a small book or pamphlet

book´mak·er *n.* one who accepts wagers on races, athletic contests, etc. —**book´mak·ing** *n.*

book´mark *n.* a device to keep the reader's place in a book

book´mo·bile´ *n.* a vehicle that serves as a mobile library

book´plate *n.* a label in or on a book that identifies the owner

book review a verbal or written commentary about a book

book´worm *n.* one who spends considerable time reading or studying

boom *n.* a deep sound, as of thunder; an upturn in business activity —*vi.* to make a deep sound

boo´me·rang *n.* a flat, bent stick that, when thrown, returns to the thrower; anything that acts differently than planned, creating the opposite effect of that intended

boon *n.* good fortune

boon´dog·gle *n.* a pointless project, often undertaken with public funds; a no-win situation

boor *n.* one who is vulgar or unrefined —**boor´ish** *adj.* —**boor´ish·ly** *adv.* —**boor´ish·ness** *n.*

boost *n.* assistance; an increase —*vt.* to push upward; to increase; to support or promote —**boost´er** *n.*

boot *n.* a covering for the foot and lower leg —*vt.* to kick; to dismiss from a job

booth *n.* a stall for the display or sale of goods, as at a fair; partially isolated seating in a restaurant

boot´leg´ *adj.* illegal —*vi., vt.* to transport or sell illegally —**boot´leg·ger** *n.*

boo´ty *n.* loot; spoils of war

booze *n.* any alcholic beverage — **booz´er** *n.* —**booz´y** *adj.*

bor´der *n.* a boundary; margin —*vt.* to extend along the boundary

bor´der·line *adj.* marginal; of questionable value —*n.* an edge or line of demarcation

bore *n.* a round hole; a dull person or event —*vt.* to make a round hole; to make weary by being dull —**bor´er** *n.*

bore´dom *n.* lack of interest; listlessness

bor´ing *adj.* uninteresting, tiresome, or dull —**bor´ing·ly** *adv.* —**bor´ing·ness** *n.*

bor´ough *n.* in Britain and some US states, an incorporated town

bor´row *vi., vt.* to take something with agreement to return or repay in kind or equivalent; to adopt, as an idea —**bor´row·er** *n.*

bos´om *n.* the human breast; closeness, likened to being clasped to ones breast —**bos´om·y** *adj.*

boss *n.* supervisor; a person in charge —*vi., vt.* to supervise

boss´y *adj.* acting like a boss; domineering —**boss´i·ness** *n.*

boss´ism *n.* control of a political district by an autocratic leader

bot´a·ny *n.* the study of plants —**bo·tan´i·cal** *adj.* —**bo·tan´i·cal·ly** *adv.* —**bot´a·nist** *n.*

botch *n.* a shoddy piece of work —*vt.* to bungle; to do a shoddy job —**botched** *adj.* —**botch´er** *n.* —**botch´y** *adj.*

both´er *n.* a cause of irritation; vexation —*vi.* to be concerned with; to fuss over —*vt.* to disturb or trouble; to inconvenience —**both´er·some** *adj.*

bot´tle *n.* a glass container with a narrow neck; the amount a bottle can hold —*vt.* to put into bottles —**bot´tler** *n.*

bot´tle·neck´ *n.* a place where progress is obstructed

bot´tom *adj.* of the lowest point —*n.* the lowest part of anything; the seat of a chair

bouf·fant´ *adj.* puffed out, as a hairdo

bough *n.* the branch of a tree

boul´der *n.* a large rock or stone worn smooth by weather or water

bou´le·vard´ *n.* a broad paved street, often landscaped

bounce *n.* a rebound; the capacity to rebound; zest, spirit —*vi.* to rebound; to spring; to return a check for insufficient funds —*vt.* to throw so as to cause a rebound; to eject an undesirable person; to dismiss from employment —**bounc´er** *n.*

bound *adj.* obligated; determined; tied or restricted in some way —*n.* a leap —*vi.* to leap; to border on another area —*vt.* to cause to leap or bounce; to mark or provide with boundaries

bound´a·ry *n.* a border or limit

bound´less *adj.* without end; unlimited —**bound´less·ly** *adv.* —**bound´less·ness** *n.*

boun´te·ous *adj.* plentiful —**boun´ti·ful** *adj.* —**boun´ti·ful·ly** *adv.* —**boun´ti·ful·ness** *n.*

boun´ty *n.* a profusion; a reward or inducement

bou·quet´ *n.* a bundle of cut flowers; fragrance

bour´bon *n.* a whiskey distilled mainly from corn —*adj.* made from or with bourbon

bour·geois *adj.* of the middle class; conventional —*n.* a member of the middle class

bour·geoi·sie´ *n.* the middle class as a whole

bout *n.* a struggle; an incident, as of an illness

bou·tique´ *n.* a small specialty shop

bou·ton·niere´ *n.* a flower worn in the buttonhole of a lapel

bo´vine *adj.* of oxen; exhibiting the qualities of an ox

bow *n.* a bending of the head or body; the front of a vessel; a curve; a device for shooting arrows; a decorative knot —*vi., vt.* to bend the body in greeting; to yield

bow´el *n.* an intestine —*pl.* **bow´els** the intestines collectively; the inside of anything perceived as deep and dark: *the bowels of the earth*

bowl *n.* a deep, rounded dish for food; anything similar in shape —*vt.* to participate in the game of bowling

bow´leg·ged *adj.* having legs that are bowed

bowl´er *n.* one who bowls; a derby

bowl´ing *n.* a game of tenpins

box *n.* a container made of cardboard, wood, etc.

box´car (*US*) *n.* a rail freight car

box´er *n.* a prizefighter

box office location where tickets are sold, as for a sporting event

box score detailed statistics of a sporting event

box seat premium seats at a theater, sports staduim, etc.

boy *n.* a male youth —**boy´hood** *n.* —**boy´ish** *adj.* —**boy´ish·ly** *adv.* — **boy´ish·ness** *n.*

boy´cott´ *n.* a refusal to have dealings with —*vt.* to avoid dealings with

bra *n.* a brassière; the top part of a two–piece swimsuit

brace *n.* a support or fastener; a pair of marks { } to connect elements or lines; a pair of like things —*vt.* to support; to fit out with braces; to steady oneself for an impact — **brac´er** *n.*

brace´let *n.* a piece of jewelry worn on the wrist or ankle

brack´et *n.* a support projecting from a wall; an angled support; a pair of marks [ ] to enclose words; a group of associated elements within a larger array —*vt.* to support or enclose with brackets; to group associated elements

brack´ish *adj.* slightly salty; disagreeable in taste

brad *n.* a small finishing nail

brag *vi., vt.* to say boastfully —*n.* a boast; something boasted about; a boaster

brag·ga·do´ci·o *n.* bravado; a swaggering manner

brag´gart, brag´ger *n.* one who boasts; a blowhard —**brag´gart·ly** *adv.*

braid (*US*) *n.* a strip of interwoven hair; a band of woven decorative material —*vt.* to interweave; to trim with interwoven material — **braid´er** *n.* —**braid´ing** *n.*

braille *n.* a method of writing that the blind can read by touch

brain *n.* a mass of tissue in the skull; the center of thought; mental ability; an intelligent person

brain´child *n.* that produced by one's own creative powers

brain´less *adj.* lacking common sense; mindless

brain´pow·er *n.* the ability to think; intellect

brain´storm *n.* inspiration —*vi.* to take part in a freewheeling session designed to generate ideas — **brain´storm·er** *n.*

brain´wash´ *vt.* to indoctrinate to a new set of beliefs

brain´y *adj.* extremely intelligent; quick–witted —**brain´i·ness** *n.*

braise *vt.* to simmer in liquid

brake *n.* any device for slowing or stopping motion —*vi., vt.* to slow or stop

bran *n.* the outer husk of grain

branch *n.* any extension from a main part or course —*vi.* to extend from the main part

brand *n.* a burning stick; a mark of ownership, stigma, etc.; a trademark —*vt.* to mark, as with a brand

bran´dish *vt.* to wave menacingly

brand´-new *adj.* recently introduced or acquired; not used

bran´dy *n.* an alcoholic beverage distilled from wine

brash *adj.* impetuous; insolent — **brash´ly** *adv.* —**brash´ness** *n.*

brass *n.* an alloy of copper and zinc; fittings, instruments, etc. made from the alloy; boldness, impudence; high–ranking officers, executives, etc. —*adj.* pertaining to or made from brass

brass´y *adj.* brazen; impudent

—**brass´i·ly** adv. —**brass´i·ness** n.

brat n. a badly behaved child —**brat´ty** adj.

bra·va´do n. pretended courage; bluster

brave adj. courageous; bold —vt. to face courageously —**brave´ness** n. —**brave´ly** adv.

brav´er·y n. courage

bra·vu´ra n. a showy display; ostentation

brawl n. a noisy quarrel —vi. to quarrel noisily —**brawl´er** n.

brawn n. muscle; muscular strength —**brawn´i·ness** n. —**brawn´y** adj.

bray n. the harsh cry of a donkey; any similar noise

bra´zen adj. of or like brass; bold, impudent —**bra´zen·ly** adv. —**bra´zen·ness** n.

bra´zier n. a coal heater or cooker; a worker in brass

breach n. a break or opening; a violation of a contract; a disagreement —vt. to break through; to violate an agreement

bread n. a baked or fried food made from grain; food in general; money

bread and butter the essentials; primary, as of an important or profitable product line of a company

bread line a place where free food is distributed; those waiting for free food

breadth n. width; the distance from one side to the other

bread´win·ner n. the one who works to support others in a family or group

break n. a breach or fracture; a stopping or pause; an interval of rest; luck or opportunity: to get a break; a sudden move —vi. to split, come apart; to become inoperable; to sever relations; to appear or happen suddenly; to run away —vt. to part by force; to ruin or cause to fail; to violate the

terms of a contract —**break´a·ble** adj.

break´age n. things broken; an allowance for things broken

break dance a style of acrobatic dance —**break dancer, break dancing**

break´down n. a failure to work, as of a machine; a separation into parts for analysis

break´er n. a wave that strikes against the shore

breakfast n. the first meal of the day —vi. to eat breakfast

break´-in adj. of a period of trial, adjustment or training —n. unauthorized entry, as to rob

breaking point the maximum level of stress that can be tolerated by a person or object

break´neck adj. of travel at a high rate of speed; dangerous

break´through´ n. an important finding

break´up n. a tearing down or disintegration; a separation

break´wa·ter n. a barrier outside a harbor to shield against the impact of waves

breast n. the front of the chest

breast´plate n. a piece of armor to protect the chest

breath n. air taken into and expelled from the lungs; the act of breathing; a light breeze; a whisper

breathe vi., vt. to take air into the lungs; to whisper —**not breathe a word** promise to keep a secret

breath´er n. a break; a brief rest period

breath´tak·ing adj. exciting; awe-inspiring

breeches pl. n. tapered trousers ending just below the knee; any trousers

breed n. a group descended from common ancestors; a particular type —vi. to originate; to reproduce —vt. to bring forth young; to raise,

breed´er n.

breed´ing n. the production of off-spring; good manners, courtesy

breeze n. a gentle wind; something easy to do —vi. to move quickly — **breez´i·ly** adv. —**breez´i·ness** n. —**breez´y** adj.

breeze´way n. an enclosed passage-way between buildings or parts of a building

breth´ren pl. n. brothers

brev´i·ty n. the quality of being brief

brew vi., vt. to make beer, coffee, etc; to formulate a plan —**brew´er** n.

brew´age n. the brewing process; something brewed

brew´er·y n. a place where beers are made

bribe n. a payment to influence an-other —vi. to influence with a payment —**brib´a·ble** adj. —**brib´er** n. —**brib´er·y** n.

brick n. a clay building block; any-thing shaped like a brick; a reli-able person —vt. to build with brick —**hit the bricks** go on strike

brick´bat n. a harshly critical com-ment; an aspersion

brid´al adj. of a bride or wedding

bride n. a woman recently or about to be married

bride´groom n. a man recently or about to be married

brides´maid n. a bride's attendant

bridge n. a structure spanning an obstacle; any similar structure or link

bridge´work n. dentures

bri´dle n. a harness for guiding a horse; anything that restrains —vi. to take offense —vt. to control, as with a bridle

brief adj. momentary; concise —n. a summary —**brief´ly** adv. —**brief´ness** n.

brief´case n. a piece of hand luggage for carrying documents

brief´ing n. a short summary of a

situation; a set of instructions

brig n. short for brigantine; a mili-tary guardhouse

bri·gade´ n. a group organized for a common purpose

brig´an·tine n. a two-masted square-rigged vessel

bright adj. full of light or color; quick-witted; lively, animated; auspicious, encouraging —**bright´ly** adv. —**bright´ness** n.

bright´en vi., vt. to make bright, as by polishing —**bright´en·er** n.

bril´liant adj. full of light; dazzling; ingenious; talented —n. a gem of fine cut —**bril´liance, bril´lian·cy** n. —**bril´liant·ly** adv.

brim n. the topmost edge of a con-tainer, a projecting rim, as of a hat —vt., vi. to fill or be full —**brim´ful** adj.

brim´less adj. without a projecting brim, especially of a hat

brim´stone n. sulphur

brine n. a salt solution; the sea or its water —**brin´i·ness** n. —**brin´y** adj.

bring vt. to convey to a designated place; to influence —**bring about** cause to happen

brink n. the edge, especially of a precipice

bri´oche n. a light, rich bread

brisk adj. quick; active; stimulating —**brisk´ly** adv. —**brisk´ness** n.

bris´tle n. short, stiff hair —vi. to become tense; to take offense — **bris´tly** adj. —**bris´tli·ness** n.

brittle adj. easily broken; fragile; unbending —**brit´tle·ness** n.

broach vt. to bring up for discussion

broad adj. wide in scope; open, obvi-ous; general —**broad´en** vi., vt. — **broad´ly** adv. —**broad´ness** n.

broad´cast´ adj. of radio or television —vi., vt. to make known over a wide area

broad´cloth´ n. a fine, smooth cloth

broad´–mind´ed adj. open to unconventional ideas or actions **broad´–mind·ed·ly** adv.; **broad´–mind·ed·ness** n.

bro·cade´ n. a heavy fabric covered with a raised design

bro·chure´ n. a small booklet or folder

brogue n. a type of accent

broil n. a thing cooked by broiling — vt. to cook by direct exposure to intense heat **—broil´er** n.

bro´ken adj. in pieces; out of order; imperfect; ill or dispirited

bro´ker n. one who trades as agent for another, as of stock

bro´ker·age n. the office of a broker; fees charged by a broker

bron´co n. a horse of the western plains, often wild

bronze n. an alloy of copper and tin

brooch n. a large decorative pin, usually worn on a woman's dress

brood adj. of an animal kept for breeding —n. all the offspring hatched at once; all of the children in a family —vi., vt. to sit on eggs; to meditate morbidly; to pine or grieve **—brood´er** n. **—brood´i·ness** n. **—brood´y** adv.

brook n. a small stream

broom n. a bundle of stiff fibers for sweeping

broth n. a clear, thin meat or vegetable soup

broth´el n. a place of prostitution

broth´er n. a male sibling; a close friend; a fellow member of a fraternity, etc. **—broth´er·hood** n.

broth´er–in–law n. a brother by marriage

brow n. the forehead; the projecting top of a steep bank

brow´beat vt. to intimidate; to harangue **—brow´beat·er** n.

brown´–bag (US) vi., vt. to bring one's own lunch; to bring liquor to a restaurant that is not licensed to sell it **—brown–bag´ger** n.

brown´out n. a dimming of lights

during an electrical shortage

brown´stone n. a house with a front of brown stone, especially one in a row of like houses

browse vi., vt. to feed on young shoots or leaves; to examine casually **—brows´er** n.

bruise n. a slight injury —vt. to wound without breaking the skin; to damage one's ego, etc.

bruis´er n. a large, strong man, often a prize fighter

brunch n. a late, often elaborate, first meal of the day

brunet, bru·nette´ adj. having dark hair or eyes —n. a person with dark hair or eyes

brunt n. the main shock or impact

brush n. bristles attached to a handle for cleaning, etc.; a dense growth of bushes, etc.; a light touch; a brief encounter —vi., vt. to use a brush; to touch lightly

brusque adj. abrupt in manner; discourteous; curt **—brusque´ly** adv. **—brusque´ness** n.

bru´tal adj. extremely cruel **—bru·tal´i·ty** n. **—bru´tal·ly** adv.

bru´tal·ise (Brit.), **bru´tal·ize** (US) vt. to degrade or demean; to humiliate **—bru·tal·i·sa´tion, bru·tal·i·za´tion** n.

brute adj. unreasoning; savage; carnal —n. a beast; a barbarian; a monster

brut´ish adj. bestial; savage — **brut´ish·ly** adv. **—brut´ish·ness** n.

bub´ble n. a tiny ball of gas trapped in a liquid or a film of liquid; anything shaped like a bubble —vi., vt. to make or form bubbles **—bub´bly** adj.

buc·ca·neer´ n. a pirate

buck n. a male animal —vi., vt. to move in an effort to throw a rider

buck´et n. a container for dipping or carrying water, coal, etc.; anything that looks or functions like a bucket

buck´le *n.* a device for connecting the ends of a strap; a decoration that looks like a buckle —*vi., vt.* to join with a buckle; to bend under heat or pressure

buck´ram *n.* a coarse cotton or linen cloth

buck´shot *n.* heavy shot for bringing down large game

buck up to encourage or cheer up

bu·col´ic *adj.* of a country or farm setting —**bu·col´i·cal·ly** *adv.*

bud *n.* a small growth on a plant that precedes a leaf or flower —**nip in the bud** to stop in the early stages —**bud´like** *adj.*

bud´dy *n.* a close friend; a comrade

buddy system a pairing of comrades for mutual protection

budge *vi.* to move a little

budg´et *n.* a projection of anticipated need or use, often financial —*vi., vt.* to plan future needs —**bud´get·ar·y** *adj.;* **bud´get·er** *n.*

buff *vt.* to shine, polish; to burnish —**in the buff** naked

buf´fet *n.* a blow —*vt.* to strike repeatedly

buf·fet´ a sideboard for storing tableware and from which food is served; an informal meal at which guests serve themselves

buff´er *n.* a machine, person or device that polishes; padding or another device to lessen the shock of contact

buf·foon´ *n.* a clown or jester; a fool, jerk —**buf·foon´er·y** *n.* —**buf·foon´ish** *adj.*

bug *n.* any insect or similar organism; a disease-causing microorganism; an annoying defect; a small microphone for eavesdropping —*vt.* to hide a microphone for eavesdropping; to annoy

bug´a·boo *n.* a gremlin; something that causes difficulty, fear, or anxiety

bug´-eyed *adj.* amazed; astonished

bug´gy *adj.* infested with bugs; eccentric, crazy —*n.* a light, one-horse carriage

bu´gle *n.* a hunting or military horn —*vi., vt.* to signal with a bugle call —**bu´gler** *n.*

build *n.* the physical form of a person —*vi.* to put up a building; to increase in amount, intensity, etc. —*vt.* to construct; to cause to grow; to establish as a basis — **build´er** *n.*

build´ing *n.* a structure with sidewalls and a roof

build´up *n.* information designed to promote; puffery; a gradual increase: *an inventory buildup*

built´-in *adj.* installed as part of the structure, such as for cabinets or appliances

built´-up *adj.* of land covered by buildings in close proximity to each other

bulb *n.* the tuberous root of a plant; anything similar in shape

bul´bous *adj.* round; shaped like a bulb; rotund, corpulent

bulge *n.* an outward swelling; a projection —*vi., vt.* to swell out; to project —**bulg´i·ness** *n.*

bulk *adj.* of the aggregate; not broken down —*n.* the main part —*vi., vt.* to enlarge, expand; to buy in bulk; to purchase a large quantity, not broken down for resale

bulk´head *n.* a wall, as of a ship or airplane

bulk´y *adj.* of significant size; awkward or difficult to handle, more because of size than weight — **bulk·i·ness** *n.*

bull *n.* the adult male of certain large animals; a speculator who anticipates higher prices

bull´doz´er *n.* a powerful earth-moving machine; one who aggressively promotes an idea, cause, etc. —**bull´doze** *vt.*

bul´le·tin *n.* a brief statement; a

timely report; a newsletter

bul´let·proof *adj.* unable to pierce with bullets; of an agreement or contract that cannot be broken

bull´frog´ *n.* a large North American frog

bull´head·ed *adj.* stubborn; obstinate **—bull´head·ed·ly** *adv.* **—bull´head·ed·ness** *n.*

bull´horn *n.* a hand–held amplifier

bul´lion *n.* bulk gold or silver

bull´ock *n.* a steer; a castrated bull

bull´pen *n.* an area where the members of a baseball team wait when they are not playing; any waiting or holding area; those not participating who are available to be called on

bull's´eye *n.* the center of a target; the achievement of a goal

bul´ly *n.* one who intimidates those who are smaller or weaker **—vi., vt.** to intimidate

bul´wark *n.* a fortification; the side of a ship above the deck

bum *adj.* of inferior quality; erroneous or worthless **—n.** a tramp or derelict; a loafer; one addicted to a pursuit to the neglect of all else **— vi.** to live as a vagrant or by begging **—vt.** to get by begging or freeloading

bum´mer *n.* a bad experience; a washout

bump *n.* a blow; a bulge or swelling **—vi., vt.** to hit or collide with

bump´er *adj.* remarkably large: *a bumper crop* **—n.** a guard to absorb the shock of collision

bump´kin *n.* an unrefined person; a country boy

bump´tious *adj.* arrogantly conceited **—bump´tious·ly** *adv.* **— bump´tious·ness** *n.*

bump´y *adj.* marked by bulges; rough; irregular **—travel a bumpy road** undertake a difficult task **— bump´i·ness** *n.*

bun *n.* a small bread roll

bunch *n.* a cluster of like things attached or together **—vi., vt.** to gather together **—bunch´i·ness** *n.* **—bunch´y** *adj.*

bun´dle *n.* a number of things bound together **—vt.** to make into bundles; to dress warmly

bung *n.* a stopper in a barrel or cask

bun´ga·low´ *n.* a small house

bun´gee, bun´gee cord *n.* an elastic cord used to secure cargo

bungee jumping the sport of leaping from a height with an elastic cord attached to one's ankles so as to break the fall before hitting the surface

bun´gle *vi., vt.* to make or work clumsily **—n.** an imperfect performance **—bun´gler** *n.* **—bun´gling·ly** *adv.*

bun´ion *n.* an inflammation on the big toe

bunk *n.* a bed attached to the wall; any sleeping place; meaningless or misleading information **—vi.** to sleep in a bunk or makeshift bed

bunk´er *n.* a fortified position

bunk´house *n.* sleeping quarters to accommodate a number of workers such as field hands

bunk mate, bunk´mate *n.* one who shares quarters or lives in the same bunkhouse

bun´ny *n.* a rabbit

bunt *vi., vt.* to hit a pitched baseball lightly so as to keep it in the infield **—n.** **—sacrifice bunt** a strategy that will likely result in an out for the batter with the intention of advancing another base runner **— bunt´er** *n.*

bun´ting *n.* cloth used to make flags, banners, etc.; a decorative banner; a baby's garment or wrapping

buoy *n.* a fixed float in water to mark a navigable channel, a hazard, etc. **—vt.** to keep afloat; to encourage **—buoy´an·cy** *n.* **—buoy´ant** *adj.*

bur´den *n.* a heavy or difficult load;

a responsibility —*vt.* to weigh down —**bur´den·some** *adj.*

bu´reau (*US*) *n.* a chest of drawers; an office, department, or agency

bu·reau´ra·cy *n.* governing through a number of departments or sections, each with limited jurisdiction or authority —**bu´reau·crat** *n.*

bu·reau·crat´ic *adj.* to act strictly according to the rules —**bu·reau·crat´i·cal·ly** *adv.*

bu·reau´cra·tise (*Brit.*), **bu·reau´cra·tize** (*US*) *vi., vt.* to make into or develop into a bureaucrat or bureaucracy —**bu·reau·cra·ti·sa´tion, bu·reau·cra·ti·za´tion** *n.*

burg *n.* a small town or village, usually inferring one that is quiet or backward

bur´geon *vi.* to grow rapidly or profusely; to flourish

burg´er *n.* a ground meat, fish or vegetable patty; a sandwich made with such a patty

bur´gla·ry *n.* the act of breaking in to commit a crime —**bur´glar** *n.* —**bur´glar·ize** *vi.*

bur´i·al *n.* the act of burying

bur´lap (*US*) *n.* a coarse cloth used in the making of sacks and as a backing for upholstry or carpeting

bur·lesque´ *n.* broad comedy; satire; a type of theatrical entertainment —*vt.* to imitate with mockery or satire

bur´ly *adj.* strong and muscular —**bur´li·ness** *n.*

burn *n.* an injury caused by fire —*vi.* to be on fire; to emit light or heat; to be injured by fire; to be heated, as with emotion —*vt.* to set on fire; to injure, change or consume by fire —**burn´er** *n.* —**burnt** *adj.*

bur´nish *n.* a smooth luster —*vt.* to polish —**bur´nish·er** *n.*

bur·noose´, bur·nous´ *n.* a long hooded cloak

burp *n.* belch

burp gun an automatic weapon

bur´ro *n.* a donkey

bur´row *n.* a hole dug by an animal for shelter —*vi., vt.* to make or hide in a burrow —**bur´row·er** *n.*

bur´sar *n.* one dealing with money, especially the comptroller of a college or university

bur´sa·ry *n.* a treasury or repository for funds, especially for a college or university

burst *n.* a sudden action, as an explosion or eruption —*vi.* to break apart suddenly; to cxpress sudden emotion or action —*vt.* to cause to break apart

bur´y *vt.* to place in the ground; to cover so as to hide; to remove from one's conscious mind; to completely absorb oneself

burying ground a cemetary, especially of ancient origin

bus *n.* a motor vehicle designed to carry a large number of passengers; an omnibus; (*Brit.*) a large, often double-decker, passenger vehicle that operates locally

bus´boy *n.* a restaurant worker whose duty it is to clear tables

bush *n.* a woody plant with a profusion of low branches; an area with many such plants; anything like such a plant —**beat around the bush** to talk around an issue without committing oneself —**bush´i·ness** *n.* —**bush´y** *adj.*

bushed *adj.* tired; fatigued

bush´el *n.* a dry measure of 4 pecks or 32 dry quarts

bush´ing *n.* a sleeve for reducing friction between machine parts

bush´whack *vi., vt.* to attack from ambush —**bush´whack·er** *n.*

busi´ness *n.* commerce; the buying and selling of goods and services; one's occupation; any activity or matter for concern: *the business of planning a party, mind your own business* —**got the business** subjected to rough treatment, hazing, teasing, etc. —**to mean business** to be sincere or resolute

busi·ness·like adj. of a professional; manner; systematic, orderly

buss n. a kiss; a smack on the lips —vi., vt. to kiss playfully

bust n. a sculpture of a person from head to the upper chest; the chest; an undertaking that is a failure; a severe economic downturn —vi., vt. to break; to make or become bankrupt

bus·tle n. brisk activity —vi. to move briskly —**bus·tling·ly** adv.

bus·y adj. active; occupied —**bus·i·ly** adv. —**bus·y·ness** n.

bus·y·bod·y n. one who is overly concerned with or meddles in the affairs of others

bus·y·work n. useless activity intended to appear worthwhile

butch·er n. one who processes and sells meat; a murderer —vt. to kill animals or process their meat; to massacre; to do sloppy work —**butch·er·y** n.

but·ler n. a manservant usually in charge of food service

butler's pantry a station between the kitchen and dining room where the table service is kept

but·ter n. edible fat obtained from churning cream; any spread used like butter —**but·ter·y** adj.

but·ter·ball n. affectionately, a chubby person

but·ter·fat n. the fat in milk that is churned into butter

but·ter·fin·gered adj. of one who is clumsy —**but·ter·fin·ger** n.

but·ter·fly adj. of or like a butterfly —n. an insect noted for its colorful wings

butterfly bandage an adhesive plaster shaped like a butterfly with wings extended, used to keep a wound tightly closed

but·ter·milk n. the liquid remains left after churning butter

but·ter·scotch adj. of a flavoring of brown sugar and butter —n. the flavoring; a candy made with this flavor

but·ton n. a small device for fastening clothing; a thing resembling a button —vi., vt. to fasten with buttons —**button down** to finalize, take care of the last detail —**button up** don't speak; keep a secret —**on the button** on time, in place, etc.; precise

but·ton–down adj. of a shirt or jacket collar whose tips are buttoned to the garment; conservative

but·ton·hole n. an opening in clothing designed to receive a button —vt. to compel one to listen

but·tress n. a structure that extends out from a wall to reinforce it; reinforcement —vt. to reinforce, support —**flying buttress** a buttress built away from a wall and connected to it by an arch

bux·om adj. full–figured —**bux·om·ly** adv. —**bux·om·ness** n.

buy n. anything purchased; a bargain —vt. to obtain for money; accept as valid —**buy·a·ble** adj. —**buy·er** n.

buy off to bribe

buy time to stall

buzz n. a droning sound; a low murmur; a telephone call —vi. to make a droning sound, like that of a bee; to talk excitedly in a low tone —vt. to speak rapidly in a low tone; to make a telephone call; to signal with a buzzer

buzz·er n. a device that signals with a buzzing sound, as for a timer

by prep. proximity in space or time; at the hand of; through the medium of —adv. near

by·-and-by n. at some time in the future

bye law (Brit.) the rules governing an association or organization

by·gone adj. past —**let bygones be**

bygones forgive a past indiscretion

by´law (US) n. the rules governing an association or organization

by´-line n. an attribution; a naming of the author, as for a newspaper or magazine article —**by´-lin·er** n.

by´pass´ n. an alternative or auxilliary route; that which provides an auxilliary route —vt. to detour; to circumvent

by´-path n. a route seldom taken

by´-play n. events taking place aside from the main activity, as in a play or office politics

by´-prod´uct n. material, often waste, accumulated as the result of processing; a secondary product, often from the waste created by primary manufacturing or processing

by´stand·er n. one who is present, but not involved

byte n. a set of binary digits that is transferred as a unit in a computer; a computer word

by´way n. a side road, often branching from a main road

c, C n. third letter of the English alphabet; third-rate; in Roman characters, the symbol for 100

cab n. a taxicab; a separate area for the operator of a vehicle or heavy machinery

cab´driv·er, cab´by n. one who operates a taxicab

ca·bal´ n. a group of plotters; a secret plot

cab´a·la, cab·ba´la n. mystical teachings of Hebrew origin; any mystical or esoteric doctrine — **cab·a·lis´tic** adj.

ca·ba´na n. a shelter for changing at a beach or pool

cab·a·ret´ n. a nightclub

cab´in n. a small house; a room on a boat, plane, etc.

cabin boy an apprentice seaman who performs menial tasks on board ship

cab´i·net n. an article of furniture used for storage; a body of advisors

cab´i·net·mak·er n. a craftsman in making wood articles —**cab´i·net·ry, cab´i·net·work** n.

cabin fever anxiety, agitation or boredom as the result of living in a confined space

ca´ble n. a heavy rope, often of metal; a bundle of insulated conductors; a cablegram; cable television —vt. to connect with cable; to send a cablegram

cable car a vehicle for the transport of passengers or freight, drawn by a cable up a sharp incline, across a ravine, etc.

ca´ble·gram n. a message carried by undersea cable

cable television a system that provides for the transmission of television signals to subscribers outside of a normal viewing area

ca´ble·vi·sion n. cable television

ca·boo´dle n. a batch or group

ca·boose´ (US) n. the last car on a freight train; the trainmen's car

cab·ri·o·let´ n. a small horse-drawn carriage

cab´stand n. a place designated for taxicabs or carriages to wait for fares

ca·ca´o n. a tropical tree that bears the seeds for making chocolate; the seeds of the cacao tree

cache n. a place for storing food or supplies; the material thus stored; in a computer, a memory location set aside to store data for quick retrieval

ca·chet´ n. a mark attesting to authenticity, quality, approval, etc.

ca·coph´o·ny n. dissonance; a harsh noise —**ca·coph´o·nous** adj. —**ca·coph´o·nous·ly** adv.

cac´tus n., pl. **cac´ti, cac´tus·es** a desert plant with spiney leaves

cad *n.* one who exhibits coarse or crude behavior; a nasty person; a rogue

ca·dav´er (*US*) *n.* a dead body

ca·dav´er·ous *adj.* pale, gaunt; like a corpse —**ca·dav´er·ous·ly** *adv.* —**ca·dav´er·ous·ness** *n.*

ca´dence, ca´den·cy *n.* a rhythmic flow of sound, as of poetry; a measured beat, as in marching —**ca´denced, ca´dent** *adj.*

ca·den´tial *adj.* pertaining to a cadence or a cadenza

ca·den´za *n.* an intricate flourish in a musical solo

ca·det´ *n.* a student in a military school

cadge *vi., vt.* to beg or acquire by begging; to freeload —**cadg´er** *n.*

ca´dre *n.* staff; key personnel charged with training or leading others

ca·du´ce·us *n.* a winged staff with coiled serpents that is the emblem of the medical profession —**ca·du´ce·an** *adj.*

cae·sar´e·an, caesarean section *n.* a technique for delivering a baby by surgery

ca·fe´, ca·fé´ *n.* a coffeehouse or restaurant

café au lait a beverage of equal parts dark coffee and scalded milk

caf·e·te´ri·a *n.* a self-service or limited service restaurant; (*US*) a facility where employee meals are served

caf·feine´ *n.* a stimulant occurring naturally in coffee and tea, and that is added to some sodas, diet pills, medications, etc. —**caf·fein·at·ed** *adj.*

caf´tan *n.* a long-sleeved robe; a long, loose dress

cage *n.* a place of confinement —*vt.* to put in confinement

ca´gey *adj.* cunning; shrewd, clever —**ca´gi·ly** *adv.* —**cag´i·ness** *n.*

cai´man, cay´man *n.* a Central or

South American reptile similar to the alligator

cais´son *n.* an ammunition chest; a wagon for transporting ammunition

caisson disease a painful condition caused by the formation of nitrogen bubbles in the bloodstream, such as for a deep sea diver who surfaces too quickly

cai´tiff *adj.* cowardly, despicable —*n.* one who is mean or vulgar

ca·jole´ *vi., vt.* to press with repeated appeals; to wheedle by flattery —**ca·jole´ment, ca·jol´er·y** *n.* —**ca·jol´er** *n.;* **ca·jol´ing·ly** *adv.*

cake *n.* a sweet, bread-like pastry; something molded into a patty, block, or brick —*vi., vt.* to harden or form a crust —**icing on the cake** something extra; an unexpected bonus —**piece of cake** easy to do

cake´walk *n.* a strutting dance; a thing easily accomplished

ca·lam´i·ty *n.* extreme misfortune; tragedy —**ca·lam´i·tous** *adj.* —**ca·lam´i·tous·ly** *adv.* —**ca·lam´i·tous·ness** *n.*

cal´ci·fy *vi., vt.* to turn to stone or a stone-like mass —**cal·cif´ic** *adj.* —**cal·ci·fi·ca´tion** *n.*

cal´ci·mine *n.* a white liquid used to cover plastered walls

cal´ci·um *n.* a mineral essential to the growth of bones, teeth, etc.

cal´cu·late´ *vt.* to determine by using mathematics; to estimate; to intend: calculated to handle most of the traffic —**cal·cu·la´tion** *n.* —**cal´cu·la·tive** *adj.* —**cal´cu·la·tor** *n.*

cal´cu·lat·ed *adj.* arrived at by computation or reckoning; deliberate —**cal´cu·lat·ed·ly** *adv.* —**cal´cu·lat·ed·ness** *n.*

cal´cu·lat·ing *adj.* scheming; shrewd or crafty —**cal´cu·lat·ing·ly** *adv.*

cal´cu·lous *adj.* relating to or having

a stony deposit

cal´cu·lus *n., pl.* **cal´cu·li, cal´cu·lus·es** a stone–like deposit, as in the kidney or gallbladder; a system of computation employing symbolic notation

cal´dron, caul´dron *n.* a large kettle

cal´en·dar *n.* a system for arranging the months, weeks, and days of the year; a list of appointments

calf *n., pl.* **calves** the young of certain animals; the cured hide of a young cow: calfskin; the fleshy back of the leg below the knee

cal´i·ber *n.* the diameter of a cylindrical object, as a gun; the quality of a person

cal´i·brate *vt.* to regulate or adjust a measuring instrument or device — **cal·i·bra´tion** *n.* —**cal´i·bra·tor** *n.*

cal´i·co´ *n.* a printed cotton cloth

cal´i·per *n.* a device for measuring thickness or diameter

ca´liph, ca´lif *n.* an Islamic leader or ruler

ca´liph·ate *n.* land ruled by a caliph

cal´is·then´ics *pl. n.* exercises to develop the body

cal·lig´ra·phy *n.* handwriting as an art form; embellished handwriting —**cal·lig´ra·pher** *n.* —**cal·li·graph´ic** *adj.*

call´ing *n.* the act of one who calls; one's profession or vocation

calling card a small card containing one's name and other information appropriate to its use, such as address, profession, etc.; a business card

cal·li´o·pe´ *n.* a keyboard instrument similar to the organ that uses steam whistles to create tones

cal´lous *adj.* heartless; indifferent — **cal´lous·ly** *adv.* —**cal´lous·ness** *n.*

cal´low *adj.* young and inexperienced; immature —**cal´low·ness** *n.*

cal´lus *n.* a thickened formation of skin

call waiting a feature of some telephone systems that alerts one who is on the phone of another incoming call

calm *adj.* still; tranquil; composed — *n.* stillness; tranquility —*vi., vt.* to soothe or pacify —**calm´ly** *adv.* —**calm´ness** *n.*

calm´a·tive *n.* a sedative

cal´o·rie *n.* one of two measures of heat, the small or *gram calorie* and the large or *kilogram calorie*; the large calorie, used to measure the energy produced by food —**ca·lor´ic** *adj.* —**ca·lor´i·cal·ly** *adv.*

cal·o·rif´ic *adj.* producing heat; of high calorie foods —**cal·o·rif´i·cal·ly** *adv.*

cal·o·rim´e·ter *n.* a device for measuring quantities of heat

ca·lum´ni·ate *vi., vt.*; to spread slanderous rumors —**ca·lum·ni·a´tion** *n.* —**ca·lum´ni·a·tor** *n.*

ca·lum´ni·ous *adj.* slanderous —**ca·lum´ni·ous·ly** *adv.*

cal´um·ny *n.* slander; defamation

calve *vi., vt.* to give birth to a calf

ca·lyp´so *n.* the rhythmic music of Trinidad —*adj.*

ca·ma·ra´de·rie *n.* good fellowship

cam´ber *n.* arching; curvature

cam´bist *n.* one who deals in foreign exchange; a publication that lists rates of exchange —**cam´bist·ry** *n.*

cam´bric *n.* a fine linen fabric

cam´cord·er *n.* a portable video camera

cam´el *n.* a common beast of burden in the deserts of Asia and Africa — **cam´el·eer´** *n.*

cam´e·o´ *n.* a shell or gem carved in relief; a brief appearance by a noted performer

cam´er·a *n.* a device for recording visual images —**cam´er·a·man** *n.*

cam´er·a lu´ci·da *n.* an optical device for projecting an image on a flat surface

cam´ou·flage´ *n.* the art of protection through the deceptive use of color and form; any device employed to conceal or deceive

camp *n.* an area of temporary living, as for soldiers or vacationers; something flamboyant, outdated, artificial, etc. —*vi., vt.* to live temporarily outdoors —**camp´er** *n.* — **camp´ground, camp´site** *n.*

cam·paign´ *n.* an undertaking organized to achieve a specific objective —*vi.* to participate in such an undertaking —**cam·paign´er** *n.*

cam·pa·ni´le *n.* a bell tower

cam·pa·nol´o·gy *n.* the art of designing and making bells —**cam·pa·nol´o·gist** *n.*

camp´fire *n.* an outdoor fire for cooking, warmth, or as a gathering place for campers

cam´pus *adj.* of a school or its buildings, grounds, etc. —*n.* the grounds or buildings of a complex, such as for a school, hospital, etc.

ca·nal´ *n.* an artificial waterway; a waterway improved so as to be navigable; a duct or channel —*vt.* to build a canal

can·a·pé *n.* an appetizer comprised of bread or crackers spread with meat, cheese, etc.

ca·nard´ *n.* a misleading story; a hoax

can´cel *vt.* to invalidate; to rescind; to delete —**can´cel·a·ble** *adj.* — **can´cel·er** *n.* —**can·cel·la´tion** *n.*

can´cer *n.* a malignant growth; any infectious evil —**can´cer·ous** *adj.* —**can´cer·ous·ly** *adv.*

can·de·la´brum *n., pl.* **can·de·la´bra** a large, branching candle holder

can´did *adj.* straightforward, honest; impartial —**can´did·ly** *adv.* —**can´did·ness** *n.*

can´di·date *n.* a nominee for office, an award, etc.

can´died *adj.* cooked in or coated with sugar

can´dle *n.* a wax or tallow cylinder

surrounding a wick that can be burned to give off light; anything similar in form or use —*vt.* to examine, as eggs, by placing in front of a bright light —**burn the candle at both ends** to work or play so hard as to burn up one's energy — **not hold a candle to** to be in some way inferior

can´dle·light *adj.* lighted by candles, as *a candlelight supper;* of the soft light of candles —*n.* subdued light

can´dle·pow·er *n.* an expression of the intensity of a light

can´dle·stick *n.* a candle; a candle holder; a candelabrum

can´dor *n.* frankness or honesty of expression; impartiality

can´dy (US) *n.* a confection made primarily from sugar and flavoring —*vt.* to glaze with a sugar syrup

candy striper a hospital volunteer worker

cane *n.* the stem of certain woody plants; the plants themselves; split rattan used in weaving; a walking stick; a rod used for flogging —*vt.* to beat, as with a cane —**can´er** *n.*

cane´brake *n.* a stand of sugar cane

cane sugar sugar obtained from cane

ca´nine´ *adj.* of or like a dog —*n.* a dog; a sharp-pointed tooth

can´is·ter *n.* a small storage container; any similar container

can´ker *n.* an ulcerous sore; something that tends to corrupt —*vi., vt.* to infect or corrupt —**can´ker·ous** *adj.*

canned *adj.* of food that has been processed and sealed in metal containers; material recorded for later broadcast; prepared ahead; contrived

can´ner *n.* a person or company involved in the processing and packaging of food

can´ner·y *n.* an industrial plant where raw food is processed

can·ni·bal *n.* any creature that eats its own kind —**can´ni·bal·ism** *n.* —**can·ni·bal·is´tic** *adj.*

can·ni·bal·ise (*Brit.*), **can´ni·bal·ize** (*US*) *vi., vt.* to devour one's own kind; to take parts from to use in repairing or building another

can´ny *adj.* cautious, watchful; shrewd —**can´ni·ly** *adv.* —**can´ni·ness** *n.*

ca·noe´ *n.* a light, narrow boat —*vi., vt.* to travel or carry by canoe

can´on *n.* the laws of a church; an established principle, a standard

ca·non´ic, ca·non´i·cal *adj.* according to church law; accepted, as a standard —**ca·non´i·cal·ly** *adv.* —**can·on·ic´i·ty** *n.*

can´on·ist *n.* an authority in canon law —**can·on·is´tic** *adj.*

can´on·ize *vt.* to sanctify or consecrate; to glorify, venerate —**can·on·i·za´tion** *n.* —**can´on·ry** *n.*

canon law the precepts that govern a church

can´o·py *n.* a protective, roof-like covering; anything similar in form or function —*vt.* to create an overhead covering

cant *n.* a sloping surface; the terminology peculiar to a particular group; insincere speech —*vi., vt.* to slope or cause to slope; to speak in a particular jargon

can´ta·loupe´ *n.* a variety of melon

can·tan´ker·ous *adj.* quarrelsome, disagreeable

caf·e·te´ri·a *n.* a self-service or limited service restaurant; (*US*) a facility where employee meals are served

can·teen´[1] *n.* a small sealed container for drinking water; a place where food is served to workers

can·teen´[2] (*Brit.*) a collection of cutlery

can´ti·cle *n.* a hymn

can´ti·lev·er *n.* a projection anchored only by the wall from which

it emerges

can´tor *n.* a choir leader; a leader in prayer or scripture reading

can´vas *n.* a heavy cloth used for sails, tents, oil paintings, etc.; an oil painting

can´vass *vi., vt.* to blanket an area for opinions, votes, etc. —**can´vass·er** *n.*

can´yon *n.* a narrow gorge

cap *n.* a tight-fitting covering for the head; any cover, as for a bottle, jar, etc. —*vt.* to place a top on; to cover

ca´pa·ble *adj.* having the necessary skill —**ca·pa·bil´i·ty, ca´pa·ble·ness** *n.* —**ca´pa·bly** *adv.*

ca·pa´cious *adj.* spacious; massive; having the space to hold much —**ca·pa´cious·ly** *adv.* —**ca·pa´cious·ness** *n.*

ca·pac´i·ty *n.* the ability to hold; having the necessary aptitude; properly qualified or authorized

cape *n.* a sleeveless outer garment, a cloak; a point of land extending into a body of water

caper *n.* a playful leap; a silly action or prank —*vi.* to leap in a playful manner: frolic

cap´il·lar´y *adj.* like a hair; of the hair-like blood vessels of the body —*n.* any of the tiny blood vessels of the body —**cap·il·la´ceous** *adj.*

cap·il·lar´i·ty *n.* the interaction between contacting surfaces of a liquid and a solid that encloses it

cap´i·tal *adj.* punishable by death; most significant; first-rate —*n.* the center of an industry, government, etc.; assets, as money or property; an uppercase letter; the top of a column

cap´i·tal·ism *n.* an economic system in which most means for the production of goods and services are privately owned —**cap´i·tal·ist** *n.* —**cap·i·tal·is´tic** *adj.* —**cap·i·tal·is´ti·cal·ly** *adv.*

cap·i·tal·ise (*Brit.*), **cap·i·tal·ize** (*US*) *vt.* to write the first letter or all of the letters of a word in uppercase; to finance; to exploit or turn to a profit —**cap·i·tal·i·sa'tion**, **cap·i·tal·i·za'tion** *n.*

capital punishment a penalty of death

Capitol the building in which the US Congress meets —**capitol** the building housing a state legislature in the US

ca·pit'u·late *vi.* to surrender, often conditionally —**ca·pit·u·la'tion** *n.*

ca·pote' *n.* a long, hooded cloak

ca·price' *n.* a sudden impetuous action; a tendency to unpredictable change —**ca·pri'cious** *adj.* —**ca·pri'cious·ly** *adv.* —**ca·pri'cious·ness** *n.*

cap'size *vt.* to upend —**cap'siz·a·ble** *adj.*

cap'stan *n.* a shipboard apparatus for hoisting an anchor; a spindle that drives magnetic tape

cap'sule' *n.* a small container, such as a seed pod or that used to hold a single dose of medicine; a closed compartment, as for personnel and instruments in a spacecraft —**cap'su·lar**, **cap'su·late**, **cap'su·lat·ed** *adj.*

cap'sul·ize *vt.* to summarize; to furnish in an abbreviated form

cap'tain *n.* an officer in a military or quasi–military hierarchy; a group leader in some enterprise, as *captain of the team*

cap'tion *n.* a heading or title, as of a legal document or a composition; descriptive matter

cap'tious *adj.* intended to be critical; fond of finding fault —**cap'tious·ly** *adv.* —**cap'tious·ness** *n.*

cap'ti·vate *vt.* to attract, as by charm; to fascinate or bewitch —**cap'ti·vat·ing·ly** *adv.* —**cap'ti·va'tion** *n.* —**cap'ti·va·tor** *n.*

cap'tive *adj.* held prisoner; restricted; fascinated —*n.* a prisoner —**cap'tiv'i·ty** *n.* —**cap'tor** *n.*

captive audience an audience held by one's charm or charisma; an audience that cannot leave, as at a business meeting

cap'ture *n.* the act of taking or being taken prisoner; that taken —*vt.* to take and hold; to captivate, as by charm —**cap'tor**, **cap'tur·er** *n.*

car *n.* an automobile; a space or area for passengers, as on an elevator; (*US*) a railway passenger vehicle

ca·rafe' *n.* a container for serving beverages

car'a·mel *n.* burnt sugar used as a flavoring; a candy of this flavor; the color of burnt sugar —**car'a·mel·ize** *n.*, *vt.*

car'at *n.* a unit of weight for gems

car'a·van[1] *n.* a company of travelers; a file of vehicles or pack animals —**car'a·van·er**, **car'a·van·ner** *n.*

car'a·van[2] *n.* (*Brit.*) a mobile home

car'a·van'sa·ry *n.* an inn with a large center courtyard; a haven for caravans

car'a·vel *n.* a small, 15th century sailing ship

car'a·way *n.* a seed used for flavoring; the herb that produces such seeds

car'bine *n.* a light rifle

car'bo·hy'drate *n.* an organic compound composed of carbon, hydrogen, and oxygen

car'bon *n.* a nonmetallic chemical element present in all organic compounds —**car·bo·na'ceous**, **car·bon'ic**, **car·bon·if'er·ous** *adj.*

car'bo·nate *vt.* to infuse with carbon dioxide, as *carbonated water* —**car·bon·a'tion** *n.*

carbon dating determination of the age of a relic by measurement of the amount of carbon 14 remaining in it —**car'bon–date** *vt.*

car'bon di·ox·ide *n.* a colorless,

odorless gas released by respiration and absorbed by plants

carbon 14 a radioactive isotope of carbon used to date relics

car·bon·ize vt. to convert to carbon; to coat or combine with carbon

car·bon mon·ox·ide n. a colorless, odorless, poisonous gas

carbon paper a thin paper placed between sheets of writing paper to transfer an image from the top sheet to the sheet below

carbon copy an exact duplicate

car·bon tet·ra·chlo·ride n. a colorless liquid solvent commonly used as a cleaning fluid

car·bun·cle n. a deep red gemstone; a large painful skin eruption similar to a boil —**car·bun´cu·lar** adj.

car·bu·re·tor n. a device for mixing air and gas to feed an internal combustion engine —**car´bu·ret** vt. **car·bu·ri·za´tion** n.

car´cass n. a dead animal; the human body

car·cin´o·gen n. a cancer-causing substance —**car·ci·no·gen´e·sis** n. —**car·cin·o·gen´ic** adj.

car·ci·no´ma n. a cancerous growth —**car·ci·nom´a·tous** adj.

car·ci·no·ma·to´sis n. the spread of a carcinoma throughout the body

card n. a small, stiff sheet of paper, plastic, etc.; a witty or amusing person —**business card** a card that identifies one in business, especially a salesperson —**credit card** identification signifying that the bearer is authorized to purchase on credit —**playing card** a set of cards containing numbers, pictures, etc. used as elements in a game —**trading card** any of a series of cards depicting noted personalities, events, etc.

car´da·mom n. a spice

card´board n. a stiff paper-like material —adj. of or like cardboard

card-carrying adj. of one who is a

member; of one who espouses a cause, as a *card-carrying environmentalist*

car´di·ac´ adj. of the heart

car´di·gan a long-sleeved sweater that buttons down the front

car´di·nal adj. primary; foremost — **car´di·nal·ly** adv.

cardinal number a number that designates quantity, in contrast to an *ordinal number* that denotes relative position

car·di·ol´o·gy n. the branch of medicine that deals with the heart, its function, and diseases —**car·di·o·log´ic, car·di·o·log´i·cal** adj.

car·di·ol´o·gist n. one who specializes in diseases of the heart

card shark an expert player at cards, often, one who cheats

card table a felt-topped table designed for card playing; a utility table with folding legs

care n. having concern; acting with caution; having responsibility —vi., vt. to feel concern —**couldn't care less** of no concern

ca·reen´ vi., vt. to lean sideways; to swerve

ca·reer´ n. one's progress through life; a line of work —**ca·reer´ism** n. —**ca·reer´ist** n.

care´free adj. without concern or worry; lighthearted

care´ful adj. cautious; attentive to detail; frugal —**care´ful·ly** adv. — **care´ful·ness** n.

care´giv·er n. an individual or organization charged with the health and well-being of another

care´less adj. reckless, lacking reasonable caution; inattentive to detail —**care´less·ly** adv. —**care´less·ness** n.

ca·ress´ vt. to touch lightly, as by a breeze; to stroke lovingly —n. an expression of affection; a gentle touching —**ca·ress´ing·ly** adv. — **ca·ress´ive** adj.

car´et n. a mark (^) used to show where something is to be inserted

care´tak·er n. one hired to maintain or preserve, as of a house or grounds; one temporarily filling a position pending a permanent appointment

care´worn adj. weary; showing the effects of a burden

car´fare n. the price of a ride, as on a public conveyance

car´go n. freight

car´i·ca·ture n. an exaggerated likeness; something so inferior as to be absurd —vt. to ridicule; to create a distorted likeness —**car´i·ca·tur·ist** n.

car´ies n. the decay of teeth

car´il·lon n. an instrument that sounds musical passages with the use of bells —**car·il·lon·neur´** n.

car´load n. the amount that can be carried by a freight or passenger vehicle

car´mine n. deep red

car´nage n. a massacre; the remains of a slaughter

car´nal adj. of the flesh; of worldly pleasures; temporal —**car·nal´i·ty** n. —**car´nal·ly** adv.

car´ni·val n. a time of merrymaking; a local festival, as a summer carnival; (US) a traveling show

car´ni·vore n. any creature that consumes the flesh of another

car·niv´o·rous adj. flesh-eating

car´ol n. a song of joy —vi. to sing —**car´ol·er, car´ol·ler** n.

car´o·tene, car´o·tin n. a food substance that is converted to vitamin A in the liver

ca·rot´e·noid adj. of a pigment in the yellow to red range —n.

ca·rot´id adj. of the two main arteries of the neck —n.

ca·rouse´ n. drunken revelry —vi. to engage in drunken revelry —**ca·rous´al** n. —**ca·rous´er** n.

car·ou·sel´, car·rou·sel´ n. a merry-go-round; a revolving device that feeds in a continuous stream, as for viewing slides or in a baggage claim area

carp vi. to find fault; to complain regularly of petty grievances

car´pen·ter n. a worker in wood —vi. to work with wood as a builder or fabricator —**car´pen·try** n.

car´pet n. a thick covering for a floor —**car´pet·ing** n.

car´pet·bag n. a type of luggage made from carpeting

carpetbagger a derogatory term for politicians, swindlers, etc. from northern states who migrated south the take advantage of conditions following the Civil War

car pool a group of individuals who share driving, as to work, school, etc. —**car´pool** vi.

car´port n. a permanent structure, usually beside a house, for protecting an automobile

car n. an automobile; a space or area for passengers, as on an elevator

car´riage n. one's bearing; a horse-drawn vehicle —**baby carriage** a small vehicle for transporting the very young

car´riage n. (Brit.) a railway passenger vehicle

car´ri·er n. a person or vehicle that transports; one infected by a disease without exhibiting symptoms —**common carrier** an individual or company that contracts for the transfer of goods

car´ri·on n. decaying flesh

car´ry vt. to convey from one place to another; to support or sustian

carried away caught up in events, emotion, etc.

carry on to operate or manage, as a business; to remain firm in the face of adversity; to behave childishly

car´ry·o·ver n. something left from a

previous time, as a staff member from a previous administration

car´ry-out, car´ry·out *adj.* of restaurant food that is to be eaten off the premises

cart *n.* a small wheeled conveyance that is pulled or pushed —*vt.* to transport by cart —**cart´er** *n.*

cart off to take away

cart´age *n.* the act of transporting, usually for a fee; a charge for transporting, as freight

carte blanche full authority to do as one wishes

car´tel´ *n.* an alliance of individual businesses, formed to fix prices and production; any coalition for a common cause

car·tog´ra·phy *n.* the art of making maps —**car·tog´ra·pher** *n.* —**car·to·graph´ic, car·to·graph´i·cal** *adj.*

car´ton *n.* a cardboard box

car´toon´ *n.* a caricature; a line drawing —*vi., vt.* to make or draw cartoons —**animated cartoon** a series of drawings that can be viewed quickly to create the impression of movement —**car·toon´ist** *n.*

car´tridge´ *n.* a small carrier for material to be inserted into a larger device, as for film, tape, etc.

cart´wheel *n.* an acrobatic maneuver that involves supporting the body by each hand and foot in quick succession while remaining perpendicular to the surface so as to create the impression of a turning wheel

carve *vt.* to shape or fashion by cutting; to divide by cutting or as if by cutting —**carve up** to divide into portions; to share —**carv´er** *n.*

carv´ing *n.* a figure or design, often in wood, formed by cutting

cas·cade´ *n.* a succession of steep waterfalls; a number of devices connected in series —*vi., vt.*

case *n.* an instance or occurrence; a legal action; a container —**just in case** in reserve for a contingency —**on his/her case** critical, fault-finding

case book a reference work

case study an analysis of a specific unit, as the progression of a disease in particular individuals

case´work·er *n.* a social worker who is charged with the investigation and oversight of specific clients — **case´work** *n.*

cash *n.* money in hand; currency; liquid assets —*vt.* to convert into cash, as *to cash in stocks and bonds* —**petty cash** a small amount of money kept in an office for incidental purchases —**cash´a·ble** *adj.*

cash-and-carry terms of a sale: no credit and no delivery

cash bar a facility where beverages may be purchased, such as at a reception, banquet, etc.

cash´book *n.* a record of cash transactions; a cash journal

cash box storage for cash receipts, petty cash, etc.

cash crop produce, etc. grown to sell in contrast to that grown for feed

cash discount a rebate for paying cash

cash´ew *n.* a type of edible nut; the tree on which it grows

cash·ier´ *n.* one who handles cash transactions; one responsible for the receipt and disbursement of cash in a business

cash´mere *n.* a type of fine wool; cloth made from the wool

cash reg·is·ter *n.* a machine for recording sales and storing cash, checks, etc. received

cas´ing *n.* framework, as for a tire, door, etc.; the outer covering of sausage

cask *n.* a barrel

cas´ket *n.* a small chest; a coffin

cas´se·role *n.* an earthenware pot with bulging sides and a tight-fitting lid; the slow baking of food in such a pot; a combination of foods cooked and served in a single dish

cas·sette *n.* a small case for film, magnetic tape, etc.

cas´sock *n.* a clergyman's robe

cast *n.* the act or technique of throwing or projecting, as an object or a glance; a thing formed, as in a mold; all of the actors in a theatrical production; the appearance of a thing —*vi., vt.* to throw with vigor; to select performers for roles

cast´a·way *n.* one who is shipwrecked; a thing that has been relinquished or abandoned

caste *n.* social position or status based on wealth, birth, etc.

cas·tel·lat·ed *adj.* built like a castle —**cas·tel·la´tion** *n.*

cas´ti·gate´ *vt.* to criticize severely —**cas´ti·ga´tion** *n.* —**cas´ti·ga·tor** *n.*

cast´ing *n.* that formed in a mold

cast iron an alloy of iron

cas´tle *n.* a fortification

cast´off *adj.* discarded —*n.* discarded material, a remnant

castor oil an oil extracted from castor beans, used for lubrication and as a medication

cas´trate *vt.* to remove the testicles from; to spay; to make ineffectual, as by depriving of authority —**cas·tra´tion** *n.*

cas´u·al *adj.* without plan; haphazard; careless or unconcerned —**cas´u·al·ly** *adv.* —**cas´u·al·ness** *n.*

cas´u·al·ty *n.* a serious accident; anyone harmed as the result of an accident or incident

cat·a·bol´ic *adj.* of the conversion of living tissue to energy —**cat·a·bol´i·cal·ly** *adv.* —**ca·tab´o·lism** *n.*

cat´a·clysm *n.* a major disturbance —**cat·a·clys´mal, cat·a·clys´mic** *adj.* —**cat·a·clys´mi·cal·ly** *adv.*

cat´a·comb´ *n.* an underground cemetery

cat´a·lep·sy *n.* an abnormal condition characterized by muscular rigidity and a trancelike state —**cat·a·lep´tic** *adj.*

cat´a·log´, cat´a·logue´ *n.* a book advertising merchandise for sale; any extensive listing of related material —*vi., vt.* to list or classify —**cat´a·log·er, cat´a·log·ist** *n.*

ca·tal´y·sis *n.* the changing of the rate of a chemical reaction by the addition of another substance

cat´a·lyst *n.* a substance that changes the rate of a chemical reaction; a person or thing that serves to bring about a conclusion or resolution —**cat·a·lyt´ic** *adj.* —**cat·a·lyt´i·cal·ly** *adv.*

catalytic converter a device that acts on automobile exhaust fumes so as to reduce pollution

cat´a·lyze *vt.* to bring about with the use of a catalyst —**cat´a·lyz·er** *n.*

cat´a·ma·ran´ *n.* a sailboat with twin hulls

cat´a·mount *n.* a wildcat

cat´a·pult *n.* an ancient seige weapon; a device for launching airplanes from the deck of a ship —*vi., vt.*

cat´a·ract´ *n.* a large waterfall; a disease of the eye

ca·tarrh´ *n.* inflammation of a mucous membrane —**ca·tarrh´al** *adj.* —**ca·tarrh´al·ly** *adv.*

ca·tas´tro·phe *n.* any great or sudden disaster; a complete failure —**cat·a·stroph´ic, cat·a·stroph´i·cal** *adj.* —**cat·a·stroph´i·cal·ly** *adv.*

cat burglar a thief who enters through the upper stories of a building

cat´call *n.* a sound of disapproval, directed at a speaker, actor, etc. —*vi., vt.* to utter or jeer with catcalls

catch *n.* a prize; that captured; a drawback; a fastener —*vi.* to take hold —*vt.* to take hold; to deceive; to take unawares; to overtake

catch·all *n.* a place where a variety of things are kept or left; a useless item

catchall phrase meaningless drivel

catch'ing *adj.* contagious

catch on to understand, comprehend; to become popular

catch phrase a slogan or motto designed to capture the attention of the listener

catch'y *adj.* attention–getting; easily remembered —**catch'i·ness** *n.*

cat·e·chise (*Brit.*), **cat·e·chize** (*US*) *vt.* to teach, especially religion, by the use of questions and answers —**cat·e·chi·sa'tion, cat·e·chi·za'tion** *n.*

cat'e·chism *n.* a set of questions and answers for teaching fundamentals, as of a religion —**cat·e·chis'mal** *adj.*

cat'e·chist *n.* one who teaches using questions and answers —**cat·e·chis'tic, cat·e·chis'ti·cal** *adj.*

cat·e·chu'men *n.* one being instructed in fundamentals

cat'e·gor'i·cal *adj.* without qualification; absolute —**cat·e·gor'i·cal·ly** *adv.*

cat'e·go·rize *vt.* to classify or type; to arrange —**cat·e·go·ri·za'tion** *n.*

cat'e·go'ry *n.* a classification

cat·e·na'tion *n.* formed in succession; a continuity —**cat'e·nate** *vt.*

ca'ter *vi.* to provide food or entertainment; to indulge the wishes of another —**ca'ter·er** *n.*

cat'er·waul *n.* a wail, as of a rutting cat; discordant screeching —*vi.*

cat'gut *n.* a tough line used for stringing musical instruments, tennis rackets, etc.

ca·thar'sis *n.* a cleansing or purgation —**ca·thar'tic, ca·thar'ti·cal** *adj.*

ca·the'dral *n.* a large church

cathedral ceiling a vaulted dome

cath'e·ter *n.* a slender tube passed through a body opening for examination, passing fluid, etc. —**cath'e·ter·ize** *vt.*

cath'ode–ray tube a vacuum tube that displays images by the projection of electrons on its surface

cath'o·lic *adj.* broad in scope or taste —**ca·thol'i·cal·ly** *adv.* —**cath·o·lic'i·ty** *n.* —**ca·thol'i·cise** (*Brit.*), **ca·thol'i·cize** (*US*) *vi., vt.*

cat'nap *n.* a light sleep —*vi.* to doze

cat'nip *n.* a type of mint

cat-o'–nine'tails *n.* a whip comprised of nine knotted cords

cat'tle *n.* livestock

cat'ty *adj.* catlike, cunning; malicious, vindictive, spiteful

catty–corner, catty–cornered *adj.* diagonal —*adv.* at a diagonal

cat'walk *n.* a narrow walkway allowing access to remote parts of equipment, buildings, etc. for the purpose of monitoring or maintenance

cau'cus *n.* a closed conference; a faction within a political party

cau'dal *adj.* of or like a tail; near the tail —**cau'dal·ly** *adv.*

cau·date *adj.* having a tail

caul *n.* the membrane surrounding a fetus

caul'dron *n.* a large kettle

caulk *n.* a malleable sealer for seams in wood, tile, etc. —*vt.* to apply a sealer

caulking compound a sealant for wood, tile, etc.

caus'al *adj.* of, or relating to, cause and effect —**caus'al·ly** *adv.* —**cau·sal'i·ty** *n.*

cau·sa'tion *n.* the act of causing —**caus'a·tive** *adj.*

cause *n.* any source or agent of change; an objective or goal —*vt.* to make something happen —**caus'er** *n.*

cause'way *n.* an elevated road, as across water or a swamp

caus´tic *adj.* corrosive; biting or sarcastic —**caus´ti·cal·ly** *adv.*

cau·ter·ise (*Brit.*), **cau´ter·ize** (*US*) *vt.* to destroy unwanted tissue or seal a wound by burning

cau´tion *n.* discretion; prudence; a warning —*vt.* to warn; to admonish —**cau´tion·ar·y** *adj.* —**cau´tious** *adj.* —**cau´tious·ly** *adv.* —**cau´tious·ness** *n.*

cav´al·cade´ *n.* a procession; a series of events

cav´a·lier´ *adj.* casual; carefree or nonchalant; hauty or arrogant —*n.* an armed horseman; a gentleman —**cav·a·lier´ly** *adv.* —**cav·a·lier´ness** *n.*

cav´al·ry *n.* mounted soldiers —**cav´al·ry·man** *n.*

cave *n.* a hollow area under the earth

ca´ve·at *n.* a formal notice or warning

cave´–in a place where the surface gives way, as over a cave or sink hole

cave man prehistoric man; a rough or crude individual

cav´ern *n.* a hollow place in the earth, a large cave —**cav´ern·ous** *adj.*

cav´i·ar *n.* the eggs of a fish: roe

cav´il *n.* a trivial objection —*vi.* to quibble or make trivial objections —**cav´il·er** *n.*

cav´i·ty *n.* a hole or hollow place

ca·vort´ *vi.* to frolic; to prance

caw *n.* the call of a crow —*vi.*

cay *n.* an offshore island, reef, etc.

cay·enne´ *n.* a hot red pepper

CD *n.* a compact disc

cease *vi., vt.* to stop —**ces·sa´tion** *n.*

cease–fire agreement to a temporary cessation of hostilities

cease´less *adj.* without end; never stopping; constant —**cease´less·ly** *adv.*

cede *vt.* to surrender, as one's rights or the possession of something

ce·dil´la *n.* a mark under the letter *c* (ç) to indicate that it is to be pronounced like an *s*

ceil´ing *n.* the top of a room; an upper limit —**hit the ceiling** to grow excited; to lose one's temper

cel´e·brant *n.* one who celebrates —**cel´e·bra·tor** *n.*

cel´e·brate´ *vt.* to commemorate with ceremony or rejoicing; to praise publicly; to make widely known —**cel·e·bra´tion** *n.* —**cel´e·bra·tive** *adj.* —**cel´e·bra·to·ry** *adj.*

cel´e·brat·ed *adj.* widely known and praised

ce·leb´ri·ty *n.* one who is famous

ce·ler´i·ty *n.* quickness of action; dispatch

ce·les´tial *adj.* of the sky or the bodies seen in the sky, as the sun, moon, etc. —**ce·les´tial·ly** *adv.*

celestial navigation laying a course by sighting on the stars

cel´i·ba·cy *n.* abstinence from sexual intercourse; the state of being unmarried

cel´i·bate *adj.* unmarried; abstaining from sexual intercourse —*n.* one who abstains from sexual intercourse; one unmarried, esp. to comply with religious vows

cell *n.* a small plain room; the fundamental component of all organisms; a basic unit of a storage battery —**celled**, **cel´lu·lar** *adj.*

cel´lar *n.* an underground area, often used for storage —**in the cellar** the lowest possible standing, as of an athletic team

cell division the means by which cells reproduce

cel´lo *n.* a stringed instrument of the violin family —**cel´list** *n.*

cel´lo·phane´ *n.* a thin, transparent material made from cellulose

cell phone, **cellular phone** (*US*) a mobile telephone

cel´lu·lar *adj.* like a cell; consisting of cells —**cel·lu·lar´i·ty** *n.*

cel´lule *n.* a small cell

cel´lu·lite *n.* fatty deposits, esp. around the thighs

cel´lu·lose *n.* a complex carbohydrate found in the cell walls of plants and used in the manufacture of a number of products

Cel´si·us *adj.* of a thermometer on which the freezing point of water is 0° and the boiling point is 100°.

ce·ment´ *n.* a building material used as a solid section or as mortar to bind other materials; an adhesive —*vt.* to join with cement; to unite firmly —**ce·men·ta´tion** *n.* —**ce·ment´er** *n.*

cem´e·ter´y *n.* a place set aside for for burial of the dead

ce´no·bite *n.* a member of a religious order living communally, as in a monastery or nunnery —**cen´o·bit´ic, cen´o·bit´i·cal** *adj.*

cen´o·taph *n.* a monument to a dead person whose remains are elsewhere; an empty tomb

cen´ser *n.* an incense holder

cen´sor *n.* one authorized to examine printed matter, sound or motion picture recordings, etc. for objectionable material —*vt.* to review so as to ban that found objectionable —**cen´sor·a·ble** *adj.* — **cen·so´ri·al** *adj.* —**cen´sor·ship** *n.*

cen·so´ri·ous *adj.* expressing censure; faultfinding; tending to be critical —**cen·so´ri·ous·ly** *adv.* — **cen·so´ri·ous·ness** *n.*

cen´sur·a·ble *adj.* subject to reprimand; at fault, blameful —**cen´sur·a·bly** *adv.*

cen´sure *n.* disapproval; an official rebuke —*vt.* to express disapproval —**cen´sur·er** *n.*

cen´sus *n.* a count of the population

cen´taur *n.* a mythical creature, half man and half horse

cen·te·nar´i·an *n.* one who has lived to the age of 100 years

cen·ten´a·ry *adj.* a period of 100 years; a one–hundredth anniversary

cen·ten´ni·al *adj.* of a hundred —*n.* a one–hundredth anniversary

cen´ter (*US*) *n.* a point equally distant from all others; the middle point or part of anything; a hub of activity, influence, etc. —*vi.* to focus or concentrate —*vt.* to place on or at a point of focus

cen´ter·board *n.* a sheet of wood or steel that descends below the keel of a sailing vessel —**retractable centerboard** a centerboard that can be raised for traversing shallow water

centered (*US*) *adj.* focused or concentrated; self–confident; being at the center

center of gravity (*US*) the point at which the weight of a thing is concentrated

cen´ter·piece *n.* the dominating decoration or display on a buffet or dining table

cen·tes´i·mal *adj.* of a hundredth part —**cen·tes´i·mal·ly** *adv.*

cen´ti·grade´ *adj.* divided into one hundred degrees; of the Celsius thermometer

cen´ti·gram *n.* one hundredth part of a gram

cen´ti·me´ter *n.* one hundredth part of a meter

cen´tral *adj.* at or near the center; of basic or significant importance; of a single source of control —**cen·tral´i·ty** *n.* —**cen´tral·ly** *adv.*

central heating a single, centralized heating plant that serves an entire building or group of buildings

cen´tral·ism *n.* a system in which all power and authority is concentrated at or near one place —**cen´tral·ise** (*Brit.*), **cen´tral·ize** (*US*) *vi., vt.* —**cen·tral·i·sa´tion, cen·tral·i·za´tion** *n.*

central nervous system the brain and spinal cord of the body

central processing unit (CPU) the primary chip that controls a computer

cen´tre (*Brit.*) *n.* a point equally distant from all others; the middle point or part of anything; a hub of activity, influence, etc. —*vi.* to focus or concentrate —*vt.* to place on or at a point of focus

centred (*Brit.*) *adj.* focused or concentrated; self-confident; being at the centre

centre of gravity (*Brit.*) the point at which the weight of a thing is concentrated

cen´trif´u·gal *adj.* moving away from a center —**cen·trif´u·gal·ly** *adv.*

centrifugal force the tendency of anything revolving around a center to move outward, away from the center

cen´tri·fuge *n.* a device that pushes matter outward by revolving at a high rate of speed, as a laboratory machine that separates particles of varying density

cen·trip´e·tal *adj.* moving toward a center —**cen·trip´e·tal·ly** *adv.*

cen·tu´ri·on *n.* a soldier in ancient Rome who commanded one hundred men

cen´tu·ry *n.* a period of one hundred years; a group of one hundred

ce·phal´ic *adj.* of the head

ce·ram´ic *adj.* of objects made from baked clay, such as pottery —**ce·ram´ist** *n.*

ce·ram´ics *n.* the art of making objects from baked clay; ceramic products

ce´re·al *n.* a grain used as food; a food prepared from grain —*adj.*

cer´e·bral *adj.* of the brain or the intellect —**cer·e´bral·ly** *adv.*

cerebral palsy a disorder resulting from damage to the central nervous system

cer´e·brum *n.* the front part of the brain

cer´e·ment *n.* a shroud; a burial garment

cer·e·mo´ni·al *adj.* of a ritual; stately or solemn —*n.* a formal system of ritual associated with a particular event —**cer·e·mo´ni·al·ism** *n.* —**cer·e·mo´ni·al·ist** *n.* —**cer·e·mo´ni·al·ly** *adv.*

cer·e·mo´ni·ous *adj.* with great formality; devoted to ritual or ceremony —**cer·e·mo´ni·ous·ly** *adv.* —**cer·e·mo´ni·ous·ness** *n.*

cer´e·mo´ny *n.* a formal rite or ritual; a formality

ce·rise´ *adj.* bright red

cer´tain *adj.* definite; reliable; inevitable; of an indefinite quality, as *a certain something* —**cer´tain·ly** *adv.*

cer·tain·ty *n.* without doubt

cer·tif´i·cate *n.* an official document attesting to something, as of birth or completion of a course of study —**cer´ti·fi·a·ble** *adj.* —**cer´ti·fi·a·bly** *adv.*

certificate of deposit a document confirming the deposit of funds with a bank or other financial institution, usually to earn interest for a fixed period

cer´ti·fi·ca´tion *n.* affirmation, acceptance

cer´ti·fied *adj.* authorized; approved; vouched for

certified check an instrument for the transfer of funds that confirms the existence of those funds

certified mail mail that is confirmed as to time deposited and delivered

certified public accountant an accountant recognized as having complied with the laws of the state as to knowledge of his trade

cer´ti·fy *vt.* to make known as certain; to declare in writing —**cer´ti·fi·er** *n.*

cer´ti·tude *n.* conviction; with absolute confidence

ce·ru´le·an *adj.* azure blue in color

cer′vi·cal *adj.* of the cervix

cer′vix *n.* the neck or a neck-like part of the body

ces·sa′tion *n.* an ending or stopping

ces′sion *n.* a surrender or renunciation; a waiver

cess′pool *n.* a large receptical for receiving effluence from a household; a place that is corrupted

chad *n.* bits of paper removed from perforated tape or punch cards used in computer processing

chafe *n.* tenderness or wear from friction —*vi.* to rub; to become irritated —*vt.* to irritate by rubbing; to annoy —**chafe at the bit** to show impatience —**chaf′er** *n.*

chaff *n.* the waste from threshing; anything worthless

chaf′ing dish′ *n.* a serving dish with a heat source for cooking or keeping food warm

cha·grin′ *n.* embarrassment —*vt.* to embarrass

chain *n.* a flexible series of links; any series of logically connected elements; a thing that binds —*vt.* to bind or restrain, as with a chain

chain gang a prison work party

chain letter a letter containing a request, and asking that the same request be passed on to others

chain lightning a stroke of lightning seen as having many branches; of a person who seems to move quickly in many directions at once

chain reaction a series of events in which each incident influences the next

chain saw a portable power saw with teeth attached to a chain

chain-smoke to smoke cigarettes continuously, one after another — **chain smoker**

chain store a retail outlet that is one of many operating under the same name

chair *n.* a place for sitting; a position of authority —*vt.* to preside over, as a meeting

chair′lift *n.* a type of conveyance for transporting skiers up a hill

chair′man *n.* one who officiates, as over a committee or a meeting — **chair′man·ship** *n.*

chair′person *n.* one who officiates; often used to avoid the gender connotation of *chairman*

chaise longue, chaise lounge *n.* a long chair with support for the legs and back

cha·let′ *n.* a style of Swiss house

chal′ice *n.* a goblet

chalk *n.* a type of limestone; a marker for writing on a blackboard, etc. —*vt.* to write with chalk —**chalk′i·ness** *n.* —**chalk′y** *adj.*

chalk′board *n.* a blackboard or slate; a surface for writing with chalk

chal′lenge *n.* a difficult task; an invitation to compete; a calling into question —*vt.* to invite one to compete; to call into question — **chal′lenge·a·ble** *adj.* —**chal′leng·er** *n.*

chal′leng·ing *adj.* difficult, formidable; intriguing, fascinating

cham′ber *n.* a room, bedroom; a meeting room; a board or council; any enclosed space or compartment

cham′ber·maid *n.* one who cleans rooms, as in a hotel

chamber music light music for performance by a small musical group

chamber of commerce an organization dedicated to the promotion of business

champ *n.* a champion —*vt.* to chew —**champ at the bit** be impatient

cham·pagne′ *n.* a sparkling wine from the Champagne region of France; commonly, a wide variety of light, sparkling wines; the yellowish color of the wine

cham′pi·on *n.* one who supports a cause; one with the attributes of a winner —*vt*. to fight for; to support —**cham´pi·on·ship** *n*.

chance *adj*. fortuitous, unplanned — *n*. a happening without discernible cause; an unexpected occurrence; a wager; an opportunity —*vi*. to occur accidentally —*vt*. to risk — **chanc´i·ness** *n*. —**chanc´y** *adj*.

chance´ful *adj*. full of outstanding events; momentous

chan´cel·ler·y *n*. the office of chancellor

chan´cel·lor *n*. president of a university; in some countries, the prime minister —**chan´cel·lor·ship** *n*.

chan´de·lier´ *n*. an elaborate hanging light fixture

change *n*. the process of altering; a substitution; a transformation; coins —*vi*., *vt*. to make or become different; to exchange; to transform

change´a·ble *adj*. able to be altered; temporary; adaptable or flexible; unstable, flighty, or fickle — **change·a·bil´i·ty, change´a·ble·ness** *n*. —**change´a·bly** *adv*.

change´ful *adj*. unstable; likely to change; variable; **change´ful·ly** *adv*.; **change´ful·ness** *n*.

change´less *adj*. constant; permanent —**change´less·ly** *adv*. — **change´less·ness** *n*.

change of heart a shift in thinking or attitude

change of pace something dissimilar; a difference or respite from the usual

change´o·ver *n*. passing from one to another; a transformation; an altering of configuration, as of industrial equipment altered to manufacture a different product

chang´er *n*. one who changes; that which changes records, disks, etc.

chan´nel *n*. the bed of a flowing body of water; a passageway for liquid; a band or route for communications —*vt*. to wear into grooves or ruts; to send through a channel; to direct —**chan´nel·ize** *vt*. —**chan·nel·i·za´tion** *n*.

chan·nel·ing *n*. the concept that one may be a conduit for another, such as for a spiritual force — **chan´nel·er** *n*.

chant *n*. a primitive musical form; a rhythmic recitation as of a slogan —*vi*., *vt*. —**chant´er** *n*.

cha´os *n*. extreme confusion or disorder —**cha·ot´ic** *adj*. —**cha·ot´i·cal·ly** *adv*.

chap *n*. a male, man or boy —*vi*., *vt*. to roughen the skin, as from the wind

cha·pa·re´jos *n*. leather leg protectors worn by cowboys; chaps

chap·ar·ral *n*. a thicket

cha·pa´ti *n*. a skillet bread indigenous to India

cha·peau´ *n*., *pl*. **cha·peaus´, cha·peaux´** a hat

chap´el *n*. a small room set aside for worship; a small church

chap´er·on´ *n*. one who escorts or oversees, especially the activities of a young unmarried female —*vt*. to overseer or supervise —**chap´er·on·age** *n*.

chap´lain *n*. a clergyman, especially one appointed to service in an institution, organization, etc. — **chap´lain·cy, chap´lain·ship** *n*.

chap´let *n*. prayer beads

chaps *n*. leather leg protectors worn by cowboys; chaparejos

chap´ter *n*. a main division of a book; a distinct period; a branch of an organization

char *vi*., *vt*. to scorch; to reduce to charcoal

char´ac·ter *n*. any mark or symbol used in writing or printing; a distinctive quality; moral or ethical strength; a particular person in a book, play, history, etc.; an odd person

character actor an actor or actress who specializes in portraying unusual individuals

character assassination slander with intent to destroy credibility

char·ac·ter·is´tic *adj.* typical; distinguishing —*n.* a distinctive attribute or style —**char·ac·ter·is´ti·cal·ly** *adv.*

char´ac·ter·ize *vt.* to depict, typify —**char·ac·ter·i·za´tion** *n.*

cha·rade´ *n.* a game in which common sayings, titles, etc. are acted out; a thinly disguised deception; a sham

char´broil *vt.* to broil over charcoal; to barbecue —**char´broiled** *adj.*

char´coal´ *n.* charred wood used as fuel; a stick for sketching —*vt.* to charbroil; to sketch with charcoal

charge *n.* asking price; a financial obligation; an assigned duty; one given into the care of another; a call to attack; mild excitement —*vt.* to set a price; to incur a financial obligation; to command; to hold liable; to accuse; to attack —*vi.* to set a price —**charge´a·ble** *adj.*

charge account an agreement with a merchant or financial institution that allows one to purchase on credit

charge card identification for one who has a charge account

char·gé d'af·faires´ *n.* a diplomatic officer

char´i·ot *n.* a two-wheeled, horse-drawn vehicle; the family car —*vi., vt.* to convey, ride or drive in a chariot —**char´i·o·teer´** *n.*

cha·ris´ma *n.* leadership quality; charm, appeal

char·is·mat´ic *adj.* having charisma; of certain religious groups —*n.* one reputed to have divine powers

char´i·ta·ble *adj.* generous; forgiving —**char´i·ta·ble·ness** *n.* —**char´i·ta·bly** *adv.*

char´i·ty *n.* almsgiving; an institution for providing aid to those in need

char·la·tan *n.* a fake; one who falsely claims to have certain knowledge or skill —**char´la·tan·ism, char´la·tan·ry** *n.*

charley horse a muscle cramp

charm *n.* something assumed to have magical power; a quality that attracts or pleases —*vt.* to attract or please —**charm´er** *n.*

charmed fortunate, lucky —**live a charmed life** protected from misfortune

charm´ing *adj.* captivating; appealing or attractive —**charm´ing·ly** *adv.*

chart *n.* a map, as for navigation; a graphic representation of data —*vt.* to make a map or graph —**chart´er** *n.* —**char´tist** *n.*

char´ter *n.* a document that attests to or authorizes formation, sets forth aims, grants specific rights, etc., as a *corporate* or *city charter*; to lease, as a boat or plane —*vt.* to establish by charter; to lease

charter member one who joins an organization at the time of its inception

char·treuse´ *n.* a pale green color; a type of liqueur —*adj*

char´y *adj.* cautious

chase *n.* pursuit —*vt.* to pursue; to drive away —*vi.* to follow in pursuit —**chas´er** *n.*

chasm *n.* a narrow gorge or ravine; any sharp division —**chas´mal** *adj.*

chaste *adj.* virtuous, pure in thought or conduct —**chaste´ly** *adv.* —**chaste´ness, chas´ti·ty** *n.*

chas´ten *n.* to correct by punishing —**chas´ten·er**

chas·tise´ *vt.* to punish; to scold sharply —**chas·tise´ment** *n.* —**chas·tis´er** *n.*

chas·ti·ty *n.* purity; innocence

chat *n.* casual conversation —*vi.* to

converse in a easygoing manner —
chat·ti·ly *adv.* **—chat´ti·ness** *n.*
—chat´ty *adj.*

cha·teau´ *n.* a country house

chat´tel *n.* moveable personal property

chat´ter *n.* foolish talk —*vi.* to speak rapidly and foolishly; to click rapidly or rattle

chat´ter·box *n.* one who talks constantly

chauf´feur *n.* a hired driver; anyone who drives for another —*vt.* to drive for another

chau·vin·ism *n.* fanatical patriotism; irrational belief in the superiority of one's sex, race, etc. **—chau´vin·ist** *n.* **—chau·vin·is´tic** *adj.* **—chau·vin·is´ti·cal·ly** *adv.*

cheap *adj.* inexpensive; of little value **—cheap´ly** *adv.* **—cheap´ness** *n.*

cheap´en *vt.* to depreciate; to debase or degrade

cheap shot an underhanded remark

cheap·skate *n.* one unwilling to spend money

cheat *n.* a swindle; one who defrauds —*vi.*, *vt.* to defraud; to be dishonest **—cheat´er** *n.*

check *n.* a stop or slowing; an examination for quality, etc.; a bill, as at a restaurant; a negotiable instrument for the transfer of money; a pattern made up of squares —*vt.* to slow or stop, as forward progress; to examine for errors, etc. **—check´er** *n.*

check·er·board *adj.* of a pattern of squares —*n.* a game board consisting of alternating dark and light squares used to play checkers and chess

checking account (*US*) a monetary deposit that permits the transfer of funds by writing checks

check´list *n.* a reference list for checking tasks, names, etc.

check´mate *n.* a winning move in chess; any action that frustrates

the aims of another

check´off *n.* a system for the collection of union dues through payroll deduction

check´-out, check´out *n.* the tallying of purchases; a time by which a hotel room must be vacated without penalty; examination or verification

check´point *n.* a location for inspection or verification, as in a roadrace or at a border

check´room *n.* a place for hanging coats, storing luggage, etc.

check´up *n.* an examination, as by a doctor

ched´dar *n.* a type of cheese

cheek *n.* the side of the face; impertinence, rudeness

cheek´bone *n.* a bone at the side of the face near the top of the cheek

cheek´y *adj.* brazen, bold; impertinent **—cheek´i·ly** *adv.* **—cheek´i·ness** *n.*

cheer *n.* a pleasant mood; a source of pleasure; a shout of approval or encouragement —*vi.*, *vt.* to gladden; to sound approval — **cheer´ful** *adj.* **—cheer´ful·ly** *adv.* **—cheer´ful·ness** *n.*

cheer´lead·er *n.* one of a group who leads cheering for an athletic team; one who is seen as overzealous in promoting a person, company, cause, etc.

cheer´less *adj.* dreary; dismal; barren **—cheer´less·ly** *adv.* **—cheer´less·ness** *n.*

cheer´y *adj.* happy; light–hearted; jaunty **—cheer´i·ly** *adv.* **—cheer´i·ness** *n.*

cheese *n.* a food made from the pressed curds of soured milk

cheese´cake *n.* a pie–like dessert based on creamed cottage or ricotta cheese; a picture of a scantily clad man or woman

cheese´cloth *n.* a loosely woven cotton cloth used for cleaning, straining, etc.

chees´y *adj.* of or like **cheese** in texture, taste, etc.; lacking in quality —**chees´i·ness** *n.*

chef *n.* a cook; one in charge of a kitchen

chem´i·cal *adj.* of chemistry; made from chemicals —*n.* a substance used in or made by a chemical process —**chem´i·cal·ly** *adv.*

chemical warfare the use of chemicals, such as poison gas, to defeat an enemy

che·mise´ *n.* a type of dress or an undergarment for women

chem´is·try *n.* the study of the properties of matter —**chem´ist** *n.*

chem·o·ther´a·py *n.* the treatment of illness or disease by the use of chemicals —**chem·o·ther´a·pist** *n.*

cheque *n.* (*Brit.*) a bill, as at a restaurant; a negotiable instrument for the transfer of money; a pattern made up of squares

cher´ish *vt.* to hold dear; to protect; to harbor, as an idea —**cher´ish·er** *n.* —**cher´ish·ing·ly** *adv.*

che·root´ *n.* a type of cigar

cher·vil *n.* an herb used for flavoring

chess *n.* a board game for two players; —**chess´board**, **chess´man**, **chess´men** *n.*

chest *n.* the front of the body between the neck and the abdomen; a box for strorage; a cabinet

chest´nut *n.* a type of edible nut or the tree on which it grows; a reddish-brown horse —*adj.* the brown color of the nut —pull chestnuts out of the fire to recover from a potentially difficult situation

chest of drawers a piece of furniture containing several drawers for storage, as for clothing

chest´y *adj.* having a large chest; buxom

chev´ron *n.* a uniform insignia worn on the sleeve to denote rank

chew *vt.*, *vi.* to grind with the teeth; to consider —**chew** out to scold; upbraid —**chew** the fat, **chew** the rag to talk; converse —**chew´a·ble** *adj.* —**chew´er** *n.*

chew´y *adj.* of food, such as meat, that is tough or difficult to **chew** —**chew´i·ness** *n.*

chic *adj.* stylish; smartly dressed —*n.* refinement in style or manner

chi·can´er·y *n.* deception by means of crafty speech or action; trickery

chi´chi *adj.* elegant in style or manner; of a style that is overdone; of one haughty in manner

chick *n.* a young bird; a young woman

chick´en *n.* a common domestic fowl; a coward —*adj.* fearful, timid; overly strict or severe —**chicken** out to back down —no spring chicken no longer young

chicken feed an inconsequential amount, usually of money; insignificant

chick´en–heart´ed *adj.* fearful; fainthearted

chicken pox a childhood disease

chicken wire a light fencing made of wire intertwined to form geometric patterns

chic´le *n.* substance used in the making of chewing gum

chic´o·ry *n.* a type of flowering plant; its leaves, used in salad; its root, used to flavor coffee

chide *vi.*, *vt.* to scold quietly —**chid´ing·ly** *adv.*

chief *adj.* most significant, as *the chief ingredient* —*n.* a leader

Chief Executive President of the United States

chief executive, **chief executive officer** the highest ranking administrator of an organization

chief justice the official head of a judicial body

chief´ly *adj.* of or like a **chief** —*adv.* especially, mainly, primarily

chief of staff the leading director of

an organization

chief of state a head of government

chief′tain *n.* a chief

chif·fon′ *n.* a lightweight cloth

chif·fo·nier′ *n.* a chest of drawers

child *n., pl.* **chil′dren** an infant; offspring —**child's play** easy

child′bear·ing *n.* the process of carrying an unborn child and giving birth —*adj.*

child′birth *n.* the act of bringing forth a baby

child′hood *n.* the years from infancy to puberty; a time of growth and development

child′ish *adj.* acting like a child; immature; silly —**child′ish·ly** *adv.* —**child′ish·ness** *n.*

child′less *adj.* having no offspring

child′like *adj.* exhibiting the attributes or temperament of a child; innocent; adolescent

chil′i *n.* a type of pepper; a dried red pepper used for seasoning

chill *adj.* slightly cold —*n.* coldness; shivering caused by a disease —*vt.* to make cold —**chill′ness** *n.*

chill′er *n.* that shocks or frightens, as a book, movie, etc.

chill′y *adj.* of a discernibly cold, uncomfortable environment; uncomfortable from the cold; of discourteous, unfriendly behavior, as *a chilly reception* —**chill′i·ness** *n.*

chill′ing *adj.* frightening; causing concern —**chill′ing·ly** *adv.*

chime *n.* a bell; the sound of bells tuned to a musical scale —*vi., vt.* to sound in harmony —**chime in** to interrupt or take part in —**chim′er** *n.*

chi·me′ra *n.* an imaginary monster; a wild fancy —**chi·mer′ic, chi·mer′i·cal** *adj.* —**chi·mer′i·cal·ly** *adv.*

chim′ney *n.* a channel for smoke to escape

chimney sweep one whose profession is cleaning chimneys

chin *n.* the front of the lower jaw — *vi.* to idly chat or gossip

chi′na *n.* procelain or a similar material, originally made in China; fine dinnerware —**chi′na·ware** *n.*

china cabinet, china closet a cupboard for storing and displaying fine dinnerware

chine *n.* a backbone or spine

chink *n.* a crack or slit —*vt.* to fill in a crack —**a chink in one's armor** a weakness

chi′no *n.* a cotton cloth —**chinos** casual slacks make from the cloth

chi·noi·se·rie′ *n.* an oriental style of decoration, as for furniture, textiles, etc.

chintz′y *adj.* cheap; gawdy, vulgar; of poor quality

chip *n.* a small piece; a thin slice; a spot where a small piece has been removed; a marker or token used as a game piece —*vi., vt.* to break off a small piece —**a chip off the old block** a son who is much like his father —**chip in** to contribute —**have a chip on one's shoulder** to be testy or quarrelsome —**in the chips** wealthy

chipped beef dried beef, sliced very thin; thinly sliced dried beef served in a sauce

chip′per *adj.* light-hearted; cheerful —*n.* a tool for chipping

chi·rop′o·dist *n.* a podiatrist; a specialist in disorders of the foot —**chi·rop′o·dy** *n.*

chi·ro·prac′tor *n.* one who treats disorders of the body by manipulating the joints —**chi′ro·prac′tic** *adj., n.*

chis′el *n.* a tool for cutting and shaping wood —*vt.* to cut with a chisel; to cheat; to obtain by deception —**chis′el·er** *n.*

chit *n.* a bill, usually for a small amount; a marker

chit′chat *n.* idle, often meaningless, talk

chiv´al·ry *n.* the qualities attributed to knighthood, such as fine manners, bravery, etc —**chiv´al·rous** *adj.* —**chiv´al·rous·ly** *adv.* —**chiv´al·rous·ness** *n.*

chive *n.* an herb used for flavoring

chlo´ri·nate *vt.* to treat with chlorine, as water for purification — **chlo·rin·a´tion** *n.*

chlo´rine *n.* a chemical used for water purification, as a cleaning and bleaching agent, etc.

chock *n.* a block used as a stopper or wedge, as to keep a wheeled vehicle from rolling; a device on the deck of a ship through which rope is guided

chock-full *adj.* filled to the brim

choc´o·hol·ic *n.* one who is extremely fond of chocolate

choc´o·late *n.* a flavoring made from cacao beans —*adj.* flavored with chocolate —**choc´o·lat·ey** *adj.*

choice *adj.* preferred; superior —*n.* the act or right of choosing; a thing chosen; an alternative; a favored part; the finest part

choir *n.* an organized group of singers; a part of a church set aside for singers: *a choir loft*

choir´boy *n.* one who sings in the choir; one who cultivates the image of being well-behaved

choke *n.* the sounds made by one choking; a device that alters the flow of air to an engine —*vi.* to have difficulty breathing; to have difficulty performing, as *to choke under pressure* —*vt.* to throttle or strangle; to obstruct or restrict, as the flow of air to a combustion engine

choke back to suppress, as tears

choke´ber·ry *n.* a fruit reputed to cause choking if eaten; the bush on which the berries grow

choke´bore *n.* a shotgun bore configuration that maintains a tight pattern of shot

choke´cher·ry *n.* a fruit reputed to cause choking if eaten; the tree or bush on which the berries grow

choke collar a collar, as for a dog, that tightens as strain is put on the leash; a tight leather collar with metal studs

choke chain a leash that is part of a choke collar

choke down to eat with difficulty, as of a food that is not to one's liking

chok´er *n.* one who throttles another; jewelry or furs that fit closely around the neck

choke up to block or clog; to be overcome by emotion

chol´er *n.* a state of irritation; anger or rage —**chol´er·ic** *adj.*

cho´line *n.* a B vitamin

choose *vi., vt.* to select; to prefer as an option

choos´y *adj.* selective; fastidious

chop *n.* a cut of meat that includes the rib; a sharp blow —*vt.* to cut with a sharp blow; to cut into small pieces

chop´per *n.* a helicopter

chop´py *adj.* characterized by quick starts and stops or direction changes; discordant —**chop´pi·ly** *adv.* —**chop´pi·ness** *n.*

chop´sticks *n.* a pair of relatively small straight rods used in the orient to manipulate food in cooking, eating, etc.

chop su´ey a quasi-oriental dish of meat and vegetables in a sauce, usually served over rice

cho´ral *adj.* of a performance by a choir or chorus; of the work performed —**cho´ral·ly** *adv.*

cho·rale´ *n.* a choir or chorus; a musical work performed by a choir or chorus

chord *n.* a set of musical tones sounded together; anything harmonious, as of thought or emotion; a straight line joining two points of an arc

chore *n.* a small task; a difficult or unpleasant job

cho·re′a *n.* a nervous disorder characterized by spastic motions

cho′re·o·graph *vi., vt.* to create and direct a dance; to carefully plan and direct the execution of any activity

cho′re·og′ra·phy *n.* creation and direction of dances —**cho·re·og′ra·pher** *n.* —**cho·re·o·graph′ic** *adj.* —**cho·re·o·graph′i·cal·ly** *adv.*

chor′tle *n.* a quiet laugh; a chuckling sound —*vi., vt.* to chuckle or snicker

chorus *n.* a group that performs as a unit, as singers or dancers; the part performed by a chorus; a group or action that is in accord, as *a chorus of dissension*; the refrain of a song —*vi., vt.* to perform in unison —**cho′ris·ter** *n.*

chos′en *adj.* of one selected, often for a special honor; favored, as by good fortune

chow *n.* a breed of dog, short for *chow chow*; food —**chow′** time meal time

chow′der *n.* a type of soup; a hodgepodge —**chowderhead** one whose thinking is muddled

chow mein′ a quasi-oriental stew of meat and vegetables, served with fried noodles and rice

chris′ten *vt.* to baptize or name; to bring into service; to use for the first time —**chris′ten·ing** *n.*

chris′ten·dom *n.* the time of Christianity; that portion of the earth populated by Christians; all of the known or inhabited world

Christian *adj.* of those who follow the teachings of Christ —*n.* a follower of Christ

Chris·ti·an′i·ty *n.* the Christian religion; Christians generally

Christian name one's given name as distinguished from a family name

Christian Science of those who believe in the healing power of the teachings of Christianity

chro·mat′ic *adj.* of colors; progressing by semitones in music — *n.* a modified musical tone —**chro·mat′i·cal·ly** *adv.*

chro′ma·tin *n.* the substance in cells that forms chromosomes

chrome *n.* chromium used for plating —*vt.* to plate with chromium

chro′mi·um *n.* a metallic element that resists corrosion

chro′mo·some′ *n.* a strand of DNA that carries hereditary information

chron′ic *adj.* continuous or recurring often; habitual, as *a chronic eater* —**chron′i·cal·ly** *adv.*

chron′i·cle *n.* an ordered record of events; a detailed report —*vt.* to record or narrate events —**chron′i·cler** *n.*

chro·nol′o·gy *n.* the study of the fixing of dates and the order of events; an ordered record of events —**chron·o·log′ic,** **chron·o·log′i·cal** *adj.* —**chron·o·log′i·cal·ly** *adv.* —**chro·nol′o·gist** *n.*

chro·nom′e·ter *n.* a device for measuring time with great precision —**chron·o·met′ric,** **chron·o·met′ri·cal** *adj.* —**chron·o·met′ri·cal·ly** *adv.*

chro·nom′e·try *n.* the study and implementation of methods for the extremely accurate measuring of time

chub′by *adj.* round and plump

chuck *n.* an adjustable device for securing a tool, as a drill in a bit; a shim —*vt.* to throw; to throw away or discard

chuck′le *n.* a quiet laugh —*vi.* to laugh quietly —**chuck′ler** *n.*

chuck′le·head *n.* a silly or foolish person

chum *n.* a friend or associate; bits of fish or fish entrails used as bait — *vi.* to hang about together; to scatter fish parts on the water in an effort to attract game fish — **chum´mi·ly** *adv.* —**chum´mi·ness** *n.* —**chum´my** *adj.*

chump *n.* one who is gullible; the victim of a con game; a stupid or foolish person

chunk *n.* a lump; a substantial amount —*vt.* to cut or form into lumps

chunk´y *adj.* stocky, especially of a person; containing solid bits, as *chunky peanut butter* —**chunk´i·ness** *n.*

church *n.* a place set apart for worship; a group of worshippers who ascribe to similar beliefs — **church´go·er** *n.*

church´ly *adj.* of one who is pious, worshipful; of a church or its offices

church´war·den *n.* a long clay pipe

church´y *adj.* of one who is unusually preoccupied with religion or the affairs of a church

church´yard *n.* the grounds about a church, often serving as a burial plot for its members

churl *n.* a bumpkin; a grouch or curmudgeon

churl´ish *adj.* crude, vulgar; grouchy, surly —**churl´ish·ly** *adv.* —**churl´ish·ness** *n.*

churn *n.* a container in which cream is made into butter —*vi., vt.* to make butter in a churn; to agitate violently —**churn´er** *n.*

chute *n.* an inclined trough

chut´ney *n.* a relish of fruit and spices

chutz´pah, chutz´pa *n.* brazenness; audacity; insolence

cic´a·trix *n., pl.* **cic´a·tri·ces, cic´a·trix·es** fibrous tissue that forms at the healing of a wound; a scar

cic´a·trise (*Brit.*), **cic´a·trize** (*US*) *vi., vt.* to heal by forming a scar —**cic·a·tri·sa´tion, cic·a·tri·za´tion** *n.*

ci´der *n.* a juice from apples

ci·gar´ *n.* a roll of cured tobacco for smoking

cig´a·ret´, cig´a·rette´ *n.* finely cut cured tobacco rolled in paper for smoking

cil´i·a *n. pl., sing.* **cil´i·um** small hair or hair-like projections in or on a life form —**cil´i·ar·y** *adj.* —**cil´i·ate** *adj.*

cinch *n.* a wide belt used to secure a saddle or pack; a task that is easy to do —*vt.* to secure a saddle or pack with a cinch; to make certain

cinc´ture *n.* a belt or sash; something that encircles —*vt.* to bind or encircle

cin´der *n.* a rough, rock-like material formed by exposure to great heat, as lava or slag; material that has been burned, but not turned to ash

cinder block a concrete block for building

cin´e·ma *n.* a movie theater; the making of films; the motion-picture industry

cin·e·ma·tog´ra·pher *n.* one who operates a motion-picture camera; one who produces or directs the making of films

cin·e·ma·tog´ra·phy *n.* the art of motion picture photography —**cin·e·mat·o·graph´ic** *adj.* —**cin·e·mat·o·graph´i·cal·ly** *adv.*

cin·e·rar´i·um *n.* a place where the ashes of cremated bodies are kept —**cin´er·ar·y** *adj.*

cin´na·bar *n.* mercuric sulphide, the source of mercury; bright red

ci´pher *n.* the character zero; a thing of no value; a system for coding messages; an encoded message

cir´ca *prep.* about, esp. of an approximate date, as *circa 1500*

cir·ca·di´an *adj.* of the biological rhythms associated with the twenty-four hour day

cir´cle *n.* a round figure, ring, or orb; a group of people; an extent, as of influence; a revolution or

cycle —vi. to revolve; to move in a circle —vt. to move around; to encircle, surround

cir´clet n. a small circle

cir´cuit n. a somewhat circular or continuous route; a journey over such a route made in the exercise of a calling, as for a judge or preacher; the course of an electric current —cir´cuit·ry n.

circuit board an insulated board to which the elements of a circuit are affixed and connected

circuit breaker a safety device that interrupts an electrical circuit in the event of an overload

circuit court a judicial forum that sits periodically in various places throughout an area

cir·cu´i·tous adj. roundabout or devious —cir·cu´i·tous·ly adv.

cir´cu·lar adj. round; of that which is moving in a circle; circuitous — n. a printed advertisement that is widely distributed —cir·cu·lar´i·ty, cir´cu·lar·ness n. —cir´cu·lar·ly adv.

cir´cu·late´ vi., vt. to move about freely, as a guest at a party; to move on a predetermined course, as blood through the body — cir´cu·la´tion n. —cir´cu·la·tor n. —cir´cu·la·to·ry adv.

cir·cum´fer·ence n. the boundary of a circle or an area —cir·cum·fer·en´tial adj. —cir·cum·fer·en´tial·ly adv.

cir´cum·lo·cu´tion n. an evasive, lengthly means of expression — cir·cum·loc´u·to·ry adj.

cir´cum·nav´i·gate vt. to travel completely around —cir·cum·nav·i·ga´tion n.

cir´cum·scribe vt. draw a line around; to define the limits of — cir·cum·scrib´a·ble adj. —cir´cum·scrip´tion n.

cir´cum·spect´ adj. cautious; prudent —cir·cum·spec´tion,

cir´cum·spect·ness n. —cir·cum·spec´tive adj. —cir·cum·spect´ly adv.

cir´cum·stance´ n. a related fact or condition; a happening; a ceremonial display

cir´cum·stan´tial adj. based on circumstances; of little importance; inconclusive —cir·cum·stan·ti·al´i·ty n. —cir·cum·stan´tial·ly adv.

circumstantial evidence in a court of law, information that is not conclusive, but that may infer proof

cir·cum·stan´ti·ate vt. to verify — cir·cum·stan·ti·a´tion n.

cir´cum·vent vt. to go around, or bypass; to avoid by craft —cir´cum·vent·er n. —cir·cum·ven´tion n. —cir·cum·ven´tive adj.

cir´cus n. a traveling show featuring trained animals, clowns, acrobats, etc.; frantic activity or disorder

cis´tern n. a storage tank for water; a container for catching rain water; a reservoir

cit´a·del n. a fortress or stronghold; a place of refuge

ci·ta´tion n. a quotation or reference; a summons to appear in court; formal acknowledgment; a commendation

cite vt. to quote; to summon before a court of law —cit´a·ble adj.

cit´ied adj. of an area having cities; of or like a city

cit´i·fy vt. to build up and make like a city; to become like a city person in manner, dress, etc. —cit´i·fied adj.

cit´i·zen n. one who is entitled to the full protection of the state; an inhabitant of any place; cit´i·zen·ship n.

cit´i·zen·ry n. citizens collectively

citizen's arrest apprehension or citation by one who is not an officer of the law

cit´ric adj. pertaining to citrus fruit;

the acid of such fruit; citric acid

cit·ron·el´la *n.* a pungent oil used in the making of perfumes, insect repellent, etc.

cit´rus *n.* trees that bear fruit such as oranges, lemons, limes, etc.; the fruit of these trees —*adj.*

citrus fruit oranges, lemons, limes, grapefruit, etc.

cit´y (*US*) *n.* an incorporated area that is self-governing according to the laws of its state

cit´y (*Brit.*) *n.* an urban area with a cathedral or that has been designated a city by royal warrant

city council elected members of the governing body of a city

city father anyone who wields power in the running of a city

city hall the seat of government in a city —can't fight city hall expressing the futility of opposing established authority or dogma

city manager a professional administrator hired by a city to oversee the operation of its departments

city planning the science and process of regulating growth and change in a city

cit´y·scape *n.* a view of a city, its skyline, etc.

city slicker one who is perceived as being too suave or urbane

civ´ic *adj.* of a city or its citizens — civ´i·cal·ly *adv.*

civ´ic-mind´ed *adj.* inclined to act in the best interests of a city or its citizens —civ´ic-mind´ed·ly *adv.* —civ´ic-mind´ed·ness *n.*

civics *n.* the study of the rights and duties of citizenship

civ´il *adj.* of citizens; civilized in manner; formally polite; of matters that pertain to the rights of individuals —ci·vil´ian *n.* —civ´il·ly *adv.*

civil defense a program for recruiting, organizing, and training a group of volunteers to be called on

for the protection of and to civilians in the event of enemy attack or natural disaster

civil disobedience a tactic for opposing government action or policy through noncompliance

civil engineer an engineer who specializes in the concept and development of construction projects for a community, such as roads, bridges, etc.

ci·vil´ian *n.* persons not associated with the military, law enforcement, etc. —*adj.* of civilians or civil life

ci·vil´ian·ize *vt.* to revert or place under civilian control —ci·vil·ian·i·za´tion *n.*

ci·vil´i·ty *n.* good breeding; courteous behavior

civ·i·li·sa´tion (*Brit.*), civ·i·li·za´tion (*US*) *n.* the state of being or becoming civilized; the aggregate culture of a people; the comforts and protection of a civilized state

civ´i·lise (*Brit.*), civ´i·lize (*US*) *vi., vt.* to convert from a savage state — civ´i·lis·a·ble, civ´i·liz·a·ble *adj.* —civ´i·lised, civ´i·lized *adj.*

civil law the law that pertains to the rights of individuals

civil liberty the right of an individual to act without interference from the government except as required for public safety

civil rights rights granted by the Constitution

civil service of those employed by the government, excepting the military or elected officials

civil war war between opposing factions within a nation

clab´ber *n.* thick sour milk —*vi., vt.* to curdle

clad *adj.* clothed; covered, as by a layer of metal

clad´ding *n.* a layer of metal covering another; the procedure for affixing one layer of metal to another

claim *vt.* to request or demand as a

right; to state as fact —n. a demand; the basis for a demand; a
thing demanded; an assertion —
claim´a·ble adj. —claim´ant,
claim´er n.

claiming race a horse race in which
the participating horses are made
available for sale

clair·voy´ant adj. of the ability to
sense or perceive that which is not
apparant —n. one with such ability —clair·voy´ance n. —clair·
voy´ant·ly adv.

cla´mant adj. crying out noisily;
insistent —cla´mant·ly adv.

clam´bake n. an outing featuring
raw, steamed, or baked clams

clam´ber vi. to climb with much
action of the hands and feet

clam´my adj. unpleasantly cold and
damp —clam´mi·ly adv. —clam´
mi·ness n.

clam´or n. a loud, sustained outcry
—vi. to make insistant demands —
clam´or·er n. —clam´or·ous adj.
—clam´or·ous·ly adv. —clam´or·
ous·ness n.

clamp n. a device used to join or
hold —vt. to join with a clamp

clamp´down n. the imposition of
restrictions or regulations —clamp
down to grow more restrictive; to
forbid or prohibit

clan n. a family, group of families, or
tribe; a group with common interests —clan´nish adj. —clan´nish·
ly adv. —clan´nish·ness n. —
clans´man n.

clan·des´tine adj. kept secret or
hidden —clan·des´tine·ly adv. —
clan·des´tine·ness n.

clang n. a loud, harsh, metallic
sound —vi. to make such a sound

clang´or n. a repeated or persisting
clanging sound —vi. to make such
a noise —clang´or·ous adj. —
clang´or·ous·ly adv.

clap n. a sudden sharp sound; a
blow —vi., vt. make a sharp sound;

to applaud —clap´per n.

clap´board n. wood siding —vt. to
apply wood siding

clap´trap n. idle words

clar´et n. a dry red wine

clar´i·fy vi., vt. to make or become
clear, as a liquid; to make or become easier to understand —clar·
i·fi·ca´tion n.

clar´i·net´ n. a single-reed wood-
wind instrument —clar·i·net´ist n.

clar´i·on adj. clear, sharp, distinct
—n. a medieval trumpet; the
sound made by a clarion —vt. to
proclaim clearly and distinctly

clar´i·ty n. the quality of being clear

clash n. a harsh clanging noise; a
conflict between hostile forces or
ideas —vi. to collide with a harsh
noise; to come into conflict

clasp n. a fastener; an embrace —vt.
to fasten as with a clasp; to embrace

class n. a distinct type or category;
social rank; quality, especially of
manners or dress —vt. to grade or
rank

class action, class action suit a
legal action on behalf of a large
group of people, such as against
the manufacturer of a defective
product

clas´sic adj. of the highest order;
famous; traditional; uncomplicated
—n. a work of the highest order; a
thing, that is famous or traditional
—clas´si·cal adj. —clas´si·cal·ly
adj. —clas´si·cal·ness n.

clas´si·cism n. the qualities associated with the art of ancient Greece
or Rome; classical scholarship —
clas´si·cist n. —clas´si·cize vi., vt.

clas´si·fied adj. arranged in suitable
categories; secret

classified ad, classified advertisement small advertisements in a
periodical, usually arranged according to subject matter

clas´si·fy vt. to arrange according to

a **system** of categories; to restrict the use or distribution of —**clas´-si·fi·a·ble** adj. —**clas´si·fi·ca´tion** n. —**clas´si·fi·er** n.

class´ism n. consciousness of the differences in station between persons; discrimination based on social standing —**class´ist** adj., n.

class´mate n. one who is in the same class in school; one who graduates in the same year as another, whether or not attending the same classes

class´room n. any room where classes are taught

class´y adj. of one with fine manners or style; elegant; splendid —**class´i·ness** n.

clat´ter n. noise; a racket or hubbub —vi. to rattle or reverberate —**clat´ter·er** n. —**clat´ter·ing·ly** adv. —**clat´ter·y** adj.

clause n. a part of a sentence; a section of a legal document —**claus´al** adj.

claus·tro·pho´bi·a n. a fear of confined or restricted spaces —**claus·tro·pho´bic** adj.

cla´vier, cla·vier´ n. any stringed instrument that has a keyboard; the keyboard of such an instrument

claw n. a curved appendage, often sharp-pointed, used for grasping; anything that resembles a claw

clay n. a type of earth that becomes malleable when moistened; a material used in the making of pottery, models, etc. —**clay´ey** adj.

clay´more n. a broadsword

clay pigeon n. a clay disk used as a target in skeet shooting; one who is unknowingly open to attack, especially in office politics

clean adj. free of contamination; pure, undefiled; distinct, readable; smooth or well proportioned; flawless —adv. neatly; entirely —vi. to be cleansed —vt. to wash or scrub;

to disinfect; to prepare food for cooking or eating —**clean´a·ble** adj. —**clean´er** n. —**clean´ness** n.

clean´-cut adj. clear, precise; of a pleasing appearance

clean´ly adj. kept clean —adv. in a clean manner —**clean´li·ness** n.

cleanse vt. to make clean; to absolve; to free from sin —**cleans´er** n. —**cleans´ing** adj., n.

clean-shaven without facial hair

clean´up n. the process of cleaning; the ridding of corruption, vice, etc.

clear adj. bright, unclouded; distinct, unmistakable; calm, untroubled, as a clear conscience; unencumbered, as from debt or lien —adv. obviously, completely —vi. to become clear; to be absolved —vt. to set or make free, unblock; to wipe clean; to absolve; to jump over —**clear** the air to discuss freely, as a difference of opinion —**clear up** to explain —in the clear absolved of guilt or suspicion —**clear´ly** adv. —**clear´ness** n.

clear´ance n. exoneration; permission, official sanction; the space between two objects in close proximity

clear´-cut adj. without ambiguity; denuded of trees —vt. to cut down all of the trees in an area

clear headed adj. discerning; reasonable, sensible —**clear´head·ed·ly** adv. —**clear´head·ed·ness** n.

clear´ing n. an area devoid of trees

clear´ing·house n. a facility for collection, processing, etc., of information or negotiable instruments such as bank drafts

clear´-sight·ed adj. shrewd; keenly perceptive —**clear´-sight·ed·ly** adv. —**clear´-sight·ed·ness** n.

cleat n. a small projection on furniture, footwear, etc.; a device on the deck or gunnel of a ship for securing lines

cleave vi., vt. to split; to separate

—cleav´a·ble *adj.*

clem´en·cy *n.* leniency, mercy

clench *n.* a rigid hold —*vt.* to make a fist; to grit one's teeth

cler´gy *n.* collectively, those ordained for religious service

cler´i·cal *adj.* of a clerk in an office or a member of the clergy —cler´i·cal·ly *adv.*

clerical collar a stiff white collar worn by certain members of the clergy as a sign of office

clerk *n.* an office worker or official in charge of records; a counter person, as a hotel or sales clerk

clev´er *adj.* skillful; intelligent; witty —clev´er·ly *adv.* —clev´er·ness *n.*

cli·ché´ *n.* a trite phrase —cli·ched´ *adj.*

cli´ent *n.* a customer; one who is dependent on or served by another —cli·en´tal *adj.*

cli·en·tele´ *n.* all the clients of a business as a group

cliff *n.* a high, steep face of rock

cliff´-hang·er, cliff´hang·er *n.* a story that is full of suspense

cli´mate *n.* the prevailing weather conditions of an area; any condition that may influence, as *the climate for change* —cli·mat´ic *adj.*

cli·ma·tol´o·gy *n.* the study of climate —cli·ma·to·log´i·cal *adj.* —cli·ma·tol´o·gist *n.*

cli´max´ *n.* the final, forceful, or significant element in a series; a turning point or crisis

climb *n.* the act of scaling, as a mountain; advancement or improvement, as *the climb up the corporate ladder* —*vi., vt.* to mount by use of the hands and feet; any ascension, as through the offices of a company —climb´a·ble *adj.* —climb´er *n.*

clinch *n.* a fastening; a hug —*vt.* to fasten; to conclude —clinch´er *n.*

cling *vi.* to hold fast, adhere; to remain near, be emotionally

attached —cling´er *n.* —cling´i·ness *n.* —cling´ing·ly *adv.* —cling´y *adj.*

clinging vine one who is inclined to great dependence on others

cling´stone *adj.* of a fruit with pulp firmly attached to the pit —*n.*

clin´ic *n.* a place for the medical treatment of ambulatory patients; an infirmary or dispensary; an intensive learning session, as *a sales clinic*

clin´i·cal *adj.* of a clinic; of an atmosphere like a clinic: sterile; scientific or objective —clin´i·cal·ly *adv.*

clinical thermometer a thermometer used to measure body temperature

clip *n.* a thing cut, as hair or a piece of film; a fast pace; a sharp blow; a fastener —*vi.* to cut off; kto move rapidly —*vt.* to cut or cut off; to shorten by cutting, as vowels or syllables from a word, when speaking; to strike with a sharp blow; to cheat; to fasten

clip´board *n.* a writing surface of pressed board or plastic with a clamp at the top to hold papers

clip joint an establishment that regularly overcharges

clip´-on *adj.* having a fastener for attaching as *a clip-on tie*

clip´per *n.* a person who cuts or trims; a tool for such cutting, as *hedge clippers*; a type of sailing ship

clip´ping *n.* the act of cutting off; that cut off, as trimmings; an item cut from a periodical

clique *n.* a small exclusive group — cli´quey, cli´quish *adj.* —cli´quish·ly *adv.* —cli´quish·ness *n.*

cloak *n.* a long cape; that which covers or conceals —*vt.* to cover or conceal; to camouflage

cloak´-and-dag´ger *adj.* of the activities of secret agents, spies, etc.

cloak´room n. a place for the safe-keeping of coats, hats, etc.

clob´ber vt. to hit forcefully; to win by a wide margin

clock n. a mechanism for calibrating and marking time; any device similar to a clock in function —vt. to measure the time taken to perform a task; to measure output, distance, etc. —time clock a device that records the arrival and departure of employees

clock´wise adj., adv. in the direction of the hands of a clock

clock´work n. the moving parts of a clock; any mechanism that is similar to that of a clock like clockwork precise; according to plan

clod n. a lump of earth; a dull or stupid person —clod´dish adj. —clod´dish·ly adv. —clod´dish·ness n.

clod´hop·per n. an unrefined person: a country bumpkin; a heavy shoe, as worn by a farmer

clog vi. to become obstructed —vt. to obstruct or impede —n. an obstruction; a shoe with a wooden sole —clog´gi·ness n. —clog´gy adv.

clois´ter n. a covered walk around a courtyard; a place of seclusion —vt. to seclude or protect —clois´tered adj. —clois´tral adj.

close adj. nearby; like in form, thought, emotion, etc.; confining; restrictive; limited —close´ly adv. —close´ness n.

close n. an ending, conclusion —vi., vt. to conclude; to shut; to connect —clos´a·ble adj.

close by near; beside

close call, close shave a near miss; a narrow escape

closed captioned of a television broadcast that displays printed dialogue for the benefit of the hearing impaired

closed shop designating of an employer who agrees to hire only those who belong to or agree to join a particular union or unions

close´fist·ed adj. stingy, miserly —close´fist·ed·ness n.

close´out n. the selling of goods at a discount, to dispose of discontinued items or to liquidate the business —vi., vt. to close or sell out a business interest

close quarters a crowded space

clos´et (US) n. a small room for storage —vt. to consult privately in a closed room: closeted with one's attorney

close´up an intimate or near view to show detail, emphasis, etc.

clos´ing adj. of the final stages, as closing arguments in a trial —n. the ending or finalization, as of a speech, letter, etc.

closing costs monies exchanged as agreed at the finalizing of a contract, esp. for the purchase of property

clo´sure n. a conclusion; anything that closes

clot n. a soft mass —vi. to thicken or coagulate

cloth n. a fabric

clothe vt. to cover, as with clothing, to furnish with clothing —clothes n. pl. wearing apparel

clothes´horse n. one who is inordinately fond of clothes

clothes´line n. a cord, rope, etc. on which clothing is hung out to dry

clothes peg n. (Brit.) a device for securing clothing to a line for drying

clothes´pin (US) n. a device for securing clothing to a line for drying

clothes tree an upright post with hooks near the top for hanging hats and coats

cloth´ier n. one who manufactures or sells clothes

cloth´ing n. all of one's garments;

wearing apparel in general

clo´ture n. a parliamentary maneuver for closing debate and putting the matter to an immediate vote

cloud n. a mist of water droplets suspended in the atmosphere; a cloud–like mass of smoke, dust, etc.; anything in the air that resembles a cloud, as *a cloud of locusts*; anything that casts a shadow or gloom —*vi., vt.* to obscure or overshadow —have one's head in the clouds daydream —living under a cloud under suspicion; depressed —cloud´i·ness n. —cloud´y adj.

cloud´burst a sudden heavy rain

cloud´less adj. without clouds; clear, sunny —cloud´less·ly adv. —cloud´less·ness n.

cloud nine a state of bliss

clout n. a blow; power or influence —vt. to strike

clove n. a fragrant spice; a segment of a bulb, as of garlic

clo´ven adj. split; cleft

clo´ver·leaf n. a complex highway interchange

clown n. a performer who entertains with broad humor; one who acts like a fool; one clumsy or incompetent —vi. to perform or act like a fool —clown´ish adj. —clown´ish·ly adv. —clown´ish·ness n.

cloy vi., vt. to make unpleasant by excess, esp. of something very rich or sweet —cloy´ing·ly adv.

club n. a heavy stick used as a weapon; a group of persons organized for a common purpose —vt. to strike with a club

club´foot´ n. a congenital deformity of the foot

club´house n. the meeting place or facilities used by the members of an organization

cluck n. the sound of a hen; a foolish person

clue n. information that may help to solve a puzzle —clue in to inform or provide with information

clum´sy adj. awkward; poorly fashioned —clum´si·ly adv. —clum´si·ness n.

clus´ter n. a group of similar or like things gathered together —vi., vt. to grow or come together —clus´ter·y adj.

clutch n. a grasping, as with a hand or claw; a mechanical device that grabs and holds —vt. to grasp and hold closely

clut´ter n. a number of items scattered in disarray —vt. to scatter, litter

coach (US) n. the main passenger compartment of a train or plane; an instructor or trainer —vt. to teach or train

coach (Brit.) n. a large motor vehicle designed to carry passengers between cities or towns; an instructor or trainer —vt. to teach or train

co·ag´u·late vi., vt. to change from a liquid state to a thick, soft mass —co·ag·u·la´tion n. —co·ag´u·la·tive adj. —co·ag´u·la·tor n.

coal n. a combustible mineral; an ember

co´a·lesce´ vi. to unite or merge into a single unit —co·a·les´cence n. —co·a·les´cent adj.

co·a·li´tion n. a temporary union of persons, groups, etc. for some special purpose —co·a·li´tion·al adj. —co·a·li´tion·ist n.

co–an´chor n. one who shares the duties of anchorperson on a news program —vi., vt.

coarse adj. of a rough surface, manner, etc.; of a person or thing that is vulgar or obscene —coarse´ly adv. —coarse´ness n.

coarse´-grained´ adj. having a rough texture

coars´en vi., vt. to make rough

coast n. land near the sea —vi. to

move pulled by the force of gravity or momentum; to slack off or proceed with little effort, relying on past success —coast´al adj. —coast´al·ly adv.

coast´er n. a flat bottomed conveyance for sliding down hill, usually on snow or ice; a sled; a mat, etc. placed under a container to protect the surface beneath it

coast guard a naval force charged with the protection of a nation's coast

coast´line n. a strip of land where a body of water touches the shore

coat n. an outer garment; protective covering; a layer, as a coat of paint

coat´dress n. a long frock that buttons down the front similar to a coat

coat´ing n. a layer, as a coating of wax; material for making coats

coat of arms an insignia or emblem that identifies a family, clan, nation, etc.; armorial bearings

coat of mail a medieval garment intended to protect the upper body

coat´rack n. an upright post with hooks near the top for hanging hats and coats; a series of hooks for hanging coats, hats, etc., attached to a wall

coat´room n. a place for safekeeping coats, hats, etc.

coat´tail n. the bottom of a coat at the back —on someone's coattails to attain success by identifying with someone who is successful

co–au´thor n. one who writes or creates in collaboration with another

coax vi. to cajole —vt. to persuade by cajolery or wheedling —coax´er n. —coax´ing·ly adv.

co·ax´i·al adj. having a common axis; of a transmission line that has a central conductor insulated from a surrounding conductor

coaxial cable n. cable used to transmit telephone, television, etc. signals

cob n. the cylindrical core from which the kernels of corn grow; a male swan

co´balt n. a metallic chemical element

cobalt blue dark blue

cob´ble vt. to repair shoes

cob´bler n. one who makes or repairs shoes; a fruit pie

cob´ble-stone n. rounded stone used for paving

COBOL n. COmmon Business Oriented Language; a computer programming language with vocabulary and syntax similar to everyday English

cob´web´ n. a spider web; something similar to a spider web

co´ca n. a family of tropical plants, the dried leaves of which are the source for cocaine

co´caine´ n. a narcotic made from dried coca leaves

co·cain´ism n. addiction to cocaine

co·cain´ize vt. to treat with cocaine —co·cain·i·za´tion n.

coc´cyx n. a small bone at the lower end of the spine

co·chair´ n. one who shares the duties of a chairperson —vi.

cock n. the male of certain birds; a device for regulating the flow of liquid or gas; the striking part of the lock of a gun; small pile of hay; a jaunty angle —vt. to set for release, as of a fist, a gun, a camera, etc.; to set at a jaunty angle

cock-a-leek´ie n. a Scottish soup based on chicken and leeks

cock´a·ma·mie adj. fictional; fabricated; ridiculous

cock-and–bull story a fabrication

cocked hat a three-cornered hat knock into a cocked hat to spoil; to reveal as false

cock´eyed adj. out of alignment;

ridiculous; of a concept or reasoning that is awry

cock´ney *n.* a rhyming dialect from the East End of London; a native speaker of the dialect —*adj.* of the dialect or those who speak it

cock´sure *adj.* arrogantly self-confident

cock´tail´ *n.* a beverage or food served before or at the start of a meal

cock´y *adj.* overconfident; flamboyant

co´coa´ *n.* a powder made from processed cacao beans; a beverage made from this powder; a brown color

cocoa butter a fat derived from cacao seeds

co·co·nut *n.* the fruit of the coconut palm

coconut milk the thin liquid from the center of the coconut

coconut oil an oil obtained from coconut meat

coconut palm a tropical tree that produces coconuts

co·coon´ *n.* a protective cover spun by certain insect larvae; any similar cover

cod *n.* a type of food fish that is also the source of cod-liver oil

co´da *n.* a phrase or section added to a musical composition to signal its end

cod´dle *vt.* to overindulge; to pamper or treat gently; to cook by poaching in water that is kept just below the boiling point

code *n.* a systematic arrangement of a body of law, regulations, etc.; a system of symbols or signs for sending messages —*vt.* to translate into representative symbols, as *to code a computer program* — **cod´er** *n.*

co·de·fend´ant *n.* one who, with another or others, is accused of a crime or wrongdoing

co´deine *n.* a narcotic derivative of opium

codg´er *n.* an old man, often eccentric or senile

cod´i·cil *n.* an addendum, as to a contract or a will

cod´i·fy *vt.* to arrange according to an established system —**cod´i·fi·ca´tion** *n.* —**cod´i·fi·er** *n.*

cod´-liv·er oil *n.* oil from the liver of codfish, rich in vitamins A and D

co´ed´ *adj.* coeducational —*n.* a female student

co·ed´it *vt.* to work with another in preparing a book, journal, etc. for publication —**co·ed´i·tor** *n.*

co·ed·u·ca´tion·al *adj.* of an institution of learning that caters to both male and female students —**co·ed·u·ca´tion** *n.* —**co·ed·u·ca´tion·al·ly** *adv.*

co·erce´ *vt.* to bring about by force; to compel under duress —**co·erc´i·ble** *adj.*

co·er´cion *n.* the use of threats or force to compel —**co·er´cive** *adj.* —**co·er´cive·ly** *adv.* —**co·er´cive·ness** *n.*

co·ex·ist´ *vi.* to exist at the same time, place, etc.; to live side by side in harmony —**co·ex·is´tence** *n.* —**co·ex·is´tent** *adj.*

cof´fee *n.* a beverage made from the ground seeds of a tropical plant; the plant or its seeds; an informal gathering; a light brown color

coffee beans the seeds of the coffee plant

coffee break a brief rest period for workers

cof´fee·cake *n.* a bread-like pastry usually served as a light repast with coffee

cof´fee·house *n.* a café that serves coffee and light refreshments

coffee maker an appliance, often electric, for making coffee; a coffee pot

cof´fee·pot *n.* a utensil of metal,

glass, etc. for the making and serving of coffee

coffee shop a coffeehouse; a retail shop that sells exotic coffee and utensils for making and serving coffee

coffee table a low table, usually part of a living room set

cof´fer *n.* a strongbox; a reinforced shelter; a cofferdam

cof´fer·dam *n.* a barrier to hold back water for construction or repairs taking place below water level

cof´fin *n.* a box for burial

cog *n.* any of the teeth on a gear; a minor, but necessary, functionary

co´gent *adj.* forceful or compelling, as of an argument —co´gen·cy *n.*

cog´i·tate´ *vi.* to consider carefully —cog´i·ta´tion *n.* —cog´i·ta·tive *adj.* —cog´i·ta·tor *n.* —cog´i·ta·tive·ly *adv.*

cog´nac *n.* a brandy produced in the Cognac region of France, distilled from wine

cog´nate´ *adj.* of common ancestry —cog·na´tion *n.*

cog·ni´tion *n.* the mental processes generally, such as perception, reasoning and judgement —cog·ni´tion·al *adj.* —cog´ni·tive *adj.*

cog´ni·zance *n.* knowledge, especially that gained through observation; awareness —cog´ni·za·ble *adj.* —cog´ni·zant *adj.*

cog´no´men *n.* a family name; any name

cog´wheel *n.* a wheel with teeth around the rim

co·hab´it *vi.* to live together in a sexual relationship —co·hab´i·tant *n.* —co·hab·i·ta´tion *n.*

co´here´ *vi.* to hold together naturally or logically —co´her´ence *n.*

co·her´ent *adj.* congruous; logically connected; understandable —co·her´ent·ly *adv.*

co·he´sive *adj.* adhesive; sticking together; co·he´sion *n.*; co·he´-

sive·ly *adv.*; co·he´sive·ness *n.*

co´hort *n.* a colleague or friend; a contemporary

coif *vt.* to style hair —*n.* coiffure

coif·fure´ *n.* a hair style

coin *n.* a metal piece of fixed monetary value —*vt.* to mint coins; to make or invent, as *to coin a phrase* —coin´er *n.*

coin´age *n.* the process of minting coins; the money system of a country

co´in·cide´ *vi.* to correspond exactly, as in form, space, time, etc.; to be in accord

co·in´ci·dence *n.* the condition of coinciding; a series of chance events that seem to have been planned —co·in´ci·dent *adj.*

co·in·ci·den´tal *adj.* of that which coincides; accidental; characterized by chance —co·in·ci·den´tal·ly *adv.*

coin-op´er·at·ed *adj.* of a device that is made to function by inserting coins, as *a coin-operated game*

co·i´tus, **co·i´tion** *n.* sexual intercourse; co´i·tal *adj.*

col´an·der *n.* a perforated container used in cooking for draining off liquid

cold *adj.* of a low temperature; lacking heat or warmth; unfeeling or unfriendly —*n.* the absence of heat; a viral infection of the respiratory tract —go in cold without preparation —have cold feet to be reticent, afraid —have down cold know thoroughly —in the cold left out or ignored —turn a cold shoulder to scorn or ignore

cold´blood´ed *adj.* of a creature with a low body temperature; unfeeling, callous —cold´blood´ed·ly *adv.* —cold´blood´ed·ness *n.*

cold chisel a hardened steel tool for cutting or breaking metal

cold cream a cosmetic skin cleanser

cold cuts any of a variety of processed meats, usually served cold

cold front the leading edge of a cold air mass that influences the weather in the areas it approaches

cold″heart″ed adj. unresponsive to affection; lacking compassion — **cold″heart″ed·ly** adv. —**cold″heart″ed·ness** n.

cold″ly adv. in a cool fashion: coldly polite —**cold″ness** n.

cold pack a cool, wet compress applied to an injury, such as a sprain; a chemical ice pack used in first aid

cold snap a sudden bout of cold weather

cold sore a viral infection of small blisters about the mouth, usually following a cold, fever, etc.

cold storage a storage area for refrigerating food, safekeeping of furs during the off-season, etc.

cold turkey suddenly, without preparation, often of quitting a habit, as smoking

cold war a state of unfriendly relations between countries without actual fighting

cole″slaw n. a salad of shredded cabbage and dressing

col″ic n. persistent discomfort experienced by an infant, characterized by constant crying —**col″ick·y** adj.

col″i·se″um n. a building for sporting events, shows, etc.

co·li″tis n. an inflammation of the large intestine

col·lab″o·rate″ vi. to work together; to cooperate in an undertaking —**col·lab·o·ra″tion** n. —**col·lab″o·ra·tive** adj. —**col·lab″o·ra·tive·ly** adv. —**col·lab″o·ra″tor** n.

col·lage″ n. an artistic composition constructed of odd bits of material —**col·lag″ist** n.

col·lapse″ vi. to fall or break down suddenly; to fold into a compact unit —**col·laps·i·bil″i·ty** adv. —**col·laps″i·ble** adj.

col″lar n. the part of a garment that rests on or near the neck; a decorative or functional band worn around the neck

col″lards, col″lard greens n. a green leafy vegetable

col″late vt. to gather together in order, as typed pages or sections of a book —**col·la″tor** n.

col·lat″er·al adj. similar; of a thing pledged as a guarantee for fulfillment of an obligation —n. that pledged as a guarantee —**col·lat″er·al·ly** adv.

col·lat″er·al·ize vt. to pledge as security; to guarantee by pledging security

col″league″ n. an associate, usually in business

col·lect″ vi., vt. to gather together; to secure payment —**col·lect″a·ble, col·lect″i·ble** adj. —**col·lec″tion** n. —**col·lec″tor** n.

col·lect″ed adj. gathered together, accumulated; self-possessed: calm and composed

col·lect″ive adj. as a group; consolidated; of a venture characterized by people working together as a group —n. a cooperative organization —**col·lec″tive·ly** adv.

collective bargaining negotiations between employees as a group and their employer

col″lege n. an institution of learning; an association of individuals for a special purpose: electoral college

col·le″gi·an n. a student at a college —**col·le″gi·ate** adj.

col·lide″ vi. to come together violently

col·li″sion n. a coming together violently; a clash of opinions, etc.

col″lo·cate vt. to arrange; categorize

col·lo″qui·al adj. conversational; of a word or phrase used informally —**col·lo″qui·al·ly** adv.

col·lo″qui·al·ism n. a word or phrase

used informally

col´lo·quy *n.* a formal discussion

col·lu´sion *n.* a conspiracy; a plot to act, especially for some illegal purpose —**col·lu´sive** *adj.* —**col·lu´sive·ly** *adv.*

co´lon *n.* a puncutation mark (:); the large intestine from the cecum to the rectum

colo´nel *n.* a military officer —**col´o·nel·cy** *n.*

co·lo´ni·al *adj.* of an outpost of a government or society

co·lo´ni·al·ism *n.* a government policy of settling new lands, especially for exploitation —**co·lo´ni·al·ist** *adj., n.*

col´o·nist *n.* one who establishes or lives in a colony —**col´o·nise´** (*Brit.*), **col´o·nize´** (US) *vt.* —**col´o·ni·sa´tion**, **col´o·ni·za´tion** *n.*

col·on·nade´ *n.* a series of upright columns

col´o·phon *n.* a printed emblem, as of a publisher or trade union

col´or (US) *n.* the separation of white light into varying wavelengths; the sensation created in the eye by light waves of varying lengths; any substance used to dye, tint, etc. —*vi., vt.* to give or change color

col·or·a´tion *n.* the shades and tones that make up the color of a thing

col´or·blind (US) *adj.* incapable of distinguishing between certain colors; without racial prejudice —**col´or·blind·ness** *n.*

col´ored (US) *adj.* having color; of a non-caucasian race; biased, as *colored by one's belief*

col´or·fast (US) *adj.* of a garment or material that will not bleed color or fade when washed

col´or·ful (US) *adj.* bright; picturesque; quaint or unusual —**col´or·ful·ly** *adv.* —**col´or·ful·ness** *n.*

color guard (US) those who carry and accompany the flag or flags

col´or·ing (US) *n.* the process of applying color; the color applied

col´or·ist (US) *n.* one who applies color, especially to black and white drawings or motion pictures

col´or·ize (US) *vt.* to add color to a photograph or motion picture that was shot in black and white —**col·or·i·za´tion** *n.*

col´or·less (US) *adj.* bland; uninteresting

col´ors (US) *n.* a banner or flag that identifies a nation, clan, fighting unit, etc.

co·los´sal *adj.* amazingly large —**co·los´sal·ly** *adv.*

co·los´sus *n.* an extremely large structure, statue, etc.; one who is bigger than life

co·los´to·my *n.* surgery that creates an opening in the colon for disposal of body waste

col´our (*Brit.*) *n.* the separation of white light into varying wavelengths; the sensation created in the eye by light waves of varying lengths; any substance used to dye, tint, etc. —*vi., vt.* to give or change color

col´our·blind (*Brit.*) *adj.* incapable of distinguishing between certain colors; without racial prejudice —**col´our·blind·ness** *n.*

col´oured *adj.* (*Brit.*) having color; of a non-caucasian race; biased, as *colored by one's belief*

col´our·ful *adj.* (*Brit.*) bright; picturesque; quaint or unusual —**col´our·ful·ly** *adv.* —**col´our·ful·ness** *n.*

col´our·ing *n.* (*Brit.*) the process of applying color; the color applied

col´our·ist *n.* (*Brit.*) one who applies color, especially to black and white drawings or motion pictures

col´our·ise *vt.* (*Brit.*) to add color to a photograph or motion picture that was shot in black and white —**col·our·i·sa´tion** *n.*

col´our·less *adj.* (*Brit.*) bland; uninteresting

col´ours (*Brit.*) *n.* a banner or flag that identifies a nation, clan, fighting unit, etc.

colt *n.* a young horse, donkey, etc.

col´umn *n.* a slender support; any similar formation; a vertical strip on a written or printed page made up of horizontal lines —**col·um´nar** *adj.*

co·lum·ni·a´tion *n.* the use of columns in architecture

col´um·nist *n.* a writer of commentary in a magazine or newspaper

co´ma *n.* a state of deep sleep caused by illness or injury

com´bat *n.* armed conflict, a battle; a struggle —**com·bat´** *vt.* to fight against; to contend

com·bat´ant *n.* one who takes part in a war or struggle

combat fatigue mental illness brought on by prolonged exposure to combat conditions

com·ba´tive *adj.* inclined to fight —**com·bat´iv·ly** *adv.* —**com·bat´ive·ness** *n.*

com´bi·na·tion *n.* a union created by the blending or merging of divers things —**com·bi·na´tion·al** *adj.*

com´bine *n.* a machine for harvesting grain; an association, as of businesses, for a common purpose —**com·bine´** *vi.*, *vt.* to join forces; unite —**com·bin´a·ble** *adj.* —**com·bin·a·bil´i·ty** *n.*

com´bo *n.* a small instrumental ensemble

com·bus´ti·ble *adj.* easily ignited and burned; excitable —*n.* a material that is easily ignited —**com·bus·ti·bil´i·ty** *n.* —**com·bus´ti·bly** *adv.*

com·bus´tion *n.* the process of burning

come´back *n.* a return or attempt to return to a previous state, as in politics or show business; a sharp retort

co·me´di·an *n.* one who writes or performs comedy

co·me´dic *adj.* pertaining to comedy —**co·me´di·cal·ly** *adv.*

come´down *n.* a reversal of fortune

com´e·dy *n.* any writing, acting, etc. designed to make others laugh

comedy of errors a series of mistakes that are more humorous than tragic

come´ly *adj.* attractive; pleasing in appearance —**come´li·ness** *n.*

come´on *n.* an enticement; something offered as an incentive

co·mes´ti·ble *n.* food

come·up´pance *n.* a humbling penalty that is deserved; retaliation

com´fort *n.* a feeling of contentment; any attempt to relieve pain or stress; one who provides relief —*vt.* to relieve from pain or stress; to aid or assist

com´fort·a·ble *adj.* at ease; free from pain or stress; adequate, as *a comfortable living* —**com´fort·a·ble·ness** *n.* —**com´fort·a·bly** *adv.*

com´fort·er *n.* one who consoles; (*US*) a heavy bed covering

com´ic *adj.* funny, silly, or humorous —*n.* a comedian

com´i·cal *adj.* amusing, humorous; facetious —**com´i·cal·ly** *adv.* —**com´i·cal·ness** *n.*

comic book a book of stories illustrated with cartoon characters

comic opera a humorous work in the style of grand opera

comic relief a humorous incident that punctuates an otherwise serious situation in life or the theater

comic strip a series of cartoons that tell a story

com´ing *adj.* drawing near; full of promise —**have it coming** deserve, as punishment

com´ing–out´ *n.* a debut, often as one comes of age for courting

com´ma *n.* a punctuation mark (,)

com·mand´ *n.* the authority to lead or direct; an order, the ability to use well, as *command of the language* —*vt.* to direct or order —**com·mand´a·ble** *adj.*

com´man·dant *n.* a commanding officer

com·man·deer´ *vt.* to take without permission, especially to take for official use

com·mand´er *n.* one who is in charge; a leader

commander in chief the senior commanding officer

com·mand´ing *adj.* having power or authority; impressive; compelling —**com·mand´ing·ly** *adv.*

commanding officer one who is in charge of a military unit or post

com·mand´ment *n.* a rule or regulation

com·man´do *n.* a warrior trained to operate inside enemy territory

command post temporary headquarters for one directing a military operation

com·mem´o·rate´ *vt.* to honor the memory of, as by a memorial —**com·mem·o·ra´tion** *n.* —**com·mem´o·ra·tive** *adj., n.* —**com·mem´o·ra·to·ry** *adj.*

com·mence´ *vi., vt.* to begin

com·mence´ment *n.* an induction or beginning; a school graduation ceremony

com·mend´ *vt.* to praise; to entrust, as *commend to one's care* —**com·men´da·to·ry** *adj.*

com·mend´a·ble *adj.* worthy of praise; admirable —**com·mend´a·bly** *adv.*

com·men·da´tion *n.* a medal, plaque, etc. that designates one as worthy of praise

com·men´su·ra·ble *adj.* to the same degree; proportionate —**com·men´su·ra·bly** *adv.*

com·men´su·rate *adj.* equivalent or comparable; corresponding in size or degree —**com·men´su·rate·ly** *adv.* —**com·men´su·rate·ness** *n.*

com·men·su·ra´tion *n.* the consideration of things by resemblance to one another

com´ment *n.* a note or remark of explanation, observation, criticism, etc. —*vi.* to speak or write about —**com´men·tar´y** *n.* —**com·men·tar´i·al** *adj.*

com´men·ta·tor *n.* one who reports on and expresses an opinion of current events —**com´men·tate** *vi., vt.*

com´merce *n.* the buying and selling of goods and services

com·mer´cial¹ *adj.* of commerce; undertaken for profit —*n.* paid advertising, as on television, radio, etc. —**com·mer´cial·ly** *adv.*

com·mer´cial² (*Brit.*) *n.* a traveling salesman

commercial art advertising art and design as distinguished from art that is purely decorative

com·mer´cial·ism *n.* operating mainly for profit

com·mer´cial·ize *vt.* to operate for profit or in the manner of a commercial venture, often of something that heretofore was operated for the public good —**com·mer´cial·i·za´tion** *n.*

commercial traveler a traveler on business, as a salesman

com·min´gle *vi., vt.* to mix together; to combine

com·mis´er·ate *vi., vt.* to feel or express sorrow or pity —**com·mis·er·a´tion** *n.* —**com·mis´er·a·tive** *adj.* —**com·mis´er·a·tive·ly** *adv.* —**com·mis´er·a·tor** *n.*

com´mis·sar´y *n.* a store or cafeteria

com·mis´sion *n.* the authority to carry out certain duties; the duties so authorized; a group given such authority —*vt.* to grant authority to perform some function or duty

com·mis´sion·er *n.* one given authority by a commission to act; the head of a government department

com·mis´sion·a·ble *adj.* of sales for which a fee is to be paid, as to a salesman, stock broker, etc.

com·mit´ *vt.* to do; to give, as for safekeeping or confinement; to bind or obligate —**com·mit´tal** *n.*

com·mit´ment *n.* a pledge or promise; dedication

com·mit´tee *n.* a group appointed for a special purpose

com·mo´di·ous *adj.* spacious — **com·mo´di·ous·ly** *adv.* —**com·mo´di·ous·ness** *n.*

com·mod´i·ty *n.* anything useful that can be traded

com´mon *adj.* ordinary; basic; widespread; shared by many —*n.* a public square —**com·mon·al´i·ty, com´mon·al·ty** *n.* —**com´mon·ly** *adv.* —**com´mon·ness** *n.*

common carrier a company or person that transports passengers or freight

common denominator a multiple that is common to the denominators of all of the fractions in a set of two or more; a feature that is shared by two or more things under consideration

com´mon·er *n.* one who is not of noble blood

common ground an area of agreement

common law the law based on tradition or usage

common law marriage a marriage without legal sanction

com´mon·place *adj.* ordinary —*n.* anything that is ordinary or trite

com´mon·sense *adj.* sound, rational, as *a commonsense decision*

common sense reasonable judgement

common touch having empathy for the average citizen

com´mon·weal *n.* the welfare of the general public

com´mon·wealth *n.* the people of a state, nation, etc.; a government so designated

com·mo´tion *n.* a disturbance; confusion

com·mu´nal·ize *vt.* to make into a commune; to transfer or add property to a commune

com´mune *n.* a group of people banded together for a common purpose, to share labor and its rewards, etc.; a cooperative —**com·mu´nal** *adj.* —**com·mu´nal·ly** *adv.* —**com·mu´nal·ism** *n.* —**com·mu´nal·ist** *n.* —**com·mu·nal·is´tic** *adj.*

com·mune´ *vi.* to converse with; be in harmony with, as *to commune with nature*

com·mu´ni·ca·ble *adj.* able to be passed on; infectious or contagious, as a disease —**com·mu·ni·ca·bil´i·ty, com·mu´ni·ca·ble·ness** *n.* —**com·mu´ni·ca·bly** *adv.*

com·mu´ni·cate´ *vi.* to share information; be understood —*vt.* to convey information; to make known; to transmit, as an illness

com·mu·ni·ca´tion *n.* a letter, news; the act of communicating

com·mun´ion *n.* a close fellowship; an intimate association; a group who comprise such a fellowship, as of a Christian denomination — **com·mu´ni·cant** *n.*

com´mu·nism *n.* the concept of a classless society with common ownership of property —**com´mu·nist** *n.* —**com´mu·nis´tic** *adj.* —**com´mu·nis´ti·cal·ly** *adv.*

com·mu´ni·ty *n.* society in general; the members of a political unit; collectively, those who share a common interest, as *the community of artists*

community college an educational institution, often providing vocational training or the first two years of a liberal arts education

community property property held in common by a married couple or by a community at large

community service voluntary work for a charitable or government organization; work in the community assigned as punishment for wrongdoing

com·mu·nize vt. to place in ownership and control of the community at large

com·mu·ta´tion n. a substitution or exchange; the act of traveling to and from work, often on public transportation

com·mute´ vi. to travel to and from work; to make an exchange —vt. to substitute or replace —**com·mut´er** n.

com´pact´ adj. requiring little space, small or light —n. a covenant; a small automobile

com·pact´ adj. tightly packed —vt. to pack tightly —**com·pact´ly** adv. —**com·pact´ness** n. —**com·pac´tor** n.

compact disk n. device for storing data, as to create sound or for computer files

com·pan·ion n. one who accompanies another; a thing that is a part of a set —**com·pan´ion·ship** n.

com·pan·ion·a·ble adj. cordial, congenial; having the qualities of a good companion —**com·pan´ion·a·ble·ness** n. —**com·pan´ion·a·bly** adv.

companion piece an item of furniture, decor, etc. that fits with others to make a set

com·pan´ion·way n. a hall or stairway aboard ship

com·pa·ny n. an assembly or association of persons for some purpose; a guest; companionship —ship's company the crew of a ship

company store a retail establishment operated by a company for its employees

company union an employee bargaining unit that is not affiliated with any other union; often describing a bargaining unit that is controlled by the employer

com´pa·ra·ble adj. able to be compared; similar —**com·pa·ra·bil´i·ty, com´pa·ra·ble·ness** n. —**com´pa·ra·bly** adv.

com·par´a·tive adj. relative to another or others, as comparative philosophy; corresponding —**com·par´a·tive·ly** adv.

com·pare´ vt. to examine for similarities or differences —**com·par´i·son** n.

com·part´ment n. a section into which a larger space is divided —**com·part·men´tal** adj. —**com·part·men·tal·i·za´tion** n. —**com·part·men´tal·ize** vt.

com·pas´sion n. concern for the troubles of another; pity; sympathy —**com·pas´sion·ate** adj. —**com·pas´sion·ate·ly** adv.

com·pas´sion·less adj. without pity; unfeeling

com·pat´i·ble adj. capable of existing or working well together —**com·pat·i·bil´i·ty, com·pat´i·ble·ness** n. —**com·pat´i·bly** adv.

com·pa´tri·ot n. a colleague or associate

com·peer´ n. a comrade or friend; a peer; one's equal

com·pel´ vt. to force or bring about by force —**com·pel´lent** adj.

com·pel´ling adj. forceful; impressive —**com·pel´ling·ly** adv.

com·pen´di·ous adj. of that summarized briefly

com·pen´di·um n. a synopsis; an abridgement

com·pen·sate´ vt. to offset; to pay, as for services or for damages —**com·pen´sa·ble** adj. —**com´pen·sa·tive, com·pen´sa·to·ry** adj.

com·pen·sa´tion n. payment, as

restitution for a wrong or remu-
neration for services rendered —
com·pen·sa´tion·al *adj.*

com·pete´ *vi.* to work against; to
contend

com´pe·tence, com´pe·ten·cy *n.*
adequate qualification; fitness

com´pe·tent *adj.* qualified; suitable;
adequate —**com´pe·tent·ly** *adv.*

com·pe·ti´tion *n.* rivalry in business, sports, etc.; a rival

com·pet´i·tive *adj.* inclined to rivalry —**com·pet´i·tive·ly** *adv.* —
com·pet´i·tive·ness *n.*

com·pet´i·tor *n.* a rival, as an individual or team; one who competes

com·pile´ *vt.* to gather and arrange
in some order, as of data or a series of literary works —**com´pi·la´**
tion *n.*

com·pil´er *n.* one who compiles; a
computer program that translates
high-level program instructions
into machine language

com·pla´cence, com·pla´cen·cy *n.*
contentment;   self-satisfaction;
apathy —**com·pla´cent** *adj.* —
com·pla´cent·ly *adv.*

com·plain´ *vi.* to express dissatisfaction —**com·plain´er** *n.* —**com·**
plain´ing·ly *adv.*

com·plain´ant *n.* in law, one who
files a complaint

com·plaint´ *n.* an expression of
dissatisfaction

com·plai´sant *adj.* striving to please;
accommodating; obliging —**com·**
plai´sance *n.* —**com·plai´sant·ly**
adv.

com·plect´ed *adj.* of skin coloring,
as *light complected*

com´ple·ment *n.* that which completes —*vt.* to make complete

com·ple·men´ta·ry *adj.* of a part
that completes; corresponding —
com·ple·men´tal *adj.*

complementary angle an angle
that, when added to its comple-
ment, equals 90°

com´plete´ *adj.* lacking nothing —*vt.*
to conclude; to accomplish successfully —**com·ple´tion** *n.* —
com·plete´ly *adv.* —**com·plete´**
ness *n.*

com·plex´ *adj.* complicated —**com´**
plex *n.* a group of related elements
taken as a single entity, as *an
apartment complex* —**com·plex´**
i·ty *n.* —**com·plex´ness** *n.*

com·plex´ion *n.* appearance of the
skin; the general nature of a thing
—**com·plex´ioned** *adj.*

com·pli´ance *n.* a tendency to yield;
conformity —**com·pli´a·ble, com·**
pli´ant *adj.* —**com·pli´ant·ly** *adv.*

com´pli·cate´ *vt., vi.* to make or
grow difficult

com´pli·cat·ed *adj.* made up of
many parts; intricate, tangled; difficult   to   understand   —**com´**
pli·cat·ed·ly *adv.* —**com´pli·cat·**
ed·ness *n.* —**com·pli·ca´tion** *n.*

com·plic´i·ty *n.* involvement in
wrongdoing

com´pli·ment *n.* a statement of
praise; an act of courtesy —*vt.* to
praise or congratulate —**com´pli·**
men´ta·ry *adj.*; **com·pli·men´ta·**
ri·ly *adv.*

com·ply´ *vi.* to act on another's
request

com·po´nent *n.* an integral part

com·port´ *vt.* to conduct oneself in a
particular manner —**com·port´**
ment *n.*

com·pose´ *vt.* to form by combining;
to put in order; to create, as of
music; to calm oneself; to arrange
elements on a page for printing

com·posed´ *adj.* calm, deliberate

com·pos´er *n.* one who creates,
especially of music

com·pos´ite *adj.* made up of several
parts —*n.* a material made from a
joining of several materials —**com·**
pos´ite·ly *adv.*

com´po·si´tion *n.* the act of forming
or combining; the placement of

combined elements; a thing formed or composed

com·pos´i·tor n. one who sets type for printing

com´post n. decomposed organic matter used as potting soil —vt. to transform into compost

com·po´sure n. tranquillity, self-control

com´pote n. a dessert of fruit marinated in syrup; a stemmed serving dish

com´pound´ adj. made up of two or more elements —n. a mixture

com·pound´ vt. to combine; to increase or intensify by adding to, as compound interest, compounding a problem

compound fracture a broken bone that pierces the skin

compound interest interest on a loan that is calculated on the principal plus accrued interest

com´pre·hend´ vt. to understand; to take in, include —com·pre·hend´i·ble, com·pre·hen´si·ble adj. —com·pre·hend´ing·ly adv. —com´pre·hen´sion n.

com´pre·hen´sive adj. taking in much; broad in scope —n. a detailed layout, as for an advertisement —com´pre·hen´sive·ly adv. —com·pre·hen´sive·ness n.

com´press n. a pad of cloth or gauze used medically to apply heat, cold, pressure, etc. to a wound or injury —com·press´ vt. to press together; to squeeze; to make compact —com·press´i·ble adj. —com·pres´sor n. —com·pres´sion n.

com·prise´ vt. to include; to consist of

com´pro·mise n. a settlement resulting from concessions —vt. to settle by concession; to expose to danger or difficulty, as by carelessness: his actions have compromised our position

comp·trol´ler n. one who overseees

the financial affairs of an organization

com·pul´sion n. a driving force; an irrational impulse —com·pul´sive adj. —com·pul´sive·ly adv.

com·pul´so·ry adj. required; obligatory

com·punc´tion n. uneasiness or doubt aroused by the prospect of wrongdoing

com·pute´ vt. to calculate —com·put´a·ble adj. —com´pu·ta´tion n.

com·put´er n. an electronic device for processing data —computer literate familiar with the operation of a computer

com·put·er·ese´ n. terminology used by those involved with computers or computer programs

computer graphics artwork produced with the aid of a computer

com·put´er·ise (Brit.), com·put´er·ize (US) vt. to operate or enable to operate with the aid of or under the control of a computer —com·put·er·i·sa´tion (Brit.), com·put·er·i·za´tion (US) n.

computer virus a program that causes malfunction in a computer or computer program

com´rade´ n. a friend or companion —com´rade·ly adj. —com´rade·ship n.

con adv. against; of an opposing view —n. an opposing position; a swindle; a convict —vt. to swindle; to trick, especially by lies or smooth talk

con·cat´e·nate vt. to join; to link together —con·cat·e·na´tion n.

con´cave´ adj. curved like the inner surface of a sphere —n. —con·cave´ly adv.

con·ceal´ vt. to cover; to keep secret —con·ceal´a·ble adj. —con·ceal´er n. —con·ceal´ment n.

con·cede´ vt. to acknowledge reluctantly; to grant, as a privilege

con·ceit´ n. an overly high opinion

of oneself —con·ceit´ed *adj.* —con·ceit´ed·ly *adv.* —con·ceit´ed·ness *n.*

con·ceiv·a·ble *adj.* able to be believed or understood —con·ceiv´a·bly *adv.*

con·ceive´ *vt.* to imagine; to understand

con´cen·trate´ *n.* a substance that has been made more dense or intense, often by the removal of water —*vi., vt.* to increase in density or intensity —con´cen·tra´tion *n.*

concentration camp a place for the internment of prisoners of war, political prisoners, etc.

con·cen´tric, con·cen´tri·cal *adj.* having a common center —con·cen´tri·cal·ly *adv.* —con·cen·tric´i·ty *n.*

con´cept´ *n.* a theory; a broad understanding

con·cep´tion *n.* a beginning; an impression or understanding —con·cep´tion·al *adj.*

con·cep´tu·al *adj.* theoretical or abstract; ideal —con·cep´tu·al·ly *adv.*

con·cep´tu·al·ize *vt.* to form a theory or opinion —con·cep·tu·al·i·za´tion *n.*

con·cern´ *n.* a matter of interest; a feeling of anxiety; a business firm —*vt.* to show interest; to cause anxiety —con·cerned´ *adj.*

con´cert *n.* mutual understanding; a program of music —con·cert´ *vt.* to arrange or resolve by mutual understanding

con·cert´ed *adj.* harmoniously; unified, as *a concerted effort* —con·cert´ed·ly *adv.*

concert grand a large piano intended for a concert hall

con·cer·ti´na *n.* a small musical instrument with a bellows and keys to change pitch

con·cer´to *n.* a musical composition arranged for an orchestra and a solo instrument

con·ces´sion *n.* the act of conceding; a thing conceded; space leased for a business venture on the land of another, as *a food concession*

con·ces´sion·aire´ *n.* one who operates a business on the property of another for some consideration

conch *n.* a large marine mollusk with a spiral shell

con·cil´i·ate´ *vt.* to appease, placate —con·cil´i·a´tion *n.* —con·cil´i·a·tor *n.* —con·cil´i·a·to·ry *adj.*

con·cise´ *adj.* succinct; brief and to the point —con·cise´ly *adv.* —con·cise´ness *n.*

con´clave *n.* a large gathering; a secret meeting

con·clude´ *vt.* to bring to a close; to deduce by reasoning —con·clu´sion *n.*

con·clu´sive *adj.* final; convincing —con·clu´sive·ly *adv.* —con·clu´sive·ness *n.*

con·coct´ *vt.* to make or devise from a variety of elements —con·coc´tion *n.*

con·com´i·tant *adj.* associated with; connected —con·com´i·tance, con·com´i·tan·cy *n.*

con´cord *n.* harmony or agreement; a treaty to establish peaceful relations

con·cord´ance *n.* an agreement; an index of leading words in a text

con·cor´dant *adj.* agreeing; harmonious

con´course´ *n.* a broad walkway; an open area for passing or congregating as at an airline terminal

con´crete´ *adj.* formed into a solid mass; precise —*n.* a building material formed of cement, sand, and gravel —*vi., vt.* to solidify —con·crete´ly *adv.* —con·crete´ness *n.*

con·cre´tion *n.* a hardened mass

con·cu´pis·cence *n.* intense desire; lustfulness —con·cu´pis·cent *adj.*

con·cur´ *vi.* to correspond or coincide; to agree —con·cur´rence, con·cur´ren·cy n.

con·cur´rent adj. in agreement; occurring or existing together; convergent —con·cur´rent·ly adv.

con·cus´sion n. a shock, as from an impact; an injury caused by an impact

con·demn´ vt. to disapprove; to find one guilty; to impose punishment; to declare unfit for use —con·dem´na·ble adj. —con´dem·na´tion n. —con·demn´er n.

con´den·sa´tion n. compression or compaction; an abridgement

con·dense´ vt. to make dense; to compress; to abridge or summarize —con·den·sa·bil´i·ty n. —con·dens´a·ble adj.

condensed milk a thick, sweet milk processed from fresh cow's milk

con´de·scend´ vi. to do that considered beneath one's dignity or station —con·de·scend´ence, con´de·scen´sion n.

con·de·scend´ing adj. patronizing; disdainful; smug —con·de·scend´ing·ly adv.

con·dign´ adj. suitable, especially of punishment

con´di·ment n. a seasoning or relish for food

con·di´tion n. a requirement; a circumstance; anything that modifies something else —vt. to modify or influence

con·di´tion·al adj. contingent on circumstances; true only if certain requirements are satisfied —con·di´tion·al·ly adv.

con·di´tioned adj. in a proper or desired state of being

con·dole´ vi. to sympathize; to console; to comfort

con·do´lence n. an expression of sympathy

con´do·min´i·um[1] (Brit.) n. a territory governed by two or more nations

con´do·min´i·um[2] (US) n. an apartment owned by the tenant; a building in which such an apartment is located

con·done´ vt. to forgive; to disregard without protest —con·don´a·ble adj.

con´dor n. a large vulture

con·duce´ vi. to assist or contribute

con·du´cive adj. contributing or leading to —con·du´cive·ness n.

con·duct n. the way one acts —con·duct´ vt. to lead; to behave in a certain manner; to convey

con·duc´tor n. a leader; a guide; a person in charge; material which transmits heat or electricity

con·duct´ance n. the ability to transmit electricity —con·duc´tive adj. —con·duc·tiv´i·ty n. —con·duc´tor n.

con·duc´tion n. conveyance, as of electricity through a wire

con´duit n. a channel, as to carry water, electric lines, etc.

cone n. a geometric solid created by a circle and a surface that runs from the diameter of the circle to the end of a line extending from the center of the circle and perpendicular to its base

con´fab n. a discussion; confabulation —vi.

con·fab·u·la´tion n. a conversation or informal discussion —con·fab´u·late vi. —con·fab´u·la·tor n. —con·fab´u·la·to·ry adj.

con·fec´tion n. any sweet edibles, such as candied fruit, cookies, etc. —con·fec´tion·ar·y adj. —con·fec´tion·er n.

confectioners' sugar finely ground sugar

con·fec´tion·er·y n. a shop where confections are made or sold

con·fed´er·a·cy n. an alliance of people, states, etc. joined for a common purpose —con·fed´er·a´tion n.

con·fed´er·ate *n.* an associate or
accomplice —*vt.* to unite

con·fer´ *vi.* to meet for discussion —
vt. to grant, as an honorary degree
—con´fer·ee´ *n.*

con·fer·ence *n.* a formal meeting for
discussion

conference call a telephone connection for more than two persons

con·fess´ *vt.* to acknowlege

con·fes´sion *n.* an admission of guilt

con·fes´sion·al *n.* a small enclosure
in a church where parishioners
confess their sins to a priest

con·fes´sor *n.* one who confesses; a
priest who hears confessions

con·fet´ti *n.* small bits of colored
paper tossed in the air during festivities

con´fi·dant *n.* a trusted friend

con·fide´ *vi., vt.* to share a secret

con·fi·dence *n.* trust or faith in
anything; self-assurance; that
confided as a secret

confidence game a swindle

confidence man a swindler

con´fi·dent *adj.* self-assured —con´
fi·dent·ly *adv.*

con·fi·den´tial *adj.* secret —con·fi·
den·ti·al´i·ty *n.* —con·fi·den´tial·
ly *adv.*

con·fid´ing *adj.* trusting —con·fid´
ing·ly *adv.*

con·fig´ure *vt.* to set up or arrange
in a particular way

con·fig´u·ra´tion *n.* arrangement of
the parts that make up a thing;
the structure of a thing based on
the arrangement of its parts —
con·fig´u·ra´tion·al·ly *adv.* —con·
fig´u·ra´tion·al *adj.*

con´fine *n.* an enclosure —con·fine´
vt. to restrict; to shut in —con·
fin´a·ble *adj.* —con·fine´ment *n.*

con·firm´ *vt.* to prove; to validate, as
by formal approval —con´fir·ma´
tion *n.*

con·firmed´ *adj.* resolved; proved

con´fis·cate *vt.* to seize, usually by

authority —con·fis·ca´tion *n.* —
con·fis´ca·to·ry *adj.*

con´fla·gra´tion *n.* a large destructive fire

con´flict *n.* a clash of ideas, interests, etc.; open warfare —con·
flict´ *vi.* to clash

conflict of interest a situation that
occurs when one is in a position of
moral obligation that is at variance
with personal interest

con´flu·ence *n.* a flowing together,
as of two rivers or a crowd of people —con´flu´ent *adj.*

con·form´ *vi.* to adapt; to follow
custom or tradition —con·form´er,
con·form´ist *n.* —con·form´i·ty *n.*

con·for·ma´tion *n.* the symmetry or
form of a structure

con·found´ *vt.* to confuse, bewilder
—con·found´ed *adj.*

con·fra·ter´ni·ty *n.* a brotherhood; a
group associated for a common
purpose, as religious or charitable
—con·fra·ter´nal *adj.*

con·front´ *vt.* to come or bring face
to face —con·fron·ta´tion *n.* —
con·fron·ta´tion·al *adj.*

con·fuse´ *vt.* to bewilder; to mistake,
as one thing for another; to mingle
indiscrimately —con·fus´ing *adj.*
—con·fus´ing·ly *adv.*

con·fu´sion *n.* bewilderment; a state
of chaos or disorder

con·fute´ *vt.* to prove in error —con´
fu·ta´tion *n.*

con´ga *n.* a Latin American dance or
its music

con·geal´ *vi., vt.* to thicken or solidify by cooling —con·geal´a·ble *adj.*
—con·geal´ment *n.*

con·gen´ial *adj.* friendly; compatible
—con·ge·ni·al´i·ty *n.* —con·ge´
nial·ly *adv.*

con·gen´i·tal *adj.* existing at birth;
hereditary —con·gen´i·tal·ly *adv.*

con·gest´ *vt.* to clog or obstruct, as
nasal passages; to overcrowd, as a
highway —con·ges´tive *adj.*

con·ges'ted *adj.* overcrowded —con·ges'tion *n.*

con·glom'er·ate *adj.* gatherered together in a mass or group —*n.* an agglomeration; a corporation made up of a number of smaller diversified companies —*vi., vt.* to form or cause to form in a mass —con·glom·er·a'tion *n.*

con·grat'u·late *vt.* to compliment; to express joy —con·grat'u·la·tor *n.* —con·grat'u·la·to·ry *adv.*

con·grat·u·la'tions *n.* an expression of pleasure at the good fortune of another

con'gre·gate *vi.* to gather; to as·semble —con'gre·ga'tion *n.* —con·gre·ga'tion·al *adj.*

con·gre·ga'tion·al·ism *n.* a church society in which local assemblies are autonomous —con·gre·ga'tion·al·ist *n.*

con'gress *n.* a coming together; a formal assembly —Congress the federal legislature of the U.S. —con·gres'sion·al *adj.*

con·gru'ence, con·gru'en·cy *n.* a state of agreement; harmony, ac·cord —con'gru·ent *adj.* —con·gru'ent·ly *adv.* —con·gru'i·ty *n.*

con'gru·ous *adj.* appropriate, seemly; suitable or fitting to the circumstances —con'gru·ous·ly *adv.* —con'gru·ous·ness *n.*

con'i·cal *adj.* shaped like a cone —con'i·cal·ly *adv.*

co'ni·fer *n.* an evergreen tree or shrub —co·nif'er·ous *adj.*

con·jec'tur·al *adj.* based on specu·lation —con·jec'tur·al·ly *adv.*

con·jec'ture *n.* speculation; a judgement based on incomplete information —*vt.* to speculate

con·join' *vi., vt.* to unite or connect

con'ju·gal *adj.* of or pertaining to marriage —con·ju·gal'i·ty *n.* —con'ju·gal·ly *adv.*

con'ju·gate *adj.* joined together —*vt.* join; to give the inflections of a

verb —con·ju·ga'tion *n.* —con·ju·ga'tion·al, con'ju·ga·tive *adj.* —con·ju·ga'tion·al·ly *adv.* —con'ju·ga·tor *n.*

con·junct' *adj.* collective —*n.* that joined with another

con·junc'tion *n.* a joining together; a word that connects other words, phrases, or clauses —con·junc'tion·al *adj.*

con·junc'tive *adj.* connective; serv·ing as a conjunction —*n.* a con·junction

con·junc·ti·vi'tis *n.* an inflamma·tion of the eyelid

con·jure' *vi., vt.* to summon a spirit, as by magic —con·jur·a'tion *n.* —con'jur·er, con'ju·ror *n.*

conk *n.* a blow —*vt.* to strike —conk out to suddenly fail or quit, as a machine or a person

con man a confidence man; swindler

con·nect' *vi.* to become linked —*vt.* to link together —con·nect'er, con·nec'tor *n.*

con·nect'a·ble *adj.* able to be con·nected —con·nect·a·bil'i·ty *adv.*

con·nect'ed *adj.* linked; joined in order; having important social or business contacts —con·nect'ed·ly *adv.* —con·nect'ed·ness *n.*

con·nec'tive *adj.* serving to join or link —*n.* a bond; anything that joins or links —con·nec'tive·ly *adv.* —con·nec·tiv'i·ty *n.*

con·nec'tion *n.* a joining; a part that joins; a relationship; an important contact

con·nip'tion *n.* a fit; a frenzy; ex·citement or rage

con·niv'ance *n.* secret involvement; wrongdoing

con·nive' *vi.* to cooperate secretly in wrongdoing —con·niv'er *n.*

con·nois·seur' *n.* one with expert knowledge, especially of the arts; a person of discriminating taste

con·no·ta'tion *n.* an implied mean·ing; an insinuation —con'no·ta·

tive *adj.* —con'no·ta·tive·ly *adv.*

con·note' *vt.* to suggest or imply

con·nu'bi·al *adj.* of marriage

con'quer *vi., vt.* to overcome con'quer·a·ble *adj.* —con'quer·or *n.* —con'quest *n.*

con·san'guine, con·san·guin'e·ous *adj.* of common ancestry —con·san·guin'e·ous·ly *adv.*

con'san·guin'i·ty *n.* related through a common ancestor; a close association

con'science *n.* a sense of right and wrong

conscience–stricken *adj.* feeling remorse for wrong–doing

con·sci·en'tious *adj.* guided by conscience; thorough —con·sci·en'tious·ly *adv.* —con·sci·en'tious·ness *n.*

conscientious objector one who, because of religious or moral beliefs, refuses to serve in combat

con'scious *adj.* awake; aware of one's own and other's existence, actions, etc. —con'scious·ly *adv.* —con'scious·ness *n.*

con'script *n.* one drafted into the military

con·script' *vt.* to draft into military service

con'se·crate' *vt.* to set apart as sacred; to dedicate to a worthy cause —con'se·cra'tion *n.*

con·sec'u·tive *adj.* proceeding in logical order —con·sec'u·tive·ly *adv.* —con·sec'u·tive·ness *n.*

con·sen'su·al *adj.* mutually consenting —con·sen'su·al·ly *adv.*

con·sen'sus *n.* general agreement

con·sent' *n.* permission —*vi.* to grant permission —con·sent'er *n.*

con'se·quence *n.* something that logically follows an action; relative significance, as *of little or no consequence*

con'se·quent *adj.* following as a result —*n.* anything that follows

con·se·quen'tial *adj.* having significance; that creates an effect or is an effect —con·se·quen'tial·ly *adv.* —con·se·quen'tial·ness *n.*

con'se·quent·ly *adv.* as a result

con·serv'an·cy *n.* a group or society devoted to the preservation of natural resources

con·ser·va'tion *n.* the protection of natural resources

conservation of energy the scientific principal that in a closed system energy may be converted to another form, but is never diminished

con·serv'a·tism *n.* a policy that advocates moderation, or opposition to change

con·serv'a·tive *adj.* typified by a lack of flamboyance; cautious; reserved or moderate —*n.* one who is reserved or moderate in manner —con·serv'a·tive·ly *adv.*

con·serv'a·to·ry *n.* a greenhouse for the display of plants; a school of music or drama

con·serve' *n.* a type of fruit preserve —*vt.* to guard against damage or waste; to make a fruit preserve

con·sid'er *vt.* to carefully contemplate; to bear in mind; to be respectful of; to deem, believe

con·sid'er·a·ble *adj.* large, extensive; substantial —con·sid'er·a·bly *adv.*

con·sid'er·ate *adj.* having regard for others; con·sid'er·ate·ly *adv.* —con·sid'er·ate·ness *n.*

con·sid'er·a'tion *n.* careful contemplation; payment for services

con·sid'ered *adj.* given careful thought

con·sid'er·ing *adv., prep.* taking into account

con·sign' *vt.* to give over to another

con·sign·ee' *n.* one to whom goods are transferred

con·sign'ment *n.* goods transferred to another for sale or safekeeping —con·sign'or *n.*

con·sist´ *vi.* to be made up of

con·sist´ence, con·sist´en·cy *n.* uniformity; texture

con·sist´ent *adj.* constant; unwavering; harmonious —con·sist´ent·ly *adv.*

con·sis´to·ry *n.* a church council

consolation prize a reward for one who participates in a contest, but does not win

con·sole´ *vt.* to comfort —con·sol´a·ble *adj.* —con´so·la´tion *n.*

con·sol´i·date´ *vi., vt.* to combine; to strengthen by combining or compacting —con·sol·i·da´tion *n.*

con·som·mé´ *n.* a clear broth

con´so·nance, con´so·nan·cy *n.* harmony; a pleasant blending of a combination of sounds

con´sort *n.* a spouse or associate —con·sort´ *vi., vt.* to associate with

con·sor´ti·um *n.* an alliance, as of business firms, to promote a common interest

con·spic´u·ous *adj.* obvious, apparent; notable: *conspicuous bravery* —con·spic´u·ous·ly *adv.* —con·spic´u·ous·ness *n.*

conspicuous consumption extravagance in acquiring goods and wastefulness in their use

con·spir´a·cy *n.* a secret plan; those involved in carrying out such a plan —con·spir´a·tor *n.*

con·spir´a·to´ri·al *adj.* of or inclined to scheming or collusion; conspiring —con·spir´a·to´ri·al·ly *adv.*

con·spire´ *vi.* to plot secretly; to work together, as of circumstances

con´sta·ble *n.* an officer of the law

con·stab´u·lar·y *n.* the jurisdiction of a peace officer; law officers collectively

con´stant *adj.* unchanging; continual; steadfast —n. that which is unchanging —con´stan·cy *n.* —con´stant·ly *adv.*

con·ster·na´tion *n.* a state of confusion and distress

con·stit´u·en·cy *n.* a district or the persons in the district that an elected official represents; generally, the body of one's supporters —con·stit´u·ent *adj.*

con·sti·tute´ *vt.* to found, establish; to make up, be the parts of

con´sti·tu´tion *n.* the fundamental structure of a thing —con·sti·tu´tion·al *adj.* —con·sti·tu·tion·al´i·ty *n.* —con·sti·tu´tion·al·ly *adv.*

con·strain´ *vt.* to confine; to restrain; to compel —con·straint´ *n.*

con·strict´ *vt.* to make smaller by squeezing or contracting —con·stric´tion *n.*

con·strict´tor *n.* a thing that constricts; a snake that kills its prey by squeezing

con·struct´ *vt.* to build; to piece together —con·struc´tion *n.* —con·struc´tor *n.*

con·struc´tive *adj.* of that which is helpful or useful: *constructive criticism*; affirmative; instructive —con·struc´tive·ly *adv.* —con·struc´tive·ness *n.*

con·strue´ *vt.* to interpret or deduce; to understand —con·stru´a·ble *adj.*

con´sul *n.* an official appointed to serve a government or its citizens on foreign soil —con´su·lar *adj.*

con´su·late *n.* the offices of a consul; the authority of a consul

con·sult´ *vi.* to meet to exchange views —vt. to refer to for advice or information

con·sult´ant *n.* a professional who is hired to analyze and advise, as *a management consultant*

con·sul·ta´tion *n.* a meeting to share knowledge and plan a course of action —con·sul´ta·tive *adj.* —con·sul´ta·tive·ly *adv.*

con·sult´ing *adj.* one who acts in an advisory capacity, as *a consulting physician*

con·sum´a·ble *adj.* subject to being

expended or dissipated, as *a consumable resource* —*n.* any material that is used up or spent in the course of its use

con·sume´ *vt.* to make use of; to deplete, devour, or destroy —**con·sum´er** *n.*

consumer credit a loan or line of credit provided for the purchase of consumer goods

consumer goods possessions that satisfy the needs of individuals in contrast to those used in the production of goods and services

con·sum´er·ism *n.* a passion for acquisition of personal property; the concept that a healthy economy requires a strong consumer market; advocacy to protect consumers from false advertising, shoddy merchandise, etc.

con´sum·mate *adj.* complete or perfect; skillful —*vt.* to complete or perfect —**con·sum´mate·ly** *adv.*

con·sump´tion *n.* the using of goods or services; the amount used; a wasting of the body by disease —**con·sump´tive** *adj.* —**con·sump´tive·ly** *adv.*

con´tact *n.* the condition of touching; a communication, as by telephone or letter; one connected in some way, as *a business contact* —*vt.* to touch; to communicate with

contact lens a corrective lens worn directly over the eyeball

con·ta´gion *n.* the spread of disease by contact; the disease itself

con·ta´gious *adj.* spread by contact —**con·ta´gious·ly** *adv.* —**con·ta´gious·ness** *n.*

con·tain´ *vt.* to hold or have the capacity to hold; to keep within fixed limits —**con·tain´a·ble** *adj.* —**con·tain´er** *n.*

con·tain´er·ize *vt.* to place in a large container, often of standardized containers that ease handling in transshipment

con·tain´ment *n.* a limiting or confinement, as of the spread of a conflict, political system, etc.

con·tam´i·nate´ *vt.* to pollute; to make impure —**con·tam´i·nant, con·tam´i·na·tor** *n.* —**con·tam´i·na´tion** *n.*

con·temn´ *vt.* to view with contempt; to despise —**con·temn´er, con·tem´nor** *n.*

con´tem·plate *vt.* to study or ponder intently; to consider as a possible course of action —**con´tem·pla´tion** *n.*

con·tem´pla·tive *adj.* inclined to be reflective or thoughtful —**con·tem´pla·tive·ly** *adv.* —**con·tem´pla·tive·ness** *n.*

con·tem´po·ra´ne·ous *adj.* contemporary

con·tem´po·rar´y *adj.* of or related to the same time; current, as in style —*n.* one living at the same time or in the present time

con·tem´po·rize *vi., vt.* to make suitable to the time

con·tempt´ *n.* disdain; a show of disrespect, as for a court or legislative body —**con·tempt´i·ble** *adj.* —**con·tempt·i·bil´i·ty, con·tempt´i·ble·ness** *n.* —**con·tempt´i·bly** *adv.*

con·temp´tu·ous *adj.* disdainful —**con·temp´tu·ous·ly** *adv.* —**con·temp´tu·ous·ness** *n.*

con·tend´ *vi.* to compete; to argue or dispute —*vt.* to claim to be true —**con·tend´er** *n.*

con·tent´ *adj.* satisfied —*n.* satisfaction —**con´tent** *n.* all that is contained within

con·tent´ed *adj.* satisfied —**con·tent´ed·ly** *adv.* —**con·tent´ed·ness** *n.*

con·ten´tion *n.* an argument or dispute; an assertion

con·ten´tious *adj.* quarrelsome —**con·ten´tious·ly** *adv.* —**con·ten´tious·ness** *n.*

con·ter'mi·nous *adj.* within the same boundary —con·ter'mi·nous·ly *adv.*

con'test *n.* a competition or competing —con·test' *vt.* to dispute or challenge; to compete —con·test'a·ble *adj.* —con·test'a·bly *adv.*

con·tes'tant *n.* one who disputes, as a will; one who competes

con'text' *n.* the setting in which a thing appears or occurs —con·tex'tu·al *adj.*

con·tig'u·ous *adj.* touching; adjacent —con·tig'u·ous·ly *adv.* —con·tig'u·ous·ness *n.*

con'ti·nence *n.* moderation; self-restraint —con'ti·nent *adj.* —con'ti·nent·ly *adv.*

con'ti·nent *n.* any of the great land masses of the earth —con·ti·nen'tal *adj.* —con·ti·nen'tal·ly *adv.*

continental breakfast a light breakfast of juice, coffee, and sweet rolls

continental drift the gradual shifting of land mass on the earth's surface

continental shelf the land mass under shallow coastal waters

con·tin'gence *n.* contact; adjacency; a contingency

con·tin'gen·cy *n.* a possibility or likelihood; something that happens by chance

con·tin'gent *adj.* happening by chance; unpredictable —*n.* a contingency; a representative group

con·tin'u·al *adj.* repeated without interruption —con·tin'u·al·ly *adv.*

con·tin'u·a'tion *n.* restarting after a pause; a thing added, an extension

con·tin'ue *vi.* to endure, to remain in effect —*vt.* to persist; to remain; to resume after interruption —con·tin'u·ance *n.*

con·tin'u·i·ty *n.* the quality of being continuous

con·tin'u·ous *adj.* unbroken; connected; without interruption

—con·tin'u·ous·ly *adv.* —con·tin'u·ous·ness *n.*

con·tort' *vt.* to twist out of shape; to distort

con·tort'ed *adj.* twisted; misshapen; deformed —con·tort'ed·ly *adv.*

con·tor'tion *n.* an abnormal twisting, as of the body —con·tor'tion·ist *n.*

con'tra·band' *adj.* of goods prohibited by law from import or export —*n.* illegal merchandise

con'tra·cep'tion *n.* the prevention of pregnancy

con'tra·cep'tive *n.* a device or chemical used to prevent pregnancy —*adj.* pertaining to contraception; used to prevent pregnancy

con'tract *n.* a binding agreement, usually in writing, between two or more parties who each agree to do something —*vi., vt.* to enter into a formal agreement —con·tract' *vt.* to acquire, as a disease; to shorten or reduce in size

con·trac'tion *n.* something shortened, as a word; the shortening of a muscle under stress —con·trac'tion·al *adj.*

con·trac'tu·al *adj.* pertaining to or implying a formal agreement —con·trac'tu·al·ly *adv.*

con·trac'tor *n.* any of the parties to a contract —con'trac·tor *n.* one who agrees to perform a service for a stipulated price

contract bridge a card game in which the winning bidders establish the number of tricks to be taken

con'tra·dict' *vt.* to claim the opposite of; to be inconsistent with —con'tra·dic'tion *n.*

con'tra·dic'tive, con'tra·dic'to·ry *adj.* tending to refute; inconsistent —con'tra·dic'tive·ly, con'tra·dic'to·ri·ly *adv.* —con'tra·dic'tive·ness *n.*

con'trail *n.* a condensed vapor trail,

as from an airplane or rocket

con·trap´tion *n.* a contrivance or apparatus considered strange; a makeshift device

con·tra·pun´tal *adj.* of counterpoint or its characteristic style —**con·tra·pun´tal·ly** *adv.*

con·tra·ri´e·ty *n.;* dissension or opposition; an indication of inconsistency

con´trar·y *adj.* in opposition; disagreeable —*n.* a thing that is opposite —**con´trar·i·ness** *n.*

con´trast *n.* a significant difference —**con·trast´** *vi.* show difference when compared —*vt.* to set off so as to show difference

con·tra·vene´ *vt.* to oppose; to contradict; to interfere or infringe on —**con·tra·ven´tion** *n.*

con·tri´bute *vi., vt.* to give in common with others; to submit for publication —**con´tri·bu´tion** *n.* —**con·trib´u·tor** *n.* —**con·trib´u·to·ry** *adj.*

con·trite´ *adj.* feeling or expressing regret for an offense —**con·trite´ly** *adv.* —**con·trite´ness, con·tri´tion** *n.*

con·triv´ance *n.* a thing created, as a device or plan

con·trive´ *vt.* to create, devise or scheme —**con·trived´** *adj.* —**con·triv´er** *n.*

con·trol´ *n.* the power or authority to regulate or restrain; a device that regulates —**con·trol·la·bil´i·ty** *n.* —**con·trol´la·ble** *adj.*

controlled *adj.* kept in bounds

controlled experiment a test in which all known variables are carefully monitored

controlled substance a drug regulated by law or at the direction of a government agency

con·trol´ler *n.* a comptroller, the executive in an organization who is responsible for financial control; a device that regulates the operation of another

controlling interest the amount of investment in a company that allows unchallenged authority in directing its operation

control tower the site at an airport from which air traffic is directed

con·tro·ver´sial *adj.* subject to debate or disagreement —**con·tro·ver´sial·ly** *adv.*

con´tro·ver·sy *n.* a dispute between those holding opposing views

con´tro·vert *vt.* to dispute; to contradict —**con·tro·vert´i·ble** *adj.* —**con·tro·vert´i·bly** *adv.*

con·tu·ma´cious *adj.* obstinately disobedient

con´tu·me·ly *n.* arrogant rudeness; insolence —**con·tu·me´li·ous** *adj.* —**con·tu·me´li·ous·ly** *adv.*

con·tuse´ *vt.* to injure without breaking the skin; to bruise

con·tu´sion *n.* a bruise

co·nun´drum *n.* an enigma; a puzzle

con·va·lesce´ *vi.* to recover gradually from an illness; to regain health —**con·va·les´cence** *n.*

con·va·les´cent *adj.* regaining health after illness —*n.* one who is recovering

con·vene´ *vi., vt.* to assemble, especially for a particular purpose

con·ven´ient *adj.* accessible; suited to one's purpose —**con·ven´ience** *n.* —**con·ven´ient·ly** *adv.*

convenience store a neighborhood shop or grocery offering a limited assortment of merchandise, often open around the clock

con´vent *n.* a religious community

con·ven´tion *n.* a gathering of members, delegates, etc.; practices generally accepted as by custom or formal agreement

con·ven´tion·al *adj.* customary; adhering to tradition; not unusual —**con·ven´tion·al´i·ty** *n.* —**con·ven´tion·al·ly** *adv.*

con·ven·tion·eer´ *n.* one who attends a convention

con·verge´ *vi.* to approach a common point; to grow closer —**con·ver´gence**, **con·ver´gen·cy** *n.* —**con·ver´gent** *adj.*

con·ver´sant *adj.* familiar or knowledgeable, especially by experience or study —**con·ver´sance** *n.*

con·ver·sa´tion *n.* an informal verbal exchange —**con·ver·sa´tion·al** *adj.* —**con·ver·sa´tion·al·ly** *adv.* —**con·ver·sa´tion·al·ist** *n.*

conversation piece a unique work of art, article of furniture, etc. that is inclined to attract comment

con·verse´ *vi.* to speak familiarly —**con´verse** *adj.* reversed; transposed —*n.* interchanged; opposite

con·ver´sion *n.* a change from one form, use, etc. to another —**con·vert´** *vt.* —**con·vert´er** *n.*

con·vert´i·ble *adj.* able to be converted —*n.* anything designed to be converted; an automobile that can be changed to an open car —**con·vert´i·bil´i·ty** *n.* —**con·vert´i·bly** *adv.*

con·vex´ *adj.* curved, like the outer surface of a sphere

con·vey´ *vt.* to transport or transfer; to make known —**con·vey´er, con·vey´or** *n.*

con·vey´ance *n.* a means for transporting passengers or freight; the transfer of property, as by sale; the instrument of such a property transfer: a deed

conveyor belt a belt, chain, series of chains, etc. that transfers goods, as from one work station to another in a manufacturing plant

con·vey´or·ize *vt.* to install conveyor belts for the transfer of goods

con´vict´ *n.* one found guilty of a crime; one serving a prison sentence —**con·vict´** *vt.* to find guilty; to condemn —**con·vic´tion** *n.*

con·vince´ *vt.* to persuade; to argue

into —**con·vinc´ing** *adj.* —**con·vinc´ing·ly** *adv.*

con·viv´i·al *adj.* congenial; gregarious —**con·viv·i·al´i·ty** *n.* —**con·viv´i·al·ly** *adv.*

con·vo·ca´tion *n.* a congregation; a formal gathering —**con·vo·ca´tion·al** *adj.* —**con·vo·ca´tion·al·ly** *adv.*

con·voke´ *vt.* to convene a meeting

con·vo·lute´ *vt.* to form in a spiral; to twist or intertwine —**con·vo·lu´tion** *n.*

con´vo·lut´ed *adj.* complicated; intricate or twisted, as *convoluted logic* —**con´vo·lut·ed·ly** *adv.* —**con´vo·lut·ed·ness** *n.*

con´voy *n.* (*Brit.*) a company of travelers; a file of vehicles or pack animals

con·vulse´ *vt.* to shake violently

con·vul´sion *n.* uncontrollable muscle spasms; any severe disturbance —**con·vul´sive** *adj.* —**con·vul´sive·ly** *adv.* —**con·vul´sive·ness** *n.*

cook *n.* one who prepares food —*vi.* to act as a cook; to be changed by exposure to intense heat —*vt.* to prepare food for eating, as by dressing, subjecting to heat, etc. —**cook the books** to prepare a false set of financial records —**cook up** to devise or concoct, as a plan

cook´book *n.* a book containing instructions for the preparation of food

cook´er *n.* any of a variety of devices designed for a particular type of cooking —**pressure cooker** a tightly lidded pot that cooks using steam pressure; a job where one works under extreme pressure

cook´e·ry *n.* the art of food preparation

cook´ie (*US*) *n.* a small cake–like confection

cookie cutter a device for shaping cookies —**cookie–cutter** a project that has been precisely planned

cook´stove n. a kitchen appliance for cooking food

cook´ware n. containers for holding food and implements for manipulating food while it is being cooked or otherwise processed

cool adj. more cold than hot; calm, collected; indifferent; in a discourteous manner —**cool´ly** adv. —**cool´ness** n.

cool´ant n. a substance that resists heat, as in an automobile engine, a refrigerator, etc.

cool box (Brit.) a storage unit where things are made or kept cool

cool´er[1] (Brit.) n. a detention cell

cool´er[2] (US) n. a storage space or unit where things are made or kept cool; a wine cocktail

cool–head´ed adj. disposed to remain calm or composed

coop n. a small cage —vt. to confine —**flew the coop** escaped

coop´er n. one who makes barrels

coop´er·age n. the business of making barrels; barrels and casks collectively; the charge for making barrels

co·op´er·ate´ vi. to work together; to comply —**co·op´er·a´tion** n.

co·op´er·a·tive adj. tending to work well with others; pertaining to a communal organization —n. an organization owned by and operated for the benefit of its members —**co·op´er·a·tive·ly** adv. —**co·op´er·a·tive·ness** n. —**co·op´er·a·tor** n.

cop n. a law officer —vt. to seize; to steal —**cop out** to give up

co·pa·cet´ic adj. fine, acceptable; peaceful

cope vi. to face and deal with, as a trying situation

cop´i·er n. one who imitates; a duplicating machine

coping saw a hand saw with a very thin blade used to cut decorative pieces

co´pi·ous adj. abundant; abounding in thoughts or words —**co´pi·ous·ly** adv. —**co´pi·ous·ness** n.

cop´y n. a reproduction; a manuscript; the text of a book, letter, etc. —vt. to imitate; to reproduce

cop´y·cat n. one who imitates another

copy machine an office machine for making copies of documents

cord n. a light rope; (US) anything resembling a light rope, as an electrical cord; a measure of the volume of cut firewood

cord´age n. the amount of wood in a particular area

cor´date´ adj. heart-shaped

cor´dial adj. friendly —**cor·dial´i·ty**, **cor´dial·ness** n. —**cor´dial·ly** adv.

cord´ite n. an explosive

cord´less adj. battery–operated; having no cord

core n. the innermost part of a thing —vt. to remove the inner part, especially of fruit

cork n. the outer bark of the cork tree; anything made of cork or like cork —vt. to stop a bottle, as with a cork

cork´age n. a charge for serving a bottle of wine, liquor, etc.

cork´board n. a decorative wall panel made from cork

cork´screw n. a device for removing a cork from a wine bottle

corn n. (Brit.) wheat or oats; (US) a cereal plant with seeds growing from a center stalk and covered by an outer husk; the edible seed of the corn plant; any of a variety of hard seeds, as a peppercorn; trite humor; a painful growth of thick skin on the foot —vt. to preserve with salt, as corned beef

corn bread a bread made with cornmeal

corn´cob n. the stalk on which kernels of corn grow

cor´ner n. the angle formed by the junction of two lines or surfaces

—*adj.* located at or near a corner —*vt.* to trap in an awkward position —**around the corner** in the near future —**cut corners** cut back, as on materials, quality, proper procedure, etc., often with negative impact —**turn the corner** survive a crisis

cor′ner·stone *n.* a basic or essential element; one of the foundation stones at the corner of the building often inscribed with the construction date

cor·net′ *n.* a brass wind instrument similar to a trumpet; a piece of paper or pastry formed into a cone and filled with a confection

corn flour (*Brit.*) *n.* a starch extracted from corn, used in cooking as a thickener

cor′nice *n.* a projected molding along the top of a building or above a window

corn meal ground meal made from corn

corn′row *n.* a hairstyle pattern of small tight braids

corn′starch (*US*) *n.* a starch extracted from corn, used in cooking as a thickener

cor′nu·co′pi·a *n.* a representation of a goat's horn overflowing with fruits, flowers, etc.; a conical container

corn whiskey an alcoholic beverage distilled from corn mash

corn′y *adj.* trite; hackneyed

cor′ol·lar·y *n.* an inference that naturally follows, as a mathematical proof stemming from a concept already proven

cor′o·nar·y *adj.* regarding the arteries that supply blood directly to the heart muscle; pertaining to the heart —*n.* a coronary artery; coronary thrombosis

coronary bypass an operation that shunts the flow of blood around a damaged artery in the heart

coronary occlusion coronary thrombosis

coronary thrombosis the obstruction of a coronary artery by a blood clot

cor·o·na′tion *n.* a ceremony for the crowning of a monarch

cor′o·ner *n.* a public official whose main duty is to inquire into any death that may not be due to natural cause

cor·o·net′ *n.* a small crown

cor′po·ral *adj.* of the body —*n.* a non–commissioned officer

cor′po·rate *adj.* of a corporation

corporate raider an individual, consortium, corporation, etc. that attempts to gain control of a corporation by buying up its stock

cor·po·ra′tion *n.* a legal entity authorized to act as one individual

cor·po′re·al *adj.* of a material nature; tangible

corps *pl. n.* a body of people acting together under common direction

corpse (*Brit.*) *n.* a dead body

cor′pu·lent *adj.* excessively fat — **cor′pu·lence** *n.*

cor′pus *n.*, *pl.* **cor′por·a** the main part or substance of a fleshly structure; a comprehensive collection of a specific type of writing

cor′pus de·lic′ti substantial proof that a crime has been committed; the body of a murder victim

cor·ral′ *n.* an enclosure for livestock —*vt.* to surround and capture

cor·rect′ *adj.* accurate; proper, suitable —*vt.* to make right; to adjust —**cor·rect′a·ble** *adj.* —**cor·rec′tive** *adj.* —**cor·rect′ly** *adv.* — **cor·rect′ness** *n.* —**cor·rec′tor** *n.*

cor·rec′tion *n.* the process of making right; an amount adjusted

cor′re·late′ *vt.* to discover or establish a relationship —**cor′re·la′tion** *n.* —**cor·re·la′tion·al** *adj.*

cor·rel′a·tive *adj.* related, corresponding

cor·re·spond´ *vi.* to be similar; to conform; to communicate by letter —**cor·re·spon´dence** *n.* —**cor·re·spond´en·cy** *adv.* —**cor·re·spond´ent** *n.*

correspondence school an institution that offers instruction by mail or computer

cor´ri·dor *n.* a long passageway

cor´ri·gi·ble *adj.* able to be reformed —**cor·ri·gi·bil´i·ty** *n.* —**cor´ri·gi·bly** *adv.*

cor·rob´o·rate´ *vt.* to support or strengthen, as testimony —**cor·rob´o·ra´tion** *n.* —**cor·rob´o·ra·tive** *adj.* —**cor·rob´o·ra·tor** *n.*

cor·rode´ *vt.* destroy gradually, as by rust or chemicals —**cor·rod´i·ble** *adj.* —**cor·ro´sion** *n.*

cor·ro´sive *adj.* tending to corrode —*n.* a substance that causes corroding —**cor·ro´sive·ly** *adv.* —**cor·ro´sive·ness** *n.*

cor·rupt´ *adj.* marked by immorality; altered —*vt.* to pervert, debase; to alter, contaminate —**cor·rupt´er** *n.* —**cor·rupt´i·ble** *adj.* —**cor·rup´tion** *n.* —**cor·rupt´ly** *adv.* —**cor·rupt´ness** *n.*

cor·rup´tive *adj.* tending to make immoral or impure —**cor·rup´tive·ly** *adv.*

cor·sage´ *n.* a small flower arrangement worn on a dress or the wrist

cor´sair *n.* a buccaneer, a pirate

cor·tege´, cor·tège´ *n.* a group of attendants

cor´tex *n.* the outer layer of an internal organ

cor·us·cate´ *vi.* to give off flashes of light; to sparkle, glitter —**cor·us·ca´tion** *n.*

co·sign´ *vi., vt.* to share responsibility for the obligation of another —**co·sig´na·to·ry** *adj.* —**co´sign·er** *n.*

cos·met´ic *adj.* tending to improve the appearance; superficial improvement —*n.* any of a variety of preparations for improving one's appearance —**cos·met´i·cal·ly** *adv.* —**cos·me·ti´cian** *n.*

cos·me·tol´o·gy *n.* the art of selecting and applying cosmetics

cos´mic *adj.* of the universe; of immense proportions

cosmic dust minute particles floating in space

cosmic ray a stream of charged particles from outer space

cos·mog´o·ny *n.* the study of the theories of creation

cos·mog´ra·phy *n.* collectively, the sciences that deal with the configuration of the universe —**cos·mog´ra·pher** *n.* —**cos·mo·graph´ic, cos·mo·graph´i·cal** *adj.* —**cos·mo·graph´i·cal·ly** *adv.*

cos·mol´o·gy *n.* the study of the formation and nature of the universe —**cos·mol´o·ger** *n.* —**cos·mo·log´ic, cos·mo·log´i·cal** *adj.* —**cos·mo·log´i·cal·ly** *adv.*

cos´mo·naut *n.* an astronaut

cos´mo·pol´i·tan *adj.* of that common to the entire world; worldly —*n.* an urbane or sophisticated person —**cos·mop´o·lite** *n.*

cos´mos *n.* universal order

cost *n.* price; the value of a thing; the expense of producing or obtaining something

cost accounting a system by which a company accounts for the expense of production

cost´-ef·fec´tive *adj.* considered worth the expenditure —**cost´-ef·fec´tive·ness** *n.*

cost´ly *adj.* expensive; splendid —**cost´li·ness** *n.*

cost of living expenditures for necessities

cos´tume *n.* the mode of dress typical to a time, place, etc.; clothing appropriate to a season, occasion, etc. —**cos´tum·er** *n.*

costume jewelry fake jewelry

cot *n.* a small, folding bed

co´te·rie *n.* a close circle of friends

co·til´lion n. a formal dance

cot´tage n. a simple house

cottage cheese a soft cheese of curds

cottage industry a small business, often conducted from a home

cotter pin a split pin used to fasten machine parts

cot´ton n. a tropical plant that produces soft hairs used in the making of thread for cloth; the soft hairs of the cotton plant; the thread or cloth produced

cotton candy (US) a confection made up of fibers of spun suger

cotton floss (Brit.) a confection made up of fibers of spun suger

cotton gin a device for separating the seeds from raw cotton

cot´ton·seed n. the seed from the cotton plant, a source of cooking oil

cottonseed oil oil from the seed of the cotton plant

cot´ton·tail n. a rabbit

couch n. (US) a sofa —vt. to cause to recline; to say or express in a particular way: *couched in terms of endearment* —vi. to recline

cough n. illness marked by frequent clearing of the lungs —vi. to expel air from the lungs suddenly and noisily

cough drop a small hard candy–like tablet, medicated to relieve coughing, sore throat, etc.

cough syrup a liquid patent medicine for the relief of coughing and other cold symptoms

coun´cil n. a group elected or appointed for some task, esp. for government administration — **coun´ci·lor** n.

coun´sel n. advice or guidance; a legal adviser —vi., vt. to give advice —**coun´se·lor** n.

count vi., vt. to number in order

count´down n. the final check or preparation before an event

coun´te·nance n. appearance —vt. to express approval

coun´ter adj. opposing —adv. in an opposing manner —vi., vt. to react or respond

count´er n. a device for counting; any flat working surface as in a store, a kitchen, etc.

coun·ter·act vt. to mitigate by opposing action —**coun·ter·ac´tion** n. —**coun·ter·ac´tive** adj.

coun´ter·at·tack n. a strategic move to blunt an attack —vi., vt. to attack in retaliation

coun·ter·bal´ance n. an element that counteracts another

coun´ter·claim n. an opposing claim, as in a lawsuit

coun´ter–cul·ture n. a lifestyle that opposes traditional values

coun´ter·feit adj. forged; fraudulent —n. an imitation —vt. to make a copy with intent to defraud; to fake —vi. to practice deception —**coun´ter·feit·er** n.

coun·ter·in·tel´li·gence n. techniques designed to thwart the activity of enemy agents; those employing such techniques

coun´ter·mand vt. to cancel or reverse, as a previous order

coun´ter·meas·ure n. an action in opposition to another

coun·ter·of·fen´sive n. a counterattack

coun´ter·pane n. a bedspread

coun´ter·part n. an opposite number; anything with the same characteristics or function as another

coun´ter·point n. a thing that interacts with another; a musical form that features two simultaneous melodic lines

coun·ter·pro·duc´tive adj. serving to promote an effect opposite of that intended; detrimental

coun´ter·rev·o·lu´tion n. action against a revolutionary government; opposition to reform

—**coun´ter·rev·o·lu´tion·ar·y** *adj*.

coun´ter·sign´ *n*. a signature added to a signed document to authenticate or confirm the first signature; a secret sign or signal given as a required response —*vt*. to authenticate by signing

coun´ter·sink *vt*. to set the head of a screw in wood so that it is flush with the surface —*n*. a bit for widening the top of a hole to accept a screw head

coun´ter·weight *n*. a weight that balances another

coun´tess *n*. a woman of noble birth equal in rank to a count or earl

count´less *adj*. innumerable; a quantity that cannot be numbered

coun´tri·fied *adj*. having the characteristics of a farmer or small-town dweller

coun´try *n*. the area claimed by a particular nation or state; a rural area —*adj*. of a rural area

country club a facility that serves the needs of its members for socializing, sports, etc.

coun´try·man *n*. another citizen of one's own country

country music a musical style indigenous to the southern U.S.

country rock a musical style that combines the style of country music with rock and roll

coun´try·side *n*. the view of a rural area

coun´ty *n*. an administrative subdivision in some nations, territories, and states

county fair an annual festival featuring exhibits of farm and commercial products from a county

county seat the location of the government of a county

coup *n*. a successful feat; a splendid achievement

coup d´etat the overthrow of a government

cou·pé´ *n*. (*Brit*.) a half compartment

at the end of a railway car

coupe *n*. a closed, two-door automobile

cou´ple *n*. a pair; two people united socially; something that links two things —*vt*. to link —**coup´ler** *n*. —**coup´ling** *n*.

cou´pon *n*. a printed paper entitling the bearer to a benefit, as an interest payment for a bond or a discount on merchandise; a form of transmittal, as for ordering goods or payment on an installment loan

cour´age *n*. the quality that allows one to face danger or adversity with confidence

cou·ra´geous *adj*. brave; fearless —**cou·ra´geous·ly** *adv*. —**cou·ra´geous·ness** *n*.

cour´i·er *n*. a messenger

course *n*. the direction or route moved; a method or sequence of action; a program of study —*vi*., *vt*. to race; to move swiftly; to dash

court *n*. an open area, as a square or short street surrounded by buildings; a closed play area for certain games; a forum of justice or the building in which it sits; royal persons or their households —*vt*. to supplicate or flatter to obtain some benefit

cour´te·ous *adj*. considerate; well-mannered —**cour´te·ous·ly** *adv*. —**cour´te·ous·ness** *n*.

cour´te·san *n*. a prostitute; the mistress of a man of importance

cour´te·sy *n*. politeness; an act of consideration; furnished without charge

court´house *n*. a building that houses a court of law

court´ly *adj*. dignified; elegant —**court´li·ness** *n*.

court of appeals a state or federal court to which may be appealed the decisions of a lower court

court of law a judicial forum

court´room *n*. the room in which

legal proceedings are conducted before a judge

court´ship n. the process by which a person seeks to gain the approval of another; a wooing

court´yard n. an open space in the center of a large building

cous´in n. a relative of the same generation who is not a sibling

cou·ture´ n. the business of designing women's clothing; high–fashion clothing —**cou·tu´rier** n.

co·va´lence n. the pairs of electrons that an atom can share —**co·va´lent** n.

cove n. a small sheltered bay along a shore or in the side of a mountain; the architectural equivalent, as a recess in a wall

cov´en n. an assembly of witches

cov´e·nant n. a binding agreement; a formal contract

cov´er n. a thing that shields, shelters, protects, etc. —vt. to place something over so as to hide, shelter, etc.

cov´er·age n. the amount and type of information, protection, etc. offered

cov´er·all n. a loose outer garment that covers the entire body except for the hands, feet and head

cover charge a fixed charge at a restaurant or night club, usually for entertainment

cov´er·ing n. a thing used to protect or shield

cov´er·let n. a light bed covering

cov´ert adj. hidden; disguised —**co´vert·ly** adv. —**co´vert·ness** n.

cov´er–up n. actions designed to hide the truth

cov´et vi., vt. to desire longingly —**cov´et·ous** adj. —**cov´e·tous·ly** adv. —**cov´e·tous·ness** n.

cov´ey n. a small flock of birds

cow n. the adult female of certain mammals; often, any domestic cattle

cow´ard n. one who lacks courage —**cow´ard·ice**, **cow´ard·li·ness** n. —**cow´ard·ly** adv.

cow´bell n. a bell hung around a cow's neck

cow´boy n. a worker on a cattle ranch

cow´catch·er n. a sloping bumper on the front of a locomotive designed to fend off obstacles on a railroad track

cow college a college of agriculture

cow´er vi. to shrink back or huddle, as from fear or cold

cow´hand n. a cowboy

cow´hide n. leather made from the hide of a cow; a leather whip

cowl n. a hood or hooded garment; any similar covering, as for a chimney or engine

cow´lick n. an unruly shock of hair

cowl´ing n. a metal covering for an engine

cow´punch·er n. a cowboy

co·work´er, **co–work´er** n. an associate at work

cox´swain n. the helmsman of a small boat or racing shell

coy adj. shy, demur; affecting shyness; evasive —**coy´ly** adv.

coz´en vi., vt. to deceive; to obtain by deceit

coz´y adj. comfortable —n. a cover for a teapot —**cozy up** attempt to get in the good graces of another —**play it cozy** act cautiously or secretively —**co´zi·ly** adv. —**co´zi·ness** n.

crab n. a crustacean having eight legs and pincers; an ill-tempered person —vi. to fish for crabs; to complain

crab´by adj. grouchy; ill–humored —**crab´bi·ly** adv. —**crab´bi·ness** n.

crack adj. excelling, first–rate —n. a sharp sound; a fracture or narrow opening; a sharp blow; a type of cocaine —vi., vt. to produce a sharp sound; to strike; to split; to break down mentally —**crack the whip** to press workers for greater output; to demand strict adherence to rules

crack´down *n.* a strict enforcement or meting out of punishment —*vi.* to enforce strictly or punish more severely

crack´er *n.* a thin crisp wafer; (*US*) a country boy —**crack´ers** (*Brit.*) mentally deranged

crack´er·jack *adj.* outstanding; proficient

crack´head *n.* one who uses crack cocaine

crack´house *n.* a place where crack cocaine is processed and distributed

crack´le *n.* the finely cracked surface of some pottery —*vi.* to make a series of snapping or cracking noises, as of a fire —*vt.* to produce fine cracks on the surface of pottery

crack´pot *adj.* insane; offbeat, eccentric —*n.* a person who acts strange or eccentric

crack´–up *n.* an accident involving a moving vehicle; a mental breakdown

cra´dle *n.* a baby's bed; a place of early development, as *the cradle of civilization;* a device for supporting a heavy object

craft *n.* one's art or trade; skill in deception; ships of the sea or air —*vt.* to form with skill

crafts´man *n.* a skilled worker; an artisan —**crafts´man·ship** *n.*

craft´y *adj.* clever; scheming; deceitful —**craft´i·ly** *adv.* —**craft´i·ness** *n.*

crag *n.* a rough, steep projecting rock

crag´gy *adj.* rough and steep; irregular —**crag´gi·ness** *n.*

cram *vt.* to compress or compact; to fill beyond normal capacity

cramp *n.* a sudden involuntary

muscular contraction —*vt.* to restrict

cramped *adj.* confined; restraining

crane *n.* a large wading bird; a machine for raising heavy objects

cra´ni·al *adj.* of the cranium

cranial nerve *n.* any of a number of nerves attached to the stem of the brain

cra´ni·um *n.* the skull

crank *n.* an arm attached to a shaft for transferring motion; an eccentric or complaining person —*vi., vt.* to turn a handle, as to start or operate

crank´case *n.* the oil reservoir that encloses a crankshaft

crank´shaft *n.* a rod that drives a crank for transferring movement

crank´y *adj.* irritable; ill·tempered; testy —**crank´i·ness** *n.*

cran´ny *n.* a small opening

crap *n.* excrement; junk, trash; foolishness; anything useless

crap out to lose at craps; to drop out due to exhaustion, fear, etc.

crap´py *adj.* of inferior quality

craps *pl. n.* a game of dice

crap´shoot *n.* a venture that carries risk or that cannot be controlled

crap´u·lence *n.* excessive eating or drinking —**crap´u·lent** *adj.*

crap´u·lous *adj.* inclined to excessive eating or drinking; suffering from such excess —**crap´u·lous·ly** *adv.*

crash *n.* a sudden loud noise; a collision; a sudden financial collapse —*vi.* to make a loud noise; to collide; to fail suddenly, as of a computer; to bed down in temporary quarters —*vt.* to cause a noise or collision; to attend without an invitation

crash helmet *n.* headgear designed to protect the wearer from injury

crash´–land *vi., vt.* to set down an aircraft in an unconventional manner, as with malfunctioning equipment, etc.

crash pad temporary living quarters

crass *adj*. crude; vulgar; tasteless — **crass´ly** *adv*. —**crass´ness** *n*.

crate *n*. a box made of wood —*vt*. to pack in a wooden box —**crat´er** *n*.

cra´ter *n*. a bowl–shaped depression

cra·vat´ *n*. a scarf worn at the neck

crave *vi*., *vt*. to long for —**crav´ing** *n*.

cra´ven *adj*. cowardly

craw *n*. the crop of a bird; an animal's stomach —**stick in one's craw** to displease; irritate

craw´dad *n*. crayfish

craw´fish *n*. crayfish

crawl *n*. slow movement; a swimming stroke —*vi*. to move on hands and knees or by dragging the body along the ground; to move slowly or feebly

crawl space (*US*) a low space, as under a house, that allows access to wiring, plumbing, etc.

cray´fish *n*. a fresh–water crustacean similar to a lobster, but much smaller and without claws

cray´on *n*. a stick of colored wax for drawing, coloring, etc.

craze *n*. a current fad —*vi*., *vt*. to anger; to enrage

cra´zy *adj*. insane; foolish; overly enthusiastic —*n*. one who acts as though mentally unstable —**cra´zi·ly** *adv*. —**cra´zi·ness** *n*.

creak *n*. a squeaking sound —*vi*. to make such a sound

creak´y *adj*. squeaky —**creak´i·ly** *adv*. —**creak´i·ness** *n*.

cream *n*. a derivative of milk, rich in butterfat; a product made from cream; the color of cream; a cosmetic, medication, etc. that is the consistency of whipped cream; the best part, as *cream of the crop* — *adj*. containing or like cream —*vt*. to remove the cream from milk; to blend to a smooth consistency

cream cheese a soft cheese made from cream

cream´er *n*. a pitcher for holding

and serving cream; a nondairy product used to lighten and flavor coffee

cream´er·y *n*. adjunct to a dairy farm where milk is processed

cream puff a light pastry filled with whipped cream

cream sauce a smooth sauce made with milk or cream

cream soda a vanilla flavored soft drink

cream´y *adj*. containing cream; smooth, of the consistency of heavy cream —**cream´i·ness** *n*.

crease *n*. a line or mark made by folding, wrinkling, etc —*vt*. to make or form creases in

cre·ate´ *vt*. to originate; to bring about; to produce through artistic endeavor

cre·a´tion *n*. the act of creating; that which is created —**cre·a´tor** *n*.

cre·a´tion·ism *n*. the belief that the account of the creation in the Bible is literally correct

cre·a´tive *adj*. displaying or rousing imagination or inventiveness — **cre·a´tive·ly** *adv*. —**cre·a´tive· ness** *n*.

cre·a·tiv´i·ty *n*. inventiveness

crea´ture *n*. a living being

creature comforts those things that provide contentment for the body

cre´dence *n*. acceptance as true

cre·den´tial *n*. anything that serves to identify or attest to one's knowledge or authority

cre·den´za *n*. a sideboard

credibility gap incongruity between what is said and what is done or appears to be true

cred´i·ble *adj*. plausible; believable —**cred·i·bil´i·ty** *n*.

cred´it *n*. trust; a favorable reputation; approval or praise —*vt*. to believe in; to assign, as an attribute —**cred´i·tor** *n*.

credit card a card attesting to the bearer's line of credit for the purchase of goods or services

credit line the amount of credit one is allowed

credit rating an assessment of one's ability and prospect for repaying obligations

cre´do *n.* a creed

cre·du´li·ty *n.* an inclination to believe without good cause

cred´u·lous *adj.* inclined to believe readily —**cred´u·lous·ly** *adv.* — **cred´u·lous·ness** *n.*

creed *n.* a statement of beliefs

creek *n.* (*US*) a stream; (*Brit.*) a small inlet of the sea —**up the creek** in a difficult predicament

creel *n.* a fisherman's bag

creep *vi.* to move with the body close to the ground; to move slowly, with great stealth —**creep´er** *n.*

creep´y *adj.* apprehensive; uneasy —**creep´i·ly** *adv.* —**creep´i·ness** *n.*

cre´mate´ *vt.* to incinerate, esp. a dead body —**cre·ma´tion** *n.*

cre·ma·to´ri·um, cre´ma·to·ry *n.* a place where dead bodies are cremated

cre´o·sote *n.* a wood preservative

crêpe *n.* a thin crinkled cloth; a thin pancake, often wrapped around a filling

crepe paper a thin crinkled paper used for decoration

cres·cen´do *adj., adv.* gradually increasing —*n.* a gradual increase, as in loudness or intensity —*vi.*

crest *n.* a decorative plume, as on a helmet or the head of a bird; a device placed over a coat of arms; the highest point, as of a hill or wave —**crest´ed** *adj.*

crest´fall·en *adj.* saddened; shamed; disheartened

cre·ta´ceous *adj.* of chalk or a chalk-like substance

cre´tin *n.* a buffoon; one suffering from cretinism

cre´tin·ism *n.* a congenital disease marked by physical deformity and mental retardation

cre·vasse´ *n.* a deep fissure; a chasm

crev´ice *n.* a narrow crack or opening

crew *n.* a group of people working together

crew cut a close-cropped hair style

crew´el *n.* a type of embroidery; the thread used

crib *n.* a bed with high sides for a small child; a small building or bin for storing grain —*vi., vt.* to cheat or steal

crib´bage *n.* a card game for two to four players in which score is kept on a pegboard

crick *n.* a stiffness of the back, neck, etc.

crime *n.* an act in violation of the law; a disgraceful act

crim´i·nal *adj.* relating to or in the nature of a crime —*n.* one convicted of a crime —**crim·i·nal´i·ty** *n.* —**crim´i·nal·ly** *adv.*

criminal code the body of law that deals with criminal offenses

criminal court a court that tries criminal cases

criminal law the branch of law that deals with crime and the punishment for commision of a crime

crim·i·nol´o·gist *n.* one who engages in the study and methodical investigation of crime —**crim·i·nol´o·gy** *n.*

crimp *n.* a pleat or fold —*vt.* to crumple or crinkle; to form into wrinkles

crim´son *adj., n.* deep red

cringe *vi.* to cower or shrink, as in fear

crin´kle *vi., vt.* to form in wrinkles; to rustle, as paper —**crin´kly** *adj.*

crin´o·line *n.* a petticoat; a stiff cloth used as a lining or undergarment

crip´ple *n.* one who is deprived of normal use of a limb —*vt.* to cause to lose the use of a limb; to impair, as a device or plan —**crip´pler** n.

cri´sis n., pl. **cri´ses** a decisive or turning point; a traumatic event

crisp adj. brittle; clean and fresh; invigorating —vi., vt. to make crisp —**burned to a crisp** blackened so as to be inedible or unusable; severly sunburned —**crisp´ly** adv. — **crisp´ness** n.

crisp´y adj. brittle —**crisp´i·ness** n.

cri·te´ri·on n. a basis for judging

crit´ic n. one who reviews movies, art, etc.; one who tends to fault-finding

crit´i·cal adj. tending to find fault; marked by careful analysis; dangerous; decisive —**crit´i·cal·ly** adv.

crit´i·cise´ (Brit.), **crit´i·cize´** (US) vi., vt. to evaluate; to find fault — **crit´i·cism** n.

cri·tique´ n. a careful analysis

crit´ter n. a creature; a small animal

croak n. a deep, rough voice, as that of a frog —vi., vt. to utter a deep, rough sound; to die or cause to die

crock n. an earthenware pot; information deemed to be misleading or incorrect

crock´er·y n. pottery

croc´o·dile n. a large amphibious reptile

crocodile tears figurative tears shed in an insincere display of grief

croc´o·dil´i·an adj. like a crocodile

crois·sant n. a light breakfast roll shaped in a crescent

crone n. an old woman; a hag

cro´ny n. a close friend

cro´ny·ism n. the practice of appointing one's friends to key positions, especially in politics

crook n. an implement with a curved or bent part; one who lives by dishonest means —vi., vt. to bend

crook´ed adj. bent; dishonest

croon vi., vt. to sing in a low, soft tone, especially a romantic or sentimental ballad —**croon´er** n.

crop n. agricultural products; the

amount of products harvested; a thing similar to a harvest, as a crop of students; things cut short, as a type of haircut, a riding whip, etc. —vt. to trim; to cut short or clip —**crop up** to appear suddenly or unexpectedly

crop duster a small airplane that flies low over a cultivated field to discharge insecticide or fungicide; the pilot of the aircraft; a business that provides such a service — **crop–dusting** n.

crop´land n. land where produce is grown

crop´per n. one who farms on shares, a sharecropper; a bad experience; a failed venture

crop rotation the practice of changing crops from year to year so as to avoid depleting the soil

cro·quet´ n. a lawn game in which wooden balls are driven by mallets through a course of wickets

cro·quette´ n. a deep-fried cake of chopped meat or seafood

cross adj. angry; cranky —n. a symbol composed of a horizontal and vertical line intersecting at or near their centers; a burden, affliction; a mixture, as a hybrid plant —vt. to intersect; to travel or reach over; to oppose —**cross a palm** to pay, as a bribe

cross´beam n. a structural member

cross´bow n. a medieval weapon of war

cross´breed n. a hybrid —vi., vt. to produce a hybrid as by pairing different lines of animals or plants —**cross´bred** adj.

cross´check vi., vt. to verify

cross´-coun·try adj., adv. across a land, as a cross–country tour; through rugged country, as a cross–country race

cross´cur·rent n. a flow of water, as in the ocean, that runs across the main current; any influence that is contrary to the main thrust, as *a crosscurrent of ideas*

cross·ex·am·i·na′tion *n.* a careful questioning, especially in court to refute earlier testimony —**cross′-ex·am′ine** *vi., vt.*

cross′-eyed *adj.* of a condition in which the movements of eyes are not properly coordinated

cross′-fer·ti·li·za′tion *n.* the process of breeding with a plant or animal of a different line

cross′hatch·ing *n.* a drawing technique that creates shading with sets of crossing parallel lines —**cross′hatch** *vi., vt.*

cross′ing *n.* a place for moving from one side to the other, as of a street, river, etc.; a place where two ways cross, as of a road: an intersection

cross′ly *adv.* in a cantankerous manner

cross′-pol′li·nate *vi., vt.* to transfer pollen from a plant of one species to that of another —**cross′-pol·li·na′tion** *n.*

cross′-ref′er·ence *n.* a notation that refers to another source of information about a subject or to mention of the subject elsewhere —*vt.* to refer to another mention; to prepare a reference to other sources

cross′road *n.* an intersection of two roads; an important time or incident

crossword, crossword puzzle a word puzzle

crotch *n.* an intersection, as by the branches of a tree; the area where the legs meet at the trunk

crotch′et *n.* an odd or whimsical notion

crouch *vi.* to bend low with limbs drawn close, as though ready to spring; to cower in fear

crou′pi·er *n.* one who operates a casino gambling table

crou′ton *n.* a small piece of crisp bread garnish for soup or salad

crow′bar *n.* a metal bar designed as a prying tool

crowd *n.* a group of people gathered in one place; a number of people with something in common, as *the college crowd* —*vi., vt.* to squeeze or push —**city hall crowd** local politicians or bureaucrats

crown *n.* a head covering worn as a symbol of sovereignty; the power or office of a monarch; a symbol of distinction, as in sports —*vt.* to confer with a crown or the power, honor, etc. that it symbolizes; to be, or form, the highest part; to bring to successful completion

crow′s-feet *n.* a pattern of lines around the corner of the eyes

crow′s-nest *n.* a high platform used as a lookout, as on the mast of a sailing ship

cru′cial *adj.* extremely significant; decisive —**cru′cial·ly** *adv.*

cru′ci·fy′ *vt.* to put to death by binding or nailing to a cross; to treat cruelly, especially verbally

crud *n.* gunk; a worthless or nasty thing

crude *adj.* in an unrefined or raw state; lacking manners or tact —**crude′ly** *adv.* —**crude′ness, cru′di·ty** *n.*

cru′el *adj.* inclined to purposely inflict misery; barbarous; pleasure taken in the suffering of others; heartless —**cru′el·ly** *adv.* —**cru′el·ness, cru′el·ty** *n.*

cru′et *n.* a narrow mouth jar

cruise *n.* a pleasure voyage —*vi.* to travel about, as for pleasure —**cruis′er** *n.*

cruise control a device for automatically maintaining constant speed in an automobile

crul′ler *n.* a cake fried in melted fat; an unraised doughnut

crumb *n.* a piece or fragment

crum´ble *vi.*, *vt.* to break into small fragments; to collapse or disintegrate

crum´bly *adj.* tending to be easily broken into small pieces; consisting of fragments; dilapidated, fallen in —**crum´bli·ness** *n.*

crum´my *adj.* cheap; shoddy; shabby

crum´pet *n.* a small batter cake baked on a griddle, similar to an English muffin in the US

crum´ple *vi.*, *vt.* to crush; to collapse

crunch *n.* a difficult economic situation —*vi.*, *vt.* to grind with a crackling sound

cru·sade´ *n.* a broad campaign for a good cause —*vi.* to participate in such a campaign —**cru·sad´er** *n.*

crush *n.* a crowding together; a passing infatuation; a fruit drink —*vt.* to press so as to bruise or break into smaller pieces; to press or crowd upon; to subdue —**crush´a·ble** *adj.*

crust *n.* a hard outer surface; insolence —*vi.*, *vt.* to cover with a crisp or hard surface

crust´y *adj.* displaying a brusque, uncivil manner —**crust´i·ly** *adv.* —**crust´i·ness** *n.*

crutch *n.* any device used as an aid or support

crux *n.* a decisive factor; the heart of a matter

cry *n.* a scream or shout; weeping —*vi.* to scream or shout; to weep —*vt.* to plead or beg for —**a far cry** very different than expected

cry´ba·by *n.* one who complains excessively

cry·o·gen´ics *pl. n.* the science that deals with the creation and effects of low temperature —**cry·o·gen´ic** *adj.* —**cry·o·gen´i·cal·ly** *adv.*

crypt *n.* an underground chamber used as a burial place

crypt·a·nal´y·sis *n.* the science of deciphering codes

cryp´tic *adj.* enigmatic; having hidden meaning

cryp´to·gram *n.* a coded message

cryp´to·graph *n.* a means for the writing or deciphering of coded messages —**cryp·tog´ra·pher** *n.* —**cryp·tog´ra·phy** *n.*

crys´tal *adj.* of or like a high–quality glass or certain minerals; tranparent —*n.* a high–quality glass or a thing made of the glass; geometrically shaped particles of a mineral; the glass covering a watch face

crystal–clear without flaw, like a crystal; easily seen or understood

crys´tal·line *adj.* like or made of crystal

crys´tal·lize *vi.*, *vt.* to form or cause to form a crystal; to assume or bring to permanent form —**crys·tal·li·za´tion** *n.*

cub´by·hole *n.* a small compartment

cube *n.* a solid form having six square faces; the third power of any number —*vt.* to raise to the third power —**cu´bic** *adj.*

cube steak a piece of beef that has been tenderized by a pattern of cross cuts on the surface

cu´bi·cle *n.* a small enclosure, as for a single worker in an office

cub´ism *n.* an abstract syle of art using geometric patterns for representation —**cub´ist** *n.*

cuck´old *n.* a man whose wife has been unfaithful —**cuck´old·ry** *n.*

cud *n.* food regurgitated from the first stomach of a ruminating animal

cud´dle *n.* an embrace —*vi.*, *vt.* to embrace

cud´dly *adj.* affectionate; lovable; appealing —**cud´dle·some** *adj.*

cudg´el *n.* a short heavy stick; a club

cue *n.* a signal or hint to prompt an action —*vt.* to signal

cue ball an unmarked ball struck with the cue in pool or billiards

cuff *n.* a slap with the open hand; a fold at the end of a shirt sleeve; (*US*) turned up material at the end of a trouser leg —*vt.* to slap with the open hand

cui·sine´ *n.* a particular style of food preparation

cul´-de-sac´ *n.* a street with a single outlet and a turnabout at the closed end

cu´li·nar´y *adj.* of the kitchen or cooking

cull *n.* something selected for removal, especially for poor quality —*vt.* to select

cul´mi·nate *vi., vt.* to come or bring to completion —**cul´mi·na´tion** *n.*

cul´pa·ble *adj.* deserving blame — **cul·pa·bil´i·ty** *n.* —**cul´pa·bly** *adv.*

cul´prit *n.* one accused or guilty

cult *n.* a group considered to be extremist or obsessive in their beliefs

cul´ti·vate´ *vt.* to tend crops; to promote or nurture, as an interest in learning —**cul´ti·vat·ed** *adj.* — **cul´ti·va´tion** *n.*

cul´tur·al *adj.* of a particular culture —**cul´tur·al·ly** *adv.*

cul´ture *n.* the characteristics of a society; enlightenment, refinement

cultured pearl a pearl grown from an implanted irritant

culture shock disorientation experienced by exposure to an unfamiliar environment

cul´vert *n.* a conduit or drain passing under a road, path, etc.

cum´ber·some *adj.* unwieldy; difficult to maneuver because of size or shape; bulky; awkward

cu´mu·late *vi., vt.* to collect; to accumulate —**cu´mu·la´tion** *n.* —**cu´mu·la·tive** *adj.*

cu·mu·lo·nim´bus *n.* a cloud structure associated with thunder and lightning storms

cu´mu·lus *n.* a tall cloud structure with a dark, flat, moisture-laden base —**cu´mu·lous** *adj.*

cu·ne´i·form *adj.* wedge-shaped, as the strokes or characters in certain ancient writing —*n.*

cun´ning *adj.* sly; crafty —*n.* skillful at deceiving

cup *n.* an open container for serving a beverage, broth, etc.; a standard measure of 8 ounces

cup´board *n.* a storage place for dinnerware

cup´cake (*US*) *n.* a small cake appropriate for a single serving

cup´ful *adj.* the amount a cup can hold; a cup measure of 8 ounces

cu·pid´i·ty *n.* avarice; greed

cu·po·la *n.* a domed ceiling; a small domed structure on a roof

cur *n.* a dog, usually a mongrel; a vile person

cu´rate *n.* a clergyman who assists a rector or vicar

cu´ra·tor *n.* a custodian

curb *n.* a checking or hindrance; a curbstone —*vt.* to subdue; to check

curb service service offered to patrons in their cars, as at a fast food restaurant

curd *n.* coagulated milk

cur´dle *vi., vt.* to turn into curd; to coagulate

cu´ra·tor *n.* an overseer, as of a museum

cure *n.* a method or agent that restores health or corrects an unpleasant condition —*vt.* to effect a recovery or remedy; to preserve, as food by smoking —**cur´a·ble** *adj.* —**cur´a·tive** *adj., n.*

cure´-all *n.* a remedy for all ills or troubles

cur´few *n.* a regulation specifying a time for citizens to be off the street; the time specified; a time set for a young person to be home

cu·ri·os´i·ty *n.* a desire to learn; a rare or unusual artifact

cu´ri·ous *adj.* eager to learn; very

inquisitive; unusual —**cu´ri·ous·ly** *adv*. —**cu´ri·ous·ness** *n*.

cur´li·cue *n*. an ornate curve, as in caligraphy

curling iron a device for making curls in the hair

curl´y *adj*. having waves or ringlets; inclined to curl —**curl´i·ness** *n*.

cur´mudg´eon *n*. an ill-tempered or disparaging person

cur´ren·cy *n*. the money in use in a country or territory

cur´rent *adj*. of the present —*n*. a general tendency or movement —**cur´rent·ly** *adv*.

current account (*Brit*.) a monetary deposit that permits the transfer of funds by writing cheques

cur·ric´u·lum *n*. an established course of study; collectively, the studies offered by a particular school

cur´ry *n*. a piquant blend of spices; a dish or sauce prepared with curry —*vt*. to groom a horse

cur´sive *adj*. of handwriting in which all characters in a word are connected

cur´so·ry *adj*. hastily done; casual, as *a cursory glance*

curt *adj*. short, concise; brusque —**curt´ly** *adv*. —**curt´ness** *n*.

cur´tail´ *vt*. to cut short; to reduce; to lessen —**cur·tail´ment** *n*.

cur´tain *n*. material hung as a decoration or barrier; something that covers or obscures, as *a curtain of fog* —*vt*. to cover, as with a curtain

curtain call a performer's return to the stage to acknowledge applause

curtain raiser a brief entertainment before the main show

curt´sy *n*. a polite bow —*vi*. to make a bow

cur·va´ceous *adj*. of a woman with an attractive figure —**cur·va´ceous·ness** *n*.

cur´va·ture´ *n*. a curve or curved part

curve *n*. a line or surface that deviates in a relatively smooth fashion —*vi*., *vt*. to deviate from a straight line or surface

cush´y *adj*. easy, as *a cushy job*

cusp *n*. a point or projection; an intersection of two lines —**cus´pi·date, cus´pi·dat·ed** *adj*.

cus´pid *n*. a tooth characterized by a single projection

cuss *n*. a person or animal, often used affectionately —*vi*., *vt*. to curse

cus´tard *n*. a thick, creamy dessert

cus·to´di·an *n*. a caretaker, as of an art collection, a building, etc. —**cus·to´di·al** *adj*.

cus´to·dy *n*. the act of caring for and protecting

cus´tom *adj*. made to order —*n*. common practice; tradition

cus´tom·ar·y *adj*. usual; according to custom —**cus´tom·ar·i·ly** *adv*.

cus´tom–built´ *adj*. made to the buyer's specifications

cus´tom·er *n*. one who patronizes a business

cus´tom·house *n*. a clearing house at a port of entry for imports and exports

cus´tom·ize *vt*. to make or alter to suit the buyer's specifications

cus´tom–made *adj*. custom-built

cut *n*. an incision; a reduction; a sharp, derogatory comment —*vi*. to use a sharp instrument; to cause discomfort, as *a cutting remark*; to move quickly —*vt*. to penetrate with a sharp instrument; to reduce or trim, as *a cut in staff*; to offend with a sharp remark; to pass across or through; to discontinue or stop —**a cut above** significantly better —**cut and dried** a foregone conclusion; routine —**cut loose** to act with abandon —**cut no ice** of no influence —**cut out for** suited to —**cut through** get to the point

cu·ta´ne·ous *adj*. relating to the skin

cut´back´ *n.* a reduction in production, personnel, expenses, etc.

cu´ti·cle *n.* the outer layer of skin: the epidermis; the hardened skin around the nails

cut´ler·y *n.* utensils for cutting

cut´let *n.* a slice of meat from the rib or leg; a chopped meat patty

cut´off *adj.* of an established limit — *n.* a shortcut; a valve or other device for shutting off flow

cut´-rate *adj.* of that offered for a reduced price; of questionable quality

cut´throat *adj.* murderous; unmerciful, relentless —*n.* a murderer

cutting *adj.* of a sharp instrument; sharp or piercing, as *a cutting wit* —*n.* the act of slicing, piercing, etc.; anything cut off

cutting board a wood, plastic, etc. surface used for cutting

cutting edge the latest innovation

cut´up *n.* a joker

cu·vée´ *n.* a particular blend of wine

cy´cle *n.* the time during which an event or series of events occurs; a bicycle or motorcycle —*vi.* to occur in cycles; to pass through one occurrence; to ride a bicycle, etc.

cy´clic, cy´cli·cal *adj.* occurring in cycles —**cy´cli·cal·ly** *adv.*

cy´clist *n.* one who rides a bicycle or motorcycle

cy´clone´ *n.* a violent, rotating windstorm; a device used to separate materials by centrifigal force

cyclone cellar an underground shelter for safety from windstorms

cy´clo·tron´ *n.* a particle accelerator

cyn´ic *n.* one who suspects or denies the sincerity of others —**cyn´i·cal** *adj.* —**cyn´i·cism** *n.*

cy´no·sure *n.* a well-known personality

cy·tol´o·gy *n.* the science dealing with the study of cells

czar *n.* formerly, a male monarch; one having great power

d, D fourth letter of the English alphabet; in Roman characters, the symbol for 500

dab *n.* a small quantity —*vi., vt.* to pat lightly

dab´ble *vi.* to engage in superficially

daf´fy *adj.* silly, ridiculous

daft *adj.* insane; foolish

dai´ly *adj.* taking place each day — *adv.* every day

daily double a wager to choose winners in two specified events from a series of events

dain´ty *adj.* delicate; fragile —**dain´ti·ly** *adv.* —**dain´ti·ness** *n.*

dair´y *n.* a place for the processing or sale of milk and milk products

dairy cattle cows cultivated for their milk

dairy farm a farm that raises cattle for the production of milk products

daisy chain a connected series

dal´li·ance *n.* flirtation

dal´ly *vi.* to flirt or trifle with; to waste time

dam *n.* a barrier to hold back the flow, as of liquid; an obstruction — *vt.* to hold back as with a dam; to obstruct

dam´age *n.* breakage; injury causing a loss of value —*vt.* to mar or injure —**dam´age·a·ble** *adj.*

dam´ages *n.* compensation ordered or paid for damage or injury

dam´ask *n.* a linen fabric; a rose color —*adj.* of damask linen; rose colored

dame *n.* a matron

damp *adj.* slightly moist —*n.* humidity; moisture —*vt.* to moisten; to slow a fire by reducing the air supply; to check, as sound waves —**damp´ish** *adj.* —**damp´ly** *adv.* —**damp´ness** *n.*

damp´en *vt.* to moisten; to check or deaden, as sound; to lessen, as enthusiasm —*vi.* to become moist —**damp´en·er** *n.*

damp´er *n.* a valve for controlling air

flow in a line; a device that deadens, as the vibration of strings on a piano

lance *n.* graceful, rhythmic movement in time to music —*vi.*, *vt.* to move in rhythm to music —**danc´er** *n.*

danc´er·cise *n.* rhythmic exercise set to music

dan´der *n.* temper; anger

dan´di·fy *vt.* to dress like a dude

dan´dy *adj.* first–rate —*n.* a man who is overly attentive to his appearance —**dan´dy·ish** *adj.* —**dan´dy·ism** —**dan´di·ly** *adv.*

dan´ger *n.* that liable to cause injury or pain

dan´ger·ous *adj.* perilous; liable or able to cause injury or harm —**dan´ger·ous·ly** *adv.* —**dan´ger·ous·ness** *n.*

dan´gle *vi.*, *vt.* to hang loosely

dank *adj.* disagreeably damp; clammy —**dank´ly** *adv.* —**dank´ness** *n.*

dap´per *adj.* stylish; neatly and smartly dressed; alert, active —**dap´per·ly** *adv.* —**dap´per·ness** *n.*

dare *n.* a challenge —*vi.* to be sufficiently bold —*vt.* to have the necessary courage; to challenge —**dar´ing** *adj.* —**dar´ing·ly** *adv.* —**dar´ing·ness** *n.*

dare´dev·il *adj.* bold and adventurous —*n.* one who is willing to take chances; one who performs hazardous acts, esp. as part of a public performance —**dare´dev·il·ry**, **dare´dev·il·try** *n.*

dark *adj.* lacking light; gloomy, dismal; sinister; unenlightened: *kept in the dark* —*n.* a lack of light; night —**dark´ish** *adj.* —**dark´ly** *adv.* —**dark´ness** *n.*

dark´en *vi.* to become dark or darker —*vt.* to make dark or darker; to cause to become obscure or confusing —**dark´en·er** *n.*

dark horse one who is unexpectedly successful, as in a horse race or political contest

dark´room *n.* a room for processing photographic film

dart *n.* a pointed missile used as a weapon or for games; a sudden rapid movement —*vi.*, *vt.* to move suddenly and rapidly

dash *n.* a hasty move; a mark (-) of punctuation; a small amount —*vi.* to rush; to smash —*vt.* to thrust or smash violently; to act hastily

dash´board *n.* the panel of controls and gauges at the front of the passenger compartment of an automobile

dash´ing *adj.* adventurous, gallant; jaunty; stylishly elegant or splendid —**dash´ing·ly** *adv.*

das´tard *n.* a malicious or cowardly person —**das´tard·li·ness** *n.* —**das´tard·ly** *adj.*

da´ta *n. pl., sing.* **dat´um** information; facts or figures used in analysis

da´ta·base *n.* an orderly collection of related data, especially as stored in a computer

data processing *n.* the manipulation of data, especially by a computer

date *n.* a point in time, stated as a day, month and year; an appointment; a companion at a social function; a palm tree or its fruit —*vi.* to originate or exist from a particular time; to become obsolete: *the work rules have become dated*; to accompany socially —*vt.* to mark with or determine the date of; to arrange a meeting with

date´book *n.* an appointment book

dat´ed *adj.* marked with a date; from a previous time; out of style

daub *vi.*, *vt.* to apply crudely, as paint, plaster, etc.

daugh´ter *n.* a female offspring

daugh´ter-in-law *n.* a son's wife

daunt *vt.* to discourage

daunt´less *adj.* daring; heroic; not to

be discouraged —**daunt˘less·ly** *adv.* —**daunt˘less·ness** *n.*

dav·en·port *n.* (*Brit.*) a type of desk; (*US*) a sofa

daw˘dle *vi., vt.* to waste time

dawn *n.* the start of daylight; a beginning —*vi.* to begin, as light in the morning sky

day *n.* the daylight hours, between sunrise and sunset; a 24-hour period; an era, as *olden days*

day˘bed *n.* a lounge that can be used for a bed

day˘book *n.* a daily journal

day˘break *n.* dawn

day camp a camp program that does not provide overnight accommodations

day care the tending of children during the day or after school hours; a facility where children are cared for

day˘dream *n.* a fantasy or dreamlike thoughts experienced while awake —*vi.* to be lost in reverie

day laborer a worker who is hired and paid daily as needed

day˘light *n.* sunlight

day nursery a day care facility

day one the start of a venture or project

day room a recreation room

day school a private school that does not provide overnight accommodations

day shift the working hours from early morning until late afternoon

day˘time *n.* the hours between sunrise and sunset

day˘-to-day˘ *adj.* regular; routine

daze *n.* a stupor; bewilderment —*vt.* to stun; to bewilder —**daz˘ed·ly** *adv.*

daz˘zle *vi., vt.* to blind temporarily with bright light; to amaze, as by something exceptional —**daz˘zler** *n.* —**daz˘zling·ly** *adv.*

dea˘con, dea˘con·ess *n.* a man or woman who is a lay officer in a church; a minister's assistant

de·ac˘ti·vate *vt.* to make a thing inoperable or ineffective; to release something or someone from military service —**de·ac·ti·va˘tion** *n.* —**de·ac·ti·va˘tor** *n.*

dead *adj.* lacking life; lacking vitality or brilliance, as *dead sound* or a *dead color*; dispassionate: *dead to emotion*; numb: *my arm feels dead*; ancient or out of date: *a dead language*; no longer productive or useful; absolute: *his assessment was dead on*; exhausted —**dead˘ness** *n.*

dead˘beat *adj.* an idler; one who doesn't repay debts

dead˘bolt *n.* a latch that secures a door with a heavy bolt that can only be operated with a key

dead center at the exact center

dead˘en *vt.* to anesthetize; to reduce, as the brilliance of color or the loudness of sound

dead end a street or road without an outlet; an unprofitable venture, course, etc. —**dead˘-end˘** *adj.* offering no means for continuation or advancement: *a dead-end job*

dead˘fall *n.* a snare designed to drop a heavy object on its victim; a fallen tree and the debris it carries

dead˘head *n.* a commercial vehicle running without paying cargo or passengers; a dull or stupid person —*vi.* to travel without cargo

dead heat a race that ends in a tie

dead letter a piece of mail that cannot be delivered or returned

dead˘line *n.* a date or time established for the completion of something, as a task or a payment

dead˘lock *n.* a stalemate

dead˘ly *adj.* apt to cause serious injury or death; lethal; extremely accurate or effective: *deadly aim, deadly satire* —**dead˘li·ness** *n.*

dead˘pan *adj., adv.* without expression —*n.* a blank look

dead reckoning estimating position based on speed, travel time, and experience

dead ringer a precise match

dead′wood n. something useless

deaf adj. unable to hear; unwilling to listen or be persuaded —**deaf′ly** adv. —**deaf′ness** n.

deaf′en vt. to make deaf; to overwhelm with sound —**deaf′en·ing** adj. —**deaf′en·ing·ly** adv.

deaf–mute n. one who is unable to hear or speak

deal n. an agreement; a business transaction; a distribution —vi. to take action; to do business —vt. to distribute, as playing cards —**deal′er** n.

deal′er·ship n. a business authorized by a manufacturer or distributor to market their product in a particular area

dean n. an officer in a school or college having jurisdiction over a particular group: *dean of men, dean of faculty*; one who is senior or preeminent: *the dean of country music*

dear adj. cherished; expensive —n. a loved one —adv. with affection; at great cost —**dear′ly** adv. —**dear′ness** n.

dearth n. a lack or scarcity

death n. the termination of life

death′bed n. the final hours of a person's life; the bed or place where one dies

death benefit an insurance payment to a beneficiary on the death of the policyholder

death′blow n. an event that causes death

death certificate the official record of a person's death

death′less adj. undying; enduring —**death′less·ly** adv. —**death′less·ness** n.

death′like adj. gaunt; pale

death′ly adj. ghastly; deathlike —adv. to a deadly extent —**death′li·ness** n.

death rate a ratio of the number of deaths per thousand persons for a particular area over a specified period of time

death′trap n. an unsafe place, predicament, etc.

death warrant official authorization to put a person to death

death′watch n. attendance at the bedside of a dying person

death wish a desire for one's own death

de·ba′cle n. the total dissolution of order; a rout

de·bar′ vt. to exclude from a right or privilege; to prohibit or restrict —**de·bar′ment** n.

de·bark′ vi., vt. to leave a ship or aircraft; disembark —**de·bar·ka′tion** n.

de·base′ vt. to lower in worth or purity; to adulterate —**de·base′ment** n.

de·bate′ n. an airing of opposing views; a formal argument —vi., vt. to discuss openly; to engage in formal argumentation; to consider or contemplate —**de·bat′a·ble** adj. —**de·bat′er** n.

de·bauch′ vt. to corrupt or debase —**de·bauch′ed·ly** adv. —**de·bauch′ed·ness** n. —**de·bauch′er** n.

de·bauch′er·y, de·bauch′ment n. revelry; intemperance; excessive indulgence in sensual gratification

de·ben′ture n. a promissory note

de·bil′i·tate′ vt. to drain of strength or energy —**de·bil·i·ta′tion** n. —**de·bil′i·ta·tive** adj.

de·bil′i·ty n. weakness; an infirmity

deb·o·nair′, deb·o·naire′ adj. sophisticated, urbane; nonchalant, carefree —**deb·o·nair′ly** adv. —**deb·o·nair′ness** n.

de·brief′ vt. to examine and instruct, as for a returning agent, emissary, or ambassador

dé·bris´ *n.* scattered remains; rubble

debt *n.* something owed; an obligation

debt´or *n.* one who owes

de·bug´ *vt.* to seek out and correct errors or malfunctions, as in a computer program

de·bunk´ *vt.* to expose as false; demystify

de·but´ *n.* a first public appearance; a beginning

deb´u·tante *n.* a young woman making her first formal appearance in society

dec´ade *n.* a group of ten; ten years

dec´a·dence, dec´a·den·cy *n.* a deterioration or decline, as in moral standards; a time of decline, as in art or literature —**dec´a·dent** *adj.* —**dec´a·dent·ly** *adv.*

de·caf´fein·ate *vt.* to remove the caffeine, as from coffee or soft drinks —**de·caf´fein·at·ed** *adj.*

dec´a·gon *n.* a geometric form with ten sides

dec·a·he´dron *n.* a solid with ten surfaces

de´cal *n.* a decorative design for transferring to glass, wood, etc.

de·cal´ci·fy *vt.* to remove or reduce calcium, as from bones or teeth — *vi.* to lose calcium

de·cant´ *vt.* to pour off a liquid, as wine, to eliminate sediment; to pour from one container to another —**de·can´ta·tion** *n.* —**de·cant´er** *n.*

de·cap´i·tate *vt.* to behead —**de·cap´i·ta´tion** *n.* —**de·cap´i·ta·tor** *n.*

de·cath´lon *n.* an athletic competition comprising ten events

de·cay´ *n.* the decomposition of organic matter; a slow deterioration —*vi.* to decompose; to deteriorate slowly —*vt.* to cause decomposition or deterioration

de·cease´ *vi.* to die —**de·ceased´** *adj.* —**de·ce´dent** *n.*

de·ceit´ *n.* a misrepresentation; a dishonest action; trickery

de·ceit´ful *adj.* marked by deception; fraudulent —**de·ceit´ful·ly** *adv.* —**de·ceit´ful·ness** *n.*

de·ceive´ *vt.* to mislead, as by lying or trickery —*vi.* to practice deceit —**de·ceiv´a·ble** *adj.* —**de·ceiv´er** *n.* —**de·ceiv´ing·ly** *adv.*

de·cel´er·ate *vi., vt.* to slow; to reduce speed —**de·cel·er·a´tion** *n.* —**de·cel´er·a·tor** *n.*

de´cent *adj.* proper; respectable; conforming to accepted standards; moderately good: *a decent performance* —**de´cen·cy, de´cent·ness** *n.* —**de´cent·ly** *adv.*

de·cen´tral·ize *vt.* to disperse personnel and authority, as for a corporation or government entity —**de·cen·tral·i·za´tion** *n.*

de·cep´tion *n.* practicing deceit; being deceived; a dishonest act or misrepresentation

de·cep´tive *adj.* misleading; designed to mislead or misrepresent —**de·cep´tive·ly** *adv.* —**de·cep´tive·ness** *n.*

de·cer´ti·fy *vt.* to revoke a license, endorsement, or authorization —**de·cer´ti·fi·ca´tion** *n.*

de·cide´ *vt.* to settle, as a dispute; to bring to a decision —*vi.* to make a decision —**de·cid·a·bil´i·ty** *n.* —**de·cid´a·ble** *adj.* —**de·cid´er** *n.*

de·cid´ed *adj.* certain, clear-cut; without reservation; determined, resolute —**de·cid´ed·ly** *adv.* —**de·cid´ed·ness** *n.*

de·cid´u·ous *adj.* falling off or shed at specific seasons, as leaves or antlers; temporary, ephemeral —**de·cid´u·ous·ly** *adv.* —**de·cid´u·ous·ness** *n.*

dec´i·mal *adj.* based on the number 10 —*n.* a decimal fraction

decimal point the dot between a whole number and its fraction in base ten

decimal system a number system in

base 10

dec·i·mate *vt*. to select by lot and kill one in ten; to destroy or slaughter a large part of —**dec·i·ma´tion** *n*.

de·ci´pher *vt*. to interpret, as that which is obscure, poorly written or encoded —**de·ci´pher·a·ble** *adj*. —**de·ci´pher·er** *n*. —**de·ci´pher·ment** *n*.

de·ci´sion *n*. a conclusion or judgment made on a matter under consideration

de·ci´sive *adj*. conclusive; resolving uncertainty; determined, positive; extremely important —**de·ci´sive·ly** *adv*. —**de·ci´sive·ness** *n*.

de·claim´ *vi., vt*. to recite dramatically; proclaim; to vehemently speak out —*vi*. to recite eloquently —**dec·la·ma´tion** *n*. —**de·clam´a·to·ry** *adj*.

de·clar´a·tive *adj*. effecting to inform; making an assertion —**de·clar´a·tive·ly** *adv*.

de·clare´ *vt*. to announce formally; to state positively or emphatically; to reveal or name —*vi*. to make a positive statement —**de·clar´a·ble** *adj*. —**dec´la·ra´tion** *n*. —**de·clar´er** *n*.

de·clen´sion *n*. a declining; a slope or descent; a deviation —**de·clen´sion·al** *adj*.

dec·li·na´tion *n*. a slope or descent; deviation, as from a standard; a courteous refusal —**dec·li·na´tion·al** *adj*.

de·cline´ *n*. a downward slope or trend; deterioration or decay —*vi*. to gradually deteriorate; to refuse politely; to slope downward —*vt*. to refuse to accept; to cause to incline or slope

de·cliv´i·ty *n*. a sloping on a downward course —**de·cliv´i·tous, de·cliv´ous** *adj*.

de·code´ *vt*. to translate a coded message

de·com·mis´sion *vt*. to take out of service

de·com·pose´ *vt*. to break down into basic elements —*vi*. to disintegrate or decay —**de·com·pos·a·bil´i·ty** *n*. —**de·com·pos´a·ble** *adj*. —**de·com·po·si´tion** *n*.

de·com·press´ *vt*. to reduce pressure on, as for a deep-sea diver; to permit expansion by reducing pressure —**de·com·pres´sion** *n*.

decompression chamber an area with controlled air pressure to gradually acclimate to normal air pressure, as a deep-sea diver

decompression sickness a painful, potentially fatal condition caused by the formation of nitrogen bubbles in the blood due to a rapid reduction in pressure, as of a deep-sea diver who returns to the surface too quickly

de·con·tam´i·nate *vt*. to free from harmful matter; to make safe —**de·con·tam´i·nant** *n*. —**de·con·tam·i·na´tion** *n*. —**de·con·tam´i·na·tor** *n*.

de·cor´ *n*. a style of adornment, furnishings, etc. in an interior area

dec´o·rate´ *vt*. to adorn or beautify; to paint and refurnish a home, office, etc.; to plan and direct a refurbishing; to honor, as with a medal —**dec´o·ra´tion** *n*. —**dec´o·ra·tor** *n*.

dec´o·ra·tive *adj*. ornamental; aesthetic; artistic —**dec´o·ra·tive·ly** *adv*. —**dec´o·ra·tive·ness** *n*.

dec´o·rous *adj*. characterized by decorum —**dec´o·rous·ly** *adv*. —**dec´o·rous·ness** *n*.

de·cor´ti·cate *vt*. to peel; to remove the outer layer from —**de·cor·ti·ca´tion** *n*.

de·co´rum *n*. fine manners; propriety

de·cou·page´ *n*. a style of decoration characterized by designs or illustrations affixed to a surface and coated with varnish or laquer —*vt.*

de·coy *n.* a thing used to mislead or lure —*vi.*, *vt.* to lure, as into a trap

de·crease *vi.*, *vt.* to become or cause to become gradually less or smaller —**de·crease** *n.* the process or lessening; the amount of reduction —**de·creas·ing·ly** *adv.*

de·cree *n.* an official proclamation or order —*vt.* to order in an official capacity —*vi.* to issue a decree

de·crep·it *adj.* worn out, as by age or use —**de·crep·it·ness** *n.* —**de·crep·i·tude** *n.*

de·cry *vt.* to denounce; to criticize or condemn —**de·cri·al** *n.* —**de·cri·er** *n.*

ded·i·cate *vt.* to set apart for a special purpose; to devote oneself to a cause, course of action, etc.; to open with a ceremony, as of a building or park; to pay homage by dedicating, as of a book —**ded·i·ca·tion** *n.* —**ded·i·ca·tive** *adj.* —**ded·i·ca·tor** *n.*

ded·i·cat·ed *adj.* given over totally to a cause, a course of action, etc.; designed for a specific use: *a dedicated telephone line linking us to the Internet* —**ded·i·cat·ed·ly** *adv.*

de·duce *vt.* to conclude or infer by reasoning —**de·duc·i·bil·i·ty** *n.* —**de·duc·i·ble** *adj.*

de·duct *vt.* to take away: to subtract; to conclude by reasoning: to deduce —**de·duct·i·bil·i·ty** *n.* —**de·duct·i·ble** *adj.*

de·duc·tion *n.* a subtraction or the amount subtracted; the process of reasoning to reach a conclusion; the conclusion reached —**de·duc·tive** *adj.* —**de·duc·tive·ly** *adv.*

deed *n.* an act; a notable achievement; a legal document used to convey interest in property —*vt.* to transfer by means of a legal document

deem *vi.*, *vt.* to believe; to judge; to have as an opinion

de—em·pha·size *vt.* to reduce the importance of —**de—em·pha·sis** *n.*

deep *adj.* extending or located far from a reference point; of a specific extent: *ten inches deep*; penetrating; low in tone or pitch; abstract, difficult to comprehend; serious, earnest: *deep sorrow*; —**deep·ly** *adv.* —**deep·ness** *n.*

deep·en *vi.*, *vt.* to become or make deeper

deep·freeze *vt.* to freeze food quickly to very low temperature

deep·fry *vt.* to cook in a vat of hot grease

deep·root·ed *adj.* having deep roots; firmly established

deep·seat·ed *adj.* firmly established; difficult to change or overcome, as *deep-seated prejudice*

deep space outer space beyond the solar system

de·face *vt.* to disfigure or mar; to damage in appearance, value, etc. —**de·face·a·ble** *adj.* —**de·face·ment** *n.* —**de·fac·er** *n.*

de fac·to *Latin* existing in fact

de·fame *vt.* to damage one's reputation by slander or libel —**def·a·ma·tion** *n.* —**de·fam·a·to·ry** *adj.* —**de·fam·er** *n.*

de·fault *n.* a failure to fulfill an obligation or duty; a failure to appear, as for a competition —*vi.*, *vt.* to fail in fulfilling a duty or obligation —**de·fault·er** *n.*

de·feat *n.* the act of conqering or the state of being conquered —*vt.* to overpower or conquer; to frustrate another's efforts

de·feat·ist *n.* one who expects or readily accepts defeat —*adj.* marked by an expectation or willingness to accept misfortune —**de·feat·ism** *n.*

def·e·cate *vi.* to eliminate waste matter from the body —*vt.* to clear of impurities —**def·e·ca·tion** *n.* —**def·e·ca·tor** *n.*

de´fect, de·fect´ n. an imperfection or fault; a deficiency —**de·fect´** vi. to abandon a cause, one's country, etc., esp. to join the opposition — **de·fec´tion** n. —**de·fec´tor** n.

de·fec´tive adj. imperfect or deficient in some way —**de·fec´tive·ly** adv. —**de·fec´tive·ness** n.

de·fence´ (Brit.) n. protection from harm; a means of protection; justification for an action; in law, a defendant and his or her solicitor or the arguments they present

de·fend´ vt. to protect, as from danger; to justify, as one's actions; to contest, as a charge or suit —vi. to make a defense —**de·fend´a·ble** adj. —**de·fend´er** n.

de·fend´ant n. in law, one against whom an action is brought

de·fen·es·tra´tion n. the act of throwing out of a window

de·fense´ (US) n. protection from harm; a means of protection; justification for an action; in law, a defendant and his or her lawyer or the arguments they present

de·fense´less adj. without protection; unable to defend oneself; helpless —**de·fense´less·ly** adv. — **de·fense´less·ness** n.

de·fen´si·ble adj. capable of being justified or defended —**de·fen·si·bil·i·ty, de·fen´si·ble·ness** n. —**de·fen´si·bly** adv.

de·fen´sive adj. resistant to criticism; recalcitrant; tending to deny or justify, as one's actions —n. prepared to resist —**de·fen´sive·ly** adv. —**de·fen´sive·ness** n.

de·fer´ vi., vt. to postpone; to procrastinate; to yield in deference to the wishes or judgment of another —**de·fer´ra·ble** adj. —**de·fer´rer** n. —**de·ferred´** adj.

def´er·ence n. courteous regard

def´er·ent, def´er·en´tial adj. respectful; polite; obedient —**def´er·en´tial·ly** adv.

de·fi´ance n. bold resistance or opposition; a disposition to challenge —**de·fi´ant** adj. —**de·fi´ant·ly** adv.

de·fi´cience, de·fi´cien·cy n. a lack of something; the nature of a thing that is lacking

de·fi´cient adj. lacking in something; defective in some way — **de·fi´cient·ly** adv.

def´i·cit n. a shortage; the amount of a shortage

deficit financing borrowing to cover the excess of expenditures over income

deficit spending a condition characterized by expenditures that exceed income

de·file´ vt. to corrupt or debase; to pollute; to profane, as a reputation —**de·file´ment** n. —**de·fil´er** n. — **de·fil´ing·ly** adv.

de·fine´ vt. to give precise value or meaning, as of a word; to describe; to specify a limit or boundary — **de·fin´a·ble** adj. —**de·fin´a·bly** adv. —**de·fin´er** n.

def´i·nite adj. having exact limits; clear in meaning; certain or positive —**def´i·nite·ly** adv. —**def´i·nite·ness** n.

def·i·ni´tion n. a statement of limits or meaning; the condition of being clearly outlined

de·fin´i·tive adj. conclusive; precise; being the most authoritative or accurate —**de·fin´i·tive·ly** adv. —**de·fin´i·tive·ness** n.

de·flate´ vi., vt. to collapse or cause to collapse by the release of gas; to make smaller or less in value; to dishearten: *to deflate one's hopes* —**de·fla´tion** n. —**de·fla´tion·ar·y** adj.

de·flect´ vi., vt. turn aside or cause to turn aside —**de·flect´a·ble** adj. —**de·flec´tion** n. —**de·flec´tive** adj. —**de·flec´tor** n.

de·fo´li·ant n. a chemical that

causes a living plant to shed its leaves —de·fo´li·ate vt. —de·fo´li·a´tion n. —de·fo´li·a·tor n.

de·for´est vt. to clear an area of trees —de·for·est·a´tion n. —de·for´est·er n.

de·form´ vt. to damage the natural form or appearance of; to disfigure —vi. to become disfigured —de·form·a·bil´i·ty n. —de·form´a·ble adj. —de·for·ma´tion n.

de·formed´ adj. misshapen or disfigured —de·for´mi·ty n.

de·fraud´ vt. to take or withhold by deceit; to swindle —de·fraud·a´tion n. —de·fraud´er n.

de·fray´ vt. to provide for payment or bear the expense of —de·fray´a·ble adj. —de·fray´er, de·fray´ment n. —de·fray´er n.

de·frost´ vt. to remove frost or ice; to thaw —de·frost´er n.

deft adj. skillful; dexterous —deft´ly adv. —deft´ness n.

de·funct´ adj. no longer existing; dead —de·func´tive adj. —de·funct´ness n.

de·fy´ vt. to openly resist or oppose; to challenge; to baffle: to defy understanding

de·gen´er·ate adj. morally depraved: corrupted; having become deteriorated —n. one who is depraved or corrupted —vi. to decline in quality —de·gen´er·a·cy, de·gen´er·ate·ness n. —de·gen´er·ate·ly adv. —de·gen´er·a·tive adj.

de·gen·er·a´tion n. the process of becoming worse; the progressive deterioration of an organ or tissue

de·grad´a·ble adj. that can be reduced chemically —de·grad·a·bil´i·ty n.

de·grade´ vt. to disgrace or debase; to reduce in value, quality, rank, etc.; to reduce by erosion —vi. to degenerate —deg´ra·da´tion n.

de·grad´ed adj. reduced in rank, quality, etc.; corrupted or debased —de·grad´ed·ly adv. —de·grad´ed·ness n.

de·grad´ing adj. debasing; humiliating —de·grad´ing·ly adv.

de·grease´ vt. to cleanse or improve by removing grease: degrease a fitting, degrease the soup —de·greas´er n.

de·gree´ n. a relative ranking, as of position, intensity, etc.; a unit on a scale, as for temperature, angles, arcs, etc. —by degrees little by little —to a degree somewhat

de·hu´man·ize vt. to strip of emotion or other human attributes; to make mechanical —de·hu·man·i·za´tion n.

de·hu·mid´i·fi·er n. a device that removes moisture from the air —de·hu·mid·i·fi·ca´tion n. —de·hu·mid´i·fy vt.

de·hy´drate vi. to lose water —vt. to remove or deprive of water —de·hy·dra´tion n. —de·hy·dra´tor n.

de·ice´ vt., vi. to remove ice or prevent ice from forming

de´i·fy vt. to exalt, idealize; to look upon or worship as a god —de·if´ic adj. —de·i·fi·ca´tion n. —de´i·fi·er n.

de´ism n. the belief in creation by a supreme being who abstains from involvement in the world or its inhabitants —de´ist n. —de·is´tic, de·is´ti·cal adj. —de·is´ti·cal·ly adv.

de´i·ty n. a god; a divinity

de·ject´ vt. to make unhappy; to depress—de·jec´tion n.

de·ject´ed adj. dispirited; depressed —de·ject´ed·ly adv. —de·ject´ed·ness n.

de·lay´ vt. to postpone; to slow or detain —vi. to linger —n. that which causes lateness; the length of a postponement —de·lay´er n.

de´le vt. to take out: delete

de·lec´ta·ble adj. pleasing; delightful —de·lec·ta·bil´i·ty, de·lec´ta·ble·

ness n. —**de·lec´ta·bly** adv.

de·lec·ta´tion n. delight; entertainment

del´e·gate´ n. one authorized to speak or act for others —vt. to authorize or entrust another to act; to send as a representative —**del´e·ga´tion** n.

de·lete´ vt. to eliminate, cross out, or erase

del´e·te´ri·ous adj. harmful; injurious —**del·e·te´ri·ous·ly** adv. —**del·e·te´ri·ous·ness** n.

de·lib´er·ate adj. intentional; carefully planned; unhurried —vi., vt. to think about and consider carefully —**de·lib´er·ate·ly** adv. —**de·lib´er·ate·ness** n.

de·lib´er·a´tion n. careful consideration; discussion and consideration of all sides of an issue, as by a panel of judges

de·lib´er·a·tive adj. contemplative; attributable to deliberation —**de·lib´er·a·tive·ly** adv. —**de·lib´er·a·tive·ness** n.

del´i·ca·cy n. the quality of being beautiful or refined; frailty; requiring sensitivity: *a matter of some delicacy*; a special food

del´i·cate adj. fine or dainty; fragile; subtle; requiring or displaying remarkable tact —**del´i·cate·ly** adv. —**del´i·cate·ness** n.

del·i·ca·tes´sen n. a store where ready-to-eat foods are sold; the food sold in such a store

de·li´cious adj. pleasing to the senses —**de·li´cious·ly** adv. —**de·li´cious·ness** n.

de´light n. a thing that gives great pleasure; a quality that pleases: charm —vi. to give or take great pleasure —vt. to please or gratify —**de·light´ful** adj. —**de·light´ful·ly** adv. —**de·light´ful·ness** n.

de·lin´e·ate vt. to depict or describe with drawings or words —**de·lin·e·a´tion** n. —**de·lin´e·a·tive** adj. —**de·lin´e·a·tor** n.

de·lin´quen·cy n. failure to perform as required by duty or law; a fault or misdeed

de·lin´quent adj. of that contrary to what duty or the law requires; overdue, as an obligation —n. one who acts contrary to what duty or the law requires —**de·lin´quent·ly** adv.

de·lir´i·ous adj. marked by delirium; extremely pleased or excited —**de·lir´i·ous·ly** adv. —**de·lir´i·ous·ness** n.

de·lir´i·um n. a state of altered consciousness marked by anxiety, confused speech, hallucinations, confusion, etc. —**de·lir´i·um tre´mens** an extreme case of delirium brought on by withdrawal from or excessive ingestion of alcoholic beverages

de·liv´er vt. to carry to or give over to another; to say: *deliver a speech or lecture*; to bring forth or produce, as a baby; to rescue: *deliver from the enemy* —vi. to fulfill a promise; to perform well —**de·liv´er·a·bil´i·ty** n. —**de·liv´er·a·ble** adj. —**de·liv´er·er** n.

de·liv´er·ance n. the condition of being set free; a pardon; redemption

de·liv´er·y n. a setting free; liberation; the conveyance or transference of goods; childbirth; one's speaking ability

dell n. a small grove; a shady retreat

de·louse´ vt. to free of lice

del´ta n. the name or symbol (Δ) for the fourth letter of the Greek alphabet; something shaped like a triangle; an alluvial deposit at the mouth of a river

del´toid adj. triangular —n. a triangular muscle that covers the shoulder

de·lude´ vt. to mislead or deceive —**de·lud´er** n.

del′uge *n.* a great flood; heavy rain-fall; a thing that overwhelms —*vt.* to flood; to overwhelm

de·lu′sion *n.* a false or irrational belief —**de·lu′sion·al, de·lu′sion·ar·y** *adj.*

de·lu′sive, de·lu′so·ry *adj.* misleading; deceitful —**de·lu′sive·ly** *adv.* —**de·lu′sive·ness** *n.*

de·luxe′ *adj.* luxurious; elegant

delve *vi.* to search resolutely

de·mag′net·ize *vt.* to cancel or neutralize magnetic properties

dem′a·gogue *n.* a revolutionary; one who arouses followers by appeals to emotion or prejudice —**dem′a·gog′ic** *adj.* —**dem·a·gog′i·cal·ly** *adv.* —**dem′a·gogu·er·y, dem′a·gog·y** *n.*

de·mand′ *n.* an urgent or bold request; a thing requested; a formal request: a claim; a need —*vt.* to request boldly; to claim as due; to inquire formally; to require: *the job demands all of his time* —*vi.* to make a demand —**de·mand′a·ble** *adj.* —**de·mand′er** *n.*

de·mand′ing *adj.* difficult, challenging; hard to please —**de·mand′ing·ly** *adv.*

de·mar·ca′tion *n.* a separation or boundary; the fixing of boundaries or limits —**de·mar′cate** *vt.* —**de·mar′ca·tor** *n.*

de·mean′ *vt.* to debase or humble

de·mean′or *n.* one's behavior or appearance

de·ment′ed *adj.* mentally ill —**de·ment′ed·ly** *adv.* —**de·ment′ed·ness** *n.*

de·men′tia *n.* impairment of mental faculties; mental illness —**de·men′tial** *adj.*

de·men′tia prae′cox′ *n.* schizophrenia

dem′i·god *n.* one who is godlike

de·mise′ *n.* a termination of existence; death; a transfer of rights or authority —*vt.*, *vi.* to transfer or be

transferred as by will or abdication

dem′i·tasse *n.* literally, half a cup; strong black coffee served after a meal or the small cup in which it is served

dem′o *n.* a demonstration, such as an audio or video tape showcasing an artist, a piece of music, etc.

de·mo′bi·lize *vt.* to disband, as troops; to discharge from military service —**de·mo·bi·li·za′tion** *n.*

de·moc′ra·cy *n.* the principle of the equality of rights, opportunity, etc. for all people; political control shared by the populace

dem′o·crat′ *n.* one who advocates government by the people —**dem′o·crat′ic** *adj.* —**dem′o·crat′i·cal·ly** *n.*

de·moc′ra·tize *vt.*, *vi.* to make or become democratic —**de·moc′ra·ti·za′tion** *n.*

dem·o·graph′ics *n.* the classification of a population by age, sex, etc., especially for the marketing of consumer products —**dem·o·graph′ic, dem·o·graph′i·cal** *adj.* —**dem·o·graph′i·cal·ly** *adv.*

de·mog′ra·phy *n.* the study of the vital and social statistics within a population —**de·mog′ra·pher, de·mog′ra·phist** *n.*

de·mol′ish *vt.* to tear down, as a building; to destroy completely; to severely damage, as a person's reputation —**de·mol′ish·er** *n.* —**de·mol′ish·ment**

dem′o·li′tion *n.* the process of tearing down or destroying —**dem′o·li′tions** *n.* explosives —**dem′o·li′tion·ist** *n.*

de′mon *n.* an evil being; one who shows great energy or enthusiasm —**de·mon′ic** *adj.* —**de·mon′i·cal·ly** *adv.*

de·mo′ni·ac, de′mo·ni′a·cal *adj.* demon-possessed; fiendish; furious; frenzied —**de·mo·ni′a·cal·ly** *adv.*

de·mon·ism *n.* a belief in demons

de·mon·ol·a·try *n.* demon worship

de·mon·ol·o·gy *n.* the study of demons and demonolatry

de·mon·stra·ble *adj.* able to be shown or verified —**de·mon·stra·bil·i·ty** *n.* —**de·mon·stra·ble·ness** *n.* —**de·mon·stra·bly** *adv.*

dem·on·strate *vt.* to prove by reasoning; to illustrate by showing in operation; to make evident, as an emotion —*vi.* to take part in a protest, as by congregating or marching —**dem·on·stra·tion** *n.* —**dem·on·stra·tor** *n.*

de·mon·stra·tive *adj.* able to be proved or verified; open and outgoing; openly affectionate —**de·mon·stra·tive·ly** *adv.* —**de·mon·stra·tive·ness** *n.*

de·mor·al·ize *vt.* to dishearten; to cause confusion —**de·mor·al·i·za·tion** *n.*

de·mote *vt.* to lessen in status or rank —**de·mo·tion** *n.*

de·mount *vt.* to take down; to remove from a mounting —**de·mount·a·ble** *adj.*

de·mur *n.* a delay or objection based on doubt —*vi.* to voice an objection

de·mure *adj.* modest, reserved; affecting modesty —**de·mure·ly** *adv.* —**de·mure·ness** *n.*

de·mur·rage *n.* compensation paid to a freight company for delaying equipment, as by failure to load or unload in a timely fashion

de·mys·ti·fy *vt.* to take the mystery from; to expose, explain —**de·mys·ti·fi·ca·tion** *n.* —**de·mys·ti·fi·er** *n.*

de·my·thol·o·gize *vt.* to explain away or remove elements considered mythical, as from a creed, belief, etc. —**de·my·thol·o·gi·za·tion** *n.* —**de·my·thol·o·giz·er** *n.*

den *n.* the lair of an animal; a gathering place, as *a den of thieves*; a room in a house that serves as a

study or retreat

de·nat·u·ral·ize *vt.* to revoke one's citizenship

de·na·ture *vt.* to change the nature or properties of, as through chemical action —**de·na·tur·ant** *n.* —**de·na·tur·a·tion** *n.*

de·ni·a·ble *adj.* possible to be disputed; that can be withheld or disowned —**de·ni·a·bil·i·ty** *n.* —**de·ni·a·bly** *adv.*

de·ni·al *n.* a refusal, as to honor a request; a disavowal; an unwillingness to believe or acknowledge

de·ni·er *n.* one who denies

de·nier *n.* a measure of the fineness of thread

den·i·grate *vt.* to cast aspersions on one's character, reputation, etc. —**den·i·gra·tion** *n.* —**den·i·gra·tor** *n.* —**den·i·gra·to·ry** *adj.*

den·im *n.* a stout cloth used for work clothes

den·i·zen *n.* an inhabitant; one who frequents a particular place —**den·i·zen·a·tion** *n.*

de·nom·i·na·tion *n.* a name or designation; a specific unit of value; a religious group or sect within a larger group —**de·nom·i·na·tion·al** *adj.* —**de·nom·i·na·tion·al·ly** *adv.*

de·nom·i·na·tion·al·ism *n.* a system of separation by classification —**de·nom·i·na·tion·al·ist** *n.*

de·nom·i·na·tor *n.* one that names; an attribute common to the members of a group; the designation in a fraction that expresses the number of parts into which the whole is divided

de·note *vt.* to signify or indicate; to serve as a symbol for —**de·not·a·ble** *adj.* —**de·no·ta·tive**, **de·no·tive** *adj.* —**de·no·ta·tive·ly** *adv.*

de·nounce *vt.* to openly condemn or accuse —**de·nounce·ment** *n.* —**de·nounc·er** *n.*

dense *adj.* compact; thick; opaque;

slow to comprehend **—dense´ly** *adv.* **—dense´ness** *n.*

den´si·ty *n.* a relative concentration of mass

dent *n.* an indentation in an otherwise smooth surface; an accomplishment, as *to put a dent in a list of tasks —vi.* to get a dent *—vt.* to cause a dent

den´tal *adj.* of the teeth **—den´tal·ly** *adv.*

den´tate *adj.* having teeth

den´ti·frice *n.* any of various products for cleaning the teeth

den´tist *n.* one who specializes in the care and treatment of the teeth **—den´tis·try** *n.*

den·ti´tion *n.* the process or time of teething; the types and arrangement of the teeth

de´nu·date *adj.* naked; stripped of foliage *—vt.* to denude **—de·nu·da´tion** *n.*

de·nude´ *vt.* to strip bare, as of foliage

de·nun´ci·ate *vt.* to denounce **—de·nun´ci·a·tor** *n.* **—de·nun´ci·a´tory** *adj.*

de·nun·ci·a´tion *n.* public condemnation **—de·nun´ci·a·tive** *adj.* **—de·nun´ci·a·tive·ly** *adv.*

de·ny´ *vt.* refuse to acknowledge, believe, or allow

de·o´dor·ant *adj.* able to mask or destroy unpleasant odors *—n.* a substance applied to the body or released into the air that masks or destroys odors **—de·o´dor·i·za´tion** *n.* **de·o´dor·ize´** *vt.* **—de·o´dor·iz·er** *n.*

de·ox·y·ri´bo·nu·cle·ic ac´id DNA, that carries the genetic code within cells

de·part´ *vi., vt.* to leave **—depart from** to deviate, as from a usual course **—de·par´ture** *n.*

de·part´ment *n.* a separate operating division, as in a business, government, or school; a field of study

or knowledge; a regular section in a periodical **—de·part·men´tal** *adj.* **—de·part·men´tal·ly** *adv.* **—de·part·men´tal·ism** *n.*

de·part·men´tal·ize *vt.* to organize into separate operating units or subdivisions **—de·part·men·tal·i·za´tion** *n.*

department store a retail establishment that sells a wide variety of merchandise from various departments or sections

de·par´ture *n.* a setting out or leaving; a change or divergence from a standard course of action

de·pend´ *vi.* to rely on; to place trust or confidence in; to be contingent upon

de·pend´a·ble *adj.* reliable; trustworthy **—de·pend·a·bil´i·ty** *n.* **—de·pend´a·ble·ness** *n.* **—de·pend´a·bly** *adv.*

de·pen´dence, **de·pen´dance** *n.* reliance on another, as for subsistence; faith or trust in another; an addiction **—de·pend´en·cy, de·pend´an·cy** *n.*

de·pend´ent *adj.* relying on something or someone else; contingent; subordinate; helpless **—de·pend´ent, de·pen´dant** *n.* one who relies on another, as for moral or financial support **—de·pend´ent·ly** *adv.*

de·per´son·al·ize *vt.* to consider or act objectively, removing personal considerations; to cause the loss of a sense of distinctiveness **—de·per·son·a·li·za´tion** *n.*

de·pict´ *vt.* to portray by drawing, sculpting, etc.; to represent or describe in words or pictures **—de·pic´tion** *n.*

dep´i·late *vt.* to eliminate hair **—dep·i·la´tion** *n.* **—dep´i·la·tor** *n.* **—de·pil´a·to·ry** *adj., n.*

de·plete´ *vt.* to use completely; to lessen gradually, as by use **—de·plet´a·ble** *adj.* **—de·ple´tion** *n.* **—de·ple´tive** *adj.*

de·plor´a·ble *adj.* tragic; distressing; unfortunate —**de·plor·a·bil´i·ty** *n.* —**de·plor´a·bly** *adv.*

de·plore´ *vt.* to condemn as wrong or unjust; to regret

de·ploy´ *vt.* to position according to a plan, as personnel or equipment —*vi.* to be positioned —**de·ploy·a·bil´i·ty** *n.* —**de·ploy´a·ble** *adj.* —**de·ploy´er** *n.* **de·ploy´ment** *n.*

de·pop·u·la´tion *n.* a sharp reduction in the number of inhabitants of an area, such as caused by disease or war —**de·pop´u·late** *vt.* —**de·pop´u·la·tor** *n.*

de·port´ *vt.* to expel from a country; to conduct oneself in a particular manner

de´por·ta´tion *n.* banishment from a country —**de·port´a·ble** *adj.* —**de·port·ee´** *n.*

de·port´ment *n.* one's behavior

de·pos´it *n.* something of value placed with another for safekeeping or as security; something left behind, as silt by a flood —*vt.* to place or leave behind —**de·pos´i·tor** *n.* —**de·pos´i·to·ry** *n.*

dep·o·si´tion *n.* removal from power; the act of depositing; testimony taken under oath outside the court —**dep·o·si´tion·al** *adj.*

de´pot´ *n.* a railway or bus station; a storehouse

de·prave´ *vt.* to corrupt or pervert — **dep·ra·va´tion** *n.* —**de·praved´** *adj.* —**de·prav´ed·ly** *adv.* —**de·prav´i·ty** *n.*

dep´re·cate *vt.* to express disapproval; to belittle —**dep´re·cat·ing·ly** *adv.* —**dep·re·ca´tion** *n.* —**dep´re·ca·tor** *n.*

dep´re·ca·tive, **dep´re·ca·to·ry** *adj.* tending to express disapproval; belittling; apologetic —**dep·re·ca·to´ri·ly** *adv.*

de·pre´ci·ate´ *vi.* to fall in value —*vt.* to lessen in value; to consider of little value —**de·pre´ci·a·ble** *adj.*

—**de·pre·ci·a´tion** *n.* —**de·pre´ci·a·to·ry** *adj.*

de·press´ *vt.* to lower, as one's spirit; to lessen, as the value of a thing; to push or press down —**de·press´ing** *adj.* —**de·press´ing·ly** *adv.* —**de·pres´sor** *n.*

de·pres´sant *n.* an agent that slows the vital functions; a sedative

de·pressed´ *adj.* pressed down; downhearted, despondent; reduced in amount, value, etc.

de·pres´sion *n.* despondency; a period of economic stagnation; a sunken or indented place in a surface

de·pres´sive *adj.* inclined to despondency; tending to cause a slowing of business activity —**de·pres´sive·ly** *adv.* —**de·pres´sive·ness** *n.*

de·prive´ *vt.* to take from: dispossess; to keep from acquiring or enjoying: *to deprive of a normal home life* —**de·priv´al**, **dep·ri·va´tion·al** *adj.* —**dep·ri·va´tion** *n.* — **de·priv´a·ble** *adj.*

de·prived´ *adj.* lacking the necessities of life; lacking opportunity; underprivileged

dep´u·ty *n.* one acting in the place of another; an aide or assistant; in some countries, a member of the legislature —**dep·u·ta´tion** *n.* — **dep´u·tize** *vi., vt.*

de·rail´ *vi., vt.* to go or cause to go off the rails, as a train; to stop or cause to stop, as *a program derailed by a lack of interest* —**de·rail´ment** *n.*

de·rail´leur *n.* a device for shifting gears on a bicycle

de·range´ *vt.* to disorder or disturb the arrangement of; to make insane

de·range´ment *n.* being out of the usual order; mental illness

der´by *n.* a contest or race; a type of felt hat

de·reg´u·late vt. to void or suspend the rules; to free from government control —**de·reg·u·la´tion** n. —**de·reg´u·la·tor** n.

der´e·lict adj. abandoned; negligent or delinquent as in carrying out a duty —n. property that has been abandoned; a social outcast; a loiterer —**der·e·lic´tion** n.

de·ride´ vt. to mock or ridicule —**de·rid´er** n. —**de·rid´ing·ly** adv.

de·ri´sion n. the state of being mocked or ridiculed; a display of scorn or contempt

de·ri´sive, de·ri´so·ry adj. characterized by derision —**de·ri´sive·ly** adv. —**de·ri´sive·ness** n.

der·i·va´tion n. something derived: a derivative; the source from which something derives; the formation of a word from another word, as by adding a prefix or suffix —**der·i·va´tion·al** adj.

de·riv´a·tive adj. borrowed or learned, not original —n. something produced from another source —**de·riv´a·tive·ly** adv. —**de·riv´a·tive·ness** n.

de·rive´ vt. to obtain from a source; to arrive at by reasoning; to trace a word to its origin

der´ma n. the dermis —**der´mal** adj.

der·ma·ti´tis n. an irritation of the skin

der·ma·tol´o·gy n. the scientific study of the skin, its diseases, and their treatment —**der·ma·to·log´ic, der·ma·to·log´i·cal** adj. —**der·ma·tol´o·gist** n.

der´mis n. the layer of skin below the epidermis

de·rog´a·to´ry, de·rog´a·tive adj. disparaging; tending to belittle —**de·rog·a·to´ri·ly** adv.

der´rick n. a machine for hoisting and moving heavy objects

der´rin·ger n. a small pistol

der´vish n. a member of a Muslim sect

de·scend´ vi., vt. to progress downward; to move from a higher to lower level; to derive from a source, as an ancestor

de·scend´ant, de·scend´ent n. one who is of a particular lineage; anything traced back to an earlier form

de·scend´er n. the part of a typeset character that falls below the baseline

de·scent´ n. a downward motion; an inclined surface; a lowering, as of status; a sudden onset

de·scribe´ vt. to relay an account or impression; to represent in speech or writing; to draw or trace —**de·scrib´a·ble** adj. —**de·scrib´er** n.

de·scrip´tion n. an account or report that describes; a drawing or tracing

de·scrip´tive adj. serving to describe; illustrative —**de·scrip´tive·ly** adv. —**de·scrip´tive·ness** n.

de·scrip´tor n. an identifying emblem

des´e·crate vt. to violate that which is considered sacred; to profane —**des´e·crat·er, des´e·cra·tor** n. —**des·e·cra´tion** n.

de·sen´si·tize vt. to deaden or benumb: to make insensible, as by repeated exposure or shock; to protect from extreme reaction to an antigen —**de·sen·si·ti·za´tion** n. —**de·sen´si·tiz·er** n.

des´ert n. a dry, often sandy, barren region

des·ert´ vi., vt. to abandon —**de·ser´tion** n. —**de·sert´er** n.

de·serve´ vi., vt. be worthy of

de·served´ adj. honestly earned; justified or suitable —**de·serv´ed·ly** adv. —**de·serv´ed·ness** n.

de·serv´ing adj. worthy of assistance, praise, etc.: a subject deserving of further study —**de·serv´ing·ly** adv.

des´ic·cate vt. to dry thoroughly; to

preserve food by drying —*vi.* to become dry —**des·ic·ca'tion** *n.* — **des'ic·ca·tor** *n.* —**des'ic·ca·tive** *adj.*

de·sign' *n.* a detailed plan or schematic; a bringing together of elements so as to present a congruous whole; an artistic rendering — *vt.* to invent or devise; to make a graphic representation; to have as a purpose or goal —**de·sign'a·ble** *adj.* —**de·sign'er** *n.*

des·ig·nate *vt.* to specify or appoint; to set aside, as for a specific purpose —**des·ig·na'tion** *n.* —**des'ig·na·tive, des'ig·na·tory** *adj.* — **des'ig·na·tor** *n.*

designated driver a group member who forgoes alcoholic beverages in order to chauffer those who are drinking

designated hitter in baseball, one who hits in place of the pitcher

de·sign'ed·ly *adv.* intentionally; deliberately

des'ig·nee' *n.* one named or set apart

designer drug a synthetic drug formulated to produce certain desired effects

de·sign'ing *adj.* scheming, crafty, or treacherous; of the making of designs or patterns —*n.* the art or business of making designs or patterns —**de·sign'ing·ly** *adv.*

de·sir'a·ble *adj.* worth seeking or having; beneficial: *a desirable change*; pleasing or attractive — **de·sir·a·bil'i·ty, de·sir'a·ble·ness** *n.* —**de·sir'a·bly** *adv.*

de·sire' *n.* a longing or craving; lust —*vt.* to want or express a wish for —**de·sire'er** *n.* —**de·sir'ous** *adj.* — **de·sir'ous·ly** *adv.* —**de·sir'ous·ness** *n.*

de·sist' *vi.* to cease; to abstain from —**de·sis'tance** *n.*

desk *n.* an executive work station; a table for writing or studying with

drawers for storage

desk'top *n.* the working surface of a desk —*adj.* designed for use on a desk: *a desktop computer*

desktop publishing the use of a computer for the preparation of copy for printing

des'o·late *adj.* forsaken; dismal, dreary; disconsolate or forlorn — *vt.* to lay waste; to devastate — **des'o·late·ly** *adv.* —**des'o·late·ness** *n.* —**des'o·lat·er, des'o·la·tor** *n.* —**des'o·la'tion** *n.*

de·spair' *n.* a loss of hope —*vi.* to lose all hope —**de·spair'ing** *adj.* — **de·spair'ing·ly** *adv.*

des'per·ate *adj.* hopeless; dangerous; frantic; seeming so hopeless as to cause one to be reckless or foolhardy —**des'per·ate·ly** *adv.* — **des'per·ate·ness** *n.* —**des·per·a'tion** *n.*

des·pic'a·ble *adj.* detestable; deserving of contempt; mean or vile —**des·pic'a·bil·i·ty, de·spic'a·ble·ness** *n.* —**de·spic'a·bly** *adv.*

de·spise' *vt.* to regard with disdain or scorn; to look down on —**de·spis'a·ble** *adj.* —**de·spis'al** *n.* — **de·spis'er** *n.*

de·spite' *n.* an insult; an act of spite —*prep.* notwithstanding

de·spond' *vi.* to lose hope; to become depressed or discouraged —**de·spond'ing·ly** *adv.*

de·spon'dent *adj.* suffering a loss of courage or hope; dejected —**de·spon'dence, de·spon'den·cy** *n.* — **de·spon'dent·ly** *adv.*

des'pot *n.* an absolute ruler; a tyrant —**des·pot'ic, des·pot'i·cal** *adj.* —**des·pot'i·cal·ly** *adv.* —**des'pot·ism** *n.*

des·sert' *n.* the final course of a meal, usually something sweet

des'ti·na'tion *n.* the place to which someone or something is going or being sent

des'tine *vt.* to be determined or

seem to be determined for a special goal or purpose

des·ti·ny *n.* the seeming inevitable course of events

des·ti·tute´ *adj.* completely lacking or impoverished; without means of survival —**des´ti·tu´tion** *n.*

de·stroy´ *vt.* to ruin utterly; to make useless; to tear down or demolish —**de·stroy´er** *n.*

de·struct´ *n.* the demolition of a defective missile —*vt.* to destroy after launch —*vi.* to undergo deliberate destruction

de·struc´ti·ble *adj.* capable of being destroyed; easily broken —**de·struc·ti·bil´i·ty, de·struc´ti·ble·ness** *n.*

de·struc´tion *n.* the process or condition of being demolished or brought to ruin

de·struc´tive *adj.* producing or likely to produce destruction; tending to discourage or make ineffective: *destructive criticism* —**de·struc´tive·ly** *adv.* —**de·struc´tive·ness, de·struc·tiv´i·ty** *n.*

des´ul·to·ry *adj.* lacking direction or focus; random —**des´ul·to·ri·ly** *adv.* —**des´ul·to·ri·ness** *n.*

de·tach´ *vt.* to disconnect; remove from attachment to —**de·tach·a·bil´i·ty** *adv.* —**de·tach´a·ble** *adj.* —**de·tach´a·bly** *adv.*

de·tached´ *adj.* aloof, impartial; separated, cut off —**de·tach´ed·ly** *adv.* —**de·tach´ed·ness** *n.*

de·tach´ment *n.* the condition of being separated; impartiality or indifference; a military unit organized and trained, or sent off, for some special purpose

de·tail´ *n.* any of the minute parts that make up something; a precise account; a detachment of military personnel designated for a special mission —*vt.* to report in precise terms; to select or dispatch for a special purpose

detail person a company representative who visits distributors to tout the company's products, supervise promotions, etc.

de·tain´ *vt.* to restrain or delay; to hold in custody —**de·tain´er** *n.* —**de·tain´ment** *n.*

de·tect´ *vt.* to become aware of or search out something not readily apparent or that is hidden —**de·tect´a·ble, de·tect´i·ble** *adj.* —**de·tect´er** *n.* —**de·tec´tion** *n.*

de·tec´tive *n.* one who investigates crimes; anyone who painstakingly analyzes anything

de·tec´tor *n.* a device for discovering or disclosing the presence of something, as *a metal detector* or *smoke detector*

dé·tente´ *n.* a relaxing of tension between opposing groups

de·ten´tion *n.* a period of temporary custody or enforced delay —**de·ten´tive** *adj.*

de·ter´ *vt.* to prevent or discourage by instilling doubt or fear —**de·ter´ment** *n.* —**de·ter´ra·ble** *adj.* —**de·ter´rer** *n.*

de·ter´gent *adj.* cleansing —*n.* a substance for cleansing —**de·ter´gence, de·ter´gen·cy** *n.*

de·te´ri·o·rate´ *vi., vt.* to become or make worse —**de·te·ri·o·ra´tion** *n.* —**de·te·ri·o·ra´tive** *adj.*

de·ter´mi·na·ble *adj.* able to be ascertained or established —**de·ter´mi·na·bil´i·ty** *n.* —**de·ter´min·a·bly** *adv.*

de·ter´mi·nant *n.* a factor that fixes or limits

de·ter´mi·nate *adj.* exactly fixed or limited; conclusive —**de·ter´mi·nate·ly** *adv.* —**de·ter´mi·nate·ness** *n.*

de·ter´mi·na·tive *adj.* tending to influence in deciding or settling —*n.* that which determines —**de·ter´mi·na·tive·ly** *adv.* —**de·ter´mi·na·tive·ness** *n.*

de·ter´mine *vt.* to set bounds; to render a decision; to reach a conclusion after study and consideration —**de·ter´mi·na´tion** *n.* —**de·ter´min·er** *n.*

de·ter´mined *adj.* characterized by determination; resolved; steadfast in purpose —**de·ter´mined·ly** *adv.* —**de·ter´mined·ness** *n.*

de·ter´min·ism *n.* the belief that everything is predetermined by other events —**de·ter´min·ist** *n.* —**de·ter´min·is´tic** *adj.* —**de·ter·min·is´ti·cal·ly** *adv.*

de·ter´rent *adj.* tending to cause restraint —*n.* a thing that hinders; an obstacle —**de·ter´rence** *n.*

de·test´ *vt.* to dislike intensely; to despise; loathe —**de·tes·ta´tion** *n.* —**de·test´er** *n.*

de·test´a·ble *adj.* disgusting; abhorrent; despicable —**de·test·a·bil´i·ty, de·test´a·ble·ness** *n.* —**de·test´a·bly** *adv.*

de·throne *vt.* to remove from power —**de·throne·ment** *n.*

det´o·nate´ *vi., vt.* to explode or cause to explode —**det·o·na´tion** *n.* —**det´o·na·tor** *n.*

de·tox´i·fy *vt.* to counteract or remove poisonous properties from; to rid of the effects of poison; to treat so as to rid of dependence on alcohol or narcotics —**de·tox´i·fi·ca´tion** *n.*

de·tract´ *vt.* to take away or withdraw —*vi.* to undergo removal of a valued quality or part —**de·trac´tion** *n.* —**de·trac´tive** *adj.* —**de·trac´tive·ly** *adv.* —**de·trac´tor** *n.*

det´ri·ment *n.* damage or loss; anything that causes damage —**det´ri·ment´al** *adj.* —**det´ri·ment´al·ly** *adv.*

de·tri´tus *n.* loose particles or fragments of rock created and deposited by natural forces; disintegrated matter; debris —**de·tri´tal** *adj.* —**de·tri´tion** *n.*

deuce *n.* a playing card or die with two spots

de·val´u·ate, de·val´ue *vt.* to reduce in value or significance

de·val·u·a´tion *n.* a reducing or reduction in value, especially of the exchange rate of a currency

dev´as·tate *vt.* to lay waste, as by war, storm, or fire; to overwhelm or stun, as by harsh criticism —**dev´as·tat·ing·ly** *adv.* —**dev·as·ta´tion** *n.* —**dev´as·ta·tor** *n.*

de·vel´op *vt.* to improve by realizing potential or capability; to expand or enlarge on; to increase effectiveness —*vi.* to grow or evolve: to advance from a lower to a higher state; to become revealed —**de·vel·op·a·bil´i·ty** *n.* —**de·vel´op·a·ble** *adj.*

de·vel´oped *adj.* technologically advanced; of an area or nation seen as highly evolved in terms of industry, finance, standard of living, etc.; of land cleared of natural growth and used for farming, industry, residents, etc.

de·vel´op·er *n.* a builder or contractor; one who oversees and finances or arranges financing for construction; a chemical used in the processing of photographic film

de·vel´op·ing *adj.* of an area or nation in the process of developing its industrial and economic capabilities

de·vel´op·ment *n.* a community where numerous dwellings are located or are under construction; an occurrence, often an outgrowth of an earlier action —**de·vel·op·men´tal** *adj.* —**de·vel·op·men´tal·ly** *adv.*

de·vi·ant *adj.* contrasting with the usual or normal —*n.* one whose behavior does not conform to accepted social standards —**de·vi·ance, de´vi·an·cy** *n.*

de´vi·ate *vi.* to depart from a normal

or standard course —de·vi·a·
tion *n.* —de·vi·a·tor *n.* —de·vi·a·
to·ry *adj.*

de·vice´ *n.* anything contrived, as a
technique, a mechanical apparatus, etc.; an ornamental embellishment

dev´il *n.* an evil spirit; a wicked
person; one, often a child, who is
mischievous —poor devil an unlucky person —dev´il·ish *adj.* —
dev´il·ish·ly *adv.* —dev´il·ish·
ness *n.*

dev´il·ment *n.* mischief

dev´il·ry, dev´il·try *n.* wickedness,
sinfulness; mischief, impishness

devil's advocate a church official
assigned to find fault with those
selected for beatification; anyone
who explores the negative side of a
proposition

de´vi·ous *adj.* deceptive; crafty; not
direct, roundabout —de´vi·ous·ly
adv. —de´vi·ous·ness *n.*

de·vise´ *n.* a dividing, or giving of
real property by will; the property
given; a will or clause in a will that
bequeaths real property —*vi., vt.* to
create or contrive; to bequeath real
property —de·vis´a·ble *adj.* —de·
vis´er *n.*

dev·i·see´ *n.* one to whom real property is given in a will

de·vis´er *n.* one who contrives or
plots

dev·i´sor *n.* one who bequeaths real
property

de·vi´tal·ize *vt.* to weaken or enfee-
ble; to deprive of life —de·vi·tal·i·
za´tion *n.*

de·void´ *adj.* lacking entirely; empty

de·volve´ *vt., vi.* to pass or cause to
be passed on to another, as accountability or an obligation —de·
v·o·lu´tion, de·volve´ment *n.*

de·vote´ *vt.* to dedicate or assign for
a specific purpose; to give, as time
or effort

de·vot´ed *adj.* dedicated; loving and

faithful; thoughtful, solicitous —
de·vot´ed·ly *adv.* —de·vot´ed·
ness *n.* —dev´o·tee´ *n.*

de·vo´tion *n.* strong affection or
dedication; piety —de·vo´tion·al
adj. —de·vo´tion·al·ly *adv.*

de·vour´ *vt.* to eat or absorb completely

de·vout´ *adj.* very religious; expressing devotion; sincere —de·
vout´ly *adv.* —de·vout´ness *n.*

dew *n.* drops of moisture formed by
warm air contacting a cool surface
—dew´drop *n.*

dew´lap *n.* a loose fold of skin
hanging from the neck of certain
animals

dew point the temperature at which
moisture in the air condenses into
liquid

dew´y *adj.* moist; like dew; brisk or
exhilarating; innocence —dew´i·ly
adv. —dew´i·ness *n.*

dew´y–eyed *adj.* displaying innocence or trust

dex·ter´i·ty *n.* skill with the hands
or mind —dex´ter·ous, dex´trous
adj. —dex´ter·ous·ly, dex´trous·ly
adv. —dex´ter·ous·ness, dex´
trous·ness *n.*

dex´trose *n.* sugar formed from
starch; corn sugar

di·a·be´tes *n.* any of several diseases
characterized by excessive thirst
and frequent urination

di´a·bet´ic *n.* one who has diabetes

di·a·bol´ic, di·a·bol´i·cal *adj.* sa-
tanic; fiendish, wicked —di·a·bol´i·
cal·ly *adv.* —di·a·bol´i·cal·ness *n.*

di·ab´o·lism *n.* devil or demon worship; fiendish or wicked deeds —
di·ab´o·list *n.*

di´a·crit´ic *n.* any of the marks over
or under a letter (ñ, ç, é, ŭ) that
distinguish a change in pronunciation

di·a·crit´i·cal *adj.* helping to distinguish; marking a difference —di·a·
crit´i·cal·ly *adv.*

di´a·dem n. a crown

di´ag·nose vi., vt. to make a critical analysis —**di·ag·nos´a·ble** adj.

di´ag·no´sis n. a critical analysis to determine the nature of a thing — **di·ag·nos´tic** adj. —**di·ag·nos´ti·cal·ly** adv.

di´ag·nos·tics n. the study or application of diagnosis —**di·ag·nos·ti´cian** n.

di´a·gram n. a sketch or drawing that explains or clarifies; a chart or graph —**di´a·gram·mat´ic, di·a·gram·mat´i·cal** adj. —**di´a·gram·mat´i·cal·ly** adv.

di´al n. the face of a watch or clock; a rotating disk, as on a telephone; a gauge or indicator; a knob used to indicate or adjust: a radio dial

dialling code (Brit.) a prefix to a telephone number that identifies the locality to which a call is being placed

di´a·lect n. the language variations commonly spoken in a particular place or by a particular group; speech characteristic of a class, trade, or profession —**di·a·lec´tal** adj. —**di·a·lec´tal·ly** adv.

di·a·lec´tic n. the examining of ideas through systematic argumentation or deduction —**di·a·lec´ti·cal** adj. —**di·a·lec´ti·cal·ly** adv.

di·a·lec·toi´o·gy n. the study of variations in a spoken language — **di·a·lec´ti·cian** n.

di´a·logue´ n. conversation; an exchange of ideas; spoken lines in a play; a dissertation written in the form of a conversation

di·al´y·sis n. the means by which impurities are removed from the blood of patients suffering kidney failure

di·am´e·ter n. a line passing from one side to the other through the center of a circle or sphere; the length of such a line

di·a·met´ric, di·a·met´ri·cal adj.

pertaining to a diameter; totally different, contrary, etc. —**di·a·met´ri·cal·ly** adv.

diametrically opposed completely different or incompatible, as at the opposite ends of a diameter

di´a·mond n. an extremely hard crystal of nearly pure carbon; a geometric figure of four equal sides that is not a square

di·aph´a·nous adj. extremely fine so as to be transparent; thin and airy —**di·aph´a·nous·ly** adv. —**di·aph´a·nous·ness** n.

di´a·phragm´ n. a membrane that serves to separate

di´a·rist n. one who keeps a diary

di·ar·rhe´a n. morbid looseness of the bowels

di´a·ry n. a daily journal of events and observations

di´a·tribe n. a harsh tirade; a denunciation

dice n. pl., sing. **die** small gaming cubes marked with spots to indicate the value of a throw —vt. to cut, as vegetables, into small cubes

dic´ey adj. chancy; speculative

di·chot´o·my n. division into two, usually opposing, parts or viewpoints; in biology, a forking in pairs —**di·chot´o·mous** adj. —**di·chot´o·mous·ly** adv. —**di·chot´o·mous·ness** n.

dick´er vi. to barter; to bargain

dic·tate´ n. a command; a guiding principle —vi., vt. to command with authority; to speak for another to record —**dic·ta´tion** n. —**dic·ta´tion·al** adj.

dic´ta·tor n. a ruler with unlimited power —**dic´ta·to´ri·al** adj.

dic·ta´tor·ship n. government by a dictator

dic´tion n. the choice of words and clarity of enunciation in speech

dic´tion·ar´y n. a list of words or references arranged alphabetically to provide a definition, translation to another language, etc.

dic´tum *n., pl.* **dic´tums, dic´ta** a pronouncement

di·dac´tic, di·dac´ti·cal *adj.* instructive; inclined to sermonizing —**di·dac´ti·cal·ly** *adv.* —**di·dac´ti·cism** *n.*

die *vi.* to stop living; to stop working, as of a motor or machine —*n.* a metal stamp

die´–hard *adj.* stubborn —*n.* one firmly committed to a fundamental principle, concept, etc.

di´et *n.* the food and drink normally consumed; special food as required for health, religious belief, etc. —*vi.* to limit one's intake of food for some reason —**di´e·tar·y, di·e·tet´ic** *adj.* —**di´et·er** *n.* —**di·e·ti´cian** *n.*

di·e·tet´ics *n.* the study of diet and its effects on physical health and development

dif´fer *vi.* to disagree; to be different

dif´fer·ence *n.* a distinctive mark or characteristic; anything that differentiates one thing from another; a variance in quantity, quality, etc.; a disagreement

dif´fer·ent *adj.* unlike; changed; diverse —**dif´fer·ent·ly** *adv.* —**dif´fer·ent·ness** *n.*

dif·fer·en´tial *adj.* of a difference; able to cause varied results —*n.* a difference; a gear that alters the output of an engine —**dif·fer·en´tial·ly** *adv.*

dif·fer·en´ti·ate *vi.* to become different —*vt.* to make different; to recognize a difference; to display a difference —**dif·fer·en·ti·a´tion** *n.*

dif´fi·cult´ *adj.* requiring considerable effort; hard to accomplish, endure, please, understand, etc.; hard to deal with or satisfy —**dif´fi·cult´ly** *adv.* —**dif´fi·cul´ty** *n.*

dif´fi·dence *n.* a lack of self-confidence

dif´fi·dent *adj.* lacking confidence; shy; insecure —**dif´fi·dent·ly** *adv.*

dif·fuse´ *adj.* widely spread or dispersed; of rambling or excessively wordy speech —*vi., vt.* to spread in all directions; to disperse widely —**dif·fuse´ly** *adv.* —**dif·fuse´ness** *n.*

dif·fus´er, dif·fus´or *n.* a device that diffuses, such as frosted glass covering a light bulb, or a baffle mounted in front of a loudspeaker

dif·fus´i·ble *adj.* suitable for effecting diffusion; able to be diffused —**dif·fus´i·bly** *adv.*

dif·fu´sion *n.* the dissemination of light or sound so as to create a soft, even impression over a wide area —**dif·fu´sion·al** *adj.*

dif·fu´sive *adj.* circulating; spread about —**dif·fu´sive·ly** *adv.* —**dif·fu´sive·ness** *n.*

dig *vt.* to make a hole; to uncover, as by removing protection or by careful study —*n.* a sarcastic remark —**dig in** get to work —**digs** living quarters —**dig'ger** *n.*

di´gest *n.* a condensation of a previously published literary work; a collection of works —**di·gest´** *vt.* to condense or summarize a literary work; to convert food for absorption by the body; to study and absorb information —**di·ges´tion** *n.*

di·gest´i·ble *adj.* able or fit to be digested —**di·gest·i·bil´i·ty** *n.* —**di·gest´i·bly** *adv.*

di·ges´tive *adj.* pertaining to or conducive to the digestion of food —*n.* anything that aids digestion —**di·ges´tive·ly** *adv.* —**di·ges´tive·ness** *n.*

digestive system the chain of body organs that ingest food, process and use part for energy, then discard waste matter

dig´gings *pl. n.* material unearthed; a place where digging takes place, as a mine

dig´it *n.* a finger or toe; one of the

units of a numbering system, as 0 to 9 in base 10

dig·i·tal *adj.* discrete, having specific value; expressed in the units of a particular numbering system — **dig·i·tal·ly** *adv.*

digital computer a computer that manipulates digital data

digital data data represented in discrete values, in contrast to *analog*

dig·i·tal·is *n.* a medicine used by heart patients

dig·ni·fied *adj.* characterized by or displaying dignity; courtly or reserved —**dig·ni·fied·ly** *adv.*

dig·ni·fy *vt.* to honor; to make someone or something seem more worthy than it is: *dignify a retreat by calling it an advance to the rear*

dig·ni·tar·y *n.* one of high rank or position

dig·ni·ty *n.* a presence that commands respect; poise; stateliness

di·gress *vi.* to stray, as from the subject in speaking or writing —**di·gres·sion** *n.* —**di·gres·sion·al** *adj.*

di·gres·sive *adj.* distinguished by rambling or a departure from the main subject —**di·gres·sive·ly** *adv.* —**di·gres·sive·ness** *n.*

dike *n.* an embankment constructed to prevent flooding

di·lap·i·date *vi., vt.* to fall or cause to fall into disrepair or ruin — **di·lap·i·da·tion** *n.*

di·lap·i·dat·ed *adj.* broken down; fallen into disrepair

di·late *vi., vt.* to make or become larger; to expand —**di·lat·a·bil·i·ty** *n.* —**di·lat·a·ble** *adj.* —**di·lat·a·bly** *adv.* —**di·la·tive** *adj.*

di·lat·ed *adj.* expanded or distended —**di·lat·ed·ness** *n.*

di·la·tion *n.* a widening or expansion; the process of dilating

di·la·tor *n.* something that causes dilation, such as a muscle in the eye that dilates the pupil or a surgical instrument for spreading an opening

dil·a·to·ry *adj.* intended to delay; inclined to delay —**dil·a·to·ri·ly** *adv.* —**dil·a·to·ri·ness** *n.*

di·lem·ma *n.* a situation that calls for a choice between equally unpleasant options; any serious predicament —**on the horns of a dilemma** a choice between equally undesirable options

dil·et·tan·te *n.* one who dabbles in something for personal amusement; a lover of the arts —*adj.* characteristic of a dilettante —**dil·et·tan·tish** *adj.* —**dil·et·tan·te·ism, dil·et·tan·tism** *n.*

dil·i·gent *adj.* industous; showing painstaking effort —**dil·i·gence** *n.* —**dil·i·gent·ly** *adv.*

dill *n.* an herb whose seeds or leaves are used to flavor foods

dil·ly·dal·ly *vi.* to waste time

di·lute *adj.* thinned or weakened — *vt.* to make thinner or weaker by adding something —**di·lute·ness, di·lu·tion** *n.*

dim *adj.* faint, murky; ill defined; indistinct, as a sound; not encouraging: *dim prospects* —*vi., vt.* to grow or make faint or indistinct — **dim·ly** *adv.* —**dim·ness** *n.*

di·men·sion *n.* the measure of a thing, as its length, width or depth —**di·men·sion·al** *adj.* —**di·men·sion·al·i·ty** *n.* —**di·men·sion·al·ly** *adv.*

di·min·ish *vt., vi.* to make or become reduced in size, importance, etc. — **di·min·ish·a·ble** *adj.* —**di·min·ish·ment** *n.*

diminishing returns a lessening proportional increase, as in productivity or profitability, as more improvements or incentives are introduced

dim·i·nu·tion *n.* a lessening or reduction; something reduced — **dim·i·nu·tion·al** *adj.*

di·min´u·tive *adj.* very small; of a word or suffix expressing diminished size —*n.* something small; a word form expessing diminished size or station, as piglet for a small pig or sonny for a young son — **di·min´u·tive·ly** *adv.* —**di·min´u·tive·ness** *n.*

dim´mer *n.* a device for reducing the brightness of a lamp or light

dim´ple *n.* an indentation on the body, often on the cheek or chin; any small indentation, as a dent on a car body —*vt. vi.* to mark with or form dimples —**dim´ply** *adj.*

din *n.* a loud clamor

dine *vi.* to eat, often of a formal affair in the company of others — *vt.* to entertain at dinner

din´er *n.* one who is eating; in the US, a small informal restaurant

di·nette´ *n.* a small dining area; tables and chairs for a dining area

din´ghy *n.* a small boat, often a tender to a larger boat or ship

din´gy *adj.* drab or dirty; grimy — **din´gi·ly** *adv.* —**din´gi·ness** *n.*

dining room living space set aside for taking meals

dink´y *adj.* diminutive; small

din´ner *n.* the main meal of the day; a social event featuring a large meal

dinner jacket a man's jacket worn on formal occasions; a tuxedo jacket

dinner theater a restaurant in which theatrical entertainment accompanies or follows dinner

diph´thong´ *n.* a complex vowel sound made by sliding from one vowel to another in the same syllable

di·plo´ma *n.* a document testifying to completion of a course of study

di·plo´ma·cy *n.* the art of managing affairs between political entities; the ability to act with finesse and tact —**dip´lo·mat´** *n.* —**dip´lo·**

mat´ic *adj.* —**dip·lo·mat´i·cal·ly** *adv.*

diplomatic corps collectively, those who staff a legation

diplomatic immunity exemption for members of the diplomatic corps from the taxes, court suits, etc. in the country to which they are posted

dip´stick *n.* a rod for measuring the level of liquid in a container; a stupid or silly person

dire *adj.* serious; extremely desperate; urgent; requiring immediate action: dire necessity —**dire´ly** *adv.* —**dire´ness** *n.*

di·rect´ *adj.* straight; being the straightest course; uninterrupted in line of descent; immediate; absolute: *a direct opposite*; straightforward or sincere —*vt.* to control or manage; to point out or guide; to instruct or order; to aim: *direct one's gaze* —**di·rect·ly** *adv.* — **di·rect´ness** *n.*

direct current electricity that flows in one direction

direct deposit a system whereby all or part of one's wages are credited to a bank account

direct election the selection of candidates for office by voters directly rather than through delegates

di·rec´tion *n.* instruction; supervision; a command; the point toward which a thing is facing or moving —**di·rec´tion·al** *adj.* —**di·rec·tion·al´i·ty** *n.* **di·rec´tion·al·ly** *adv.*

di·rec´tive *n.* an official order —*adj.* serving to rule or govern

direct mail advertising or sales material posted directly to specific individuals or households

direct marketing the sale or attempted sale of goods or services to specific persons or households, as by mail, telephone, etc.

di·rec´tor *n.* one who supervises or manages

di·rec´to·rate n. the board of directors of an organization; the office and trappings of a company or corporate director —**di·rec·to´ri·al** adj. —**di·rec´tor·ship** n.

di·rec·to·ry n. an alphabetical reference, as of individuals, companies, products, etc.; a directorate

direct tax a tax assessed on the person who pays it, such as an income or sales tax, in contrast to taxes paid by others and passed on through higher prices

dirge n. a mournful musical or literary work

dir´i·gi·ble n. an airship

dirk n. a dagger

dirt adj. surfaced with earth, as a dirt road or a dirt floor —n. soil or earth; anything unclean; gossip or scandal; pornography

dirt–cheap extremely inexpensive

dirt´y adj. soiled or having a soiled appearance; vulgar, lewd; contaminated —vi., vt. to soil or stain —**dirty linen** information that could prove embarrassing if generally known —**dirty pool** unfair tactics —**dirt´i·ly** adv. —**dirt´i·ness** n.

dis·a´ble vt. to make unfit for use; to incapacitate —**dis·a·bil´i·ty** n. —**dis·a´ble·ment** n. —**dis·a´bling** adj. —**dis·a´bling·ly** adv.

dis·a´bled adj. inoperative, as of a motor vehicle; incapacitated, as of a physical impairment — n. those who are physically incapacitated, considered as a group,

dis·a·buse´ vt. to rid of a false notion; to clarify

dis´ad·van´tage n. a handicap; unfavorable circumstances —vt. to hinder —**dis´ad·van´taged** adj. —**dis´ad·van·ta´geous** adj. —**dis´ad·van·ta´geous·ly** adv. —**dis´ad·van·ta´geous·ness** n.

dis·af·fect´ vt. to cause estrangement; to alienate —**dis·af·fect´ed** adj. —**dis·af·fect´ed·ly** adv. —**dis·af·fec´tion** n.

dis´a·gree´ vi. to differ; to quarrel; to produce discomfort, as by eating certain foods —**dis·a·gree´ment** n.

dis·a·gree´a·ble adj. unpleasant; quarrelsome —**dis·a·gree´a·ble·ness** n. —**dis·a·gree´a·bly** adv.

dis·al·low´ vt. to refuse to permit; to reject —**dis·al·low´a·ble** adj. —**dis·al·low´ance** n.

dis·ap·pear´ vi. to pass from sight; to become extinct —**dis´ap·pear´ance** n.

dis·ap·point´ vt. to fail to satisfy; to prevent fulfillment of the expectation of —**dis´ap·point´ment** n.

dis·ap·point´ed adj. frustrated in a desire or expectation —**dis·ap·point´ed·ly** adv.

dis·ap·point´ing adj. frustrating; not meeting expectation —**dis·ap·point´ing·ly** adv.

dis·ap·prove´ vi., vt. to frown upon; to condemn —**dis·ap·prov´al** n. —**dis·ap·prov´er** n. —**dis·ap·prov´ing·ly** adv.

dis·arm´ vt. to take weapons from; to weaken, render powerless; to win over by charm —vi. to relinquishment arms —**dis´arm´ing** adj. —**dis´arm´ing·ly** adv.

dis·ar´ma·ment n. the relinquishing of arms; the reduction or limitation of military forces or weapons

dis·ar·ray´ n. a state of confusion or disorder — vi. to throw into confusion

dis·as·sem´ble vt. to tear down or dismantle —**dis·as·sem´bly** n.

dis·as·so´ci·ate vt. to separate; to cease to consider as allied; to withdraw from an alliance or relationship —**dis·as·so·ci·a´tion** n.

dis·as´ter n. an incidence of great harm or distress —**dis·as´trous** adj. —**dis·as´trous·ly** adv. —**dis·as´trous·ness** n.

disaster area a region officially

recognized as a victim of disaster, such as a flood or hurricane, and often eligible for government aid

dis·a·vow´ *vt.* to deny, as knowledge of or responsibility for —**dis·a·vow´a·ble** *adj.* —**dis·a·vow´al** *adj.* —**dis·a·vow´er** *n.*

dis·band´ *vi.* to cease to function as a group —*vt.* to dissolve a group or organization; to release from military service —**dis·band´ment** *n.*

dis·bar´ *vt.* to withdraw a lawyer's right to practice —**dis·bar´ment** *n.*

dis´be·lieve´ *vi., vt.* to refuse to believe; to consider as false —**dis´be·lief´** *n.* —**dis·be·liev´er** *n.*

dis·burse´ *vt.* to pay out —**dis·burs´a·ble** *adj.* —**dis·burse´ment** *n.* — **dis·burs´er** *n.*

dis´card *n.* something cast off or abandoned —**dis´card´** *vt.* to throw away; to cast aside or reject —**dis·card´a·ble** *adj.* —**dis·card´er** *n.*

dis·cern´ *vt.* to perceive with the sight or in the mind; to recognize, especially as being different —*vi.* to recognize a difference —**dis·cern´i·ble** *adj.* —**dis·cern´i·bly** *adv.* — **dis·cern´ment** *n.*

dis·cern´ing *adj.* having good judgment; discriminating —**dis·cern´ing·ly** *adv.*

dis·charge´ *vt.* to unload, as passengers or freight; to release, as from confinement or duty; to fulfill an obligation; to fire a weapon — **dis·charge´, dis´charge** *n.* the act of unloading, dismissing, etc.; that which is discharged —**dis·charge´a·ble** *adj.* —**dis·charge´er** *n.*

dis·ci´ple *n.* an active follower or adherent of a teacher or concept — **dis·ci´ple·ship** *n.*

dis·ci·pline *n.* a branch of knowledge or learning; formal training; self-control; acceptance of authority; punishment —*vt.* to train or control; to punish

dis·ci·pli·nar´i·an *n.* one who maintains or upholds strict discipline

dis´ci·pli·nar·y *adj.* relating to a branch of knowledge; punitive, as punishment for wrongdoing —**dis´ci·plin·er** *n.*

dis·claim´ *vt.* to give up or deny a claim or connection —**dis·clam´a·to·ry** *adj.*

dis·claim´er *n.* a denial of responsibility; a relinquishing of a right or claim —**dis·cla·ma´tion** *n.*

dis·close´ *vt.* to reveal or make known —**dis·clos´er** *n.* —**dis·clo´sure** *n.*

dis·col´or *vt.* to alter color, as by fading, soiling, etc. —*vi.* to become faded or soiled —**dis·col·or·a´tion, dis·col´or·ment** *n.*

dis·com·bob´u·late *vt.* to embarrass; to confuse —**dis·com·bob·u·la´tion** *n.*

dis·com´fit *vt.* to frustrate the plans or aspirations of; to make uncomfortable —**dis·com´fi·ture** *n.*

dis·com´fort *n.* physical or mental distress; uneasiness —*vt.* to make uneasy —**dis·com´fort·a·ble** *adj.* —**dis·com´fort·ing·ly** *adv.*

dis·com·mode´ *vt.* to cause inconvenience —**dis·com·mo´di·ous** *adj.* —**dis·com·mo´di·ous·ly** *adv.* —**dis·com·mo´di·ous·ness** *n.*

dis·con·cert´ *vt.* to confuse or embarrass —**dis·con·cert´ment** *n.*

dis·con·cert´ed *adj.* characterized by confusion or embarrassment — **dis´con·cert´ed·ly** *adv.* —**dis´con·cert´ed·ness** *n.*

dis·con·cert´ing *adj.* tending to cause confusion or embarrassment —**dis·con·cert´ing·ly** *adv.* —**dis´con·cert´ing·ness** *n.*

dis´con·nect´ *vt.* to detach —**dis·con·nec´tion** *n.*

dis·con·nect´ed *adj.* separated; cut off; disjointed or incoherent, as a narrative —**dis·con·nect´ed·ly** *adv.* —**dis·con·nect´ed·ness** *n.*

dis´con´so·late *adj.* dejected,

gloomy; inconsolable —**dis·con´so·late·ly** *adv.* —**dis·con´so·late·ness, dis·con·so·la´tion** *n.*

dis·con·tent´ *adj.* displeased with present circumstances —*n.* a lack of satisfaction with present circumstances —*vt.* to make displeased or dissatisfied —**dis·con·tent´ed** *adj.* —**dis·con·tent´ed·ly** *adv.* —**dis·con·tent´ed·ness, dis·con·tent´ment** *n.*

dis·con·tin´u·ance *n.* a temporary cessation or termination; a suspension of legal action —**dis·con·tin·u·a´tion** *n.*

dis·con·tin´ue *vi., vt.* to stop or end

dis·con·tin´u·ous *adj.* disordered; disconnected; irrational —**dis·con·tin´u·ous·ly** *adv.* —**dis·con·ti·nu´i·ty** *n.*

dis·cord´ *n.* a lack of harmony, disagreement; harsh sounds —**dis·cor´dance** *n.* —**dis·cord´ant** *adj.* —**dis·cor´dant·ly** *adv.*

dis´count *n.* a reduction or rebate from a standard price —**dis·count´** *vt.* to rebate or sell at a reduced price; to tender the proceeds of a loan after deducting interest; to minimize or reject as untrue or of little importance —**dis·count´a·ble** *adj.* —**dis´count·er** *n.*

discount store a shop or outlet specializing in merchandise sold at less than the usual price

dis·cour´age *vt.* to advise against; to attempt to dissuade; to dishearten —**dis·cour´age·ment** *n.* —**dis·cour´ag·ing** *adj.* —**dis·cour´ag·ing·ly** *adv.*

dis·course´ *n.* to exchange ideas in conversation; a lengthly treatment of a subject in writing or speech —**dis·course´** *vi.* to converse; to write or speak at length —**dis´course´er** *n.*

dis·cour´te·ous *adj.* impolite; rude —**dis·cour´te·ous·ly** *adv.* —**dis·cour´te·ous·ness** *n.*

dis·cour´te·sy *n.* bad manners; an impolite manner, attitude, etc.

dis·cov´er *vt.* to obtain knowledge; to detect or make known, esp. for the first time —**dis·cov´er·a·ble** *adj.* —**dis·cov´er·er** *n.*

dis·cov´er·y *n.* detection or disclosure; findings, a thing discovered

dis·cred´it *n.* damage to one's reputation; anything causing such damage —*vt.* to cast doubt upon; to damage the reputation of another —**dis·cred´it·a·ble** *adj.* —**dis·cred´it·a·bly** *adv.*

dis·creet´ *adj.* prudent; exercising caution, especially concerning the privacy and personal affairs of others —**dis·creet´ly** *adv.* —**dis·creet´ness** *n.*

dis·crep´an·cy *n.* a variance or inconsistency —**dis·crep´ant** *adj.* —**dis·crep´ant·ly** *adv.*

dis·crete´ *adj.* comprised of unconnected, distinct parts —**dis·crete´ly** *adv.* —**dis·crete´ness** *n.*

dis·cre´tion *n.* the quality of being discreet; the ability or freedom to make decisions on one's own —**dis·cre´tion·ar·i·ly** *adv.* —**dis·cre´tion·ar·y** *adj.*

dis·crim´i·nate´ *vi., vt.* to make distinction; to differentiate —**dis·crim´i·nate·ly** *adv.* —**dis·crim´i·na´tion** *n.*

dis·crim´i·nat·ing *adj.* able to differentiate; discerning —**dis·crim´i·nat·ing·ly** *adv.*

dis·crim´i·na·tive *adj.* having or forming distinctions —**dis·crim´i·na·tive·ly** *adv.*

dis·crim´i·na·to·ry *adj.* judgemental; discriminating

dis·cur´sive *adj.* rambling; wandering from one subject to another —**dis·cur´sive·ly** *adv.* —**dis·cur´sive·ness** *n.*

dis·cuss´ *vt.* to talk or write about —**dis·cuss´a·ble, dis·cuss´i·ble** *adj.* —**dis·cuss´er** *n.* —**dis·cus´sion** *n.*

dis·dain´ *n.* a show of contempt —*vt.* to treat with contempt; to deem unsuited to one's position

dis·dain´ful *adj.* showing contempt —**dis·dain´ful·ly** *adv.* **dis·dain´ful·ness** *n.*

dis·ease´ *n.* an illness of the body; any unsound or harmful condition —**dis·eased´** *n.*

dis´em·bark´ *vi., vt.* to leave or be taken from a conveyance —**dis·em·bar·ka´tion, dis·em·bark´ment** *n.*

dis·em·bod´y *vt.* to separate from physical existence —**dis·em·bod´ied** *adj.* —**dis·em·bod´i·ment** *n.*

dis·en·chant´ *vt.* to free from delusion —**dis·en·chant´er** *n.* —**dis´en·chant´ing·ly** *adv.* —**dis·en·chant´ment** *n.*

dis·en·cum´ber *vt.* to relieve of a burden or difficulty —**dis·en·cum´ber·ment** *n.*

dis·en·fran´chise *vt.* to deprive of a right or privilege; to deprive of the right to vote —**dis·en·fran´chise·ment** *n.*

dis·en·tan´gle *vt.* to unsnarl; to extricate; to free from confusion —**dis·en·tan´gle·ment** *n.*

dis·fa´vor *n.* disapproval —*vt.* to look upon with disapproval

dis·fig´ure *vt.* to spoil the appearance of —**dis·fig·u·ra´tion, dis·fig´ure·ment** *n.*

dis·fran´chise *vt.* disenfranchise

dis·gorge´ *vi., vt.* to discharge the contents of

dis·grace´ *n.* a loss of respect or honor; a thing that brings dishonor —*vt.* to bring dishonor upon; to dishonor by chastising publicly —**dis·grace´ful** *adj.* **dis·grace´ful·ly** *adv.* —**dis·grace´ful·ness** *n.*

dis·grun´tle *vt.* to make unhappy; to dissatisfy

dis·guise´ *n.* that used to conceal the identity of a person or thing —*vt.* to alter or conceal the identity of; to misrepresent —**dis·guis´a·ble** *adj.* —**dis·guised´** *adj.*

dis·gust´ *n.* a deep dislike; an aversion —*vt.* to arouse dislike; to offend —**dis·gust´ed** *adj.* —**dis·gust´ed·ly** *adv.* —**dis·gust´ed·ness** *n.*

dis·gust´ing *adj.* provoking disgust; nasty; distasteful, nauseating —**dis·gust´ing·ly** *adv.*

dish *n.* a container for food; food prepared in a particular way —*vt.* to serve up, as food

dis·ha·bille´ *n.* a condition of partial, uncoordinated, or incongruous dress

dis·har·mo·ny *n.* a lack of harmony; dissonance; discord, as between persons, colors, etc. —**dis·har·mo´ni·ous** *adj.* —**dis·har·mo´ni·ous·ly** *adv.* **dis·har´mo·nize** *vi., vt.*

dis·heart´en *vt.* to lessen the courage, resolve, enthusiasm, etc. of

dis·heart´en·ing *adj.* tending to cause a loss of courage, enthusiasm, optimism, etc. —**dis·heart´en·ing·ly** *adv.* —**dis·heart´en·ment** *n.*

di·shev´eled, di·shev´elled *adj.* untidy; rumpled; disorderly —**di·shev´el** *vt.* —**di·shev´el·ment** *n.*

dis·hon´est *adj.* lacking honesty; deceitful; untrustworthy —**dis·hon´est·ly** *adv.* —**dis·hon´es·ty** *n.*

dis·hon´or *n.* a loss of honor, respect, etc.; something causing a loss of respect —*vt.* to cause a loss of honor; to treat with disrespect; to refuse to honor or pay, as an invoice —**dis·hon´er·a·ble** *adj.* —**dis·hon´or·a·ble·ness** *n.* —**dis·hon´or·a·bly** *adv.*

dis·il·lu´sion *vt.* to free from a false sentiment; to disappoint or disenchant —**dis·il·lu´sion·ment** *n.*

dis·in·clined´ *adj.* hesitant; reluctant —**dis·in·cli·na´tion** *n.* —**dis·in·cline´** *vt., vi.*

dis´in·fect´ *vt.* to sanitize; to sterilize

—dis·in·fec´tion n.

dis·in·fec´tant adj. serving to sanitize —n. any substance used to sanitize

dis·in·fec´tive adj. disinfectant

dis·in·gen´u·ous adj. deceitful; insincere; crafty —dis·in·gen´u·ous·ly adv. —dis·in·gen´u·ous·ness n.

dis·in·her´it vt. to deprive of a right or privilege, especially the right of inheritance —dis·in·her´i·tance n.

dis·in´te·grate vi., vt. to break into fragments —dis·in´te·gra·tive adj. —dis·in·te·gra´tion n. —dis·in´te·gra·tor n.

dis·in·ter´ vt. to dig up from a grave —dis·in·ter´ment n.

dis·in´ter·est n. a lack of concern

dis·in´ter·est·ed adj. free of bias; impartial; indifferent —dis·in´ter·est·ed·ly adv. —dis·in´ter·est·ed·ness n.

dis·join´ vt. to detach or separate —vi. to become separated

dis·joint´ vt. to dismember; to cut or take apart; to separate

dis·joint´ed adj. disconnected; lacking unity; incoherent; rambling —dis·joint´ed·ly adv. —dis·joint´ed·ness n.

dis·junc´tive adj. separating; causing sharp divisions —dis·junc´tion, dis·junc´ture n. —dis·junc´tive·ly adv.

disk n. a thin flat circular object; anything similar in form

disk drive the mechanism that spins a computer storage disk

disk·ette´ n. a removable disk for computer data storage

dis·like´ n. a feeling of distaste or aversion —vt. to look upon with distaste —dis·lik´a·ble, dis·like´a·ble adj.

dis·lo´cate´ vt. to put out of proper place or position, esp. of a bone —dis´lo·ca´tion n.

dis·lodge´ vt. to force from a position —dis·lodge´ment n.

dis·loy´al adj. unfaithful —dis·loy´al·ly adv. —dis·loy´al·ty n.

dis´mal adj. dreary, bleak —dis´mal·ly adv. —dis´mal·ness n.

dis·man´tle vt. to take apart systematically; to strip of furniture, equipment, etc. —dis·man´tle·ment n.

dis·may´ n. a loss of resolve in the face of difficulty —vt. to cause alarm or loss of courage by describing impending danger or difficulty

dis·mem´ber vt. to cut up; to mutilate —dis·mem´ber·ment n.

dis·miss´ vt. to send away; to release from employment; to put out of mind —dis·mis´sal n. —dis·miss´i·ble adj.

dis·mis´sive adj. displaying a lack of concern

dis·o·be´di·ent adj. refusing to obey; insubordinate —dis·o·be´di·ence n. —dis·o·be´di·ent·ly adv.

dis·o·bey´ vi., vt. to fail or refuse to obey

dis·or´der n. a state of confusion or disarray; a public disturbance; an illness —vt. to throw into confusion or disarray —dis·or´dered adj. —dis·or´dered·ly adv. —dis·or´dered·ness n.

dis·or´der·ly adj. untidy; lacking order; rowdy, creating a disturbance —dis·or´der·li·ness n.

dis·or´gan·ize vt. to cause or create disorder; to eradicate the unity of —dis·or·gan·i·za´tion n.

dis·o´ri·ent, dis·o´ri·en·tate vt. to confuse, bewilder —dis·o´ri·en·ta´tion n.

dis·own´ vt. to refuse to acknowledge or accept; to disinherit

dis·par´age vt. to discredit; to belittle —dis·par´age·ment n. —dis·par´ag·ing adj. —dis·par´ag·ing·ly adv.

dis´pa·rate adj. dissimilar; diversified —dis·par´ate·ly adv. —dis·

par´ate·ness *n.*

dis·par´i·ty *n.* a difference, as in quality or quantity

dis·pas´sion *n.* a lack of emotional involvment; freedom from passion

dis·pas´sion·ate *adj.* free from emotional involvement; detached — **dis·pas´sion·ate·ly** *adv.* —**dis·pas´sion·ate·ness** *n.*

dis·patch´ *n.* a sending out; a message sent; promptness in action — *vt.* to send out, usually with haste; to act quickly; to kill —**dis·patch´er** *n.*

dis·pel´ *vt.* to drive away; to eliminate, as a rumor

dis·pen´sa·ble *adj.* not essential; unnecessary; that can be distributed —**dis·pens·a·bil´i·ty** *n.* —**dis·pen´sa·ble·ness** *n.*

dis·pen´sa·ry *n.* a place for obtaining medicines and medical aid

dis·pen·sa´tion *n.* a distribution; something distributed; a release or exemption, as from an obligation —**dis·pen·sa´tion·al** *adj.* —**dis´pen·sa·tor** *n.*

dis·pense´ *vt.* to distribute; give out; to administer, as justice; to absolve —**dispense with** to do without —**dis·pens´er** *n.*

dis·perse´ *vt.* to cause to scatter widely; to drive off; to cause to disappear or dissipate, as mist; to separate light into its component colors — *vi.* to scatter in various directions; to disappear —**dis·per´sal, dis·per´sion** *n.* —**dis·pers´er** *n.* —**dis·pers´i·ble** *adj.* —**dis·per´sive** *adj.*

dis·place´ *vt.* to move from a proper or usual place; to take the place of; to remove from office —**dis·plac´a·ble** *adj.* —**dis·place´ment** *n.* — **dis·plac´er** *n.*

dis·play´ *n.* a public showing —*vt.* to show publicly

dis·please´ *vi., vt.* to dissatisfy or annoy; to offend —**dis·pleas´ing·ly**

adv. —**dis·pleas´ure** *n.*

dis·pos´a·ble *adj.* designed to be discarded after a single use —**dis·pos´a·bil·i·ty** *n.*

disposable income income that remains after taxes

dis·pose´ *vt.* to place in proper order or form; to settle; to adjust mentally so as to be amenable or receptive —**dis·pos´al** *n.* —**dis·pos´er** *n.*

dis·po·si´tion *n.* one's usual temperament or inclination; a final settlement or solution

dis·pos·sess´ *vt.* to deprive of a possession —**dis·pos·sessed´** *adj.* — **dis·pos·ses´sion** *n.* —**dis·pos·ses´sor** *n.*

dis·pro·por´tion *n.* a lack of harmony or symmetry —*vt.* to make disproportionate —**dis·pro·por´tion·al** *adj.* —**dis·pro·por´tion·al·ly** *adv.*

dis·pro·por´tion·ate *adj.* out of proportion; uneven —**dis·pro·por´tion·ate·ly** *adv.* —**dis·pro·por´tion·ate·ness** *n.*

dis·prove´ *vt.* to expose as false; to refute —**dis·prov´a·ble** *adj.*

dis·pu´ta·ble *adj.* questionable; uncertain —**dis·put·a·bil´i·ty** *n.* — **dis·put´a·bly** *adv.*

dis·pu´tant *n.* one who quarrels or disagrees —*adj.* involving dispute

dis´pu·ta´tion *n.* a controversy; the act of disagreeing; a formal debate —**dis·pu·ta´tious, dis·pu´ta·tive** *adj.* —**dis·pu·ta´tious·ly** *adv.* — **dis·pu·ta´tious·ness** *n.*

dis·pute´ *n.* a quarrel or argument; a disagreement —*vi.* to argue —*vt.* to argue about; to doubt the truth of —**dis·put´er** *n.*

dis·qual´i·fy *vt.* to declare ineligible —**dis·qual·i·fi·ca´tion** *n.*

dis·qui´et *n.* anxiety —*vt.* to make anxious

dis·re·gard´ *n.* a lack of regard or respect —*vt.* to ignore or neglect

dis·re·pair´ *n.* in need of repair; a product of neglect

dis·rep´u·ta·ble *adj.* lacking in character or respectability —**dis·rep´u·ta·ble·ness** *n.* —**dis·rep´u·ta·bly** *adv.*

dis·re·pute´ *n.* a lack or loss of reputation

dis·re·spect´ *n.* discourtesy; insolence —*vt.* to treat discourteously —**dis´re·spect´ful** *adj.* —**dis´re·spect´ful·ly** *adv.* —**dis´re·spect´ful·ness** *n.*

dis·robe´ *vi., vt.* to undress —**dis·robe´ment** *n.*

dis·rupt´ *vt.* to intrude; to upset an orderly process —**dis·rupt´er, dis·rupt´or** *n.* —**dis·rup´tion** *n.*

dis·rup´tive *adj.* rebellious; unruly; intruding —**dis·rup´tive·ly** *adv.* —**dis·rup´tive·ness** *n.*

dis·sat·is·fac´to·ry *adj.* not acceptable

dis·sat´is·fy *vt.* to fail to please —**dis·sat·is·fac´tion** *n.* —**dis·sat´is·fied** *adj.*

dis·sect´ *vt.* to separate into parts; to examine closely —**dis·sect´ed** *adj.* —**dis·sec´tion** *n.* —**dis·sec´tor** *n.*

dis·sem´ble *vt.* to conceal so as to deceive —*vi.* to conceal one's true nature —**dis·sem´blance** *n.* —**dis·sem´bler** *n.*

dis·sem´i·nate´ *vt.* to scatter; to spread widely —**dis·sem´i·na´tion** *n.* —**dis·sem´i·na´tor** *n.*

dis·sen´sion *n.* a disagreeing; a difference of opinion

dis·sent´ *n.* a difference of opinion —*vi.* to express disagreement —**dis·sent´er** *n.* —**dis·sent´ing** *adj.* —**dis·sent´ing·ly** *adv.*

dis·sen´tience *n.* disagreement; opposition

dis·sen´tient *adj.* disagreeing —*n.* a dissenter

dis·sen´tious *adj.* opposing; disagreeing —**dis·sen´tious·ly** *adv.*

dis´ser·tate *vi.* speak at length

dis´ser·ta´tion *n.* a lengthly discourse —**dis·ser·ta´tion·al** *adj.*

dis·serve´ *vt.* to harm; treat badly

dis·serv´ice *n.* a harmful or thoughtless deed

dis´si·dent *adj.* hostile; opposed; of those opposing or disagreeing —*n.* one who opposes —**dis´si·dence** *n.* —**dis´si·dent·ly** *adv.*

dis·sim´i·lar *adj.* different —**dis·sim´i·lar·ly** *adv.*

dis·sim´i·lar´i·ty *n.* a difference; an instance of divergence or deviation

dis·sim´i·late´ *vt., vi.* to make or become different —**dis·sim´i·la·tive** *adj.*

dis·sim·i·la´tion *n.* making different

dis·si·mil´i·tude *n.* difference

dis·sim´u·late´ *vi., vt.* to conceal or disguise one's feelings by pretense —**dis·sim·u·la´tion** *n.* —**dis·sim´u·la·tive** *adj.* —**dis·sim´u·la·tor** *n.*

dis´si·pate *vi.* to waste one's life in debauchery; to vanish by dispersion —*vt.* to scatter, dispel, or disperse; to use recklessly, waste —**dis´si·pa´tion** *n.*

dis´si·pat·ed *adj.* scattered; depleted or destroyed; exhibiting the injurious effects of self–indulgence —**dis´si·pat·ed·ly** *adv.* —**dis´si·pat·ed·ness** *n.*

dis·so´ci·ate *vi., vt.* to separate; to sever ties —**dis·so´ci·at·ed** *adj.* —**dis·so·ci·a´tion** *n.*

dis·so´ci·a·tive *adj.* tending to produce separation

dis·sol´u·ble *adj.* able to be dissolved —**dis·sol·u·bil´i·ty, dis·sol´u·ble·ness** *n.*

dis´so·lute *adj.* lacking restraint; immoral —**dis´so·lute·ly** *adv.* —**dis´so·lute·ness** *n.*

dis·so·lu´tion *n.* a dissolving or termination, as of a meeting, a business, etc.

dis·solve´ *vi., vt.* to change or cause to change into a liquid; to pass or make pass into solution: *dissolve the cocoa in hot water,* to disintegrate or disappear; to end, as a marriage —**dis·solv·a·bil´i·ty** *adv.* —**dis·solv´a·ble** *adj.* —**dis·solv´ent** *n.*

dis´so·nance, dis´so·nan·cy *n.* a disagreeable combination of sound; a lack of agreement or harmony —**dis´so·nant** *adj.* —**dis´so·nant·ly** *adv.*

dis·suad´a·ble *adj.* able to be persuaded against

dis·suade´ *vt.* to persuade from a course of action —**dis·suad´er** *n.* —**dis·sua´sion** *n.*

dis·sua´sive *adj.* intended to discourage or prevent —**dis·sua´sive·ly** *adv.* —**dis·sua´sive·ness** *n.*

dis´tal *adj.* remote; far from origin or attachment —**dis´tal·ly** *adv.*

dis´tance *n.* the time or space between two points; reserve, remoteness —*vt.* to keep away; to act aloof

dis´tant *adj.* remote; far apart in time or space; reserved, aloof —**dis´tant·ly** *adv.*

dis·taste´ *n.* repugnance

dis·taste´ful *adj.* offensive; unpleasant —**dis·taste´ful·ly** *adv.* —**dis·taste´ful·ness** *n.*

dis·tem´per *n.* an affliction or disease; an infectious disease of animals

dis·tend´ *vi., vt.* to inflate; to stretch —**dis·ten´si·ble** *adj.* —**dis·ten´sion, dis·ten´tion** *n.*

dis·til´, dis·till´ *vt.* to extract or concentrate by distillation —**dis·til´la·ble** *adj.*

dis´til·late *n.* the result of distillation

dis·til·la´tion *n.* the process of refining by heating a substance, then cooling and collecting the condensation; something produced by distilling —**dis·till´er** *n.* —**dis·till´er·y** *n.*

dis·tinct´ *adj.* undeniably different; definite, unmistakable; clearly perceptible —**dis·tinct´ly** *adv.* —**dis·tinct´ness** *n.*

dis·tinc´tion *n.* a specific difference; a distinguishing characteristic or quality; eminence or prestige

dis·tinc´tive *adj.* characteristic; having a unique or uncommon quality —**dis·tinc´tive·ly** *adv.* —**dis·tinc´tive·ness** *n.*

dis·tin´guish *vi., vt.* to set apart; to recognize clearly; to bring prestige to: *distinguished in literary circles*

dis·tin´guish·a·ble *adj.* able to be discerned; perceptible; seen to be unique or different —**dis·tin´guish·a·bil´i·ty, dis·tin´guish·a·ble·ness** *n.* —**dis·tin´guish·a·bly** *adv.*

dis·tin´guished *adj.* celebrated, well-known; refined; extraordinary

dis·tort´ *vt.* to bend out of shape; to misrepresent; to alter so as to spoil: *poor acoustics distorted the sound of the music* —**dis·tort´ed·ness, dis·tor´tion** *n.*

dis·tor´tive *adj.* causing distortion

dis·tract´ *vt.* to divert attention away; to create confusion —**dis·tract´ing** *adj.* —**dis·tract´ing·ly** *adv.*

dis·tract´ed *adj.* diverted; confused; —**dis·tract´ed·ly** *adv.* —**dis·tract´ed·ness** *n.*

dis·trac´tion *n.* something that diverts one's attention, or that confuses or distresses; a drawing away of one's attention or concentration

dis·tract´i·ble *adj.* easily diverted or confused; —**dis·tract´i·bil·i·ty** *n.*

dis·traught´ *adj.* deeply troubled; severely distressed

dis·tress´ *n.* suffering, such as pain, anxiety, discomfort, etc.; a condition requiring immediate help: *a ship in distress* —*vt.* to cause pain, anxiety, etc.; to inflict suffering upon —**dis·tressed** adj. —**dis·tress′ing·ly** adv.

dis·tress′ful adj. causing worry or torment —**dis·tress′ful·ly** adv. —**dis·tress′ful·ness** n.

dis·trib′u·tar·y n. a channel or line of distribution flowing away from a main channel or line

dis·trib′ute vt. to disburse in more or less equal amounts, or according to a plan —**dis·trib′ut·a·ble** adj. —**dis′tri·bu′tion** n.

distribution curve a graphic representation of the concentration of elements in an array

dis·trib′u·tive adj. serving to disseminate or classify; pertaining to distribution —**dis·trib′u·tive·ly** adv. —**dis·trib′u·tive·ness** n.

dis·trib′u·tor n. one who is authorized to merchandise a particular product or brand; any merchant; a device that dispenses a measured quantity in a timely manner, as the device in an engine that feeds power to the spark plugs

dis′trict n. an area specially defined or distinguished by some chracteristic

district attorney in the US, a prosecutor for the government

dis·trust′ n. a lack of trust or confidence —vt. to lack confidence in —**dis·trust′ful** adj. —**dis·trust′ful·ly** adv. —**dis·trust′ful·ness** n.

dis·turb′ vt. to upset the serenity or order of; to interrupt; to make uneasy

dis·tur′bance n. a commotion; disorder; a deviation from the usual

dis·turbed′ adj. distressed, troubled; mentally or emotionally unstable

dis·u·nite′ vi., vt. to divide or separate —**dis·un′ion** n.

dis·use′ n. a state of neglect —vt. to take out of service; to abandon or discard

ditch n. a trench or channel used for carrying water or forming a barrier —vt. to make a ditch; to get rid of something; to deliberately leave behind

di′the·ism n. a belief in two supreme beings —**di·the·is′tic, di·the·is′ti·cal** adj.

dith′er n. a nervous or excited condition —vi. to act in a nervous or excited manner; to babble —**dith′er·y** adj.

dit′to n. the same as previous; a repetition —vt. to duplicate; make a copy; to repeat —**ditto mark** a symbol (") used in a list to indicate a repeat of the item above it

dit′ty n. a simple song

ditty bag a small bag or pouch for holding personal gear

di·u·re′sis n. excessive excretion of urine

di·u·ret′ic adj. tending to increase the output of urine —n. a substance that tends to increase the output of urine

di·ur′nal adj. happening each day; in the daytime —**di·ur′nal·ly** adv.

di·van′ n. a davenport or sofa

dive n. a headlong leap, as into water; a sudden dropping, as of prices; the descent of an airplane —vi., vt. to plunge or drop

div′er n. one who dives, esp. an underwater worker or explorer

di·verge′ vi. to move in different directions from a common point —**di·ver′gence** n. —**di·ver′gent** adj. —**di·ver′gent·ly** adv.

di′vers adj. several

div′ers n. pl. those who dive

di·verse′ adj. dissimilar; assorted —**di·verse′ly** adv. —**di·verse′ness** n.

di·ver′si·fied adj. disparate; dissimilar; sundry —**di·ver′si·ty** n.

di·ver′si·fy′ vt. to add variety; to branch out into new fields —**di·ver′si·fi·ca′tion** n.

di·ver′sion n. a turning aside; a distraction —**di·ver′sion·ar·y** adj.

di·vert′ vt. to turn aside; to distract

di·vert´ing adj. engaging; pleasing; entertaining —**di·vert´ing·ly** adv.

di·ver´tisse·ment n. an amusement or distraction, especially during an interlude in a theater performance

di·vest´ vt. to get rid of; to deprive of, as of an office —**di·vest´i·ture, di·vest´ment** n.

di·vide´ vt. to separate, as into parts or categories; to distribute in portions; to cause disagreement: *political beliefs divided them* —vi. to become separated; to share

di·vid´ed adj. separated; in disagreement —**di·vid´ed·ly** adv. — **di·vid´ed·ness** n.

divided highway (US) a road with a center strip that separates vehicles traveling in opposite directions

di·vid´er n. anything that serves to separate —**room divider** an article of furniture with open shelves, or a screen used to separate parts of a room

div´i·dend n. a bonus, often a share of profits divided among stockholders; an unexpected benefit

div·i·na´tion n. the art of prediction —**div·in´a·to·ry** adj.

di·vine´ adj. of the nature of a diety; godlike; pleasing —vt. to predict — **di·vine´ly** adv. —**di·vine´ness** n.

di·vin´er n. one who foretells the future; one who determines the presence of that not apparent, such as the location of water underground

diving bell a device used for exploring under water, supplied with air from a host vessel

diving board a springboard from which one can dive into a swimming pool

diving suit a heavy garment worn by a deep sea diver

divining rod a forked branch used by a diviner in locating water underground

di·vin´i·ty n. a divine nature; the study of theology; a type of candy

di·vis´i·ble adj. able to be separated into smaller parts; capable of being evenly divided by a particular number, leaving no remainder — **di·vis·i·bil´i·ty** n. —**di·vis´i·ble·ness** n.

di·vi´sion n. a partition; a portioning or the resulting portion; a rift or disagreement —**di·vi´sion·al, di·vi´sion·ar·y** adj. —**di·vi´sion·al·ly** adv.

di·vi´sive adj. provoking disagreement —**di·vi´sive·ly** adv. —**di·vi´sive·ness** n.

di·vi´sor n. the value by which a number is divided

di·vorce´ n. the legal dissolution of a marriage; any radical separation, as of operations within a company or the association of concepts —vt. to dissolve a marriage; to entirely separate two or more entities or concepts from association or influence —**di·vorce´ment** n.

di·vulge´ vt. to make known; reveal —**di·vulge´ment, di·vul´gence** n. —**di·vulg´er** n.

di·vulse´ vt. to tear apart —**di·vul´sion** n. —**di·vul´sive** adj.

diz´zy adj. light–headed; dazed; silly; flighty —**diz´zi·ly** adv. —**diz´zi·ness** n.

DNA n. deoxyribonucleic acid, that carries the genetic code within cells

do vi., vt. to perform; to cause; to behave —**do in** to murder —**done in** tired; murdered —**do well** to prosper

do´a·ble adj. able to be accomplished; profitable or expedient

do´cent n. a teacher or lecturer; (US) a tour guide —**do´cent·ship** n.

doc´ile adj. mild–mannered; submissive —**doc´ile·ly** adv. —**do·cil´i·ty** n.

dock n. a pier or wharf —vt. to bring a boat or ship into dock; to cut short; to deduct: *dock his wages for arriving late*

dock´et *n.* a court calendar

doc´tor *n.* one licensed to practice medicine; the highest degree awarded by a college or university —*vt.* to treat an illness or injury; to repair, especially in a makeshift fashion; to alter for some purpose —**doc´tor·al** *adj.*

doc´tor·ate *n.* a doctor's degree

doc´tri·naire´ *adj.* theoretical —*n.* one favoring theory over fact

doc´trine *n.* a statement of principals or policy —**doc´tri·nal** *adj.* —**doc´tri·nal·ly** *adv.*

doc´u·ment *n.* a written record of information or evidence —*vt.* to furnish supporting information or evidence —**doc´u·ment·a·ble** *adj.* —**doc·u·men·ta´tion** *n.*

doc·u·ment´ary *adj.* regarding a document or documents; of a factual report; based on documents —*n.* a book, movie etc. that presents a purportedly factual report —**doc·u·men·tar´i·an** *n.*

dod´der *vt.* to totter, as from age — **dod´der·ing** *adj.* —**dod´der·ing·ly** *adv.*

dodge *vt.* to sidestep; to avoid or evade by trickery —*vi.* to move suddenly; to employ trickery —*n.* a deception or ruse —**dodg´er** *n.*

do´er *n.* one who achieves

doff *vt.* to remove; to discard

dog *n.* a domesticated animal related to the wolf

dog´-ear *vt.* to turn down the corner of a page —*n.* a folded corner of a page —**dog´-eared** *adj.*

dog´ged *adj.* persistent —**dog´ged·ly** *adv.* —**dog´ged·ness** *n.*

dog´ma *n.* an authoritative statement of doctrine

dog·mat´ic, dog·mat´i·cal *adj.* adhering strictly to doctrine; dictatorial —**dog·mat´i·cal·ly** *adv.* —**dog´ma·tism** *n.* —**dog´ma·tist** *n.*

doi´ly *n.* a mat or runner used as a table decoration

dol´drums *n.* a depressed state of mind

dole *n.* a charitable gift; a thing portioned out carefully —*vt.* to give charitably; to portion out

dole´ful *adj.* mournful; full of sadness —**dole´ful·ly** *adv.* —**dole´ful·ness** *n.*

do´lor *n.* sorrow; anguish —**dol´or·ous** *adj.* —**do´lo·rous·ly** *adv.* —**do´lo·rous·ness** *n.*

doit *n.* one who is slow-witted — **dolt´ish** *adj.* —**dolt´ish·ly** *adv.* —**dolt´ish·ness** *n.*

do·main´ *n.* one's sphere of influence or control; territory controlled by a person, government, etc.

do·mes´tic *adj.* of a household; fond of caring for a home or family; pertaining to a country; of a tamed animal —*n.* a servant in the home —**do·mes´ti·cal·ly** *adv.*

do·mes´ti·cate´ *vt.* to bring under control, as a wild plant or animal; to bring and adapt to a new region or country —**do·mes·ti·ca´tion** *n.*

do·mes·tic´i·ty *n.* a fondness for home and family

dom´i·cile *n.* a place of residence; a home

dom´i·nate *vt.* to control; to have preeminence —**dom´i·nance, dom·i·na´tion** *n.* —**dom´i·nant** *adj.* —**dom´i·nant·ly** *adv.*

dom·i·neer´ *vi., vt.* to tyrannize or bully

dom·i·neer´ing *adj.* assertive; overbearing —**dom·i·neer´ing·ly** *adv.* —**dom·i·neer´ing·ness**

do·min´ion *n.* sovereignty

do´nate *vt.* to contribute, especially to a worthy cause —**do·na´tion** *n.*

done *adj.* completed

do´nor *n.* a contributor

doom *n.* inevitable ruin; condemnation —*vt.* to destine for ruination; to condemn

dooms´day *n.* a time of final judgment

door *n.* an entryway

dope *n.* a drug; information

dor´mant *adj.* temporarily inactive —**dor´man·cy** *n.*

dor´mi·to´ry *n.* a building providing living quarters, esp. at a college or university; a large room providing sleeping accommodations for many people

dor´y *n.* a small rowboat

dose *n.* an amount to be given or taken at one time, as of a medicine —*vt.* to give in measured amounts —**dos´age** *n.*

dos´si·er *n.* information relating to a particular matter or person

dot´age *n.* childish behavior caused by old age: senility; extravagant affection

do´tard *n.* a senile old person

dote *vi.* to be excessively attentive to —**dot·er** *n.* —**dot´ing·ly** *adv.*

dou´ble *adj.* twofold; duplicated; paired; made for two —*n.* anything twice as much; a look–alike —*vt.* to make twice as much; to fold and make two layers —*vi.* to increase twofold; to reverse course; to serve in more than one capacity —**dou´bly** *adv.*

dou´ble–deal´ing *adj.* treacherous — **dou´ble–deal´er** *n.*

dou´ble–deck´er *n.* a bus with two levels, a sandwich or ice cream cone made in two layers, etc.

dou´ble–en·ten´dre *n.* a word or phrase having a double meaning, often risqué

double helix the coiled structure of DNA

double standard a code that is unevenly applied

dou´blet *n.* a pair; a short, close–fitting outer garment

double take an amusing delayed reaction

doubt *n.* uncertainty; a lack of trust; skepticism —*vi., vt.* to be uncertain or skeptical —**doubt´ful** *adj.* —**doubt´ful·ly** *adv.* —**doubt´fulness** *n.*

doubt´less *adj.* without question — **doubt´less·ly** *adv.* —**doubt´lessness** *n.*

dough´ty *adj.* valiant —**dough´ti·ly** *adv.* —**dough´ti·ness** *n.*

dour *adj.* dreary; gloomy —**dour´ly** *adv.* —**dour´ness** *n.*

douse *vt.* to immerse in liquid; to wet thoroughly

dove´tail´ *n.* a cutout, usually at the end of a strip of wood, shaped like the tail of a dove, that fits into a cutout in another piece to join the two —*vi., vt.* to connect with a dovetail joint; to fit closely; to connect, as data, so as to form a logical sequence

dov´ish *adj.* peaceful —**dov´ish·ness**

dow´a·ger *n.* a dignified elderly lady

dow´dy *adj.* shabby —**dow´di·ly** *adv.* —**dow´di·ness** *n.*

dow´el *n.* a round piece of wood or metal, often used to join wooden parts

dow´er *n.* an endowment, esp. a widow's portion —*vt.* to furnish with a dower

down *adv.* from higher to lower; from a former or earlier time; to a diminshed volume or bulk: *to boil down*; to a less active state; to greater intensity: *get down to work* —*adj.* toward a lower position; in a lower place; dejected —*vt.* to subdue; to swallow —*n.* a descent; a reversal of fortune

down–and–out´ destitute

down´cast *adj.* dejected; despondent

down´fall *n.* a failure; disgrace

down´grade *vt.* to reduce or lower in status, earnings, etc.

down´heart·ed *adj.* dejected; discouraged —**down´heart·ed·ly** *adv.*

down´pour *n.* a heavy rain

down´right *adj.* absolute; straightforward —*adv.* utterly

down'trod·den *adj.* oppressed

down'turn *n.* an economic decline

down'ward *adj., adv.* toward a lower point —**down'ward·ly, down'wards** *adv.*

dow'ry *n.* property brought by a bride to her husband at the time of marriage

doze *n.* a brief, light sleep —*vi.* to sleep lightly or briefly

doz'en *n.* a set of twelve

drab *adj.* dull; colorless —**drab'ly** *adv.* —**drab'ness** *n.*

draft (*US*) *adj.* drawn from a keg —*n.* a drawing or writing, often preliminary; a current of air; an order directing the payment of money; that drawn from a keg; the selection of a person or persons for some purpose; the depth of a vessel below the water line —*vt.* to make a layout; to sketch or write; to select for service —**draft·ee'** *n.*

drafts'man *n.* one who draws, especially designs or plans requiring precision

drag *n.* the act of pulling; any of a number of devices that are normally pulled or that check motion by weight, friction, etc.; an impedence or a measure of impedence; slow laborious movement; a thing that is tiresome; influence —*vi.* to be pulled or lag behind; to move slowly —*vt.* to pull; to draw out slowly or with difficulty —**main drag** a main road

drag'on *n.* a legendary beast

dra·goon' *n.* a cavalryman

drain *n.* a duct for carrying waste water, etc.; that which gradually draws off —*vi.* to draw off, as to remove water, etc.; to cause a depletion of energy, resources, etc. —**drain'age** *n.*

drake *n.* a male duck

dram *n.* a unit of weight; a small portion

dra'ma *n.* a play, or plays collectively; a serious play or actual events that emulate such a play —**dra·mat'ic** *adj.* —**dra·mat'i·cal·ly** *adv.* —**dram'a·tist** *n.*

dra'ma·tis per·so'nae *n.* a cast of characters

dra·mat'ics *n.* the art of staging drama; histrionics

dram'a·tize' *vt.* to adapt to use in a play; to present events in an exaggerated fashion —**dram'a·tiz·a·ble** *adj.* —**dram·a·ti·za'tion** *n.* —**dram'a·tiz·er** *n.*

drape *n.* a cloth hanging in folds; the way in which cloth hangs —*vt.* to cover or decorate with cloth; to arrange cloth; to hang loosely —**dra'per·y** *n.*

dras'tic *adj.* extreme; strong and rapid —**dras'ti·cal·ly** *adv.*

draught (*Brit.*) *adj.* drawn from a keg —*n.* a drawing or writing, often preliminary; a current of air; an order directing the payment of money; that drawn from a keg; the depth of a vessel below the water line —*vt.* to make a layout; to sketch or write

draughts *n.* (*Brit.*) a board game similar to checkers in the US

draw *n.* something that attracts or entices; a conflict ending in a tie —*vi., vt.* to pull or drag; to suck; to entice; to compose or portray; to pull out —**draw the line** to set a limit

draw'back' *n.* a disadvantage or shortcoming

draw'er *n.* one who draws; a sliding container in furniture

drawl *n.* a manner of speaking characterized by drawn out vowels —*vi., vt.* to speak slowly, drawing out vowels —**drawl'er** *n.* —**drawl'ing** *adj.* —**drawl'ing·ly** *adv.*

dray *n.* a low, heavy cart —**dray'man** *n.*

dray'age *n.* a fee for hauling

dread n. fearful anticipation —vt. to anticipate with fear or reluctance

dread'ful adj. inspiring dread; unpleasant, distasteful —**dread'ful·ly** adv. —**dread'ful·ness** n.

dread'nought n. a battleship

dream n. images occurring during sleep; a visionary concept; something extremely pleasant —vi. to experience in a dream; to deem practical —vt. to envision in a dream or as in a dream; to waste time —**dream'er** n. —**dream'ful** adj. —**dream'ful·ly** adv.

dream'y adj. pleasant; soothing —**dream'i·ly** adv. —**dream'i·ness** n.

drear'y adj. bleak, dismal; dull —**drear'i·ly** adv. —**drear'i·ness** n. —**drear'i·some** adj.

dredge n. a machine for clearing waterways —vt., vi. to dig with or as with a dredge —**dredg'er** n.

dregs pl. n. residue; something that is worthless, as the dregs of humanity

drench vt. to saturate; to wet thoroughly

dress vt. to clothe; to trim, or adorn —vi. to don or wear clothing —n. apparel —**dress up** to improve the appearance of; to don one's best clothing —**dress'mak·er** n. —**dress'mak·ing** adj., n.

dress'er n. a decorator, as window dresser; one who dresses well; (US) a chest of drawers

dressing gown (Brit.) a loose, casual garment, usually closed at the front with a belt

drib'ble n. a small amount —vi., vt. to trickle; to flow a little at a time

drift n. something carried, as by wind or water; a gradual change in position; a trend —vi. to be carried by wind or water; to wander casually or aimlessly; to stray from a set course or position

drift'er n. a homeless person

drill n. practice exercises; a boring tool —vi. to use a drill —vt. to bore a hole; to train with the use of methodical exercises

drink n. a beverage —vi., vt. to ingest or absorb a liquid —**drink'a·ble** adj. —**drink'er** n.

drip n. a falling in drops; a drop of liquid; the sound of a falling drop of liquid —vi., vt. to fall or cause to fall in drops

drive n. the act of operating or propelling a motor vehicle; a trip by auto; a path for an auto; a sharp blow, as of a ball with a club, bat, etc.; an organized effort for some purpose; enthusiasm or vigor —vi., vt. to operate or propel; to hit a ball; to press toward a goal —**driv·a·bil·i·ty** n. —**driv'a·ble** adj. —**driv'er** n.

driv'el n. foolish talk —vi., vt. to utter foolishly —**driv'el·er, driv'el·ler** n.

drive'way n. a private access road

driz'zle n. a light rain —vi., vt. to fall in small or light drops; to lightly moisten —**driz'zly** adj.

droll adj. quaintly humorous —**droll'er·y** n. —**drol'ly** adv.

drone n. a loafer; a dull humming sound —vi. to speak monotonously

droop vi. to hang down; to become dejected —**droop'i·ness** n. —**droop'ing** adj. —**droop'ing·ly** adv. —**droop'y** adj.

drop n. the quantity of a liquid that can fall in one spherical mass; a small piece or amount; a sharp decline; the vertical distance between two levels; a location for depositing material for distribution; the material deposited —vi., vt. to fall or cause to fall or decline; to deposit at a specified location

drop'let n. a small drop

drop'out n. one who abandons an undertaking

dross n. waste matter

drought n. a long period of dry

weather; any prolonged shortage —**drought´y** *adj.*

drove *n.* a large number moving together, as of people or cattle — **dro´ver** *n.*

drown *vi.* to die by suffocation in liquid —*vt.* to kill by suffocation in liquid; to overwhelm

drowse *vt., vi.* to make or become sleepy

drow´sy *adj.* sleepy; sluggish — **drows´i·ly** *adv.* —**drows´i·ness** *n.*

drub *vt.* to beat with a stick; to vanquish —*n.* a heavy blow

drub´bing *n.* a one-sided defeat

drudge *n.* one engaged in menial or dull work —*vi.* to labor at a menial or dull task

drudg´er·y *n.* work that is menial or tiresome

drug *n.* any substance that alters a body function —*vt.* to give an altering substance to; to add a narcotic to food or drink

dru´id *n.* a priest or sorcerer in ancient Gaul —**dru·id´ic, dru·id´ic·al** *adj.* —**dru´id·ism** *n.*

drum *n.* a percussion instrument; a cylindrical receptacle; constant repetition —*vi., vt.* to beat constantly, as on a drum —**drum out** to expel —**drum up** to summon or seek by persistence: *drum up customers* —**drum´mer** *n.*

drunk *adj.* affected by alcoholic drink to the point of impairment; overcome by emotion —*n.* one who is legally or noticeably overcome by drink —**drunk´en** *adj.* —**drunk´en·ly** *adv.* —**drunk´en·ness** *n.* — **drunk´ard** *n.*

dry *adj.* lacking or freed of moisture; of any non-liquid substance; not sweet, as of a wine; plain, as of food served without butter or sauce; not marked by emotion; boring; unproductive —*vi., vt.* to become or make dry —**dri´ly, dry´ly** *adv.* —**dry´ness** *n.*

dry´ad *n.* a mythical wood nymph

dry cell *n.* a sealed battery

dry´dock *n.* a mooring that can be pumped free of water for the repair of ships —*vi., vt.* to go or be put into drydock

dry goods textile, fabrics

dry rot *n.* a fungal disease of wood or growing plants

dry run *n.* a rehearsal

dual *adj.* comprised of two parts — **du´al·ism** *n.* —**du·al·is´tic** *adj.* — **du·al·is´ti·cal·ly** *adv.* —**du·al´i·ty** *n.* —**du´al·ly** *adv.*

dual carriageway (*Brit.*) a road with a center strip that separates vehicles traveling in opposite directions

dub *vt.* to bestow knighthood; to confer with a title, nickname, etc.; to add music, subtitles, etc. to a film or recording

du·bi´e·ty *n.* doubt; uncertainty

du´bi·ous *adj.* questionable; suspect; causing or feeling doubt or uncertainty —**du´bi·ous·ly** *adv.* —**du´bi·ous·ness** *n.*

du·bi´ta·ble *adj.* uncertain —**du´bi·ta·bly** *adv.*

du´cal *adj.* of a duke or duchy

duch´ess *n.* the wife or widow of a duke

duch´y *n.* the realm of a duke

duck *n.* a web-footed water bird — *vi., vt.* to plunge into water; to dodge; to evade or avoid

duck´ling *n.* a small or baby duck

duct *n.* a tubular channel —**duct´work** *n.*

duc´tile *adj.* able to be hammered thin; easily led —**duc´tile·ness, duc´til´i·ty** *n.*

dude *n.* a dandy —**dud´ish** *adj.*

dud´geon *n.* sullen displeasure

due *adj.* scheduled or expected, as for arrival or payment; fitting or deserved, as *due respect* —*n.* anything owed or deserved

du´el *n.* formal combat between two

persons —*vi.*, *vt.* to fight a duel —
du´el·er, **du´el·ist** *n.*

du·et´ *n.* a musical composition for
two voices or instruments

dug´out *n.* a canoe; an underground
shelter

duke *n.* an English peer below a
prince or archbishop

duke´dom *n.* a duchy

dul´cet *adj.* pleasing to the ear;
soothing —**dul´cet·ly** *adv.*

dul´ci·mer *n.* a stringed musical
instrument

dull *adj.* mentally or physically slow;
lacking spirit; boring; blunt, as of
a knife; lacking brightness, as of
color —*vt.*, *vi.* to make or become
dull —**dull´ish** *adj.* —**dull´ness**,
dul´ness *n.* —**dul´ly** *adv.*

dul´lard *n.* a dull person

duly *adv.* in a proper manner

dumb *adj.* unable or unwilling to
speak, as from shock or emotion;
lacking intelligence —**dumb´ly**
adv. —**dumb´ness** *n.*

dumb´found, **dum´found** *vt.* to astonish; to make speechless from
shock

dumb´struck *adj.* shocked speechless

dum´my *n.* a stupid or foolish person; a representation of a person:
*a ventriloquist's dummy, a store
dummy*; a silent player, as in
bridge —*adj.* fake or counterfeit;
representational

dump *vt.*, *vi.* to empty or unload; to
get rid of —*n.* a place for refuse; a
distribution point: *fuel dump*

dump´ling *n.* a filled pastry; dough
dropped into soup or stew

dump´ster *n.* (US) a large metal
container for trash

dump´y *adj.* short and thick

dun *vt.*, *vi.* to press for payment

dunce *n.* an ignorant person

dune *n.* a hill or ridge of sand

dung *n.* animal excrement

dun·ga·ree´ *n.* a sturdy cotton cloth

—**dun·ga·rees´** work clothes

dun´geon *n.* an underground cell or
vault

dunk *vi.*, *vt.* to dip into liquid

du·o·de´num *n.* the section of the
small intestine nearest to the
stomach

dupe *n.* one easily deceived; a person
deceived or used by another —*vt.*
to deceive —**dup·a·bil·i·ty** *n.* —
dup´a·ble *adj.* —**dup´er** *n.* —**dup·
er·y** *n.*

du´plex *adj.* double —*n.* (US) two
housing units that share a common wall

du´pli·cate *adj.* copied —*n.* an exact
copy —*vt.* to make a copy; to repeat —**du·pli·ca´tion** *n.* —**du´pli·
ca·tive** *adj.* —**du´pli·ca·tor** *n.*

du·plic´i·ty *n.* deception —**du·plic´i·
tous** *adj.* —**du·plic´i·tous·ly** *adv.*

du´ra·ble *adj.* able to withstand
heavy use —**du·ra·bil´i·ty**, **du´ra·
ble·ness** *n.* —**du´ra·bly** *adv.*

durable goods products that have a
relatively long life, such as automobiles or household appliances

du·ra´tion *n.* an interval of time

du·ress´ *n.* threat or coercion

dur´ing *prep.* throughout; in the
course of

dusk *adj.* dark in tone —*n.* the early
evening darkness —**dusk´i·ly** *adv.*
—**dusk´i·ness** *n.* —**dusk´y** *adj.*

dust *n.* a substance reduced to powder —*vt.* to remove dust from; to
sprinkle with or cover lightly: *dust
the fish with flour* —**dust´y** *adj.*

dust´er *n.* a device for removing
dust; a protective garment

du´te·ous *adj.* obedient; attentive to
duty —**du´te·ous·ly** *adv.* —**du´te·
ous·ness** *n.*

du´ti·ful *adj.* having a sense of duty;
obedient —**du´ti·ful·ly** *adv.* —
du´ti·ful·ness *n.*

duty *n.* that required by custom,
law, etc.; any task assigned or required by one's work; a tax on

imported goods

dwarf n. any animal or plant notably smaller than most of its species — vt. to curb the natural growth of — **dwarf´ish** adj. —**dwarf´ish·ness** n. —**dwarf´ism** n.

dwell vi. to reside; to linger —**dwell´er** n. —**dwell´ing** n.

dwin´dle vi. to lessen gradually

dye n. coloring matter —vt., vi. to stain with liquid coloring

dy·nam´ic, dy·nam´i·cal adj. relating to force or to the study of force; marked by frequent change; forceful, intense —**dy·nam´i·cal·ly** adv. —**dy´na·mism** n.

dy·nam´ics n. the study of force; the forces that make up or cause changes in a system

dy´na·mite n. an explosive —vt. to destroy with an explosive

dy´na·mo´ n. a mechine for converting mechanical energy to electrical energy

dy´nas·ty n. a succession of rulers from the same family —**dy·nas´tic, dy·nas´ti·cal** adj. —**dy·nas´ti·cal·ly** adv.

dyne n. a unit of force

dys´en·ter·y n. an inflammation of the large intestine

dys·func´tion n. abnormal or impaired function —**dys·func´tion·al** adj.

dys·lex´i·a n. a visual impairment — **dys·lex´ic** adj.

dys·pep´si·a n. distressed digestion —**dys´pep´tic** adj.

dys·pha´gia n. difficulty in swallowing —**dys·phag´ic** adj.

dys·pha´sia n. difficulty with speech —**dys·pha´sic** adj.

dys´tro·phy n. a disorder caused by faulty nutrition —**dys·troph´ic** adj.

e, E fifth letter of the English alphabet

each adj. one of two or more —adv.

ea´ger adj. impatient or anxious — **ea´ger·ly** adv. —**ea´ger·ness** n.

ea´gle-eyed adj. having keen sight

ear n. the organ and sense of hearing; heed

ear´ful n. gossip

ear´ly adj. near the beginning; before the usual or expected time — **ear´li·ness** n.

ear´mark vt. to mark for identification; to set aside for a special purpose —n. an owner's mark

earn vt. to receive as payment for labor; to deserve for one's efforts; to yield, as a profit —**earn´er** n.

earnings pl. n. salary or wages; profit

ear´nest adj. serious; intense; important —**earnest money** a payment made in advance to seal a bargain —**ear´nest·ly** adv. —**ear´nest·ness** n.

ear´shot n. hearing distance

earth n. dry land or the soil on dry land; a place of being as contrasted to the spirit world —**Earth** the planet that supports human life; —**earth´ling** n. —**earth´ly** adj. —**earth´li·ness** n.

earth´en n. made of earth or baked clay —**earth´en·ware** n.

earth´quake´ n. a tremor caused by disturbance of the earth's surface

earth´work n. a fortification

earth'y adj. crude, unrefined; natural —**earth´i·ness** n.

ease n. comfort; a state of rest; freedom from difficulty —vi., vt. to lessen or free from, as difficulty or pain; to move slowly and carefully —**ease´ful** adj. —**ease´ful·ly** adv —**ease´ful·ness** n.

ea´sel n. a stand for displaying pictures, paintings, etc.

ease´ment n. relief, as from pain something that provides relief; the right to limited use of property

east n. the general direction from which the sun rises —**the East** ar

182

eastern region; Asia —**east´er·ly** adj., adv. —**east´ward, east´ward·ly** adj., adv.

east´ern adj. pertaining to the east —**east´ern·er** n.

eas´y adj. done without difficulty; unhurried, relaxing —**eas´i·ly** adv. —**eas´i·ness** n.

eas´y·go·ing adj. relaxed; unhurried

eat vi., vt. to take in food; to consume or destroy: eaten by rust; to annoy —**eat´a·ble** adj. —**eat´er** n.

eat´er·y n. a restaurant

eaves pl. n. the projecting edge of a roof

eaves´drop vi. to listen secretly — **eaves´drop·per** n. —**eaves´drop·ing** n.

ebb n. a decline; a receding of tide waters (also **ebb tide**) —vi. to decline; to recede

eb´on·ite n. hard rubber

eb´on·y n. a hard wood, usually black —adj. made from ebony; black

e·bul´lient adj. exuberant; full of enthusiasm **e·bul´lience, e·bul´-lien·cy** n. —**e·bul´lient·ly** adv.

ec·cen´tric adj. off center; having different centers; unconventional —n. a device for transferring recip-rocating motion; an odd or uncon-ventional person —**ec·cen´tri·cal·ly** adv. —**ec·cen·tric´i·ty** n.

ec·cle·si·as´tic n. a cleric —**ec·cle´si·as´tic ec·cle·si·as´ti·cal** adj. pertaining to the church —**ec·cle·si·as´ti·cal·ly** adv.

ec·cle·si·ol´o·gy n. the study of church function, or of church ar-chitecture and ornamentation

ec·dys´i·ast n. a stripteaser

ech´e·lon n. a military formation; a level of responsibility or function

e·chid´na n. a spiny anteater

echo n. reflected sound —vi. to re-sound; to be repeated —vt. to re-peat —**ech´o·er** n.

ech·o·lo´cate vt. to position by

means of sound waves —**ech·o·lo·ca´tion** n. —**ech·o·lo´ca·tor** n.

é´clair, e·clair´ n. a filled pastry

e´clat´ n. a dazzling display; celeb-rity or renown

ec·lec´tic adj. from a variety of sources —n. one who utilizes ma-terial from a variety of sources — **ec·lec´ti·cal·ly** adv. —**ec·lec´ti·cism** n.

e·clipse´ n. the obscuring of one celestial body by another; any dimming or diminishing —vt. to darken or diminish; to overshadow

e·clip´tic n. the plane that intersects the sun and the earth's orbit — **e·clip´tic, e·clip´ti·cal** adj. — **e·clip´ti·cal·ly** adv.

e·col´o·gy n. the study of the effects of a changing environment on or-ganisms —**ec·o·log´ic, ec·o·log´i·cal** adj. —**ec·o·log´i·cal·ly** adv. — **e·col´o·gist** n.

e·co·nom´ic adj. of the production and management of wealth

e·co·nom´i·cal adj. done or intended to be done without waste; eco-nomic; pertaining to economics — **ec·o·nom´i·cal·ly** adv.

e·co·nom´ics n. the study of the production and management of wealth —**e·con´o·mist** n.

e·con´o·my n. the management of finances; care in the use of re-sources; a system for producing or managing resources

e·con´o·mize vi. to use carefully, especially by avoiding waste — **e·con´o·miz·er** n.

ec´o·sys·tem n. a community of organisms and their environment

ec´ru adj. light brown

ec´sta·sy n. emotional rapture or delight —**ec·stat´ic** adj. —**ec·stat´i·cal·ly** adv.

ec·u·men´ic, ec·u·men´i·cal adj. general or universal; promoting unity, esp. among religions —**ec·u·men´i·cal·ly** adv. —**ec·u·me·nic´i-**

ty *n.* —**ec´u·me·nism** *n.* —**ec´u·me·nist** *n.*

ec´ze·ma *n.* a skin inflammation

e·da´cious *adj.* voracious —**e·dac´i·ty** *n.*

ed´dy *n.* a circling current —*vi., vi.* to move or cause to move in circles

e·de´ma *n.* morbid accumulation of fluid

e·den´tate *adj.* toothless

edge *n.* a border or margin; the cutting part of a blade; a dividing line —*vt.* to create a border; to sharpen; to advance gradually

edg´y *adj.* irritable; nervous —**edg´i·ly** *adv.* —**edg´i·ness** *n.*

ed´i·ble *adj.* fit to be eaten —**ed·i·bil´i·ty, ed´i·ble·ness** *n.*

e´dict *n.* a formal decree; a strict order

ed´i·fice *n.* an imposing building

ed´i·fy´ *vt.* to instruct or enlighten —**ed·i·fi·ca´tion** *n.* —**ed´i·fi·er** *n.* —**ed´i·fy·ing·ly** *adv.*

ed´it *vt.* to prepare a written work for publication; to correct or alter, as a motion picture, sound track, computer file, etc. —**ed´i·tor** *n.* —**ed´it·a·ble** *adj.*

e·di´tion *n.* the form of a published work; the number of copies issued at one time

ed´i·to´ri·al *adj.* of an editor —*n.* an article or essay expressing opinion —**ed·i·to´ri·al·ize** *vi.* —**ed·i·to´ri·al·ly** *adv.*

ed´u·cate *vt.* to teach or train, especially by formal study; to inform; to refine, as one's taste

ed´u·cat·ed *adj.* well–schooled; cultivated in speech, manner, etc.

ed·u·ca´tion *n.* the training of one's mind; knowledge attained by instruction; the art of teaching —**ed·u·ca´tion·al** *adj.* —**ed·u·ca´tion·al·ly** *adv.* —**ed´u·ca·tor** *n.*

ed´u·cat·ive *adj.* instructive

e·duce´ *vt.* to draw out; to formulate —**e·duc´i·ble** *adj.* —**e·duc´tion** *n.*

—**e·duc´tor** *n.*

ee´rie, ee´ry *adj.* weird; awesome; strange —**ee´ri·ly** *adv.* —**ee´ri·ness** *n.*

ef·face´ *vt.* to obliterate; to make oneself insignificant —**ef·face´a·ble** *adj.* —**ef·face´ment** *n.* —**ef·fac´er** *n.*

ef·fect´ *n.* something brought about; the power to influence —*vt.* to produce or cause —**ef·fec´tive** *adj.* —**ef·fec´tive·ly** *adv.* —**ef·fec´tive·ness** *n.*

ef·fec´tu·al *adj.* possessing power; in force, legal —**ef·fec·tu·al´i·ty** *n.* —**ef·fec´tu·al·ly** *adv.*

ef·fec´tu·ate *vt.* to bring about —**ef·fec·tu·a´tion** *n.*

ef·fem´i·nate *adj.* having female traits; characterized by weakness and overrefinement —**ef·fem´i·na·cy** *n.* —**ef·fem´i·nate·ly** *adv.*

ef·fer·ves´cent *adj.* emitting tiny bubbles, like champagne or soda; lively or vivacious —**ef·fer·vesce´** *vi.* —**ef·fer·ves´cence, ef·fer·ves´cen·cy** *n.* —**ef·fer·ves´cent·ly** *adv.*

ef·fete´ *adj.* unproductive; burned out by self-indulgence —**ef·fete´ly** *adv.* —**ef·fete´ness** *n.*

ef·fi·ca´cious *adj.* capable of producing a desired effect —**ef·fi·ca´cious·ly** *adv.* **ef·fi·ca´cious·ness** *n.* —**ef´fi·ca·cy** *n.*

ef·fi´cient *adj.* producing a desired effect with a minimum of effort, waste, etc. —**ef·fi´cien·cy** *n.* —**ef·fi´cient·ly** *adv.*

ef´fi·gy *n.* a representative figure

ef·flo·resce´ *vi.* to bear flowers —**ef·flo·res´cence** *n.* —**ef·flo·res´cent** *adj.*

ef´flu·ence *n.* that flowing out, especially of liquid waste

ef·flu´vi·um *n.* an invisible emanation; noxious fumes or vapor —**ef·flu´vi·al, ef·flu´vi·ous** *adj.*

ef´fort *n.* the energy expended or required to accomplish a task; an attempt; that attempted or accomplished

ef·fort·less *adj.* requiring little or no effort **—ef·fort·less·ly** *adv.* **—ef·fort·less·ness** *n.*

ef·fron·ter·y *n.* boldness; insolence

ef·ful·gence *n.* a shining forth; radiance **—ef·ful·gent** *adj.* **—ef·ful·gent·ly** *adv.*

ef·fuse *vt., vi.* to pour forth or emanate **—ef·fu·sion** *n.*

ef·fu·sive *adj.* overly demonstrative; gushing **—ef·fu·sive·ly** *adv.* **—ef·fu·sive·ness** *n.*

e·gal·i·tar·i·an *adj.* of political and social equality **—e·gal·i·tar·i·an·ism** *n.*

egg *n.* a reproductive body; a female gamete **—lay an egg** to fail **—egg on** to incite

egg·head *n.* an intellectual

e·go *n.* the conscious self

e·go·cen·tric *adj.* self-centered; caring only for one's own interests **—e·go·cen·tric·i·ty, e·go·cen·trism** *n.*

e·go·ism *n.* excessive concern with one's self; conceit; the belief that self-interest should be the primary goal of human conduct **—e·go·ist** *n.* **—e·go·is·tic, e·go·is·ti·cal** *adj.* **—e·go·is·ti·cal·ly** *adv.*

e·go·ma·ni·a *n.* excessive concentration on one's self and one's own concerns **—e·go·ma·ni·ac** *n.* **—e·go·ma·ni·a·cal** *adj.*

e·go·tist *n.* one with an overblown sense of self-importance **—e·go·tism** *n.* **—e·go·tis·tic, e·go·tis·ti·cal** *adj.* **—e·go·tis·ti·cal·ly** *adv.*

e·gre·gious *adj.* exceptionally bad **— e·gre·gious·ly** *adv.* **—e·gre·gious·ness** *n.*

e·gress *n.* a going out; an exit **— e·gres·sion** *n.*

ei·der *n.* a large sea duck

ei·ther *adj.* one of two

e·jac·u·late *vt.* to utter or eject suddenly **—e·jac·u·la·tion** *n.*

—e·jac·u·la·tor *n.*

e·ject *vt.* to cast or drive out **— e·jec·tion** *n.* **—e·jec·tive** *adj.* **— e·jec·tive·ly** *adv.* **—e·jec·tor** *n.*

eke *vt.* to supplement; to produce with difficulty

e·lab·o·rate *adj.* developed with great attention to detail; intricate **—***vi., vt.* to work out or present in great detail **—e·lab·o·rate·ly** *adv.* **—e·lab·o·rate·ness, e·lab·o·ra·tion** *n.* **—e·lab·o·ra·tive** *adj.*

é·lan *n.* dash; vivacity

e·lapse *vi.* to pass by

e·las·tic *adj.* capable of quick recovery; easily adapting **—***n.* a stretchable fabric **—e·las·tic·i·ty** *n.* **— e·las·ti·cal·ly** *adv.*

e·late *vt.* raise the spirits of **—e·lat·ed** *adj.* **—e·lat·ed·ly** *adv.* **—e·lat·ed·ness** *n.*

e·la·tion *n.* exultation

el·bow *n.* the joint at the bend of the arm; any angular joint or fitting

el·der *adj.* older; superior in rank **— ***n.* an older person

el·der·ly *adj.* somewhat old

el·dest *adj.* first-born

e·lect *adj.* chosen; singled out, exclusive **—***n.* one chosen or singled out **—***vt.* to choose or vote for **—the elect** a favored group

e·lect·a·ble *adj.* able or likely to be elected **—e·lect·a·bil·i·ty** *n.*

e·lec·tion *n.* the process of selecting for office

e·lec·tion·eer *vi.* to seek election; to canvass for votes

e·lec·tive *adj.* chosen by votes; open to choice: optional

e·lec·tor *n.* a voter; a member of the electoral college **—e·lec·tor·al** *adj.*

electoral college the people chosen by the voters of a state to formally elect the president and vice president of the U.S.

e·lec·tor·ate *n.* a body of voters

e·lec·tric, e·lec·tri·cal *adj.* of or operated by electricity; emotionally charged —e·lec´tri·cal·ly *adv.* — e·lec·tri´cian *n.*

e·lec·tric´i·ty *n.* a flow of atomic particles used as a source of energy

e·lec´tri·fy *n.* to equip for operation by electricity; to startle or thrill — e·lec·tri·fi·ca´tion *n.*

e·lec·tro·car´di·o·gram *n.* a graph showing heart activity

e·lec·tro·car´di·o·graph´ *n.* an instrument for recording activity of the heart —e·lec·tro·car·di·og´ra·phy *n.*

e·lec´tro·cute´ *vt.* to execute by electricity —e·lec·tro·cu´tion *n.*

e·lec´trode *n.* a conducting element for an electric charge

e·lec·tro·dy·nam´ics *n.* the study of the interaction of electic currents and magnetic fields

e·lec·tro·en·ceph´a·lo·gram *n.* a record of the brain's electrical activity

e·lec·tro·en·ceph´a·lo·graph *n.* a device for recording electrical activity in the brain

e·lec·trol´y·sis *n.* a means to destroy unwanted body hair

e·lec·tro·lyte *n.* a chemical compound that becomes a conductor when dissolved or molten — e·lec·tro·lyt´ic, e·lec·tro·lyt´i·cal *adj.* —e·lec·tro·lyt´i·cal·ly *adv.*

e·lec·tro·mag´net *n.* a magnet produced by the flow of electricity through an outer coil —e·lec´tro·mag·net´ic *adj.* —e·lec´tro·mag·net´i·cal·ly *adv.* —e·lec·tro·mag´net·ism *n.*

e·lec´tron *n.* a negatively charged atomic particle

e·lec´tron´ics *n.* the study of carriers of electric charge

e·lec·tro·stat´ic *adj.* of electric charges at rest —e·lec·tro·stat´i·cal·ly *adv.*

el·ee·mos´y·nar·y *adj.* charity; nonprofit

el´e·gance, el´e·gan·cy *n.* a sense of propriety, grace, or beauty; tasteful luxury; cleverly simple, as of a solution —el´e·gant *adj.* —el´e·gant·ly *adv.*

el´e·gy *n.* a classical poem with a sorrowful theme —el´e·gi´ac *adj.* —el´e·gize *vt., vi.*

el´e·ment *n.* a basic substance or component; one's natural environment —el´e·men´tal, el´e·men´tary *adj.* —el·e·men´tal·ly, el·e·men·tar´i·ly *adv.*

el´e·phant *n.* a huge mammal with a flexible trunk and tusks —el´e·phan´tine *adj.*

el´e·vate´ *vt.* to raise or lift to a higher level; to improve one's moral or intellectual awareness; to improve the spirits of —el´e·vat·ed *adj.* —el´e·va´tion *n.*

elf *n.* a mischievous sprite —elf´in, elf´ish *adj.*

e·lic´it *vt.* to draw out from, as for information; to bring out, as a reaction

e·lide´ *vt.* to omit; to ignore —e·lid´i·ble *adj.*

el´i·gi·ble *adj.* qualified or suitable to participate —el·i·gi·bil´i·ty *n.* — el´i·gi·bly *adv.*

e·lim´i·nate *vt.* to remove or reject — e·lim·i·na´tion *n.* —e·lim·i·na·tive *adj.* —e·lim´i·na·tor *n.*

e·lite´ *n.* the aristocracy; a small powerful group —e·lit´ism *n.* — e·lit´ist *n.*

e·lix´ir *n.* a medicinal preparation; a cure–all

elk *n.* a large deer with broad antlers

el·lipse´ *n.* an oval geometric form — el·lip´tic, el·lip´ti·cal *adj.* —el·lip´ti·cal·ly *adv.*

el·lip´sis *n., pl.* el·lip´ses the omission of a word or phrase to complete a thought; marks that indicate omission as ... or ***

el·o·cu´tion *n.* the art of public speaking —el·o·cu´tion·ar·y *adj.*

—**el·o·cu´tion·ist** *n.*

e·lon´gate *vt.*, *vi.* to make or grow longer —**e·lon´gate**, **e·lon´ga·ted** *adj.* made longer; slender — **e´lon·ga´tion** *n.*

e·lope´ *vi.* to run away, esp. to marry —**e·lope´ment** *n.* —**e·lop´er** *n.*

el´o·quence *n.* expressive and compelling speech or writing —**el´o·quent** *adj.* —**el´o·quent·ly** *adv.*

else *adj.* different or other; more: *we need something else* —*adv.*

e·lu´ci·date *vt.* to clarify; to explain —**e·lu·ci·da´tion** *n.* —**e·lu´ci·da·tive** *adj.*

e·lude´ *vt.* to evade or escape by cunning; to slip from memory — **e·lu´sion** *n.* —**e·lu´sive**, **e·lu´so·ry** *adj.* —**e·lu´sive·ly** *adv.* —**e·lu´sive·ness** *n.*

e·ma´ci·ate´ *vt.* to make abnormally thin, as by disease or starvation — **e·ma´ci·a´tion** *n.* —**e·ma´ci·at·ed** *adj.*

em´a·nate´ *vi.* to come forth, as from a source —**em´a·na´tion** *n.*

e·man´ci·pate´ *vt.* to release from bondage or restraint —**e·man´ci·pa´tion** *n.* —**e·man´ci·pa·tor** *n.*

e·mas´cu·late *vt.* to deprive of force —**e·mas·cu·la´tion** *n.* —**e·mas´cu·la·tive**, **e·mas´cu·la·to·ry** *adj.* — **e·mas´cu·la·tor** *n.*

em·balm´ *vt.* to treat a dead body so as to preserve it; to preserve in the memory —**em·balm´er** *n.* —**em·balm´ment** *n.*

em·bank´ment *n.* a protective mound of earth or stone —**em·bank´** *vt.*

em·bar´go *n.* an order restricting or prohibiting trade in certain goods, to certain ports, etc. —*vt.* to place a restriction on trade

em·bark´ *vi.*, *vt.* to take or go aboard as for a journey —**em´bar·ka´tion** *n.* —**em·bark´ment** *n.*

em·bar´rass *vt.* to make ill at ease or self-conscious; to involve or be involved in financial difficulties — **em·bar´rassed·ly**, **em·bar´rass·ing·ly** *adv.* —**em·bar´rass·ing** *adj.* —**em·bar´rass·ment** *n.*

em´bas·sy *n.* the post, trappings, staff, buildings, etc. of an ambassador

em·bat´tle *vt.* to equip for battle; to fortify —**em·bat´tled** *adj.*

em·bed´ *vt.* to set firmly

em·bel´lish *vt.* to add detail or adornment to: to decorate; to add particulars, often fictitious, to an account —**em·bel´lish·er** *n.* —**em·bel´lish·ment** *n.*

em´ber *n.* a live coal —**embers** *n.* a dying fire

em·bez´zle *vt.* to take illegally in violation of a trust —**em·bez´zle·ment** *n.* —**em·bez´zler** *n.*

em·bit´ter *vt.* to give rise to unhappiness or displeasure —**em·bit´ter·ment** *n.*

em·bla´zon *vt.* to adorn or decorate —**em·bla´zon·er** *n.* —**em·bla´zon·ment**, **em·bla´zon·ry** *n.*

em´blem *n.* a symbol or badge; an object representative of something else: *a cross is the emblem of the Christian church* —**em´blem·at´ic**, **em·blem·at´i·cal** *adj.* —**em·blem·at´i·cal·ly** *adv.*

em·bod´y *vt.* to collect into a whole; to include or incorporate into — **em·bod´i·ment** *n.*

em·bold´en *vt.* to give courage to

em´bo·lism *n.* stoppage in a blood vessel

em´bo·lus *n.* an object capable of obstructing a blood vessel

em·bos´om *vt.* to take in; shelter

em·boss´ *vt.* to adorn with a raised design —**em·boss´a·ble** *adj.* —**em·boss´er** *n.* —**em·boss´ment** *n.*

em·brace´ *n.* a hug; acceptance —*vi.* to join in a hug —*vt.* to hug by holding close; to accept; to surround or include —**em·brace´a·ble** *adj.*—**em·brac´er** *n.*

em·broi·der·y *n.* ornamental needlework —**em·broi·der** *vt.* —**em·broi·der·er** *n.*

em·broil *vt.* to draw into, as a conflict —**em·broil·ment** *n.*

em·bry·o *n.* the early developmental stage of an animal or plant; anything in the early stages of development —**em·bry·al, em·bry·on·ic** *adj.*

em·bry·ol·o·gy *n.* the study of embryos —**em·bry·ol·o·gist** *n.*

e·mend *vt.* to correct a literary work —**e·mend·a·ble** *adj.* —**e·men·da·tion** *n.* —**e·men·da·tor** *n.* —**e·men·da·to·ry** *adj.*

em·er·ald *n.* a bright green precious stone

e·merge *vi.* to come forth; to come into view; to form or evolve — **e·mer·gence** *n.* —**e·mer·gent** *adj.* —**e·merg·ing** *adj.*

e·mer·gen·cy *n.* a situation requiring immediate action

e·mer·i·tus *adj.* retired, but retained in a honorary position

em·er·y *n.* a very hard mineral used as an abrasive

e·met·ic *n.* a medicine used to induce vomiting —*adj.* causing vomiting

em·i·grate *vi.* to leave a country or region to settle in another — **em·i·grant** *adj., n.* —**em·i·gra·tion** *n.* —**é·mi·gré** *n.*

em·i·nent *adj.* renowned, exalted; rising high above others —**em·i·nence** *n.* —**em·i·nen·cy** *n.* —**em·i·nent·ly** *adv.*

eminent domain the right to take or purchase private property for public use

em·is·sar·y *n.* one sent on a special mission

e·mis·sion *n.* something omitted

e·mit *vt.* to give out or discharge

e·mol·u·ment *n.* compensation for office or employment

e·mote *vi.* to act melodramatically

e·mo·tion *n.* strong feeling; a state of mental agitation —**e·mo·tion·al** *adj.* —**e·mo·tion·al·ism** *n.* —**e·mo·tion·al·ly** *adv.*

e·mo·tion·a·lize *vt.* to make emotional —**e·mo·tion·al·i·za·tion** *n.*

e·mo·tive *adj.* tending to arouse emotion —**e·mo·tive·ly** *adv.* — **e·mo·tive·ness** *n.*

em·pa·thy *n.* identification with the emotions, thoughts, etc. of another —**em·pa·thet·ic, em·path·ic** *adj.* —**em·pa·thet·i·cal·ly** *adv.* —**em·pa·thize** *vi., vt.*

em·per·or *n.* ruler of an empire

em·pha·sis *n.* forcefulness; special attention or importance —**em·pha·size** *vt.*

em·phat·ic *adj.* expressed with force; definite —**em·phat·i·cal·ly** *adv.*

em·phy·se·ma *n.* a lung condition marked by shortness of breath

em·pire *n.* a vast organization under unified control

em·pir·ic, em·pir·i·cist *n.* one who seeks knowledge through experience —*adj.* empirical

em·pir·i·cal *adj.* based on experience and observation —**em·pir·i·cal·ly** *adv.* —**em·pir·i·cism** *n.*

em·ploy *vt.* to engage the services of; to use —**em·ploy·ee** *n.* —**em·ploy·er** *n.* —**em·ploy·ment** *n.*

em·ploy·a·ble *adj.* capable of being employed or put to use —**em·ploy·a·bil·i·ty** *n.*;

em·po·ri·um *n.* a marketplace

em·pow·er *vt.* to enable or permit — **em·pow·er·ment** *n.*

emp·ty *adj.* having nothing within; insincere; frivolous —*vt., vi.* to make or become empty; to transfer the contents of —**emp·ti·ly** *adv.* — **emp·ti·ness** *n.*

e·mu *n.* a flightless bird of Australia related to the ostrich

em·u·late *vt.* to imitate; to strive to equal or surpass, esp. by imitation

—em·u·la´tion n. —em´u·la·tive adj. —em´u·la·tive·ly adv. —em´u·la·tor n.

e·mul´sion n. a mixture in which small particles are suspended in a liquid —e·mul´sive adj.

e·mul´si·fy vt. to mix or whip so as to make into an emulsion —e·mul·si·fi·ca´tion n. —e·mul´si·fi·er n.

en·a´ble vt. to make possible

en·act´ vt. to make into law —en·act´ment n.

en·am´el n. a glossy protective or decorative coating —vt. to surface with a hard protective coating

en·am´or vt. to inspire love

en·cap´su·late vt. to summarize —en·cap·su·la´tion n.

en·ceph·a·li´tis n. an inflammation of the brain —en·ceph´a·lit´ic adj.

en·ceph´a·lon n. the brain

en·chant´ vt. to delight or charm as if by a magic spell —en·chant´er n. —en·chant´ing adj. —en·chant´ing·ly adv. —en·chant´ment n.

en·ci´pher vt. to translate into a secret code

en·cir´cle vt. to surround —en·cir´cle·ment n.

en´clave n. a distinct geogrphical or political area enclosed within a larger area

en·close´ vt. to surround or contain —en·clo·sure n.

en·co´mi·um n. a eulogy

en·com´pass vt. to include; to encircle or surround —en·com´pass·ment n.

en´core n. a repeat performance

en·coun´ter n. a meeting —vi., vt. to meet, especially unexpectedly or in conflict

en·cour´age vt. to support; to inspire with courage —en·cour´age·ment n. —en·cour´ag·ing adj. —en·cour´ag·ing·ly adv.

en·croach´ vi. to intrude on the possessions or rights of another

—en·croach´ment n.

en·crust´ vt. to cover with a hard coating; to decorate, as with jewels —en·crus·ta´tion n.

en·cum´ber vi. to obstruct or weigh down so as to hinder —en·cum´brance n.

en·cy´clo·pae´di·a, en·cy´clo·pe´di·a n. an authoritative reference

end n. a terminal point

en·dan´ger vt. to imperil —en·dan´ger·ment n.

en·dear´ vt. to make beloved en·dear´ing adj. —en·dear´ing·ly adv.

en·dear´ment n. an expression of affection

en·deav´or n. a sincere effort; any undertaking —vi., vt. to make a sincere effort

en·dem´ic adj. occurring in or peculiar to a particular area or people, as an endemic disease

end´less adj. boundless; without end; forming a closed loop —end´less·ly adv. —end´less·ness n.

en·dorse´ vt. to approve, support, or acknowledge —en·dors´a·ble adj. —en·dors·ee´ n. —en·dorse´ment n. —en·dors´er n.

en·dow´ vt. to provide with income; to furnish or equip —en·dow´ment n.

en·dure´ vi., vt. to continue; to bear up, as under pain —en·dur´a·ble adj. —en·dur´a·bly adv. —en·dur´ance n.

en´e·my n. one hostile to another

en·er·get´ic adj. displaying energy —en·er·get´i·cal·ly adv.

en´er·gize vt. to bring to action —en´er·giz·er n.

en´er·gy n. the power to act effectively; power derived from natural sources, as oil, water, etc. —adj. pertaining or relating to power

en´er·vate vt. to deprive of energy; weaken —en·er·va´tion n. —en´er·va·tor n.

en·fee´ble *vt.* to weaken; to render helpless —**en·fee´ble·ment** *n.* —**en·fee´bler** *n.*

en·fold´ *vt.* to embrace; to wrap

en·force´ *vt.* to compel obedience —**en·force·a·bil´i·ty** *n.* —**en·force´a·ble** *adj.* —**en·force´ment** *n.* —**en·forc´er** *n.*

en·fran´chise *vt.* to endow with rights; to free from bondage —**en·fran´chise·ment** *n.*

en·gage´ *vi., vt.* to hire; to promise to marry; to occupy oneself with —**en·gaged´** *adj.* —**en·gage´ment** *n.*

en·gag´ing *adj.* charming —**en·gag´ing·ly** *adv.*

en·gen´der *vt.* to bring about; to produce

en´gine *n.* a machine that converts energy into force

en´gi·neer´ *n.* one who plans and manages scientifically —*vt.* to contrive; to plan and supervise

en´gi·neer´ing *n.* the application of scientific knowledge to the solving of practical problems

en·grave´ *vt.* to carve or etch into a surface —**en·grav´er** *n.* —**en·grav´ing** *n.*

en·gross´ *vt.* to absorb entirely —**en·gross´ing** *adj.* —**en·gross´ing·ly** *adv.* —**en·gross´ment** *n.*

en·gulf´ *vt.* to swallow up; to overwhelm

en·hance´ *vt.* to embellish so as to improve quality or value —**en·hance´ment** *n.*

e·nig´ma *n.* something ambiguous or perplexing —**en´ig·mat´ic, e·nig·mat´i·cal** *adj.* —**e·nig·mat´i·cal·ly** *adv.*

en·join´ *vt.* to forbid or prohibit

en·joy´ *vt.* to find pleasure in; to have the use of —**en·joy´a·ble** *adj.* —**en·joy´a·ble·ness** *n.* —**en·joy´a·bly** *adv.* —**en·joy´ment** *n.*

en·kin´dle *vt.* to set on fire; to excite

en·large´ *vt., vi.* to make or become larger —**en·large·ment** *n.*

en·light´en *vt.* to inform or impart special knowledge to —**en·light´en·ment** *n.*

en·liv´en *vt.* to stimulate

en·mesh´ *vt.* to entangle

en´mi·ty *n.* hostility

en·no´ble *vt.* to confer nobility; to honor or venerate —**en·no´ble·ment** *n.* —**en·no´bler** *n.*

en·nui´ *n.* listlessness or indifference caused by boredom

e·nor´mous *adj.* of great size —**e·nor´mi·ty** *n.* —**enor´mous·ly** *adv.* —**e·nor´mous·ness** *n.*

e·nough´ *adj.* adequate; sufficient —*adv.* sufficiently —*n.* an adequate supply —*interj.*

en·rage´ *vt.* to make angry; to infuriate —**en·rage´ment** *n.*

en·rap´ture *vt.* to delight

en·rich´ *vt.* to increase the wealth or quality of —**en·rich´ment** *n.*

en·rol, en·roll´ *vt.* to register or place on record; to enlist —**en·rol´ment, en·roll´ment** *n.*

en·sconce´ *vt.* to settle snuggly

en·sem´ble *n.* a suitable or pleasing combination, as of attire; a group of performers

en·shrine´ *vt.* to hold sacred —**en·shrine´ment** *n.*

en·shroud´ *vt.* to cover or conceal

en´sign *n.* a flag, banner, or symbol; a naval officer

en´si·lage *n.* stored fodder

en·slave´ *vt.* to place in bondage; to dominate —**en·slave´ment** *n.* —**en·slav´er** *n.*

en·snare´ *vt.* to trap

en·sue´ *vi.* to result; to follow after

en·sure´ *vt.* to make safe or secure; to make certain; to guarantee

en·tail´ *vt.* to impose as a consequence —**en·tail´ment** *n.*

en·tan´gle *vt.* to complicate; to involve in difficulties —**en·tan´gle·ment** *n.* —**en·tan´gler** *n.*

en·tente´ *n.* an understanding between nations

en·ter *vt.* to gain admission; to become a member; to begin; to record, as on a list

en·ter·pris·ing *adj.* displaying initiative —**en·ter·prise** *n.* —**en·ter·pris·ing·ly** *adv.*

en·ter·tain *vt.* to amuse; to offer hospitality to; to consider, as an idea or proposal —**en·ter·tain·er** *n.* —**en·ter·tain·ing** *adj.* —**en·ter·tain·ing·ly** *adv.* —**en·ter·tain·ment** *n.*

en·thral, **en·thrall** *vt.* to charm or fascinate —**en·thrall·ment**, **en·thral·ment** *n.*

en·thu·si·asm *n.* great excitement or interest —**en·thu·si·ast** *n.* —**en·thu·si·as·tic** *adj.* —**en·thu·si·as·ti·cal·ly** *adv.*

en·tice *vt.* to attract with promises —**en·tice·ment** *n.* —**en·tic·ing** *adj.* —**en·tic·ing·ly** *adv.*

en·tire *adj.* complete; undivided —**en·tire·ly** *adv.* —**en·tire·ness**, **en·tire·ty** *n.*

en·ti·tle *vt.* to give right to; to authorize —**en·ti·tle·ment** *n.*

en·ti·ty *n.* any being; anything that exists

en·tomb *vt.* to place for burial —**en·tomb·ment** *n.*

en·to·mol·o·gy *n.* the study of insects —**en·to·mo·log·ic**, **en·to·mo·log·i·cal** *adj.* —**en·to·mo·log·i·cal·ly** *adv.* —**en·to·mol·o·gist** *n.*

en·tou·rage *n.* companions and attendants

en·trance[1] *n.* the act or means of entering —**en·trance·way** *n.*

en·trance[2] *vt.* to fill with delight or enchantment —**en·trance·ment** *n.* —**en·tranc·ing** *adj.* —**en·tranc·ing·ly** *adv.*

en·trant *n.* one who enters or takes part in, as a contest

en·trap *vt.* to catch or ensnare; to trick or lure into danger or difficulty; to lay a trap for —**en·trap·ment** *n.*

en·treat *vt.*, *vi.* to plead or implore —**en·treat·ment** *n.* —**en·treat·y** *n.*

en·trench *vt.* to fortify; to establish firmly —**en·trench·ment** *n.*

en·tre·pre·neur *n.* one who undertakes a business venture, taking both control and risk —**en·tre·pre·neur·i·al** *adj.* —**en·tre·pre·neur·ship** *n.*

en·trust *vt.* to give over for safekeeping

en·try *n.* a means or place of access; the act of entering; an item entered, as on a list; an entrant

en·twine *vt.*, *vi.* to twist together

e·nu·mer·ate *vt.* to name one by one; to count —**e·nu·mer·a·tion** *n.* —**e·nu·mer·a·tive** *adj.* —**e·nu·mer·a·tor** *n.*

e·nun·ci·ate *vt.* to pronounce distinctly; to state precisely; to proclaim —**e·nun·ci·a·tion** *n.* —**e·nun·ci·a·tive** *adj.* —**e·nun·ci·a·tor** *n.*

en·vel·op *vt.* to surround completely with or as with a covering: *enveloped in mist* —**en·vel·op·ment** *n.* —**en·vel·op·er** *n.*

en·ve·lope *n.* that which envelops or wraps around; a paper wrapper, as for a letter, documents, etc.

en·vi·a·ble *adj.* sufficiently desirable so as to provoke envy or admiration —**en·vi·a·bly** *adv.*

en·vi·ous *adj.* experiencing or expressing envy —**en·vi·ous·ly** *adv.* —**en·vi·ous·ness** *n.*

en·vi·ron·ment *n.* the combination of conditions that affect the growth and development of an organism; one's surroundings or circumstances —**en·vi·ron·men·tal** *adj.* —**en·vi·ron·men·tal·ly** *adv.*

en·vi·ron·men·tal·ist *n.* an advocate for environmental preservation —**en·vi·ron·men·tal·ism** *n.*

en·vi·rons *pl. n.* the surrounding area; the environment

en·vis·age *vt.* to visualize; to form a

mental image of **—en·vis´age·ment** n.

en·vi´sion vt. to imagine; to foresee

en´voy´ n. a diplomatic agent

en´vy n. resentment aroused by jealousy —vt. to regard jealously — **en´vi·er** n. **—en´vy·ing·ly** adv.

e´on n. an incalculable time

ep´au·let´ n. a shoulder ornament on a uniform

e·phem´er·al adj. short-lived; transitory **—e·phem´er·al·ly** adv. — **e·phem´er·al·ness** n.

ep´ic n. a literary or dramatic work having a heroic theme **—ep´ic, ep´i·cal** adj. on a grand scale; heroic or legendary

ep´i·cen·ter n. the point on the earth's surface above the source of an earthquake; a central point

ep´i·cure n. a person of discriminating taste, especially for food and drink **—ep´i·cu´re·an** adj., n. **—ep´i·cur·ism** n.

ep´i·dem´ic n. a widespread condition, situation, disease, etc. **—ep´i·dem´ic, ep·i·dem´i·cal** adj. affecting many in an area at once — **ep·i·dem´i·cal·ly** adv.

ep·i·de·mi·ol´o·gy n. the study of epidemics, their causes, and contol **—ep·i·de·mi·o·log´i·cal** adj. — **ep·i·de·mi·o·log´i·cal·ly** adv. — **ep·i·de·mi·ol´o·gist** n.

ep´i·der´mis n. the outer layer of the skin **—ep´i·der´mal, ep´i·der´mic** adj.

ep´i·gram´ n. a thought-provoking saying

ep´i·lep·sy n. a nervous disorder marked by loss of consciousness and sometimes convulsions

ep´i·logue n. a concluding section, as of a book or play

e·pis´co·pa·cy n. government of a church by bishops **—e·pis´co·pal** adj. **—e·pis´co·pa´li·an** n., adj.

e·pis´co·pate n. the office of a bishop

ep´i·sode´ n. one event in a series of related events; a notable incident **—ep·i·sod´ic, ep·i·sod´i·cal** adj. — **ep·i·sod´i·cal·ly** adv.

e·pis·te·mol´o·gy n. the philosophical study of human knowledge — **e·pis´te·mo·log´i·cal** adj. **—e·pis·te·mo·log´i·cal·ly** adv. **—e·pis·te·mol´o·gist** n.

e·pis´tle n. a letter, especially one of instruction

ep´i·taph´ n. inscription on a tomb

ep´i·thet´ n. a word or phrase used to characterize a person or thing, as *Lion–Hearted* in *Richard the Lion–Hearted* **—ep·i·thet´ic, ep·i·thet´i·cal** adj.

e·pit´o·me n. a typical example; a brief summary

e·pit´o·mize vt. to abridge; to be typical of

ep´och n. a period characterized by extraordinary events **—ep´och·al** adj.

eq´ua·ble adj. of uniform condition; not easily disturbed

e´qual adj. of the same value; fair and impartial; balanced —vt. to be or become equivalent —n. a person or thing that closely matches another **—e´qual·ly** adv.

e·qual´i·ty n. the condition of being equal **—e´qual·i·za´tion** n. — **e´qual·ize** vt. **—e´qual·iz·er** n.

e´qua·nim´i·ty n. calmness; composure

e·quate´ vt. to make equal; to compare

e·qua´tion n. a complex array of elements, as *the human equation*; a mathematical statement expressing equality

e·qua´tor n. a circle around the earth equidistant from the poles — **e´qua·to´ri·al** adj.

e·ques´tri·an adj. of horses or horsemanship

e´qui·lat´er·al adj. having all sides equal **—e·qui·lat´er·al·ly** adv.

e·qui´li·brate *vi.*, *vt.* to balance; to be or bring to a state of equilibrium

e·qui·lib´ri·um *n.* a condition in which all factors are equal or balanced

e´quine *adj.* of horses —*n.* a horse

e´qui·nox *n.* one of two times each year when day and night are of equal length throughout the earth

e·quip´ *vt.* to prepare as by outfitting with supplies or training —**e·quip´ment** *n.*

eq´ui·ta·ble *adj.* fair; impartial — **eq´ui·ta·ble·ness** *n.* —**eq´ui·ta·bly** *adv.*

eq´ui·ty *n.* fairness; impartiality; net assets

e·quiv´a·lent *adj.* equal or corresponding in value —*n.* that corresponds in value —**e·quiv´a·lence**, **e·quiv´a·len·cy** *adj.* —**e·quiv´a·lent·ly** *adv.*

e·quiv´o·cate´ *vi.* speak with intent to deceive —**e·quiv´o·cal** *adj.* — **e·quiv´o·ca´tion** *n.*

e´ra *n.* a period encompassing important dates, events, etc.

e·rad´i·cate´ *vt.* to destroy utterly — **e·rad´i·ca·ble** *adj.* —**e·rad·i·ca´tion** *n.*

e·rase´ *vt.* to wipe out; to remove — **e·ra´sure** *n.* —**e·ras´er** *n.*

e·rect´ *adj.* upright or vertical; standing —*vt.* to construct; to set in an upright or vertical position — **e·rec´tion** *n.* —**e·rect´ly** *adv.*

e·rec´tile *adj.* capable of becoming erect or being raised to an upright position —**e·rec·til´i·ty** *n.*

erg *n.* a unit of work or energy

er·go·nom´ics *n.* the science of designing equipment or a workplace with intent to minimize operator fatigue —**er·go·nom´ic** *adj.* —**er·go·nom´i·cal·ly** *adv.*

e·rode´ *vt.*, *vi.* to wear or become worn away —**e·ro´sion** *n.*

e·rog´e·nous *adj.* exciting sexually

e·rot´ic *adj.* tending to arouse sexually —**e·rot´i·cal·ly** *adv.* —**e·rot´i·cism** *n.*

e·rot´i·ca *n.* erotic materials, as books, pictures, etc.

err *vi.* to make a mistake; to sin — **er´ran·cy** *n.*

er´rand *n.* a short trip; to tend to a task, often for another

er´rant *adj.* wandering; straying from a proper course —**er´rant·ly** *adv.*

er·rat´ic *adj.* deviating from the customary or expected; lacking consistency —**er·rat´i·cal·ly** *adv.*

er·ro´ne·ous *adj.* inaccurate, incorrect —**er·ro´ne·ous·ly** *adv.* —**er·ro´ne·ous·ness** *n.*

er´ror *n.* something done wrongly; an inaccuracy

er´satz´ *n.* an inferior substitute — *adj.* substitute

erst´while *adj.* former

er´u·dite´ *adj.* scholarly; learned — **er·u·di´tion** *n.*

e·rupt´ *vi.*, *vt.* to burst forth — **e·rupt´i·ble** *adj.* —**e·rup´tion** *n.* — **e·rup´tive** *adj.* —**e·rup´tive·ly** *adv.* —**e·rup´tive·ness** *n.*

es·ca·late´ *vi.*, *vt.* to increase; to ascend or carry up

es·ca·la´tor *n.* a moving staircase

es·ca·pade´ *n.* prank

es·cape´ *n.* the act breaking free; a means of breaking free —*vi.*, *vt.* to elude, avoid, or break free

es·ca´pism *n.* a turning from unpleasant reality, as by daydreaming, etc. —**es·cap´ist** *adj.*, *n.*

es·carp´ment *n.* a steep slope

es·cha·tol´o·gy *n.* the theological study of the destiny of man —**es·cha·to·log´i·cal** *adj.* —**es·cha·to·log´i·cal·ly** *adv.* —**es·cha·tol´o·gist** *n.*

es·cheat´ *n.* reversion of property to the state in the absence of heirs — *vi.*, *vt.* to revert or cause to revert to the state —**es·cheat´a·ble** *adj.*

es·chew *vt.* to shun, as something injurious

es´cort *n.* one accompanying

es·cort´ *vt.* to accompany

es´crow *n.* a thing of value held in the care of a third party until certain conditions are satisfied

es·cutch´eon *n.* a heraldic shield

e·soph´a·gus *n.* the tube that connects the mouth to the stomach

es·o·ter´ic *adj.* intended to be understood by a limited group; confidential —**es·o·ter´i·cal·ly** *adv.*

es·pe´cial *adj.* exceptional —**es·pe´cial·ly** *adv.*

es´pi·o·nage *n.* spying

es·pla·nade´ *n.* a level public space

es·pouse´ *vt.* to give or take in marriage; to take up, as a cause — **es·pous´al** *n.*

es·pres´so *n.* coffee made from beans that have been darkly roasted and finely ground

es·py´ *vt.* to catch sight of

es·quire´ *n.* a title of courtesy; a candidate for knighthood

es´say *n.* a brief written work; a testing of the nature of a thing — *vt.* to test, as ore

es´sence *n.* the basic nature or quality of a thing

es·sen´tial *adj.* fundamental; necessary —*n.* something fundamental or required —**es·sen´tial·ly** *adv.*

es·tab´lish *vt.* to create or install; to authenticate —**es·tab´lish·er** *n.* — **es·tab´lish·ment** *n.*

es·tate´ *n.* one's entire wealth; landed property

es·teem´ *n.* respect; reverence —*vt.* to value; to regard as: *esteem the recognition as an honor*

es´ti·ma·ble *adj.* deserving of esteem —**es´ti·ma·ble·ness** *n.* —**es´ti·ma·bly** *adv.*

es´ti·mate´ *vt.* to approximate; to form an opinion —*n.* an appraisal or evaluation; an opinion —**es´ti·ma´tion** *n.*

es·top´ *vt.* to prevent

estrange´ *vt.* to alienate —**es·trange´ment** *n.*

es´tu·ar´y *n.* the mouth of a river where it meets the sea

etch *vi., vt.* to engrave with acid; to make a clear impression —**etch´ing** *n.* —**etch´er** *n.*

e·ter´nal *adj.* without end; perpetual —**e·ter´nal·ly** *adv.*—**e·ter´ni·ty** *n.*

e·the´re·al *adj.* light, airy —**e·the´re·al·ly** *adv.*

eth´ic *n.* a set of principles

eth´i·cal *adj.* morally right —**eth·i·cal´i·ty**, **eth´i·cal·ness** *n.* —**eth´i·cal·ly** *adv.*

eth´ics *n.* the accepted standard of morality

eth´nic, **eth´ni·cal** *adj.* of the customs, food, etc. characteristic to a group or culture —**eth´ni·cal·ly** *adv.* —**eth·nic´i·ty** *n.*

eth·nol´o·gy *n.* the study of human cultures

e·ti·ol´o·gy *n.* the study of origins, esp. of disease —**e·ti·o·log´i·cal** *adj.* —**e·ti·o·log´i·cal·ly** *adv.* — **e·ti·ol´o·gist** *n.*

et´i·quette´ *n.* the rules for socially acceptable behavior

e´tude *n.* a musical exercise

et´y·mol´o·gy *n.* the origin and development of words —**et´y·mo·log´i·cal** *adj.*

eu·gen´ic, **eu·gen´i·cal** *adj.* of or relating to eugenics —**eu·gen´i·cal·ly** *adv.*

eu´gen´ics *n.* the study of improvements to the human race by selective breeding —**eu·gen´i·cist** *n.*

eu´lo·gy *n.* a tribute, especially for one who has died —**eu´lo·gize** *vt.*

eu´phe·mism *n.* a word or phrase substituted for one that may be offensive —**eu´phe·mis´tic**, **eu´phe·mis´ti·cal** *adj.* —**eu´phe·mis´ti·cal·ly** *adv.*

eu·phon´ic, **eu·pho´ni·ous** *adj.* pleasant or agreeable sounding

—eu·pho´ni·ous·ly *adv.* **—eu·pho´ni·ous·ness** *n.*

eu·pho´ni·um *n.* a brass instrument similar to the baritone horn

eu´pho·ny *n.* a pleasant sounding word combination

eu·pho´ri·a *n.* a feeling of well–being **eu·phor´ic** *adj.* **—eu·phor´i·cal·ly** *adv.*

eu·ryth´mics *pl. n.* musical interpretation through rhythmic body movements **—eu·ryth´mic** *adj.*

eu·tha·na´sia *n.* ending the life of a suffering person painlessly and peacefully **—eu´tha·nize** *vt.*

e·vac´u·ate´ *vt.* to depart from; to withdraw **—e·vac´u·a´tion** *n.*

e·vade´ *vi., vt.* to avoid by cleverness or deceit

e·val´u·ate *vt.* to determine the worth of; to appraise **—e·val·u·a´tion** *n.*

ev´a·nesce´ *vt.* to vanish slowly **— ev·a·nes´cence** *n.* **—ev´a·nes´cent** *adj.* **—ev´a·nes´cent·ly** *adv.*

e´van·gel´ic, e´van·gel´i·cal *adj.* believing in and adhering closely to Christian scripture; marked by enthusiasm or ardor **— e´van·gel´i·cal·ly** *adv.* **—e·van´ge·lism** *n.* **—e·van´ge·list** *n.*

e·van·gel·is´tic *adj.* of the crusading nature of one who has taken up a cause **—e·van·gel·is´ti·cal·ly** *adv.*

e·van´gel·ize *vi., vt.* to preach the gospel **—e·van·gel·i·za´tion** *n.* **— e·van´gel·iz·er** *n.*

e·vap´o·rate *vi., vt.* to become or convert into vapor **—e·vap·o·ra´tion** *n.* **—e·vap´o·ra·tive** *adj.* **— e·vap´o·ra·tor** *n.*

e·va´sive *adj.* deliberately vague, as *an evasive answer*; intended to avoid **—e·va´sion** *n.* **—e·va´sive·ly** *adv.* **—e·va´sive·ness** *n.*

eve *n.* the night before a special event

e´ven *adj.* smooth, level; unchanging, constant; calm, tranquil;

balanced **—vt., vi.** to make or become smooth, level, etc. **—adv. — e´ven·ly** *adv.* **—e´ven·ness** *n.*

eve´ning *n.* the close of the day; nightfall

e·vent´ *n.* an important occasion; an incident; an activity or one of a series of activities

e·vent´ful *adj.* momentous **e·vent´ful·ly** *adv.* **—e·vent´ful·ness** *n.*

e·ven·tu·al *adj.* occuring in the future **—e·ven·tu·al´i·ty** *n.* **—e·ven´tu·al·ly** *adv.*

ev´er *adv.* at any time; in any way; always

e·vert´ *vt.* to turn inside out **—e·ver´sion** *n.*

eve´ry *adj.* all, taken singly

e·vict´ *vt.* to turn out legally; to dispossess **—e·vic´tion** *n.* **—e·vic´tor** *n.*

ev´i·dence *n.* that which serves to make clear or prove **—vt.** to make plain; to attest **—ev·i·den´tial** *adj.* **—ev·i·den´tial·ly** *adv.* **—ev·i·den´ti·ar·y** *adj.*

ev´i·dent *adj.* clear; obvious **—ev´i·dent·ly** *adv.*

e´vil *adj.* wicked or depraved; harmful **—n.** sinfulness; that which can harm **—e´vil·ly** *adv.* **— e´vil·ness** *n.*

e·vince´ *vt.* to demonstrate clearly **— e·vinc´i·ble** *adj.* **—e·vinc´i·bly** *adj*

e·vis´cer·ate *vt.* to disembowel **— e·vis·cer·a´tion** *n.*

e·voke´ *vt.* to call forth or summon **—ev´o·ca·ble** *adj.* **—ev·o·ca´tion** *n.* **—e·voc´a·tive** *adj.*

ev·o·lu´tion *n.* the process of evolving; gradual development or growth **—ev·o·lu´tion·al, ev·o·lu´tion·ar·y** *adj.* **—ev·o·lu´tion·al·ly, ev·o·lu´tion·ar·i·ly** *adv.*

ev·o·lu´tion·ism *n.* a theory of gradual biological change over time; a belief in biological evolution **— ev·o·lu´tion·ist** *n.*

e·volve´ *vi., vt.* to progress or

develop gradually **—e·volv´a·ble** *adj.* **—e·volve´ment** *n.*

ew´er *n.* a large pitcher

ex·ac´er·bate´ *vt.* make more intense **—ex·ac·er·ba´tion** *n.*

ex·act´ *adj.* very accurate; precise *—vt.* to obtain by force or authority **—ex·act´ing** *adj.* **—ex·act´ing·ly** *adv.* **—ex·act´ly** *adv.* **—ex·act´ ness, ex·ac´ti·tude** *n.*

ex·ac´tion *n.* extortion

ex·ag´ger·ate *vi., vt.* to describe something as greater than it actually is **—ex·ag´ger·at·ed·ly** *adv.* **—ex·ag´ger·a´tion** *n.;*

ex·alt´ *vt.* to glorify or praise **—ex´ al·ta´tion** *n.* **—ex·alt´er**

ex·am´i·ne *vt.* to inspect or test **—ex·am´in·a·ble** *adj.* **—ex·am·i·na´ tion** *n.* **—ex·am´in·er** *n.*

ex·am´ple *n.* that which typifies or serves as a model: *set a good example for the others*

ex·as´per·ate *vt.* to annoy or irritate **—ex·as´per·at·ing** *adj.* **—ex·as´ per·at·ing·ly** *adv.* **—ex·as´per·a´ tion** *n.*

ex·ca´vate *vt.* to make a hole or cavity; to uncover by digging **—ex´ ca·va´tion** *n.*

ex·ceed´ *vt.* to go beyond

ex·ceed´ing *adj.* surpassing **—ex· ceed´ing·ly** *adv.*

ex·cel´ *vi., vt.* to be better or superior; to surpass

ex·cel´lent *adj.* outstanding; of exceptional quality **—ex´cel·lence** *n.* **—ex´cel·lent·ly** *adv.*

ex·cel´si·or *n.* packing material

ex·cept´ *vt.* to exclude *—vi.* to object *—prep.* with the exception of **—ex· cept´ing** *prep.*

ex·cep´tion *n.* that which is different; that which is excluded; an objection **—ex·cep´tion·a·ble** *adj.* **—ex·cep´tion·al** *adj.* **—ex·cep´ tion·al·ly** *adv.*

ex´cerpt *n.* an extract from a book or manuscript **—ex·cerpt´** *vt.* to

remove or extract; to quote

ex·cess´ *n.* an amount greater than needed; the amount by which one is greater than another; overindulgence **—ex´cess** *adj.* surplus **—ex· ces´sive** *adj.* **—ex·ces´sive·ly** *adv.* **—ex·ces´sive·ness** *n.*

ex·change´ *vt.* to trade for something of equal value; to reciprocate; to replace *—vi.* to make a trade *—n.* an act of trading or reciprocating; a substitution; a place where something is traded, such as stocks **—ex·change·a·bil´i·ty** *n.* **—ex·change´a·ble** *adj.*

ex´cise *n.* an indirect tax or fee **—ex·cise´** *vt.* to remove, often by cutting **—ex·ci´sion** *n.*

ex·cit´a·ble *adj.* high–strung; emotional; easily excited **—ex·cit·a·bil´ i·ty** *n.* **—ex·cit´a·ble·ness** *n.* **—ex·cit´a·bly** *adv.*

ex·cite´ *vt.* to stir the emotions; to provoke **—ex·cit´ed** *adj.* **—ex·cit´ ed·ly** *adv.* **—ex·cit´ed·ness** *n.*

ex·cite´ment *n.* a state of high emotion; something that thrills

ex·cit´ing *adj.* exhilarating; intensely emotional **—ex·cit´ing·ly** *adv.*

ex·claim´ *vi., vt.* to cry out suddenly **—ex´cla·ma´tion** *n.* **—ex·clam´a· to·ry** *adj.*

ex·clude´ *vt.* to put out or leave out; to except **—ex·clud´a·ble** *adj.* **—ex·clu´sion** *n.* **—ex·clu´sion·ar·y** *adj.*

ex·clu´sive *adj.* limited to a certain person or group; regarded as incompatible; restricted **—ex·clu´ sive·ly** *adv.* **—ex·clu´sive·ness** *n.*

ex´com·mu´ni·cate´ *vt.* to expel in disgrace *—adj.* expelled or excluded **—ex´com·mu´ni·ca´tion** *n.*

ex·co´ri·ate *vt.* to abrade the skin; to denounce

ex´cre·ment *n.* refuse matter; feces

ex·cre´ta *n.* waste matter eliminated from the body **—ex·crete´** *vt.*

—**ex·cre´tion** n. —**ex´cre·to·ry** adj.

ex·cru´ci·at·ing adj. causing severe mental or physical pain; intense —**ex·cru´ci·ate** vt. —**ex·cru´ci·at·ing·ly** adv.

ex´cul·pate´ vt. to prove innocent —**ex·cul·pa´tion** n. —**ex´cul´pa·to·ry** adj.

ex·cur´sion n. a short journey; a group tour

ex·cuse´ vt. to overlook; to free from blame; to offer a reason or apology; to free from an obligation —n. justification for an offense; that which relieves of obligation —**ex·cus´a·ble** adj. —**ex·cus´a·bly** adv. —**ex·cus´er** n.

ex´e·cra·ble adj. appallingly bad —**ex´e·cra·bly** adv. —**ex´e·cra·ble·ness** n.

ex´e·crate vt. to denounce; to loathe —**ex·e·cra´tion** n.

ex´e·cute´ vt. to perform; to put into effect; to validate; to put to death —**ex´e·cut·a·ble** adj. —**ex´e·cu´tion** n.

ex·ec´u·tive n. an official exercising administrative control over a governmental or or private concern — adj. administrative; having the ability to direct or control

ex·em´plar n. a typical example

ex·em´pla·ry adj. worthy of imitation; commendable —**ex·em´pla·ri·ly** adv. —**ex·em´pla·ri·ness** n.

ex·em´pli·fy vt. to show by example —**ex·em´pli·fi·ca´tion** n.

ex·empt´ adj. freed from, as an obligation —vt. to free from a duty or obligation —**ex·emp´tion** n.

ex´er·cise n. activity designed to improve strength or endurance; something practiced to develop a skill; a ceremony —vt. to train; to make use of, as authority

ex·ert´ vt. to put forth; bring to bear —**ex·er´tion** n.

ex·fo´li·ate vt., vi. to peel off; to

remove or come off in flakes, layers, etc. —**ex·fo·li·a´tion** n. —**ex·fo´li·a·tive** adj.

ex´hale´ vi. to breathe out —**ex·ha·la´tion** n.

ex·haust´ vt. to use up; to drain of resources, energy, etc. —**ex·haust´i·bil´i·ty** n. —**ex·haust´i·ble** adj.;

ex·haust´ed adj. used up; consumed; extremely tired —**ex·haust´ed·ly** adv.

ex·haust´ing adj. producing exhaustion; tiring

ex·haus´tion n. extreme fatigue

ex·haus´tive adj. extensive or complete: exhaustive research —**ex·haus´tive·ly** adv. —**ex·haus´tive·ness** n.

ex·hib´it vt. to display; to present for inspection —vi. to place on display —n. a display; something displayed —**ex·hi·bi´tion** n.

ex·hi·bi´tion·ist n. one who behaves so as to attract attention; one driven to indecent exposure —**ex·hi·bi´tion·ism** n.

ex·hil´a·rate vt. to cheer; to stimulate or enliven —**ex·hil´a·rat·ing** adj. —**ex·hil´a·rat·ing·ly** adv.

ex·hil·a·ra´tion n. elation; excitement—**ex·hil´a·ra·tive** adj.

ex·hort´ vt. to advise strongly; to entreat —**ex·hor·ta´tion** n.

ex·hume´ vt. to disinter; to dig up or disclose —**ex·hu·ma´tion** n.

ex·i´gen·cy n. a condition that requires immediate action; an emergency; a pressing need —**ex´i·gent** adj. —**ex´i·gent·ly** adv.

ex·ig´u·ous adj. meager, sparse

ex´ile n. expulsion, banishment; one who has been banished —vt. to expel or banish, as from a country

ex·ist´ vi. to have reality; to be present; to continue to be —**ex·ist´ence** n. —**ex·ist´ent** adj.

ex·is·ten´tial·ism n. a philosophy or religion that stresses free will and the responsibility of humanity for

its actions —**ex·is·ten´tial·ist** n. —
ex·is·ten´tial adj. —**ex·is·ten´tial·
ly** adv.

ex´it n. a going out or departure; a
way out

ex´o·dus n. a departure or leaving,
especially by a large group

ex·og´a·my n. the custom of marry-
ing outside one's social unit —
ex·og´e·mous adj.

ex·on´er·ate vt. to clear of an accusation; to prove blameless —
ex·on·er·a´tion n.

ex·or´bi·tant adj. excessive, as of a
price —**ex·or´bi·tance** n. —**ex·or´
bi·tant·ly** adv.

ex´or·cise´, ex´or·cize´ vt. to drive
out an evil spirit by ritual incanta-
tions; to free from evil influence —
ex´or·cism n. —**ex´or·cist** n.

ex·ot´ic adj. foreign; strange or unusual; alluring —**ex·ot´i·cal·ly**
adv.

ex·pand´ vi., vt. to make or become
greater in size or scope; to spread
or extend —**ex·pand´a·ble** adj. —
ex·pan´sion n. —**ex·pan´sive** adj.

ex·panse´ n. unbroken space; wide
extent —**ex·pan´sion** n.

ex·pan´sive adj. extensive; amiable
or outgoing —**ex·pan´sive·ly** adv.
—**ex·pan´sive·ness** n.

ex·pa´ti·ate vi. to speak at length
and in great detail; to elaborate —
ex·pa·tri·a´tion n.

ex·pect´ vt. to anticipate as likely or
deserving —**ex·pect´a·ble** adj. —
ex·pect´a·bly adv. —**ex·pect´an·
cy** n. —**ex·pect´ant** adj. —**ex·
pect´ant·ly** adv.

ex·pec·ta´tion n. something expected; the hope for good to come

ex·pec´to·rant n. medication to help
clear mucus from the lungs

ex·pec´to·rate vi., vt. to spit —**ex·
pec·to·ra´tion** n.

ex·pe´di·ent adj. appropriate; convenient; useful —n. something
suited to a pressing need —**ex·

pe´di·ence, ex·pe´di·en·cy** n. —
ex·pe´di·ent·ly adv.

ex´pe·dite vt. to hasten; to speed the
progress of —**ex´pe·dit·er** n.

ex·pe·di´tion n. a voyage taken for
some purpose; collectively, those
who journey and their equipment
—**ex·pe·di´tion·ar·y** adj.

ex·pe·di´tious adj. rapid, speedy —
ex·pe·di´tious·ly adv. —**ex·pe·di´
tious·ness** n.

ex·pel´ vt. to drive out by force; to
eject by authority —**ex·pel´la·ble**
adj.

ex·pend´ vt. to spend or use up —
ex·pend·a·bil´i·ty n. —**ex·pend´a·
ble** adj.

ex·pend´i·ture n. an expense; a
disbursement

ex·pense´ n. an outlay in money,
time, etc.; a cost

ex·pen´sive adj. costly

ex·pe´ri·ence n. that learned from
personal observation or involvement —vt. to live through —**ex·pe·
ri·en´tial** adj. —**ex·pe·ri·en´tial·ly**
adv.

ex·per´i·ment n. a test to learn
about the unknown or verify that
which is known —vi. to try or test
—**ex·per´i·ment·er** n.

ex·per´i·men´tal adj. in a developmental state —**ex·per´i·men´tal·
ism** n. —**ex·per´i·men´tal·ist** n. —
ex·per´i·men´tal·ly adv.

ex·per·i·men·ta´tion n. the process
of testing and recording results

ex·pert´ adj. having great skill or
knowledge —n. one knowledgeable
or skilled in a particular field —
ex´pert·ly adv. —**ex´pert·ness** n.

ex·per·tise´ n. the skill, knowledge,
etc. of an expert

ex´pi·ate´ vt. make amends; to atone
—**ex´pi·a´tion** n.

ex·pire´ vi. to die; to come to an end,
as an offer —**ex´pi·ra´tion** n.

ex·plain´ vi., vt. make clear or understandable —**ex·plain´a·ble** adj.

—**ex´pla·na´tion** n.

ex´ple·tive n. an exclamation; a word or phrase that does not add meaning —**ex´ple·to·ry** adj.

ex·pli·ca·ble adj. explainable —**ex´pli·ca·bly** adv.

ex´pli·cate vt. to explain

ex·plic´it adj. distinct; clearly stated; clearly established —**ex·plic´it·ly** adv. —**ex·plic´it·ness** n.

ex·plode´ vi., vt. to blow up; to burst with a loud sound

ex´ploit, ex·ploit´ n. a remarkable or daring feat —**ex·ploit´** vt. to use to one's advantage and, often, to the disadvantage of another; to take unfair advantage of —**ex·ploit´a·ble** adj. —**ex·ploi·ta´tion** n. —**ex·ploit´a·tive, ex·ploit´ive** adj. —**ex·ploit´er** n.

ex·plore´ vi., vt. to investigate or examine exhaustively —**ex·plo·ra´tion** n. —**ex·plor´a·tive, ex·plor´a·to·ry** adj. —**ex·plor´er** n.

ex·plor´a·ble adj. able to be explored

ex·plo´sion n. a sudden, loud blowing up or bursting; a sudden outburst; a sudden increase

ex·plo´sive adj. pertaining to an explosion; liable to cause violence or an outburst —n. a substance, such as dynamite, that can explode —**ex·plo´sive·ly** adv. —**ex·plo´sive·ness** n.

ex·po´nent n. one who promotes a cause; a symbol used in mathematics to indicate the number of times a value is multiplied by itself, as in $2^3 = 2 \times 2 \times 2$ where ^{3} is the exponent

ex´port n. goods, ideas, etc. that are sent out of a country or area —**ex·port´** vt. to send out of a country or area

ex·po·sé´ n. a description or airing, as of a scandal or an illegal act

ex·pose´ vt. to lay open or leave unprotected

ex·po·si´tion n. a public exhibition;

a detailed explanation

ex·po´sure n. a revealing, as of an illegal act; the condition of being open to the elements

ex·pos´tu·late´ vi. to argue against —**ex·pos·tu·la´tion** n.

ex·press´ vt. to convey in words; to represent by symbols, as in mathematics; to press or force out, as by pressure —adj. deliberate, definite; high speed or non-stop, as of a train —adv. by fast delivery —n. a system for transporting rapidly

ex·pres´sion n. a means of conveying: an expression of good will; something conveyed; a saying

ex·pres´sive adj. demonstrative; meaningful —**ex·pres´sive·ly** adv. —**ex·pres´sive·ness** n.

ex·pul´sion n. the condition of being forced out or expelled —**ex·pul´sive** adj.

ex·punge´ vt. to erase or delete

ex´qui·site adj. beautiful; delicately crafted —**ex·quis´ite·ly** adv. —**ex·quis´ite·ness** n.

ex´tant adj. still existing

ex·tem´po·ra´ne·ous, ex·tem´po·rar´y adj. improvised; speaking without notes —**ex·tem·po·ra´ne·ous·ly** adv.

ex·tend´ vi., vt. to enlarge; to stretch out —**ex·tend´ed** adj. —**ex·ten´sion** n.

ex·ten´sive adj. great in amount, extent, etc. —**ex·ten´sive·ly** adv. —**ex·ten´sive·ness** n.

ex·tent´ n. the scope or range of a thing

ex·ten´u·ate vt. to diminish the seriousness, as of an offense, by offering an excuse for the action —**ex·tenu·a´tion** n. —**ex·ten´u·a·tive, ex·ten´u·a·to·ry** adj. —**ex·ten´u·a·tor** n.

ex·te´ri·or adj. outermost; of the outside —n. the outside; an outer surface

ex·ter´mi·nate *vt.* to destroy; to eradicate completely —**ex·termi·na´tion** *n.* —**ex·ter´mi·na·tive**, **ex·ter´mi·na·to·ry** *adj.* —**ex·ter´mi·na·tor** *n.*

ex·ter´nal *adj.* on or of the outside

ex·tinct´ *adj.* no longer in existence —**ex·tinc´tion** *n.*

ex·tin´guish *vt.* to put out or quench; to destroy —**ex·tin´guish·a·ble** *adj.* —**ex·tin´guish·er** *n.*

ex·tir´pate *vt.* to uproot; to destroy completely, exterminate —**ex·tir·pa´tion** *n.*

ex·tol´, ex·toll´ *vt.* to praise; exalt

ex·tort´ *vt.* to obtain by violence or threats —**ex·tor´tion** *n.* —**ex·tor´tion·ist** *n.*

ex´tra *adj.* being more than required; additional —*n.* something special or additional —*adv.* unusually

ex´tract *n.* a thing drawn out by distillation, etc.; a quote taken from an article, book, etc. —**ex·tract´** *vt.* to draw out, as by distillation; to quote a selection

ex·tra·cur·ric´u·lar *adj.* outside the regular course of studies or work

ex´tra·dite *vt.* to give over a person accused of a crime to another jurisdiction

ex·tra´ne·ous *adj.* not belonging; unrelated —**ex·tra´ne·ous·ly** *adv.*

ex·tra·or´di·nar·y *adj.* unusual; out of the ordinary; exceptional —**ex·tra·or·di·nar´i·ly** *adv.*

ex·trap´o·late *vt.* to project a value outside the range of available data based on what is known about that data —**ex·trap·o·la´tion** *n.*

ex·tra·sen´so·ry *adj.* outside the range of normal senses, as *extra-sensory perception*

ex·trav´a·gance *n.* excess spending; immoderation in anything —**ex·trav´a·gant** *adj.* —**ex·trav´a·gant·ly** *adv.*

ex´tra·vert, ex´tro·vert *n.* one who is active and agressive —**ex·tro·ver´sion** *n.*

ex·treme´ *adj.* most remote; utmost; to the greatest degree —*n.* a limit; a thing that is as far from another in distance, character, etc. as possible —**ex·treme´ly** *adv.* —**ex·trem´i·ty** *n.*

ex·tri´cate *vt.* to release, as from difficulty; to disentangle —**ex·tri´ca·ble** *adj.* —**ex·tri´ca·bly** *adv.* —**ex·tri·ca´tion** *n.*

ex·u´ber·ant *adj.* high spirited; enthusiastic —**ex·u´ber·ance** *n.* —**ex·u´ber·ant·ly** *adv.*

ex·ult´ *vi.* to rejoice, celebrate

ex·ur´ban·ite *n.* one who lives in the suburbs of a city, often commuting to the city for work

f, F sixth letter of the English alphabet

fa´ble *n.* a fictitious story designed to teach a lesson

fab´ric *n.* cloth; the structure of a thing

fab´ri·cate´ *vt.* to manufacture or assemble; to invent a story; to lie —**fab´ri·ca´tion** *n.*

fab´u·lous *adj.* imaginary; fictitious; incredible, astonishing

fac´et *n.* the small plane surface of a gem; any aspect of a thing

fa·ce´tious *adj.* amusing; whimsical

fac´ile *adj.* easy; accomplished with little effort —**fac´ile·ly** *adv.* —**fac´ile·ness** *n.*

fa·cil´i·tate´ *vt.* to make convenient or easier

fa·cil´i·ty *n.* the absence of difficulty; skill; a building or equipment set aside for a particular purpose

fac·sim´i·le *n.* a reproduction

facsimile, fax *n.* a device for transmitting documents over telephone lines; a copy of the document transmitted

fact *n.* the truth; reliable information; anything that happens

fac´tion n. a group within an organization, united against others in the organization —**fac´tion·al** adj. — **fac´tion·al·ism** n.

fac´tious adj. tending to cause dissension —**fac´tious·ly** adv. —**fac´tious·ness** n.

fac·ti´tious adj. forced or artificial; not genuine —**fac·ti´tious·ly** adv. —**fac·ti´tious·ness** n.

fac´tor n. one who conducts business as agent for another; any cause or condition that effects a result

fac´to·ry n. a building used for the manufacture or assembling of goods

fac´ul·ty n. the ability to act; any mental or physical ability; a body of teachers

fade vi. to lose color or distinction; to diminish in some way —**fad´ed·ness** n.

fail vi., vt. to fall short of need; to cease to function properly; to be unsuccessful, as in business — **fail´ure** n.

faint adj. lacking in strength; indistinct —vi. to swoon —**faint´ly** adv. —**faint´ness** n.

faith n. unflagging trust; belief without firm proof; belief in a supreme being: a religion; fidelity — **faith´ful** adj. —**faith´ful·ly** adv. — **faith´ful·ness** n.

fal´con n. a bird of prey, often one trained to hunt small game

fall vi. to descend; to decline; to tumble down or collapse —n. the act of falling; (US) autumn

fal´la·cy n. illogical reasoning —**fal·la´cious** adj. —**fal·la´cious·ly** adv. —**fal·la´cious·ness** n.

fal´li·ble adj. questionable; liable to err —**fal·li·bil´i·ty, fal´li·ble·ness** n. —**fal´li·bly** adv.

false adj. deceitful; unfaithful; artificial —**false´ly** adv.

fal´si·fy vt. to misrepresent; to alter a document with fraudulent intent —**fal´si·fi·ca´tion** n.

fa·mil´iar adj. intimate, informal; common; presumptuous —**fa·mil·i·ar´i·ty** n. —**fa·mil´iar·ize** vt. — **fa·mil·iar·i·za´tion** n.

fam´i·ly n. the members of one's household; close relatives; a social unit, such as a tribe; a related group, as of certain plants or animals

fam´ine n. a critical shortage of food

fam´ish vi., vt. to be or cause to be hungery; to starve or cause to starve

fa´mous adj. very well known; renowned —**fa´mous·ly** adv.

fa·nat´ic, fa·nat´i·cal adj. overly enthusiastic —n. one who is unreasonably zealous —**fa·nat´i·cal·ly** adv. —**fa·nat´i·cism** n.

fan´cy adj. elaborate; intricate —n. a whim; a delusion —vt. to imagine; to be fond of —**fan´ci·ful** adj. — **fan´ci·ful·ly** adv.

fang n. a long, pointed tooth

fan·tas´tic adj. imaginary; strange, odd; fanciful

farce n. a broad comedy or satire; empty actions or ceremony —**far´ci·cal** adj.

fare n. the price for transport; one being transported: a passenger; food —vi. to prosper; to turn out

far´ther adj. more distant —adv. more remote in time or place

fas´ci·nate vt. to charm, bewitch; to captivate —**fas´ci·nat·ing** adj. — **fas´ci·nat·ing·ly** adv. —**fas´ci·na´tion** n.

fash´ion n. a popular style of dress —vt. to make or adapt —**fash´ion·a·ble** adj. —**fash´ion·a·ble·ness** n. —**fash´ion·a·bly** adv.

fas´ten vi. to become attached —vt. to attach or secure —**fas´ten·er** n.

fas·tid´i·ous adj. particular; difficult to satisfy; oversensitive —**fas·tid´i·ous·ly** adv. —**fas·tid´i·ous·ness** n.

fa´tal adj. deadly; decisive; fateful — **fa´tal·ist** n. —**fa·tal·is´tic** adj. — **fa·tal·is´ti·cal·ly** adv.

fate n. the inescapable future; destiny —vt. to predestine —**fat´ed** adj. —**fate´ful** adj. —**fate´ful·ly** adv.

fath´om n. a measure for testing the depth of water, equal to 6 feet —vt. to comprehend

fa·tigue´ n. weariness, exhaustion — vi., vt. to make or grow exhausted

fat´u·ous adj. silly, foolish; dim-witted —**fat´u·ous·ly** adv. —**fat´u·ous·ness** n.

fau´cet (US) n. a device for regulating the flow of a liquid

fault n. a flaw in appearance or structure; a mistake; a liability — **fault´i·ness** n. —**fault´y** adj.

faux pas´ n. a socially unacceptable error; a tactless deed

fa´vour (Brit.), **fa´vor** (US) n. approval; a generous act; preferential treatment; a small gift —vt. to approve; to assist —**fa´vour·a·ble**, **fa´vor·a·ble** adj. —**fa´vour·a·ble·ness**, **fa´vor·a·ble·ness** n. —**fa´vour·a·bly**, **fa´vor·a·bly** adv.

fa´vour·ite (Brit.), **fa´vor·ite** (US) n. something regarded with fondness; one liked and granted special privileges; one considered most likely to win a contest —adj. especially liked; preferred

fawn vi. to dote on; to curry favor — **fawn´er** n. —**fawn´ing·ly** adv.

faze vt. to disturb; to confuse

fear n. a state of anxiety or dread; uneasiness or concern —vi. to be afraid —vt. to dread; to regard with awe —**fear´ful** adj. —**fear´ful·ly** adv. —**fear´ful·ness** n.

fea´si·ble adj. within reason; possible to be carried out —**fea·si·bil´i·ty** n. —**fea´si·bly** adv.

feast n. a festivity; a banquet —vi. to dine extravagantly —vt. to entertain

feat n. an extraordinary deed

fea´ture n. a property or cast of a thing; a characteristic quality; a prominent article, as in a newspaper or periodical

fe´ces´ n. pl. waste matter expelled by the body; excrement

fed´er·al adj. of a coalition of states, groups, etc.; of the government of the U.S. —**fed´er·al·ize** vt. —**fed´er·al·ly** adv.

fed´er·ate vi., vt. to unite under a common authority —**fed·er·a´tion** n. —**fed´er·a·tive** adj. —**fed´er·a·tive·ly** adv.

fee n. a charge or payment for a service, license, etc.

fee´ble adj. weak, infirm —**fee´ble·ness** n.

feed vi. to eat; to flow steadily —vt. to furnish with food; to supply with material, as for processing — n. food for animals

feel n. the sense of touch; emotional or intuitive perception —vi., vt. to sense by touch; to believe, based on emotion or intuition —**feel´ing** adj. —**feel´ing·ly** adv.

feign vi., vt. to pretend —**feign´ed·ly**, **feign´ing·ly** adv. —**feign´er** n.

feint n. a deceptive move to throw an opponent off guard —vi., vt. to make a deceptive move

feis´ty adj. lively or flamboyant; spirited —**feis´ti·ness** n.

fe·lic´i·tate vt. to congratulate; to wish one well; to make happy — **fe·lic´i·ta´tion** n. —**fe·lic´i·tous** adj. —**fe·lic´i·tous·ly** adv. —**fe·lic´i·tous·ness** n.

fe·lic´i·ty n. happiness; light–heartedness; a pleasing quality

fe´line adj. of or like a cat —n. a cat

fel´low n. an associate or colleague; a scholar

fel´on n. one guilty of a serious crime

fel´o·ny n. a serious crime — **fe·lo´ni·ous** adj. —**fe·lo´ni·ous·ly**

adv. —**fe·lo´ni·ous·ness** n.

fe´male adj. of the sex that bears offspring; of a mechanical part designed to receive a projecting connector —n. a female animal or plant

fem´i·nine adj. having the qualities of a female —**fem´i·nine·ly** adv. —**fem·i·nin´i·ty** n.

fem´i·nist n. one who advocates equal rights for women —**fem´i·nism** n.

fence n. a barrier that divides property or affords protection; one who deals in stolen goods —vi. to be evasive; to deal in stolen goods — vt. to restrict, as by a barrier; to sell to a dealer in stolen goods

fenc´ing n. the art of combat with a foil, saber, etc.

fend vi. to provide for oneself —vt. to ward off; to defend

fend´er (US) n. a guard or cushion that protects from damage by contact, as on an automobile or boat

fer·ment´ n. any substance that causes fermentation; a state of agitation —vi. to undergo fermentation; to be in an agitated state — vt. to cause fermentation; to agitate

fer·men·ta´tion n. a chemical conversion brought on by a ferment; agitation

fe·ro´cious adj. savage; unmerciful; ravenous —**fe·ro´cious·ly** adv. —**fe·ro´cious·ness, fe·roc´i·ty** n.

fer´ry vt. to convey passengers or freight by boat or aircraft —n. a vehicle used for such conveyance

fer´tile adj. productive; teeming; rich in natural resources —**fer·til´i·ty** n.

fer´vid adj. impassioned; zealous — **fer´vid·ly** adv.

fer´vour (Brit.), **fer´vor** (US) n. ardor; zeal; enthusiasm

fes´ter vi., vt. to form pus; to rankle

or embitter

fes´ti·val n. a celebration

fes´tive adj. joyous, lighthearted — **fes´tive·ly** adv. —**fes´tive·ness** n.

fes·tiv´i·ty n. a festival or celebration

fes·toon´ n. a hanging garland; a decorative molding —vt. to decorate with garlands

fete, fête n. a festival —vt. to honor with a festival or celebration

fe´tish n. an object regarded as having magical powers; an object of inordinate devotion —**fe´tish·ism** n.

fet´id adj. having an offensive smell; stinking —**fet´id·ly** adv. —**fet´id·ness** n.

fe·tol´o·gy n. the medical discipline that deals with the study and care of a fetus

fet´ter n. a chain or shackle for the feet; a restraint —vt. to constrain with shackles; to restrain

fe´tus n. an unborn young in the uterus or egg

feud n. a bitter, long–lasting quarrel, especially between families, clans, etc. —vi. to sustain a long-standing quarrel

fe´ver n. a condition characterized by increased body temperature; a state of exceptional excitement

fi·an·cé´ n. a man who is engaged to be married

fi·an·ceé´ n. a woman who is engaged to be married

fi·as´co n. a complete and utter failure; a debacle

fi´at n. a legal order; a decree

fi´ber (US), **fi´bre** (Brit.) n. a thread-like structure —**fi´bered, fi´ber·less** adj. —**fi´brous** adj.

fick´le adj. flighty or unstable in attention, affection, etc. —**fick´le·ness** n.

fic´tion n. an imaginary story; a narrative portraying imaginary characters and events —**fic´tion·al**

adj. —**fic´tion·al·ly** *adv.* —**fic´tion·al·ize** *vt.*

fic·ti´tious *adj.* pretended; made up, imaginary —**fic·ti´tious·ly** *adv.* —**fic·ti´tious·ness** *n.*

fi·del´i·ty *n.* loyalty; devotion to duty or obligation; accuracy in description, reproduction, etc.

fi·du´ci·ar·y *adj.* of one who holds something in trust for another; of that held in trust —*n.* one who holds in trust

field *n.* open land; a plot of ground set aside for crops or pasture; any unbroken expanse; an area of endeavor or knowledge, as *the computer field*

fiend *n.* an evil spirit, a demon; one who is exceptionally cruel; one addicted to a drug or activity —**fiend´ish** *adj.* —**fiend´ish·ly** *adv.* —**fiend´ish·ness** *n.*

fierce *adj.* savagely cruel; violent; passionate or intense, as *a fierce longing* —**fierce´ly** *adv.* —**fierce´ness** *n.*

fi´er·y *adj.* containing or like fire; impetuous or emotional —**fier´i·ly** *adv.* —**fi´er·i·ness** *n.*

fight *vi., vt.* to take part in a conflict or battle —*n.* any conflict or struggle; a quality of boldness; readiness to struggle —**fight´er** *n.*

fig´ur·a·tive *adj.* symbolic; not to be taken in the literal sense —**fig´u·ra·tive·ly** *adv.* —**fig´ur·a·tive·ness** *n.*

fig´ure *n.* a form or likeness; a diagram; a character that represents a value —*vi., vt.* to calculate; to consider

fil´a·ment *n.* a thin threadlike component

file *n.* a storage cabinet, folder, etc. for keeping papers; a collection of related data stored together; a line of people or things, one behind the other; a tool for smoothing, scraping, etc. —*vi.* to march in line; to formally petition or register, as to a court —*vt.* to place in order and store documents, data, etc.; to place on public record; to smooth or scrape with a tool

fil´i·al *adj.* of that expected or due of a son or daughter

fil´i·gree´ *n.* delicate ornamental work of intertwined gold or silver wire

fill *n.* anything used to take up space or make full; a section of land which has been built up; a satisfactory amount —*vt.* to bring to a desired level; to make full; to occupy; to furnish what is needed; to satisfy one's hunger

fil´ly *n.* a young mare

film *n.* a thin layer or coating; sensitized material used in photography; a motion picture —*vi., vt.* to cover with a thin layer; to shoot a motion picture

fil´ter *n.* a porous substance used for straining and separating materials —*vi., vt.* to pass through a filter —**fil´ter·er** *n.*

filth *n.* offensive dirt; grime; contamination; lewd material; an obscenity

filth´y *adj.* dirty; obscene —**filth´i·ly** *adv.* —**filth´i·ness** *n.*

fil´trate *vt.* to strain or separate —*n.* a substance that has been filtered —**fil·tra·tion** *n.*

fi´nal *adj.* at the end; conclusive —*n.* the last of a series

fi´nance, fi·nance´ *n.* the management of money —*vt.* to furnish or obtain money or credit —**fi·nan´cial** *adj.* —**fi·nan´cial·ly** *adv.*

finances the resources of a person, company, etc.

fin·an·cier´ *n.* one specializing in financial operations

find *n.* an amazing discovery; something discovered —*vt.* to discover or perceive; to experience, as *to find pleasing*

fine *adj.* of exceptional quality; small, thin, or keen —*n.* money payment imposed as a penalty —*vt.* to impose a fine

fin´ger *n.* one of the digits projecting from the hand; anything resembling a finger —*vt.* to touch with the fingers; to point out

fi´nis *n.* finish

fin´ish *n.* the end or conclusion; completion, perfection; the surface of an object; fineness of manner and speech —*vt.* bring to an end or complete; to use up; to sand, rub, or apply a final coat of paint, varnish, etc.

fi´nite *adj.* having limits that are clearly defined

fir *n.* a cone–bearing evergreen tree

fire *n.* burning; combustion; strong feeling, ardor; a discharge of firearms —*vi.* to start burning; to become excited; to discharge from a firearm —*vt.* to set afire; to bake in a kiln; to excite, inspire; to discharge a firearm; to dismiss an employee

fire´proof *adj.* not easily burned —*vt.* to treat so as to be less combustible

firm *adj.* that is solid or dense; not yielding to pressure; secure, immovable; settled, as the terms of a contract; determined —*n.* a business

fir´ma·ment *n.* the dome or arch of the heavens

first *adj.* preceding all others —*n.* one who or that which is above all others in rank, position, etc.; the beginning —*adv.*

first aid emergency treatment, esp. while awaiting professional medical attention

first´-class´, first´-rate´ *adj.* of the best quality —*adv.*

fis´cal *adj.* of taxation or public finances; of financial policy in general —**fis´cal·ly** *adv.*

fish *n.* an aquatic animal with gills —*vi.*, *vt.* to try to catch fish —*adj.* pertaining to or made from fish

fis´sion *n.* a splitting apart —**nuclear fission** the splitting of atoms to release energy —**fis´sion·a·ble** *adj.*

fis´sure *n.* a long, narrow crack

fist *n.* a hand with fingers pressed into the palm

fit *adj.* able, competent; appropriate, suitable; trim, healthy —*n.* the state of being appropriate or of the proper size; a seizure —*vi.* to be suited —*vt.* to be appropriate; to alter so as to make suitable; to insert in position —**fit´ness** *n.*

fit´ting *adj.* appropriate; suitable —*n.* the process of testing or altering for a proper fit; a part that serves to connect —**fit´ting·ly** *adv.* —**fit´ting·ness** *n.*

fix *n.* an awkward situation —*vt.* to fasten firmly; to establish with certainty; to repair —**fix´a·ble** *adj.* —**fix´er** *n.*

fix·a´tion *n.* a preoccupation; an obsession —**fix´ate** *vi.*, *vt.*

fix´ture *n.* anything firmly fastened, such as electrical fittings in a building; anything that has been in place so long as to seem permanently attached

flab´by *adj.* soft, weak; lacking good physical form —**flab´bi·ness** *n.*

flac´cid *adj.* weak, feeble, soft —**flac´cid·i·ty, flac´cid·ness** *n.* —**flac´cid·ly** *adv.*

flag *n.* a cloth banner decorated with colors or symbols —*vi.* to grow weak; to tire —*vt.* to signal with a flag or by waving as with a flag

flag´el·late *vt.* to whip —**flag·el·la´tion** *n.*

fla´grant *adj.* outragious; openly disgraceful —**fla´gran·cy** *n.* —**fla´grant·ly** *adv.* —**fla´grant·ness** *n.*

flake *n.* a small, thin piece; one who is flightly or fickle —*vi.*, *vt.* to form or chip off into flakes —**flak´i·ly** adv. —**flak´i·ness** n. —**flak´y** adj.

flame n. light from a fire —vi. to burn with a bright light; to become excited; to show the flush of excitement —**flam´ing** adj. —**flam´ing·ly** adv.

flange n. a projection at the edge of a wheel, track, etc. that serves to connect, guide, strengthen, etc.

flank n. the side —vt. to be positioned at the side of

flap n. a flat, broad piece connected at one end that hangs loose; a slapping sound made as if by a flap; a state of excitement —vi., vt. to move back and forth; to flutter

flare n. a bright light used as a signal; a sudden burst of light —vi. to emit a sudden burst of light; to spread out at one end

flash adj. happening suddenly or quickly —n. a brief gleam of light; anything that comes and goes in a brief span; ostentation —vi. to emit a sudden blaze of light; to pass by swiftly —vt. to send out or display briefly —**flash´i·ly** adv. —**flash´i·ness** n. —**flash´y** adj.

flash´back´ n. a memory or reminiscence; an interruption in the action of a story, play, etc. to protray an earlier event

flask n. a small bottle

flat¹ adj. having a relatively even surface; showing little or no variation; lying prone; bland; lacking finances —n. a level surface; a musical note lowered by a half step or the symbol to indicate this —adv. —**flat´ly** adv. —**flat´ness** n. —**flat´ten** vi., vt.

flat² n. (Brit.) a room or rooms serving as living quarters

flat´ter vt. to compliment excessively or disingenuously —**flat´ter·er** n. —**flat´ter·ing** adj. —**flat´ter·ing·ly** adv. —**flat´ter·y** n.

flaunt vi., vt. to make an osten-

tatious or impudent display —**flaunt´ing·ly** adv.

fla´vor (US) n. a quality that affects taste; anything added to impart a particular taste; a distinctive quality, as of a place —vt. to impart flavor to —**fla´vor·er** n. —**fla´vor·ous**, **fla´vor·y** adj. —**fla´vor·ous·ly** adv.

fla´vor·ful (US) adj. full of flavor; delectable —**fla´vor·ful·ly** adv.

fla´vor·ing (US) n. a substance, such as an extract, that imparts flavor

fla´vor·less (US) adj. lacking flavor; flat or insipid

fla´vour (Brit.) n. a quality that affects taste; anything added to impart a particular taste; a distinctive quality, as of a place —vt. to impart flavor to —**fla´vour·er** n.

fla´vour·ful (Brit.) adj. full of flavor; delectable

fla´vour·ing (Brit.) n. a substance, such as an extract, that imparts flavor

fla´vour·less (Brit.) adj. lacking flavor; flat or insipid

flaw n. a defect —vt., vi. to make or become defective

flay vt. to strip the skin from, as by whipping; to criticize harshly

fleck n. a small particle —vt. to cover with specks

flee vi., vt. to run away or escape

fleece n. the coat of wool that covers a sheep —vt. to clip the wool from a sheep; to defraud

fleet adj. swift; temporary —vi. to proceed swiftly —**fleet´ly** adv. —**fleet´ness** n.

fleet n. the ships, planes, trucks, etc., operating under a single authority, as a military command or a company

fleet´ing adj. passing quickly; transitory —**fleet´ing·ly** adv. —**fleet´ing·ness** n.

flesh n. the meat on the body of an animal; the edible portion of fruits and vegetables; the human body; human desires, in contrast to the spiritual

flesh´ly *adj.* pertaining to the body; sensual, not spiritual: *fleshly desires*; plump —**flesh´li·ness** *n.*

flex´i·ble *adj.* able to be bent without breaking; amenable to change —**flex´i·bil´i·ty** *n.* —**flex´i·bly** *adv.*

flex´time *n.* a system that allows employees to vary their working hours, usually to accommodate those with small children or to relieve traffic congestion

flight *n.* travel by air; fleeing, running away; a set of steps

flight´y *adj.* frivolous; whimsical —**flight´i·ly** *adv.* —**flight´i·ness** *n.*

flim´sy *adj.* easily damaged; fragile; poorly fashioned —**flim´si·ly** *adv.* —**flim´si·ness** *n.*

flinch *vi.* to wince or shrink back, as from a blow or pain

fling *vt.* to throw forcefully or violently; to act with spontaneity, as *to fling oneself into a project* —*n.* the act of throwing violently; a time of wild abandon

flint *n.* a very hard stone

flint´y *adj.* like flint; unyielding —**flint´i·ly** *adv.* —**flint´i·ness** *n.*

flip´pant *adj.* frivolous; marked by a lack of reverence; impertinent —**flip´pan·cy** *n.* —**flip´pant·ly** *adv.*

flirt *n.* a trifler; a coquette —*vi.* to trifle with the affections of another; to consider briefly —**flir´ta´tion** *n.* —**flir·ta´tious** *adj.* —**flir·ta´tious·ly** *adv.* —**flir·ta´tious·ness** *n.*

float *n.* anything that rests on the surface of a liquid; a decorated platform in a parade —*vi.* to rest on the surface of a liquid; to drift on the air —*vt.* to cause to come to rest on the surface of a liquid —**float´a·ble** *adj.*

flock *n.* a group of animals; any group or congregation —*vi.* to assemble in a group

flog *vt.* to beat with a whip

flood *n.* the covering of normally dry land with water; a deluge or glut, as of mail —*vt.* to overflow, inundate, or glut

flood control measures taken, such as the building of dams, to prevent flooding

floor *n.* the surface of a room on which one walks or stands; any bottom surface, as *the floor of a canyon*; a level of a building; recognition to speak at a formal gathering —*vt.* to build or refinish a walking surface; to defeat or astound

flo´ra *n.* the plants of a particular region

flo´ral *adj.* of or like flowers —**flo´ral·ly** *adv.*

flor´id *adj.* gaudy, ornate; of a rosy complexion —**flo·rid´i·ty, flor´id·ness** *n.* —**flor´id·ly** *adv.*

flor´ist *n.* one who cultivates or sells flowers

flo·til´la *n.* a fleet of boats or small ships

floun´der *n.* any of a variety of flatfishes —*vi.* to have difficulty; to struggle —**floun´der·ing·ly** *adv.*

flour *n.* a fine meal ground from grain —*vt.* to make into flour; to sprinkle with flour

flour´ish *n.* anything showy, as decoration or adornment; a sweeping motion of the arms; an elaborate sounding of brass, a fanfare —*vi.* to prosper —*vt.* to decorate in an ornate fashion; to wave with a sweep of the arm —**flour´ish·er** *n.*

flout *vi., vt.* to mock; to regard contemptuously —*n.* a mocking insult —**flout´ing·ly** *adv.*

flow *n.* an emanation; the amount or rate of discharge; the current or course of a river, stream, etc.; a continuous stream, as of thoughts or ideas —*vi.* to move in a stream;

to progress smoothly —**flow´ing·ly** *adv.* —**flow´ing·ness** *n.*

flow´er *n.* a bloom; a plant cultivated for its blossoms; the best part or time: *the flower of youth* —*vi.* to bloom; to attain the best level —*vt.* to decorate with blossoms — **flow´ered** *adj.* —**flow´er·i·ly** *adv.* —**flow´er·i·ness** *n.* —**flow´er·ing** *adj.* —**flow´er·y** *adj.*

fluc´tu·ate´ *vi.* to vary continuously; to waver —*vt.* to cause to waver — **fluc´tu·a´tion** *n.*

flue *n.* a passage for exhausting smoke, hot air, etc.

flu´ent *adj.* smooth flowing; able to speak or write well —**flu´en·cy** *n.* —**flu´ent·ly** *adv.*

flu´id *adj.* flowing or able to flow; marked by graceful movement; readily changed: *a fluid policy* —*n.* a substance that can flow —**flu·id´i·ty, flu´id·ness** *n.* —**flu´id·ly** *adv.*

fluke *n.* that brought about by chance

flunk *vi., vt.* to fail in school

flunk´y *n.* a servant; one engaged for menial tasks

flush *adj.* well supplied; even —*n.* a rapid flow; a warm glow; sudden exhilaration —*vi., vt.* to flow rapidly; to clean with a rapid flow of liquid; to blush

flus´ter *vi., vt.* to make or become nervous or confused

flut´ter *n.* rapid waving or fluctuation; a commotion —*vi., vt.* to wave or fluctuate rapidly; to move restlessly —**flut´ter·y** *adj.*

flux *n.* a flowing; a state of constant change

fly *n.* a flap over an opening in clothing, a tent, etc.; an insect — *vi., vt.* to travel by air; to operate an aircraft; to flee

fo´cus *n.* the point where rays of light, etc. converge; any point of concentration, activity, etc. —*vi., vt.* to adjust to produce a clear image —**fo´cal** *adj.*

foe *n.* an adversary, enemy

fog *n.* a dense mist —*vt.* to obscure —**fog´gi·ness** *n.* —**fog´gy** *adj.*

foi´ble *n.* a minor weakness

foil *n.* a thin sheet of metal; a fencing sword —*vt.* to frustrate

foist *vt.* to pass off by trickery

fold *n.* a mark made by doubling; a pen for sheep —*vi.* to close, as a business —*vt.* to double by placing one part over another; to envelop

fo´li·age *n.* a mass of plant leaves

folk *adj.* of the common people —*n.* the people generally; a tribe, family, nation, etc. —**folks·y** *adj.*

folk´lore´ *n.* the traditions of a culture

fol´low *vi.* to come next; to result — *vt.* to come next; to conform; to happen as a result; to trail or pursue —**follow through** to complete —**follow up** to study more closely —**fol´low·er** *n.* —**fol´low·ing** *adj.*

fol´low·ing *adj.* ensuing —*n.* a group of supporters; a calling

fol´ly *n.* foolishness; a frivolous act or undertaking

fo·ment´ *vt.* to advocate; to incite, as rebellion

fond *adj.* cherished: *fond memories*; doting or indulgent —**fond´ly** *adv.* —**fond´ness** *n.*

fon´dle *vt.* to caress or stroke

font *n.* one size and style of type; a water basin or fountain; a place of origin

food *n.* any substance that nourishes; something that stimulates, as *food for thought*

fool *n.* one lacking common sense; a silly person —*vi.* to act silly —*vt.* to mislead or cheat —**fool´ish** *adj.* — **fool´ish·ly** *adv.* —**fool´ish·ness** *n.*

fop *n.* one overly devoted to personal appearance

for´age *n.* food for animals, fodder; a search for food —*vi., vt.* search for food or supplies

for·ay n. a raid —vt. to raid or venture

for·bear´ vi., vt. to abstain; to restrain oneself —**for·bear´ance** n. —**for·bear´ing·ly** adv.

for·bid´ vt. to prohibit; to order against; to prevent —**for·bid´dance** n. —**for·bid´den** adj.

for·bid´ding adj. frightening; unpleasant —**for·bid´ding·ly** adv.

force n. potency, might; the power to compel; a group organized for a purpose —vt. to overpower; to compel by might —**force´ful** adj. —**force´ful·ly** adv.

fore´bear n. an ancestor

fore·bode´ vi., vt. to predict; to anticipate the unpleasant —**fore·bod´ing** n.

fore´cast n. a prediction —vi., vt. to anticipate

fore·close´ vi., vt. to take away the right to redeem mortgaged property —**fore´clo´sure** n.

fore´fa·ther n. an ancestor

fore·go´ vt. to go before

for´eign adj. from another country; unfamiliar; exotic

fore´man n. one in charge of a group

fo·ren´sic adj. pertaining to legal or formal argumentation —**fo·ren´si·cal·ly** adv.

fore·run´ner n. one sent or coming before; an ancestor; a sign of something to follow

fore·see´ vt. to predict; to foretell —**fore·see´a·ble** adj.

fore´sight´ n. the ability to anticipate

for´est n. an extensive growth of trees

fore·tell´ vi., vt. to predict

for·ev´er adv. for all time

for´feit n. that lost by neglect, etc. —vt. to give up —**for´fei·ture** n.

fore·warn´ vt. to warn beforehand

forge n. a furnace for heating metal —vi., vt. to form laboriously, as metal; to falsify in order to deceive

for·ger·y n. an illegal making or altering, as of money or a signature; an imitation or fake

for·get´ vi., vt. to lose from memory; to overlook or neglect —**for·get´a·ble, for·get´ta·ble** adj.

for·get´ful adj. losing or having lost the ability to remember; careless or neglectful —**for·get´ful·ly** adv. —**for·get´ful·ness** n.

for·give´ vt. to pardon; to overlook

fork n. a device with prongs at one end, used to hold or move something: salad fork, pitchfork; a dividing —vi. to branch —vt. to split into branches; to use a fork, as for eating —**forked** adj.

for·lorn´ adj. abandoned; wretched, without hope

form n. configuration; a mold; type; convention; method —vi. to take shape —vt. to mold or shape; to conceive in the mind

for´mal adj. according to custom; correct or suitable, as formal dress; precise in manner; stodgy —**for´mal·ly** adv.

for·mal´ity n. careful adherence to custom; an official act

for·ma´tion n. a thing formed; arrangement or configuration

for´mer adj. coming before; preceding; the first of two

for´mi·da·ble adj. awesome; threatening; overwhelming —**for´mi·da·bly** adv.

for´mu·la n. a representation using logic symbols; a precise method or specification

for´mu·late vt. to conceive or develop; to express as a formula —**for·mu·la´tion** n.

for·ni·ca´tion n. sexual intercourse between unmarried persons —**for´ni·cate** vi.

for·sake´ vt. to forgo; to leave or abandon

forte n. one's special ability

for´ti·fy vt. to make stronger

for'ti·tude *n.* strength of character; determination

fort'night *n.* two weeks time

for·tu'i·tous *adj.* occurring by chance; fortunate —**for·tu'i·tous·ly** *adv.* —**for·tu'i·tous·ness, for·tu'i·ty** *n.*

for·tu·nate *adj.* lucky; auspicious —**for'tu·nate·ly**

for'tune *n.* luck; fate; riches

fo'rum *n.* a gathering for discussion

fos'sil *n.* preserved remains —**fos'sil·ize** *vt.*

fos'ter *vt.* to promote; to nurture

foul *adj.* offensive; profane; underhanded; entangled; unpleasant, as weather —*vi., vt.* to soil; to entangle —**foul'ly** *adv.*

found *adj.* discovered —*vt.* to establish or bring into being; to cast metal

foun·da'tion *n.* a fundamental principle; an endowment for financing charitable works

foun'dry *n.* the process of casting metal; a place where metal is cast

foun'tain *n.* a natural or artificial spring; a reservoir

fox'y *adj.* crafty, cunning; attractive, seductive —**fox'i·ness** *n.*

fra'cas *n.* a brawl

frac'tion *n.* a small part; a value expressed as a numerator and denominator, as ½

frac'tious *adj.* unruly; difficult to manage; irritable or testy

frac'ture *n.* a crack or break —*vi., vt.* to crack or break

frag'ile *adj.* easily damaged; delicate —**frag'ile·ly** *adv.* —**frag'ile·ness, fra·gil'i·ty** *n.*

frag'ment *n.* a part or piece, often detached —**frag'men·tar'y** *adj.*

fra'grance, fra'gran·cy *n.* a pleasant odor —**fra'grant** *adj.* —**fra'grant·ly** *adv.*

frail *adj.* easily damaged; delicate; feeble or weak —**frail'ly** *adv.* —**frail'ness** *n.* —**frail'ty** *n.*

frame *n.* a skeletal structure; a general form; a field of view —*vt.* to shape or form; to provide a border for —**frame'a·ble** *adj.*

frame of reference a point or aspect from which something is viewed

fran'chise' *n.* any right or privilege granted by a government, organization, etc.

fran'gi·ble *adj.* fragile; brittle

frank *adj.* open and honest

frantic *adj.* distraught by anger, worry, etc.; highly emotional —**fran'ti·cal·ly** *adv.*

fra·ter'nal *adj.* brotherly

frat'er·nize *vi.* to be friendly; to have friendly relations with, esp. of those in an occupied or conquered territory —**frat·er·ni·za'tion** *n.* —**frat'er·niz·er** *n.*

fraud *n.* deception; a swindle; a faker

fraud'u·lent *adj.* deceitful; marked by fraud —**fraud'u·lence** *n.* —**fraud'u·lent·ly** *adv.*

fray *n.* a brawl —*vi., vt.* to become tattered or worn

freak *adj.* abnormal; bizarre —*n.* an abnormality —**freak'ish** *adj.*

free *adj.* not busy or in use; independent; unrestrained; unencumbered; without debt or obligation; without cost —*vt.* to release or make available —**free'ly** *adv.*

fren'zy *n.* a sudden burst of agitation or activity —**fren'zied** *adj.*

fre'quent *adj.* happening often —**fre·quent'** *vt.* to stop by often

fres'co *n.* a watercolor painting on wet plaster

fresh *adj.* newly made or obtained; natural; naive or uninitiated; impertinent or impudent —**fresh'ly** *adv.* —**fresh'ness** *n.*

fret *vt., vi.* to make or be irritated or annoyed —**fret'ful** *adj.* —**fret'ful·ly** *adv.* —**fret'ful·ness** *n.*

fri'a·ble *adj.* easily crumbled

fric'tion *n.* a rubbing or abrasion;

discord caused by differences

friend *n.* one who is known, liked, trusted, etc.; an ally or supporter

fright *n.* sudden alarm or terror; a startling sight

fright´en *vt.* to cause alarm or terror

frill *n.* gathered or pleated edging; an unnecessary adjunct —**frill´li·ness** *n.* —**frill´y** *adj.*

fringe *adj.* at the outer edge; minor or peripheral —*n.* ornamental edging; an outer edge or periphery —*vt.* to decorate with a fringe

fringe benefit indirect compensation to an employee in the form of insurance, paid leave, etc.

frisky *adj.* energetic; playful

frit´ter *n.* deep-fried fruit or vegetables coated with batter —*vt.* to waste a little at a time

friv´o·lous *adj.* trivial; not serious or sensible —**fri·vol´i·ty** *n.* —**friv´o·lous·ly** *adj.*

frol´ic *n.* merriment, play —*vi.* to play —**frol´ic·some** *adj.*

front *n.* the forward part or position; appearance or demeanor; an area of activity —**fron´tal** *adj.*

fron·tier´ *n.* the border of a country; an unexplored area

frost *n.* ice crystals; coldness of air, manner, etc. —*vt.* to coat with frost or anything resembling frost, as icing for a cake —**frost´i·ly** *adv.* —**frost´i·ness** *n.* —**frost´y** *adj.*

froth *n.* foam; something trivial —*vi., vt.* to foam

frown *n.* a stern look denoting disapproval or deep thought —*vi., vt.* to scowl; to show disapproval

frugal *adj.* thrifty; inexpensive — **fru´gal´i·ty** *n.*

fruit *n.* the edible portion of a plant; a consequence —**fruit´ful** *adj.*

fru·i´tion *n.* the yielding of results; fulfillment

frus´trate´ *vt.* to nullify, as the efforts of another —**frus´tra´tion** *n.*

fu´el *n.* anything consumed to produce energy

fu´gi·tive *n.* one who flees; something elusive

ful´crum *n.* the support on which a lever pivots

ful·fill´ *vt.* to perform or accomplish

full *adj.* containing all, or nearly all, that is possible; of the highest degree; puffed out —**full´ness** *n.* — **ful´ly** *adv.*

ful´mi·nate´ *n.* an explosive salt — *vi., vt.* to denounce loudly; to explode —**ful´mi·na´tion** *n.*

ful´some *adj.* obsequious or fawning; abundant

fum´ble *vi., vt.* to grope awkwardly; to blunder

fume *n.* vapor —*vi.* to give off vapor; to show anger

fu´mi·gate´ *vt.* to disinfect with gas —**fu´mi·ga´tion** *n.*

func´tion *n.* normal use or purpose; a ceremony or event —*vi.* to perform as designed

fund *n.* assets designated for some purpose; an institution charged with management of such assets —*vt.* to finance

fun·da·men´tal *adj.* essential; basic —*n.* a principle; an essential part

fu´ner·al *n.* a ceremony or procession concerned with the burial of the dead

fu·ne´re·al *adj.* solemn

fur´bish *vt.* to restore; to polish

fu´ri·ous *adj.* enraged; frenzied

fur´nace (*US*) *n.* an appliance for producing heat, as for warming a home or firing metal or glass

fur´nish *vt.* to supply; to provide

fur´nish·ings *pl. n.* furniture, drapes, carpets, etc. for the home; clothing and accessories

fur´ni·ture *n.* household goods such as tables, chairs, and beds

fu´ror *n.* a state of excitement

fur´row *n.* a rut, as made by a plow or a wheeled vehicle; a deep wrinkle —*vt.* to make a furrow —*vi.* to become furrowed or wrinkled

fur´ther *adj.* additional; more distant —*adv.* farther; to a greater extent; moreover —*vt.* to aid or promote —**fur´ther·more** *adv.*

fur´tive *adj.* stealthy, sneaky

fu´ry *n.* violent anger; violence

fuse *n.* a device for setting off an explosive; a device that prevents the overloading of an electrical circuit —*vi., vt.* to unite or blend

fu´sion *n.* a melting or joining by heat; a nuclear reaction

fuss *n.* a quarrel; a commotion; needless concern or attention —*vi.* to complain; to make a bother over trifles —*vt.* to worry needlessly

fu´tile *adj.* hopeless; trivial —**fu´tile·ness, fu´til´i·ty** *n.*

fu´ture *adj.* that is to come or happen; expected —*n.* a time or event to come; outlook

fuzz´y *adj.* indistinct

g, G seventh letter of the English alphabet; a slang term for 1000 dollars

gab *n.* idle talk —*vi.* to gossip

gabble *n.* meaningless chatter —*vi., vt.* to jabber or chatter

gadg´et *n.* any implement; a device of limited utility

gag *n.* a joke or hoax; something placed over or in the mouth to prevent speech; anything that restricts free speech —*vi.* to choke or retch —*vt.* to silence by force, threat, etc.

gai´e·ty *n.* mirth; festivity; gaudiness

gain *n.* an increase; an advantage —*vi., vt.* to acquire; to reach

gala *adj.* joyful —*n.* a joyful celebration

gal´ax·y *n.* a star system; any gathering of distinctive persons or things

gale *n.* a strong wind

gall *n.* bile; impertinence

gal´lant *adj.* chivalrous; noble, dashing —**gal·lant´** *n.* a lover; one who is chivalrous —**gal´lant·ly** *adv.*

gal´lon *n.* a liquid measure equal to four quarts

gam´bit *n.* a strategy designed to gain an advantage

gam´ble *n.* a risk —*vi., vt.* to take a risk

gam´bol *vi.* to jump about; to frolic

gan´der *n.* a male goose —**take a gander** have a look

gang *n.* a group associated in some way

gang´ster *n.* one belonging to a group of criminals

gaol (*Brit.*), **jail** (*US*) *n.* a place of confinement for one awaiting trial or guilty of a minor offense —*vt.* to confine in a jail

gaol´er (*Brit.*), **jail´er** (*US*) *n.* one charged with the upkeep of a jail

gape *n.* a large opening; an open-mouthed stare —*vi.* to yawn or stare in amazement with the mouth open; to open wide

ga·rage´ *n.* a building for storing or repairing an automobile

garb *n.* clothing —*vt.* to clothe

gar´ble *vt.* to confuse or distort

gar´bage (*US*) *n.* waste, trash

gar´den *n.* a plot of cultivated land —*vi., vt.* to cultivate a plot of land —**gar´den·er** *n.*

gar´gle *n.* a solution for medicating or cleansing the throat —*vi., vt.* to cleanse or medicate the throat

gar´ish *adj.* overly ornate, gaudy —**gar´ish·ly** *adv.*

gar´ment *n.* an item of clothing

gar´ner *vt.* to collect and store; to acquire

gar´nish *n.* a decoration —*vt.* to decorate

gar´ret *n.* an attic room

gar´ru·lous *adj.* chattering; wordy —**gar´ru·lous·ness** *n.*

gas *n.* vapor; a mixture of gasses as used for anesthesia, fuel, etc.;

something enjoyable; (US) gasoline

gash n. a deep cut —vt. to make a deep cut

gasket n. a washer; a seal to prevent leakage

gas·o·line´ n. a flammable liquid fuel distilled from petroleum

gasp n. a difficult catching of the breath —vi. to inhale sharply or with difficulty

gas´tric adj. pertaining to the stomach

gath´er vi., to assemble; to accumulate —vt. to convene or assemble; to accumulate; to draw together; to infer or conclude

gaud´y adj. garish; vulgar

gauge n. a standard measure or means of estimating; a measuring device —vt. to measure or estimate

gaunt adj. thin and bony; drawn; dreary, barren

gay adj. lively, merry; bright —gai´ly adv.

gaze n. a steady look —vi. to look intently; to stare

gaz´et·teer´ n. a geographical dictionary or index

gear n. personal property; equipment; a device used to transmit energy in a machine

gem n. a precious stone; anything prized for its value

gene n. any of the units in a chromosome that transmits hereditary characteristics

gen·e·al´o·gy n. a record of one's lineage; the study of lineage

gen´er·al adj. extensive and diversified; non-exclusive; imprecise —**gen·er·al´i·ty** n. —**gen´er·al·ly** adv. —**gen´er·al·ize** vt. —**gen·er·al·i·za´tion** n.

gen´er·ate´ vt. to originate or bring into being; produce

gen´er·a´tion n. the process of producing; a single stage of descent or development

ge·ner´ic adj. of a class or group;

lacking a brand name

gen´er·ous adj. gracious, unselfish; ample —**gen·er·os´i·ty** n. —**gen´er·ous·ly** adv.

gen´e·sis n. origin

ge·net´ic, ge·net´i·cal adj. of origin or ancestry —**ge·net´i·cal·ly** adv.

ge·net´ics n. the study of ancestry —**ge·net´i·cist** n.

gen´ial adj. pleasant; amiable —**ge·ni·al´i·ty** n.

gen´ius n. exceptional natural ability or mental capacity

gen´o·cide´ n. the systematic extermination of a people

gen´tle adj. kindly; temperate; courtly; tame

gen´u·ine adj. authentic; sincere and honest

ge·og´ra·phy n. the study of the earth and its inhabitants; the physical nature of an area —**ge´o·graph´ic, ge´o·graph´ic·al** adj.

ge·ol´o·gy n. the study of the earth's structure and its development —**ge´o·log´ic, ge´o·log´ic·al** adj. —**ge·ol´o·gist** n.

germ n. the basic form from which an organism sprouts; any microorganism, especially one that is harmful; a basic concept

ger´mi·nate´ vi., vt. to sprout; to begin growth —**ger·mi·na´tion** n.

ges·tic´u·late´ vi., vt. to gesture

ges´ture n. a move that emphasizes; something done for effect

get vt. to receive or acquire in some way; to understand

ghast´ly adj. shocking; terrifying; ghostlike; offensive

ghet´to n. a district to which a minority group is restricted

ghost n. a disembodied spirit; a faint suggestion

gi´ant adj. of great size —n. anything of exceptional size

gibe n. a taunting remark —vi., vt. to taunt or ridicule

gift n. something freely given; a

natural ability: *the gift of gab*

gi·gan´tic *adj.* enormous

gig´gle *n.* a silly nervous laugh —*vi.* to laugh nervously

gild *vt.* to coat with gold; to make attractive; to make seem attractive

gilt *adj.* gilded —*n.* gilding

gim´mick *n.* a thing designed to deceive; a device to gain attention —**gim´mick·ry** *n.*

gird *vt.* to encircle with a belt or band

gird´er *n.* a large supporting beam

gist *n.* the primary concept

give *vi., vt.* to contribute; to impart; to yield to pressure

glad *adj.* happy; pleased —**glad´den** *vt.* —**glad´ly** *adv.*

glade *n.* an open space in a wooded area

glance *n.* a brief look; a deflecting —*vi.* to strike and fly off at an angle; to look briefly

glare *n.* an intense light; a fixed stare —*vi.* to shine intensely; to stare —**glar´ing** *adj.*

glaze *n.* a glassy finish —*vt.* to give a glassy coating or finish; to fit with glass

gleam *n.* a flash of light; a faint display —*vi.* to appear briefly

glean *vt.* to collect grain left by reapers; to obtain piecemeal, as information —**glean´ings** *n.*

glee *n.* gaiety, merriment

glib *adj.* fluency that often implies insincerity —**glib´ly** *adv.*

glide *n.* a smooth, flowing movement —*vi.* to move in a smooth, flowing manner

glim´mer *n.* a faint light; a trace —*vi.* to appear faintly

glimpse *n.* a quick view —*vi.* to glance —*vt.* to view briefly

glis´ten *vi.* to sparkle or shine

glit´ter *n.* a sparkling light; bits of decorative material —*vi.* to sparkle; to be brilliant —**glit´ter·y** *adj.*

gloat *vi.* to view with malicious

pleasure

glob´al *adj.* world–wide; comprehensive

globe *n.* a sphere; the earth

glob´ule *n.* a tiny globe; a drop

gloom *n.* dimness or darkness; despondency —**gloom´y** *adj.*

glo·ri·ous *adj.* splendid; pleasant; famed —**glo·ri·ous·ly** *adv.*

glo´ry *n.* splendor; fame; a state of well–being —*vi.* to be proud of or rejoice in —**glo´ri·fy´** *vt.* —**glo´ri·ous** *adj.* —**glo´ri·ous·ly** *adv.*

gloss *n.* shine or luster; a superficial image —*vt.* to make shiny; to pass over or cover up, as a fault or error —**gloss´i·ness** *n.* —**gloss´y** *adj.*

glos´sa·ry *n.* a list of terms with definitions

glow *n.* light produced by heat; a feeling of warmth —*vi.* to give off light; to be flushed from emotion, good health, etc.

glow´er *n.* a scowl —*vi.* to scowl

glue *n.* an adhesive —*vt.* to affix, as with an adhesive

glum *adj.* sullen, dejected

glut *n.* an oversupply —*vt.* to oversupply; to overburden

glut´ton *n.* an overeater; one with unusual capacity

gnaw *vi., vt.* to wear away, as with the teeth; to worry

goad *vt.* to prod or urge; to provoke

goal *n.* an objective toward which one strives

gob´ble·dy·gook *n.* wordy and ambiguous language

gob´let *n.* a stemmed drinking glass

gob´lin *n.* a mischievous elf

gone *adj.* departed; used up

gon´er *n.* a person or thing that is beyond help

gore *n.* blood from a wound —*vt.* to wound with a horn

gorge *n.* a ravine; the throat or gullet —*vi., vt.* to devour

gor´geous *adj.* exceptionally beautiful; delightful

gos´sip *n.* idle chatter; a rumor; one who gossips —*vi.* to engage in idle chatter

gouge *n.* a type of chisel; an overcharging —*vt.* to cut into; to cheat by overcharging

gour´mand *n.* one fond of good food; a glutton

gour´met´ *n.* a good judge of fine food and drink

gov´ern *vi., vt.* to control or influence; to regulate or restrain

gov´ern·ment *n.* a system of administration, its personnel and agencies

gown *n.* a long flowing garment

grab *vt.* to seize roughly; to take by deceit; to attract one's attention; to impress

grace *n.* an attractive or pleasing quality; good will; the temporary extension of a due date; a blessing —*vt.* to adorn; to dignify

grace´ful *adj.* having elegance of form or movement —**grace´ful·ly** *adv.* —**grace´ful·ness** *n.*

gra´cious *adj.* courteous and affable; compassionate; comfortable or luxurious: *gracious living* —**gra´cious·ly** *adv.* —**gra´cious·ness** *n.*

gra·da´tion *n.* a gradual progression

grade *n.* any of the levels in a progression; a rating; a degree of slope —*vt.* to rate or classify according to level; to change the level or slope of

gradient *adj.* sloping —*n.* a slope, or degree of slope

grad´u·al *adj.* progressing in slow or regular steps —**grad´u·al·ly** *adv.* —**grad´u·al·ness** *n.*

grad´u·ate´ *n.* one who has completed a course of study; a container for measuring —*vi.* to complete a course of study —*vt.* to award a diploma; to mark a container for measuring —**grad·u·a´tion** *n.*

graf·fi´to *n., pl.* **graf·fi´ti** a crudely-drawn inscription

graft *n.* the joining of living tissue; the tissue so joined; profit gained by extortion —*vi., vt.* to join tissue; to obtain by extortion

gram´mar *n.* the structure of a language; the rules for use of a language —**gram·mar´i·an** *n.* —**gram·mat´i·cal** *adj.*

grand *adj.* higher in rank; imposing; luxurious; noble —**grandeur** *n.*

gran·dil´o·quent *adj.* spoken pretentiously —**gran·dil´o·quence** *n.*

gran·di·ose *adj.* pompous

grant *n.* something given, as a favor or privilege —*vt.* to give

gran´u·lar *adj.* grainy

gran´ule *n.* a small particle

graph´ic, graph´i·cal *adj.* explicit; described clearly; regarding anything written or pictorial

grap´ple *vi.* to struggle with —*vt.* to seize

grasp *n.* a firm hold; the ability to hold or comprehend —*vt.* to take hold; to comprehend

grasp´ing *adj.* greedy

grate *n.* a framework of metal bars —*vt.* to make a harsh sound by scraping; to irritate; to shred, as cheese —*vi.* to make a harsh sound; to irritate

grate´ful *adj.* appreciative —**grate´ful·ly** *adv.*

grat´i·fy´ *vt.* to afford pleasure; to indulge —**grat·i·fi·ca´tion** *n.*

grat´i·tude´ *n.* appreciation

gra·tu´i·tous *adj.* given freely; without cause: *gratuitous violence* —**gra·tu´i·tous·ly** *adv.*

gra·tu´i·ty *n.* a gift for services

grave *adj.* serious; somber —*n.* a place for burial

grav´el *n.* crushed rock

grav´i·tate´ *vi.* to be inclined or attracted towards —**grav·i·ta´tion** *n.*

grav´i·ty *n.* seriousness; the attraction between celestial bodies

graze *vi., vt.* to feed on; to touch

lightly in passing

grease *n.* melted animal fat; a lubricant —*vt.* to lubricate or coat with a lubricant —**greas´y** *adj.*

great *adj.* large; extensive; important; skillful

greed *n.* excessive desire —**greed´i·ness** *n.* —**greed´y** *adj.*

greet *vt.* to welcome; to acknowledge in a particular way —**greet´ing** *n.*

gre·gar´i·ous *adj.* sociable; tending to join or associate in groups

grid *n.* a network of horizontal and vertical parallel lines, bars, etc.

grid´dle *n.* a flat iron pan for baking or frying

grief *n.* sadness, sorrow; a difficulty, or its cause

griev´ance *n.* a wrong; a complaint based on a wrong

grieve *vt., vi.* to cause or express grief

grim *adj.* stern; forbidding

grime *n.* dirt; filth —**grim´y** *adj.*

grin *n.* a broad smile —*vi.* to smile broadly

grind *vt.* to crush; to shape by rubbing; to oppress

grip *n.* a tight hold; a device for grasping; a small suitcase —*vi., vt.* to hold

gripe *n.* a complaint —*vi.* to complain

gris´ly *adj.* horrible, ghastly

grit *n.* small, hard particles; determination or pluck —*vt.* to clench or grind the teeth —**grit´ty** *adj.*

groan *n.* a deep sound expressing pain or distress; a moan —*vi.* to make a low moaning sound

grog´gy *adj.* sluggish or dazed

grom´met *n.* reinforcement for a hole punched in cloth or other light material

groom *n.* a bridegroom; one who tends horses —*vt.* to make attractive; to train for a purpose

groove *n.* a channel; a settled pattern —*vt.* to cut a channel

grope *vi.* to feel around or search uncertainly —*vt.* to fondle —**grop´er** *n.* —**grop´ing** *adj.*

gross *adj.* coarse, unrefined; offensive; flagrant; total, as *gross income* —*n.* total; twelve dozen —*vi., vt.* to earn in total

gro·tesque´ *adj.* bizarre; distorted; hideous —**gro·tesque´ly** *adv.* —**gro·tesque´ness** *n.*

grot´to *n.* a cavern

grouch *n.* one prone to complaining; a discontented person —*vi.* to grumble or complain; to sulk —**grouch´i·ly** *adv.* —**grouch´i·ness** *n.* —**grouch´y** *adj.*

ground *n.* the surface, as of the earth, floor, etc.; soil; an area set aside for a special use: *playground, burial ground*; a basis or foundation —*vt.* to place on the surface; to provide a basis

grounds *pl. n.* land around an estate

ground´less *adj.* without cause

group *n.* a number of persons or things taken together —*vi., vt.* to form or arrange together

group´ie *n.* an avid fan

grouse *n.* a game bird; a complaint —*vi.* to complain

grove *n.* a stand of trees without undergrowth

grov´el *vi.* to cower; to fawn over; to humble oneself

grow *vi.* to come to be; to increase —*vt.* to cultivate —**growth** *n.*

grown *adj.* mature; cultivated in a certain way

grub´by *adj.* filthy; wretched

grudge *n.* ongoing resentment for a real or imagined wrong

gru·el·ing *adj.* extremely demanding; exhausting

grue´some *adj.* frightful; hideous; grotesque

gruff *adj.* brusque; surly —**gruff´ly** *adv.*

grum·ble *vi.* complain; rumble

grump´y *adj.* grouchy

grun´gy *adj.* filthy; shabby

guar´an·tee´ *n.* assurance; surety — *vt.* to assure —**guar´an·tor** *n.*

guard *n.* any person or thing that protects against loss or harm —*vt.* to keep watch; to protect

guard´ed *adj.* protected; cautious; *guarded optimism* —**guard´ed·ly** *adv.* —**guard´ed·ness** *n.*

gu·ber·na·to´ri·al *adj.* relating to the office of governor

guess *n.* an estimate —*vi., vt.* to estimate; to presume

guest *n.* a visitor; one receiving hospitality; a visiting artist

guide *n.* that leads or directs —*vt.* to lead or direct —**guid´ance** *n.*

guild *n.* an association formed for the mutual aid and benefit of its members

guile *n.* craftiness, cunning

guilt *n.* liability for a wrong —**guilt´y** *adj.*

guise *n.* outward appearance; pretense

gulch *n.* a ravine

gulf *n.* a large inlet partially hemmed in by land; a wide gap or expanse

gul´li·ble *adj.* easily deceived —**gul·li·bil´i·ty** *n.* —**gul´li·bly** *adv.*

gul´ly *n.* a small ravine worn by erosion —*vt.* to form a gully

gump´tion *n.* initiative; nerve

gu´ru *n.* a spiritual advisor; a prominent leader

gush *n.* a strong flow —*vi.* to surge forth; to be overly enthused —**gush´y** *adj.*

gust *n.* a sudden burst or rush, as of wind —**gust´y** *adj.*

gus·ta·to´ry *adj.* pertaining to the sense of taste

gus´to *n.* enthusiasm, ardor

gut´tur·al *adj.* of a harsh or throaty sound

guz´zle *vi., vt.* to drink greedily

gyp *n.* a swindle or swindler —*vi., vt.* to swindle or cheat

gy´rate´ *vi.* to revolve in a circle or spiral —**gy´ra´tion** *n.*

h, H eighth letter of the English alphabet

hab´er·dash·er *n.* (*Brit.*) a seller of cloth and sewing needs; one who sells men's clothing —**hab´er·dash·er·y** *n.*

hab´it *n.* a customary behavior pattern; an addiction; a special manner of dress —**ha·bit´u·al** *adj.* —**ha·bit´u·al·ly** *adv.* —**ha·bit´u·al·ness** *n.*

hab´i·tat *n.* a creature's native environment

hab·i·ta´tion *n.* a dwelling

ha·bit´u·é *n.* a habitual visitor or frequenter of a place

hack´neyed *adj.* commonplace; made trite by overuse

hag *n.* an ugly old woman; a witch

hag´gard *adj.* drawn or gaunt —**hag´gard·ly** *adv.* —**hag´gard·ness** *n.*

hag´gle *vi.* to bargain

hail *n.* frozen rain; a shout of greeting; a barrage —*vi.* to fall as frozen rain —*vt.* to greet with cheers; to call out; to pour

hair grip (*Brit.*) a metal hair pin

hair slide (*Brit.*) a small appliance for keeping hair in place

hal´cy·on *adj.* tranquil

hale *adj.* healthy

half *adj.* being one of two equal or nearly equal parts; partial —*adv.* partly —*n.* one of two equal or nearly equal parts

half´heart´ed *adj.* lacking enthusiasm —**half´heart´ed·ly** *adv.*

hal´i·to´sis *n.* stale breath

hall *n.* a large room, as *a dance hall*; a passageway —**hall´way** *n.*

hall´mark *n.* a mark indicating quality; a distinctive feature

hal´low *vt.* to make or regard as holy

hal·lu´ci·nate *vi., vt.* to see or sense that which is not real; to fantasize —**hal·lu´ci·na´tion** *n.* —**hal·lu´ci·na´to·ry** *adj.*

hal·lu·ci·no·gen *n.* a substance that causes one to hallucinate

halt *n.* a stop, often temporary —*vi.* to stop; to hesitate or be uncertain —*vt.* to cause to stop

halve *vt.* to divide; to reduce by half

ham'let *n.* a small village

ham'per *n.* a large basket —*vt.* to prevent from moving freely

hand *n.* the part of the body at the end of the arm; anything designating of the hand's function, as gripping, fashioning, etc. —*vt.* to offer or provide

hand'book *n.* a manual

hand'ful *n.* all the hand can hold; a small amount; something or someone difficult to manage

hand'i·cap' *n.* a hindrance —*vt.* to hinder

hand'i·work' *n.* that done by one's own efforts

han'dle *n.* that part of an object designed for gripping —*vt.* to touch, hold, use, etc.; to manage or deal with; to trade in

hand'out *n.* a charitable gift; a promotional flyer

hand'pick' *vt.* to choose with care — **hand'picked'** *adj.*

hand'some *adj.* attractive; impressive —**hand'some·ly** *adv.* —**hand'some·ness** *n.*

hand-to-mouth *adj.* barely subsisting

hand'y *adj.* easily accessible; useful; skillful —**hand'i·ly** *adv.*

hang *vi., vt.* to suspend or be suspended

hang'ing *adj.* suspended —*n.* a decorative device for a wall

hang-up *n.* a difficulty or inhibition

hap'haz'ard *adj.* random —*adv.* by chance

hap'less *adj.* unlucky

hap'pen *vi.* to occur

hap'pen·ing *n.* an important event

hap'py *adj.* fortunate; pleased — **hap'pi·ly** *adv.* —**hap'pi·ness** *n.*

ha·rangue' *n.* a bombastic lecture — *vi., vt.* to lecture in a harsh and severe manner

har'ass *vt.* to pester or worry

har'bin·ger *n.* a precursor —*vt.* to herald

har'bor *n.* a place of refuge —*vt.* to provide shelter; to entertain or cling to, as an idea or impression

hard *adj.* physically or mentally inflexible; intense; unyielding; difficult —*adv.* with difficulty; diligently; with force; to a solid state

hard-bitten *adj.* tough

hard'en *vi.* to toughen —*vt.* to make tough or tougher

hard'head'ed *adj.* practical; obstinate

hard'ly *adv.* barely; probably not

hard'-nosed' *adj.* stubborn; practical

hard'ship *n.* any difficulty

har'dy *adj.* strong; resolute

harm *n.* damage —*vt.* to cause damage to —**harm'ful** *adj.*

harm'less *adj.* not likely to cause damage or distress —**harm'less·ly** *adv.* —**harm'less·ness** *n.*

har'mo·ny *n.* agreement; a pleasing combination —**har'mo'ni·ous** *adj.* —**har·mo'ni·ous·ly** *adv.* —**har·mo'ni·ous·ness** *n.*

har'row·ing *adj.* distressing

har'ry *vt.* to raid or harass

harsh *adj.* disagreeably coarse or rough; stern —**harsh'ly** *adv.* —**harsh'ness** *n.*

har'vest *n.* a season's crop; the gathering of a crop; the time for gathering; the outcome of any action —*vi., vt.* to get as the result of effort

has'-been *n.* one no longer famous, productive, etc.

has'sle *n.* a quarrel; difficulty —*vi.* to quarrel —*vt.* to annoy

haste *n.* quickness; fast action, often implying carelessness

has'ten *vi.* to be quick; to accelerate

hast´y *adj.* overly quick; done or made in a hurry; impetuous — **hast´i·ly** *adv.*

hate *n.* intense dislike —*vi., vt.* to dislike intensely —**hate´ful** *adj.* —**ha´tred** *n.*

haugh´ty *adj.* proud, arrogant; contemptuous of others

haul *n.* the act of pulling or carrying; that carried; the distance traveled —*vi., vt.* to pull or carry

haunt *n.* a place often visited —*vt.* to visit often; to pervade

have *vt.* to possess; to gain; to control or be controlled by

ha´ven *n.* a shelter; a refuge

hav´oc *n.* chaos or destruction

haz´ard *n.* an uncertainty, a danger —*vt.* to endanger; to venture — **haz´ard·ous** *adj.* —**haz´ard·ous·ly** *adv.* —**haz´ard·ous·ness** *n.*

haze *n.* a light mist or smog; a vagueness of mind —**haz´i·ly** *adv.* —**haz´i·ness** *n.* —**haz´y** *adj.*

head *n.* the part of the body that contains sensory organs for sight, smell, taste, and hearing, and through which an animal feeds; intellect or aptitude; the foremost part; a leader —*vt.* to lead or direct

head´ing *n.* forming a head; direction of motion

head´long *adj.* uncontrollable; reckless —*adv.* recklessly

head´-on´ *adj.* direct —*adv.* directly

heal *vi., vt.* to become or make healthy

health *n.* soundness of body or mind —**health´y** *adj.*

heap *n.* an accumulation; a mound; a large amount —*vt.* to amass in one place; to give in large amounts: *heap compliments on*

hear *vi.* be able to sense sound; to be informed —*vt.* to sense sound; to be informed of; to heed; to consider formally

hear´say *n.* rumor

heart *n.* the body organ that pumps blood; the essence or core of anything

heart´en *vt.* to encourage

heart´felt *adj.* sincere

heart´less *adj.* insensitive

heart´rend·ing *adj.* distressing

heart´y *adj.* enthusiastic; robust; unreserved —**heart´i·ly** *adv.* —**heart´i·ness** *n.*

heat *n.* warmth; warming —*vi., vt.* to become or make hot; to become or cause to become aroused

heat´ed *adj.* intense

heav´y *adj.* weighty; over-weight; serious or intense; greater than normal —**heav´i·ly** *adv.* —**heav´i·ness** *n.*

heav´y-hand´ed *adj.* tactless

heav´y-heart´ed *adj.* sad

heck´le *vt.* to taunt —**heck´ler** *n.*

hec´tic *adj.* frenzied

hedge *n.* a boundary of bushes or trees —*vi.* to be evasive; to make compensating investments in order to lessen risk —*vt.* to set a border of bushes; to surround, as with restrictions; to lessen a risk

heed *n.* close attention —*vi., vt.* to pay attention

heft´y *adj.* large; weighty

height *n.* extreme: *the height of indecency*; an elevation; the distance from bottom to top

height´en *vi., vt.* to become or make higher or more intense

hein´ous *adj.* atrocious

help *n.* aid; a remedy; employees — *vi., vt.* to assist; to remedy or improve —**help´ful** *adj.* —**help´ful·ly** *adv.* —**help´ful·ness** *n.*

help´less *adj.* powerless to help oneself; incapable of aiding another —**help´less·ly** *adv.* —**help´less·ness** *n.*

hence *adv.* from this place or time; therefore

hence´forth´ *adv.* from now on

her´ald *n.* a harbinger —*vt.* to foretell or publicize

her·biv·ore *n.* an animal that feeds mainly on plants —**her·biv·o·rous** *adj.*

herd *n.* a large group —*vi., vt.* to gather or move a large group; to tend a group of animals

he·red·i·tar·y *adj.* inherited

he·red·i·ty *n.* inherited characteristics

her·e·sy *n.* rejection of an accepted or established concept or belief

her·e·tic *n.* one who rejects an established belief —**he·ret·i·cal** *adj.*

her·it·age *n.* that is or can be inherited; culture, tradition, etc. that is handed down

her·mit *n.* a recluse

he·ro *n.* one noted for courage, greatness, etc.; the central figure in a story —**he·ro·ic, he·ro·i·cal** *adj.* —**he·ro·i·cal·ly** *adv.*

hes·i·tant *adj.* uncertain, doubtful —**hes·i·tan·cy** *n.*

hes·i·tate *vi.* to pause or waver; to be uncertain —**hes·i·ta·tion** *n.*

hes·si·an *n.* (*Brit.*) a coarse cloth used in the making of sacks and as a backing for upholstry or carpeting

hew *vt.* to chop or hack

hex (*US*) *n.* a spell —*vt.* to cast a spell

hi·a·tus *n.* a break in continuity; an interruption

hic·cup, hic·cough *n.* an involuntary sound made by a sudden closing of the respiratory tract

hid·den *adj.* concealed; secret

hide *vi., vt.* to conceal

hide·bound *adj.* opinionated

hid·e·ous *adj.* repulsive; terrifying

high *adj.* elevated; prominent; greater than normal, as in size, intensity, importance, etc. —**high and mighty** haughty; snobbish

high·er-up *n.* one superior in rank or position

high·hand·ed *adj.* haughty

high·-spir·it·ed *adj.* lively

high·-strung *adj.* nervous

high·way (*US*) *n.* a main road

hi·jack *vt.* to take by force

hike *n.* a long walk; a rise, as in prices —*vi.* to walk —*vt.* to raise; to pull up

hi·lar·i·ous *adj.* very funny

hill *n.* a plot of ground higher than its surroundings; a pile or mound

hill·ock *n.* a small hill

hin·der *vi., vt.* to delay or obstruct

hin·drance *n.* an obstacle

hinge *n.* a flexible joint —*vi. vt.* to be or to make contingent on something else

hint *n.* a slight indication —*vi., vt.* to intimate

hire *vt.* to employ for payment

hir·sute *adj.* hairy

his·tor·ic, his·tor·i·cal *adj.* relating to the past; notable —**his·tor·i·cal·ly** *adv.* —**his·tor·i·cal·ness** *n.*

his·to·ry *n.* an account of the past —**his·to·ri·an** *n.*

hit *n.* a blow; a success —*vi., vt.* to strike; to discover

hoard *n.* a hidden supply —*vt.* to obtain and store in reserve

hoarse *adj.* harsh sounding

hoar·y *adj.* grayish–white; old

hoax *n.* a deception

hob·by *n.* a favored pastime

hob·nob *vi.* to socialize

ho·bo (*US*) *n.* a vagrant

hod *n.* a V–shaped trough for hauling bricks or mortar; a coal scuttle

hog·wash *n.* nonsense

hoist *n.* the act of lifting; a device for raising heavy loads —*vt.* to lift or pull up

ho·kum *n.* nonsense

hold *n.* the act of grasping; an influence or controlling force —*vi.* to maintain a grasp; to remain in a particular state —*vt.* to grasp; to sustain; to contain

hole *n.* an opening; a hollow; a crude or squalid shelter

hol·i·day *adj.* festive: *a holiday*

mood —*n.* a day of rest, commemoration, etc.

hol´ler *n.* a yell —*vi., vt.* to call out

hol´low *adj.* empty inside, not solid; sunken or indented —*n.* a recess —*vi., vt.* to become or make hollow

hol´o·caust´ *n.* great destruction

hom´age *n.* a profession of fealty or loyalty; worship

home *n.* the place where one lives; one's native state, country, or land —*adj.* of or relating to a place of residence or origin —*adv.* at or in the direction of home; toward the point directed

home´ly *adj.* plain; simple; unpretentious

home´stead´ *n.* buildings and land that constitute a home

home´y *adj.* simple; comfortable

hom´i·cide *n.* the killing of one person by another; one who kills another —**hom´i·ci´dal** *adj.*

hom·i·let´ics *n.* the art of sermonizing

hom´i·ly *n.* a sermon or lecture, often to teach a practical lesson

hom´i·ny *n.* hulled and dried corn

ho·mo·ge´ne·ous *adj.* of a similar kind or type; uniform throughout

ho·mog´e·nize *vt.* to make homogeneous; to disperse particles evenly throughout a liquid

homogenized milk milk that has been processed to break up fat globules and distribute them evenly throughout

ho·mol´o·gous *adj.* corresponding or similar in many aspects

hom´o·nym *n.* a word that sounds like another, but that differs in meaning and often in spelling

Ho´mo sa´pi·ens *n.* the human race

ho´mo·sex´u·al *n.* one attracted to persons of the same sex

hone *vt.* to sharpen —*n.* a stone for sharpening

hon´est *adj.* free from deceit; marked by integrity; respectable;

trustworthy; fair —**hon´es·ty** *n.* —**hon´est·ly** *adv.*

hon´ey *n.* a thick, sweet liquid produced from nectar for food by bees and certain other insects; something good —*vt.* to sweeten with honey

hon´ey·comb *n.* a network of wax cells made by bees; any similar structure —*vt.* to permeate with small holes

hon´ey·moon *n.* a wedding trip; any brief period of accord

honk *n.* the call of a wild goose; any similar sound —*vi., vt.*

hon´or *n.* great respect; a mark of special recognition; reputation; an exalted rank —*vt.* to esteem or respect; to afford special recognition; to recognize or pay as a due debt —**hon´or·a·ble** *adj.* —**hon´or·a·bly** *adv.* —**hon´or·a·ble·ness** *n.*

hon·o·rar´i·um *n.* a fee paid to a speaker or lecturer

hon´or·ar·y *adj.* conferred without duties or pay

hon·or·if´ic *adj.* that which confers or shows respect —*n.* an honorary title

hon´our (*Brit.*) *n.* great respect; a mark of special recognition; reputation; an exalted rank —*vt.* to esteem or respect; to afford special recognition; to recognize or pay as a due debt

hood *n.* a covering, as for the head, an engine, or a stove; a hoodlum —*vt.* to cover with a hood

hood´lum *n.* a young rowdy; a gangster

hood´wink *vt.* to deceive

hoof *n.* a horny substance that covers the feet of certain mammals —*vi., vt.* to walk or dance

hoof´er *n.* one who dances for a living

hook *n.* a bent device used to snag or hang; a fishhook; a means of attracting or snaring —*vt.* to catch, connect, or suspend by means of a hook; to steal

hoo´li·gan *n.* a hoodlum

hoop *n.* a band of metal or wood as used to secure the staves of a cask or to hold embroidery; anything similar in the form of a hoop, as earrings or a plaything —*vt.* to secure with a band

hoot´e·nan´y *n.* an informal gathering of folk musicians

hop *vi.* to jump on one foot; to move quickly —*n.* a short distance; a quick trip

hope *vi.* to desire or anticipate with expectation of fulfillment —*n.* confident expectation —**hope´ful** *adj.* —**hope´ful·ly** *adv.* —**hope´ful·ness** *n.*

hop´per *n.* a container, especially one emptied through a gate at the bottom; a person or insect that hops

horde *n.* a great crowd; a throng

ho·ri´zon *n.* a line where earth and sky appear to converge; the extent of one's perception or interest

hor´i·zon´tal *adj.* level with or parallel to the horizon

hor´mone *n.* any of a number of substances produced in the body to regulate physiological activity

horn *n.* a hard projection that grows from the head of certain animals; material which coats the surface of an animal horn; something having the shape of a horn; a wind instrument made from a horn; a brass wind instrument

hor´net *n.* a type of wasp

ho·rol´o·gy *n.* the study of time; the art of creating timepieces

hor´o·scope *n.* an aspect of the heavens by which astrologers attempt to foretell the future

hor·ren´dous *adj.* dreadful

hor´ri·ble *adj.* inspiring horror; dreadful

hor´rid *adj.* hideous; shocking

hor·ri·fy´ *vt.* to overwhelm with terror —**hor·ri·fi·ca´tion** *n.*

hor´ror *n.* great revulsion or fear

hors d´oeu·vre *pl. n.* appetizers, usually served before a meal

horse *n.* a hoofed mammal domesticated for riding or hauling; a carpenter's frame for holding wood; cavalry: *horse soldiers* —*adj.* of or relating to a horse —*vt.* to provide with a horse

horse´play *n.* rough boisterous play

horse´pow·er *n.* a unit used to express the power of an engine

hor´ta·to·ry *adj.* expressing encouragement

hor´ti·cul´ture *n.* the science of cultivating plants —**hor´ti·cul´tur·ist** *n.*

hose *n.* socks or stockings: hosiery; a flexible pipe for conveying fluids —*vt.* to wet down or wash with a hose; to deceive

ho´sier·y *n.* socks and stockings

hos´pice *n.* a lodging or shelter

hos´pi·ta·ble *adj.* cordial, helpful, or generous; suitable or favorable for habitation —**hos´pi·ta·ble·ness** *n.* —**hos´pi·ta·bly** *adv.* —**hos´pi·tal´i·ty** *n.*

hos´pi·tal *n.* a building or location for the care of the sick and injured —**hos·pit·tal·i·za´tion** *n.* —**hos´pit·tal·ize** *vt.*

host *n.* one who receives guests, either socially or as an employee of a business; a master of ceremonies; a throng or multitude; an organism on which another lives

hos´tage *n.* one held as security for the fulfillment of a pledge or against the threat of harm

hos´tel *n.* lodging, esp. for hikers

host´ess *n.* a female host; a greeter at a restaurant or club

hos´tile *adj.* feeling or displaying ill will; threatening; antagonistic; detrimental to health or well–being —*n.* an enemy —**hos´til´i·ty** *n.*

hot *adj.* of a relatively high temperature; burning to the taste or touch; marked by passion; angry —*adv.* in a hot manner —**hot˝ly** *adv.*

hot˝-blood´ed *adj.* passionate

hot˝dog´ *n.* a frankfurter; a frankfurter served on a long roll; a daredevil or showoff

ho·tel´ *n.* an establishment that offers lodging and often meals to paying guests

hot˝house *n.* a greenhouse with heat and humidity controlled for the cultivation of plants

hot˝line *n.* a direct channel of communication for handling crises or problems

hot´-rod´ *n.* a car that has been modified to increase acceleration or running speed

hound *n.* a dog commonly used in hunting; one diligent in the pursuit of an interest —*vt.* to badger or annoy

hour *n.* a period of time equal to sixty minutes; the customary or set period for an activity; a significant time: *the hour of reckoning* —**hour˝ly** *adv.*

house *n.* a building that serves as a dwelling or shelter; a family or lineage; a business establishment; a branch of the legislature —*vt.* to provide living space; to shelter or store

house˝hold *n.* all of the persons who share a dwelling —*adj.* pertaining to or used in a dwelling; commonplace

hov´el *n.* a wretched dwelling

hov´er *vi.* to remain over, in, or near

how *adv.* in what manner; by what means; to what extent

how·ev´er *adv.* by whatever means

howl *n.* the plaintive wail of a beast; something very funny —*vi., vt.* to utter a plaintive wail

hoy˝den *n.* a boisterous woman

hub *n.* the center of a wheel or similar rotating object; a center of interest or activity

hub˝bub´ *n.* uproar, bustle

hub˝cap´ *n.* the covering for a hub

huck˝ster *n.* a peddler or pitchman; one who sells or promotes with overblown claims

hud´dle *vi., vt.* to crowd together; to crouch —*n.* a dense crowd; a quick, informal meeting

hue *n.* a gradation of color; a color or tint

huff *vt.* to offend —*vi.* to be indignant or offended —*n.* a feeling of anger or annoyance

huff´y *adj.* easily offended

hug *vt.* to embrace or hold close; to keep close to: *the boat hugged the shore;* to hold fast —*n.* an embrace

huge *adj.* exceedingly large; of great extent

hulk *n.* an old unwieldy or unseaworthy ship; an abondoned hull; anything bulky or unwieldy

hull *n.* a husk: the outer covering of a seed or fruit; the body of a ship —*vt.* to remove the husk from, as of peas

hum *vi., vt.* to make a low, droning sound, as that made by a bee; to sing without voicing words —*n.* a low, droning sound

hu´man *adj.* of, relating to, or having the form or characterstics of a human being; of human attributes as distinguished from those of the animals —*n.* a human being — **hu´man·ly** *adv.* —**hu´man·ness** *n.*

hu·mane´ *adj.* characterized by compassion; pertaining to human values

hu·man´i·tar´i·an *n.* one concerned with the welfare of others

hu´man´i·ty *n.* the human race; the quality of being human or humane

hu´man·ize *vt., vi.* to make or or become human or humane

hum˝ble *adj.* meek; submissive;

unpretentious —*vt.* to humiliate; to abase

hum´bug *n.* foolish talk; something intended to deceive

hu´mid *adj.* moist or damp

hu´mid·i·fi·er *n.* a device for adding moisture to the air

hu´mid´i·ty *n.* dampness; a measure of the amount of moisture in the surrounding air

hu´mi·dor *n.* a tobacco container that retains moisture

hu·mil´i·ate´ *vt.* to embarrass or shame —**hu·mil·i·a´tion** *n.*

hu·mil´i·ty *n.* the quality of being humble; modesty

hum´ming·bird´ *n.* a very small bird with brilliant plumage, notable for very rapid wing movement that allows the bird to hover and dart

hu´mor (*US*) *n.* an amusing quality; that intended to incite laughter; one's disposition —*vt.* to indulge the whims of another

hu´mor·ist *n.* an entertainer or writer who specializes in relating amusing stories

hu´mor·ous *adj.* expressing humor; amusing —**hu´mor·ous·ly** *adv.* — **hu´mor·ous·ness** *n.*

hu´mour (*Brit.*) *n.* an amusing quality; that intended to incite laughter; one's disposition —*vt.* to indulge the whims of another

hu´mus *n.* organic matter in soil

hun´ger *n.* a desire or craving —*vi.* to have a strong desire, especially for food —**hun´gry** *adj.* —**hun´gri·ly** *adv.* —**hun´gri·ness** *n.*

hunk *n.* a large piece of something

hunt *vi.*, *vt.* to seek or search —*n.* the act of seeking wild game; a hunting expedition; a diligent search

hur´dle *n.* a barrier over which competitors leap; any obstacle to a goal —*vt.*, *vi.* to surmount an obstacle or obstacles

hurl *vt.* to throw violently; to utter

vehemently; to vomit

hur´ri·cane *n.* a violent storm accompanied by high winds

hur´ry *vi.*, *vt.* to move or cause to move with haste —*n.* haste

hurt *vt.* to injure physically or mentally; to impair or lessen: *hurt one's chances* —*n.* something painful or that causes suffering — **hurt´ful** *adj.* —**hurt´ful·ly** *adv.* — **hurt´ful·ness** *n.*

hur´tle *vt.*, *vi.* to throw or move violently

hus´band *n.* a married man —*vt.* to conserve or use economically: *to husband one's resources*

hus´band·ry *n.* the study of agriculture or livestock breeding; careful management

husk *n.* the outer covering of some seeds, fruits, or vegetables —*vt.* to remove the covering from

husk´y *adj.* of a voice with a hoarse or rough quality; sturdily built

hus´sy *n.* a saucy female

hus´tle *vi.*, *vt.* to move or cause to move energetically or roughly; to shove or jostle; to convince by questionable means

hut *n.* a crude dwelling

hy´brid *n.* a thing produced by combining dissimilar species or elements —*adj.* pertaining to a hybrid —**hy´brid·ize** *vt.*, *vi.* —**hy·brid·i·za´tion** *n.*

hy´dra *n.* a freshwater polyp; persistent evil

hy´drant *n.* an outlet from a water main, used to draw water for fighting fires, cleaning streets, etc.

hy´drate *n.* a compound of water and other molecules or atoms —*vt.*

hy·drau´lic *adj.* operated by fluid under pressure

hy·drau´lics *n.* the science of the dynamics of fluid in motion

hy´dro·e·lec´tric *adj.* of electricity generated by water power

hy´dro·foil *n.* a structure that holds

the hull of a boat out of the water when it is in motion; a boat equipped with hydrofoils, also called a *hydroplane*

hy·dro·gen *n.* a flammable gas, lightest of all the elements

hydrogen bomb a powerful explosive device activated by the fusion of hydrogen isotopes

hy·drom´e·ter *n.* a device to measure the specific gravity of a liquid

hy´dro·pho´bi·a *n.* rabies

hy´dro·plane *n.* a seaplane; a small boat that skims the surface of water; a hydrofoil —*vt.* to skim the surface of water

hy·dro·pon´ics *n.* the cultivation of plants without soil

hy·e´na *n.* a scavenging carnivorous mammal of Africa and Asia

hy´giene *n.* the science of the preservation of health; any practice that serves to promote good health —**hy·gi·en´ic** *adj.* —**hy·gi·en´i·cal·ly** *adv.*

hymn *n.* a song of praise

hym´nal *n.* a book or collection of hymns

hy·per´bo·la *n.* a type of geometric curve

hy·per´bo·le *n.* a figure of speech in which exaggeration is used for emphasis: *I could eat a horse*

hy·per·bol´ic *adj.* representing or shaped like a hyperbola; exaggerated: containing hyperbole

hy·per·crit´i·cal *adj.* excessively exacting

hy·per·sen´si·tive *adj.* excessively tense or delicate

hy´per·son´ic *adj.* moving, or capable of moving, at several times the speed of sound

hy´per·ten´sion *n.* high blood pressure

hy·per·thy´roid·ism *n.* a disorder caused by an overly active thyroid gland

hy´phen *n.* a punctuation mark (-)

used to separate syllables, parts of a compound word, or phrases —**hy´phen·ate** *vt.*

hyp·no´sis *n.* a sleep–like state that may open one's mind to suppressed memories

hyp·not´ic *adj.* of hypnosis; spellbinding

hyp´no·tism *n.* the act of inducing hypnosis —**hyp´no·tize´** *vt.*

hy·po·chon´dri·a *n.* excessive anxiety about one's health —**hy·po·chon´dri·ac** *n.*

hy·poc´ri·sy *n.* pretending to a belief that one does not hold —**hyp´o·crite** *n.* —**hyp·o·crit´i·cal** *adj.* —**hyp·o·crit´i·cal·ly** *adv.*

hy´po·der´mic *adj.* of the layer of tissue beneath the skin; of injection beneath the skin —*n.* a hypodermic injection, needle, or syringe

hy´po·ten´sion *n.* low blood pressure

hy·pot´e·nuse´ *n.* the side that is opposite the right angle of a right triangle

hy·poth´e·sis *n.*, *pl.* **hy·poth´e·ses** a theory based on fact, put forth for further testing —**hy´po·thet´ic**, **hy·po·thet´i·cal** *adj.* —**hy·po·thet´i·cal·ly** *adv.*

hys·ter·ec´to·my *n.* surgical excision of part or all of the uterus

hys·te´ri·a *n.* excessive, uncontrollable emotion; a neurosis marked by physical ailment without apparent cause

hys·ter´ic, hys·ter´ic·al *adj.* characterized by hysteria

hys·ter´ics *n.* an attack of hysteria

i, I ninth letter of the English alphabet; in Roman characters, the symbol for one

ice *n.* frozen water; a dessert comprised of crushed or shaved ice and a sweet flavoring —*vt.* to cool, as with ice; to cover and decorate a cake with a sugar mixture

ice′berg′ *n.* a huge mound of floating ice

ice′box *n.* a refrigerator; an insulated cabinet used to cool food

ice′cap *n.* a mass of ice covering a large tract of land

ice sheet *n.* a large continental glacier

ich·thy·ol′o·gy *n.* the study of fishes

i′ci·cle *n.* a hanging taper of ice formed by dripping water

i′ci·ly *adv.* in a cold or haughty manner

ic′ing *n.* a sugar mixture used to coat and decorate a cake

i′con *n.* an image; a sacred picture; one who is revered; a small image on a computer screen that represents a command, data type, etc.

i′con·o·clast *n.* a destroyer of sacred images; one who attacks traditional institutions

i′cy *adj.* covered with ice; cold or slippery; cold and unfriendly — **ic′i·ness** *n.*

id *n.* that part of the subconscious concerned with instinctive or primitive impulses

i·de′a *n.* a mental image; a scheme; a concept or opinion

i·de′al *adj.* perfect or excellent; typical; existing in theory or in the mind — *n.* a thing considered a model for perfection — **i·de′al·ly** *adv.*

i·de′al·ism *n.* the practice of seeking the best in everything; the belief that all is for good

i·de′al·ist *n.* a visionary; one inspired by that which is ideal — **i·de·al·is′tic, i·de·al·is′ti·cal** *adj.* — **i·de·al·is′ti·cal·ly** *adv.*

i·de′al·ize′ *vt.* to envision as ideal

i·den′ti·cal *adj.* alike in every way

i·den·ti·fi·ca′tion *n.* the act of recognition or classification; credentials that establish one's identity

i·den′ti·fy *vt.* to establish the identity of — *vi.* to establish a unity

with certain others — **i·den′ti·fi·a·ble** *adj.*

i·den′ti·ty *n.* characteristics by which a person or thing is recognized or defined

id′e·ol′o·gy *n.* a set of beliefs or doctrines — **i·de·ol′o·gist** *n.*

id′i·o·cy *n.* folly; mental retardation

id′i·om *n.* an expression or usage peculiar to a particular language or region — **id′i·o·mat′ic, id′i·o·mat′i·cal** *adj.* — **id′i·o·mat′i·cal·ly** *adv.*

id·i·o·syn′cra·sy *n.* a characteristic peculiar to a person or group

id′i·ot *n.* one who is foolish or stupid; formerly, a classification for mental retardation, now considered offensive in that context

id·i·ot′ic *adj.* foolish or stupid

i′dle *adj.* not busy or in use; tending to avoid work — *vt.* to waste time — **i′dly** *adv.*

i′dol *n.* an image; an object of worship; one who is revered or adored

i·dol′a·try *n.* the worship of idols; excessive devotion — **i·dol′a·ter** *n.* — **i·dol′a·trous** *adj.*

i′dol·ize′ *vt.* to make the object of excessive devotion

i′dyl, i′dyll *n.* a short narrative or poem describing a pastoral or romantic scene

if *conj.* on condition that; whether or not — *n.* a supposition or condition

ig′ne·ous *adj.* pertaining to fire; formed by fire

ig′nite′ *vt.* to set afire; to arouse passion — *vi.* to burn

ig·ni′tion *n.* the act of setting or being set on fire; a system for igniting the fuel in an internal-combustion engine

ig·no′ble *adj.* base; vulgar; of low birth

ig′no·min·y *n.* disgrace; shame — **ig·no·min′i·ous** *adj.* — **ig·no·min′i·ous·ly** *adv.* — **ig·no·min′i·ous·ness** *n.*

ig·no·ra´mus *n.* an ignorant person

ig´no·rance *n.* a lack of experience or knowledge; the state of being uninformed

ig´no·rant *adj.* lacking knowledge; uninformed

ig·nore´ *vt.* to disregard

ilk *n.* type or kind

ill *adj.* sick; harmful; of a hostile nature —*n.* harmful; the cause of suffering or misfortune

ill–ad·vised´ *adj.* unwise; evidencing a lack of careful thought

ill´–bred´ *adj.* crude or impolite

il·le´gal *adj.* prohibited by law —*n.* one who enters the country illegally —**il´le·gal´i·ty** *n.*

il·leg´i·ble *adj.* difficult or impossible to decipher; unreadable —**il·leg·i·bil´i·ty** *n.*

il·le·git´i·mate *adj.* contrary to law; illegal; born out of wedlock —**il·le·git´i·ma·cy** *n.* —**il·le·git´i·mate·ly** *adv.*

ill´–fat´ed *adj.* likely to end badly

ill´–got´ten *adj.* obtained dishonestly

il·lib´er·al *adj.* selfish; bigoted; vulgar, ill–bred

il·lic´it *adj.* unlawful; prohibited

il·lit´er·a·cy *n.* the state of being unable to read or write

il·lit´er·ate *adj.* lacking formal education; lacking comprehension of a particular branch of art or knowledge —*n.* one who is unable to read and write

ill´ness *n.* a sickness or disease

il·log´i·cal *adj.* contrary to reason; unreasonable or unreasoning

ill´–tem´pered *adj.* querulous; irritable —**ill´–tem´pered·ly** *adv.* —**ill´–tem´pered·ness** *n.*

il·lum´i·nate, il·lu´mine *vi., vt.* to light or make brighter; to clarify, as by example or illustration; to decorate a printed page

il·lu·mi·na´tion *n.* lighting; clarification or instruction

il·lu´sion *n.* an erroneous or deceptive impression

il·lu´so·ry *adj.* based on illusion; deceptive; not real

il´lus·trate *vt.* to clarify or explain, as by example; to decorate with pictures

il·lus·tra´tion *n.* an example or explanation; a picture

il·lus´tra·tive *adj.* serving to illustrate or explain; symbolic

il·lus´tri·ous *adj.* distinguished; eminent

ill will *n.* malevolence; hostility

im´age *n.* a likeness; something that closely resembles another; a concept or mental picture; the way in which one is perceived

im´a·ger·y *n.* a mental image; the use of imaginative language to describe

im·ag´i·na·ble *adj.* that can be imagined; conceivable; plausible

im·ag´i·na·ry *adj.* fanciful; theoretical; nonexistent

im·ag·i·na´tion *n.* the ability to hypothesize; creativity; the formation of mental images

im·ag´i·na·tive *adj.* inventive; creative —**im·ag´i·na·tive·ly** *adv.* —**im·ag´i·na·tive·ness** *n.*

im·ag´ine *vi., vt.* to picture or create in the mind

im·bal´ance *n.* a state of unevenness

im´be·cile, im·be·cil´ic *adj.* silly; foolish

im´be·cile *n.* a foolish person; one lacking intellect; formerly, a classification for mental retardation, now considered offensive —**im´be·cil´i·ty** *n.*

im·bibe´ *vt.* to drink —*vi.* to consume an alcoholic beverage

im·bro´glio *n.* an entanglement; confusion

im·bue´ *vt.* to permeate

im´i·tate *vt.* to copy or impersonate, as in appearance or style, generally in a flattering way; to mimic, often with exaggeration and in an unflattering manner

im·i·ta´tion *n.* the act of imitating; a copy or likeness; a substitute of lesser quality

im´i·ta·tive *adj.* involving imitation; not original or genuine; deceptive

im·mac´u·late *adj.* absolutely pure or clean; without blemish

im·ma´nent *adj.* existing within; deep-seated —**im´ma·nence** *n.*

im·ma·te´ri·al *adj.* lacking importance; not significant; lacking substance

im·ma·ture´ *adj.* not yet ripe; not fully grown; childish: wanting in adult qualities

im·meas´ur·a·ble *adj.* boundless; incapable of being measured

im·me´diate *adj.* at this instant; near the present time; near at hand —**im·me´di·a·cy** *n.*

im·me·mo´ri·al *adj.* before memory or recorded history

im·mense´ *adj.* extremely large; seeming boundless

im·merse´ *vt.* to submerge in liquid; to become deeply involved; to baptize by submersing the body completely in water —**im·mer´sion** *n.*

im´mi·grant *n.* one newly-arrived in a country with intent to settle

im´mi·grate *vi.* to newly enter a country with intent to settle

im·mi·gra´tion *n.* settlement in a land to which one is not native

im´mi·nent *adj.* impending; about to occur

im·mo·bil´i·ty *n.* the state of being motionless or unable to move —**im·mo´bile** *adj.*

im·mod´er·ate *adj.* excessive

im·mod´est *adj.* bold; egotistical; lacking modesty

im´mo·late *vt.* to sacrifice —**im·mo·la´tion** *n.*

im·mor´al *adj.* characterized by a lack of virtue; contrary to accepted standards of morality

im·mo·ral´i·ty *n.* a lack of virtue; an immoral act

im·mor´tal *adj.* of that which cannot die; everlasting; enduring —*n.* a god; a person worth remembering

im·mor·tal´i·ty *n.* the condition of living or being remembered forever

im·mov´a·ble *adj.* fixed in place; unable to be moved

im·mune´ *adj.* not subject to or affected by; exempt

im·mu´ni·ty *n.* exemption or freedom from certain restrictions; protection from disease

im´mu·nize *vt.* to protect, as from disease, prosecution, etc.

im·mu·nol´o·gy *n.* the science dealing with the immune system and means of preventing disease

im·mure´ *vt.* to confine within a wall; to protect or imprison

im·mu´ta·ble *adj.* not subject to change

imp *n.* a small demon; a michievous child

im´pact *n.* a collision; the force of a collision; an effect: *the negative impact of television on book sales* —**im·pact´** *vt.* to strike with force; to pack firmly; to have effect on — **im·pact´ed** *adj.*

im·pair´ *vt.* to cause to diminish, as in quantity or value—*poor materials impair our ability to create a quality product*

im·pale´ *vt.* to thrust a pale or sharp stake through the body; to render helpless

im·pal´pa·ble *adj.* not perceived by touch; not easily grasped by the mind

im·pan´el *vt.* to prepare a list, as for jury duty

im·part´ *vt.* to give or confer; to convey, as knowledge

im·par´tial *adj.* not biased; without prejudice —**im·par´tial·ly** *adv.* — **im·par´tial·ness** *n.*

im·par·ti·al´i·ty *n.* objectivity; not

partial or biased

im·pass´a·ble adj. unable to be travelled over or through —**im·pass·a·bil´i·ty**, **im·pass´i·ble·ness** n. —**im·pass·a·bly** adv.

im´passe n. a situation that leaves no room for compromise; a stalemate

im·pas´si·ble adj. apathetic; not easily aroused emotionally —**im·pas·si·bil´i·ty**, **im·pas´si·ble·ness** n. —**im·pas´si·bly** adv.

im·pas´sioned adj. ardent; designed to arouse passion

im·pas´sive adj. insensible to pain; showing no emotion —**im·pas´sive·ly** adv. —**im·pas´sive·ness** n.

im·pa´tience n. restlessness; intolerance

im·pa´tient adj. unable to wait; restless; anxious; intolerant —**im·pa´tient·ly** adv. —**im·pa´tient·ness** n.

im·peach´ vt. to accuse or charge with misconduct in office; to attempt to discredit

im·pec´ca·ble adj. nattily attired; without flaw or imperfection —**im·pec´ca·bly** adv.

im·pe·cu´ni·ous adj. lacking means; penniless —**im·pe·cu´ni·ous·ly** adv. —**im·pe·cu´ni·ous·ness** n.

im·pede´ vt. to slow the progress of; to obstruct

im·ped´i·ment n. an obstruction; a condition that prevents clear articulation, as a *speech impediment*; in law, an obstacle that bars the making of a legal contract

im·pel´ vt. to drive or urge forward; to spur to action

im·pend´ vi. to be about to happen; to approach and threaten, as an *impending storm*

im·pen´e·tra·ble adj. unable to be penetrated; incomprehensible —**im·pen´e·tra·ble·ness** n. —**im·pen´e·tra·bly** adv.

im·pen´i·tent adj. without regret or

remorse —**im·pen´i·tence** n. —**im·pen´i·tent·ly** adv.

im·per´a·tive adj. pressing; obligatory —n. an order or obligation —**im·per´a·tive·ly** adv. —**im·per´a·tive·ness** n.

im·per·cep´ti·ble adj. that cannot be perceived —**im·per·cep´ti·ble·ness** n. —**im·per·cep´ti·bly** adv.

im·per´fect adj. deficient; flawed —**im·per´fect·ly** adv. —**im·per´fect·ness** n.

im·per·fec´tion n. a flaw

im·pe´ri·al adj. of a ruler or empire; majestic; of great size —**im·pe´ri·al·ly** adv.

im·pe´ri·al·ism n. the policy of extending an empire by acquiring new territory or establishing dominance over other nations

im·per´il vt. to endanger

im·pe´ri·ous adj. arrogant; overbearing —**im·pe´ri·ous·ly** adv. —**im·pe´ri·ous·ness** n.

im·per´ma·nent adj. not lasting; transient —**im·per´ma·nence** n. —**im·per´ma·nent·ly** adv.

im·per´me·a·ble adj. not subject to penetration, as by moisture —**im·per·me·a·bil´i·ty** n. —**im·per´me·a·bly** adv.

im·per´son·al adj. not referring or relating to a particular person or thing: *an impersonal view*; cold or indifferent —**im·per´son·al·ly** adj.

im·per´son·ate´ vt. to fraudulently pretend to be another; to mimic another for the purpose of entertaining —**im·per·son·a´tion** n.

im·per´ti·nent adj. disrespectful or insolent —**im·per´ti·nence** n. —**im·per´ti·nent·ly** adv.

im·per·turb´a·ble adj. calm; not disposed to becoming disturbed or agitated

im·per´vi·ous adj. impenetrable; not influenced, as by emotion, fear, flattery, etc. —**im·per´vi·ous·ly** adv. —**im·per´vi·ous·ness** n.

im·pet´u·ous *adj.* marked by sudden impulse or passion; spontaneous —**im·pet´u·ous·ly** *adv.* —**im·pet´u·ous·ness** *n.*

im·pe·tus *n.* a stimulus; action associated with or caused by a stimulus; momentum

im·pinge´ *vi.*, *vt.* to touch or encroach upon

im´pi·ous *adj.* lacking piety; blasphemous —**im´pi·ous·ly** *adv.* —**im´pi·ous·ness** *n.*

im·pla´ca·ble *adj.* unable to be placated; unbending —**im·pla´ca·bly** *adv.* —**im·pla´ca·ble·ness** *n.*

im·plant´ *vt.* to establish or instill; to plant surgically —*n.* a thing inserted by surgery

im·plau´si·ble *adj.* not believable — **im·plau´si·bly** *adv.*

im´ple·ment *n.* a tool or device —*vt.* to use or put into force

im´pli·cate´ *vt.* to incriminate; to imply; to entangle or involve

im´pli·ca´tion *n.* something implied; a link or involvement

im·plic´it *adj.* understood or implied; absolute —**im·plic´it·ly** *adv.* —**im·plic´it·ness** *n.*

im·plode´ *vt.*, *vi.* to burst inward

im·plore´ *vt.* to beg or plead

im·ply´ *vt.* to infer by logic; to signify indirectly

im·po·lite´ *adj.* rude; discourteous —**im·po·lite´ly** *adv.* —**im·po·lite´ness** *n.*

im·pol´i·tic *adj.* imprudent or unwise

im·pon´der·a·ble *adj.* impossible to evaluate —**im·pon·der·a·bil´i·ty** *n.* —**im·pon´der·a·bly** *adv.*

im·port´ *vt.* to bring in from another country; to transfer computer data between applications or platforms —*vi.* to be of significance —**im´port** *n.* a thing brought in; meaning or significance —**im´por·ta´tion** *n.*

im·port´ed *adj.* foreign; brought

from elsewhere

im·por´tance *n.* significance; personal distinction or standing

im·por´tant *adj.* significant — **im·por´tant·ly** *adv.*

im·por´tu·nate *adj.* persistently pleading; urgently requesting — **im·por´tu·nate·ly** *adv.* —**im·por´tu·nate·ness** *n.*

im´por·tune´ *vi.*, *vt.* to plead persistently

im·pose´ *vt.* to apply with authority or as if by authority; to force on others; to lay out a publication for printing —*vi.* to take advantage of

im·pos´ing *adj.* impressive by virtue of size or power

im´po·si´tion *n.* something burdensome or that has been forced upon; advantage taken; a graphic representation of the layout of a publication

im·pos´si·bil´i·ty *n.* that which is unattainable or likely to end in failure

im·pos´si·ble *adj.* unattainable or impractical to accomplish; not believable of existing; difficult to cope with: unacceptable, as *impossible manners* —**im·pos·si·bil´i·ty** *n.* — **im·pos´si·bly** *adv.*

im·pos´tor *n.* one who assumes a false identity

im·pos´ture *n.* deception using an assumed identity

im´po·tence *n.* a condition marked by weakness; the inability to have sexual intercourse

im´po·tent *adj.* lacking strength or power; ineffective; unable to have sexual intercourse —**im´po·tence**, **im´po·ten·cy** *n.* —**im´po·tent·ly** *adv.*

im·pound´ *vt.* to legally seize and hold

im·pov´er·ish *vt.* to deprive of, as wealth or resources

im·pov´er·ished *n.* devoid of wealth or resources; poverty–stricken

im·prac´ti·cal *adj.* not effective, prudent, or economical; unable to function in an orderly or efficient manner —**im·prac·ti·cal´i·ty** *n.*

im´pre·cate´ *vt.* to call evil down upon; to curse —**im´pre·ca´tion** *n.*

im·preg´na·ble *adj.* impossible to take by assault; impossible or nearly impossible to contest or challenge, as an assertion —**im·preg·na·bil´i·ty** *n.* —**im·preg´na·bly** *adv.*

im·preg´nate´ *vt.* to saturate; to make pregnant

im·pre·sa´ri·o *n.* an organizer or manager of musical entertainment

im·press´ *vt.* to find favor; to attract notice; to plant in the mind; to mark, as if by pressure; to force into service

im·pres´sion *n.* a firm image in the mind; a vague notion; a mark or image on a surface made by or as if by pressure; a printed image; all of the copies of a publication printed at one time

im·pres´sion·a·ble *adj.* receptive to outside influence

im·pres´sion·ism *n.* a school of art and literature that focuses on quick concept or perception of the subject

im·pres´sive *adj.* stirring; tending to impress

im·pri·ma´tur *n.* approval; sanction

im´print *n.* a distinguishing mark or emblem —**im·print´** *vt.* to produce a mark or sensory impression on

im·pris´on *vt.* to confine

im·prob´a·ble *adj.* unlikely or doubtful —**im·prob·a·bil´i·ty** *n.* —**im·prob´a·bly** *adv.*

im·promp´tu *adj.* spontaneous; unrehearsed —*adv.* extemporaneously

im·prop´er *adj.* unsuitable or inappropriate to a particular need or use; not in compliance with standards of common decency or

accepted mores —**im·prop´er·ly** *adv.* —**im´pro·pri´e·ty** *n.*

im·prove´ *vt., vi.* to make or become more useful or valuable

im·prove´ment *n.* something that has been enhanced or added to; an enhanced condition

im·prov´i·dent *adj.* not exercising due caution; rash —**im·prov´i·dence** *n.* —**im·prov´i·dent·ly** *adv.*

im´pro·vise´ *vt.* to perform without advance preparation; to create from materials at hand —**im·prov·i·sa´tion** *n.* —**im·prov·i·sa´tion·al** *adj.*

im·pru´dent *adj.* unwise —**im·pru´dence** *n.* —**im·pru´dent·ly** *adv.*

im´pu·dent *adj.* marked by audacity; impertinent; bold —**im´pu·dence** *n.* —**im´pu·dent·ly** *adv.*

im·pugn´ *vt.* to challenge as false

im´pulse´ *n.* a surge; a sudden urge that leads to action; a stimulus

im·pul´sive *adj.* tending to act on a whim; characterized by impulsive action —**im·pul´sive·ly** *adv.* —**im·pul´sive·ness** *n.*

im·pun´i·ty *n.* immunity or deliverance from punishment or loss

im·pure´ *adj.* contaminated; adulterated; lewd or obscene —**im·pure´ly** *adv.* —**im·pure´ness** *n.*

im·pu·ta´tion *n.* an insinuation

im·pute´ *vt.* to assign, as a quality or blame

in·a·bil´i·ty *n.* a lack of power or capability

in·ac·ces´si·ble *adj.* not approachable; remote; unattainable —**in·ac·ces´si·bly** *adv.* —**in·ac·ces´si·ble·ness** *n.*

in·ac´cu·ra·cy *n.* an instance of being incorrect or inexact

in·ac´cu·rate *adj.* incorrect; not exact; misleading —**in·ac´cu·rate·ly** *adv.* —**in·ac´cu·rate·ness** *n.*

in·ac´tion *n.* a state of immobility or idleness

in·ac´tive *adj.* immobile or idle; not

currently in use; retired from service —**in·ac´tiv·ly** adv. —**in´ac·tiv´i·ty** n.

in·ad´e·qua·cy n. a weakness; ineptitude

in·ad´e·quate adj. not sufficient for the intended purpose —**in·ad´e·quate·ly** adv.

in·ad·mis´si·ble adj. not allowed —**in·ad·mis·si·bil´i·ty** n.

in´ad·vert´ent adj. careless or thoughtless; not intentional —**in´ad·vert´ent·ly** adv.

in·al´ien·a·ble adj. not allowing of change or transfer —**in·al·ien·a·bil´i·ty** n. —**in·al´ien·a·bly** adv.

in·am·o·ra´ta n. a woman whom one loves

in·ane´ adj. pointless; lacking substance; empty of meaning —**in·ane´ly** adv. —**in·an´i·ty** n.

in·an´i·mate adj. lacking the qualities associated with a living organism; lacking spirit or energy —**in·an´i·mate·ly** adv. —**in·an´i·mate·ness** n.

in·ap·pro´pri·ate adj. unsuitable —**in·ap·pro´pri·ate·ly** adv. —**in·ap·pro´pri·ate·ness** n.

in·apt´ adj. inept; inappropriate —**in·apt´ly** adv. —**in·apt´ness** n.

in·ar·tic´u·late adj. unable to speak or express in words; unable to speak distinctly; incomprehensible —**in·ar·tic´u·late·ly** adv. —**in·ar·tic´u·late·ness** n.

in·at·ten´tive adj. indifferent, preoccupied —**in·at·ten´tive·ly** adv. —**in·at·ten´tion** n.

in·au´gu·rate´ vt. to begin or bring into use with ceremony, as an induction into office or the dedication of a facility; to cause to begin

in·au´gu·ra´tion n. a ceremony of installation or induction —**in·au´gu·ral** n.

in·aus·pi´cious adj. unfavorable —**in·aus·pi´cious·ly** adv. —**in·aus·pi´cious·ness** n.

in´born adj. present at birth; innate

in´bred adj. inborn

in·cal´cu·la·ble adj. that cannot be calculated or assessed; unpredictable

in·can·des´cent adj. glowing as a direct result of being heated; shining brilliantly —**in·can·des´cence** n. —**in·can·des´cent·ly** adv.

in·can·ta´tion n. a chant or recitation reputed to invoke magic; a ritual supplication or prayer

in·ca´pa·ble adj. lacking qualification or competence —**in·ca·pa·bil´i·ty, in·ca´pa·ble·ness** n. —**in·ca´pa·bly** adv.

in·ca·pac´i·tate´ vt. to deprive of potential or capability; to invalidate or disqualify

in·ca·pac´i·ty n. a lack of potential or ability; something that disqualifies

in·car´cer·ate´ vt. to imprison; to confine —**in·car·cer·a´tion** n.

in·car´nate adj. manifest, especially in human form; personified —vt. to manifest or personify —**in·car·na´tion** n.

in·cen´di·ar´y adj. capable of causing fire; inclined to inflame, as emotions —n. a device intended to cause fire; one who starts a fire with malicious intent; one who stirs emotion to incite rebellion

in´cense n. a substance burned to create a pleasing aroma —**in·cense´** vt. to excite to anger

in·cen´tive n. something that serves to encourage or inspire; the prospect of penalty or reward that spurs to action

in·cep´tion n. a beginning —**in·cep´tive** adj.

in·ces´sant adj. continuous; without interruption —**in·ces´sant·ly** adv.

in´cest n. sexual intercourse between closely related persons

in´ci·dence n. the act of occurring; a

rate of occurrence

in·ci·dent *n.* a single event or occurrence; a relatively minor occurrence

in·ci·den·tal *adj.* occurring as a minor adjunct; accidental, unplanned —*n.* a minor item of expense —**in·ci·den·tal·ly** *adv.*

in·cin·er·ate *vi., vt.* to burn or cause to burn entirely —**in·cin·er·a·tor** *n.*

in·cip·i·ent *adj.* starting to come into being —**in·cip·i·ence** *n.* —**in·cip·i·ent·ly** *adv.*

in·cise *vt.* to cut into or carve, as with a sharp implement; to engrave

in·ci·sion *n.* a cut, especially into tissue during surgery; a mark or scar left by surgery

in·ci·sive *adj.* keen or sharp, as in thought or language —**in·ci·sive·ly** *adv.* —**in·ci·sive·ness** *n.*

in·ci·sor *n.* a front cutting tooth

in·cite *vt.* to provoke to action; to instigate

in·clem·ent *adj.* stormy; cruel or merciless —**in·clem·en·cy** *n.* —**in·clem·ent·ly** *adv.*

in·cli·na·tion *n.* a disposition or preference of one thing over another; an inclined surface

in·cline *vi.* to slope or lean; to tend toward or show a preference; to deviate —*vt.* to cause to slope or lean —*n.* a slope

in·clined *adj.* sloping or leaning; tending toward as a preference

in·clude *vt.* to take in, embrace, or contain as a part —**in·clu·sion** *n.*

in·clu·sive *adj.* incorporating most or all; including all in the range specified —**in·clu·sive·ly** *adv.* —**in·clu·sive·ness** *n.*

in·cog·ni·to *adj., adv.* with identity hidden or obscured

in·co·her·ence *n.* a lack of order; the inability to communicate clearly

in·co·her·ent *adj.* lacking order or

agreement; disjointed; unable to communicate in a distinct or organized manner; inarticulate —**in·co·her·ent·ly** *adv.*

in·come *n.* something of value received in exchange, such as for goods or labor; earnings

in·com·ing *adj.* coming in; about to come in

in·com·men·su·ra·ble *adj.* not to be measured or compared —**in·com·men·su·ra·bil·i·ty, in·com·men·su·ra·ble·ness** *n.* —**in·com·men·su·ra·bly** *adv.*

in·com·men·su·rate *adj.* disproportionate; inadequate —**in·com·men·su·rate·ly** *adv.* —**in·com·men·su·rate·ness** *n.*

in·com·mo·dious *adj.* inconvenient or uncomfortable —**in·com·mo·dious·ly** *adv.* —**in·com·mo·dious·ness** *n.*

in·com·pa·ra·ble *adj.* exceptional; so remarkable or unusual as to be beyond comparing —**in·com·pa·ra·bil·i·ty, in·com·pa·ra·ble·ness** *n.* —**in·com·pa·ra·bly** *adv.*

in·com·pat·i·bil·i·ty *n.* the inability to exist harmoniously

in·com·pat·i·ble *adj.* unsuited for affiliating or blending; contradictory; mutually exclusive; irreconcilable; mutually repelling; incongruous —**in·com·pat·i·bil·i·ty** *n.* —**in·com·pat·i·bly** *adv.*

in·com·pe·tence *n.* a lack of ability

in·com·pe·tent *adj.* inadequate or unsuited as by lack of certain qualities or abilities; not legally qualified, such as by mentality —*n.* one who is unable to function in certain circumstances —**in·com·pe·tence, in·com·pe·ten·cy** *n.* —**in·com·pe·tent·ly** *adv.*

in·com·plete *adj.* not finished; missing an integral part; designation in lieu of a grade for failure to complete the requirements of a course of study —**in·com·plete·ly**

adv. —**in·com·plete´ness** *n.*

in·com·pre·hen´si·ble *adj.* difficult or impossible to understand or accept —**in·com·pre·hen·si·bil´i·ty, in·com·pre·hen´si·ble·ness** *n.* —**in·com·pre·hen´si·bly** *adv.*

in·con·ceiv´a·ble *adj.* impossible to grasp or accept; so improbable as to be considered impossible — **in·con·ceiv´a·bly** *adv.*

in·con·gru´i·ty *n.* inconsistency; something inconsistent

in·con´gru·ous *adj.* inappropriate or incompatible; inconsistent —**in·con´gru·ous·ly** *adv.* —**in·con´gru·ous·ness** *n.*

in·con·se·quen´tial *adj.* of little importance —**in·con·se·quen´tial·ly** *adv.*

in·con·sid´er·a·ble *adj.* trivial —**in·con·sid´er·a·ble·ness** *n.* —**in·con·sid´er·a·bly** *adv.*

in·con·sid´er·ate *adj.* thoughtless of others; insensitive; lacking consideration —**in·con·sid´er·ate·ly** *adv.* —**in·con·sid´er·ate·ness** *n.*

in·con·sist´en·cy *n.* a discrepancy

in·con·sis´tent *adj.* lacking agreement or harmony; not logical; erratic or unpredictable —**in·con·sis´tent·ly** *adv.*

in·con·spic´u·ous *adj.* not easily seen; hardly noticeable —**in·con·spic´u·ous·ly** *adv.* —**in·con·spic´u·ous·ness** *n.*

in·con´stant *adj.* fickle —**in·con´stan·cy** *n.* —**in·con´stant·ly** *adv.*

in·con·test´a·ble *adj.* unquestionable —**in·con·test´a·bly** *adv.*

in·con´ti·nent *adj.* lacking self-control; unable to control bodily discharges —**in·con´ti·nence, in·con´ti·nen·cy** *n.* —**in·con´ti·nent·ly** *adv.*

in·con·tro·vert´i·ble *adj.* not subject to question; not able to deny or disprove —**in·con·tro·vert´i·bil´i·ty, in·con·tro·vert´i·ble·ness** *n.* —**in·con·tro·vert´i·bly** *adv.*

in·con·ven´ience *n.* that which is not convenient; a source of bother —*vt.* to cause difficulty or annoyance

in·con·ven´ient *adj.* unsuited to one's comfort or needs; difficult to use; poorly timed —**in·con·ven´ient·ly** *adv.*

in·cor´po·rate *vi., vt.* to become or cause to become united or combined; (*US*) to form or cause to form a legal corporation

in·cor·po·ra´tion *n.* a thing added; the act of including; (*US*) legally incorporating

in·cor·po´re·al *adj.* lacking physical or material form; spiritual —**in·cor·po´re·al·ly** *adv.*

in·cor·rect´ *adj.* inaccurate; unsuitable or improper —**in·cor·rect´ly** *adv.* —**in·cor·rect´ness** *n.*

in·cor´ri·gi·ble *adj.* incapable of being changed or reformed; difficult to control or restrain: *an incorrigible liar* —*n.* one who cannot be changed or reformed —**in·cor·ri·gi·bil´i·ty, in·cor´ri·gi·ble·ness** *n.* —**in·cor´ri·gi·bly** *adv.*

in·crease´ *vt., vi.* to make or become more or larger —**in´crease** *n.* the amount or rate by which something is augmented

in·cred´i·ble *adj.* so inconceivable or unlikely as to cause disbelief: *an incredible story*; amazing or startling: *an incredible performance* — **in·cred´i·bil´i·ty, in·cred´i·ble·ness** *n.* —**in·cred´i·bly** *adv.*

in·cred´u·lous *adj.* not inclined to believe; showing disbelief: *an incredulous look* —**in·cre·du´li·ty** *n.* —**in·cred´u·lous·ly** *adv.*

in´cre·ment *n.* a steady growth of or addition to; a slight increase; one of a series —**in·cre·men´tal** *adj.*

in·crim´i·nate *vt.* to accuse of involvement, especially in a wrongful act; to implicate by inference —**in·crim·i·na´tion** *n.*

in·cu·bate *vt.* to provide an environment suitable for growth and development, as of eggs or living tissue; to hatch —*vi.* to develop and hatch —**in·cu·ba´tion** *n.*

in·cu·ba·tor *n.* equipment that maintains a controlled environment, as for hatching eggs or as life support for a premature baby

in·cu·bus *n.* a nightmare; a male demon

in·cul´cate *vt.* to teach or indoctrinate by frequent or repeated instruction —**in´cul·ca´tion** *n.*

in·cul´pate *vt.* incriminate —**in´cul·pa´tion** *n.*

in·cum´bent *adj.* exacted as a duty; obligatory; lying or resting upon something else; presently in office —*n.* one who presently holds an office —**in·cum´ben·cy** *n.*

in·cur´ *vt.* to become liable or responsible for

in·cur´a·ble *adj.* incapable of being remedied or relieved —**in·cur´a·ble·ness** *n.* —**in·cur´a·bly** *adv.*

in·cur´sion *n.* an act of entering, usually into another's territory; an invasion

in·debt´ed *adj.* obligated —**in·debt´ed·ness** *n.*

in·dec´ent *adj.* contrary to the prevailing standard of good taste or modesty —**in·dec´ent·ly** *adv.*

in·de´cen·cy *n.* immodesty, lewdness

in·de·ci´sion *n.* the inability to make a determination

in·de·ci´sive *adj.* prone to doubt or uncertainty; inconclusive, as *an indecisive victory* —**in·de·ci´sive·ly** *adv.* —**in·de·ci´sive·ness** *n.*

in·de·fat´i·ga·ble *adj.* tireless

in·de·fen´si·ble *adj.* unable to be defended —**in·de·fen·si·bil´i·ty, in·de·fen´si·ble·ness** *n.* —**in·de·fen´si·bly** *adv.*

in·def´i·nite *adj.* lacking precise limits; uncertain or undecided; vague —**in·def´i·nite·ly** *adv.* —**in·def´i·nite·ness** *n.*

in·del´i·ble *adj.* impossible to remove, as certain inks or stains; unable to forget: *the horror left an indelible impression* —**in·del´i·bly** *adv.*

in·dem´ni·fy *vt.* to compensate for loss or damage

in·dem´ni·ty *n.* protection, exemption, or compensation from loss or injury

in·dent´ *vt., vi.* to make or form a blank space between a margin and printed or written matter

in·den·ta´tion *n.* an indent; a dent, notch, etc.

in·den´ture *n.* a contract; a legal instrument binding a servant to his master

in·de·pend´ence *n.* autonomy; freedom

in·de·pend´ent *adj.* free from the control of others; self-supporting —**in·de·pend´ent·ly** *adv.*

in–depth´ *adj.* detailed

in·de·struct´i·ble *adj.* permanent; unable to be destroyed —**in·de·struct·i·bil´i·ty** *n.* —**in·de·struct´i·bly** *adv.*

in·de·ter´mi·nate *adj.* not precisely fixed; indefinite —**in·de·ter´mi·nate·ly** *adv.*

in´dex *n., pl.* **in´dex·es, in´di·ces** a list of material contained within a printed work; any list or directory; an indicator that characterizes a set of data, as *the Consumer Price Index* —*vt.* to provide with an index; to list, catalog, or otherwise arrange

in´di·cate *vt.* to point out or signify; to comment briefly

in·di·ca´tion *n.* a hint or suggestion; something suggested as necessary or practical for treatment of an illness or condition

in·dic´a·tive *adj.* serving to designate; characteristic

in·di·ca·tor *n.* any mechanism, index, etc. that serves to measure or quantify a value; (*Brit.*) a turn signal on a car

in·dict *vt.* to accuse or charge with wrongdoing

in·dict·ment *n.* a formal accusation of offense as decided by a grand jury

in·dif·fer·ence *n.* unconcern or detachment; coldness, aloofness

in·dif·fer·ent *adj.* not involved; neutral or unconcerned; of little consequence or quality —**in·dif·fer·ent·ly** *adv.*

in·dig·e·nous *adj.* native; natural; inherent —**in·dig·e·nous·ly** *adv.* —**in·dig·e·nous·ness** *n.*

in·di·gence *n.* poverty

in·di·gent *adj.* impoverished —*n.* one who is poor or needy

in·di·gest·i·ble *adj.* impossible or difficult to digest

in·di·ges·tion *n.* discomfort caused by difficulty in digesting

in·dig·nant *adj.* angry over a wrong or injustice —**in·dig·nant·ly** *adv.*

in·dig·na·tion *n.* righteous anger

in·dig·ni·ty *n.* an affront; humiliation

in·di·go *n.* a blue dye

in·di·rect *adj.* in a roundabout manner; devious —**in·di·rect·ly** *adv.* —**in·di·rect·ness** *n.*

in·dis·creet *adj.* tactless; imprudent; thoughtless —**in·dis·creet·ly** *adv.* —**in·dis·creet·ness** *n.*

in·dis·crete *adj.* undivided; tightly bound; that can not be divided

in·dis·cre·tion *n.* tactlessness

in·dis·crim·i·nate *adj.* random; without order —**in·dis·crim·i·nate·ly** *adv.* —**in·dis·crim·i·na·tion** *n.*

in·dis·pen·sa·ble *adj.* essential; definitely needed —**in·dis·pen·sa·bly** *adv.*

in·dis·posed *adj.* reluctant or unwilling, as to honor a request; ill or ailing —**in·dis·pose** *vt.*

in·dis·put·a·ble *adj.* not to be denied; incontestable —**in·dis·put·a·bly** *adv.*

in·dis·sol·u·ble *adj.* that cannot be destroyed; perpetually binding

in·dis·tinct *adj.* not clear; dim or faded; not easily understood —**in·dis·tinct·ly** *adv.* —**in·dis·tinct·ness** *n.*

in·di·vid·u·al *adj.* relating to one only; by or for one; distinctive —*n.* a lone person or thing considered apart from its group; one marked by a special quality —**in·di·vid·u·al·ism** *n.* —**in·di·vid·u·al·ly** *adv.*

in·di·vid·u·al·i·ty *n.* the qualities that make one distinctive; the quality of being unique —**in·di·vid·u·al·ize** *vt.*

in·doc·tri·nate *vt.* to instruct or propagandize, especially in a particular doctrine or ideology; to acquaint, as with a new employer's rules and policies

in·doc·tri·na·tion *n.* instruction or training

in·do·lent *adj.* habitually lazy; slothful —**in·do·lence** *n.* —**in·do·lent·ly** *adv.*

in·dom·i·ta·ble *adj.* unable to be subdued; unconquerable —**in·dom·i·ta·ble·ness** *n.* —**in·dom·i·ta·bly** *adv.*

in·du·bi·ta·ble *adj.* undeniable; too obvious to be doubted —**in·du·bi·ta·ble·ness** *n.* —**in·du·bi·ta·bly** *adv.*

in·duce *vt.* to persuade to action; to cause or bring about

in·duce·ment *n.* an incentive; something that inspires or persuades

in·duct *vt.* to formally place into office or a position; to acquaint with or instruct in, as to a new position

in·duc·tion *n.* entrance into office; a ceremony for inducting into office;

the process of reasoning that draws broad conclusions from specific facts

in·duc´tive *adj.* relating to logical induction —**in·duc´tive·ly** *adv.* —**in·duc´tive·ness** *n.*

in·dulge´ *vt.* to yield to desires, especially those that are unreasonable or outrageous —*vi.* to gratify one's desires; to take part in

in·dul´gence *n.* an act of gratification; intemperance

in·dus´tri·al *adj.* of or relating to manufacturing and trade —**in·dus´tri·al·ly** *adv.*

in·dus´tri·al·ize *vt.* to convert the economy of a country or area to one based on industry; to make into an industry —**in·dus·tri·al·i·za´tion** *n.*

in·dus´tri·ous *adj.* dedicated to a task or cause —**in·dus´tri·ous·ly** *adv.* —**in·dus´tri·ous·ness** *n.*

in·dus´try *n.* manufacture and trade in commercial goods; active dedication to a task

in·e´bri·ate *vt.* to intoxicate; to exhilarate as if intoxicated —**in·e´bri·ate, in·e´bri·a·ted** *adj.* intoxicated; drunk —**in·e·bri·a´tion** *n.*

in·ef´fa·ble *adj.* indescribable; taboo to utter —**in·ef´fa·bly** *adv.*

in·ef·fec´tive *adj.* not creating an intended effect; inadequate —**in·ef·fec´tive·ly** *adv.* —**in·ef·fec´tive·ness** *n.*

in·ef·fec´tu·al *adj.* fruitless —**in·ef·fec´tu·al·ly** *adv.*

in·ef·fi´cient *adj.* wasteful; incompetent —**in·ef·fi´cien·cy** *n.* —**in·ef·fi´cient·ly** *adv.*

in·el´i·gi·ble *adj.* precluded, as by restrictions or lack of ability —**in·el´i·gi·bil´i·ty** *n.* —**in·el´i·gi·bly** *adv.*

in·ept´ *adj.* displaying a lack of ability; incompetent; clumsy —**in·ept´i·tude, in·ept´ness** *n.* —**in·ept´ly** *adv.*

in·e·qual´i·ty *n.* a difference or disparity

in·eq´ui·ta·ble *adj.* unfair —**in·eq´ui·ta·bly** *adv.*

in·eq´ui·ty *n.* an injustice

in·ert´ *adj.* motionless; inactive; unable to move; lethargic —**in·ert´ly** *adv.* —**in·ert´ness** *n.*

in·er´tia *n.* in physics, the tendency of a body at rest to remain at rest and of one in motion to continue moving in the same direction; reluctance to move or change

in·ev´i·ta·ble *adj.* impossible to change or prevent; unavoidable; inescapable —**in·ev·i·ta·bil´i·ty, in·ev´i·ta·ble·ness** *n.* —**in·ev´i·ta·bly** *adv.*

in·ex´o·ra·ble *adj.* unyielding; implacable; not to be persuaded to change —**in·ex·o·ra·bil´i·ty, in·ex´o·ra·ble·ness** *n.* — **in·ex´o·ra·bly** *adv.*

in·ex·pe´ri·ence *n.* a lack of skill

in·ex·pe´ri·enced *adj.* lacking the skill customarily gained from practical experience

in·ex´pert *adj.* unskilled —**in·ex´pert·ly** *adv.* —**in·ex´pert·ness** *n.*

in·ex´pi·a·ble *adj.* that may not be atoned for

in·ex·pli·ca·ble *adj.* impossible to explain or understand —**in·ex·pli·ca·bil´i·ty, in·ex´pli·ca·ble·ness** *n.* —**in·ex´pli·ca·bly** *adv.*

in·ex·press´i·ble *adj.* that cannot be described —**in·ex·press·i·bil´i·ty** *n.* —**in·ex·press´i·bly** *adv.*

in·ex´tri·ca·ble *adj.* that cannot be disentangled or undone; impossible to resolve —**in·ex´tri·ca·bly** *adv.*

in·fal´li·ble *adj.* incapable of failure or error —**in·fal·li·bil´i·ty** *n.* — **in·fal´li·bly** *adv.*

in´fa·mous *adj.* having a bad reputation; deserving of low regard — **in´fa·mous·ly** *adv.* —**in´fa·mous·ness** *adv.*

in´fa·my *n.* disgrace

in´fan·cy *n.* childhood; the early stages of development

in´fant *n.* a young child; in law, a minor —*adj.* pertaining to a young or early state

in´fan·tile *adj.* relating to infancy; childlike

in´fan·try *n.* soldiers trained to fight on foot

in·fat´u·ate *vt.* to provoke unreasoning affection or passion; to incite foolish behavior —**in·fat·u·a´tion** *n.*

in·fect´ *vt.* to contaminate or corrupt, especially with organisms that cause disease

in·fec´tion *n.* invasion of the body by disease-causing microorganisms; an infectious disease

in·fec´tious *adj.* caused by infection; tending to spread from one to another —**in·fec´tious·ly** *adv.* —**in·fec´tious·ness** *n.*

in·fer´ *vt.* to presume or conclude from available evidence; to insinuate or hint

in´fer·ence *n.* the process of reaching a conclusion from information available —**in´fer·en´tial** *adj.* —**in´fer·en´tial·ly** *adv.*

in·fe´ri·or *adj.* of a lesser quality; lower in value; subordinate —*n.* one who is lower in rank or station

in·fe·ri·or´i·ty *n.* the state of being lower in quality, rank, etc.

in·fer´nal *adj.* fiendish

in·fer´no *n.* a place of fiery heat

in·fest´ *vt.* to inhabit in overwhelming numbers

in´fi·del *n.* a non-believer

in·fi·del´i·ty *n.* sexual unfaithfulness; a lack of loyalty

in´fight·ing *n.* a bitter struggle or dissension, esp. between rivals in the same organization

in´fil·trate *vt.* to secretly enter and take up position; to permeate, as by a liquid

in´fi·nite *adj.* without limit —**in´fi·nite·ly** *adv.* —**in´fi·nite·ness** *n.*

in·fin·i·tes´i·mal *adj.* minuscule; immeasureably small —**in´fin·i·tes´i·mal·ly** *adv.*

in·fin´i·ty *n.* a limitless expanse, time, or quantity

in·firm´ *adj.* feeble or weak, as from old age or disease; irresolute

in·fir´ma·ry *n.* a small clinic or dispensary

in·fir´mi·ty *n.* an ailment or weakness, as from old age

in·flame´ *vi., vt.* to become or cause to become excited or aroused; to redden and swell as of a sore; to catch or set on fire

in·flam´ma·ble *adj.* combustible; easily excited —**in·flam·ma·bil´i·ty, in·flam´ma·ble·ness** *n.*

in·flam·ma´tion *n.* redness or swelling caused by irritation or infection

in·flam´ma·to·ry *adj.* intended to arouse passion, violence, etc.; causing inflammation

in·flate´ *vt.* to fill with air and cause to swell; to enlarge or expand improperly: *to inflate the price of scarce goods* —*vi.* to become enlarged or swelled —**in·fla´tion** *n.*

in·flect´ *vt.* to modify in tone or pitch —**in·flec´tion** *n.*

in·flex·i·bil´i·ty *n.* unwillingness or inability to change

in·flex´i·ble *adj.* not easily bent or changed; inelastic; rigid — **in·flex·i·bil´i·ty, in·flex´i·ble·ness** *n.* **in·flex´i·bly** *adv.*

in·flict´ *vt.* to impose on, as punishment or hardship —**in·flic´tion** *n.*

in´flu·ence *n.* a power that effects; an effect shaped by control or persuasion —*vt.* to effect by persuasion

in·flu·en´tial *adj.* having the power to influence

in·flu·en´za *n.* a contagious viral disease marked by infection of the respiratory tract, fever and muscular ache

in´flux *n.* a flowing in

in·form´ *vi.*, *vt.* to make known; to provide information; to reveal

in·for´mal *adj.* casual; unofficial —**in·for´mal·ly** *adv.*

in·for·mal´ity *n.* casualness; the absence of ceremony or formality

in·form´ant *n.* a person who testifies against others

in·for·ma´tion *n.* a body of knowledge or data

in·for·ma´tive *adj.* providing information; revealing —**in·for´ma·tive·ly** *adv.*

in·frac´tion *n.* a violation of rules

in·fran´gi·ble *adj.* incapable of being smashed

in·fra·red´ *adj.* pertaining to radiation between red and microwave on the spectrum

in´fra·struc·ture *n.* the elements of a structure, system, etc.

in·fre´quent *adj.* at large intervals of time or space —**in·fre´quen·cy** *n.* —**in·fre´quent·ly** *adv.*

in·fringe´ *vi.*, *vt.* to intrude upon; to transgress —**in·fringe´ment** *n.*

in·fu´ri·ate *vt.* to enrage

in·fuse´ *vt.* to introduce into; to inspire; to steep without boiling in order to extract something —**in·fu´sion** *n.*

in·gen´ious *adj.* resourceful, clever —**in·gen´ious·ly** *adv.* —**in·gen´ious·ness** *n.*

in·ge·nu´i·ty *n.* resourcefulness

in·gen´u·ous *adj.* innocent; lacking sophistication; straightforward —**in·gen´u·ous·ly** *adv.* —**in·gen´u·ous·ness** *n.*

in·gest´ *vt.* take into the body for digestion; to eat

in·glo´ri·ous *adj.* marked by failure or disgrace —**in·glo´ri·ous·ly** *adv.* —**in·glo´ri·ous·ness** *n.*

in´got *n.* a lump of cast metal

in·grain´ *vt.* to fix or instill, as in the mind —**in·grained´** *adj.*

in´grate *n.* one who is ungrateful

in·gra´ti·ate *vt.* to curry favor

in·gre´di·ent *n.* one of the elements in a mixture

in·hab´it *vt.* to occupy or reside in; to fill —**in·hab´it·ant** *n.*

in·hal´ant *n.* medicine inhaled as a vapor —**in´ha·la·tor** *n.*

in·hale´ *vt.* to draw into the lungs; to take in quickly, as food —*vi.* to breathe in —**in·hal´er** *n.*

in·her´ent *adj.* inherited; intrinsic —**in·her´ent·ly** *adv.*

in·her´it *vt.* to receive, acquire, or take over from another —**in·her´it·ance** *n.*

in·hib´it *vt.* to hold back or restrain

in·hi·bi´tion *n.* a restraint; something that inhibits

in·hos·pi´ta·ble *adj.* unfriendly; barren: offering little to promote life or growth

in·hu´man, **in·hu·mane´** *adj.* lacking human qualities, as pity or compassion

in·im´i·cal *adj.* unfriendly

in·im´i·ta·ble *adj.* that cannot be imitated

in·iq´ui·ty *n.* wickedness; evil; a wicked or evil act —**in·iq´ui·tous** *adj.*

in·i´tial *adj.* the first instance of; appearing at the beginning —*n.* the first letter or letters of a proper name —*vt.* to sign with initials

in·i´ti·ate *vt.* to introduce; to start; to induct into, as a club —*n.* one newly allowed or soon to be allowed into membership; an inductee

in·i·ti·a´tion *n.* a ceremony or ritual for induction; the act of bringing into being

in·i´ti·a·tive *n.* the quality or motivation that drives one to begin or pursue an action; a first move; the power to originate, as legislation

in·ject´ *vt.* to insert or introduce into

in·ju·di·cious *adj.* unwise; lacking judgement —**in·ju·di·cious·ly** *adv.* —**in·ju·di·cious·ness** *n.*

in·junc·tion *n.* a command or directive; a legal order prohibiting a course of action

in·jure *vt.* to cause harm to; to wound

in·jur·i·ous *adj.* harmful

in·ju·ry *n.* damage or harm; an injustice for which one may seek legal redress

in·jus·tice *n.* an instance of wrongdoing; a violation of rights

ink *n.* colored liquid used for writing or printing —*vt.* to mark with ink

ink·ling *n.* a hint, suggestion, or notion

in·lay *vt.* to set decorative material into —*n.* —**in·laid** *adj.*

in·let *n.* a recess along a coast; an access from the sea to inland waters

in·mate *n.* one confined to an institution

in·most *adj.* furthest from the exterior; secret or intimate

inn *n.* a lodging for travelers, usually serving food and drink; a tavern or restaurant

in·nate *adj.* inborn

in·ner *adj.* further inside; private or secret

in·ner·most *adj.* most intimate

inn·keep·er *n.* one who operates a public hostelry

in·no·cence *n.* freedom from guilt; a lack of cunning or guile

in·no·cent *adj.* uncorrupted; blameless; unsophisticated; harmless — *n.* a guileless or unsophisticated person

in·noc·u·ous *adj.* inoffensive; unlikely to stimulate; having no harmful qualities —**in·noc·u·ous·ly** *adv.* —**in·noc·u·ous·ness** *n.*

in·no·vate *vi., vt.* to introduce or change

in·no·va·tion *n.* something new; the process of introducing something new

in·nu·en·do *n.* an insinuation, often derogatory

in·nu·mer·a·ble *adj.* incalculable; too many to count —**in·nu·mer·a·bly** *adv.*

in·oc·u·late *vt.* to immunize, esp. by vaccination —**in·oc·u·la·tion** *n.*

in·of·fen·sive *adj.* harmless; without fault

in·op·er·a·ble *adj.* unable to be made to function; inappropriate for a surgical procedure

in·op·er·a·tive *adj.* not working; no longer in force

in·op·por·tune *adj.* ill–timed —**in·op·por·tune·ly** *adv.* —**in·op·por·tune·ness** *n.*

in·or·di·nate *adj.* excessive; exceeding reasonable bounds —**in·or·di·nate·ly** *adv.* —**in·or·di·nate·ness** *n.*

in·put *n.* that directed into, as power or energy to drive a machine; data entered into a computer

in·quest *n.* an investigation or inquiry into a matter

in·qui·e·tude *n.* a state of unrest

in·quire *vi., vt.* to investigate or ask about

in·quir·y *n.* an investigation in search of the truth; a question

in·qui·si·tion *n.* an investigation

in·quis·i·tive *adj.* overly curious; eager to learn —**in·quis·i·tive·ly** *adv.* —**in·quis·i·tive·ness** *n.*

in·quis·i·tor *n.* an examiner

in·road *n.* an encroachment or invasion

in·sane *adj.* psychotic; characterized by immoderate or foolish action —**in·sane·ly** *adv.* —**in·sane·ness** *n.*

in·san·i·ty *n.* mental disorder; an extremely foolish action

in·sa·ti·a·ble, in·sa·ti·ate *adj.* unable to be satisfied —**in·sa·ti·a·bly** *adv.* —**in·sa·ti·a·ble·ness** *n.*

in·scribe´ *vt.* to write or carve on a surface; to engrave; to dedicate a book, treatise, etc. to someone

in·scrip´tion *n.* words written or engraved, as on a plaque or the flyleaf of a book; a dedication

in·scru´ta·ble *adj.* incomprehensible

in´sect *n.* a usually small animal characterized by a segmented body and three pairs of legs

in·sec´ti·cide *n.* a chemical used to kill insects

in·se·cure´ *adj.* uncertain; lacking stability —**in·se·cur´i·ty** *n.* — **in·se·cure´ly** *adv.*

in·sem´i·nate *vt.* to impregnate by injecting semen —**in·sem·i·na´tion** *n.*

in·sen´sate *adj.* inanimate: incapable of sensation; lacking reason; hard–hearted

in·sen´si·ble *adj.* unconscious; indifferent

in·sen´si·tive *adj.* incapable of feeling: numb; unconcerned with the feelings of others —**in·sen·si·tiv´i·ty, in·sen´si·tive·ness** *n.* —**in·sen´si·tive·ly** *adv.*

in·sen´ti·ent *adj.* inanimate: totally lacking in life or consciousness —**in·sen´ti·ence** *n.*

in·sep´a·ra·ble *adj.* indivisible; closely associated: *inseparable playmates*

in·sert´ *vt.* to place into or among —**in´sert** *n.* an enclosure, as a card or flyer placed in a magazine

in·ser´tion *n.* something added; the act of adding or inserting

in·side´ *adj.* inner; select or confidential, as *inside information* —*adv.* into —*n.* an interior surface or part —**in·sid´er** *n.*

in·sid´i·ous *adj.* harmful and subtly conveyed or accumulated —**in·sid´i·ous·ly** *adv.* —**in·sid´i·ous·ness** *n.*

in´sight *n.* the ability to recognize the true nature of a situation

in·sig´ni·a *n.* a badge or emblem, as of office or rank

in·sig·nif´i·cance *n.* unimportance

in·sig·nif´i·cant *adj.* unimportant; having little force or value; of small size or quantity —**in·sig·nif´i·cant·ly** *adv.*

in·sin·cere´ *adj.* pretentious; deceitful or hypocritical

in´sin·cer´i·ty *n.* deceit; hypocrisy

in·sin´u·ate *vt.* to convey, as a notion or opinion, in a subtle manner

in·sin·u·a´tion *n.* a subtle hint

in·sip´id *adj.* uninteresting; dull; lacking flavor —**in·sip´id·ly** *adv.* —**in·sip´id·ness** *n.*

in·sist´ *vi.* to be firm or persistent —*vt.* to demand firmly or persistently

in·so·bri´e·ty *adj.* drunkenness

in´so·lent *adj.* rude or disrespectful; insulting —**in´so·lence** *n.*

in·sol´u·ble *adj.* not able to be dissolved; insolvable —**in·sol´u·bil´i·ty** *n.*

in·solv´a·ble *adj.* difficult or impossible to solve or explain

in·sol´vent *adj.* unable to pay one's debts; of or relating to bankruptcy —*n.* a person who is bankrupt

in·som´ni·a *n.* the persistent inability to sleep

in·spect´ *vt.* to examine carefully or critically

in·spec´tion *n.* an examination

in·spec´tor *n.* one whose job it is to examine; a police officer

in·spi·ra´tion *n.* stimulation to a high level of creativity; a sudden creative idea

in·spire´ *vt.* to invigorate or encourage

in·spir´it *vt.* to exhilarate; to instill with courage

in·stall´ *vt.* to set up, attach, or build into; to admit into office

in·stal·la´tion *n.* the placement of fixtures or equipment; something installed

in·stall´ment *n.* one of a series, as of periodic payments

in·stance *n.* an occurrence; an example or illustration

in·stant *adj.* immediate; designed for easy or quick preparation —*n.* a particular point in time —**in·stan·ta·ne·ous** *adj.*

in·stant·ly *adv.* immediately

in·stead *adv.* alternatively

in·sti·gate *vt.* to initiate, incite, or urge —**in·sti·ga·tion** *n.*

in·still *vt.* to implant or infuse, as an idea; to teach or indoctrinate

in·stinct *n.* inborn or natural behavior

in·stinc·tive *adj.* intuitive; natural

in·sti·tute *n.* an established organization; buildings and land occupied by an organization —*vt.* to enact or establish

in·sti·tu·tion *n.* the act of founding or establishing; a custom or tradition; an established organization or the buildings and land it occupies —**in·sti·tu·tion·al** *adj.* —**in·sti·tu·tion·al·ly** *adv.*

in·struct *vt.* to educate or edify; to order or direct firmly —*vi.* to discharge the duties of an instructor

in·struc·tion *n.* guidance; the imparting of knowledge; a direct order —**in·struc·tion·al, in·struc·tive** *adj.* —**in·struc·tive·ly** *adv.*

in·struc·tor *n.* a teacher; one who passes on knowledge

in·stru·ment *n.* an implement or tool; a device for producing musical sounds; a legal contract —**in·stru·men·ta·list** *n.*

in·stru·men·tal *adj.* serving as an agency for; partly responsible; of music written for a particular instrument

in·stru·men·tal·i·ty *n.* agency

in·stru·men·ta·tion *n.* a musical arrangement; a group of instruments

in·sub·or·di·nate *adj.* rebellious; hesitant or unwilling to obey

in·sub·or·di·na·tion *n.* rebellion against authority

in·suf·fer·a·ble *adj.* intolerable; difficult to endure —**in·suf·fer·a·bly** *adv.* —**in·suf·fer·a·ble·ness** *n.*

in·suf·fi·cient *adj.* not enough; lacking —**in·suf·fi·cient·ly** *adv.*

in·su·lar *adj.* detached; isolated

in·su·late *vt.* to isolate; to separate or protect with a barrier

in·su·la·tion *n.* a protective covering; protection from external influence —**in·su·la·tor** *n.*

in·sult *vi., vt.* to offend or treat offensively —**in·sult** *n.* an offensive act or utterance

in·su·per·a·ble *adj.* impossible to be overcome —**in·su·per·a·bly** *adv.*

in·sup·port·a·ble *adj.* intolerable; that cannot be justified

in·sur·ance *n.* protection against loss

in·sure *vt.* to make certain; to protect with an insurance policy

in·sur·ed *adj.* protected

in·sur·gent *n.* one who rebels against constituted authority —*adj.* rebellious

in·sur·mount·a·ble *adj.* that cannot be passed over or overcome —**in·sur·mount·a·bil·i·ty** *n.* —**in·sur·mount·a·bly** *adv.*

in·sur·rec·tion *n.* an act of open rebellion

in·sus·cep·ti·ble *adj.* not vulnerable

in·tact *adj.* complete; not damaged or diminished in any way

in·tan·gi·ble *adj.* indefinable by the senses —**in·tan·gi·ble·ness** *n.* —**in·tan·gi·bly** *adv.*

in·te·ger *n.* a whole number

in·te·gral *adj.* necessary to make complete; essential

in·te·grate *vt.* to bring together; to unify

in·te·gra·tion *n.* a unifying or blending

in·teg·ri·ty *n.* strict compliance to an ethical standard; the state of being whole or sound

in·tel·lect *n.* the capacity for reason or understanding

in·tel·lec·tu·al *adj.* relating or appealing to the intellect; intelligent —*n.* one given to intellectual pursuits

in·tel·li·gence *n.* the capacity for knowledge; information or news, especially that which is secret

in·tel·li·gent *adj.* having knowledge or the ability to acquire knowledge —**in·tel·li·gent·ly** *adv.*

in·tel·li·gent·si·a *n.* the intellectual elite

in·tel·li·gi·ble *adj.* able to be understood

in·tem·per·ance *n.* excessive indulgence

in·tend *vt.* to have in mind, as for a particular use or plan of action

in·tend·ed *adj.* intentional

in·tense *adj.* extreme, as in force or magnitude; emotional —**in·tense·ly** *adv.* — **in·tense·ness, in·ten·si·ty** *n.*

in·ten·si·fy *vi., vt.* to grow or make stronger

in·ten·sive *adj.* characterized by a sense of vigor or concentration — **in·ten·sive·ly** *adv.* —**in·ten·sive·ness** *n.*

in·tent *adj.* firmly fixed in the mind —*n.* something intended —**in·tent·ly** *adv.*

in·ten·tion *n.* aim; purpose

in·ten·tion·al *adj.* deliberate; planned —**in·ten·tion·al·ly** *adv.*

in·ter *vt.* to bury or entomb

in·ter·act *vi.* to relate or act mutually —**in·ter·ac·tion** *n.*

in·ter·cede *vt.* to plead on behalf of another

in·ter·cept *vt.* to interrupt the progress of —**in·ter·cep·tion** *n.*

in·ter·ces·sion *n.* a plea for another; mediation

in·ter·change *vi., vt.* to change or cause to change successively, as the elements in a design —**in·ter·change** *n.* a system of ramps that allows access to intersecting highways

in·ter·course *n.* communication between persons; sexual relations

in·ter·de·pen·dence, in·ter·de·pend·en·cy *n.* mutually dependent —**in·ter·de·pen·dent** *adj.* —**in·ter·de·pen·dent·ly** *adv.*

in·ter·dict *vt.* to prohibit by law or by order of the church —*n.* a legal prohibition; censure by the church —**in·ter·dic·tion** *n.*

in·ter·est *n.* curiosity about something in particular; the right to a share in something; a fee for the loan of money —*vt.* to hold one's attention

in·ter·est·ed *adj.* connected or affected in some way, as *an interested party*

in·ter·est·ing *adj.* inviting attention —**in·ter·est·ing·ly** *adv.*

in·ter·fere *vt.* to invene

in·ter·fer·ence *n.* something that obstructs; an act of interrupting or obstructing

in·ter·ga·lac·tic *adj.* existing between galaxies

in·ter·im *n.* a time between events —*adj.* effective for a time

in·te·ri·or *adj.* of the inside; situated away from the coast —*n.* the internal part; the internal affairs of a political entity

in·ter·ject *vt.* to insert between other components —**in·ter·jec·tion** *n.*

in·ter·lace *vt.* to weave or entwine; to unite

in·ter·leaf *n.* a blank sheet placed between pages in a book —**in·ter·leave** *vt.*

in·ter·lock *vt., vi.* to join together; to link

in·ter·lop·er *n.* one who meddles in the affairs of others

in·ter·lude *n.* a lull or intervening time

in·ter·me´di·ar·y *n.* an agent or mediator

in·ter·me´di·ate *adj.* occurring between

in·ter´ment *n.* burial

in·ter´mi·na·ble *adj.* without terminus; endless; tiresome —**in·ter´mi·na·bly** *adv.*

in·ter·min´gle *vt., vi.* to combine or become mingled together

in·ter·mis´sion (*US*) *n.* a pause between events, as the acts of a play

in·ter·mit´tent *adj.* not continuous —**in·ter·mit´tent·ly** *adv.*

in·ter·mix´ *vt., vi.* to mix or become mixed together

in´tern *n.* one who is apprenticed — **in·tern´** *vt.* to confine, as in prison —*vi.* to serve as an apprentice — **in·tern·ee´** *n.* —**in´tern·ship** *n.*

in·ter´nal *adj.* of the area inside or within borders —**in·ter´nal·ly** *adv.*

in·ter·na´tion·al *adj.* worldwide; between nations —**in·ter·na´tion·al·ism** *n.* —**in·ter·na´tion·al·ly** *adv.*

in·ter·nec´ine *adj.* of a struggle within an organization; mutually destructive

in·tern´ment *n.* confinement, as in prison

in·ter´nist *n.* a physician specializing in internal medicine

in·ter·per´son·al *adj.* between persons

in´ter·play *n.* interaction between parties

in·ter´po·late *vt.* to insert new material derived from that which precedes and that which follows it — **in·ter·po·la´tion** *n.*

in·ter·pose´ *vt.* to inject into or between elements

in·ter´pret *vt.* to translate, explain, or illuminate

in·ter·pre·ta´tion *n.* an explanation; a presentation marked by a particular style or point of view

in·ter´pret·er *n.* one who translates or explains

in·ter·re·late´ *vt., vi.* to bring or come into interdependent association —**in·ter·re·la´tion·ship** *n.*

in·ter´ro·gate *vt.* to cross–examine

in·ter·ro·ga´tion *n.* a formal questioning —**in·ter´ro·ga·tor** *n.* —**in·ter·rog´a·tive** *adj.*

in·ter·rupt´ *vt.* to break in or interfere with the continuity of

in·ter·rup´tion *n.* a delay or intrusion

in·ter·sect´ *vt., vi.* to cross or abut; to form an intersection

in·ter·sec´tion *n.* the point where two or more lines, streets, etc. abut or cross

in·ter·sperse´ *vt.* to place at regular intervals throughout

in·ter·twine´ *vt., vi.* to unite by interlacing

in´ter·val *n.* space or time between

in·ter·vene´ *vi.* to come between; to interfere

in·ter·ven´tion *n.* interference in the affairs of another, as a person or state

interview *n.* a meeting in which one person elicits information from another, as for publication, or in which information is exchanged, as in a *job interview*

in·tes´tine *n.* the long passage between the stomach and the anus that plays a major role in digestion and the subsequent evacuation of waste —**in·tes´ti·nal** *adj.*

in·ti·ma·cy *n.* closeness

in´ti·mate *adj.* marked by one's innermost thoughts, feelings, etc.; closely associated; of informality and privacy —*n.* a close associate —*vt.* to hint —**in´ti·mate·ly** *adv.*

in·ti·ma´tion *n.* information communicated subtly and indirectly; a hint

in·tim´i·date *vt.* to frighten; to pressure by threatening —**in·tim·i·da´tion** *n.*

in·tol´er·a·ble *adj.* unbearable;

grossly offensive —**in·tol´er·a·bly**
adv.

in·tol´er·ant *adj.* bigoted or prejudiced; unwilling to accept: *intolerant of evil* —**in·tol´er·ance** *n.* —
in·tol´er·ant·ly *adv.*

in·to·na´tion *n.* modulation of the
voice

in·tone´ *vt.*, *vi.* to recite or chant in
a monotone

in·tox´i·cant *n.* a means of intoxica-
tion, as an alcoholic beverage or a
narcotic

in·tox´i·cate *vt.* to inebriate or be-
fuddle, as by strong drink; to
stimulate, as by good news, beautiful scenery, etc.

in·tox·i·ca´tion *n.* drunkenness;
stimulation

in·trac´ta·ble *adj.* obstinate or undisciplined; difficult to control, as
an intractable disease —**in·trac·ta·
bil´i·ty, in·trac´ta·ble·ness** *n.* —
in·trac´ta·bly *adv.*

in·tran´si·gence *n.* a refusal to compromise, even from an untenable
position; obstinacy; stubborness

in·tran´si·gent *adj.* intolerant and
uncompromising; obstinate

in·tra·ve´nous *adj.* injected into or
situated within a vein —**in·tra·ve´
nous·ly** *adv.*

in·trep´id *adj.* fearless —**in·trep´id·
ly** *adv.* —**in·trep´id·ness** *n.*

in´tri·ca·cy *n.* something extremely
complex

in´tri·cate *adj.* elaborately complex
or involved —**in´tri·cate·ly** *adv.* —
in´tri·cate·ness *n.*

in·trigue´ *n.* a secret scheme or plot
—*vi.* to plot secretly —*vt.* to arouse
interest

in·trin´sic *adj.* of an inborn quality
—**in·trin´si·cal·ly** *adv.*

in·tro·duce´ *vt.* to present for consideration; to acquaint one person
with another

in·tro·duc´tion *n.* the presentation
of a person, idea, etc.; a time or

ceremony of presentation

in·tro·duc´to·ry *adj.* of the presentation of something new

in·tro·spec´tion *n.* contemplation
and self-examination

in´tro·vert *n.* one whose interests
are directed inward —**in·tro·ver´
sion** *n.* —**in·tro·ver´sive** *adj.*

in·trude´ *vi.*, *vt.* to intervene or
cause to intervene where one is
not wanted

in·trud´er *n.* one who meddles or
enters improperly

in·tru´sion *n.* an interruption; unwarranted meddling —**in·tru´sive**
adj. —**in·tru´sive·ly** *adv.* —**in·tru´
sive·ness** *n.*

in·tu·i´tion *n.* an instinctive feeling
that something has happened or is
about to happen

in·tu´i·tive *adj.* instinctive; perceived or concluded without the
benefit of reason —**in·tu´i·tive·ly**
adv. —**in·tu´i·tive·ness** *n.*

in´un·date *vt.* to overwhelm, especially with flood waters

in·un·da´tion *n.* a flooding or overflowing

in·ure´ *vt.* to acclimate or accustom
to something unpleasant

in·vade´ *vt.* to attack, as of an act of
war; to enter and remain, as of an
infestation —**in·vad´er** *n.*

in·val´id *adj.* not legal; not legally
binding; faulty —**in´va·lid** *n.* one
who is disabled by illness or injury

in·val´i·date *vt.* to revoke or nullify

in·val´u·a·ble *adj.* priceless

in·var´i·a·ble *adj.* unchanging —**in·
var´i·a·bly** *adv.*

in·va´sion *n.* an attack by a hostile
force; an infestation

in·va´sive *adj.* tending to invade or
intrude

in·vec´tive *adj.* characterized by
abusive language —*n.* abusive language or discourse; a denunciation

in·veigh´ *vt.* to protest vigorously

in·vei´gle *vt.* to entice or trick by

coaxing or flattery

in·vent′ *vt.* to create something new; to misrepresent, as by way of an excuse —**in·ven′tor** *n.*

in·ven′tion *n.* something newly created

in·ven′tive *adj.* clever; creative; resourceful —**in·ven′tive·ly** *adv.* —**in·ven′tive·ness** *n.*

in′ven·to·ry *n.* a list of goods in stock; an accounting —*vt.* to count and record goods on hand

in·verse′ *adj.* reversed —**in·verse′ly** *adv.*

in·vert′ *vt.* to reverse position, as to turn inside out or upside down

in·ver′te·brate *adj.* lacking a backbone —*n.* an animal that has no backbone

in·vest′ *vt.* to buy in anticipation of future profit; to charge with authority; to formally install in office

in·ves′ti·gate *vi., vt.* to make careful inquiry

in·ves·ti·ga′tion *n.* a detailed inquiry

in·vest′ment *n.* the placing of resources in the hope of profit —**in·ves′tor** *n.*

in·vet′er·ate *adj.* well-established; persisting

in·vid′i·ous *adj.* expressing ill-will; malicious —**in·vid′i·ous·ly** *adv.* —**in·vid′i·ous·ness** *n.*

in·vig′o·rate *vt.* to enliven; to energize —**in·vig·o·ra′tion** *n.*

in·vig′o·rat·ing *adj.* tending to energize; refreshing or stimulating —**in·vig′o·rat·ing·ly** *adv.*

in·vin·ci·bil′i·ty *n.* the quality of being invulnerable

in·vin′ci·ble *adj.* unconquerable

in·vi′o·la·ble *adj.* that cannot be profaned; invincible —**in·vi·o·la·bil′i·ty** *n.* —**in·vi′o·la·bly** *adv.*

in·vi′o·late *adj.* not violated; pure

in·vis′i·ble *adj.* unseen; not open to view —**in·vis′i·bly** *adv.*

in·vi·ta′tion *n.* a formal request for one to be present; an allurement or temptation

in·vi·ta′tion·al *n.* an event limited to those invited, as a celebrity golf tournament —*adj.* restricted to invited participants

in·vite′ *vt.* to formally request, as the presence of another; to tempt

in·vit′ing *adj.* attractive; enticing

in·vo·ca′tion *n.* an appeal; a prayer, especially at the start of a religious ceremony —**in′vo·ca·tor** *n.* —**in·voc′a·to·ry** *adj.*

in′voice *n.* a statement of charges for goods or services —*vt.* to tender a bill for goods or services

invoke′ *vt.* to call up, as a spirit; to beseech or appeal earnestly

in·vol′un·tar·y *adj.* unintentional; instinctive —**in·vol·un·tar′i·ly** *adv.*

in·vo·lu′tion *n.* involvement; complexity

in·volve′ *vt.* to include or connect to; to implicate or incriminate; to become engrossed in; to complicate

in·volved′ *adj.* complicated; engrossed; emotionally committed

in·volve′ment *n.* participation; entanglement

in·vul′ner·a·ble *adj.* invincible; impossible to harm or damage —**in·vul·ner·a·bil′i·ty** *adv.*

in′ward *adj.* related to the inside —*adv.* toward the inside —**in′ward·ly** *adv.*

i·o′ta *n.* a small amount

i·ras′ci·ble *adj.* irritable; quick to anger; marked by anger —**i·ras′ci·bly** *adv.*

i′rate, i·rate′ *adj.* incensed; marked by anger: *an irate caller* —**i·rate′ly** *adv.*

ire *n.* anger

irk *vt.* to vex or annoy

irk′some *adj.* annoying; disturbing

i′ron *n.* a metallic element used extensively in structural materials;

something made from iron; a symbol of unyielding strength —*vt.*, *vi.* to smooth clothing —*adj.* made of or containing iron; strong and unyielding

i·ron´ic, i·ron´i·cal *adj.* paradoxical; mocking; displaying irony —**i·ron´i·cal·ly** *adv.*

i´ro·ny *n.* a paradox between what happens and what might be expected to happen; a literary syle often used to mock or satirize convention

ir·ra´di·ate *vt.* to clarify or illuminate; to expose to radiation —**ir·ra·di·a´tion** *n.*

ir·rad´i·ca·ble *adj.* impossible to destroy —**ir·rad´i·ca·bly** *adv.*

ir·ra´tion·al *adj.* not subject to reason; illogical; silly —**ir·ra·tion·al´i·ty** *n.* —**ir·ra´tion·al·ly** *adv.*

ir·rec·on·cil´a·ble *adj.* that cannot be reconciled or justified —**ir·rec·on·cil´a·ble·ness** *n.* —**ir·rec·on·cil´a·bly** *adv.*

ir·re·deem´a·ble *adj.* that cannot be redeemed; impossible to recover or reform —**ir·re·deem´a·bly** *adv.*

ir·re·fut´a·ble *adj.* indisputable; not subject to argument or dispute

ir·reg´u·lar *adj.* contrary to that which is normal or conventional; not symmetrical or uniform —**ir·reg´u·lar·ly** *adv.*

ir·reg·u·lar´i·ty *n.* an abnormality or oddity

ir·rel´e·vance, ir·rel´e·van·cy *n.* the quality of being trivial, unconnected, or not pertinent to the matter at hand

ir·rel´e·vant *adj.* not pertinent —**ir·rel´e·vant·ly** *adv.*

ir·re·li´gious *adj.* not religious: hostile to religion

ir·re·mis´si·ble *adj.* incurable; unpardonable

ir·rep´a·ra·ble *adj.* hopeless; impossible to mend or correct —**ir·rep´a·ra·bly** *adv.*

ir·re·place´a·ble *adj.* priceless; that cannot be replaced

ir·re·press´i·ble *adj.* that cannot be controlled; overly enthusiastic —**ir·re·press´i·ble·ness** *n.* —**ir·re·press´i·bly** *adv.*

ir·re·proach´a·ble *adj.* blameless

ir·re·sist´i·ble *adj.* overwhelming; compelling —**ir·re·sist´i·ble·ness** *n.* —**ir·re·sist´i·bly** *adv.*

ir·res´o·lute *adj.* lacking in purpose or resolution; wavering —**ir·res´o·lute·ly** *adv.* —**ir·res´o·lute·ness, ir·res·o·lu´tion** *n.*

ir·re·spec´tive *adj.* regardless —**ir·re·spec´tive·ly** *adv.*

ir·re·spon´si·ble *adj.* thoughtless; unpredictable; lacking a sense of duty —**ir·re·spon´si·ble·ness** *n.* —**ir·re·spon´si·bly** *adv.*

ir·rev´er·ence *n.* a lack of respect

ir·rev´er·ent *adj.* disrespectful of that which is considered proper —**ir·rev´er·ent·ly** *adv.*

ir·rev´o·ca·ble *adj.* that cannot be retracted or changed —**ir·rev´o·ca·bly** *adv.*

ir´ri·gate *vt.* to furnish water for growing plants; to cleanse, as a wound, with liquid —**ir´ri·ga·ble** *adj.*

ir·ri·ga´tion *n.* a system for supplying water; the process of providing water for plants or liquid for cleansing

ir´ri·ta·ble *adj.* ill-tempered; easily provoked or offended —**ir´ri·ta·ble·ness** *n.* —**ir´ri·ta·bly** *adv.*

ir´ri·tant *n.* something that annoys

ir´ri·tate *vt.* to provoke to anger; to chafe or abrade, as the skin —**ir´ri·tat·ing·ly** *adv.*

ir´ri·tat·ed *adj.* troubled or disturbed

ir·ri·ta´tion *n.* something that troubles or vexes; an irritant

is´land *n.* a body of land surrounded completely by water; a structure or area similarly isolated

i′so·late *vt.* to detach and set apart

i·so·la′tion *n.* separation; seclusion

i·so·la′tion·ist *n.* one who believes in minimal involvement in the affairs of other nations

is′sue *n.* the act of flowing out; something published or distributed; an edition —*vi.*, *vt.* to flow or cause to flow out; to orginate from a source; to distribute

itch *n.* a skin irritation; a desire —*vi.* to sense an irritation or desire — **itch′i·ness** *n.* —**itch′y** *adj.*

i′tem *n.* a single element that is part of a whole, such as a clause in a document, an article in a book or newspaper, etc.

i′tem·ize *vt.*, *vi.* to enumerate, one by one —**i′tem·i·za′tion** *n.*

it·er·ance, it·er·a′tion *n.* repetition

it′er·ate *vt.* to repeat

i·tin′er·ant *adj.* roving —*n.* a wanderer —**i·tin′er·ant·ly** *adv.*

i·tin′er·ar·y *n.* a travel plan

i′vied *adj.* coated with ivy

i′vy *n.* a climbing or trailing plant

j, J tenth letter of the English alphabet

jab *n.* a quick poke or punch —*vi.*, *vt.* to poke, especially with a sharp instrument; to punch with a short, quick movement

jab′ber *vi.*, *vt.* to speak rapidly or nonsensically —*n.* senseless talk —**jab′ber·er** *n.*

ja·bot′ *n.* ornamental ruffles on the front of a shirt or blouse

jack *n.* a device for raising heavy objects; a type of food fish; (*US*) a plug for connecting electronic devices —*vt.* to raise with the aid of a jack; to raise, as prices

jack′al *n.* a wild dog

jack′ass *n.* the male ass; a stupid person

jack′boot *n.* a heavy boot reaching above the knee

jack′daw *n.* a small black bird related to the crow

jack′et *n.* a short coat; an outer covering or container —*vt.* to cover with a jacket

jack′et·ed *adj.* covered with a jacket

jack′knife *n.* a pocket knife designed in such a way that the blade folds into the handle

jack′pot *n.* a prize or pool of money; winnings; a bonanza or reward

jack′rab·bit *n.* a large American hare

jade *vt.*, *vi.* to wear out or become worn by overindulgence —*n.* a shrewish woman; a gemstone, usually pale green

jad′ed *adj.* world–weary; pretentiously indifferent —**jad′ed·ly** *adv.* —**jad′ed·ness** *n.*

jag′ged *adj.* characterized by an irregular edge —**jag′ged·ly** *adv.* — **jag′ged·ness** *n.*

jag′uar *n.* a large spotted cat

jail (*US*), **gaol** (*Brit.*) *n.* a place of confinement for one awaiting trial or guilty of a minor offense —*vt.* to confine in a jail

jail′er (*US*), **gaol′er** (*Brit.*) *n.* one charged with the upkeep of a jail

ja·la·pe′ño *n.* a pungent tropical pepper having red or green fruit

ja·lop′y *n.* an old, broken–down car

jal′ou·sie *n.* a door or window covering having adjustable horizontal slats

jam *n.* a preserve of sugar and fruit; a crush of people; a difficult situation —*vt.*, *vi.* to cram or become crammed in a tight space

jamb *n.* a vertical piece that forms the side of a door or window

jam·ba·lay′a *n.* a spicy Creole dish of rice with a variety of seafood or meat

jam′bo·ree′ *n.* a large gathering; a festive celebration

jam session an unrehearsed gathering or meeting, especially of musicians

jan´gle n. a discordant metallic sound —vi., vt. to make or cause such a sound —**jan´gler** n.

jan·i·tor (US) n. one charged with the maintenance of a building —**jan·i·to´ri·al** adj.

ja·pan´ n. a hard glossy coating; an item coated or decorated in the Japanese manner —vt. to coat with japan

jape n. a jest or prank —vi. to joke or jest —**jap´er** n. —**jap´er·y** n.

jar n. a small cylindrical container; a jolt or bump —vi., vt. to shake or cause to shake; to irritate or shock

jar·di·niere´ n. an ornamental pot or stand for flowers

jar´gon n. a patois or dialect; the specialized terms of a profession or trade

jar·gon·is´tic adj. of the nature of a jargon

jar´gon·ize vt., vi to translate into or speak in a dialect

jas´mine n. any of a species of flowering shrubs, some of which are used in making fragrances and tea; a fragrance or tea produced from the jasmine flower

jas´per n. a type of yellow, red, or brown quartz

jaun´dice n. abnormal yellowing of the skin, eyeballs, etc.; hostility, such as caused by envy or distrust —vt. to affect with jaundice; to be influenced by envy or distrust

jaunt n. an excursion; a short pleasure trip —vi. to make a short trip

jaun´ty adj. in a free and easy manner; buoyant; self-confident —**jaun´ti·ly** adv. —**jaun´ti·ness** n.

jav´e·lin n. a short light spear

jaw n. one of two bony structures forming the frame for the mouth; anything that grips like a jaw —vi., vt. to talk or scold

jaw´bone n. a bone of the jaw —vt., vi. to urge or argue vigorously

jazz n. an American musical form marked by syncopated rhythm, disonance, etc. —adj. pertaining to jazz —**jazz´man** n.

jeal´ous adj. envious; fearful of competition; protective, as jealous of one's social standing —**jeal´ous·ly** adv. —**jeal´ous·ness** n.

jeal´ou·sy n. possessive envy

jeer n. an abusive or mocking remark —vi., vt. to mock or ridicule —**jeer´ing·ly** adv.

je·june´ adj. dull or lifeless; childlike —**je·june´ly** adv.

jell vi., vt. to become firm or cause to become firm; to take shape

jel´ly n. a sweet or savory gelatinous food

jeop´ar·dize vt. to expose to danger

jeop´ar·dy n. risk of loss; danger

jerk n. a sudden, quick action; a silly or foolish person —vt. to pull with a sudden snap —vi. to make a lurching or quivering move —**jerk´i·ly** adv. —**jerk´i·ness** n.

jer´kin n. a short jacket

jerk´y adj. marked by abrupt jolts or lurching, as a jerky ride; marked by short, abrupt movement, as jerky handwriting

jer´ky n. cured meat

jer·o·bo´am n. a wine bottle with a capacity of 3 liters

jer´ry-built adj. shoddily constructed; improvised

jer´sey n. a knitted fabric; clothing made from this fabric; a pullover shirt or sweater

jest n. a joke or prank —vi. to tease or mock; to speak in fun

jest´er n. a professional comedian; one given to light banter

jet n. a flow of fluid or gas forced through a small opening at high pressure; a device that creates such a flow; a vehicle propelled by this flow; a dense, black color —vi. to travel in a jet-propelled aircraft

jet engine n. an engine that develops thrust by forcing fluid exhaust through a nozzle

jet´sam *n.* material jettisoned by a ship in distress

jet´ti·son *vt.* to throw overboard, as from a ship; to discard

jet´ty *n.* a structure that extends out from shore to protect a harbor or shoreline

jew´el *n.* a precious stone; an ornament set with precious stones; something highly prized —**jew´el·er, jew´el·ler** *n.*

jew´el·ler·y (*Brit.*) **jew´el·ry** (*US*) *n.* ornaments made of precious metals and set with precious stones

jif´fy *n.* a brief span of time

jig *n.* a lively dance or its music; a device for holding or guiding a tool or material being worked —*vi.* to dance a jig

jig´ger *n.* a 1½ ounce measure; 1½ ounces

jig´gle *vi.* to bounce lightly up and down or from side to side —**jig´gly** *adj.*

ji·had´ *n.* a holy war or pious quest

jilt *vi.* to reject suddenly, as a lover

jim´my *n.* a short crowbar —*vt.* to force, as with a crowbar

jin´gle *n.* a short rhyme or song; a light metallic tinkling sound —*vi., vt.* to make or cause to make such a sound —**jin´gly** *adj.*

jin´go *n.* one who aggressively supports his or her nation

jin´go·ism *n.* extreme nationalism

jinx *n.* a hex or spell; a person or thing that brings bad luck —*vt.* to bring bad luck

jit´ney *n.* a small passenger vehicle; a delapidated vehicle

jive *n.* the jargon of jazz; nonsensical talk —*vt., vi.* to talk nonsensically

job *n.* work for pay; the type of work one does; a task or duty; something worked on or at

job´ber *n.* one who buys in large quantities from manufacturers or distributors and sells to retailers

job´less *adj.* out of work

jock´ey *n.* one who rides horses professionally; one associated with a particular vehicle, profession, etc., as a *jet jockey* or a *disc jockey* —*vi., vt.* to ride, as a horse; to manuever: *jockey for position*

jo·cose´ *adj.* given to humor —**jo·cose´ly** *adv.* —**jo·cose´ness, jo·cos´i·ty** *n.*

joc´u·lar *adj.* given to joking —**joc·u·lar´i·ty** *n.* —**joc´u·lar·ly** *adv.*

joc´und *adj.* lighthearted —**jo·cun´di·ty** *n.* —**joc´und·ly** *adv.*

jodh´purs *n.* riding pants, wide at the hips and closefitting below the knee

jog *n.* a slow, steady trot; a slight jostling or nudge —*vi., vt.* to move or cause to move at a slow run; to jostle or nudge

jog´gle *vt., vi.* to shake lightly

join *vt., vi.* to bring or come together; to connect

join´er *n.* a carpenter; a tool designed to fashion joints

joint *n.* a place where two pieces come together; a seedy establishment, such as a tavern; a marijuana cigarette —*adj.* shared —**joint´ed** *adj.* —**joint´ly** *adv.*

joist *n.* a horizontal beam

joke *n.* an amusing story or act —*vi.* to speak or act in fun —**jok´ing·ly** *adv.*

jok´er *n.* a jester or prankster

jol´li·ty *n.* merriment

jol´ly *adj.* cheerful, exhibiting good humor —**jol´li·ly** *adv.*

jolt *n.* a jarring bump; a shock or surprise —*vt.* to jar with or as if by a sharp blow; to shock —**jolt´y** *adj.*

josh *vi.* to joke; to tease playfully —**josh´er** *n.*

jos´tle *vt.* to push or bump while walking by —**jos´tler** *n.*

jot *n.* a small amount —*vt.* to write hastily

jot´ted *adj.* written hastily

jot´ting *n.* a short note

jounce *n.* a jolting movement —*vi.*, *vt.* to move or cause to move with a jolt

jour´nal *n.* an account, as of one's finances or activities; a newspaper or periodical —**jour´nal·ize** *vt.*

jour´nal·ism *n.* the writing and editing of news items

jour´nal·ist *n.* one who writes for a newspaper or periodical —**jour·nal·is´tic** *adj.* —**jour·nal·is´ti·cal·ly** *adv.*

jour´ney *n.* the act of traveling or the distance traveled —*vi.*, *vt.* to travel

jour´ney·man *n.* one who has completed an apprenticeship

joust *n.* medieval combat between mounted opponents; a competition; a confrontation suggestive of such rivalry —*vi.* to compete; to engage in a battle of words or wits —**joust´er** *n.*

jo´vi·al *adj.* extremely cordial and sociable —**jo´vi·al·ly** *adv.*

jowl *n.* the flesh of the cheek or jaw

jowl´y *adj.* having loose hanging flesh about the cheeks and jaws

joy *n.* intense happiness or pleasure; the cause of such pleasure

joy´ful *adj.* expressing or feeling joy —**joy´ful·ly** *adv.* —**joy´ful·ness** *n.*

joy´less *adj.* lacking joy; sad —**joy´less·ly** *adv.* —**joy´less·ness** *n.*

joy´ous *adj.* causing or expressing joy —**joy´ous·ly** *adv.* —**joy´ous·ness** *n.*

joy´stick *n.* a cursor control for playing computer games

ju´bi·lant *adj.* extremely happy; rapturous —**ju´bi·lance** *n.* —**ju´bi·lant·ly** *adv.*

ju´bi·late *vi.* to rejoice

ju·bi·la´tion *n.* rapture; a manifestation of joy

ju´bi·lee *n.* a celebration; an occasion for rejoicing

judge *n.* an officer of the court; one

appointed to arbitrate or decide the relative worth of something —*vt.* to decide after argument, as in a court of law; to form an opinion, usually based on careful study

judg·mat´ic, **judg·mat´i·cal** *adj.* judicious —**judg·mat´i·cal·ly** *adv.*

judge´ship *n.* the office and authority of a judge

judge´ment, **judg´ment** *n.* the ability to discern; the process of forming an opinion based on observation and consideration; an opinion so formed

judg·men´tal *adj.* tending to judge; relating to judgment

ju·di´cial *adj.* relating to a court of law; pronouncing judgment —**ju·di´cial·ly** *adv.*

ju·di´ciar·y *n.* the court system; those who administer justice

ju·di´cious *adj.* marked by prudence; careful; discreet; sensible —**ju·di´cious·ly** *adv.* —**ju·di´cious·ness** *n.*

ju´do *n.* a form of hand-to-hand combat developed in Japan

jug *n.* a large, rounded container with a small mouth and a handle

jug´ger·naut *n.* an overwhelming force, esp. one that seems able to destroy everything in its path

jug´gle *vt.* to keep objects in the air by alternately tossing them up and catching them; to experience difficulty holding several objects or moving between activities; to alter so as to deceive, as *to juggle the books* —**jug´gler** *n.*

jug´u·lar *adj.* about the neck or throat

juice *n.* liquid derived from plant or animal tissue —**juic´er** *n.*

juic´y *adj.* full of juice; mouthwatering; having substance or special meaning, as *a juicy story* —**juic´i·ness** *n.*

juke´box *n.* a coin-operated phonograph

ju·li·enne´ *n.* a broth containing strips of vegetable —*adj.* cut into long, thin strips

jum´ble *n.* a confusing mixture —*vt., vi.* to mix or be mixed in a haphazard fashion

jum´bo *adj.* large in size

jump *n.* a leap; the distance covered by a leap —*vi., vt.* to move or cause to move or change suddenly

jump´er *n.* one who jumps or is likely to jump; a cable used to shunt an electrical circuit; (*Brit.*) a sweater; (*US*) a loose sleeveless dress worn over a blouse

jump´i·ness *n.* nervousness

jump´suit *n.* a one–piece garment that covers the entire body

jump´y *adj.* nervous

junc´tion *n.* a place where two things meet or join, such as roads or power lines —**junc´tion·al** *adj.*

junc´ture *n.* a junction; a place where two things are joined

jun´gle *n.* a wilderness characterized by tangled undergrowth; a jumbled or confusing accumulation, as *a jungle of statutes*; an environment characterized by intense rivalry

jun´ior *adj.* younger in age; lower in rank —*n.* the younger of two; one lower in rank; a third year student

junk *n.* objects cast off; something of poor quality or meaningless —*vt.* to discard —*adj.* worthless

junk bond a high yield corporate bond that entails a high risk

junk´er *n.* an old, beat–up car

jun´ket *n.* an outing; a trip at public expense or to influence a potential benefactor —**jun´ke·teer´** *n.*

junk food snack food that lacks nutritional value

jun´ta *n.* a small group of legislators or rulers of a country, often after seizing power

ju´ral *adj.* relating to the law

ju´rat *n.* certification on an affidavit

ju·rid´ic, ju·rid´i·cal *adj.* relating to

administration of the law —**ju·rid´i·cal·ly** *adv.*

ju·ris·dic´tion *n.* the range or extent of one's authority

ju·ris·dic´tion·al *adj.* relating to the limits of one's rights or authority —**ju·ris·dic´tion·al·ly** *adv.*

ju·ris·pru´dence *n.* the science of law —**ju·ris·pru´dent** *adj., n.* —**ju·ris·pru·den´tial** *adj.*

ju´rist *n.* one experienced in the law

ju·ris´tic *adj.* relating to a jurist or to matters of the law —**ju·ris´ti·cal·ly** *adv.*

ju´ror *n.* one serving on a jury

ju´ry *n.* a group of persons sworn to hear both sides of an issue and to pass judgment

ju´ry-rig *vt.* to rig for emergency use; to improvise

just *adj.* fair and fitting; conforming to what is right; impartial —*adv.* precisely; barely —**just´ly** *adv.* —**just´ness** *n.*

jus´tice *n.* adhering to what is right or just —**jus´tice·ship** *n.*

jus·ti·fi·a·ble *adj.* able to be proved correct; warranted —**jus·ti·fi·a·bil´i·ty, jus´ti·fi·a·ble·ness** *n.* —**jus´ti·fi·a·bly** *adv.*

jus·ti·fi·ca´tion *n.* defense; explanation —**jus´ti·fi·ca·tive** *adj.*

jus´ti·fy *vt.* to prove to be correct; to absolve of blame

jut *vi., vt.* to extend or cause to extend outward

ju´ve·nile *adj.* young; relating to young people; characterized by immature behavior —**ju´ve·nile·ly** *adv.* —**ju´ve·nile·ness** *n.*

jux´ta·pose *vt.* to place side by side, especially for comparison —**jux·ta·po·si´tion** *n.* —**jux·ta·po·si´tion·al** *adj.*

k, K eleventh letter of the English alphabet

ka·lei´do·scope *n.* an optical device that produces changing colored patterns by means of small bits of glass and mirrors; something that is constantly changing —**ka·lei·do·scop´ic, ka·lei·do·scop´i·cal** *adj.* —**ka·lei·do·scop´i·cal·ly** *adv.*

kan·ga·roo´ *n.* an Australian leaping marsupial

kan´ji *n.* Japanese picture writing

ka´pok *n.* a cottonlike fiber used to stuff mattresses

ka·put´ *adj.* not working; used up or gone bad

ka·ra´te *n.* a system of self–defense that originated in Japan

kar´ma *n.* one's destiny as determined by conduct

katz´en·jam·mer *n.* a hangover; a bewildered state

kay´ak *n.* an enclosed canoe with a small opening for its occupant who propells it with a double–ended paddle

ka·zoo´ *n.* an instrument with a vibrating membrane that produces a humming sound

ke·bob´ *n.* a bit of food that is broiled or barbequed on a skewer; a shish kebob

kedge *n.* a light anchor

keel *n.* the lowest point along the length of a vessel —*vi.* to roll over

keen *adj.* sharp, as a knife blade; intelligent and perceptive; sensitive, as *a keen eye*; eager for, as *keen on sailing* —**keen´ly** *adv.* — **keen´ness** *n.*

keep *vt.* to retain as a possession; to tend or care for; to cause to continue without change; to restrain or prevent —*vi.* to continue; to remain unchanged —*n.* care or support; a stronghold, as in a castle

keep´er *n.* an overseer

keep´sake *n.* a memento

ke·fir´ *n.* a drink made from fermented cow's milk

keg *n.* a small barrel; a 100 pound measure, used for nails

keg´ler *n.* one who bowls

kelp *n.* a type of seaweed

kempt *adj.* neat; orderly

ken´nel *n.* an animal shelter; a business that boards or breeds dogs

ker´a·tin *n.* a tough protein that forms nails, horns, etc. —**ke·rat´i·nous** *adj.*

ker´chief *n.* large handkerchief worn on the head or tied around the neck; a bandanna

kerf *n.* a cut made by an axe or saw

ker´nel *n.* a grain or seed; the most significant or central part

ker´o·sene (*US*) *n.* a fuel distilled from petroleum

ketch *n.* a two–masted vessel

ket´tle *n.* a metal pot, often with a handle and a lid; a teakettle

key *n.* a notched device that fits into a hole for unlocking, winding, etc.; a critical element or clue; the pitch of a musical tone

key´board *n.* a set of keys as on a typewriter, piano, etc.

key´board·ist *n.* one who plays a piano, synthesizer, etc.

keycard *n.* a small rigid card that opens a lock by means of a coded electronic strip

key club a private club to which members gain entrance with a real or symbolic key

keynote address an opening speech that sets the theme for a meeting, conference, etc.

key´pad *n.* a device for inputting data as to a computer

key´stone *n.* the topmost stone in an arch; a fundamental element

khak´i *n.* a tannish brown color; a cloth of this color —*adj.*

kib´itz *vi.* to chat informally; to intrude; to offer unwanted advice —**kib´itz·er** *n.*

kick *n.* a sharp blow with the foot; a thrust of the foot, as in swimming or dancing; vigor or stimulation as though from a kick: *we get a kick* *from dancing —vi., vt.* to strike out with the foot

kick´back *n.* a payback for part of monies received: a bribe; a violent reaction; a backlash

kick´er *n.* one who kicks; an important contingency that may be a detraction or a benefit

kick´off *n.* a traditional or ceremonial beginning

kid *n.* the young of certain animals, especially the goat; the meat or hide of a young goat; a young person —*vi., vt.* to engage in good–natured banter —**kid´der** *n.*

kid´nap *vt.* to abduct or hold illegally, esp. for ransom —**kid´nap·er, kid´nap·per** *n.*

kid´ney *n.* one of a pair of organs that filter body fluids

kid´skin *n.* leather from the skin of a young goat

kill *vt.* to put to death; to destroy, extinguish, exhaust, or end in some way; to overwhelm: *the pace is killing me, his act killed the crowd* —*n.* the act of killing or that which has been killed, as in hunting —**kill´er** *n.*

kill´joy *n.* one who undermines the pleasure of others

kiln *n.* an oven used for baking or drying, especially to fire ceramics

kil´o·byte *n.* a computer unit equal to 1,024 bytes

kil´o·cal·o·rie *n.* a unit of potential energy contained in food; a nutritionist's calorie, commonly called a large calorie

kil´o·cy·cle *n.* one thousand cycles

ki·lom´e·ter *n.* one thousand meters —**kil·o·met´ric** *adj.*

ki·mo´no *n.* a robe–like outer garment indigenous to Japan

kin *adj.* of the same ancestry —*n.* those to whom one is related

kind *adj.* benevolent, compassionate, and humane in nature —*n.* a class or type unified by common traits; something similar, as *a kind of colonial house*

kin´der·gar·ten *n.* school for young children —**kin´der·gart·ner** *n.*

kind´heart·ed *adj.* having a kind and sympathetic nature —**kind´heart·ed·ly** *adv.* —**kind´heart·ed·ness** *n.*

kin´dle *vt., vi.* to set or catch on fire; to stimulate, as emotion —**kin´dling** *n.*

kind´ly *adj.* of a kind disposition — *adv.* pleasantly or politely —**kind´li·ness** *n.*

kind´ness *n.* the state of being kind or acting in a kind manner; a courtesy or act of charity

kin´dred *adj.* of common origins or nature

ki·net´ic *adj.* depending on or producing motion —**ki·net´i·cal·ly** *adv.*

kinetic energy the energy of a body attributable to its motion

ki·net´ics *n.* the study of the dynamics of material bodies

king *n.* a male sovereign; one superior in a particular field —*adj.* preeminent

king´dom *n.* the domain of a king; a broad domain, as *the animal kingdom*

king´ly *adj.* regal; in the manner of a king —*adv.* —**king´li·ness** *n.*

king´pin *n.* a leader; the most important person

kink *n.* a tight curl; a cramp; a quirk or impediment

kink´y *adj.* tightly curled; strange or quirky —**kink´i·ness** *n.*

kin´ship *n.* relationship by blood

ki´osk *n.* a small, free-standing structure, such as a gazebo or newsstand

kip´per *n.* a fish that has been cured by salting and smoking —*vt.* to cure by salting or smoking

kir *n.* dry white wine flavored with crème de cassis

kirk *n.* a Scottish church

kirsch *n.* a clear brandy made from fermented cherry juice

kiss *n.* an affectionate or respectful touching of the lips; a light, fleeting touch —*vi., vt.* to touch with the lips; to touch lightly —**kiss´a·ble** *adj.*

kit *n.* a collection of articles or equipment, as *a tool kit*; the container for such a collection

kitch´en *n.* an area where food is prepared; a staff or a collection of implements for preparing food

kitch·en·ette´ *n.* a small kitchen, often an adjunct to a larger eating or living area

kitch´en·ware *n.* collectively, the implements used in the preparation of food

kite *n.* a type of hawk; a light frame covered with paper that is flown in the wind; a counterfeit negotiable instrument used to obtain funds —*vt., vi.* to issue or obtain money with a counterfeit instrument

kit´ty *n.* money that has been pooled for some purpose

klep·to·ma´ni·ac *n.* one with an obsessive urge to steal regardless of need —**klep·to·ma´ni·a** *n.*

klutz *n.* one who is clumsy or lacking in social grace —**klutz´i·ness** *n.* —**klutz´y** *adj.*

knack *n.* a special talent or skill

knap´sack *n.* a sturdy bag with shoulder straps, usually for carrying camping gear

knave *n.* one of humble birth; commonly, a rascal or rogue —**knav´ish** *adj.* —**knav´ish·ly** *adv.* —**knav´ish·ness** *n.*

knav´er·y *n.* deceitful or underhanded transactions

knead *vt.* to fold and press with the hands, as dough; to massage —**knead´er** *n.*

knee *n.* the joint between the thigh and lower leg; the part of a garment that covers the knee —*vt.* to strike with the knee

knee´-jerk *adj.* involuntary, as a reaction; unthinking acceptance

kneel *vi.* to rest on one or both knees —**kneel´er** *n.*

knell *n.* the slow, solemn tolling of a bell

knick´er·bock·ers [US] *n.* full trousers that are cut off and tied just below the knee

knick´knack *n.* a small curio or ornamental piece

knife *n.* a tool consisting of a thin blade attached to a handle, used for cutting or spreading

knight *n.* a medieval high–born mounted soldier; one who champions a cause —**knight´li·ness** *n.* —**knight´ly** *adj.*

knight–er´rant *n.* a knight who seeks adventure to prove himself; an adventure–seeker

knight´hood *n.* a rank conferred by a sovereign for outstanding service

knish *n.* a savory pastry filled with potato, meat, etc. and baked or fried

knit *vt., vi.* to make by intertwining strands of yarn; to join or become joined tightly, as a bone fracture; to draw or come together in wrinkles, as a furrowed brow —**knit´ter** *n.*

knit´ting, knit´wear *n.* garments made by knitting

knob *n.* a stubby projection; a rounded handle, as on a door or drawer

knobbed *adj.* having a knob

knob´by *adj.* have the appearance of a knob, as *knobby knees*

knock *vi., vt.* to strike solidly; to collide or cause to collide; to criticize —*n.* a sharp blow

knock´off *adj.* a cheap imitation

knoll *n.* a low, rounded hill; a hillock

knot *n.* a fastener or decoration made by tying; a tight group, as of people; a tight feeling; the joint of a tree trunk from which a branch grows; one nautical mile; a speed of one nautical mile per hour —*vt.*, *vi.* to fasten with or form into a knot; to tangle or become entangled

knot′ty *adj.* snarled, as a rope; containing many knots, as a board; difficult to resolve, as a problem or puzzle

know *vt., vi.* to possess information and understanding; to comprehend —**know′a·ble** *adj.*

know′-how *n.* expertise

know′ing *adj.* knowledgeable; shrewd; secretly aware; deliberate or intentional —**know′ing·ly** *adv.* —**know′ing·ness** *n.*

knowl′edge *n.* information or awareness gained from study or experience

knowl′edge·a·ble *adj.* possessing learning or experience —**knowl′edge·a·bly** *adv.*

knuck′le *n.* a bulge formed by the bones in a joint

knurl *n.* a protuberance; small ridges employed as an aid to gripping —**knurled, knurl′y** *adj.*

ko·a′la *n.* an Australian arborial marsupial

ko′an *n.* a Zen riddle in the form of a paradox

kook *n.* an unconventional person — **kook′y** *adj.*

ko′sher *adj.* conforming to Jewish dietary laws; broadly used to describe that which is valid or legitimate

ko′to *n.* a Japanese stringed instrument

kraut *n.* sauerkraut

kris *n.* a Malaysian dagger

kryp′ton *n.* an inert gas used in fluorescent bulbs

ku′chen *n.* yeast dough coffee cake

ku′dos *n.* aclaim for achievement

küm′mel *n.* caraway seed liqueur

kum′quat *n.* a small, orange–like fruit

kung fu *n.* Chinese martial art similar to karate

l, L twelfth letter of the English alphabet

lab *n.* laboratory

la′bel *n.* a tag or stamp that serves to identify, instruct, etc.; a distinguishing appellation —*vt.* to attach or ascribe with a label —**la′bel·er, la′bel·ler** *n.*

la′bor (*US*) *n.* physical or mental effort; workers collectively; the exertion of childbirth —*vi.* to expend energy; to toil conscientiously; to move with difficulty; to experience childbirth —**la′bor·er** *n.*

lab′o·ra·to·ry *n.* a place of research or learning

la′bored (*US*) *adj.* accomplished with great effort

la′bor–inten·sive *adj.* requiring a disproportionate amount of physical labor

la·bo′ri·ous *adj.* difficult or exhausting —**la·bo′ri·ous·ly** *adv.* —**la·bo′ri·ous·ness** *n.*

la′bour (*Brit.*) *n.* physical or mental effort; workers collectively; the exertion of childbirth —*vi.* to expend energy; to toil conscientiously; to move with difficulty; to experience childbirth —**la′bour·er** *n.*

la′boured (*Brit.*) *adj.* accomplished with great effort

lab′y·rinth *n.* a maze; something intricate —**lab·y·rin′thi·an, lab·y·rin′thine** *adj.*

lace *n.* a cord used to draw together or fasten; a delicate fabric —*vt.* to put in place by threading or intertwining; to spread throughout: *a soup laced with sherry, a speech laced with technical terms* —**lace into** to assail verbally —**lac′ing** *n.*

lac·er·ate vt. to cut or tear, as flesh —adj. torn

lac·er·a'tion n. a jagged wound

lach'ry·mose adj. tearful; tending to cause tears —**lach'ry·mal** adj. —**lach·ry·mose·ly** adv. —**lach·ry·mos'i·ty** n.

lack n. a deficiency, as in substance or quality —vi., vt. to have little; to be in need of something

lack·a·dai'si·cal adj. languid; lacking spirit —**lack·a·dai'si·cal·ly** adv. —**lack·a·dai'si·cal·ness** n.

lack'ey n. a menial; a fawning attendant

lack'lus·ter adj. wanting in vitality

la·con'ic, la·con'i·cal adj. not wordy; disinclined to converse —**la·con'i·cal·ly** adv.

lac'quer n. a clear, protective coating —vt. to coat with lacquer

la·crosse' n. a type of field hockey

lac'tate vi. to produce milk

lac·ta'tion n. the production of milk in the mammary glands; the period of such production —**lac·ta'tion·al** adj.

lac'te·al adj. relating to milk —**lac'te·al·ly** adv.

lac'tic adj. relating to or derived from milk

lac·tif'er·ous adj. producing milk —**lac·tif'er·ous·ness** n.

lac'y adj. resembling lace; flimsy —**lac'i·ly** adv. —**lac'i·ness** n.

lad n. a young man

lad'der n. a framework of parallel sides joined by rungs used for climbing; an analogous means of ascent or descent: the corporate ladder

lade vt. to load with cargo; to dip or ladle, as soup

lad'en adj. weighed down; oppressed

lad'ing n. cargo

la'dle n. a deep-bowled serving spoon —vt. to serve or apportion, as with a ladle —**la'dle·ful** adj. —**la'dler** n.

la'dy n. a well-mannered woman; the female head of a household

la'dy·fin·ger n. a small oval cake

lady in waiting a female attendant

lady-killer a man who is extremely attractive to women

la'dy·like adj. having the manners or bearing of a lady

lady's maid a personal servant to a lady

lag vi. to fall behind; to falter

la'ger n. a type of beer

lag'gard n. one who falls behind; a straggler —adj. slow —**lag'gard·ly** adv. —**lag'gard·ness** n.

la·goon' n. a shallow body of water, especially near the sea

la'ic, la'i·cal adj. secular —n. a layperson

laid'-back' adj. serene or casual

lair n. an animal's den; one's habitat or domain

lais'sez-faire' n. a policy of noninterference

la'i·ty n. those who are not members of the clergy

lake n. a large inland body of water

lake'front, lake'shore, lake'side n. land along the shore of a lake

la'ma n. a Tibetan or Mongolian Buddhist monk

la'ma·ser·y n. a monastery for lamas

lam·baste' vt. to rebuke sharply; to reprimand

lame adj. disabled; halting; weak or ineffective: a lame excuse —vt. to injure so as to disable —**lame'ly** adv. —**lame'ness** n.

la·mé' n. a fabric containing metallic thread

lame'brain n. a stupid or silly person

lame duck a person in office awaiting installation of a successor

la·ment' n. an expression of sorrow or affliction —vi., vt. to express grief, sorrow, or remorse —**lam'en·ta·ble** adj. —**la·men'ta·ble·ness** n. —**lam'en·ta·bly** adv.

lam·en·ta´tion *n.* a lament

lam´i·na *n.* a thin sheet or layer — **lam´i·nal, lam´i·nar** *adj.*

lam´i·nate *n.* a thin material, often an outer covering for protection or embellishment —*vt.* to cover with a thin layer of material; to form from thin layers —**lam´i·na·tor** *n.*

lam´i·nat·ed *adj.* coated with or formed from thin layers

lam·i·na´tion *n.* the process of coating or joining; material formed from such process

lamp *n.* a device that provides light or heat

lamp´black *n.* fine carbon used as a pigment

lam·poon´ *n.* a satirical work that ridicules convention —*vt.* to satirize —**lam·poon´er, lam·poon´ist** *n.* —**lam·poon´er·y** *n.*

la·nai´ *n.* a roofed porch or patio, often enclosed

lance *n.* a weapon comprised of a long shaft with a pointed end —*vt.* to pierce, as with a pointed weapon or instrument —**lanc´er** *n.*

lan´cet *n.* a surgical knife

land *n.* a piece of property; real estate; a nation or country —*vi., vt.* to come or bring to a place — **land´less** *adj.* —**land´own·er** *n.*

land bridge dry ground that joins two land masses

land´ed *adj.* possessing property

land´fall *n.* the place where one alights after a journey by sea or air

land´fill *n.* property used for or created by depositing solid waste between layers of soil

land grant property deeded by a government, usually for a special purpose or requiring that certain conditions be met

land´hold·er *n.* a property owner

land´ing *n.* a termination, as of a sea or air voyage; a place for transferring cargo; the termination of a staircase

land´la·dy, land´lord *n.* one who owns or manages rental property

land´locked *adj.* without access to the sea

land´mark *n.* a boundary marker; a prominent feature that serves as a guide; an important building or area preserved for posterity

land´scape *n.* a scenic view —*vt.* to beautify property by contouring, planting, etc. —*vi.* to beautify property as a vocation —**land´scap·er, land´scap·ist** *n.*

lands´man *n.* one who works the land; one who is from the same area or country

lane *n.* a narrow byway; a specific channel defined for certain use: *a highway passing lane, a sea lane*

lan´guage *n.* a system of sounds, symbols, gestures, etc. by which humans and other creatures communicate

lan´guid *adj.* lacking vitality or force; sluggish —**lan´guid·ly** *adv.* —**lan´guid·ness** *n.*

lan´guish *vi.* to be or to become weak or neglected —**lan´guish·er** *n.* —**lan´guish·ing·ly** *adv.* —**lan´guish·ment** *n.*

lan´guor *n.* a lack of energy; a lethargic condition

lan´guor·ous *adj.* lacking energy; lethargic —**lan´guor·ous·ly** *adv.* — **lan´guor·ous·ness** *n.*

lank *adj.* lean and gaunt —**lank´ness** *n.* —**lank´ly** *adv.*

lank´y *adj.* tall and thin, often awkward —**lank´i·ness** *n.*

lan´tern *n.* a lamp with a protective, often decorative, case

lantern jaw a protruding lower jaw —**lantern-jawed** *adj.*

lan´yard *n.* a short rope, such as used for securing a ship's rigging or for firing a cannon; a decorative cord attached to a small utensil, such as a knife

lap *n.* the flat surface formed by the

upper legs when a person is seated; the amount by which one piece lies over another; the act or sound of taking in liquid with the tongue —*vi., vt.* to lie or cause to lie over something; to overlap; to take in or make the sound of taking in liquid with the tongue

lap belt a safety harness worn across the lap

la·pel´ *n.* an extended collar that folds back against the front of a garment

lap´i·dar·y *n.* one who finishes or deals in gems

lapse *n.* a minor, temporary fault or break; a deterioration; the termination of a right —*vi.* to deteriorate or deviate from an accepted course; to lose a right

lap´top *n.* a portable computer

lar´ce·nous *adj.* given to larceny —**lar´ce·nous·ly** *adv.*

lar´ce·ny *n.* the unlawful taking of another's property —**lar´ce·ner, lar´ce·nist** *n.*

lard *n.* rendered fat —*vt.* to prepare meat for cooking by injecting with strips of fat

lar´der *n.* a store of food; a pantry

large *adj.* of greater than average size or scope; extensive; important; significant —**large´ly** *adv.* —**large´ness** *n.*

lar·gess´ *n.* generosity; gifts given generously

lar´i·at *n.* a lasso

lark *n.* a songbird; a spontaneous escapade —**lark´er** *n.*

lark´y *adj.* spontaneous; silly

lar´va *n., pl.* **larvae** the form of an insect before metamorphosis —**lar´val** *adj.*

lar´vi·cide *n.* a poison that destroys larvae —**lar´vi·cid·al** *adj.*

la·sa´gna *n.* a baked dish comprised of wide, flat pasta layered with sauce, meat, cheese, etc.

las·civ´i·ous *adj.* lewd; arousing

sexual desire —**las·civ´i·ous·ly** *adv.* —**las·civ´i·ous·ness** *n.*

lash *n.* a whip; a sudden blow or impact; a stinging attack of words, as *a tongue-lashing*; an eyelash —*vi., vt.* to strike suddenly as if with a whip; to attack with words

lash´ing *n.* a ritualized beating; a flogging; a rope or cord used to bind or secure

lass, las´sie *n.* a young woman

las´si·tude *n.* lethargy; a feeling of apathy or fatigue

las´so *n.* a rope with a noose at one end used mainly to control livestock —*vt.* to catch with a noose or as if with a noose —**las´so·er** *n.*

last *n.* the end or one at the end —*adj., adv.* final: *last place*; the only one left: *the last honest man*; most recent but one: *last year* —*vi., vt.* to continue; to endure or persist —**last´ly** *adv.*

last hurrah a final effort

last´ing *adj.* permanent; enduring for a long time —**last´ing·ly** *adv.* —**last´ing·ness** *n.*

last name (*US*) a surname; a family name

last word the final say in a dispute; the latest or most modern

latch *n.* a catch or lock, as for a door —*vi., vt.* to close or lock as with a latch

latch´key *n.* a key for a latch or lock

latchkey child a child of working parents left at home unsupervised for at least part of the day

late *adj.* occurring after the usual or expected time; well on in time: *the late show, late in life*; recent: *late-breaking news*; former or deceased: *our late chairman, the late Mr. Jones* —*adv.* after the usual or expected time; recently —**late´ness** *n.*

late´ly *adv.* recently

lat´en *vi., vt.* to become or cause to become late

la´tent *adj.* potential, but not evident; undeveloped —**la´ten·cy** *n.* —**la´tent·ly** *adv.*

lat´er·al *adj.* to the side; sideways: *a lateral move* —**lat´er·al·ly** *adv.*

lat´est *n.* newest; most recent

lath *n.* a thin wood strip

lathe *n.* a machine for cutting and shaping wood or metal

lath´er *n.* foam —*vt., vi.* to coat or become coated with lather —**lath´er·er** *n.* —**lath´er·y** *adj.*

lat´ish *adj.* somewhat late

lat´i·tude *n.* an angular distance as from the earth's equator or a celestial body; a range in which to function, especially outside normal constraints: *a greater latitude of tolerance* —**lat·i·tu´di·nal** *adj.* —**lat·i·tu´di·nal·ly** *adv.*

lat´ke *n.* a potato pancake

la·trine´ *n.* a communal toilet

lat´ter *adj.* the second of two; nearer the end —**lat´ter·ly** *adv.*

lat´tice *n.* an open panel of crisscrossed slats of wood, metal, etc. —**lat´ticed** *adj.* —**lat´tice·work** *n.*

laud *vt.* to praise —**laud·a·bil´i·ty, laud·a´ble·ness** *n.*

laud´a·ble *adj.* worthy of praise —**laud´a·bly** *adv.* —**lau·da´tion** *n.*

laud´a·tive, lau´da·to·ry *adj.* bestowing praise —**laud·a·to´ri·ly** *adv.*

laugh *vi.* to express amusement by making an impromptu, inarticulate sound; to mock with such sounds —**laugh´er** *n.*

laugh´a·ble *adj.* disdainful —**laugh´a·ble·ness** *n.* —**laugh´a·bly** *adv.*

laugh´ing *adj.* expressing amusement —**laugh´ing·ly** *adv.*

laughing gas nitrous oxide, used as an anesthetic

laugh´ing·stock *n.* something to be ridiculed

laugh´ter *n.* the sound of laughing; sounds indicating merriment or derision

launch *vt.* to set in motion —*vi.* to begin, as a new venture

launch pad a platform and scaffold for launching a spacecraft

launch vehicle a rocket for launching a spacecraft

launch window the space of time during which a spacecraft can be launched to achieve a desired trajectory

laun´der *vt.* to wash, as clothing; to conceal or obscure, as the origin of money or information —**laun´der·er** *n.*

laun·der·ette´ *n.* a commercial self-service laundry

laun´dress, laun´dry·man *n.* one who takes in laundry

Laun´dro·mat® a launderette

laun´dry *n.* clothes to be washed; a place for washing clothes

lau´re·ate *adj.* decked with laurel; distinguished —*n.* one deserving of special honor for achievement

la´va *n.* molten rock from a volcano; the rock formed when molten rock cools and hardens

lav·a·liere´ *n.* jewelry consisting of a necklace and pendant

lav´a·to·ry *n.* a public bathroom; a washbasin with running water; a toilet

lave *vt.* to bathe

lav´ish *adj.* extravagant; profuse —*vt.* to furnish in abundance —**lav´ish·er** *n.* —**lav´ish·ly** *adv.* —**lav´ish·ness** *n.*

law *n.* a code or system of conduct established by custom or authority

law´-a·bid´ing *adj.* faithful to the law

law´break·er *n.* one who violates the law

law´ful *adj.* sanctioned by law —**law´ful·ly** *adv.* —**law´ful·ness** *n.*

law´less *adj.* not founded in law; without sanction; disregarding the constraints of law —**law´less·ly** *adv.* —**law´less·ness** *n.*

law´mak·er *n.* a legislator

law´man *n.* an officer who enforces the law

lawn *n.* a tended tract of grass

lawn tennis the game of tennis played on a grassy surface

law´suit *n.* a court action

law´yer *n.* one who gives counsel and support in legal matters

lax *adj.* slack, indifferent; not exacting or demanding —**lax´i·ty** *n.*

lax´a·tive *n.* something that causes evacuation of the bowels

lay *vt.* to place or arrange in a particular way —*adj.* of the laity; not of a particular profession

lay´a·bout *n.* a loafer

lay´er *n.* a single thickness, as of material; a hen kept for egg production —*vi., vt.* to form in layers

lay´man, lay´per·son, lay´wom·an *n.* one who is not of the clergy; an outsider, not associated with a specified profession

lay´off *n.* a suspension for lack of work; a period of inactivity

laze *vi., vt.* to loaf

la´zy *adj.* inclined to inactivity; inviting idleness: *a lazy day* —**la´zi·ly** *adv.* —**la´zi·ness** *n.*

la´zy·bones *n.* a loafer

lea *n.* a meadow

lead *vt., vi.* to guide or direct; to go first —*n.* the first position; the amount by which one is ahead; a clue or suggestion

lead´en *adj.* heavy, as lead; dull or listless, as *a leaden color* —**lead´en·ly** *adv.* —**lead´en·ness** *n.*

lead´er *n.* one who guides or is in command; one in a position of influence or importance; a strip of material that precedes or joins, as on a film strip or fishing line

lead´er (*Brit.*) *n.* a newspaper or magazine article expressing editorial opinion

lead´er·ship *n.* guidance; the capacity to guide or command

lead´-in *n.* an introduction

lead´ing *adj.* most prominent; situated at the front; designed to elicit a particular response, as *a leading question*; directing or guiding

leading edge the foremost or latest trend

leading lady, leading man the principal character in a work of fiction

lead´off *n.* an opening move; one who starts first

leaf *n.* a usually flat appendage issuing from the stem of a plant; a thin sheet of material, as *gold leaf*; a page of a book —*vi., vt.* to browse through, as papers or the pages of a book

leaf´age *n.* foliage

leaf´let *n.* a pamphlet or flier

leaf´y *adj.* having or consisting of leaves; producing leaves —**leaf´i·ness** *n.*

league *n.* an association, joined to further a common interest —*vi., vt.* to come or bring together in association

leak *n.* a small opening that allows a substance such as gas or water to escape; the substance that has escaped —*vi., vt.* to allow a substance to escape; to become known or disclosed through unauthorized channels

leak´age *n.* a substance that has escaped through a leak; the amount lost through a leak

leak´y *adj.* inclined to leak —**leak´i·ness** *n.*

lean *adj.* having little fat, as meat; thin or spare, as in body build; without excess or waste, as in business or financial matters —*vi., vt.* to incline or cause to incline —**lean´ly** *adv.* —**lean´ness** *n.*

lean´ing *n.* a tendency or preference

lean´-to *n.* a makeshift shelter; a structure with a roof that slopes from a high point on one side to the ground on the opposite side

leap *vi.*, *vt.* to jump or cause to jump or act abruptly

learn *vi.*, *vt.* to acquire knowledge or understanding; to be informed or find out; to memorize —**learn´er** *n.*

learn´ed *adj.* scholarly —**learn´ed·ly** *adv.* —**learn´ed·ness** *n.*

learn´ing *n.* knowledge or understanding acquired by study

learning curve a representation of the time needed to acquire a skill

lease *n.* a contract that grants the use of property for a fee —*vt.* to use or grant the use of property by contract —**leas´a·ble** *adj.*

lease´back *n.* a contract for leasing sold property back to the seller

lease´hold *n.* property controlled by a lease

leash *n.* a length of chain, rope, etc. used as a restraint —*vt.* to restrain

least *adj.* lowest in rank, importance, or magnitude —*adv.*

leath´er *n.* the dressed hide of an animal; a thing made from leather

leath´er·work *n.* things made from leather; decorative work on leather —**leath´er·work·er** *n.* — **leath´er·work·ing** *n.*

leath´er·y *adj.* having the texture or consistency of leather; tough — **leath´er·i·ness** *n.*

leave *n.* consent; a departure —*vt.* to depart; to abandon or overlook, as to *leave behind* or to *leave something out*

leav´en, **leav´en·ing** *n.* a substance such as yeast that causes fermentation

leav´ings *n.* the remains or residue

lech´er·y *n.* a preoccupation with sex; lust —**lech´er** *n.* —**lech´er·ous** *adj.* —**lech´er·ous·ly** *adv.* — **lech´er·ous·ness** *n.*

lec´tern *n.* a stand with a sloping top for holding a speaker's notes

lec´ture *n.* an address to a group intended to enlighten; a reprimand —*vi.*, *vt.* to expound on a subject; to deliver a series of talks; to admonish —**lec´tur·er** *n.*

lec´tur·er (*Brit.*) *n.* an educator; an instructor, especially at a college or university

le´der·ho·sen *n.* leather shorts

ledge *n.* a horizontal projection that forms a shelf

ledg´er *n.* a book for recording financial transactions

lee *n.* the side away from the wind

leech *n.* a worm that feeds on blood; a parasite —*vi.* to oneself like a parasite —*vt.* to draw off the resources of

leer *n.* a sly look expressing lust — *vi.* to view with lust or maliciousness —**leer´ing·ly** *adv.*

leer´y *adj.* wary; distrustful —**leer´i·ness** *n.*

lee´way *n.* a margin of space or latitude

left *adj.* of the left side of the body; at or toward the left

left field the left side of a baseball field as viewed from home plate; a radical view

left´ist *n.* a radical —*adj.* liberal or radical

leg *n.* a limb on a vertebrate that supports and propels; any similar appendage; the part of clothing that covers the leg; a segment, as of a journey or a contest

leg´a·cy *n.* something passed on from an ancestor or predecessor

le´gal *adj.* based on, established by, or in conformity with the law —**le´gal·ly** *adv.* —**le·gal´i·ty** *n.*

le·gal·ese´ *n.* the jargon of the legal profession

le´gal·ism *n.* overly strict interpretation or adherence to the law —**le´gal·is´tic** *adj.* —**le·gal·is´ti·cal·ly** *adv.*

le´gal·ize *vt.* to make legal; to sanction by law —**le·gal·i·za´tion** *n.*

legal pad a writing tablet of ruled sheets, 8½ x 14 inches

le´gal–size *adj.* of paper that is 8½ x 14 inches; an envelope, folder, etc. sized to hold legal paper

legal tender currency authorized and that must be accepted for the payment of debts

leg´end *n.* a popular, often heroic, fable; a celebrated individual or deed; an inscription

leg´end·ar·y *adj.* of the nature of a legend; celebrated

leg´er·de·main´ *n.* sleight of hand; trickery

leg´gy *adj.* having long legs

leg´i·ble *adj.* clear; able to be read — **leg·i·bil´i·ty, leg´i·ble·ness** *n.* — **leg´i·bly** *adv.*

le´gion *n.* a large number; a multitude

leg´is·late *vi., vt.* to write or enact laws —**leg´is·la·tor** *n.* —**leg·is·la·to´ri·al** *adj.*

leg·is·la´tion *n.* a law or set of laws

leg´is·la·tive *adj.* of a governing body; of the making of law —**leg´is·la·tive·ly** *adv.*

leg´is·la·ture *n.* a governing body charged with the making of laws

le·git´ *adj.* legitimate

le·git´i·mate *adj.* complying with the law or recognized standards; reasonable or logical: *a legitimate objection, a legitimate conclusion* — **le·git´i·ma·cy** *n.* —**le·git´i·mate·ly** *adv.*

leg´man *n.* one whose job it is to gather information, run errands, etc. for others

leg´room *n.* space to stretch the legs; room in which to act or maneuver

leg´ume *n.* a pod, as of a bean, that splits to reveal seeds —**le·gu´mi·nous** *adj.*

lei *n.* a crown or wreath of flowers

lei´sure *n.* time free of pressing obligations

lei´sure·ly *adj.* characterized by an unhurried or deliberate pace

—*adv.* in an unhurried way —**lei´sure·li·ness** *n.*

lemon law a law that provides for the repair or replacement of defective products, especially of motor vehicles

lend *vt.* to permit the temporary use of; to offer or impart, as *to lend a sense of security* —**lend´er** *n.*

length *n.* a measure of distance or duration from beginning to end — **go to great length** to make a significant effort; do all that is necessary

length´en *vi., vt.* to become or make longer

length´y *adj.* somewhat long in duration; longer than seems necessary —**length´i·ly** *adv.* — **length´i·ness** *n.*

le´ni·ent *adj.* indulgent; not strict — **le´nience, le´nien·cy** *n.* —**le´ni·ent·ly** *adv.*

lens *n.* transparent material that has been shaped to bend light rays so as to form an image

le´o·nine *adj.* having lion–like qualities

le´o·tard *n.* a close-fitting one–piece garment worn by gymnasts, dancers, etc.

lep´er *n.* one afflicted with leprosy; one shunned as though afflicted — **lep´er·ous** *adj.*

lep´re·chaun *n.* a fairy cobbler of Irish folklore

lep´ro·sy *n.* a mildly contagious tropical disease that can cause paralysis, numbness, and deformity —**lep·rot´ic** *adj.*

lep´rous *adj.* having leprosy —**lep´rous·ly** *adv.* —**lep´rous·ness** *n.*

les´bi·an *n.* a homosexual woman — **les´bi·an·ism** *n.*

le´sion *n.* a wound or abrasion

less, less´er *adj.* smaller or not as important

les·see´ *n.* one who leases from another

less´en *vt., vi.* to make or become less

les´son *n.* something learned or to be learned; a formal course of instruction; a part of a course of instruction

les´sor *n.* one who leases to another

let *vt.* to permit or allow; to rent or lease —*vi.* to be rented or leased

let´down *n.* disappointment

le´thal *adj.* harmful; able to cause death —**le´thal·ly** *adv.*

le·thar´gic, le·thar´gi·cal *adj.* sluggish; listless; apathetic —**le·thar´gi·cal·ly** *adv.*

leth´ar·gy *n.* dullness; apathy

let´ter *n.* a written symbol; a written communication

letter bomb an explosive device sent through the mail

let´tered *adj.* learned; inscribed with letters

let´up *n.* a pause or lull

leu·ke´mi·a *n.* a disease of the blood

lev´ee *n.* an embankment along a river or around an irrigated field to prevent runoff

lev´el *n.* a relative ranking: *a level of understanding, the upper level of management;* a flat surface; any of a variety of devices for determining deviation from the horizontal — *adj.* having the same relative ranking; determined to be horizontal —*vt.* to make horizontal or flat; to measure deviation from the horizontal, as with a surveyor's instrument —**on the level** honest; fair —**lev´el·ly** *adv.*

lev´el·head´ed *adj.* having common sense —**lev´el·head´ed·ly** *adv.* — **lev´el·head´ed·ness** *n.*

lev´er *n.* a simple machine used to transfer energy, composed of a rigid rod pivoting on a fulcrum; a protruding handle

lev´er·age *n.* an advantage, as provided by a lever; political or financial prominence or power

leveraged buyout the use of a company's own assets to finance debt incurred in its acquisition

le·vi´a·than *n.* a monster; an exceptionally large specimen

lev´i·tate *vi., vt.* to float or cause to float in the air with no visible means of support —**lev·i·ta´tion** *n.* —**lev·i·ta´tion·al** *adj.* —**lev´i·tator** *n.*

lev´i·ty *n.* frivolity; flippancy

lev´y *vt.* to assess and collect, as taxes or fines —*n.* monies collected

lewd *adj.* obscene; depraved —**lewd´ly** *adv.* —**lewd´ness** *n.*

lex·i·cog´ra·phy *n.* the work or method of compiling a dictionary —**lex·i·cog´ra·pher** *n.* —**lex´i·cograph´ic, lex·i·co·graph´i·cal** *adj.* —**lex·i·co·graph´i·cal·ly** a*dv.*

lex´i·con *n.* a dictionary; a collection of terms peculiar to a particular discipline

li·a·bil´i·ty *n.* a debt or obligation for which one is responsible

li´a·ble *adj.* legally responsible; at risk: *you are liable to get hurt;* extremely likely: *if I see it, I'm liable to eat it*

li´ai·son *n.* a connection or link, especially for communication between groups; one who serves as a link: *the company liaison with the press;* a clandestine affair

li´ar *n.* one who deceives by lying

li·ba´tion *n.* a beverage —**li·ba´tionar·y** *adj.*

li´bel *n.* in law, a malicious falsehood, written or printed, that defames —*vt.* —**li´bel·er** *n.*

li´bel·ous, li´bel·lous *adj.* based on libel —**li´bel·ous·ly, li´bel·lous·ly** *adv.*

lib´er·al *adj.* open to new ideas and concepts; not strict; lavish in gift giving —**lib´er·al·ly** *adv.* —**lib´eral·ness** *n.*

lib´er·al·ize *vi., vt.* to become or make more liberal: *we need*

lib·er·al·i·za´tion *n.*
liberalize out trade policies —**lib·er·al·i·za´tion** *n.*

lib´er·ate *vt.* to set free, as from bondage or onerous convention — **lib´er·a·tor** *n.*

lib·er·a´tion *n.* the act of freeing or being set free; the process of seeking equal rights or status — **lib·er·a´tion·ist** *n.*

lib·er·tar´i·an *n.* one who believes in freedom of the individual from government intervention

lib´er·tine *n.* one who lacks a sense of moral restraint; a reprobate — **lib´er·tin·ism** *n.*

lib´er·ty *n.* freedom from restraint or restriction; certain rights granted by custom or legislation

li·bid´i·nous *adj.* displaying lust; salacious —**li·bid´i·nous·ly** *adv.* — **li·bid´i·nous·ness** *n.*

li·bi´do *n.* the energy associated with inherent biological impulses; sexual appetite —**li·bid´i·nal** *adj.* —**li·bid´i·nal·ly** *adv.*

li´brar·y *n.* a collection, as of printed matter, sound or video recordings, computer programs, etc.; the place where such a collection is kept — **li·brar´i·an** *n.*

li·bret´to *n.* words set to music or a publication containing those words, such as for an opera —**li·bret´tist** *n.*

li´cence (*Brit.*) *n.* legal authorization or a document attesting to such authorization; lack of restraint or adherence to common practice — **li´cense** *vt.* to grant authorization to or for something; to formally permit

li´cense (*US*) *n.* legal authorization or a document attesting to such authorization; lack of restraint or adherence to common practice — *vt.* to grant authorization to or for something; to formally permit — **li´cens·a·ble** *adj.* —**li´cens·er**, **li´cen·sor** *n.* —**li´cens·ee´** *n.*

li·cen´tious *adj.* lacking restraint or regard for accepted morality —**li·cen´tious·ly** *adv.* —**li·cen´tious·ness** *n.*

lic´it *adj.* legal

lick *n.* the act of stroking or touching with, or as with, the tongue; a small amount: *he hasn't a lick of sense*; a blow: *get in your licks* — *vt.* to stroke with the tongue; to touch, as with the tongue: *flames licked the walls*; to overcome: *lick the problem*; to punish by striking

lick´ing *n.* a spanking; a hard loss: *the team took a licking*

lid *n.* a cover for a container

lie *n.* something meant to deceive; the manner in which something is positioned —*vi.* to pass on false information or create a false impression; to recline; to be in a certain place: *the river lies between two hills*

lien *n.* the right to property as security for a debt

lieu·ten´ant *n.* an officer in a military or quasi-military organization; a deputy or assistant who may act in place of a superior —**lieu·ten´an·cy** *n.*

life *n.* the condition of a functioning creature; the time, or any portion of the time, between birth and death; a group of living things, as *plant life*; a particular segment of one's existence, as *social life, artistic life*

life´-and–death´ *adj.* critical

life cycle the stages of development of a living creature

life expectancy statistically, the length of time a creature can be expected to live

life´less *adj.* dead; inanimate; lacking spirit —**life´less·ly** *adv.* —**life´less·ness** *n.*

life´like *adj.* precisely imitating life: *a lifelike portrait*

life´sav·er *n.* a person or thing that

serves in a crisis

life style a mode of living that reflects the values of an individual or group

lift *vi.* to rise; to disperse: *the ban was lifted* —*vt.* to raise; to give a ride to; to steal —*n.* an instance of rising; a ride offered a pedestrian; a rise in condition or attitude

lift (*Brit.*) *n.* a structure for raising or lowering people or freight, as in a building; an elevator

lig´a·ment *n.* connective tissue of the body; any connective bond — **lig´a·men´ta·ry, lig´a·men´tous** *adj.*

lig´a·ture *n.* a cord, thread, bandage, etc. that serves to unite or bind; a symbol created from two or more characters, such as æ

light *n.* illumination, or its source; clarification: *shed new light*; a source of fire —*vi.* to give off illumination; to start to burn; to dismount, as from a vehicle —*vt.* to cause to give off light; to cause to start to burn —*adj.* illuminated; of color that is less dark; relatively little, as of weight: *a light load*, quantity: *light rain*, force: *a light slap*, etc.; insubstantial: *a light step, light armor* —*adv.*

light´en *vi., vt.* to become or make brighter; to become or make less heavy or oppressive

light´-fin·gered *adj.* inclined to steal; adept at petty theft

light´head´ed *adj.* giddy or faint — **light´head´ed·ly** *adv.* —**light´-head´ed·ness** *n.*

light´heart·ed *adj.* free of care — **light´heart·ed·ly** *adv.* —**light´heart·ed·ness** *n.*

light´ing *n.* the style or fixtures for artificial illumination; the light provided

light´ly *adv.* with little exertion; delicately; in a free and easy way

light´ning *n.* a natural electric discharge or the flash it makes —*adj.* quick or abrupt

light pen an input device for a computer

light show a brilliant display of laser light

light table a glass–topped table illuminated from below, used to view and work with film, etc.

light´weight *n.* a weight class in sports, as boxing; a person lacking in knowledge, ability, etc. —*adj.* relatively light in substance or weight: *a lightweight sweater*

light´-year *n.* the distance traveled by light in one earth year

lig´ne·ous *adj.* resembling wood

like *vt.* to enjoy or be inclined toward —*vi.* to show preference for —*n.* a preference —*adj.* similar — *prep.* in the same or a similar manner —**lik´a·ble, like´a·ble** *adj.* — **lik´a·ble·ness, like´a·ble·ness** *n.*

like´li·hood *n.* probability

like´ly *adj.* possible or believable

like´-mind´ed *adj.* in agreement

lik´en *vt.* to compare

like·ness *n.* a representation, as a portrait or bust

like´wise *adj.* also: *we are likewise interested in the painting*

lik´ing *n.* a fondness or preference

lilt *n.* a light, cheerful style of speech or song; a jaunty walk —*vi., vt.* to speak or sing in a light, cheerful style

limb *n.* an appendage, as the branch of a tree or extremity of an animal

lim´ber *adj.* flexible; supple —**lim´ber·ly** *adv.* —**lim´ber·ness** *n.*

limber up to flex or make flexible, as a warm–up before heavy exercise

lime´light *n.* a center of attention (from an early stage light produced by heating lime)

lim´er·ick *n.* a light verse of five lines with the rhyming sequence *aabba*

lim´it *n.* the boundary of an area;

restriction or condition; an amount that may not be exceeded: *to the limit of our ability* —*vt.* to confine within a boundary; to firmly establish, as a requisite —**lim′it·a·ble** *adj.*

lim·i·ta′tion *n.* a restriction; a deficiency

lim′it·ed *adj.* restricted or deficient in some way: *a limited victory*; cramped or confined —*n.* a train that makes only express stops

limited edition a work of which only a specified number of copies are produced, as of literature or art, often signed by the maker

limited war a conflict to achieve a specific goal short of total conquest

lim′it·ing *adj.* serving to limit

lim′it·less *adj.* unbounded; without limit; infinite —**lim′it·less·ly** *adj.* —**lim′it·less·ness** *n.*

lim′o, lim′ou·sine *n.* a large, elegant automobile, usually chauffeur-driven

limp *n.* a hesitant or hobbling gait — *vi.* to move haltingly: *despite cutbacks, we limped along with the remaining staff*; to hobble —*adj.* lacking rigidity; lacking strength or vigor: *a limp handshake* —**limp′ly** *adv.* —**limp′ness** *n.*

lim′pid *adj.* of a clear and serene liquid, as *a limpid pool*; logical and lucid, as *a limpid account* —**lim′pid·ly** *adv.* —**lim′pid·ness** *n.*

line *n.* a stripe made by a writing instrument; any similar mark; a real or imaginary stripe between fixed points: *a firing line*; things formed in a row or a series; a sequence; the material used to form a connection: *phone line*, *electric line*; a transportation system; an area of competence or employment: *a line of work*; a row of words or symbols; a brief note; a concept or notion: *thinking along*

another line —*vt.* to cover the interior: *to line a jacket*

lin′e·age *n.* ancestry

lin′e·al *adj.* directly descended from an ancestor; relating to a particular lineage —**lin′e·al·ly** *adv.*

lin′e·ar *adj.* in a line; one–dimensional —**lin′e·ar·ly** *adv.*

lin′en *n.* cloth or articles made from flax thread —*adj.* made of or resembling linen

linen closet a storage area for bedding, tablecloths, etc.

lin′er *n.* material that covers the inside, as of a coat; a large passenger ship or airplane

lines′man *n.* a sports official who judges from the sideline

line′up *n.* persons assembled for identification; a group of people identified with a common purpose: *a lineup of backers, a lineup of players*

lin′ger *vi.* to remain longer than anticipated; to be slow to act —**lin′ger·er** *n.* —**lin′ger·ing·ly** *adv.*

lin·ge·rie′ *n.* women's underclothing

lin′go *n.* an unfamiliar or specialized language or vocabulary

lin′guist *n.* one who speaks several languages; an authority in linguistics

lin·guis′tics *n.* the study of human speech —**lin·guis′tic** *adj.* —**lin·guis′ti·cal·ly** *adv.*

lin′i·ment *n.* a liquid rubbed on the skin to relieve pain or tension

lin′ing *n.* material that covers the inside, as of a coat

link *n.* one of a series: *a link in a chain*; a connector: *a communications link* —*vi., vt.* to connect

linked *adj.* connected in some way

li·no′le·um *n.* a durable floor covering

lint *n.* bits of fiber shed from woven material; downy fibers from linen, used to dress wounds —**lint′y** *adj.*

lin′tel *n.* the brace at the top of a

window or door frame

li´on *n.* a large carniverous feline; a person distinguished for bravery; a celebrity

li´on·heart·ed *adj.* extremely brave —**li´on·heart·ed·ness** *n.*

li´on·ize *vt.* to treat as a celebrity —**li·on·i·za´tion** *n.*

lip *n.* the fleshy structure surrounding the mouth; a part that surrounds an opening; impertinent speech

lip service professed agreement without supporting action

liq´ue·fy *vi., vt.* to become or make liquid

li·queur´ *n.* an alcoholic beverage, usually sweet and flavored with fruit, herbs, or spices

liq´uid *adj.* flowing or capable of flowing; of assets readily convertible into cash —**li·quid´i·ty** *n.*

liq´ui·date *vt.* to discharge, as an obligation; to convert into cash; to destroy —*vi.* to close out a business, etc. by disposing of its assets; —**liq´ui·da´tion** *n.* —**liq´ui·da·tor** *n.*

li´quor (*US*) *n.* a distilled alcoholic beverage; liquid obtained from cooking

lisle *n.* a fine cotton fabric

lisp *n.* a speech defect typified by difficulty in articulating the sounds of s and z —*vi., vt.* to speak with a lisp —**lisp´er** *n.*

list *n.* a catalog or roster of items, as for shopping, things to do, etc.; a tilting to one side —*vt.* to itemize; to cause to tilt —*vi.* to tilt to one side

lis´ten *n.* to be attentive; to heed —**lis´ten·er** *n.*

lis·ten·a·ble *adj.* reasonably pleasing to the ear: *despite its flaws the recording is listenable* —**lis·ten·a·bil´i·ty** *n.*

list´less *adj.* lacking vitality or spirit; apathetic, indifferent —**list´less·ly**

adv. —**list´less·ness** *n.*

list price the selling price of an item as recommended by the manufacturer

lit´a·ny *n.* a responsive prayer; something often repeated: *a litany of acclamation*

li´ter (*US*) *n.* a unit of volume equal to approximately 33.8 ounces

lit´er·a·cy *n.* education, as the ability to read and write

lit´er·al *adj.* precise in interpretation; verbatim —**lit´er·al·ness** *n.*

lit´er·al·ly *adv.* precisely; word for word

lit´er·ar·y *adj.* relating to or fond of literature —**lit´er·ar·i·ly** *adv.* —**lit´er·ar·i·ness** *n.*

lit´er·ate *adj.* educated; well-informed —**lit´er·ate·ly** *adv.* —**lit´er·ate·ness** *n.*

lit·e·ra´ti *n. pl.* cultivated or well-educated people collectively

lit´er·a·ture *n.* printed matter; a collection of writings

lithe, lithe´some *adj.* supple or graceful —**lithe´ly, lithe´some·ly** *adv.* —**lithe´ness, lithe´some·ness** *n.*

lith´o·graph *n.* a print made by lithography —*vt.* to print by lithography —**lith´o·graph´ic, lith·o·graph´i·cal** *adj.* —**lith·o·graph´i·cal·ly** *adv.*

li·thog´ra·phy *n.* a process for printing fine reproductions —**li·thog´ra·pher** *n.*

lit´i·gant *n.* one involved in a lawsuit —*adj.* engaged in a lawsuit

lit´i·gate *vi., vt.* to take part in or bring about legal action —**lit´i·ga·ble** *adj.* —**lit·i·ga´tion** *n.* —**lit´i·ga·tor** *n.*

li·ti´gious *adj.* tending to be involved in legal action —**li·ti´gious·ly** *adv.* —**li·ti´gious·ness** *n.*

litmus test a chemical test using litmus to determine acidity; a test that uses a single determinant to reach a conclusion

li´tre (*Brit*.) *n*. a unit of volume equal to approximately 33.8 US ounces

lit´ter *n*. heedlessly discarded trash; the animal young from a single birth; material used to line the cage of an animal; a framework for transporting goods or a person — *vi*., *vt*. to scatter, as trash

lit´tle *n*. a small amount —*adj*. modest in size or amount; unimportant —*adv*. slightly; not at all —**lit´tle·ness** *n*.

little theater an experimental theater or community playhouse

lit´ur·gy *n*. a set form for worship or ritual —**li·tur´gi·cal** *adj*. —**li·tur´gi·cal·ly** *adv*.

liv´a·ble, live´a·ble *adj*. suitable for habitation; acceptable or tolerable —**liv´a·ble·ness, live´a·ble·ness** *n*.

live *vi*. to possess life; to exist —*adj*. having life; useable, having potential, as *live ammunition, live wires, live copy*; physically present, as *a live show, a live audience*

live´-in *adj*. having lodging in one's place of employment; living with another

live´li·hood *n*. one's means of support

live´ly *adj*. marked by energy and spirit; active: *a lively imagination* —*adv*. —**live´li·ness** *n*.

liv´en *vi*., *vt*. to become or make lively

liv´er·ied *adj*. uniformed

liv´er·wurst *n*. a sausage made of ground liver

liv´er·y *n*. a uniform; the care and boarding of horses; a service that rents out vehicles, such as boats or automobiles

live´stock *n*. domestic animals

live wire *n*. an electric wire attached to a power source; a person who is dynamic or energetic

liv´id *adj*. extremely angry —**li·vid´i·ty, liv´id·ness** *n*. —**liv´id·ly** *adv*.

liv´ing *adj*. having life or existence; pertaining to existence: *living conditions* —*n*. the condition of being alive; the means to support life

living wage earnings sufficient to provide the necessities of life

living will *n*. a will stipulating action to be taken if the maker is alive but unable to respond on his or her own behalf

load *n*. weight or volume that is carried, supported, etc.; a burden of work or responsibility —*vi*., *vt*. to put or place into or on

load´ed *adj*. having or carrying a full load; having a troublesome or hidden meaning

loaf *n*. an oblong mass, as *a loaf of bread* or *meat loaf*

loaf´er *n*. one who is frequently inactive or unemployed —**loaf** *vi*.

loan *n*. something given or received for temporary use —**loan´er** *n*.

loan shark one who lends money at a high rate of interest

loath *adj*. hesitant or reluctant

loathe *vt*. to despise —**loath´er** *n*. —**loath´ing·ly** *adv*.

loath´ing *n*. profound aversion

loath´some *adj*. arousing intense dislike —**loath´some·ly** *adv*. —**loath´some·ness** *n*.

lob´by (*US*) *n*. an entryway or waiting room; persons attempting to influence others to support a cause — *vi*., *vt*. to attempt to influence, as legislators —**lob´by·ist** *n*.

lo´cal *adj*. of a specific, relatively small area or political subdivision; contained, not widespread —*n*. a regional chapter of a lodge, labor union, etc.; a train that stops at every station —**lo´cal·ly** *adv*.

lo·cale´ *n*. a location, as a site or setting for an event

lo·cal´i·ty *n*. a particular place

lo´cal·ize *vt*. to restrict to a particular area —**lo·cal·i·za´tion** *n*.

local option a provision of a law

that permits a local jurisdiction to adopt or reject enforcement within its jurisdiction

lo·cate *vi.* to situate, as a home or business —*vt.* to learn the position of; to assign to a place —**lo·cat´a·ble** *adj.* —**lo·cat´er** *n.*

lo·ca´tion *n.* a place or position; a place designated for a specific use

lock *n.* a device or means of securing; a closed section of a channel where the water level can be raised or lowered to match the level of the next section; a piece of hair —*vi.*, *vt.* to become or make secure, as with a lock; to become or make immobile; to link together

lock´er *n.* a storage compartment

lock´et *n.* a small hinged case haning on a necklace

lock´out *n.* the closing of a workplace to striking employees

lo·co·mo´tion *n.* the act of moving from one place to another

lo·co·mo´tive *adj.* able to move from place to place —*n.* a self-proprelled engine

lo·cu´tion *n.* a manner of speech

lode *n.* a mineral deposit; an abundant source

lodge *n.* a rustic dwelling; a meeting hall —*vi.*, *vt.* to temporarily live in or provide living space; to place or plant, as for safekeeping

lodg´ing *n.* a place to live, usually temporary —**lodg´er** *n.*

loft *n.* a large, open storage area directly under the roof of a building; a gallery or alcove: *choir loft*

loft´y *adj.* tall or towering; arrogant or haughty —**loft´i·ly** *adv.* —**loft´i·ness** *n.*

log *n.* a roughly trimmed tree trunk or large branch; a record, as of performance or progress —*vt.* to set down in writing; to accumulate, as time or distance: *logged 2000 miles on the trip*

log´book *n.* a book for recording

official data relating to the operation of a ship, aircraft, etc.

loge *n.* the front rows of the mezzanine or a box in a theater

log´ic *n.* the fundamentals of reasoning, without regard to content or effectiveness; sound reasoning; the comparable functions in a computer program

log´i·cal *adj.* capable of analytical thought; reasonable, based on the information available —**log·i·cal´i·ty, log´i·cal·ness** *n.* —**log´i·cal·ly** *adv.*

lo·gis´tics *n.* planning and managing the details of an operation

lo´go, log´o·type *n.* the symbol or trademark of a business or organization

lo´gy *adj.* lethargic; muddled, as though awakening from sleep

loi´ter *vi.* to loll or linger about; to waste time —**loi´ter·er** *n.* —**loi´ter·ing·ly** *adv.*

loll *vi.* to move or lie about in a relaxed fashion —**loll´ing·ly** *adv.*

lone *adj.* without anyone or anything else; lacking companionship

lone´ly *adj.* saddened by being alone; deserted: *a lonely wasteland* —**lone´li·ly** *adv.* —**lone´li·ness** *n.*

lon´er *n.* one who works alone or shuns the company of others

lone´some *adj.* lonely —**lone´some·ly** *adv.* —**lone´some·ness** *n.*

lone wolf one who works alone; one who avoids the company of others

long *vi.* to have a craving or desire —*adj.* relatively lengthy, as of distance, height, time, etc.; of specific length or duration: *six inches long, two hours long* —*adv.*

lon·gev´i·ty *n.* long life or duration —**lon·ge´vous** *adj.*

long face a gloomy expression

long´hair *n.* one with a refined taste in art, especially music —**long´hair, long´haired** *adj.*

long´hand *n.* cursive writing

long haul a significant length of time or distance —**long´-haul´** adj.

long´ing n. a craving or desire —**long´ing·ly** adv.

lon´gi·tude n. an angular distance, as from the prime meridian or a celestial body

lon·gi·tu´di·nal adj. of longitude; running lengthwise —**lon·gi·tu´di·nal·ly** adv.

long´-last´ing, long´-lived´ adj. continuing a long time

long´-range´ adj. of a long span of time or distance: long-range planning

long´shore·man n. a dock worker

long shot a venture that holds little prospect of success

long´-stand´ing adj. lasting; of long duration

long´-suf´fer·ing adj. uncomplaining; patiently enduring hardship —**long´-suf´fer·ing·ly** adv.

long suit one's greatest asset

long´-term adj. involving an extended span of time: long-term planning

long´-wind·ed adj. wordy or tiresome —**long´-wind·ed·ly** adv. — **long´-wind·ed·ness** n.

loo´fa, loo´fah n. the dried spongelike part of the fruit of a tropical vine, used for cleansing the skin

look n. a gaze, stare, glance, etc.; appearance or fashion —vi. to use eyesight; to occupy one's attention: look after the dog; to seek out or search; to appear to be: look happy —vt. to turn one's eyes to; to appear to be: looks the part

loom vi. to appear and hover over; to menace

loon, loo´ny n. a foolish or insane person

loo´ny adj. foolish or insane

loop n. a length of material formed into a circular pattern; the shape so described; a circle —vi., vt. to form or fasten into a circle; to move in a circular pattern — **looped** adj.

loop´hole n. an oversight, as in the law, that provides a means of escape or avoidance

loose adj. not attached or confined; poorly attached or fitted: a loose screw, loose clothing; lacking discipline: loose morals; vague: a loose interpretation —vi. vt. to become or make less restrained; to release —**loose´ly** adv. —**loose´ness** n.

loose end an unresolved detail

loos´en vi., vt. to become or make loose or looser

loot n. stolen goods —vi., vt. to plunder —**loot´er** n.

lop vt. to cut off or eliminate

lope n. a leisurely gait —vi.

lop´sid·ed adj. bulkier or heavier on one side; tipped to one side —**lop´sid·ed·ly** adv. —**lop´sid·ed·ness** n.

lo·qua´cious adj. talkative —**lo·qua´cious·ly** adv. —**lo·qua´cious·ness, lo·quac´i·ty** n.

lord n. one of high rank or power; a god —vi. to domineer

lord´ly adj. majestic or noble; pretentious or arrogant; domineering —**lord´li·ness** n.

lore n. collected traditions or wisdom, as of a culture; knowledge

lor·gnette´ n. corrective lenses mounted on a short handle

lose vt. to be deprived of, as through carelessness, theft, or legal action; unable to keep: lose one's life, lose respect; to rid oneself of: lose weight, lose a pursuer —vi. to endure loss —**los´er** n.

loss n. deprivation; something taken away, misplaced, wasted, etc.

loss leader something offered at a low price to attract customers

lost adj. no longer in one's possession; no longer in evidence

lot n. a group of associated things; a large amount; one of a quantity of tokens used for selecting at random; one's fate as though chosen by lot; a plot or parcel of land, especially one occupied by or intended for a residence

lo´tion *n.* a liquid applied externally as medication or cosmetic

lot´ter·y *n.* a selection made by lot

loud *adj.* designating of high amplification; of bright colors or glaringly bad design, as clothing —**loud´ly** *adv.* —**loud´ness** *n.*

loud´en *vi., vt.* to become or make louder

loud´mouth *n.* one who speaks loudly or thoughtlessly —**loud´ mouthed** *adj.*

lounge *n.* a waiting room; a tavern or café attached to a hotel or restaurant; a type of couch with no back and a headrest at one end —*vi., vt.* to recline or pass time leisurely —**loung´er** *n.*

loupe *n.* a small, powerful magnifying glass used by printers, jewelers, etc.

louse *n.* a tiny, parasitic insect; a disreputable person —*vt.* to botch or fumble

lous´y *adj.* infested, as with lice; of poor quality or taste; unpleasant —**lous´i·ly** *adv.* —**lous´i·ness** *n.*

lout *n.* one regarded as ill-mannered or tiresome —**lout´ish** *adj.* —**lout´ish·ly** *adv.* —**lout´ish·ness** *n.*

lou´ver *n.* an opening for ventilation having angled slats to keep out rain

lov´a·ble, love´a·ble *adj.* having qualities that invite affection —**lov´a·bil´i·ty, lov´a·ble·ness** *n.* —**lov´a·bly** *adv.*

love *n.* a strong attraction brought about by affection or desire; an object of affection or desire; sexual intercourse —*vt.* to have an affection or desire for; to engage in sexual intercourse

love affair an intimate relationship; a strong attraction: *America's love affair with the automobile*

love child a child born out of wedlock

love feast a symbolic meal intended to promote friendship

love´-in *n.* a symbolic gathering intended to promote love and understanding

love´lorn *adj.* deprived of love or a lover

love´ly *adj.* beautiful and charming; something attractive or appealing —*adv.* —**love´li·ness** *n.*

lov´er *n.* one who is devoted to another person, activity, etc.; a sexual partner

love seat a seat for two people

love´sick *adj.* distracted by love — **love´sick·ness** *n.*

lov´ing *adj.* affectionate —**lov´ing·ly** *adv.*

loving cup a decorative urn, often one given as an award

low *adj.* of less than usual or acceptable height, amount, quality, etc. —*adv.*

low´ball *vi., vt.* to understate or underbid —*adj.*

low blow an unfair or unprincipled attack

low´born *adj.* of humble birth

low´boy *n.* a low chest of drawers

low´bred *adj.* unrefined

low´brow *n.* one having unrefined tastes —*adj.* suited to an unrefined person

low´-budg´et *adj.* produced at little cost; inferior, second-rate

low´-cal´ *adj.* having less than the normal amount of calories

low comedy burlesque or slapstick comedy

low´down *n.* gossip; latest information

low´-down *adj.* base; contemptible

low´-end *adj.* among the lowest in price or quality

low´er *adj.* less in price, quality,

position, etc. —*n.* a menacing look —*vi., vt.* to become or make less; to appear or look menacing —**low˝er·ing·ly** *adv.*

lowest common denominator the lowest number evenly divisible by a group of fractions; that which is understood or accepted by most of the people in a population

low˝-grade˝ *adj.* of poor quality

low˝-key˝ *adj.* restrained; subdued

low˝-lev˝el *adj.* of little importance, intensity, etc.

low˝life *n.* a disreputable person

low˝ly *adj.* unpretentious; humble in nature or rank —*adv.* —**low˝li·ness** *n.*

low˝-pres·sure *adj.* relaxed; easygoing

low˝-pro˝file *adj.* of a deed or activity performed quietly so as to avoid undue attention

low˝-spir·it·ed *adj.* depressed; lacking vitality —**low˝-spir·it·ed·ly** *adv.* —**low˝-spir·it·ed·ness** *n.*

low-tech, low-technology *adj.* of a device, system, etc. that does not employ or require a modern system or technique

low˝-tick˝et *adj.* relatively inexpensive

lox *n.* smoked salmon

loy˝al *adj.* marked by allegiance to a person, organization, etc.; faithful —**loy˝al·ist** *n.* —**loy˝al·ly** *adv.* —**loy˝al·ty** *n.*

loz˝enge *n.* a medicated candy

lu˝au *n.* a traditional Hawaiian feast

lube *vt.* to lubricate

lu˝bri·cate *vt.* to apply a substance to moving parts to reduce friction —**lu˝bri·cant** *n.* —**lu·bri·ca˝tion** *n.*

lu˝cent *adj.* clear or transparent; luminous —**lu˝cen·cy** *n.* —**lu˝cent·ly** *adv.*

lu˝cid *adj.* clear; easily understood; sane or rational —**lu·cid˝i·ty, lu˝cid·ness** *n.* —**lu˝cid·ly** *adv.*

luck *n.* the chance events that act

upon one's life

luck˝i·ly *adv.* by good fortune

luck˝y *adj.* having or bringing good fortune —**luck˝i·ness** *n.*

lu˝cra·tive *adj.* profitable —**lu˝cra·tive·ly** *adv.* —**lu˝cra·tive·ness** *n.*

lu˝cre *n.* money

lu˝di·crous *adj.* incongruous; laughable —**lu˝di·crous·ly** *adv.* —**lu˝di·crous·ness** *n.*

lug *vi., vt.* to pull or carry with difficulty

luge *n.* a racing sled

lug˝gage *n.* bags for carrying a traveler's personal effects; all of the effects carried by a traveler

lu·gu˝bri·ous *adj.* extravagantly melancholy or somber; mournful —**lu·gu˝bri·ous·ly** *adv.* —**lu·gu˝bri·ous·ness** *n.*

luke˝warm *adj.* slightly warm; lacking enthusiasm: *a lukewarm response* —**luke˝warm·ly** *adv.* —**luke˝warm·ness** *n.*

lull *n.* a period of relative quiet or calm —*vt.* to calm or quiet, as one's fears

lull˝a·by *n.* a song that soothes or quiets, especially for a child

lum˝ber (*Brit.*) *n.* unwanted items —*vi.* to move clumsily; to plod

lum˝ber (*US*) *n.* wooden boards, molding, etc. used in construction —*vi.* to move clumsily; to plod

lu˝mi·nar·y *n.* one who is distinguished; one who serves as a model for others

lu·mi·nes˝cence *n.* light accompanied by relatively little heat —**lu·mi·nes˝cent** *adj.*

lu˝mi·nous *adj.* giving off light; brightly illuminated; easily understood —**lu·mi·nos˝i·ty, lu˝mi·nous·ness** *n.* —**lu˝mi·nous·ly** *adv.*

lump *n.* a bulge or swelling; a clump or piece of something, often oddly shaped; a total amount —*adj.* complete: *a lump sum* —*vt.* to compile or consider as a whole:

they lump all expenses into a single category

lump´y *adj.* not smooth, as of a sauce; not comfortable, as of a mattress —**lump´i·ness** *n.*

lu´na·cy *n.* madness; foolishness or silliness —**lu´na·tic** *n.*, *adj.*

lu´nar *adj.* involving the moon

lunar eclipse an obscuring of the moon caused by the earth passing between the sun and the moon

lunar month the average time between new moons

lunatic fringe fanatical members of a group

lunch *n.* a midday meal —*vi.* to eat a midday meal —**lunch´er** *n.*

lunch´eon *n.* a midday gathering for a light meal

lunch´eon·ette´ *n.* an eatery where light, simple meals are served

luncheon meat, lunchmeat processed meat served cold, usually on a sandwich

lunge *n.* a sudden thrust —*vi.*, *vt.* to thrust or cause to thrust forward suddenly

lunk´head *n.* someone regarded as slow or stupid

lurch *n.* a sudden jerking movement; an unsteady gait —*vi.* to move jerkily; to walk with an unsteady gait —**lurch´ing·ly** *adv.*

lure *n.* an attraction or enticement —*vt.* to attract or entice, especially with an inducement

lu´rid *adj.* gruesome or ghastly; pale or sallow —**lu´rid·ly** *adv.* —**lu´rid·ness** *n.*

lurk *vi.* to prowl stealthily; to lie in wait unnoticed —**lurk´er** *n.* —**lurk´ing·ly** *adv.*

lus´cious *adj.* sweet and juicy; beautiful or sensuous —**lus´cious·ly** *adv.* —**lus´cious·ness** *n.*

lush *adj.* characterized by abundance, as of vegetation; luxurious or extravagant —**lush´ly** *adv.* —**lush´ness** *n.*

lust *n.* an intense craving —*vi.* to have an intense desire, especially sexual —**lust´ful** *adj.* —**lust´ful·ly** *adv.* —**lust´ful·ness** *n.*

lus´ter (*US*), **lus´tre** (*Brit.*) *n.* radiance; brilliance; the gloss on pottery achieved by glazing —*vt.* to apply a glaze —*vi.* to become glossy —**lus´trous** *adj.* —**lus´trous·ly** *adv.* —**lus´trous·ness** *n.*

lust´y *adj.* robust; boisterous —**lust´i·ly** *adj.* —**lust´i·ness** *n.*

lux·u´ri·ant *adj.* marked by abundant growth; characterized by extravagance —**lux·u´ri·ance** *n.* —**lux·u´ri·ant·ly** *adv.*

lux·u´ri·ate *vi.* to revel in pleasure or luxury

lux·u´ri·ous *adj.* charcterized by extravagance or indulgence —**lux·u´ri·ous·ly** *adv.* —**lux·u´ri·ous·ness** *n.*

lux´u·ry *n.* something that is not a necessity, but that contributes to one's comfort and enjoyment

lynch *vt.* to execute by hanging without due process of law —**lynch´ing** *n.*

lyr´ic *adj.* of poetry or verse set to music that expresses deep emotion

lyr´i·cal *adj.* melodious or poetic —**lyr´i·cal·ly** *adv.* —**lyr´i·cal·ness** *n.*

lyr´i·cist, lyr´ist *n.* one who writes song lyrics

m, M thirteenth letter of the English alphabet; the symbol for 1000 in Roman characters

ma·ca´bre *adj.* gruesome; horrible; associated with death

mac·ad´am *n.* a type of road covering consisting of stones bound with asphalt —**mac·ad·am·i·za´tion** *n.* —**mac·ad·am·ize** *vt.*

mac·a·ro´ni *n.* a type of pasta formed into short, hollow tubes

mac·a·roon´ *n.* a cookie flavored with almond or coconut

mace *n.* a medieval war club; a

ceremonial scepter; an aromatic spice obtained from the outer shell of the nutmeg seed

mac′er·ate *vi.*, *vt.* to become or make soft by soaking —**mac·er·a′tion** *n.* —**mac′er·a·tor** *n.*

ma·chet′e *n.* a large knife used mainly for cutting brush, etc.

Mach·i·a·vel′li·an *adj.* marked by cunning and duplicity

mach′i·nate *vt.* to plot —**mach·i·na′tion** *n.* —**mach′i·na·tor** *n.*

ma·chine′ *n.* a mechanical device that modifies and transfers energy; broadly, any contrivance that aids in performing a task; anything or anyone that performs in a standardized or predictable manner — *adj.* of or like a mechanical device —*vi.*, *vt.* to fashion or be fashioned by a mechanical device —**ma·chin′er·y** *n.* —**ma·chin′ist** *n.*

machine language basic computer instructions

machine shop a workshop for fashioning or repairing machines

machine tool a power–driven tool

ma·chis′mo *n.* an inflated notion or display of masculinity

ma·cho *adj.* characterized by excessively masculine behavior —*n.* a male overly impressed with displays of masculinity or virility

mack′i·naw *n.* a heavy woolen coat

mack′in·tosh *n.* a raincoat

mac·ra·mé′ *n.* coarsely knotted thread or cord

mac′ro *n.* a macroinstruction: a single computer command that triggers a series of actions

mac·ro·bi·ot′ics *n.* the promotion of good health and well–being by regulation of the diet —**mac·ro·bi·ot′ic** *adj.* —**mac·ro·bi·ot′ic·al·ly** *adv.*

mac′ro·cosm *n.* the universe; any large, multifaceted aggregate — **mac′ro·cos′mic** *adj.*

mac′ro·scop′ic, **mac·ro·scop′i·cal** *adj.* large enough to be seen with the naked eye —**mac·ro·scop′i·cal·ly** *adv.*

mad *adj.* angry; insane or acting as though insane; lacking sound judgment; expressing strong emotion, especially anger

mad′am *n.* a polite form for addressing a woman

mad′cap *adj.* wild and reckless; uninhibited

mad′den *vi.*, *vt.* to become or make angry

mad′den·ing *adj.* tending to cause anger —**mad′den·ing·ly** *adv.*

made *adj.* fashioned or produced, often in combined form: *American–made, handmade*

made′-to-or′der *adj.* fashioned according to furnished instructions or specifications; well–suited: *a made–to–order solution*

made′-up′ *adj.* fictitious; complete

mad′house *n.* a place of disorganization and chaos

mad′ly *adj.* in a foolish or frenzied manner

mad′man *n.* one who acts in an insane manner

mad′ness *n.* insanity; excessive enthusiasm

ma·dras′ *n.* a cotton cloth woven in a variety of colors and designs

mad′ri·gal *n.* a vocal composition for several voices —**mad′ri·gal·ist** *n.*

mael′strom *n.* a large whirlpool; a turbulent situation

mae′stro *n.* a master, especially a renowned musician

mag′a·zine′ *n.* a printed periodical; a storehouse; a storage compartment, as for film or tape

mag′got *n.* an insect larva; a grub

mag′ic *n.* a display of supernatural power; sorcery; entertainment using sleight of hand, misdirection, illusion, etc.; a mystifying quality or ability: *the magic of her music* — *adj.* relating to the supernatural;

mystical —**mag′i·cal** *adj.* —**mag′i·cal·ly** —*adv.* **ma·gi′cian** *n.*

mag·is·trate *n.* a local official such as a justice of the peace —**mag·is·te′ri·al** *adj.* —**mag·is·te′ri·al·ly** *adv.* —**mag′is·tral** *adj.*

mag·is·tra·cy *n.* the office of a magistrate; the area under the jurisdiction of a magistrate

mag′ma *n.* molten rock that forms part of the earth's core

mag·na·nim′i·ty *n.* an act of generosity or forgiveness

mag·nan′i·mous *adj.* generous and noble of spirit; inclined to forgive —**mag·nan′i·mous·ly** *adv.* —**mag·nan′i·mous·ness** *n.*

mag′nate *n.* a prominent industrialist

mag′net *n.* an object surrounded by a magnetic field; anything that tends to attract

mag·net′ic *adj.* having power to attract —**mag·net′i·cal·ly** *adv.*

magnetic field the area of force surrounding a magnet

magnetic north the direction of one of the earth's magnetic poles; the direction in which the arrow on a magnetic compass points

magnetic pole one of two areas on a magnet where the force is most concentrated

mag′net·ism *n.* the energy of a magnet; the power to attract

mag′net·ize *vt.* to make magnetic; to fascinate or attract, as if by a magnet: *magnetized by her beauty* —**mag′net·iz·a·ble** *adj.* —**mag·net·i·za′tion** *n.*

mag·ne′to *n.* a device that converts direct current to alternating current

mag′ne·tron *n.* a tube that produces microwave radiation, used in cooking

mag·ni·fi·ca′tion *n.* an enlarged image; the amount by which an image has been made larger

mag·nif′i·cence *n.* grandeur or luxuriousness

mag·nif′i·cent *adj.* majestic or noble, as in appearance, word, or deed; exceptionally good: *a magnificent day* —**mag·nif′i·cent·ly** *adv.*

mag′ni·fy *vt.* to make larger or make appear larger —**mag′ni·fi·er** *n.*

mag′ni·tude *n.* size or extent; importance

mag′num *n.* a wine bottle that holds 1.5 liters

magnum opus a masterpiece

maid′en *n.* an unmarried woman —*adj.* pertaining to or befitting a maiden; unmarried; original or beginning: *a maiden voyage* —**maid′en·ly** *adj.*

mail (*US*) *n.* letters, packages, etc. accepted for delivery by the postal system —*vi.*, *vt.* to send via the postal system —**mail·a·bil′i·ty** *adv.* —**mail′a·ble** *adj.*

mail drop a place where mail is delivered and held for an addressee, usually referring to a place other than one's home or business

mail′er *n.* one who uses the mails, especially in large volume for advertising, solicitation, etc.; a person or company that prepares mail in volume for delivery to the postal service; a container for items to be mailed, as a tube, padded envelope, etc.; a piece or package of commercial mail

mail′ing *n.* a large volume of like pieces sent at one time

mail order the business of buying or selling by mail

maim *vt.* to mutilate or disable

main *adj.* most significant —*n.* the dominant part; a large pipe or conduit; the open sea —**might and main** physical strength

main drag (*US*) the principal street or road in an area

main´frame *n.* a large computer designed to serve numerous terminals

main´land *n.* a large body of land; a continent, as distinguished from an island —**main´land·er** *n.*

main´ly *adv.* largely; predominantly

main´stream *n.* the dominant or accepted views of a community or group —*adj.* conventional or traditional

main·tain´ *vt.* to uphold; to preserve in an existing or desired state, as *to maintain order* —**main·tain´a·ble** *adj.*

main´te·nance *n.* the care required to preserve in good order

maî´tre d', maî´tre d'hô·tel´ *n.* a headwaiter

ma·jes´tic, ma·jes´ti·cal *adj.* stately or dignified in manner; magnificent —**ma·jes´ti·cal·ly** *adv.* —**ma·jes´ti·cal·ness** *n.*

maj´es·ty *n.* the grandeur and nobility of a sovereign; elegance or splendor: *"...purple mountains' majesty..."*

ma·jol´i·ca *n.* a type of Italian pottery

ma´jor *n.* a rank in a military or quasi–military organization —*adj.* among the most important: *a major talent*; of exceptional scope, size, etc.

ma·jor–do´mo *n.* the chief steward of a household; a butler

ma·jor´i·ty *n.* a number greater than half; a political group that controls more than half the votes on an issue; legally of age

make *vi., vt.* to assemble or fashion; to create or produce; to cause — **mak´er** *n.*

make´–be·lieve *n.* a flight of fancy — *adj.* fanciful

make´–do, make´shift *n.* a convenient substitute —*adj.* temporary; provisional

make´up *n.* the manner in which something is arranged or constituted; cosmetics; a school assignment or test that compensates for missing or unsatisfactory work

make´–work *n.* low priority tasks intended to fill a worker's idle time

mal´ad·just´ed *adj.* poorly adjusted, especially to the stresses of life — **mal´ad·just´ment** *n.*

mal´a·droit´ *adj.* inept; unskilled — **mal·a·droit´ly** *adv.* —**mal·a·droit´ness** *n.*

mal´a·dy *n.* an ailment or affliction

mal·aise´ *n.* a feeling of uneasiness or despondency

mal´a·prop·ism *n.* incorrect use of a word by mistaking it for another that sounds similar

ma·lar´ia *n.* an infectious disease characterized by alternating chills and fever —**ma·lar´i·al** *adj.*

mal´con·tent *n.* one who is habitually disgruntled; an agitator —*adj.* disgruntled; discontent

male *adj.* of the sex that fertilizes the eggs of the female; masculine; of a coupling device designed to fit into a recess or socket —*n.* a male person, animal, or plant

mal·e·dic´tion *n.* a curse —**mal·e·dic´to·ry** *adj.*

mal´e·fac´tor *n.* a criminal —**mal´e·fac´tion** *n.*

ma·lef´ic *adj.* evil

ma·lef´i·cence *n.* a hurtful or wicked quality; doing mischief

ma·lef´i·cent *adj.* harmful or hurtful; wicked

ma·lev´o·lence *n.* malicious or spiteful behavior

ma·lev´o·lent *adj.* malicious or spiteful; signifying or giving rise to evil: *a malevolent omen* —**ma·lev´o·lent·ly** *adv.*

mal·fea´sance *n.* misconduct or an impropriety, especially by a public official —**mal·fea´sant** *adj.*

mal´for·ma´tion *n.* a deformity — **mal·formed´** *adj.*

mal·func'tion n. a failure to function properly —vi. to perform poorly or not at all; break down

mal'ice n. a desire to deliberately harm; spite —**ma·li'cious** adj. — **ma·li'cious·ly** adv. —**ma·li'cious·ness** n.

ma·lign' vt. to speak ill of; to slander —**ma·lign'er** n. —**ma·lign'ly** adv.

ma·lig'nant adj. extremely harmful, as a disease; malevolent —**ma·lig'nance, ma·lig'nan·cy** n. —**ma·lig'nant·ly** adv.

ma·lin'ger vi. to avoid work by feigning illness —**ma·lin'ger·er** n.

mall (US) n. a shaded walk, often lined with shops; a large enclosed shopping complex; a park–like public area

mal'le·a·ble adj. flexible or adaptable; able to be molded —**mal'le·a·bil'i·ty, mal'le·a·ble·ness** n. — **mal'le·a·bly** adv.

mal'let n. a type of hammer, especially one with a soft head

mal·nour'ished adj. lacking proper food; showing signs of such lack — **mal·nu·tri'tion** n.

mal·o'dor·ous adj. foul smelling — **mal·o'dor·ous·ly** adv. —**mal·o'dor·ous·ness** n.

mal·prac'tice n. improper treatment by or conduct of a professional, as a doctor or lawyer

malt n. a grain that has germinated and dried for use in brewing or as a nutrient; a beverage brewed from or flavored with malt —vi., vt. to become or cause to become malt

mal'treat' vt. to abuse —**mal'treat'ment** n.

mam'bo n. a Latin American dance or music for the dance —vi. to dance the mambo

mam'mal n. any of a class of warm–blooded vertebrates that suckle their young —**mam·ma'li·an** adj.

mam·mal'o·gy n. the study of mammals

mam'mon n. wealth deemed to exert a harmful influence

mam'moth n. a large elephant, now extinct; anything very large —adj. huge; enormous

man n. an adult male human; humans in general; one endowed with qualities associated with maleness, as strength or stamina; a male underling or assistant —vt. to assign or take a position; to staff —**manned** adj.

man'a·cle n. a restraint, especially one attached at the wrists —vt. to constrain

man'age vi., vt. to direct or control; to administer; to bring about; to have charge of —**man'ag·er** n. — **man'a·ge'ri·al** adj.

man'age·a·ble adj. compliant; submissive; able to be controlled or accomplished: a manageable task —**man'age·a·bil'i·ty, man'age·a·ble·ness** n. —**man'age·a·bly** adv.

man'age·ment n. those who guide or direct a business

man'date n. an order or declaration; an assignment, as by the electorate: the people's mandate; a charge —vt. to assign or require —**man'da·tor** n.

man'da·to·ry adj. required; compulsory

man'–day' n. the work of one person for one day

man'do·lin' n. a small stringed instrument —**man'do·lin'ist** n.

mane n. long hair growing about the neck of some animals; long human hair

man'–eat·er n. an animal that feeds or is professed to feed on human flesh; a predatory woman —**man'–eat·ing** adj.

ma·neu'ver (US) n. a change in speed, direction, etc. as of an aircraft; a move or series of moves to fulfill a purpose —vi., vt. to change course; to perform moves that influence people or events —**ma·neu´ver·a·bil´i·ty** n. —**ma·neu´ver·a·ble** adj. —**ma·neu´ver·er** n.

man´ful·ly adv. in a manner characteristic of a man

mange n. a skin disease of domestic animals

man´ger n. a feeding trough for livestock

man´gle vt. to disfigure by cutting, pounding, etc.; to ruin through ignorance or ineptness: he mangled the introductions —**man´gler** n.

man´gy adj. shabby or rundown; affected with mange —**man´gi·ly** adv. —**man´gi·ness** n.

man´han·dle vt. to treat roughly

man´-hour´ n. the work of one person for one hour

man´hunt n. an extensive search, as for a fugitive

ma´nia n. an obsession; irrational behavior —**man´ic** adj.

ma·ni·ac n. an insane person; one who acts in an irrational or capricious manner —**ma·ni´a·cal** adj. —**ma·ni´a·cal·ly** adv.

man´i·cure n. a trimming and polishing of the fingernails —vt. to care for the fingernails; to crop closely and evenly: a manicured lawn —**man´i·cur·ist** n.

man´i·fest adj. evident; obvious —n. a list of cargo, passengers, etc. —vt. to reveal or become evident —**man´i·fest·ly** adv.

man·i·fes·ta´tion n. evidence or proof of something; the embodiment of a spirit

man·i·fes´to n. a statement of beliefs or aims

ma·nip´u·la·ble, ma·nip´u·lat·a·ble adj. that can be manipulated —**ma·nip·u·la·bil´i·ty** n.

ma·nip´u·late vt. to control or shape; to persuade or alter by devious means —**ma·nip·u·la´tion** n. —**ma·nip´u·la·tor** n. —**ma·nip´u·la·to·ry** adj.

ma·nip·u·la´tion n. the controlling or altering of something; sly, often deceitful, persuasion

ma·nip´u·la·tive adj. tending to persuade or alter: the use of manipulative reasoning —**ma·nip´u·la·tive·ly** adv. —**ma·nip´u·la·tive·ness** n.

man´kind´ n. humanity; the human race

man´ly adj. masculine —**man´li·ness** n.

man´-made´ adj. manufactured; artificial

man´ne·quin n. a model of the human body used to display clothing

man´ner n. a style or mode, as of conduct or carriage —**man´nered** adj.

man´ner·ism n. a distinctive trait; an affectation; an artistic style marked by distortion —**man´ner·ist** n. —**man·ner·is´tic** adj.

man´ner·ly adj. having excellent manners —adv. politely —**man´ner·li·ness** n.

man´nish adj. affecting the style of a man —**man´nish·ly** adv. —**man´nish·ness** n.

ma·noeu´vre (Brit.) n. a change in speed, direction, etc. as of an aircraft; a move or series of moves to fulfill a purpose —vi., vt. to change course; to perform moves that influence people or events

man of God, man of the cloth a clergyman

man of letters a scholar

man of the world a sophisticate

man´or n. a landed estate or the main house on an estate —**ma·no´ri·al** adj.

man´pow·er n. the laborers, soldiers, etc. that are available or required

man´sard n. a roof with a double pitch

manse n. a clergyman's house

man´sion n. a large house

man·slaugh·ter *n.* murder by accident

man·teau´ *n.* a cloak

man´tel, man´tel·piece *n.* a shelf over a fireplace

man·til´la *n.* a light lace scarf or head–covering

man´tle *n.* a cloak; something that covers or conceals: *a mantle of fog* —*vt., vi.* to cover or be covered or concealed

man´tra *n.* a word or phrase chanted as an aid to meditation — **man´tric** *adj.*

man´u·al *adj.* referring to the hands or work performed by hand —*n.* a reference or instruction book — **man´u·al·ly** *adv.*

manual training training in practical arts such as woodworking

man·u·fac´ture *vi., vt.* to fashion, fabricate, or assemble, either by hand or with the aid of machinery; to create, a usually false, story or report —*n.* the production of goods —**man·u·fac´tur·a·ble** *adj.* — **man·u·fac´tur·er** *n.* —**man·u·fac´ tur·ing** *n.*

man·u·mit´ *vt.* to liberate, as a slave —**man·u·mis´sion** *n.*

ma·nure´ *n.* dung or decaying matter used to fertilize crops —*vt.* to add fertilizer to, as crops —**ma·nur´er** *n.* —**ma·nu´ri·al** *adj.*

man´u·script *n.* text lettered by hand; an unpublished text

man·y *n., pron.* a large number — *adj.* numerous

man´y·fold *adv.* a large number of times

man´y-sid´ed *adj.* having many sides, perspectives, etc. —**man´y-sid´ed·ness** *n.*

map *n.* a depiction of an area, as of a city, the earth, etc. —*vt.* to survey and depict graphically; to set out in detail: *map a strategy for sales* —**map´mak·er, map´per** *n.* — **map´pa·ble** *adj.*

mar *vt.* to damage by marking; to deface

mar·a·schi´no *n.* a sweet liqueur made from cherries

mar´a·thon *n.* a competition requiring endurance, as a long–distance race —**mar´a·thon·er** *n.*

ma·raud´ *vi., vt.* to attack and plunder —**ma·raud´er** *n.*

mar´ble *n.* a type of multicolored stone —**mar´ble, mar´ble·ize** *vt.* to streak with color, imitating marble —**mar´bled** *adj.* —**mar´bly** *adj.*

marble cake a cake streaked with batters of different colors

mar´bling *n.* a streaking resembling that of marble; the creation of marble–like streaks, as in a design

march *n.* an orderly forward movement; a gathering to protest or champion a cause —*vi., vt.* to move or cause to move forward in an orderly, methodical manner — **march´er** *n.*

marching orders instructions or permission to proceed, as with a business plan

mar´ga·rine *n.* a butter substitute

mar´gin *n.* a limit, as the blank space around a printed page; an allowance for variation

mar´gin·al *adj.* barely acceptable — **mar·gin·al´i·ty** *n.* —**mar´gin·al·ly** *adv.* —**mar´gin·al·ize** *vt.*

ma·ri·a´chi *n.* a Mexican street band

ma·ri´na *n.* a docking area for small boats

mar´i·nade´ *n.* a seasoned liquid for steeping food before cooking

mar´i·nate *vi., vt.* to soak in a marinade —**mar·i·na´tion** *n.*

ma·rine´ *adj.* relating to the sea or seamen —**mar´i·ner** *n.*

mar´i·o·nette´ *n.* a puppet moved by strings or wires

mar´i·tal *adj.* relating to marriage — **mar´i·tal·ly** *adv.*

mar´i·time *adj.* at or near the sea; pertaining to the sea or seamen

mark *n.* a random impression, as a scratch, blotch, etc.; a representative symbol or sign; a rating; an objective —*vt.* to imprint; to scratch of blotch; to identify by or as if by a symbol; to label, as with a price; to notice —*vi.* to make a mark; to notice —**make a mark** to be successful or notable —**mark down** to lower the price of —**mark time** to pause or wait for a propitious moment —**mark up** to increase the price of —**wide of the mark** a failure

mark´down *n.* a discount

marked *adj.* noticeable; prominent —**mark´ed·ly** *adv.* —**mark´ed·ness** *n.*

mark´er *n.* something that serves to identify; an implement used to imprint or write; an IOU

mar´ket *n.* the business of buying and selling; a place where goods are available for sale; trading in a commodity —*vi., vt.* to buy or sell —**mar·ket·abil´i·ty** *n.* —**mar´ket·a·ble** *adj.*

mar´ket·er *n.* one who deals in a commodity

mar´ket·place *n.* a place where goods are bought and sold; a domain recognized as a distinct area of trade: *the literary marketplace*

market research the accumulation and analysis of consumer-related data

market share the portion of total trade in a particular commodity that a company controls or may expect to control

market value the price at which a commodity may reasonable be expected to be bought or sold

mark´ing *n.* a distinctive feature or pattern, as on an animal

mark´up *n.* the amount by which the cost of a marketable product is increased to arrive at a selling price

mar´ma·lade *n.* a thick preserve made from fruit

mar´riage *n.* the uniting of a man and woman as husband and wife; the joining of two elements: *the marriage of flavors that make a food unique, the marriage of wit and beauty*

mar´riage·a·ble *adj.* suited or able to be married: *of marriageable age* — **mar·riage·a·bil´i·ty**, **mar´riage·a·ble·ness** *n.*

marriage of convenience a union arranged for practical reasons, such as for political or economic benefit

mar´ry *vt.* to join as husband and wife; to combine or closely unite two entities —*vi.* to take as a husband or wife —**mar´ried** *adj.*

marsh *n.* land that is wet and muddy —**marsh´land** *n.*

mar´shal *n.* an officer in a law enforcement or similar agency —*vt.* to gather or arrange: *marshal forces for an attack*

marsh´mal·low *n.* a soft, spongy confection —**marsh´mal·low·y** *adj.*

marsh·y *adj.* wet and muddy — **marsh´i·ness** *n.*

mar·su´pi·al *n.* a mammal that bears its young in an external pouch —*adj.* having a pouch

mart *n.* a market

mar´tial *adj.* referring to war or warriors —**mar´tial·ism** *n.* —**mar´tial·ist** *n.* —**mar´tial·ly** *adv.*

martial art any technique of combat or war

martial law government by military authority

mar´ti·net´ *n.* a strict disciplinarian

mar·ti´ni *n.* a cocktail of gin or vodka and dry vermouth

mar´tyr *n.* one who endures suffering or death for a belief or cause; one who suffers without complaint; one who exaggerates discomfort in order to elicit sympathy —*vt.* to persecute or put to death

for devotion to a belief or cause —
mar´tyr·dom n.

mar´vel n. something that fills with
awe or wonder —vi., vt. to wonder
at; to be amazed

mar´vel·ous adj. wonderous; impressive —**mar´vel·ous·ly** adv. —
mar´vel·ous·ness n.

mar´zi·pan n. an almond–flavored
confection

mas·car´a n. eye makeup

mas´cot n. a symbol, usually an
animal, believed to bring good luck

mas´cu·line n. characteristic of a
male; attributes associated with a
male —**mas´cu·line·ly** adv. —**mas·
cu·lin´i·ty** n.

mash n. a pulpy mass —vt. to reduce to a pulpy mass

mash´er n. a utensil for crushing or
pulverizing; one who makes unwanted sexual advances

mask n. a covering for the face, as to
conceal identity or for protection; a
representation of a face hung as a
wall ornament —vi., vt. to conceal
or cover, esp. of the face —**masked**
adj.

mas´och·ist n. one who derives
pleasure from being abused —
mas´och·ism n. — **mas´och·is´tic**
adj. —**mas·och·is´ti·cal·ly** adv.

ma´son n. one who works with stone
—**ma´son·ry** n.

mas´quer·ade´ n. a costume party; a
deception —vi. to wear or assume
a disguise

mass n. a clump; physical bulk; an
undetermined number or amount
—vi., vt. to assemble or be assembled into a mass —adj. large in
number or scale

mas´sa·cre n. indiscriminate
slaughter —vt. to slaughter —**mas´
sa·crer** n.

mas·sage´ n. a rubdown —vt. to
relax the muscles by rubbing or
kneading; to manipulate, as data
—**mas·sag´er** n.

mas·seur´, **mas·seuse´** n. a man or
woman, respectively, trained in the
art of massage

mas´sive adj. large or bulky; imposing; cumbersome —**mas´sive·
ly** adv. —**mas´sive·ness** n.

mass–market adj. produced for
general consumption

mass media collectively, those
communication systems that attract a large audience

mass´–pro·duce´ vt. to manufacture
in large quantities using assembly–line techniques —**mass´–pro·
duc´tion** n.

mass transit collectively, the transportation systems that carry large
numbers of passengers on a regular basis

mas´ter adj. primary or controlling:
a master plan; proficient or knowledgeable: a master electrician —n.
one who owns or controls; a
teacher; one proficient in a craft;
one who possesses exception
knowledge or ability in a particular
field —vt. to control; to acquire
knowledge or ability —**mas´tery** n.

mas´ter·ful adj. domineering; having
or exhibiting skill: a masterful
painting —**mas´ter·ful·ly** adv. —
mas´ter·ful·ness n.

master key a passkey

mas´ter·ly adj. having or exhibiting
the skill of a master —adv.

mas´ter·mind n. one with the ability
to conceive or direct a complex operation —vt. to plan and direct
skillfully

master of ceremonies one presiding
over a banquet or entertainment,
charged with introductions

mas´ter·piece n. an outstanding
work, as of art

mas´ter·stroke n. a singular action
or achievement

mas´ter·work n. a masterpiece

mast´head n. the name of a periodical or newspaper as it appears on

a cover, a first, or a leading page; the listing in a publication of its ownership, staff, circulation, etc.

mas´ti·cate *vi., vt.* to chew food; to reduce to a pulp —**mas·ti·ca´tion** *n.* —**mas´ti·ca·tor** *n.*

mas´to·don *n.* an extinct elephant–like animal

mas·tur·ba´tion *n.* stimulation of the genitals to orgasm by means other than sexual intercourse — **mas´tur·bate** *vi., vt.* —**mas·tur·ba´ tion·al, mas´tur·ba·to·ry** *adj.* —**mas´tur·ba·tor** *n.*

mat *n.* a flat section of material used for a bed, a covering, protection, etc.; a protective border placed over a picture —*vi., vt.* to press or tangle into a mat

mat´a·dor *n.* a bullfighter

match *n.* a small strip of material used to produce fire; something that is exactly or nearly like another; something compatible or harmonious; a sporting contest — *vt.* to give or get something identical, comparable, or compatible — **match´able** *adj.*

match´less *adj.* without equal — **match´less·ly** *adv.* —**match´less· ness** *n.*

match´mak·er *n.* one who arranges marriages —**match´mak·ing** *n.*

mate *n.* one of a pair; a close friend or ally —*vi., vt.* to pair, as in marriage or for breeding

ma·te´ri·al *adj.* relevent; tangible — *n.* unprocessed matter, information, etc.: *building material, material for a book or play, material for a dress,* etc.

ma·te´ri·al·ism *n.* excessive concern for worldly matters or possessions —**ma·te´ri·al·ist** *n.* —**ma·te´ri·al· is´tic** *adj.* —**ma·te´ri·al·is´ti·cal·ly** *adv.*

ma·te´ri·al·ize *vi.* to appear suddenly —*vt.* to cause to come forth —**ma·te·ri·al·i·za´tion** *n.*

ma·te´ri·al·ly *adv.* to a meaningful extent

ma·ter´nal *adj.* of a mother or motherhood —**ma·ter´nal·ism** *n.* —**ma· ter´nal·is´tic** *adj.* —**ma·ter´nal·ly** *adv.*

ma·ter´ni·ty *n.* the emotions associated with motherhood —*adj.* relating to pregnancy or childbirth

math, math·e·mat´ics *n.* the science of numbers

math·e·mat´i·cal *adj.* pertaining to numbers —**math·e·mat´i·cal·ly** *adv.* —**math·e·ma·ti´cian** *n.*

mat´i·nee´ *n.* an afternoon performance

ma´tri·arch *n.* a woman who heads a family; a respected woman — **ma´tri·ar´chal, ma·tri·ar´chic** *adj.* —**ma·tri·ar´chal·ism** *n.*

ma´tri·ar·chy *n.* a society that traces its lineage through women

ma·tric´u·late *vt., vi.* to permit or be permitted into, as a course of study —**ma·tric´u·lant** *n.* —**ma· tric·u·la´tion** *n.*

ma·tri·lin´e·age *n.* maternal lineage —**ma·tri·lin´e·al** *adj.* —**ma·tri·lin´ e·al·ly** *adv.*

mat´ri·mo·ny *n.* the union of two persons in marriage; the state of being married —**mat´ri·mo´ni·al** *adj.* —**mat´ri·mo´ni·al·ly** *adv.*

ma´trix *n.* a mold or pattern

ma´tron *n.* a mature woman; a female supervisor —**ma´tron·li·ness** *n.* —**ma´tron·ly** *adj.*

matte *n.* a soft or dull finish —*adj.* having a soft or dull finish

mat´ter *n.* substance; something of interest or focus: *a financial matter* —*vi.* to be important

mat´ter-of-fact´ *adj.* objective; unemotional; unimaginative — **mat´ter-of-fact´ly** *adv.* —**mat´ ter-of-fact´ness** *n.*

mat´ting *n.* a rough fabric, as used for floor covering; an accumulation of material that forms a covering

mat´tress n. a pad or mat used for sleeping

mat·u·rate vi. to mature or ripen — **mat·u·ra´tion** n. —**mat·u·ra´tion·al, mat´u·ra·tive** adj.

ma·ture´ adj. fully developed; characteristic of full development; ripe —vi., vt. to ripen or cause to ripen; to become due, as a debt —**ma·ture´ly** adv. —**ma·ture´ness, ma·tur´i·ty** n.

mat´zo n. unleavened bread

maud´lin adj. tearful; nauseatingly sentimental

maul n. a heavy hammer; a sledgehammer —vt. to beat or batter; to mangle by rough treatment — **maul´er** n.

mau·so·le´um n. a tomb; a tomblike room or building

ma´ven n. an expert

mav´er·ick adj. independent; radical —n. a nonconformist; one who acts independently

mawk´ish adj. overly sentimental — **mawk´ish·ly** adv. —**mawk´ish·ness** n.

max´im n. an adage or motto

max´i·mal adj. of a maximum; largest —**max´i·mal·ly** adv.

max´i·mize vt. to increase or emphasize as much as possible — **max·i·mi·za´tion** n. —**max´i·miz·er** n.

max´i·mum adj. of the largest possible or allowed —n. the largest amount or extent

may´be adv. possibly —n. a possibility

may´hem n. deliberate injury to a person; reckless damage or destruction; a state of turmoil

may´o, may·on·naise´ n. a thick, rich white sauce or dressing

may´or n. a municipal administrator —**may´or·al** adj. —**may´or·al·ty** n.

maze n. a complex pattern, as of paths or lines; a network of complicated or confusing elements: an intricate maze of building codes — **maz´i·ness** n. —**maze´like, maz´y** adj.

mead´ow n. an expanse of pasture or grassland —**mead´owy** adj.

mea´ger (US), **mea´gre** (Brit.) adj. scant; lacking, as in quality — **mea´ger·ly, mea´gre·ly** adv. — **mea´ger·ness, mea´gre·ness** n.

meal n. edible grain, whole or ground; the food eaten at a sitting

meal´y adj. containing or resembling meal —**meal´i·ness** n.

meal´y-mouthed adj. tending to avoid direct and honest discourse

mean adj. cruel or malicious; low, as in quality or amount; selfish or miserly —n. midway between extremes —vt. to indicate or intend: this means war, I mean to win

me·an´der vi. to wander aimlessly; to travel a winding course —n. a winding course —**me·an´der·er** n. —**me·an´der·ing·ly** adv. —**me·an´drous** adj.

mean´ing adj. revealing; having purpose —n. significance or purpose; that which is understood — **mean´ing·ful** adj. —**mean´ing·ful·ly, mean´ing·ly** adv. —**mean´ing·ful·ness** n.

mean´ing·less adj. without purpose; insignificant —**mean´ing·less·ly** adv. —**mean´ing·less·ness** n.

mean´ly adv. in a shabby way

mean´ness n. cruelty or malice; a lack, as in quality or amount; selfishness

mean´-spir´it·ed adj. characterized by pettiness —**mean´-spir´it·ed·ly** adv. —**mean´-spir´it·ed·ness** n.

mea´sur·a·ble adj. that can be quantified; finite; significant — **mea·sur·a·bil´i·ty, mea´sur·a·ble·ness** n. —**mea´sur·a·bly** adv.

mea´sure n. a standard unit, such as an inch or a pound, used to express size, weight, etc.; a device calibrated to such a standard; an unspecified amount: *enjoying a measure of fame*; an unspecified action: *time to take corrective measures* —*vi.*, *vt.* to express or gauge, as size or capacity, in terms of a standard unit —**beyond measure** incalculable —**in some measure** to an unspecified extent—**measure up** to fulfill expectations —**mea´sur·er** *n.*

mea´sured *adj.* steady and deliberate: *spoke in measured tones* —**mea´sured·ly** *adv.* —**mea´sured·ness** *n.*

mea´sure·less *adj.* without limit — **mea´sure·less·ly** *adv.* —**mea´sure·less·ness** *n.*

mea´sure·ment *n.* a determination of size, capacity, etc.; a system for such determination

meat *n.* the edible flesh of an animal or plant; a main idea: *the meat of the discussion*

meat-and-potatoes *adj.* basics

meat´ball *n.* ground meat formed into a sphere and baked or fried; a foolish person

meat´y *adj.* containing meat; important or significant —**meat´i·ness** *n.*

me·chan´ic *n.* one who repairs machines

me·chan´i·cal *adj.* relating to or driven by mechanical action or a machine; in a perfunctory manner —**me·chan´i·cal·ly** *adv.* —**me·chan´i·cal·ness** *n.*

mechanical advantage the ratio of the output of a mechanism to the input energy required or expended

me·chan´ics *n.* the study of force acting on a material body; the study of machinery

mech´a·nism *n.* the parts, action, or operation of a mechanical device

mech´a·nize *vt.* to equip with machines; to automate —**mech·a·ni·za´tion** *n.*

med´al *n.* a small, flat article of ornamented metal recognizing a person, event, etc. —**med´al·ist** *n.*

me·dal´lion *n.* a large medal or emblem that serves as an ornament, identification, etc.; food cut or formed in circles

med´dle *vi.* to interfere in the affairs of another —**med´dler** *n.*

med´dle·some *adj.* tending to interfere —**med´dle·some·ly** *adv.* — **med´dle·some·ness** *n.*

med´e·vac *n.* medical evacuation: the transporting of injured by air to a medical facility

me´di·a *n.* plural of *medium*; the forms of mass communication collectively, as newpapers, television, etc.

media event an occurrence that prompts wide coverage by the news media

me´di·al *adj.* median —**me´di·al·ly** *adv.*

me´di·an *adj.* relating to the middle —*n.* a middle part —**me´di·an·ly** *adv.*

me´di·ate *vt.* to resolve a dispute between two or more parties —*vi.* to act as the agent of reconciliation —**me´di·ate·ly** *adv.* —**me·di·a´tion** *n.* —**me·di·a´tive** *adj.* —**me´di·a·tor** *n.*

med´ic *n.* a physician, especially in the military

med´i·cal *adj.* of the science of healing: *medical treatment* —**med´i·cal·ly** *adv.*

me·dic´a·ment *n.* a medicine

med´i·cate *vt.* to treat with medicine —**med·i·ca´tion** *n.* —**med´i·ca·tive** *adj.*

me·dic´i·nal *adj.* of or like medicine —**me·dic´i·nal·ly** *adv.*

med´i·cine *n.* the science or practice of healing; something prescribed to treat an illness

medicine show a sophisticated sales pitch reminiscent of traveling shows in the past that attracted audiences for the selling of patent, often ineffective, medicines

me·di·e´val *adj*. of the Middle Ages; antiquated; barbaric —**me·di·e´val·ly** *adv*.

me·di·e´val·ism *n*. the study of life in the Middle Ages; a custom or practice of the Middle Ages —**me·di·e´val·ist** *n*.

me´di·o´cre *adj*. unexceptional; barely acceptable; inferior —**medi·oc´ri·ty** *n*.

med´i·tate *vi., vt*. to deliberate or consider; to spend time in quiet contemplation —**med·i·ta´tion** *n*. —**med´i·tat·or** *n*.

med´i·ta·tive *adj*. characterized by quiet contemplation; thoughtful or reflective —**med´i·ta·tive·ly** *adv*. —**med´i·ta·tive·ness** *n*.

me´di·um *adj*. between extremes — *n*. something approximately midway between limits; a substance or means by which something is attained: *oil paint is the medium for this portrait, a credit card is the preferred medium for shoppers*

medium of exchange the accepted currency in a particular society or circumstance, as dollars, pounds, pesos, shells, etc.

med´ley *n*. an assortment; a conglomeration

meek *adj*. subdued or submissive; humble —**meek´ly** *adv*. —**meek´ness** *n*.

meet *vt*. to come upon or confront; to make the acquaintance of; to gather, as for discussion; to satisfy: *meet the requirements for a job* —*vi*. to come together; to assemble; to be introduced —*n*. a gathering, as for athletic competition

meet´ing *n*. an encounter or confrontation; a gathering; an intersecting, as of two roads

meg´a·dose *n*. a large measure, as of medicine

meg´a·hertz *n*. one million cycles per second, as of a radio frequency or computer speed

meg´a·lith *n*. a large stone monument —**meg´a·lith´ic** *adj*.

meg·a·lo·ma´ni·a *n*. obsession with wealth or power —**meg·a·lo·ma´ni·ac** *n*. —**meg·a·lo·ma·ni´a·cal, meg·a·lo·man´ic** *adj*.

meg·a·lop´o·lis *n*. an area of closely joined cities and their surrounding areas — **meg´a·lo·pol´i·tan** *adj*.

meg´a·phone *n*. a device that amplifies the voice —**meg·a·phon´ic** *adj*. —**meg·a·phon´i·cal·ly** *adv*.

mel´a·mine *n*. a type of plastic

mel·an·cho´lia *n*. a mental disorder marked by depression —**mel·an·cho´li·ac** *n*.

mel´an·choly *adj*. sadly quiet and contemplative —*n*. a condition marked by sadness or gloom and a quiet attitude, as though deep in thought —**mel´an·chol´ic** *adj*. —**mel´an·chol´i·cal·ly** *adv*.

me·lange´ *n*. a collection or jumble

mel·a·no´ma *n*. a darkly-colored growth, usually occurring on the skin and often malignant

meld *n*. a blending together —*vi., vt*. to become or cause to become mingled: *cook lightly so that the flavors can meld*

me´lee *n*. a violent clash or mingling

mel´io·rate *vi., vt*. to improve, as a condition —**mel´io·ra·ble** *adj*. — **me·lio·ra´tion** *n*. —**me´lio·ra·tive** *adj*. —**me·lio·ra´tor** *n*.

mel·lif´lu·ent *adj*. mellifluous — **mel·lif´lu·ence** *n*. —**mel·lif´lu·ent·ly** *adv*.

mel·lif´lu·ous *adj*. smooth and mellow, as of a voice or musical tone —**mel·lif´lu·ous·ly** *adv*. —**mel·lif´lu·ous·ness** *n*.

mel´low *adj*. soft and rich, as a flavor or sound; pleasant and unhurried, as of a conversation —*vi., vt*. —**mel´low·ly** *adv*. —**mel´low·ness** *n*.

me·lod´ic *adj.* tuneful —**me·lod´i·cal·ly** *adv.*

me·lo´di·ous *adj.* harmonious; pleasing to the ear —**me·lo´di·ous·ly** *adv.* —**me·lo´di·ous·ness** *n.*

mel´o·dra·ma *n.* a theatrical work characterized by overdrawn characterizations and exaggerated emotion —**mel´o·dra·mat´ic** *adj.* —**mel´o·dra·mat´i·cal·ly** *adv.*

mel´o·dy *n.* a musical strain; a series of tones comprising a tune that expresses the theme of a musical composition

melt *vi., vt.* to transform from a solid to a liquid state; to soften, dissolve, or disappear: *as we rode away, the scene melted in the distance* —**melt·a·bil´i·ty** *n.* —**melt´a·ble** *adj.* —**melt´er** *n.* —**melt´ing·ly** *adv.*

mem´ber *n.* one who belongs or is a part of: *a club member, a member of the band*; part of an organism, as a limb; a distinct part of something, as a structure

mem´ber·ship *n.* affiliation with an organization; collectively, those who are affiliated

mem´brane *n.* a thin sheet of tissue that serves as a cover or lining

me·men´to *n.* a keepsake

mem´o, mem·o·ran´dum *n.* a written communication

mem´oir *n.* an autobiography —**mem´oir·ist** *n.*

mem·o·ra·bil´ia *pl. n.* souvenirs or mementos associated with a person, place, event, etc.

mem´o·ra·ble *adj.* worth remembering; unusual —**mem·o·ra·bil´i·ty, mem´o·ra·ble·ness** *n.* —**mem´o·ra·bly** *adv.*

me·mo´ri·al *adj.* commemorative —*n.* a monument, ceremony, etc. that serves as a remembrance —**me·mo´ri·al·ly** *adv.*

me·mo´ri·al·ize *vt.* to commemorate —**me·mo·ri·al·i·za´tion** *n.*

mem´o·rize *vt.* to commit to memory —**mem´o·riz·a·ble** *adj.* —**mem·o·ri·za´tion** *n.* —**mem´o·riz·er** *n.*

mem´o·ry *n.* the ability to remember and recall; something remembered

men´ace *n.* a threat —*vt.* to threaten —**men´ac·ing·ly** *adv.*

me·nag´er·ie *n.* an assortment of animals; a place where animals are confined; a collection

mend *vi., vt.* to make or become better; to correct, repair, or heal —**mend´a·ble** *adj.* —**mend´er** *n.*

men·da´cious *adj.* lying or deceitful, as of a person, statement, etc. —**men·da´cious·ly** *adv.* —**men·da´cious·ness, men·dac´i·ty** *n.*

men´di·cant *adj.* pertaining to a beggar; depending on alms —*n.* a beggar —**men´di·can·cy, men·dic´i·ty** *n.*

me´ni·al *adj.* servile or humble; befitting a servant —*n.* a servant —**me´ni·al·ly** *adv.*

men´su·ra·ble *adj.* that can be measured —**men·su·ra·bil´i·ty, men´su·ra·ble·ness** *n.*

men·su·ra´tion *n.* the process of measuring —**men´su·ra·tive** *adj.*

men´tal *adj.* relating to the mind —**men´tal·ly** *adv.*

men´tal·ism *n.* the concept that some mental phenomena are beyond explanation; parapsychological events, such as telepathy —**men´tal·ist** *n.* —**men·tal·is´tic** *adj.*

men·tal´i·ty *n.* one's intellectual capacity; a manner of thinking: *an optimistic mentality*

mental retardation a deficiency in mental development

men´tion *n.* a casual reference; a tribute, as *honorable mention* —*vt.* to refer to —**men´tion·a·ble** *adj.* —**men´tion·er** *n.*

men´tor *n.* a trusted advisor or teacher

men´u *n.* a list of available food

items; any list of options

me῾nu–driv·en *adj.* of a computer program that offers lists of options for the operator to select

mer῾can·tile *adj.* relating to the marketing of goods; commercial —**mer·can·til·ism** *n.* —**mer·can·til·is῾tic** *adj.*

mer῾ce·nar·y *n.* a soldier in the pay of a foreign government; one motivated mainly by personal gain —*adj.* influenced by desire for gain —**mer·ce·nar῾i·ly** *adv.* —**mer῾ce·nar·i·ness** *n.*

mer῾chan·dise *n.* goods that are bought and sold —*vi., vt.* to sell or promote the sale of —**mer῾chan·dis·er** *n.* —**mer῾chan·dis·ing** *n.*

mer῾chant *adj.* pertaining to commercial trade —*n.* one who makes a business of selling for profit —**mer῾chant·able** *adj.*

merchant marine merchant ships or their crews

mer῾ci·ful *adj.* showing mercy —**mer῾ci·ful·ly** *adv.* —**mer῾ci·ful·ness** *n.*

mer῾ci·less *adj.* showing no mercy; lacking compassion —**mer῾ci·less·ly** *adv.* —**mer῾ci·less·ness** *n.*

mer·cu῾ri·al *adj.* volatile; fluctuating; likely to change abruptly —**mer·cu῾ri·al·ly** *adv.* —**mer·cu῾ri·al·ness** *n.*

mer῾cy *n.* compassion; an act of foregiveness or compassion

mere *adj.* insignificant; inconsequential —**mere῾ly** *adv.*

mer·e·tri῾cious *adj.* gaudy; insincere —**mer·e·tri῾cious·ly** *adv.* —**mer·e·tri῾cious·ness** *n.*

merge *vt., vi.* to combine or become combined —**mer῾gence** *n.*

merg῾er *n.* a combining, as of companies or interests

me·ringue῾ *n.* egg whites, beaten until stiff and sometimes sweetened, then baked, usually used as a topping or dessert shell

mer῾it *n.* a worthwhile quality —*vt.* to be worthy of; to deserve

mer·i·toc῾ra·cy *n.* a hierarchy based on ability —**mer·i·to·crat῾ic** *adj.*

mer·i·to῾ri·ous *adj.* praiseworthy; commendable —**mer·i·to῾ri·ous·ly** *adv.* —**mer·i·to῾ri·ous·ness** *n.*

mer῾maid, mer῾man *n.* a mythical creature that is half fish and half human

mer῾ri·ment *n.* lively fun; gaiety

mer῾ry *adj.* joyous; happy; marked by laughter or mirth —**mer῾ri·ly** *adv.* —**mer῾ri·ness** *n.*

mer῾ry–go–round *n.* a revolving platform ridden for pleasure

mer῾ry·mak·er *n.* a participant in a festive event; a reveler —**mer῾ry·mak·ing** *n.*

me῾sa *n.* a broad plateau with steep sides

mesh *n.* a loose, open fabrication of thread, wire, etc. —*vi., vt.* to fit or make fit together: *meshing gears, meshing ideas* —**mesh῾work** *n.*

mes῾mer·ize *vt.* to fascinate; to hypnotize —**mes῾mer·ism, mes·mer·i·za῾tion** *n.*

mess *n.* disordered clutter; a jumble; a large quantity: *a mess of data* —*vi., vt.* to clutter; to make untidy

mes῾sage *n.* a communication; the underlying lesson or guidance contained in a communication

mes῾sen·ger *n.* one who carries or delivers messages or small packages; a courier —*vt.* to send by courier

mess῾y *adj.* disorderly; unpleasant: *a messy divorce* —**mess῾i·ly** *adv.* —**mess῾i·ness** *n.*

met·a·bol῾ic *adj.* pertaining to or relating to metabolism —**met·a·bol῾i·cal·ly** *adv.*

me·tab῾o·lism *n.* the process by which a living organism converts food into energy, synthesizes substances necessary to life, manufactures tissue, etc.

me·tab´o·lize vt., vi. to change or undergo change by metabolism — **me·tab´o·liz·able** adj.

met´al n. any of the elements or a combination of elements that are usually shiny, good conductors, and ductile — **me·tal´lic** adj. — **me·tal´li·cal·ly** adv.

met´al·lur·gy n. the technique for extracting metals from ore or combining them to produce alloys — **met´al·lur´gic, met´al·lur´gi·cal** adj. — **met·al·lur´gi·cal·ly** adv. — **met´al·lur·gist** n.

met·a·mor´pho·sis n. a transformation, especially one that seems miraculous, as that of a caterpillar into a butterfly — **met·a·mor´phic** adj. — **met·a·mor´phism** n. — **met·a·mor´phose** vi., vt.

met´a·phor n. a figure of speech in which one thing is used to designate something different: all the world's a stage — **met·a·phor´ic, met·a·phor´i·cal** adj. — **met·a·phor´i·cal·ly** adv.

met´a·phys´ics n. the branch of philosophy that deals with the essential nature of reality — **met·a·phys´i·cal** adj. — **met·a·phys´i·cal·ly** adv.

mete vt. to measure and distribute

me´te·or n. a bright streak in the heaven produced when a meteoroid enters the earth's atmosphere

me·te·or´ic adj. pertaining to meteors; pertaining to atmospheric phenomenon; swift, as a meteoric rise to power — **me·te·or´i·cal·ly** adv.

me´te·or·ite n. an object from space that has fallen into the earth's atmosphere — **me·te·or·it´ic, me·te·or·it´i·cal** adj.

me´te·or·oid n. any of the small particles of matter moving through space

me·te·o·rol´o·gy n. the study of atmospheric phenomenon, esp.

relating to weather — **me·te·or·o·log´ic, me·te·or·o·log´i·cal** adj. — **me·te·or·o·log´i·cal·ly** adv. — **me·te·o·rol´o·gist** n.

me´ter (Brit.) n. a device for measuring

me´ter (US) n. a rhythmic pattern, as in poetry or music; a device for measuring; a unit of length in the metric system — vt. to measure with a meter; to provide in measured amounts

meth´od n. a systematic procedure; orderliness in manner or mode

me·thod´i·cal adj. in a systematic or orderly fashion — **me·thod´i·cal·ly** adv. — **me·thod´i·cal·ness** n.

meth·od·ol´o·gy n. the body of systematic procedures that characterize a particular area of study or investigation — **meth·od·o·log´i·cal** adj. — **meth·od·o·log´i·cal·ly** adv. — **meth·od·ol´o·gist** n.

me·tic´u·lous adj. precise; marked by unusual attention to detail — **me·tic´u·lous·ly** adv. — **me·tic´u·lous·ness** n.

me´tre (Brit.) n. a rhythmic pattern, as in poetry or music; a unit of length in the metric system — vt. to measure with a meter; to provide in measured amounts

metric system n. a decimal system of weights and measure — **met´ric** adj.

met´ro adj. metropolitan

met´ro·nome n. a device used to mark time in music — **met´ro·nom´ic** adj.

me·trop´o·lis n. a major urban area

met´ro·pol´i·tan adj. of a major urban area

met´tle n. courage; strength of character — **met´tle·some** adj.

mez´za·nine´ n. a balcony; a landing or balcony between two main floors of a building

mi·as´ma n. foul air; a corrupting influence spread as though carried in the air —**mi·as´mal, mi·as·mat´ic, mi·as´mic** adj.

mi´crobe n. a microorganism —**mi·cro´bi·al, mi·cro´bic** adj.

mi·cro·bi·ol´o·gy n. the study of microorganisms —**mi´cro·bio·log´i·cal** adj. —**mi´cro·bi·ol´o·gist** n.

mi´cro·com·put·er n. a portable computer such as a laptop or notebook computer

mi´cro·cosm n. a small representation of a much larger system —**mi´cro·cos´mic, mi·cro·cos´mi·cal** adj.

mi·crom´e·ter n. a device for making small measurements

mi·cro·min´i·a·tur·i·za´tion n. reduction to extremely small size or scale —**mi·cro·min´i·a·ture** adj. —**mi·cro·min´i·a·tur·ize** vt.

mi·cro·or´ga·nism n. a microscopic creature

mi´cro·phone n. a device for converting sound waves into electronic impulses —**mi´cro·phon´ic** adj.

mi´cro·proc·es·sor n. an integrated circuit that comprises the central processing unit of a computer

mi´cro·pro´gram n. any of the individual computer instructions that together comprise a complete command

mi´cro·scope n. a device for magnifying objects that cannot be seen with the naked eye —**mi´cro·scop´ic** adj. —**mi·cro·scop´i·cal·ly** adv.

mi´cro·wave n. an electromagnetic energy wave; a microwave oven — vt. to cook in a microwave oven

mid´dle adj. positioned approximately midway between extremes —n. a center or midpoint

mid´dle·man n. a go–between; one who buys in large volume from a few sources and distributes in smaller quantities to retailers or consumers; a jobber

middle management administrators and supervisors who deal mainly with the day–to–day operation of a business

mid´land n. the central part of a country

mid´riff n. the part of the body between the chest and the abdomen

midst n. positioned in or among; located at or near the midpoint

mid´way n. an assortment of carnival sideshows, games, etc.; halfway

mid´wife n. one trained to assist in childbirth —**mid·wife´ry** n.

mien n. one's appearance or demeanor

miff vi., vt. to be or cause to be offended or annoyed

might n. strength or power

might´y adj. strong or powerful; imposing; impressive —**might´i·ly** adv. —**might´i·ness** n.

mi´graine n. a severe headache —**mi·grain´ous** adj.

mi´grant adj. migratory —n. one who moves frequently, often in search of work

mi´grate vi. to move frequently and often, regularly; to move from one area, country, etc. to another

mi·gra´tion n. a move, especially of a group moving together

mi·gra·to·ry adj. tending to move often, especially with the change of seasons

mild adj. gentle or moderate —**mild´ly** adv. —**mild´ness** n.

mil´dew n. a type of fungus; a coating caused by this fungus

mile n. a measure of distance

mile´age n. distance traveled; an amount paid or allowed for business travel

mile´post, mile´stone n. a distance marker set beside a road; anything that is a mark of progress: *graduation from college is a milepost on the way to a successful career*

mi·lieu´ n. environment; surroundings

mil´i·tant *adj.* belligerent or aggressive in nature —**mil´i·tance, mil´i·tan·cy** *n.* —**mil´i·tant·ly** *adv.*

mil´i·ta·rism *n.* an emphasizing of the need for military preparedness; a philosophy that emphasizes military spirit or values —**mil´i·ta·rist** *n.* —**mil´i·ta·ris´tic** *adj.* —**mil·i·ta·ris´ti·cal·ly** *adv.*

mil´i·ta·rize *vt.* to prepare for war or for use by armed forces —**mil·i·ta·ri·za´tion** *n.*

mil´i·tar·y *adj.* related to armed forces or to war —**mil·i·tar´i·ly** *adv.*

mi·li´tia *n.* a citizen army —**mi·li´tia·man** *n.*

milk *n.* fluid produced by mammals to feed their young; any similar fluid, as from a plant —*vt.* to draw off or extract milk from; to take advantage of —**milk´i·ness** *n.* —**milk´y** *adj.*

mill *n.* a place for grinding grain; a factory; a device or machine that transforms by grinding, shaping, etc.; something that functions or seems to function methodically: *the rumor mill* —*vt.* to transform by a machine or other device —*vi.* to move about in a disorderly fashion —**mill´er** *n.*

mil·len´ni·um *n.* a period of a thousand years; a thousand–year period of joy and plenty as foretold in the Christian Bible —**mil·len´ni·al** *adj.* —**mil·len´ni·al·ist** *n.* —**mil·len´ni·al·ly** *adv.*

mil´li·ner *n.* one who makes or sells women's hats —**mil´li·ner·y** *n.*

mi´lion·aire´ *n.* a wealthy person; one who possesses over a million dollars worth of assets

mill´stone *n.* a large, heavy stone used in milling grain; a burden: *debt can be a millstone around one's neck*

milque´toast *n.* a timid person

mime *n.* one who performs without words; a pantomime —*vi., vt.* to communicate with gestures —**mim´er** *n.*

mim´e·o·graph *n.* a machine that duplicates or prints documents from a stencil; copies made with such a machine —*vi., vt.*

mim´ic *n.* one who portrays another, often with exaggeration —*vt.* to imitate closely —**mim´ick·er** *n.* —**mim´ic·ry** *n.*

min´a·ret´ *n.* a tower on a mosque from which Muslims are summoned to prayer

min´a·to·ry, min·a·to´ri·al *adj.* threatening —**min·a·to´ri·al·ly, min´a·to·ri·ly** *adv.*

mince *vi.* to walk or speak in an affected manner —*vt.* to chop into small pieces; to lessen or cushion so as to be polite: *to mince words* —**minc´er** *n.*

mince´meat *n.* a thick, spicy concoction of fruit and meat used especially as a pie filling

mind *n.* consciousness or awareness of being; the intellect that comprises such elements as memory, original thought, and emotion; the ability to think —*vi., vt.* to behave; to notice or give heed to; to be concerned about

mind´–al·ter·ing *adj.* that distorts the consciousness or intellect

mind´–bog·gling *adj.* overwhelming; extremely impressive —**mind´–bog·gler** *n.*

mind´–expand·ing *adj.* creating greater awareness: *education is mind–expanding*; psychedelic: creating distorted perception

mind´ful *adj.* careful, attentive; maintaining awareness —**mind´ful·ly** *adv.* —**mind´ful·ness** *n.*

mind´less *adj.* without reason or purpose; lacking care or caution; indifferent —**mind´less·ly** *adv.* —**mind´less·ness** *n.*

mind·set, mind´–set *n.* a fixed

attitude or response; a predilection

mind's eye imagination or memory

mine *n.* a hole in the ground or a tunnel, especially to extract minerals; any source, as of material or information: *the library is a mine for knowledge*; an explosive device used in warfare —*vi., vt.* to dig a tunnel; to extract minerals from the earth; to set a hidden explosive device

mine´field *n.* an area seeded with explosive devices; something potentially dangerous or unpleasant: *the minefield of morality in politics*

min·er·al *n.* naturally occurring inorganic matter —*adj.* of or containing inorganic matter

min·er·al·o·gy *n.* the study of minerals —**min·er·al·og´ic, min´er·al·og´i·cal** *adj.* —**min·er·al·og´i·cal·ly** *adv.* —**min·er·al´o·gist** *n.*

mineral oil a colorless, tasteless oil derived from petroleum

mineral water water that contains mineral salts, produced naturally or artificially

min·e·stro´ne *n.* an Italian soup of beans, pasta, and vegetables

min´gle *vi., vt.* to combine or mix together

min´i·a·ture *adj.* small or smaller — *n.* something small for its type; a copy or model of something larger —**min´i·a·tur·ist** *n.*

min´i·a·tur·ize *vt.* to make smaller without loss of utility: *to miniaturize computer components*; to make a model or copy in miniature — **min·i·a·tur·i·za´tion** *n.*

min´i·bus *n.* a small bus; a public conveyance used especially on routes traveled by few passengers

min´i·cam *n.* a portable video camera

min·i·com·put·er *n.* a computer that is smaller than a mainframe, but not easily portable; a desktop computer

min´i·mal *adj.* the smallest possible; barely adequate —**min´i·mal·ly** *adv.*

min´i·mal·ism *n.* a style of art characterized by simplicity of form, color, etc. —**min´i·mal·ist** *n.*

min´i·mize *vt.* to make with the smallest practical investment of resources; to downplay: *they minimized the extent of the loss* — **min´i·miz·er** *n.*

min´i·mum *n.* the least possible or allowable —*adj.*

min´ion *n.* a subordinate; a toady

min´i·se·ries *n.* a television program aired in a specific number of episodes

min´is·ter *n.* a clergyman; a government official —*vi.* to care for others

min´is·te´ri·al *adj.* of a clergyman or government official, or their offices —**min·is·te´ri·al·ly** *adv.*

min·is·tra´tion *n.* the act of caring for another —**min´is·tra´tive** *adj.*

min´is·try *n.* the office and duties of a minister; a department of government or the building in which it is housed; the care of others

min´now *n.* a type of small fish

mi´nor *adj.* of less significance —*n.* something less by comparison; one who is not of legal age

mi·nor´i·ty *n.* the smaller of two groups that comprise a whole; the time before one is of legal age

min´strel *n.* a wandering singer and poet; a minstrel show

minstrel show a variety show performed by singers, comics, etc. in blackface

mint *adj.* new in appearance, as if freshly made: *in mint condition* —*n.* a place where coins are struck; a plentiful amount —*vt.* to make or strike coins —**mint´er** *n.*

min·u·et´ *n.* a type of formal dance

min´us·cule *adj.* tiny

min´ute *n.* a small span of time;

1/60th of an hour —**mi·nute´** *adj.* very small; detailed or exacting, as of an examination —**mi·nute´ly** *adv.* —**mi·nute´ness** *n.*

mi·nu´ti·a *n., pl.* **mi·nu´ti·ae** a small often insignificant detail

minx *n.* a flirtatious or defiant woman —**minx´ish** *adj.*

mir´a·cle *n.* an event that seems to be scientifically unexplainable; a supernatural occurrence

miracle drug a medicine that is unusually effective or that can be used to treat a variety of illnesses

mi·rac´u·lous *adj.* of the nature of a miracle —**mi·rac´u·lous·ly** *adv.* —**mi·rac´u·lous·ness** *n.*

mi·rage´ *n.* an illusion, such as the sight of water in the desert when there is none; something flimsy or fanciful

mire *n.* an expanse of wet, muddy ground; a swamp; a difficult situation —*vi., vt.* to become stuck, as if in a mire: *they were mired in paperwork* —**mir´y** *adj.*

mir´ror *n.* a surface that reflects a visual image; something thought of as presenting an image: *auto sales mirror the strength of the economy*

mirror image a reverse image, as presented in a mirror

mirth *n.* lighthearted merriment

mirth´ful *adj.* expressing lighthearted gaiety —**mirth´ful·ly** *adv.* —**mirth´ful·ness** *n.*

mirth´less *adj.* lacking gaiety; somber —**mirth´less·ly** *adv.* —**mirth´less·ness** *n.*

mis·ad·ven´ture *n.* misfortune

mis·an´thrope, mis·an´thro·pist *n.* one who dislikes or distrusts people; a recluse —**mis·an·throp´ic, mis·an·throp´i·cal** *adj.* —**mis·an·throp´i·cal·ly** *adv.*

mis·an´thro·py *n.* hatred or distrust of people in general

mis·ap·pre·hend´ *vt.* to misunderstand — **mis·ap·pre·hen´sion** *n.*

mis·ap·pro´pri·ate *vt.* to take or use improperly or illegally —**mis·ap·pro·pri·a´tion** *n.*

mis·be·have´ *vt.* to conduct oneself badly or improperly —*vi.* to behave badly —**mis·be·hav´er** *n.* —**mis·be·hav´ior** *n.*

mis·cal´cu·late *vi., vt.* to plan, judge, or tally inaccurately —**mis·cal·cu·la´tion** *n.*

mis·car´riage *n.* the premature birth of a nonviable fetus; a spontaneous abortion; a failure or malfunction: *a miscarriage of justice* —**mis·car´ry** *vi.*

mis·ceg·e·na´tion *n.* a mixing of races, as by marriage

mis·cel·la´ne·a *pl. n.* a collection of written works or items

mis·cel·la´ne·ous *adj.* comprising a variety —**mis·cel·la´ne·ous·ly** *adv.* —**mis·cel·la´ne·ous·ness** *n.*

mis´cel·la·ny *n.* a collection

mis·chance´ *n.* misfortune

mis´chief *n.* a deliberate act that causes damage or distress; a tendency to perform such acts; one who engages in such acts —**mis´chief–mak·er** *n.*

mis´chie·vous *adj.* inclined to playful action such as teasing, or bothersome behavior such as being distructive or spreading rumors —**mis´chie·vous·ly** *adv.* —**mis´chie·vous·ness** *n.*

mis·con·cep´tion *n.* a misunderstanding —**mis·con·ceive´** *vt.*

mis·con´duct *n.* action contrary to accepted standards; wrongdoing, especially by a public official or one charged with protecting the interests of another —**mis´con·duct´** *vt.* to behave improperly; to mismanage the assets of another

mis´con·strue´ *vt.* to misinterpret

mis´cre·ant *n.* a villain; a criminal —*adj.* villainous

mis·deed´ *n.* the violation of a rule or law

mis´de·mean´or *n.* a minor crime

mis·di·rect´ *vt.* to improperly instruct or inform; to deliberately draw attention away from —**mis·di·rec´tion** *n.*

mi´ser *n.* one who hoards money

mis´er·a·ble *adj.* wretched; unpleasant —**mis´er·a·ble·ness** *n.* —**mis´er·a·bly** *adv.*

mi´ser·ly *adj.* stingy —**mi´ser·li·ness** *n.*

mis´er·y *n.* suffering or distress; anything that causes suffering

mis´fit´ *n.* one who does not harmonize or conform; a maladjusted person

mis·for´tune *n.* bad luck; adversity or a condition brought on by adversity

mis·giv´ing *n.* a feeling of doubt or uncertainty

mis·guide´ *vt.* to guide or direct improperly; to mislead; to lead astray —**mis·guid´ance** *n.* —**mis·guid´er** *n.*

mis·guid´ed *adj.* improperly directed; based on improper information or logic: *misguided efforts* —**mis·guid´ed·ly** *adv.*

mis·han´dle *vt.* to mismanage; to treat roughly or clumsily

mis´hap *n.* an accident

mish´mash *n.* a jumble of miscellaneous things; a poorly assembled or organized collection: *a mishmash of information*

mis·in·form´ *vt.* to advise inadequately or inaccurately; to mislead —**mis·in·form´ant,** **mis·in·form´er** *n.* —**mis·in·for·ma´tion** *n.*

mis·in·ter´pret *vt.* to misunderstand; to explain incorrectly —**mis´in·ter·pre·ta´tion** *n.* —**mis·in·ter´pret·er** *n.*

mis·judge´ *vt.* to form an opinion wrongly or unfairly —*vi.* to err in judging —**mis·judg´ment** *n.*

mis·lay´ *vt.* to place and forget

mis·lead´ *vt.* to direct wrongly or improperly; to lead astray —**mis·lead´er** *n.*

mis·lead´ing *adj.* deceptive —**mis·lead´ing·ly** *adv.*

mis·man´age *vt.* to conduct or supervise carelessly or wrongfully —**mis·man´age·ment** *n.*

mis·match´ *n.* an incompatible or unfit pairing —*vt.*

mis·no´mer *n.* an inappropriate name or designation

mi´so *n.* a thick fermented paste used especially in soup

mis·og´a·mist *n.* one who hates marriage —**mis·o·gam´ic** *adj.* —**mis·og´a·my** *n.*

mis·og´y·nist *n.* one who hates women —**mis·og´y·nis´tic,** **mis·og´y·nous** *adj.* —**mi·sog´y·ny** *n.*

mis·place´ *vt.* to mislay or lose; to put in the wrong place —**mis·place´ment** *n.*

mis´print *n.* a printing error —*vt.*

mis·pri´sion *n.* concealment of a crime

mis·pro·nounce´ *vt.* to enunciate incorrectly —**mis·pro·nun·ci·a´tion** *n.*

mis·quote´ *vt.* to cite incorrectly —**mis·quo·ta´tion** *n.*

mis·read´ *vt.* to read or interpret incorrectly; to misunderstand

mis·re·mem´ber *vt.* to recall incorrectly; to fail to recall

mis·rep·re·sen·ta´tion *n.* a false or misleading depiction —**mis´rep·re·sent´** *vt.*

miss *n.* a failing; a form of address for an unmarried woman —*vi.,* *vt.* to fail to make contact, as in hitting or catching a ball; to exclude or allow to pass: *miss an opportunity*; to discover or endure the loss of: *I miss my friends*

mis´sal *n.* a prayer book

mis·shape´ *vt.* to fashion badly; to deform or distort —**mis·shap´en·ly** *adv.*

mis´sile *n.* a projectile

miss´ing *adj.* absent or lacking; gone

missing link something lacking in a sequence, as in the evolutionary chain of a creature

mis´sion *n.* a group or organization established for a special purpose, as of a diplomatic or religious nature; the function or task of such a group —**mis´sion·ar·y** *n., adj.*

mis´sive *n.* a letter or memo; any written message

mis·speak´ *vi., vt.* to speak incorrectly or out of turn

mis·spend´ *vt.* to squander

mis·step´ *n.* a slipping or stumbling; a mistake or blunder

mist *n.* minute droplets that form a haze; something that obscures — *vt., vi.* to make or become dim: *to mist over*; to rain in fine droplets —**mist´i·ly** *adv.* — **mist´i·ness** *n.* —**mist´y** *adj.*

mis·tak´a·ble *adj.* susceptible to misunderstanding —**mis·tak´a·bly** *adv.*

mis·take´ *n.* an error; a misunderstanding —*vi.* to make a mistake —*vt.* to misinterpret; to wrongly identify a person

mis·tak´en *adj.* misinformed or misguided; wrong —**mis·tak´en·ly** *adv.*

mis´ter *n.* a form of address for a man

mis·treat´ *vt.* to handle roughly or clumsily —**mis·treat´ment** *n.*

mis´tress *n.* a woman in authority; one who owns or controls; a teacher; one who possesses exception knowledge or ability in a particular field; a female who is companion to and supported by a man not her husband

mis·tri´al *n.* a trial in which a verdict is not rendered or that is declared invalid

mis·trust´ *n.* uncertainty, doubt, or suspicion —*vi., vt.* to regard with doubt or suspicion —**mis·trust´ful** *adj.* —**mis·trust´ful·ly** *adv.* —**mis·trust´ful·ness** *n.*

mist´y-eyed *adj.* sentimental; tearful

mis·un·der·stand´ *vt.* to misinterpret

mis·un·der·stand´ing *n.* a calm disagreement or quarrel; a misinterpretation

mis·un·der·stood´ *adj.* misinterpreted; misjudged; not appreciated

mis·use´ *n.* an improper use; abuse —*vt.* to use wrongly or improperly; to abuse —**mis·us´age** *n.*

mi´ter *n.* a tall ornamental headdress worn by church leaders; the office of a bishop; one of the bevels that make up a miter joint —*vt.* to raise to the rank of bishop; to join with a miter

miter box a guide designed to assist in the cutting of a miter

miter joint a coupling of two angled pieces, as at the corner of a picture frame

mit´i·gate *vi., vt.* to become or make less intense or severe —**mit´i·ga·ble** *adj.* —**mit·i·ga´tion** *n.* —**mit´i·ga·tive, mit´i·ga·to·ry** *adj.* —**mit´i·ga·tor** *n.*

mitt *n.* a glove, especially one worn for protection: *catcher's mitt, oven mitt*

mit´ten *n.* a glove with one pocket for the thumb and another for the four fingers

mix *n.* a combination of ingredients —*vi., vt.* to become or cause to become combined; to blend in; to confuse: *the waiter mixed up their orders* —**mix´a·ble** *adj.*

mixed *adj.* combined; consisting of differing elements: *of mixed blood*

mixed´-up´ *adj.* confused or befuddled

mix´er *n.* a device that combines or blends; the non-alcoholic beverage in a cocktail; a type of gathering;

one who meets easily with others

mix´ture *n.* a mix; anything that results from mixing or combining;

mix´-up *n.* a state of turmoil or confusion

mne·mon´ics *n.* any formula or technique used as a memory aid — **mne·mon´i·cal·ly** *adv.* —**mne· mon´ic, mne·mon´i·cal** *adj.*

moan *n.* a low, doleful sound — **moan´er** *n.*

moat *n.* a protective ditch

mob *n.* a large crowd, often disorderly; a group of criminals —*vt.* to crowd or overwhelm

mo´bile *adj.* movable; easily moved —*n.* a piece of hanging art made up of balanced pieces that move freely

mo·bil´i·ty *n.* movement; the ability to move easily

mo´bi·lize *vt.* to make moveable; to organize and deploy, as for a cause —**mo·bi·li·za´tion** *n.*

mob´ster *n.* a criminal

moc´ca·sin *n.* footwear similar to a slipper, often of leather

mo´cha *n.* a rich coffee; a flavoring of coffee and chocolate

mock *adj.* imitation; false —*vi., vt.* to ridicule or imitate derisively — **mock´er** *n.* —**mock´ery** *n.* — **mock´ing·ly** *adv.*

mock´-up *n.* a scale model; a layout for a printed page

mode *n.* a particular manner or fashion —**mod´al** *adj.*

mod´el *n.* a copy or prototype; one who poses for an artist or displays clothing, etc.; an ideal: *a model of virtue* —*vi., vt.* to make a model; to pose; to display by wearing

mod´el·ing *n.* the art of sculpting; the act of posing, as for an artist

mo´dem *n.* a device that converts data from digital to analog and back

mod´er·ate *adj.* not extreme or excessive —*n.* one who is not

inclined to extreme views, as in politics —*vi., vt.* to become or make less extreme; to preside as moderator —**mod´er·ate·ly** *adv.* — **mod´er·ate·ness** *n.* —**mod·er·a´ tion** *n.*

mod´er·a·tor *n.* one who mediates or officiates, as at a meeting

mod´ern *adj.* of recent time or development —**mod´ern·ly** *adv.* —**mod´ ern·ness** *n.*

mod´ern·ize *vi., vt.* to become or make contemporary —**mod·ern·i· za´tion** *n.*

mod´est *adj.* unpretentious; diffident; conforming to convention; not given to extremes: *a modest proposal* —**mod´est·ly** *adv.* — **mod´es·ty** *n.*

mod´i·cum *n.* a small amount

mod·i·fi·ca´tion *n.* a change or alteration; the result of such change —**mod´i·fi·ca·to·ry** *adj.*

mod´i·fy *vt.* to change or alter, especially to make less extreme —**mod· i·fi·a·bil´i·ty** *n.* —**mod´i·fi·a·ble** *adj.* —**mod´i·fi·er** *n.*

mod´ish *adj.* smart or trendy; in the current style —**mod´ish·ly** *adv.* — **mod´ish·ness** *n.*

mod´u·lar *adj.* of a module; based on the use of or made up of modules —**mod´u·lar·ize** *vt.* —**mod´u· lar·ized** *adj.*

mod´ule *n.* a self-contained component that may be attached as or where needed, sucn as a part of a furniture grouping, a sound system, or a computer program

mo´dus ope·ran´di *n.* a manner of operating

mo´dus vi·ven´di *n.* a manner of living

mo´gul *n.* one who is rich or powerful

moi´e·ty *n.* a half; a portion

moist *adj.* slightly wet; damp — **moist´ly** —*adv.* —**moist´ness** *n.*

moist´en *vi., vt.* to become or make

slightly wet —**moist´en·er** n.

mois´ture n. slight wetness, as dampness in the air or condensation on a surface

mois´tur·ize vt. to add wetness to — **mois´tur·iz·er** n.

mo´lar n. a large tooth used to grind foods

mo·las´ses n. a thick, sweet syrup

mold¹ (US) n. a form for casting an image —vi. to be shaped in or as if in a form —vt. to form or shape — **mold´able** adj. —**mold´er** n.

mold² (US) n. a type of fungal growth — vt. to be marked or damaged by a fungal growth

mold, mold´ing n. a decorative strip used as trim, as around a door or window

mold´er (US) vi. to gradually decay

mold´y (US) adj. damaged or spoiled by a fungal growth; having a musty odor —**mold´i·ness** n.

mol´e·cule n. the smallest particle of matter having distinctive chemical and physical properties; a tiny particle —**mo·lec´u·lar** adj.

mo·lest´ vt. to disturb or annoy; to accost improperly in a sexual manner —**mo·les·ta´tion** n. —**mo·lest´er** n.

mol´li·fy vt. to soothe or pacify; to soften —**mol·li·fi·ca´tion** n. — **mol´li·fy·ing·ly** adv.

mol´lusk n. a marine invertebrate with a soft body and a hard protective shell —**mol·lus´coid** adj.

molt (US) vi., vt. to shed, as feathers or an outer skin —**molt´er** n.

mol´ten adj. extremely hot and melted or liquified

mo´ment n. a brief interval: he'll be along in a moment; importance: a breakthrough of great moment

mo´men·tary adj. existing for a brief time —**mo´men·tar´i·ly** adv. — **mo´men·tar·i·ness** n.

mo·men´tous adj. of great importance —**mo·men´tous·ly** adv. —**mo·men´tous·ness** n.

mo·men´tum n. a measure of the force of a body in motion; the force or energy generated by ideas or events

mon´arch n. an absolute ruler — **mo·nar´chal, mo·nar´chic, mo·nar´chi·cal** adj. —**mo·nar´chal·ly** adv.

mon´ar·chism n. advocacy of a monarchy —**mon´ar·chist** n. — **mon·ar·chist´ic** adj.

mon´ar·chy n. government by a sovereign, usually selected by hereditary succession and for life — **mo·nar´chi·al** adj.

mon´as·ter·y n. a religious community, often secluded —**mon´as·te´ri·al** adj.

mo·nas´tic adj. typical of a monastery, as an austere or disciplined environment —**mo·nas´ti·cal·ly** adv.

mon·au´ral adj. monophonic: of sound directed through a single channel —**mon·au´ral·ly** adv.

mon´e·ta·rism n. the management of an economy by adjustment of the domestic money supply — **mon´e·ta·rist** n.

mon´e·tary adj. regarding money or finances —**mon·e·tar´i·ly** adv.

mon´ey n. legal tender; the currency, notes, etc. issued by a government; an expression of wealth: in the money

mon´ey·bags n. a wealthy person; a spendthrift

mon´eyed adj. wealthy

mon´ey·grub´ber n. one intent on amassing wealth —**mon´ey·grub´bing** adj.

mon´ey·mak·ing adj. profitable — **mon´ey·mak·er** n.

mon´ger n. a tradesman: a fishmonger; a promoter or advocate of something: a peacemonger, a scandalmonger

mon´grel adj. of mixed breed —n. a

plant or animal that is the result of interbreeding —**mon·grel·i·za´tion** n. —**mon´grel·ize** vt.

mon´i·tor n. a device that controls or provides a overview of a system; an adviser or assistant; an overseer —vt. to oversee or regulate —**mon·i·to´ri·al** adj. —**mon·i·to´ri·al·ly** adv. —**mon´i·tor·ship** n.

mon´i·to·ry adj. admonishing; cautionary

monk n. a member of a religious order, residing in a monastary —**monk´hood** n.

monk´ish adj. characteristic of a monk or a monastic life; austere or disciplined —**monk´ish·ly** adv. —**monk´ish·ness** n.

mon·o·chro·mat´ic adj. having one color —**mon·o·chro·mat´i·cal·ly** adv. —**mon·o·chro·ma·tic´i·ty** n.

mon´o·chrome n. a picture or image in one color —adj. monochromatic —**mon·o·chro´mic** adj.

mon´o·cle n. a corrective lens for one eye —**mon´o·cled** adj.

mo·noc´ra·cy n. government by a single person —**mon´o·crat** n. —**mon·o·crat´ic** adj.

mo·nog´a·my n. the practice of having one spouse or mate at a time; the practice of taking one spouse or mate for a lifetime —**mo·nog´a·mist** n. —**mo·nog´a·mous** adj. —**mo·nog´a·mous·ly** adv.

mon´o·gram n. a letter or letters designed as a distinguishing emblem —vt. to adorn with a monogram —**mon´o·gram·mat´ic** adj.

mon´o·graph n. a scholarly dissertation —**mo·nog´ra·pher** n. —**mon´o·graph´ic** adj.

mon´o·lith n. a large block of stone that forms a column or monument; something massive and solid —**mon·o·lith´ic** adj. —**mon·o·lith´i·cal·ly** adv.

mon´o·log, mon´o·logue n. an informal discourse by a single person that may be dramatic or comedic —**mo·nol´o·gist** n.

mon·o·pho´bi·a n. fear of being alone

mon·o·phon´ic adj. monaural; of a musical composition that is mainly a single line of melody —**mon·o·phon´i·cal·ly** adv. —**mo·noph´o·ny** n.

mo·nop´o·lize vt. to dominate, as a conversation; to control, as the market in certain goods —**mo·nop·o·li·za´tion** n.

mo·nop´o·ly n. absolute control of a market by a limited number; those having control, or the commodity or service thereby controlled; any control, as if by a monopoly: they act as if they have a monopoly on integrity —**mo·nop´o·list** n. —**mo·nop·o·lis´tic** adj. —**mo·nop·o·lis´ti·cal·ly** adv.

mon´o·rail n. a train that travels on or is suspended from a single rail

mon·o·syl·lab´ic adj. pertaining to a word of one syllable —**mon·o·syl·lab´i·cal·ly** adv.

mon´o·the·ism n. belief in a single god —**mon´o·the·ist** n. —**mon´o·the·is´tic, mon·o·the·is´ti·cal** adj. —**mon·o·the·is´ti·cal·ly** adv.

mon´o·tone —n. an instrumentation or vocalization in a single tone; an illustration in a single color; a listless or boring delivery: he droned on in a monotone —**mon·o·ton´ic** adj. —**mon·o·ton´i·cal·ly** adv.

mo·not´o·nous adj. tedious or tiresome; spoken in a monotone —**mo·not´o·nous·ly** adv. —**mo·not´o·ny** n.

mon´ster n. a frightening creature; someone abnormally cruel; a deformed organism; something very large

mon´strous adj. frightening; abnormally cruel; deformed; huge —**mon·stros´i·ty** n. —**mon´strous·ly**

adv. —**mon´strous·ness** *n.*

mon·tage´ *n.* a work of art made up of a number of separate designs or pictures

month *n.* a period approximating one cycle of the moon; one-twelfth of a year

month´ly *adj.* occurring every month —*n.* a periodical that is published every month

mon´u·ment *n.* a memorial, such as a structure or plaque; a structure or plate anchored in the ground as a boundry or survey marker; an outstanding example: *the decor is a monument to bad taste*

mon·u·men´tal *adj.* impressive, as in size or significance —**mon·u·men´tal·ly** *adv.*

mooch *vi., vt.* to freeload or get by begging —**mooch´er** *n.*

mood *n.* one's state of mind or attitude

mood´y *adj.* sullen; susceptible to depression; temperamental —**mood´i·ly** *adv.* —**mood´i·ness** *n.*

moon *n.* a satellite of a planet; the bared buttocks —*vi.* to languish about as though distracted —*vt.* to bare the buttocks in a playful manner

moon´light *n.* light reflected from the moon —*vi.* to work at a second job, often at night

moon´shine *n.* illegal whiskey —**moon´shin·er** *n.*

moon´struck *adj.* beguiled by romantic notions

moor *vi., vt.* to secure or anchor, as a boat or plane

moor´age, moor´ing *n.* a place where a boat or plane may be secured; the charge for use of such a place

moot *adj.* that can be disputed; of no significance

mop *n.* a clump or mass of soft material, usually attached to a handle and used for cleaning; something resembling a soft clump or mass: *a mop of hair* —*vi., vt.* to wash or wipe by rubbing; to make clean; to complete a task: *mop up the details of the contract* —**mop´–up** *n.*

mope *vi.* to act dejected; to sulk —**mop´er** *n.* —**mop´ey, mop´ish** *adj.* —**mop´ish·ly** *adv.*

mop´pet *n.* a child

mo·raine´ *n.* debris deposited by a glacier, as rocks or boulders —**mo·rain´ic** *adj.*

mor´al *adj.* conforming to what is right or just —*n.* a truth or principle, as contained in a story or saying —**mor´al·ly** *adv.*

mo·rale´ *n.* one's attitude or sense of enthusiasm, resolve, or confidence

mor´al·ist *n.* one overly concerned with morals; one inclined to impose his or her values on others —**mor´al·ism** *n.* —**mor´al·is´tic** *adj.* —**mor·al·is´ti·cal·ly** *adv.*

mo·ral´i·ty *n.* a system or sense of what is right or just; conduct that is true to such a system

mor´al·ize *vi., vt.* to pronounce judgement or lecture on morals —**mor·al·iz·a´tion** *n.*

mo·rass´ *n.* a wetland; a marsh or bog; something that impedes: *a morass of regulations*

mor·a·to´ri·um *n.* a suspension or delay: *a moratorium on nuclear testing* —**mor´a·to·ry** *adj.*

mor´bid *adj.* diseased; caused by disease; gruesome; abnormally preoccupied by that which is gruesome —**mor´bid·ly** *adv.* —**mor´bid·ness** *n.*

mor·da´cious *adj.* sharp or caustic; sarcastic —**mor·da´cious·ly** *adv.* —**mor·dac´i·ty** *n.*

mor´dant *adj.* sharp or incisive; caustic —*n.* a corrosive substance used in etching —**mor´dan·cy** *n.* —**mor´dant·ly** *adv.*

more *adj.* greater, as in number or degree; enhanced or extended —*n.*

an additional amount —*adv.*

mo´res *n.* the accepted standards of a society, as in customs, manners, or morals

morgue *n.* a place where dead bodies are kept awaiting identification, autopsy, burial, etc.; a library or reference file, especially in a news office

mor·i·bund *adj.* nearing death; outdated —**mor·i·bun´di·ty** *n.* —**mor´ i·bund·ly** *adv.*

morn *n.* daybreak; the daylight hours of morning

morn´ing *n.* that part of the day from midnight to noon or from sunrise to noon; a beginning

mo´ron *n.* someone regarded as stupid or very foolish —**mo·ron´ic** *adj.* —**mo·ron´i·cal·ly** *adv.*

mo·rose´ *adj.* surly or gloomy —**mo· rose´ly** *adv.* —**mo·rose´ness** *n.*

mor·phol´o·gy *n.* the scientific study of the form and structure of things, as of organisms or of words —**mor´pho·log´ic, mor·pho·log´i· cal** *adj.* —**mor·pho·log´i·cal·ly** *adv.* —**mor·phol´o·gist** *n.*

mor´row *n.* the next day

mor´sel *n.* a bit of food, especially a delicacy; a small amount: *a morsel of kindness*

mor´tal *adj.* of the physical person in contrast to the spiritual or supernatural; susceptible to death; deadly —*n.* a human being — **mor´tal·ly** *adv.*

mor·tal´i·ty *n.* the limits to being mortal; a rate of death or failure

mor´tar *n.* a bonding material used in construction; something that bonds: *the star is the mortar that holds the show together*; a type of cannon; a container in which material such as spice or chemicals are ground with a pestle

mor´tar·board *n.* a board used for carrying mortar; a flat-topped graduation cap

mort´gage *n.* the pledge of property as security for payment of a debt; a contract stipulating the terms of such a pledge —*vt.* to pledge property —**mort´gage·a·ble** *adj.*

mort·ga·gee´ *n.* one who lends and holds a mortgage

mort´ga·gor *n.* one who borrows and mortgages

mor·ti´cian *n.* one who prepares the dead for burial; an undertaker

mor·ti·fi·ca´tion *n.* humiliation or shame; discipline or pennance as by self-denial

mor´ti·fy *vi.* to undergo discipline through self-denial —*vt.* to humiliate or shame; to discipline oneself through self-denial

mor´tise *n.* a slot designed to accept a tenon and form a joint in a piece of wood or other material

mor´tu·ary *n.* a place where dead bodies are kept in preparation for burial

mo·sa´ic *n.* a design made on a surface by joining small colored pieces, such as tiles; something resembling a mosaic —**mo·sa´i· cal·ly** *adj.*

mosque *n.* a Muslim house of worship

most *adj.* of the greatest number or amount —*n.* the larger part; the greatest amount —*adv.* to the greatest degree, extent, etc.

most´ly *adv.* frequently; largely

mot *n.* a witty remark

mote *n.* a speck

mo·tel´ *n.* a lodging for travelers

moth´-eat·en *adj.* passé; shabby, as though attacked by moths

moth´er *adj.* being of a source or derived from: *English is our mother tongue* —*n.* a female parent; one who gives birth —*vt.* to give birth; to rear

moth´er·board *n.* a panel that contains the primary circuitry for a computer

moth´er·in·law *n.* the mother of one's spouse

mother lode an abundant source

moth´er·ly *adj.* nurturing; having the qualities of a mother

mother tongue one's native language

mo·tif´ *n.* a recurring theme, as in art or decorating

mo´tile *adj.* having the power of motion —**mo·til´i·ty** *n.*

mo·tion *n.* a movement; the act of moving; a proposal, as put before a court or in a formal meeting —*vi.*, *vt.* to gesture or guide

mo´tion·less *adj.* immobile; still — **mo´tion·less·ly** *adv.* —**mo´tion·less·ness** *n.*

mo´ti·vate *vt.* to rouse to action — **mo´ti·va´tor** *n.*

mo·ti·va´tion *n.* an inducement — **mo·ti·va´tion·al** *adj.* —**mo·ti·va´tion·al·ly** *adv.*

mo·tive *n.* an urge that induces one to act

mot´ley *adj.* varied; marked by variety or incongruity; multicolored — *n.* a multi-colored garment as worn by court jesters of old; an incongruous mixture

mo´tor *adj.* of motion or things associated with motion —*n.* a device that produces mechanical energy —*vi.*, *vt.* to travel or convey by motor vehicle

mo´tor·cade *n.* a parade of motor vehicles

motor vehicle a free-wheeling conveyance, such as a car or truck, powered by a built-in engine

mot´tled *adj.* spotted with a variety of colors or tints —**mot´tle** *vt.* — **mot´tling** *n.*

mot´to *n.* a word or phrase that expresses a worthwhile thought

mould¹ (*Brit.*) *n.* a form for casting an image —*vi.* to be shaped in or as if in a form —*vt.* to form or shape —**mould´er** *n.*

mould² (*Brit.*) *n.* a type of fungal growth — *vt.* to be marked or damaged by a fungal growth

mould´er (*Brit.*) *vi.* to gradually decay

mould´y (*Brit.*) *adj.* damaged or spoiled by a fungal growth; having a musty odor —**mould´i·ness** *n.*

moult (*Brit.*) *vi.*, *vt.* to shed, as feathers or an outer skin —**moult´er** *n.*

mound *n.* a pile or heap; a knoll or small hill —*vt.* to make into a heap

mount *n.* a riding horse; a device that holds something, as for display —*vi.*, *vt.* to ascend, as stairs; to get onto, as a horse; to fix in place, as pictures in an album; to increase, as cost —**mount´a·ble** *adj.* —**mount´er** *n.*

mount, moun´tain *n.* elevated land of substantial height and mass; a large amount: *we faced a mountain of work*

mountain dew moonshine

moun´tain·ous *adj.* resembling a mountain: extremely large; full of mountains —**moun´tain·ous·ly** *adv.*

mountain range a string of connected mountains

moun´te·bank *n.* a charlatan; originally, a fast-talking seller of useless medicine or tonic

mourn *vi.*, *vt.* to express grief or sorrow —**mourn´er** *n.*

mourn´ful *adj.* expressing or suggesting grief or sorrow: *a mournful sound* —**mourn´ful·ly** *adv.* — **mourn´ful·ness** *n.*

mourn´ing *n.* a period of grieving for the dead; the signs of grieving, as black clothing or arm band

mouse *n.* a small rodent; a timid person; a computer control device —**mous´ey, mous´y** *adj.* —

mousse *n.* any of a number of light desserts or savory dishes bound by whipped cream and gelatin and served cold; a preparation used to style the hair

mous´tache *n.* hair grown on the upper lip

mouth *n.* the body opening for taking in food; any restricted opening, as of a river, a bottle, or a cave — *vi., vt.* to speak; to form words without sound

mouth´y *adj.* given to excessive or offensive speech; annoyingly talkative —**mouth´i·ly** *adv.* — **mouth´i·ness** *n.*

move *vi., vt.* to advance, or cause to advance from one place to another; to alter position; to act or be active; to be or cause to be emotionally aroused; to propose a course, as in court or a formal meeting — **mov·a·bil´i·ty, mov´a·ble·ness** *n.* —**mov´a·ble** *adj.* —**mov´a·bly** *adv.*

move´ment *n.* a change in position; a steady or gradual change

mov´er *n.* one who transports goods; one purposeful in seeking advancement

mov´ing *adj.* in motion; of the transfer of goods; tending to arouse an emotional response — **mov´ing·ly** *adv.*

mow *n.* a place in a barn for the storage of feed; the feed stored — *vi., vt.* to cut down, as grain — **mow´er** *n.*

much *adj.* considerable, as in quantity or extent —*n.* a considerable amount —*adv.* to a great degree; approximately

mu´ci·lage *n.* an adhesive —**mu´ci·lag´i·nous** *adj.*

muck *n.* a wet sticky mixture; filth; something offensive —*vt.* to soil; to botch: *he mucked up the deal* — **muck´y** *adj.*

muck´rak·er *n.* one who exposes the shortcomings of those in the public eye —**muck´rake** *vi.*

mud *n.* a mixture of soil and water; plaster or mortar; charges of wrongdoing or indiscretion

mud´dle *n.* confusion or disorder; a predicament —*vi., vt.* to be or make confused; to mismanage — **mud´dler** *n.* —**mud´dle-head·ed** *adj.*

mud´dy *adj.* stained with mud; murky or hazy: *muddy coffee, muddy thinking* —**mud´di·ly** *adv.* —**mud´di·ness** *n.*

mud´sling·er *n.* one who levels charges of wrongdoing or indiscretion, especially at a political opponent —**mud´sling·ing** *n.*

muff *vi., vt.* to perform badly; to bungle

muf´fin *n.* a type of quick bread

muf´fle *vt.* to suppress or deaden sound; to maintain secrecy, as if by covering

muf´fler *n.* a heavy scarf; (*US*) a device for deadening sound, as from an engine

mug *n.* a heavy cup; one's face or expression; a gangster —*vi.* to contort the face for comic effect — *vt.* to assault

mug´ger *n.* one who makes comical faces; one who assaults

mug´gy *adj.* warm and humid — **mug´gi·ness** *n.*

mulch *n.* ground cover placed around plants to protect them — *vt.* to distribute ground cover

mul´ish *adj.* obstinate —**mul´ish·ly** *adv.* —**mul´ish·ness** *n.*

mull *vi., vt.* to ponder

mul´ti·col´ored *adj.* made up of a variety of colors

mul·ti·cul´tur·al *adj.* involving a diversity of cultures —**mul·ti·cul´tur·al·ism** *n.*

mul´ti·di·men´sion·al *adj.* diverse; varied in proportions and scope — **mul´ti·di·men·sion·al´i·ty** *n.*

mul·ti·fac´et·ed *adj.* diverse; having many aspects; versatile

mul´ti·far´i·ous *adj.* having great variety; diverse —**mul·ti·far´i·ous·ly** *adv.* —**mul·ti·far´i·ous·ness** *n.*

mul´ti·form *adj.* having many forms —**mu´ti·form´i·ty** *n.*

mul´ti·lat´er·al *adj.* involving several groups or nations; having many sides —**mul·ti·lat´er·al·ly** *adv.*

mul·ti·lin´gual *adj.* proficient in several languages —**mul·ti·lin´gual·ism** *n.* —**mul·ti·lin´gual·ly** *adv.*

mul´ti·me´di·a *n.* the mingling of several means of communication, such as visual images and sound on the computer, or the use of newspapers, radio, and television for an advertising campaign —*adj.* of the combining of media: *a multimedia presentation*

mul´ti·na´tion·al *adj.* involving several nations, such as for a trade agreement —*n.* a company with operations in several countries

mul´ti·ple *adj.* relating to several

mul´ti·plex *n.* a single building that contains a number of similar units, such as movie theaters

mul·ti·pli·ca´tion *n.* the process of increasing a number by adding it to itself a given number of times; animal or plant reproduction —**mul·ti·pli·ca´tion·al** *adj.*

mul·ti·plic´i·ty *n.* a large or varied collection: *a multiplicity of styles*

mul´ti·ply *vi., vt.* to increase or grow in numbers —**mul´ti·pli·able, mul´ti·plic´a·ble** *adj.*

mul´ti·task´ing *adj.* of a computer or computer application capable of performing several tasks at the same time

mul´ti·tude *n.* a large number; the general public

mul·ti·tu´di·nous *adj.* of a large number —**mul·ti·tu´di·nous·ly** *adv.* —**mul·ti·tu´di·nous·ness** *n.*

mum´ble *n.* an indistinct articulation or utterance —*vi., vt.* to speak indistinctly —**mum´bler** *n.* —**mum´bling·ly** *adv.* —**mum´bly** *adj.*

mum´bo jum´bo *n.* gibberish

mum´mer *n.* one who masquerades, esp. for certain festivals; an actor —**mum´mery** *n.*

mum·mi·fi·ca´tion *n.* preparation of a body for burial in the manner of the ancient Egyptians; the drying and preservation of a cadaver by natural conditions —**mum´mi·fy** *vi., vt.* —**mum´my** *n.*

mumps *pl. n.* a viral disease manifested mainly in the swelling of the salivary glands

munch *vi., vt.* to chew food —**munch´a·ble** *adj.*

munch´ies *n.* snack food

munch´kin *n.* a small person, especially a child

mun·dane´ *adj.* common or ordinary; not exceptional: *a mundane performance* —**mun·dane´ly** *adv.* —**mun·dane´ness** *n.*

mu·nic´i·pal *adj.* relating to a municipality or to local government —**mu·nic´i·pal·ly** *adv.*

mu·nic·i·pal´i·ty *n.* a local governmental unit, as for a city or town

mu·nic´i·pal·ize *vt.* to bring under municipal authority or ownership —**mu·nic·i·pal·i·za´tion** *n.*

mu·nif´i·cent *adj.* generous —**mu·nif´i·cence** *n.* —**mu·nif´i·cent·ly** *adv.*

mu·ni´tions *pl. n.* arms and ammunition

mu´ral *n.* a painting or photograph applied directly to a wall or ceiling —**mu´ral·ist** *n.*

mur´der *n.* an unlawful killing; something arduous or unpleasant: *this chemistry test is murder* —*vt.* to kill or destroy; to corrupt: *he murders the language* —**mur´der·er** *n.*

mur´der·ous *adj.* capable of killing; menacing; unpleasant: *murderous weather* —**mur´der·ous·ly** *adv.* —**mur´der·ous·ness** *n.*

murk´y *adj.* dark or gloomy; hazy

—**murk´i·ly** *adv.* —**murk´i·ness** *n.*

mur´mur *n.* a low-pitched, indistinct sound —*vi., vt.* to complain or utter in a low tone

mus´cle *n.* fibrous tissue that serves to achieve movement in the body; strength or force —*vi.* to crowd or intrude: *they muscled their way into our group*

mus´cu·lar *adj.* relating to the muscles; inferring power —**mus·cu·lar´i·ty** *n.* —**mus´cu·lar·ly** *adv.*

muse *n.* a spiritual or intellectual guide —*vi.* to ponder or meditate —**mus´ing** *n.* —**mus´ing·ly** *adv.*

mu·se´um *n.* a place dedicated to preservation, as of art or historical objects

mush *n.* porridge; a pasty mass; exaggerated affection —**mush´y** *adj.* —**mush´i·ly** *adv.* —**mush´i·ness** *n.*

mush´room *n.* a type of fungus, esp. those which are edible; something in the umberella shape characteristic of mushrooms —*vi.* to grow rapidly or in the shape of a mushroom —*adj.* pertaining to or like a mushroom

mu´sic *n.* a contrived or natural sound that is pleasant to the ear; a musical score

mu´si·cal *adj.* relating to or resembling music; able to produce music; set to music —*n.* a musical comedy show —**mu·si·cal·ly** *adv.* —**mu·si·cal´i·ty** *n.*

musical chairs a game in which players are eliminated as they compete for a limited number of chairs; a reorganizing that is more of form than of substance, often in an attempt to confuse

musical comedy a theatrical work dominated by music and dance; a light opera

mu·si´cian *n.* one who composes or performs music

music of the spheres harmonious music in outer space, thought at one time to be produced by the motion of heavenly bodies

mu·si·col´o·gy *n.* the study of music —**mu·si·co·log´i·cal** *adj.* —**mu·si·co·log´i·cal·ly** *adv.* —**mu·si·col´o·gist** *n.*

mus´lin *n.* a type of fabric

muss *n.* a mess —*vt.* to make a mess; tousle: *don't muss my hair* —**muss´i·ly** *adv.* —**muss´i·ness** *n.* —**muss´y** *adj.*

mus´sel *n.* a type of marine or freshwater mollusk

must *n.* something required — *aux. verb* a requirement: *you must be a member to attend*; a command: *you must leave now*; a likelihood: *they must have seen the notice*; a certainty: *all good things must end*; intention: *I must go now*

mus´tache *n.* a moustache

mus´ter *n.* a gathering —*vi.* to assemble —*vt.* to call together; to summon or marshal: *muster the courage to ask*

must´y *adj.* stale, as of a smell; old or out of date —**mus´ti·ly** *adv.* —**must´i·ness** *n.*

mu·ta·ble *adj.* changeable —**mu·ta·bil´i·ty, mu·ta·ble·ness** *n.* —**mu´ta·bly** *adv.*

mu·ta´tion *n.* a change or modification; the process of changing; something created by change, especially genetic —**mu´tant** *n.* —**mu´tate** *vi., vt.* —**mu·ta´tion·al** *adj.* —**mu·ta´tion·al·ly** *adv.*

mute *adj.* unable or unwilling to speak; expressed without sound: *mute admiration* —*n.* one who cannot speak —**mute´ly** *adv.* —**mute´ness** *n.*

mut´ed *adj.* indistict; subdued

mu´ti·late *vt.* to maim or cripple; to disfigure —**mu·ti·la´tion** *n.* —**mu´ti·la·tor** *n.*

mu´tiny *n.* open rebellion against authority; revolt —**mu´ti·nous** *adj.*

—mu´ti·nous·ly adv.

mutt n. a dog of mixed breed

mut´ter n. a low, mumbling utterance —vi., vt. to utter in a low voice; to quietly grumble or complain —**mut´ter·er** n. —**mut´ter·ing·ly** adj.

mu´tu·al adj. reciprocal or common: mutual respect, mutual interest —**mu·tu·al´i·ty** n. —**mu´tu·al·ly** adv.

muu´muu n. a long, loose dress

muz´zle n. the snout of an animal; a device that covers a snout; something that prevents free speech —vt. to restrain with a muzzle; to prevent from speaking

my·o´pi·a n. nearsightedness —**my·op´ic** adj. —**my·op´i·cal·ly** adv.

myr´i·ad adj. innumerable —n. a large number

mys·te´ri·ous adj. marked by mystery; puzzling or enigmatic —**mys·te´ri·ous·ly** adv. —**mys·te´ri·ous·ness** n.

mys´ter·y n. something not immediately or easily understood, or that is ultimately beyond comprehension; a work of fiction

mys´tic n. one involved in mysticism

mys´tic, mys´ti·cal adj. of mysticism; mysterious; incomprehensible to the senses —**mys´ti·cal·ly** adv. —**mys´ti·cal·ness** n.

mys´ti·cism n. a belief in a reality beyond the understanding or comprehension of the senses

mys´ti·fy vt. to puzzle or perplex —**mys´ti·fy·ing** adj. —**mys´ti·fy·ing·ly** adj.

mys·tique´ n. a special quality attributed to someone or something

myth n. a legend or folk tale; a fictitious tale; something that is untrue or only partly true: the myth of upward mobility —**myth´ic, myth´i·cal** adj. —**myth´i·cal·ly** adv.

myth´i·cize vt. to fashion a myth about: mythicizing the American dream

myth·o·log´i·cal adj. of mythology; imaginary —**myth·o·log´i·cal·ly** adv.

my·thol´o·gy n. a collection of myths; the study of myths —**my·thol´o·gist** n. —**my·thol´o·gize** vi., vt.

n, N fourteenth letter of the English alphabet; in mathematics, an indefinite number

nab vt. to snatch or seize; to arrest —**nab´ber** n.

na´bob n. a rich or distinguished person

na´dir n. the lowest point

nag n. one given to complaining or chastising; a horse, often, old or inferior —vi., vt. to scold or annoy by scolding; to torment or be a source of torment

nail n. a metal fastener; a hard covering at the end of a finger or toe; to fasten or secure —**nail´er** n.

na·ive´ adj. unsophisticated; guileless; gullible —**na·ive´ly** adv. —**na·ive´ness** n.

na·ive·té´ n. inexperience; ingenuousness

na´ked adj. uncovered or unprotected —**na´ked·ly** adv. —**na´ked·ness** n.

nam´by–pam´by adj. sentimental or weak —n. one given to sentimentality or perceived as weak

name n. a word by which something is known; a designation or title; a disparaging epithet —vt. to give a distinctive designation to: name the baby; to appoint or assign, as to a rank or position —**name´able** adj. —**nam´er** n.

name brand a trademark or unique symbol that identifies a product —**name´–brand** adj.

name´–drop·ping n. an attempt to amplify one's importance by

suggesting association with well–
known persons —**name´-drop** vi.
—**name´-drop·per** n.

name´less adj. countless; unnamed;
anonymous: the nameless poor;
indescribably offensive: the nameless horrors of war —**name´less·ly**
adv. —**name´less·ness** n.

name´ly adv. specifically

nan´ny n. a nursemaid

nap n. a brief sleep; a soft raised
surface as on a carpet —vi. to
sleep briefly

nape n. the back of the neck

na´per·y pl. n. household linens

nap´kin n. a cloth or paper towelette
used when dining

nar´cis·sism n. excessive concern
with or devotion to one's self or
one's appearance —**nar´cis·sist** n.
—**nar·cis·sis´tic** adj. —**nar·cis·sis´·
ti·cal·ly** adv.

nar·co·lep´tic n. one given to uncontrolled seizures of deep sleep
—**nar´co·lep·sy** n.

nar·co´sis n. stupor produced by a
narcotic

nar·cot´ic adj. soothing or addictive
—n. an addictive drug; something
soothing or seemingly addictive —
nar·cot´i·cal·ly adv.

nar´rate vi., vt. to recite or describe;
to give an account of; to provide
commentary, as for a documentary
—**nar·rat·a·bil´i·ty** n. —**nar´rat·a·
ble** adj. —**nar´rat·er, nar´ra·tor** n.

nar·ra´tion n. an act or process of
recounting events; that which is
recounted —**nar·ra´tion·al** adj. —
nar·ra´tion·al·ly adv.

nar´ra·tive n. a story; an account of
an event or series of events —adj.
having the qualities of a narration
—**nar´ra·tive·ly** adv.

nar´row adj. small in width; confined or limited: a narrow opening,
a narrow margin; extremely close:
a narrow margin —n. a confined
passage —vi., vt. to become or

make confined or restricted —**nar´
row·ly** adv. —**nar´row·ness** n.

nar´row-mind´ed adj. limited in
belief or opinion; biased; prejudiced —**nar´row-mind´ed·ly** adv.
—**nar´row-mind´ed·ness** n.

na´sal adj. of the nose —**na·sal´i·ty**
n. —**na´sal·ly** adv.

nas´cent adj. beginning; emerging —
nas´cence, nas´cen·cy n.

nas´ty adj. offensive; unpleasant —
nas´ti·ly adv. —**nas´ti·ness** n.

na´tal adj. of birth

na´tion n. a group of people bound
by a common government, heritage, etc.; the land occupied by
such a group; a government —**na´
tion·al** adj. —**na´tion·al·ly** adv.

na´tion·al·ism n. loyalty or devotion
to one's government or heritage;
patriotism; a movement for inde-
pendence —**na´tion·al·ist** n. —**na·
tion·al·is´tic** adj. —**na·tion·al·is´
ti·cal·ly** adv.

na·tion·al´i·ty n. one's affiliation
with a particular government or
heritage

na´tion·al·ize vt. to convert to government ownership; to make na-
tionwide in scope —**na·tion·al·i·
za´tion** n.

na´tion-wide´ adj. throughout the
nation

na´tive adj. of or associated with a
particular place; connected by
birth; natural or inherited: native
talent —n. one connected by birth
—**na´tive·ly** adj. —**na´tive·ness** n.

na·tiv´i·ty n. birth

nat´ter vi. to chatter idly

nat´ty adj. dapper; smart or stylish
in appearance —**nat´ti·ly** adv. —
nat´ti·ness n.

nat´u·ral adj. occurring in nature;
usual, typical, or characteristic;
simple and unrehearsed —n. one
who is well-suited —**nat´u·ral·ly**
adv. —**nat´u·ral·ness** n.

natural history the study of things

that exist in nature, especially regarding their development

nat·u·ral·ist *n.* one who studies natural history; one in harmony with nature —**nat·u·ral·is'tic** *adj.* —**nat·u·ral·is'ti·cal·ly** *adv.*

nat·u·ral·iza'tion *n.* the process of becoming accepted or acclimated —**nat'u·ral·ize** *vi., vt.*

natural law principles that derive from nature

natural resource wealth that occurs in nature

natural science the study and classification of things that exist in nature

natural selection the theory that organisms best adapted to an environment will survive and improve with succeeding generations

na'ture *n.* the realm of living things; the processes and power that control living organisms; the quality of something: *a quiet nature*

naught *n.* nothing

naugh'ty *adj.* disobedient; mischievous; playfully improper: *a naughty story* —**naugh'ti·ly** *adv.* —**naugh'ti·ness** *n.*

nau'sea *n.* illness marked by a queasy stomach; revulsion, as though to make one vomit

nau'se·ate *vi., vt.* to have or cause a quesy stomach; to disgust —**nau'se·at·ing** *adj.* —**nau'se·at·ing·ly** *adv.*

nau'seous *adj.* causing nausea; disgusting; affected by nausea —**nau'seous·ly** *adv.* —**nau'seous·ness** *n.*

nau'ti·cal *adj.* of ships or shipping —**nau'ti·cal·ly** *adv.*

na'val *adj.* applicable to a navy; of ships or shipping

nave *n.* the central aisle of a church

na'vel *n.* the process on a mammal left by removal of the umbilical cord

nav'i·ga·ble *adj.* suitable for passage through or over —**nav·i·ga·bil'i·ty, nav'i·ga·ble·ness** *n.* —**nav'i·ga·bly** *adv.*

nav'i·gate *vi., vt.* to plot or direct the course of; to travel by means of ship or aircraft

nav·i·ga'tion *n.* the charting of a course; shipping or transport collectively —**nav·i·ga'tion·al** *adj.*

nav'i·ga·tor *n.* one skilled in navigation; one who plots or directs a course, as of a ship or aircraft

na'vy *n.* the branch of the military that operates on the sea

nay *adv.* no —*n.* a negative vote

nay'say·er *n.* one inclined to be negative; one who disagrees

ne·an'der·thal *n.* Neanderthal man, an extinct species; one exhibiting characteristics that might be attributable to a cave man: brutish or uncouth

near *adj., adv.* approaching or close to; almost: *a near miss* —*vi., vt.* to come or draw near —**near'ly** *adv.* —**near'ness** *n.*

near'by' *adj. , adv.* not far from

near'sight·ed *adj.* unable to see clearly at a distance —**near'sight·ed·ly** *adv.* —**near'sight·ed·ness** *n.*

neat *adj.* orderly or tidy; clever or adroit; undiluted —**neat'ly** *adv.* —**neat'ness** *n.*

neat'en *vt.* to put in order or make tidy

neb'bish *n.* a timid person —**neb'bish·y** *adj.*

neb'u·lous *adj.* hazy or indistinct; vague or confused: *a nebulous promise* —**neb'u·lous·ly** *adv.* —**neb'u·lous·ness** *n.*

nec'es·sar·y *adj.* essential; required: *fill out the necessary paperwork* —**nec'es·sar'i·ly** *adv.*

ne·ces'si·tate *vt.* to require or make unavoidable; to make compulsory —**ne·ces·si·ta'tion** *n.* —**ne·ces'si·ta·tive** *adj.*

ne·ces'si·ty *n.* something essential

or required

neck n. a narrow body part that joins, as between the head and the trunk; a narrow section, as *a neck of land, neck of a bottle,* etc. —vi., vt. to kiss and caress

neck´band n. a strip of cloth sewn inside a collar; a type of necklace

neck´er·chief n. a kerchief designed to be worn around the neck

neck´lace n. an ornamental loop worn around the neck

neck´line n. the shape or form of that portion of a garment that goes around the neck

neck´piece n. an article of clothing worn loosely around the neck, as a strip of fur

neck´tie n. a strip of cloth worn around the neck, usually under the collar and tied in front

neck´wear n. any article of clothing or jewelry worn about the neck

nec·ro·man·cy n. communication with the dead; black magic —**nec´ro·man·cer** n. —**nec·ro·man´tic** adj.

nec·ro·phil´i·a n. obsession with death and dead bodies —**nec´ro·phile** n. —**nec·ro·phil´i·ac** adj., n. —**nec·ro·phil´ic** adj.

nec·ro·pho´bi·a n. an abnormal fear of death and dead bodies —**nec·ro·pho´bic** adj.

ne·crop´o·lis n. a place of burial, especially one that belongs to an ancient city

nec´tar n. a sweet liquid secreted by certain plants; an especially delicious drink —**nec·tar´e·an, nec´tar·ous** adj.

need n. a lack of something; a thing required or desired; a necessity; a state of poverty —vt. to have want of; to require —vi. to be in want; to be obliged or compelled: *I need to leave* —**need´er** n.

need´ful adj. needed or required; needy —**need´ful·ly** adv. —**need´**

ful·ness n.

nee´dle n. a slender device, tapered to a point at one end: *sewing needle, hypodermic needle, knitting needle*

nee´dle·craft n. things made with the use of a needle, as for sewing or knitting; the art of creating with the use of a needle

nee´dle·point n. decorative needlework

needless adj. unnecessary; useless: *spent needless hours daydreaming* —**need´less·ly** adv. —**need´less·ness** n.

nee´dle·work n. needlecraft

need´y adj. poor; overly dependent on the support of others

ne´er´–do–well n. a capricious or unreliable person

ne·far´i·ous adj. extremely wicked —**ne·far´i·ous·ly** adv. —**ne·far´i·ous·ness** n.

ne·gate´ vt. to nullify or retract —**ne·ga´tor, ne·gat´er** n. —**ne·ga´tion** n. —**ne·ga´tion·al** adj.

neg´a·tive adj. expressing opposition or denial; lacking any affirmative quality: *a negative philosophy* —**neg´a·tive·ly** adv. —**neg´a·tive·ness, neg·a·tiv´i·ty** n.

neg´a·tiv·ism n. a tendency to reject or ignore the suggestions of others —**neg´a·tiv·ist** n. —**neg´a·tiv·is´tic** adj.

ne·glect n. indifference or carelessness —vt. to disregard or be indifferent to; to be careless or irresponsible —**ne·glect´er** n.

ne·glect´ful adj. marked by carelessness or disregard —**ne·glect´ful·ly** adv. —**ne·glect´ful·ness** n.

neg·li·gee´ n. a woman's dressing gown

neg´li·gent adj. tending to neglect; careless —**neg´li·gence** n. —**neg´li·gent·ly** adv.

neg´li·gi·ble adj. insignificant; inconsequential —**neg·li·gi·bil´i·ty**

neg´li·gi·ble·ness *n.* —**neg´li·gi·bly** *adv.*

ne·go´ti·a·ble *adj.* that can be bargained for; transferrable by delivery or endorsement, such as cash, a promissory note or a bond —**ne·go´ti·a·bly** *adv.* —**ne·go·ti·a·bil´i·ty** *n.*

ne·go´ti·ate *vi.* to confer in an attempt to reach agreement —*vt.* to compromise or agree, as to price, terms, etc.; to transfer ownership, as of a security —**ne·go·ti·a´tion** *n.* —**ne·go´ti·a·tor** *n.* —**ne·go´ti·a·to·ry** *adj.*

neigh´bor (*US*) *n.* one who lives near; anything near or adjacent —*vi.*, *vt.* to live or be situated near —*adj.* near to; adjacent

neigh´bor·hood (*US*) *n.* collectively, those who live near one another or the area in which they live; a proximity: *it will cost in the neighborhood of ten dollars*

neigh´bor·ly (*US*) *adj.* friendly or helpful —**neigh´bor·li·ness** *adv.*

neigh´bour (*Brit.*) *n.* one who lives near; anything near or adjacent —*vi.*, *vt.* to live or be situated near —*adj.* near to; adjacent

neigh´bour·hood (*Brit.*) *n.* collectively, those who live near one another or the area in which they live; a proximity: *it will cost in the neighborhood of ten pounds*

neigh´bour·ly (*Brit.*) *adj.* friendly or helpful —**neigh´bour·li·ness** *adv.*

nei´ther *adj.* not either; not one or the other

nem´e·sis *n.* an enemy, especially one seeking retribution or revenge; something harmful

ne·o·clas´sic, ne·o·clas´si·cal *adj.* pertaining to the revival of earlier forms, as in classical music or literature —**ne·o·clas´si·cism** *n.* —**ne·o·clas´si·cist** *n.*

ne·o·con·serv´a·tism *n.* a reactionary or traditionalist philosophy that arises in response to excessive liberalism of an earlier period —**ne·o·con·serv´a·tive** *n.*

ne·ol´o·gism, ne·ol´o·gy *n.* a new word; a new meaning for a word or expression; the creation of a new word, meaning, or expression —**ne·ol´o·gist** *n.* —**ne·ol·o·gis´tic, ne·ol·o·gis´ti·cal** *adj.*

ne´o·phyte *n.* a novice; a recent convert

neph´ew *n.* the son of one's sibling

nep´o·tism *n.* favoritism to a relation, as by granting employment —**nep´o·tist** *n.* —**nep·o·tis´tic, nep·o·tis´ti·cal** *adj.*

nerd *n.* one engrossed in scholarly pursuits to the exclusion of regard for personal appearance or the social graces —**nerd´y** *adj.*

nerve *n.* any of the fibers that transmit signals throughout the body; courage; impudence —**nerv´y** *adj.* —**nerv´i·ness** *n.*

nerve center a set of nerve cells that perform a specific function in the body; a control center: *the CPU is the nerve center of the computer*

nerve´less *adj.* lacking courage; cool in a crisis, as though not affected by natural fear or caution —**nerve´less·ly** *adv.* —**nerve´less·ness** *n.*

nerve´-rack·ing *adj.* irritating, difficult, or wearisome

ner´vous *adj.* of the nerve system; high-strung or excitable; agitated or apprehensive —**ner´vous·ly** *adv.* —**ner´vous·ness** *n.*

ne´science *n.* ignorance; a lack of knowledge or awareness —**ne´scient** *adj.*

nest *n.* a cozy shelter, especially for rearing young; a refuge; a group of objects that fit together: *a nest of boxes* —*vi.*, *vt.* to fit or place together snugly —**nest´a·ble** *adj.*

nest egg money or investments set aside for future use

nes´tle *vi.*, *vt.* to lie or place snugly

or comfortably

net *adj.* remaining after deductions, as for waste or expenses: *net profit, net weight* —*n.* the amount remaining, as for profit or yield; a mesh of fabric or rope, usually to catch or hold something —*vt.* to produce, as profit; to catch, as in a net —**net´ta·ble** *adj.*

net´tle *n.* a prickly plant —*vt.* to annoy or irritate

net´tle·some *adj.* irritating

net´work *n.* a system or structure with interconnecting bonds: *communications network, old boy network*

net´work·ing *n.* the exchange of information or assistance among those having mutual interests

neu´ral *adj.* regarding the nerves or nervous system

neu·ral´gia *n.* pain associated with a nerve —**neu·ral´gic** *adj.*

neu·ri´tis *n.* inflammation of a nerve —**neu·rit´ic** *adj.*

neu·rol´o·gy *n.* the study of the workings and disorders of the nervous system —**neu·ro·log´ic, neu·ro·log´i·cal** *adj.* —**neu·ro·log´i·cal·ly** *adv.* —**neu·rol´o·gist** *n.*

neu´ron *n.* a nerve cell —**neu´ro·nal, neu·ron´ic** *adj.*

neu·ro´sis *n.* a mental or emotional disorder —**neu·rot´ic** *adj., n.* —**neu·rot´ic·al·ly** *adv.*

neu´tral *adj.* not supporting either position in a controversy; unbiased or disinterested; drab or colorless —**neu´tral·ism, neu·tral´i·ty** *n.* —**neu´tral·ist** *n.* —**neu·tral·is´tic** *adj.*

neu´tral·ize *vt.* to make neutral; to nullify or cancel out —**neu·tral·i·za´tion** *n.* —**neu´tral·iz·er** *n.*

nev´er *adv.* not ever

nev´er·the·less´ *adv.* disregarding that: *he has failed twice, nevertheless he plans to try again*

new *adj.* recently formed or discov-

ered; previously unused; different: *a new style*; inexperienced: *a new employee* —**new´ness** *n.*

New Age *adj.* characteristic of a less traditional approach to spirituality, healing, the arts, etc.

new´found *adj.* recently acquired or cognizant of: *newfound freedom*

new´ish *adj.* relatively new

new´ly *adv.* recently; freshly

news *pl. n.* new information, especially that reported by the print or electronic media; information of interest to the general public or to a particular group

news´cast *n.* a broadcasting of the news on radio or television —**news´cast·er** *n.*

news´let·ter *n.* a publication containing information for a select audience

news´mag·a·zine *n.* a slick periodical, usually weekly, devoted to current events

news´pa·per *n.* a daily or weekly periodical that reports on current events; newsprint

news´print *n.* inexpensive paper used for short-lived publications such as newspapers

news´wor·thy *adj.* considered to be of interest to the readers of a publication —**news´wor·thi·ness** *n.*

news´y *adj.* containing fresh news or gossip —**news´i·ness** *n.*

next *adj.* following immediately in sequence: *the next minute*; close by: *the next room* —*n.* that which comes immediately after —*adv.*

next of kin one's closest relative or relatives

nib´ble *n.* a small bite —*vi. , vt.* to take or eat in small bites —**nib´bler** *n.*

nice *adj.* pleasing; courteous or considerate; delicate or subtle: *a nice sense of tact* —**nice´ly** *adv.* —**nice´ness** *n.*

ni´ce·ty *n.* a precise, subtle, or

refined quality

niche *n.* a recess or alcove; a special area, as of activity or interest

nick *n.* a small cut or indentation — *vt.* to make a small cut in

nick´name *n.* a familiar name, as a short form of a proper name or one that is descriptive

niece *n.* the daughter of one's sibling, or a wife or husband's sibling

nif´ty *adj.* very good; clever

nig´gard·ly *adj.* closefisted; reluctant to give or spend —**nig´gard** *n.* —**nig´gard·li·ness** *n.*

nig´gle *vi.* to constantly nag or complain over trifles —**nig´gling** *adj.*, *n.* —**nig´gling·ly** *adv.*

nigh *adj., adv.* near; nearly

night *n.* the period between sunset and sunrise; the evening hours before midnight

night´cap *n.* a beverage taken at the end of an evening or just before going to bed

night´club *n.* an eating and drinking establishment that offers entertainment in the evening

night´fall *n.* dusk; the approaching darkness of night

night´gown *n.* a woman's frock worn for sleeping

night´ly *adj.* occurring every night; occurring during the night —*adv.* by night; every night

night´mare *n.* a frightening dream; a terrifying experience —**night´mar·ish** *adj.* —**night´mar·ish·ly** *adv.*

night´spot *n.* a nightclub

night´stand *n.* a small table situated at the side of a bed

night´stick (*US*) *n.* a staff carried by a uniformed police officer

night table a nightstand

night´time *adj.* during the night — *n.* the time from sunset to sunrise or from dark to dawn

ni´hi·lism *n.* a philosophy that denies all existence; the rejection of religion and morality; the concept

that conditions can be improved only by destroying the existing political and social structure —**ni´hi·list** *n.* —**ni´hi·lis´tic** *adj.*

ni·hil´i·ty *n.* nothingness

nil *n.* nothing

nim´ble *adj.* quick and agile; sharp witted —**nim´ble·ness** *n.* —**nim´bly** *adv.*

nim´bus *n.* a halo or disk of light encircling the head

nin´com·poop *n.* a silly or foolish person

nin´ja *n.* a 14th century Japanese assassin

nin´ny *n.* a nincompoop

nip *n.* a sip, especially of liquor; a small bite or particle; a sharp or stinging quality, as of cold air or spicy food —*vt.* to sip; to bite or pinch off; to sting

nip´per *n.* a tool for grasping or for making small cuts, such as pliers

nip´ping *adj.* stinging, as from cold or spiced food —**nip´ping·ly** *adv.*

nip´ple *n.* a small projection on a mammary gland from which milk is released; any similar projection used to release or eject a liquid

nip´py *adj.* biting or sharp; somewhat chilly —**nip´pi·ly** *adv.* —**nip´pi·ness** *n.*

nir·va´na *n.* an ideal state —**nir·va´nic** *adj.*

nit´pick *vi.* to find fault or quarrel over trifles —**nit´pick·er** *n.* —**nit´pick·ing** *n.*

nit´ty-grit´ty *n.* the essence of something —*adj.* basic

nit´wit *n.* one regarded as silly or foolish

nix *vt.* to negate or put an end to

no *adj.* not any: *there is no time left;* absolutely not: *he's no leader* —*n.* a negative response

no´-account *adj.* valueless; useless

no·bil´i·ty *n.* the state of being exalted; a class of persons of high rank or status; noteworthy moral excellence

no·ble *adj.* pertaining to or having qualities attributable to nobility, as regal bearing, courage, generosity, etc. —**no·ble·ness** *n.* —**no·bly** *adv.*

no·blesse· oblige· the obligation of high ranking persons to behave honorably and generously

no·body *n.* a person of no importance —*pron.* no one

no·cent *adj.* harmful

noc·tur·nal *adj.* occurring in the night —**noc·tur·nal·ly** *adv.*

noc·turne *n.* a painting of a night scene; a gentle, dreamy musical composition

noc·u·ous *adj.* harmful or detrimental —**noc·u·ous·ly** *adv.*

nod *n.* assent or agreement —*vi., vt.* to move the head up and down, especially as an assent or acknowledgement; to briefly drift off to sleep

nod·ule *n.* a small lump —**nod·u·lar** *adj.*

no·-fault *adj.* of insurance or a legal action that honors a claim without assigning blame

no·-frills· *adj.* lacking any special features or amenities

no·-go· *n.* a termination

no·-good· *adj.* lacking value

noise *n.* a loud or unpleasant sound; a complaint; interference on a transmisssion line; unwanted or meaningless data —*vt.* to spread information, especially gossip or rumors

noise·less *adj.* silent —**noise·less·ly** *adv.* —**noise·less·ness** *n.*

noise·mak·er *n.* one who makes noise; a device for making raucous sounds at a celebration —**noise· mak·ing** *n.*

noi·some *adj.* disgusting, especially of an odor; dangerous or deadly, as fumes —**noi·some·ly** *adv.* — **noi·some·ness** *n.*

nois·y *adj.* making or marked by noise —**nois·i·ly** *adv.* —**nois·i· ness** *n.*

no·mad *n.* a wanderer; one who lacks a permanent home —**no·mad·ic** *adj.* —**no·mad·i·cal·ly** *adv.*

no man's land a strip of land marking a division between warring parties; land that is unclaimed or unexplored

nom de guerre an assumed name

nom de plume a pen name; a name assumed by a writer

no·men·cla·ture *n.* a name or designation; a system of names, as used in a scientific discipline

nom·i·nal *adj.* of a name or designation; of a small or token amount; of the face value of a security; existing in name only — **nom·i·nal·ly** *adv.*

nom·i·nate *vt.* to name as a candidate for office; to appoint to office —**nom·i·na·tion** *n.* —**nom·i·na·tor** *n.*

nom·i·nee· *n.* one named as a candidate

non·age *n.* the time during which one is legally underage

non·cha·lant· *adj.* seemingly casual or indifferent —**non·cha·lance·** *n.* —**non·cha·lant·ly** *adv.*

non·com·mit·tal *adj.* guarded about one's feelings or opinions —**non·com·mit·tal·ly** *adv.*

non·com·pli·ance *n.* a failure to conform or accede, as to a court order or ordinance —**non·com·pli· ant** *adj., n.*

non com·pos men·tis legally incompetent; not of sound mind

non·con·form·ist *n.* one in opposition to accepted customs or practices —**non·con·form·i·ty** *n.*

non·de·script *adj.* lacking any distinctive characteristics

none *adv.* not at all —*pron.* no one

non·en·ti·ty *n.* something of no importance; something that does not exist

non·e·vent´ *n.* a minor function or gathering promoted out of proportion to its importance

non·ex·is´tent *adj.* not real; imaginary —**non·ex·is´tence** *n.*

non·fea´sance *n.* failure to discharge a duty or obligation

non´fic´tion *n.* writing that is factual or professed to be so — **non·fic´tion·al** *adj.*

non´pa·reil´ *adj.* without equal

non·par´ti·san *adj.* neutral; not aligned with any particular group or cause —*n.* —**non·par´ti·san·ship** *n.*

non´plus´ *vt.* to bewilder; to put at a loss for words

non·pro·duc´tive *adj.* not profitable or useful; not involved directly in producing, as of supervisory or management personnel

non·prof´it *adj.* of an organization that operates to serve, rather than for profit

non·pro·lif·er·a´tion *adj.* stemming growth or acquisition, as of nuclear weapons

non   pro·se´qui·tur judgement against a plaintiff who fails to appear in court

non´sense *n.* something having no meaning or that is of no value; foolishness

non·sen´si·cal *adj.* unintelligible; without meaning; absurd —**non·sen·si·cal´i·ty,   non·sen´si·cal·ness** *n.* —**non·sen´si·cal·ly** *adv.*

non·vi´o·lence *n.* reliance on peaceful means to achieve objectives

nook *n.* a cranny or compartment; a hiding place; a recess or corner of a room, often offering a measure of privacy

noon *n.* midday; the time when the sun is at or near its highest point

no one *pron.* nobody; not one person

noose *n.* a rope loop

norm *n.* a standard

nor´mal *adj.* typical, usual, or standard;   sane —**nor´mal·cy,   nor·mal´i·ty** *n.* —**nor´mal·ly** *adv.*

nor´mal·ize *vt.* to make normal — **nor·mal·i·za´tion** *n.* —**nor´mal·iz·er** *n.*

north *n.* the direction to the left of the sunrise, roughly perpendicular to the path of the sun; an area located in that general direction

nose *n.* the organ at the front of the face for detecting odors; the sense of smell; an aroma, as of a wine; the ability to find, as if by smell: *a nose for news*; the front, as of an aircraft, rocket, etc.

nose´–dive *vi.* to suddenly plummet: *our sales took a nose–dive* — **nose´dive** *n.*

nose job rhinoplasty: plastic surgery on the nose

nosh *n.* a snack —*vi.*

no´–show *n.* one who does not arrive as promised

nos·tal´gia *n.* a sentimental longing for the past —**nos·tal´gic** *adj.* —**nos·tal´gi·cal·ly** *adv.*

nos´tril *n.* one of the openings in the nose

nos´trum *n.* an untested medicine or remedy

nos´y *adj.* curious or prying —**nos´i·ly** *adv.* —**nos´i·ness** *n.*

not *adv.* in no way

no´ta·ble *adj.* distinctive or remarkable, as of an event; important or distinguished, as of a person; deserving   notice   —**no·ta·bil´i·ty, no´ta·ble·ness** *n.* —**no´ta·bly** *adv.*

no·ta·ri·za´tion *n.* certification by a notary public, as of a signature — **no´ta·rize** *vt.*

no´ta·ry, no´ta·ry pub´lic *n.* one authorized to perform certain legal duties —**no·tar´i·al** *adj.* —**no·tar´i·al·ly** *adv.*

no·ta´tion *n.* a note or comment, often added to existing text; a system of symbols used for a particular purpose, as in mathematics or computer programming —**no·ta´tion·al** adj.

notch n. a small cut or nick

note n. a short, informal letter; a written record, as of the main points of a lecture, annotations in a publication, a reminder, etc.; currency or a document convertible to currency —vt. to make a written record of; to take notice of

not´ed adj. distinguished; famous — **not´ed·ly** adv.

note´wor·thy adj. deserving of notice —**note´wor·thi·ly** adv. — **note´wor·thi·ness** n.

noth´ing adj. meaningless: a nothing day —n. something of no value — pron. not anything

noth´ing·ness n. a void

no´tice n. an announcement or warning; observation or attention —vt. to observe or become aware of —**no·tice·a·bil´i·ty** n. —**no´tice·a·ble** adj. —**no´tice·a·bly** adv.

no´ti·fy vt. to serve notice; to inform or make known —**no´ti·fi·ca´tion** n. —**no´ti·fi·er** n.

no´tion n. an idea or opinion; a theory; a disposition toward — **no´tion·al** adj.

no·to·ri´e·ty n. fame; reputation

no·to´ri·ous adj. infamous; well-known —**no·to´ri·ous·ly** adv. — **no·to´ri·ous·ness** n.

not·with·stand´ing prep. in spite of —adv.

noun n. a word that names a person, place, thing, etc.

nour´ish vt. to promote the development of; to provide with food or other necessities for life and growth —**nour´ish·ment** n.

nou·veau´ riche one who flaunts newly acquired wealth

nou·velle´ cui·sine´ a style of cooking that stresses fresh ingredients and light sauces

nov´el adj. new and unusual —**nov´el·ly** adj.

nov´el n. a book-length, fictional story —**nov´el·ist** n. —**nov·el·is´tic** adj. —**nov·el·is´ti·cal·ly** adv.

nov´el·ette´ n. a short novel

nov´el·ize vt. to write a fictional account based on a true story, a historical event, a play or movie, etc.

no·vel´la n. a short novel; a short story

nov´el·ty n. the quality of being original or fresh; something unique; a fad; a trinket

nov´ice n. one new to a trade or activity; an apprentice

now adj. at this time —adv. immediately; promptly

no way interj. absolutely not

no´where adv. not anywhere —n. remote

no´-win´ adj. stalemated or deadlocked

no´wise adv. in no way

nox´ious adj. harmful —**nox´ious·ly** adv. —**nox´ious·ness** n.

noz´zle n. a spout or outlet for controlling the flow of a liquid

nu´ance n. a subtlety; a slight variation

nub n. a knob or protuberance; the gist or substance of something — **nub´bly, nub´by** adj.

nu´bile adj. of marriageable age; sexually mature —**nu·bil´i·ty** n.

nu´cle·ar adj. of a nucleus; atomic

nuclear energy energy created by nuclear reaction

nuclear power power such as electricity generated by nuclear fission or fusion

nuclear reactor a device for harnessing nuclear energy

nu´cle·us n. the center or essence of something

nude adj. unclothed or uncovered — n. a naked body, especially a statue or painting —**nude´ly** adv. —**nude´ness, nu´di·ty** n.

nudge *n.* a light push; one who persists in annoying or complaining —*vt.* to touch or push gently

nud´ism *n.* a belief in the practice of living in the nude to promote health and well-being —**nud´ist** *n.,* *adj.*

nug´get *n.* a small lump or portion

nui´sance *n.* a bother or annoyance; an illegal action that interferes with the rights of others

nuke *vt.* to use a nuclear bomb; to microwave

null *adj.* nonexistent or insignificant; invalid

nul´li·fy *vt.* to invalidate or neutralize —**nul·li·fi·ca´tion** *n.* —**nul´li·fi·er** *n.*

numb *adj.* lacking physical or emotional feeling —*vt., vi.* to make or become numb —**numb´ly** *adv.* —**numb´ness** *n.*

num´ber *n.* an integer; one of a series in a normal progression; a set of numerals that represent something unique: *telephone number, house number* —*vt.* to assign a position in a series; to count or total —**num´ber·er** *n.*

num·ber-crunch·ing *n.* performing complex calculations —**num´ber-crunch·er** *n.*

num´ber·less *adj.* innumerable; limitless

numb´skull *n.* a numskull

nu´mer·a·ble *adj.* that can be enumerated

nu´mer·al *n.* a symbol representing a number

nu·mer´ic, nu·mer´i·cal *adj.* of a number or numbers —**nu·mer´i·cal·ly** *adv.*

nu·mer·ol´o·gy *n.* the belief that there is secret meaning associated with number values, as of a date or the number of letters in a name —**nu·mer·o·log´i·cal** *adj.* —**nu·mer·ol´o·gist** *n.*

nu´mer·ous *adj.* many; a large number —**nu´mer·ous·ly** *adv.* —**nu´mer·ous·ness** *n.*

nu·mis·mat´ics *n.* the collection or study of coinage —**nu·mis·mat´ic** *adj.* —**nu·mis·mat´i·cal·ly** *adv.* —**nu·mis´ma·tist** *n.*

num´skull *n.* a simpleton or fool

nup´tial *adj.* of marriage or a marriage ceremony —**nup´tial·ly** *adv.*

nup´tials *n.* a wedding ceremony

nurse *n.* one trained in ministering to the sick; one in charge of young children —*vt.* to tend or care for another; to sustain or conserve —**nurs·er** *n.*

nur´ser·y *n.* a place set aside for children; a place where plants are grown

nurse's aide one who assists a registered or practical nurse

nurs´ing *n.* the profession of a nurse; the care of a nurse

nursing home a residence for the elderly or those very ill

nur´ture *vt.* to care for; to aid in growth and improvement —**nur´tur·ance** *n.* —**nur´tur·ant** *n.* —**nur´tur·ing** *adj.*

nut *n.* a seed contained in a hard shell; one considered to be insane or eccentric; a fanatic

nu´tri·ent *adj.* providing nutrition; nourishing —*n.* a source of nourishment

nu´tri·ment *n.* food; anything that promotes growth and development —**nu·tri·men´tal** *adj.*

nu·tri´tion *n.* the study of food and nourishment; the process by which food is digested and used in the body —**nu·tri´tion·al** *adj.* —**nu·tri´tion·al·ly** *adv.* —**nu·tri´tion·ist** *n.*

nu·tri´tious *adj.* nourishing —**nu·tri´tious·ly** *adv.* —**nu·tri´tious·ness** *n.*

nu´tri·tive *adj.* nutritious; pertaining to nutrition —**nu´tri·tive·ly** *adv.* —**nu´tri·tive·ness** *n.*

nut´ty *adj.* nut–like; crazy; wild and foolish —**nut´ti·ly** *adv.* —**nut´ti·ness** *n.*

nuz´zle *vi.*, *vt.* to nestle; to push gently with the nose

o, O fifteenth letter of the English alphabet

oaf *n.* one who is slow–witted or clumsy —**oaf´ish** *adj.* — **oaf´ish·ly** *adv.* —**oaf´ish·ness** *n.*

oa´sis *n.*, *pl.* **oa´ses** a haven of greenery in the midst of a wasteland; a place of refuge or one that differs from its surroundings: *an oasis of excellence in the midst of mediocrity*

oast *n.* an oven for drying grain or tobacco

oath *n.* a solemn promise; an irreverent or blasphemous use of a sacred name

ob´du·rate *n.* hardhearted; stubborn —**ob´du·ra·cy** *n.* —**ob´du·rate·ly** *adj.* —**ob´du·rate·ness** *n.*

o·be´di·ent *adj.* deferential to authority; submissive —**o·be´di·ence** *n.* —**o·be´di·ent·ly** *adv.*

o·bei´sant *adj.* respectful —**o·bei´sance** *n.* —**o·bei´sant·ly** *adv.*

ob´e·lisk *n.* a tall stone shaft

o·bese´ *adj.* extremely overweight — **o·bese´ly** *adv.* —**o·be´si·ty** *n.*

o·bey´ *vi.*, *vt.* to accept or comply with

ob·fus´cate *vt.* to make confused — **ob·fus·ca´tion** *n.* —**ob·fus´ca·tor** *n.* —**ob·fus´ca·to·ry** *adj.*

o·bit´ *n.* an obituary

o·bit´u·ar·y *n.* a published account of a death, often including highlights of the person's life, information about family, etc.

ob´ject *n.* a thing that can be perceived by the senses; a goal or objective; a recipient: *the object of our attention* —**ob·ject´** *vi.*, *vt.* to oppose or dissent —**ob·jec´tor** *n.*

ob·jec´tion *n.* the act of opposing; remarks made in opposition; a reason for opposing

ob·jec´tion·a·ble *adj.* offensive —**ob·jec´tion·a·bly** *adv.* —**ob·jec´tion·a·ble·ness** *n.*

ob·jec´tive *adj.* fair and unbiased — *n.* a tangible goal —**ob·jec´tive·ly** *adv.* —**ob·jec´tive·ness**, **ob·jec·tiv´i·ty** *n.*

object lesson a concrete example

ob´jet d'art an art object

ob·la´tion *n.* a solemn offering, especially as an act of worship —**ob·la´tion·al**, **ob´la·to·ry** *adj.*

ob´li·gate *adj.* essential —*vt.* to bind or compel as by indebtedness, a sense of morality, etc. —**ob´li·ga·tor** *n.*

ob·li·ga´tion *n.* a responsibility dictated by conscience or law; a debt —**ob·li·ga´tion·al** *adj.*

o·blig´a·to·ry *adj.* required; morally or legally binding —**o·blig´a·to´ri·ly** *adv.*

o·blige´ *vt.* to require, as a legal or moral matter; to accommodate or assist

o·blig´ing *adj.* disposed to be accommodating —**o·blig´ing·ly** *adv.* —**o·blig´ing·ness** *n.*

o·blique´ *adj.* inclined or slanting; angled; indirect, as *an oblique reference* —**o·blique´ly** *adv.* —**o·blique´ness** *n.*

ob·liq´ui·ty *n.* inclination or the amount of inclination from a horizontal or vertical —**ob·liq´ui·tous** *adj.*

ob·lit´er·ate *vt.* to remove completely —**ob·lit·er·a´tion** *n.* —**ob·lit´er·a·tive** *adj.* —**ob·lit´er·a·tor** *n.*

ob·liv´i·on *n.* obscurity; nonexistence; the condition of being completely forgotten

ob·liv´i·ous *adj.* preoccupied; lacking awareness —**ob·liv´i·ous·ly** *adv.* —**ob·liv´i·ous·ness** *n.*

ob´long *adj.* elongated

ob´lo·quy *n.* severe denunciation

ob·nox′ious *adj.* offensive or objectionable; impolite —**ob·nox′ious·ly** *adv.* —**ob·nox′ious·ness** *n.*

o′boe *n.* a double–reed wind instrument —**o′bo·ist** *n.*

ob·scene′ *adj.* contrary to accepted morality or propriety —**ob·scene′ly** *adv. n.*

ob·scen′i·ty, ob·scene′ness *n.* something that is offensive or indecent; an obscene remark

ob·scu′rant *adj.* tending to make indistinct: *an obscurant mist*; marked by opposition to improvement or enlightenment —*n.* one who opposes education or enlightenment —**ob·scu′ran·tism** *n.* —**ob·scu′rant·ist** *n.*

ob·scure′ *adj.* not clearly perceived; indistinct —*vt.* to conceal or make indistinct —**ob·scure′ly** *adv.* —**ob·scure′ness** *n.*

ob·scu′ri·ty *n.* the condition of being unknown or indistinct

ob·se′qui·ous *adj.* groveling or subservient; fawning —**ob·se′qui·ous·ly** *adv.* —**ob·se′qui·ous·ness** *n.*

ob·serv′a·ble *adj.* noticeable; that can be perceived by sight —**ob·serv′a·bly** *adv.*

ob·serv′ance *n.* a traditional rite or celebration; an act of compliance, as to custom or law

ob·serv′ant *adj.* quick to comprehend or obey; attentive; strict in complying, as to duty or the law —**ob·serv′ant·ly** *adv.*

ob·ser·va′tion *n.* the act of complying, as to custom or law; a record of careful study; a comment or mention —**ob·ser·va′tion·al** *adj.* —**ob·ser·va′tion·al·ly** *adv.*

ob·serv′a·to·ry *n.* a place with a commanding view, especially one equipped to study the heavens

ob·serve′ *vt.* to notice or watch carefully; to celebrate a traditional rite; to abide by custom or law; to mention —*vi.* to make a casual remark; to take notice —**ob·serv′er** *n.* —**ob·serve′ing·ly** *adv.*

ob·sess′ *vt.* to be totally preoccupied —**ob·sess′ing·ly** *adv.*

ob·ses′sion *n.* an unnatural or irrational fascination or compulsion; the focus or subject of this fascination —**ob·ses′sion·al** *adj.* —**ob·ses′sion·al·ly** *adv.*

ob·ses′sive *adj.* compulsive —**ob·ses′sive·ly** *adv.* —**ob·ses′sive·ness** *n.*

ob·so·les′cence *n.* the process of going out of use; the condition of being out–dated —**ob·so·lesce′** *vi.* —**ob·so·les′cent** *adj.* —**ob·so·les′cent·ly** *adv.*

ob·so·lete′ *adj.* no longer in use or useful; out–of–date —**ob·so·lete′ly** *adv.* —**ob·so·lete′ness** *n.*

ob′sta·cle *n.* a hindrance; a barrier or obstruction

ob·ste·tri′cian *n.* a physician who specializes in obstetrics

ob·stet′rics *n.* the care of women during and immediately following pregnancy —**ob·stet′ri·cal** *adj.* —**ob·stet′ri·cal·ly** *adv.*

ob′sti·nate *adj.* stubborn; defying control or treatment, as an illness —**ob′sti·na·cy, ob′sti·nate·ness** *n.* —**ob′sti·nate·ly** *adv.*

ob·strep′er·ous *adj.* unruly; defiant —**ob·strep′er·ous·ly** *adv.* —**ob·strep′er·ous·ness** *n.*

ob·struct′ *vt.* to interfere or hinder; to block the view of —**ob·struct′er, ob·struc′tor** *n.* —**ob·struc′tive** *adj.* —**ob·struc′tive·ness** *n.*

ob·struc′tion *n.* an act, thing, etc. that blocks or hinders —**ob·struc′tion·ism** *n.*

ob·struc′tion·ist *n.* one who delays or blocks, especially the introduction of new ideas

ob·tain′ *vt.* to gain possession of —**ob·tain′a·ble** *adj.*

ob·trude′ *vi., vt.* to attempt to press one's person or opinions on another —**ob·trud´er** n. —**ob·tru´sion** n.

ob·tru´sive adj. interfering; overly conspicuous —**ob·tru´sive·ly** adv. —**ob·tru´sive·ness** n.

ob·tuse´ adj. dull or ignorant; lacking understanding —**ob·tuse´ly** adv. —**ob·tuse´ness** n.

ob·vert´ vt. to turn over

ob´vi·ate vt. to make unnecessary: the alarm system obviated the need for a guard —**ob·vi·a´tion** n. —**ob´vi·a·tor** n.

ob´vi·ous adj. clearly seen or understood —**ob´vi·ous·ly** adv. —**ob´vi·ous·ness** n.

oc·ca´sion n. an event or opportunity —vt. to cause

oc·ca´sion·al adj. occurring infrequently —**oc·ca´sion·al·ly** adv.

oc´ci·dent n. the west; countries west of the orient —**oc´ci·den´tal** adj.

oc·cult´ adj. obscured or hidden; mysterious; relating to the supernatural —**oc·cult´ly** adv. —**oc·cult´ness** n.

oc·cult´ism n. belief in the supernatural —**oc·cult´ist** n.

oc´cu·pan·cy n. the possession of an office, home, etc.; the period of such possession

oc´cu·pant n. one who fills a position or inhabits a place

oc·cu·pa´tion n. an activity, esp. as a means of livlihood; occupancy —**oc·cu·pa´tion·al** adj. —**oc·cu·pa´tion·al·ly** adv.

oc´cu·py vt. to fill, as time or space; to hold one's attention; to control, as by conquest —**oc´cu·pi·er** n.

oc·cur´ vi. to happen; to present itself, as an idea —**oc·cur´rence** n. —**oc·cur´rent** adj.

o´cean n. a large body of salt water; a large amount: an ocean of paperwork —**o·ce·an´ic** adj.

o·cea·nog´ra·pher n. one engaged in scientific study of the ocean and its phenomena —**o·cea·no·graph´ic, o·cea·no·graph´i·cal** adj. —**o·cea·no·graph´i·cal·ly** adv. —**o·cean·og´ra·phy** n.

o·cea·nol´o·gist n. an oceanographer —**o·cea·no·log´ic, o·cea·no·log´i·cal** adj. —**o·cea·nol´o·gy** n.

oc´ta·gon n. an eight–sided polygon —**oc·tag´o·nal** adj. —**oc·tag´o·nal·ly** adv.

oc´tal adj. a number system based on units of eight

oc·tet´ n. a group of eight; music written for eight instruments

oc´u·lar adj. of the eye or the sense of sight

oc´u·list n. a physician who specializes in treating the eyes; an optomotrist or opthalmologist

odd adj. strange or different; unusual or unexpected: taking place at an odd hour; of a remainder or uneven amount —**odd´ly** adv. —**odd´ness** n.

odd´ball n. an eccentric

odd´i·ty n. something unusual

odds n. pl. a ratio or other expression of probability: the odds are two–to–one he'll take the job

ode n. a lyric poem —**od´ic** adj. —**od´ist** n.

o´di·ous adj. offensive; engendering aversion —**o´di·ous·ly** adv. —**o´di·ous·ness** n.

o´di·um n. hatred or aversion

o·dom´e·ter n. a device for measuring distance traveled

o´dor (US) n. something perceived by smell; an aroma

o·dor·if´er·ous adj. having an aroma —**o·dor·if´er·ous·ly** adv. —**o·dor·if´er·ous·ness** n.

o´dor·less adj. lacking aroma

o´dor·ous adj. having a distinctive aroma —**o´dor·ous·ly** adv. —**o´dor·ous·ness** n.

o´dour (Brit.) n. something perceived by smell; an aroma

off adj., adv., prep. away from; at a

distance; removed

of´fal n. waste, especially the inedible parts of an animal

off´beat adj. unconventional

off´-col´or adj. in poor taste; obscene

of·fence´ (Brit.) n. a violation, as of custom or law; that which arouses disapproval

of·fend´ vi., vt. to effect or arouse disapproval —**of·fend´er** n.

of·fense´ (US) n. a violation, as of custom or law; that which arouses disapproval

of·fen´sive adj. disagreeable; vulgar or insulting —**of·fen´sive·ly** adv. —**of·fen´sive·ness** n.

of´fer n. something submitted for consideration —vt. to present or submit

of´fer·ing n. a gift; something presented, as for sale

of´fice n. a place for conducting business; a position of authority

of´fi·cer n. one in authority

of·fi´cial adj. relating to a particular office or position; authorized —n. one who holds a position of authority —**of·fi´cial·dom** n. —**of·fi´cial·ly** adv.

of·fi´ci·ar·y n. officials, collectively

of·fi´ci·ate vt. to preside, as a chairperson; to perform the duties of an office —**of·fi´ci·a·tor** n.

of·fi´cious adj. overly eager to offer assistance or advice —**of·fi´cious·ly** adv. —**of·fi´cious·ness** n.

off´shoot n. anything that branches off from a main source

off´spring n. progeny, descendants

oft adv. often

of´ten adv. frequently

of´ten·times adv. frequently

o´gle vi., vt. to look or stare rudely —**o´gler** n.

o´gre n. a mythical monster; one deemed to be barbaric or terrifying —**o´gre·ish** adj.

•il n. a generally liquid or liquifiable substance used in cooking, as a lubricant, or for fuel —**oil´i·ness** n. —**oil´y** adj.

oint´ment n. a salve

old adj. aged or elderly; of a specific age: ten years old; showing signs of age or wear; seasoned or matured

old´-fash´ioned adj. out-of-date; tending to outdated styles or concepts

old hat commonplace or hackneyed

old money inherited wealth

old school a commitment to tradition

old wives' tale superstition; a traditional belief

o´leo n. oleomargarine

o´le·o·mar´ga·rine n. margarine, a substitute for butter

ol·fac´to·ry adj. of the sense of smell

ol´i·gar·chy n. a governmental system controlled by a small group of people —**ol·i·gar´chic, ol·i·gar´chi·cal** adj.

ol·i·gop´o·ly n. a market dominated by few suppliers —**ol·i·gop´o·lis´tic** adj.

ol·i·gop´so·ny n. a market dominated by few buyers —**ol·i·gop·so·nis´tic** adj.

o´li·o n. a type of stew; a mixture or collection

om´buds·man n. an investigator and mediator, especially one who settles disputes between citizens and governmental or private organizations

o´men n. a sign or indication that supposedly predicts good or evil, or that is seen to predict the future

om´i·nous adj. threatening; inauspicious; characterized by an evil omen —**om´i·nous·ly** adv. —**om´i·nous·ness** n.

o·mis´sion n. something omitted or neglected

omit´ vt. to leave out; to fail to include or perform

om·ni·bus *adj.* including many things: *an omnibus bill that provides for both taxes and welfare* — *n.* a large passenger vehicle: a bus

om·nip·o·tent *adj.* having unlimited power —**om·nip·o·tence** *n.* —**om·nip·o·tent·ly** *adv.*

om·nis·cient *adj.* having unlimited knowledge —**om·nis·cience** *n.* —**om·nis·cient·ly** *adv.*

om·niv·o·rous *adj.* taking both plants and animals for food —**om·niv·o·rous·ly** *adv.* —**om·niv·o·rous·ness** *n.*

on·com·ing *adj.* approaching

on·er·ous *adj.* difficult or troublesome —**on·er·ous·ly** *adv.* —**on·er·ous·ness** *n.*

one'-sid·ed *adj.* prejudiced; unfair; favoring one person, argument, etc. over another —**one'-sid·ed·ly** *adv.* —**one'-sid·ed·ness** *n.*

one'-up·man·ship *n.* an attempt to outdo another in the matter of possessions or accomplishments

on·go·ing *adj.* continuous; in progress

on·set *n.* a beginning

on·slaught *n.* an attack; an outpouring

o·nus *n.* responsibility; burden

on·ward *adj., adv.* forward

ooze *n.* something that leaks out; slimy mud —*vi.* to flow or leak out slowly; to give off, as a particular quality: *she oozes charisma* —*vt.* to give off

o·pac·i·ty *n.* a lack of clarity or transparency

o·paque' *adj.* not transparent; impervious to light; ambiguous or obscure: *opaque reasoning* —**o·paque'ly** *adv.* —**o·paque'ness** *n.*

o·pen *adj.* accessible; unlocked or unobstructed; unrestricted; available; candid and straightforward; lacking prejudice: *open-minded* —*vi., vt.* to become or make accessible; to begin, as of a meeting or a

business —**o·pen·ly** *adv.* —**o·pen·ness** *n.*

o·pen·ing *n.* a clear passage or space; a beginning; an opportunity or vacancy

o·pen-mind·ed *adj.* receptive to new ideas; able to be reasoned with —**o·pen-mind·ed·ly** *adv.* —**o·pen-mind·ed·ness** *n.*

op·er·a *n.* a musical drama —**op·er·at·ic** *adj.* —**op·er·at·i·cal·ly** *adv.*

op·er·a·ble *adj.* able to be put to use; that can be corrected by surgery —**op·er·a·bil·i·ty** *n.* —**op·er·a·bly** *adv.*

op·er·ate *vi.* to function, as of a machine; to perform surgery —*vt.* to control or cause to function; to manage, as a business

op·er·a·tion *n.* the condition or an instance of functioning: *a manufacturing operation*; a procedure or method; surgery —**op·er·a·tion·al** *adj.* —**op·er·a·tion·al·ly** *adv.*

op·er·a·tive *adj.* functioning well —**op·er·a·tive·ly** *adv.*

op·er·a·tor *n.* one who controls or runs, as a machine or a business

op·er·et·ta *n.* a light opera

oph·thal·mol·o·gy *n.* the branch of medicine that deals with the study of the eye, its diseases, and treatment —**oph·thal·mo·log·ic, oph·thal·mo·log·i·cal** *adj.* —**oph·thal·mol·o·gist** *n.*

o·pi·ate *n.* a sedative; anything that dulls the senses

o·pin·ion *n.* a belief or judgment that may be based on knowledge or simple emotion

o·pin·ion·at·ed *adj.* having strong, often radical, beliefs —**o·pin·ion·at·ed·ly** *adv.* —**o·pin·ion·at·ed·ness** *n.*

o·pi·um *n.* a narcotic derived from the opium poppy

op·po·nent *adj.* acting in opposition —*n.* one who opposes

op·por·tune' *adj.* timely or suitable

—**op·por·tune´ly** *adv.* —**op·por· tune´ness** *n.*

op·por·tun´ist *n.* one who makes the most of an advantage, often unmindful of others —**op·por·tun·is´ tic** *adj.* —**op·por·tun·is´ti·cal·ly** *adv.*

op·por·tu´ni·ty *n.* an advantageous occasion or time

op·pos´a·ble *adj.* capable of being opposite or reversed, esp. of the thumb; that can be confronted or countered —**op·pos·a·bil´i·ty** *n.* — **op·pos´a·bly** *adv.*

op·pose´ *vt.* to act in conflict with; to place across from —**op·pos´er** *n.* —**op·pos´ing·ly** *adv.*

op´po·site *adj.* positioned or placed across from; facing or moving away; facing or moving the wrong way; contrary —**op´po·site·ly** *adv.* —**op´po·site·ness** *n.*

op·po·si´tion *n.* the state of conflicting; those in disagreement — **op·po·si´tion·al** *adj.*

op·press´ *vt.* to suppress by maltreatment or abuse; to overburden; to depress mentally —**op·pres´ sion** *n.* —**op·pres´sor** *n.*

op·pres´sive *adj.* marked by persecution, hardship, etc.; producing depression —**op·pres´sive·ly** *adv.* —**op·pres´sive·ness** *n.*

op·pro´bri·ous *adj.* contemptuous or reproachful; shameful —**op·pro´ bri·ous·ly** *adv.* —**op·pro´bri·ous· ness** *n.*

op·pro´bri·um *n.* shameful conduct; a cause of shame or disgrace

opt *vi.* to choose

op´tic *adj.* relating to the eye —**op´ ti·cal·ly** *adv.*

op´ti·cal *adj.* relating to vision

optical illusion a deceptive or misleading image

op·ti´cian *n.* one who makes or sells eyeglasses or other optical devices

op´tics *pl. n.* the branch of science dealing with vision and light

op´ti·mal *adj.* most favorable —**op´ ti·mal·ly** *adv.*

op´ti·mism *n.* an inclination to expect a favorable outcome —**op´ti· mist** *n.* —**op´ti·mis´tic** *adj.* —**op´ ti·mis´ti·cal·ly** *adv.*

op´ti·mize *vt.* to maximize effectiveness —**op·ti·mi·za´tion** *n.*

op´ti·mum *adj.* most favorable

op´tion *n.* a choice; a right to choose or elect

op´tion·al *adj.* discretionary

op·tom´e·try *n.* the technology involved in examining, diagnosing problems, and prescribing treatment for the eyes —**op·to·met´ric, op·to·met´ri·cal** *adj.* —**op·tom´e· trist** *n.*

op´u·lent *adj.* marked by wealth or abundance; profuse —**op´u· lence, op´u·len·cy** *n.* —**op´u·lent· ly** *adv.*

o´pus *n.* a creative literary or musical composition

or´a·cle *n.* a prophet; a visionary; one considered a source of great wisdom

o·rac´u·lar *adj.* prophetic; obscure or ambiguous, as the prophesies of an oracle —**o·rac·u·lar´i·ty** *n.* — **o·rac´u·lar·ly** *adv.*

o´ral *adj.* spoken; relating to speech or the mouth —**o´ral·ly** *adv.*

o·rate´ *vi.* to speak formally —**o·ra´ tion** *n.* —**o·ra´tor** *n.*

or·a·tor´i·cal *adj.* pertaining to an orator or oratory —**or·a·tor´i·cal· ly** *adv.*

or´a·to·ry *n.* the art of public speaking

orb *n.* a sphere

or´bit *n.* the path traveled by one body around another, as of a satellite around the earth; a sphere of influence —*vi.* to travel in an orbit —*vt.* to place in an orbit —**or´ bit·al** *adj.*

or´chard *n.* trees grown for their produce, such as fruit, nuts, etc.

or·ches·tra *n.* a large group of musicians; the area of a theater directly in front of the stage —**or·ches´tral** *adj.* —**or·ches´tral·ly** *adv.*

or·ches·trate *vt.* to arrange music; to coordinate an activity: *orchestrate a corporate buyout* —**or·ches·tra´tion** *n.* —**or´ches·tra·tor** *n.*

or·dain´ *vt.* to charge with holy orders; to decree or dictate —**or·dain´ment** *n.*

or´deal *n.* a trying experience

or´der *n.* a logical sequence or arrangement; a command or request; a group or organization —*vt.* to arrange; to instruct or direct —**or´der·er** *n.*

or´der·ly *adj.* neat; systematic or methodical; peaceful and law-abiding —*n.* a hospital attendant; a soldier assigned to attend an officer —**or´der·li·ness** *n.*

or´di·nance *n.* a law, especially a local regulation or statute

or´di·nary *adj.* common; unexceptional —*n.* that which is usual or normal —**or·di·nar´i·ly** *adv.* —**or·di·nar´i·ness** *n.*

ord´nance *n.* military arms and equipment

ore *n.* mineral rock from which a useful substance can be extracted

or´gan *n.* a musical instrument; a body part; a controlled–circulation publication

or·gan´ic *adj.* of or relating to living tissue or things —**or·gan´i·cal·ly** *adv.*

or´ga·nism *n.* a life form

or´gan·ist *n.* one who plays an organ

or·ga·ni·za´tion *n.* the process of bringing together or making functional; an entity so formed; an association of persons united for a common purpose —**or·ga·ni·za´tion·al** *adj.* —**or·ga·ni·za´tion·al·ly** *adv.*

or´ga·nize *vt.* to make orderly or functional; to bring together or establish —**or´ga·niz·er** *n.*

or´ga·nized *adj.* established; functional; orderly

or´gasm *n.* sexual climax —**or·gas´mic, or·gas´tic** *adj.*

or´gy *n.* revelry; uncontrolled indulgence —**or·gi·as´tic** *adj.* —**or·gi·as´ti·cal·ly** *adv.*

o´ri·ent *vt.* to position according to the points of the compass or some other point of reference; to familiarize, as with a company's policies and procedures

o´ri·en·tate *vt.* to orient —**o·ri·en·ta´tion** *n.*

or´i·fice *n.* an opening —**or·i·fi´cial** *adj.*

or´i·gin *n.* a beginning; a source

o·rig´i·nal *adj.* first or new; different or imaginative —*n.* a thing from which others are derived; a prototype

o·rig·i·nal´i·ty *n.* creativeness; innovation

o·rig´i·nal·ly *adv.* first; initially

o·rig´i·nate *vi., vt.* to come or bring into existence —**o·rig·i·na´tion** *n.* —**o·rig´i·na·tor** *n.*

or´na·ment *n.* a decoration or embellishment —*vt.* to decorate or embellish

or·na·men´tal *adj.* decorative —**or·na·men´tal·ly** *adv.* —**or·na·men·ta´tion** *n.*

or·nate´ *adj.* elaborately styled or decorated —**or·nate´ly** *adv.* —**or·nate´ness** *n.*

or´ner·y *adj.* surly or irritable —**or´ner·i·ness** *n.*

or·ni·thol´o·gy *n.* the study of birds —**or·nith·o·log´ic, or·nith·o·log´i·cal** *adj.* —**or·ni·thol´o·gist** *n.*

or´phan *adj.* lacking parents; unsupported, as *the orphan concept of cold fusion* —*n.* a child without parents —*vt.* to deprive of one or both parents

or´phic *adj.* mystical

ort *n.* a scrap, especially of food left

after a meal

or·tho·don´tia, or·tho·don´tics *n.* dentistry involved in the prevention and correction of irregularities in teeth **—or·tho·don´tic** *adj.* **—or·tho·don´tist** *n.*

or´tho·dox *adj.* adhering to traditional or established ways **—or´tho·dox·y** *n.*

or·tho·pe´dics *n.* the branch of medicine concerned with ailments of the skeletal system **—or·tho·pe´dic** *adj.* **—or·tho·pe´di·cal·ly** *adv.* **—or´tho·pe´dist** *n.*

os´cil·late *vi.* to move back and forth; to vibrate **—os·cil·la´tion** *n.*

os´cu·late *vi.* to come together **—vt.** to kiss **—os·cu·la´tion** *n.*

os·mo´sis *n.* the tendency of fluid to pass through a thin membrane until it is of equal density on both sides; a gradual, often unnoticed, process of absorbing or learning **—os´mose** *vi., vt.* **—os·mot´ic** *adj.* **—os·mot´i·cal·ly** *adv.*

os·si·fi·ca´tion *n.* the process of forming bone; the process of becoming hardened or the material so formed **—os·sif´ic** *adj.* **—os´si·fy** *vi., vt.*

os·ten´si·ble *adj.* appearing as; professed or pretended: *his ostensible goal is progress, but he really means to sow dissent* **—os·ten´si·bly** *adv.*

os·ten´sive *adj.* apparent or seeming **—os·ten´sive·ly** *adv.*

os·ten·ta´tion *n.* a pretentious display intended to impress

os·ten·ta´tious *adj.* overly showy **—os·ten·ta´tious·ly** *adv.* **—os·ten·ta´tious·ness** *n.*

os´tra·cize *vt.* to isolate or banish, as from a group **—os´tra·cism** *n.*

oth´er *adj.* distinct from; remaining from those indicated

oth´er·wise *adv.* differently; in a different setting or circumstance

oth´er–world´ly *adj.* mystical;

unconcerned with the present **—oth´er–world´li·ness** *n.*

o´ti·ose *adj.* idle, indolent **—o´ti·ose·ly** *adv.* **—oti·os´i·ty** *n.*

oust *vt.* to eject or force out **—oust´er** *n.*

out *adj., adv.* exterior; away or apart from; distinct from that which is usual or accepted

out´age *n.* a shortage or variance; a temporary interruption, as of electrical power

out´break *n.* an outset or beginning, as of sudden violence or disease

out´burst *n.* an abrupt discharge or disturbance

out´cast *n.* one who has been expelled or rejected **—adj.** rejected

out´come *n.* a consequence or result

out´cry *n.* a protest or clamor

out·dat´ed *adj.* antiquated; no longer popular or stylish **—out·dat´ed·ness** *n.*

out·do´ *vt.* to surpass

out·doors´ *n.* outside; away from civilization **—out´door´** *adj.*

out´er *adj.* external or exterior

outer space beyond the limits of a planet's atmosphere

out´fit *n.* a set of clothing or equipment **—vt.** to furnish with clothing or equipment **—out´fit·ter** *n.*

out·fox´ *vt.* to outsmart

out´go *n.* expenditures

out´go´ing *adj.* sociable; leaving, as from a place or position

out´grow´ *vt.* to become too large for, as clothing; to overcome or depart from, as immature habits

out´growth *n.* something produced as a result

out´ing *n.* an airing or excursion

out·land´ish *adj.* foreign or unconventional **—out·land´ish·ly** *adv.* **—out·land´ish·ness** *n.*

out´law *n.* a criminal; a rebel or radical **—vt.** to prohibit

out´lay *n.* an expenditure

out´let *n.* an opening, as for egress

or escape; a shop that sells goods or services, especially a specific brand or at reduced prices; a connector, as for electricity or a telephone

out´line *n.* a plan or general description; a line drawing that defines the shape of an object —*vt.* to provide a general description; to create a line drawing

out´look *n.* a particular viewpoint; an assessment of future prospects

out´ly·ing *adj.* distant; far removed

out´mod´ed *adj.* no longer practical or fashionable

out´-of-date´ *adj.* outmoded

out´-of-doors´ *n.* outdoors

out´-of-pock´et *adj.* of a cash expenditure

out´-of-the-way´ *adj.* remote

out·pace´ *vt.* to exceed, as in growth or expectations: *the cost to operate the business could quickly outpace our income*

out´pa·tient *n.* one treated at a hospital or clinic without an ovenight stay

out·per·form´ *vt.* to achieve better results than another

out´put *n.* an amount produced; that which is produced

out´rage *n.* an offensive act; anger caused by such an act —*vt.* to make violently angry

out·ra´geous *adj.* extremely offensive; excessive or unconventional: *charged an outrageous price* — **out·ra´geous·ly** *adv.* —**out·ra´geous·ness** *n.*

out´right *adj., adv.* direct and without reservation; completely and entirely

out´set *n.* a beginning

out·side´ *adj.* of the outer limit —*n.* the outer surface or limit —*adv.*

out·sid´er *n.* one who does not belong or fit in

out·smart´ *vt.* to outwit or outmaneuver; to deceive

out·spo´ken *adj.* candid —**out´spo´ken·ly** *adv.* —**out´spo´ken·ness** *n.*

out·stand´ing *adj.* notable or exceptional; unsettled, as an unpaid debt —**out·stand´ing·ly** *adv.*

out´strip´ *vt.* to outrun or exceed

out´ward *adj., adv.* toward the outside; external —**out´ward·ly** *adv.* —**out´ward·ness** *n.*

out´wit´ *vt.* to trick or deceive

o´val *adj.* elliptical; egg-shaped —*n.* —**o´val·ly** *adv.* —**o´val·ness** *n.*

o´vate *adj.* oval, as of a leaf — **o´vate·ly** *adv.*

o·va´tion *n.* spirited applause — **o·va´tion·al** *adj.*

ov´en *n.* a closed compartment for baking or drying

o´ver *adj.* extreme; extra —*adv.* above; across: *he jumped over the puddle*; as far as: *move over to the table*; completed or done —*prep.*

o·ver·a·chieve´ *vi.* to be more successful than anticipated; to accomplish more than expected — **o·ver·a·chieve´ment** *n.* —**o·ver·a·chiev´er** *n.*

o·ver·act´ *vi., vt.* to overplay or exaggerate a role

o·ver·ac´tive *adj.* more active than normal or expected —**o·ver·ac·tiv´i·ty** *n.*

o´ver·age *n.* an excess

o·ver·all *adj.* all–inclusive

o´ver·alls *n.* (*Brit.*) a one–piece garment customarily worn over street clothes to protect them; (*US*) loose trousers with a bib front and shoulder straps

o·ver·awe´ *vt.* to inspire great wonderment or veneration

o·ver·bear´ *vt.* to dominate

o·ver·bear´ing *adj.* domineering or arrogant —**o´ver·bear´ing·ly** *adv.*

o·ver·blown´ *adj.* excessive

o´ver·build´ *vi., vt.* to fill an area with more structures than necessary or practical

o´ver·bur´den *vt.* to overload or

overwork

o·ver·cast *adj.* cloudy or misty; gloomy

o·ver·charge´ *vt.* to request an excessive price for —*n.* an excessive charge

o·ver·coat *n.* a heavy coat that covers most of the body

o·ver·come´ *vt.* to defeat or prevail over —*vi.* to win

o·ver·com·mit´ *vt.* to obligate beyond one's ability to perform — **o·ver·com·mit´ment** *n.*

o·ver·com·pen·sate *vt.* to react immoderately to a real or imagined error or shortcoming —*vi.* to make too great a compensation for — **o´ver·com·pen´sa·to·ry** *adj.* — **o´ver·com·pen·sa´tion** *n.*

o·ver·crowd´ *vi., vt.* to crowd or cause to crowd excessively

o·ver·de·vel´op *vt.* to improve or expand excessively —**o·ver·de·vel´op·ment** *n.*

o·ver·do´ *vi., vt.* to overreach or carry to extremes

o´ver·dose *n.* an excessive dosage or amount —*vt.* to take or administer an excessive dose

o´ver·draft *n.* an amount drawn from an account in excess of available funds

o·ver·draw´ *vt.* to withdraw from an account in excess of available funds; to exaggerate

o·ver·dress´ *vi., vt.* to wear attire that is too elaborate or out of place

o´ver·due´ *adj.* being beyond the time when expected or due

o·ver·es´ti·mate *vt.* to esteem or appraise too highly

o·ver·ex·pose´ *vt.* to exhibit or allow excessive access to

o·ver·ex·tend´ *vt.* to obligate or use beyond a reasonable limit —**o·ver·ex·ten´sion** *n.*

o´ver·flow *n.* an excessive amount; a device that allows excess to escape —*vi., vt.* to spill over; to abound

o´ver·growth *n.* luxurious or excessive growth, especially of plants — **o·ver·grow´** *vi., vt.* —**o·ver·grown´** *adj.*

o´ver·hang´ *vi., vt.* to extend beyond, as the edge of a roof over the walls below

o´ver·haul´ *vt.* to renovate or make extensive repairs

o´ver·head *n.* the cost of operating a business such as the rent and utilities, excluding the cost of producing a product or service —*adj.* —**o·ver·head´** *adv.* above the level of the head

o·ver·hear´ *vi., vt.* to hear without the speaker's knowledge

o·ver·in·dulge´ *vt.* to partake excessively —**o´ver·in·dul´gence** *n.* — **o´ver·in·dul´gent** *adj.* —**o·ver·in·dul´gent·ly** *adv.*

o´ver·joyed *adj.* delighted —**o´ver·joy´** *vt.*

o´ver·kill *n.* an excess of that required

o´ver·lay *n.* something spread over to cover or embellish —*vt.*

o´ver·look *n.* a vantage point — **o´ver·look´** *vt.* to watch over or supervise; to disregard or omit

o´ver·ly *adv.* excessively

o·ver·much´ *adj., adv.* excessive

o·ver·night´ *adj.* extending over one night or throughout the night

o·ver·night´er *n.* a trip of more than a single day; one making an overnight stay; a suitcase

overnight bag a suitcase to carry clothing, etc. for a short trip

o´ver·pass (*US*) *n.* a passageway over a road, walkway, etc.

o·ver·pay´ *vi.* to pay in excess of what is required or necessary — **o·ver·pay´ment** *n.*

o·ver·play´ *vt.* to stress excessively

o´ver·pop·u·la´tion *n.* overcrowding that causes depletion of resources —**o·ver·pop´u·late** *vi., vt.*

o·ver·pow´er *vt.* to overwhelm

o·ver·price´ *vt.* to price or value too highly

o´ver·print *n.* an image printed over an existing image —**o·ver·print´** *vt.*

o·ver·pro·duce´ *vt.* to manufacture more than is required —**o·ver·pro·duc´tion** *n.*

o·ver·qual´i·fied *adj.* possessing education or experience beyond that required for a particular job

o·ver·rate´ *vt.* to rank or appraise too highly

o·ver·reach´ *vt.* to go beyond that which is right or prudent

o·ver·re·act´ *vi.* to react excessively or inappropriately —**o·ver·re·ac´tion** *n.*

o·ver·rule´ *vt.* to rule against an earlier decision

o·ver·run´ *vi., vt.* to spread or extend over a reasonable or normal limit

o·ver·seas´ *adj.* of places across the sea

o·ver·see´ *vt.* to supervise —**o´ver·seer** *n.*

o·ver·sell´ *vt.* to contract to sell more than is available; to praise or promote too highly

o·ver·shad´ow *vt.* dominate

o·ver·shoot´ *vi., vt.* to exceed or go beyond

o´ver·sight *n.* supervision; an unintentional error

o·ver·sim´pli·fy *vi., vt.* to explain in terms so simple as to cause misunderstanding —**o·ver·sim´pli·fi·ca´tion** *n.*

o·ver·size, o´ver·sized *adj.* larger than usual or necessary

o·ver·spend´ *vi., vt.* to spend in excess; to tire

o·´ver·state´ *vt.* to exaggerate —**o·ver·state´ment** *n.*

o·vert´ *adj.* open and public; sanctioned: *an overt military operation* —**o·vert´ly** *adv.*

o·ver·tax´ *vt.* to burden excessively

o´ver-the-count´er *adj.* of medicine

that can be sold without a doctor's prescription

o·ver·throw´ *vt.* to overturn, as a government; to throw, as a ball, past its intended mark —**o·ver·throw´er** *n.*

o´ver·time *n.* time past an established norm, as work beyond a normal eight hour day

o´ver·tone *n.* an inference or hint: *an explanation with overtones of condescension*

o´ver·ture *n.* a musical introduction; an approach that signals readiness to negotiate

o´ver·view *n.* a general view; a summary

o·ver·wea´ry *adj.* exhausted

o·ver·whelm´ *vt.* to defeat; to astonish; to inundate —**o·ver·whelm´ing** *adj.* —**o·ver·whelm´ing·ly** *adv.*

o·ver·work´ *vi., vt.* to work or use too much

o·ver·wrought´ *adj.* overexcited or agitated; overly ornate

o´vine *adj.* pertaining to sheep; sheeplike

o´void *adj.* shaped like an egg

owe *vi., vt.* to be indebted

ow´ing *adj.* unpaid

own *adj.* of one's possession —*vt.* to possess or control —*vi., vt.* to admit or acknowledge —**own´er** *n.* —**own´er·ship** *n.*

ox·i·da´tion *n.* the combining of oxygen with another substance

ox´i·dize *vt.* to combine with oxygen —**ox´i·diz´able** *adj.* —**ox·i·di·za´tion** *n.* —**ox´i·diz·er** *n.*

ox´y·gen *n.* a nonmetallic element that mixes readily with most other elements, is necessary for plant and animal respiration, and is required for most combustion

ox´y·gen·ate *vt.* to combine with oxygen —**ox·y·gen·a´tion** *n.*

ox·y·mo´ron *n.* a descriptive phrase that incorporates seemingly contradictory terms, as *a sweet* *sadness* or *the silence was deafening* —**ox·y·mo·ron´ic** *adj.*

p, P sixteenth letter of the English alphabet

pace *n.* a manner of walking; the speed at which one walks or at which an event takes place; a stride of about 30 inches —*vt., vi.* to walk; to measure by paces

pace´mak·er *n.* a device used to regulate the heartbeat

pach´y·derm *n.* any of a variety of large animals with thick hides such as the elephant or rhinoceros —**pach·y·der´mal,   pach·y·der´ma·tous** *adj.*

pa·cif´ic *adj.* peaceful, tranquil — **pa·cif´i·cal·ly** *adv.*

pac·i·fi·ca´tion *n.* appeasement — **pac´i·fi·ca·tor** *n.* —**pa·cif´i·ca·to·ry** *adj.*

pac´i·fism *n.* the rejection of the use of violence in the settling of conflicts —**pac´i·fist** *n.* —**pac·i·fis´tic** *adj.* —**pac·i·fis´ti·cal·ly** *adv.*

pac´i·fy *vt.* to ease anger or conflict —**pac´i·fi·a·ble** *adj.*

pack *n.* a small package; a set of like items: *a pack of cards*; a closed bag with straps for carrying necessary items for hiking, camping, etc.; a group, generally functioning as a unit —*vt., vi.* to place in a container or containers; to press together or compress —**pack´a·ble** *adj.*

pack´age *n.* a container holding items for storage or transport; a combination of elements taken together: *a package deal* —*vt.* to make into or offer as a combination —**pack´ag·er** *n.*

pack´ag·ing *n.* material used to form a package or to protect or cushion a packaged item; the way in which something is presented

pack´et *n.* a small package

pack´ing *n.* material used to protect or cushion a packaged item

pact *n.* an agreement; a contract

pad *n.* a thin protective cushion; sheets of writing paper glued together at one end —*vt.* to protect with soft material; to increase deceitfully: *pad a speech with irrelevant stories, pad an expense account* —**pad´ding** *n.*

pad´dle *n.* any of a variety of flattened implements used for such things as mixing, propelling a boat, spanking, etc. —*vi., vt.* to propel with a paddle; to spank — **pad´dler** *n.*

pa´gan *adj.* without religion; heathenish —*n.* a nonreligious person —**pa´gan·dom** *n.* —**pa´gan·ish** *adj.* —**pa´gan·ism** *n.*

page *n.* one side of a sheet of paper —*vt.* to summon by calling aloud or with a beeper

pag´eant *n.* an elaborate procession or celebration —**pag´eant·ry** *n.*

pag´i·nate *vt.* to number the pages of a publication —**pag·i·na´tion** *n.*

pa·go´da *n.* an ornate multi-storied tower that serves as a Buddhist shrine

pail *n.* a cylindrical container with a handle used for carrying liquids

pain *n.* a disagreeable sensation caused by injury, etc.; suffering — *vi., vt.* to cause pain —**take pains** to exercise great care —**pain´ful** *adj.* —**pain´ful´ly** *adv.* —**pain´ful·ness** *n.*

pain´kill·er *n.* a medication that relieves pain —**pain´kill·ing** *adj.*

pain´less *adj.* free from pain; causing no pain —**pain´less·ly** *adj.* — **pain´less·ness** *n.*

pains´tak·ing *adj.* requiring great care; careful —*n.* very careful work —**pains´tak·ing·ly** *adv.*

paint *n.* liquid coloring used to decorate or protect; the coating formed when the liquid dries —*vi., vt.* to cover with paint; to create an

image with paint or with words —
paint´a·ble *adj.* —**paint´er** *n.*

paint´ing *n.* the process or business of covering surfaces with paint; a picture or design created with paint

pair *n.* two persons or things sharing something in common —*vi., vt.* to come or bring together in a pair

pal *n.* a friend

pal´ace *n.* a grand and sumptuous residence —**pa·la´tial** *adj.* —**pa·la´tial·ly** *adv.* —**pa·la´tial·ness** *n.*

pal´at·a·ble *adj.* edible; acceptable: *a palatable solution* —**pal´at·a·bil´i·ty,** —**pal´at·a·ble·ness** *n.* —**pal´at·a·bly** *adv.*

pal´ate *n.* the roof of the mouth; the sense of taste

pale *adj.* light in color; pallid; dim — *vt., vi.* to make or become pale — **pale´ly** *adv.* —**pale´ness** *n.* —**pal´ish** *adj.*

pal´ette *n.* a flat panel for mixing artist's colors; the colors used by an artist

pal´i·mo·ny *n.* financial support for a former companion

pal´in·drome *n.* a word, phrase, etc. that can be read backward or forward, such as *a man, a plan, a canal, Panama* —**pal´in·drom´ic** *adj.*

pal·i·sade´ *n.* a steep cliff, often overlooking a body of water

pall *n.* gloom; a dark cover, as of clouds or smoke

pal´li·ate *vt.* to excuse; to relieve or ease as symptoms of an illness — **pal·li·a´tion** *n.* —**pal´li·a·tor** *n.*

pal´li·a·tive *adj.* serving to relieve the symptoms of an illness —**pal´li·a·tive·ly** *adv.*

pal´lid *adj.* extremely pale; ashen — **pal´lid·ly** *adv.* —**pal´lid·ness, pal´lor** *n.*

palm´is·try *n.* the telling of fortunes from the patterns on the palm of the hands —**palm´ist** *n.*

pal´pa·ble *adj.* obvious; tangible

—**pal·pa·bil´i·ty, pal´pa·ble·ness** *n.* —**pal´pa·bly** *adv.*

pal´pi·tate *vi.* to tremble or quiver; to pulsate —**pal´pi·tat·ing·ly** *adv.* —**pal´pi·ta´tion** *n.*

pal´try *adj.* trivial; insignificant; of little worth —**pal´tri·ly** *adv.* — **pal´tri·ness** *n.*

pam´per *vt.* to cater to excessively; to indulge —**pam´per·er** *n.*

pamph´let *n.* a leaflet or brochure — **pam´phlet·ar·y** *adj.* —**pam´phle·teer** *n.*

pan *n.* a shallow metal container used for cooking; any similar container such as a *dishpan*; harsh critcism —*vi., vt.* to seek out or separate by rinsing: *to pan for gold*; to criticize

pan·a·ce´a *adj.* a cure-all —**pan·a·ce´an** *adj.*

pa·nache´ *n.* spirit or zest

pan·chro·mat´ic *adj.* sensitive to all colors: *panchromatic film* —**pan·chro´ma·tism** *n.*

pan·dem´ic *adj.* general; universal

pan·de·mo´ni·um *n.* noisy confusion

pan´der *vi.* to cater to or exploit the baser tastes of others; to procure for sexual affairs —*n.* a procurer or pimp

pane *n.* a panel of glass for a window; a flat piece or surface

pan´el *n.* a flat decorative section set off from the rest of the object of which it is a part: *a door panel;* any similar section: *an instrument panel*; a group formed for some specific purpose: *a panel of judges* —*vt.* to provide with panels

pan´el·ing *n.* a wall covering

pan´el·ist *n.* a member of a group formed for a specific purpose, as to judge a contest or discuss an issue

pang *n.* a sudden sharp pain or emotion: *a pang of guilt*

pan´han·dle (*US*) *vi.* to beg for food etc. —**pan´han·dler** *n.*

pan´ic *n.* sudden fear; genera

hysteria —*vi.*, *vt.* to become or cause to become fearful —**pan´ick·y** *adj.*

pan´icked, pan·ick·ing *adj.* driven by fear

pan´ic-strick·en *adj.* overcome by fear or dread

pan´o·ply *n.* an extensive or impressive display

pan·o·ram´a *n.* an extensive view —**pan·o·ram´ic** *adj.* —**pan·o·ram´i·cal·ly** *adv.*

pant *vi.* to take short rapid breaths

pan´to·graph *n.* a mechanical device used to make a copy of a drawing, diagram, etc. —**pan·tog´ra·pher** *n.* —**pan·to·graph´ic** *adj.*

pan´to·mime *n.* communication by means of gestures; a performance that expresses ideas without speech —*vt.*, *vi.* to express in pantomime —**pan·to·mim´ic** *adj.* —**pan´to·mimist** *n.*

pan´try *n.* a closet for storing food and food service items; an area where foods are plated or otherwise prepared for serving

pap *n.* soft food, as for infants or the infirm; a thing of little significance

pa´per *adj.* formed of or resembling paper; lacking substance: *paper shuffling, paper profits* —*n.* a thin material made from wood or cloth pulp; a formal dissertation or document of value; a daily newspaper —*vt.* to cover with paper

pa´per·back *n.* a book with a thick paper cover —*adj.*

pa´per-push·er *n.* an inconsequential bureaucrat

paper tiger one who is weak or ineffectual while pretending to be strong and forceful

pa·pier-mâ·ché´ *n.* paper pulp, easily shaped when wet, that dries to a hard surface

par *adj.* normal —*n.* an established standard or level for comparison; the face value of a negotiable instrument, such as a stock or bond

par´a·ble *n.* a story with a moral

par´a·chute *n.* a cloth canopy attached with cords to a person or object to slow the rate of descent from a high altitude —*vi.*, *vt.* to descend or land by parachute —**par´a·chut·ist** *n.*

pa·rade´ *n.* a procession, that can be formal such as a *Thanksgiving Day parade*, or informal as for *a parade of shoppers*; a series of things or events: *a parade of sitcoms on television* —**pa·rad´er** *n.*

par´a·digm *n.* an example or model —**par·a·dig·mat´ic** *adj.* —**par´a·dig·mat´i·cal·ly** *adv.*

par´a·dise *n.* a perfect place of peace and beauty —**par·a·di·sa´ic, par·a·di·sa´i·cal, par·a·di·si´a·cal** *adj.* —**par·a·di·sa´i·cal·ly, par·a·di·si´a·cal·ly** *adv.*

par´a·dox *n.* a statement that seems contradictory, but that may nevertheless be true such as *standing in one place is more tiring than walking*; an enigma, as a person or thing that possesses contradictory qualities —**par·a·dox´i·cal** *adj.* —**par·a·dox´i·cal·ly** *adv.* —**par·a·dox´i·cal·ness** *n.*

par´a·gon *n.* an example of perfection: *a paragon of virtue*

par´a·graph *n.* a section of prose that typically deals with a single topic or quotation —*vt.* to divide into paragraphs —**par·a·graph´ic, par·a·graph´i·cal** *adj.* —**par·a·graph´i·cal·ly** *adv.*

par·a·jour´nal·ism *n.* reporting that embodies some fictional license, as a study of student life that features a character who is a composite of several individuals —**par·a·jour´nal·ist** *n.* —**par·a·jour·nal·is´tic** *adj.*

par·a·le´gal *n.* one trained to assist an attorney

par·al·lax *n.* apparent displacement of an object caused by a change in the observer's position —**par·al·lac´tic** *adj.* —**par·al·lac´ti·cal·ly** *adv.*

par·al·lel *adj.* being of equal distance from each other at all points; being or moving in concert: *the story of parallel careers* —*n.* a resemblance or likeness; comparable —*vt.* to make parallel; to extend parallel to; to resemble or correlate —**par·al·lel·ism** *n.*

par·a·lyse (*Brit.*) *vt.* to render unable to move or function

pa·ral´y·sis *n.* a loss of ability to move or function

par·a·lyt´ic *adj.* paralyzed —**par·a·lyt´i·cal·ly** *adv.*

par·a·lyze (*US*) *vt.* to render unable to move or function —**par·a·ly·za´tion** *n.* —**par´a·lyz·ing·ly** *adv.*

par·a·med´ic *n.* one trained to provide emergency medical treatment and to assist a doctor —**par·a·med´i·cal** *adj.*

pa·ram´e·ter *n.* a boundry or limitation —**par´a·met´ric, par·a·met´ri·cal** *adj.*

par´a·mount *adj.* of primary importance; dominant —**par´a·mount·cy** *n.* —**par´a·mount·ly** *adv.*

par´amour *n.* a lover

par·a·noi´a *n.* irrational fear or distrust —**par´a·noi´ac, par´a·noid** *adj., n.*

par´a·nor´mal *adj.* outside the realm of normal knowledge or description —**par´a·nor´mal·ly** *adj.*

par·a·pher·na´lia *n.* the implements customarily used for a particular activity; equipment: *an artist's paraphernalia*

par´a·phrase *n.* a retelling in different words, usually to simplify or to clarify —*vi., vt.* to retell; restate —**par´a·phras·a·ble** *adj.* —**par´a·phras·er** *n.*

para·ple´gia *n.* paralysis of the lower part of the body —**par´a·ple´gic** *n., adj.*

par·a·pro·fes´sion·al *n.* one trained to assist another in a particular profession

par·a·psy·chol´o·gy *n.* the study of paranormal activity —**par´a·psy·cho·log´i·cal** *adj.* —**par´a·psy·chol´o·gist** *n.*

par´a·site *n.* an organism that is supported by another organism without providing anything to its host; one who relies on the generosity of others —**par´a·sit´ic, par´a·sit´i·cal** *adj.* —**par·a·sit´i·cal·ly** *adv.*

par´a·sol *n.* a small umbrella used as cover or protection from the sun

par´boil *vt.* to boil food briefly before cooking by some other method

par´cel *n.* a package; a section of land —*vt.* to divide and portion out

parch *vt., vi.* to make or become extremely dry or shriveled with heat; to make or become thirsty

parch´ment *n.* originally, animal skin used as a writing surface; paper made to resemble cured or treated animal skin

par´don *n.* foregiveness, as from punishment for a crime or for a social blunder —*vt.* to release from punishment; to forgive —**par´don·a·ble** *adj.* —**par´don·a·bly** *adv.* —**par´don·er** *n.*

pare *vt.* to remove the outer part by cutting; to trim

par´ent *n.* an ancestor; a mother or father: a source: *the automobile is parent to urban blight* —**pa·ren´tal** *adj.* —**pa·ren´tal·ly** *adv.* —**par´ent·hood** *n.*

par´ent·age *n.* one's lineage

pa·ren´the·sis *n., pl.* **pa·ren´the·ses** either of the curved symbols ( ) used to set apart a word or words as in a sentence or parts of a mathematical formula

par·en·thet´ic, par·en·thet´i·cal

adj. an aside; a comment apart, as though set off by parenthesis — **par·en·thet´i·cal·ly** *adv.*

par´ent·ing *n.* performance of the duties of a parent

par ex´cel·lence *adj.* preeminent; beyond comparing

pa·ri´ah *n.* an outcast

par´ish *n.* a district in the charge of a clergyman; a church congregation; a civil district that corresponds to a township or county — **pa·rish´ion·er** *n.*

par´i·ty *n.* equality or equivalence

park *n.* a section of land set aside usually for recreation or for its natural beauty; an area set aside for a particular purpose as *an industrial park* —*vt.* to place or leave temporarily, as a car

park´way (*US*) *n.* a wide landscaped road

par´lance *n.* a style of speech; jargon: *the parlance of a printer*

par´ley *n.* a conference, especially between adversaries —*vi.* to hold a conference

par·lia·ment *n.* a legislative body

par·lia·men´ta·ry *adj.* of a parliament, or its customs and rules — **par·lia·men·tar´i·an** *n.* —**par´lia·men·ta´ri·ly** *adv.*

par´lor *n.* a room set aside for a special purpose, as the entertainment of visitors

pa·ro´chi·al *adj.* relating to a local parish; local or conservative; provincial —**pa·ro´chi·al·ism** *n.* — **pa·ro´chi·al·ist** *n.* —**pa·ro´chi·al·ly** *adv.*

par´o·dy *n.* a comic work that ridicules the style of another; something so bad as to be a mockery — *vt.* to ridicule; to make a travesty of —**pa·rod´ic, pa·rod´i·cal, par´o·dis´tic** *adj.* —**par´o·dist** *n.*

par´ox·ysm *n.* a sudden emotional outburst, as of laughter or anger; a sudden attack or worsening of a disease —**par´ox·ys´mal** *adj.* — **par´ox·ys´mal·ly** *adv.*

par·quet´ *n.* a floor of inlaid wood formed in geometric patterns

par´ri·cide *n.* the murdering of a close relative, especially of one's parents —**par´ri·ci´dal** *adj.*

parry *n.* evasion, as of a blow or an embarrassing question —*vi., vt.* to ward off or avoid

parse *vt.* to examine in detail by separating into components

par·si·mo´ni·ous *adj.* extremely frugal —**par·si·mo´ni·ous·ly** *adv.* —**par·si·mo´ni·ous·ness, par´si·mo·ny** *n.*

part *adj.* incomplete; partial —*n.* a portion of a whole —*vt., vi.* to separate or become separated — **part´ly** *adv.*

par·take´ *vt., vi.* to take or receive a share in —**par·tak´er** *n.*

par´tial *adj.* incomplete; involving a part only; prejudiced or biased — **par´tial·ness** *n.*

par·tial´i·ty *n.* fondness or preference; bias

par´tial·ly *adv.* not completely

par·tic´i·pate *vi.* to engage in; to share in —**par·tic´i·pant, par·tic´i·pa·tor** *n.* —**par·tic´i·pa´tion** *n.* — **par·tic´i·pa·tive** *adj.*

par´ti·cle *n.* a tiny piece; the least possible amount: *not a particle of decency in him*

par·tic´u·lar *adj.* fussy, attentive to detail; of a specific thing; noteworthy: *a gem of particular fineness* —*n.* a detail or specific: *fill me in on the particulars*

par·tic·u·lar´i·ty *n.* attention to detail; distinctiveness or individuality

par·tic´u·lar·ly *adv.* especially

par´ti·san *adj.* biased —*n.* an ardent supporter —**par´ti·san·ship** *n.*

par´tite *adj.* divided

par·ti´tion *n.* a separation; something that separates —*vt.* to divide

or separate into parts —**par·ti·
tion·er** n.

part·ner n. one allied with another,
as in business or marriage; an associate —**part´ner·ship** n.

par´ty adj. of a group: party politics;
of a social gathering: a party mood
—n. a group or gathering: a political party, a cocktail party; a participant: party to the action —vi. to
carouse —**party line** the standards or ideals of a particular
group —**party pooper** one who
shuns or avoids involvement —
par´ty·er n.

pass n. a passageway; a ticket or
permit; a kind of throw; a sexual
overture —vi., vt. to move by or
beyond; to transfer: pass the salt;
to bandy: words passed between
them; to be satisfactory: he passed
the exam

pass´a·ble adj. accessible or navigable, as a road; generally acceptable; adequate —**pass´a·ble·ness**
n. —**pass´a·bly** adv.

pas´sage n. a journey; a path or
road; movement, transition, or
progress: the passage of time; an
excerpt from literature, music,
etc.; enactment, as of a law

pas´sage·way n. a walkway; a corridor or hallway that permits movement between rooms, buildings,
etc.

pas·sé´ adj. no longer fashionable

pas´sen·ger n. a rider

pas´ser·by´ n., pl. **pas´sers·by´** one
who passes by chance

pas´sion n. intense emotion —**pas´
sion·al, pas´sion·ate** adj. —**pas´
sion·ate·ly** adv. —**pas´sion·ate·
ness** n.

pas´sion·less adj. lacking emotion;
detached —**pas´sion·less·ly** adv.
—**pas´sion·less·ness** n.

pas´sive adj. accepted without reaction; complacent —**pas´sive·ly**
adv. —**pas´sive·ness** n.

pas´siv·ist n. one who shuns violence as means to achieve an end
—**pas´siv·ism** n. —**pas·siv´i·ty** n.

past adj. former or prior; gone by: in
years past —n. a former time or
event —prep. beyond: they drove
past their destination

paste n. a thick smooth compound
as of food: tomato paste; an adhesive —vt. to fasten with paste

pas·tel´ adj. of a pale color —n. a
pale color; a chalk–like artist's
medium for producing such colors
—**pas·tel´ist** n.

pas·teur·ize vt. to process food so as
to retard spoilage —**pas·teur·i·
za´tion** n.

pas´time n. an amusement or diversion

pas´to·ral adj. of the country or
country life; rustic —n. an artistic
work that emulates country life, in
music, called a pas·to·rale´ —
pas·to·ral·ism n. —**pas·to·ral·ist**
n. —**pas·to·ral·ly** adv.

pas´ture n. vegetation eaten by
grazing animals; the land on which
such vegetation grows; the grazing
of animals —vt. to put an animal
out to graze —**pas´tur·a·ble** adj.
—**pas´tur·age** n.

past´y adj. appearing pale or sickly;
the consistency of paste —**past´i·
ness** n.

pat adj. to the point: a pat answer —
n. a light tap or caress; a bit of
food, a small piece: a pat of butter
—vt. to lightly tap or caress; to
flatten or compress by patting —vi.
to tap lightly

patch n. a small piece or part: an
elbow patch, a patch of land —vt.
to apply a patch of material, as for
mending or decoration —**patch´a·
ble** adj. —**patch´er** n.

patch´work n. something, such as a
quilt, made from patches

patch´y adj. described by patches;
uneven or variable: a patchy

performance —**patch´i·ly** *adv.* —
patch´i·ness *n.*

pate *n.* the top of the head

pat´ent[1] *adj.* protected by patent or
trademark —*n.* a right granted an
inventor to alone profit from his or
her work for a specified period —
vt. to apply for or grant a patent —
pat·ent·a·bil´i·ty *n.* —**pat´ent·a·
ble** *adj.* —**pat´ent·ed** *adj.* —**pat´
en·tee´** *n.* —**pat´en·tor** *n.*

pat´ent[2] *adj.* obvious or apparent —
pat´ent·ly *adv.*

pa·ter´nal *adj.* relating to fatherhood
—**pa·ter´nal·ly** *adv.*

pa·ter´nal·ism *n.* governing in a
benevolent or fatherly fashion —
pa·ter´nal·is´tic *adj.* —**pa·ter·nal·
is´ti·cal·ly** *adv.*

pa·ter´ni·ty *adj.* of the verification of
fatherhood and establishment of
responsibility for support of offspring —*n.* fatherhood

path *n.* a route along which something travels or progresses —
path´way *n.*

pa·thet´ic, pa·thet´i·cal *adj.* deserving of pity; inspiring contempt
—**pa·thet´i·cal·ly** *adv.*

path·o·log´i·cal *adj.* relating to pa-
thology; of behavior that is habitual or obsessive —**path·o·log´i·
cal·ly** *adv.*

pa·thol´o·gy *n.* the study of diseases
pa·thol´o·gist *n.*

pa´thos *n.* feelings of sympathy or
sorrow

pa´tience *n.* the ability to accept
without complaint, as inconvenience or delay

pa´tient *adj.* accepting of inconvenience or difficulty; tolerant —*n.* one
under the care of a physician,
dentist, chiropractor, etc. —**pa´
tient·ly** *adv.*

pat·i·na, pat·i´na *n.* change brought
about by age and exposure, as the
greenish layer that forms on copper or the delicate luster of old

wood —**pat´i·naed, pat·i´naed** *adj.*
—**pat´i·nate** *vt., vi.*

pat´io *n.* outdoor living space adjacent to a dwelling

pa·tis´se·rie *n.* a French bakery

pa´tois *n.* a provincial dialect; the
vernacular of a particular group

pa´tri·arch *n.* a man who heads a
family or group, or considered its
founder; an elder; the oldest member of a group —**pa´tri·ar´chal,
pa´tri·ar´chic** *adj.* —**pa´tri·ar´
chal·ly** *adv.*

pa´tri·archy *n.* a society that traces
its lineage through men

pa·tri´cian *n.* an aristocrat; one of
refined manners and taste —*adj.*
aristocratic; pertaining to aristocracy —**pa·tri´cian·ly** *adj.*

pat´ri·cide *n.* the murdering of one's
father —**pat´ri·cid´al** *adj.*

pat·ri·lin´e·age *n.* ancestry traced
through men —**pat·ri·lin´e·al** *adj.*
—**pat·ri·lin´e·al·ly** *adv.*

pat´ri·mo·ny *n.* inheritance from a
father —**pat·ri·mo´ni·al** *adj.* —**pat·
ri·mo´ni·al·ly** *adv.*

pa´tri·ot *n.* one who supports his or
her country —**pa´tri·ot´ic** *adj.* —
pa´tri·ot´i·cal·ly *adv.* —**pa´tri·ot·
ism** *n.*

pa·trol´ *n.* a person or persons who
move about and monitor an area
—*vt., vi.* to go about an area for
the purpose of guarding or inspecting —**pa·trol´ler** *n.*

pa´tron *n.* a customer; one who
supports an institution or cause —
pa´tron·age *n.*

pa´tron·ize *vt.* to frequent, as of a
customer; to support, as a cause;
to treat condescendingly —**pa·
tron·i·za´tion** *n.* —**pa´tron·iz·ing**
adj. —**pa´tron·iz·ing·ly** *adv.*

pat´ter *n.* a prepared spiel, as of a
salesperson or entertainer; meaningless chatter; a soft tapping
sound —*vt., vi.* to speak glibly

pat´tern *n.* a model or drawing used

as a guide in making something: *a dress pattern*; a reoccurring feature or characteristic: *a pattern of behavior* —*vt.* to make after a model or plan

pat´ty *n.* a flat round portion of food: *a hamburger patty*; a small pastry shell

pau´ci·ty *n.* a lack or scarcity

paunch *n.* a protruding abdomen — **paunch´i·ness** *n.* —**paunch´y** *adj.*

pau´per *n.* an impoverished person —**pau´per·ism** *n.* —**pau´per·ize** *vt.*

pause *n.* a temporary halt, as by indecision; a deliberate hesitation for effect: *a dramatic pause for emphasis* —*vi.* to temporarily cease speech or action

pave´ment (*US*) *n.* a durable surface as for covering a walkway or roadway —**pave** *vt.* —**pav´er** *n.* —**pav´ing** *n.*

pa·vil´ion *n.* a somewhat open, often temporary, shelter as at a picnic, campground, or fair

pawn *n.* something held as security against a loan; one held hostage — *vt.* to use or give as security — **pawn´a·ble** *adj.* —**pawn´bro·ker** *n.* —**pawn´er** *n.* —**pawn´shop** *n.*

pay *vt.* to give something of value in return for goods or services; to reward or punish: *they have to pay for disloyalty*; to render, as a compliment —*vi.* to make payment; to be profitable: *it pays to be ready* — *n.* compensation —**pay´a·ble** *adj.* —**pay·ee´** *n.* —**pay´er** *n.* —**pay´ment** *n.*

peace *n.* freedom from hostility; serenity —**peace´ful** *adj.* —**peace´ful·ly** *adv.* —**peace´ful·ness** *n.*

peace´a·ble *adj.* disposed to peace; tranquil —**peace´a·ble·ness** *n.* — **peace´a·bly** *adv.*

peace´keep·er *n.* one who assures or maintains peace —**peace´keep·ing** *adj.*

peace´mak·er *n.* a settler of disputes

—**peace´mak·ing** *adj.*

peak *adj.* at or near the upper limit —*n.* a pointed top; the height of development —*vi.* to bring to a climax or high level of development

peaked *adj.* pointed

peak´ed *adj.* appearing sickly — **peak´ed·ness** *n.*

peal *n.* a ringing —*vi.*, *vt.* to sound or ring

peas´ant *n.* a rustic; an uncouth person —**peas´ant·ry** *n.*

peb´ble *n.* a small stone —**peb´bly** *adj.*

pec´ca·ble *adj.* likely to sin —**pec´ca·bil´i·ty** *adj.*

pec·ca·dil´lo *n.* a petty sin; a minor indiscretion

pec´cant *adj.* sinful —**pec´can·cy** *n.* —**pec´cant·ly** *adv.*

peck *vi.* to strike with a beak; to nibble; to kiss lightly —*n.*

peck´ish *adj.* irritable

pec´u·late *vt.* to wrongfully appropriate, as funds entrusted to one's care; to embezzle —**pec·u·la´tion** *n.* —**pec´u·la·tor** *n.*

pe·cu´liar *adj.* odd or unusual; unique; characteristic of a particular person, group, etc. — **pe·cu·liar´i·ty** *n.* —**pe·cu´liar·ly** *adv.*

pe·cu´ni·ar·y *adj.* monetary —**pe·cu´ni·ar´i·ly** *adv.*

ped·a·gog´ics, ped·a·go·gy *n.* the teaching profession —**ped·a·gog´ic, ped·a·gog´i·cal** *adj.* —**ped·a·gog´i·cal·ly** *adv.*

ped´a·gogue *n.* an instructor; a narrow-minded teacher

ped´al *adj.* relating to the foot —*n.* a small pad for the foot that attaches to a device such as a bicycle or organ —*vt.*, *vi.* to operate or propel by means of a pedal

pe·dan´tic *adj.* overly concerned with scholarship and formality — **ped´ant** *n.* —**pe·dan´ti·cal·ly** *adv.* —**ped´ant·ry** *n.*

ped′dle *vi.* to travel about selling — *vt.* to offer for sale; to promote or attempt to sell, as an idea — **ped′dler** *n.*

ped·es′tal *n.* a foundation or base, as for a statue

pe·des′tri·an *adj.* of travel by foot; ordinary or trite —*n.* one moving on foot —**pe·des′tri·an·ism** *n.*

pe·des′tri·an·ize *vt.* to convert to use for foot travel —**pe·des·tri·an·i·za′tion** *n.*

pe·di·a·tri′cian *n.* a physician who specializes in treating infants — **pe′di·at′ric** *adj.* —**pe·di·at′rics** *n.*

ped′i·gree *n.* a list of ancestors; lineage

pe·do·phile, pe·do·phil′i·ac *n.* an adult who is sexually attracted to children —**pe·do·phil′i·a** *n.* —**pe·do·phil′ic** *adj.*

peek *n.* a momentary view or glance —*vi.* to view quickly as from hiding; to emerge, as though hiding: *tips of flowers peek through the underbrush*

peel *n.* the outer covering of certain fruits and vegetables —*vi., vt.* to come off or strip off, as bark or skin —**peel′er** *n.*

peep *n.* a short high-pitched sound, as of a bird; a sly glance —*vi.* to utter a weak cry; to glance furtively —**peep′er** *n.*

peer *vi.* to stare —*n.* an equal before the law; a person of noble birth — **peer′age** *n.*

peer′less *adj.* unequaled; incomparable

peeve *vi., vt.* to become or cause to become annoyed —*n.* a complaint or grievance

pee′vish *adj.* disagreeable; fretful; showing discontent —**pee′vish·ly** *adv.* —**pee′vish·ness** *n.*

peg *n.* a wooden pin used to join two pieces; a marker —*vt.* to fasten or mark with pegs

peign·oir′ *n.* a dressing gown

pej·o·ra′tion *n.* a process of degeneration; the course by which a word becomes degenerated, such as that of *silly* which once meant *blessed*

pe·jo′ra·tive *adj.* disparaging or derisive —*n.* a derisive word or phrase —**pe·jo′ra·tive·ly** *adv.*

pelf *n.* money or riches; ill-gotten gains or spoils

pel′let *n.* a small solid bit of matter, such as a pill

pell′-mell′ *adv.* in a disorderly manner; hurriedly; in confused haste; impetuously

pelt *n.* an animal skin —*vt.* to strike repeatedly

pen *n.* a writing instrument; a coop or similar enclosure —*vt.* to write; to confine or cage

pe′nal *adj.* relating to punishment —**pe′nal·ly** *adv.*

pe′nal·ize *vt.* to punish; to impose a penalty on —**pe·nal·iza′tion** *n.*

pen′al·ty *n.* a punishment dictated by law or rules; consequences: *they suffered the penalty of failure to plan properly*

pen′ance *n.* an action to show remorse for wrongdoing

penchant *n.* an inclination or tendency; a predisposition

pen′cil *n.* a writing instrument —*vt.* to write

pencil pusher *n.* a clerk

pen′dant *n.* a hanging ornament

pen′dent *adj.* hanging or projecting —**pend′ent·ly** *adv.*

pend′ing *adj.* awaiting settlement — *prep.*

pen′du·lous *adj.* hanging so as to swing freely; dangling —**pen′du·lous·ly** *adv.* —**pen′du·lous·ness** *n.*

pen′du·lum *n.* a hanging weight that swings cyclically to control a device such as a clock

pen′e·tra·ble *adj.* accessible; able to penetrate —**pen·e·tra·bil′i·ty** *n.* — **pen′e·tra·bly** *adv.*

pen′e·trate *vt.* to gain entrance; to pierce; to affect profoundly —**pen·e·tra′tion** *n.* —**pen′e·tra·tor** *n.*

pen′e·trat·ing *adj.* piercing; perceptive or shrewd; intrusive —**pen′e·trat·ing·ly** *adv.*

pen′e·tra·tive *adj.* having power to penetrate —**pen′e·tra·tive·ly** *adv.*

pe·nin′su·la *n.* a point of land that projects into a body of water —**pe·nin′su·lar** *adj.*

pen′i·tence *n.* remorse for misdeeds

pen′i·tent *adj.* sorrowful or atoning for guilt —*n.* —**pen′i·tent·ly** *adv.*

pen·i·ten′tial *adj.* suffering remorse —**pen·i·ten′tial·ly** *adv.*

pen·i·ten′tia·ry (*US*) *n.* a prison

pen′nant *n.* a tapered streamer used for recognition or signaling

pen′ni·less *adj.* poverty-stricken —**pen′ni·less·ly** *adv.* —**pen′ni·less·ness** *n.*

pen′ny (*US*) *n.* a coin of small value; a cent

penny ante of little consequence; trivial

pe·nol′o·gy *n.* the study of prisons and rehabilitation —**pe′no·log′i·cal** *adj.* —**pe·nol′o·gist** *n.*

pen′sion *n.* money paid or to be paid regularly during retirement —*vt.* to grant a pension to —**pen′sion·a·ble** *adj.* —**pen′sion·er** *n.*

pen′sive *adj.* inclined to thought; thoughtful —**pen′sive·ly** *adv.* —**pen′sive·ness** *n.*

pent′house *n.* a residence on the roof or upper floors of a building

pent′–up′ *adj.* held in or repressed: *pent-up anxiety*

pe·nu′ri·ous *adj.* frugal or miserly; unproductive or barren, as land —**pe·nu′ri·ous·ly** *adv.* —**pe·nu′ri·ous·ness** *n.*

pen′u·ry *n.* poverty; barrenness

peo′ple *n.* human beings in general; a group of persons with something in common: *people of Asian descent* —*vt.* to populate

pep *n.* energy —*vt.* to enervate

pep′py *adj.* full of energy —**pep′pi·ly** *adv.* —**pep′pi·ness** *n.*

per *adv., prep.* for each

per cap′i·ta *adv.* per person

per·ceive′ *vt., vi.* to understand; to become aware of —**per·ceiv′a·bil′i·ty** *n.* —**per·ceiv′a·ble** *adj.* —**per·ceiv′a·bly** *adv.* —**per·ceiv′er** *n.*

per·cent′ *n.* parts per hundred

per·cep′ti·ble *adj.* able to be perceived or discerned —**per·cep·ti·bil′i·ty** *n.* —**per·cep′ti·bly** *adv.*

per·cep′tion *n.* discernment or judgment; insight gained from observation —**per·cep′tion·al** *adj.* —**per·cep′tu·al** *adj.* —**per·cep′tu·al·ly** *adv.*

per·cep′tive *adj.* discerning; observant —**per·cep′tive·ly** *adv.* —**per·cep′tive·ness, per·cep·tiv′i·ty** *n.*

perch *n.* a roost for a bird; a lofty position —*vi., vt.* to alight or set on a perch —**perch′er** *n.*

per·chance′ *adv.* possibly; conceivably

per′co·late *vi., vt.* to pass or cause to pass through a filter —*n.* a filtered liquid —**per·co·la′tion** *n.* —**per′co·la·tor** *n.*

per·cus′sion *n.* a striking together or colliding —**per·cus′sive** *adj.* —**per·cus′sive·ly** *adv.* —**per·cus′sive·ness** *n.*

per·di′tion *n.* damnation

per′e·gri·nate *vi.* to travel or roam, especially on foot —*vt.* to travel over or through —**per·e·gri·na′tion** *n.* —**per′e·gri·na·tor** *n.*

pe·remp′to·ry *adj.* decisive or final; dictatorial —**pe·remp′to·ri·ly** *adv.* —**pe·remp′to·ri·ness** *n.*

pe·ren′ni·al *adj.* long-lasting or enduring; recurring often —**per·en′ni·al·ly** *adv.*

per′fect *adj.* complete; free of faults; well-suited; capable —**per′fect·ly** *adv.* —**per′fect·ness** *n.*

per·fect′ *vt.* to further develop or

complete; to make flawless —**per·**
fect´er n.

per·fect´i·ble adj. able to become or
to be made flawless —**per·fect´i·**
bil´i·ty n.

per·fec´tion n. the state of being
perfect

per·fec´tion·ism n. an abnormal
obsession with idealistic goals —
per·fec´tion·ist n. —**per·fec´tion·**
is´tic adj.

per·fid´i·ous adj. deliberately unfaithful or treacherous —**per·fid´i·**
ous·ly adv. —**per´fid·y** n.

per´fo·rate vt. to pierce; to mark
with rows of holes for ease of separating —**per´for·a·ble** adj. —**per´**
fo·rat·ed adj. —**per·fo·ra´tion** n.
—**per´fo·ra·tor** n.

per·form´ vt., vi. to act on and complete; to function; to present in
public for entertainment —**per·**
form´able adj. —**per·form´ance** n.
—**per·form´er** n.

per´fume n. an ingredient that gives
off a pleasant aroma; a pleasant
aroma

per·fum´er·y n. a concern that
makes or sells perfume; the art of
making and marketing perfume —
per·fum´er n.

per·func´to·ry adj. indifferent; done
mechanically, casually, or carelessly —**per·func´to·ri·ly** adv. —
per·func´to·ri·ness n.

per·haps´ adv. conceivably; possibly

per´il n. exposure to danger —vt. to
expose to danger —**per´il·ous** adj.
—**per´il·ous·ly** adv. —**per´il·ous·**
ness n.

pe·rim´e·ter n. the boundary or
border of an area —**per·i·met´ric**,
per·i·met´ri·cal adj. —**per·i·met´**
ri·cal·ly adv.

pe´ri·od n. a span of time; (US) a
punctuation mark that indicates
the end of a sentence

pe·ri·od´ic adj. cyclical; recurring at
regular intervals —**pe·ri·od·i·cal·**

ly adv. —**pe·ri·o·dic´i·ty** n.

pe·ri·od´i·cal n. a publication issued
at regular intervals —adj. pertaining to a publication, such as a
magazine or journal, that is published at regular intervals

per·i·pa·tet´ic adj. roaming about;
itinerant —n. one given to roaming
—**per·i·pa·tet´i·cal·ly** adv.

pe·riph´er·al adj. pertaining to an
outer area; of minor significance —
pe·riph´er·al·ly adv.

pe·riph´ery n. a line or area that
forms a perimeter

per´ish vi. to decay or die; to pass
from existence —**per·ish·a·bil´i·ty**,
per·ish·a·ble·ness n. —**per·ish·a·**
ble adj. —**per·ish·a·bly** adv.

per´jure vt. to testify falsely; to violate an oath or a promise —**per´**
jur·er n. —**per·ju´ri·ous** adj. —
per·ju´ri·ous·ly adv. —**per´jury** n.

perk´y adj. lively; proud or haughty
—**perk´i·ly** adv. —**perk´i·ness** n.

per´ma·nent adj. durable; enduring;
unchanging —**per´ma·nence, per´**
ma·nen·cy, per´ma·nent·ness n.
—**per´ma·nent·ly** adv.

per´me·a·ble adj. pervious; that can
be infiltrated or saturated —**per·**
me·a·bil´i·ty, per·me·a·ble·ness
n. —**per´me·a·bly** adv.

per´me·ate vt. to spread completely
throughout —vi. to penetrate and
spread throughout —**per·me·a´**
tion n. —**per´me·a·tive** adj.

per·mis´si·ble adj. that can be allowed —**per·mis·si·bil´i·ty, per·**
mis´si·ble·ness n. —**per·mis´si·**
bly adv.

per·mis´sion n. approval or authorization

per·mis´sive adj. that grants permission; likely to allow: lenient —
per·mis´sive·ly adv. —**per·mis´**
sive·ness n.

per·mit´ vt. to allow or authorize —
per´mit n. a document that grants
permission, such as a license

—per´mit·tee´ n.

per·mu·ta´tion n. an alteration or transformation —**per·mu·ta´tion·al** adj.

per·ni´cious adj. likely to be harmful or injurious —**per·ni´cious·ly** adv. —**per·ni´cious·ness** n.

per´o·rate vi. to speak at length: lecture; to summarize at the end of a speech —**per·o·ra´tion** n. —**per·o·ra´tion·al** adj.

per·pen·dic´u·lar adj. at right angles to the horizon —n. a line, plane, etc. that is at right angles to another —**per·pen·dic·u·lar´i·ty** n. —**per·pen·dic´u·lar·ly** adv.

per´pe·trate vt. to commit, as a crime —**per·pe·tra´tion** n. —**per´pe·tra·tor** n.

per·pet´u·al adj. continuing indefinitely; recurrent —**per·pet´u·al·ly** adv.

per·pet´u·ate vt. to endure indefinitely —**per·pet·u·a´tion** n. —**per·pet´u·a·tor** n.

per·pe·tu´i·ty n. endlessness; the quality of continuing indefinitely

per·plex´ vt. to confound or confuse —**per·plexed´** adj. —**per·plex´ed·ly, per·plex´ing·ly** adv.

per´qui·site n. an allowance or benefit associated with position: *comfort is a perquisite of the moneyed class*

per´se·cute vt. to oppress or abuse, particularly because of race, religion, etc.; to harass —**per·se·cu´tion** n. —**per·se·cu´tion·al, per´se·cu·tive, per´se·cu·to·ry** adj. —**per´se·cu·tor** n.

per·se·ver´ance n. patience and persistence; determination —**per´se·vere´** vi. —**per·se·ver´ing·ly** adv.

per´si·flage n. good–natured banter

per·sist´ vi. to persevere in spite of obstacles; to endure —**per·sist´ence, per·sist´en·cy** n. —**per·sist´ent** adj. —**per·sist´ent·ly** adv.

—per·sist´er n.

per´son n. an individual; the character, appearance, or characteristics of an individual; a living human body

per´son·a·ble adj. agreeable or pleasant in appearance or manner —**per´son·a·ble·ness** n. —**per´son·a·bly** adv.

per´son·age n. an eminent person

per´son·al adj. relating to a particular person; done by or for a particular person; intimate —**per´son·al·ly** adv.

per·son·al´i·ty n. the character, characteristics, and other qualities of a particular person; distinctive attributes; a famous person —**per´son·al·ize** vt. —**per·son·al·i·za´tion** n.

per·son´i·fy vt. to represent by or endow with human qualities —**per·son·i·fi·ca´tion** n. —**per·son´i·fi·er** n.

per´son·nel´ n. the employees of an organization; persons collectively

per·spec´tive n. a particular view or viewpoint; a panorama; a device that gives a flat rendering the impression of three dimensions —**per·spec´tiv·al** adj. —**per·spec´tive·ly** adv.

per·spi·ca´cious adj. demonstrating unusual insight —**per·spi·ca´cious·ly** adj. —**per·spi·ca´cious·ness, per·spi·cac´i·ty, per·spi·cu´ity** n.

per·spire´ vi., vt. to expel through the pores —**per·spi·ra´tion** n. —**per·spir´a·to·ry** adj.

per·suade´ vt. to convince by reason or pleas —**per·suad´a·ble, per·sua´si·ble** adj. —**per·suad´er** n.

per·sua´sion n. the power to convince another; a firm opinion or conviction —**per·sua´sive** adj. —**per·sua´sive·ly** adv. —**per·sua´sive·ness** n.

pert adj. vivacious; impudently

saucy or forward —**pert´ly** adv. —
pert´ness n.
per·tain´ vi. to belong or relate to; to
be pertinent to
per´ti·na´cious adj. persistent; obstinate —**per´ti·na´cious·ly** adv.
—**per´ti·na´cious·ness, per·ti·**
nac´i·ty n.
per´ti·nent adj. relevant; applicable
—**per´ti·nence, per´ti·nen·cy** n.
—**per´ti·nent·ly** adv.
per·turb´ vt. to disquiet or worry —
per·turb´a·ble adj. —**per·tur·ba´**
tion n.
pe·ruse´ vt. to study thoroughly; to
scrutinize —**pe·rus´able** adj. —**pe·**
rus´al n. —**pe·rus´er** n.
per·vade´ vt. to penetrate or permeate —**per·va´sion** n. —**per·va´sive**
adj. —**per·va´sive·ly** adv. —**per·**
va´sive·ness n.
per·verse´ adj. evil or wicked; contrary or obstinate —**per·verse´ly**
adv. —**per·verse´ness, per·ver´**
sity n.
per·ver´sion n. deviation from what
is normal, especially of sexual desire or activity; something perverted —**per·ver´sive** adj.
per·vert´ vt. to use improperly; to
distort the meaning of; to corrupt
or lead away from approved or accepted conduct —**per´vert** n. —
per·vert´er n. —**per·vert´i·ble** adj.
per·vert´ed adj. characterized by
perversion —**per·vert´ed·ly** adv. —
per·vert´ed·ness n.
per´vi·ous adj. permeable; capable
of being penetrated; open to argument —**per´vi·ous·ly** adv. —**per´**
vi·ous·ness n.
pes´ky adj. annoying; troublesome
—**pesk´i·ly** adv. —**pesk´i·ness** n.
pes´si·mist n. one who tends to a
negative view —**pes´si·mism** n. —
pes·si·mis´tic adj. —**pes·si·mis´ti·**
cal·ly adv.
pest n. a nuisance; something that
is harmful, as a virus

pes´ter vt. to harass or annoy —
pes´ter·er n.
pes´ti·cide n. a chemical used to
destroy weeds or insects —**pes´ti·**
ci·dal adj.
pes´ti·lence n. a widespread disease: an epidemic; any dangerous
or harmful agent —**pes´ti·lent,**
pes´ti·len´tial adj. —**pes·ti·len´**
tial·ly adv.
pes´tle n. a device used for crushing
or blending, as in a mortar
pet n. a tame animal treated with
affection; a person treated affectionately —adj. regarded as favored or a favorite —vt. to indulge;
to caress
pe·tite´ n. small
pe·ti´tion n. an appeal or request to
a higher authority —vi., vt. to
make an appeal —**pe·ti´tion·a·ble**
adj. —**pe·ti´tion·ar·y** adj. —**pe·ti´**
tion·er n.
pet´ri·fy vt. to fossilize; to paralyze
with fright
pet´rol (Brit.) n. fuel for a motor
vehicle
pe·tro´le·um (US) n. crude oil
pet´ti·fog vi. to quibble over trifles
—**pet´ti·fog´ger** n. —**pet´ti·fog·**
ger·y n.
pet´tish adj. irritable; peevish —**pet´**
tish·ly adv. —**pet´tish·ness** n.
pet´ty adj. trivial or unimportant;
mean or miserly; narrow-minded
—**pet´ti·ly** adv. —**pet´ti·ness** n.
pet´u·lant adj. ill-tempered; irritable
—**pet´u·lance, pet´u·lan·cy** n. —
pet´u·lant·ly adv.
phan´tasm n. an apparition; an
illusion —**phan·tas´mal, phan·**
tas´mic adj.
phan·tas·ma·go´ri·a n. bizarre im-
agery as in artwork or as in a
dream —**phan·tas·ma·gor´ic,**
phan·tas´ma·gor´i·cal adj. —
phan·tas´ma·gor´i·cal·ly adv.
phan´tom adj. illusory; imaginary —
n. an apparition or ghost

phar·ma·ceu´tic, phar·ma·ceu´ti·cal adj. pertaining to pharmacy or pharmacists —n. a drug —**phar·ma·ceu´ti·cal·ly** adv.

phar·ma·ceu´tics pl. n. the science of preparing medicinal compounds; medicinal compounds collectively

phar´ma·cist n. a qualified druggist

phar·ma·col´o·gy n. the study of drugs and their uses; the properties of a drug —**phar·ma·co·log´ic, phar·ma·co·log´i·cal** adj. —**phar·ma·co·log´i·cal·ly** adv. —**phar·ma·col´o·gist** n.

phar´ma·cy n. a drugstore

phase n. a particular stage or state of progress —**pha´sic** adj.

phe·nom´e·nal adj. extraordinary or remarkable —**phe·nom´e·nal·ly** adv.

phe·nom´e·non n. an unusual or extraordinary person, thing, or event

phi´al n. a vial

phi·lan´der vi. to make love casually, without intent to marry —**phi·lan´der·er** n.

phi·lan´thro·py n. charity or benevolence for the good of others; a humanitarian endeavor —**phil·an·throp´ic, phil·an·throp´i·cal** adj. —**phil·an·throp´i·cal·ly** adv. —**phi·lan´thro·pist** n.

phi·lat´e·ly n. stamp collecting —**phil·a·tel´ic, phil·a·tel´i·cal** adj. —**phil·a·tel´i·cal·ly** adv. —**phi·lat´e·list** n.

phi·lol´o·gy n. classical studies, especially to ascertain meaning or certify the authenticity of literary works —**phil·o·log´ic, phil·o·log´i·cal** adj. —**phil·o·log´i·cal·ly** adv. —**phi·lol´o·gist** n.

phi·los´o·phy n. the study of knowledge; a fundamental principle; a system of beliefs —**phi·los´o·pher** n. —**phil´o·soph´ic, phil´o·soph´i·cal** adj. —**phil´o·soph´i·cal·ly** adv.

—phi·los´o·phize vi. —**phi·los´o·phiz·er** n.

phil´ter n. a magic potion

phleg·mat´ic, phleg·mat´i·cal adj. impassive; composed; unemotional —**phleg·mat´i·cal·ly** adv.

pho´bia n. an irrational fear or aversion —**pho´bic** adj.

phone n. a telephone

pho·net´ics n. the sounds of speech or of a specific language —**pho·net´ic, pho·net´i·cal** adj. —**pho·net´i·cal·ly** adv.

phon´ics n. the sounds of speech in relation to spelling; phonetics —**phon´ic** adj. —**phon´i·cal·ly** adv.

pho´ny adj. imitation or artificial; fake —n. an imitation; a fake

pho´to·cop·y n. a duplicate made by the use of photography —vt. to reproduce by means of a photocopy machine

pho·tog´ra·phy n. the art of reproducing images by means of photosensitive coatings —**pho·to·graph´ic, pho·to·graph´i·cal** adj. —**pho·to·graph´i·cal·ly** adv.

pho´to, pho´to·graph n. an image captured by means of photography —vt. to capture by photography —**pho´to·graph·a·ble** adj. —**pho·tog´ra·pher** n.

pho·to·sen´si·tive adj. sensitive or reactive to light rays —**pho·to·sen·si·tiv´i·ty** n. —**pho·to·sen·si·ti·za´tion** n. —**pho·to·sen´si·tize** vt.

pho·to·syn´the·sis n. the process by which plants derive nourishment using light as an energy source —**pho·to·syn·thet´ic** adj. —**pho·to·syn·thet´i·cal·ly** adv.

phrase n. a group of words that express a thought, but that do not comprise a complete sentence —vt., vi. to express in a certain way, as to phrase tactfully —**phras´a·ble** adj. —**phras´al** adj. —**phras´al·ly** adv.

phra·se·ol´o·gy n. the way in which

a thought or idea is expressed; one's style of speaking or writing —**phra·se·o·log´i·cal** adj. — **phra·se·ol´o·gist** n.

phre·nol´o·gy n. the belief that character and intelligence can be determined by the configuration of the skull —**phre·nol´o·gist** n.

phys´i·cal adj. applicable to the body or to tangible matter as distinguished from the mental or spiritual —**phys·i·cal´i·ty** n. — **phys´i·cal·ly** adv.

phy·si´cian n. a doctor of medicine; one devoted to healing

phys´ics n. the study of matter and energy —**phys´i·cist** n.

phys·i·ol´o·gy n. the study of living organisms —**phys´i·o·log´i·cal** adj. —**phys´i·o·log´i·cal·ly** adv. — **phys·i·ol´o·gist** n.

phy·sique´ n. the structure and appearance of the body

pic·a·yune´ adj. of little value; trivail; unimportant

pick vt. to select or separate; to gather or pluck —**pick´er** n.

picked adj. chosen carefully

pick´et n. a protester, often with a sign stating a grievance; a pointed stake —**pick´et·er** n.

pick´y adj. extremely fussy —**pick´i·ness** n.

pic´nic n. an outing or an outdoor meal; something seen as easy to do; an enjoyable experience —**pic´nick·er** n.

pic·to´ri·al adj. pertaining to pictures; containing pictures —n. a publication containing mostly pictures —**pic·to´ri·al·ly** adj.

pic·to´ri·al·ize vt. to illustrate — **pic·to·ri·al·i·za´tion** n.

pic´ture n. an illustration; a visual or oral depiction; a mental image; a motion picture —vt. to visualize; to describe vividly

pic·tur·esque´ adj. striking or impressive —**pic·tur·esque´ly** adv.

—**pic´tur·esque´ness** n.

pid´dling adj. trivial

piece n. a part or portion; something of a type: a piece of music, a piece of furniture —vt. to join together

pièce de ré´sis·tance´ n. a primary or outstanding element, especially of a meal

piece´meal adj. accomplished in stages —adv. gradually

pierce vt. to penetrate —**pierc´er** n. —**pierc´ing** adj. —**pierc´ing·ly** adv.

pi´e·ty n. devotion or reverence — **pi´etism** n. —**pi·etis´tic** adj.

pig´head·ed adj. stubborn; obstinate —**pig´head·ed·ly** adv. —**pig´head·ed·ness** n.

pig´ment n. a dye or coloring —**pig´men·tary** adj.

pig·men·ta´tion n. a characteristic color

pik´er n. a cheapskate

pile n. a heap; an accumulation, as of money —vt., vi. to make or form a heap

pil´fer vt., vi. to steal —**pil´fer·age** n.

pil´grim n. a traveler, especially one who is on a sacred journey —**pil´grim·age** n.

pill n. a capsule of medicine; someone who is annoying or disagreeable

pil´lage vt. to take by force; to plunder —**pil´lag·er** n.

pil´lar n. a supporting column; a responsible person: a pillar of the community

pil´low n. a cushion used for resting the head or for decoration —**pil´low·y** adj.

pi´lot n. one who operates or guides a craft; that which guides or directs on a course: a pilot hole for a screw, a television pilot

pim´ple n. a small swelling of the skin; a similar bulge on a hard surface —**pim´pled, pim´ply** adj.

pin n. a thin rod of metal, wood, etc.

used for fastening; a decorative jewel attached with a pin; something that attaches in place, as a *hairpin* or *clothespin*; something long and slender, as a *rolling pin*; (*Brit.*) the contact points for an electrical connector —*vt.* to fasten, attach, or hold as with a pin; to fix, as for liability: *don't pin the blame on me, pin him down to get a decision*

pinch *n.* a sprinkling or dash: *a pinch of salt*; a predicament —*vt.* to squeeze so as to cause discomfort; to arrest; to steal —*vi.* to squeeze; to be stingy; to become constricted —**pinch´a·ble** *adj.* —**pinch´er** *n.*

pinch´pen·ny *adj.* miserly —*n.* a penny pincher

pin´na·cle *n.* a crest or summit

pi´o·neer´ *adj.* early or experimental; brave or adventurous —*n.* an explorer or settler of new territory —*vt., vi.* to take the lead; to prepare the way

pi·os´i·ty *n.* exaggerated piety

pi´ous *adj.* devout, reverent —**pi´ous·ly** *adv.* —**pi´ous·ness** *n.*

pipe *n.* a hollow tube used to convey liquid, etc.; a smoking implement —*vt.* to convey, as liquid, through a pipe

pip´ing *n.* a network of pipes; trimming, as on a uniform; decoration on a cake or pastry

pi´quant *adj.* spicy; interesting or charming —**pi´quan·cy, pi´quant·ness** *n.* —**pi´quant·ly** *adv.*

pique *n.* a sense of indignation or ire —*vt.* to irritate; to excite or arouse, as one's curiosity

pi´ra·cy *n.* robbery or blackmail; the illegal selling of protected material —**pi´rate** *n., vt., vi.* —**pi·rat´ic, pi·rat´i·cal** *adj.* —**pi·rat´i·cal·ly** *adv.*

pis´tol *n.* a handgun

pit *n.* a hole in the ground; a small indentation; an area set aside for a special purpose: *an orchestra pit* —*vt., vi.* to mark or become marked with indentations; to place in conflict: *an individual pitted against the system*

pitch *vt.* to throw; to set up: *pitch camp*; to set at an angle; to promote: *pitch the benefits, not the product* —*n.* a sales talk

pitch´er *n.* one who throws; (*US*) a container for liquids: a jug

pitch´man *n.* one who attempts to sell, especially aggressively

pit´e·ous *adj.* pitiful; stirring or deserving pity —**pit´e·ous·ly** *adv.* —**pit´e·ous·ness** *n.*

pit´fall *n.* a hazard

pith *n.* the core or essence

pith´y *adj.* meaningful; brief —**pith´i·ly** *adv.* —**pith´i·ness** *n.*

pit´i·ful *adj.* arousing pity or contempt; pathetic —**pit´i·ful·ly** *adv.* —**pit´i·ful·ness** *n.*

pit´i·less *adj.* unfeeling; having no mercy —**pit´i·less·ly** *adv.* —**pit´i·less·ness** *n.*

pit´tance *n.* a trifling sum

pit´y *n.* compassion or sympathy aroused by the suffering of another —**pit´i·a·ble** *adj.* —**pit´i·a·ble·ness** *n.* —**pit´i·a·bly** *adv.*

piv´ot *n.* the thing or point on which something turns —*vi.* to turn on a pivot —**piv´ot·al** *adj.* —**piv´ot·al·ly** *adv.*

pix´i·lat·ed *adj.* frivolous or whimsical —**pix·i·la´tion** *n.*

plac´a·ble *adj.* inclined to tolerance or acceptance —**placa·bil´i·ty, plac´a·ble·ness** *n.*

pla´cate *vt.* to appease or pacify —**pla´cat·er** *n.* —**pla·ca´tion** *n.* —**pla´ca·tive, pla´ca·to·ry** *adj.*

place *n.* a particular position, space, or locality; one's status, rank, or job —*vt.* to situate in a particular location; to appoint to a position; to find a home or job for —**place´ment** *n.*

pla·ce´bo *n.* a fake or phony medication; a sugar pill

plac´id *adj.* peaceful or calm —**pla·cid´i·ty, plac´id·ness** *n.* —**plac´id·ly** *adv.*

pla´gia·rism *n.* misappropriation of the works or ideas of another —**pla´gia·rist** *n.* —**pla´gia·ris´tic** *adj.* —**pla´gia·rize** *vi., vt.*

plague *n.* a sudden spread of disease; a disaster; a sudden outbreak; an annoyance —*vt.* to annoy; to afflict with disease or disaster

plain *adj.* unadorned; simple; open or obvious; ordinary —**plain´ly** *adv.* —**plain´ness** *n.*

plaint *n.* a complaint

plain´tiff *n.* one who accuses in a court of law

plain´tive *adj.* mournful; lamenting —**plain´tive·ly** *adv.* —**plain´tive·ness** *n.*

plan *n.* a strategy worked out in advance of an action; an outline or diagram —*vt.* to work out the means for doing something; to have as an intention —**plan´ner** *n.*

plane *adj.* level —*n.* a flat surface —**pla´nar** *adj.*

plan´et *n.* a heavenly body that revolves around a star —**plan´e·tar·y** *adj.*

plan·e·tar´i·um *n.* a room or building equipped for viewing images of the heavens

plank *n.* a piece of lumber; a component of a political platform —**plank´ing** *n.*

plant *n.* an organism that grows from the ground, etc.; a manufacturing facility —*vt.* to sow seeds; to set firmly in place —**plant´er** *n.*

plan·ta´tion *n.* land under cultivation; an estate

plaque *n.* a flat decorative panel or plate

plas´ter *n.* a compound used to coat or patch walls —*vt.* to cover with or as with plaster; to affix —**plas´ter·er** *n.*

plas´tic *adj.* malleable; artificial —*n.* a flexible synthetic material that can be hardened and adapted to a variety of uses —**plas´ti·cal·ly** *adj.* —**plas·tic´i·ty** *n.*

plat *n.* a plot of land; a map showing existing or planned building lots, streets, etc. —*vt.* to make an area map showing this detail

plate *n.* a flat piece of material, such as for holding food, for decoration, or as part of a machine; food service for one —*vt.* to overlay or coat —**plat´ed** *adj.*

pla·teau´ *n.* a flat-topped hill

plat´form *n.* a raised landing such as a stage; a statement of beliefs or goals, especially political

plat´i·tude *n.* a trite expression; a cliché —**plat·i·tu´di·nal, plat·i·tu´di·nous** *adj.* —**plat·i·tu´di·nous·ly** *adv.*

pla·ton´ic *adj.* spiritual; ideal

pla·toon´ *n.* a small group set on a common purpose

plat´ter *n.* a large plate

plau´dit *n.* acclamation; praise

plau´si·ble *adj.* probable; convincing; seeming to justify belief —**plau·si·bil´i·ty, plau´si·ble·ness** *n.* —**plau´si·bly** *adv.*

play *vi., vt.* to act out a role; to perform; to participate, as in a game —*n.* a dramatic performance; the looseness of a machine part —**play´er** *n.*

play´ful *adj.* frolicsome or mischievous —**play´ful·ly** *adv.* —**play´ful·ness** *n.*

play´wright *n.* a writer of plays

plaz´a *n.* a public square

plea *n.* a request or appeal

plead *vi., vt.* to beseech; to offer an excuse or justification —**plead´a·ble** *adj.* —**plead´er** *n.* —**plead´ing·ly** *adv.*

pleas´ant *adj.* providing pleasure

—**pleas´ant·ly** *adv.* —**pleas´ant·ness** *n.*

pleas´ant·ry *n.* a polite or humorous remark

please *vi., vt.* to give pleasure —*adv.* —**pleas´ing** *adj.* —**pleas´ing·ly** *adv.*

plea·sur·a·ble *adj.* enjoyable; pleasing —**plea´sur·a·ble·ness** *n.* —**plea´sur·a·bly** *adv.*

plea´sure *n.* a feeling of delight; that which brings happiness or enjoyment; a preference —**plea´sure·ful** *adj.*

plea´sure·less *adj.* devoid of humor or amusement —**plea´sure·less·ly** *adv.*

ple·be´ian *adj.* common; unrefined —**ple·be´ian·ism** *n.* —**ple·be´ian·ly** *adv.*

pleb´i·scite *n.* choosing by vote of the complete electorate —**ple·bis´ci·tar·y** *adj.*

pledge *n.* a binding promise; security for payment of a debt —*vt.* —**pledge´a·ble** *adj.* —**pledg·ee´** *n.* —**pledg´er** *n.*

ple´na·ry *adj.* complete and unrestricted —**ple´na·ri·ly** *adv.*

plen´i·tude *n.* an abundance —**plen´i·tu´di·nous** *adj.*

plen·te·ous *adj.* abundant; plentiful —**plen´te·ous·ly** *adv.* —**plen´te·ous·ness** *n.*

plen´ti·ful *adj.* abundant; bountiful —**plen´ti·ful·ly** *adv.* —**plen´ti·ful·ness** *n.*

plen´ty *adj.* abundant —*adv.* extremely —*n.* an adequate amount; an abundance

pleth´o·ra *n.* an excess —**ple·thor´ic** *adj.* —**ple·thor´i·cal·ly** *adv.*

pli´a·ble *adj.* flexible; readily shaped or influenced; impressionable —**pli·a·bil´i·ty, pli´a·ble·ness** *n.* —**pli´a·bly** *adv.*

pli´ant *adj.* yielding; docile; adaptable —**pli´an·cy, pli´ant·ness** *n.* —**pli´ant·ly** *adv.*

pli´ers *n.* a hand tool for grasping or turning

plight *n.* a predicament or difficulty; a condition or state; a promise —*vt.* to promise or pledge

plod *vi., vt.* to move or work steadily and painstakingly —**plod´der** *n.* —**plod´ding·ly** *adv.*

plot *n.* a parcel of land, especially one occupied by or intended for a residence; a story line; a plan or conspiracy —*vt.* to locate, as on a map or chart; to take part in a conspiracy —*vi.* to conspire —**plot´ter** *n.*

plow *n.* an implement for breaking ground, moving snow, etc. —*vi., vt.* to break up or move with a plow; to move forcefully, as with a plow —**plow´a·ble** *adj.* —**plow´er** *n.*

pluck *n.* boldness or determination —*vt.* to pull out; to remove brusquely —**pluck´er** *n.*

pluck´y *adj.* spirited; couageous —**pluck´i·ly** *adv.* —**pluck´i·ness** *n.*

plug *n.* material that closes or obstructs; an electrical connector; casual mention of a product —*vt.* to stop up or close off; to advertise a product —*vi.* to become stopped up or closed off

plumb *adj.* precisely vertical —*adv.* vertical; squarely —*n.* a weight attached to a line used to establish a precise vertical —*vt.* to make vertical; to check with a plumb

plume *n.* an ornamental feather or clump of feathers; a feather-like form —**plu´mage** *n.*

plum´met *vi.* to fall rapidly

plump *adj.* having a full rounded figure —*vt., vi.* to make or become plump

plun´der *n.* stolen property —*vt. vi.* to take by force —**plun´der·a·ble** *adj.* —**plun´der·er** *n.* —**plun´der·ous** *adj.*

plunge *vi., vt.* to fall or thrust vigorously

plu·ral *adj.* comprising more than one

plu·ral·ism *n.* the condition of a society made up of diverse groups —**plu·ral·i·ty** *n.*

plus *adj.* positive; added —*conj.* added to —*n.* something added

plush *adj.* sumptuous; opulent — **plush·i·ness plush·ness** *n.* — **plush·ly** *adv.* —**plush·y** *adj.*

plu·toc·ra·cy *n.* government by the wealthy —**plu·to·crat** *n.* —**plu·to·crat·ic** *adj.* —**plu·to·crat·i·cal·ly** *adv.*

ply *n.* one of two or more layers —*vt.* to regularly practice or provide, as a trade or service

pneu·mat·ic *adj.* relating to air; operated by the use of air —**pneu·mat·i·cal·ly** *adv.*

poach *vt.* to cook in boiling liquid; to trespass and take unlawfully, as fish or game —*vi.* to trespass — **poach·er** *n.*

pock·et *n.* a small pouch, such as attaced to a garment; an opening or cavity —*adj.* pertaining to a pocket; small enough to fit a pocket, as *a pocket calculator* —*vt.* to take —**pock·et·a·ble** *adj.* — **pock·et·er** *n.*

po·di·a·try *n.* the branch of medicine dealing with the feet —**po·di·a·trist** *n.*

po·di·um *n.* a speaker's platform

po·em *n.* a literary work in verse — **po·e·sy** *n.* —**po·et** *n.*

po·et·ic, po·et·i·cal *adj.* typifying the traits of poetry as lyrical, romantic, or idyllic —**po·et·i·cal·ly** *adv.*

po·et·ry *n.* poetic works; the traits of a poem

po·grom *n.* systematic persecution

poi·gnant *adj.* mentally intense; distressing or moving —**poi·gnance, poi·gnan·cy** *n.* —**poi·gnant·ly** *adv.*

point *n.* a sharp end; a projection: *a point of land*; a dot; a particular spot: *at some point in time*; a distinct element, quality, or condition: *the point of the discussion* — *vi., vt.* to direct attention to — **point·ed** *adj.* —**point·ed·ly** *adv.* —**point·y** *adj.*

point·less *adj.* without meaning; ineffective —**point·less·ly** *adv.* — **point·less·ness** *n.*

poise *n.* an attitude of grace, dignity, and composure —*vt., vi.* to balance or hover

poi·son *n.* a chemical that can cause illness or death; something similarly harmful —*vt.* to administer a harmful substance; to have a harmful effect —*adj.* lethal — **poi·son·er** *n.* —**poi·son·ous** *adj.* —**poi·son·ous·ly** *adv.* —**poi·son·ous·ness** *n.*

poke *n.* a punch or jab —*vt.* to thrust or jab; to punch —*vi.* to meddle; to pry; to putter or dawdle

poke·y, pok·y *adj.* slow; hesitant — **pok·i·ly** *adv.* —**pok·i·ness** *n.*

po·lar·ize *vt.* to consolidate according to differing views —**po·lar·iz·a·ble** *adj.* —**po·lar·iz·a·tion** *n.*

po·lem·ic *n.* a contentious view — **po·lem·ic, po·lem·i·cal** *adj.* —**po·lem·i·cal·ly** *adv.*

po·lem·ics *n.* the art of debate — **po·lem·i·cist** *n.*

po·lem·i·cize *vi.* to involve in debate or disputation

po·lice *n.* a department or persons charged with enforcement of the laws of a community —*vt.*

pol·i·cy *n.* a plan or procedure; an insurance contract

pol·ish *n.* luster or sheen; refinement —*vt.* to make smooth and bright; to make refined or elegant —**pol·ish·er** *n.*

po·lite *adj.* considerate and tactful; courteous or elegant —**po·lite·ly** *adv.* —**po·lite·ness** *n.*

pol·i·tic *adj.* discreet; shrewd or

crafty —**pol´i·tic·ly** adv.

po·lit´i·cal adj. relating to government or politics, or to the tactics for gaining power —**po·lit·i·cal·i·za´tion** n. —**po·lit´i·cal·ize** vt. —**po·lit´i·cal·ly** adv.

po·lit´i·cize vt. to act in the interest of political gain

pol´i·tics n. the science of government; tactics for gaining and holding power —**pol·i·ti´cian** n.

poll n. voting; a survey of public opinion —vt. to cast or record votes; to question for a survey —**poll´er, poll´ster** n.

pol·lute´ vt. to contaminate or make unfit to use —**pol·lu´tant** n. —**pol·lut´er** n. —**pol·lu´tion** n.

pol´ter·geist n. a supernatural being that creates noises and disorder

po·lyg´a·mous adj. relating to the circumstance of having more than one spouse at a time —**po·lyg´a·mist** n. —**po·lyg´a·mous·ly** adv. —**po·lyg´a·my** n.

pol´y·the·ism n. belief in more than one god —**pol´y·the·ist** n. —**pol·y·the·is´tic, pol·y·the·is´ti·cal** adj. —**pol·y·the·is´ti·cal·ly** adv.

pomp n. pageantry; a magnificent display

pomp´ous adj. pretentious; boastful and arrogant —**pom·pos´i·ty, pomp´ous·ness** n. —**pomp´ous·ly** adv.

pond n. a small body of water

pon´der vt. to consider carefully —vi. to meditate —**pon´der·a·ble** adj. —**pon´der·a·bil´i·ty** n.

pon´der·ous adj. weighty; dull or lifeless —**pon´der·ous·ly** adv. —**pon´der·ous·ness** n.

pon·tif´i·cate vi. to speak dogmatically —**pon·tif´i·ca·tor** n. —**pon·tif·i·ca´tion** n.

pool n. an accumulation of liquid; a small body of water; an assemblage of persons or resources —vi., vt. to merge resources

poor adj. lacking wealth; lacking basic needs; inferior in quality or quantity —**poor´ness** n.

pop´u·lace n. the general public

pop´u·lar adj. generally accepted; well-liked —**pop´u·lar·ly** adv.

pop·u·lar´i·ty n. general acceptance; the quality of being liked

pop´u·lar·ize vt. to make generally acceptable —**pop·u·lar·i·za´tion** n.

pop´u·late vt. to inhabit; to furnish with inhabitants

pop·u·la´tion n. the people of an area or of a particular grouping —**pop´u·list** n.

pop´u·lous adj. well-populated —**pop´u·lous·ly** adv. —**pop´u·lous·ness** n.

por´ce·lain n. a fine glazed ceramic; china

porch n. an open or partly open area connected to a building at an entryway

por·nog´ra·phy n. sexually explicit material —**por·nog´ra·pher** n. —**por·no·graph´ic** adj. —**por·no·graph´i·cal·ly** adv.

po·ros´i·ty n. the quality of being porous; a measure of the level of absorbency of a substance

po´rous adj. having pores; absorbent; penetrable —**po´rous·ly** adv. —**po´rous·ness** n.

port n. a place for docking ships; the left side of a ship; an opening; a fortified wine

por´ta·ble adj. designed to be easily carried or moved —**por·ta·bil´i·ty, por´ta·ble·ness** n. —**por´ta·bly** adv.

por´tal n. an entryway

por·tend´ vt. to predict or foretell

por´tent n. a sign or omen

por·ten´tous adj. ominous or foreboding —**por·ten´tous·ly** adv. —**por·ten´tous·ness** n.

port·fo´li·o n. a briefcase or folder for holding papers; a collection of documents: *an artist's portfolio, a* *stock portfolio*

por´ti·co *n.* an open porch

por´tion *n.* a part or share; the amount of food served to one person —*vt.* to separate into parts; to distribute —**por´tion·a·ble** *adj.* — **por´tion·er** *n.*

port´ly *adj.* stout —**port´li·ness** *n.*

por´trait *n.* a formal painting or photograph of a person; a verbal picture —**por´trait·ist** *n.* —**por´trai·ture** *n.*

por·tray´ *vt.* to represent in a picture, through words, or as an actor —**por·tray´a·ble** *adj.* —**por·tray´al** *n.* —**por·tray´er** *n.*

pose *n.* a feigned attitude; an affectation —*vi.* to assume or hold a position; to feign an attitude; to misrepresent: *to pose as an expert* —*vt.* to cause to sit, as for a portrait; to put forth, as a question or threat —**pos´er** *n.*

posh *adj.* comfortable

po·si´tion *n.* a specific place; a particular viewpoint; social or professional status —*vt.* to place especially or appropriately —**po·si´tion·al** *adj.* —**po·si´tion·er** *n.*

pos´i·tive *adj.* certain, absolutely sure; decisive; direct —**pos´i·tive·ly** *adv.* —**pos´i·tive·ness** *n.*

pos·sess´ *vt.* to have, as goods, traits, or emotions; to dominate — **pos·ses´sor** *n.*

pos·ses´sion *n.* a thing owned or in one's custody

pos·ses´sive *adj.* jealous; exhibiting a desire to control —**pos·ses´sive·ly** *adv.* —**pos·ses´sive·ness** *n.* — **pos·ses´so·ry** *n.*

pos·si·bil´i·ty *n.* something likely

pos´si·ble *adj.* likely or able to be — **pos´si·bly** *adv.*

post *n.* a shaft or rod of wood, metal, etc. used as a support or connection; a place of appointment or assignment; mail —*vt.* to announce publicly, as by hanging a sign; to

appoint or assign; (*Brit.*) to send via the postal system —**post´al** *adj.*

pos·te´ri·or *adj.* situated behind —*n.* the buttocks —**pos·te·ri·or´i·ty** *n.* —**pos·te´ri·or·ly** *adv.*

pos·ter´i·ty *n.* succeeding generations

post´hu·mous *adj.* occurring after a person's death —**post´hu·mous·ly** *adv.* —**post´hu·mous·ness** *n.*

post´-mor´tem *adj.* after death —*n.* an autopsy

post·pone´ *vt.* put off to a future time —**post·pon´a·ble** *adj.* —**post·pone´ment** *n.*

post´script *n.* something added to a written or printed document

pos´tu·late *n.* a presumption or supposition —*vt.* to presume without proof or confirmation —**pos·tu·la´tion** *n.*

pos´ture *n.* characteristic bearing, manner, or attitude —*vi.* to affect an attitude —**pos´tur·al** *adj.*

po´ta·ble *adj.* suitable for drinking —*n.* a beverage —**po·ta·bil´i·ty,** **po´ta·ble·ness** *n.*

po´tent *adj.* strong; powerful — **po´ten·cy** *n.* —**po´tent·ly** *adv.*

po´ten·tate *n.* a sovereign; one who dominates

po·ten´tial *adj.* possible —*n.* an unrealized capacity or capability — **po·ten·ti·al´i·ty** *n.* —**po·ten´tial·ly** *adv.*

poth´er *n.* a disturbance —*vi.,* *vt.* to be or cause to be concerned about inconsequential things

po´tion *n.* a medicine or drug

pot´pour·ri´ *n.* a mixture or medley; a conglomeration

pot´sherd *n.* a fragment of pottery

pot´tage *n.* a thick soup or stew

pot´ter·y *n.* baked clay vessels

pouch *n.* a bag or recepticle for carrying: *tobacco pouch, mail pouch* —**pouch´y** *adj.*

pounce *vi.* to attack or seize

347

suddenly —**pounc´er** *n.*

pound *n.* a unit of weight or currency; a place of confinement —*vt.* to strike repeatedly; to tread heavily; to confine

pour *vi., vt.* to flow or make to flow in a steady stream; to rain profusely —**pour´er** *n.*

pout *n.* a facial expression denoting displeasure —*vi.* to be sullen — **pout´er** *n.* —**pout´ing·ly** *adv.* — **pout´y** *adj.*

pov´er·ty *n.* a state of want; lacking means; inadequacy

pow´der *n.* material made up of fine particles —*vi., vt.* to become or cause to become granular or pulverized —**pow´der·er** *n.* —**pow´ der·y** *adj.*

pow´er *n.* strength, energy; the energy or ability to act effectively; the authority to act —*vt.* to provide with a means of propulsion —*adj.* operated by a motor or by electricity —**pow´er·ful** *adj.* —**pow´er·ful· ly** *adv.* —**pow´er·ful·ness** *n.*

pow´er·bro·ker *n.* one who controls through political or financial connections

pow´er·less *adj.* helpless; lacking strength or authority —**pow´er· less·ly** *adv.* —**pow´er·less·ness** *n.*

power of attorney authority to act as agent for another

prac´ti·ca·ble *adj.* achievable; attainable —**prac·ti·ca·bil´i·ty** *n.* — **prac´ti·ca·bly** *adv.*

prac´ti·cal *adj.* useful or usable; workable or sensible —**prac·ti·cal´ i·ty, prac´ti·cal·ness** *n.*

prac´ti·cal·ly *adv.* in a practical manner; almost

prac´tice *n.* repetition to improve competence; a usual mode or manner of functioning; a profession —**prac´tice** (*US*), **prac´tise** (*Brit.*) *vt., vi.* to repeat an action in order to acquire skill; to perform according to custom; to work at a

profession —**prac´ticed** *adj.* — **prac´tic·er** *n.*

prac·ti´tion·er *n.* one who follows a particular course, such as a profession or a lifestyle

prag·mat´ic *adj.* practical; concerned with facts and logic —**prag· mat´i·cal·ly** *adv.* —**prag·mat´i· cism** *n.* —**prag´ma·tism** *n.* —**prag´ ma·tist** *n.* —**prag·ma·tis´tic** *adj.*

praise *n.* an expression of admiration or approval —*vt.* to express approval of; to honor or glorify, as of a god

praise´wor·thy *adj.* deserving praise; commendable —**praise´ wor·thi·ly** *adv.* —**praise´wor·thi· ness** *n.*

prance *vi.* to strut and frolic in a spirited manner —**pranc´er** *n.* — **pranc´ing·ly** *adv.*

prank *n.* a practical joke; a playful escapade —**prank´ish** *adj.* — **prank´ish·ly** *adv.* —**prank´ish· ness** *n.* —**prank´ster** *n.*

prate *n.* idle chatter —*vi., vt.* to talk idly and frivolously —**prat´er** *n.* — **prat´ing·ly** *adv.*

prat´tle *n.* childlike or foolish talk — *vi., vt.* to speak in a childish manner —**prat´tler** *n.* —**prat´tling·ly** *adv.*

prayer *n.* an earnest appeal or supplication —**pray** *vi., vt.* —**prayer´ ful** *adj.* —**prayer´ful·ly** *adv.* — **prayer´ful·ness** *n.*

pray´er *n.* one who prays

preach *vi., vt.* to lecture or sermonize, especially in a dull and dogmatic fashion —**preach´er** *n.* — **preach´ing·ly** *adv.*

preach´i·fy *vi.* to lecture in a dull, didactic fashion —**preach·i·fi·ca´ tion** *n.*

preach´y *adj.* overly given to preaching or moralizing

pre·am´ble *n.* a preface to a formal document

pre·ar·range´ *vt.* to set up or organize in advance —**pre·ar·range´ ment** n.

pre·car´i·ous adj. uncertain or unstable —**pre·car´i·ous·ly** adv. — **pre·car´i·ous·ness** n.

pre·cau´tion n. care taken to avoid hazards —**pre·cau´tion·ary** adj.

pre·cede´ vt., vi. to come or go before

prec´e·dence, prec´e·den·cy n. priority; superiority

prec´e·dent n. an example or pattern

pre´cept n. a rule or principle that defines a policy; an instruction — **pre·cep´tive** adj. —**pre·cep´tive·ly** adv.

pre·cinct n. a minor territorial or jurisdictional district

pre´cious adj. valuable; cherished; overly refined or nice —adv. —**pre´cious·ly** adv. —**pre´cious·ness** n.

prec´i·pice n. a cliff's edge; the edge or threshold of danger

pre·cip´i·tant adj. impulsive; sudden or rash —**pre·cip´i·tance, pre·cip´i·tan·cy** n. —**pre·cip´i·tant·ly** adv.

pre·cip´i·tate adj. hasty or rash — vi., vt. to fall or cause to fall, as rain; to hasten the occurrence of —**pre·cip´i·tate·ly** adv. —**pre·cip´i·tate·ness** n. —**pre·cip´i·ta·tive** adj. —**pre·cip´i·ta·tor** n.

pre·cip·i·ta´tion n. haste or rashness; falling moisture, such as rain, snow, or sleet

pre·cip´i·tous adj. steep —**pre·cip´i·tous·ly** adv. —**pre·cip´i·tous·ness** n.

pré·cis´ n. a synopsis or summary of a text

pre·cise´ adj. exact; well–defined — **pre·cise´ly** adv. —**pre·cise´ness** n. —**pre·ci´sion** n., adj.

pre·clude´ vt. to exclude or prohibit —**pre·clu´sion** n. —**pre·clu´sive** adj. —**pre·clu´sive·ly** adv.

pre·co´cious adj. exhibiting early maturity; mature beyond what

may be expected for the subject's chronological age —**pre·co´cious·ly** adv. —**pre·co´cious·ness, pre·coc´i·ty** n.

pre·cog·ni´tion n. foresight; prescience —**pre·cog´ni·tive** adj.

pre´con·ceive´ vt. to reach a conclusion without complete information —**pre·con·cep´tion** n.

pre·con·di´tion n. a requisite for further action

pre·cur´sor n. a forerunner or harbinger —**pre·cur´sive, pre·cur´so·ry** adj.

pred´a·tor n. one that preys on others —**pred·a·to´ri·ly** adv. —**pred´a·to·ri·ness** n. —**pred´a·to·ry** adj.

pre·des·ti·na´tion n. the belief that one's destiny is determined in advance —**pre·des´ti·nate, pre·des´tine** vt.

pre·des·ti·nar´i·an adj. relating to or believing in predestination —n. one who believes in predestination —**pre·des·ti·nar´i·an·ism** n.

pre·de·ter´mine vt. to ascertain an outcome in advance —**pre·de·ter´mi·nate** adj. —**pre·de·ter·mi·na´tion** n.

pre·dic´a·ment n. a difficult situation

pred´i·cate vt., vi. to assert or profess —**pred·i·ca´tion** n. —**pred·i·ca´tion·al** adj. —**pred´i·ca·tive** adj. —**pred´i·ca·tive·ly** adv.

pre·dict´ vt. to assert in advance on the basis of theory or experience — vi. to foretell or prophesy —**pre·dict·a·bil´i·ty** adv. —**pre·dict´a·ble** adj. —**pre·dict´a·bly** adv. — **pre·dic´tive** adj. —**pre·dic´tive·ly** adv. —**pre·dic´tive·ness** n. —**pre·dic´tor** n.

pre·dic´tion n. a thing predicted

pred´i·lec´tion n. a tendency

pre´dis·pose´ vt. to influence or make susceptible —**pre·dis·po·si´tion** n.

pre·dom´i·nant adj. most important

or widespread —**pre·dom´i·nance** n. —**pre·dom´i·nant·ly** adv.

pre·dom´i·nate vi. to be superior to all others in some way —**pre·dom´i·nat·ing·ly** adv. —**pre·dom´i·nate·ly** adv. —**pre·dom·i·na´tion** n. —**pre·dom´i·na·tor** n.

pre·em´i·nent adj. distinguished; outstanding —**pre·em´i·nence** n. —**pre·em´i·nent·ly** adv.

pre·empt´ vt. to usurp or confiscate; to take precedence, as in a right to purchase —**pre·emp´tor** n. —**pre·emp´to·ry** adj.

pre·emp´tion n. the right to purchase before others; seizure or appropriation —**pre·emp´tive** adj. —**pre·emp´tive·ly** adv.

preen vt. to groom carefully; to gloat —vi. to primp; to gloat

pref´ace n. an introduction or opening message, as in a book —vt. to furnish with an opening message; to serve as an introductory message

pre·fer´ vt. to favor over another; to like better —**pref´er·ence** n.

pref´er·a·ble adj. more desirable —**pref·er·a·bil´i·ty**, **pref´er·a·ble·ness** n. —**pref´er·a·bly** adv.

pref·er·en´tial adj. favored; granting assistance —**pref·er·en´tial·ism** n. —**pref·er·en´tial·ly** adv.

preg´na·ble adj. pervious; vulnerable —**preg·na·bil´i·ty** adv.

preg´nant adj. carrying a developing offspring; significant or meaningful —**preg´nan·cy** n. —**preg´nant·ly** adv.

pre·hen´sile adj. adapted for grasping, as a monkey's tail —**pre·hen·sil´i·ty** adv.

pre·hen´sion n. apprehension, understanding

pre·his·tor´ic, pre´his·tor´i·cal adj. belonging to the time before recorded history —**pre´his·tor´i·cal·ly** adv. —**pre·his´to·ry** n.

prej´u·dice n. prejudgment; opinion

founded on bias —vt. to influence another to prejudge; to wrong by opinion or action —**prej´u·di´cial** adj. —**prej´u·di´cial·ly** adv.

pre·lim´i·nar·y adj. introductory or preceding —n. an introduction; something that precedes —**pre·lim·i·nar´i·ly** adv.

pre·mar´i·tal adj. before marriage —**pre·mar´i·tal·ly** adv.

pre·ma·ture´ adj. before the correct or proper time —**pre·ma·ture´ly** adv. —**pre·ma·ture´ness** n. —**pre·ma·tur´i·ty** n.

pre·med´i·tate vt. vi. to plan or consider in advance —**pre·med´i·ta·tive** adj. —**pre·med´i·ta·tor** n.

pre·med´i·tat·ed adj. characterized by deliberate intention —**pre·med´i·tat·ed·ly** adv. —**pre·med·i·ta´tion** n.

pre·mier´ adj. foremost —n. a chief administrative officer

pre·miere´ n. an introductory public performance —vt., vi. to present publicly for the first time

prem´ise n. an assumption that is the basis for debate or resolution

pre´mi·um adj. excellent; superior; —n. a reward or bonus; an excess amount by which something is valued or paid

pre·mo·ni´tion n. foreboding; a sign or omen —**pre·mon·i·to´ri·ly** adv. —**pre·mon´i·to·ry** adj.

pre·nup´tial adj. before marriage

pre·oc´cu·pied adj. distracted; immersed in thought; troubled —**pre·oc·cu·pa´tion** n. —**pre·oc´cu·py** vt.

pre·or·dain´ vt. to predetermine; to destine —**pre·or·di·na´tion** n.

prep·a·ra´tion n. arrangements made in advance; readiness; a mixture made for some purpose —**pre·par´a·tive** adj., n. —**pre·par´a·tive·ly** adv.

pre·par´a·to·ry adj. introductory or preliminary, as a course of study

—*adv.* in making ready for —**pre·par·a·to´ri·ly** *adv.*

pre·pare´ *vt.* to arrange in advance; to provide what is needed; to make complete —**pre·par´ed·ness** *n.* —**pre·par´er** *n.*

pre·pay´ *vt.* to pay in advance —**pre·pay´ment** *n.*

pre·pon´der·ant *adj.* superior; dominant —**pre·pon´der·ance** *n.* —**pre·pon´der·ant·ly** *adv.*

pre·pos´ter·ous *adj.* absurd; irrational —**pre·pos´ter·ous·ly** *adv.* —**pre·pos´ter·ous·ness** *n.*

pre´quel *n.* a story recounting events that lead up to those in a work published earlier

pre·req´ui·site *n.* a requirement or condition for further action —*adj.* required or necessary

pre·rog´a·tive *n.* a right or privilege, such as granted by virtue of rank or birth

pres´age *n.* an omen or intuition —*vt., vi.* —**pres´age·ful** *adj.*

pre´sci·ence *n.* foreknowledge of coming events —**pre´scient** *adj.* —**pre´scient·ly** *adv.*

pre·scribe´ *vt.* to direct or order —**pre·scrib´er** *n.*

pre·scrip´tion *n.* directions or instructions; a formula, as for preparing a medicine

pres´ence *n.* attendance, proximity, or influence: *their presence at the meeting is vital;* one's appearance or bearing: *a commanding presence*

pres´ent *adj.* at this moment; current; existing; here; near at hand —*n.* now

pres´ent *n.* a gift —**pre·sent´** *vt.* to offer or give, as a gift

pre·sent´a·ble *adj.* suitable for offering or giving —**pre·sent·a·bil´i·ty, pre·sent´a·ble·ness** *n.* —**pre·sent´a·bly** *adv.*

pre·sen·ta´tion *n.* something offered or given —**pre·sen·ta´tion·al** *adj.*

pres´ent·ly *adv.* soon

pres·er·va´tion·ist *n.* one who supports the protection of natural areas —**pres·er·va´tion·ism** *n.*

pre·serv´a·tive *n.* a substance that keeps food from spoiling —*adj.*

pre·serve´ *n.* an area set aside to be kept in its natural state —*vt.* to protect; to save in a natural state; to prepare food so as to prevent spoilage —**pre·serv´a·ble** *adj.* —**pres·er·va´tion** *n.* —**pre·serv´er** *n.*

pre·side´ *vi.* to officiate, as at a meeting; to direct or control —**pre·sid´er** *n.*

pres´i·dent *n.* a chief officer or executive; one who presides —**pres´i·den·cy** *n.* —**pres·i·den´tial** *adj.* —**pres·i·den´tial·ly** *adv.*

press *n.* journalism or journalists; a machine for printing; any device used to apply pressure; urgency —*vt., vi.* to apply pressure

pres´sure *n.* the applying of constant physical or mental forces —*vt.* to persuade

pres´sur·ise (*Brit.*) *vt.* to apply mental pressure; to persuade

pres·ti·dig·i·ta´tion *n.* sleight-of-hand —**pres·ti·dig´i·ta·tor** *n.*

pres·tige´ *n.* distinction or renown; esteem —**pres·tig´i·ous** *adj.* —**pres·tig´i·ous·ly** *adv.* —**pres·tig´i·ous·ness** *n.*

pre·sume´ *vt.* to take for granted; to undertake without proper authorization —*vi.* to make excessive demands on —**pre·sum´a·bly, pre·sum´ed·ly** *adv.* —**pre·sum´er** *n.*

pre·sump´tion *n.* something taken for granted; arrogance

pre·sump´tive *adj.* based on probability; providing reasonable cause for belief —**pre·sump´tive·ly** *adv.*

pre·sum´ing *adj.* presumptuous —**pre·sum´ing·ly** *adv.*

pre·sump´tu·ous *adj.* impudent or rude; overly forward —**pre·sump´tu·ous·ly** *adv.* —**pre·sump´tu·ous·ness** *n.*

pre·sup·pose´ *vt.* to take for granted —**pre·sup·po·si´tion** *n.*

pre·tend´ *vt.*, *vi.* to feign or mimic; to make believe; to be deceitful or attempt to deceive —**pre·tence´** (*Brit.*), **pre·tense´** (*US*) *n.*

pre·tend´ed *adj.* insincere; feigned or counterfeit —**pre·tend´ed·ly** *adv.*

pre·ten´tious *adj.* presumptuous or arrogant; pompous or showy —**pre·ten´sion**, **pre·ten´tious·ness** *n.* —**pre·ten´tious·ly** *adv.*

pre´text *n.* subterfuge; an alleged reason

pret´ti·fy *vt.* to make attractive

pret´ty *adj.* attractive; considerable: *a pretty mess*; insubstantial: *pretty words* —*adv.* quite; somewhat — **pret´ti·ly** *adv.* —**pret´ti·ness** *n.*

pre·vail´ *vi.* to overcome; to influence or effect —**pre·vail´er** *n.*

pre·vail´ing *adj.* dominant; generally accepted —**pre·vail´ing·ly** *adv.*

prev´a·lent *adj.* common or widespread —**prev´a·lence** *n.* —**prev´a·lent·ly** *adv.*

pre·var´i·cate *vi.* to lie —**pre·var·i·ca´tion** *n.* —**pre·var´i·ca·tor** *n.*

pre·vent´ *vt.* to keep from happening; to prohibit or hamper —**pre·vent´a·ble** *adj.* —**pre·vent´er** *n.* — **pre·ven´tion** *n.*

pre·vent´a·tive, pre·ven´tive *adj.* hindering; precautionary —*n.* something that prevents, as protection from disease —**pre·ven´tive·ly** *adv.* —**pre·ven´tive·ness** *n.*

pre´view *n.* an advance view; a survey or inspection —*vt.* to view in advance

pre´vi·ous *adj.* former; having occurred earlier —**pre´vi·ous·ly** *adv.*

prey *n.* one that is hunted; a victim —*vi.* to hunt; to victimize

price *n.* the cost or value of something —*vt.* to set a value for

price´less *adj.* of immeasurable value

pric´ey *adj.* expensive

prick *n.* a sharp pain; a puncture — *vt.*, *vi.*

pride *n.* self-esteem; haughtiness or disdain —**pride´ful** *adj.* —**pride´ful·ly** *adv.* —**pride´ful·ness** *n.*

prig *n.* a prude; one who is overly correct or formal —**prig´ger·y** *n.* —**prig´gish** *adj.* —**prig´gish·ly** *adv.* —**prig´gish·ness** *n.*

prim *adj.* overly exacting or proper; demur; orderly —**prim·ly** *adv.* — **prim´ness** *n.* —**pri´ma·cy** *n.*

pri´mal *adj.* primitive; original; primary

pri´mary *adj.* first; earliest; fundamental; principal —**pri·mar´i·ly** *adv.*

prime *adj.* excellent; of the finest quality; original —*n.* the age of full perfection or vigor: *the prime of life*; the best of anything —*vt.* to prepare or make ready: *prime a pump*; to apply an initial coating — **prime´ly** *adv.* —**prime´ness** *n.*

pri·me´val *adj.* ancient; primitive — **pri·me´val·ly** *adv.*

prim´i·tive *adj.* simple; ancient; uncivilized —**prim´i·tive·ly** *adv.* —**prim´i·tive·ness** *n.*

pri·mor´di·al *adj.* primitive; original —**pri·mor´di·al·ly** *adv.*

primp *vt.*, *vi.* to groom with care

prince *n.* a nobleman; one who is outstanding —**prince´li·ness** *n.* — **prince·ly** *adj.*

prin´cess *n.* a noblewoman

prin´ci·pal *adj.* first or leading —*n.* a person of importance —**prin´ci·pal·ly** *adv.*

prin´ci·ple *n.* a fundamental rule or concept; an ideal —**prin´ci·pled** *adj.*

print *n.* a duplicate made by transferring an image to a receptor such as paper; an indentation made by pressure —*vi.*, *vt.* —**print´er** *n.* — **print´ing** *n.* —**print´mak·er** *n.*

pri´or *adj.* preceding

pri·or´i·tize vt. to organize in order of importance —**pri·or´i·ty** n. —**pri·or·i·ti·za´tion** n.

pris´on n. a place of confinement —**pris´on·er** n.

pris´sy adj. unduly proper —**pris´si·ly** adv. —**pris´si·ness** n.

pris´tine adj. unspoiled

pri´vate adj. not open to the public; not public: private ownership; secluded —**pri´va·cy** n. —**pri´vate·ly** adv. —**pri´vate·ness** n.

pri·va´tion n. abject poverty

priv´i·lege n. a special right

priv´i·leged adj. invested with a special right or advantage

prize n. an award; something desired —adj. greatly valued —vt. to value highly

prob´a·ble adj. likely; worth believing although unproven —**prob·a·bil´i·ty** n. —**prob´a·bly** adv.

pro·ba´tion n. a trial period —**pro·ba´tion·al** adj. —**pro·ba´tion·ary** adj. —**pro·ba´tion·er** n.

pro·bi´ty n. honesty; integrity

prob´lem adj. difficult to manage: a problem child —n. something to be considered; a puzzle or dilemma

prob´lem·at´ic,　　prob´lem·at´i·cal adj. difficult; doubtful —**prob´lem·at´i·cal·ly** adv.

pro·ce´dure n. a manner of doing something; a system for doing —**pro·ce´dur·al** adj. —**pro·ce´dur·al·ly** adv.

pro·ceed´ vi. to move forward

pro´ceeds n. money received; yield

pro·ceed´ing n. a process or procedure

proc´ess n. a set of actions; a system

pro·ces´sion n. an orderly progression; a parade

proc´es·sor n. a device for manipulating: a food processor, a data processor

pro·claim´ vt. to announce; to praise —**pro·claim´er** n. —**proc·lam´a·to·ry** adj.

proc·la·ma´tion n. a formal announcement or edict

pro·cliv´i·ty n. an inherent inclination or tendency

pro·cras´ti·nate vi. to put off taking action —vt. to postpone or delay —**pro·cras·ti·na´tion** n. —**pro·cras´ti·na·tor** n.

pro·cure´ vt. to acquire —**pro·cur´a·ble** adj. —**pro·cure´ment** n. —**pro·cur´er** n.

prod vt. to goad or provoke —n. anything that incites to action

prod´i·gal adj. wasteful —**prod·i·gal´i·ty** n. —**prod´i·gal·ly** adv.

pro·di´gious adj. extraordinary or impressive —**pro·di´gious·ly** adv. —**pro·di´gious·ness** n.

prod´i·gy n. one with exceptional talent; a genius

prod´uce n. that which is made; farm products —**pro·duce´** vt. to make or manufacture; to create —**pro·duc´er** n. —**prod´uct** n.

pro·duc´tion n. output or yield

pro·duc´tive adj. fruitful or prolific; effective —**pro·duc´tive·ly** adv.

pro·duc·tiv´i·ty n. the speed or effectiveness for generating output

pro·fane´ adj. sacrilegious or irreverent; vulgar or base —vt. to desecrate or debase —**prof·a·na´tion** n. —**pro·fan´a·to·ry** adj. —**pro·fane´ly** adv. —**pro·fan´er** n.

pro·fane´ness, pro·fan´i·ty n. irreverence; the use of abusive or vulgar language

pro·fess´ vt. to claim or declare; to pretend or feign —**pro·fess´ed·ly** adv.

pro·fes´sion n. an occupation, especially one requiring special training; a declaration of faith

pro·fes´sion·al adj. skillful —n. one skilled or specially trained —**pro·fes´sion·al·ly** adv.

pro·fes´sor n. (Brit.) a distinguished teacher at a college or university; (US) an educator, especially at a college or university —**pro·fes·so´ri·al** adj. —**pro·fes·so´ri·al·ly** adv.

prof´fer vt. to offer

pro·fi´cient adj. competent or able —**pro·fi´cien·cy** n. —**pro·fi´cient·ly** adv.

pro´file n. a summary; a side view

prof´it n. gain from a business venture —vt., vi. to realize gain or benefit; to be of benefit to —**prof´it·a·bil´i·ty** n. —**prof´it·a·ble** adj. —**prof´it·a·bly** adv.

prof´i·teer´ vi. to make an unreasonable profit —n.

prof´li·gate adj. extravagant or wasteful —**prof´li·ga·cy** n. —**prof´li·gate·ly** adv.

pro·found´ adj. deep or penetrating; scholarly —**pro·found´ly** adv. —**pro·found´ness** n.

pro·fun´di·ty n. the quality of being profound; a scholarly paper, theory, etc.

pro·fuse´ adj. abundant —**pro·fuse´ly** adv. —**pro·fuse´ness** n.

pro·fu´sion n. an abundance or outpouring

prog´e·ny n. an offspring; a descendant

prog·no´sis n. a forecast or prediction

prog·nos´ti·cate vt. to predict —**prog·nos·ti·ca´tion** n. —**prog·nos´ti·ca·tor** n.

pro´gram (US) n. a schedule or agenda; a radio or television broadcast; a set of computer instructions —vt. to prepare a schedule or agenda; to write computer instructions —**pro´gram·ma·ble** adj. —**pro´gram·mer** n.

pro´gramme (Brit.) n. a schedule or agenda; a radio or television broadcast —vt. to prepare a schedule or agenda

prog´ress n. a moving forward; advancement, development, or improvement —**pro·gress´** vi. to move forward; to advance; to grow

or improve —**pro·gres´sion** n.

pro·gres´sive adj. receptive to fresh ideas or concepts —**pro·gres´sive·ly** adv. —**pro·gres´sive·ness** n.

pro·hib´it vt. to forbid or ban —**pro·hi·bi´tion** n.

pro·hib´i·tive adj. forbidding —**pro·hib´i·tive·ly** adv.

proj´ect n. a plan; a serious undertaking —**pro·ject´** vt. to extend or thrust forward —**pro·jec´tile** n.

pro·jec´tion n. a bulge or protuberance; an extended part; a forecast based on historical data

pro·le·tar´i·at n. the working class —**pro·le·tar´i·an** adj.

pro·lif´er·ate vi., vt. to increase rapidly —**pro·lif·er·a´tion** n.

pro·lif´ic adj. producing or capable of producing in abundance —**pro·lif´i·ca·cy** n. —**pro·lif´i·cal·ly** adv.

pro·lix´ adj. excessively wordy

pro´logue n. an introductory text

pro·long´ vt. to extend or lengthen

prom´e·nade´ n. a public walkway —vi., vt. to take a leisurely walk

prom´i·nent adj. clearly discernable; well-known or celebrated —**prom´i·nence** n. —**prom´i·nent·ly** adv.

pro·mis´cu·ous adj. tending to casual relationships; indiscriminate; random —**prom·is·cu´i·ty** n. —**pro·mis´cu·ous·ly** adv. —**pro·mis´cu·ous·ness** n.

prom´ise n. a pledge or vow —vt. —**prom´is·er** n. —**prom´is·ing** adj. —**prom´is·so·ry** adj.

pro´mo n. a promotional message or campaign

prom´on·to·ry n. a high point of land extending out into a body of water

pro·mote´ vt. to advance to a higher level; to attempt to make more popular or prominent —**pro·mot´a·ble** adj. —**pro·mot´er** n.

pro·mo´tion n. an elevation in status or position; a program to improve the perception of a

354

person, product, or concept —**pro·mo´tion·al** adj.

prompt adj. punctual; timely —vt. to arouse or provoke; to remind —**prompt´er** n. —**prompt´ly** adv. —**prompt´ness** n.

prom´ul·gate vt. to announce publicly or officially —**prom·ul·ga´tion** n. —**prom´ul·ga·tor** n.

prone adj. lying face downward; disposed to or likely —**prone´ly** adv.

prong n. a slender pointed extension; (US) the contact points for an electrical connection

pro´noun n. a designation that substitutes for a noun

pro·nounce´ vt., vi. to utter or speak clearly; to announce officially —**pro·nounce´a·ble** adj. —**pro·nounce´ment** n.

pro·nounced´ adj. distinctive; obvious —**pro·nounc´ed·ly** adv. —**pro·nounc´ed·ness** n.

pro·nun·ci·a´tion n. the generally accepted sound of a spoken word

proof n. evidence; a demonstration of authenticity; verification or validation

proof´read vt., vi. to review copy for errors —**proof´read·er** n.

prop n. a support —vt. to support or assist

prop·a·gan´da n. information designed to promote a cause or point of view —**prop·a·gan´dist** n. —**prop·a·gan·dis´tic** adj. —**prop·a·gan´dize** vi., vt.

prop´a·gate vt. to breed or multiply; to spread or extend —**prop·a·ga´tion** n. —**prop´a·ga·tor** n.

pro·pel´ vt. to drive forward

pro·pel´lant, pro·pel´lent n. a substance that serves to push or thrust —adj. serving to propel

pro·pen´si·ty n. an inclination or tendency

prop´er adj. appropriate; fitting; according to convention —**prop´er·ly** adv. —**prop´er·ness** n.

prop´er·tied adj. having assets, especially land as a source of income

prop´er·ty n. one's belongings or possessions; a section of land; a characteristic or quality

proph´e·cy n. a prediction or forecast

proph´e·sy vt. to predict or foretell

proph´et n. one who pronounces or interprets by divine inspiration; a spokesperson —**pro·phet´ic, pro·phet´i·cal** adj. —**pro·phet´i·cal·ly** adv.

pro·phy·lac´tic adj. protective, as against disease —n.

pro·pin´qui·ty n. nearness; similarity

pro·pi´ti·ate vt. to appease

pro·pi´tious adj. promising or favorable, as of circumstances; kindly disposed —**pro·pi´tious·ly** adv. —**pro·pi´tious·ness** n.

pro·po´nent n. an advocate or defender; a supporter

pro·por´tion n. a share; relative magnitude; symmetry —**pro·por´tion·al** adj. —**pro·por´tion·ate** adj.

pro·pos´al n. an offer or proposition; a plan or scheme

pro·pose´ vt. to suggest or recommend; to put forth for consideration; to intend —vi. to make an offer, as of marriage —**pro·pos´er** n.

prop·o·si´tion n. something offered for consideration —**prop·o·si´tion·al** adj.

pro·pound´ vt. to put forth, as for consideration or solution —**pro·pound´er** n.

pro·pri´e·tar·y adj. pertaining to a proprietor; protected, as by copyright or patent —n. ownership —**pro·pri·e·tar´i·ly** adv.

pro·pri´e·tor n. an owner; one having exclusive right to —**pro·pri´e·tor·ship** n.

pro·pri·e·ty *n.* the mark of good breeding; conformity to society's standards

pro·rate´ *vt., vi.* to distribute or divide proportionally

pro·sa´ic *adj.* commonplace; mundane, humdrum, or dull —**pro·sa´ i·cal·ly** *adv.* —**pro·sa´ic·ness** *n.*

pro·scribe´ *vt.* to condemn or forbid —**pro·scrip´tion** *n.* —**pro·scrip´ tive** *adj.* —**pro·scrip´tive·ly** *adv.*

prose *n.* the style of ordinary conversation, in contrast to poetry

pros´e·cute *vt.* to initiate legal proceedings; to pursue or carry on so as to complete —**pros´e·cut·a·ble** *adj.* —**pros·e·cu´tion** *n.* — **pros´e·cu·tor** *n.* —**pros·e·cu·to´ri· al** *adj.*

pros´e·lyte *n.* one who has been converted —*vt., vi.* to proselytize

pros´e·lyt·ize *vt., vi.* to convert, as to a religion, doctrine, or political view —**pros´e·lyt·iz·er** *n.*

pros´pect *n.* an expectation or possibility —*vt., vi.* to search or explore

pro·spec´tive *adj.* hoped for —**pro· spec´tive·ly** *adv.*

pro·spec´tus *n.* a summary, as of the details concerning a venture or investment

pros´per *vi.* to thrive; to be financially successful

pros·per´i·ty *n.* affluence or wellbeing

pros´per·ous *adj.* successful; flourishing —**pros´per·ous·ly** *adv.* — **pros´per·ous·ness** *n.*

pros´the·sis *n.* a device intended to replace a missing body part — **pros·thet´ic** *adj.* —**pros·thet´i· cal·ly** *adv.* —**pros·thet´ics** *n.*

pros´ti·tute *n.* one who accepts money or other consideration for sex or other base end —*vt.* to use or offer for base purposes —**pros´ ti·tu´tion** *n.*

pros´trate *adj.* lying prone; submissive; overcome or exhausted —*vt.* to bow down or lie flat, as in submission; to overcome

pros·tra´tion *n.* a state of exhaustion or collapse

pro·tag´o·nist *n.* the principal or leading character in a story

pro·tect´ *vt.* to safeguard against damage or harm —**pro·tect´ing·ly** *adv.* —**pro·tec´tion** *n.*

pro·tec´tive *adj.* suited to or intended to safeguard —*n.* something that protects —**pro·tec´tive· ly** *adv.* —**pro·tec´tive·ness** *n.*

pro·tec´tion·ism *n.* a system of tariffs or quotas designed to protect domestic business from an influx of imported goods; the advocacy of such a system —**pro·tec´ tion·ist** *n.*

pro·tec´tor *n.* a person or thing that safeguards or protects

pro´té·gé *n.* one endorsed by a person of influence

pro tem *adv.* pro tempore

pro tem´po·re *adv.* temporarily; for the time being

pro´test *n.* a declaration or display of disapproval —**pro·test´** *vt.* to object strongly and solemnly — **prot´es·ta´tion** *n.* —**pro·test´er** *n.*

pro´to·col *n.* a code of conduct; proper etiquette; ceremony

pro´to·type *n.* a model —**pro·to·typ´ ic, pro·to·typ´i·cal** *adj.*

pro·tract´ *vt.* to draw out or prolong —**pro·tract´ed·ly** *adv.* —**pro· tract´ed·ness** *n.* —**pro·trac´tion** *n.* —**pro·trac´tive** *adj.*

pro·trude´ *vt., vi.* to jut or thrust outward —**pro·trud´ent** *adj.* — **pro·tru´sion** *n.*

pro·tu´ber·ance *n.* something that protrudes, as a knob or a swelling —**pro·tu´ber·ant** *adj.* —**pro·tu´ ber·ant·ly** *adv.*

proud *adj.* full of self-esteem; of vain or arrogant conceit; dignified — **proud´ly** *adv.* —**proud´ness** *n.*

prove *vt.* to establish by argument or evidence —**prov·a·bil´i·ty** *n.* —**prov´a·ble** *adj.* —**prov´a·bly** *adv.*

prov´en *adj.* verified

prov´en·der *n.* supplies or provisions

prov´erb *n.* a saying or adage

pro·ver´bi·al *adj.* widely alluded to or believed —**pro·ver´bi·al·ly** *adv.*

pro·vide´ *vt.* to supply or furnish; to stipulate —**pro·vid´er** *n.*

prov´i·dence *n.* advance preparation; divine guidance —**prov´i·dent, prov·i·den´tial** *adj.* —**prov·i·den´tial·ly, prov´i·dent·ly** *adv.*

prov´ince *n.* an outlying area

pro·vin´cial *adj.* crude or unsophisticated —**pro·vin´cial·ism, pro·vin·ci·al´i·ty** *n.* —**pro·vin´cial·i·za´tion** *n.* —**pro·vin´cial·ly** *adv.*

pro·vi´sion *n.* an act of providing; supplies provided; a requirement —*vt.* to supply —**pro·vi´sion·er** *n.*

pro·vi´sion·al *adj.* temporary —**pro·vi´sion·al·ly** *adv.*

pro·vi´so *n.* a stipulation —**pro·vi´so·ry** *adj.*

prov·o·ca´tion *n.* something that provokes —**pro·voc´a·tive** *adj.* —**pro·voc´a·tive·ly** *adv.* —**pro·voc´a·tive·ness** *n.*

pro·voke´ *vt.* to induce, as to action or anger

pro·vok´ing *adj.* troubling or vexing —**pro·vok´ing·ly** *adv.*

prow´ess *n.* notable skill or daring

prowl *vt., vi.* to move stealthily —**prowl´er** *n.*

prox´i·mal *adj.* adjacent; nearest —**prox´i·mal·ly** *adv.*

prox´i·mate *adj.* approximate —**prox´i·mate·ly** *adv.* —**prox´i·mate·ness** *n.*

prox·im´i·ty *n.* nearness

prox´y *n.* an agent; the authority to act as agent

prude *n.* one overly concerned with propriety —**prud´er·y** *n.* —**prud´ish** *adj.* —**prud´ish·ly** *adv.*

—**prud´ish·ness** *n.*

pru´dence *n.* caution or good judgement in the conduct of one's business —**pru´dent, pru·den´tial** *adj.* —**pru·den´tial·ly, pru´dent·ly** *adv.*

prune *n.* a partially dried plum —*vt., vi.* to trim or excise that which is superfluous or excessive —**prun´er** *n.*

pru´ri·ent *adj.* overly interested in or attracted by sexual matters —**pru´ri·ence, pru´ri·en·cy** *n.* —**pru´ri·ent·ly** *adv.*

pry *vi.* to snoop or meddle —*vt.* to force open —*n.* a lever or bar, as for prying open

pseu´do·nym *n.* an alias; an artist's fictitious name —**pseu·don´y·mous** *adj.* —**pseu·don´y·mous·ly** *adv.*

psy´che *n.* the subconscious mind; the soul

psych·e·del´ic *adj.* characterized by hallucination or distortion —*n.* a substance that alters awareness —**psych·e·del´i·cal·ly** *adj.*

psy·chi´a·try *n.* the diagnosis and treatment of mental disorders —**psy·chi·at´ric** *adj.* —**psy·chi·at´ri·cal·ly** *adv.* —**psy·chi´a·trist** *n.*

psy´chic *adj.* mental; relating to exceptional mental processes such as ESP —*n.* a spiritualist —**psy´chi·cal·ly** *adv.*

psy´cho *adj.* mentally ill; deranged; psychopathic —*n.* a psychopath

psy·cho·anal´y·sis *n.* a type of treatment for mental or emotional disorders —**psy·cho·an´a·lyst** *n.* —**psy´cho·an·a·lyt´ic, psy·cho·an·a·lyt´i·cal** *adj.* —**psy·cho·an·a·lyt´i·cal·ly** *adv.* —**psy·cho·an´a·lyze** *vt.*

psy´cho·bab·ble *n.* psychological terminology, used especially in derogation

psy·cho·log´i·cal *adj.* touching on the mind or emotions —**psy·cho·**

log′i·cal·ly *adv.* —**psy·chol′o·gist** *n.* —**psy·chol′o·gy** *n.*

psy·cho·path′ic *adj.* antisocial, agressive, or perverted —**psy′cho·path** *n.* —**psy·cho·path′i·cal·ly** *adv.*

psy·cho′sis *n.* a mental disorder

psy·cho·so·mat′ic *adj.* of an illness caused by mental or emotional disorder —**psy·cho·so·mat′i·cal·ly** *adv.*

psy·cho·ther′a·py *n.* treatment for a mental or emotional disorder —**psy·cho·ther′a·pist** *n.*

psy·chot′ic *adj.* mentally deranged

pub *n.* a public house; a tavern

pub′lic *adj.* common or shared; of a community —**pub′lic·ly** *adv.*

pub·li·ca′tion *n.* printed material; the communication of information

public house (*Brit.*) a tavern

pub·lic′i·ty *n.* information distributed widely, usually of a promotional nature —**pub′li·cist** *n.* —**pub′li·cize** *vt.*

pub′lish *vt.* to promote or broadcast widely; to print and issue —*vi.* to engage in the business of publishing; to have one's work published —**pub′lish·a·ble** *adj.* —**pub′lish·er** *n.*

puck′er *n.* a wrinkle —*vt.*, *vi.* to gather or become gathered into small folds

puck′ish *adj.* impish —**puck′ish·ly** *adv.* —**puck′ish·ness** *n.*

pud′dle *n.* a small pool of liquid —**pud′dly** *adj.*

pudg′y *adj.* chubby; fat —**pudg′i·ness** *n.*

pu′er·ile *adj.* childish or juvenile —**pu′er·ile·ly** *adv.* —**pu·er·il′i·ty** *n.*

puff *n.* a short breath; a brief gust of air —*vi.*, *vt.* to puff —**puff′i·ness** *n.* —**puff′y** *adj.*

puff′er·y *n.* exaggerated praise; promotion

pu′gi·lism *n.* the sport of boxing —**pu′gi·list** *n.* —**pu′gi·lis′tic** *adj.*

pug·na′cious *adj.* belligerent —**pug·na′cious·ly** *adv.* —**pug·na′cious·ness, pug·nac′i·ty** *n.*

pul′chri·tude *n.* great beauty —**pul·chri·tu′di·nous** *adj.*

pule *vi.* to whine or whimper

pull *n.* allure; influence —*vt.* to apply force to draw toward; to tug; to attract —*vi.* to use force in hauling, dragging, etc.

pul′ley *n.* a simple machine for multiplying effort

pulp *n.* soft, moist matter —*vt.* to reduce to pulp —**pulp′i·ness** *n.* —**pulp′y** *adj.*

pul′pit *n.* a lectern, especially for religious services

pul′sate *vi.* to vibrate rhythmically —**pul·sa′tion** *n.* —**pul′sa′tor** *n.* —**pul′sa·to·ry** *adj.*

pulse *n.* a rhythmic beating

pul′ver·ize *vt.* to crush; to reduce to powder —**pul′ver·iz·able** *adj.* —**pul·ver·i·za′tion** *n.* —**pul′ver·iz·er** *n.*

pum′mel *vt.* to beat, especially with the fists

pump *n.* a device for moving liquid —*vi.*, *vt.* to pull or push as with a pump; to move up and down as though with a pump handle —**pump′er** *n.*

pun *n.* a play on words —*vi.* —**pun′ster** *n.*

punch *n.* a tool for piercing or stamping; a fruit beverage —*vt.* to strike, as with a fist

punc·til′i·ous *adj.* attentive to detail; precise —**punc·til′i·ous·ly** *adv.* —**punc·til′i·ous·ness** *n.*

punc′tu·al *adj.* on time; prompt —**punc·tu·al′i·ty, punc′tu·al·ness** *n.* —**punc′tu·al·ly** *adv.*

punc·tu·a′tion *n.* marks in writing to indicate pauses, separations, etc.; a pause or emphasis in speaking —**punc′tu·ate** *vi.*, *vt.* —**punc′tu·a·tor** *n.*

punc′ture *vt.* to pierce —*n.* a hole

made by piercing

pun´dit *n.* a critic or scholar —**pun´dit·ry** *n.*

pun´gent *adj.* sharp or biting —**pun´gen·cy** *n.* —**pun´gent·ly** *adv.*

pun´ish *vt.* to penalize for an offense —**pun·ish·a·bil´i·ty** *n.* —**pun´ish·a·ble** *adj.* —**pun´ish·er** *n.* —**pun´ish·ment** *n.*

pu´ni·tive, pu´ni·to·ry *adj.* inflicting or designed to inflict punishment —**pu´ni·tive·ly** *adv.* —**pu´ni·tive·ness** *n.*

pu´ny *adj.* weak or frail —**pu´ni·ness** *n.*

pu´pil *n.* a student

pup´pet *n.* a small figure with jointed parts moved by strings, the hands, etc.; one controlled by another —**pup´pe·teer´** *n.* —**pup´pet·ry** *n.*

pup´py *n.* a small dog

pur´chase *n.* a thing bought —*vt.* to buy through exchange —**pur´chas·a·ble** *adj.* —**pur´chas·er** *n.*

pure *adj.* free of dirt or pollutants; without fault —**pure´ly** *adv.* —**pure´ness** *n.* —**pu´ri·ty** *n.*

pu·rée´ *n.* a smooth or blended food product —*vt.* to reduce to a thick smooth paste

pur´ga·tive *adj.* tending to cleanse —*n.* a medication used in purging the bowels: a laxative —**pur·ga´tion** *n.*

pur·ga·to·ry *n.* a place of banishment or suffering; in theology, a place where the soul is purged of sin —**pur·ga·to·ri·al** *adj.*

purge *vt.* to cleanse or purify; to rid of impurities or individuals considered undesirable; —*n.* an act of purification; an action to rid of undesirable elements, as in a government or private organization; to cause evacuation of the bowels

pu·ri·fi·ca´tion *n.* an act of cleansing

pu´ri·fy *vt.* to free of impurities or defilement —**pu´ri·fi·er** *n.*

pur´ist *n.* one committed to being exact or correct —**pu·ris´tic** *adj.*

pu·ri·tan´i·cal *adj.* marked by strict morality —**pu·ri·tan´i·cal·ly** *adv.* —**pu·ri·tan´i·cal·ness** *n.*

pur·loin´ *vi., vt.* to steal

pur·port´ *vt.* to claim or have intention —**pur·port´ed** *adj.* —**pur·port´ed·ly** *adv.*

pur´pose *n.* an aim or goal; an intention

pur´pose·ful *adj.* having intent —**pur´pose·ful·ly** *adv.* —**pur´pose·ful·ness** *n.*

pur´pose·ly *adv.* with specific intent

pur´pos·ive *adj.* serving a purpose —**pur´pos·ive·ly** *adv.* —**pur´pos·ive·ness** *n.*

purse *n.* (*Brit.*) a small receptacle used by women to carry currency, credit cards, etc.; (*US*) a woman's handbag; an award of money —*vt.* to gather in small folds, as the lips to show disapproval

purs´er *n.* a ship's officer responsible for accounts, tickets, freight, etc.

pur·sue´ *vt.* to chase or hunt; to aspire or strive for —**pur·su´a·ble** *adj.* —**pur·su´er** *n.*

pur·suit´ *n.* a hunt or chase; an activity, such as a hobby

pu´ru·lent *adj.* containing pus —**pu´ru·lence** *n.* —**pu´ru·lent·ly** *adv.*

pur·vey´ *vt., vi.* to provide —**pur·vey´ance** *n.* —**pur·vey´or** *n.*

pur´view *n.* extent, as of capability or authority; range of view or understanding

push *vt., vi.* to apply force to; to press —*n.* energy; drive

push´y *adj.* aggressive

pu·sil·lan´i·mous *adj.* cowardly —**pu·sil·la·nim´i·ty** *n.* —**pu·sil·lan´i·mous·ly** *adv.*

put *vt.* to place; to cause to be placed, as by propelling or thrusting: *put an arrow in the bull's-eye*; to cause or impose: *put them to* *work* —*vi.* to proceed: *put to sea*

pu´ta·tive *adj.* supposed —**pu´ta·tive·ly** *adv.*

pu·tre·fac´tion *n.* decomposed organic matter —**pu´tre·fac´tive** *adj.* —**pu´tre·fy** *vi.*, *vt.*

pu´trid *adj.* decaying; corrupt; vile or offensive —**pu·trid´i·ty, pu´trid·ness** *n.* —**pu´trid·ly** *adv.*

put´ter *n.* a golf club —*vt.* to proceed or work in a dawdling or ineffective manner; to poke about —*vi.* to waste time —**put´ter·er** *n.*

putz *n.* a dolt —*vi.* to putter

puz´zle *n.* a mystery —*vt.* to baffle or bewilder —**puz´zler** *n.*

pyre *n.* a formation of material for burning a dead body

q, Q seventeenth letter of the English alphabet

quack *n.* the sound of a duck; a bogus or incompetent doctor —**quack´er·y** *n.*

quad´ran·gle *n.* a plane figure with four sides; an area enclosed by buildings —**quad·ran´gu·lar** *adj.*

quad´rant *n.* a 90° arc; one fourth of a circle

quad·ra·phon´ic, quad·ri·phon´ic *adj.* of a four channel sound system

quad·ri·lat´er·al *n.* a figure bounded by four sides —*adj.*

quad·ri·ple´gi·a *n.* paralysis of the body from the neck down —**quad·ri·ple´gic** *adj.*, *n.*

quad´ru·ped *n.* a four-footed animal —**quad´ru·pe·dal** *adj.*

quad·ru´ple *adj.* involving four parts —*vt.*, *vi.* to multiply by four —**quad·ru´ply** *adv.*

quad·rup´let *n.* one of four born at the same time

quad´ru·plex *n.* a dwelling made up of or divided into four living units

quaff *vt.*, *vi.* to drink —**quaff´er** *n.*

quag´mire *n.* a slough or swamp; a difficult situation

quaint *adj.* curious or uncommon; picturesque —**quaint´ly** *adv.* —**quaint´ness** *n.*

quake *n.* an earthquake —*vi.* to tremble or shake —**quak´y** *adj.*

qual´i·fied *adj.* capable; with limitations, as *qualified approval* —**qual´i·fied·ly** *adv.*

qual´i·fi·er *n.* that which limits or modifies

qual´i·fy *vi.*, *vt.* to be or make eligible; to describe; to limit —**qual·i·fi·ca´tion** *n.*

qual´i·ty *n.* a characteristic or trait; excellence —**qual´i·ta·tive** *adj.* —**qual´i·ta·tive·ly** *adv.*

qualm *n.* uneasiness or uncertainty —**qualm´ish** *adj.* —**qualm´ish·ly** *adv.* —**qualm´ish·ness** *n.*

quan´da·ry *n.* a dilemma; uncertainty

quan´ti·fy *vt.* to express in terms of quantity; to set or devise a limit —**quan·ti·fi´a·ble** *adj.* —**quan·ti·fi´a·bly** *adv.* —**quan·ti·fi·ca´tion** *n.* —**quan´ti·fi·er** *n.*

quan´ti·tate *vt.* to determine the quantity of

quan·ti·ta·tive *adj.* measurable —**quan´ti·ta·tive·ly** *adv.* —**quan´ti·ta·tive·ness** *n.*

quan´ti·ty *n.* an amount; a considerable volume

quar´an·tine *n.* a period of isolation, especially to prevent the spread of disease —*vt.* to place or order to be placed in isolation —**quar´an·tin´a·ble** *adj.*

quar´rel *n.* a disagreement; an argument —*vt.* —**quar´rel·er, quar´rel·ler** *n.* —**quar´rel·some** *adj.*

quar´ry *n.* something pursued; an excavation —*vt.* to dig up, as stone

quart *n.* a liquid measure equal to 32 ounces

quar´ter *n.* one-fourth; a U.S. or Canadian coin —*vt.* to divide into four parts; to furnish lodging

quar´ter·ly *adj.* occurring ever-three months

quar·tet´ *n.* a group of four

quar´to *n.* a page or book size equal to one–quarter of a sheet

quash *vt.* to suppress

qua´si *adj.* resembling

qua´train *n.* a poem of four lines

qua´ver *vi.* to tremble —**qua´ver·ing· ly** *adv.* —**qua´ver·y** *adj.*

quea´sy *adj.* nauseated; uneasy or troubled —**quea´si·ly** *adv.* —**quea´ si·ness** *n.*

queen *n.* a female ruler; wife of a king; the breeding member of a colony of ants, bees, etc. —**queen´ ly** *adj., adv.*

queer *adj.* strange, unusual; unconventional —**queer´ly** *adv.* —**queer´ ness** *n.*

quell *vt.* to suppress; to ease or calm

quench *vt.* to end or extinguish; to moisten or drench —**quench´a·ble** *adj.* —**quench´er** *n.*

quer´u·lous *adj.* complaining; peevish; disgruntled —**quer´u·lous·ly** *adv.* —**quer´u·lous·ness** *n.*

que´ry *n.* a question or inquiry —*vt.* to question —**que´ri·er, que´rist** *n.*

quest *n.* a search; a journey of exploration —*vi.* to go on a search — **quest´er** *n.*

ques´tion *n.* an inquiry; something open to discussion —*vt.* to interrogate; to doubt; to challenge —*vi.* to ask —**ques´tion·er** *n.* —**ques´tion· ing·ly** *adv.*

ques´tion·a·ble *adj.* open to question; suspect —**ques·tion·a·bil´i· ty, ques´tion·a·ble·ness** *n.* — **ques´tion·a·bly** *adv.*

ques´tion·naire´ *n.* a list of questions, as for a survey

queue *n.* a waiting line, as of people

quib´ble *n.* a petty argument —*vi.* to fret over a trivial matter —**quib´ bler** *n.*

quick *adj.* swift and abrupt; alert, intelligent —**quick´ly** *adv.* — **quick´ness** *n.*

quick´en *vt.* to stimulate; to hasten —*vi.* to move more briskly; to come to life —**quick´en·er** *n.*

quick´–tem´pered *adj.* easily angered

quick´–wit´ted *adj.* alert; quick to discern —**quick´–wit´ted·ly** *adv.* —**quick´–wit´ted·ness** *n.*

quid pro quo an equal exchange

qui·es´cent *adj.* still; inactive —**qui· es´cence** *n.* —**qui·es´cent·ly** *adv.*

qui´et *adj.* silent; calm; tranquil — *vt.* to still noise; to make serene — *vi.* to become still —**qui´et·ly** *adv.* —**qui´et·ness** *n.*

qui´e·tude *n.* a state of tranquillity —**qui·e´tus** *n.*

quilt *n.* a thick covering, especially one stuffed with cotton, down, etc. —*vi.* to make such a cover —**quilt´ er** *n.*

qui´nine *n.* an alkaloid used to treat malaria

quin·tes´sence *n.* the essence of a thing —**quin·tes·sen´tial** *adj.* — **quin·tes·sen´tial·ly** *adv.*

quin·tet´ *n.* a group of five

quip *n.* a witty remark, usually spontaneous —**quip´ster** *n.*

quirk *n.* an idiosyncrasy —**quirk´i·ly** *adv.* —**quirk´i·ness** *n.* —**quirk´y** *adj.*

quit *vi.* to resign; to cease; to leave —*vt.* to discontinue; to relinquish; to leave

quite *adv.* totally; absolutely; to a great extent, as *quite nice*

quiv´er *n.* vibration —*vi.* to shudder or tremble —**quiv´er·y** *adj.*

quix·ot´ic *adj.* idealistic —**quix·ot´ i·cal·ly** *adv.*

quiz *n.* a short test —*vt.* to question

quiz´zi·cal *adj.* curious; puzzling — **quiz´zi·cal·ly** *adv.*

quo·ta´tion *n.* a citing of the words or work of another

quote *n.* a quotation —*vt.* to repeat the words of another; to cite; to state a price —**quot·a·bil´i·ty** *n.*

—**quot´a·ble** adj. —**quot´er** n.

quo·tid´i·an adj. commonplace; daily

quo´tient n. the result of dividing one number by another

r, R eighteenth letter of the English alphabet

rab´bet n. a groove into which an opposing piece fits to form a joint

rab´bi n. a Jewish scholar —**rab·bin´ic, rab·bin´i·cal** adj.

rab·bin·ate n. the office or function of a rabbi

rab´ble n. an unruly mob; riffraff

rab´ble-rous·er n. a troublemaker

rab´id adj. fanatical; frenzied —**ra·bid´i·ty, rab´id·ness** n. —**rab´id·ly** adv.

race[1] n. a group of people linked by appearance, geographical location, etc. —**ra´cial** adj. —**ra´cial·ly** adv.

race[2] n. a sporting event decided by speed; any similar rivalry or motion toward an end —vi. to take part in a race; to proceed at great speed —**rac´er** n.

rac´ism n. discrimination based on race —**rac´ist** n.

rack n. a frame, stand, etc. to hold something; an instrument of torture; a cut of meat —vt. to cause severe distress: *racked by pain*

rack´et n. a disturbing noise; a criminal activity; an effortless task or job —**rack´ety** adj.

rack´e·teer´ n. one operating an illegal business

rac´on·teur n. a skilled storyteller

rac´y adj. spirited; risqué or suggestive; lewd —**rac´i·ly** adv. —**rac´i·ness** n.

ra´dar n. a device that uses high frequency radio waves to determine the position, speed, etc. of a distant object

ra´di·ant adj. emitting heat or light; bright, glowing —**ra´di·ance** n. —**ra´di·ant·ly** adv.

ra´di·ate vi., vt. to extend from a

central point; to emit —**ra·di·a´tion** n.

rad´i·cal adj. deviating from the usual; extreme —n. one who advocates extreme change —**rad´i·cal·ism** n. —**rad·i·cal·i·za´tion** n. —**rad´i·cal·ize** vt. —**rad´i·cal·ly** adv.

ra´di·o·ac·tiv´i·ty n. the presence or emission of radiation —**ra·di·o·ac´tive** adj.

ra·di·ol´o·gy n. the medical use of radioactive materials to diagnose and treat disease —**ra·di·o·log´i·cal** adj. —**ra·di·ol´o·gist** n.

raff´ish adj. jaunty, fun-loving —**raff´ish·ly** adv. —**raff´ish·ness** n.

raft n. a flat-bottomed float; a large number —vi. to travel by raft

raft´er n. one who travels by raft

raf´ter n. a beam that supports a roof or upper story of a building

rag adj. made from bits of cloth or a cloth pulp —n. a piece of cloth

rag´a·muf·fin n. a squalid or pitiful child

rage n. violent anger; passion —vi. to speak or act violently

rag´ged adj. tattered; worn or frayed; rough or uneven —**rag´ged·ly** adv. —**rag´ged·ness** n. —**rag´ged·y** adj.

ra·gout´ n. a spicy stew

rag´time n. an American music form marked by syncopation

raid n. an unexpected assault as by an armed force or a business competitor —vi., vt. —**raid´er** n.

rail n. a horizontal bar

rai´ment n. clothing

rain n. drops of water condensed from the air; anything falling like rain —vi. to fall like rain; to furnish in profusion —**rain´y** adj.

raise vt. to move or make higher; to increase; to build —**rais´er** n.

rai·son d'ê´tre a reason for being

rake[1] n. a garden tool —vt. to scrape smooth, etc. with a rake; to search carefully

rake[2] n. a womanizer; a lewd man

—**rak´ish** adj. —**rak´ish·ly** adv. —
rak´ish·ness n.

ral´ly n. an assemblage —vi. to assemble; to recover from a difficulty

ram n. a device used to batter or
crush —vt. to strike heavily; to
force or cram into place

ram´ble n. a leisurely stroll —vi. to
wander aimlessly —**ram´bler** n. —
ram´bling adj. —**ram´bling·ly** adv.

ram·bunc´tious adj. restive; disorderly —**ram·bunc´tious·ly** adv. —
ram·bunc´tious·ness n.

ram·i·fi·ca´tion n. a consequence of
an action, problem, etc.

ramp n. a generally sloping surface
that links two levels

ram´page n. savage or frenzied behavior —vi. to act violently —**ram´
pag·er** n.

ram´pant adj. uncontrolled; without
restraint —**ramp´an·cy** n. —**ram´
pant·ly** adv.

ram´part n. a fortification or barricade

ranch n. a large farm for raising
stock —**ranch´er** n.

ran´cid adj. of stale or tainted fats
—**ran·cid´i·ty, ran´cid·ness** n.

ran´cor n. harsh resentment; animosity —**ran´cor·ous** adj. —**ran´
cor·ous·ly** adv. —**ran´cor·ous·
ness** n.

ran´dom adj. lacking order; haphazard —**ran´dom·ly** adv. —**ran´dom·
ness** n.

ran´dom·ize vt. to arrange haphazardly —**ran·dom·i·za´tion** n. —
ran´dom·iz·er n.

rand´y adj. lascivious; lecherous —
rand´i·ness n.

range n. reach or scope; the area or
extent of an activity, thing, etc.;
limits of travel, variation, etc. —vi.
to wander; to vary within limits

rang´y adj. tall and thin —**rang´i·
ness** n.

rank adj. having an offensive odor;
utter or complete as a rank

amateur —n. one's station or position —vt. to arrange or place in position

ran´kle vt. to irritate

ran´sack vt. to search or seek aggressively

ran´som n. a payment for release —
vt. —**ran´som·er** n.

rant vi., vt. to speak wildly, often
incoherently —**rant´er** n.

rap n. a light blow; a tapping noise;
informal dialogue —vt. to strike
lightly; to discuss

ra·pa´cious adj. avaricious or
greedy; ravenous —**ra·pa´cious·ly**
adv. —**ra·pa´cious·ness, ra·pac´i·
ty** n.

rap´id adj. swift; occurring with
unusual speed —**ra·pid´i·ty** n. —
rap´id·ly adv.

rap·pel´ vi. to descend along a vertical surface by means of a rope

rap·port´ n. understanding

rap·proche·ment´ n. reconciliation;
the establishing of harmonious
relations

rapt adj. enthralled or engrossed;
spellbound —**rapt´ly** adv.

rap´ture n. joy, ecstasy

rap´tur·ous adj. transported by
emotion —**rap´tur·ous·ly** adv. —
rap´tur·ous·ness n.

rare adj. uncommon, unusual; excellent, incomparable —**rare´ly**
adv. —**rar´i·ty** n.

rar´e·fy vi., vt. to filter or purify; to
make less dense

ras´cal n. a playful rogue; a scoundrel —**ras´cal·ly** adj.

rash adj. impulsive or impetuous;
reckless —**rash´ly** adv. —**rash´
ness** n.

rasp n. a coarse file; a harsh sound
—vt., vt. to abrade; to speak in a
hoarse voice —**rasp´er** n. —**rasp´i·
ness** n. —**rasp´ing·ly** adv. —**rasp´
ish, rasp´y** adj.

ratch´et n. a mechanism that limits
movement of a wheel or bar to a

single direction

rate *n.* a relative value, as *rate of speed, birth rate,* etc.; a charge or value per unit —*vt.* to place a value on —**rat·a·bil´i·ty, rat´a·ble·ness** *n.* —**rat´a·ble** *adj.* —**rat´a·bly** *adv.* —**rat´ing** *n.*

rath´er *adv.* preferably; to some extent; more accurately

rat´i·fy *vt.* to approve; to sanction — **rat·i·fi·ca´tion** *n.*

ra´tio *n.* a proportional relationship between two similar things

ra´tion *n.* an assigned measure, as of food or fuel for a particular undertaking —*vt.* to allot or distribute

ra´tion·al *adj.* sane; able to reason —**ra´tion·al·ly** *adv.* —**ra·tio·nal´i·ty** *n.*

ra·tio·nale´ *n.* grounds for reasoning; interpretation

ra´tion·al·ize *vt.* to reason; to explain away —**ra·tio·nal·iza´tion** *n.*

rat´tle *n.* a chattering sound; a device that produces such a sound —*vi.* to make a chattering sound; to speak rapidly, often carelessly

rat´ty *adj.* squalid or shabby

rau´cous *adj.* loud and rowdy; boisterous —**rau´cous·ly** *adv.* —**rau´cous·ness** *n.*

raun´chy *adj.* sloppy; lewd or obscene —**raun´chi·ly** *adv.* —**raun´chi·ness** *n.*

rav´age *n.* devastation —*vi., vt.* to destroy —**rav´ag·er** *n.*

rave *vi., vt.* to babble incoherently; to praise

rav´el *vi.* to fray or unravel; to become tangled —**rav´el·er** *n.*

rav´en·ous *adj.* hungry; insatiable; greedy —**rav´en·ous·ly** *adv.* —**rav´en·ous·ness** *n.*

raw *adj.* uncooked; natural, not processed; inexperienced; exposed —**raw´ly** *adv.*

ray *n.* a beam or shaft, as of light

reach *n.* an extent or range

—*vi., vt.* to extend to; to arrive at

re·act´ *vi.* to respond or reply —**re·ac´tion** *n.*

re·ac´tion·ar·y *adj.* in opposition to progress

re·ac´tive *adj.* readily responsive to stimulus, especially of chemistry or physics —**re·ac´tive·ly** *adv.* —**re·ac´tive·ness** *n.* —**re·ac´tor** *n.*

read *vi., vt.* to study and understand, as written characters or symbols —**read·a·bil´i·ty, read´a·ble·ness** *n.* —**read´a·ble** *adj.* —**read´a·bly** *adv.* —**read´er** *n.*

read´er·ship *n.* collectively, the subscribers to a publication

read´y *adj.* prepared and available; eager —**read´i·ly** *adv.* —**read´i·ness** *n.*

re´al *adj.* genuine; not imaginary —**re´al·ism** *n.* —**re´al·ist** *n.*

re´al·is´tic *adj.* practical; truly representative —**re·al·is´ti·cal·ly** *adv.*

re·al´i·ty *n.* the state of being true; acceptance of that which is true

re´al·ize *vt.* to recognize as true; to make true: *to realize an objective* —**re·al·iza´tion** *n.*

re´al·ly *adv.* truly; exceptionally

realm *n.* one's sphere or domain

re´al·ty *n.* real estate

reap *vi., vt.* to harvest; to gain, as a reward for effort —**reap´er** *n.*

rear *n.* back; the position farthest from the front —*vt.* to care for or raise, as a child

rea´son *n.* explanation, as for an action; intellect; a cause to believe —*vi., vt.* to consider logically; to persuade by logic —**rea´son·er** *n.*

rea´son·a·ble *adj.* able to reason; governed by reason —**rea´son·a·ble·ness** *n.* —**rea´son·a·bly** *adv.*

re·as·sure´ *vt.* to encourage; to restore confidence —**re·as·sur´ance** *n.* —**re·as·sur´ing·ly** *adv.*

re´bate *n.* a discount or deduction — *vt.* —**re´bat·er** *n.*

reb´el *n.* one who defies authority — **re·bel´** *vt.* to resist authority or influence

re·bel´lion *n.* a show of defiance — **re·bel´lious** *adj.* —**re·bel´lious·ly** *adv.* —**re·bel´lious·ness** *n.*

re·bound´ *vi.* to bounce back; to recover, as from illness or defeat

re·buff´ *n.* a rejection or rebuke; a slight or snub —*vt.*

re·buke´ *n.* a reprimand —*vt.*

re·but´ *vt.* to answer by opposing — **re·but´tal** *n.* —**re·but´ter** *n.*

re·cal´ci·trant *adj.* stubbornly defiant —**re·cal´ci·trance, re·cal´ci·tran·cy** *n.*

re·call´, re´call *n.* the ability to remember; a calling back, as of workers or a defective product — **re·call´** *vt.* —**re·call´a·ble** *adj.*

re·cant´ *vt.* to take back, as of a former belief

re´cap *n.* a summary —*vt.* to reccapitulate

re·ca·pit´u·late *vt.* to summarize — **re·ca·pit´u·la´tion** *n.*

re·cede´ *vi.* to move back

re·ceipt´ *n.* proof of payment; a receiving —*vt., vi.*

re·ceiv´a·ble *adj.* awaiting payment; unpaid —*n.* an outstanding account

re·ceive´ *vt.* to get, take possession of; to experience or undergo; to make welcome, as a guest —**re·ceiv´er** —**re·ceiv´er·ship**

re´cent *adj.* at a time just earlier than now —**re´cen·cy, re´cent·ness** *n.* —**re´cent·ly** *adv.*

re·cep´ta·cle *n.* a container

re·cep´tion *n.* a greeting; a social gathering; acceptance

re·cep´tive *adj.* able or willing to receive; open-minded —**re·cep´tive·ly** *adv.* —**re·cep´tive·ness, re·cep·tiv´i·ty** *n.*

re´cess *n.* a hollow or nook, as in a wall; an intermission —*vt.* to create a nook —*vi.* to take a break

re·ces´sion *n.* a receding or withdrawal; an economic downturn — **re·ces´sion·ar·y** *adj.*

re·cid´i·vism *n.* a reversion to earlier conduct, especially of a criminal — **re·cid´i·vist** *n.* —**re·cid·i·vis´tic, re·cid´i·vous** *adj.*

rec´i·pe *n.* instructions, especially for the preparation of food or medication

re·cip´i·ent *n.* one who receives — **re·cip´i·ence** *n.*

re·cip´ro·cal *adj.* complementary; interdependent —**re·cip´ro·cal·ly** *adv.* —**re·cip´ro·cal·ness** *n.*

re·cip´ro·cate *vi., vt.* to give or take in return; to move back and forth —**re·cip·ro·ca´tion** *n.* —**re·cip´ro·ca·tive** *adj.* —**re·cip´ro·ca·tor** *n.*

rec·i·proc´i·ty *n.* a mutually beneficial interchange

re·cit´al *n.* a public performance, as of music or dance; a detailed chronicling —**re·cit´al·ist** *n.*

re·cite´ *vt.* to repeat a memorized text; to recount in detail —**rec·i·ta´tion** *n.* —**re·cit´er** *n.*

reck´less *adj.* rash; heedless of consequences —**reck´less·ly** *adv.* — **reck´less·ness** *n.*

reck´on *vt.* to calculate or consider —**reck´on·er** *n.*

re·claim´ *vt.* to recover by returning to a prior condition, such as for land, or by processing, such as waste that is recycled for a new use —**re·claim´able** *adj.* —**rec·la·ma´tion** *n.*

re·cline´ *vi.* to lean back or lie down

rec´luse *n.* one who lives in seclusion —**re·clu´sion** *n.* —**re·clu´sive** *adj.*

rec´og·nize *vt.* to distinguish or identify; to acknowledge, as a claim —**rec·og·ni´tion** *n.* —**rec´og·niz·a·ble** *adj.* —**rec´og·niz·a·bly** *adv.* —**rec´og·niz·er** *n.*

re·coil´ *vi.* to draw back, as in alarm or fright

rec·ol·lect´ *vi.*, *vt.* to remember —**rec·ol·lec´tion** *n.*

rec·om·mend´ *vt.* to advise or endorse —**rec·om·mend´a·ble** *adj.* —**rec·om·men·da´tion** *n.* —**rec·om·mend´er** *n.*

rec´om·pense *n.* compensation, as for services rendered or for damages —*vt.* to repay, as for damages

rec·on·cile *vt.* to resolve differences, as between associates, accounts, one's own misgivings, etc. —**rec·on·cil·a·bil´i·ty, rec·on·cil·a·ble·ness** *n.* —**rec´on·cil·a·ble** *adj.* —**rec´on·cil·a·bly** *adv.* —**rec´on·cil·er** *n.* —**rec·on·cil·i·a´tion** *n.*

rec´ord *n.* a document, registry, etc. used to retain information; the information so retained —**re·cord´** *vt.* to set down information by some permanent means

re·coup´ *vt.* to regain, as to make up for a loss —**re·coup´a·ble** *adj.* —**re·coup´ment** *n.*

re·cov´er *vt.* to regain; to return to a former state —**re·cov´er·a·ble** *adj.* —**re·cov´ery** *n.*

rec´re·ant *adj.* disloyal; cowardly —**rec´re·ance, rec´re·an·cy** *n.* —**rec´re·ant·ly** *adv.*

rec·re·a´tion *n.* diversion or amusement —**rec·re·a´tion·al** *adj.*

re·crim·i·na´tion *n.* the countering of one charge with another —**re·crim´i·na·tive, re·crim´i·na·to·ry** *adj.* —**re·crim´i·na·tor** *n.*

re·cruit´ *n.* a new member —*vt.*, *vi.* to secure new members, as for the military or for volunteer work —**re·cruit´er** *n.* —**re·cruit´ment** *n.*

rec´tan·gle *n.* a plane figure of four sides at right angles to each other —**rec·tan´gu·lar** *adj.*

rec´ti·fy *vt.* to correct —**rec´ti·fi·a·ble** *adj.* —**rec·ti·fi·ca´tion** *n.*

rec´ti·tude *n.* righteousness

rec´to *n.* the right–hand page of a book

re·cum´bent *adj.* resting or reclining

—**re·cum´bence, re·cum´ben·cy** *n.* —**re·cum´bent·ly** *adv.*

re·cu´per·ate *vt.*, *vi.* to recover, as from illness or adversity; to recover after losing, as of money —**re·cu·per·a´tion** *n.* —**re·cu´per·a·tive** *adj.*

re·cur´ *vi.* to occur again —**re·cur´rence** *n.* —**re·cur´rent** *adj.* —**re·cur´rent·ly** *adv.*

re·cuse´ *vt.* to seek disqualification from judging or decision-making because of a percived prejudice or the possibility of conflict of interest

re·cy´cle *vt.* to reuse or prepare for reuse —**re·cy´cla·ble** *adj.*

re·deem´ *vt.* to reclaim or retrieve, as by fulfilling a pledge; to convert, as for stocks or bonds —**re·deem´a·ble** *adj.* —**re·demp´tion** *n.* —**re·demp´tion·al, re·demp´tive, re·demp´to·ry** *adj.*

re·de·ploy´ *vt.* to move, as men and materiel, to improve efficacy —**re·de·ploy´ment** *n.*

red´o·lent *adj.* suggesting or reminiscent —**red´o·lence, red´o·len·cy** *n.* —**red´o·lent·ly** *adv.*

re·doubt´a·ble *adj.* formidable; awe–inspiring —**re·doubt´a·bly** *adv.*

re·dress´ *n.* remedy for a wrong —*vt.* to set right, as by compensation or punishment —**re·dress´er** *n.*

re·duce´ *vt.* to diminish or decrease, as in rank, size, strength, etc. —**re·duc´er** *n.* —**re·duc·i·bil´i·ty** —**re·duc´i·ble** *adj.* —**re·duc´i·bly** *adv.* —**re·duc´tion** *n.*

re·dun´dant *adj.* superfluous; unnecessary —**re·dun´dan·cy** *n.* —**re·dun´dant·ly** *adv.*

reek *vi.* to emit a stench; to be offensive: *testimony reeking of bias*

reel *n.* a device to hold flexible material such as tape or rope; (*Brit.*) a device to hold cotton or thread; a lively dance —*vt.* to wind around a reel —*vi.* to lurch or stagger

re·fer´ *vt.* to direct to; to assign or

attribute to —*vi.* to mention; to make reference to —**refer´a·ble** *adj.* —**re·fer´ral** *n.* —**ref´er·ence** *n.*

ref·er·en´dum *n.* submission of a public matter to popular vote

re·fine´ *vt., vi.* to make or become pure, rid of unsuitable elements; to make or become more elegant or polished —**re·fined´** *adj.* —**re·fine´ment** *n.* —**re·fin´er** *n.*

re·fin´er·y *n.* an industrial installation for purifying sugar, coal, petroleum, etc.

re·flect´ *vt.* to mirror; to cast back an image —*vi.* to ponder —**re·flec´tion** *n.* —**re·flec´tion·al** *adj.*

re·flec´tive *adj.* tending to cast back an image; given to deep thought —**re·flec´tive·ly** *adv.* —**re·flec´tive·ness** *n.*

re´flex *adj.* instinctive —*n.* an involuntary response

re·form´ *adj.* advocating change: *a reform movement* —*n.* a correction or improvement —*vt.* to correct or improve —**re·form´a·ble** *adj.* —**ref·or·ma´tion** *n.* —**re·for´ma·tive** *adj.* —**re·form´er** *n.*

re·frac´tion *n.* the bending of a wave, such as light or sound, from its usual course —**re·frac´tion·al, re·frac´tive** *adj.* —**re·frac´tive·ly** *adv.* —**re·frac´tive·ness** *n.*

re·frain´ *n.* an oft repeated phrase or subject —*vi.* to abstain; to hold back from

re·fresh´ *vt.* to revive or restore —**re·fresh´ing** *adj.* —**re·fresh´ing·ly** *adv.*

re·fresh´ment *n.* that refreshes, as food or drink

re·frig´er·ant *n.* that which serves to cool

re·frig´er·ate *vt.* to make cold; to preserve by cooling —**re·frig·er·a´tion** *n.*

ref´uge *n.* a place of safety or shelter —**ref´u·gee** *n.*

re·ful´gent *adj.* radiant; glorious **re·ful´gence, re·ful´gen·cy** *n.* —**re·ful´gent·ly** *adv.*

re´fund *n.* a return or repayment —**re·fund´** *vt. vi.* to repay —**re·fund´a·ble** *adj.*

re·fur´bish *vt.* to restore or renovate —**re·fur´bish·ment** *n.*

re·fuse´ *vt. vi.* to decline or deny —**ref´use** *n.* trash or waste —**re·fus´al** *n.*

re·fute´ *vt.* to disprove; to contradict —**re·fut´a·ble** *adj.* —**re·fut´a·bly** *adv.* —**re·fut´al, ref·u·ta´tion** *n.* —**re·fut´er** *n.*

re´gal *adj.* befitting royalty; stately; splendid —**re·gal´i·ty** *n.* —**re´gal·ly** *adv.*

re·gale´ *vt.* to entertain lavishly —**re·gale´ment** *n.*

re·ga´lia *n.* the trappings of royalty; an impressive array

re·gard´ *n.* respect or admiration; deliberate heed —*vt.* to admire; to observe carefully; to deem to be —*vi.* to heed; to gaze

re·gard´less *adj.* disregarding —*adv.* despite

re·gime´ *n.* a specific government, management, order, etc.

reg´i·men *n.* a system, as of diet, exercise, etc.

re´gion *n.* an area with natural or appointed boundaries —**re´gion·al** *adj.* —**re´gion·al·ly** *adv.*

reg´is·ter *n.* a record of data; alignment of printed matter; a musical range —*vt., vi.* to record officially or formally; to show: *register disbelief*

reg·is·tra´tion *n.* an official recording —**reg´is·trant** *n.* —**reg´is·trar** *n.* —**reg´is·try** *n.*

re·gress´ *vi.* to move backward; to degenerate —**re·gres´sion** *n.* —**re·gres´sive** *adj.* —**re·gres´sive·ly** *adv.* —**re·gres´sor** *n.*

re·gret´ *n.* a feeling of sorrow or remorse about something past

—*vt.* to feel remorse —**re·gret´ful** *adj.* —**re·gret´ful·ly** *adv.* —**re·gret´ful·ness** *n.*

re·gret´ta·ble *adj.* unfortunate —**re·gret´ta·bly** *adv.* —**re·gret´ter** *n.*

reg·u·lar *adj.* normal or usual; methodical; periodic; conforming to expectations —**reg·u·lar´i·ty** *n.* —**reg·u·lar·ly** *adv.*

reg·u·late *vt.* to control or direct; to adjust —**reg·u·la´tion** *n.* —**reg´u·la·tive, reg·u·la·to·ry** *adj.* —**reg´u·la·tor** *n.*

re·gur´gi·tate *vt.* to disgorge; to throw up —**re·gur·gi·ta´tion** *n.*

re·ha·bil´i·tate *vt.* to restore to a former state; to restore to health —**re·ha·bil´i·tant** *n.* —**re·ha·bi´i·ta´tion** *n.*

re·hearse´ *vt.* to practice —**re·hears´al** *n.*

re·im·burse´ *vt.* to pay back, as for expense or loss —**re·im·burs´a·ble** *adj.* —**re·im·burse´ment** *n.*

re·in·car·na´tion *n.* the belief that after death the soul is reborn in another body

re·in·force´ *vt.* to strengthen —**re·in·force´ment** *n.*

re·in·state´ *vt.* to restore, as to use, a former state, etc.

re·it´er·ate *vt.* to repeat —**re·it·er·a´tion** *n.* —**re·it´er·a·tive** *adj.* —**re·it´er·a·tive·ly** *adv.*

re·ject *n.* one that has been discarded —**re·ject´** *vt.* to refuse; to discard —**re·ject´er, re·jec´tor** *n.* —**re·jec´tion** *n.*

re·joice´ *vi., vt.* to feel or express joy

re·join´der *n.* a response, especially to a challange

re·ju´ve·nate *vt.* to refresh and revitalize —**re·ju·ve·na´tion** *n.* —**re·ju´ve·na·tor** *n.*

re·lapse´ *n.* regression to a former state, such as a recurrence of an illness during recuperation or after recovery —*vi.* to lapse back, as into illness or addiction

re·late´ *vt.* to recount or describe; to connect or associate —**re·lat´a·ble** *adj.* —**re·lat´er, re·la´tor** *n.*

re·lat´ed *adj.* associated or connected

re·la´tion *n.* an association, or one associated, by birth or marriage; a connection, such as cause and effect —**re·la´tion·al** *adj.* —**re·la´tion·ship** *n.*

rel´a·tive *adj.* connected or affiliated; comparable —*n.* a family member —**rel´a·tive·ly** *adv.* —**rel·a·tiv´i·ty** *n.*

re·lax´ *vi., vt.* to ease tension or stress; to be or make less stringent or intense —**re·lax·a´tion** *n.* —**re·lax´ed** *adj.*

re´lay, re·lay´ *vt.* to transmit; to send forward

re·lease´ *n.* liberation; a mechanical catch —*vt.* to set free; to issue for publication —**re·leas´er** *n.*

rel´e·gate *vt.* to assign, as a task or position, often in the sense of limiting or downgrading —**rel·e·ga´tion** *n.*

re·lent´ *vi.* to surrender or soften, as a harsh attitude

re·lent´less *adj.* unyielding; persistent —**re·lent´less·ly** *adv.*

rel´e·vant *adj.* applicable to the matter at hand —**rel´e·vance, rel´e·van·cy** *n.* —**rel´e·vant·ly** *adv.*

re·li´a·ble *adj.* dependable —**re·li·a·bil´i·ty, re·li´a·ble·ness** *n.* —**re·li´a·bly** *adv.*

re·li´ance *n.* confidence or trust —**re·li´ant** *adj.* —**re·li´ant·ly** *adv.*

rel´ic *n.* an artifact; a thing of historical value

re·lief´ *n.* aid or assistance; alleviation from distress, pain, etc. —**re·liev´a·ble** *adj.* —**re·lieve´** *vt.* —**re·liev´er** *n.*

re·li´gion *n.* the belief in a controlling power outside oneself; a system of belief; an order of worship; an obsessive pursuit or cause

—**re·li´gious** adj. —**re·li´gious·ly** adv. —**re·li´gious·ness** n.

re·lin´quish vt. to give up or abandon —**re·lin´quish·er** n. —**re·lin´quish·ment** n.

rel´ish n. an appreciation or particular liking; a condiment —vt. to enjoy —vi. to gratify

re·luc´tant adj. hesitant or unwilling —**re·luc´tance** n. —**re·luc´tant·ly** adv.

re·ly´ vi. to trust completely; to depend on, as for help or support —**re·li´er** n.

re·main´ vi. to continue unchanged; to stay

re·main´der n. that left after part has been removed

re·mark´ n. a comment —vt. to comment briefly; to notice

re·mark´a·ble adj. noteworthy; striking or exceptional —**re·mark´a·ble·ness** n. —**re·mark´a·bly** adv.

re·me´di·a·ble adj. that can be corrected —**re·me´di·a·ble·ness** n. —**re·me´di·a·bly** adv.

re·me´di·al adj. intended to correct —**re·me´di·al·ly** adv. —**re·me·di·a´tion** n.

rem´e·dy n. something that corrects —vt. to make right

re·mem´ber vi. to keep in the mind; to retain —vt. to recall to mind

re·mem´brance n. recollection or reminiscence; something that serves to commemorate

re·mind´ vt. to prompt recall —**re·mind´er** n.

rem·i·nisce´ vi. to dwell on the past —**rem·i·nis´cence** n. —**rem·i·nis´cent** adj. —**rem·i·nis´cent·ly** adv. —**rem·i·nis´cer** n.

re·miss´ adj. negligent or careless in attention to duty —**re·miss´ly** n. —**re·miss´ness** n.

re·mis´sion n. a lessening or relief as from pain, etc.

re·mit´ vt. to transfer, as money, for deposit or payment —**re·mit´ta·ble** adj. —**re·mit´tance** n. —**re·mit´ter** n.

re·mit´tent adj. having temporary relief, as of a disease —**re·mit´tence, re·mit´ten·cy** n. —**re·mit´tent·ly** adv.

rem´nant n. a scrap or piece, especially of fabric; a remaining trace or indication

re·mon´strate vi. to protest —vt. to argue against —**re·mon´strance, re·mon·stra´tion** n. —**re·mon´stra·tive** adj. —**re·mon´stra·tive·ly** adv. —**re·mon´stra·tor** n.

re·morse´ n. repentance; sorrow for misconduct —**re·morse´ful** adj. —**re·morse´ful·ly** adv.

re·morse´less adj. lacking pity —**re·morse´less·ly** adv.

re·mote´ adj. distant; secluded —**re·mote´ly** adv. —**re·mote´ness** n.

re·move´ vt. to take away —vi. to relocate —**re·mov´a·ble** adj. —**re·mov´al** n. —**re·moved´** adj. —**re·mov´er** n.

re·mu´ner·ate vt. to compensate or make payment, as for goods or services —**re·mu´ner·a·ble** adj. —**re·mu·ner·a´tion** n. —**re·mu´ner·a·tive** adj. —**re·mu´ner·a·tive·ly** adv. —**re·mu´ner·a·tor** n.

ren´ais·sance n. a revival or rebirth

rend vt. to tear apart

ren´der vt. to give or provide, as for payment or approval; to depict, as by drawing; to express, as by performing; to melt down fat —**ren´der·able** adj. —**ren´der·ing** n.

ren´dez·vous n. an arranged meeting; a meeting place —vi., vt. to meet or cause to meet at a specific place and time

ren·di´tion n. performance or interpretation, as of a piece of music

ren´e·gade n. a rebel or traitor; a defector

re·nege´ vi. to fail to live up to a commitment —**re·neg´er** n.

re·new´ vt. to restore; to make new

again; to reaffirm or extend, as a license, a contract, etc. —**re·new´a·ble** *adj.* —**re·new´al** *n.*

re·nounce´ *vt.* to repudiate or deny; to forsake, as a right —**re·nounce´ment, re·nun·ci·a´tion** *n.*

ren´o·vate *vt.* to restore or redecorate —**ren·o·va´tion** *n.* —**ren´o·va·tor** *n.*

re·nowned´ *adj.* celebrated; distinguished —**re·nown´** *n.*

rent *n.* payment for occupancy or use —*vi.* to hire out —*vt.* to grant or obtain temporary use for payment —**rent·a·bil´i·ty** *n.* —**rent´a·ble** *adj.* —**rent´al** *n.* —**rent´er** *n.*

re·nun·ci·a´tion *n.* a renouncing —**re·nun´ci·a·tive, re·nun´ci·a·to·ry** *adj.*

re·pair´ *vt.* to restore to good or useable condition; to rectify or make up for —*n.* an assessment of condition: *the house seems to be in good repair* —**re·pair´a·ble** *adj.* —**re·pair´er** *n.*

rep´a·ra·ble *adj.* repairable; worthwhile to repair —**rep´a·ra·bly** *adv.*

rep·a·ra´tion *n.* compensation for a loss; atonement

rep·ar·tee´ *n.* witty conversation

re·past´ *n.* food; a meal

re·pa´tri·ate *n.* one returned or reconciled to citizenship, a country, etc. —*vt., vi.* to return or be returned to one's country —**re·pa·tri·a´tion** *n.*

re·pay´ *vt.* to reimburse or pay back; to refund —**re·pay´a·ble** *adj.* —**re·pay´ment** *n.*

re·peal´ *vt.* to revoke, as a law —**re·peal´a·ble** *adj.* —**re·peal´er** *n.*

re·peat´ *vt., vi.* to say or do again —**re·peat´a·ble** *adj.* —**re·peat´ed·ly** *adv.* —**re·peat´er** *n.*

re·pel´ *vt.* to repulse or ward off; to disgust or offend —**re·pel´lent** *adj.*

re·pent´ *vi., vt.* to feel remorse or regret; to change one's feelings

about —**re·pent´ance** *n.* —**re·pent´ant** *adj.* —**re·pent´ant·ly** *adv.*

re·per·cus´sion *n.* backlash; an unexpected consequence of an action —**re·per·cus´sive** *adj.*

rep´er·toire *n.* a list of works adopted by a performer or group of performers

rep·e·ti´tion *n.* reiteration; the process of repeating —**rep·e·ti´tious, re·pet´i·tive** *adj.* —**rep·e·ti´tious·ly, re·pet´i·tive·ly** *adv.* —**rep·e·ti´tious·ness, re·pet´i·tive·ness** *n.*

re·place´ *vt.* to put back in place; to substitute or supplant; to return or restore —**re·place´a·ble** *adj.* —**re·place´ment** *n.*

re·plen´ish *vt.* to refill —**re·plen´ish·er** *n.* —**re·plen´ish·ment** *n.*

re·plete´ *adj.* abundant; lavish —**re·plete´ness** *n.* —**re·ple´tion** *n.*

rep´li·ca *n.* a copy, often on a reduced scale

rep´li·cate *vt.* to repeat or duplicate, as an experiment; to make copies of —**rep·li·ca´tion** *n.* —**rep´li·ca·tive** *adj.*

re·ply´ *n.* a response —*vi.* to give an answer; to respond —**re·pli´er** *n.*

re·port´ *n.* a precise account; a rumor —*vt.* to inform; to present an account of —**re·port´a·ble** *adj.* —**re·port´age** *n.* —**re·port´er** *n.* —**rep·or·to´ri·al** *adj.* —**rep·or·to´ri·al·ly** *adv.*

re·port´ed·ly *adv.* according to rumor or hearsay

re·pose´ *n.* sleep; calm; peacefulness —*vi.* to lie prone —**re·pos´er** *n.* —**re·pose´ful** *adj.* —**re·pose´ful·ly** *adv.*

re·pos´i·to·ry *n.* a place for safekeeping; a container

re·pos·sess´ *vt.* to reclaim, as for nonpayment —**re·pos·ses´sion** *n.*

rep·re·hen´si·ble *adj.* deserving blame; wicked —**rep·re·hen·si·bil´i·ty, rep·re·hen´si·ble·ness** *n.*

370

—rep·re·hen´si·bly *adv.*

rep·re·sent´ *vt.* to present a likeness of; to stand in place of, as an agent —rep·re·sent·a·bil´i·ty *n.* —rep·re·sent´a·ble *adj.* —rep·re·sen·ta´tion *n.* —rep·re·sen·ta´tion·al *adj.*

rep·re·sent´a·tive *adj.* typical; characteristic —*n.* an example; an agent or delegate —rep·re·sent´a·tive·ly *adv.*

re·press´ *vt.* to restrain or control; to quell or curb —re·press´er, re·pres´sor *n.* —re·press´i·ble *adj.* —re·pres´sion *n.*

re·pres´sive *adj.* tending to restrain or control excessively, such as by a dictator or governement —re·pres´sive·ly *adv.* —re·pres´sive·ness *n.*

re·prieve´ *n.* relief; deferment or repeal, as from punishment —*vt.* to suspend temporarily

rep´ri·mand *n.* censure; condemnation —*vt.* to admonish or censure

re·pri´sal *n.* retaliation

re·proach´ *n.* condemnation; disgrace —*vt.* to criticize or rebuke —re·proach´a·ble *adj.* —re·proach´a·bly *adv.* —re·proach´ful *adj.* —re·proach´ful·ly *adv.* —re·proach´ful·ness *n.*

rep´ro·bate *adj.* perverted —*n.* an immoral person —rep·ro·ba´tion *n.* —rep´ro·ba·tive *adj.*

re·pro·duce´ *vt.* to copy or duplicate; to propagate —re·pro·duc´tion *n.* —re·pro·duc´tive *adj.*

re·proof´ *n.* disapproval

re·prove´ *vt.* to criticize; to admonish —re·prov´al *n.* —re·prov´ing *adj.* —re·prov´ing·ly *adv.*

re·pub´lic *n.* a government controlled by the people or their representatives —re·pub´li·can *adj.*, *n.* —re·pub´li·can·ism *n.*

re·pu´di·ate *vt.* to reject or disavow; to disown —re·pu·di·a´tion *n.* —re·pu´di·a·tive *adj.* —re·pu´di·a·tor *n.*

re·pug´nance, re·pug´nan·cy *n.* a

feeling of dislike or repulsion

re·pug´nant *adj.* offensive; revolting —re·pug´nant·ly *adv.*

re·pulse´ *vt.* to fend off or repel, as an attack; to spurn by insolence or indifference —re·pul´sion *n.*

re·pul´sive *adj.* offensive; repugnant —re·pul´sive·ly *adv.* —re·pul´sive·ness *n.*

rep´u·ta·ble *adj.* of good reputation —rep·u·ta·bil´i·ty *n.* —rep´u·ta·bly *adv.*

rep·u·ta´tion *n.* one's standing; the way in which one is regarded by others; prominence or notoriety

re·pute´ *n.* reputation —*vt.* to deem or consider as —re·put´ed *adj.* —re·put´ed·ly *adv.*

re·quest´ *n.* an entreaty; something asked for —*vt.* to express a desire for —re·quest´er *n.*

re·quire´ *vt.* to need; to demand or oblige: *we require a deposit* —re·quire´ment *n.* —re·quir´er *n.*

req´ui·site *adj.* required —*n.* that which is necessary or obligatory —req´ui·site·ly *adv.*

req·ui·si´tion *n.* a formal request —req·ui·si´tion·er *n.*

re·quite´ *vt.* to repay or compensate; to return in kind —re·quit´a·ble *adj.* —re·quit´al *n.*

re·scind´ *vt.* to repeal; to nullify —re·scind´a·ble *adj.* —re·scind´ment *n.*

res´cue *vt.* to liberate; to set free —res´cu·a·ble *adj.* —res´cu·er *n.*

re·search´ *n.* scientific examination; deliberate study —re·search´a·ble *adj.* —re·search´er *n.*

re·sem´blance *n.* similarity to —re·sem´ble *vt.*

re·sent´ *vt.* to take offense, as at an insult or slight —re·sent´ful *adj.* —re·sent´ful·ly *adv.* —re·sent´ful·ness *n.* —re·sent´ment *n.*

res·er·va´tion *n.* something withheld; an agreement to hold, as a table at a restaurant; something set aside, as land for special use; hesitance or misgivings

re·serve′ *n.* restraint; caution; something set aside —*vt.* to set aside — **re·serv′a·ble** *adj.* —**re·serv′ed** *adj.* —**re·serv′ed·ly** *adv.* —**re·serv′ed·ness** *n.*

res′er·voir *n.* a reserve supply, as of water or oil

re·side′ *vi.* to inhabit; to live in

res′i·dence *n.* one's home —**res′i·den·cy** *n.* —**res′i·dent** *adj., n.* —**res′i·den′tial** *adj.*

res′i·due *n.* a remainder —**re·sid′u·al** *adj., n.* —**re·sid′u·al·ly** *adv.*

re·sign′ *vt.* to renounce or give up; to accept as unavoidable —**res·ig·na′tion** *n.*

re·signed *adj.* complacent; submissive —**re·sign′ed·ly** *adv.* —**re·sign′ed·ness** *n.*

re·sil′ience, re·sil′ien·cy *n.* flexibility —**re·sil′ient** *adj.* —**re·sil′ient·ly** *adv.*

re·sist′ *vt.* to defy or oppose; to withstand —**re·sist′er** *n.* —**re·sist′i·ble** *adj.* —**re·sist′i·bly** *adv.*

re·sis′tive *adj.* tending to or marked by resistance: *plants resistive to drought* —**re·sis′tive·ly** *adv.* —**re·sis′tive·ness** *n.*

re·sist′ance *n.* any force tending to hinder or oppose; the capacity of an organism to ward off harmful substances —**re·sist′ant** *adj.*

res′o·lute *adj.* determined —**res′o·lute·ly** *adv.* —**res′o·lute·ness** *n.*

res·o·lu′tion *n.* determination; an outcome; a formal pronouncement; visual clarity

re·solve′ *n.* a sense of purpose; determination —*vt.* to decide: *resolve to be neater*; to solve; to end successfully —**re·solv·a·bil′i·ty** *n.* —**re·solv′a·ble** *adj.* —**re·solv′ed·ly** *adv.* —**re·solv′er** *n.*

res′o·nant *adj.* sonorous; resounding —**res′o·nance** *n.* —**res′o·nant·ly** *adv.* —**res′o·nate** *vi.*

—**res·o·na′tion** *n.*

re·sort′ *n.* a vacation retreat; a resource —*vt.* to fall back on

re·sound′ *vi.* to echo; to reverberate —**re·sound′ing** *adj.* —**re·sound′ing·ly** *adv.*

re′source *n.* that available for use, as means for production, inner strength, property, etc.

re·source′ful *adj.* clever or imaginitive —**re·source′ful·ly** *adv.* —**re·source′ful·ness** *n.*

re·spect′ *n.* esteem or admiration; consideration: *a respect for power*; a feature or detail: *alike in many respects* —*vt.* to admire or esteem; to consider —**re·spect′er** *n.* —**re·spect′ful** *adj.* —**re·spect′ful·ly** *adv.* —**re·spect′ful·ness** *n.*

re·spect′a·ble *adj.* worthy of esteem; conventional —**re·spect·a·bil′i·ty, re·spect′a·ble·ness** *n.* —**re·spect′a·bly** *adv.*

re·spec′tive *adj.* specific or distinct —**re·spec′tive·ly** *adv.*

res·pi·ra′tion *n.* the process of breathing —**re·spi·ra·to·ry** *adj.*

res′pite *n.* a short rest

re·splen′dent *adj.* brilliant, sparkling —**re·splen′dence, re·splen′den·cy** *n.* —**re·splen′dent·ly** *adv.*

re·spond′ *vi.* to answer; to react: *respond to treatment* —**re·spon′dence, re·spon′den·cy** *n.* —**re·spon′dent** *adj.*

re·sponse′ *n.* a reply or reaction

re·spon′si·ble *adj.* accountable for one's actions; capable of acting alone —**re·spon·si·bil′i·ty** *n.* —**re·spon′si·ble·ness** *n.* —**re·spon′si·bly** *adv.*

re·spon′sive *adj.* tending to respond or react, as to advice, learning, etc. —**re·spon′sive·ly** *adv.* —**re·spon′sive·ness** *n.*

rest *n.* relaxation; a pause; a remainder —*vi., vt.* to relax; to lie against or on —**rest′ful** *adj.* —**rest′ful·ly** *adv.* —**rest′ful·ness** *n.*

res·tau·rant n. a public eating place —**res´tau·ra·teur´** n.

res·ti·tu´tion n. restoration; compensation

res´tive adj. impatient —**res´tive·ly** adv. —**res´tive·ness** n.

rest´less adj. uneasy; impatient; unable or unwilling to rest —**rest´less·ly** adv. —**rest´less·ness** n.

re·stor·a·tive adj. having power to restore; corrective —n. a substance that restores health or well–being: a tonic —**re·stor´a·tive·ly** adv. —**re·stor´a·tive·ness** n.

re·store´ vt. to return to a former condition, position, etc.; to make amends —**res·to·ra´tion** n. —**re·stor´er** n.

re·strain´ vt. to check or hold back; to confine —**re·strain´a·ble** adj.

re·straint´ n. control or restriction

re·strict´ vt. to limit —**re·strict´ed** adj. —**re·stric´tion** n.

re·stric´tive adj. serving to restrict or limit—**re·stric´tive·ly** adv. —**re·stric´tive·ness** n.

re·sult´ n. an effect, as of an action —vi. to follow as an outcome of —**re·sult´ant** adj.

re·sume´ vt. to begin again after an interruption —**re·sum´a·ble** adj. —**re·sump´tion** n.

ré´su·mé n. (Brit.) a summary or summing up; (US) a description of one's qualifications for employment

re·sur´gence n. a renewal or reawakening —**re·sur´gent** adj.

res·ur·rect´ vt. to restore or revive, as a past strategy or custom —**res·ur·rec´tion** n. —**res·ur·rec´tion·al** adj. —**res·ur·rec´tor** n.

re·sus·ci·tate vt., vi. to revive —**re·sus·ci·ta·ble** adj. —**re·sus·ci·ta´tion** n.

re´tail n. the sale of goods directly to consumers —vt. to sell in small quantity, direct to the consumer —adj., adv. —**re´tail·er** n.

re·tain´ vt. to keep in one's possession; to remember; to hire, as an attorney, by paying a fee —**re·tain´a·ble** adj.

re·tain´er n. a fee paid to engage or reserve services; a servant

re·tal´i·ate vi., vt. to repay in kind; to avenge —**re·tal·i·a´tion** n. —**re·tal´i·a·tive, re·tal´i·a·to·ry** adj. —**re·tal´i·a·tor** n.

re·tard´ n. a slowing —vt. to impede the course of —**re·tard´er** n.

re·ten´tion n. memory; the ability to keep and hold —**re·ten´tive** adj. —**re·ten´tive·ly** adv. —**re·ten´tive·ness** n.

ret´i·cent adj. restrained or reserved; hesitant —**ret´i·cence** n. —**ret´i·cent·ly** adv.

ret´i·nue n. a group of followers

re·tire´ vi., vt. to withdraw or be removed, as from a field of battle, from an occupation, or at the end of a day —**re·tired´** adj. —**re·tir·ee´** n. —**re·tire´ment** n.

re·tir´ing adj. withdrawn

re·tort´ n. a sharp reply —vt., vi. to respond —**re·tort´er** n.

re·tract´ vt., vi. to take back, as an accusation —**re·tract·a·bil´i·ty, re·tract·i·bil´i·ty** n. —**re·tract´a·ble, re·tract´i·ble** adj. —**re·trac´tion** n.

ret·ri·bu´tion n. compensation; reward or punishment

re·trieve´ vt. to regain —**re·triev·a·bil´i·ty** n. —**re·triev´a·ble** adj. —**re·triev´al** n. —**re·triev´er** n.

ret´ro adj. of things past; retroactive

ret·ro·ac´tive adj. applying to a prior period —**ret´ro·ac´tion** n. —**ret·ro·ac´tive·ly** adv.

ret´ro·grade adj. opposite; regressing to a prior state

ret´ro·gress vi. to revert to an earlier state —**ret·ro·gres´sion** n. —**ret·ro·gres´sive** adj. —**ret·ro·gres´sive·ly** adv.

ret´ro·spect n. a reflection of things

past; a look back —**ret·ro·spec'·tion** n. —**ret·ro·spec'tive** adj. —**ret·ro·spec'tive·ly** adv.

re·turn' adj. of a coming back or reciprocating —n. a thing brought or sent back; a profit —vi., vt. to go or send back; to yield, as a profit; to revert to a former owner —**re·turn'a·ble** adj. —**re·turn·ee'** n.

re·un'ion n. a gathering of former members: a class reunion

re·vamp' vt. to reorganize or renovate

re·veal' vt. to expose or disclose

rev'el vi. to delight in; to carouse —n. a celebration —**rev'el·er, rev'el·ler** n. —**rev'el·ry** n.

rev·e·la'tion n. something revealed; sudden inspiration or understanding

re·venge' n. reprisal or retribution —vt. to retaliate —**re·venge'ful** adj. —**re·venge'ful·ly** adv.

rev'e·nue n. income; gross receipts

re·ver'ber·ant adj. tending to or characterized by reverberation —**re·ver'ber·ant·ly** adv.

re·ver'ber·ate vt. to resound or echo repeatedly —**re·ver·ber·a'tion** n. —**re·ver'ber·a·tive** adj. —**re·ver'ber·a·tor** n.

re·vere' vt. to regard with awe; to venerate —**rev'er·ence** n. —**rev'er·ent** adj. —**rev'er·en'tial** adj. —**rev'er·ent·ly** adv.

rev'er·ie n. idle contemplation; daydreaming

re·verse' adj. backward; opposite —n. an opposite side, condition, etc.; misfortune —vt. to change to the opposite, as of a movement, a decision, etc. —**re·ver'sal** n. —**re·vers·i·bil'i·ty, re·vers'i·ble·ness** n. —**re·vers'i·ble** adj. —**re·vers'i·bly** adv.

re·vert' vi. to return to previous condition —**re·ver'sion** n. —**re·vert'er** n. —**re·vert'i·ble** adj.

re·view' n. a reexamination; a critique or criticism —vt. to reconsider or restudy —**re·view'a·ble** adj. —**re·view'er** n.

re·vile' vt. to berate verbally —**re·vile'ment** n. —**re·vil'er** n. —**re·vil'ing·ly** adv.

re·vise' vt. to change or modify —**re·vis'a·ble** adj. —**re·vis'al** n. —**re·vis'er** n. —**re·vi'sion** n. —**re·vi'sion·ar·y** adj.

re·vive' vt., vi. to restore to consciousness or life; to bring or come back into use —**re·viv'al** n.

re·voke' vt. to nullify or repeal —**rev'o·ca·ble, re·vok'a·ble** adj. —**rev·o·ca'tion** n. —**re·vo·ca·to·ry** adj. —**re·vok'er** n.

re·volt' n. a rebellion —vi. to oppose or rebel; to disgust —**re·volt'er** n. —**re·volt'ing** adj. —**re·volt'ing·ly** adv.

rev·o·lu'tion n. rotation; an abrupt, radical change —**rev·o·lu'tion·ar'i·ly** adv. —**rev·o·lu'tion·ar·y** adj. —**rev·o·lu'tion·ist** n., adj. —**rev·o·lu'tion·ize** vt.

re·volve' vi. to rotate; to turn on an axis

re·vue' n. a musical comedy show

re·vul'sion n. a sudden aversion or abhorrence —**re·vulsed'** adj. —**re·vul'sive** adj.

re·ward' n. compensation, as for a commendable act —vt. to recompense —**re·ward'a·ble** adj. —**re·ward'ing** adj.

rhap'so·dy n. a state of ecstasy; excessive enthusiasm; an elegant literary or musical work —**rhap·sod'ic, rhap·sod'i·cal** adj. —**rhap·sod'i·cal·ly** adv. —**rhap'so·dist** n. —**rhap'so·dize** vt., vi.

rhet'o·ric n. the art of effective speaking or writing; pretentious, vacuous speech —**rhe·tor'i·cal** adj. —**rhe·tor'i·cal·ly** adv. —**rhet·o·ri'cian** n.

rhyme n. a similarity in the sounds of words; verse with lines ending in words that sound similar —*vi.*, *vt.* —**rhym´er** *n.*

rhythm *n.* regular cadence or accent; the harmonious pattern of a work —**rhyth´mic, rhyth´mi·cal** *adj.* —**rhyth´mi·cal·ly** *adv.*

rib´ald *adj.* marked by vulgar humor —**rib´al·dry** *n.*

rib´bon *n.* a thin strip of material used for tying, for decoration, etc. —**rib´boned** *adj.* —**rib´bon·y** *adj.*

rich *adj.* wealthy; plentiful; elegant or lavish —**rich´es** *n.* —**rich´ly** *adv.* —**rich´ness** *n.*

rick´et·y *adj.* wobbly

rid *vt.* to release or free from —**rid´dance** *n.* —**rid´der** *n.*

rid´dle *n.* a puzzle —*vt.* to perforate

ride *vi.* to be conveyed; seeming to be conveyed: *riding on a cloud* —**rid´er** *n.* —**rid´ing** *n.*

rid´i·cule *n.* words or action intended to mock; derision —*vt.* to make fun of

ri·dic´u·lous *adj.* absurd; deserving of ridicule —**ri·dic´u·lous·ly** *adv.* —**ri·dic´u·lous·ness** *n.*

rife *adj.* abundant

ri´fle *n.* a firearm —*vt.* to search through or plunder

rift *n.* a fracture or tear

right *adj.* fitting and proper; equitable; accurate; lawful —*adv.* exactly; quite —*n.* that which is proper; privilege —*vt.* to correct —**right´ful** *adj.* —**right´ful·ly** *adv.* —**right´ful·ness** *n.* —**right´ly** *adv.*

right´eous *adj.* moral; virtuous —**righ´teous·ly** *adv.* —**righ´teous·ness** *n.*

rig´id *adj.* stiff; inflexible —**ri·gid´i·ty** *n.* —**rig´id·ly** *adv.* —**rig´id·ness** *n.*

rig´or (*US*) *n.* harshness; hardship —**rig´or·ous** *adj.* —**rig´or·ous·ly** *adv.* —**rig´or·ous·ness** *n.*

rig´our (*Brit.*) *n.* harshness; hardship —**rig´or·ous** *adj.* —**rig´or·ous·ly** *adv.* —**rig´or·ous·ness** *n.*

rile *vt.* to anger; to irritate or vex

rim *n.* a border or edge

rind *n.* a firm covering, as on fruit or bacon

ring *n.* a circular object, area, shape, etc.; a group or gang: *an extortion ring*

ring´let *n.* a lock of hair

rinse *n.* a liquid used in washing, to remove soap, to color the hair, etc. —*vt.* —**rins´a·ble, rins´i·ble** *adj.* —**rins´er** *n.*

ri´ot *n.* a public disturbance involving a large group of people; an eruption, as of merriment or revelry —*vi.* —**ri´ot·er** *n.* —**ri´ot·ous** *adj.* —**ri´ot·ous·ly** *adv.* —**ri´ot·ous·ness** *n.*

rip *n.* a tear or split —*vt.*

ripe *adj.* mature; fully developed —**ripe´ly** *adv.* —**rip´en** *vt.*, *vi.* —**ripe´ness** *n.*

rip´ple *n.* a small wave or wave–like motion —*vi.* —**rip´ply** *adj.*

rise *vi.* to move or proceed upward; to increase, as in price, intensity, etc.; to get up, as from a chair or bed; to emerge or originate —**ris´er** *n.* —**ris´ing** *adj.*

risk *n.* possible hazard or danger; the probability for loss, as by an investor, a lender, an insurer, etc. —**risk´i·ness** *n.* —**risk´y** *adj.*

ris·qué´ *adj.* lewd or suggestive

rite *n.* a ritual or ceremony

rit´u·al *n.* an observance; a formality; an orderly procedure —*adj.* —**rit´u·al·ism** *n.* —**rit´u·al·ist** *n.* —**rit´u·al·is´tic** *adj.* —**rit´u·al·is´ti·cal·ly, rit´u·al·ly** *adv.* —**rit´u·al·ize** *vt.* —**rit·u·al·i·za´tion** *n.*

ri´val *n.* one in competition with another —*vt.* to equal or exceed —*adj.* competing —**ri´val·rous** *adj.* —**ri´val·ry** *n.*

rive *vt.* to split or tear apart

riv´er *n.* a large body of naturally flowing water; an abundant flow —**sell down the river** to betray

riv´et *n.* a fastener used to join metal plates —*vt.* to join with a rivet; to fasten firmly; to attract and hold the attention of —**riv´et·er** *n.*

road *n.* a course for the passage of vehicles, etc.; any real or imagined course: *the road to ruin* —**road´way** *n.*

roam *vt., vi.* to wander or move about —**roam´er** *n.*

roar *n.* a deep, prolonged cry; a burst of laughter —*vi., vt.*

roar´ing *adj.* flourishing or robust —**roar´ing·ly** *adv.*

roast *vt.* to cook with dry heat; to subject to excessive heat; to deride —*n.* (*US*) a cut of meat; a gathering; derision —*adj.* —**roast´er** *n.*

rob *vt.* to take or withhold unjustly —**rob´ber** *n.* —**rob´ber·y** *n.*

robe *n.* a loose flowing garment; a dressing gown

ro´bot *n.* a device that can be programmed to perform a variety of tasks; one who functions mechanically —**ro·bot´ic** *adj.*

ro·bot´ics *n.* the scientific study of robots; the creation of robots

ro·bust´ *adj.* strong and healthy —**ro·bust´ly** *adv.* —**ro·bust´ness** *n.*

rock *n.* a hard natural formation; a firm support: *he's been a rock in these difficult times* —*vi., vt.* to wobble or sway

rock´y *adj.* containing or suggesting rock; unsteady; difficult or discouraging, as though moving over rocks —**rock´i·ness** *n.*

ro·co´co *n.* an ornate style of architecture, music, etc.

rod *n.* a thin straight shaft

rogue *n.* a scoundrel; a mischievous person; an abnormal plant or animal —**rogu´er·y** *n.* —**rogu´ish** *adj.* —**rogu´ish·ly** *adv.* —**rogu´ish·ness** *n.*

roil *vt.* to disturb or stir up —**roil´y** *adj.*

role *n.* a part for an actor; the behavior or attention to duty expected of a person

roll *n.* a cylinder, as of film, tape, etc.; a small piece of baked bread; a registry; a rocking motion —*vi., vt.* to move or cause to move by turning; anything that suggests such movement: *get the program rolling, the clouds rolled by* —**roll´er** *n.*

rol´lick·ing *adj.* playful; boisterous —**rol´lick·ing·ly** *adv.* —**rol´lick·some, rol´lick·y** *adj.*

ro·mance´ *n.* a passionate fondness, such as infatuation or love; a fascination; a fantasy or fictional account —*vi. vt.* —**ro·manc´er** *n.*

ro·man´tic *adj.* characterized by thoughts or feelings of infatuation, idealism, etc.; visionary; impractical —*n.* —**ro·man´ti·cal·ly** *adv.*

ro·man´ti·cize *vt.* to regard as romantic —**ro·man·ti·ci·za´tion** *n.*

romp *vi.* to frolic or play —*n.* noisy frolic; an easy victory —**romp´er** *n.*

roof *n.* a top covering; an upper surface —*vt.* —**roof´er** *n.*

room *n.* adequate space; a divided area within a structure —*vi.* to occupy a room —**room´er** *n.*

room´y *adj.* spacious; having adequate space —**room´i·ness** *n.*

root *n.* the base of a plant that usually grows underground; a base, source, or core; a mental or emotional attachment —*vi., vt.* —**root´er** *n.*

ros´ter *n.* a list

ros´trum *n.* a speaker's platform

ros´y *adj.* bright and flushed, as a rose; optimistic

rot *n.* decomposition; silliness —*vi.* to decay or disintegrate —**rot´ten** *adj., adv.* —**rot´ten·ly** *adv.* —**rot´ten·ness** *n.*

ro·tate´ *vt., vi.* to revolve; to proceed by turns —**ro·tat´a·ble** *adj.* —**ro·ta´tion** *n.* —**ro·ta´tion·al** *adj.*

rote *n.* a method for learning by repetition

ro·tund *adj.* round; plump —**ro·tun·di·ty** *n.*

rough *adj.* of a coarse or irregular surface; crude or impolite; difficult; disorderly —**rough·en** *vt.* —**rough·en·er** *n.* —**rough·ly** *adv.* —**rough·ness** *n.*

round *adj.* curved; of a curved shape, as a circle, globe, cylinder, etc.; full-toned; approximate: *a round number* —*n.* an accumulation, as *a round of drinks, a round of activities,* etc. —**round·ed** *adj.* —**round·ed·ness, round·ness** *n.*

round·a·bout *adj.* circuitous or indirect: *a roundabout answer*

rouse *vi., vt.* to awaken or cause to wake; to excite to action —**rous·er** *n.* —**rous·ing** *adj.* —**rous·ing·ly** *adv.*

rout *n.* a defeat; disorderly flight —*vt.* to defeat or put to flight

route *n.* a road or course; an itinerary —*vt.* to send or direct by a certain course —**rout·er** *n.*

rou·tine *adj.* usual or customary —*n.* a regular procedure —**rou·tine·ly** *adv.* —**rou·tin·ize** *vt.*

rove *vi., vt.* to wander —**rov·er** *n.*

row *n.* a continuous line; a disturbance —*vt.*

row·dy *adj.* clamorous; disorderly —*n.* a ruffian —**row·di·ly** *adv.* —**row·di·ness** *n.* —**row·dy·ism** *n.*

rub *vi., vt.* to stroke using pressure —*n.* a pitfall

rub·bish *n.* trash; nonsense —**rub·bish·y** *adj.*

rub·ble *n.* stone fragments —**rub·bly** *adj.*

rub·down *n.* a massage

rude *adj.* ill-mannered; unrefined; crude, primitive —**rude·ly** *adv.* —**rude·ness** *n.*

ru·di·ment *n.* a basic component —**ru·di·men·tal** *adj.*

ru·di·men·ta·ry *adj.* fundamental; embryonic —**ru·di·men·ta·ri·ly** *adv.* —**ru·di·men·ta·ri·ness** *n.*

rue *vi., vt.* to regret —**rue·ful** *adj.* —**rue·ful·ly** *adv.* —**rue·ful·ness** *n.*

ruf·fi·an *n.* a hoodlum or tough

ruf·fle *n.* a frilled trim —*vi.* to rumple or wrinkle; to irritate or annoy

rug·ged *adj.* sturdy; strong; tempestuous —**rug·ged·ly** *adv.* —**rug·ged·ness** *n.*

ru·in *n.* total destruction —*vt.* to destroy utterly —**ru·in·ous** *adj.* —**ru·in·ous·ly** *adv.*

rule *n.* a governing authority; regulation; a generally accepted condition or course of action —*vi., vt.* to direct and control; to judge or decree —**rul·a·ble** *adj.* —**rul·er** *n.*

rum·ble *n.* a deep undulating sound —*vi.* —**rum·bler** *n.* —**rum·bling·ly** *adv.* —**rum·bly** *adj.*

ru·mi·nate *vi., vt.* to ponder; consider intensely —**ru·mi·na·tion** *n.* —**ru·mi·na·tive** *adj.* —**ru·mi·na·tive·ly** *adv.* —**ru·mi·na·tor** *n.*

rum·mage *vt.* to search thoroughly; to disorganize while inspecting —**rum·mag·er** *n.*

ru·mor *n.* gossip; unconfirmed news —**ru·mor·mon·ger** *n.*

rum·ple *vt.* to wrinkle —**rum·ply** *adj.*

run *n.* an indefinite period: *for the run of the play;* ordinary: *run of the mill* —*vi.* to move swiftly; to move or operate: *the motor runs smoothly;* to flow, as liquid from a container; to extend: *the road runs up to the house, the trees run along the road,* etc. —**run·ner** *n.* —**run·ning** *adj., n.*

rup·ture *n.* a break —*vt., vi.* to break apart

ru·ral *adj.* of the country —**ru·ral·ly** *adv.*

ruse *n.* a ploy or stratagem

rush *n.* abrupt motion; haste; a swell of emotion —*vi.* to move quickly

rus·tic *adj.* rural; unsophisticated

—rus´ti·cal·ly *adv.*

rus´tle *vt.*, *vi.* to make a soft crackling sound

rut *n.* a groove worn into a path or roadway —**rut´ty** *adj.*

ruth´less *adj.* lacking pity or compassion —**ruth´less·ly** *adv.* —ruth´less·ness *n.*

s, S nineteenth letter of the English alphabet

sab·bat´i·cal *n.* a leave of absence, often a paid leave for travel and research

sa´ber *n.* a curved sword

sa·bot´ *n.* a wooden shoe

sab´o·tage *n.* destructive action to obstruct or defeat an enemy —*vi. vt.* —**sab´o·teur´** *n.*

sa´chem *n.* a Native American chieftan

sa·chet´ *n.* a small perfumed parcel used to freshen the clothing in drawers or closets

sack *n.* a bag for holding loose articles; dismissal from a job —*vt.* to plunder; to dismiss

sac´ra·ment *n.* a traditional religious rite —**sac·ra·men´tal** *adj.* —**sac·ra·men´tal·ly** *adv.*

sa´cred *adj.* deserving of reverence or respect —**sa´cred·ly** *adv.* —**sa´ cred·ness** *n.*

sac´ri·fice *n.* an offering —*vt.* to give something valued for a thing considered more valuable: *she sacrificed her career to raise a family* —**sac´ri·fi·cer** *n.* —**sac·ri·fi´cial** *adj.* —**sac·ri·fi´cial·ly** *adv.* —**sac´ri·fic· ing·ly** *adv.*

sac´ri·lege *n.* desecration or disrespect of that considered sacred —**sac·ri·le´gious** *adj.* —**sac·ri·le´ gious·ly** *adv.* —**sac·ri·le´gious· ness** *n.*

sac´ro·sanct *adj.* sacred or hallowed —**sac´ro·sanc´ti·ty** *n.*

sad *adj.* unhappy; sorrowful or downhearted; somber; dire or

unfortunate: *a sad state of affairs* —**sad´den** *vt.*, *vi.* —**sad´ly** *adv.* —sad´ness *n.*

sa´dism *n.* the achieving of satisfaction by inflicting pain on others; a psychological disorder —**sa´dist** *n.* —**sa·dis´tic** *adj.* —**sa·dis´ti·cal·ly** *adv.*

sa·fa´ri *n.* a journey, especially for hunting

safe *adj.* free from risk or danger — *n.* a repository for protecting property —**safe´ly** *adv.* —**safe´ty** *n.*

safe´guard *n.* something that protects, as a mechanism, a preventive measure, a clause in a contract, etc. —*vt.* to protect

sag *vi.* to droop or slump

sa·ga´cious *adj.* discerning; wise — **sa·ga´cious·ly** *adv.* —**sa·ga´cious· ness** *n.* —**sa·gac´i·ty** *n.*

sage *adj.* wise and discerning — **sage´ly** *adv.* —**sage´ness** *n.*

saint *n.* one recognized as being extremely virtuous —**saint´ed** *adj.* —**saint´li·ness** *n.* —**saint´ly** *adj.*

sake *n.* reason or purpose: *for the sake of argument;* self-interest: *for the sake of his career*

sal´a·ble, sale´a·ble *adj.* marketable

sa·la´cious *adj.* arousing sexual desire; lascivious —**sa·la´cious·ly** *adv.* —**sa·la´cious·ness, sa·lac´ i·ty** *n.*

sal´a·ry *n.* fixed wages —**sal´a·ried** *adj.*

sale *n.* the exchange of goods or services for money —**sales´man, sales´per·son, sales´wom·an** *n.*

sa´li·ent *adj.* important or conspicuous; protruding —**sa´lience** *n.* — **sa´li·ent·ly** *adv.*

sa´line *adj.* consisting or or characteristic of salt; salty —**sa·lin´i·ty** *n.*

sal´low *adj.* of a sickly or pasty complexion —**sal´low·ness** *n.*

sal´ly *n.* a sudden assault; an excursion; a witty remark —*vi.* to rush out suddenly or energetically

sa·lon´ *n.* a large room or gallery for receiving guests; a fashionable social or intellectual gathering

sal´sa *n.* a spicy sauce

salt *n.* a crystalline substance used to season or preserve food, or as medication; table salt —*vt.* to add salt; to treat with a salt; to disperse throughout: *salted the report with statistics*

salt´y *adj.* containing too much salt; spirited or risqué, as *salty language* —**salt´i·ly** *adv.* —**salt´i·ness** *n.*

sa·lu´bri·ous *adj.* healthy or wholesome —**sa·lu´bri·ous·ly** *adv.* —**sa·lu´bri·ous·ness, sa·lu´bri·ty** *n.*

sal´u·tar·y *adj.* beneficial —**sal·u·tar´i·ly** *adv.* —**sal´u·tar·i·ness** *n.*

sal·u·ta´tion *n.* a greeting —**sal·u·ta´tion·al** *adj.*

sa·lute´ *n.* an act or form of greeting; a gesture of welcome or honor: *a salute to a great poet* —*vt.* to greet; to honor, as with a gesture of respect

sal´vage *n.* property saved from destruction —*vt.* to retrieve for future use —**sal´va·ble, sal´vage·a·ble** *adj.* —**sal·vage·a·bil´i·ty** *n.* —**sal´vag·er** *n.*

salve *n.* an ointment —*vt.* to alleviate or remedy, as by soft words or apology

same *adj.* identical

same´ness *n.* monotony; a lack of diversity

sam´ple *n.* a representative part; an example —*vt.* to test by tasting

sa´mu·rai *n.* a Japanese warrior class

san·a·tar´i·um, san·a·to´ri·um *n.* a hospital or retreat for therapy or fitness

sanc·ti·mo´ni·ous *adj.* pretentiously pious —**sanc·ti·mo´ni·ous·ly** *adv.* —**sanc·ti·mo´ni·ous·ness** *n.* —**sanc´ti·mo·ny** *n.*

sanc´tion *n.* authorization or permission; a penalty for nonconformity —*vt.* to approve; to punish for transgression

sanc´tu·ar·y *n.* a sacred place; an asylum

san´dal *n.* an open shoe held on with straps

sane *adj.* having a sound mind —**sane´ly** *adv.* —**sane´ness** *n.*

san´guine *adj.* optimistic; confident; of a red or ruddy color —**san´guine·ly** *adv.* —**san´guine·ness** *n.*

san´i·tar´i·um *n.* a sanatorium

san´i·tar·y *adj.* uncontaminated; free of germs

san·i·ta´tion *n.* the process of maintaining sanitary conditions; a local agency responsible for the removal of garbage

san´i·tize *vt.* to make sanitary

san´i·ty *n.* soundness of mind

sans *prep.* without

sap´i·ent *adj.* wise —**sap´i·ence** *n.* —**sap´i·ent·ly** *adv.*

sar´casm *n.* a caustic rejoinder intended to ridicule —**sar·cas´tic** *adj.* —**sar·cas´ti·cal·ly** *adv.*

sar·coph´a·gus *n.* a stone coffin

sar·don´ic *adj.* sarcastic —**sar·don´i·cal·ly** *adv.*

sar·to´ri·al *adj.* of a clothier or clothing —**sar·to´ri·al·ly** *adv.*

sash *n.* a band of cloth worn as a belt or a mark of rank; a frame for a window pane

sa·shay´ *n.* an overly casual or showy style of movement —*vi.*

sas´sy *adj.* insolent, disrespectful; spirited, jaunty —**sass** *n.*, *vt.*

sa·tan´ic, sa·tan´i·cal *adj.* wicked; diabolic —**sa·tan´i·cal·ly** *adv.*

sate *vt.* satiate

sat´el·lite *n.* a celestial body that orbits a planet; a dependency, as a community or nation that is dominated or dependent on another

sa´ti·a·ble *adj.* that can be satisfied —**sa·ti·a·bil´i·ty** *n.* —**sa´ti·a·bly** *adv.*

sa·ti·ate *vt.* to satisfy completely — **sa·ti·a·tion** *n.*

sat·ire *n.* a literary work that uses mockery or ridicule to expose human frailty —**sa·tir·ic, sa·tir·i·cal** *adj.* —**sa·tir·i·cal·ly** *adv.* —**sat·i·rist** *n.* —**sat·i·rize** *vt.*

sat·is·fac·tion *n.* gratification; fulfillment, as of an obligation — **sat·is·fac·to·ri·ly** *adv.* —**sat·is·fac·to·ry** *adj.*

sat·is·fy *vt.* to fulfill, as a desire or promise; to convince or persuade; to pacify —*vi.* to be sufficient — **sat·is·fied** *adj.* —**sat·is·fi·er** *n.* — **sat·is·fy·ing·ly** *adv.*

sa·trap *n.* a petty official

sat·u·rate *vt.* to soak or fill completely —**sat·u·rant** *n.* —**sat·u·rat·ed** *adj.* —**sat·u·ra·tion** *n.* —**sat·u·ra·tor** *n.*

sa·tyr *n.* a mythical creature, part man and part goat —**sa·tyr·ic, sa·tyr·i·cal** *adj.*

sauce *n.* a seasoned liquid or condiment served with food; a gravy

sau·cy *adj.* impudent; pert —**sau·ci·ly** *adv.* —**sau·ci·ness** *n.*

saun·ter *vi.* to stroll leisurely — **saun·ter·er** *n.*

sau·té *vt.* to fry lightly

sav·age *adj.* uncivilized; vicious, ferocious —*n.* a rude or unruly person —*vt.* to attack —**sav·age·ly** *adv.* —**sav·age·ness** *n.* —**sav·age·ry** *n.*

save *vt.* to rescue from danger or destruction; to set aside for the future; to conserve —**sav·able** *adj.* —**sav·er** *n.*

sa·vor *n.* a characteristic flavor or quality —*vt.* to season; to taste; to relish, enjoy —**sa·vor·er** *n.* —**sa·vor·y** *adj.*

say *vt.* to speak; to express in words; to allege —*vi.* to speak

saying *n.* a maxim or axiom

scab·bard *n.* a sheath for a weapon

scab·rous *adj.* roughened; difficult to handle tactfully; salacious — **scab·rous·ly** *adv.* —**scab·rous·ness** *n.*

scaf·fold *n.* a raised platform; a temporary structure for workmen —**scaf·fold·ing** *n.*

scal·a·wag *n.* a worthless person; a rascal

scald *vt., vi.* to burn or become burned or cleaned with hot liquid or steam —*n.*

scale[1] *n.* a protective plate covering certain fish, reptiles, etc. —*vt., vi.* to strip of scales; to form scales — **scal·y** *adj.* —**scal·i·ness** *n.*

scale[2] *vt., vi.* to ascend; to climb — **scal·er** *n.* —**scal·a·ble** *adj.*

scal·lop *n.* any of various hinged shell mollusks; an ornamental edging —**scal·loped** *adj.* —**scal·lop·er** *n.*

scalp *n.* the skin at the top and back of the head —*vt.* to buy and resell tickets for a profit —**scalp·er** *n.*

scal·pel *n.* a surgical knife

scamp *n.* a rogue or rascal; a scalawag; an impish child —**scamp·ish** *adj.* —**scamp·ish·ness** *n.*

scam·per *vi.* to run quickly

scan *vt.* to examine closely; to glance at —**scan·ner** *n.*

scan·dal *n.* injury to one's reputation; malicious gossip —**scan·dal·ous** *adj.* —**scan·dal·ous·ly** *adv.* — **scan·dal·ous·ness** *n.*

scan·dal·ize *vt.* to shock; to outrage morally —**scan·dal·i·za·tion** *n.*

scant *adj.* meager; a bit less than — **scant·ly** *adv.* —**scant·ness** *n.*

scant·y *adj.* too little; insufficient; less than necessary —**scant·i·ly** *adv.* —**scant·i·ness** *n.*

scar *n.* a mark left after healing

scarce *adj.* rare, unusual; insufficient —**scar·ci·ty, scarce·ness** *n.* —**scarce·ly** *adv.*

scare *vt.* to frighten —*vi.* to take fright —**scar·i·ly** *adv.* —**scar·y** *adj.*

scarf *n.* a cloth band worn as a garment; a table runner

scarp *n.* a steep slope

scathe *vt.* to criticize severely; to denounce —**scath´ing** *adj.* — **scath´ing·ly** *adv.*

sca·tol´o·gy *n.* the study of excrement —**scat·o·log´ic, scat·o·log´i·cal** *adj.*

scat´ter *vt.* to throw about; to disperse —*vi.* to separate and depart —**scat´tered** *adj.* —**scat´ter·er** *n.*

scav´enge *vt.* to forage; to scrounge —**scav´eng·er** *n.*

sce·nar´io *n.* an outline of a dramatic work

scene *n.* a locality or area; a setting for a drama

sce´ner·y *n.* landscape; a theater backdrop

sce´nic *adj.* of a beautiful natural vista —**sce´ni·cal·ly** *adv.*

scent *n.* an odor or aroma; a fragrance —**scent´ed** *adj.*

scep´ter *n.* a wand or staff denoting authority

sched´ule *n.* (*US*) a timetable; (*Brit.*) a plan or list of appointments, social activities, etc.; a detailed plan —*vt.* to plan to take place at a specified time

sche´ma *n.* a summary or diagram

sche·mat´ic *adj.* relating to a scheme —*n.* a diagram —**sche·mat´i·cal·ly** *adv.*

scheme *n.* a plan or program; a plot —*vt., vi.* to plan or plot —**schem´er** *n.*

schism *n.* a division into factious groups —**schis·mat´ic** *adj.* — **schis·mat´i·cal·ly** *adv.*

schol´ar *n.* a learned person; an authority —**schol´ar·ly** *adj.*

schol´ar·ship *n.* learning; financial or other aid to a student

scho·las´tic, scho·las´ti·cal *adj.* pertaining to education —**scho·las´ti·cal·ly** *adv.*

school *n.* an educational institution; a congregation of fish —*vi.* to come together in a school

school´ing *n.* formal instruction; classroom instruction

sci´ence *n.* knowledge gained by observation and experiment —**sci·en·tif´ic** *adj.* —**sci·en·tif´i·cal·ly** *adv.* —**sci´en·tist** *n.*

scim´i·tar *n.* a curved saber

scin·til´la *n.* a trace

scin´til·late *vi.* to be witty; to sparkle —**scin´til·lat·ing** *adj.* —**scin´til·lat·ing·ly** *adv.* —**scin·til·la´tion** *n.*

sci´on *n.* a descendant

scoff *vi.* to address scornfully — **scoff´er** *n.*

scold *vt., vi.* to find fault —*n.* a nag —**scold´er** *n.*

sconce *n.* an ornamental bracket

scoop *n.* an implement for measuring or dipping; a ladle —*vt.* to dip with a scoop

scope *n.* a range of view or action

scorch *vt.* to burn slightly —*n.* the mark of a burn

score *n.* points in a game or test; written music; a group of 20

scorn *n.* a feeling of contempt —*vt.* to treat with contempt —**scorn´ful** *adj.* —**scorn´ful·ly** *adv.* —**scorn´ful·ness** *n.*

scotch *vt.* to wound; to suppress

scoun´drel *n.* an unscrupulous person; a villain

scour *vt.* to clean thoroughly; to brighten by rubbing

scourge *n.* a whip; severe punishment; anything causing suffering —*vt.* to flog or otherwise punish — **scourg´er** *n.*

scout *n.* one sent out to get information —*vt.* to spy upon

scowl *n.* an angry or gloomy aspect —*vi.* to wrinkle the brow; to look threatening or angry —*vt.* to express by scowling —**scowl´er** *n.* —**scowl´ing·ly** *adv.*

scrag´gly *adj.* uneven, irregular

scram´ble *vi.* to move in a disorderly manner —*vt.* to mix hurriedly or haphazardly —*n.* a struggle — **scram´bler** *n.*

scrap *n.* a fragment; a quarrel —*vt.* to discard —*vi.* to quarrel —*adj.* waste; fragmentary

scrape *vt.* to rub so as to abrade; to gather with effort —*n.* the act, effect, or noise of scraping; a difficult situation; a fight —**scrap´er** *n.*

scrap´py *adj.* very competitive; tough —**scrap´pi·ly** *adv.* —**scrap´pi·ness** *n.*

scratch *vt.* to mark with something sharp; to scrape lightly as to relieve itching; to write hurriedly; to cancel or withdraw —*vi.* to manage with difficulty —*n.* a mark or sound of scratching —*adj.* hasty or haphazard —**scratch´er** *n.* — **scratch´i·ly** *adv.* —**scratch´i·ness** *n.* —**scratch´y** *adj.*

scrawl *n.* irregular or illegible writing —*vt.*, *vi.* to write hastily —**scrawl´er** *n.*

scrawn´y *adj.* lean and bony — **scrawn´i·ness** *n.*

scream *n.* a piercing cry —*vt.*, *vi.* to cry out, as in pain or terror — **scream´er** *n.* —**scream´ing·ly** *adv.*

screech *n.* a shrill cry; any similar sound: the screech of brakes — **screech´er** *n.* —**screech´i·ness** *n.* —**screech´y** *adj.*

screed *n.* a prolonged tirade; a harangue

screen *n.* a light partition; a fine mesh; something that conceals or protects; a curtain for projecting images —*vt.* to conceal; to sift; to classify —**screen´er** *n.*

screw *n.* a threaded mechanical device for joining or affixing —*vt.*, *vi.* to tighten or fasten

scrib´ble *vt.* to write hastily —*n.* — **scrib´bler** *n.*

scribe *n.* a clerk or public writer

scrim *n.* a lightweight fabric

scrimp *vt.*, *vi.* to be economical; to skimp

scrip *n.* writing; an instrument of entitlement, as to stock, property, or money

script *n.* cursive writing; the text of a play —**script´er** *n.*

scrip´ture *n.* sacred writings — **scrip´tur·al** *adj.* —**scrip´tur·al·ly** *adv.*

scriv´en·er *n.* a scribe or notary

scroll *n.* a parchment roll

scrounge *vt.*, *vi.* to scavenge; to forage —**scroung´er** *n.*

scrub *vt.*, *vi.* to rub vigorously —*n.* stunted growth —**scrub´bi·ness** *n.* —**scrub´by** *adj.*

scruff *n.* the nape of the neck

scruff´y *adj.* shabby, seedy

scrump´tious *adj.* delicious; elegant —**scrump´tious·ly** *adj.* —**scrump´tious·ness** *n.*

scru´ple *n.* reluctance fostered by disapproval —**scru´pu·lous** *adj.* — **scru´pu·lous·ly** *adv.* —**scru´pu·lous·ness** *n.*

scru´ti·nize *vt.* to examine carefully; to observe —**scru´ti·niz·er** *n.* — **scru´ti·ny** *n.*

scuf´fle *n.* a disorderly struggle —*vi.* to struggle; to drag one's feet

sculp´ture *n.* a three–dimensional work of art —*vt.* to fashion or manufacture such a work —**sculp´tor** *n.*

scum *n.* impure matter on the surface of a liquid; a low, contemptible person —**scum´mi·ness** *n.* — **scum´my** *adj.*

scur´ril·ous *adj.* grossly offensive; abusive: *a scurrilous attack* — **scur´ril·ous·ly** *adv.* —**scur´ril·ous·ness** *n.*

scur´ry *vi.* to move hurriedly; to scamper

scut´tle *n.* a small covered opening or hatchway —*vt.* to wreck or destory; to sink a ship; to move like a crab

sea *n.* a great body of salt water; the ocean; anything vast

seal *n.* an impression made on a document attesting to its authenticity; a decorative stamp —*vt.* to close securely or permanently — **seal´able** *adj.* —**seal´er** *n.*

seam *n.* a visible junction between parts

seam´y *adj.* unpleasant; depraved or base; squalid —**seam´i·ness** *n.*

sé´ance *n.* a sitting; a meeting to seek communication from the spirit of the dead

sear *vt.* to dry up or wither; to scorch —*adj.* withered

search *vt.* to look through thoroughly; to seek out —*n.* —**search´a·ble** *adj.* —**search´er** *n.*

search´ing *adj.* examining thoroughly: *a searching investigation;* observant or penetrating: *a searching look* —**search´ing·ly** *adj.* —**search´ing·ness** *n.*

sea´son¹ *n.* a division of the year; a time of special activity, as *baseball season* —**sea´son·al** *adj.* —**sea´son·al·ly** *adv.*

sea´son² *vt.* to add spices, etc. to food; to improve or make fit by aging —**sea´son·ing** *n.*

sea´son·a·ble *adj.* in keeping with or usual for the season or time; practical for the season —**sea´son·a·ble·ness** *n.* — **sea´son·a·bly** *adv.*

seat *n.* something to sit on; the place where a thing is situated: *the seat of government* —*vt.* to put in a sitting position or on a seat; to accommodate: *the room will seat 30 people;* to set firmly or establish in a place

seat´ing *n.* the seats available: *seating for fifty;* the arrangement of seats, as in a theater: *balcony seating* —**seat´er** *n.*

sea´wor·thy *adj.* of a boat that is in fit condition and ready for use — **sea´wor·thi·ness** *n.*

se·cede´ *vt.* to formally withdraw — **se·ced´er** *n.*

se·ces´sion *n.* the act of seceding — **se·ces´sion·al** *adj.* —**se·ces´sion·ism** *n.* —**se·ces´sion·ist** *n.*

se·clude´ *vt.* to set or keep apart; to isolate

se·clud´ed *adj.* separated; protected —**se·clud´ed·ly** *adv.* —**se·clud´ed·ness** *n.*

se·clu´sion *n.* solitude; retirement — **se·clu´sive** *adj.* —**se·clu´sive·ly** *adv.* —**se·clu´sive·ness** *n.*

sec´ond *n.* a unit of time; an angular measure; a formal attendant, as in a duel; something of inferior quality —*adj.* of a brief time; next in order; of lesser value —*vt.* to formally support

sec´ond·ar·y *adj.* of second rank — **sec´on·dar·ily**

se´cret *adj.* kept hidden; esoteric; not revealed, as *a secret partner;* mysterious —*n.* a mystery; something known to only a few —**se´cre·cy,** **se´cret·ness** *n.* —**se´cret·ly** *adv.*

sec´re·tary *n.* one who deals with correspondence and clerical business; an official responsible for record keeping in a business or other organization; the head of a government department; a type of writing desk —**sec´re·tar´i·al** *adj.*

se·crete´ *vt.* to conceal; to hide away; to form and release, as digestive fluids —**se·cre´tion** *n.*

se·cre´tive *adj.* disposed to secrecy —**se´cre·tive·ly** *adv.* —**se´cre·tive·ness** *n.*

sect *n.* a separate group, especially a religious or philosophical faction broken away from a larger order — **sec·tar´i·an** *adj.* —**sec·tar´i·an·ism** *n.*

sec´tion *n.* a separate part; the act of separating by cutting —*vt.* to divide into parts —**sec´tion·al** *adj.*

sec´tor *n.* a section, especially of a

military position

sec´u·lar *adj.* worldly; temporal; not controlled by or concerned with religion —**sec´u·lar·ism** *n.* —**sec´u·lar·ist** *n.* —**sec·u·lar·is´tic** *adj.*

sec´u·lar·ize *vt.* to convert from sacred to secular use

se·cure´ *adj.* unlikely to be threatened or overcome; confident —*vt.* to protect; to make certain; to obtain —**se·cur´a·ble** *adj.* —**se·cur´er** *n.* —**se·cure´ly** *adv.* —**se·cure´ness** *n.*

se·cur´i·ty *n.* the state of being secure; persons responsible for the protection of others, as in a building, shopping mall, etc.; measures calculated to provide for protection; something pledged for payment of a debt

se·dan´ *n.* a closed automobile — **sedan chair** a closed chair with poles at the side for carrying

se·date´ *adj.* composed; dignified — *vt.* to calm with medication —**se·date´ly** *adv.* —**se·date´ness** *n.*

sed´a·tive *adj.* tending to calm —*n.* a medicine that serves to calm — **se·da´tion** *n.*

sed´en·tar·y *adj.* inactive; characterized by sitting —**sed´en·tar´i·ly** *adv.* —**sed´en·tar´i·ness** *n.*

sed´i·ment *n.* matter that settles to the bottom of a liquid; fragmentary material deposited by water, ice, etc. —**sed´i·men´ta·ry** *adj.* —**sed·i·men·ta´tion** *n.*

se·di´tion *n.* resistance or action against lawful authority —**se·di´tious** *adj.* —**se·di´tious·ly** *adv.* —**se·di´tious·ness**

se·duce´ *vt.* to lead astray: *seduced by quick profit*; to tempt or entice into a wrong —**se·duc´er** *n.* —**se·duc´a·ble, se·duc´i·ble** *adj.* —**se·duc´tion** *n.*

se·duc´tive *adj.* tending to seduce — **se·duc´tive·ly** *adv.* —**se·duc´tive·ness** *n.*

sed´u·lous *adj.* diligent; industrious —**sed´u·lous·ly** *adv.* —**sed´u·lous·ness** *n.*

see *vt.* to view with the eyes; to perceive with the mind; to encounter: *I often see her*; to be certain: *see that you go* —*vi.* to exercise the power of sight; to comprehend; to be attentive

seed *n.* the ovule that produces a plant; the origin of anything; any small granular fruit —*vt.* to plant; to spread, as with seeds; to remove the seeds from —**seed´er** *n.*

seed´y *adj.* overflowing with seeds; gone to seed; shabby —**seed´i·ly** *adv.* —**seed´i·ness**

seek *vt.* to go in search of; to strive for —**seek´er** *n.*

seem *vi.* to appear to be

seem´ing *adj.* projecting a false appearance: *her seeming indifference hides her pain* —*n.* outward appearance —**seem´ing·ly** *adj.* —**seem´ing·ness** *n.*

seem´ly *adj.* proper; decorous — **seem´li·ness** *adv.*

seep *vi.* to gradually diffuse; to penetrate through small openings —**seep´age** *n.*

se´er *n.* a prophet; one who foretells the future

seethe *vi.* to boil; to be agitated, as by rage

seg´ment *n.* a distinct part; a part cut off —*vt.*, *vi.* to cut or separate into parts —**seg·men´tal** *adj.* — **seg·men´tal·ly** *adv.* —**seg´men·tar·y** *adj.*

seg´re·ga·ble *adj.* that can be separated: *segregable expenses*

seg´re·gate *vt.* to isolate or separate from a larger group —*adj.* separated or set apart —**seg·re·ga´tion** *n.* —**seg´re·ga·tive** *adj.*

seg·re·ga´tion·ist *n.* one who believes in the separation of races, as in housing, schools, and work

se´gue *vi.* to move smoothly from

one element to another, as *the segue from daylight to dusk*

seis′mic, **seis′mi·cal** *adj*. pertaining to earthquakes

seis′mo·graph *n*. an instrument for recording movements in the earth's crust —**seis′mo·graph′ic** *adj*. —**seis·mog′ra·pher** *n*. —**seis·mog′ra·phy** *n*.

seis·mol′o·gy *n*. the study of earthquakes and related phenomena —**seis·mo·log′ic**, **seis·mo·log′i·cal** *adj*. —**seis·mo·log′i·cal·ly** *adv*. —**seis·mol′o·gist** *n*.

seize *vt*. to grasp suddenly and forcefully; to understand; to take possession by force; to take immediate advantage —**seiz′a·ble** *adj*. —**seiz′er** *n*.

sei′zure *n*. the act of seizing; a sudden attack or incapacitation, as by an illness

sel′dom *adv*. infrequently; at widely spaced intervals —*adj*. infrequent or rare —**sel′dom·ness** *n*.

se·lect′ *vt.*, *vi*. to choose —*adj*. superior to others of its type; particular in choosing —**se·lec′tion** *n*.

se·lec′tive *adj*. very particular; choosy —**se·lec′tive·ly** *adv*. —**se·lec′tive·ness**, **se·lec·tiv′i·ty** *n*. —**se·lec′tor** *n*.

self *n*. the distinct identity and individuality of a person or thing; personal advantage —*adj*. of the same quality or kind

self′-cen′tered *adj*. concerned exclusively with one's own needs and desires —**self′-cen′tered·ly** *adv*. —**self′-cen′tered·ness** *n*.

self-con′fi·dence *n*. belief in one's own ability, judgement, etc. —**self-con′fi·dent** *adj*. —**self-con′fi·dent·ly** *adv*.

self-con′scious *adj*. uncomfortable under the scrutiny of another; ill at ease in a particular situation —**self-con′scious·ly** *adv*. —**self-con′scious·ness** *n*.

self–con′trol′ *n*. command of one's impulses, emotions, etc.

self-dis′ci·pline *n*. control of oneself, especially for personal betterment

self-es·teem′ *n*. a just opinion of oneself; an overestimate of oneself; conceit

self-im·por′tance *n*. an overestimation of one's prominence; conceit —**self-im·por′tant** *adj*. —**self-im·por′tant·ly** *adv*.

self–in·dul′gence *n*. excessive gratification of one's desires —**self′–in·dul′gent** *adj*. —**self′–in·dul′gent·ly** *adv*.

self′ish *adj*. motivated by personal desires while disregarding the feelings of others' —**self′ish·ly** *adv*. —**self′ish·ness** *n*.

self′less *adj*. having little concern for oneself; unselfish —**self′less·ly** *adv*. —**self′less·ness** *n*.

self-pos·ses′sion *n*. complete control of one's powers or faculties —**self-pos·sessed′** *adj*.

self-pres·er·va′tion *n*. the instinctive drive to avoid harm

self-re·li′ance *n*. dependence on one's own ability, resources, etc. —**self-re·li′ant** *adj*. —**self-re·li′ant·ly** *adv*.

self-right′eous *adj*. confident of one's own moral superiority —**self-right′eous·ly** *adv*. —**self-right′eous·ness** *n*.

self-suf·fi′cien·cy *n*. the ability to maintain oneself without the assistance of others —**self-suf·fi′cient** *adj*. —**self-suf·fi′cient·ly** *adv*.

sell *vt*. to transfer property for a consideration; to offer for sale —*vi*. to work in sales —**sell′er** *n*.

sel′vage *n*. the edge of a fabric finished so as not to ravel

se·man′tics *pl. n*. the study of the structure, meanings, changes, etc. of speech forms; a deliberate distortion of meaning —**se·man´tic** *adj.* —**se·man´ti·cal´ly** *adv.* —**se·man´ti·cist** *n.*

sem´blance *n.* a likeness or resemblance; the barest trace

sem´i- *prefix* partly: *semiautomatic*; exactly half: *semicircle*; occurring twice in the period: *semiannual*

sem´i·nar *n.* an informal meeting to address a particular topic

sem´i·nary *n.* a school of theology —**sem·i·nar´i·an** *n.*

sen´ate *n.* a legislative body —**sen´a·tor** *n.* —**sen·a·to´ri·al** *adj.* —**sen´a·tor·ship** *n.*

send *vt.* to transmit; to cause or enable to go: *send to school*; to drive or impel —**send´er** *n.*

se´nile *adj.* of old age, especially when accompanied by mental infirmity —**se´nile·ly** *adv.* —**se·nil´i·ty** *n.*

sen´ior *adj.* older in years or time of service —*n.* any elderly person; one more advanced in rank, dignity, etc.; a member of a graduating class —**se·nior´i·ty** *n.*

sen´sate *adj.* having physical sensation; perceived by the senses —**sen´sate·ly** *adv.*

sen·sa´tion *n.* stimulation of a sense organ, as hearing or taste; the capacity to respond to such stimulation; a state of mind induced by indeterminate stimuli, as *a sensation of fear*

sen·sa´tion·al *adj.* of the senses or sensation; causing excitement —**sen·sa´tion·al·ly**

sen·sa´tion·al·ism *n.* the theory that all knowledge has a sensory basis; techniques intended to shock or startle —**sen·sa´tion·al·ist** *n.* —**sen·sa´tion·al·is´tic** *adj.* —**sen·sa´tion·al·ize** *vt.*

sense *n.* any of the faculties of a sentient being to respond to stimuli, as sound, hunger, etc.; a special capacity to appreciate, as a

sense of humor; a vague perception, as *a sense of danger*; the power to reason —*vt.* to perceive; to become aware

sense´less *adj.* unconscious; incapable of feeling; lacking good sense; without apparent reason: *a senseless crime* —**sense´less·ly** *adv.* —**sense´less·ness** *n.*

sen´si·ble *adj.* possessing good mental perception; perceptible through the senses or to the mind —**sen·si·bil´i·ty** *n.* —**sen´si·ble·ness** *n.* —**sen´si·bly** *adv.*

sen´si·tive *adj.* acutely responsive to certain sensation; responsive to the feelings and attitudes of others; appreciative of aesthetic or intellectual qualities; easily irritated or offended —**sen´si·tive·ly** *adv.* —**sen´si·tive·ness, sen·si·tiv´i·ty** *n.*

sen´si·tize *vt.* to make sensitive

sen´sor *n.* a device that responds to stimuli, as an electric eye

sen·so´ri·al, sen´so·ry *adj.* of the senses or sensation

sen´su·al *adj.* unduly indulgent to the appetites or senses —**sen´su·al·ly** *adv.* —**sen´su·al·ize** *vt.* —**sen·su·al·i·za´tion** *n.*

sen´su·al·ism *n.* excessive indulgence in sensual pleasures; the philosophical concept that sensual pleasures represent the highest good —**sen´su·al·ist** *n.* —**sen·su·al·is´tic** *adj.*

sen·su·al´i·ty *n.* the state of being sensual; lewdness; lasciviousness

sen´su·ous *adj.* appealing to the senses —**sen´su·ous·ly** *adv.* —**sen´su·ous·ness** *n.*

sen´tence *n.* a determination or judgement; a penalty pronounced in court; in grammar, a group of words that express a thought

sen´tient *adj.* possessing powers of perception —**sen´tience** *n.* —**sen´tient·ly** *adv.*

sen´ti·ment n. delicate sensibility; a complex of feelings used as a basis for judgement —**sen·ti·men´tal** adj. —**sen·ti·men´tal·ism** n. —**sen·ti·men´tal·ist** n. —**sen·ti·men´tal·ly** adv.

sen·ti·men·tal´i·ty n. the quality of being overly sentimental

sen´ti·nel n. a guard

sen´try n. a guard, especially a soldier

sep´a·ra·ble adj. capable of being divided —**sep´a·ra·ble·ly** adv. —**sep´a·ra·ble·ness** n.

sep´a·rate vt. to set apart or divide; to isolate —vi. to become divided; to draw apart —adj. distinct; apart from others; detached; existing independently —**sep´a·rate·ly** adv. —**sep´a·rate·ness** n. —**sep´a·ra·tive** adj. —**sep´a·ra·tor** n.

sep·a·ra´tion n. the state of being apart; a gap or dividing line

sep´a·rat·ist n. one who advocates separation, as of races or religions, or by political boundaries —**sep´a·rat·ism** n.

sep´ul·cher n. a burial place; a tomb or vault

se·pul´chral adj. of a sepulcher; dismal in aspect —**se·pul´chral·ly** adv.

se´quel n. something that follows; a narrative that develops from a previous one; a consequence

se´quence n. the process of following in order —**se·quen´tial** adj. —**se·quen·ti·al´i·ty** n. —**se·quen´tial·ly** adv.

se·ques´ter vt. to place apart; to seclude, as a jury during the course of a trial; property taken into custody pending settlement of a claim —**se·ques´tered** adj.

ser´e·nade´ n. a love song —vi., vt. to sing, especially to one's love —**ser´e·nad´er** n.

ser·en·dip´i·ty n. the faculty of making fortunate discoveries by accident —**ser·en·dip´i·tous** adj. —**ser·en·dip´i·tous·ly** adv.

se·rene´ adj. untroubled; tranquil —**se·rene´ly** adv. —**se·rene´ness**, **se·ren´i·ty** n.

se´ri·al adj. arranged in a series; presented at regular intervals —n. a story presented in regular installments, as in a periodical or on television —**se´ri·al·ize** vt. —**se´ri·al·ly** adv.

se´ries n. an arrangement or succession of related things

ser´if n. a light stroke crossing or projecting from the main stroke in a letter

se´ri·ous adj. thoughtful; sober; involving much work or difficulty; of grave importance; grim or critical, as a serious accident —**se´ri·ous·ly** adv. —**se´ri·ous·ness** n.

ser´mon n. a lecture; a serious talk; a discourse, especially on a text from the Bible —**ser·mon´ic** adj. —**ser´mon·ize** vt., vi.

ser´pent n. a snake

ser´pen·tine adj. winding, like a serpent

ser´rate, **ser´rat·ed** adj. having sawlike teeth, as the edge of certain leaves —**ser·ra´tion** n.

se´rum n. the fluid constituent of blood; a fluid that confers immunity

ser´vant n. one employed to assist in domestic matters

serve vt. to work as a servant; to be of service to; to satisfy the requirements of; to perform the duties of an office; to satisfy, as a term of enlistment or incarceration —vi. to be a servant; to perform the duties of employment, office, etc.; to wait on others; be useful or suitable —**serv´er** n.

serv´ice n. the act of serving; the manner in which one is served; a business or occupational category, as a delivery service; maintenance

387

and repair; an act of public worship —*vt.* to maintain or repair — *adj.* pertaining to the act of serving; designated for those who serve or supply: *service entrance*

serv´ice·a·ble *adj.* useful; beneficial; durable —**serv·ice·a·bil´i·ty, serv´ice·a·ble·ness** *n.* —**serv´ice·a·bly** *adv.*

ser´vile *adj.* submissive; befitting a servant; abject —**ser´vile·ly** *adv.* —**ser´vile·ness, ser·vil´i·ty** *n.*

ses´sion *n.* the meeting of a legislative assembly, court, etc.; a time of specified activity: *a bull session*

set *vt.* to place; to fix in place; to bring to a specified condition: *set a fire, set at ease*; to restore: *set a broken bone*; to establish: *set boundaries*; to mount, as a gem; to value: *set a price* —*vi.* to wane, as *the setting sun*; to solidify; to begin: *set out, set to work* —*n.* a group regarded as associated: *the jet set*; a number of things belonging together

set´tle *vt.* to put in order; to set to rights; to establish in place: *settle in*; to calm or quiet; to sink to the bottom; to decide or determine finally; to pay, as a debt —*vi.* to come to rest; to sink gradually; to become established; to pay a bill

set´tle·ment *n.* the condition of being settled; an area newly colonized; an agreement or adjustment —**set´tler** *n.*

sev´er *vt.* to separate; to cut or break into parts; to break off, as a relationship —*vi.* to break or come apart —**sev´er·a·ble** *adj.* —**sev´er·ance** *n.*

sev´er·al *adj.* more than two, but not a large number; individually different, diverse —**sev´er·al·ly** *adv.*

se·vere´ *adj.* harsh; extremely strict; austere in disposition or manner; plain and simple —**se·vere´ly** *adv.* —**se·vere´ness** *n.* —**se·ver´i·ty** *n.*

sew *vt.* to make, mend, or fasten with needle and thread — *vi.* to work with needle and thread

sex *n.* the division, male or female, by which organisms are distinguished with reference to the reproductive functions; activity concerned with sexual desire or reproduction

sex´ism *n.* discrimination against one of the opposite sex —**sex´ist** *n., adj.*

sex´less *adj.* having no sex; without sexual interest or distinction — **sex´less·ly** *adv.* —**sex´less·ness** *n.*

sex´ton *n.* a church officer responsible for maintenance

sex´u·al *adj.* pertaining to sex and its functions; characterized by or having sex —**sex·u·al´i·ty** *n.* — **sex´u·al·ly** *adv.*

sex´y *adj.* provocative; stimulating —**sex´i·ly** *adv.* —**sex´i·ness** *n.*

shab´by *adj.* threadbare; characterized by worn or ragged garments; paltry —**shab´bi·ly** *adv.* —**shab´bi·ness** *n.*

shack *n.* a crudely built dwelling — **shack up** (*US*) to live somewhere temporarily; to live together as husband and wife without benefit of matrimony

shade *vt.* to screen from light or heat; to represent by gradation of color —*n.* relative darkness caused by interruption of light; a darkened gradation of color; a minute variation: *shade of meaning*; a screen that partly obscures light: *a lamp shade*

shad´ow *n.* comparative darkness caused by interruption of light; the image produced by that which interrupts light; the shaded portion of a picture; a trace: *not a shadow of evidence* —*vt.* to cast a shadow; to follow —**shad´ow·y** *adj.*

shad´y *adj.* shaded or sheltered; morally or legally suspect: *a shady* *deal* —**shad´i·ly** *adv.* —**shad´i·ness** *n.*

shaft *n.* a long narrow rod; a long handle; a beam of light; any long, narrow, relatively straight structure or opening, as *an elevator shaft* or *an air shaft*

shag *n.* a coarse cloth or coat; a once popular dance —*vt.*, *vi.* to make or become coarse or rough

shag´gy *adj.* resembling rough hair or wool; unkempt —**shaggy-dog story** a long involved story with a meaningless punch line —**shag´gi·ly** *adv.* —**shag´gi·ness** *n.*

shake *vt.*, *vi.* to vibrate with short, rapid movements; to agitate or rouse —**shak´a·ble** *adj.*

shak´y *adj.* not solid or well founded; not reliable; marked by weakness or shaking —**shak´i·ly** *adv.* —**shak´i·ness** *n.*

shal´low *adj.* lacking depth or extent: *a shallow closet;* superficial or unintelligent, especially of a person —**shal´low·ly** *adv.* —**shal´low·ness** *n.*

sham *adj.* false; pretended —*n.* a hoax; a counterfeit; artificiality or pretension

sham´ble *vi.* to walk with shuffling or unsteady gait

shame *n.* a sense of guilt or unworthiness; disgrace or humiliation; a disappointment: *it's a shame they can't go* —*vt.* to cause to feel shame; to bring shame upon; to impel through a sense of shame

shame´ful *adj.* disgraceful; scandalous; indecent —**shame´ful·ly** *adv.* —**shame´ful·ness** *n.*

shame´less *adj.* brazen; immodest; done without shame —**shame´less·ly** *adv.* —**shame´less·ness** *n.*

shan´ty *n.* a small, poorly built dwelling; a shack

shape *n.* outward form; final form: *put into shape* —*vt.* to give form to; to adapt or modify; to put in final form —*vi.* to develop or take shape —**shap´a·ble** *adj.* —**shaped** *adj.* —**shap´er** *n.*

shape´less *adj.* lacking form or symmetry —**shape´less·ly** *adv.* —**shape´less·ness**

shape´ly *adj.* having a pleasing form —**shape´li·ness** *adv.*

shard *n.* a broken piece, as of pottery

share *n.* a portion due or contributed; stock in a company —*vt.*, *vi.* to participate in; to divide into equal parts —**shar´er** *n.*

sharp *adj.* having a keen edge; capable of cutting or piercing; abrupt: *a sharp curve;* well-defined: *sharp contrast;* quick to perceive; shrewd; intense: *a sharp wit, a sharp temper* —*adv.* —**sharp´ly** *adv.* —**sharp´ness** *n.*

sharp´en *vt.*, *vi.* to make or become sharp —**sharp´en·er** *n.*

shat´ter *vt.* to break into pieces suddenly; to damage or demolish: *the loss shattered her hopes* —*vi.* to burst —**shat´ter·ing·ly** *adv.*

shave *vt.* to remove hair with a razor; to trim closely; to slice thinly; to graze or come close —*n.* the act of cutting with a razor; a thin slice —**shav´en** *adj.* —**shav´er** *n.*

shawl *n.* a cloth wrap worn over the head or shoulders

sheaf *n.* bound stalks of cut grain; a collection of things banded or tied; a quantity: *a sheaf of papers*

sheath *n.* a case, as for a sword or knife —*vt.* to place or enclose in or as in a sheath or covering

sheathe *vt.* put into a sheath; to protect or conceal, as by covering —**sheath´ing** *n.*

shed *vt.* to pour forth, as tears; to radiate: *the sun shed its rays;* to repel, as rain; to cast off by natural process, as a snake's skin; to get rid of: *he shed 10 pounds just by exercising* —*vi.* to cast off by natural process —*n.* a small storage building —**shed light on** to explain or make clear

sheen *vi.* to glisten —*n.* a glossy finish; luster

sheep *n.* a wooly ruminant, especially those domesticated for their fleece, flesh, and hide

sheep´ish *adj.* embarrassed; meek or timid —**sheep´ish·ly** *adv.* — **sheep´ish·ness**

sheet *n.* a thin, broad piece of material; a broad, flat expanse; cloth used as bedding; a piece of paper —*vt.* to form or cut into sheets —*adj.* formed or cut into sheets

shelf *n.* a platform or ledge designed to hold articles; a projecting rock ledge —**shelv´ing** *n.*

shell *n.* a hard outer covering; anything like a shell, as the framework of a building, a hollow pastry, etc.; a projectile containing explosives, etc.; a psychological barrier: *come out of one's shell* —*vt.* to remove the outer covering from; to bombard

shel´ter *n.* that which covers or protects —*vt.* to provide cover — **shel´ter·er** *n.*

shib´bo·leth *n.* a test word; a watchword

shield *n.* a relatively flat plate of defensive armor, usually carried on the arm; anything that protects; a shield-like badge or emblem; a heraldic escutcheon —*vt.* to guard or protect; to hide from view

shift *vt., vi.* to change position —*n.* a change in attitude, position, loyalty, etc.; a dress that is unbelted or fitted at the waist

shift´less *adj.* unwilling to work; lazy; incompetent —**shift´less·ly** *adv.* —**shift´less·ness** *n.*

shift´y *adj.* characterized by deceit or trickery; resourceful —**shift´i·ly** *adv.* —**shift´i·ness**

shim´mer *vi.* to shine faintly; to glimmer —*n.* a gleaming —**shim´mer·y** *adj.*

shim´my *n.* a jazz dance; an undesirable vibration

shine *vi.* to emit light; to glow; to excel —*vt.* to brighten by rubbing —*n.* radiance; sheen; a liking or fancy —**shin´er** *n.*

shin´gle *n.* a thin tapering piece used in courses to cover a roof; a sign outside the office of a doctor, lawyer, etc. —*vt.*

shin´y *adj.* glistening; polished — **shin´i·ness** *n.*

ship *n.* a deep-water vessel; an aircraft or spacecraft —*vt.* to transport

ship´ment *n.* goods transported — **ship´per** *n.*

shirk *vt., vi.* to avoid work or obligation —**shirk´er** *n.*

shirt *n.* a garment for the upper part of the body

shirt´ing *n.* material used for making shirts, blouses, etc.

shiv´er *vi.* to tremble, as with cold or fear —**shiv´er·y** *adj.*

shoal *n.* a shallow place in a body of water

shock *n.* a violent blow; a jolt to the mind or emotions; trauma associated with injury —*vt.* to horrify or disgust —**shock´er** *n.*

shock´ing *adj.* causing sudden surprise or horror —**shock´ing·ly** *adv.*

shod´dy *adj.* poorly made —**shod´di·ly** *adv.* —**shod´di·ness** *n.*

sho´gun *n.* former hereditary leader of the Japanese militia

shoot *vt.* to wound with a projectile from a weapon; to fire a weapon; to send forth, as a glance; to pass over swiftly, as rapids; to photograph —*vi.* to discharge; to move swiftly; to put forth buds —*n.* the act of shooting; early growth — **shoot´er** *n.*

shop *n.* a place where goods and services are sold, manufactured, or repaired —*vi.* to inspect and purchase goods —**shop assistant** (*Brit.*) one who works in a retail shop —**shop´per** *n.*

shore *n.* land adjacent to a body of water

short *adj.* of less than average or usual length, height, or extent; of brief duration; of a limited distance; less than required: *short of the mark* —**short´ness** *n.*

short´age *n.* an inadequate supply; the amount of a deficiency or shortfall

short´com·ing *n.* a defect

short´en *vt., vi.* to make or become reduced in length

short´ly *adv.* soon

shout *n.* a sudden, loud outcry —*vt., vi.* to utter loudly —**shout´er** *n.*

shove *vt., vi.* to push; to press forcibly against —**shov´er** *n.*

shov´el *n.* a flattened scoop with a handle —*vt., vi.* to take up with a shovel; to toss hastily —**shov´el·er** *n.* —**shov´el·ful** *n.*

show *vt.* to present to view; to explain or prove; to lead: *show them in*; to enter in a show or exhibition —*vi.* to become visible; to appear — *n.* a production, as a movie or live performance; an exhibition; a competition for displaying and judging; ostentation: *mere show*

show´er *n.* one who exhibits at a show; a brief rain; a sudden or liberal outpouring: *a shower of accolades*; a party honoring an event as *a bridal shower* or *baby shower*; a means for cleansing the body with a fine spray of water or the bathroom appliance used for such cleansing — *vt., vi.* to make wet or bathe, as in a shower

show´man *n.* one skilled in the art of performing or of managing performances —**show´man·ship** *n.*

show´place *n.* an extremely attractive or well-ordered site

show´y *adj.* flamboyant; ostentatious —**show´i·ness** *n.*

shred *n.* a fragment —*vt.* to cut or tear into fragments —**shred´der** *n.*

shrew *n.* a tiny mouselike creature; a vexatious or nagging woman — **shrew´ish** *adj.* —**shrew´ish·ly** *adv.* —**shrew´ish·ness** *n.*

shrewd *adj.* having keen insight; calculating —**shrewd´ly** *adv.* — **shrewd´ness** *n.*

shriek *n.* a shrill cry —*vi.*

shrill *adj.* high-pitched and piercing —*vi., vt.* to make or cause to make a piercing sound —**shrill´ness** *n.* —**shril´ly** *adv.*

shrine *n.* a sacred place; a place of worship; a site or structure respected for its importance; a memorial dedicated to a person, event, etc.

shrink *vi.* to contract; diminish; to recoil, as in disgust —*vt.* to cause to shrink —**shrink´a·ble** *adj.* — **shrink´age** *n.*

shriv´el *vt., vi.* to contract into wrinkles; to make or become helpless

shroud *n.* cloth used to wrap a corpse; something that covers or conceals —*vt.* to cover or conceal

shrug *vt., vi.* to draw up the shoulders, as in doubt or indifference

shuck *n.* a covering, such as a husk, shell, or pod —*vt.* to remove an outer covering, as *to shuck peas* or *shuck one's garments*

shud´der *vi.* to tremble, as from fright or cold

shuf´fle *vt., vi.* to move with a dragging gait; to mix, as a deck of playing cards; to move, change, or rearrange —*n.* a trick or deception

shunt *vt., vi.* to turn aside; to divert —*n.* a railroad switch; a connector that diverts power, etc.

shut *vt.* to close, as a door or window; to collapse after use, as an umbrella; to exclude: *they shut out the riffraff*

shut´-in *n.* an invalid; one who is unable to leave —*adj.*

shy *adj.* uneasy in the company of others; timid; easily startled; expressing reserve, as *a shy look* — *vt.* to draw back, as *to shy away* — **shy´ly** *adv.* —**shy´ness** *n.*

shy´ster *n.* an unscrupulous businessman

sib´i·lant *adj.* hissing; in grammar, expressing a consonant, as *s, z, sh,* and *zh,* uttered with a hissing sound —**sib´i·lance** *n.* —**sib´i·lant·ly** *adv.*

sib´ling *n.* a brother or sister

sick *adj.* ill; affected by disease; weak; nauseated; emotionally upset: *sick with grief;* monotonous: *sick of dining alone* —**sick´ness** *n.*

sick´en *vt., vi.* to make or become sick or repelled —**sick´en·ing** *adj.* —**sick´en·ing·ly** *adv.*

sick´le *n.* a cutting implement with a long, curved blade mounted on a short handle

sick´ly *adj.* habitually ailing; characterized by sickness; weak or unconvincing: *a sickly excuse* —*adv.* —**sick´li·ness** *n.*

side *n.* the boundary of a surface or an object; the lateral half of a surface or object; an aspect or point of view; a group competing together

si·de´re·al *adj.* relating to the stars

si´dle *vi.* to move sideways — *n.* a sideways movement

siege *n.* the surrounding of a place so as to sieze it; a prolonged bout, as *a siege of illness* —*vt.* to besiege or assault

sieve *n.* a utensil such as a wire mesh attached to a rigid frame for separating out coarse particles — *vt., vi.* to force or pass through a sieve; to sift

sift *vt.* to examine carefully; to separate out; to filter, as *to sift fact from fiction* —**sift´er** *n.*

sigh *n.* a deep audible breath — *vi.* to make a sound to express sorrow, weariness, etc.; to make a sound suggestive of a sigh —*vt.* to express with a sigh

sight *n.* vision; an image perceived by the eye; mental perception: *don't lose sight of our objective;* a device for aiming; observation with a telescope —*vt.* to catch sight of; to observe through a telescope or similar device —*vi.* to take aim; to make an observation —*adj.* performed without previous preparation: *sight reading;* due when presented: *a sight draft* —**sight´ed** *adj.*

sight´less *adj.* blind; invisible — **sight´less·ly** *adv.* —**sight´less· ness** *n.*

sign *n.* a telltale mark or indication: *a sign of aging, the first sign of spring;* an action used to communicate; a symbol: *black armbands are a sign of grief;* a structure containing advertising, directions, etc. —*vt., vi.* to write one's signature; to indicate or signal — **sign´er** *n.*

sig´nal *n.* an agreed upon sign or event; that used to convey information —*adj.* out of the ordinary notable —*vt.* to convey or communicate by a sign

sig´na·to·ry *n.* one bound by a signed document —*adj.* being a signer

sig´na·ture *n.* the name of a person written by himself; any identifying mark or sign; a folded sheet that constitutes a part of a book; symbols at the beginning of a piece of music that indicate time and key

sig·nif´i·cant *adj.* rich in meaning important —**sig·nif´i·cance, sig nif´i·can·cy** *n.* —**sig·nif´i·cant·l** *adv.*

sig´ni·fy *vt.* to represent; to mak

known by signs or words —*vi.* to have meaning or importance

si′lent *adj.* not making any sound; mute; taciturn, disinclined to talk; not audible; free from disturbance; the absence of comment: *he was silent on the issues* —**si′lence** *n.* — **si′lent·ly** *adv.*

sil·hou·ette′ *n.* a profile drawing or portrait filled in with uniform color

sil′ly *adj.* foolish; frivolous —*adv.* — **sil′li·ness** *n.*

silt *n.* extremely fine particles carried by water; a deposit of such particles —**silt′y** *adj.*

sim′i·an *n.* an ape or monkey —*adj.*

sim′i·lar *adj.* bearing resemblance; having like characteristics —**sim·i·lar′i·ty** *n.* —**sim′i·lar·ly** *adv.*

sim′i·le *n.* a figure of speech expressing likeness

si·mil′i·tude *n.* similarity

sim′mer *vi.* to boil gently; to be near to showing emotion —*vt.* to cook by boiling gently —*n.*

si′mo·ny *n.* the buying or selling of that which is sacred

sim′per *vi.* to smirk —*vt.* to say with a smirk —*n.* a silly, self-conscious smile

sim′ple *adj.* easy to understand or do; plain and unadorned, as clothing or food; having nothing added: *the simple truth*; free from affectation; silly or foolish; ordinary —**sim′ple·ness** *n.*

sim·plic′i·ty *n.* the state of being simple

sim′pli·fy *vt.* to make easy to understand or do —**sim·pli·fi·ca′tion** *n.* —**sim′pli·fi·er** *n.*

sim·plis′tic *adj.* overly simple; tending to overlook potential complications —**sim·plis′ti·cal·ly** *adv.*

sim′ply *adv.* in a simple manner; really: *simply adorable*

sim′u·late *vt.* to make a pretense of; to assume the appearance of — **sim·u·la′tion** *n.* —**sim′u·la·tive**

adj. —**sim′u·la·tive·ly** *adv.* —**sim′ u·la·tor** *n.*

si·mul·ta′ne·ous *adj.* occurring or existing at the same time — **si·mul·ta′ne·ous·ly** *adv.* —**si·mul· ta′ne·ous·ness** *n.*

sin *n.* a transgression against moral or religious law —*vi.* to do wrong —**sin′ful** *adj.* —**sin′ful·ly** *adv.* — **sin′ful·ness** *n.*

since *adv.* from a past time to the present; at some time before the present: *he has since recovered* — *prep.* from a time in the past: *since you left* —*conj.* inasmuch as

sin·cere′ *adj.* genuine; free from hypocrisy or deceit —**sin·cere′ly** *adv.* —**sin·cer′i·ty** *n.*

sin′e·cure *n.* a position that provides compensation with little or no effort

sing *vi.* to produce musical sounds with the voice or as with the voice —*vt.* to perform vocally; to chant —**sing′a·ble** *adj.* —**sing′er** *n.*

singe *vt.* to burn slightly —*n.* a superficial burn

sin′gle *adj.* consisting of one; solitary; unmarried —**sin′gle·ness** *n.* —**sin′gly** *adv.*

sin′gu·lar *adj.* unique; remarkable; uncommon —**sin·gu·lar′i·ty** *n.* — **sin′gu·lar·ly** *adv.* —**sin′gu·lar· ness** *n.*

sin′is·ter *adj.* of the left side; evil; ominous; threatening misfortune —**sin′is·ter·ly** *adv.* —**sin′is·ter· ness** *n.*

sin′is·tral *adj.* of or facing the left — **sin′is·tral·ly** *adv.*

sink *vi.* to go beneath the surface; to descend slowly; to slope gradually; to approach death; to lessen: *his voice sank* —*vt.* to cause to go beneath the surface; to cause to drop or lessen; to defeat —*n.* a basin with running water and a drain; a depression in a land surface; a device that absorbs or dissipates

energy: *a heat sink* —**sink´a·ble**
adj. —**sink´er** *n.*

sin´u·ous *adj.* winding or undulating; devious —**sin´u·ous·ly** *adv.* —
sin´u·ous·ness *n.*

sip *vt., vi.* to drink in small quantities —*n.* a small drink —**sip´per** *n.*

si´phon *n.* a tube or device for
transferring liquid —*vt.* to draw off

sir *n.* respectful address to a man; a
title for barons or knights

sire *n.* the male parent of an animal

si´ren *n.* an enticing woman; a device that warns by producing a
loud distinctive sound —*adj.* seductive

sis´sy *n.* an effeminate man; a
weakling

sis´ter *n.* a female sibling

sit *vi.* to rest on the buttocks or
haunches; to perch or roost; to
pose; to meet or hold a session; to
be situated or located —*vt.* to seat
oneself

si´tar´ *n.* a long-necked stringed
instrument similar to a lute, used
for Hindu music —**si·tar´ist** *n.*

site *n.* a specific place or location

sit´u·ate *vt.* to place or locate

sit·u·a´tion *n.* the way in which a
thing rests; a condition as modified or determined by circumstance; a salaried post; a state of
affairs, especially one that is difficult or significant —**sit·u·a´tion·al**
adj. —**sit·u·a´tion·al·ly** *adv.*

siz´a·ble *adj.* comparatively large —
siz´a·ble·ness *n.* —**siz´a·bly** *adv.*

size *n.* the dimensions of a thing;
one of a series of standard measures, as for shoes, hats, etc.

siz´zle *vi.* to emit a hissing sound —
n. a hissing sound caused by heat

skate *n.* a runner or wheels attached
to a shoe for gliding over ice,
pavement, etc. —*vi.* to glide over a
smooth surface —**skat´er** *n.*

skel´e·ton *n.* the supporting framework of a vertebrate; the main

supporting parts of a structure; a
mere sketch or outline —**skel´e·tal**
adj. —**skel´e·tal·ly** *adv.*

skep´ti·cal *adj.* doubtful or suspi-
cious —**skep´ti·cal·ly** *adv.* —**skep´**
ti·cal·ness *n.*

skep´ti·cism *n.* the belief that absolute knowledge is unattainable;
a doubting or incredulous state;
doubt about basic religious doctrines —**skep´tic** *n.*

sketch *n.* a rough drawing; a preliminary study; a brief description;
a short play —**sketch´er** *n.*

sketch´y *adj.* lacking detail; superficial —**sketch´i·ly** *adv.* —**sketch´**
i·ness *n.*

skew´er *n.* a long rod for holding
food while roasting —*vt.* to run
through or fasten as with a skewer

skiff *n.* a light rowboat or sailing
vessel

skill *n.* proficiency; a specific craft or
trade —**skilled, skill´ful** *adj.* —
skill´ful·ly *adv.* —**skill´ful·ness** *n.*

skil´let *n.* a frying pan

skim *vt.* to remove matter from the
surface of a liquid; to move lightly
over a surface; to cover with a thin
film; to read over hastily —*vi.* to
move lightly over a surface; to
glance over; to become covered
with a thin film —*n.* a thin coating
—**skim´mer** *n.*

skimp *vi., vt.* to do poorly or carelessly; to provide too little —
skimp´ing·ly *adv.*

skimp´y *adj.* scanty; barely enough;
insufficient —**skimp´i·ly** *adv.* —
skimp´i·ness *n.*

skin *n.* the outer covering of an
animal body; a container made
from the skin of an animal; any
outer layer, as the rind of fruit

skin´flint *n.* one obsessed with sav-
ing money

skin´ny *adj.* overly thin —**skin´ni**
ness *n.*

skip *vi.* to move by a series of ligh

hops; to ricochet —*vt.* to leap over
or bypass; to fail to attend — *n.*

skir´mish *n.* a minor encounter; an
unimportant dispute —*vi.* to battle
—**skir´mish·er** *n.*

skirt *n.* a woman's garment or that
part of a garment that hangs from
the waist; anything that hangs or
covers like a skirt; the border of an
area: *outskirts* —*vt.* to form the
border of; to avoid: *skirt the town*
—*vi.* to pass along the border

skit *n.* a short play

skit´tish *adj.* easily frightened, as a
horse; playful —**skit´tish·ly** *adv.*
—**skit´tish·ness** *n.*

skulk *vi.* to move about furtively —
skulk´er *n.*

sky *n.* heaven; the upper atmosphere

slab *n.* a thick, flat slice

slack *adj.* hanging loosely; listless;
careless; lacking activity —**slack´
en** *vi.*, *vt.* —**slack´ness** *n.*

slack´er *n.* idler; one who shirks

slake *vt.* to quench: *slake one's thirst*

slam *vt.* to shut violently; to dash; to
criticize —*vi.* to shut with force —
n. severe criticism

slan´der *vt.*, *vi.* to utter false state-
ments; to defame —*n.* a false
statement —**slan´der·er** *n.* —**slan´
der·ous** *adj.* —**slan´der·ous·ly**
adv. —**slan´der·ous·ness**

slang *n.* the special language of a
particular group; words or phrases
derived from unconventional use
of standard vocabulary —**slang´
i·ly** *adv.* —**slang´i·ness** *n.* —
slang´y *adj.*

slant *vt.* to cause to slope; to write
from a biased point of view —*adj.*
sloping —*n.* an incline; an opinionated view —**slant´ing** *adj.* —
slant´ing·ly *adv.*

slap *vt.* to strike with the open hand;
to insult —*n.* a blow; an insult —
slap´per *n.*

slash *vt.* to cut violently; to strike

with a whip; to reduce sharply —
vi. to make a long sweeping stroke
—*n.* a cut or gash; an ornamental
slit in a garment; a forest clearing
covered with debris —**slash´er** *n.*

slat *n.* a thin strip of wood

slaugh´ter *vt.* to kill for food; to
murder savagely —*n.* a savage
killing —**slaugh´ter·er**

slave *n.* one owned by another; one
completely subject to another or to
some habit or influence; a device
controlled by another device —*vi.*
to toil ceaselessly

slav´er *n.* a person or vessel engaged
in slave trade

slav´ery *n.* the holding of persons as
property; submission to a habit or
influence; constant toil

slay *vt.* to kill violently —**slay´er** *n.*

slea´zy *adj.* shoddy or shabby; vulgar or tawdry —**slea´zi·ness**

sled (*US*) *n.* a vehicle with runners
designed to carry loads over snow
and ice —*vt.*, *vi.* to convey or ride
on a sled —**sled´der** *n.*

sledge (*Brit.*) *n.* a vehicle mounted on
low runners to carry loads over
frozen or rough terrain, especially
one pulled by draft animals —*vt.*,
vi. to transport or travel by sledge

sleek *adj.* smooth and glossy; well-
groomed; slick —**sleek´ly** *adv.*
—**sleek´ness** *n.*

sleep *n.* a period of rest characterized by cessation of voluntary
movement and indifference to external stimuli —*vt.*, *vi.* to rest or
fall asleep

sleep´er *n.* one who sleeps; a railway
sleeper car; something or someone
that unexpectedly excels; (*Brit.*) a
section of concrete or timber that
separates and supports railway
tracks

sleep´less *adj.* unable to sleep; always active —**sleep´less·ly** *adv.* —
sleep´less·ness *n.*

sleep´y *adj.* drowsy; lethargic or

sluggish —**sleep´i·ly** *adv.* —**sleep´ i·ness** *n.*

sleet *n.* partly frozen rain —*vi.* to fall as frozen rain —**sleet´y** *adj.*

sleeve *n.* the part of a garment that covers the arm; a covering or wrapper

sleigh *n.* a horse-drawn vehicle with runners for transporting people or goods over snow or ice —*vi.* to ride in a sleigh

sleight *n.* dexterity; a deception — **sleight of hand** trickery or deception performed by deft manipulation of small objects

slen´der *adj.* long and thin; attractively slim —**slen´der·ly** *adv.* — **slen´der·ness** *n.*

slen´der·ize *vt.*, *vi.* to make or become slender

sleuth *n.* a detective —*vi.* to work as a detective

slice *n.* a thin piece cut from a larger one; a portion —*vt.* to cut from a larger piece; to divide into parts — *vi.* to cut, as with a knife —**slice´ a·ble** *adj.* —**slic´er** *n.*

slick *adj.* smooth or sleek; deceptively clever —*n.* a film of oil

slide *vi.* to move smoothly over a surface; to slip from a position —*n.* an inclined plane for moving persons or materiel; a glass plate for mounting microscope specimens; a transparency; a part or mechanism that slides; the slipping of a mass of earth or snow —**slid´er** *n.*

slight *adj.* of small importance; slender in build; frail —*vt.* to do carelessly or thoughtlessly; to treat as trivial —*n.* an act of disrespect —**slight´ly** *adv.* —**slight´ness** *n.*

slim *adj.* lacking girth; meager: *a slim chance* —*vt.*, *vi.* to make or become slimmer —**slim´ly** *adv.* — **slim´ness** *n.*

slime *n.* moist, adhesive mud or earth; a mucous discharge from certain organisms —*vt.* to smear with slime

slim´y *adj.* covered with slime; filthy or foul —**slim´i·ly** *adv.* —**slim´i· ness** *n.*

sling *n.* a strap for hurling a stone; a device for holding an injured arm; a strap for lifting heavy objects — *vt.* to throw or fling

slink *vi.* to move furtively

slink´y *adj.* stealthy; graceful, serpentine: *a slinky dress* —**slink´i·ly** *adv.* —**slink´i·ness** *n.*

slip *vt.* to put on or off easily; to convey slyly; to pass unobserved —*vi.* to slide so as to lose one's footing; to fall into error; to escape; to move stealthily; to overlook —*n.* a sudden slide; an error; a woman's undergarment; a pillowcase; undesired motion: *the problem is caused by slip in the gears*

slip´per *n.* a light, casual shoe

slip´per·y *adj.* being so smooth as to make sliding likely; elusive; unreliable —**slip´per·i·ness** *n.*

slit *n.* a long, narrow opening —*vt.* to cut lengthwise

slith´er *vi.* to glide like a snake —*n.* a sinuous gliding movement — **slith´er·y** *adj.*

slob *n.* a careless or ill-kempt person

slob´ber *vt.* to ooze from the mouth; to shed or spill from the mouth, as in eating —*vi.* to slaver; to talk or act gushingly —*n.* sentimental talk

slog *vt.*, *vi.* to plod

slo´gan *n.* a catchword or motto

slo·gan·eer´ *vi.* to coin or use slogans —*n.* one who creates or uses slogans

sloop *n.* a small sailboat

slop *vi.*, *vt.* to splash or cause to splash or spill —*n.* waste food; swill

slope *vi.* to slant —*n.* a slanting surface; the degree of inclination of a line or surface

slop´py *adj.* watery or pulpy; messy; marked by carelessness: *a sloppy* *job*; overly sentimental —**slop´pi·ly** *adv.* —**slop´pi·ness** *n.*

slosh *vi.* to splash; to flounder —**slosh´y** *adj.*

slot *n.* a narrow groove or opening: *a coin slot, mail slot*; a narrow cut designed to receive a corresponding part; an opening, as for a job or an event —*vt.* to cut a slot; to assign: *slot a job interview*

sloth *n.* a slow-moving mammal; laziness

sloth´ful *adj.* inclined to idleness or inactivity —**sloth´ful·ly** *adv.* —**sloth´ful·ness** *n.*

slouch *n.* a drooping movement or appearance; an incompetent person —*vi.* to sit or move in an ungraceful, drooping manner —**slouch´i·ly** *adv.* —**slouch´i·ness** *n.* —**slouch´y** *adj.*

slough *n.* a stagnant swamp or backwater —**slough´y** *adj.*

slov´en·ly *adj.* untidy and careless in appearance —*adv.* —**slov´en·li·ness** *n.*

slow *adj.* taking a long time; not hasty; dull in comprehending; tedious; not brisk —*vt.*, *vi.* to make or become slow or slower; to delay —*adv.* at less than normal speed —**slow´ly** *adv.* —**slow´ness** *n.*

sludge *n.* soft mud or slush —**sludg´y** *adj.*

slug´gard *n.* a slow or lazy person; an idler —**slug´gard·ly** *adv.* —**slug´gard·ness** *n.*

slug´gish *adj.* inactive; habitually slow and lazy —**slug´gish·ly** *adv.* —**slug´gish·ness** *n.*

sluice *n.* an artificial channel for conducting water; a device for controlling flow

slum *n.* a squalid street or section of the city

slum´ber *vi.* to sleep lightly —*n.* quiet sleep —**slum´ber·ous** *adj.*

slump *vi.* to fall or fail suddenly; to stand or walk in a stooped manner; to slouch —*n.* a collapse or decline, as in business activity

slur *vt.* to slight or disparage; to pronounce indistinctly —*n.* a disparaging remark

slush *n.* soft, sloppy material; sentimental words —**slush´i·ness** *n.* —**slush´y** *adj.*

slut *n.* a slatternly woman; a promiscuous woman —**slut´tish** *adj.* —**slut´tish·ly** *adv.* —**slut´tish·ness** *n.*

sly *adj.* stealthily clever; roguish —**sly´ly** *adv.* —**sly´ness** *n.*

smack *n.* a quick, sharp sound; a noisy kiss; a slap

small *adj.* not as large as others of its kind; little; unimportant; having little body or volume; mean-spirited: *a small person* —*n.* a petite or slender part: *the small of the back* —*adv.* —**small´ish** *adj.* —**small´ness** *n.*

smart *n.* a stinging sensation —*vi.* to cause or experience a stinging sensation; to experience remorse —*vt.* to cause a stinging pain; to feel such a pain; to feel anguish: *their cruel remarks smart* —*adj.* intelligent; clever or shrewd; impertinent; brisk: *a smart pace*; fashionable —**smart´ly** *adv.*

smart´en *vt.*, *vi.* to improve one's appearance; to make or become more knowledgeable

smash *vt.* to break into pieces; to crush; to strike —*n.* an outstanding success —**smash´er** *n.*

smat´ter·ing *n.* a little bit; superficial knowledge

smear *vt.* to soil; to apply in a thick coat; to slander

smell *vt.* to perceive through the nose; to examine or discover by odor —*n.* an unpleasant odor; a faint suggestion —**smell´i·ness** *n.* —**smell´y** *adj.*

smile *n.* a pleased expression —*vi.* to appear cheerful; to show approval

—**smil´ing·ly** adv.

smirch vt. to soil; to defame or dishonor —n. a smear

smirk n. a sarcastic or derisive grin —vi. to grin —**smirk´er** n.

smite vt. to strike hard; to afflict or kill with a sudden blow

smock n. a loose outer garment

smog n. a noxious mist caused by the action of sunlight on atmospheric pollutants —**smog´gy** adj.

smoke n. the vaporous byproduct of combustion; something resembling this; something to smoke: a tobacco product —vi. to give off smoke; to make use of tobacco products — vt. to flavor food by treating with smoke; to force out as with smoke —**smok´er** n.

smok´y adj. containing or emitting smoke; discolored by smoke; being the gray color of smoke —**smok´i·ly** adv. —**smok´i·ness** n.

smol´der vi. to burn slowly; to have suppressed feelings or emotions

smooth adj. of an even surface; without lumps; sauve and flattering, especially deceitfully —vt., vi. to make or become even; to make free of lumps —**smooth´ly** adv. —**smooth´ness** n.

smoth´er vt. to prevent from breathing; to suffocate; to stifle or overwhelm: smother with kindness

smudge vt., vi. to smear or become smeared —n. a stain; heavy smoke designed to drive away insects or protect plants from frost —**smudg´i·ness** n. —**smudg´y** adj.

smug adj. self–satisfied; complacent —**smug´ly** adv. —**smug´ness** n.

smug´gle vt. to take in or out of a country illegally —**smug´gler** n.

smut n. blackening made by soot or smoke; something obscene; a fungal disease of plants

smut´ty adj. stained with soot; obscene —**smut´ti·ly** adv. —**smut´ti·ness** n.

snack n. a light meal; a small amount of food —vi. to eat a small amount

snag n. a jagged bulge; an obstacle or difficulty —vt. to catch, as clothing, on something jagged or protruding

snap n. a sharp sound; a quick, sharp closing of the jaws; a sudden breaking or release; a fastener; brisk energy; an easy task —adj. done suddenly: made a snap judgement; that fastens with a snap —vi., vt. to grasp suddenly; to speak sharply; to move quickly and smartly

snap´pish adj. apt to speak crossly; disposed to snap or bite, as a dog —**snap´pish·ly** adv. —**snap´pish·ness** n.

snap´py adj. smart or stylish; snappish —**snap´pi·ly** adv. —**snap´pi·ness** n.

snare n. a trap for catching animals; something that misleads —vt. to trap; to entrap by trickery

snarl n. a growl; a tangle, as of hair —vi. to growl; to speak harshly; to become entangled —**snarl´er** n. —**snarl´y** adj.

snatch vt. to seize suddenly or eagerly; to obtain as opportunity allows: snatch a little sleep between calls —**snatch´er** n.

sneak vi., vt. to move or act in a stealthy manner —n. a stealthy movement; a dishonest person — adj. stealthy —**sneak´i·ly, sneak´ing·ly** adv. —**sneak´i·ness** n. —**sneak´y** adj.

sneak´er (US) n. a flexible sports shoe with a soft rubber sole

sneer n. a scornful grimace —vi. to show or express contempt —**sneer´ing·ly** adv.

snick´er n. a smothered laugh —vi., vt. to laugh derisively

sniff vi. to breath audibly in short bursts through the nose —vt. to inhale; to smell —n.

snif´fle vi. to breathe with difficulty; to snivel —n. **—snif´fler** n.

snif´ter n. a roundish goblet for serving brandy

snip vt., vi. to cut with short, quick strokes —n. a small cut

snip´pet n. a small clipping

snip´py adj. abrupt; insolent; rude —**snip´pi·ly** adv. —**snip´pi·ness** n.

snitch vt. to steal —vi. to inform on

sniv´el vi. to whine tearfully —n. —**sniv´el·er** n.

snob n. one preoccupied with wealth and station; one who affects to be superior —**snob´ber·y**, **snob´bish·ness** n. —**snob´bish·ly** adv.

snood n. a hairnet

snoop vi. to pry —n. —**snoop´er** n. —**snoop´y** adj.

snoot´y adj. haughty; snobbish — **snoot´i·ly** adv. —**snoot´i·ness** n.

snooze vi. to sleep lightly —n. a brief, light sleep

snore vi. to breathe with snorting noises while sleeping —n. —**snor´er** n.

snow n. precipitation in the form of ice crystals —vi., vt. to fall or cause to fall as snow

snub vt. to treat with disdain — n. a deliberate slight —**snub´ber** n.

snug adj. cozy; close-fitting —**snug´ly** adv. —**snug´ness** n.

snug´gle vt., vi. to nestle or cuddle

soak vt. to saturate; to drench

soap n. a sudsy cleansing agent — **soap opera** an ongoing, usually daytime, radio or television drama, originally sponsored by companies that made and sold soap —**soap´i·ness** n. —**soap´y** adj.

soar vi. to float aloft; to glide through the air —**soar´er** n. —**soar´ing·ly** adv.

sob vi., vt. to weep audibly

so´ber adj. unaffected by an alcoholic beverage; temperate or rational; solemn or serious —vt., vi.

to make or become sober —**so´ber·ly** adv. —**so´ber·ness** n.

so·bri´e·ty n. the state or being unaffected by drink; composure or seriousness

so´bri·quet n. a nickname

so´cia·ble adj. inclined to prefer company; friendly; characterized by friendly conversation —**so·cia·bil´i·ty**, **so´cia·ble·ness** n. —**so´cia·bly** adv.

so´cial adj. of society or its mores; friendly; pertaining to public welfare; existing in communities —n. an informal gathering

so´cial·ite n. one prominent in fashionable society

so´cial·ize vi. take part in social activities —vt. to control or adapt for the needs of society —**so·cial·i·za´tion** n. —**so´cial·iz·er** n.

so´cial·ly adv. with regard to society: socially acceptable

so·ci´e·tal adj. of the function, structure, etc. of society —**so·ci´e·tal·ly** adv.

so·ci´e·ty n. a group of people sharing certain characteristics, as language, customs, etc.; the fashionable members of a community; an association joined for a common purpose, shared interest, etc.

so·ci·ol´o·gy n. the study of the origin, evolution, etc. of human society —**so´ci·o·log´ic**, **so´ci·o·log´i·cal** adj. —**so´ci·o·log´i·cal·ly** adv. —**so·ci·ol´o·gist** n.

so´ci·o·path n. one who is antisocial or hostile to society —**so´ci·o·path´ic** adj.

sock´et n. a depression into which a corresponding part fits, as a light socket that holds a bulb; (Brit.) a connector for electricity or a telephone

sod n. grassy surfaced soil —vt. to cover with sod

sodden adj. saturated; drenched; dull, as from drink —**sod´den·ly**

adv. **—sod´den·ness** *n.*

soft *adj.* easily changed by pressure; easily worked; less hard than others of the same kind; smooth and delicate; expressing mildness or sympathy **—soft, soft´ly** *adv.* **—soft´ness** *n.*

soft´en *vt., vi.* to make or become soft **—soft´en·er** *n.*

sog´gy *adj.* soaked with moisture; heavy and wet **—sog´gi·ly** *adv.* **—sog´gi·ness** *n.*

soil *n.* a layer of rock particles mixed with decaying matter that forms the outer crust of the earth; a spot or stain **—vt., vi.** to make or become dirty

soi·rée´ *n.* an evening reception

so´journ *vi.* to stay temporarily **—n.** a short stay **—so´journ·er** *n.*

sol´ace *vt.* to comfort; to alleviate or soothe **—n.** that which furnishes comfort in grief **—sol´ac·er** *n.*

so´lar *adj.* pertaining to the sun, as *solar energy*

so·lar´i·um *n.* a place, often glassed in, where one can sit in the sun

sole *adj.* only; being the only one, as *the sole survivor* **—n.** the bottom surface of the foot or a shoe; a flat fish

sol´e·cism *n.* a grammatical error; any incongruity **—sol´e·cist** *n.* **—sol´e·cis´tic** *adv.*

sole´ly *adv.* by oneself alone; entirely

sol´emn *adj.* sacred; marked by ceremonial observance, majesty, or power **—sol´emn·ly** *adv.* **—sol´emn·ness** *n.*

so·lem´ni·ty *n.* a solemn rite

sol´em·nize *vt.* to perform according to ritual, as *to solemnize a marriage* **—sol·em·ni·za´tion** *n.*

so·lic´it *vt.* to ask for earnestly; to entice to an immoral act **—so·lic´i·ta´tion** *n.*

so·lic´i·tor *n.* one who seeks money for charity, merchandise, etc.; the chief law officer of a municipality

so·lic´i·tous *adj.* full of concern **— so·lic´i·tous·ly** *adv.* **—so·lic´i·tous·ness** *n.*

so·lic´i·tude *n.* care or concern, as for another; that which makes one concerned or anxious

sol´id *adj.* having shape and volume; resistant to pressure; filling a space; of the same substance throughout: *solid gold*; well-built; financially sound; reliable, as *a solid citizen* **—n.** a three-dimensional object **—sol´id·ly** *adv.* **—so·lid´i·ty, sol´id·ness** *n.*

so·i·dar´i·ty *n.* unity of purpose

so·lid´i·fy *vt., vi.* to make or become solid **—so·lid·i·fi·ca´tion** *n.* **—so·lid´i·fi·er** *n.*

so·lil´o·quy *n.* a speech by which a lone actor reveals his thoughts to an audience **—so·lil´o·quist, so·lil´o·quiz·er** *n.* **—so·lil´o·quize** *vi.*

sol´ip·sism *n.* the philosphy that only knowledge of the self is verifiable and is therefore the only reality **—sol´ip·sist** *n.* **—sol·ip·sis´tic** *adj.*

sol´i·taire *n.* a gem set alone; a card game for one

sol´i·tar·y *adj.* alone; remote or excluded **—sol´i·tar·i·ly** *adv.* **—sol´i·tar·i·ness** *n.*

sol´i·tude *n.* seclusion; loneliness

so´lo *n.* anything accomplished without assistance, especially of a performance **—adj.** performed alone **—vi.** to perform alone; to pilot an aircraft for the first time without an instructor on board **—so´lo·ist** *n.*

sol´stice *n.* either of the times each year when the sun is farthest from the celestial equator

sol´u·ble *adj.* capable of being solved or explained; capable of being dissolved **—sol´u·ble·ness** *n.* **—sol´u·bly** *adv.*

so·lu´tion *n.* a mixture of varying proportions; the answer to or resolution of a problem

solve *vt.* to work out a correct solution or answer —**solv·a·bil´i·ty** *n.* —**solv´a·ble** *adj.* —**sol´ver** *n.*

sol´vent *adj.* financially sound; capable of dissolving —*n.* a substance capable of dissolving other substances —**sol´ven·cy** *n.*

som´ber *adj.* dark, gloomy; melancholy —**som´ber·ly** *adv.* —**som´ber·ness** *n.*

some *adj.* of an indeterminate number —*pron.* a certain undetermined number: *take some, some prefer it* —*adv.*

some´body *pron.* an unknown or unnamed person —*n.* a person of importance

some´day *adv.* at some future time

some´how *adv.* in some unspecified way

some´one *pron.* some unspecified person

song *n.* a short musical composition for voice; any melodic utterance

son´ic *adj.* relating to sound

son´net *n.* a poem of 14 lines —**son´ne·teer´** *n.*

so·no´rous *adj.* of a deep rich sound; lofty sounding —**so·no´rous·ly** *adv.* —**so·no´rous·ness** *n.*

soon *adv.* in the near future; early: *it came too soon;* willingly: *I would as soon go as not*

soot *n.* a fine black deposit from incomplete combustion —**soot´i·ness** *n.* —**soot´y** *adj.*

soothe *vt.* to calm; to relieve, as pain —*vi.* to afford relief —**sooth´er** *n.* —**sooth´ing** *adj.* —**sooth´ing·ly** *adv.*

sooth´say·er *n.* one who claims to be able to foretell the future —**sooth´say·ing** *n.*

soph´ism *n.* a misleading argument; a fallacy —**soph´is·try** *n.*

soph´ist *n.* a learned person; one who argues deviously

so·phis´ti·cate *n.* one presumed to be worldly–wise

so·phis´ti·cat·ed *adj.* cultured; refined; complex —**so·phis·ti·ca´tion** *n.*

soph´o·more (US) *n.* a second–year student —*adj.* of a second–year student or the second year of school

soph·o·mor´ic (US) *adj.* of a sophomore; shallow, pretentious; immature —**soph·o·mor´i·cally** *adv.*

sop·o·rif´ic *adj.* tending to cause sleep; sleepy

sop´ping *adj.* drenched

so·pra´no *n.* a voice or music of the highest range; one who sings such music —*adj.*

sor´cer·er *n.* a wizard or magician

sor´cer·ess *n.* a female wizard; a witch

sor´cer·y *n.* magic; witchcraft —**sor´cer·ous** *adj.* —**sor´cer·ous·ly** *adv.*

sor´did *adj.* degrading; vile; squalid —**sor´did·ly** *adv.* —**sor´did·ness** *n.*

sore *n.* a place on the body that is bruised, inflamed, etc.; anything causing pain or trouble —*adj.* tender; pained or distressed —**sore´ness** *n.*

sore´ly *adv.* distressingly; extremely: *sorely needed*

so·ror´i·ty *n.* a woman's organization

sor´row *n.* pain or sadness because of loss, etc.; an event that causes distress; the expression of grief —**sor´row·ful** *adj.* —**sor´row·ful·ly** *adv.* —**sor´row·ful·ness** *n.*

sor´ry *adj.* feeling regret or remorse; affected by sorrow; paltry or worthless: *a sorry piece of work* —**sor´ri·ly** *adv.* —**sor´ri·ness** *n.*

sort *vt.* to arrange by kind, size, etc. —*n.* a collection characterized by similar qualities; a particular kind: *that sort of person* —**sort´a·ble** *adj.* —**sor´ter** *n.*

soul *n.* the moral or spiritual part of man; emotional or spiritual depth or vitality; the essence of something; embodiment: *the soul of generosity*; the disembodied spirit of one who has died

soul´ful *adj.* full of emotion —**soul´ful·ly** *adv.* —**soul´ful·ness** *n.*

sound *n.* energy perceptible by the hearing; noise of a particular quality: *the sound of a door slamming*; significance: *a sinister sound* —*vi., vt.* to give forth or cause to give forth a sound —*adj.* healthy; free from flaw, decay, etc.; correct or logical: *sound advice*; financially solvent; thorough: *a sound thrashing* —**sound´ly** *adv.* —**sound´ness** *n.*

sound´less *adj.* silent; noiseless —**sound´less·ly** *adv.* —**sound´less·ness** *n.*

soup *n.* food cooked and served in a liquid

soup·çon´ *n.* a small quantity; a taste

sour *adj.* sharp, acid, or tart to the taste; pertaining to fermentation —**sour´ly** *adv.* —**sour´ness** *n.*

source *n.* that from which something originates or is derived

souse *vt., vi.* to dip or steep in a liquid; to pickle —*n.* pickled meat; a drunkard

south *n.* the general direction to the right of sunrise —*adj.* in a southerly direction —**south´ern** *adj.*

sou·ve·nir´ *n.* a memento

sov´er·eign *adj.* exersizing supreme jurisdiction; autonomous: *a sovereign state* —*n.* one who possesses supreme authority —**sov´er·eign·ty** *n.*

sow *vt., vi.* to scatter, as seed

space *n.* the expanse considered to be an integral part of the universe; a specific distance or area; an area designated for a particular use: *living space* —*adj.*

spa´cial *adj.* spatial

spa´cious *adj.* roomy; containing

more than adequate space —**spa´cious·ly** *adv.* —**spa´cious·ness** *n.*

span *vt.* to measure; to extend across or over —*n.* the distance between two points; a part that extends between two points

span´gle *n.* a small bit of brilliant decoration —*vi., vt.* to glitter or cause to glitter —**span´gly** *adj.*

spank *vt.* to strike as punishment —**spank´er** *n.*

spar *n.* a pole supporting a sail —*vi.* to box; to bandy words

spare *vt.* to treat mercifully; to relieve from, as pain or expense; to use frugally —*adj.* over and above what is needed; held in reserve; lean; scanty —*n.* something saved for future use —**spare´ness** *n.*

spar´ing *adj.* scanty; frugal or stingy —**spar´ing·ly** *adv.*

spark *n.* a glistening or brilliant point or particle; a trace: *a spark of wit* —*vi.* to give off sparks —*vt.* to activate: *spark a revolution*

spar´kle *vi.* to glitter; to emit sparks; to effervesce, as certain wines; to be brilliant or vivacious —*n.* brilliance, vivacity —**spar´kler** *n.*

sparse *adj.* scattered; not dense —**sparse´ly** *adv.* —**sparse´ness**, **spar´si·ty** *n.*

spasm *n.* a sudden, involuntary muscular contraction; a sudden action or effort

spas·mod´ic, **spas·mod´i·cal** *adj.* temporary; transitory —**spas·mod´i·cal·ly** *adv.*

spas´tic *adj.* characterized by spasms —*n.* a person afflicted with a disability that causes spasms —**spas´ti·cal·ly** *adv.*

spate *n.* an overflow; a sudden outpouring, as of words

spa´tial *adj.* relating to space —**spa´tial·ly** *adv.*

spat´ter *vi., vt.* to throw off or scatter in drops —*n.* a mark caused by spattering

speak *vi.* to utter; to express or convey, as in speech; to deliver an address; to converse —*vt.* to make known, as in speech; to utter in speech; to be capable of conversing, especially in a foreign language —**speak′a·ble** *adj.* —**speak′er** *n.*

spear *n.* a weapon consisting of a pointed head on a long shaft; a slender stalk

spe′cial *adj.* out of the ordinary; uncommon; designed for a specific purpose: *a special permit*; notable: *a special occasion* —*n.* something designated for a specific service, occasion, etc. —**spe′ci·al·ly** *adv.*

spe′cial·ist *n.* one devoted to a particular discipline

spe·ci·al′i·ty, spe′ci·al·ty *n.* something in which one specializes

spe′ci·al·ize *vi.* to concentrate on one particular activity, branch of learning, etc. —*vt.* to adapt for a particular use or purpose —**spe·ci·al·i·za′tion** *n.*

spe′cie *n.* coined money

spe′cies *n.* a category of animals or plants

spe·cif′ic *adj.* distinctly set forth; explicit —*n.* a medicine affecting a specific condition; a particular item or detail —**spe·cif′i·cal·ly** *adv.* —**spec·i·fic′i·ty**

spec·i·fi·ca′tion *n.* a detailed description of a device, part, project, etc.

spec′i·fy *vt.* to state in full and explicit detail —**spec′i·fi·a·ble** *adj.* —**spec′i·fi·er** *n.*

spec′i·men *n.* a person or thing regarded as representative of a class or type; a sample for laboratory anyalysis

spe′cious *adj.* apparently plausible, but actually without merit: *specious reasoning* —**spe′cious·ly** *adv.* —**spe′cious·ness** *n.*

speck *n.* a small spot or stain; a tiny particle or trace

speck′le *vt.* to mark with specks —*n.* a speck

spec′ta·cle *n.* a grand display, as a pageant, natural phenomenon, etc.; a deplorable exhibition

spec·tac′u·lar *adj.* wonderfully exciting —*n.* something lavish —**spec·tac·u·lar′i·ty** *n.* —**spec·tac′u·lar·ly** *adv.*

spec′ta·tor *n.* one who views; an eyewitness

spec′ter *n.* an apparition —**spec′tral** *adj.* —**spec′tral·ly** *adv.*

spec′trum *n.* the band of colors observed when a beam of white light is diffracted; a band of wave frequencies; a range: *a wide spectrum of activities*

spec′u·late *vi.* to ponder or theorize; to involve in an endeavor or make an investment that involves risk —**spec·u·la′tion** *n.* —**spec′u·la·tor** *n.* —**spec′u·la·to·ry** *adj.*

spec′u·la·tive *adj.* pertaining to conjecture; strictly theoretical; relating to financial risk; risky or doubtful —**spec′u·la·tive·ly** *adv.* —**spec′u·la·tive·ness** *n.*

speech *n.* the faculty of expressing with the spoken word; the power to speak; that which is spoken; a public address or lecture; a characteristic manner of speaking —**speech′i·fi·er** *n.* —**speech′i·fy** *vi.*

speech′less *adj.* mute; temporarily mute due to a physical disorder, emotion, etc.; inexpressible in words: *speechless wonder* —**speech′less·ly** *adv.* —**speech′less·ness** *n.*

speed *n.* rapidity of motion; the rate of movement —*vi.* to move or go rapidly —*vt.* to promote the forward progress of —**speed′er** *n.*

speed′y *adj.* characterized by speed; without delay —**speed′i·ly** *adv.* —**speed′i·ness** *n.*

spell *vt.* to pronounce or write the

letters of a word; to relieve temporarily, as from work —*n.* a period of time; a turn of duty in relief of another; an incantation; a state of enchantment

spell´bind *vt.* to enthrall, as if by a spell —**spell´bind·ing·ly** *adv.* — **spell´bound** *adj.*

spell´er *n.* one who spells; a spelling book

spe·lunk´er *n.* one who explores and studies caves

spend *vt.* to pay out or disburse; to use up; to use wastefully or squander —**spend´a·ble** *adj.* — **spend´er** *n.*

spend´thrift *n.* one who is wasteful of money —*adj.* excessively lavish

spent *adj.* worn out or exhausted

sperm *n.* the male fertilizing fluid: semen; a male reproductive cell: spermatozoon

spew *vi.* to come or issue forth —*vt.* to eject or send forth

sphere *n.* a round body in which every point on the surface is equidistant from the center; a field of activity, influence, etc. —**spher´ic, spher´i·cal** *adj.* —**spher´i·cal·ly** *adv.*

sphe´roid *n.* a body approximating the form of a sphere

sphinx *n.* a mythical monster; a mysterious person

spice *n.* an aromatic substance used to flavor; that which gives zest or adds interest —*vi.* to season with spice; to add zest to —**spic´er** *n.*

spic´y *adj.* flavored or fragrant with spice; full of spirit; somewhat improper or risqué —**spic´i·ly** *adv.* — **spic´i·ness** *n.*

spig´ot *n.* a plug for a cask; a faucet or the valve by which it functions

spike *n.* a large, thick nail; a pointed projection, as on an iron fence or on the soles of shoes; a high slender heel of a woman's shoe; an ear of grain —*vt.* to fasten with a

spike; to pierce with a spike

spill *vi., vt.* to run over or cause to run over —*n.* that which is spilled —**spill´age** *n.* —**spill´er**

spill´way *n.* a passage by which excess water escapes or is released

spin *vt.* to draw out and twist fiber into thread, yarn, etc.; to produce a web; to tell, as a story or yarn — *vi.* to make thread or yarn; to whirl rapidly —*n.* a ride, as in an automobile; the uncontrolled spiral descent of an airplane

spin´dly *adj.* of a slender, lanky form, suggesting weakness

spine *n.* the spinal column of a vertebrate; a hard, pointed outgrowth on the bodies of certain animals; a thorny projection on the stem of a plant; the back of a bound book — **spin´y** *adj.*

spine´less *adj.* lacking courage; weak or irresolute; having no backbone; having a flexible backbone —**spine´less·ly** *adv.* —**spine´less·ness** *n.*

spin´et *n.* a small harpsichord or upright piano

spin´ster *n.* a woman who has never married —**spin´ster·hood** *n.* — **spin´ster·ish** *adj.*

spi´ral *n.* a curve that winds like a screw thread; a continuously developing increase or decrease: *a price spiral* —*vi., vt.* to take or cause to take a spiral form or course —*adj.*

spire *n.* the tapering roof of a tower or steeple; a slender stalk

spir´it *n.* the animating principle of life and energy in man and animals; that part of a human characterized by intelligence, emotion, etc.; a supernatural being; mood or disposition; vivacity or energy; unspecified intent: *the spirit of the law* —*vt.* to carry off mysteriously —*adj.* of ghosts or disembodied entities

spir´it·ed *adj.* lively, animated; having a specific characteristic: *mean–spirited* —**spir´it·ed·ly** *adv.* —**spir´it·ed·ness** *n.*

spir´it·less *adj.* lacking enthusiasm or courage —**spir´it·less·ly** *adv.* —**spir´it·less·ness** *n.*

spir´i·tu·al *adj.* pertaining to the highest moral or intellectual qualities of man; sacred or religious; supernatural —**spir·i·tu·al´i·ty, spir´i·tu·al·ness** *n.* —**spir´i·tu·al·ly** *adv.*

spir´i·tu·al·ism *n.* the belief that the spirits of the dead can communicate with the living; a philosophy that identifies the ultimate reality as basically spiritual —**spir´i·tu·al·ist** *n.* —**spir·i·tu·al·is´tic** *adj.*

spite *n.* malicious bitterness or resentment —*vt.* to vex maliciously —**spite´ful** *adj.* —**spite´ful·ly** *adv.* —**spite´ful·ness** *n.*

splash *vt.* to spatter a liquid about; to display prominently: *splashed over the front page* —*n.* the act or noise of spattering; a small amount: *a splash of bitters*; a brilliant or ostentatious display —**splash´i·ly** *adv.* —**splash´i·ness** *n.* —**splash´y** *adj.*

splat´ter *vt., vi.* to spatter or splash in small drops: *a spatter of grease* —*n.* the mark or stain of a spatter; a small amount

splay *vt., vi.* to spread or extend outward —*adj.* spread or turned outward

spleen *n.* an organ of most vertebrates which modifies, filters, and stores blood; ill temper or spitefulness

splen´did *adj.* magnificent, imposing; conspicuously great or illustrious —**splen´did·ly** *adv.* —**splen´did·ness** *n.*

splen´dor *n.* magnificence; grandeur —**splen´dor·ous, splen´drous** *adj.*

splice *vt.* to unite, as two pieces of rope to form a continuous piece; to connect, as timbers, by beveling, scarfing, or overlapping —*n.* a joint made by splicing —**splic´er** *n.*

splint *n.* a thin, flexible strip used for basket weaving, chair bottoms, etc.; an appliance to support or immobilize a part of the body —*vt.* to apply a splint

splin´ter *n.* a thin, sharp piece split or torn off; a sliver; a faction that has broken away from a larger group —*vt., vi.* to break into fragments; to separate into a smaller group —**splin´ter·y** *adj.*

split *vt.* to separate into two or more parts; to divide and distribute —*vi.* to break or divide lengthwise; become divided by disagreement; share with others —*n.* the act or result of splitting; a separation into factions; a share or portion —*adj.* divided or separated

splurge *vi.* to spend money lavishly or wastefully —*n.* a showy or extravagant display

spoil *vt.* to damage or destory; to overindulge another —*vi.* to become tainted or decayed, as food

spoil´age *n.* that which is spoiled; the extent of waste or loss

spoils *n.* plunder seized by violence; government jobs awarded to the faithful supporters of a party

spoke *n.* one of the members of a wheel that connect it to the hub

spo´ken *adj.* uttered aloud; of a specific kind of speech: *soft–spoken*

spokes·man *n.* one who speaks on behalf of another

sponge *n.* an underwater, plantlike animal having a fibrous skeleton; the light, absorbent skeleton of such animals used for bathing, cleaning, etc.; any absorbent substance used to clean, soak up liquids, etc.; leavened dough —*vt.* to wipe with a sponge; to impose on

another —spon´gi·ness n. —
spong´y adj.

spong´er n. one who uses a sponge;
one who gathers sponges from the
sea; one who takes advantage of
the generosity of others

spon´sor n. one who acts as surety
for another; a person or group who
establishes or finances something
—vt. to act as a sponsor —spon·
so´ri·al adj. —spon´sor·ship n.

spon·ta´ne·ous adj. arising naturally
and without constraint or
prompting; produced without human involvement —spon·ta·ne´
i·ty n. —spon·ta´ne·ous·ly adv. —
spon·ta´ne·ous·ness n.

spoof vt., vi. to deceive; to satirize in
a good-natured manner —n. a
hoax; a playful parody

spook vt. to haunt; to frighten or
disturb; to startle or frighten, as
an animal, into flight

spook´y adj. ghostly, eerie; frightened, nervous —spook´i·ly adv. —
spook´i·ness n.

spool (US) n. a cylinder for holding
thread, wire, etc.

spoon n. an eating or serving utensil
having a shallow oval bowl and a
handle —vt. to lift up or out with a
spoon

spoon´ful n. as much as a spoon will
hold

spoor n. footprints or other traces of
a wild animal

spo·rad´ic, spo·rad´i·cal adj. occurring infrequently; not widely diffused —spo·rad´i·cal·ly adv.

spore n. the reproductive body in
plants that have no seeds; any minute organism

sport n. a diversion; a particular
game or activity pursued for diversion; a spirit of raillery; a laugh-
ingstock —vi. to participate in
games; to jest —adj. pertaining to
sports; of casual wear

sport´ing adj. conforming to the

spirit of sportsmanship

spor´tive adj. playful; interested in
athletic games —spor´tive·ly adv.
—spor´tive·ness n.

sport´y adj. colorful, as in dress —
sport´i·ly adv. —sport´i·ness n.

spot n. a particular place; a mark,
blot, stain, etc.; a mark on a playing card —vt. to mark or stain; to
see and identify —adj. available at
once: spot cash

spot´less adj. free from dirt, etc.;
unblemished, as a spotless reputation —spot´less·ly adv. —spot´
less·ness n.

spot´ty adj. having many spots;
uneven, as in quality or performance —spot´ti·ness n.

spouse n. a partner in marriage

spout vi., vt. to pour out or cause to
pour out, as a liquid under pressure; to utter angrily or at length

sprawl vi. to sit or lie ungracefully;
to spread out, as vines, etc. —
sprawl´er n.

spray n. a device for dispersing liquid in fine particles or the liquid
dispelled; any similar dispersal, as
a cluster of flowers —vt., vi. to disperse or send forth in fine particles
—spray´er n.

spread vt. to open or unfold; to force
apart; to distribute over a surface;
to distribute over time or among a
group; to disperse widely: spread a
rumor —vi. to be extended or expanded; to be spread apart; to be
dispersed —spread´er n.

spread´sheet n. a document with
information arranged in rows and
columns, often a computer program for processing numerical
data

spree n. a period of heavy drinking;
any boisterous fun

sprig n. a shoot or sprout of a plant

spring vi. to move or jump suddenly;
to occur suddenly; to proceed as
from a source —vt. to cause to

move or occur suddenly —n. a device that yields under stress and returns to normal when the stress is removed; a flow of water; the season that precedes summer —adj. resilient —**spring´er** n.

spring´y adj. elastic; resiliant

sprin´kle vt. to scatter in drops or small particles —vi. to fall in scattered drops —n. a small quantity; a light rain —**sprin´kler** n.

sprint n. a short race —vi. to run fast, especially for a short distance —**sprint´er** n.

sprite n. a fairy; a small elflike person

sprout vi. to put forth shoots; to begin to grow; to develop or grow rapidly —n. a new shoot on a plant

spruce adj. smart and neat in appearance —n. a type of pine tree or its wood —**spruce up** make neat and trim

spry adj. quick; agile —**spry´ly** adv. —**spry´ness** n.

spume n. froth or foam —vi. to foam

spunk n. slow-burning tinder; courage, pluck

spunk´y adj. spirited; daring —**spunk´i·ly** adv. —**spunk´i·ness** n.

spur n. a pointed device worn on a horseman's boot; any similar device, as climbing irons used by linemen; anything that incites or urges; a ridge extending laterally from a mountain; a railroad branch —vt. to prick or urge, as with spurs

spu´ri·ous adj. not genuine; illegitimate, as of birth —**spu´ri·ous·ly** adv. —**spu´ri·ous·ness** n.

spurn vt., vi. to reject with disdain

spurt n. a sudden gush or outbreak, as of liquid or energy —vi. to gush forth; to make a sudden, forceful effort

sput´ter vi. to make crackling or popping sounds while throwing off small particles, like burning wood

or frying fat —vi., vt. to speak excitedly and incoherently —**sput´ter·er** n.

spy n. one hired to get secret information; one who watches secretly —vi. to watch closely or secretly; to examine carefully or pry into —vt. to observe stealthily; to catch sight of

squab´ble vi. to engage in a petty quarrel —n. a petty argument —**squab´bler** n.

squad n. a small group organized for a special purpose

squal´id adj. dirty, neglected, or poverty-stricken —**squal´id·ly** adv. —**squal´id·ness, squal´or** n.

squall n. a screaming outcry; a brief commotion; a sudden burst of wind, often accompanied by rain or snow —vi.

squan´der vt. to spend wastefully, as money or time —n. wastefulness —**squan´der·er** n. —**squan´der·ing·ly** adv.

square n. a plane figure having four equal sides and four right angles; a device used to test or lay out right angles; an open area bordered by intersecting streets —adj. of or like a square; perfectly adjusted; honest, fair —vt. to make square; to test for squareness; to adjust or make satisfactory: to square accounts; to reconcile or set right —vi. to be at right angles; to conform or harmonize —**square´ness** n. —**squar´er** n.

square, square´ly adv. honestly, fairly; direct; at right angles

squash vt. to crush; to suppress —vi. to be smashed or crushed; to make a sucking sound —n. the sudden fall or sound made by a bursting body; the sound made by walking through ooze or muck; an indoor game played with rackets and a ball; an edible gourd

squat vi. to crouch or cower; to settle

on land illegally; to settle on government land in accordance with regulations —*adj.* short and thick —*n.* a crouching position —**squat´er** *n.*

squat´ty *adj.* short and thickset

squeak *n.* a thin penetrating sound —*vi.*, *vt.* —**squeek through** narrowly avert failure —**squeak´i·ly** *adv.* —**squeak´i·ness** *n.* — **squeak´y** *adj.*

squeal *vi.* to utter a sharp, shrill cry; to betray an accomplice or a plot —*n.* a shrill cry, as of a pig — **squeal´er** *n.*

squeam´ish *adj.* easily shocked or nauseated; overly scrupulous — **squeam´ish·ly** *adv.* —**squeam´ish·ness** *n.*

squeeze *vt.* to extract by pressure; to embrace —*vi.* to apply pressure; to yield to pressure —*n.* pressure; an embrace; a time of difficulty; pressure exerted for extortion — **squeeze by** avoid failure by the narrowest of margins —**squeez´a·ble** *adj.* —**squeez´a·bly** *adv.* — **squeez´er** *n.*

squelch *vt.* to squash; to silence, as with a crushing retort —*vi.* to make or move with a sucking noise —*n.* a noise as made by wet boots; a crushing reply —**squelch´er** *n.*

squint *vi.* to peer with half-closed eyes —*vt.* to hold the eyes half shut as in glaring light —*n.* — **squint´er** *n.* —**squint´y** *adj.*

squire *n.* a knight's attendant; in England a prominent landowner; in the U.S. a village lawyer or justice of the peace; a gentleman escort or suitor

squirm *vi.* to bend and twist the body; wriggle; show signs of distress —*n.* a twisting motion

squirt *vi.*, *vt.* to come forth or eject in a thin stream —*n.* a jet of liquid

stab *vt.*, *vi.* to thrust or wound, as with a pointed weapon —*n.* a

wound; a sharp pain; an effort

sta·bil´i·ty *n.* the condition of being stable; steadfastness of purpose

sta´bi·lize *vt.* to make stable; to keep from fluctuating —*vi.* to become stable —**sta·bi·li·za´tion** *n.* —**sta´bi·liz·er** *n.*

sta´ble *adj.* standing firmly in place; not easily moved or changed; having permanence; resistant to chemical change —*n.* a building for lodging horses or cattle; the racehorses of a particular owner; performers, writers, etc. under the same agency —**sta´ble·ness** *n.* — **sta´bly** *adv.*

stack *n.* a pile arranged in a somewhat orderly fashion; a large amount —*vt.* to gather into a pile; to arrange dishonestly so as to assure a certain result —**stack´a·ble** *adj.* —**stack´er** *n.*

sta´di·um *n.* a large structure for sporting events

staff *n.* a stick or rod carried as a cane; a cudgel; an emblem of authority; a pole that supports, as *a flagstaff;* a group of assistants or advisors; a group working together, as *a hospital staff* —**staff´er** *n.*

stag *n.* a male deer; an unaccompanied male; a gathering for men only —*adj.* for men only

stage *n.* a platform or area from which performances are given; a distinct step or level in a process; a portion of a journey —*vt.* to exhibit on the stage; to plan and carry out, as *to stage a protest;* to simulate: *stage for publicity* —**the stage** the acting profession; any activity or profession associated with theater or drama

stag´ger *vi.* to move unsteadily as if carrying something heavy —*vt.* to cause to stagger; to overwhelm, as with surprise or grief; to place in alternating positions —*n.* an

unsteady walk —**stag´ger·er** n. —
stag´ger·ing·ly adj.

stag´nant adj. not flowing; foul from
standing; sluggish —**stag´nant·cy**
n. —**stag´nant·ly** adv.

stag´nate vi. to become stagnant —
stag·na´tion n.

staid adj. sedate; serious —**staid´ly**
adv. —**staid´ness** n.

stain n. discoloration from foreign
matter; a dye or pigment; a moral
blemish —vt. to discolor; to color
with a dye; to blemish —vi. to take
or impart a stain —**stain´a·ble** adj.
—**stain´er** n.

stair n. one of a set of steps for as-
cending or descending

stake n. a sharpened stick or post;
something wagered, as betting
money; an interest or share, as in
an enterprise —vt. to mark a
boundary with stakes; to wager; to
back with money, equipment, etc.

stale adj. having lost freshness;
deteriorated; lacking effectiveness,
spontaneity, etc. —**stale´ness** n.

stale´mate n. a tie or deadlock —vt.
bring to a standstill

stalk n. a supporting part, as the
stem of a plant —vi., vt. to approach stealthily —**stalk´er** n.

stall n. a compartment for the confinement of an animal; any small
compartment; a delaying action; a
condition in which an engine stops
functioning — vt. to place or keep
in a stall; to halt the progress of —
vi. to come to a standstill; to make
delays

stal´wart adj. strong and robust;
determined; courageous —n. an
uncompromising partisan —**stal´
wart·ly** adv. —**stal´wart·ness** n.

stam´i·na n. endurance, as in withstanding hardship or difficulty

stam´mer vt., vi. to speak or utter
with nervous repetitions, involuntary pauses, etc. —**stam´mer·er** n.

stamp vt. to strike heavily and

noisily with the sole of the foot; to
affect as by crushing with the foot:
stamp out opposition; to cut or imprint with a die; to affix or impress
with a die or as with a die —vi. to
strike the foot heavily on the
ground; to walk heavily and noisily
—n. a machine or tool that cuts or
shapes; an implement for im-
printing or the imprint; printed
proof that a tax or fee has been
paid: *a postage stamp*; a specific
quality: *the stamp of genius* —
stamp´er n.

stam·pede´ n. a sudden, impulsive
rush, as of a herd of cattle or a
crowd of people; a spontaneous
trend, as to support a political
candidate —vt., vi. to cause or
participate in a sudden rush

stance n. a mode of standing; a
point of view

stanch vt. to stop or check; to put
an end to

stand vi. to maintain an upright
position; to take a position: *stand
aside*; to have position: *it stands
on a hill*; to assume or maintain an
attitude: *stand and fight*; to leave
unchanged: *use the letter as it
stands* —vt. to place upright; to
endure —n. a designated place or
position: *a taxi stand*; an opinion
or attitude; a structure upon
which persons may sit or stand; a
stall, etc. where merchandise is
traded; a vertical growth of trees —
stand for to represent; symbolize

stan´dard n. a flag or banner; an
emblem or symbol; that generally
accepted as a model; an established reference for weight, quality,
value, etc. —adj. serving as a criterion or gauge; of recognized excellence, popularity, etc.; not special
in any way; typical

stan´dard·ise (*Brit.*), **stan´dard·ize**
(*US*) vt. to make conform to, regulate, or test by a standard

—**stan·dard·i·za´tion** n.

stand´off n. a draw or tie

stand·off´ish adj. aloof; cool — **stand·off´ish·ly** adv. —**stand·off´ ish·ness** n.

sta´ple n. a principal commodity or product of a country or region; a product universally traded or used —adj. regularly traded, consumed, etc.

star n. a celestial object that emits radiant light; a conventional figure having radiating points; a person of outstanding accomplishment; the lead performer in a play, motion picture, etc. —vi. to be prominent or brilliant; to play a leading role —adj. exceptional or outstanding: *the star player on our team*; of the stars: *a star-gazer*

star´dom n. the status of an outstanding performer

stare vi., vt. to gaze fixedly —n. a steady, fixed gaze

stark adj. barren, bleak; severe; lacking ornamentation, color, etc.; grim, pitiless: *stark reality* —adv. utterly: *stark naked* —**stark´ly** adv. —**stark´ness** n.

star´ry adj. marked with or abounding in stars; shining like a star —**star´ri·ness** n.

start vi. to make a quick, involuntary movement; to begin an action, undertaking, etc.; to become active, operative, etc. —vt. to set in motion; to begin or commence; to set up or establish —n. a quick, startled movement; a beginning or commencement; a time or place of beginning

start´er n. a member at the beginning; one giving the signal to begin, as a race; one who sends out at intervals or at particular times, as trains or busses; a mechanical device, as for an engine; a substance that initiates a chemical reaction

star´tle vt., vi. to arouse or be aroused or excited suddenly — **star´tling** adj.

star·va´tion adj. insufficient to sustain life —n. the act of starving

starve vi. to perish from lack of food; to suffer extreme hunger; to suffer from lack: *starved for friendship* — vt. to cause to die of hunger; to deprive of something

stash vt. to hide or conceal for future use —n. a place where things are hidden; things hidden

state n. a mode or condition of existence: *a state of war*; an extreme mental condition; social status or position; a grand, ceremonious, or luxurious style: *to arrive in state*; a sovereign political unit —adj. of a government; intended for ceremonial use —vt. to set forth in speech or writing

state´ly adj. dignified; majestic — adv. loftily —**state´li·ness** n.

stat´ic adj. pertaining to bodies at rest or forces in equilibrium; at rest; not active —n. electrical noise, especially that which interferes with radio communication

sta´tion n. an assigned place, as of a guard; a headquarters; a place for accommodating passengers or freight on a bus or train line; social rank or standing —vt. to assign to a place; to set in position

sta´tion·ar·y adj. remaining in one place; fixed

sta´tio·ner n. a dealer in office supplies

sta´tion·er·y n. office supplies, as pens, paper, etc.

sta·tis´tic n. a number or value based on a representative sampling, as of opinion, income, preference, etc. —**sta·tis´tic, sta·tis´ ti·cal** adj. —**sta·tis´ti·cal·ly** adv.

stat·is·ti´cian n. one skilled in collecting, tabulating, and analyzing data

sta·tis´tics *n.* the collection and analysis of quantitative data

stat´u·ary *n.* statues collectively — *adj.* of statues

stat´ue *n.* a three–dimensional representation

stat·u·esque´ *adj.* resembling a statue, as in proportion or dignity; attractive —**stat·u·esque´ly** *adv.* —**stat·u·esque´ness** *n.*

stat·u·ette´ *n.* a small statue

stat´ure *n.* natural height; status or reputation

sta´tus *n.* state or condition; relative position or rank

stat´ute *n.* an established law or regulation

stat´u·to·ry *adj.* pertaining to a statute; based on legislative enactment —**stat´u·to·ri·ly** *adv.*

staunch *adj.* firm in principle; constant —**staunch´ly** *adv.* —**staunch´ness** *n.*

stay *vi.* to stop, halt; to remain: *stay at home, stay healthy* —*vt.* to bring to a halt; to hinder; to postpone — *n.* an act or time of staying; a suspension, as of judicial proceedings

stead *n.* the place of another as assumed by a substitute

stead´fast *adj.* firmly fixed, as in faith or devotion to duty —**stead´fast·ly** *adv.* —**stead´fast·ness** *n.*

stead´y *adj.* stable; not likely to shake or totter; unfaltering, constant; regular, as *a steady customer* —*vt., vi.* to make or become steady —**stead´i·ly** *adv.* —**stead´i·ness** *n.*

steal *vt.* to take unlawfully; to obtain subtly: *he has stolen her heart* —*vi.* to move quietly and stealthily; to commit theft —*n.* a bargain

stealth *n.* secret or furtive movement or behavior

stealth´y *adj.* marked by stealth; intended to avoid notice —**stealth´i·ly** *adv.* —**stealth´i·ness** *n.*

steam *n.* water vapor; the visible mist formed by the sudden cooling of hot steam —*vi.* to emit vapor; to move by the power of steam —*vt.* to treat with steam, as of cooking —*adj.* of, driven, or operated by steam; producing of containing steam —**steam´i·ness** *n.* —**steam´y** *adv.*

steam´er *n.* a steamship or steamboat; a utensil for steaming food

steed *n.* a spirited horse

steel *n.* any of various alloys of iron; hardness of character —*adj.* made of steel; firm, unyielding —**steel´i·ness** *n.* —**steel´y** *adj.*

steep[1] *adj.* sloping sharply; precipitous; costly —**steep´ly** *adv.* —**steep´ness** *n.*

steep[2] *vt.* to soak in a liquid; to infuse, as with liquid for cooking

stee´ple *n.* the lofty structure above the roof of a church

steer *vt., vi.* to direct the course of

steer´age *n.* that part of an ocean vessel allotted to passengers paying the lowest fares

stem *n.* the main axis or a subsidiary stalk of a plant; the slender upright support of a goblet, vase, etc.; the rod used for winding a watch; the bow of a boat —*vt.* to stop or hold back

stench *n.* an offensive odor

sten´cil *n.* an openwork pattern through which paint, etc. can penetrate to create a design on the surface beneath

step *n.* a move accomplished by lifting the foot and putting it down in a different place; the distance moved; a stair or ladder rung; one of a series of moves toward accomplishing something; the sound of a footfall —*vi., vt.*

stere *n.* a cubic meter

ster´e·o *n.* a stereophonic sound system

ster´e·o·type *n.* a hackneyed expression, custom, or mode of thought; a metal printing plate — **ster′e·o·typed** adj. —**ste′reo·typ·er** n.

ster′ile adj. having no reproductive power; lacking productiveness; containing no microorganisms; lacking vigor: *sterile prose* —**ste·ril′i·ty** n.

ster′i·lize vt. to render incapable of reproduction; to destroy microorganisms —**ster·i·liza′tion** n. —**ster′i·liz·er** n.

stern adj. marked by severity or harshness; having an austere disposition; resolute: *showing stern resolve* —**stern′ly** adv. —**stern′ness** n.

ste′ve·dore n. one who loads or unloads ships —vt., vi.

stew′ard n. one entrusted with the management of the affairs of others; one in charge of services for a club, ship, etc. —**stew′ard·ship** n.

stick n. a rigid shoot or branch from a tree or bush; any relatively long and thin piece of wood —vt. to pierce with a pointed object; to fasten, as with an adhesive —vi. to be or become fixed in place; to persevere or remain faithful

stick′er n. a gummed label; a prickly stem or bur

stick′ler n. one with exacting standards; a baffling problem

stick′y adj. tending to adhere; covered with adhesive; warm and humid; difficult: *a sticky situation* —**stick′i·ness** n.

stiff adj. rigid; resistant to bending; not easily moved: *a stiff bolt*; not natural or graceful: *a stiff bow*; strong and steady: *a stiff breeze*; thick, viscous: *a stiff batter*; harsh: *a stiff penalty*; stubborn, unyielding; difficult, arduous —n. an awkward or unresponsive person —**stiff′ly** adv. —**stiff′ness** n.

stiff′en vt., vi. to make or become stiff or stiffer —**stiff′en·er** n.

sti′fle vt. to kill by stopping respiration; to hold back or suppress, as sobs —vi. to die of suffocation; to have difficulty breathing, as in a stuffy room —**sti′fler** n. —**sti′fling·ly** adv.

stig′ma n. a mark of disgrace; a spot or scar on the skin —**stig·mat′ic** adj. —**stig′ma·tize** vt.

stile n. a set of steps that span a fence or wall

sti·let′to n. a small dagger with a slender blade

still adj. motionless; free from disturbance or agitation; silent; hushed; soft or subdued —n. the absence of sound or noise —adv. up to this time; in spite of; in increasing degree —conj. nevertheless —vt. to silence or hush; to allay, as fears —vi. to become still — **still′ness** n.

stim′u·lant n. a drug that stimulates; anything that rouses one to activity

stim′u·late vt. to rouse to activity; to affect by intoxicants —vi. to act as a stimulus or stimulant —**stim′u·lat·er, stim′u·la·tor** n. —**stim·u·la′tion** n.

stim′u·lus n., pl. **stim′u·li** anything that rouses to activity

sting vt. to pierce or prick painfully; to cause to suffer sharp, smarting pain; to cause to suffer mentally —vi. to suffer a sharp, smarting pain; to suffer mental distress —n.

stin′gy adj. extremely miserly; meager: *a stingy portion* —**stin′gi·ly** adv. —**stin′gi·ness** n.

stink n. a strong foul odor —vi., vt. to give forth or cause to give forth a foul odor —**stink′er** n. —**stink′y** adj.

stint vt. to limit, as in amount —vi. to be frugal or sparing —n. a restriction or limit; a specified task or time: *a weekly stint* —**stint′er** n. —**sting′ing·ly** adv.

sti´pend *n.* a regular, fixed allowance

stip´ple *vt.* to depict an image with dots —*n.* a method of representing light and shadow using dots; stippled work

stip´u·late *vt.* to specify as the terms or requirements for an agreement —*vi.* to demand something as a requirement —**stip·u·la´tion** *n.* —**stip´u·la·tor** *n.*

stir *vt.* to mix thoroughly by a circular motion; to cause to move; to rouse, as from sleep or inactivity; to provoke —*vi.* to move; to be active —*n.* movement; public interest or excitement

stitch *n.* a single link of thread, yarn, etc. in a line of sewn material; a specific arrangement of thread, etc. as *a chain stitch*; a sudden sharp pain —*vi.* to sew — *vt.* to join or ornament with stitches —**stitch´er** *n.*

sto·chas´tic *adj.* characterized by conjecture; involving probability — **sto·chas´ti·cal·ly** *adv.*

stock *n.* the goods a merchant has on hand; the original from which others are descended or derived; the trunk or main stem of a plant; shares in a corporation; raw material; the broth from boiled vegetables, meat, etc. —*vt.* to supply with cattle, as for a farm; to supply with merchandise; to keep on hand to sell; to supply with wildlife: *stock a pond*; to put aside for future use — *adj.* commonplace: *a stock item*; employed in tending to merchandise: *a stock clerk*

stock·ade´ *n.* a defensive barrier or the area it encloses; an area used to confine prisoners —*vi.* to fortify with a stockade

stock´y *adj.* short and stout — **stock´i·ness** *n.*

stodg´y *adj.* dull or boring; heavy, as a feeling —**stodg´i·ly** *adv.*

— **stodg´i·ness** *n.*

sto´ic *n.* one apparently unaffected by emotion, such as pleasure or pain —**sto´ic, sto´i·cal** *adj.* impassive or indifferent to pain or suffering —**sto´i·cal·ly** *adv.* —**sto´i·cism** *n.*

stoke *vt.* to supply a furnace with fuel; to stir up —*vi.* to tend a fire —**stok´er** *n.*

stol´id *adj.* without feeling; impassive —**stol´id·ly** *adv.* —**stol´id·ness** *n.*

stom´ach *n.* a pouchlike dilation of the alimentary canal that serves as one of the principal organs of digestion; the abdomen; a desire — *vt.* to put up with; to endure

stomp *vt., vi.* to tread heavily upon —*n.* a jazz dance

stone *n.* a small piece of rock; a shaped rock, as *a gravestone*; something small and hard; the pit of a fruit —*adj.* made of stone —*vt.* to hurl stones at; to remove pits from

ston´y *adj.* abounding in stone; unfeeling: *hard as stone* —**ston´i·ly** *adv.* —**ston´i·ness** *n.*

stooge *n.* one who acts as or is the dupe of another

stool *n.* a backless and armless seat; a low bench for the feet or for kneeling; feces

stoop *vi.* to lean the body forward and down; to walk with the upper body bent forward; to lower or degrade oneself —*vt.* to bend forward —*n.* a habitual forward inclination of the head and shoulders; a small porch

stop *vt.* to bring to a halt; to prevent the completion of; to withhold or cut off; to cease doing; to check or stanch; to fill in or close, as with a cork —*vi.* to come to a halt —*n.* the act of stopping; an obstruction

stop´per, stop´ple *n.* a cork, plug, etc. —*vt.* to close with a cork, etc.

stor´age n. the placing of articles for safekeeping; a space or a charge for storing

store vt. to put away for safekeeping or future use —n. that which is put away; a place where merchandise is kept for sale —**set store by** to value or esteem; to believe — **store´house** n. —**store´keep·er** n.

sto´rey (Brit.) n. one level of a building

sto´ried adj. having a notable history

storm n. an atmospheric disturbance marked by strong winds, precipitation, etc.; heavy prolonged winds and precipitation; a violent emotional outburst; political or social disturbance: a storm of protest —vi. to blow or rage like a storm — vt. to attack

storm´y adj. characterized by storms; turbulent; violent — **storm´i·ly** adv. —**storm´i·ness** n.

sto´ry n. a narrative of an event, either true or invented; an account of facts; an anecdote; the plot of a fictional account; a falsehood; (US) one level of a building

stout adj. thick-set; firmly built; courageous —n. a strong dark beer —**stout´ly** adv. —**stout´ness** n.

stout´-heart´ed adj. brave, courageous —**stout´-heart´ed·ly** adv. —**stout´-heart´ed·ness** n.

stove n. an appliance for heating or cooking

stow vt. to pack; to store —**stow away** to hide for safekeeping; to hide so as not to pay passage

stow´age n. the space or charge for stowing goods; goods stowed

strad´dle vt. to stand, sit, etc. with legs on either side of; to spread the legs wide apart; to appear to favor both sides of an issue —n. the act of straddling; a position of noncommittal —**strad´dler** n. —**strad´dling·ly** adv.

strag´gle vi. to stray or wander; to fall behind; to occur at irregular intervals —**strag´gler** n. —**strag´gling·ly** adv. —**strag´gly** adj.

straight adj. extending without curve or bend; erect; fair and honest; correctly arranged; conforming to what is accepted as normal or conventional —n. an unbent piece or section —adv. in a direct course; at once, directly; without qualification —**straight´ness** n.

straight´en vt., vi. to make or become straight —**straight´en·er** n.

strain vt. to exert to the utmost; to injure by overexertion; to pass through a filter; to remove with a filter —vi. to make a violent effort; to become wrenched or twisted; to filter —n. any taxing demand on resources; any violent effort; an injury caused by excessive effort

strain´er n. a device that filters or sifts

strait n. a narrow passage of water that connects two larger bodies of water

strand n. fibers, wires, etc., singly or twisted together to form a rope, cable, etc.; a ropelike object —vt., vi. to leave or be left in a difficult or helpless situation

strange adj. unfamiliar; peculiar; out of the ordinary; out of place — **strange´ly** adv. —**strange´ness** n.

stran´ger n. an unfamiliar person; one who is ignorant of or oblivious to something: a stranger to good manners

stran´gle vt. to choke to death; to suppress —vi. to suffer or die from choking —**stran´gler** n.

stran·gu·late vt. to constrict so as to cut off circulation of the blood — **stran·gu·la´tion** n.

strap n. a long, narrow, flexible strip of a material such as leather —vt. to fasten, as with a strap; to beat, as with a strap

strap´ping *adj.* large and muscular; robust

stra·te´gic, stra·te´gi·cal *adj.* based on strategy; of that which is vital or essential —**stra·te´gi·cal·ly** *adv.*

strat´e·gy *n.* a broad–based plan; the use of artifice in striving for an objective —**strat´e·gist** *n.*

strat´i·fy *vt., vi.* to arrange or be formed in layers —**strat´i·fi·ca´tion** *n.*

stray *vi.* to wander from a proper course; to deviate from right or goodness —*adj.* wandering: *a stray dog*; out of place: *a stray hair* —*n.* a domestic animal that has wandered —**stray´er** *n.*

streak *n.* a long, narrow strip; a contrasting mark or characteristic: *a steak of kindness* —*vi., vt.* to form a streak or streaks; to move at great speed; to run by naked, as for a thrill —**streak´er** *n.* — **streak´y** *adj.* —**streak´i·ly** *adv.* —**streak´i·ness** *n.*

stream *n.* a flow of water; any uninterrupted flow: *a stream of laughter* —*vi.* to pour forth or issue; to proceed without interruption

street *n.* a public walkway or road —*adj.* taking place on the street: *a street musician*

strength *n.* the quality of being physically strong; the capacity to apply or withstand force; intensity, as of light, sound, medication, etc.

strength´en *vt., vi.* to make or become strong or stronger —**strength´en·er** *n.*

stren´u·ous *adj.* marked by great effort or exertion —**stren´u·ous·ly** *adv.* —**stren´u·ous·ness** *n.*

stress *n.* physical or emotional tension; emphasis; pressure —*vt.* to subject to stress; to give emphasis or accent, as in speech —**stress´ful** *adj.* —**stress´ful·ly** *adv.*

stretch *vt.* to extend or draw out; to strain to the utmost; to adapt to circumstances: *stretch the truth* —*vi.* to extend from one place to another; to be extended beyond normal limits; to extend one's limbs —*n.* a continuous extent of space or time —*adj.* capable of being easily distended, as *stretch socks* —**stretch´a·ble** *adj.* —**stretch´a·bil´i·ty, stretch´i·ness** *n.* —**stretch´y** *adv.*

strew *vt.* to spread about at random; to be scattered over

stri´ate *vt.* to mark with grooves, stripes, etc. —**stri´ate, stri´at´ed** *adj.* —**stri·a´tion** *n.*

strick´en *adj.* affected by injury, disease, sorrow, etc.

strict *adj.* containing or enforcing severe rules or provisions; harsh, stern, exacting; absolute: *in strict confidence* —**strict´ly** *adv.* — **strict´ness** *n.*

stric´ture *n.* something that restricts; a narrowing or closure of a duct of the body

stride *n.* a long, often measured, step —*vi., vt.* to walk with long steps —**strid´er** *n.*

stri´dent *adj.* loud and harsh sounding —**stri´dence, stri´den·cy** *n.* —**stri´dent·ly** *adv.*

strife *n.* angry contention; a rivalry

strike *vt.* to hit; to crash into; to affect suddenly or in a specified manner; to cease work or interfere with the work of others as a protest: *a sit–down strike*; to make and confirm, as a bargain —*vi.* to come into violent contact; to sound from a blow; to cease work —*n.* a blow; a sudden success: *a lucky strike*; a work stoppage by employees —**strik´er** *n.*

string *n.* a slender line for tying parcels, etc.; a cord or wire for a musical instrument, tennis racket, etc.; a connected series of things on a cord or as on a cord

—*vt.* to thread, as beads; to replace a cord, as on a musical instrument, racket, etc. —*vi.* to extend, proceed, or form in a series

strin´gent *adj.* rigid or severe, as regulations; convincing —**strin´gen·cy, strin´gent·ness** *n.* —**strin´gent·ly** *adv.*

string´y *adj.* like string, as of hair; forming or formed in strings; tall and wiry —**string´i·ness** *n.*

strip *n.* a narrow piece, often long; a set of cartoon drawings —*vt.* to lay bare; to deprive of something; to damage, as of gears or a bolt —*vi.* to undress

stripe *n.* a band that differs in color, texture, etc. from its surroundings; a distinctive quality; a blow struck with a whip or rod —*vt.* to mark with a contrasting band

strip´ling *n.* a lad

strive *vi.* to make an effort; to fight —**striv´er** *n.*

stroll *vi.* to walk in a casual manner —*n.* a leisurely walk —**stroll´er** *n.*

strong *adj.* physically powerful; healthy, robust; especially competent or able; firm, tenacious —*adv.* in a firm manner —**strong´ly** *adv.*

struc´tur·al *adj.* of or pertaining to construction —**struc´tur·al·ly** *adv.*

struc´ture *n.* that which is constructed; something based on a plan or design; a manner of design: *a wood frame structure*; the arrangement and relationship of the parts of a whole: *hierarchical structure* —*vt.* to build; to conceive as a structural whole

strug´gle *n.* an arduous effort; a war —*vt.* to contend with an adversary; to strive —**strug´gler** *n.* —**strug´gling·ly** *adv.*

strut *n.* a pompous walk; a supporting member of a framework —*vi.* to walk pompously —*vt.* to support or separate with a brace —**strut´ter** *n.* —**strut´ting·ly** *adv.*

stub *n.* a short remnant, as of a pencil, candle, etc. —*vt.* to strike, as the toe, against an obstacle accidently

stub´ble *n.* the remnants of plants in the ground after reaping; a short, bristly beard —**stub´bly** *adj.*

stub´born *adj.* inflexible; determined to have one's own way; not easily overcome —**stub´born·ly** *adv.* —**stub´born·ness** *n.*

stub´by *adj.* short and thick —**stub´bi·ness** *n.*

stud *n.* a short, ornamental knob or button; an upright member of a building frame —*vt.* to set thickly with ornamental buttons; to scatter over: *flowers stud the valley*

stu´dent *n.* one engaged in a course of study; a careful observer

stu´dio *n.* a working area for an artist, photographer, etc.

stu´di·ous *adj.* devoted to study; careful or attentive —**stu´di·ous·ly** *adv.* —**stu´di·ous·ness** *n.*

stud´y *n.* the process of acquiring knowledge; a branch of knowledge; a room set aside for reading or studying —*vt.* to acquire knowledge of; to examine thoroughly —*vi.* to apply the mind to learning; to be a student

stuff *vt.* to fill completely; to plug or stop up —*n.* a fundamental element: *the stuff of genius*; personal possessions generally; unspecified matter; a miscellaneous collection

stuff´y *adj.* poorly ventilated; filled up so as to impede respiration; strait–laced, stodgy —**stuff´i·ly** *adv.* —**stuff´i·ness** *n.*

stul´ti·fy *vt.* to cause to appear absurd; to make useless or futile —**stul·ti·fi·ca´tion** *n.* —**stul´ti·fi·er** *n.*

stum´ble *vi.* to miss one's step and almost fall; to speak in a halting manner; to happen upon by chance; to do wrong —*vt.* to cause to stumble —*n.* the act of stumbling —**stum´bler** *n.* —**stum´bling·ly** *adv.*

stump *n.* that portion left when a part is cut off, as of a limb; a place where a political speech is made —*adj.* pertaining to political campaigning —*vt.* to make a political speech

stun *vt.* to render incapable of action; to astound, daze, or overwhelm

stun´ning *adj.* impressive; beautiful —**stun´ning·ly** *adv.*

stunt *vt.* to check the natural development of —*n.* a check in growth or development

stu·pe·fa´cient *adj.* stupefying —*n.* a drug that induces stupor

stu·pe·fy *vt.* to dull the senses or faculties; to amaze or astound —**stu·pe·fac´tion** *n.* —**stu´pe·fi·er** *n.*

stu·pe·fac´tive *adj., n.* stupefacient

stu·pen´dous *adj.* astonishing; of immense size, breadth, etc. —**stu·pen´dous·ly** *adv.* —**stu·pen´dous·ness** *n.*

stu´pid *adj.* lacking intelligence; dull-witted; tiresome or annoying —**stu·pid´i·ty**, **stu´pid·ness** *n.* —**stu´pid·ly** *adv.*

stu´por *n.* abnormal lethargy or intellectual dullness

stur´dy *adj.* robust and powerful; firm and resolute —**stur´di·ly** *adv.* —**stur´di·ness** *n.*

stut´ter *vt., vi.* to speak with spasmodic repetition —*n.* halting or repetitious speech —**stut´ter·er** *n.* —**stut´ter·ing·ly** *adv.*

sty *n.* a pen for swine; any filthy habitation; a pustule on the edge of an eyelid

style *n.* a fashionable appearance; a particular or distinctive fashion, form, or manner —*vt.* to give a name or title: *Richard I, styled "the Lion–Hearted"*; to cause to conform to a specific form

styl´ish *adj.* fashionable —**styl´ish·ly** *adv.* —**styl´ish·ness** *n.*

styl´ist *n.* a master of style; a creator of style —**sty·lis´tic** *adj.* —**sty·lis´ti·cal·ly** *adv.*

styp´tic *adj.* tending to halt bleeding —*n.* an astringent —**styp´ti·cal** *adj.*

sua´sion *n.* persuasion —**sua´sive** *adj.* —**sua´sive·ly** *adv.* —**sua´sive·ness** *n.*

suave *adj.* smoothly pleasant and courteous —**suave´ly** *adv.* —**suave´ness**, **suav´i·ty** *n.*

sub·con´scious *adj.* not attended by full awareness —*n.* mental activity not in the focus of consciousness —**sub·con´scious·ly** *adv.* —**sub·con´scious·ness** *n.*

sub·cul·ture *n.* a group with behavioral characteristics that set it off from others within a culture —**sub·cul´tur·al** *adj.*

sub´di·vide *vt., vi.* to separate into smaller pieces; to divide a parcel of land into lots for individual sale

sub´di·vi·sion *n.* a tract of land made up of subdivided lots; a group of usually similar houses in an area

sub·due´ *vt.* to gain dominion over; to repress —**sub·du´a·ble** *adj.* —**sub·du´er** *n.*

sub´ject *adj.* under the power of; having a tendency —*n.* one under the power of another; one employed or treated in a specified way; a theme or topic; a branch of learning —**sub·ject´** *vt.* to bring under control; to make liable or responsible for

sub·jec´tive *adj.* relating to personal feeling or opinion; influenced by emotion or prejudice —**sub·jec´tive·ly** *adv.* —**sub·jec´tive·ness**, **sub·jec·tiv´i·ty** *n.*

sub·join´ *vt.* to add at the end —**sub·join´der** *n.*

sub·ju·gate *vt.* to conquer; to make

subservient —**sub·ju·ga´tion** n. —
sub´ju·ga·tor n.

sub´li·mate vt. to convert inappropriate behavior to that which is
socially acceptable —**sub·li·ma´
tion** n.

sub·lime´ adj. characterized by
grandeur —**sub·lime´ly** adv. —
sub·lime´ness n.

sub·lim´in·al adj. below the threshold of consciousness; too slight to
be perceived —**sub·lim´in·al·ly**
adv.

sub·merge´ vt. to place under water
—vi. to sink beneath the surface —
sub·mer´gence n.

sub·merse´ vt. submerge —**sub·mer´
sion** n.

sub·mers´i·ble adj. that may be
submerged —n. a warship designed to operate both on the surface and under water; a small underwater craft used for observation, rescue, etc. —**sub·mers·i·bil´
i·ty** adv.

sub·mis´sion n. yielding to another;
the act of presenting for consideration, arbitration, etc.; something submitted, as a manuscript

sub·mis´sive adj. inclined to submit
—**sub·mis´sive·ly** adv. —**sub·mis´
sive·ness** n.

sub·mit´ vt. to yield to another; to
present for consideration —vi. to
surrender; obey

sub·or´di·nate adj. lower in rank;
secondary —n. a person of lower
rank; a helper or assistant —vt. to
assign a lower rank; to make subservient —**sub·or´di·nate·ly** adv.
—**sub·or·di·na´tion** n.

sub·orn´ vt. to bribe someone to
commit perjury; to incite to commit an unlawful act —**sub·or·na´
tion** n.

sub·poe´na n. a writ requiring a
court appearance

sub´ro·gate vt. to substitute one for
another, especially of a creditor

—**sub·ro·ga´tion** n.

sub·scribe´ vt. to sign one's name to
as an expression of assent; to
promise to pay or contribute; to
give approval; to agree; to promise
to contribute money; to pay in advance, as for a periodical, tickets,
etc. —**sub·scrib´er** n. —**sub·scrip´
tion** n.

sub´se·quent adj. following in time,
order, etc. —**sub´se·quence** n. —
sub´se·quent·ly adv.

sub·ser´vi·ent adj. servile or obsequious —**sub·ser´vi·ence, sub·ser´
vi·en·cy** n. —**sub·ser´vi·ent·ly**
adv.

sub·side´ vi. to sink to a lower level;
to become calm or quiet —**sub·sid´
ence** n.

sub·sid´i·ar·y adj. supplementary or
auxiliary; pertaining to a subsidy
—n. a business with over half its
assets owned by another —**sub·
sid´i·ar·i·ly** adv.

sub´si·dize vt. to furnish with financial aid —**sub´si·diz·er** n.

sub´si·dy n. a financial grant given
by one person or government to
another

sub·sist´ vi. to continue to exist; to
maintain life

sub·sist´ence n. that by which one
subsists, as for food or earnings —
sub·sist´ent adj.

sub´stance n. the material of which
something is made; the essential
component of anything; wealth or
property; the quality of being constant or solid

sub·stan´tial adj. firm and solid;
tangible; of significant worth or
importance —**sub·stan´tial·ly** adv.
—**sub·stan´tial·ness** n.

sub·stan´ti·ate vt. to verify by evidence; to prove —**sub·stan·ti·a´
tion** n.

sub´stan·tive n. a noun or pronoun;
a verbal form, phrase, etc. used in
place of a noun —adj. that can be

used as a noun; denoting existence; having substance —**sub'stan·tive·ly** adv. —**sub'stan·tive·ness** n.

sub'sti·tute vt. to put in place of another; to take the place of —vi. to act as a substitute —n. an alternate or replacement —adj. alternative; temporary: a substitute teacher —**sub·sti·tut·a·bil'i·ty** n. —**sub'sti·tut·a·ble** adj.

sub·sti·tu'tion n. the act of replacing; the state of being a replacement; a substitute —**sub·sti·tu'tion·al** adj. —**sub·sti·tu'tion·al·ly** adv.

sub'ter·fuge n. a deception

sub·ter·ra'ne·an adj. below the surface of the earth

sub'til·ize vt., vi. to make or become subtle; to argue with careful differentiation —**sub·til·i·za'tion** n.

sub'tle adj. not easily detected, as a subtle aroma; not obvious; skillful or ingenious —**sub'tle·ness** n. —**sub'tly** adv.

sub'tle·ty n. the quality of being subtle; a small differentiation

sub·tract' vt., vi. to take away or deduct —**sub·trac'tion** n. —**sub·trac'tive** adj.

sub'urb n. an area adjacent to a city; an outlying district —**sub·ur'ban** adj.

sub·ur'ban·ite n. a resident of a suburb

sub·ur'bi·a n. the suburbs or suburbanites collectively; the cultural world of suburbanites

sub·ver'sive n. one desiring to weaken or overthrow, as a government —adj. tending to undermine or weaken —**sub·ver'sion** n. —**sub·ver'sive·ly** adv.

sub·vert' vt. to corrupt; to destroy utterly

sub'way n. an underpass; an underground railway

suc·ceed' vi. to accomplish what is intended; to turn out as intended: the plan succeeded; to come next in a sequence —vt. to come after in time or order

suc·cess' n. a favorable process or termination; the gaining of fame, wealth, etc.; the scale or level of gain

suc·cess'ful adj. ending in success —**suc·cess'ful·ly** adv.

suc·ces'sion n. the act of following in order; the right to a predecessor's office, possessions, etc. —**suc·ces'sor** n.

suc·ces'sive adj. following in order —**suc·ces'sive·ly** adv.

suc·cinct' adj. presented clearly and concisely; marked by brevity —**suc·cinct'ly** adv. —**suc·cinct'ness** n.

suc'cu·lent adj. juicy; having thick fleshy leaves; interesting —n. a succulent plant —**suc'cu·lence** n. —**suc'cu·lent·ly** adv.

suc·cumb' vi. to yield, as to force or persuasion; to die

such adj. being the same or similar: times such as these; extreme: such an uproar —pron. the same as implied or indicated —adv. especially: in such good spirits

suck vt. to draw in by a partial vacuum; to pull or draw in as if by suction: the lure of profit sucked him in —vi. to draw in by suction; to suckle; to make a suckling sound

suc'tion n. the production of a partial vacuum —adj. creating or operating by suction

sud'den adj. happening quickly without warning; hasty, rash —**sud'den·ly** adv. —**sud'den·ness** n.

suds pl. n. froth, foam —**suds'y** adj.

sue vt. to take legal action in order to redress a wrong; to prosecute —vi. to institute legal proceedings; to seek to persuade by entreaty: to sue for peace —**su·a·bil'i·ty** n.

—**su´a·ble** *adj.* —**su´er** *n.*

suede *n.* hide or fabric having a napped surface

suf·fer *vi.* to feel pain or distress; to sustain loss or injury; to undergo punishment —*vt.* to sustain or have inflicted on one; to endure; to allow —**suf´fer·a·ble** *adj.* —**suf´fer·a·bly** *adv.* —**suf´fer·er** *n.* —**suf´fer·ing** *adj.* —**suf´fer·ing·ly** *adv.*

suf·fer·ance *n.* permission granted or implied by failure to permit; the capacity for suffering

suf·fice´ *vi.* to be sufficient or adequate

suf·fi·cien·cy *n.* that which is sufficient

suf·fi·cient *adj.* being all that is needed; enough —**suf·fi´cient·ly** *adv.*

suf·fix *n.* an addition to a word that modifies it or forms a new word —*vt.* to add as a suffix

suf·fo·cate *vt.* to kill by obstructing respiration; to cause distress by depriving of adequate oxygen; to smother, as a fire; to stifle: *suffocated by affection* —*vi.* to be distressed or to die by deprivation of oxygen; to become or feel stifled —**suf´fo·cat´ing·ly** *adv.* —**suf·fo·ca´tion** *n.* —**suf´fo·ca·tive** *adj.*

suf·frage *n.* the privilege of voting; a vote —**suf´frag·ist** *n.*

suf´frag·ette´ *n.* a female advocate of women's right to vote

suf·fuse´ *vt.* to spread over, as with a liquid, light, etc. —**suf·fu´sion** *n.* —**suf·fu´sive** *adj.*

sug·gest´ *vt.* to present for consideration; to associate: *gold suggests wealth*; to imply: *her gesture suggests indifference*

sug·gest´i·ble *adj.* that can be recommended; easily lead —**sug·gest´i·bil´i·ty** *n.*

sug·ges´tion *n.* something offered for consideration; a small amount, a trace

sug·ges´tive *adj.* that stimulating thought or reflection; hinting at something improper —**sug·ges´tive·ly** *adv.* —**sug·ges´tive·ness** *n.*

su´i·cide *n.* the taking of one's own life; ruin brought on by one's own actions —**su´i·ci´dal** *adj.* —**su´i·ci´dal·ly** *adv.*

suit *n.* a garment or set of garments; a grouping or set of compatible things: *a bedroom suit*; a court proceeding; the courting of a woman —*vt.* to meet the requirements of; to satisfy; to adapt; to furnish with clothes —*vi.* to prove satisfactory —**suit´or** *n.*

suit´a·ble *adj.* appropriate or fitting —**suit·a·bil´i·ty**, **suit´a·ble·ness** *n.* —**suit´a·bly** *adv.*

suite *n.* a set of things intended for use together, as connecting rooms in a hotel; a set of matched furniture, a *suit*

sulk *vi.* to be sullen and withdrawn —*n.* a sullen mood

sulk´y *n.* a light, horse–drawn vehicle for one —*adj.* sullen and withdrawn —**sulk´i·ly** *adv.* —**sulk´i·ness** *n.*

sul´len *adj.* ill–humored; glum; depressing; slow or sluggish —**sul´len·ly** *adv.* —**sul´len·ness** *n.*

sul´ly *vt.* to soil; to shame or defile

sul´try *adj.* hot and humid; arousing passion; sensual —**sul´tri·ly** *adv.* —**sul´tri·ness** *n.*

sum *n.* the entire amount; a summary

sum´ma·rize *vt.* to prepare or present as an outline or summary —**sum´ma·ri·za´tion** *n.* —**sum´ma·ri·zer** *n.*

sum´ma·ry *n.* a brief account —*adj.* containing the essential details; performed without ceremony or delay —**sum·mar´i·ly** *adv.*

sum·ma´tion *n.* the act of adding numbers; a final review of the main points of an argument

sum´mit *n.* the highest point or part; the highest level or office

sum´mon *vt.* to send for; to call together; to rouse to action —**sum´ mon·er** *n.*

sum´mons *n.* a notice to appear in court; any call to appear

sump´tu·ous *adj.* lavish; luxurious —**sump´tu·ous·ly** *adv.* —**sump´tu· ous·ness** *n.*

sunk´en *adj.* lying at the bottom; lower than the surrounding area: *a sunken garden*

sun *n.* the star at the center of the solar system; any star —*vt.* to expose to the sun —*vi.* to bask in the sun

sun´ny *adj.* filled with sunlight; bright, cheerful —**sun´ni·ly** *adv.*

sun´set *n.* the time at which the sun falls below the horizon; a final period or decline

sup *vi.* to eat

su´per *adj.* surpassing others of its kind; outstanding —*n.* a superintendent

su´per·a·ble *adj.* that can be overcome —**su´per·a·bil´i·ty, su´per·a· ble·ness** *n.* —**su´per·a·bly** *adv.*

su·perb´ *adj.* extraordinarily good —**su·perb´ly** *adv.* —**su·perb´ness** *n.*

su·per·cil´i·ous *adj.* haughtily disdainful; arrogant —**su·per·cil´ i·ous·ly** *adv.* —**su·per·cil´i·ous· ness** *n.*

su·per·fi´cial *adj.* on or near the surface: *a superficial wound;* trivial, not profound; hasty: *a superficial examination;* apparent rather than real: *a superficial resemblance* —**su´per·fi·ci·al´i·ty** *n.* — **su·per·fi´cial·ly** *adv.*

su·per´flu·ous *adj.* surplus; exceeding what is needed; unnecessary or irrelevant: *a superfluous comment* —**su·per·flu´i·ty** *n.* —**su·per´ flu·ous·ly** *adv.*

su·per·in·tend´ *vt.* to direct or supervise   —**su·per·in·tend´ence,**

su·per·in·tend´en·cy *n.*

su·per·in·tend´ent *n.* one who has charge; one responsible for maintenance and repair

su·pe´ri·or *adj.* higher in rank, quality, etc.; affecting an attitude of indifference or disdain —*n.* one who is higher in rank —**su· pe·ri·or´i·ty** *n.* —**su·pe´ri·or·ly** *adv.*

su·per´la·tive *adj.* of the highest degree; most excellent; exaggerated —*n.* something of the highest grade —**su·per´la·tive·ly** *adv.* — **su·per´la·tive·ness** *n.*

su·per·nat´u·ral *adj.* existing outside the forces of nature; miraculous or divine; of ghosts, demons, etc. —*n.* unnatural phenomena —**su·per· nat´u·ral·ly** *adv.* —**su·per·nat´u· ral·ness** *n.*

su·per·nat´u·ral·ism *n.* a belief in the supernatural; belief in a divine force that directs the universe — **su·per·nat´u·ral·ist** *adj., n.* —**su· per·nat´u·ral·is´tic** *adj.*

su·per·sede´ *vt.* to set aside and replace with something newer or better; to take the place of —**su· per·sed´er** *n.*

su·per·son´ic *adj.* moving faster than the speed of sound

su·per·sti´tion *n.* an irrational belief; any practice inspired by such belief

su·per·sti´tious *adj.* influenced by superstition; based on superstition —**su·per·sti´tious·ly** *adv.* —**su· per·sti´tious·ness** *n.*

su´per·vise *vt.* to have charge of; to oversee or manage—**su·per·vi´sion** *n.* —**su´per·vi·sor** *n.* —**su´per·vi´ so·ry** *adj.*

su·pine´ *adj.* lying face up —**su· pine´ly** *adv.* —**su·pine´ness** *n.*

sup´per *n.* the evening meal; the last meal of the day

sup·plant´ *vt.* to displace, as of something outdated; to displace by treachery —**sup·plant´er** n.

sup´ple adj. flexible; agile or grace-ful; yielding readily, compliant; adaptable —vt., vi. to make or be-come supple —**sup´ple·ness** n.

sup´ple·ment n. something added to correct or augment —vt. to make an addition to —**sup·ple·men´tal,** **sup´ple·men·ta·ry** adj. —**sup·ple·men´tal·ly** adv.

sup´pli·cate vt. to ask for humbly or by earnest prayer —vi. to make an earnest request —**sup´pli·cant** n. —**sup·pli·ca´tion** n.

sup·ply´ vt. to make available or furnish; to provide for adequately —vi. to take the place of another temporarily —n. a quantity on hand; the amount available —**sup·pli´er** n.

sup·port´ vt. to bear the weight of; to hold in position; to provide with necessities; to substantiate or de-fend; to provide with the means to endure —n. someone or something that supports

sup·port´er n. one who provides with necessities; a device that braces

sup·port´ive adj. contributing sig-nificantly to one's physical or emotional health —**sup·por´tive·ly** adv. —**sup·port´ive·ness** n.

sup·pose´ vt. to believe to be possi-ble; to expect; to imply —**sup·pos´a·ble** adj. —**sup·pos´a·bly** adv. —**sup·pos´er** n.

sup·posed´ adj. accepted as genu-ine; imagined —**sup·pos·ed´ly** adv.

sup·po·si´tion n. a conjecture or assumption —**sup´po·si´tion·al** adj. —**sup´po·si´tion·al·ly** adv.

sup·press´ vt. to end or stop; to hold back or repress; to check —**sup·pres´sant** n. —**sup·press´er, sup·pres´sor** n. —**sup·press´i·ble, sup·pres´sive** adj.

sup·pres´sion n. an instance of suppressing; the exclusion of

unpleasant ideas, memories, etc. from consciousness

su·prem´a·cy n. supreme power or authority

su·preme´ adj. dominant; highest in degree, etc.; ultimate —**su·preme´ly** adv.

sur·cease´ n. a cessation —vt., vi. to end

sure adj. without doubt; positive —**sure´ly** adv. —**sure´ness** n.

sur´e·ty n. security against loss or damage

surf n. the swelling of the sea as it breaks on the shore —vi. to ride a surfboard —**surf´er** n.

sur´face n. the exterior; a superficial aspect —vt. to apply or improve an exterior; to cause to rise —vi. to rise; to come to public notice —**sur´fac·er** n.

sur´feit vt. to supply to excess —vi. to overindulge in food or drink —n. any excessive amount

surge vi. to roll with a swelling mo-tion, as waves; to move in a wave-like motion; to increase or vary suddenly —n. a great swelling or rolling motion; any sudden in-crease

sur´ger·y n. medical treatment by manual and operative means; the branch of medicine concerned with treatment by surgery; an operating room —**sur´geon** n. —**sur´gi·cal** adj. —**sur´gi·cal·ly** adv.

sur´ly adj. ill-humored; gruff or insolent —**sur´li·ness** n.

sur·mise´ vt., vi. to infer on slight evidence —n. a supposition

sur·mount´ vt. to overcome; to mount or pass over, as an obsta-cle; to place above —**sur·mount´a·ble** adj.

sur´name´ n. a family name; a cog-nomen or nickname —vt. to fur-nish with a nickname

sur·pass´ vt. to go beyond or past in degree or amount —**sur·pass´a·ble**

adj. —**sur·pass´er** *n.*

sur´plus *n.* that over what is used or required —*adj.* an excess

sur·prise´ *vt.* to cause to feel wonder or astonishment; to take unawares —*n.* astonishment; something that causes astonishment —**sur·pris´ing** *adj.* —**sur·pris´ing·ly** *adv.*

sur·re´al *adj.* having a dreamlike quality —**sur·re´al·ly** *adv.*

sur·re´al·ism *n.* an art movement characterized by the incorporation of dreamlike elements —**sur·re´al·ist** *adj.,* *n.* —**sur·re·al·is´tic** *adj.* —**sur·re·al·is´ti·cal·ly** *adv.*

sur·ren´der *vt.* to yield; to give up in favor of another; to give oneself over to, as passion —*vi.* to give oneself up, as to an enemy —*n.* the act of surrendering —**sur·ren´der·er** *n.*

sur·rep·ti´tious *adj.* accomplished by secret means; acting with stealth —**sur·rep·ti´tious·ly** *adv.* —**sur·rep·ti´tious·ness** *n.*

sur´ro·gate *n.* someone taking the place of another; a probate court judge —*vt.* to deputize or substitute —**sur´ro·ga·cy** *n.*

sur·round´ *vt.* to encircle or enclose

sur·round´ings *n.* that which constitutes one's environment

sur·veil´lance *n.* discreet observation of someone or something

sur·vey´, sur´vey *vt.* to look at carefully; to scrutinize; to conduct a land survey so as to determine accurately the area, boundaries, etc. —*vi.* to survey land —*n.* the process of surveying land; the systematic collection and analysis of data; a general or overall view —**sur´vey´or** *n.*

sur·viv´a·ble *adj.* that can be survived —**sur·viv·a·bil´i·ty** *adv.*

sur·vive´ *vi.* to remain alive or in existence; to live past the death of another —*vt.* to outlast; to go on living in spite of —**sur·viv´al** *n.*

—**sur·vi´vor** *n.*

sus·cep´ti·ble *adj.* readily affected; vulnerable; capable of being influenced —**sus·cep·ti·bil´i·ty, sus·cep´ti·ble·ness** *n.* —**sus·cep´ti·bly** *adv.*

sus·pect´ *vt.* to think guilty without proof; to distrust or doubt —*vi.* to have suspicions —**sus·pect´, sus´pect** *adj.* inspiring suspicion —**sus´pect** *n.* one who may be guilty of a crime

sus·pend´ *vt.* to bar for a time as punishment; to cease or interrupt for a time; to defer action on; to move freely while hanging from a support or in the air

sus·pense´ *n.* anxiety caused by uncertainty —**sus·pense´ful** *adj.*

sus·pen´sion *n.* a temporary removal from office, withholding of privilege, etc.; an interruption or cessation; a deferment; hanging freely; dispersion in a liquid or gas

sus·pi´cion *n.* an uncertain belief in the liklihood of another's guilt, wrongdoing, etc.; a slight amount

sus·pi´cious *adj.* questionable; disposed to doubt —**sus·pi´cious·ly** *adv.* —**sus·pi´cious·ness** *n.*

sus·tain´ *vt.* to keep up or maintain; to maintain by providing with necessities; to endure or withstand; to suffer or undergo; to uphold or prove as being true or just —**sus·tain´a·ble** *adj.*

sus´te·nance *n.* maintenance of life or health; that which sustains, as food

svelte *adj.* slender; smart or chic —**svelte´ly** *adv.* —**svelte´ness** *n.*

swab *n.* a soft, absorbent substance on the end of a short stick, used to apply medication, cleanse, etc.; a specimen taken for medical examination; a mop for cleaning floors, etc. —*vt.* to clean or apply medication with a swab —**swab´ber** *n.*

swad′dle *vt.* to wrap a newborn in strips of cloth; to wrap, as with a bandage —*n.* a band or cloth used as swaddling

swag *n.* a decorative hanging, such as a curtain or drape covering the top of a window and gathered in sections; a similar carved motif; stolen property; (*Austral.*) a bundle of personal belongings

swag′ger *vi.* to walk with an air of self-confidence; to behave or boast in a self-satisfied manner —*n.* a self-confident gait —*adj.* showy — **swag′ger·ing·ly** *adv.*

swal′low *vt.* to cause to pass from the mouth into the stomach; to take in or engulf; to submit to, as insults; to suppress: *swallow one's pride* —*n.* the amount taken in at one time; a mouthful; a small bird —**swal′low·er** *n.*

swamp *n.* a tract of low land saturated with water —*vt.* to drench with water; to overwhelm, as with work —*vi.* to sink in water — **swamp′land** *n.* —**swamp′y** *adj.*

swank *n.* an ostentatious display; stylishness —*adj.* stylish or smart

swank′y *adj.* ostentatiously fashionable —**swank′i·ly** *adv.* —**swank′i·ness** *n.*

swap *vt., vi.* to exchange or trade — *n.* something traded —**swap meet** a gathering in which goods are traded

swarm *n.* a large crowd or mass, especially one moving together — *vi.* to come together or move in great numbers; to be overrun: *swarming with tourists* —*vt.* to fill with a crowd

swarth′y *adj.* dark complected — **swarth′i·ness** *n.*

swat *vt.* to strike with a quick blow —*n.* —**swat′ter** *n.*

swath *n.* a strip or row, as of cut grain

swathe *vt.* to bind or wrap, as with bandages —*n.* a bandage

sway *vi.* to swing from side to side; to incline, as in opinion, sympathies, etc.; to control —*vt.* to cause to swing or lean; to influence —*n.* power or influence; a turning from side to side

swear *vi.* to make a solemn affirmation; to make a vow; to use profanity —*vt.* to assert solemnly; to vow; to declare emphatically

sweat *vi.* to exude salty moisture from the pores; to condense moisture in drops on a surface; to work hard; to suffer, as from anxiety —*vt.* to exude or condense drops of moisture; to cause to sweat; to force to work for low wages, etc.; to join metal with solder; to subject to rigorous interrogation —*n.* —**sweat′i·ness** *n.* — **sweat′y** *adj.*

sweep *vt.* to clear or clean away, as with a broom, brush, etc.; to pass over swiftly; to win overwhelmingly —*vi.* to clean a surface with a broom, etc.; to move quickly; to extend: *the road sweeps along the lake* —*n.* a long stroke or movement; the act of clearing; an unbroken stretch; an overwhelming victory; one who cleans chimneys, streets, etc.; a flowing contour — **sweep′er** *n.*

sweet *adj.* having a flavor like that of sugar; pleasing to the senses —*n.* someone or something agreeable or pleasing —**sweet′ly** *adv.* — **sweet′ness** *n.*

sweet′en *vt.* to make agreeable or pleasing —**sweet′en·er** *n.*

swell *vi.* to increase in size or volume, as by inflation or absorption; to increase in amount, etc.; to arise in waves, as the sea; to bulge —*vt.* to cause to increase, as in size, volume, amount, etc.; to cause to bulge; to puff with pride —*n.* an expansion; a rise or undulation; a bulge; a long continuous wave —*adj.* fashionable, elegant —**swell´ing** *n., adj.*

swel´ter *vi., vt.* to suffer or cause to suffer from oppressive heat —*n.* oppressive heat —**swel´ter·ing** *adj.* —**swel´ter·ing·ly** *adv.*

swerve *vi., vt.* to turn or cause to turn aside —*n.* a sudden turning

swift *adj.* moving or capable of moving with great speed; happening without delay —**swift´ly** *adv.* —**swift´ness** *n.*

swill *vt., vi.* to drink greedily or to excess —*n.* semiliquid food for animals; unappetizing food; garbage

swim *vi.* to move through water by moving the limbs; to move with a flowing motion; to be flooded —*vt.* to traverse by swimming; to cause to swim —*n.* the action or pastime of swimming; the distance swum —**swim´mer** *n.*

swin´dle *vt.* to cheat or defraud; to obtain by fraud —*vi.* to practice fraud —*n.* the act of defrauding —**swin´dler** *n.*

swing *vi.* to move to and fro rhythmically; to pivot; to be suspended; to be contemporary and sophisticated —*vt.* to cause to move to and fro; to brandish; to lift, hoist, or hang; to bring to a successful conclusion: *swing a deal* —*n.* a free swaying motion; a hanging seat; a trip or tour: *a swing through the low country;* a type of jazz music —**swing´er** *n.*

swirl *vi., vt.* to move or cause to move with a whirling motion —*n.*

switch *n.* a small flexible rod or whip; an act or mechanism for shifting or changing —*vt.* to whip or lash; to turn aside or divert; to exchange —*vi.* to turn aside; to change —**switch´er** *n.*

swiv´el *n.* a pivot that permits parts to rotate independently; anything that turns on a pivot —*vt., vi.* to turn, as on a swivel

swoon *vi.* to faint —*n.* a fainting spell

swoop *vi.* to descend suddenly; to pounce —*vt.* to seize suddenly —*n.* a sudden violent descent

sword *n.* a weapon consisting of a long blade fixed in a hilt

syc´o·phant *n.* a servile flatterer — **syc´o·phan·cy** *n.* —**syc´o·phan´tic, syc´o·phan´ti·cal** *adj.* —**syc´o·phan´ti·cal·ly** *adv.*

syl·lab´ic *adj.* pertaining to syllables; having every syllable distinctly pronounced —**syl·lab´i·cal·ly** *adv.*

syl·lab´i·cate, syl·lab´i·fy *vt.* to form or divide into syllables —**syl·lab·i·ca´tion** *n.*

syl´la·ble *n.* a word or part of a word uttered in a single vocal impulse

syl´la·bus *n.* a concise description, as of a course of study

syl´lo·gism *n.* a form of reasoning in which a conclusion is derived from a commonality within two premises —**syl·lo·gis´tic, syl·lo·gis´ti·cal** *adj.* —**syl·lo·gis´ti·cal·ly** *adv.* —**syl´lo·gize** *vi., vt.*

syl´van *adj.* of a forest or wooded area; of a creature that lives in the woods; wooded

sym·bi·o·sis *n.* a mutually advantageous relationship between dissimilar organisms —**sym·bi·ot´ic, sym·bi·ot´i·cal** *adj.* —**sym·bi·ot´i·cal·ly** *adv.*

sym´bol *n.* a mark, character, emblem, etc. chosen to represent something else —**sym·bol´ic, sym·bol´i·cal** *adj.* —**sym·bol´i·cal·ly** *adv.*

sym´bol·ism *n.* the art of investing with symbolic meaning; a system of symbolic representation; symbolic meaning or character —**sym´bol·ist** *n.* —**sym·bol·is´tic** *adj.* — **sym·bol·is´ti·cal·ly** *adv.*

sym·bol·ize *vt.* to represent symbolically; to represent by a symbol; to use symbols

sym·me·try *n.* a balancing of parts or elements; the beauty and harmony that results from balance — **sym·met'ric, sym·met'ri·cal** *adj.* —**sym·met'ri·cal·ly** *adv.* —**sym·met'ri·cal·ness** *n.*

sym·pa·thet'ic, sym·pa·thet'i·cal *adj.* pertaining to sympathy; having compassion for others; being in accord or harmony; relating to sounds produced by responsive vibrations —**sym·pa·thet'i·cal·ly** *adv.*

sym'pa·thize *vi.* to understand the sentiments of another; to feel or express compassion; to be in harmony or agreement —**sym'pa·thiz·er** *n.* —**sym'pa·thiz'ing·ly** *adv.*

sym'pa·thy *n.* an agreement of feeling; compassion for another's suffering; agreement or accord; support or approval

sym·pho'ni·ous *adj.* in a state of accord; harmonious —**sym·pho'ni·ous·ly** *adv.*

sym'pho·ny *n.* an agreeable mingling of sounds; any agreeable blending, as of color; a composition for orchestra —**sym·phon'ic** *adj.* —**sym·phon'i·cal·ly** *adv.*

sym·po'si·um *n.* a meeting for discussion of a particular subject; a collection of writing on a particular subject

symp'tom *n.* a condition indicating the presence of disease; an indication that serves to point out something else: *a symptom of civil unrest* —**symp·to·mat'ic, symp·to·mat'i·cal** *adj.* —**symp·to·mat'i·cal·ly** *adv.*

syn'a·gogue *n.* a place of meeting for Jewish worship and religious instruction; a Jewish congregation

syn'apse *n.* the junction of two neurons across which a nerve impulse passes —**syn·ap'tic** *adj.* — **syn·ap'ti·cal·ly** *adv.*

syn·chron'ic *adj.* synchronous; pertaining to the study of events of a particular time —**syn·chron'i·cal·ly** *adv.*

syn'chro·nism *n.* concurrence; a grouping of historic persons or events according to their dates — **syn·chro·nic'i·ty** *n.* —**syn·chro·nis'tic, syn·chro·nis'ti·cal** *adj.* — **syn·chro·nis'ti·cal·ly** *adv.*

syn'chro·nize *vi.* to occur at the same time; to operate in unison — *vt.* to cause to operate together; to assign the same date or period — **syn·chro·ni·za'tion** *n.*

syn'chro·nous *adj.* occurring at the same time —**syn'chro·nous·ly** *adv.* —**syn'chro·nous·ness** *n.*

syn'co·pate *vt.* to modify by syncopation

syn·co·pa'tion *n.* the suppression of an expected rhythmic accent in music

syn'di·cate *n.* an association united to engage in an enterprise —*vt.* to combine into a syndicate —**syn·di·ca'tion** *n.* —**syn'di·ca·tor** *n.*

syn'drome *n.* the combined symptoms characteristic of a specific disease; traits regarded as being characteristic of a condition, etc. —**syn'drom·ic** *adj.*

syn'er·gism *n.* the reinforcing action of separate organs, agents, etc. which produce a greater effect than any acting singly —**syn·er·gis'tic, syn·er·gis'ti·cal** *adj.*

syn'er·gy *n.* synergism

syn'od *n.* an ecclesiastical council

syn'o·nym *n.* a word having the same or almost the same meaning as another

syn·on'y·mous *adj.* being equivalent or similar in meaning —**syn·on'y·mous·ly** *adv.*

syn·op'sis *n.* a condensation, as of a

story, book, etc.; a summary

syn·op´tic *adj.* giving a general view; offering a similar point of view

syn´tax *n.* the arrangement of words in grammatical construction — **syn·tac´tic, syn·tac´ti·cal** *adj.* — **syn·tac´ti·cal·ly** *adv.*

syn´the·sis *n., pl.* **syn´the·ses** the assembling of subordinate parts into a new form; the resulting complex form created

syn´the·size *vt.* to produce by synthesis

syn´the·siz·er *n.* an electronic device used to create musical tones

syn·thet´ic, syn·thet´i·cal *adj.* produced artificially, as by chemical synthesis; artificial —**syn·thet´i·cal·ly** *adv.*

sy·ringe´ *n.* a device used to remove or inject fluids —*vt.* to cleanse or inject with a syringe

syr´up *n.* a thick, sweet liquid —**syr´up·y** *adj.*

sys´tem *n.* a group or arrangement of parts, facts, etc. that relate to or interact with each other; a group of logically related facts, beliefs, etc.; a method of classication, arrangement, etc. —**sys·tem·at´ic, sys·tem·at´i·cal** *adj.* —**sys·tem·at´i·cal·ly** *adv.*

sys´tem·a·tize *vt.* to organize methodically —**sys·tem·a·ti·za´tion** *n.* —**sys´tem·a·tiz·er** *n.*

sys·tem´ic *adj.* of or pertaining to a system; affecting the body as a whole: *a systemic poison* —**sys·tem´i·cal·ly** *adv.*

sys´tem·ize *vt.* systematize —**sys·tem·i·za´tion** *n.*

t, T *n.* 20th letter of the English alphabet —**to a T** perfectly, precisely

tab *n.* a flap, projection, etc. as on a garment or file card —*vt.* to provide with a tab

tab´er·na·cle *n.* a house of worship; the ornamental receptacle for the eucharistic elements; formerly, the portable sanctuary used by the Israelites —**tab´er·nac´u·lar** *adj.*

ta´ble *n.* an article of furniture with a flat top and legs; the surface on which food is served, or the food served; an array of elements arranged in rows and columns for easy reference; a listing: *table of contents*; a tablet or slab —*vt.* to postpone discussion

tab´leau *n., pl.* **tab´leaux** or **tab´leaus** a picturesque representation

table d'hôte a complete meal served at a fixed price

ta´ble·spoon *n.* a measure equal to three teaspoons; a tablespoonful

ta´ble·spoon·ful *n.* the amount a tablespoon will hold; ½ fluid ounce

tab´let *n.* a pill; a pad of paper; a flat surface intended for an inscription or design

ta´ble·ware *n.* dishes and implements for dining

tab´loid *n.* a newspaper in which news is presented concisely and often sensationally

ta·boo´, ta·bu´ *n.* a restriction or ban based on religious belief, custom, or convention —*adj.* restricted or prohibited —*vt.* to place under taboo

tab´u·lar *adj.* arranged in a table or list —**tab´u·lar·ly** *adv.*

tab´u·late *vt.* to arrange in a table or list —**tab·u·la´tion** *n.* —**tab´u·la·tor** *n.*

ta·chom´e·ter *n.* a device for indicating speed of rotation, as for an engine

tach´y·car´di·a *n.* an abnormally rapid heartbeat

tac´it *adj.* not spoken; inferred or implied without being directly stated —**tac´it·ly** *adv.*

tac·i·turn *adj.* habitually reserved — **tac·i·tur´ni·ty** *n.* —**tac´i·turn·ly** *adv.*

tack *n.* a small nail or pin with a broad flat head; a policy or course of action; a temporary fastening — *vt.* to fasten with a tack or tacks; to secure temporarily — *vi.* to change one's course of action: *take a different tack*

tack´le *n.* a combination of ropes and pulleys used for hoisting or moving objects; the rigging of a ship; sport or work gear — *vt.* to undertake, as to *tackle a problem*; to seize suddenly and forcefully — **tack´ler** *n.*

tack´y *adj.* slightly sticky; in poor taste — **tack´i·ness** *n.*

ta´co *n.* a fried tortilla folded around a filling

tact *n.* the ability to say or do the proper thing — **tact´ful** *adj.* — **tact´ful·ly** *adv.* — **tact´ful·ness** *n.*

tac´ti·cal *adj.* pertaining to tactics; adept at planning and maneuvering — **tac´ti·cal·ly** *adv.* — **tac·ti´cian** *n.*

tac´tics *n.* strategy; the art of maneuvering to gain an end

tac´tile *adj.* relating to the sense of touch; that may be touched or perceived by touch — **tac´til´i·ty** *n.*

tact´less *adj.* characterized by a lack of tact — **tact´less·ly** *adv.* — **tact´less·ness** *n.*

taf·fe·ta *n.* a fine, somewhat stiff fabric used for women's garments — *adj.* made of taffeta

taf´fy *n.* a chewy confection of brown sugar or molasses

tag *n.* an attachment that identifies, shows price, etc.; a children's game — *vt.* to fit with a tag; to follow closely; to touch, as in the game of tag

Ta·ga´log *n.* a Philippine native; the official language of the Philippines

ta·hi´ni *n.* sesame seed butter

tail *n.* the flexible appendage at the hind end of an animal; anything resembling a tail, as the luminous cloud extending from a comet; the hind or back portion — *vt.* to be at the end of; to follow stealthily — *vi.* to follow closely; to diminish gradually — *adj.* rearmost; coming from behind

tail´gate *n.* a hinged gate at the back of a motor vehicle — *vt., vi.* to follow too closely for safety

tai´lor *n.* one who makes or repairs garments — *vi.* to do a tailor's work — *vt.* to fit with garments; to adapt to meet a need — **tai´lor·ing** *n.*

tai´lored *adj.* custom–made; severe or tight–fitting

tai´lor–made´ *adj.* made by a tailor; perfectly suited to fill a need

taint *vt., vi.* to affect or be affected by contamination or corruption — *n.* a cause or result of contamination

take *vt.* to lay hold of or gain possession of; to choose; to steal; to undergo or submit to: *take a beating*; to accept; to charm or captivate: *take advantage of*; to perform, as an action; to feel — *vi.* to gain possession; to acquire; to be captivated: *taken with her beauty*; to require: *the cake takes two eggs*; to enter upon: *take a job*; to assume: *take the blame*; to have an intended effect — *n.* something taken; something received or the amount received: *the day's take for ticket sales* — **tak´a·ble** *adj.* — **tak´er** *n.*

tale *n.* a story; a narrative of events; idle or malicious gossip; a lie

tale´bear·er *n.* one who gossips or spreads rumors — **tale´bear·ing** *adj.*

tal´ent *n.* natural ability; a particular aptitude; collectively, those with special abilities — **tal´ent·ed** *adj.*

tal´is·man *n.* an object supposed to ward off evil or bring good luck; anything with seeming magical power —**tal·is·man´ic, tal·is·man´i·cal** *adj.*

talk *vi.* to express audibly; to communicate by means other than the voice: *money talks*; to make sounds suggestive of speech —*vt.* to express in words —*n.* conversation or speech; a conference or discussion; sounds suggesting speech —**talk´er** *n.*

talk´a·thon *n.* a prolonged discussion, debate, etc.

talk´a·tive *adj.* given to much talk —**talk´a·tive·ly** *adv.* —**talk´a·tive·ness** *n.*

talk´y *adj.* talkative; given overly to talk: *a talky movie* —**talk´i·ness** *n.*

tall *adj.* of more than average height; of a specified height; exaggerated, as *a tall story*; extensive, as *a tall order* —*adv.* proudly: *to walk tall* —**tall´ish** *adj.* —**tall´ness** *n.*

tal´low *n.* rendered animal fat

tal´ly *n.* a score or mark; a reckoning; a mark indicating a number —*vt.* to score; to reckon; to cause to correspond —*vi.* to make a tally; to keep score; to agree precisely

tal´on *n.* the claw of an animal

ta·ma´le *n.* a Mexican food of seasoned ground beef rolled in corn meal, then wrapped in leaves and steamed

tame *adj.* domesticated; docile, subdued; lacking spirit, uninteresting —*vt.* to domesticate; to tone down —**tam´a·ble, tame´a·ble** *adj.* —**tame´ly** *adv.* —**tame´ness** *n.* —**tam´er** *n.*

tamp *vt.* to pack down

tam´per *vi.* to meddle in or interfere with; to make potentially harmful changes; to use improper measures, as bribery —**tam´per·er** *n.*

tan *vt.* to convert into leather; to darken by exposure to sunlight —*vi.* to become tanned —*n.* a yellow-brown color; a dark coloring of the skin —**tan´ner** *n.*

tan´dem *adv.* one behind the other —*n.* a team of horses harnessed one behind the other or the carriage they pull; a bicycle with two or more seats —*adj.*

tang *n.* a sharp, penetrating taste or odor —**tang´i·ness** *n.* —**tang´y** *adj.*

tan´gent *adj.* touching without intersecting —**tan´gen·cy** *n.*

tan·gen´tial *adj.* pertaining to a tangent; touching lightly —**tan·gen·ti·al´i·ty** *n.* —**tan·gen´tial·ly** *adv.*

tan´ger·ine´ *n.* a variety of orange

tan´gi·ble *adj.* perceptible by touch; real or concrete —*n.* assets having value that can be appraised —**tan·gi·bil´i·ty, tan´gi·ble·ness** *n.* —**tan´gi·bly** *adv.*

tan´gle *vt.* to twist into a mass; to ensnare or enmesh; to involve in such a way as to confuse —*vi.* to be or become tangled —*n.* a confused intertwining —**tan´gler** *n.* —**tan´gly** *adj.*

tan´go *n.* a Latin American dance; the music for such a dance —*vi.*

tank *n.* a large receptacle for fluid; an armored combat vehicle —*vt.* to store in a tank

tan´kard *n.* a large, handled drinking cup, often with a cover

tan´ner·y *n.* a place where leather is tanned

tan´ta·lize *vt.* to torment by promising something, then withholding it —**tan´ta·li·za´tion** *n.* —**tan´ta·liz·er** *n.* —**tan´ta·liz·ing·ly** *adv.*

tan´ta·mount *adj.* equivalent to

tan´trum *n.* a fit of temper

tap *n.* the act or sound of striking gently; a spout through which liquid is drawn; a plug or stopper —*vt.* to touch or strike gently; to provide with a spigot; to open so as to draw liquid; to draw upon

tape *n.* a long narrow strip —*vt.* to secure with tape —**tap´er** *n.*

ta´per *n.* a slender candle; a wick used to light candles; a cone; a gradual decrease —*vt.*, *vi.* to make or become thin toward one end; to lessen gradually —*adj.*

tap´es·try *n.* a heavy woven textile with a pictorial design —*vt.* to adorn with tapestry

tape´worm *n.* a parasitic worm

tap·i·o·ca *n.* a starchy food obtained from cassava

tar·an·tel´la *n.* a lively Neopolitan dance

ta·ran´tu·la *n.* a large hairy spider

tar´dy *adj.* not coming or happening as anticipated; moving ahead slowly —**tar´di·ly** *adv.* —**tar´di·ness** *n.*

tar´get *n.* something shot at; the object of an action, as ridicule, criticism, etc. —*vt.* to establish as a goal —**tar´get·a·ble** *adj.*

tar´iff *n.* a schedule of duties to be paid, or those imposed, on imports and exports; a price schedule —*vt.* to fix a price on

tarn *n.* a small mountain lake

tar´nish *vt.* to dim the luster of; to sully or debase —*vi.* to become tarnished —**tar´nish·a·ble** *adj.*

ta´ro *n.* a tropical plant having a starchy edible rootstock

ta´rot *n.* a set of cards used mainly for fortunetelling

tar·pau´lin *n.* a waterproof material used as a protective covering

tar´pon *n.* a large game fish

tar´ra·gon *n.* a European plant with leaves used for seasoning

tar´ry *vi.* to put off going; to linger; to remain temporarily

tar´sal *adj.* pertaining to the ankle

tar´sus *n.* the ankle

tart *n.* a small filled pastry —*adj.* having a sharp sour taste; caustic, as a remark —**tart´ly** *adv.* —**tart´ness** *n.*

tar´tan *n.* a woolen fabric, especially one with a pattern distinctive to a particular Scottish clan

task *n.* a designated job, especially one required; a difficult assignment —*vi.* to assign a task; to overburden

task´mas·ter *n.* one who assigns tasks, especially burdensome ones

tas´sel *n.* a tuft of loose hanging cords such as used to ornament cushions, etc. —*vt.* to adorn with tassels —*vi.* to put forth tassels, as on corn

taste *vt.* to perceive the flavor of; to eat or drink a little; to experience —*vi.* to recognize a flavor; to take a small amount; to experience: *taste the fruits of victory*; to have a specific flavor —*n.* the sensation associated with stimulation of the taste buds; a small quantity or sample; a special fondness or appreciation: *a taste for music*; a respect for propriety and refinement —**taste´a·ble** *adj.*

taste buds receptors on the tongue stimulated by sweet, salt, sour, or bitter substances

taste´ful *adj.* conforming to good taste —**taste´ful·ly** *adv.* —**taste´ful·ness** *n.*

taste´less *adj.* without flavor; lacking tact or decorum —**taste´less·ly** *adv.* —**taste´less·ness** *n.*

tast´y *adj.* having a fine flavor —**tast´i·ly** *adv.* —**tast´i·ness** *n.*

tat´ter *n.* a torn shred —*vt.*, *vi.* to make or become ragged —**tat´ters** ragged clothing

tat·ter·de·ma´lion *n.* one wearing ragged clothing; a ragamuffin —*adj.*

tat´ter·sall *n.* a pattern of intersecting dark lines on a light background; cloth of this design —*adj.*

tat´tle *vi.*, *vt.* to gossip or reveal by gossiping —*n.* idle chatter —**tat´tler** *n.* —**tat´tling·ly** *adv.*

tat´tle·tale *n.* one who tattles —*adj.* revealing: *tattletale signs*

tat·too´ *vt.* to mark the skin with patterns —*n.* a pattern or design on the skin; a continuous drumbeat; the sounding of a drum or bugle to signal a return to quarters —**tat·too´er, tat·too´ist** *n.*

tat´ty *adj.* somewhat worn or shabby

taunt *n.* a sarcastic remark; a jibe —*vt.* to provoke with derision or insults —**taunt´er** *n.* —**taunt´ing·ly** *adv.*

[...]ownish gray color

[...]hed tight; tidy —**taut´** **taupe** **taut** [...]ness *n.*

[...] the unnecessary [...] concept in

[...] *n.* the —**tau·to·log´ic**, [...]ating at a —**tau·to·log´i·** television, **ol´o·gize** *vi.* —

m·mu´ni· **mu´ni·ca·** place licensed to [...]ages

[...]ractice of [...] and showy; [...]rough a [...]uality —**taw´dri·** **mute´** [...]ness *n.*

[...]olored —*n.* tan — [...] *n.*

tax ge levied for the support **tax** of [...]ent; a heavy demand, as [...]'s powers or resources — **tax** *vt.* y a tax on; to impose a **bur**[...]on —**tax shelter** a financ·[...]nipulation designed to re· **duc**[...]x liability —**tax·a·bil´i·ty** *n.* **tax·a** **·a·ble** *adj.*

[...] **tion** *n.* the process of taxing; [...]amount levied; revenue raised from taxes

tax´i *n.* a taxicab —*vi.* to ride in a taxicab; to move along the surface, as of an airplane preparing to take off

tax´i·cab *n.* a passenger vehicle for hire

tax´i·der·my *n.* the art of stuffing and mounting animals —**tax·i·der´mal, tax·i·der´mic** *adj.* —**tax´i·der·mist** *n.*

tax´ing *adj.* difficult, trying —**tax´ing·ly** *adv.*

tax·on´o·my *n.* the laws and principles of classification, as of plant and animal life into successive subgroups —**tax·o·nom´ic, tax·o·nom´i·cal** *adj.* —**tax·o·nom´i·cal·ly** *adv.* —**tax·on´o·mist** *n.*

T cell *n.* a type of white blood cell that performs various functions in the immune system

tea *n.* an Asian plant or its leaves, used in preparing a beverage; a beverage prepared from leaves, an animal extract, etc.; a social gathering —**tea service** a set of matching cups and saucers, a creamer, etc. used for serving tea

teach *vt.* to provide instruction to; to instruct in: *teach French*; to train —*vi.* to act as teacher —**teach·a·bil´i·ty, teach´a·ble·ness** *n.* —**teach´a·ble** *adj.* —**teach´a·bly** *adv.* —**teach´er** *n.*

teaching machine an interactive computer that presents material to a student and provides corrective feedback

teak *n.* an extremely durable wood or the tree from which it comes

team *n.* a group working together as a unit —*vi.* to work as a team — **team player** one who identifies with and cooperates in a team — **team´work** harmony of action among the members of a group

team´ster *n.* one who drives a team of horses or a motor vehicle

tear *n.* a drop of fluid from the eye; a break or rip, as in a fabric; a violent outburst —*vt.* to pull apart; to wound or lacerate; to distress or disrupt: *torn by dissension* —*vi.* to become torn; to move with haste or energy

tear´ful *adj.* causing tears; accompanied by tears —**tear´ful·ly** *adv.* —**tear´ful·ness** *n.*

tear´ing *adj.* with great haste

tearˊjerkˎer *n.* a book, play, etc. designed to evoke tears

tearˊy *adj.* filled or wet with tears; sentimental; overemotional —**tearˊiˎly** *adv.* —**tearˊiˎness** *n.*

tease *vt.* to annoy or vex; to coax or beg; to comb —*vi.* to annoy in a petty way —*n.* one who teases —**teasˊer** *n.* —**teasˊingˎly** *adv.*

teaˊspoon *n.* a small spoon for measuring, stirring, etc. —**teaˊspoon, teaˊspoonˎful** *n.* the amount a teaspoon will hold

techˊniˎcal *adj.* pertaining to or characteristic of a particular art, trade, etc.; exhibiting technique; according to an accepted body of rules —**techˊniˎcalˎly** *adv.*

technical foul a violation of a rule that does not necessarily involve physical contact

techˎniˎcalˊiˎty *n.* a technique or approach peculiar to an art, trade, etc.; a petty detail

techˎniˊcian *n.* one skilled in a particular field

techˊnics *n.* the study or principles of an art, trade, etc.

techˎniqueˊ *n.* the way in which one works; the degree of skill one exhibits; any method of accomplishing something

techˎnocˊraˎcy *n.* a government dominated by technicians —**techˊnoˎcrat** *n.* —**techˊnoˎcratˎic** *adj.*

techˎnolˊoˎgy *n.* the technical means employed to meet the needs of a society; technical terms —**techˎnoˎlogˊic, techˎnoˎlogˊiˎcal** *adj.* —**techˎnoˎlogˊiˎcalˎly** *adv.* —**techˎnolˊoˎgist** *n.*

tecˎtonˊics *n.* the science or art of construction; the study of the movements of the earth's crust —**tecˎtonˊic** *adj.* —**tecˎtonˊiˎcalˎly** *adv.*

teˊdiˎous *adj.* boring or repetitious —**teˊdiˎousˎly** *adv.* —**teˊdiˎousˎness** *n.*

teˊdiˎum *n.* the quality of being boring, monotonous, etc.

teem *vi.* to be full or overflowing —**teemˊingˎly** *adv.*

teenˊage, teenˊ-age, teenˊaged, teenˊ-aged *adj.* of the ages from 13 to 19 —**teen, teenˊager, teenˊager** *n.*

teeˊter *vi.* to walk unsteadily; to vacillate or waver

teethe *vi.* to develop teeth

teeˎtoˊtal *adj.* advocating abstention from the consumption ... holic beverages —**teeˊt**... —**teeˎtoˊtalˎism** *n.*

telˊeˎcast *vt., vi.* to bro... television —*n.* —**telˊeˎca**...

telˎeˎcomˎmuˎniˎcaˊtion technology of communic... distance as by radio, ... telephone, etc. —**telˎeˎco**... **cate** *vt., vi.* —**telˎeˎcom**... **tor** *n.*

telˊeˎcomˎmutˎing *n.* the p... working from home th... computer link —**telˊeˎco**... *vi.* —**telˊeˎcomˎmutˎer** *n.*

telˊeˎconˊferˎence *n.* a m... people located at a dis... means of a telephone h... closed circuit television ... participate in a teleconfe... **telˊeˎconˊferˎencˎing** ...

telˊeˎgraph *n.* a system fo... mitting messages over a ... —**telˊeˎgram** *n.* —**teˎlegˊra**... —**teˎlegˊraˎphy** *n.*

telˎeˎkiˎneˊsis *n.* the unexplained movement of objects, as by occult power —**telˎeˎkiˎnetˊic** *adj.*

telˊeˎmarˎketˎing *n.* the selling of products by telephone or television —**telˊeˎmarˎketˎer** *n.*

teˎlemˊeˎtry *n.* the automatic measurement and transmission of data from a distance —**telˊeˎmeˎter** *n.*, *vt.* —**telˎeˎmetˊric, telˎeˎmetˊriˎcal** *adj.* —**telˎeˎmetˊriˎcalˎly** *adv.*

telˎeˎolˊoˎgy *n.* the study of final

causes; the explanation of natural phenomenon in terms of design and purpose —**tel·e·o·log´ic, tel·e·o·log´i·cal** *adj.* —**tel·e·o·log´i·cal·ly** *adv.* —**tel·e·ol´o·gist** *n.*

te·lep´a·thy *n.* communication by other than normal sensory means —**tel·e·path´ic** *adj.* —**tel·e·path´i·cal·ly** *adv.* —**te·lep´a·thist** *n.*

tel´e·phone *n.* a device for transmitting sound or speech over a distance —*vt., vi.* to communicate by telephone —**tel·e·phon´ic** *adj.* —**tel·e·phon´i·cal·ly** *adv.*

te·leph´o·ny *n.* the technology of telephone communication

tel´e·pho´to *adj.* of a system of lenses which produces a near view of a distant object

tel·e·pho·tog´ra·phy *n.* the technique for producing magnified photographs of distant objects — **tel·e·pho·to·graph´ic** *adj.*

tel´e·scope *n.* an instrument for viewing distant objects —**tel´e·scop´ic** *adj.* —**tel´e·scop´i·cal·ly** *adv.*

tel´e·thon *n.* a television show intended to raise funds for charity

tel·e·van´ge·lism *n.* the broadcasting of religious shows intended to attract new adherents —**tel·e·van´ge·list** *n.*

tel´e·vise *vt., vi.* to transmit a television signal

tel´e·vi·sion *n.* a system, industry, etc. involved with the transmission of visual images and sound; a device for receiving such transmissions

tell *vt.* to narrate or relate in detail; to express in words; to ascertain or distinguish, as *to tell who is at fault* —*vi.* to give an account; to serve as an indication: *their rags told of their poverty* —**tell´a·ble** *adj.*

tell´er *n.* one who narrates, as a story; (*US*) a bank employee

tell´ing *adj.* producing a marked effect —**tell´ing·ly** *adv.*

tell´tale *adj.* revealing —*n.* one who tells on others, a tattler; an outward sign or indication

tem·er·ar´i·ous *adj.* daring or reckless —**tem·er·ar´i·ous·ly** *adv.* —**tem·er·ar´i·ous·ness** *n.*

te·mer´i·ty *n.* foolish disregard for danger

tem´peh *n.* a high–protein food made from fermented soybeans

tem´per *n.* a fit of anger; a tendency to quick anger; temperament; the hardness of a metal —*vt.* to moderate, as by adding something; to toughen, as by hardship —*vi.* to be or become tempered —**tem·per·a·bil´i·ty** *n.* —**tem´per·a·ble** *adj.*

tem´per·a *n.* a type of paint; a method of painting

tem´per·a·ment *n.* the nature or disposition of a person; an overly dramatic or moody disposition

tem·per·a·men´tal *adj.* pertaining to temperament; overly excitable, capricious, etc.; unpredictable — **tem·per·a·men´tal·ly** *adv.*

tem´per·ance *n.* moderation and self–control, especially in the indulgence of an appetite —*adj.* restraint

tem´per·ate *adj.* characterized by moderation or the absence of extremes; calm, restrained; practicing moderation in all things; of a climate that is not extreme: not overly hot or cold —**tem´per·ate·ly** *adv.* —**tem´per·ate·ness** *n.*

tem´per·a·ture *n.* a measure of the relative heat or cold as in the atmosphere, the body, etc.; an excess of heat in a body

tem´pered *adj.* of a particular temperament, as *even–tempered* or *quick–tempered*; modified by the addition of something else: *discipline tempered with love*; having a desired quality: *tempered steel*

tem´pest *n.* a violent wind; a violent disturbance

tem·pes´tu·ous *adj.* stormy, turbulent —**tem·pes´tu·ous·ly** *adv.* — **tem·pes´tu·ous·ness** *n.*

tem´plate *n.* a pattern used in the making or design of something

tem´ple *n.* a place dedicated to worship; an imposing structure dedicated to a special purpose, as *a temple of learning*

tem´po *n.* relative speed and rhythm, as of music

tem´po·ral *adj.* worldly; material as contrasted to spiritual; transitory; of or related to time —**tem·po·ral´i·ty, tem´po·ral·ness** *n.* —**tem´po·ral·ly** *adv.*

tem´po·rar·y *adj.* lasting for a time only; not permanent —*n.* a worker hired as seasonal help, to fill in for a permanent employee who is ill or on vacation, etc. —**tem´po·rar´i·ly** *adv.* —**tem´po·rar·i·ness** *n.*

tem´po·rize *vi.* to act evasively so as to gain time or defer commitment; to give in to the situation, circumstances, etc.; to compromise — **tem·po·ri·za´tion** *n.* —**tem´po·riz·er** *n.* —**tem´po·riz·ing·ly** *adv.*

tempt *vt.* to try to persuade to do, as by promises; to risk provoking: *to tempt fate*; to influence: *they were tempted by the promise of profit* — **tempt´a·ble** *adj.* —**tempt´er, tempt´ress** *n.*

temp·ta´tion *n.* that which tempts; the state of being tempted

tempt´ing *adj.* attractive; seductive —**tempt´ing·ly** *adv.* —**tempt´ing·ness** *n.*

tem´pu·ra *n.* a Japanese dish of vegetables or seafood fried in a light batter

ten´a·ble *adj.* capable of being maintained or defended, as a concept, position, etc. —**ten·a·bil´i·ty, ten´a·ble·ness** *n.* —**ten´a·biy** *adv.*

te·na´cious *adj.* obstinate or persis-

tent, as in a belief; adhesive or sticky; strongly retentive, as of memory —**te·na´cious·ly** *adv.* — **te·na´cious·ness, te·nac´i·ty** *n.*

ten´an·cy *n.* the holding of property by any form of title; the period of tenancy

ten´ant *n.* one who rents or has title to property belonging to another; an occupant —*vt., vi.* to hold as, or to be, a tenant —**ten´ant·a·ble** *adj.* —**ten´ant·ry** *n.*

tend *vi.* to have an aptitude or inclination; to be in attendance, to serve; to give attention or care — *vt.* to take care of; to watch over

tend´en·cy *n.* an inclination; movement, as toward some end or result

ten·den´tious, ten·den´cious *adj.* disposed to a particular view — **ten·den´tious·ly** *adv.* —**ten·den´tious·ness** *n.*

ten´der[1] *adj.* delicate or fragile; youthful: *of a tender age*; marked by gentleness and consideration; expressing affection: *a tender look*; emotionally sensitive —**ten´der·ly** *adv.* —**ten´der·ness** *n.*

tend´er[2] *vt.* to present for acceptance, as an invitation or offer, the payment of a debt, etc. —*n.* an offer; that which is offered, especially money; a boat that services a larger vessel, as by ferrying passengers or supplies; a railway car attached to a steam locomotive to carry fuel and water; a person who tends or ministers

ten´der·foot *n.* a newcomer or beginner —*adj.* inexperienced

ten´der·heart·ed *adj.* responsive to another's troubles; compassionate; sympathetic —**ten´der·heart·ed·ly** *adv.* —**ten´der·heart·ed·ness** *n.*

ten´der·ize *vt.* to make meat tender —**ten·der·i·za´tion** *n.* —**ten´der·iz·er** *n.*

ten´der·loin *n.* a tender cut of meat;

a city district known for crime and corruption

ten·di·ni´tis, ten·do·ni´tis *n.* inflammation of a tendon

ten´don *n.* a band of tough, fibrous tissue that attaches muscle to bone —**ten´di·nous** *adj.*

ten´dril *n.* a delicate, curling extension by which certain plants attach themselves —**ten´dril·ed, ten´drill·ed, ten´dril·ous** *adj.*

ten´e·ment *n.* a rented room or set of rooms; commonly, a low–rent run–down apartment building; property held by a renter —**ten·e·men´tal, ten·e·men´ta·ry** *adj.*

ten´et *n.* a principle, doctrine, etc. held by a group or profession

ten´on *n.* a projection on the end of a timber for inserting into a mortise to form a joint

ten´or *n.* general character or nature; a general course or tendency; a male voice or singing part higher than a baritone —*adj.* of a voice, singing part, or musical instrument in the tenor range

tense *adj.* stretched tight; under mental stress; providing suspense —*vt., vi.* to make or become tense —*n.* the quality of a verb that denotes time or state of being: *past tense, present tense*, etc. —**tense´ly** *adv.* —**tense´ness** *n.*

ten´sile *adj.* pertaining to tension; capable of being stretched —**ten´sile·ly** *adv.* —**ten´sile·ness** *n.*

tensile strength resistance of a material to any force that may tend to rupture it

ten´sion *n.* the act of stretching or the condition of being stretched; mental strain or anxiety; a device on a machine that regulates stress —**ten´sion·al** *adj.*

ten´sor *n.* a muscle that tenses or stretches —**ten·so´ri·al** *adj.*

tent *n.* a portable shelter of canvas or similar material —*vi.* to pitch a tent; to camp

ten´ta·cle *n.* a long, flexible appendage of certain animals that functions as the organ of touch or for grasping; a similar organ on the leaves of certain plants, such as for trapping insects —**ten´ta·cled, ten·tac´u·lar** *adj.*

ten´ta·tive *adj.* not finalized, subject to change; somewhat uncertain —**ten´ta·tive·ly** *adv.* —**ten´ta·tive·ness** *n.*

ten´ter *n.* a frame for stretching cloth to dry

ten´ter·hook *n.* a sharp pin for holding cloth on a tenter —**be on tenterhooks** to be in a state of anxiety

ten´u·ous *adj.* weak, lacking substance, as of an argument or reasoning; thin: lacking density, such as air at high altitudes —**ten´u·ous·ly** *adv.* —**ten´u·ous·ness** *n.*

ten´ure *n.* the right, condition, etc. of holding something, as property, office, or a position —**ten´ured, ten·u´ri·al** *adj.* —**ten·u´ri·al·ly** *adv.*

tep´id *adj.* moderately warm; unenthusiastic —**te·pid´i·ty, tep´id·ness** *n.* —**tep´id·ly** *adv.*

te·qui´la *n.* an alcoholic beverage of Mexican origin

te·rat´o·gen *n.* an agent that causes malformation, as in a developing fetus —**te·rat·o·gen´e·sis** *n.* —**te·rat·o·gen´ic** *adj.*

ter´i·ya´ki *n.* a Japanese dish of broiled marinated fish or meat

term *n.* a word or expression used to name something, convey a concept, etc.; the conditions of an agreement; a fixed period; a prescribed period —*vt.* to designate by means of a name

term insurance life insurance that is active for a specific period, as five years or ten years after which it can be renewed at a revised rate

ter˘ma·gant *n.* a scolding woman — *adj.* abusive or quarrelsome

ter˘mi·na·ble *adj.* that may be terminated —**ter·mi·na·bil´i·ty, ter˘ mi·na·ble·ness** *n.* —**ter˘mi·na·bly** *adv.*

ter˘mi·nal *adj.* pertaining to an end, as of an action, life, etc.; situated at or forming an end or limit —*n.* an intermediate or terminating point, as of a passenger station; an electrical junction; a station from which one communicates to or through a computer —**ter˘mi·nal· ly** *adv.*

ter˘mi·nate *vt.* to put an end to; to bound or limit —*vi.* to come to an end —**ter˘mi·na·tive** *adj.* —**ter˘ mi·na·tive·ly** *adv.*

ter·mi·na˘tion *n.* an ending, outcome, or conclusion; the condition of being terminated; that which bounds or limits —**ter·mi·na˘ tion·al** *adj.*

ter˘mi·na·tor *n.* one who or that which terminates

ter·mi·nol´o·gy *n.* the terms relating to a particular discipline, as in art, science, etc. —**ter·mi·no·log´i·cal** *adj.* —**ter·mi·no·log´i·cal·ly** *adv.* —**ter·mi·nol´o·gist** *n.*

ter˘mi·nus *n.* the final point or end; a terminal

ter·mi·tar´i·um *n.* a termite nest

ter˘mite *n.* an insect resembling the ant, noted for boring into wood

terp˘si·cho·re˘an *adj.* of or relating to dancing

ter˘race *n.* a raised level space with sloping sides; a raised street supporting a row of houses; an open paved area connected to a house —*vt.* to form into or provide with a terrace —**terrace house** (*Brit.*) a house, usually of more than one storey, situated in a row of dwellings that share a common wall with one or more adjoining houses

ter˘ra cot˘ta reddish–brown clay pottery; a reddish–brown color — **ter˘ra–cot˘ta** *adj.*

ter˘ra fir˘ma solid ground

ter·rain˘ *n.* a land area described by a particular characteristic

ter·rane˘ *n.* a series of similar rock formations

ter˘ra·pin *n.* a type of tortoise

ter·rar´i·um *n.* a glass enclosure for growing small plants

ter·raz˘zo *n.* a flooring of stone chips set in mortar

ter·res˘tri·al *adj.* belonging to the planet Earth; pertaining to earth; of land as distinct from water — **ter·res˘tri·al·ly** *adv.*

ter˘ri·ble *adj.* causing fear or dread; severe or extreme, as *a terrible headache*; dreadful, as *a terrible meal* —**ter˘ri·ble·ness** *n.* —**ter˘ri· bly** *adv.*

ter˘ri·er *n.* a breed of small energetic dogs

ter·rif˘ic *adj.* arousing fear or terror; unusually good —**ter·rif´i·cal·ly** *adv.*

ter˘ri·fy *vt.* to fill with terror

ter·rine˘ *n.* a dish for cooking and serving food

ter·ri·to˘ri·al *adj.* of a territory; restricted to a particular territory —**ter·ri·to˘ri·al·ly** *adv.*

territorial waters coastal waters under the jurisdiction of a particular government

ter·ri·to˘ri·al·ize *vt.* to organize as a territory; to create or extend a territory —**ter·ri·to·ri·al·i·za˘tion** *n.*

ter˘ri·to·ry *n.* the domain over which a government exercises jurisdiction; a distinctive area, as *a sales territory*; a region self-governed but lacking the status of a state or province

ter˘ror *n.* great fear or something that causes such fear; a difficult child

ter·ror·ism *n.* violence committed to

achieve a political end —**ter´ror·ist** n. —**ter·ror·is´tic** adj.

ter´ror·ize vt. to terrify, especially by acts of violence; to intimidate through terrorism —**ter·ror·i·za´tion** n. —**ter´ror·iz·er** n.

ter´ry, ter´ry·cloth n. an absorbent pile fabric

terse adj. short and to the point —**terse´ly** adv. —**terse´ness** n.

ter´ti·ar·y adj. third in importance, rank, etc.

test vt. to subject to examination —vi. to undergo or give an examination —n. an examination; a criterion or standard —**test·a·bil´i·ty** n. —**test´a·ble** adj.

tes´ta·ment n. the written statement of one's last will; a statement testifying to some belief; proof —**tes´ta·men´ta·ry** adj.

tes´tate adj. having a will —**tes´ta·cy** n. —**tes´ta·tor** n.

tes´ter n. one who administers tests; a canopy, as over a bed

tes´ti·cle n. one of the two sex glands of the male —**tes·tic´u·lar** adj.

tes´ti·fy vi. to make a solemn declaration; to bear witness; to serve as evidence —**tes·ti·fi·ca´tion** n. —**tes´ti·fi·er** n.

tes·ti·mo´ni·al n. a statement endorsing character, value, etc.; public acknowledgment to show respect or appreciation

tes´ti·mo·ny n. a statement of a witness under oath; any public acknowledgment; any evidence or proof: *the dinner bore testimony to her skill as a cook*

tes´ty adj. irritable —**tes´ti·ly** adv. —**tes´ti·ness** n.

tet´a·nus n. an often fatal bacterial disease marked by spasmodic muscular contractions —**te·tan´ic** adj.

tête´-à-tête´ adj. confidential —n. a private conversation

teth´er n. a line for restricting the movements of an animal; the limit of one's power, etc.

te·tral´o·gy n. a series of four novels, plays, etc.

text n. the words of an author or speaker; the main body of matter in a book; any of the written or printed versions of a piece of writing; the words of a song, opera, etc.

text´book n. a book used as a standard or basis of instruction

tex´tile n. a fabric —adj. of weaving, woven fabric, or that which may be woven

tex´tu·al adj. of or relating to a text —**tex´tu·al·ly** adv.

tex´tu·al·ism n. the strict interpretation of a text, especially religious —**tex´tu·al·ist** n.

tex´ture n. the surface characteristic of a fabric; the characteristic of anything, especially in regard to appearance or tactile qualities: *the texture of bread*; the structure, form, etc. of a work of art, as *the tightly-knit texture of his prose*; the basic nature of something —**tex´tur·al** adj. —**tex´tur·al·ly** adv. —**tex´tured** adj.

thal´a·mus n. matter at the base of the brain involved in sensory transmission —**tha·lam´ic** adj.

than·a·tol´o·gy n. the study of death and dying —**than·a·to·log´i·cal** adj. —**than·a·tol´o·gist** n.

thane n. in Anglo-Saxon England, one granted the land of a king or noble in exchange for military service; the chief of a Scottish clan

thank vt. to express gratitude

thank´ful adj. feeling or expressing gratitude —**thank´ful·ly** adv. —**thank´ful·ness** n.

thank´less adj. unlikely to elicit approval; unappreciated —**thank´less·ly** adv. —**thank´less·ness** n.

thanks´giv´ing n. the act of giving

437

thanks; a means of expressing thanks, as by prayer or celebration

that *adj.* pertaining to something previously mentioned, understood, or pointed out; denoting something more remote than the one with which it is being compared —*pron.* something mentioned, understood, etc.; the thing more remote —*adv.* to the extent required: *I can't see that far* —*conj.*

thatch *n.* a covering of leaves, reeds, etc. arranged so as to shed water; material used for such a covering —*vt.* to cover with a thatch — **thatch´er** *n.* —**thatch´y** *adj.*

thaw *vi.* to melt, as ice or snow; to rise in temperature so as to melt ice; to become less aloof —*vt.* to cause to thaw —*n.* the act of melting; warmth of temperature; progression toward sociability

the·a·ter *n.* a structure or area for the presentation of plays, operas, etc.; a similar place used for lectures, demonstrations, etc.; the world of the legitimate stage; a place that is the scene of action: *a theater of war*

the·at´ric, the·at´ri·cal *adj.* pertaining to any aspect of the theater, as script, actors, costumes, etc.; dramatically compelling; pretentious —**the·at´ri·cal·ism, the· at·ri·cal´i·ty** *n.* —**the·at´ri·cal·ly** *adv.*

the·at´rics *n.* undue dramatization

theft *n.* an act of stealing; that which is stolen

the´ism *n.* belief in a god or gods — **the´ist** *n.* —**the·is´tic, the·is´ti· cal** *adj.* —**the·is´ti·cal·ly** *adv.*

theme *n.* a main subject or topic, as of a work of art, speech, etc.; a short essay —**the·mat´ic, the· mat´i·cal** *adj.* —**the·mat´i·cal·ly** *adv.*

the·oc´ra·cy *n.* government by religious authority —**the·o·crat´ic,**

the·o·crat´i·cal *adj.* —**the·o·crat´ i·cal·ly** *adv.*

the·od´o·lite *n.* a surveying instrument

the·og´o·ny *n.* a chronicle of the geneology of gods —**the·o·gon´ic** *adj.*

the·o·lo´gi·an *n.* one trained in or engaged in the study of religious belief

the·o·log´ic, the·o·log´i·cal *adj.* relating to religious matters —**the· o·log´i·cal·ly** *adv.*

the·ol´o·gy *n.* the study of religion and religious doctrine

the´o·rem *n.* a proposition or theory that is demonstrably true or generally considered to be true

the·o·ret´ic, the·o·ret´i·cal *adj.* relating to theory; existing in theory only; disposed to speculation —**the·o·ret´i·cal·ly** *adv.*

the´o·rize *vi.* to speculate; to put forth as a theory —**the·o·ri·za´ tion** *n.* —**the´o·riz·er** *n.* —**the´o· rist** *n.*

the´o·ry *n.* conjecture or speculation; a body of fundamental or abstract principles underlying an art, science, etc.; a proposed explanation

the·os´o·phy *n.* religious philosophy based on mystical insight — **the·o·soph´ic, the·o·soph´i·cal** *adj.* —**the·o·soph´i·cal·ly** *adv.* — **the·os´o·phist** *n.*

ther´a·peu´tic, ther´a·peu´ti·cal *adj.* having curative powers — **ther´a·peu´ti·cal·ly** *adv.*

ther·a·peu´tics *n.* the study of medical treatment and cures for illness and disease

ther´a·py *n.* the treatment of illness and disease; a type of treatment, as *physical therapy* or *psychotherapy* —**ther´a·pist** *n.*

there *adv.* in or at that place; yonder; in that respect —*n.* a position removed from that of the speaker

there·a·bout, there·a·bouts *adv.* approximately

there·af·ter *adv.* from that time on

there·by *adv.* through the agency of

there·fore *adv., conj.* for that reason; consequently

there·in *adv.* in that respect

there·in·af·ter *adv.* in a subsequent part

ther·e·min *n.* an electronic instrument for producing musical tones

there·upon *adv.* following or in consequence of

there·with *adv.* thereupon

ther·mal, ther·mic *adj.* relating to or caused by heat; warm — *n.* a rising current of warm air

ther·mo·dy·nam·ics *n.* the study of the relationship between heat and other sources of energy —**ther·mo·dy·nam·ic, ther·mo·dy·nam·i·cal** *adj.* —**ther·mo·dy·nam·i·cal·ly** *adv.* —**ther·mo·dy·nam·i·cist** *n.*

ther·mo·e·lec·tric·i·ty *n.* electricity generated by heat —**ther·mo·e·lec·tric, ther·mo·e·lec·tri·cal** *adj.* —**ther·mo·e·lec·tri·cal·ly** *adv.*

ther·mo·gram *n.* the record made by a thermograph

ther·mo·graph *n.* a device for recording temperature as it is registered

ther·mog·ra·phy *n.* a process for producing raised letters on paper, such as business cards or stationery; the process of recording temperature variations with a thermograph —**ther·mo·graph·ic** *adj.* —**ther·mo·graph·i·cal·ly** *adv.*

ther·mom·e·ter *n.* a device for measuring temperature —**ther·mo·met·ric, ther·mo·met·ri·cal** *adj.* —**ther·mo·met·ri·cal·ly** *adv.*

ther·mo·nu·cle·ar *adj.* pertaining to the fusion of atomic particles at high temperatures

ther·mo·plas·tic *adj.* becoming soft when heated —*n.* a thermoplastic resin —**ther·mo·plas·tic·i·ty** *n.*

ther·mo·stat *n.* a device used to maintain a desired temperature range —**ther·mo·stat·ic** *adj.* —**ther·mo·stat·i·cal·ly** *adv.*

ther·mo·trop·ic *adj.* tending to grow or move toward a heat source, as of certain plants —**ther·mot·ro·pism** *n.*

the·sau·rus *n.* a collection of words with their synonyms; a collection of words or concepts relating to a specific subject

the·sis *n., pl.* **the·ses** a proposition advanced and defended by argumentation; an unproved premise; a formal treatise on a specific subject

thes·pi·an *adj.* relating to drama — *n.* an actor or actress

they *pron.* persons or things previously mentioned; people in general: *you know what they say*

thi·am·in, thi·am·ine *n.* vitamin B_1

thick *adj.* relatively large in depth or extent; being of a specified dimension; having constituent elements closely packed: *a field thick with flowers*; viscous: *a thick sauce*; dense: *a thick fog*; very noticeable: *a thick accent* —*n.* the most dense or intense part: *the thick of battle* —*adv.* —**thick·ish** *adj.* —**thick·ly** *adv.* —**thick·ness** *n.*

thick·en *vt., vi.* to make or become thick or thicker —**thick·en·ing** *n.*

thick·et *n.* a dense growth, as of underbrush

thick·-head·ed *adj.* slow to learn or react; dumb —**thick·-head·ed·ness** *n.*

thick·set *adj.* short and stocky; closely planted

thick·-skinned *adj.* slow to anger; indifferent to insults

thief *n.* one who takes something belonging to another without permission

thieve *vt.* to steal —*vi.* to be a thief

thiev·er·y *n.* the act of stealing

—**thiev´ish** *adj.* —**thiev´ish·ly** — *adv.* —**thiev´ish·ness** *n.*

thigh *n.* the part of the leg between the hip and the knee

thin *adj.* of little depth or width; lean and slender; lacking density: *a thin sauce* —*vt.*, *vi.* to make or become thin or thinner —*adv.* —**thin´ly** *adv.*

thing *n.* that which exists as a separate entity; a matter or circumstance: *things have changed*; an act or event: *the right thing to do*; an idea or notion: *don't put things in her head*; an unexplainable or mysterious quality or attraction: *he has a thing for tall women*

think *vt.* to conceive mentally; to determine by reasoning; to believe to be true; to remember or recall; to intend —*vi.* to engage in rational thought; to weigh in the mind; to have a particular opinion, feeling, etc.; to recall —**think better of** to reconsider —**think little of** consider to be inconsequential — **think the world of** to venerate or admire —**think´er** *n.*

think´a·ble *adj.* possible; worth considering —**think´a·bly** *adv.*

think´ing *adj.* intellectually active — *n.* a result of thought; one's opinion or bias

think tank *n.* a group, as of scientists, business executives, etc., organized for the study of a particular problem

thin´-skinned´ *adj.* easily offended

third *adj.*, *adv.* next in order after the second; being one of three equal parts —*n.*

third´-rate´ *adj.* of poor quality

third world an underdeveloped nation

thirst *n.* a need for water; any craving, as *a thirst for alcohol* or *a thirst for glory* —*vi.* to have a desire or craving

thirst´y *adj.* lacking moisture; parched; eagerly desirous —**thirst´i·ly** *adv.* —**thirst´i·ness** *n.*

this *adj.* that near or present, understood, or just mentioned — *pron.* a person or thing near or present, etc. —*adv.*

this´tle *n.* a prickly plant —**this´tly** *adj.*

thong *n.* a narrow strip, as for fastening; a lash of a whip; a type of sandal; a type of beach wear

tho·rac´ic *adj.* relating to the thorax

tho´rax *n.* the part of the body between the neck and the abdomen, enclosed by the ribs; the middle segment of an insect

thorn *n.* a sharp outgrowth from a plant; a source of discomfort or annoyance

thorn´y *adj.* full of thorns; difficult or perplexing, as a problem — **thorn´i·ly** *adv.* —**thorn´i·ness** *n.*

thor´ough *adj.* attentive to details; complete or exhaustive, as *a thorough search* —**thor´ough·ly** *adv.* —**thor´ough·ness** *n.*

thor´ough·bred *adj.* bred from pure stock; possessing excellence —*n.* a horse bred for racing

thor´ough·fare (*US*) *n.* a main road

thor´ough·go·ing *adj.* characterized by thoroughness

though *conj.* notwithstanding; even if; and yet —*adv.*

thought *n.* the process or product of thinking; the concepts identified with a particular time, place, discipline, etc.: *modern political thought*; consideration or attention; preoccupation

thought´ful *adj.* contemplative or reflective; attentive or considerate; preoccupied —**thought´ful·ly** *adv.* —**thought´ful·ness** *n.*

thought´less *adj.* marked by a lack of care or regard; inconsiderate; flighty —**thought´less·ly** *adv.* — **thought´less·ness** *n.*

thrall *n.* a person or idea in bondage

—**thrall´dom** n.

thrash vt. to thresh, as grain; to beat, as with a flail; to defeat utterly —vi. to move about with violent motions —**thrash´er** n.

thread n. a slender cord or line; a filament; something that runs through —vt., vi.

thread´bare adj. worn; commonplace —**thread´bare·ness** n.

threat n. a declaration of intent to inflict harm; a danger

threat´en vt., vi. to utter threats; to be or appear to be menacing — **threat´en·er** n. —**threat´en·ing·ly** adv.

thresh vt. to beat so as to separate grain from the husks —vi. to thrash about —**thresh´er** n.

thresh·old n. a doorsill; an entering point or beginning

thrift n. care in the management of one's resources —**thrift´less** adj. —**thrift´less·ly** adv. —**thrift´less·ness** n.

thrift´y adj. practicing good management; prosperous —**thrift´i·ly** adv. —**thrift´i·ness** n.

thrift´shop a shop that deals in used articles

thrill vi., vt. to feel or cause to feel excitement —n. a feeling of excitement —**thrill´ing·ly** adv.

thrill´er n. an exciting book, play, movie, etc.

thrive vi. to be succesful; to prosper; to flourish —**thriv´er** n. —**thriv´ing·ly** adv.

throat n. the front part of the neck; the passage extending from the back of the mouth; any narrow passage

throat´y adj. guttural or husky, as of a voice —**throat´i·ly** adv. — **throat´i·ness** n.

throb vi. to pulsate rhythmically; to show emotion by trembling —n. a pulsation —**throb´bing·ly** adv.

throe n. a violent pain, as in death

or childbirth

throm·bo´sis n. the formation of a blood clot, as in the heart or an artery —**throm·bot´ic** adj.

throm´bus n. a clot formed in the heart or an artery

throne n. the authority of a ruler; a chair symbolizing authority

throng n. a closely crowded group of people —vi., vt. to gather or crowd together in large numbers

throt´tle n. a valve controlled the flow of fuel to an engine —vt. to choke or strangle; to silence or suppress; to change speed by means of a throttle —**throt´tler** n.

through prep. from end to end, side to side, etc.; permeating; by way of —adv.

through·out´ adv. in every part — prep. all through

throw vt. to propel or hurl; to place carelessly; to direct or project —vi. to cast or fling something —n. an act of casting or flinging; the distance flung; a scarf or other light covering

thrust vt. to push or shove with force; to pierce —vi. to make a sudden push; to force oneself through —n. a sudden forceful push; a vigorous attack; a force that drives or propels; a salient force: *the thrust of his remarks* — **thrust´er** n.

thud n. a dull, heavy sound; a blow or fall —vi.

thug n. a hoodlum or ruffian; formerly, a professional assassin in India —**thug´ger·y** n. —**thug´gish** adj.

thumb n. the short, thick digit of the human hand or a similar part of some animals

thumb index a series of indentations along the edge of a book to indicate its sections

thumb´screw n. a screw that can be turned with the fingers; an instrument of torture

thumb´tack *n.* a broad–headed tack

thump *n.* a blow made with a blunt object; the sound of such a blow — *vt., vi.* to beat or strike —**thump´er** *n.*

thun´der *n.* the sound that accompanies lightning; any similar noise —*vi., vt.* to make a noise reminiscent of thunder —**thun´der·er** *n.*

thun´der·bolt *n.* a lightning flash accompanied by thunder; a forceful person

thun´der·clap *n.* the sharp sound of thunder

thun´der·cloud *n.* a large, dark cloud

thun´der·ous *adj.* of a loud sound — **thun´der·ous·ly** *adv.*

thun´der·show·er *n.* rain accompanied by thunder and lightning

thun´der·storm *n.* a heavy blowing rain accompanied by thunder

thun´der·strick·en,   thun´der· struck *adj.* astonished, amazed

thwack *vt.* to strike heavily with something flat —*n.*

thwart *vt.* to frustrate or foil by some means, as of a plan or scheme; to extend across —*n.* a seat or brace extending across a small boat or canoe —*adj.* extending or passing across —**thwart´er** *n.*

thyme *n.* a small plant of the mint family; the leaves of the plant, used for seasoning —**thy´mic, thym´y** *adj.*

thy´mus *n.* a ductless glandlike structure at the base of the neck

thy´roid *n.* cartilage of the larynx which form the Adam's apple; a large, ductless gland located near the larynx —*adj.*

ti·ar´a *n.* a jeweled head ornament or crown

tib´ia *n.* the larger of two leg bones extending below the knee; the shinbone —**tib´i·al** *adj.*

tic *n.* an habitual involuntary

muscular spasm

tick´et *n.* a printed paper showing entitlement, as to transportation, entrance to a show, etc.; a tag or label; a list of candidates on a ballot; a court summons, as for a traffic violation —*vt.* to attach a label to; to furnish with a ticket

tick´le *vt.* to cause to laugh, especially by touching; to amuse or entertain —*vi.* to have or cause a tingling sensation —*n.*

tick´ler *n.* one who tickles; a book, file, etc. that serves as a reminder of things to be done at a certain time in the future

tick´lish *adj.* responsive to tickling; easily offended; requiring tact or delicate handling —**tick´lish·ly** *adv.* —**tick´lish·ness** *n.*

tid´al *adj.* pertaining to or influenced by the tide; dependent on the tide

tidal wave a great incoming rise of water; a surge, as of public opinion

tid´bit *n.* a delicacy

tide *n.* the periodic rise and fall of the ocean corresponding to the phases of the moon

tide´land *n.* land periodically covered by a rising tide

tide´wa·ter *n.* water near the coast that is affected by the movements of the tide

ti´dings *n.* news

ti´dy *adj.* neat and orderly —*vt., vi.* to put in order —**ti´di·ly** *adv.* —**ti´di·ness** *n.*

tie *vt.* to draw together or fasten with a cord, rope, etc.; to make a knot; to fasten or join; to equal another in score or achievement — *vi.* to make a connection; to make the same score —*n.* a fastener; any bond or connection; (*US*) a timber that supports railroad tracks

tie´-in *n.* something that connects or associates —*adj.*

tier *n.* one of a series arranged one

above another, such as rows of seats in a sports arena

tiff *n.* a spat; a small argument —*vi.* to take part in a spat

ti´ger *n.* a large striped carnivorous feline; a fiercely determined or energetic person —**ti´ger·ish** *adj.*

ti´ger-eye *n.* a yellow and brown semiprecious stone

tight *adj.* firmly fixed or secure; fully stretched; difficult or demanding: *a tight schedule, a tight spot*; closely fitted; scarce; stingy; intoxicated —*adv.* securely —**tight´ly** *adv.* —**tight´ness** *n.*

tight´en *vt., vi.* to make or become tight or tighter —**tight´en·er** *n.*

tight´-fist´ed *adj.* stingy —**tight´-fist´ed·ness** *n.*

tight´-lipped *adj.* uncommunicative; secretive

tights *n.* a close-fitting garment, worn by dancers, gymnasts, etc.

tight´wad *n.* a miser

til´de *n.* a diacritical mark (~) used in Spanish and Portuguese to indicate a change in the pronunciation of certain letters

tile *n.* a thin piece used as an ornament and for covering roofs, floors, walls, etc. —*vt.* to cover with tiles —**til´er** *n.* —**til´ing** *n.*

till *vt., vi.* to work soil for the cultivation of crops —*n.* a money drawer; available cash

till´age *n.* the cultivation of land —**till´a·ble** *adj.*

tilt *vi., vt.* to incline or cause to incline at an angle

tim´bal *n.* a kettledrum

tim´bale *n.* a custard containing cheese, fish, vegetables, etc. and baked in a pastry mold

tim´ber *n.* (*Brit.*) wood dressed for use in construction; standing trees

tim´ber·land *n.* land covered with trees

tim´ber·line *n.* the imaginary line beyond which trees do not grow,

as on a mountainside or the northern and southern tips of the planet

tim´bre *n.* the distinctive quality of a sound

time *n.* the concept of continuous existence: the past, present, and future; a distinct moment or period; a period considered as having distinct quality: *times are hard, have a good time*; a system for measuring duration; musical tempo —*adj.* relating to time; payable at a future date; designed to be active at a specified time —*vt.* to record the speed or duration of; to mark the rhythm of

time´-hon´ored *adj.* accepted as customary or traditional

time´less *adj.* eternal; not limited to a specific time —**time´less·ly** *adv.* —**time´less·ness** *n.*

time´ly *adj.* occurring at the proper or a convenient time —**time´li·ness** *n.*

time´ous *adj.* timely —**time´ous·ly** *adv.*

time´-shar·ing *n.* access to a large central computer by many users; the use of vacation property by several owners in turn based on an arranged schedule —**time´-share** *vt. vi.*

time´ta·ble *n.* a schedule showing the arrival and departure time of busses, trains, etc.; a plan for the completion of the parts of a project

time´worn *adj.* made ineffective by time or overuse, as a motto or maxim

tim´id *adj.* fearful; lacking self-confidence —**ti·mid´i·ty, tim´id·ness** *n.* —**tim´id·ly** *adv.*

tim´ing *n.* the art of regulating occurance to insure maximum effect

tim´o·rous *adj.* fearul; anxious —**tim´o·rous·ly** *adv.* —**tim´o·rous·ness** *n.*

tim´o·thy *n.* a perennial grass grown

mainly for cattle feed

tim´pa·ni *n.* kettledrums —**tim´pa· nist** *n.*

tin *n.* a metallic element used in making alloys

tinc´ture *n.* a medicinal solution; a coloring substance; a slight trace

tin´der *n.* any dry substance that ignites easily —**tin´der·y** *adj.*

tin´der·box *n.* a container of material for starting a fire; highly flammable material; an extremely excitable person

tine *n.* a prong, as on a fork

tinge *n.* a faint trace, as of color — *vt.* to tint or color lightly

tin´gle *vi., vt.* to experience or cause to experience a prickly, stinging sensation —*n.* a stinging sensation —**tin´gler** *n.* —**tin´gly** *adv.*

tin´kle *vi., vt.* to produce or cause to produce light metallic sounds, as of a bell —**tin´kly** *adj.*

tin·ni´tus *n.* a ringing or buzzing sound in the ears

tin´ny *adj.* made of or containing tin; flimsy; of a flat sound —**tin´ ni·ly** *adv.* —**tin´ni·ness** *n.*

tin´sel *n.* thin glittering bits used for ornamentation; something that is showy, but of little value —*adj.* decorated with tinsel; gaudy or showy —*vt.* to decorate with tinsel —**tin´sel·ly** *adv.* —**tin´sel·ry** *n.*

tin´smith *n.* one who works with tin or tin plate

tint *n.* a pale color; a shading or gradation of color —*vt.* to apply color —**tint´er** *n.*

tin·tin·nab·u·la´tion *n.* the ringing of bells —**tin·tin·nab´u·lar, tin· tin·nab´u·lous** *adj.*

ti´ny *adj.* very small —**ti´ni·ness** *n.*

tip *n.* a light tap; a gift of money for service; a helpful hint; confidential information; an extremity; a piece made to cap an extremity —*vt.* to cause to lean; to overturn; to strike lightly; to adorn the tip of

—*vi.* to become tilted; to overturn

tip´off *n.* a warning

tip´ple *vt., vi.* to drink frequently and habitually

tip´sy *adj.* unsteady; intoxicated — **tip´si·ly** *adv.* —**tip´si·ness** *n.*

ti·rade´ *n.* a prolonged denunciation

tire *vt.* to reduce the strength of, as by exertion; to make weary or impatient —*vi.* to become weary; to lose patience —*n.* (US) a flexible covering for a wheel

tired *adj.* weary; fatigued —**tired´ ness** *n.*

tire´less *adj.* not easily fatigued; energetic —**tire´less·ly** *adv.* — **tire´less·ness** *n.*

tire´some *adj.* tedious or boring; mundane —**tire´some·ly** *adv.* — **tire´some·ness** *n.*

tis´sue *n.* an aggregate of organic cells and associated matter having a particular function; a light fabric, as gauze; tissue paper; a light disposable sheet of paper used as a wipe

tissue culture tissue kept alive and growing in a culture medium

tissue paper thin paper for wrapping or protecting

ti´tan *n.* a giant

tithe *n.* one tenth; a tax or contribution for the support of the clergy and the church; any tax or levy — *vt.* to give or pay a tithe —**tith´a· ble** *adj.* —**tith´er** *n.*

tit´il·late *vt.* to cause a tickling sensation; to stimulate or excite, often erotically —**tit´il·lat·er** *n.* — **tit´il·lat·ing·ly** *adv.* —**tit·il·la´tion** *n.* —**tit´il·la·tive** *adj.*

ti´tle *n.* a descriptive name; the name of a book, song, etc.; a designation, as of rank, profession, etc.; the legal right to property — *vt.* to give a name or designation; to entitle to

ti´tled *adj.* having a title, especially one denoting nobility

tit´ter n. a suppressed laugh —vi. — **tit´ter·er** n. —**tit´ter·ing·ly** adv.

tit´tle n. the tiniest amount

tit´u·lar adj. existing in name or title only —**tit´u·lar·ly** adv.

tiz´zy n. a bewildered state of mind

toad n. a jumping amphibian resembling the frog; a loathsome person

toad´y adj. an obsequious flatterer; one who acts without scruples in order to gain favor —vt., vi. to flatter or serve without question — **toad´y·ism** n.

toast vt., vi. to make or become warm or browned; to drink to the health of another —n. a tribute of words followed by a drink; one who is well-known and greatly admired: *the toast of the town*

toast´mas·ter n. one who presides at a public banquet, calling the toasts, announcing speakers, etc.

toast´y adj. comfortably warm

to·bog´gan n. a long sledlike vehicle without runners for traveling over snow or ice —vi. to ride on a toboggan —**to·bog´gan·er, to·bog´gan·ist** n.

tod´dle vi. to walk unsteadily —n. a shaky walk —**tod´dler** n.

tod´dy n. whiskey, rum, or other spirits mixed with hot water, spices, and sugar

to-do´ n. a fuss

toe n. a digit of the foot; the forward part of the foot; part of a covering for the foot

to´fu n. a cheese–like food made from soybeans

to´ga n. a loose flowing robe — **to´gaed** adj.

to·geth´er adv. in the company of others; collectively, as one unit: spent more money that all the others together —**to·geth´er·ness** n.

tog´ger·y n. clothing

toil n. strenuous labor —vi. to work hard —vt. to accomplish with great effort —**toil´er** n.

toi´let n. a bathroom fixture for disposing of body waste; the process of grooming —adj. used in grooming, as *toilet articles*

toi´let·ry n. something such as soap, cologne, etc. used in personal grooming

toil´some adj. involving hard work; difficult —**toil´some·ly** adv. —**toil´some·ness** n.

to´ken n. tangible evidence, as of affection, authority, etc.; a metal piece issued in place of currency —adj. nominal or minimal; partial

to´ken·ism n. an attempt to meet an obligation or condition with a symbolic gesture

tol´er·a·ble adj. endurable; barely satisfactory —**tol´er·a·bil´ity, tol´er·a·ble·ness** n. —**tol´er·a·bly** adv.

tol´er·ance n. freedom from prejudice; the ability to bear hardship; an allowance for variation; resistance to the effects of a substance

tol´er·ant adj. long–suffering; indulgent —**tol´er·ant·ly** adv.

tol´er·ate vt. to allow or concede; to bear —**tol·er·a´tion** n. —**tol´er·a·tive** adj. —**tol´er·a·tor** n.

toll n. a tax or charge, as for passage; a charge for a special service; the sound of a bell rung slowly and regularly —vi., vt. to take or exact a charge; to sound or cause to sound, as a bell

tomb n. a burial place —vt. to entomb or bury

tom´boy n. a very active young girl —**tom´boy·ish** adj. —**tom´boy·ish·ly** adv. —**tom´boy·ish·ness** n.

tomb´stone n. a stone that marks a place of burial

tome n. a large heavy book

tom·fool´er·y adj. nonsensical behavior; foolishness

to·mor´row n. the next day after today —adv.

ton n. a measure of weight, such as:

—short ton 2000 pounds **—long ton** 2240 pounds **—metric ton** 1000 kilograms

to´nal *adj.* pertaining to tone or tonality —**to´nal·ly** *adv.*

to·nal´i·ty *n.* a system or scheme of tones as in music or visual art

tone *n.* a musical sound or its quality; a characteristic tendency or quality: mode of one's writing or speech; style or elegance; the effect of light and color —*vt.* to impart a desired tone, as of sound or color —**tone down** to quiet or soften

tone´less *adj.* lifeless or flat —**tone´less·ly** *adv.* —**tone´less·ness** *n.*

tongue *n.* a muscular organ attached to the floor of the mouth; a manner of speaking; a language or dialect; something resembling a tongue —**tongue twister** a phrase difficult to repeat quickly

tongue´-in-cheek *adj.* said jokingly

tongue´-lashing *n.* a scolding

tongue´-tied *adj.* speechless

ton´ic *n.* something that promotes health or well-being; quinine water —*adj.* pertaining to tone; tending to stimulate or refresh

ton´nage *n.* weight expressed in tons; capacity

ton´sil *n.* either of two lymphoid masses located in the opening between the mouth and larynx

ton·sil·lec´to·my *n.* surgical removal of the tonsils

ton·sil·li´tis *n.* inflammation of the tonsils

ton·so´ri·al *adj.* of a barber or barbering

ton´sure *n.* shaving of the head, like that of a monk —*vt.* to shave part or all of the hair on the head

ton´tine *n.* an agreement by which an investment held in trust reverts to the survivor or survivors

too *adv.* also; excessive; extremely

tool *n.* any implement used in work or the performance of a task:

books are the tools of learning; a person used to carry out the designs of another —*vt.* to form or shape with a tool; to scribe a motif or design on leather

tool´ing *n.* ornamental work, especially on leather

tool´mak·er *n.* a machinist who makes or repairs tools

tooth *n.* a hard structure in the mouth used for seizing and chewing food; a small projection, as on a saw or gear; a rough surface, as of paper; an appetite or taste for something

tooth´ache *n.* pain in or near a tooth

tooth´less *adj.* lacking teeth; lacking effectiveness —**tooth´less·ly** *adv.* —**tooth´less·ness** *n.*

tooth´some *adj.* pleasant tasting — **tooth´some·ly** *adv.* —**tooth´some·ness** *n.*

tooth´y *adj.* showing the teeth; having prominent or projecting teeth —**tooth´i·ly** *adv.* —**tooth´i·ness** *n.*

top *n.* the uppermost or highest part; an upper surface; a lid; the highest degree; the best —*adj.* relating to the top; most important or best —*vt.* to remove the uppermost part; to form or provide a top; to surmount or surpass

top´coat *n.* a light overcoat

top´-heavy *adj.* unstable due to excessive weight at the top; of an organization with an overly large executive staff —**top´-heav·i·ly** *adv.* —**top´-heav·iness** *n.*

to´pi·ar·y *n.* live bushes or trees trimmed or formed in decorative shapes —*adj.* pertaining to the art of topiary

top´ic *n.* the subject matter or substance, as for a speech, discussion, etc.

top´i·cal *adj.* relating to matters of local or current interest; pertaining to a topic **—top·i·cal´i·ty** *n*. **—top´i·cal·ly** *adv*.

top´knot *n*. a tuft or knot of hair or feathers at the top of the head; an ornament worn as a headdress

top´less *adj*. lacking a top; nude above the waist **—top´less·ness** *n*.

top´-lev´el *adj*. of the highest rank or importance

to·pog´ra·phy *n*. the physical features of a region or a representation of them; topographic surveying **—to·pog´ra·pher** *n*. **—top·o·graph´ic, top·o·graph´i·cal** *adj*. **—top·o·graph´i·cal·ly** *adv*.

top·o´nym *n*. a place name **—top·o·nym´ic, top·o·nym´i·cal** *adj*.

to·pon´y·my *n*. the study of the place names of a region or of a language

top´ple *vi*. to fall, as by its own weight **—***vt*. to cause to fall; to overthrow

top´soil *n*. the surface soil of land

top´sy-tur´vy *adj*., *adv*. upside down; in utter disarray **—***n*. a state of disorder **—top´sy-tur´vi·ly** *adv*. **—top´sy-tur´vi·ness** *n*.

tor *n*. a rocky peak

torch *n*. a flame at the end of a stick or rod; anything that brightens; a device producing an intense flame as for welding, removing paint, etc.

torch´bear·er *n*. one who carries a torch; one who conveys truth or knowledge, etc.; leader of a cause

to·re·a·dor *n*. a bullfighter

tor´ment *n*. intense pain or anguish; a source of pain or anguish **—tor·ment´** *vt*. to subject to torture; to harass **—tor·men´ter, tor·men´tor** *n*. **—tor·ment´ing·ly** *adv*.

tor·na´do *n*. a whirling wind of exceptional force

tor·pe´do *n*. a self-propelled underwater missile **—***vt*. to damage or sink with a torpedo; to sabotage or destroy utterly

tor´pid *adj*. dormant; sluggish; apathetic **—tor·pid´i·ty, tor´pid·ness** *n*. **—tor´pid·ly** *adv*.

tor´por *n*. loss of sensibility or power of motion; apathy, listlessness **—tor´por·if´ic** *adj*.

torque *n*. a turning or twisting force; a measure of the tendency to cause rotation

tor´rent *n*. a rapid, turbulent stream of liquid; any violent flow: *a torrent of abuse* **—tor·ren´tial** *adj*. **—tor·ren´tial·ly** *adv*.

tor´rid *adj*. intensely hot and dry; passionate **—tor´rid·ly** *adv*. **—tor´rid·ness** *n*.

tor´so *n*. the trunk of the human body

tort *n*. a civil wrong not involving breach of contract **—tor´tious** *adj*.

tor´te *n*. a rich cake

tor·tel·li´ni *n*. small ring–shaped pasta stuffed with cheese, spinach, meat, etc.

tor·ti´lla *n*. a small, flat bread made of corn meal and baked on a skillet

tor´toise *n*. a land turtle

tor´tu·ous *adj*. twisting, as a road; devious, as *tortuous logic* **—tor´tu·ous·ly** *adv*. **—tor´tu·ous·ness** *n*.

tor´ture *n*. intense physical or mental suffering; something that causes pain **—***vi*. to inflict pain upon; to cause to suffer **—tor´tur·er** *n*.

tor´tur·ous *adj*. pertaining to torture **—tor´tur·ous·ly** *adv*.

toss *vt*. to throw or cast; to pitch or fling about; to interject casually; to turn over and mix **—***vi*. to be thrown about, as by the sea; to roll about restlessly, as in sleep **—***n*. a throw; a quick movement: *a toss of the head* **—toss´er** *n*.

toss´pot *n*. a drunkard

tos·ta´da *n*. a crisp tortilla

tot *n*. a small child

to´tal *n*. the entire amount **—***adj*. complete **—***vt*. to ascertain the full amount **—to´tal·ly** *adv*.

to·tal·i·tar·i·an *adj.* of an oppressive government with absolute power — *n.* —**to·tal·i·tar·i·an·ism** *n.*

to·tal·i·ty *n.* a total amount; the state of being whole

tote *vt.* to carry —*n.* something carried —**tot´a·ble** *adj.* —**tot´er** *n.*

to´tem *n.* a natural object or representation believed to be ancestrally related and that serves as an emblem for a group, tribe, etc. — **to·tem´ic** *adj.* —**to´tem·ism** *n.*

tot´ter *vi.* to tremble or waver as if about to fall; to seem near to collapse; to walk unsteadily —*n.* an unsteady or wobbly manner of walking —**tot´ter·er** *n.* —**tot´ter·ing·ly** *adv.* —**tot´ter·y** *adj.*

tou´can *n.* a tropical bird with colorful plumage and a very large beak

touch *vt.* to perceive by feeling; to be in or come into contact with; to affect; to impress emotionally —*vi.* to come into or be in contact —*n.* a coming into contact; a sensation conveyed by contact; a distinctive manner or style: *the master's touch*; a trace or hint; the manner in which something is fingered, as piano keys —**touch on** to concern or relate to —**touch up** to add final corrections —**touch´a·ble** *adj.* —**touch´a·ble·ness** *n.*

touched *adj.* effected emotionally; mentally unbalanced; peculiar or eccentric

touch´ing *adj.* appealing to emotion —*prep.* with regard to; concerning —**touch´ing·ly** *adv.* —**touch´ing·ness** *n.*

touch´y *adj.* apt to take offense; liable to cause offense or contention —**touch·i·ly** *adv.* —**touch´i·ness** *n.*

tough *adj.* capable of bearing stress or strain; difficult to cut or chew; requiring intense effort; unyielding; severe or harsh —*n.* a rowdy

—**tough´ly** *adv.* —**tough´ness** *n.*

tough´en *vt., vi.* to make or become tough or tougher —**tough´en·er** *n.*

tough´-mind´ed *adj.* facing difficulty with strength and resolve; unsentimental —**tough´-mind´ed·ly** *adv.* —**tough´-mind´ed·ness** *n.*

tou·pee´ *n.* a small wig

tour *n.* a journey or excursion; a fixed period of service —*vt.* to make a trip; to take a show on the road —*vi.* to go on a trip

tour´ism *n.* recreational travel; the travel industry

tour´ist *n.* one who travels for pleasure —*adj.* relating to or suitable for recreational travelers — **tour·is´tic** *adj.* —**tour´ist·y** *adj.*

tour´na·ment *n.* a series of competitive events

tour´ni·quet *n.* a device to control severe external bleeding, as from a wound

tou´sle *vt.* to dishevel, as hair —*n.* mussed hair

tout *vt.* to solicit; to praise highly; to sell information about —*vi.* to solicit customers, patronage, etc.; to sell information —*n.* one who sells information —**tout´er** *n.*

tow *vt.* to pull or drag, as by rope, etc. —*n.* something being towed — **in tow** drawn or brought along: *she arrived with friends in tow* — **tow´a·ble** *adj.* —**tow´age** *n.*

to´ward *prep.* in the direction of; for the purpose of; near, approaching

tow´el *n.* cloth, paper, etc. used for wiping or polishing

tow´el·ing *n.* material used to make towels

tow´er *n.* a tall structure or part of a structure; a place of security —*vi.* to extend to a great height

tow´er·ing *adj.* very tall: *a towering figure*; very great: *a towering rage*

town (*US*) *n.* an incorporated populated area larger than a village and smaller than a city; a city; collectively, the inhabitants or government of a town —*adj.* pertaining to or characteristic of a town or its population

town house (*US*) a house, usually of more than one story, situated in a row of dwellings that share a common wall with one or more adjoining houses

tow′path *n.* a narrow road along a waterway, used by men or animals towing boats

tox·e′mi·a *n.* the presence of toxins in the blood —**tox·e′mic** *adj.*

tox′ic *adj.* poisonous; caused by poison or a toxin —**tox′i·cal·ly** *adv.* —**tox·ic′i·ty** *n.*

tox′i·cant *n.* a poison —*adj.* poisonous

tox·i·col′o·gy *n.* the study of poisons, their detection, antidotes, etc. —**tox·i·co·log′ic, tox·i·co·log′i·cal** *adj.* —**tox·i·co·log′i·cal·ly** *adv.* —**tox·i·col′o·gist** *n.*

tox′in *n.* a poisonous substance

toy *n.* something designed for or serving as a plaything; something trifling or ineffectual —*vi.* to consider without conviction: *toy with an idea*; to use someone or something for one's own amusement —*adj.* designed as a toy; resembling a toy, as of a miniature

trace *n.* a vestige or mark left by someone or something no longer present; a barely detectable quality, characteristic, etc. —*vt.* to find or find out by investigation; to copy onto an overlay —*vi.* to follow a track, course of development, etc. —**trace·a·bil′i·ty, trace′a·ble·ness** *n.* —**trace′a·ble** *adj.* —**trace′a·bly** *adv.*

trac′er·y *n.* delicate ornamentation

tra′chea *n.* the windpipe; an air passage —**tra′che·al** *adj.*

tra·che·ot′o·my, tra·che·os′to·my *n.* a surgical incision into the trachea

tra·cho′ma *n.* a contagious viral disease of the eye —**tra·chom′a·tous** *adj.*

track *n.* a mark left by the passage of anything; a path beaten down by repeated use; any path, especially one describing movement; a trail or roadway; the act of following or tracing, as *keeping track of expenses*; a continuous belt by which some vehicles are moved; metal rails that control the course of a train or trolley car —*vt.* to follow the course of; to trail; to make tracks —*vi.* to leave tracks; to be in agreement: *thinking along the same track* —**track′a·ble** *adj.* —**track′er** *n.*

track record a history of achievement

tract *n.* an extended area; a short discourse or pamphlet

trac′ta·ble *adj.* easily led; malleable —**trac·ta·bil′i·ty, trac′ta·ble·ness** *n.* —**trac′ta·bly** *adv.*

trac′tion *n.* the act of pulling; the state of being pulled or drawn; pulling power; rolling friction, as of tires on the road —**trac′tion·al, trac′tive** *adj.*

trac′tor *n.* a vehicle used to pull farm machinery; a motor vehicle used to haul trailers, etc.

trade *n.* a business or craft; the people or companies engaged in a particular business; the buying and selling, or exchange of commodities; a firm's customers; an exchange of one thing for another —*vt.* to give in exchange; to barter —*vi.* to engage in commerce —*adj.* —**trad′a·ble** *adj.* —**trad′er** *n.*

trade′mark *n.* a name, symbol, etc. used to distinguish a product from all others; any distinctive feature —*vt.* to legally protect, as a name, symbol, etc.

tra·di′tion *n.* the body of knowledge, customs, etc. transmitted down through generations —**tra·di´tion·al** *adj.* —**tra·di´tion·al·ly** *adv.*

tra·di´tion·al·ism *n.* adherence to tradition —**tra·di´tion·al·ist** *n.* — **tra·di´tion·al·is´tic** *adj.*

tra·duce´ *vt.* to willfully harm through misrepresentation; to defame or slander —**tra·duce´ment** *n.* —**tra·duc´er** *n.* —**tra·duc´ing·ly** *adv.*

traf´fic *n.* the passing of people, vehicles, messages, etc. through a limited space or between certain points; those which are moving; the business of buying and selling: *to traffic in household items*; the business of transportation —**traf´fick·er** *n.*

tra·ge´di·an *n.* an actor or writer of tragedies

trag´e·dy *n.* drama in which the protagonist comes to an unhappy end; a tragic incident

trag´ic *adj.* of the nature of a tragedy; causing or likely to cause suffering —**trag´i·cal·ly** *adv.*

trag·i·com´e·dy *n.* drama having characteristics of both comedy and tragedy; an incident of this nature —**trag·i·com´ic, trag·i·com´i·cal** *adj.* —**trag·i·com´i·cal·ly** *adv.*

trail *vt.* to draw or drag lightly over a surface; to follow the track of; to be behind; to follow behind —*vi.* to hang or extend loosely so as to drag; to grow along the ground; to be behind; to lag behind —*n.* the track or traces left by something that has passed; something that follows, as vapor from a jet plane; (*US*) a worn path, such as one through a wilderness area

trail´blaz·er *n.* one that breaks a new trail; an innovator or pioneer

trail´er (*US*) *n.* a drawn vehicle equipped as living quarters or used to haul freight

train *n.* a series of connected rail cars; anything drawn along or

following behind: *the train of a dress*; a set of connected things: *a train of thought* —*vt.* to make skillful or proficient; to teach; to point in an exact position: *train your eyes on the action* —*vi.* to undergo a course of instruction or preparation —**train·a·bil´i·ty** *adv.* —**train´a·ble** *adj.* —**train·ee´** *n.*

train´er *n.* one who trains or coaches, as an athlete or show animal; a device used to improve physical fitness or skill; (*Brit.*) a flexible sports shoe with a soft rubber sole: a sneaker

train´ing *n.* systematic instruction

traipse *vi.* to walk or wander about

trait *n.* a distinguishing quality

trai´tor *n.* one who betrays a trust; a person found guilty of treason

trai´tor·ous *adj.* constituting or resembling treason; characteristic of a traitor —**trai´tor·ous·ly** *adv.* —**trai´tor·ous·ness** *n.*

tra·jec´to·ry *n.* the path described by a body moving in space

tramp *vi., vt.* to wander; to walk heavily —*n.* one who wanders, living by odd jobs or charity; a long walk; the sound of a heavy tread —**tramp´er** *n.*

tram´ple *vi.* to tread heavily; to injure or crush, as by treading heavily on —*vt.* to tread heavily or ruthlessly on —**tram´pler** *n.*

trance *n.* a dreamlike state as induced by hypnosis or a supernatural force; profound concentration —**trance´like** *adj.*

tran´quil *adj.* calm; quiet and motionless —**tran´quil·ly** *adv.* — **tran´quil·ness** *n.*

tran´quil·ize *vt., vi.* to make or become tranquil

tran´quil·iz·er *n.* a drug that calms without impairing consciousness

tran·quil´li·ty *n.* the state of being tranquil

trans·act´ *vt.* to accomplish —*vi.* to

carry on or conduct business —
trans·ac′tion n. —**trans·ac′tion·al** adj. —**trans·ac′tor** n.

tran·scend′ vt. to go beyond the limits of: *knowledge that transcends reason*; to rise above —vi. to excel

tran·scen′dent adj. transcendental; existing apart from the material universe —**tran·scen′dence, tran·scen′den·cy** adj. —**tran·scen′dent·ly** adv.

tran·scen·den′tal adj. beyond ordinary limits; supernatural; pertaining to transcendentalism —**tran·scen·den′tal·ly** adv.

tran·scen·den′tal·ism n. the philosophy that one can attain knowledge that transcends sensory phenomena —**tran·scen·den′tal·ist** n.

tran·scribe′ vt. to copy or make a record of —**tran·scrib′er** n.

tran′script n. a copy; something recorded, as from a stenographer's notes —**tran·scrip′tion** n. —**tran·scrip′tion·al** adj.

tran·sect′ vt. to divide by cutting across —**tran·sec′tion** n.

trans·fer, trans·fer′ vt. to convey from one person or place to another —**trans′fer** n. that which is transferred, as a design; assignment of title or property —**trans·fer·a·bil′i·ty** n. —**trans·fer′a·ble** adj. —**trans·fer′al** n.

trans·fig·u·ra′tion n. a change in appearance

trans·fig′ure vt. to change the appearance of; to make splendid —**trans·fig′ure·ment** n.

trans·fix′ vt. to pierce through; to impale; to render motionless, as with amazement

trans·form′ vt. to change the form or appearance of; to change the nature or character of —vi. to be or become changed —**trans·form′a·ble** adj. —**trans·for·ma′tion** n.

trans·fuse′ vt. to cause to flow from

one person or thing to another; to pass into, permeate —**trans·fus′i·ble** adj. —**trans·fu′sion** n.

trans·gress′ vt. to overstep the bounds of, as propriety or good taste —vi. to break a law; to sin —**trans·gress′i·ble** adj. —**trans·gres′sion** n. —**trans·gres′sive** adj. —**trans·gres′sive·ly** adv. —**trans·gres′sor** n.

tran′sient adj. not permanent; transitory: *a transient thought*; residing temporarily —n. a temporary resident, as at a hotel; a visitor; a tramp —**tran′sience, tran′sien·cy** n. —**tran′sient·ly** adv.

tran′sit n. the act of passing over or through; the process of change; the act of carrying across or through; transportation; a surveying instrument

tran·si′tion n. passage from one place, condition, etc. to another —**tran·si′tion·al, tran·si′tion·a·ry** adj. —**tran·si′tion·al·ly** adv.

tran′si·to·ry adj. existing only briefly; ephemeral —**tran·si·to′ri·ly** adv. —**tran′si·to·ri·ness** n.

trans·late′ vt. to change into another language; to explain in other words —**trans·lat′a·ble** adj. —**trans·lat′a·ble·ness** n. —**trans·la′tion** n. —**trans·la′tor** n.

trans·lu′cent adj. allowing the passage of light, but not transparent —**trans·lu′cence, trans·lu′cen·cy** n. —**trans·lu′cent·ly** adv.

trans·mi′grate vi. to move, as from one country to another; to pass into another body, as of the soul at death —**trans·mi·gra′tion** n. —**trans·mi′gra·tor** n. —**trans·mi′gra·to·ry** adj.

trans·mis′si·ble adj. capable of being transmitted —**trans·mis′si·bil′i·ty** n.

trans·mit′ vt. to send or pass on from one place, person, etc. to another; to serve as a medium of

passage —**trans·mis´sion** n. —
trans·mit´ta·ble adj. —**trans·mit´-
tal, trans·mit´tance** n. —**trans·
mit´ter** n.

trans·mog´ri·fy vt. to transform
radically; to make into something
completely different —**trans·mog·
ri·fi·ca´tion** n.

tran´som n. a horizontal piece over
an opening: a lintel; a small window over a door

trans·par´en·cy n. the quality of
being transparent; a section of
photographic film

trans·par´ent adj. that can be seen
through; easy to understand; obvious —**trans·par´ent·ly** adv. —
trans·par´ent·ness n.

trans·plant´ vt. to uproot a plant in
order to replant it in another
place; to move people or animals
from one place to be resettled in
another; to implant living tissue
from one person or part of the
body to another —n. that which is
relocated —**trans·plant´a·ble** adj.
—**trans·plant·ta´tion** n. —**trans·
plant´er** n.

trans·port´ vt. to carry or convey; to
carry away with emotion —**trans´
port** n. a means or system of conveyance; a state of emotional bliss
—**trans·port·a·bil´i·ty** n. —**trans·
port´a·ble** adj.

trans·por·ta´tion n. a means of
transporting or traveling; the conveyance of passengers or freight

trans·pose´ vt. to reverse in order —
trans·pos´a·ble adj. —**trans·pos´
er** n. —**trans·po·si´tion** n. —
trans·po·si´tion·al adj.

trans·sex´u·al n. a person psycho-
logically disposed to identify with
the opposite sex —**trans·sex´u·al·
ism** n. —**trans·sex·u·al´i·ty** n.

tran·sub·stan´ti·ate vt. to transform
from one substance into another
—**tran·sub·stan·ti·a´tion** n.

trans·verse´ adj. lying across —n.

something that lies across, from
side to side, as a beam —**trans·
ver´sal** adj. —**trans·verse´ly** adv.

trans·ves´tite n. one who wears the
clothes of the opposite sex

trap n. a device for catching animals;
a devious plan by which a person
may be caught unawares; a device
that collects residue or prevents a
return flow —vt. to catch —vi. to
set traps for game —**trap´per** n.

tra·peze´ n. a suspended bar for
exercise or acrobatics

trap´e·zoid n. a four-sided plane
figure with two parallel sides —
trap·e·zoi´dal adj.

trap´pings n. adornment or ornamentation; goods or privileges associated with something: the trappings of wealth

trash n. (US) waste material; foolish
talk; anything worthless —
trash´i·ness n. —**trash´y** adj.

trat·to·ri´a n. an informal Italian
restaurant

trau´ma n. physical injury or emotional shock —**trau·mat´ic** adj. —
trau·mat´i·cal·ly adv. —**trau´ma·
tize** vt.

tra·vail´ n. pain or anguish encoun-
tered in the course of effort; labor
in childbirth —vi. to suffer the
pangs of childbirth; to toil

trav´el vi. to make a journey; to
proceed; to go from place to place
—vt. to move or journey across or
through —n. passage to or over a
certain place; distance moved, as
by a machine part —**trav´el·er** n.

trav´eled adj. having made many
journeys; frequented by travelers:
a well-traveled path

trav´el·og, trav´el·ogue n. a film
documenting a traveled place; an
illustrated lecture on travel

tra·verse´ vt. to pass over, across, or
through —vi. to move across; to
move back and forth —**trav´erse**
n. a crosspiece; a screen or barrier

—*adj.* lying across —**tra·vers'a·ble** *adj.* —**tra·vers'al** *n.*

trav'es·ty *n.* an absurd rendering, as if in mockery: *the judge's decision was a travesty of justice* —*vt.* to parody

trawl *n.* a large fishing net; an anchored line from which many lines are strung —*vi.* to fish with a trawl —*vt.* to drag, as a net or line, to catch fish —**trawl'er** *n.*

treach'er·ous *adj.* likely to betray; potentially dangerous or unreliable, as *treacherous footing* — **treach'er·ous·ly** *adv.* —**treach'er· ous·ness** *n.*

treach'er·y *n.* violation of confidence; treason

trea'cle *n.* molasses; overly sentimental speech —**trea'cly** *adj.*

tread *vt.* to step or walk; to trample; to oppress harshly —*vi.* to walk; to press beneath the feet —*n.* the act or sound of treading or trampling; the part of a wheel that comes in contact with the surface; the impression made by a tire, foot, etc.; the length of a step

trea'dle *n.* a foot-operated lever —*vi.*

tread'mill *n.* a mechanism rotated by a walking animal; a monotonous routine

trea'son *n.* betrayal; a breech of faith —**trea'son·ous** *adj.* —**trea' son·ous·ly** *adv.*

trea'son·a·ble *adj.* involving or characteristic of treason —**trea' son·a·bly** *adv.*

trea'sure *n.* accumulated riches; something very precious —*vt.* to set a high value on

trea'sur·er *n.* one responsible for the receipt, care, and disbursement of revenues

trea'sure–trove *n.* hidden treasure; a rich or rewarding discovery

trea'sur·y *n.* a government department concerned with finances; a place where funds are received and disbursed —**Treasury** a government department in charge of collecting and managing revenues of the state; a security issued by the US Treasury

treat *vt.* to look upon or regard in a particular manner; to provide medical attention; to deal with in writing or speaking; to buy for another —*vi.* to deal with in writing or speaking; to pay for another, as the cost of dinner —**treat'er** *n.*

treat'a·ble *adj.* responsive to treatment

trea'tise *n.* a formal critique of a serious subject

treat'ment *n.* the act, manner, or process of dealing with something; a measure or measures designed to heal or alleviate

trea'ty *n.* a formal agreement between nations

treb'u·chet *n.* a medieval catapult

tree *n.* a woody perennial having a distinct trunk with branches and foliage well above the ground; something resembling a tree as a diagram, certain shrubs, etc. —*vt.* to force to take refuge in a tree

trek *vi.* to move along slowly or with effort; to journey —*n.* a journey — **trek'ker** *n.*

trel'lis *n.* a lattice used to support plants, etc.

trem'ble *vi.* to shake involuntarily; to vibrate —*n.* a perceptible shaking of a part of the body — **trem'bler** *n.* —**trem'bling·ly** *adv.* —**trem'bly** *adj.*

tre·men'dous *adj.* extraordinarily large; awe-inspiring; marvelous — **tre·men'dous·ly** *adv.* —**tre·men' dous·ness** *n.*

trem'or *n.* a sudden shaking or vibration; a state of agitation or excitement

trem'u·lant *adj.* tremulous; trembling

trem'u·lous *adj.* characterized by

trembling; showing timidity — **trem´u·lous·ly** *adv.* —**trem´u·lous·ness** *n.*

trench *n.* a long, narrow ditch; a long, narrow area much deeper than that which surrounds it, as on the ocean floor —*vt., vi.* to dig a ditch

tren´chant *adj.* clear and effective; cutting or caustic —**tren´chan·cy** *n.* —**trench´ant·ly** *adv.*

trench´er *n.* a wooden board for cutting or serving food

trench´er·man *n.* a hearty eater

trend *n.* a prevailing tendency; a probable course; a popular preference —*vi.* to follow a general course; to exhibit a tendency

trend´y *adj.* of the latest styles; fashionable; inclined to adopt the current fashion —**trend´i·ly** *adv.* —**trend´i·ness** *n.*

trep´id *adj.* timid; timorous; trembling —**trep´id·ly** *adv.*

trep·i·da´tion *n.* agitation caused by fear or apprehension

tres´pass *vt.* to violate the rights of another; to go beyond the bounds of what is right or proper —*n.* a transgression of law or moral duty; an intrusion —**tres´pass·er** *n.*

tress *n.* a lock of hair —**tressed** *adj.*

tres´tle *n.* a framework used to support a table, platform, etc.; a framework bridge supporting a road or railway

tri´ad *n.* a group of three —**tri·ad´ic** *adj.*

tri·age´ *n.* a system used to allocate a scarce commodity; the selection of persons for medical treatment based on immediate need

tri´al *n.* examination in a court of law; the process of testing; hardship —*adj.*

tri·an´gle *n.* a three-sided figure; something involving three persons —**tri·an´gu·lar** *adj.* —**tri·an·gu·lar´i·ty** *n.* —**tri·an´gu·lar·ly** *adv.*

tri·an·gu·la´tion *n.* a technique for surveying an area by dividing it into triangles and, working from a known baseline, determining its dimensions using trigonometry — **tri·an´gu·late** *vt.*

tri·ath´lon *n.* an ahtletic contest comprising three events

tribe *n.* a group of people united by ancestry, language, or culture — **trib´al** *adj.* —**trib´al·ism** *n.* —**trib´al·ly** *adv.*

trib·u·la´tion *n.* distress or suffering; a cause for distress

tri·bu´nal *n.* a court of justice or other judicial body; the seat set apart for judges, magistrates, etc.

trib´u·tar·y *adj.* flowing into or feeding a larger body; owing tribute —*n.*

trib´ute *n.* that paid to another for peace or protection; any obligatory payment

tri·chi´na *n.* a roundworm whose larvae cause trichinosis

trich·i·no´sis *n.* an affliction caused by eating undercooked meat — **trich´i·nous** *adj.*

trick *n.* a deception or practical joke; a malicious act; a peculiar trait or skill —*vt., vi.* to deceive or practice deceit —**trick´er, trick´ster** *n.* — **trick´er·y** *n.*

trick´le *vi.* to flow or move in a thin stream —*vt.* to cause to trickle —*n.* a thin stream

trick´y *adj.* deceitful; requiring adroitness or skill —**trick´i·ly** *adv.* —**trick´i·ness** *n.*

tri·cus´pid, tri·cus´pi·dal *adj.* having three points, as a molar; having three segments, as a heart valve

tri´dent *n.* a three-pronged spear used as a weapon or for fishing — *adj.* three-pronged —**tri·den´tate** *adj.*

tried *adj.* tested; freed of impurities

tri·en´nial *adj.* taking place every

tri·en´ni·al·ly *adv.*

third year; lasting three years — **tri·en´ni·al·ly** *adv.*

tri´fle *vi.* to treat as of no value or importance; to toy with —*vt.* to spend idly and purposelessly —*n.* a thing of little value or importance; a small amount —**tri´fler** *n.*

tri´fling *adj.* frivolous; insignificant —**tri´fling·ly** *adv.*

tri·fo´li·ate *adj.* having three leaves

tri·fur´cate, tri·fur´cat·ed *adj.* having three forks or branches —**tri·fur·ca´tion** *n.*

trig´ger *n.* any of various devices designed to activate

trig·o·nom´e·try *n.* the branch of mathematics dealing with the relationships between the sides and angles of a triangle —**trig·o·no·met´ric, trig·o·no·met´ri·cal** *adj.* —**trig·o·no·met´ri·cal·ly** *adv.*

tri·lat´er·al *adj.* having three sides —**tri·lat´er·al·ly** *adv.*

trill *vt.* to sing or play in a quavering tone —*n.* an utterance of successive quavering tones; a warble

tril´o·gy *n.* a literary work made up of three parts, each complete by itself

trim *vt.* to remove by cutting; to ornament; to smooth or make neat —*n.* good physical condition; the molding or ornamentation of a building —**trim´ly** *adv.* —**trim´ness** *n.*

tri·mes´ter *n.* a three–month period —**tri·mes´tral, tri·mes´tri·al** *adj.*

trin´ket *n.* a small ornament; a trifle

tri´o *n.* a group of three

trip *n.* a journey; a misstep; a nimble step; a blunder —*vi.* to stumble; to move quickly and lightly; to make an error —*vt.* to cause to stumble or make a mistake

tri´ple *vt., vi.* to make or become three times as many or as large

trip´let *n.* any of three children from one birth

trip´li·cate *n.* one of three similar things —*vt.* —**trip´li·cate·ly** *adv.* —**trip·li·ca´tion** *n.*

tri´pod *n.* a three–legged stand — **trip´o·dal, tri·pod´ic** *adj.*

trip´ping *adj.* light, nimble —**trip´ping·ly** *adv.*

trip´tych *n.* a work of art on three adjacent panels

tri´reme *n.* an ancient warship with three banks of oars

tri·sect´ *vt.* to divide into three equal parts —**tri·sec´tion** *n.* —**tri·sec´tor** *n.*

trite *adj.* made commonplace or hackneyed by frequent use — **trite´ly** *adv.* —**trite´ness** *n.*

trit´u·rate *vt.* to reduce to a fine powder; to pulverize —*n.* a pulverized pharmaceutical —**trit´u·ra·ble** *adj.* —**trit´u·ra´tion** *n.* —**trit´u·ra·tor** *n.*

tri´umph *vi.* to win a victory; to be successful —*n.* an important success —**tri·um´phal** *adj.* —**tri·um´phal·ly** *adv.*

tri·um´phant *adj.* victorious; exultant, as in victory —**tri·um´phant·ly** *adv.*

tri·um´vi·rate *n.* a coalition of three

triv´et *n.* a three–legged stand for holding a cooking vessel in a fireplace or a heated container on a tabletop

triv´ia *n.* insignificant matters

triv´i·al *adj.* of little importance; insignificant —**triv´i·al·ism** *n.* —**triv·i·al´i·ty** *n.* —**triv´i·al·ly** *adv.*

triv´i·al·ize *vt.* to regard as unimportant; to make trivial —**triv´i·al·i·za·tion** *n.*

tro´che *n.* a medicated lozenge

trog´lo·dyte *n.* a prehistoric man; a person considered to be primitive —**trog·lo·dyt´ic, trog·lo·dyt´i·cal** *adj.*

trol´lop *n.* an untidy woman

troop *n.* a gathering; a flock or herd; a unit of cavalry —*vi.* to move as a group —**troop´er** *n.*

trope *n.* a figure of speech

tro´phy *n.* something displayed as proof of victory

trot *n.* a slow running gait —*vi.*, *vt.* to go or cause to go at a trot —**trot´ter** *n.*

trou·ba·dour *n.* a wandering minstrel

trou´ble *n.* distress or worry; something that causes difficulty; a difficult situation; a disease or ailment; effort; general unrest —*vt.* to distress or worry; to inconvenience or annoy; to cause physical pain or discomfort —*vi.* to take pains —**trou´bler** *n.*

trou´ble·mak·er *n.* one who habitually causes distress to others

trou´ble·shoot·er *n.* one adept at analyzing problems and devising solutions; one assigned to resolve problems, mediate disputes, etc.

trou´ble·some *adj.* difficult or trying; pertaining to a source of difficulty —**trou´ble·some·ly** *adv.* —**trou´ble·some·ness** *n.*

trough *n.* a container for food or water for animals; a long, narrow depression, as between waves

trounce *vt.* to beat or thrash severely

troupe *n.* a company of performers —*vi.* to travel as a performer —**troup´er** *n.*

trous´seau *n.* clothing and linens assembled by a bride

trove *n.* a collection of valuable items

trow´el *n.* an implement for digging, applying or smoothing plaster, etc. —*vt.* to dig or smooth with a trowel —**trow´el·er, trow´el·ler** *n.*

tru´ant *n.* a pupil who is absent without permission; one who shirks a responsibility —*adj.* a juvenile offender; a loafer —*vi.* to shirk responsibility —**tru´an·cy** *n.*

truce *n.* an agreement to suspend hostilities; a respite, as from pain

truck *n.* (*US*) a vehicle designed to transport heavy loads; a two-wheeled vehicle for moving loads a short distance: *a hand truck* —*vi.* to carry goods; to drive a truck —**truck´er** *n.*

truck´age (*US*) *n.* the conveyance of goods by truck; the charge for moving goods

truck´ing (*US*) *n.* the business of operating trucks

truck´le *vi.* to yield or submit weakly; to move on rollers or casters —*vt.* to cause to move on rollers or casters —*n.* a small wheel —**truck´ler** *n.*

truc´u·lent *adj.* of savage character; inclined to ferocity —**truc´u·lence, truc´u·len·cy** *n.* —**truc´u·lent·ly** *adv.*

trudge *vi.* to walk wearily or laboriously —*n.* a tiresome walk —**trudg´er** *n.*

true *adj.* faithful to reality; real or genuine; faithful or dependable, as to friends, promises, etc. —*vt.* to bring to conformity with a standard —*adv.* in truth, truly; within tolerance —**true´ness** *n.*

truf´fle *n.* an edible fungus, similar to a mushroom, regarded as a delicacy; a chocolate confection

tru´ly *adv.* conforming to fact; with accuracy; with loyalty

trump *n.* in card games, a card or suit selected to rank above all others; a hidden advantage —*vt.* to take with a trump; to surpass or beat; to outdo or outmaneuver —*vi.* to play a trump —**trump up** to invent for fraudulent purposes

trump´er·y *n.* worthless finery; nonsense

trum´pet *n.* a brass wind instrument of the upper register; something resembling the flaring bell of a trumpet; a loud penetrating sound —*vt.* to sound or publish abroad —*vi.* to blow a trumpet; to sound forth, like an elephant — **trum´pet·er** n.

trun´cate vt. to cut the top from — adj. ending abruptly, as though cut off —**trun´cate·ly** adv. — **trun·ca´tion** n.

trun´cheon n. a short, thick stick or club; a mark of office or authority; (Brit.) a policeman's nightstick — vt. to beat; to cudgel

trunk n. the main stem of a tree; the central part of an animal or human body; a main passage, as for blood, transportation, communication, etc.; a large container

truss n. a supporting framework, as for a roof or bridge —vt. to support or brace; to tie or bind

trust n. reliance on the integrity of a person or thing; something committed to one's care: to hold funds in trust; confident expectation; an affiliation of business firms to control output, prices, etc. —vt. to rely on; to commit to the care of another; to expect or believe —vi. to place confidence in —adj. held in trust

trust·ee´ n. one entrusted with the management of property or affairs of another —**trust·ee´ship** n.

trust´ful adj. inclined to believe; showing trust —**trust´ful·ly** adv. —**trust´ful·ness** n.

trust fund assets held in trust

trust´ing adj. having or showing trust —**trust´ing·ly** adv. —**trust´ing·ness** n.

trust´wor·thy adj. deserving of confidence; reliable —**trust´wor·thi·ly** adv. —**trust´wor·thi·ness** n.

trust´y adj. faithful to duty —**trust´i·ly** adv. —**trust´i·ness** n.

truth n. conformity to fact; that which is true

truth´ful adj. conforming to fact; telling the truth —**truth´ful·ly** adv. —**truth´ful·ness** n.

try vt. to make an attempt; to make experimental use of; to subject to a test; to put severe strain on; to subject to stress; to extract by rendering —vi. to make an attempt; to put forth effort; to make a test —n. an attempt; a test

try´ing adj. difficult to endure —**try´ing·ly** adv. —**try´ing·ness** n.

tryst n. an appointment to meet; a meeting —vi.

tsu·nam´i n. an immense wave generated by an earthquake under the ocean

tub n. a large round flat-bottomed vessel, such as for washing or storage; (US) a bath or bathtub

tu´ba n. a large brass instrument of the lower register

tub´by adj. round and fat; resembling a tub

tube n. a long, hollow cylinder

tu´ber n. a short, thickened portion of an underground stem, as a potato; a tubercle

tu´ber·cle n. a small rounded eminence

tu·ber´cu·lar adj. affected with tubercles; tuberculosis

tu·ber·cu·lo´sis n. a communicable disease marked by tubercles in the lungs —**tu·ber´cu·lous** adj.

tu´ber·ous adj. bearing projections or prominences

tub´ing n. tubes collectively; a piece of tube or material for tubes

tu´bu·lar adj. having the form of a tube; consisting of tubes —**tu·bu·lar´i·ty** n. —**tu´bu·lar·ly** adv.

tuck vt. to press in the edges of; to wrap or cover snugly; to make folds by gathering or stitching —vi. to draw together; to make tucks — n. a fold sewn into a garment; something inserted or folded — **tuck´er** n.

tuft n. a clump, as of hair, feathers, etc. —vt. to provide with tightly drawn buttons, as on upholstery or pillows; to cover or adorn with

tufts — *vi.* to form or grow in tufts —**tuft´ed** *adj.* —**tuft´er** *n.*

tug *vt., vi.* to pull with effort —*n.* a violent pull; a strenuous effort

tu·i´tion *n.* a charge or payment for instruction; the business of teaching —**tu·i´tion·al, tu·i´tion·ar·y** *adj.*

tum´ble *vi.* to toss about; to perform acrobatics —*vt.* to cause to fall

tum´bler *n.* a drinking glass; an acrobat; a revolving cage or cylinder for tossing like the tumbler on a clothes dryer

tum´brel *n.* a rude cart

tu´me·fy *vi., vt.* to swell or cause to swell —**tu´me·fa´cient** *adj.* —**tu·me·fac´tion** *n.*

tu·mes´cent *adj.* swelling; somewhat timid —**tu·mes´cence** *n.*

tu´mor *n.* a local swelling on or in the body —**tu´mor·ous** *adj.*

tu´mult *n.* a commotion or disturbance by a multitude; any violent commotion; mental or emotional agitation

tu·mul´tu·ous *adj.* characterized by tumult; greatly disturbed; stormy, tempestuous —**tu·mul´tu·ous·ly** *adv.* —**tu·mul´tu·ous·ness** *n.*

tun *n.* a large cask —*vt.* to put into a cask

tu´na *n.* a large food or game fish

tun´a·ble, tune´a·ble *adj.* that can be tuned, as a musical instrument —**tun·a·bil´i·ty, tun´a·ble·ness** *n.* —**tun´a·bly** *adv.*

tun´dra *n.* a rolling treeless plain

tune *n.* a coherent succession of musical tones; correct musical pitch; harmony; fine adjustment — *vt.* to adjust —**tun´er** *n.*

tune´ful *adj.* melodic —**tune´ful·ly** *adv.* —**tune´ful·ness** *n.*

tune´less *adj.* not in tune; lacking a melody —**tune´less·ly** *adv.* — **tune´less·ness** *n.*

tu´nic *n.* a loose outer garment gathered at the waist; a short coat

tun´nel *n.* an underground passageway —*vt.* to dig; to make a passageway through or under — **tun´nel·er, tun´nel·ler** *n.*

tun´ny *n.* tuna

tur´ban *n.* a head covering —**tur´baned** *adj.*

tur´bid *adj.* muddy; dense or opaque; confused —**tur·bid´i·ty, tur´bid·ness** *n.* —**tur´bid·ly** *adv.*

tur´bine *n.* a rotary engine

tur´bot *n.* a large European flatfish

tur´bu·lent *adj.* violently disturbed or agitated; tending to disturb — **tur´bu·lence, tur´bu·len·cy** *n.* — **tur´bu·lent·ly** *adv.*

tu·reen´ *n.* a large covered bowl, as used for serving soup

turf *n.* a section or plot of grass; an area regarded possessively —*vt.* to cover with sod

tur·ges´cent *adj.* being or becoming swollen —**tur·ges´cence, tur·ges´cen·cy** *n.* —**tur·ges´cent·ly** *adv.*

tur´gid *adj.* unnaturally distended; swollen —**tur·gid´i·ty, tur´gid·ness** *n.* —**tur´gid·ly** *adv.*

tur´key *n.* a large North American bird; something lacking quality

tur´moil *n.* disturbance; tumult

turn *vi., vt.* to revolve or cause to revolve or rotate; to change the direction of; to give finished form; to bend, curve, twist, etc.; to transform; to translate; to change —*n.* the act of turning or being turned; a change of direction —**turn´er** *n.*

turn´ing *n.* the art of shaping on a lathe

turn´pike *n.* a toll road

tur´pi·tude *n.* depravity

tur´ret *n.* a small projecting tower — **tur´ret·ed** *adj.*

tur´tle *n.* a four–limbed reptile with a soft body encased in a shell

tusk *n.* a long projecting tooth —*vt.* to gore, root, etc. with a tusk

tus´sle *vt., vi.* to scuffle or struggle —*n.* a scuffle

tu´te·lage *n.* being under the care of a tutor or guardian; the office of a guardian; the act of tutoring

tu´te·lar, tu´te·lar·y *adj.* watching over; protecting

tu´tor *n.* a private teacher —*vt., vi.* to act as a tutor —**tu·to´ri·al** *adj.*

tu´tu *n.* a ballet skirt

tux·e´do *n.* formal dinner or evenng attire

twad´dle *n.* pretentious, silly talk — *vt., vi.* —**twad´dler** *n.*

twang *vt., vi.* to make or cause to make a sharp, vibrant sound; to speak with a nasal sound —*n.* a sharp vibrating or nasal sound — **twang´y** *adj.*

tweak *vt.* to pinch or twist sharply; to fine–tune —*n.* a pinch

tweed *n.* a woolen fabric

tweet *vi.* to utter a thin, chirping note —*n.*

tweez´ers *n.* small pincers —**tweeze** *vt.*

twid´dle *vt.* to twirl idly —*vi.* to be busy about trifles

twig *n.* a small shoot or branch

twi´light *n.* the period after sunset and before sunrise; any faint light; a period of waning glory, decline in achievements, etc.

twin *n.* either of two young from the same birth; one greatly similar to another

twine *vt.* to twist together; to coil about something —*vi.* to interlace; to proceed on a winding course — *n.* string; the act of entwining

twinge *n.* a sudden sharp pain; a mental pang —*vi., vt.* to feel or cause to feel a sudden pain

twin´kle *vi.* to shine intermittently; to sparkle; to move lightly and rapidly; to wink or blink —*vt.* to cause to flicker; a quick movement of the eyelids —*n.* a glimmer — **twin´kler** *n.*

twin´kling *n.* the act of something that twinkles; an instant, a

moment; a wink

twirl *vt., vi.* to whirl or rotate rapidly; to twist or curl —*n.* a whirling motion; a curl or twist

twist *vt.* to wind around each other; to form by winding; to deform or distort —*vi.* to become twisted; to move in a winding course; to squirm or writhe —*n.* a curve or bend; a strain, as of a joint; an unnatural inclination; an unexpected turn or development — **twist´able** *adj.* —**twist´ing·ly** *adv.* —**twist´y** *adj.*

twist´er *n.* one or that which twists; a tornado or cyclone

twit *vt.* to taunt —*n.* a reproach or taunt; a foolish person

twitch *vt., vi.* to pull or move with a quick spasmodic jerk —*n.* a sudden involuntary muscle contraction

two´–faced *adj.* double–dealing; insincere —**two´–fac·ed·ly** *adv.* — **two´–fac·ed·ness** *n.*

tycoon´ *n.* a wealthy, powerful businessman or financier

tyke *n.* a small child

type´ *n.* a group having traits in common; a standard or model; a block of raised characters or other medium used for printing —*vt.* to represent; to typify; to classify

type´set *vt.* to make written material ready for printing —**type´set·ter** *n.* —**type´set·ting** *n.*

type´writ·er *n.* a machine for producing characters on paper; a typist —**type´write** *vi., vt.*

ty·phoi´dal *adj.* pertaining to typhoid fever

typhoid fever a serious infectious disease contracted from contaminated water or food

ty·phoon´ *n.* a violent tropical storm

ty´phus *n.* a contagious disease spread by fleas, lice, etc. —**ty´phous** *adj.*

typ´i·cal *adj.* characteristic of a

group or type —**typ′i·cal·ly** *adv.* — **typ′i·cal·ness** *n.*

typ′i·fy *vt.* to represent by a type; to serve as an example —**typ·i·fi·ca′ tion** *n.*

typ′ist *n.* one who operates a keyboard, as on a typewriter, typesetting machine, or computer word processor

ty′po *n.* an error in typing or printing

ty·pog′ra·pher *n.* one who sets written material into type suitable for printing

ty·po·graph′ic,   **ty·po·graph′i·cal** *adj.* relating to typesetting or printing —**ty·pog′ra·phy** *n.*

ty·ran′nic, ty·ran′ni·cal *adj.* of or like a tyrant; despotic or arbitrary —**ty·ran′ni·cal·ly** *adv.*

tyr′an·nize *vi.* to exercise power cruelly; to rule as a tyrant — *vt.* to treat cruelly; to domineer —**tyr′ an·niz·er** *n.*

tyr′an·nous *adj.* despotic; cruel — **tyr′an·nous·ly** *adv.* —**tyr′an· nous·ness** *n.*

ty′rant *n.* one who rules oppressively or cruelly; one who exercises power or authority in a harsh, cruel manner —**tyr′an·ny** *n.*

tyre (*Brit.*) *n.* a flexible covering for a wheel

ty′ro *n.* a novice or beginner

u, U twenty–first letter of the English alphabet

u·biq′ui·tous *adj.* seeming to be everywhere at once; omnipresent —**ubiq′ui·tous·ly** *adv.* —**ubiq′ui· tous·ness, ubi′qui·ty** *n.*

ud′der *n.* a pendulous, milk–secreting gland of a mammal for the feeding of offspring

ug′ly *adj.* distasteful to the senses; repulsive; morally revolting —**ug′ li·ness**

uku·le′le *n.* a small guitar–like instrument having four strings

ul′cer *n.* an open sore on the skin or internally; a corrupt condition — **ul′cer·ate** *vi.*, *vt.* **ul·cer·a′tion** *n.* —**ul′cer·a·tive** *adj.* —**ul′cer·ous** *adj.*

ul′na *n.* the larger of the two bones of the forearm —**ul′nar** *adj.*

ul′ster *n.* a long, loose overcoat

ul·te′ri·or *adj.* intentionally unrevealed; secondary in importance — **ul·te′ri·or·ly** *adv.*

ul′ti·ma *n.* the last syllable of a word

ul′ti·mate *adj.* last or final; beyond all others, as in size, quality, etc.; fundamental —*n.* the best, latest, most fundamental, etc. —**ul′ti· mate·ness** *n.*

ul′ti·mate·ly *adv.* in the end; finally

ul·ti·ma′tum *n.* final terms for settlement accompanied by a threat

ul′tra *adj.* extreme

ul′tra·light *n.* a lightweight airplane

ul·tra·mod′ern *adj.* extremely fresh and new —**ul·tra·mod′ern·ism** *n.* —**ul·tra·mod′ern·ist** *n.*

ul·tra·son′ic *adj.* pertaining to inaudible sound waves —**ul·tra·son′i· cal·ly** *adv.*

ul·tra·sound′ *n.* the use of ultrasonic waves for medical diagnosis

ul·tra·vi′o·let *adj.* having a wavelength between visible violet and those of X–rays

ul′u·late *vi.* to howl or wail —**ul′u· lant** *adj.* —**ul′u·la′tion** *n.*

um′ber *n.* a brown iron oxide used as a pigment; a color made from umber —*adj.* pertaining to umber or its color

um·bil′i·cal *adj.* pertaining to or situated near the naval —*n.* a tube that serves as a connecting device for an astronaut or aquanaut outside the craft

umbilical cord the structure connecting a fetus with the placenta

um·bil′i·cus *n.* the naval

um′brage *n.* a feeling of anger or resentment; shade or shadow

—**um·bra´geous** *adj.* —**um·bra´geous·ly** *adv.* —**um·bra´geous·ness** *n.*

um·brel´la *n.* a portable canopy on a folding frame that protects from sun or rain; something serving as a cover or shield

um´laut *n.* an altered vowel sound; two dots over a vowel, as ä, ë, etc., used to mark the change in sound

um´pire *n.* a person called on to settle a disagreement or dispute; one chosen to enforce the rules of certain games

un·a·bat´ed *adj.* maintaining original force or intensity: *the storm continued unabated for two hours*

un·a´ble *adj.* incompetent; ineffectual

un·a·bridged´ *adj.* containing all of the original text; complete

un·ac·cept´a·ble *adj.* not satisfactory —**un·ac·cept·a·bil´i·ty** *n.* —**un·ac·cept´a·bly** *adv.*

un·ac·count´a·ble *adj.* impossible to explain —**un·ac·count·a·bil´i·ty**, **un·ac·count´a·ble·ness** *n.* —**un·ac·count´a·bly** *adv.*

un·ac·cus´tomed *n.* not familiar with; uncommon, strange —**un·ac·cus´tomed·ly** *adv.* —**un·ac·cus´tomed·ness** *n.*

un·a·chiev´a·ble *adj.* impossible or unlikely to attain

un·ac·quaint´ed *adj.* not having met; not informed: *unacquainted with the situation*

un·a·dorned´ *adj.* plain; lacking embellishment

un·a·dul´ter·at·ed *adj.* pure; not dilute; complete, utter: *the unadulterated truth*

un·ad·vised´ *adj.* rash or imprudent; uninformed —**un·ad·vis´ed·ly** *adv.* —**un·ad·vis´ed·ness** *n.*

un·af·fect´ed *adj.* natural or sincere; not influenced or changed — **un·af·fect´ed·ly** *adv.* —**un·af·fect´ed·ness** *n.*

un·a·fraid´ *adj.* showing no fear

un·aid´ed *adj.* without assistance: *he prepared the dinner unaided*

un·al·loyed´ *adj.* pure, not mixed; complete, unqualified —**un·al·loy´ed·ly** *adv.*

un·al´ter·a·ble *adj.* that cannot be changed: *the unalterable onset of winter* —**un·al´ter·a·ble·ness** *n.* —**un·al´ter·a·bly** *adv.*

u·nan´i·mous *adj.* being in complete agreement; without dissent — **u·na·nim´i·ty**, **u·nan´i·mous·ness** *n.* —**u·nan´i·mous·ly** *adv.*

un·ap·peal´ing *adj.* lacking attraction; not inviting or tempting

un·ap·proach´a·ble *adj.* aloof; reserved; inaccessible —**un·ap·proach·a·bil´i·ty**, **un·ap·proach´a·ble·ness** *n.* —**un·ap·proach´a·bly** *adv.*

un·a·shamed´ *adj.* feeling or showing no embarrassment: *unashamed to show emotion*

un·asked´ *adj.* not asked, invited, or requested

un·as·sail´a·ble *adj.* not possible to contest or disprove; resistant to attack —**un·as·sail·a·bil´i·ty**, **un·as·sail´a·ble·ness** *n.* —**un·as·sail´a·bly** *adv.*

un·as·sum´ing *adj.* modest; unpretentious —**un·as·sum´ing·ly** *adv.* —**un·as·sum´ing·ness** *n.*

un·at·tached´ *adj.* independent; not affiliated with any group; unmarried

un·at·tain´a·ble *adj.* impossible or unlikely to be accomplished — **un·at·tain·a·bil´i·ty**, **un·at·tain´a·ble·ness** *n.* —**un·at·tain´a·bly** *adv.*

un·a·vail´a·ble *adj.* not obtainable; not accessible —**un·a·vail·a·bil´i·ty** *n.*

un·a·vail´ing *adj.* ineffective; futile —**un·a·vail´ing·ly** *adv.*

un·avoid´a·ble *adj.* inevitable —**un·avoid·a·bil´i·ty**, **un·avoid´a·ble·ness** *n.* —**un·avoid´a·bly** *adv.*

un·a·ware´ *adj.* carelessly unmindful; inattentive; not informed — *adv.* unawares —**un·a·ware´ly** *adv.* —**un·a·ware´ness** *n.*

un·a·wares´ *adv.* unexpectedly; without premeditation

un·bal´ance *vt.* to disturb or derange mentally

un·bal´anced *adj.* lacking mental stability; unequal; wobbly

un·bear´a·ble *adj.* intolerable; insufferable —**un·bear´a·ble·ness** *n.* —**un·bear´a·bly** *adv.*

un·beat´a·ble *adj.* not to be defeated; first-rate —**un·beat´a·bly** *adv.*

un·be·com´ing *adj.* inappropriate; not decorous, improper —**un·be·com´ing·ly** *adv.* —**un·be·com´ing·ness** *n.*

un·be·liev´a·ble *adj.* incredible; too astonishing to be believed —**un·be·liev´a·bly** *adv.*

un·be·liev´er *n.* a doubter or skeptic; one without religious faith —**un·be·liev´ing** *adj.* —**un·be·liev´ing·ly** *adv.* —**un·be·liev´ing·ness** *n.*

un·bend´ *vt.* to relax, as from exertion; to dispense with formality — *vi.* to become free of restraint, formality, etc.

un·bend´ing *adj.* resolute; firm; not relaxed or able to relax —**un·bend´ing·ly** *adv.* —**un·bend´ing·ness** *n.*

un·bi´ased *adj.* impartial; not prejudiced —**un·bi´ased·ly** *adv.*

un·bid´den *adj.* spontaneous, done without asking; not commanded or invited

un·blem´ished *adj.* lacking fault: *an unblemished record*

un·blink´ing *adj.* without emotion; fearless —**un·blink´ing·ly** *adv.*

un·bound´ed *adj.* having no limits; unrestrained —**un·bound´ed·ly** *adv.* —**un·bound´ed·ness** *n.*

un·bowed´ *adj.* not broken or subdued by adversity

un·break´a·ble *adj.* impossible or extremely difficult to break —**un·break´a·ble·ness** *n.* —**un·break´a·bly** *adv.*

un·bri´dled *adj.* unrestrained; uncontrolled

un·bro´ken *adj.* uninterrupted; continuous; not tamed —**un·bro´ken·ly** *adv.* —**un·bro´ken·ness** *n.*

un·bur´den *vt.* to relieve from cares or worries; to make known so as to gain relief

un·can´ny *adj.* unnatural; weird; seeming to be almost supernatural —**un·can´ni·ly** *adv.* —**un·can´ni·ness** *n.*

un·car´ing *adj.* lacking concern or sympathy

un·ceas´ing *adj.* without stopping; continuous; eternal —**un·ceas´ing·ly** *adv.* —**un·ceas´ing·ness** *n.*

un·cen´sored *adj.* not reviewed or examined for the purging of inappropriate material; complete, with nothing removed or struck out

un·cer·e·mo´ni·ous *adj.* casual, informal; without preamble; rude or discourteous —**un·cer·e·mo´ni·ous·ly** *adv.* —**un·cer·e·mo´ni·ous·ness** *n.*

un·cer´tain *adj.* not yet determined; unpredictable; doubtful or dubious; tenuous —**un·cer´tain·ly** *adv.* —**un·cer´tain·ty** *n.*

un·change´a·ble *adj.* that cannot be altered or modified —**un·change·a·bil´i·ty, un·change´a·ble·ness** *n.* —**un·change´a·bly** *adv.*

un·chang´ing *adj.* constant; enduring —**un·chang´ing·ly** *adv.* —**un·chang´ing·ness** *n.*

un·char·ac·ter·is´tic *adj.* unusual; strange or exceptional: *we were surprised by his uncharacteristic generosity* —**un·char·ac·ter·is´ti·cal·ly** *adv.*

un·char´i·ta·ble *adj.* not forgiving; unkind; lacking generosity —**un·char´i·ta·ble·ness** *n.* —**un·char´i·ta·bly** *adv.*

un·chart´ed *adj.* unknown; unexplored

un·civ´il *adj.* discourteous; ill-bred —**un·civ´il·ly** *adv.* —**un·civ´il·ness** *n.*

un·civ´il·ized *adj.* barbarous; rude and uncouth; remote from civilization —**un·civ´il·iz·ed·ly** *adv.*

un·clad´ *adj.* without clothes; naked

un·clean´ *adj.* soiled, squalid; morally or ceremonially impure —**un·clean´li·ness** *n.* —**un·clean´ly** *adv.*

un·com´fort·a·ble *adj.* ill at ease; causing uneasiness —**un·com´fort·a·ble·ness** *n.* —**un·com´fort·a·bly**

un·com´mon *adj.* remarkable; strange —**un·com´mon·ly** *adv.* —**un·com´mon·ness** *n.*

un·com·mu´ni·ca·tive *adj.* not disposed to talking; reserved —**un·com·mu´ni·ca·tive·ly** *adv.* —**un·com·mu´ni·ca·tive·ness** *n.*

un·com´pli·cat·ed *adj.* relatively simple or easy; fundamental or basic

un·com´pro·mis·ing *adj.* inflexible; strict —**un·com´pro·mis·ing·ly** *adv.*

un·con·ceiv´a·ble *adj.* that cannot be imagined or understood; unbelievable —**un·con·ceiv´a·ble·ness** *n.* —**un·con·ceiv´a·bly** *adv.*

un·con·cerned´ *adj.* lacking interest; indifferent; not worried —**un·con·cern´** *n.* —**un·con·cern´ed·ly** *adv.* —**un·con·cern´ed·ness** *n.*

un·con·di´tion·al *adj.* absolute; without prerequisite or provision —**un·con·di´tion·al·ly** *adv.* —**un·con·di´tion·al·ness** *n.*

un·con·di´tioned *adj.* not restricted

un·con´quer·a·ble *adj.* that cannot be overcome or defeated —**un·con´quer·a·bly** *adv.*

un·con´scion·a·ble *adj.* unscrupulous; unbelievably bad or wrong —**un·con´scion·a·ble·ness** *n.*

—un·con´scion·a·bly *adv.*

un·con´scious *adj.* lacking consciousness; not produced by conscious effort —*n.* that part of the mind that retains memories, compulsions, etc. not readily accessible to one's consciousness —**un·con´scious·ly** *adv.* —**un·con´scious·ness** *n.*

un·con·sti·tu´tion·al *adj.* violating the precepts of a constitution —**un·con·sti·tu·tion·al´i·ty** *n.* —**un·con·sti·tu´tion·al·ly** *adv.*

un·con·trol´la·ble *adj.* that cannot be governed or restrained; unmanageable —**un·con·trol·la·bil´i·ty, un·con·trol´la·ble·ness** *n.* —**un·con·trol´la·bly** *adv.*

un·con·ven´tion·al *adj.* not adhering to traditional rules, practices, etc. —**un·con·ven·tion·al´i·ty** *n.* —**un·con·ven´tion·al·ly** *adv.*

un·co·or´di·nat·ed *adj.* lacking muscular coordination; lacking planning or organization —**un·co·or´di·nat·ed·ly** *adv.*

un·count´ed *adj.* beyond counting; innumerable

un·cou´ple *vt.* to disconnect or unfasten

un·couth´ *adj.* coarse, boorish, or unrefined —**un·couth´ly** *adv.* —**un·couth´ness** *n.*

un·cov´er *vt.* to remove a covering from; to make known; to discover or disclose —*vi.* to remove a covering

unc´tion *n.* the act of anointing; a substance, as oil, used for anointing; something that soothes; excessive or affected sincerity

unc´tu·ous *adj.* greasy or soapy to the touch; marked by excessive or affected sincerity; overly smooth or suave —**unc´tu·ous·ly** *adv.* —**unc´tu·ous·ness** *n.*

un·daunt´ed *adj.* fearless; intrepid —**un·daunt´ed·ly** *adv.* —**un·daunt´ed·ness** *n.*

un·de·cid´ed adj. uncertain; unsettled —**un·de·cid´ed·ly** adv. —**un·de·cid´ed·ness** n.

un·de·ni´a·ble adj. indisputable; unquestionable —**un·de·ni´a·ble·ness** n. —**un·de·ni´a·bly** adv.

un´der prep. beneath; covered by; lower than; less in value, amount, etc.; inferior to; subordinate to; being the subject of; by virtue of; having regard to —adv. underneath; in an inferior position; less in amount, value, etc. —adj.

un·der·a·chieve´ vi. to perform below one's capability —**un·der·a·chieve´ment** n. —**un·der·a·chiev´er** n.

un·der·age´ adj. not of a requisite legal age

un´der·brush n. small trees, shrubs, etc. growing beneath forest trees

un´der·car·riage n. the framework supporting the body of a structure

un·der·class´man n. a freshman or sophomore

un·der·coat, un´der·coat·ing n. a protective coating, as a primer, applied over bare wood or metal — vt. to apply a protective coating

un·der·cov´er adj. secret; engaged in spying

un´der·cur·rent n. a flowing layer of air or water beneath another layer or beneath the surface; a concealed or secret force or tendency

un´der·done n. not completely cooked

un·der·es´ti·mate vt. to place too low a value on; to misjudge or underrate —**un·der·es·ti·ma´tion** n.

un´der·foot´ adv. beneath the feet; in the way

un·der·go´ vt. to be subject to; to bear up under; to endure

un·der·grad´u·ate n. a college or university student who has not yet earned a degree

un´der·ground adj. situated or operating beneath the surface; done in

secret —n. that which is beneath the surface; organized resistance against leadership, convention, etc. —adv.

underground railway (Brit.) a rapid transit system of trains running underground: a subway; (US) before 1861, a system for assisting fugitive slaves in the U.S.

un´der·growth n. underbrush

un·der·hand´ed adj., adv. done in a sly or treacherous manner —**un´der·hand·ed·ly** adv. —**un´der·hand·ed·ness** n.

un·der·ly´ing adj. positioned under; basic or fundamental, as underlying principles; not obvious, but implied

un·der·mine´ vt. to excavate beneath; to weaken or impair secretly or insidiously

un·der·nour´ish vt. to provide food in insufficient quantity or quality to sustain health —**un·der·nour´ished** adj. —**un·der·nour´ish·ment** n.

un´der·pass n. a road, walkway, etc. that runs beneath another road, track, etc.

un´der·pin·ning n. material or framework supporting a structure from below; something seen as a basis or foundation: the underpinnings of guilt in our society

un´der·priv´i·leged adj. deprived socially and economically

un·der·rate´ vt. to underestimate

un´der·score vt. to underline; to emphasize —n. a line drawn under type for emphasis

un´der·signed n. one who signs or attests to a document

un·der·stand´ vt. to come to know the meaning or import of; to perceive the nature or character of; to have comprehension of; to suppose or believe; to accept as a condition —vi. to comprehend; to believe to be the case; to have sympathy or

un·der·stand·a·bil´i·ty *n.* —**un·der·stand´a·ble** *adj.* —**un·der·stand´a·bly** *adv.*

un·der·stand´ing *n.* comprehension; the capacity to think, retain knowledge, etc.; an agreement; a viewpoint, interpretation, or opinion; sympathy or tolerance for others —*adj.* characterized by comprehension, sympathy, tolerance, etc. —**un·der·stand´ing·ly** *adv.*

un·der·state´ *vt.* to relate or describe in a deliberately restrained manner —**un´der·state·ment** *n.*

un·der·stat´ed *adj.* marked by restraint; showing good taste: *understated elegance* —**un·der·stat´ed·ly** *adv.*

un·der·stood´ *adj.* comprehended; taken for granted without utterance; agreed upon by all

un´der·study *n.* one prepared to fill in for another in an emergency, such as an actor —*vt., vi.* to learn, practice, etc. so as to be able to stand in for another

un´der·take *vt.* to agree to attempt; to contract to do

un´der·tak·er *n.* one who sets out to do something; one who prepares the dead for burial

un´der·tak´ing *n.* an effort or endeavor; the business of preparing the dead for burial

un´der·tone *n.* a subdued sound, color, etc.; a meaning, quality, etc. implied but not expressed

un·der·val´ue *vt.* to rate something below its real worth; to regard as being of little value —**un·der·val·u·a´tion** *n.*

un´der·world *n.* the mythical abode of the dead; the realm of organized crime and vice

un´der·write *vt.* to sign; to assume liability; to guarantee, as of the shares in a new company —*vi.* to act as a guarantor, especially of insurance —**un´der·writ·er** *n.*

un·de·served´ *adj.* not earned or deserved: *an undeserved honor;* unwarranted or unfair: *an undeserved punishment* —**un·de·serv´ed·ly** *adv.*

un·de·sir´a·ble *adj.* objectionable; not wanted —*n.* an objectionable person —**un·de·sir·a·bil´i·ty** *n.* —**un·de·sir´a·bly** *adv.*

un·do´ *vt.* to cause to be as if never done; to loosen; to bring to ruin; to disturb emotionally —**un·do´ing** *n.* —**un·done´** *adj.*

un·doubt´ed *adj.* assured or certain; unsuspected —**un·doubt´ed·ly** *adv.*

un·dress´ *vt.* to strip or disrobe; to remove the dressing from, as of a wound —*vi.* to remove one's clothing —*n.* the state of being nude or only partially attired

un´du·lant *adj.* moving like a wave; fluctuating

un´du·late *vi., vt.* to move or cause to move like a wave —**un´du·late, un´du·lat·ed** *adj.* having a wavelike appearance

un·du·la´tion *n.* a waving or sinuous motion —**un´du·la·to·ry** *adj.*

un·du´ly *adv.* excessively; improperly or unjustly

un·dy´ing *adj.* immortal; eternal

un·earned´ *adj.* not earned through one's efforts; undeserved

un·earth´ *vt.* to dig up; to discover

un·earth´ly *adj.* seemingly not of this world; supernatural; terrifying —**un·earth´li·ness** *n.*

un·eas´y *adj.* disturbed; disquieted; causing discomfort; not stable or secure, as *an uneasy peace* —**un·eas´i·ly** *adv.* —**un·eas´i·ness** *n.*

un·em·ploy´a·ble *adj.* not useful; unable to keep a job, as by lack of skills, illness, etc. —*n.* an unskilled or disabled person

un·em·ployed´ *adj.* not having work; not put to use; idle —**un´em·ploy´ment** *n.*

un·e´qual *adj.* not alike, as in size or ability; inadequate; not uniform — **un·e´qual·ly** *adv.*

un·e´qualed, un·e´qualled *adj.* not to be matched or compared; without rivals

un·e·quiv´o·cal *adj.* understandable in only one way; not ambiguous — **un·e·quiv´o·cal·ly** *adv.* —**un·e·quiv´o·cal·ness** *n.*

un·err´ing *adj.* making no mistakes; certain —**un·err´ing·ly** *adv.*

un·es·sen´tial *adj.* not important; not required

un·e´ven *adj.* not smooth or level; rough; not balanced or matched; not uniform —**un·e´ven·ly** *adv.* —**un·e´ven·ness** *n.*

un·e·vent´ful *adj.* quiet; lacking unusual activity —**un·e·vent´ful·ly** *adv.* —**un·e·vent´ful·ness** *n.*

un·ex·cep´tion·a·ble *adj.* not open to question or objection; irreproachable —**un·ex·cep´tion·a·ble·ness**—**un·ex·cep´tion·a·bly**

un·ex·cep´tion·al *adj.* ordinary; not unusual —**un·ex·cep´tion·al·ly** *adv.*

un·ex·pect´ed *adj.* coming without warning; not foreseen —**un·ex·pect´ed·ly** *adv.* —**un·ex·pect´ed·ness** *n.*

un·fail´ing *adj.* fulfilling requirements or expectations; sure, infallible —**un·fail´ing·ly** *adv.* —**un·fail´ing·ness** *n.*

un·fair´ *adj.* marked by injustice; biased; not honest or ethical — **un·fair´ly** *adv.* —**un·fair´ness** *n.*

un·faith´ful *adj.* disloyal; not abiding by a vow, duty, etc.; unreliable; adulterous —**un·faith´ful·ly** *adv.* —**un·faith´ful·ness** *n.*

un·fa·mil´iar *adj.* not versant in; outside the sphere of one's knowledge; not previously known or seen, as *an unfamiliar face* —**un·fa·mil·i·ar´i·ty** *n.* —**un·fa·mil´iar·ly** *adv.*

un·fath´om·a·ble *adj.* incomprehensible; difficult or impossible to understand

un·fa´vor·a·ble *adj.* not propitious; detrimental —**un·fa´vor·a·ble·ness** *n.* —**un·fa´vor·a·bly** *adv.*

un·feel´ing *adj.* not sympathetic; showing no emotion —**un·feel´ing·ly** *adv.* —**un·feel´ing·ness** *n.*

un·feigned´ *adj.* sincere —**un·feign´ed·ly** *adv.*

un·fit´ *adj.* unsuitable for a given purpose; not physically or mentally sound —**un·fit´ly** *adv.* —**un·fit´ness** *n.*

un·flag´ging *adj.* not diminishing; tireless —**un·flag´ging·ly** *adv.*

un·flap´pa·ble *adj.* impassive; imperturbable —**un·flap·pa·bil´i·ty** *n.* —**un·flap´pa·bly** *adv.*

un·fledged´ *adj.* inexperienced or immature

un·flinch´ing *adj.* steadfast; resolute —**un·flinch´ing·ly** *adv.*

un·fold´ *vt.* to open or spread; to disclose gradually; to develop —*vi.* to expand; to develop fully

un·fore·seen´ *adj.* unexpected; unpredicted; without warning

un·for·get´ta·ble *adj.* memorable; not likely to be forgotten —**un·for·get´ta·ble·ness** *n.* —**un·for·get´ta·bly** *adv.*

unforgiving *adj.* not willing to excuse or absolve; having little tolerance for error: *sailing over an unforgiving sea*

un·for´tu·nate *adj.* unlucky; resulting from misfortune; regrettable — *n.* a victim —**un·for´tu·nate·ly** *adv.* —**un·for´tu·nate·ness** *n.*

un·found´ed *adj.* not based on fact; not established —**un·found´ed·ly** *adv.* —**un·found´ed·ness** *n.*

un·fre´quent·ed *adj.* rarely visited

un·friend´ly *adj.* not amiable or sympathetic; not favorable or propitious —**un·friend´li·ness** *n.*

un·furl´ *vt., vi.* to unroll or spread

out —**un·furled´** *adj.*

un·gain·ly *adj.* awkward; clumsy; poorly proportioned —**un·gain´li·ness** *n.*

un·god·ly *adj.* lacking reverence; sinful; outrageous —*adv.* outrageously —**un·god´li·ness** *n.*

un·gov·ern·a·ble *adj.* that cannot be governed or controlled —**un·gov´ern·a·ble·ness** *n.* —**un·gov´ern·a·bly** *adv.*

un·gra·cious *adj.* lacking manners; offensive —**un·gra´cious·ly** *adv.* —**un·gra´cious·ness** *n.*

un·grate·ful *adj.* lacking gratitude; disagreeable —**un·grate´ful·ly** *adv.* —**un·grate´ful·ness** *n.*

un·guard·ed *adj.* unprotected; thoughtless or careless; without guile —**un·guard´ed·ly** *adv.* —**un·guard´ed·ness** *n.*

un·guent *n.* an ointment or salve —**un´guen·tar·y** *adj.*

un´gu·late *adj.* having hoofs —*n.* a hoofed animal

un·hand´ *vt.* to remove one's hand from; to release

un·hand·y *adj.* inconvenient; lacking manual skill —**un·hand´i·ly** *adv.* —**un·hand´i·ness** *n.*

un·hap·py *adj.* sad or depressed; unfortunate; inappropriate; displeased —**un·hap´pi·ly** *adv.* —**un·hap´pi·ness** *n.*

un·health·y *adj.* sickly; injurious to health; dangerous or risky —**un·health´i·ly** *adv.* —**un·health´i·ness** *n.*

un·heard´-of *adj.* unprecedented; outrageous

un·hinge´ *vt.* to detach, as from hinges; to throw into confusion or derange

un·ho·ly *adj.* wicked; sinful

u·ni·cel·lu·lar *adj.* consisting of a single cell, as a protozoan —**u·ni·cel·lu·lar´i·ty** *n.*

u´ni·corn *n.* a mythical creature resembling a horse with a single

horn growing from its head

u´ni·form *adj.* being always alike; consistent —*n.* similar clothing worn by members of an organization, service, etc. —*vt.* to make comparable; to clothe with a uniform —**u·ni·form´i·ty, u´ni·form·ness** *n.* —**u´ni·form·ly** *adv.*

u´ni·fy *vt.* to bring together or unite; to make alike —**u´ni·fi·a·ble** *adj.* —**u·ni·fi·ca´tion** *n.* —**u´ni·fi·er** *n.*

u·ni·lat´er·al *adj.* relating to or affecting one side only; undertaken or obligating only one of two or more parties involved; having only one side; recognizing only one aspect as of an argument or discussion —**u·ni·lat´er·al·ly** *adv.*

un·im·peach´a·ble *adj.* beyond question; blameless —**un·im·peach´a·bly** *adv.*

un·im·proved´ *adj.* having no improvement or progress made, as *an unimproved road;* not cleared or cultivated; unused

un·in·spired´ *adj.* dull or boring; indifferent

un·in·tel´li·gi·ble *adj.* incomprehensible —**un·in·tel·li·gi·bil´i·ty, un·in·tel´li·gi·ble·ness** *n.* —**un·in·tel´li·gi·bly** *adv.*

un·in·ten´tion·al *n.* not deliberate or planned; inadvertent —**un·in·ten´tion·al·ly** *adv.*

un·in´ter·est·ed *adj.* indifferent; unconcerned —**un·in´ter·est·ed·ly** *adv.* —**un·in´ter·est·ed·ness** *n.*

un´ion *n.* a joining of two or more things; something formed by joining or combining; a device for joining mechanical parts —*adj.* pertaining to or involving a union

un´ion·ism *n.* labor unions collectively, their principles and practices —**un´ion·ist** *n.*

un´ion·ize *vi., vt.* to join or cause to join a labor union; to organize a union

u·nique´ *adj.* being the only one of

its kind; without equal; very unusual or remarkable —**u·nique′ly** *adv.* —**u·nique′ness** *n.*

u′ni·sex *adj.* appropriate to or characteristic of either sex —*n.* the integration of clothing, hair style, etc. so as to be appropriate for either sex

u·ni·sex′u·al *adj.* of only one sex; having to do with unisex —**u·ni·sex·u·al′i·ty** *n.* —**u·ni·sex′u·al·ly** *adv.*

u′ni·son *n.* a condition of perfect agreement; speaking or singing together as one

u′nit *n.* a value used as a standard of comparison or measurement; a measure of requirements for a scholastic degree; the quantity required to produce a desired effect; persons or things considered as constituent parts of a whole —*adj.* being a distinct part —**u′ni·tar·y** *adj.*

u·nite′ *vt.* to join together; to bring into close connection; to possess in combination; to combine —*vi.* to be merged into one; to join together —**u·nit′ed** *adj.*

u′ni·ty *n.* the state or quality of being united; singleness of purpose; mutual understanding

u·ni·ver′sal *adj.* common everywhere; including all things, persons, etc. without exception; adapted to a variety of uses —*n.* any general notion or idea; a trait common to all men or cultures — **u·ni·ver′sal·ism** *n.* —**u·ni·ver′sal·ly** *adv.* —**u·ni·ver′sal·ness** *n.*

u·ni·ver′sal·ize *vt.* to make universal; to generalize —**u·ni·ver·sal·i·za′tion** *n.*

u′ni·verse *n.* the aggregate of all existing things; something extensive, as in a field of thought or activity

u·ni·ver′si·ty *n.* an institute of higher learning including its buildings, grounds, students, faculty, etc.

un·just′ *adj.* not fair; wrongful —**un·just′ly** *adv.* —**un·just′ness** *n.*

un·kempt′ *adj.* not neat or tidy

un·kind′ *adj.* lacking sympathy; harsh or cruel —**un·kind′li·ness, un·kind′ness** *n.* —**un·kind′ly** *adv.*

un·known′ *adj.* not apprehended; not recognized or identified —*n.* an unfamiliar person or thing

un·law′ful *adj.* illegal; not moral or ethical —**un·law′ful·ly** *adv.* —**un·law′ful·ness** *n.*

un·learned′ *adj.* illiterate; marked by lack of knowledge; acquired by means other than training —**un·learn′ed·ly** *adv.*

un·leash′ *vt.* to set free from or as from a leash

un·less′ *conj.* except that —*prep.* excepting

un·like′ *adj.* having little or no similarity —*prep.* different from; not characteristic of —**un·like′ness** *n.*

un·like′ly *adj.* improbable; contrary to expectation; not promising — *adv.* improbably —**un·like′li·hood, un·like′li·ness** *n.*

un·lim′it·ed *adj.* not restricted; having no boundaries

un·load′ *vt.* to discharge, as cargo; to unburden; to dispose of by selling —*vi.* to discharge freight

un·loose′ *vt.* to set free

un·loos′en *vt.* to undo or release

un·luck′y *adj.* not favored or favorable; unfortunate; likely to prove unfortunate —**un·luck′i·ly** *adv.* — **un·luck′i·ness** *n.*

un·make′ *vt.* to restore to a previous condition; to ruin; to deprive of rank, power, etc.

un·mask′ *vt.* to expose the true nature of —*vi.* to remove one's disguise

un·men′tion·a·ble *adj.* not fit for discussion; too embarrassing to mention or discuss —**un·men´tion·a·ble·ness** n. —**un·men´tion·a·bly** adv.

un·mer´ci·ful adj. showing no mercy; cruel or pitiless; extreme or exorbitant —**un·mer´ci·ful·ly** adv. —**un·mer´ci·ful·ness** n.

un·mis·tak´a·ble adj. evident; obvious —**un·mis·tak´a·bly** adv.

un·mit´i·gat·ed adj. not relieved or lessened; absolute or thoroughgoing —**un·mit´i·gat·ed·ly** adv. —**un·mit´i·gat·ed·ness** n.

un·nat´u·ral adj. contrary to accepted standards of morality and decency; contrived or artificial —**un·nat´u·ral·ly** adv. —**un·nat´u·ral·ness** n.

un·nec´es·sar·y adj. not required —**un·nec·es·sar´i·ly** adv. —**un·nec·es·sar´i·ness** n.

un·nerve´ vt. to deprive of resolve, courage, etc.; to make nervous —**un·nerve´ing·ly** adv.

un·oc´cu·pied adj. empty, uninhabited; idle, unemployed

un·of·fi´cial adj. not authorized or sanctioned; acting without authority —**un·of·fi´cial·ly** adv.

un·op·posed´ adj. without opposition; not challenged: *the candidate for mayor ran unopposed*

un·or´ga·nized adj. without form or structure; not unionized

un·or·tho·dox adj. contrary to convention or tradition —**un·or´tho·dox·ly** adv. —**un·or´tho·dox·y** n.

un·pal´at·a·ble adj. not pleasing to the taste: *unpalatable food*; disagreeable or difficult to accept: *unpalatable criticism* —**un·pal·at·a·bil´i·ty** n. —**un·pal´at·a·bly** adv.

un·par´al·leled adj. unmatched; unprecedented

un·pleas´ant adj. disagreeable —**un·pleas´ant·ly** adv. —**un·pleas´ant·ness** n.

un·plumbed´ adj. not fully measured or explored

un·pop´u·lar adj. generally disliked —**un·pop·u·lar´i·ty** n. —**un·pop´u·lar·ly** adv.

un·prac´ticed adj. not experienced; not used or tried

un·prec´e·dent·ed adj. being without precedent; new or novel

un·pre·dict´a·ble adj. unforeseen; that cannot be anticipated; tending to rash or unexpected action —**un·pre·dict·a·bil´i·ty, un·pre·dict´a·ble·ness** n. —**un·pre·dict´a·bly** adv.

un·prej´u·diced adj. free from bias; impartial

un·prin´ci·pled adj. unscrupulous; lacking a standard of morality

un·print´a·ble adj. profane or obscene

un·pro·fes´sion·al adj. violating the code, standards, etc. of a profession —**un·pro·fes´sion·al·ly** adv.

un·prof´it·a·ble adj. contributing nothing; lessening the profits of a business; serving no useful purpose —**un·prof·it·a·bil´i·ty** —**un·prof´it·a·ble·ness** n. —**un·prof´it·a·bly** adv.

un·qual´i·fied adj. lacking qualifications; without limitation or restriction —**un·qual´i·fied·ly** adv.

un·ques´tion·a·ble adj. beyond doubt; indisputable —**un·ques´tion·a·ble·ness** n. —**un·ques´tion·a·bly** adv.

un·rav´el vt. to separate, as something tangled; to unfold or explain, as a plot —vi. to become untangled; to grow apparent

un·read´ adj. uninformed; unlearned; not yet examined

un·read´a·ble adj. illegible; poorly written

un·read´y adj. not prepared; ill-prepared

un·re´al adj. having no substance; fanciful, imaginary; not true or sincere —**un·re·al´i·ty** n.

un·rea´son·a·ble adj. acting contrary

to reason; immoderate, exorbitant —**un·rea´son·a·ble·ness** *n.* —**un·rea´son·a·bly** *adv.*

un·rea´son·ing *adj.* irrational —**un·rea´son·ing·ly** *adv.*

un·re·gen´er·ate *adj.* not changed spiritually; sinful; stubbornly recalcitrant —**un·re·gen´er·a·cy** *n.* —**un·re·gen´er·ate·ly** *adv.*

un·re·lent´ing *adj.* determined; unyielding; not diminishing in pace, effort, etc. —**un·re·lent´ing·ly** *adv.*

un·re·li´a·ble *adj.* not dependable —**un·re·li·a·bil´i·ty**, **un·re·li´a·ble·ness** *n.* —**un·re·li´a·bly** *adv.*

un·re·mit´ting *adj.* not stopping or relaxing; incessant —**un·re·mit´ting·ly** *adv.*

un·re·quit´ed *adj.* not returned in kind

un·re·served´ *adj.* without qualification; informal —**un·re·serv´ed·ly** *adv.* —**un·re·serv´ed·ness** *n.*

un·rest´ *n.* restlessness; dissatisfaction bordering on revolt

un·right´eous *adj.* wicked, sinful, inequitable —**un·right´eous·ly** *adv.* —**un·right´eous·ness** *n.*

un·ri´valed *adj.* having no equal

un·ruf´fled *adj.* calm; undisturbed

un·ru´ly *adj.* tending to resist regulation; difficult to control —**un·ru´li·ness** *n.*

un·sa´vor·y *adj.* having a disagreeable taste or odor; lacking flavor; morally distasteful or offensive —**un·sa´vor·i·ly** *adv.* —**un·sa´vor·i·ness** *n.*

un·scathed´ *adj.* not injured

un·scru´pu·lous *adj.* lacking restraint; unprincipled —**un·scru´pu·lous·ly** *adv.* —**un·scru´pu·lous·ness** *n.*

un·sea´son·a·ble *adj.* not suited or customary for the time of year; untimely —**un·sea´son·a·ble·ness** *n.* —**un·sea´son·a·bly** *adv.*

un·seat´ *vt.* to depose or vote out

un·seem´ly *adj.* unbecoming; inappropriate —**un·seem´li·ness** *n.*

un·set´tle *vt.* to confuse, upset, or disturb —*vi.* to become unsettled

un·shak´a·ble *adj.* unable to be disturbed or agitated

un·sight´ly *adj.* offensive to the eyes; ugly

un·skilled´ *adj.* lacking training or experience; requiring no special skill or training

un·skill´ful *adj.* awkward; incompetent —**un·skill´ful·ly** *adv.* —**un·skill´ful·ness** *n.*

un·snarl´ *vt.* to disentangle

un·so´cia·ble *adj.* not inclined to the company of others; not conducive to friendly interchange or association —**un·so´cia·ble·ness** *n.* —**un·so´cia·bly** *adv.*

un·so·phis´ti·cat·ed *adj.* inexperienced, artless; genuine; not complicated —**un·so·phis´ti·cat·ed·ly** *adv.* —**un·so·phis´ti·cat·ed·ness**, **un·so·phis·ti·ca´tion** *n.*

un·sound´ *adj.* not strong or solid; unhealthy; faulty or unfounded, as of reasoning —**un·sound´ly** *adv.* —**un·sound´ness** *n.*

un·spar´ing *adj.* generous or lavish; showing no mercy —**un·spar´ing·ly** *adv.* —**un·spar´ing·ness** *n.*

un·speak´a·ble *adj.* that cannot be expressed, as of something very good or very bad —**un·speak´a·ble·ness** *n.* —**un·speak´a·bly** *adv.*

un·spoiled´ *adj.* not changed, as *an unspoiled wilderness*

un·sta´ble *adj.* lacking firmness or durability; easily influenced; emotionally unsettled; liable to change —**un·sta´ble·ness** *n.* —**un·sta´bly** *adv.*

un·stead´y *adj.* not steady; liable to move or sway; fluctuating; unreliable —**un·stead´i·ly** *adv.* —**un·stead´i·ness** *n.*

un·struc´tured *adj.* loosely organized

un·strung´ *adj.* having string removed, as of beads, etc.; emotionally upset

un·sub·stan´tial *adj.* lacking substance or strength; having no valid basis in fact; fanciful **—un·sub·stan·ti·al´i·ty** *n.* **—un·sub·stan´tial·ly** *adv.*

un·suit´a·ble *adj.* inappropriate; unfitting **—un·suit·a·bil´i·ty, un·suit´a·ble·ness** *n.* **—un·suit´a·bly** *adv.*

un·sung´ *adj.* not honored or celebrated; overlooked, as *an unsung hero*

un·tan´gle *vt.* to free from snarls; to clear up, as a confusing situation

un·taught´ *adj.* lacking instruction or knowledge; learned or known without instruction

un·ten´a·ble *adj.* impossible to defend, save, preserve, etc. **—un·ten·a·bil´i·ty, un·ten´a·ble·ness** *n.*

un·think´ing *adj.* lacking thoughtfulness, care, or attention **—un·think´ing·ly** *adv.* **—un·think´ing·ness** *n.*

un·ti´dy *adj.* messy; disorderly **—un·ti´di·ly** *adv.* **—un·ti´di·ness** *n.*

un·tie´ *vt.* to free from that which binds or restrains **—vi.** to loosen or undo

un·til´ *prep.* up to the time of **—conj.** to the time when; to the place or degree that

un·time´ly *adj.* coming before; not at the proper time; premature or inopportune **—adv.** before time; inopportunely **—un·time´li·ness** *n.*

un·told´ *adj.* not revealed; too great to be counted or measured

un·touch´a·ble *adj.* out of reach; beyond culpability or blame; forbidden; unpleasant or dangerous to touch **—un·touch·a·bil´i·ty** *n.* **—un·touch´a·bly** *adv.*

un·true´ *adj.* false or incorrect; disloyal; not conforming to standard: not even, level, etc.

un·truth´ful *adj.* not telling the truth; inconsistent with the truth **—un·truth´ful·ly** *adv.* **—un·truth´ful·ness** *n.*

un·tu´tored *adj.* not educated

un·u´su·al *adj.* odd, rare, or extraordinary **—un·u´su·al·ly** *adv.* **—un·u´su·al·ness** *n.*

un·ut´ter·a·ble *adj.* too great, profound, etc. to be expressed in words **—un·ut´ter·a·ble·ness** *n.* **—un·ut´ter·a·bly** *adv.*

un·var´nished *adj.* not coated with varnish; not embellished or adorned: *the unvarnished truth*

un·veil´ *vt.* to remove the covering from; to disclose to view; to reveal **—vi.** to remove one's veil

un·war´rant·a·ble *adj.* that cannot be justified or excused; indefensible **—un·war´rant·a·bly** *adv.*

un·war´rant·ed *adj.* without justification

un·war´y *adj.* careless or incautious **—un·war´i·ly** *adv.* **—un·war´i·ness** *n.*

un·whole´some *adj.* detrimental to physical or mental health; unhealthy in appearance **—un·whole´some·ly** *adv.* **—un·whole´some·ness** *n.*

un·wield´y *adj.* difficult to move or control **—un·wield´i·ness** *n.*

un·will´ing *adj.* reluctant; done, said, granted, etc. with reluctance **—un·will´ing·ly** *adv.* **—un·will´ing·ness** *n.*

un·wind´ *vt.* to disentangle **—vi.** to become disentangled; to relax

un·wise´ *adj.* showing a lack of wisdom or good sense **—un·wise´ly** *adv.*

un·wit´ting *adj.* having no knowledge; not intentional **—un·wit´ting·ly** *adv.*

un·wor´thy *adj.* not deserving; not befitting or becoming **—un·wor´thi·ly** *adv.* **—un·wor´thi·ness** *n.*

un·writ´ten *adj.* based on tradition,

as *an unwritten law*; understood, as an agreement or arrangement between friends

up *adv.* toward a higher place; in or on a higher place; to or at that which is or is deemed to be higher —*adj.* moving or directed upward; at or to a high level, condition, etc. —*prep.* toward or at a higher point; to or at a point farther above or along —*n.* an ascent; a state of prosperity

up′beat *n.* an unaccented beat in music —*adj.* optimistic; confident

up′braid *vt.* to reproach

up′end′ *vt.*, *vi.* to stand on end; to overturn

up′grade *n.* an upward slope —*vt.* to modernize or improve as in value, performance, etc.

up·heav′al *n.* a violent change, as in the established social order

up·hold′ *vt.* to keep from falling or sinking; to aid, encourage, etc.

up·hol′ster *vt.* to fit with coverings, cushions, etc. —**up·hol′ster·er** *n.*

up·hol′ster·y *n.* the covering or repairing of furniture; material for covering furniture

up′keep *n.* the act, state, or cost of maintaining in good condition

up·lift′ *vt.* to elevate; to put on a higher plane mentally, morally, culturally, etc. —**up′lift** *n.* the act of raising; elevation to a higher plane; a social movement aiming to improve

up′per *adj.* higher, as in position, rank, authority, etc. —*n.* something that is above another

upper hand an advantage

up′per·most *adj.* highest in rank, authority, etc.; foremost —*adv.*

up′right *adj.* erect; righteous —*n.* the state of being erect; something erect —*adv.* in an upright or vertical position —**up′right·ly** *adv.* —**up′right·ness** *n.*

up·ris·ing *n.* a revolt or insurrection; an upward slope

up′roar *n.* a state of confusion, disturbance, excitement, etc.

up·roar′i·ous *adj.* accompanied by a commotion; tumultuous; loud and boisterous; provoking laughter —**up·roar′i·ous·ly** *adv.* —**up·roar′i·ous·ness** *n.*

up′root *vt.* to tear up by the roots; to destroy utterly; to leave

up·set′ *vt.* to overturn; to throw into confusion or disorder; to disconcert or disquiet; to defeat, especially to best a favored opponent —**up·set′**, **up′set** *adj.* overturned; disturbed —**up′set** *n.* the act of overturning; a physical or emotional disorder; defeat of a favored opponent —**up·set′ter** *n.* —**up·set′ting·ly** *adv.*

up′shot *n.* outcome or result

up′side *n.* the upper part; an advantage; an upward trend, as in business

up·stand′ing *adj.* honest or straightforward; upright; placed erect —**up·stand′ing·ness** *n.*

up′start *n.* one who attains sudden power, importance, etc.

up′swing *n.* a swinging upward; an increase or improvement, as in business climate

up·tight′ *adj.* anxious or nervous; angry; conventional or conservative —**up′tight′ness** *n.*

up′ward *adv.* in or toward a higher place; in the upper parts; toward a better condition —*adj.* directed toward or located in a higher place —**upward mobility** the opportunity or ability to improve one's income, status, etc. —**up′ward·ly** *adv.* —**up′wards** *adv.*

ur′ban *adj.* pertaining to a city or city life; living or located in a city —**ur′ban·ite** *n.*

ur·bane′ *adj.* refined; suave —**ur·bane′ly** *adv.* —**ur·bane′ness** *n.* —**ur·ban·i·ty** *n.*

ur'ban·ism *n.* life in a city; the study of city life —**ur'ban·ist** *n.* —**ur'ban·is'tic** *adj.*

ur'ban·ize *vt.* to cause to assume the characteristics of a city; to cause to adopt an urban life style

ur·ban·ol'o·gy *n.* the study of cities and their problems —**ur·ban·ol'o·gist** *n.*

urban renewal a program for revitalizing cities

urban sprawl the spread of population, shopping centers, etc. into rural or undeveloped areas

u·re'mi·a *n.* a toxic condition caused by the presence in the blood of substances ordinarily excreted by the kidneys —**u·re'mic** *adj.*

urge *vt.* to drive or force forward; to entreat earnestly —*vi.* to present arguments, claims, etc. —*n.* a strong impulse; the act of urging

ur'gent *adj.* requiring prompt action; insistent —**ur'gen·cy** *n.* —**ur'gent·ly** *adv.*

u·ri·nal'y·sis *n.* chemical analysis of the urine

u·ri·nate *vi.* to pass urine —**u·ri·na'tion** *n.*

u'rine *n.* fluid filtered by the kidneys and passed off as waste —**u'ri·nar·y** *adj.*

urn *n.* a footed receptacle

u·rol'o·gy *n.* the study of the diseases, treatment, etc. of the urinary system —**u·ro·log'ic, u·ro·log'i·cal** *adj.* —**urol'o·gist** *n.*

us'a·ble, use'a·ble *adj.* that can be used; that may be useful —**us'a·ble·ness** *n.* —**us'a·bly** *adv.*

us'age *n.* the act or manner of using; customary or habitual practice; the accepted manner of using words

use *vt.* to put into service; to take advantage of —*n.* the act of using or the state of being used; function; advantage or usefulness; the purpose for which something is used —**us'er** *n.*

use'ful *adj.* serviceable; helpful —**use'ful·ly** *adv.* —**use'ful·ness** *n.*

use'less *adj.* having no use; serving no function —**use'less·ly** *adv.* —**use'less·ness** *n.*

ush'er *n.* one who escorts theater patrons to their seats; an official doorkeeper; a male attendant in a wedding party —*vi., vt.* to serve as an usher

u'su·al *adj.* customary or common —**u'su·al·ly** *adv.* —**u'su·al·ness** *n.*

u·su'ri·ous *adj.* practicing usury; of the nature of or pertaining to usury —**u·su'ri·ous·ly** *adv.* —**u·su'ri·ous·ness** *n.*

u·surp' *vt.* to seize without authority; to take possession by force —**u·sur·pa'tion** *n.* —**u·surp'er** *n.*

u'su·ry *n.* lending money at excessive or unlawful interest rates; excessive or unlawful interest —**u'su·rer** *n.*

uten'sil *n.* an implement that serves a useful purpose

u'tile *adj.* useful

u·til'i·ty *n.* fitness for a practical purpose

u'ti·lize *vt.* to make use of —**u'ti·li·za'tion** *n.* —**u'ti·liz·er** *n.*

ut'most *adj.* of the highest or greatest degree; being at the furthest limit; extreme —*n.* the most or best possible

ut'ter *vt.* to say, express, give out, or send forth; to put in circulation —*adj.* complete; unqualified —**ut'ter·er** *n.* —**ut'ter·ly** *adv.*

ut'ter·ance *n.* a manner of speaking; a thing uttered

ut'ter·most *adj., n.* utmost

v, V twenty-second letter of the English alphabet; in Roman characters, the symbol for 5

va'cant *adj.* containing nothing; empty; not being used; having no incumbent, officer, etc., as of a

post or office —**va´can·cy** *n.* —
va´cant·ly *adv.* —**va´cant·ness** *n.*

va´cate *vt.* to make vacant; to set
aside, as a ruling —*vi.* to leave an
office, dwelling, etc.

va·ca´tion (*US*) *n.* time away from
work for recreation or rest; a holiday —*vi.* to take a holiday —
va·ca´tion·er, va·ca´tion·ist *n.*

vac´ci·nate *vt.* to innoculate as a
preventive measure —**vac·ci·na´**
tion *n.* —**vac´ci·na·tor** *n.*

vac·cine´ *n.* a preparation used to
provide immunity

vac´il·iate *vi.* to waver; to be irresolute —**vac·il·la´tion** *n.* —**vac´il·la·**
tor *n.* —**vac´il·la·to·ry** *adj.*

va·cu´i·ty *n.* emptiness; vacant
space; a lack of intelligence;
something inane or stupid

vac´u·ous *adj.* empty; lacking intelligence; lacking substance; devoid of
meaning or expression: *a vacuous
stare* —**vac´u·ous·ly** *adv.* —**vac´u·**
ous·ness *n.*

vac´u·um *n.* a space nearly devoid of
matter; a reduction of pressure
below that of the surrounding atmosphere

vag´a·bond *n.* one who wanders
without visible means of support;
a shiftless, irresponsible person —
adj. wandering; aimless; irresponsible —**vag´a·bond·age** *n.*

va´gar·y *n.* a wild fancy or extravagant notion

va´grant *n.* one without an established home or job; a tramp —*adj.*
wandering aimlessly; wayward —
va´gran·cy *n.* —**va´grant·ly** *adv.*

vague *n.* lacking definition; indistinct; not clearly stated —**vague´ly**
adv. —**vague´ness** *n.*

vain *adj.* showing excessive pride in
oneself; unproductive or useless —
in vain to no purpose —**vain´ly**
adv. —**vain´ness** *n.*

vain´glo·ry *n.* excessive vanity; ostentation —**vain·glo´ri·ous** *adj.*

—**vain·glo´ri·ous·ly** *adv.* —**vain·**
glo´ri·ous·ness *n.*

val´ance (*US*) *n.* decorative drapery
hanging from the tester of a bed-
stead or across the top of a window; a decorative panel that serves
to cover the fixtures along the top
of a window

vale *n.* a valley

val·e·dic´tion *n.* a farewell

val·e·dic·to´ri·an *n.* a student selected to give the farewell address
at a graduation ceremony

val·e·dic´to·ry *adj.* of a leave–taking
—*n.* a parting address

va´lence *n.* in chemistry, the capacity of an atom or radical to combine with another atom or radical

val´et *n.* a man's personal servant; a
hotel employee who performs personal services for guests, such as
cleaning and pressing clothes —
vt., vi. to serve as a valet

val·e·tu·di·nar´i·an *n.* a chronic
invalid —*adj.* infirm or ailing;
overly concerned about one's
health —**val·e·tu·di·nar´i·an·ism**
n. —**val·e·tu´di·nar·y** *adj.*

val´iant *adj.* strong and courageous;
performed with valor —**val´iance,
val´ian·cy** *n.* —**val´iant·ly** *adv.*

val´id *adj.* based on facts or evidence; well–founded; effective: *a
valid system*; legally binding —**va·**
lid´i·ty, val´id·ness *n.* —**val´id·ly**
adv.

val´i·date *vt.* to confirm as true; to
declare to be legally binding; to
mark or stamp so as to give sanction or make official —**val·i·da´**
tion *n.*

va·lise´ *n.* a traveling bag

val´ley *n.* an area drained by a river;
low land lying between mountains
or hills; a hollow

val´or *n.* remarkable courage; bravery —**val´or·ous** *adj.* —**val´or·ous·**
ly *adv.*

val´u·a·ble *adj.* having significant

worth or value; costly —**val´u·a· bles** n. expensive or treasured articles, such as jewelry —**val´u·a· ble·ness** n. —**val´u·a·bly** adv.

val·u·a´tion n. an estimate of worth; an estimated value —**val·u·a´tion· al** adj. —**val´u·a·tor** n.

val´ue n. the worth of a thing; something regarded as desirable or worthy; market price; a bargain; a number represented by a symbol; the relative lightness or darkness of a color — vt. to assess or appraise; to regard highly; to consider relatively important: *the value of good health* —**val´u·er** n.

val´ued adj. hightly esteemed, as *a valued friend*; having a specific worth: *valued at ten dollars*

val´ue·less adj. worthless

valve n. a device that controls the movement or flow of a fluid —**val´ vu·lar** adj.

vam´pire n. in folklore, a reanimated corpse that feeds on human blood; a person who preys on those of the opposite sex; a bat that feeds on the blood of mammals, also called a *vampire bat* —**vam·pir´ic, vam´ pir·ish** adj. —**vam´pir·ism** n.

van n. a large, enclosed wagon or truck used to transport goods; (Brit.) a railroad car used to transport freight or baggage; (Brit.) a caravan; (US) a motor vehicle somewhat like a small bus, designed to transport passengers

van´dal·ism n. the willful defacement or destruction of property — **van´dal** n. —**van·dal·is´tic** adj.

van´dal·ize vt. to willfully deface or destroy the property of others — **van·dal·i·za´tion** n.

vane n. a thin plate, pivoted on a rod, to indicate wind direction; an arm or plate, as of a windmill, propeller, etc.

van´guard n. the forward part of an advancing army; the foremost

position; leaders of a movement, trend, etc.

va·nil´la n. a climbing orchid of tropical America; flavoring extracted from the seed capsule of the orchid; a vanilla flavoring made synthetically —**va·nil´lic** adj.

van´ish vi. to disappear; to pass out of existence —**van´ish·ing·ly** adv. —**van´ish·ment** n.

van´i·ty n. excessive pride in one's talents, looks, etc.; something worthless or futile; a dressing table —**vanity case** a traveling case for cosmetics, etc.

van´quish vt. to defeat in battle; to suppress, or overcome, as fear — **van´quish·a·ble** adv. —**van´quish· er** n. —**van´quish·ment** n.

van´tage n. superiority or advantage; a position or condition that offers an advantage; a position that affords an overall view

vap´id adj. flat or dull; lacking flavor or attraction —**va·pid´i·ty, vap´id· ness** n. —**vap´id·ly** adv.

va´por n. moisture in the air; any cloudy substance; something insubstantial and fleeting —vt. to vaporize —vi. to emit or pass off in vapor

va´por·ize vt., vi. to convert or be converted into vapor —**va´por·iz· a·ble** adj. —**va·por·iza´tion** n.

va´por·ous adj. misty, like a vapor; emitting or forming vapor; whimsical —**va´por·ous·ly** adv. —**va´por· ous·ness** n.

va´por·ware n. computer software that is marketed before it is complete or ready for sale

var´i·a·ble adj. having the capacity to change; tending or likely to change; of no fixed size, amount, etc. —n. something liable or able to change —**var·i·a·bil´i·ty, var´i· a·ble·ness** n. —**var´i·a·bly** adv.

var´i·ance n. a discrepancy or difference; license or permission to do something contrary to local custom or ordinance

var'i·ant *adj.* differing, as from a standard or type —*n.* something that differs in form, as an alternate spelling or pronunciation

var·i·a'tion *n.* a difference or modification; the extent to which a thing differs; something that differs from others of the same type —**var·i·a'tion·al** *adj.*

var'ied *adj.* consisting of diverse sorts; modified or altered —**var'ied·ly** *adv.*

var'i·e·gat·ed *adj.* varied in color

va·ri'e·tal *adj.* describing a variety —*n.* a wine named for the variety of grape from which it is made —**va·ri'e·tal·ly** *adv.*

va·ri'e·ty *n.* diversity or difference; sort or kind: *a variety of mustard*; a collection or assortment

var'i·ous *adj.* different from one another; several; separate, identifiable; multifaceted —**var'i·ous·ly** *adv.* —**var'i·ous·ness** *n.*

var'nish *n.* a finish for furniture, etc.; outward show —*vt.* to coat with varnish; to hide or gloss over: *varnish the truth* —**var'nish·er** *n.*

var'y *vt.* to change or modify; to diversify —*vi.* to become changed; to deviate —**var'y·ing·ly** *adv.*

vas'cu·lar *adj.* pertaining to body vessels or ducts

vast *adj.* immense; great in quantity, importance, etc.; extensive —**vast'ly** *adv.* —**vast'ness** *n.*

vat *n.* a large open vessel or tub

vaude'ville *n.* theatrical entertainment consisting of short sketches, songs, dances, etc.; a variety show —**vaude·vil'lian** *n.*

vault *n.* an arched roof or ceiling; a room or compartment for storage or safekeeping; a burial chamber —*vi.*, *vt.* to leap

vault'ing *n.* the construction that

forms a vault

vaunt *vi.*, *vt.* to boast —*n.* a brag or boast —**vaunt'ing·ly** *adv.*

veer *vi.* to turn; to shift as from an opinion, belief, etc. —*vt.* to change the direction of

veg'an *n.* a vegetarian whose diet is limited to food derived from plants

veg'e·ta·ble *n.* a plant cultivated for food; the edible part of a plant —*adj.* relating to or derived from plants: *vegetable oil*; made from edible plants: *vegetable soup*

veg'e·tal *adj.* pertaining to plants or vegetables

veg·e·tar'i·an *n.* one who does not eat meat; one who subscribes to any of a variety of diets that exclude meat and sometimes seafood or animal products such as eggs and milk —*adj.* relating to vegetarians or vegetarianism; consisting only of vegetables, grains, fruit, nuts, and seeds —**veg·e·tar'i·an·ism** *n.*

veg'e·tate *vi.* to grow, as a plant; to exist in a monotonous, passive state

veg·e·ta'tion *n.* plant life —**veg'e·ta·tive** *adj.*

ve'he·ment *adj.* marked by strong feeling or passion; acting with great force —**ve'he·mence** *n.* —**ve'he·ment·ly** *adv.*

ve'hi·cle *n.* any conveyance for transporting people or freight —**ve·hic'u·lar** *adj.*

veil *n.* a thin fabric for covering the face; anything that conceals or covers —*vt.* to cover, conceal, disguise, etc.

veil'ing *n.* a covering, such as a veil; material for making a veil

vein *n.* a tubular vessel that conveys blood; a branching structure such as the ribs in a leaf or the wing of an insect; a colored streak as in wood, stone, etc.; a distinctive tendency or disposition —*vt.* to extend or mark throughout like veins —**veined** *adj.*

veld, veldt *n.* a South African plain

vel´lum *n.* fine parchment

ve·loc´i·pede *n.* an early form of the bicycle with pedals attached to a large front wheel

ve·loc´i·ty *n.* speed; quickness of motion

ve·lour´ *n.* a soft fabric having a short, thick pile

vel´vet *n.* a fabric with a short, smooth pile on one side and a plain underside —*adj.* made of velvet; smooth and soft to the touch —**vel´vet·y** *adj.*

ve´nal *adj.* open to or characterized by corruption or bribery —**ve·nal´i·ty** *n.* —**ve´nal·ly** *adv.*

vend *vt.* to sell as an occupation; to sell through a vending machine — *vi.* to be employed in selling — **vend´er, ven´dor** *n.*

ven·det´ta *n.* a private feud in which the relatives of a slain or wronged person seek revenge; any bitter quarrel

vend´i·ble, vend´a·ble *adj.* salable; marketable —*n.* something for sale —**vend·i·bil´i·ty** *n.* —**vend´i·bly** *adv.*

ve·neer´ *n.* a thin layer; surface or show, as *a veneer of civility* —*vt.* to cover with veneer; to conceal, as something disagreeable or coarse —**ve·neer´er** *n.*

ven´er·a·ble *adj.* worthy of respect because of dignity, age, etc. —**ven·er·a·bil´i·ty, ven´er·a·ble·ness** *n.* —**ven´er·a·bly** *adv.*

ven´er·ate *vt.* to regard with respect or awe —**ven·er·a´tion** *n.* —**ven´er·a·tor** *n.*

ve·ne´re·al *adj.* pertaining to or proceeding from sexual intercourse

ve·ne·re·ol´o·gy *n.* the study of sexually transmitted disease —**ve·ne·re·o·log´i·cal** *adj.* —**ve·ne·re·ol´o·gist** *n.*

ven´geance *n.* infliction of a deserved penalty; retribution —**with a vengeance** with remarkable intensity or force; in the extreme

venge´ful *adj.* seeking revenge; unforgiving —**venge´ful·ly** *adv.* —**venge´ful·ness** *n.*

ve´ni·al *adj.* slight or trivial, as a fault —**ve·ni·al´i·ty** *n.* —**ve´ni·al·ly** *adv.*

ven´i·son *n.* the flesh of a wild animal, especially of a deer, used for food

ven´om *n.* poison secreted by certain reptiles, insects, etc.; ill will —**ven´om·ous** *adj.* —**ven´om·ous·ly** *adv.* —**ven´om·ous·ness** *n.*

ve´nous *adj.* pertaining to or carried by veins; designating blood returning to the heart and lungs; having veins —**ve´nous·ly** *adv.* —**ve´nous·ness** *n.*

vent *n.* an outlet or opening; a slit in a garment —*vt.* to give expression to; to permit escape, as a gas; to make a vent in

ven·ti·la´tion *n.* the free circulation of air; exposure to examination and discussion; oxygenation, as of blood —**ven´ti·late** *vt.* —**ven´ti·la·tive** *adj.*

ven´tral *adj.* toward or at the abdomen; situated near the abdomen —**ven´tral·ly** *adv.*

ven´tri·cle *n.* a small cavity in the body, such as the lower chambers of the heart or interconnecting cavities in the brain —**ven·tric´u·lar** *adj.*

ven·tril´o·quism, ven·tril´o·quy *n.* the art of speaking so that the sound seems to come from another source —**ven·tri·lo´qui·al, ven·tril´o·quis´tic** *adj.* —**ven·tri·lo´qui·al·ly** *adv.* —**ven·tril´o·quist** *n.* —**ven·tril´o·quize** *vi., vt.*

ven´ture *vt.* to expose to risk —*vi.* to take risk —*n.* an undertaking marked by risk; that which is risked, as *venture capital* **—ven´tur·er** *n.*

venture capital investment in a new, untried business; an investment that is at risk

ven´ture·some *adj.* bold or daring; involving risk **—ven´ture·some·ly** *adv.* **—ven´ture·some·ness** *n.*

ven´tur·ous *adj.* adventurous; risky **—ven´tur·ous·ly** *adv.* **—ven´tur·ous·ness** *n.*

ven´ue *n.* the place or setting of an action or event; in law, a place where a crime has been committed, where a cause of action arises, or where a trial must be held

ve·ra´cious *adj.* truthful; accurate **—ve·ra´cious·ly** *adv.* **—ve·ra´cious·ness** *n.*

ve·rac´i·ty *n.* honesty; accuracy

ve·ran´da *n.* an open porch along the side of a building

verb *n.* a word that expresses action, existence, or occurence

ver´bal *adj.* pertaining to words: *a verbal image*; concerned with words rather than ideas: literal — *n.* in grammar, a noun directly derived from a verb **—ver´bal·ly** *adv.*

ver´bal·ist *n.* one skilled in the use of words; one more concerned with words than with facts or ideas **— ver·bal·is´tic** *adj.*

ver´bal·ize *vt.* to express in words — *vi.* to speak or write in a wordy fashion **—ver·bal·i·za´tion** *n.* **— ver´bal·iz·er** *n.*

ver·ba´tim *adj., adv.* exactly, word for word

ver´bi·age *n.* the use of too many words; a manner of verbal expression

ver·bose´ *adj.* overly wordy; repetitive or redundant; containing too many or unnecessary words **—ver·bose´ly** *adv.* **—ver·bose´ness, ver·bos´i·ty** *n.*

ver´dant *adj.* covered with green vegetation: *the verdant country-*

side; inexperienced **—ver´dan·cy** *n.* **—ver´dant·ly** *adv.*

ver´dict *n.* the decision of a jury; a conclusion or opinion

ver´dure *n.* the fresh greenness of growing vegetation; lush vegetation **—ver´dur·ous** *adj.* **—ver´dur·ous·ness** *n.*

verge *n.* the extreme edge; a boundary **—vi.** to be contiguous or adjacent; to approach: *familiarity verging on insolence* **—vt.** to be in the process of change: *wilderness verging into farmland*

ver·i·fi·ca´tion *n.* a proof or confirmation

ver´i·fi·a·ble *adj.* that can be confirmed or proven **—ver·i·fi·a·bil´i·ty** *n.* **—ver´i·fi·a·bly** *adv.*

ver´i·fy *vt.* to prove; to test the accuracy or truth of

ver·i·si·mil´i·tude *n.* the appearance of truth or reality; that which has only the appearance of truth or reality: a likeness

ver´i·ta·ble *adj.* genuine or real; actual **—ver´i·ta·ble·ness** *n.* **— ver´i·ta·bly** *adv.*

ver´i·ty *n.* truth; the quality of being true or real

ver·mi·cel´li *n.* a slender, wormlike pasta

ver´mi·form *adj.* shaped like a worm

ver´min *n.* destructive small animals or parasitic insects; a repulsive person **—ver´min·ous** *adj.* **—ver´min·ous·ly** *adv.*

ver·mouth´ *n.* a fortified wine

ver·nac´u·lar *n.* the language peculiar to a locality; common daily speech; the specialized vocabulary of a trade or profession **—adj.** of a native tongue; spoken or written in a particular language or argot; relating to a locality **—ver·nac´u·lar·ism** *n.* **—ver·nac´u·lar·ly** *adv.*

ver´nal *adj.* appropriate to spring; fresh or youthful **—ver´nal·ly** *adv.*

ver´sa·tile *adj.* having many talents;

having many uses —**ver´sa·tile·ly** *adv.* —**ver·sa·til´i·ty** *n.*

verse *n.* poetry, as distinguished from prose; a line or group of lines, as of poetry, scripture, etc.

versed *adj.* skilled; knowledgeable

ver´si·fy *vt.* to turn into poetry —*vi.* to write poetry —**ver·si·fi·ca´tion** *n.* —**ver´si·fi·er** *n.*

ver´sion *n.* a translation or rendition; an adaptation, as *the film version of a novel*; a personal account or view —**ver´sion·al** *adj.*

ver´so *n.* a left-handed page; the reverse of a coin or medallion

ver´sus *prep.* against; considered as the alternative of

ver´te·bra *n.*, *pl.* **ver´te·brae** a bone of the spinal column —**ver´te·bral** *adj.*

ver´te·brate *adj.* having a backbone; pertaining to or characteristic of creatures that have a backbone

ver´ti·cal *adj.* upright or erect; directly overhead; situated at right angles to the horizon —*n.* something upright —**vertical integration** a business structure that develops or grows by adding to its level of processing from a raw material to a finished product —**ver´ti·cal´i·ty**, **ver´ti·cal·ness** *n.* —**ver´ti·cal·ly** *adv.*

ver·tig´i·nous *adj.* affected by vertigo; spinning —**ver·tig´i·nous·ly** *adv.* —**ver·tig´i·nous·ness** *n.*

ver´ti·go *n.* dizziness; disorientation; a disorder in which, subject to certain stimuli, a person or his surroundings seem to whirl about

verve *n.* energy; enthusiasm

ver´y *adv.* to a high degree; exactly —*adj.* suitable; identical; the thing itself: *the very point I wanted to make*

ves´i·cle *n.* a small cavity or cyst; a blister —**ve·sic´u·lar** *adj.* —**ve·sic´u·late** *vi.*, *vt.* —**ve·sic·u·la´tion** *n.*

ves´pers *n.* evening worship service

ves´sel *n.* an open container capable of holding liquid; a physical process that holds or carries a fluid: *a blood vessel*; a ship or aircraft

vest *n.* (*Brit.*) an undergarment worn under a shirt; (*US*) a short, sleeveless outer garment —*vt.* to confer, as ownership or authority —*vi.* to become legally vested

vest´ed *adj.* inalienable or absolute, as *a vested right*

ves´ti·bule *n.* a small entryway or antechamber; an enclosed passageway between cars of a passenger train —**ves·tib´u·lar** *adj.*

ves´tige *n.* a discernible trace; a remnant of an organ that is no longer functional —**ves·tig´ial** *adj.* —**ves·tig´ial·ly** *adv.*

vest´ment *n.* an article of clothing; a ritual garment

ves´try *n.* a room in a church used for storing vestments, conducting meetings, etc.; a church's administrative body

ves´try·man *n.* a member of a church vestry

vet´er·an *n.* someone long experienced, as in the military or an occupation

vet´er·i·nar·y *adj.* of the prevention and treatment of diseases and injuries of animals: *veterinary medicine* —**vet·er·i·nar´i·an** *n.*

ve´to *vt.* to refuse, as approval or consent —*n.* the right to cancel, prohibit, or postpone; the exercising of such a right —**ve´to·er** *n.*

vex *vt.* to annoy; to trouble or afflict; to baffle or confuse —**vex·a´tion** *n.* —**vex´ed·ly** *adv.* —**vex´ed·ness** *n.*

vexed *adj.* annoyed or disturbed; baffled

vex·a´tious *adj.* annoying; disturbing —**vex·a´tious·ly** *adv.* —**vex·a´tious·ness** *n.*

vi´a *prep.* by way of; by means of

vi´a·ble *adj.* capable of living and developing normally; workable or practicable, as a plan **—vi·a·bil´i·ty** *n.* **—vi´a·bly** *adv.*

vi´a·duct *n.* a bridgelike structure of arched masonry that carries a road, pipeline, etc.

vi´al *n.* a small bottle

vi´and *n.* an article of food

vi´brant *adj.* vigorous or enthusiastic: *a vibrant personality*; energetic, powerful: *vibrant color* **—vi´bran·cy** *n.* **—vi´brant·ly** *adv.*

vi´brate *vi., vt.* to move or cause to move back and forth rapidly **—vi·bra´tion** *n.* **—vi·bra´tion·al**, **vi´bra·to·ry** *adj.* **—vi´bra·tor** *n.*

vi·bra´to *n.* a cyclical variation in the pitch of a musical tone

vic´ar *n.* one authorized to perform in the stead of another; a church representative

vic´ar·age *n.* the office of a vicar; a vicar's residence

vi·car´i·ous *adj.* suffered or done in place of another; identifying with the experience of another; delegated **—vi·car´i·ous·ly** *adv.* **—vi·car´i·ous·ness** *n.*

vice *n.* moral depravity; an immoral action, trait, etc.; a habitual failing or shortcoming; (*Brit.*) a clamping device, as used to hold material for woodworking

vice´roy *n.* one who rules by the authority of a sovereign

vi·chys·soise´ *n.* a cream soup of potato and leeks, usually served cold

vi·cin´i·ty *n.* nearness; proximity; a nearby area, region, etc.

vi´cious *adj.* dangerous; marked by evil intent: *a vicious rumor*; depraved or immoral; forceful or intense **—vi´cious·ly** *adv.* **—vi´cious·ness** *n.*

vi·cis´si·tude *n.* a change or alteration **—vi·cis´si·tudes** *pl. n.* irregular changes, as of conditions or fortune **—vi·cis·si·tu´di·nar·y**, **vi·cis·si·tu´di·nous** *adj.*

vic´tim *n.* one harmed in some way, as by injury, disease, fraud, trickery, etc.

vic´tim·ize *vt.* to cause to suffer; to cheat or dupe **—vic·tim·i·za´tion** *n.* **—vic´tim·iz·er** *n.*

vic´tor *n.* one who wins a struggle or contest **—vic´tor**, **vic·to´ri·ous** *adj.* **—vic´to·ry** *n.*

vict´uals *pl. n.* food prepared for consumption

vid´e·o *adj.* pertaining to television; producing a signal convertible into a television picture **—n.** a television image

vid´e·o·con·fer·ence *n.* a meeting between participants at a distance from each other via closed–circuit television

vie *vi.* to put forth effort; to compete in an athletic contest; to contend for superiority: *to vie for position*

view *n.* the act of seeing or examining; range of vision; something seen; one's opinion or belief **—vt** to look at; to examine; to consider; to regard in a certain way **—view´a·ble** *adj.* **—view´er** *n.*

vig´il *n.* an act or period of keeping watch

vig´i·lant *adj.* alert to danger; wary **—vig´i·lance** *n.* **—vig´i·lant·ly** *adv.*

vig·i·lan´te *n.* a member of a vigilance committee; one who advocates preempting the law **—vig·i·lan´tism** *n.*

vi·gnette´ *n.* a picture that shades off gradually into the background; a brief literary sketch; a decorative design, as at the beginning of a book, chapter of a book, etc.

vig´or *n.* energy; vital or natural growth; intensity **—vig´or·ous** *ad* **—vig´or·ous·ly** *adv.* **—vig´or·ous ness** *n.*

vile *adj.* morally base; corrupt loathsome; very bad, as *vile tastin* **—vile´ly** *adv.* **—vile´ness** *n.*

vil´i·fy *vt.* to speak of abusively; to defame —**vil·i·fi·ca´tion** *n.* —**vil´i·fi·er** *n.*

vil´lage *n.* in the US, a residential area smaller than a town but larger than a hamlet; the inhabitants of a village collectively —**vil´lag·er** *n.*

vil´lain *n.* a scoundrel

vil´lain·ous *adj.* wicked; evil —**vil´lain·ous·ly** *adv.* —**vil´lain·y** *n.*

vim *n.* force or vigor; energy

vin´ci·ble *adj.* easily overcome; that can be conquered or defeated —**vin·ci·bil´i·ty** *n.* —**vin´ci·bly** *adv.*

vin´di·cate *vt.* to clear of suspicion; to maintain, as a right or claim; to justify —**vin·di·ca´tion** *n.* —**vin´di·ca·tive, vin´di·ca·to·ry** *adj.* —**vin´di·ca·tor** *n.*

vin·dic´tive *adj.* having a vengeful spirit —**vin·dic´tive·ly** *adv.* —**vin·dic´tive·ness** *n.*

vine *n.* a climbing plant

vin´e·gar *n.* a variously flavored condiment and preservative; ascerbity, as of speech —**vin´e·gar·y** *adj.*

vine´yard *n.* an area devoted to the cultivation of grapes

vin´i·cul·ture *n.* the cultivation of grapes for wine —**vin´i·cul´tur·al** *adj.* —**vin´i·cul´tur·ist** *n.*

vin´i·fy *vt.* to convert into wine —**vin·i·fi·ca´tion** *n.*

vi´nous *adj.* pertaining to or characteristic of wine

vin´tage *n.* the yield of grapes or wine for one season; the region and year in which a wine is produced —*adj.* of a fine wine; of a good year for wine

vint´ner *n.* a wine maker; a wine merchant

vi´nyl *n.* a type of plastic

vi·o´la *n.* a musical instrument similar to a violin, slightly larger and with a deeper tone

vi´ol·a·ble *adj.* that can be or is likely to be violated —**vi·o·la·bil´i·ty, vi´ol·a·ble·ness** *n.* —**vi´ol·a·bly** *adv.*

vi´o·late *vt.* to break, as a law, agreement, etc.; to ravish or rape; to offend —**vi·o·la´tion** *n.* —**vi´o·la·tive** *adj.* —**vi´o·la·tor** *n.*

vi´o·lence *n.* physical force used to injure, damage, or destroy; intensity, severity; injury or damage, as by distortion or alteration

vi´o·lent *adj.* marked by great physical force or intense emotional excitement; characterized by intensity of any kind —**vi´o·lent·ly** *adv.*

vi´o·let *n.* a bluish–purple color; a plant or herb bearing violet–colored flowers

vi·o·lin´ *n.* a stringed instrument of the highest register, usually played with a bow; a violinist

vi·o·lin´ist *n.* one who plays the violin

vi´ol·ist *n.* one who plays the viola

vi·o·lon·cel´lo *n.* a cello —**vi·o·lon·cel´list** *n.*

vi´per *n.* a kind of snake; a treacherous or spiteful person —**vi´per·ine** *adj.*

vi´per·ish *adj.* malicious or spiteful

vi´per·ous *adj.* pertaining to vipers or snakes; treacherous or spiteful —**vi´per·ous·ly** *adv.*

vi·ra´go *n.* an ill–tempered woman; a shrew

vi´ral *adj.* pertaining to or caused by a virus —**vi´ral·ly** *adv.*

vi·res´cent *adj.* greenish —**vi·res´cence** *n.*

vir´gin *n.* one who has never had sexual intercourse; an unmarried woman —*adj.* being a virgin; pertaining or suited to a virgin; uncorrupted, pure; not hitherto used or processed, as *virgin wool, virgin forest* —**vir´gin·al** *adj.* —**vir´gin·al·ly** *adv.* —**vir·gin´i·ty** *n.*

vir´gule *n.* a diagonal mark (/)

vir·i·des´cent *adj.* greenish; turning green —**vir·i·des´cence** *n.*

vir´ile *adj.* having the vigor or strength of manhood; able to procreate —**vi·ril´i·ty** *n.*

vi·rol´o·gy *n.* the study of viruses — **vi·rol´o·gist** *n.*

vir´tu·al *adj.* existing in essence or effect, but not in actual form —**vir·tu·al´i·ty** *n.* —**vir´tu·al·ly** *adv.*

vir´tue *n.* moral excellence; any admirable quality

vir·tu·os´i·ty *n.* technical mastery, as of a musical instrument

vir·tu·o´so *n.* a master of technique, especially in the arts —*adj.* capable of or displaying extraordinary skill: *a virtuoso violinist*

vir´tu·ous *adj.* righteous; pure and chaste —**vir´tu·ous·ly** *adv.* —**vir´tu·ous·ness** *n.*

vir´u·lent *adj.* extremely harmful; very infectious; full of hatred —**vir´u·lence** *n.* —**vir´u·lent·ly** *adv.*

vi´rus *n.* a parasite capable of reproduction only within living cells; a disease caused by a parasite; any evil influence

vi´sa *n.* official endorsement on a passport that permits the bearer to enter a country

vis´age *n.* appearance; aspect —**vis´aged** *adj.*

vis´cer·a *n.* the internal organs of the body

vis´cer·al *adj.* pertaining to the viscera; instinctive or emotional — **vis´cer·al·ly** *adv.*

vis·cos´i·ty *n.* a property of fluids by which they offer resistance to flow or change

vis´cous *adj.* resistant to flow; of high viscosity —**vis´cous·ly** *adv.* —**vis´cous·ness** *n.*

vise (*US*) *n.* a clamping device, as used to hold material for woodworking —*vt.* to hold or squeeze, as in a vise

vis´i·ble *adj.* capable of being seen;

that can be perceived —**vis·i·bil´i·ty, vis´i·ble·ness** *n.* —**vis´i·bly** *adv.*

vi´sion *n.* the sense of sight; that which is seen; something beautiful; a mental image; foresight; imagination —**vi´sion·al** *adv.*

vi´sion·ar·y *adj.* existing in the imagination; affected by fantasies; speculative; impractical —*n.* one who has visions; one whose plans or projects are impractical or unrealistic —**vi´sion·ar·i·ness** *n.*

vis´it *vt.* to look in on a person out of friendship, to meet in order to conduct business; to go or come to a place; to be a guest of; to inflict upon —*vi.* to pay a call; to stay with temporarily —*n.* a social call; a short stay —**vis´i·tor** *n.*

vis´i·tant *n.* a visitor; a migratory bird

vis·it·a´tion *n.* the act of visiting; an official inspection or examination —**vis·it·a´tion·al** *adj.*

vi´sor *n.* a projection, as on a hat, to shield the eyes

vis´ta *n.* a view; a mental image

vi´su·al *adj.* pertaining to the sense of sight; perceptible by sight; done or perceived only by sight —*n.* pictures, charts, etc. used to enhance a presentation —**vis´u·al·ly** *adv.* —**vis·u·al´i·ty** *n.*

vis´u·al·ize *vt., vi.* to form a mental image; to picture in the mind — **vis·u·al·i·za´tion** *n.* —**vis´u·al·iz·er** *n.*

vi´tal *adj.* pertaining to life; essential to or supporting life; of the utmost importance; dynamic and full of life —**vi´tal·ly** *adv.* —**vi´tal·ness** *n.*

vi´tal·ism *n.* the belief that a living organism is sustained by a vital force independent of all chemical and physical processes —**vi´tal·ist** *n.* —**vi·tal·is´tic** *adj.*

vi·tal´i·ty *n.* the power to live and develop; physical or mental energy

vi´tal·ize *vt.* to endow with life or energy; to make more spirited or energetic —**vi·tal·i·za´tion** *n.*

vi´ta·min *n.* any of a group of naturally occurring organic substances essential to the body's normal health and growth

vi´ti·ate *vt.* to impair the use or value of; to render weak or ineffective; to make legally invalid —**vi·ti·a´tion** *n.* —**vi´ti·a·tor** *n.*

vit´i·cul·ture *n.* the cultivation of grapes —**vit·i·cul´tur·al** *adj.* —**vit´i·cul·tur·ist** *n.*

vit´re·ous *adj.* glassy; obtained from glass; of the vitreous humor —*n.* the vitreous humor —**vit·re·os´i·ty, vit´re·ous·ness** *n.*

vitreous humor the clear jelly–like substance that fills the eyeball

vit´ri·fy *vt., vi.* to change or become changed into a glass or glass–like substance —**vit·ri·fi·a·bil´i·ty** *n.* —**vit´ri·fi·a·ble** *adj.* —**vit·ri·fi·ca´tion** *n.*

vit´ri·ol *n.* a sulfate of metal; sulfuric acid; harshness or bitterness of thought or expression; reproach

vit·ri·ol´ic *adj.* acrimonious; harsh or bitter, as a *vitriolic critique*

vi·tu´per·ate *vt.* to fault abusively; to berate or scold —**vi·tu´per·a·tive** *adj.* —**vi·tu´per·a·tive·ly** *adv.*

vi·tu·per·a´tion *n.* harsh or abusive language; the use of such language —**vi·tu´per·a·tor** *n.*

vi·va´cious *adj.* full of life and spirit —**vi·va´cious·ly** *adv.* —**vi·va´cious·ness, vi·vac´i·ty** *n.*

viv´id *adj.* strong or intense, as of color; suggesting lifelike images; producing a sharp impression on the senses —**viv´id·ly** *adv.* —**viv´id·ness** *n.*

viv´i·fy *vt.* to give life to; to animate; to make more vivid or striking —**viv·i·fi·ca´tion** *n.* —**viv´i·fi·er** *n.*

vi·vip´a·rous *adj.* bringing forth live young that have developed within the mother's body —**viv·i·par´i·ty, vi·vip´a·rous·ness** *n.* —**vi·vip´a·rous·ly** *adv.*

viv·i·sec´tion *n.* cutting or dissection on a living animal —**viv´i·sect** *vt.* —**viv·i·sec´tion·al** *adj.* —**viv·i·sec´tion·ist** *n.*

vix´en *n.* a female fox; a quarrelsome or malevolent woman —**vix´en·ish** *adj.* —**vix´en·ly** *adj., adv.*

vo·cab´u·lar·y *n.* all the words of a language; all the words understood by an individual

vo´cal *adj.* pertaining to the voice; able to speak or utter sounds; speaking freely —**vo´cal·ly** *adv.* —**vo´cal·ness** *n.*

vo´cal·ise (*Brit.*) *vt.* to voice or make vocal —*vi.* to speak or sing

vo´cal·ism *n.* the use of the voice; a particular singing style

vo´cal·ist *n.* a singer; one who sings as a profession —**vo·cal·is´tic** *adj.*

vo´cal·ize (*US*) *vt.* to voice or make vocal —*vi.* to speak or sing —**vo·cal·i·za´tion** *n.* —**vo´cal·iz·er** *n.*

vo·ca´tion *n.* a regular job or profession; a career

vo·ca´tion·al *adj.* pertaining to a job or profession; of training designed to provide specific useful skills or those being trained: *vocational school* —**vo·ca´tion·al·ly** *adv.*

vo·cif´er·ant *adj.* vociferous

vo·cif´er·ate *vt., vi.* to cry out with a loud voice; to protest boisterously —**vo·cif·er·a´tion** *n.* —**vo·cif´er·a·tor** *n.*

vo·cif´er·ous *adj.* characterized by a loud outcry; noisy; clamorous —**vo·cif´er·ous·ly** *adv.* —**vo·cif´er·ous·ness** *n.*

vogue *n.* a fashion or style; popularity —**vogu´ish** *adj.* —**vogu´ish·ly** *adv.* —**vogu´ish·ness** *n.*

voice *n.* sound produced by the vocal organs; the quality of a sound; the right to expression, as of opinion, choice, etc.; the agency by which something is expressed: *our newspaper is the voice of the community* —*vt.* to put into speech; to give expression to —**voiced** *adj.* —**voiced′ness** *n.*

voice′less *adj.* having no voice or vote; having no means of expression —**voice′less·ly** *adv.* —**voice′less·ness** *n.*

void *adj.* containing nothing; completely lacking; having no legal force; useless —**void′a·ble** *adj.* —**void′ance** *n.*

voile *n.* a fine, sheer fabric

vol′a·tile *adj.* evaporating rapidly; prone to change suddenly and sharply; fleeting —**vol′a·tile·ness**, **vo·a·til′i·ty** *n.*

vol′a·til·ize *vi., vt.* to pass off or cause to pass off as vapor; to become or make volatile —**vol′a·til·iz·a·ble** *adj.* —**vo·a·til·i·za′tion** *n.* —**vol′a·til·iz′er** *n.*

vol·can′ic *adj.* pertaining to or produced by a volcano or volcanoes; like a volcano; explosive or violent —**vol·can′i·cal·ly** *adv.* —**vol·can·ic′i·ty** *n.*

vol·ca′no *n.* an opening in the earth from which hot matter is or has been ejected; a mound or mountain formed by ejected material

vol·can·ol′o·gy *n.* the study of volcanoes —**vol·can·o·log′ic**, **vol·can·o·log′i·cal** *adj.* —**vol·can·ol′o·gist** *n.*

vo·li′tion *n.* exercise of the will; willpower; the power to make a choice —**vo·li′tion·al**, **vo·li′tion·ar·y**, **vol′i·tive** *adj.* —**vo·li′tion·al·ly** *adv.*

vol′ley *n.* a simultaneous discharge; a discharge of many things, as bullets, stones, etc. —*vt., vi.* to discharge or be discharged in large numbers

volt *n.* a unit of electric and electromotive potential

volt′age *n.* electromotive force

expressed in volts

volt′me·ter *n.* an instrument for measuring differences of electric potential

vol′u·ble *adj.* having fluency in speaking; talkative —**vo′u·bil′i·ty**, **vol′u·ble·ness** *n.* —**vol′u·bly** *adv.*

vol′ume *n.* a book, especially one that is part of a set; a bound set of periodicals; an amount, as of number, space, sound, etc.; a capacity or space occupied, as of a container or area

vo·lu′mi·nous *adj.* sufficient to fill volumes; large or extensive —**vo·lu·mi·nos′i·ty**, **vo·lu′mi·nous·ness** *n.* —**vo·lu′mi·nous·ly** *adv.*

vol′un·ta·rism *n.* the use of volunteer labor to achieve an end, such as for staffing phones or raising funds; willing participation; the philosophy that free will is fundamental to individual action or experience —**vol′un·ta·rist** *n.* —**vol·un·ta·ris′tic** *adj.*

vol′un·tar·y *adj.* done of one's own free will; acting without constraint; intentional; able to choose or elect: optional; supported by charitable donations of money or time —**vol·un·tar′i·ly** *adv.* —**vol′un·tar·i·ness** *n.*

vol·un·teer′ *n.* an unpaid worker; one who enters into or performs of his own free will —*adj.* pertaining to or composed of volunteers —*vt.* to offer or give voluntarily —*vi.* to enter or offer to enter into a service without pay

vol·un·teer′ism *n.* the practice of being a volunteer or using unpaid volunteer workers, such as in a charitable organization

vo·lup′tu·ar·y *n.* one addicted to luxury and indulgence —*adj.* pertaining to or marked by luxury and extravagance

vo·lup′tu·ous *adj.* pertaining to sensuous or sensual gratification;

suggesting the satisfaction of sensual desire —**vo·lup´tu·ous·ly** *adv.* —**vo·lup´tu·ous·ness** *n.*

vom´it *vi., vt.* to disgorge the contents of the stomach —*n.* matter ejected in vomiting —**vom´it·er** *n.*

voo´doo *n.* a religion characterized by belief in sorcery and the use of charms, etc.; a charm or spell believed to have magical powers —*vt.* to bewitch —*adj.* —**voo´doo·ism** *n.* —**voo´doo·ist** *n.* —**voo·doo·is´ tic** *adj.*

vo·ra´cious *n.* eager, insatiable; eating greedily —**vo·ra´cious·ly** *adv.* —**vo·ra´cious·ness, vo·rac´i· ty** *n.*

vor´tex *n., pl.* **vor´tex·es, vor´ti·ces** a mass of rotating or whirling fluid; something resembling a vortex, as a situation difficult to escape —**vor´ti·cal** *adj.* —**vor´ti· cal·ly** *adv.*

vo·ta·rist, vo·ta·ry *n.* one bound by vows, as a nun or priest; one who is intensely devoted, as a believer or ardent disciple; one devoted to a particular pursuit or study

vote *n.* a formal expression of choice; a ballot or other means of expressing choice; the number of ballots cast; the right to vote; a voter —*vt.* to determine by vote; to cast one's vote for —*vi.* to cast one's vote

vo´tive *adj.* performed in fulfillment of a vow —**vo´tive·ly** *adv.* —**vo´ tive·ness** *n.*

vouch *vi.* to give assurance or guarantee; to support or justify —*vt.* to bear witness to; to declare; to provide or disclose as support or justification

vouch´er *n.* a document that serves to authorize or attest; one who vouches for another

vouch·safe´ *vt.* to permit or grant — *vi.* to condescend or deign

vow *n.* a solemn promise; an emphatic affirmation —*vt.* to promise solemnly; to make a solemn promise or threat —*vi.* to make a vow

voy´age *n.* a long journey —*vi.* to make a voyage —**voy´ag·er** *n.*

vo·yeur´ *n.* one who is sexually gratified by observing sexual objects or acts; one obsessed with the viewing of sensational or sordid events —**vo·yeur´ism** *n.* —**voy· eur·is´tic** *adj.* —**voy·eur·is´ti· cal·ly** *adv.*

vul´can·ize *vt., vi.* to process, as rubber, in order to increase strength and elasticity —**vul·can· i·za´tion** *n.* —**vul´can·iz·er** *n.*

vul´gar *adj.* lacking manners, taste, etc.; offensive or obscene; of or pertaining to the common people; pertaining to a common language or dialect —**vul·gar´i·ty** *n.* —**vul´ gar·ly** *adv.*

vul·gar´i·an *n.* a person of vulgar taste or manners, especially a wealthy person prone to ostentatious display

vul´gar·ism *n.* a word or expression generally considered to be in poor taste

vul´gar·ize *vt.* to make common or coarse; to popularize —**vul´gar·i· za´tion** *n.*

vul´ner·a·ble *adj.* open to attack or injury; open to criticism; susceptible to temptation —**vul·ner·a·bil´ i·ty, vul´ner·a·ble·ness** *n.* —**vul´ ner·a·bly** *adv.*

vul´ture *n.* a large bird that feeds on carrion; someone who preys on others —**vul´tur·ous** *adj.*

vy´ing *adj.* that vies or competes

w, W twenty–third letter of the English alphabet

wack´y, whacky *adj.* extremely irrational; erratic —**wack´i·ly** *adv.* —**wack´i·ness** *n.*

wad *n.* a small, compact mass; a

large amount, especially of a roll of currency: *a wad of cash* —*vt.* to press, roll, fold, etc. into a wad — *vi.* to form into a wad

wad´dle *n.* a clumsy, rocking walk like that of a duck —*vi.* to walk or move awkwardly —**wad´dler** *n.* — **wad´dly** *adj.*

wade *vi.* to walk through something that offers resistance, such as water, snow, or brush; to proceed slowly or laboriously: *wade through a mountain of paperwork* —*vt.* to walk through or cross by walking on the bottom, as of a river or stream

wad´er *n.* one who wades—**wad´ers** *n.* high waterproof boots

wader, wading bird a variety of long-legged bird that feeds in shallow water, such as a crane or stork

wa´fer *n.* a thin, crisp cookie, cracker, etc.; a disk of gummed material used for sealing or attaching, as papers, mailers, etc.: *a wafer seal*

waf´fle *n.* a crisp batter cake, similar to a pancake —*vi.* to be evasive — **waf´fler** *n.* —**waf´fling·ly** *adv.* — **waf´fly** *adj.*

waft *vt.* to bear gently through the air or over water —*vi.* to float, as on the wind; to blow gently, as a breeze —*n.* lightly passing air, sound, or aroma —**waft´er** *n.*

wag *vi., vt.* to move or cause to move rapidly, as a dog's tail or the tongue in talking —*n.* a wagging motion; a droll person; a wit

wage *n.* payment for service; reward or consequence, as *the wages of sin* —*vt.* to engage in, as *to wage war*

wa´ger *vt., vi.* to gamble —*n.* a bet; the thing bet on or the amount of a stake

wag´ger·y *n.* mischievous joking

wag´gish *adj.* humorous; said or

done as a joke —**wag´gish·ly** *adv.* —**wag´gish·ness** *n.*

wag´gle *vt.* to wag or swing with short quick motions —*vi.* to move unsteadily —**wag´gling·ly** *adv.* — **wag´gly** *adj.*

wag´on *n.* a four-wheeled vehicle for carrying heavy loads; a child's cart; a small food or beverage cart; a vehicle that goes from place to place selling prepared food: *a lunch wagon*

waif *n.* a homeless child; a stray animal

wail *vi.* to make a mournful, crying sound —*vt.* to mourn or lament; to cry out in sorrow —**wail´er** *n.* — **wail´ful** *adj.* —**wail´ful·ly, wail´ ing·ly** *adv.*

wain´scot, wain´scot·ing *n.* paneling for inner walls

wain´wright *n.* a maker of wagons

waist *n.* the middle of the body; the middle of an object, especially one that is narrowed

waist´coat (*Brit.*) *n.* a short, sleeveless garment worn over a shirt; (*US*) a vest —**waist´coat·ed** *adj.*

wait *vi.* to anticipate: *waiting for a package to arrive*; to pause: *wait for the others to catch up*; to delay or postpone: *dinner will have to wait*; to remain expectant or in readiness: *wait for the right moment to act*; to serve, especially as a waiter or waitress —*vt.* to remain in expectation of: *wait your turn*; to delay: *wait for us*; to work as a waiter or waitress: *to wait tables* — *n.* (*Brit.*) musicians employed to play at a public function; street carolers or musicians

wait´er *n.* a man employed to serve, as in a restaurant; one who awaits; a tray for serving food

wait´ing *n.* expectant; an instance of remaining inactive or expectant

wait´ress *n.* a woman employed to serve, as in a restaurant

waive *vt.* to relinquish or forego a claim to; to put off temporarily

waiv´er *n.* voluntary relinquishment; the instrument which evidences relinquishment

wake[1] *vi.* to emerge from sleep; to become aware or alert —*vt.* to rouse from sleep; to make aware of or alert to —*n.* a watch or vigil, especially over the body of a deceased person; (*Brit.*) an annual parish festival; (*Brit.*) an annual vacation from work —**wak´er** *n.*

wake[2] *n.* the track or trail left by a vessel moving through the water; the track or turbulence left by anything that has passed: *the truck left a cloud of dust in its wake* —**in the wake of** following immediately after: *cheers were heard in the wake of the announcement*; a result or consequence: *only ruins were left in the wake of the fire*

wake´ful *adj.* not sleepy; watchful, alert; restless —**wake´ful·ly** *adv.* —**wake´ful·ness** *n.*

wak´en *vt.* to rouse from sleep; to rouse or stir up: *the speech wakened his patriotic fervor* —*vi.* to cease sleeping; to wake up: *I expect to waken at six in the morning*; to become active or animated —**wak´en·er** *n.*

wak´ing *adj.* characterized by consciousness or awareness

wale *n.* a ridge or rib on cloth —*vt.* to raise welts by striking; to manufacture cloth with ridges

walk *vi.* to advance by moving the feet; to move or progress on foot; to behave in a certain manner: *to walk in peace*; to leave abruptly: *they walked out* —*vt.* to pass through at a walk; to force or help to walk: *walk the bicycle uphill*; to accompany or escort on a walk; to direct or cause to move in a manner reminiscent of walking: *walk the refrigerator away from the wall, walk them through the procedure* —*n.* the act of walking; a distinctive manner of walking; a place for walking; status or position in society: *she was supported by people of all walks* —**walk all over** to mistreat or use badly —**walk off with** to steal —**walk on air** to feel exhilarated or euphoric —**walk out on** to abandon —**walk´er** *n.*

walk´out *n.* a labor strike

walk´-up *n.* an apartment located above the ground floor in a building with no elevator

wall *n.* a structure designed to enclose or divide an area; something resembling the nature or function of a wall: *a wall of water, a wall of silence* —*vt.* to provide with a wall; to enclose or separate with a wall —*adj.* attached to or built into a wall —**drive up a wall** to frustrate or distress —**off the wall** unconventional; eccentric —**wall´less** *adj.* —**wall´like** *adj.*

wal´la·by *n.* a small kangaroo

wall´eye *n.* an eye with a light-colored iris; a condition in which the eyes diverge; a type of fish — **wall´eyed** *adj.*

wall´flow·er *n.* one who is shy or unpopular

wal´lop *vt.* to beat soundly; to strike a hard blow —*n.* a hard blow — **wal´lop·er** *n.*

wal´lop·ing *adj.* very large —*n.* a beating; a crushing defeat

wal´low *vi.* to roll about in mud, snow, etc.; to be plentiful: *wallowing in profits*; to indulge oneself: *he wallowed in self-pity* —*n.* the act of wallowing; a depression or hollow —**wal´low·er** *n.*

wall´-to-wall´ *adj.* completely covered: *wall-to-wall carpeting*; completely filled: *wall-to-wall people, wall-to-wall flowers*

waltz *n.* a ballroom dance —*vi.* to

dance a waltz; to move quickly —
waltz´er *n.*

wan *adj.* pale, as from sickness;
faint or feeble —**wan´ly** *adv.* —
wan´ness *n.*

wand *n.* a slender rod waved by a
conjurer; a staff symbolizing
authority; a musician's baton

wan´der *vi.* to roam; to go casually
or by an indirect route; to twist or
meander; to stray —*vt.* to meander
across or through —**wan´der·er** *n.*
—**wan´der·ing·ly** *adv.*

wan´der·lust *n.* an impulse to travel;
restlessness

wane *vi.* to diminish; to decline or
decrease gradually —*n.* a de-
creasing; a period of decline

wan´gle *vt.* to obtain by indirect or
dishonest means —*vi.* to resort to
indirect or irregular methods —
wan´gler *n.*

want *vt.* to feel a wish for; to desire;
to lack or be deficient in; to request or require: *wanted on the
phone* —*vi.* to have need; to be
needy or destitute —*n.* a lack,
scarcity, or shortage; poverty or
destitution —**want´er** *n.* —**want"
less** *adj.* —**want´less·ness** *n.*

want´ing *adj.* missing or lacking; not
coming up to some standard,
need, or expectation

wan´ton *adj.* licentious or lewd;
heartless or malicious; unrestrained; capricious or unprovoked
—*vi.* to act in a wanton manner —
vt. to waste or squander —*n.* a
lewd or licentious person —**wan´
ton·ly** *adv.* —**wan´ton·ness** *n.*

wap´i·ti *n.* the American elk

war *n.* armed strife between nations,
states, etc.; any conflict or struggle; warfare —*vi.* to wage war; to
fight or take part in war; to be in
opposition or contention —*adj.*
pertaining to war or its aftermath:
war orphans

war´ble *vi., vt.* to sing with trills,

tremulo, etc. —*n.* the act or sound
of warbling —**war´bler** *n.*

war chest a fund set aside for a
purpose, such as for a political
campaign

ward *n.* a section of a hospital: *ma-
ternity ward*; an administrative division of a city; one in the charge
of a guardian or the state; the act
of guarding or being guarded —*vt.*
to repel or turn aside

war´den *n.* a supervisor or custodian; (*Brit.*) an executive or administrative officer, such as a
crown officer, a hospital or college
official, or a church trustee; (*US*)
the chief administrative officer of a
prison

ward´er *n.* a person who guards or
protects; (*Brit.*) a prison guard —
ward´er·ship *n.*

ward´robe *n.* a cabinet or closet for
storing wearing apparel; the costumes belonging to a theater or
theater group; the room where
theater costumes are kept; collectively, all the garments that belong
to a person, or those suited to a
particular season: *winter wardrobe*

ward´room *n.* eating or living quarters for commissioned officers
aboard a warship

ward´ship *n.* the state of being a
ward or a guardian; custody

ware *n.* articles of the same type
collectively, as *glassware, hard-
ware*, etc.; dishes or pottery, especially those of a particular kind;
merchandise displayed for sale

ware´house *n.* a place where goods
are kept awaiting sale or use; a
storehouse; (*Brit.*) a large cut-rate
or retail store —*vt.* to place or keep
in a warehouse —**ware´house·
man** *n.*

war´fare *n.* the waging of war; struggle or strife

war horse a veteran of many strug-
gles, as a politician

war´like *adj.* fond of war; threatening war

war´lock *n.* a male witch; a sorcerer

war´lord *n.* a military commander who governs; a militaristic head of state —**war´lord·ism** *n.*

warm *adj.* moderately or relatively hot; imparting or preserving warmth: *warm clothing*; heated, as from exertion; cordial or friendly; recently made, as *warm from the oven*; suggesting warmth, as of a color —*vt.*, *vi.* to make or become heated, interested, or excited: *she warmed to the idea of redecorating*; to become friendly; to fill with or feel pleasure: *it warms the heart* —**warm´er** *n.* —**warm´ly** *adv.* —**warm´ness** *n.*

warm´-blood´ed *adj.* having a nearly constant, warm body temperature; ardent or passionate —**warm´-blood´ed·ness** *n.*

warmed´-o´ver *adj.* reheated, as of leftover food; stale or hackneyed; made ineffectual by overuse

warm´-heart·ed *adj.* kind; sympathetic; generous —**warm´heart·ed·ly** *adv.* —**warm´heart·ed·ness** *n.*

warm´ish *adj.* somewhat warm

war´mon·ger *n.* one who tries to provoke war —**war´mon·ger·ing** *adj.*, *n.*

warmth *n.* a sense of being warm or comfortable; ardor or excitement; friendliness or understanding

warn *vt.* to alert to danger; to advise; to give notice to go or stay away —*vi.* to give warning —**warn´er** *n.*

warn´ing *n.* the act of giving notice or being alerted; that which alerts or advises —*adj.* serving to give notice or warn: *a warning light* —**warn´ing·ly** *adv.*

warp *vt.* to twist out of shape, as for a piece of wood; to corrupt or pervert; to divert from a proper course; to arrange strands for weaving so as to run lengthwise —*vi.* to become twisted or distorted; to turn aside from a proper course; to go astray —*n.* a condition of being twisted out of shape; a distortion; an abnormality; a mental or moral aberration; woven strands that run the length of a fabric —**warp´er** *n.* —**warp´ing** *n.*

war´rant *n.* an order that provides legal authorization for arrest, search, etc.; a guarantee or warrantee; a sanction or justification —*vt.* to assure or guarantee the quality or condition of; to guarantee a consumer against loss if a product does not perform as advertised; to give legal authority; to guarantee clear title to property —**war·rant·a·bil´i·ty**, **war´rant·a·ble·ness** *n.* —**war´rant·a·ble** *adj.* —**war´rant·a·bly** *adv.*

war´rant·ee´ *n.* the person to whom a warranty is given

war´ran·tor´, **war´rant·er** *n.* one who makes or issues a warrant or who gives a warranty to another

war´ran·ty *n.* a guarantee by a seller that whatever is sold is as represented; an official authorization or warrant; justification for a course of action; legal assurance by a seller of property that the title is free and clear

war´ren *n.* a place where rabbits are kept; an enclosure for small animals; an overcrowded living space

war´ri·or *n.* one engaged or experienced in warfare

wart *n.* a small, hard growth on the skin; any of various natural growths on certain plants and animals —**wart´ed**, **wart´y** *adj.*

war´y *adj.* watchful: *be wary of easy money*; marked by caution; shrewd or wily —**war´i·ly** *adv.* —**war´i·ness** *n.*

wash *vt.* to cleanse or remove with a liquid; to cover with liquid; to soak or rinse; to flow against or over; to

coat with a thin layer of pigment —
vi. to bathe or launder; to be removed or drawn off by a liquid; to
bear close scrutiny: *his alibi won't
wash* —n. the process of wetting
or cleaning with liquid; clothes set
aside to be laundered; a surge of
water or the turbulence caused by
rushing water: *wash from a boat's
propeller;* removal or deposit of
topsoil by rushing water; an area
periodically covered by water; a
preparation for washing or coating;
a thin coating of pigment: a tint —
come out in the wash to be revealed —**wash one's hands of** to
reject or renounce —**wash out** to
be removed, damaged, or destroyed by moving water; to be
eliminated, as from school or a
sports team

wash'a·ble *adj.* that can be laundered without damage —**wash·a·
bil'i·ty** *n.*

wash'ba·sin, wash'bowl *n.* a water
container for washing the hands
and face

wash'board *n.* a board having a
corrugated surface for scrubbing
laundry

washed'–out' *adj.* lacking intensity
or faded; exhausted

washed'–up' *adj.* finished; no longer
capable or needed

wash'er *n.* one or that which
washes; a small, flat disk used to
tighten a nut or a joint

wash'out *n.* erosion by the action of
water; a failure

wash'room *n.* a lavatory

wash'stand *n.* a cabinet for holding
a pitcher, washbowl, etc.; a bathroom sink

wash'tub *n.* a large vessel used for
laundry

wasp *n.* an insect with a slender
segmented body, related to the bee

wasp'ish *adj.* like a wasp: having a
slender figure; irritable or bad-

tempered —**wasp'ish·ly** *adv.* —
wasp'ish·ness *n.*

wasp waist a slim, narrow waist —
wasp-waist·ed *adj.*

was'sail *n.* an ancient toast; a spiced
drink of ale and wine; a celebration —*vi.* to revel or carouse —*vt.*
to drink to the health of —**was'
sail·er** *n.*

wast'age *n.* that lost by leakage, etc.

waste *vt.* to use thoughtlessly; to
squander; to make weak or feeble;
to fail to use or take advantage of;
to devastate —*vi.* to lose vigor,
bulk, etc.; to diminish; to pass
gradually, as time —*n.* thoughtless
or unnecessary consumption; failure to benefit; a desolate place; a
gradual wearing away; something
discarded —**wast'er** *n.*

wast'ed *adj.* squandered or needlessly depleted; useless or excessive: *wasted effort;* frail or feeble,
as from illness; inebriated or under the influence of a narcotic

waste'ful *adj.* prone to or causing
waste; extravagant —**waste'ful·ly**
adv. —**waste'ful·ness** *n.*

waste'land *n.* a barren or desolate
land

waste pipe a conduit for carrying off
waste

wast'er *n.* a spendthrift or squan-
derer; an idler

wast'ing *adj.* destructive; enfeebling
—**wast'ing·ly** *adv.*

was'trel *n.* a spendthrift; an idler

watch *vi.* to observe closely; to be on
the alert; to wait expectantly; to
function as a guard or sentinel; to
keep a religious vigil —*vt.* to look
at attentively; to keep informed
about: *watch the course of the election campaign;* to be alert for; to
guard —*n.* careful observation; an
attitude of alertness or vigilance;
one in service as a guard; the time
of being on guard duty; a small
timepiece, as worn on the wrist or

carried in a pocket; a religious vigil —**watch´er** n.

watch´case n. a covering for a watch

watch´dog n. a guard dog; a person who serves to protect against waste, unlawful or prohibited acts, etc.

watch´ful adj. vigilant; alert — **watch´ful·ly** adv. —**watch´ful·ness** n.

watch´man n. one who guards and protects

watch´word n. a password; a slogan

wa´ter n. the colorless liquid that is an essential constituent of all organisms; a body of water; a supply of water; a liquid or preparation of water holding a substance in solution, such as urine or saliva —vt. to provide with water; to dilute with water —vi. to secrete or discharge water —**keep one's head above water** to stay out of difficulty, especially financial —**water down** to reduce or dilute in some manner, such as by increasing shares in a corporation without adding to assets —**watered–down** adj. —**water under the bridge** a past event that is to be forgiven or forgotten —**wa´ter·er** n.

wa´ter·bed n. a bed with a water-filled mattress

wa´ter·borne adj. floating on water; transported on a ship, etc.

water clock a timepiece operated by water

water closet (Brit.) a toilet

wa´ter·col·or n. a water–soluble pigment or coloring matter; a painting rendered in watercolors — adj. painted with watercolors — **wa´ter·col·or·ist** n.

wa´ter·course n. a flow of water, as a river, stream, etc.; a channel for water

wa´ter·fowl n. a swimming game bird

wa´ter·front n. property abutting or overlooking a body of water; an area of docks, warehouses, etc.

water gap a deep ravine permitting passage of water, usually the course of a river or stream

wa´ter·glass n. a drinking vessel; a gauge for indicating water level; a device somewhat like a bucket with a glass bottom, used for examining objects under water

watering hole a pond or pool frequented by wildlife; a tavern or pub

wa´ter·ish adj. resembling water: clear; watery or diluted

water level n. the relative elevation of the surface of a body of water; a ship's waterline

wa´ter·line n. a line on the hull of a ship which shows where the water surface reaches; a mark showing the level to which water has risen, as during a flood

wa´ter·logged adj. soaked with water; so saturated as to be unmanageable and barely able to float

water main a primary conduit for carrying water

wa´ter·mark n. a waterline; a design impressed into paper when it is made —vt. to impress with a watermark

water mill a mill with equipment operated by water power

water nymph a mythical being that dwells in a stream, lake, etc.

water pipe a conduit for water; a tobacco pipe designed so that the smoke is filtered and cooled by water

wa´ter·pow·er n. energy derived from flowing or falling water

wa´ter·shed n. the region from which a river receives its supply of water; a decisive turning point

wa´ter·spout n. a moving, whirling column of water; a pipe for discharging water

water table the upper level of saturated subterranean rock

wa´ter·tight *adj.* so closely made that water cannot leak through; that cannot be misunderstood, found illegal, or in error —**wa´ter·tight·ness** *n.*

water tower a tank used as a reservoir to maintain water pressure

water vapor moisture below the boiling point mixed in the air

wa´ter·way *n.* a river, channel, etc., especially when navigable

water wheel a wheel turned by flowing water, used for power or for raising water

wa´ter·works *n.* a system of pumps, pipes, etc. for furnishing a water supply

wa´ter·worn *adj.* worn smooth or eroded by running or falling water

wa´ter·y *adj.* like water; diluted; insipid —**wa´ter·i·ness** *n.*

watt *n.* a unit of electrical power

watt´age *n.* a measure of power expressed in watts

wat´tle *n.* a woven framework of poles and twigs; a fold of skin hanging from the throat of a bird or lizard

wave *vi.* to move freely, as a flag in the wind; to greet or signal with the hand; to have the shape of a series of curves or curls, as of the hair —*vt.* to cause to move freely; to flourish; to signal by waving; to give a curved appearance to; to form into curves or curls —*n.* a ridge or undulation, as on the surface of a liquid: *the ocean waves pounded the shore*; a motion with the hand; a series of curves, as *a hair wave*; an upsurge, as *a wave of nausea* or *a wave of patriotic fervor*; a somewhat prolonged condition, as *a heat wave*; the pattern formed by the transfer of energy, as *a sound wave* —**wav´er** *n.*

wave´form *n.* the curve produced by

recording the movement of a wave of energy

wave´length *n.* the distance between two like points, such as the crests or troughs, in consecutive cycles of an energy wave

wa´ver *vi.* to move one way and the other; to be uncertain; to falter —*n.* a wavering —**wa´ver·er** *n.* —**wa´ver·ing·ly** *adv.*

wav´y *adj.* full of curves, as *wavy hair*; undulating —**wav´i·ly** *adv.* —**wav´i·ness** *n.*

wax *n.* a pliable substance that is insoluble in water and that burns in the air; a waxlike product, as paraffin, furniture polish, etc. —*adj.* made with or from wax —*vt.* to coat or polish with wax —*vi.* to gradually increase, as in size or intensity; to express oneself: *he waxed poetic on the joys of love*

wax´en *adj.* consisting of or covered with wax; pale or pallid; malleable or pliant

wax´er *n.* a person or machine that applies wax

wax museum a place that exhibits life–size wax figures

wax paper paper coated with wax, used in the preparation and preservation of food

wax´work *n.* something sculpted in wax —**wax´work·er** *n.*

wax´works *n.* an exhibit of wax sculptures

wax´y *adj.* resembling wax; abounding in wax; pale or pallid —**wax´i·ness** *n.*

way *n.* a direction: *let's go that way*; a course or passage from one place to another; space or room: *make way for the king*; a process or means: *a way to solve the problem*; a customary or habitual manner: *the way we live, do it your way*; a condition: *in a bad way* —**go out of the way** to be inconvenienced —**in a way** to some extent —**out of**

the way taken care of; completed; remote —*adv.*

way′bill *n.* a document providing particulars about a shipment of goods

way′far·er *n.* one who travels, usually aimlessly and on foot —**way′far·ing** *n., adj.*

way′lay *vt.* to lie in ambush; to meet on the way —**way′lay·er** *n.*

ways and means methods for defraying costs or accomplishing something

way station an intermediate station, as on a railroad

way′ward *adj.* willful, headstrong; not predictable —**way′ward·ly** *adv.* —**way′ward·ness** *n.*

weak *adj.* lacking strength, energy, vigor, etc.; not effective or forceful, as of an argument; lacking mental power; lacking skill or experience; deficient in something

weak′en *vt., vi.* to make or become weak or weaker —**weak′en·er** *n.*

weak′fish *n.* any of various marine food fishes

weak′ling *n.* a feeble person or animal

weak′ly *adj.* sick or feeble —*adv.* in a weak manner —**weak′li·ness** *n.*

weak′-mind′ed *adj.* not resolute; lacking conviction; foolish; unable to comprehend —**weak′mind′ed·ly** *adv.* —**weak′mind′ed·ness** *n.*

weak′ness *n.* the quality of being fragile or delicate; a slight failing or fault; a strong liking; something that strongly attracts

weal *n.* a welt, as from a blow

wealth *n.* riches: an abundance of assets or goods; the state of being rich; great abundance of anything: *a wealth of knowledge*

wealth′y *adj.* possessing riches; characterized by abundance; more than sufficient —**wealth′i·ly** *adv.* —**wealth′i·ness** *n.*

wean *vt.* to end dependence on

mother's milk for nourishment; to withdraw from a detrimental habit or association

wean′ling *adj.* freshly weaned —*n.* a child or animal freshly weaned

weap′on *n.* any implement, means, defensive organ, etc. that may be used against an adversary —**weap′on·ry** *n.*

wear *vt.* to have on the person, as a garment or ornament; to display, as an aspect; to damage by constant or prolonged use; to exhaust —*vi.* to be diminished gradually by use; to withstand the effects of use, time, etc.: *to wear well*; to have a tiring effect: *the trip was wearing* —*n.* the act of wearing or being worn; articles of dress; destruction from use or time; durability —**wear′er** *n.*

wear′a·ble *adj.* suitable for wear

wear·a·bil′i·ty *n.* the ability to withstand the effects of use or time

wear′ing *adj.* tiresome; exhausting; designed to be worn —**wear′ing·ly** *adv.*

wea′ry *adj.* tired; fatigued; discontented or bored; indicating fatigue —*vt., vi.* to make or become weary —**wea′ri·ly** *adv.* —**wea′ri·ness** *n.*

wea′ri·some *adj.* causing fatigue; tiresome —**wea′ri·some·ly** *adv.* —**wea′ri·some·ness** *n.*

wea′sel *n.* a small, slender carnivorous animal; a sly or treacherous person —*vi.* to renege, as on a promise: *weaseled out of the deal*; to equivocate

weath′er *n.* general atmospheric conditions, as temperature, moisture, wind, etc.; unpleasant conditions — *vt.* to expose to the elements; to show the effects of exposure; to pass through and survive —*vi.* to undergo changes from exposure; to resist the action of weather —*adj.* facing the direction of the wind

weath´er·beat·en, weath´er·worn *adj.* showing the effects of exposure to weather

weath´ered *adj.* worn or damaged by or as if by the elements; visibly improved by exposure or intended to emulate exposure, as *weathered brick* or *weathered siding*

weath´er·ing *n.* the process by which materials exposed to the elements undergo changes in appearance or integrity; the appearance of materials that have been exposed to the elements, often produced artificially for effect

weath´er·proof *adj.* capable of withstanding the effects of exposure to harsh weather —*vt.* to make weatherproof —**weath´er·proof·ness** *n.*

weather station a place from which meteorological observations are made

weath´er·strip, weath´er·strip·ping *n.* material applied in or over crevices to exclude drafts, rain, etc. —*vt.* to attach or apply weatherstripping

weave *vt.* to interlace or make something by interlacing thread, yarn, cane, reeds, etc.; to produce by interlacing elements: *weave a tale*; to advance by moving from one side to another —*vi.* to make by weaving; to become interlaced; to make one's way by weaving —**weav´er** *n.*

web *n.* the network spun by a spider; an artfully contrived trap; an entanglement: *a web of deceit*; any complex network: *the world–wide web for computers*; the membrane connecting the digits of aquatic birds, frogs, etc. — *vt.* to create a web; to trap in a web

webbed *adj.* of or having a web

wed *vt., vi.* to marry

wed´ding *n.* the rite of marriage; the anniversary of a marriage

wedge *n.* a tapered piece of metal, wood, etc. used to create pressure in a fissure, such as to split a log or tighten a joint; something in the form of a wedge; something that facilitates entry, intrusion, etc. — *vt.* to force apart or fix in place with a wedge; to crowd or squeeze —*vi.* to force oneself in

wed´lock *n.* the state of being married

wee *adj.* very small

weed *n.* an unwanted or unsightly plant, especially of growth among cultivated plants—*vt., vi.* to remove unwanted growth; to remove anything considered undesirable: *weed out the useless information* —**weed´er** *n.*

weed´y *adj.* abounding in weeds: *a weedy garden*; of a weed or weeds; gawky or lanky —**weed´i·ly** *adv.* —**weed´i·ness** *n.*

week *n.* a period of seven calendar days, customarily Sunday through Saturday; a period described by an event or cause: *Christmas week, Teacher Recognition week*; the portion of a week dedicated to business: *a five–day week*

week´end *n.* the end of a week; the time at the end of a work week, customarily Friday evening to Sunday evening —*vi.* to visit over the weekend: *we'll weekend at the beach house*

week´end·er *n.* a vacationer or weekend visitor; a small bag designed to carry clothing and incidentals sufficient for a few day's needs

week´ly *adj., adv.* occurring every week or once a week; pertaining to a week: *a weekly wage* —*n.* a periodical issued once a week

weep *vt.* to show grief or remorse by shedding tears; to form liquid in drops, as condensation —*vt.* to weep for; to shed liquid —*n.* the act of weeping; an exhudation of liquid, as from a running sore — **weep´er** n.

weep´ing adj. that weeps; shedding tears; having branches that curve downward

weeping willow a tree notable for long drooping branches

weep´y adj. weeping or inclined to weep

wee´vil n. a small destructive beetle —**wee´vil·ly, wee´vil·y** adj.

weigh vt. to determine the weight of; to measure according to weight; to consider carefully: to weigh the consequences —vi. to have a specified weight; to have importance: to weigh heavy on one's mind; to be burdensome: weighed down with guilt —**weigh´er** n.

weight n. heaviness; a measure of heaviness; a piece used as a standard in weighing; a unit of heaviness; burden or pressure: the weight of responsibility; importance or consequence; a heavy object used in competition or for exercise; an object used to hold something down: a paperweight — vt. to make heavy; to oppress or burden;

weight´ed adj. adjusted so as to correctly reflect the ratio of elements, as a weighted average

weight´less adj. having or experiencing little or no heaviness; free from the pull of gravity, as of a traveler in outer space —**weight´less·ly** adv. —**weight´less·ness** n.

weight´y adj. of great importance: a weighty decision; effectual: a weighty argument; oppressive; heavy —**weight´i·ly** adv. — **weight´i·ness** n.

weir n. a dam across a waterway to raise or divert the water; a fence in a stream, used to catch fish

weird adj. odd or bizarre; pertaining to the supernatural or a super-

natural occurrence —**weird´ly** adv. —**weird´ness** n.

wel´come vt. to greet pleasantly or hospitably; to receive with pleasure —n. a warm reception —adj. received cordially; producing satisfaction or pleasure; free to use or enjoy —**wel´come·ly** adv. —**wel´come·ness** n. —**wel´com·er** n.

weld vt. to unite, as two pieces of metal, by the application of heat; to bring into close association —n. the joining of metal by welding; the joint formed by welding —**weld´a·ble** adj. —**weld´er** n.

wel´fare n. well-being; prosperity; money or other assistance given to those in need

welfare state a system by which the state assumes responsibility for the welfare of its citizens, as for health insurance, retirement, etc.

well n. a shaft sunk into the earth; a source of continued supply; a depression or cavity used to hold or collect water; a vertical opening through a building for light, ventilation, stairs, etc. —vi. to rise to the surface —vt. to gush or pour forth —adv. satisfactorily: performed well; in a correct manner; to a considerable extent: well known; quite, positively: well worth the money —adj. suitable or proper; fortunate; in good health; prosperous: well off

well´-ad·just·ed adj. suitably adapted to surroundings or circumstances; mentally sound

well´-appoint´ed adj. properly equipped

well-bal´anced adj. correctly proportioned; mentally sound

well´-be´ing n. health, happiness, or prosperity

well´born adj. of good family; titled; aristocratic

well´-de·fined´ adj. having distinct features or limits; unambiguous

well´-done *adj.* performed skillfully; thoroughly cooked

well´-fa´vored *adj.* attractive; comely

well´-found´ed *adj.* based on fact

well´-ground´ed *adj.* properly schooled or taught

well´-in·ten´tioned *adj.* meaning well; having good intentions

well´-man´nered *adj.* courteous; polite

well´-mean´ing *adj.* having good intentions

well´-nigh´ *adv.* almost

well´-off´ *adj.* in comfortable circumstances; wealthy

well´-round´ed *adj.* having many interests, abilities, etc.

well´spring *n.* the source of a stream, spring, etc.; a source of continual supply

well´-timed´ *adj.* happening at a propitious or favorable time

well´-wish·er *n.* a supporter —**well´-wish·ing** *adj., n.*

welt *n.* a raised mark on the skin resulting from a blow; a strip of material used to cover or strengthen a seam —*vt.* to decorate with a welt; to flog so as to raise welts

wen *n.* a cyst

wend *vt.* to go on; to proceed

were´wolf *n.* in folklore, a person changed into a wolf or able to take the form of a wolf

west *n.* the general direction in which the sun sets —*adj.*

west´er·ly *adj., adv.* in, toward, or of the west —**west´er·li·ness** *n.*

west´ern *adj.* of, in, directed toward, or facing the west; from the west —**west´ern·er** *n.*

west´ern·ize *vt.* to adapt to the customs of a western nation, such as the US or Europe; to adopt the trappings of the American west, especially in manner of dress —**west·ern·i·za´tion** *n.*

wet *adj.* moistened or covered with a liquid; marked by rainfall; not yet dry, as paint —*n.* moisture; rainy weather —*vt., vi.* to make or become wet —**all wet** completely wrong —**wet behind the ears** inexperienced —**wet´ness** *n.*

wet blanket one who discourages or disparages taking part in festivities; one whose presence diminishes the enjoyment of others

wet´land *n.* a land area such as a swamp or marsh that is saturated or partly under water

whack *vt., vi.* to strike sharply —*n.* a resounding blow

whale *n.* a very large marine mammal; something very good, large, or impressive: *a whale of a party* —*vi.* to engage in hunting whales —**whal´er** *n.*

wharf *n., pl.* **wharfs, wharves** a place or structure for the docking and loading or unloading of ships; a pier or dock

what *pron.* which specific thing, amount, circumstance, etc.: *what is this?, what does it cost?, what happened?* that which: *take only what is yours*; whatever situation or contingency: *able to take what comes* —*adj.* which one: *what color is it? what show did you watch?* —*adv.* how much: *what does it matter?* —**what for** a strong reproof or denunciation —**what it boils down to** the gist of the matter; essentially

what´not *n.* an article of furniture designed to hold and display small objects; a small decorative object

wheal *n.* a small pimple on the skin

wheat *n.* a cereal grass, esp. one cultivated and ground into flour

wheat germ the nutricious embryo of the wheat kernel

whee´dle *vt.* to persuade by flattery, cajolery, etc.; to obtain by cajoling or coaxing —*vi.* to use flattery or cajolery **—whee´dier —whee´dling·ly** adv.

wheel n. a disk or rim that turns on a central axis; a turning or rotating movement; a person of influence —vt. to move or convey on wheels; to cause to turn, as though on an axis; to provide with wheels —vi. to turn, as on an axis; to change one's course; to move on wheels

wheel´bar·row n. a one-wheeled vehicle with opposing handles used to move small loads —vt. to convey in a wheelbarrow

wheel´chair n. a chair mounted between large wheels, for the use of one unable to walk

wheel´er-deal´er n. one who acts freely, aggressively, and often unscrupulously, as in arranging a business or political bargain

wheel´wright n. a man whose business is making or repairing wheels

wheeze vt., vi. to breathe with a husky, whistling sound —n. a wheezing sound **—wheez´i·ly, wheez´ing·ly** adv. **—wheez´i·ness** n. **—wheez´y** adj.

whelp n. one of the young of a dog, wolf, etc.; a worthless young fellow —vt., vi. to give birth

when adv. at what or which time; at an earlier time; under what circumstances —conj.

whence adv. from what place or source —conj.

where adv. at or in what place or situation; to or from what place — conj.

where´a·bouts n. an unspecified location: we don't know his whereabouts

where´with·al n. the necessary means or resources

whet vt. to sharpen, as a knife; to excite or stimulate: the smell of food will whet your appetite

whet´stone n. a fine stone for the sharpening of knives, etc.

whey n. a clear liquid that separates from the curd when milk is curdled, as in the making of cheese — **whey´ey, whey´ish** adj.

which pron. what thing: which is larger? that previously indicated: take the red car, which is mine — adj. what specific one: which car do you want to take?

whiff n. a gust of air; an aroma; a puff

while vt. to pass time pleasantly —n. a span or amount of time —conj. during the time that; at the same time; whereas

whim n. a sudden, capricious idea or notion

whim´per vi., vt. to cry or utter with a plaintive sound **—whim´per·er** n. **—whim´per·ing·ly** adv.

whim´si·cal adj. capricious; marked by erratic or unpredictable conduct; odd or quaint **—whim·si·cal´i·ty, whim´si·cal·ness** n. **—whim´si·cal·ly** adv.

whim´sy n. a whim or caprice; odd or quaint humor

whine vi. to utter a high, plaintive, nasal sound expressive of grief or distress; to complain in a fretful or childish way; to make a steady high-pitched sound, as of a machine —vt. to utter with a whine — n. **—whin´er** n. **—whin´ing·ly** adv. **—whin´y** adj.

whip vt. to strike with a lash, rod, etc.; to buffet in the manner of a whip; to beat to a froth; to seize, jerk, throw, etc. with a sudden motion —vi. to move or turn suddenly; to thrash about —n. a lash attached to a handle; a whipping or thrashing motion; a legislator appointed to enforce discipline, attendance, etc.; a dessert containing whipped cream or beaten egg whites

whip´lash n. the end of a whip; a

neck injury caused by a sudden snapping of the head

whip'per·snap·per *n.* a pretentious but insignificant young person

whipping boy one who receives undeserved blame or punishment

whir *vt., vi.* to fly or move with a buzzing sound —*n.* a whizzing sound; confusion or bustle

whirl *vi.* to turn or revolve rapidly; to move or go swiftly; to have a spinning sensation —*vt.* to cause to turn or revolve rapidly —*n.* a swift rotating motion; a state of confusion; a round of activities: *the social whirl* —**whirl'er** *n.*

whirl'pool *n.* an eddy or vortex of rapidly whirling water

whirl'wind *n.* a rapidly spinning column of air such as a tornado or waterspout; a destructive force —*adj.* extremely swift or impetuous: *a whirlwind tour*

whisk *vt.* to brush or sweep off lightly; to beat with quick movements —*vi.* to move quickly and lightly —*n.* a light sweeping motion; a kitchen untensil made up of wire loops for whipping or blending cream, egg whites, sauces, etc.

whisk broom a small hand broom

whisk'er *n.* the hair of a man's beard; long bristly hair near the mouth of some animals —**whisk'ered, whisk'er·y** *adj.*

whis'key, whis'ky *n.* an alcoholic beverage —*adj.* pertaining to or made with whiskey

whis'per *n.* hushed speech; a secret communication; a low, rustling sound —*vi.* to speak in hushed tones; to speak furtively; to make a low, rustling sound —*vt.* to utter or speak in a low tone —**whis'per·er** *n.* —**whis'per·ing·ly** *adv.* —**whis'per·y** *adv.*

whist *n.* a card game similar to bridge

whis'tle *vi.* to make a sharp, shrill sound; to sound a whistle —*vt.* to produce a sound by whistling —*n.* a sharp, shrill sound; a device for making such a sound: *a steam whistle* —**whis'tler** *n.*

whis'tle-blow'er *n.* a person who exposes wrongdoing, often one with strong links to the organization cited such as an employee — **whis'tle-blow·ing** *n.*

whistle stop a town along the course of a railway where a train stops only when signaled to do so: a small town, or one of little importance; a brief stop in the course of a political candidate's tour

whit *n.* the smallest bit

white *n.* the color produced by reflection of all the visible colors of the spectrum; the condition of being white; anything white or nearly white; the white part of something, as of an egg; the lighter-colored pieces, as of chess men, or the one playing those pieces —*adj.* lacking hue, as new snow; relatively light in color, as *white wine, white hair,* or *white skin*; relatively unmarked or clean: *white paper*; relatively harmless or innocuous: *white noise* —**white'ness** *n.*

white blood cell cells of the blood that help the body stave off infection and disease

white'-col'lar *adj.* designating salaried or office employees

white dwarf an extremely dense star that glows faintly due to its relatively small size

white elephant anything that is a burden and expensive to maintain; something of uncertain value

white flag a symbol of surrender

white heat the temperature at which heated metal turns white; a state of intense emotion —**white hot** *adj.*

white knight a rescuer; a person or

organization that buys or merges with a company in order to rescue it from a hostile takeover

white´-knuck´le *adj.* marked by or causing severe uneasiness or apprehension: *a white-knuckle flight*

white lie a harmless, trivial fib

whit´en *vt., vi.* to make or become white, as by bleaching —**whit´en·er** *n.*

white paper an authoritative report on an important topic, especially one prepared by a government agency

white sauce a sauce of cream or broth, thickened with a butter and flour mixture, used especially as a base for a variety of flavored sauces

white´wash *n.* a thin mixture of lime, water, sizing, etc. used for coating walls or other structures; a suppressing or concealing of faults or failure —*vt.* to coat with whitewash; to suppress or gloss over, as wrongdoing —**white´wash·er** *n.*

whit´ish *adj.* somewhat white or nearly white —**whit´ish·ness** *n.*

whit´tle *vt.* to make or shape by cutting bits from; to reduce or wear away a little at a time: *he whittled away at his inheritance until there was nothing left* —*vi.* to cut or shape wood —**whit´tler** *n.*

whiz *vi., vt.* to make or cause to make a hissing and humming sound while passing rapidly through the air —*n.* a whizzing sound; a person of extraordinary ability

whiz kid a relatively young person who is extremely clever, talented, or successful

who·dun´it *n.* a mystery story

whole *adj.* complete or entire: *she read the whole book*; not broken or defective: *a whole walnut*; being the full amount: *tell us the whole story* —*n.* collectively, all the parts

or elements that make up a thing —**whole´ness** *n.*

whole´heart·ed *adj.* complete and unreserved enthusiasm, energy, dedication, etc. —**whole´heart·ed·ly** *adv.* —**whole´heart·ed·ness** *n.*

whole´sale *n.* the sale of goods in bulk, usually to a person or company that resells to consumers —*adj.* pertaining to the buying or selling of goods in bulk; made or done on a large scale —*adv.* in bulk or quantity; extensively or indiscriminately: *wholesale slaughter* —**whole´sal·er** *n.*

whole´some *adj.* tending to promote health; advocating mental or moral righteousness: *wholesome entertainment* —**whole´some·ly** *adv.* —**whole´some·ness** *n.*

whol´ly *adv.* completely, totally; exclusively, only

whoop *vi.* to utter loud cries —*vt.* to call or chase away with loud cries —*n.* a shout of excitement, joy, derision, etc.

whooping cough a contagious respiratory disease marked by violent coughing

whop´per *n.* something large or remarkable; an outrageous lie

whop´ping *adj.* unusually large or remarkable

why *adv.* for what cause, purpose, or reason —*n.* a cause or reason

wick *n.* a cord or strand that conveys fuel to a flame, as of a candle or oil lamp —*vt., vi.* to convey or be conveyed by capillary action —**wick´ing** *n.*

wick´ed *adj.* evil; mischievous or roguish; mean or troublesome —**wick´ed·ly** *adv.* —**wick´ed·ness** *n.*

wide *adj.* relatively broad; spacious; distant from the desired point: *wide of the mark*; having great scope —*adv.* extensively —**wide´ly** *adv.* —**wide´ness** *n.*

wid´en *vt., vi.* to make or become

wide or wider —**wid´en·er** n.

wide´spread´ adj. extending over a large area; happening or accepted extensively

wid´ow n. a woman whose husband has died

wid´ow·er n. a man whose wife has died

width n. the dimension of an object from side to side

wield vt. to use, as a weapon or tool; to exercise authority, power, influence, etc. —**wield´a·ble** adj. — **wield´er** n.

wield´y adj. easily handled or managed

wie´ner, **wie´ner·wurst** n. a kind of smoked sausage

wife n. a woman who is joined to a man in marriage —**wife´dom**, **wife´hood** n.

wife´ly adj. of or suitable to a wife — **wife´li·ness** n.

wig n. a head covering that replaces part or all of the wearer's hair, constructed from real or artificial hair —vt. to furnish with a wig

wig´gle vi., vt. to move or cause to move from side to side —n. —**wig´ gler** n. —**wig´gly** adj.

wild adj. living or growing in a natural state; uncivilized; undisciplined; reckless or imprudent; extremely odd, strange, or bizarre; disorderly or disarranged; far from the mark: a wild throw —n. an uninhabited or uncultivated place —adv. in a wild manner —**wild´ly** adv. —**wild´ness** n.

wild´cat n. any of various feral cats, as the lynx, cougar, etc.; an aggressive, quick–tempered person; a tricky or unsound business venture —adj. unsound or risky; unofficial or unauthorized —vt., vi. to drill for oil —**wild´cat·ter** n.

wildcat strike an unauthorized walkout

wil´der·ness n. an uncultivated or uninhabited area

wild´fire n. a raging fire, difficult to extinguish

wild´fowl n. a wild game bird

wild-goose chase pursuit of the unknown or unattainable

wild´life n. wild animals collectively

wild rice an aquatic grass of North America or its edible grain

wild´wood n. natural forest land

wile n. a trick or artifice —vt. to lure, beguile, or mislead

will n. the power to make deliberate choices; a specific purpose, choice, etc.; strong determination; self-control —vt. to choose; to resolve upon as an action or course; to decree —vi. to wish or desire

will´ful adj. deliberate, intentional; stubborn or headstrong —**will´fully** adv. —**will´ful·ness** n.

will´ing adj. favorably disposed; readily and gladly acting, responding, giving, etc. —**will´ing·ly** adv. —**will´ing·ness** n.

wil´low n. a tree or shrub with flexible shoots often used in basketry —adj. made of willow wood

wil´low·y adj. tall and graceful; lithe or flexible; supple; abounding in willow trees —**wil´low·i·ness** n.

will´pow·er n. strength to control one's actions or desires; determination

wilt vi. to lose freshness; to droop — vt. to cause to lose freshness, energy, etc.

wil´y adj. sly or cunning —**wil´i·ly** adv. —**wil´i·ness** n.

wimp n. a person regarded as a weakling: a sissy; one who whimpers —**wimp´ish**, **wimp´y** adj.

win vi. to be victorious — vt. to be successful in; to gain victory; to influence —n. a victory

wince vi. to shrink back; to be startled; to recoil, as in pain —n. a startled motion —**winc´er** n.

wind n. any movement of air; breath;

idle chatter —*vt.* to catch a scent of; to exhaust the breath of: *the short run winded him*

wind *vt., vi.* to coil or twine

wind´bag *n.* an overly talkative person

wind´break *n.* anything, such as a hedge, fence, etc., that protects from the wind

wind´break·er *n.* an outer jacket with close-fitting waistband and cuffs

wind´ed *adj.* out of breath

wind´fall *n.* something, as ripened fruit, brought down by the wind; unexpected good fortune

wind gauge a device for measuring the speed of the wind

wind´ing *adj.* turning about an axis or core; having bends or turns —*n.* a bend or turn

wind instrument a musical instrument sounded by blowing

wind´jam·mer *n.* a sailing vessel

wind´lass *n.* a device for hoisting or hauling

wind´mill *n.* a mill turned by the wind to power a pump, etc.

win´dow *n.* an opening to admit light or air

window dressing an arrangement in a store window; a means by which something is made to seem more attractive or plausible than it actually is

win´dow-shop *vi.* to look over goods without intention of buying —**win´dow-shop·per** *n.*

win´dow·sill *n.* the ledge beneath a window opening

wind´shear *n.* a strong rapid change in wind direction

wind´swept *adj.* exposed to or brushed by wind

wind tunnel a device that artificially produces winds, used to study the effects of the force of wind on the design of airplane wings, etc.

wind´up *n.* a conclusion

wind´ward *adj.* toward the direction from which the wind blows; being on the side exposed to the wind — *n.* the direction facing the wind — *adv.* against the wind

wind´y *adj.* stormy; tempestuous; boastful or talkative —**wind´i·ly** *adv.* —**wind´i·ness** *n.*

wine *n.* fermented juice, especially of the grape; the color of red wine — *vt.* to entertain or treat with wine

wine cellar a storage space for wines

wine´press *n.* an apparatus for extracting grape juice; a place where grape juice is extracted

win´er·y *n.* an establishment where wine is made

wing *n.* an organ of flight; anything resembling or suggesting a wing; an attachment or extension, as of a building, a stage, an organization, etc. —*vt.* to pass over in flight; to accomplish by flying; to disable by wounding slightly —*vi.* to fly

winged *adj.* having wings; sublime, lofty

wink *vi., vt.* to blink or cause to blink; to signal by closing the eyelid of one eye; to twinkle —*n.* a fleeting time; a twinkle; a hint conveyed by winking —**forty winks** a short nap —**wink´er** *n.*

win´na·ble *adj.* attainable; possible to accomplish —**win·na·bil´i·ty** *n.*

win´ner *n.* one who prevails; a victor; someone or something likely to succeed

win´ning *adj.* successful; charming —**win´ning·ly** *adv.* —**win´ning·ness** *n.*

win´now *vt.* to separate, as grain from chaff; to eliminate that which is bad —*vi.* to separate grain from chaff —*n.* a device used to separate grain —**win´now·er** *n.*

win´some *adj.* charming; attractive —**win´some·ly** *adv.* —**win´some·ness** *n.*

win´ter *n.* the coldest season, between autumn and spring; a year: *a man of ninety winters* —*vi.* to pass the winter —*vt.* to protect during the winter —*adj.* suitable for or characteristic of winter

win´ter·green *n.* a small evergreen plant or the flavoring oil extracted from its leaves

win´ter·ize *vt.* to prepare for winter —**win´ter·i·za´tion** *n.*

win´ter·y, win´try *adj.* of or like winter: cold, stormy, bleak, etc. —**win´tri·ly** *adv.* —**win´tri·ness** *n.*

win´y *adj.* having the taste, color, etc. of wine

wipe *vt.* to rub; to remove or apply by rubbing —*n.* the act of wiping —**wip´er** *n.*

wipe out to destroy utterly

wire *n.* a slender rod or strand of metal; something made of wire; a telegram —*vt.* to fasten with wire; to equip with wiring, as for providing a building with electricity; to telegraph —*vi.* to telegraph —**wir´er** *n.*

wired *adj.* fitted out for electricity, telephones, etc.; keyed up or excited

wire´less *adj.* having no wires; requiring no wires —*n.* a device such as a telephone or computer mouse that operates without wires; (*Brit.*) a radio

wire´tap *n.* a device for listening in on or recording a telephone conversation —*vt.* to connect or listen with a wiretap —*vi.* to use a wiretap —**wire´tap·per** *n.*

wir´ing *n.* a network of wires such as installed within a building to provide electricity, telephone service, etc.; the process of connecting or installing wires

wir´y *adj.* lean, but tough and sinewy; stiff or bristly, like wire —**wir´i·ly** *adv.* —**wir´i·ness** *n.*

wis´dom *n.* the ability to make sound judgements; insight or intuition; extensive knowledge; an accumulated body of knowledge

wise *adj.* having insight, common sense, or knowledge; shrewd and calculating —**wise´ly** *adv.*

wise´a·cre *n.* one who claims to know everything; a smart aleck or jokester

wise´crack *n.* an insolent or supercilious remark —*vi.* to utter a wisecrack

wish *n.* a desire or longing; something desired —*vt.* to have a desire or longing for; to request or entreat —*vi.* to feel a desire; to express a desire —**wish´er** *n.*

wish´ful *adj.* having or indicating a desire —**wish´ful·ly** *adv.* —**wish´ful·ness** *n.*

wishful thinking believing that what one wants to be true is true

wish´y-wash´y *adj.* lacking in purpose; indecisive or ineffective

wisp *n.* a small bunch, as of straw or hair; a mere indication: *a wisp of perfume*; a slight, delicate thing: *a wisp of a child* —**wisp´y** *adj.* —**wisp´i·ly** *adv.* —**wisp´i·ness** *n.*

wist´ful *adj.* wishful, yearning; musing, pensive —**wist´ful·ly** *adv.* —**wist´ful·ness** *n.*

wit *n.* intelligence; mental acuity; guile: *to live by one's wits*; a clever or amusing person

witch *n.* a woman who practices sorcery; an ugly or cruel old woman; a fascinating woman —*vt.* to work a spell upon; to fascinate or charm —**witch´y** *adj.*

witch´craft *n.* black magic, sorcery; extraordinary influence or charm

witch´er·y *n.* witchcraft; the power to fascinate

witch hazel any of a genus of small trees and shrubs; a mild astringent containing an extract from the bark and leaves of the witch hazel plant

witch hunt investigation or harassment of dissenters

witch´ing *adj.* able to enchant; bewitching —**witch´ing·ly** *adv.*

with·draw´ *vt.* to take away or remove; to take back or rescind, as an offer; to prevent from using, selling, etc. —*vi.* to retreat; to remove oneself —**with·draw´a·ble** *adj.* —**with·draw´er** *n.*

with·draw´al *n.* an instance of taking back, removing, retreating, etc.; the process or effects of overcoming an addiction

with·drawn´ *adj.* not responsive; introverted; isolated

with´er *vi.* to become limp or dry, like cut flowers; to waste, as flesh —*vt.* to cause to become limp or dry; to disconcert or humble, as by a scornful glance

with·hold´ *vt.* to hold back; to refuse to grant, permit, etc. —*vi.* to refrain —**with·hold´er** *n.*

with·stand´ *vt.*, *vi.* to resist, oppose, or endure

wit´less *adj.* lacking intelligence; fatuous; silly or foolish —**wit´less·ly** *adv.* —**wit´less·ness** *n.*

wit´ness *n.* one who is competent to testify by virtue of having seen or learned something; one who attests to the authenticity of a document, signature, etc. —*vt.* to see or know personally; to give testimony; to subscribe to the authenticity of a document, signature, etc. —*vi.* to testify

wit´ti·cism *n.* a clever or humorous remark

wit´ting *adj.* knowing; aware; purposely done —**wit´ting·ly** *adv.*

wit´ty *adj.* displaying cleverness or humor —**wit´ti·ly** *adv.* —**wit´ti·ness** *n.*

wiz´ard *n.* a sorcerer; one exceptionally skillful or clever —*adj.* (*Brit.*) extraordinary: *he's a wizard pianist* —**wiz´ard·ly** *adv.*

wiz´ard·ry *n.* the practice or methods of a wizard

wiz´ened *adj.* shriveled; dried up

wob´ble *vi.* to sway unsteadily; to show indecision —*vt.* to cause to wobble —*n.* unsteadiness; instability —**wob´bler** *n.* —**wob´bli·ness** *n.* —**wob´bly** *adj.*

woe *n.* overwhelming sorrow; suffering

woe·be·gone *adj.* mournful; sorrowful

woe´ful *adj.* accompanied by or causing sorrow; paltry or mean —**woe´ful·ly** *adv.* —**woe´ful·ness** *n.*

wolf *n.* a wild, carnivorous mammal related to the dog; a cruel or rapacious person; a man devoted to the pursuit of women

wolf´ish *adj.* rapacious, savage; suggestive of a wolf —**wolf´ish·ly** *adv.* —**wolf´ish·ness** *n.*

wom´an *n.* an adult human female; a female attendant or servant —*adj.* of or characteristic of women; female

wom´an·ish *adj.* characteristic of a woman; feminine or effeminate —**wom´an·ish·ly** *adv.* —**wom´an·ish·ness** *n.*

wom´an·ize *vi.* to aggressively pursue women —*vt.* to endow with female characteristics —**wom´an·iz·er** *n.*

wom´an·kind *n.* women collectively

wom´an·ly *adj.* having qualities suited to a woman —**wom´an·li·ness** *n.*

womb *n.* a place where anything is engendered or brought into life; a sheltering space or area

wom´bat *n.* a burrowing marsupial of Australia

won´der *n.* a feeling of mingled surprise, admiration, and astonishment; something causing wonder —*vt.* to have a feeling of curiosity or doubt —*vi.* to marvel; to be curious or doubtful —*adj.* spectacularly successful —**won´der·er** n. — **won´der·ing·ly** adv.

won´der·ful adj. astonishing; very good —**won´der·ful·ly** adv. —**won´der·ful·ness** n.

won´der·ment n. astonishment or awe; something marvelous; puzzlement

won´drous adj. wonderful; marvelous; extraordinary —adv. surprisingly —**won´drous·ly** adv. — **won´drous·ness** n.

wont adj. accustomed —n. an ordinary manner of doing or acting

wont´ed adj. commonly used or done; accustomed —**wont´ed·ly** adv. —**wont´ed·ness** n.

woo vt. to seek the affection or approval of; to entreat earnestly —vi. to pay court —**woo´er** n.

wood n. the hard fibrous material that constitutes the bulk of a tree; a forest —adj. made of or using wood; living or growing among trees

wood´craft n. knowledge of survival in the wild as to making shelter, finding food, etc.; the art of fashioning articles of wood —**wood´crafts·man** n.

wood´cut n. an engraved block of wood used for making prints; a print made from a woodblock engraving

wood´ed adj. abounding with trees

wood´en adj. made of wood; stiff or awkward —**wood´en·ly** adv. —**wood´en·ness** n.

wood´land n. land covered with trees; timberland —adj. belonging to or dwelling in the woods

wood nymph a forest sprite

woods´y adj. of, pertaining to, or like a woodland —**woods´i·ness** n.

wood´wind n. a musical instrument that uses a wood or woodlike reed

wood´work n. things made of wood; the interior trim in a house, such as door and window frames or molding —**wood´work·er** n. — **wood´work·ing** n.

wood´y adj. made of or containing wood; resembling wood; wooded — **wood´i·ness** n.

wool n. a soft, durable fiber from the fleece of certain animals; yarn, fabric, or garments made from the fibers —adj. made of or pertaining to wool or woolen material

wool´en adj. of or pertaining to wool; made of wool —n. cloth or clothing made of wool

wool´gath·er·ing n. idle daydreaming

wool´ly, wool´y adj. consisting of or resembling wool; not clear or sharply detailed —**wool´i·ness, wool´li·ness** n.

wooz´y adj. befuddled; nauseous — **wooz´i·ly** adv. —**wooz´i·ness** n.

word n. the smallest meaningful unit of a language; speech; a brief remark, message, comment, command, etc.; a promise

word´age n. words collectively; verbiage

word´ing n. a style or arrangement of words; phraseology

word´less adj. unspoken; silent — **word´less·ly** adv. —**word´less·ness** n.

word of mouth oral communication —**word-of-mouth** adj.

word´play n. clever repartee

word´y adj. expressed in too many words; verbal —**word´i·ly** adv. — **word´i·ness** n.

work n. physical or mental exertion; labor; employment; one's profession, trade, etc.; the place where one is employed —vi. to perform work; to be employed; to prove effective —vt. to cause or bring about; to make or shape by toil or skill; to cause to be productive; to make or achieve by effort — **work´er** n.

work´a·ble adj. capable of being

worked, developed, etc.; practicable, as a plan —**work·a·bil´i·ty** *adv.* —**work´a·ble·ness** *n.*

work´ing *adj.* employed; occupied by work; that performs its function; sufficient for use or action: *a working agreement*

working capital the finances of a business available for its operation

working class those who work for wages

work´man·like *adj.* like or befitting a skilled workman; skillfully done

work´man·ship *n.* the art or skill of a workman; the quality of work; the work accomplished

work of art something considered to be fine art, as painting or sculpture; anything made or done with great beauty or skill

work´out *n.* an activity to improve skills, physical fitness, etc.; any instance of strenuous or intense activity

work sheet a schedule or record of an employee's work times; a copy of preliminary notes or calculations; a spreadsheet

work´shop *n.* a room or building set aside for light tasks or projects; a meeting or seminar for training or discussion in a specialized field or on a specific subject

world *n.* the earth; the universe; a celestial body; a part of the earth: *the Third World*; a division of time, things, etc.: *the ancient world, the animal world*; a large amount: *a world of knowledge*

world´ly *adj.* pertaining to the world; devoted to secular, earthly things; sophisticated —**world´li·ness** *n.*

world´ly-wise *adj.* schooled in the ways of the world; sophisticated

world´-wea·ry *adj.* dissatisfied or discontented with life and its conditions —**world´-wea·ri·ness** *n.*

worm *n.* an elongated, limbless, soft–bodied creature; a despicable

or despised person; something seen to be like a worm —*vt.* to proceed in a wormlike manner; to draw forth by artful means: *worm the information out of him*; to rid of intestinal worms —*vi.* to progress slowly and stealthily

worm gear a toothed wheel that meshes with a shaft having a spiral prominence

worn *adj.* frayed, damaged, etc. by wear; showing the effects of worry, anxiety, etc.; hackneyed

worn–out *adj.* having lost all value or effectiveness, especially from long use; tired or exhausted

wor´ri·ment *n.* a source of concern or anxiety

wor´ri·some *adj.* causing concern or anxiety —**wor´ri·some·ly** *adv.*

wor´ry *vi.* to be uneasy; to feel anxiety —*vt.* to cause to feel uneasy; to bother or pester; to bite, pull at, or shake with the teeth —*n.* a state of anxiety or uneasiness; something causing such a state —**wor´ri·er** *n.*

worse *adj.* bad or ill to a greater degree; less favorable, as conditions, circumstances, etc. —*adv.* in a less favorable manner, way, etc.; with greater intensity, severity, etc.

wors´en *vt., vi.* to make or become less favorable

wor´ship *n.* adoration, homage; rituals, prayers, etc. used in paying tribute to a diety; excessive or ardent admiration —*vt.* to venerate; to have intense admiration or love for —*vi.* to perform acts of veneration —**wor´ship·er, wor´ship·per** *n.*

wor´ship·ful *adj.* feeling or showing great love, reverence, etc. —**wor´ship·ful·ly** *adv.* —**wor´ship·ful·ness** *n.*

worst *adj.* extremely bad or ill; least favorable —*adv.* to the extreme degree of inferiority, badness, etc.

—*vt.* to defeat, vanquish

wor´sted *n.* a type of woolen yarn, or a fabric made from such yarn — *adj.* made from worsted

worth *n.* the value of something; the quality that makes a thing estimable or desirable; the amount obtainable for a specific sum: *two dollars worth of gas*; wealth —*adj.* equal in value to; deserving of

worth´less *adj.* having no value — **worth´less·ly** *adv.* —**worth´less·ness** *n.*

worth´while´ *adj.* sufficiently important to occupy the time; of sufficient value to repay the effort — **worth´while´ness** *n.*

wor´thy *adj.* possessing valuable or useful qualitites; deserving —*n.* a person of eminent worth —**wor´thi·ly** *adv.* —**wor´thi·ness** *n.*

would´–be *adj.* desiring, professing, or intending

wound *n.* an injury; any cause of pain or grief, as to feelings, honor, etc. —*vt.*, *vi.* to inflict a wound; to injure the feelings or pride of — **wound´ed·ly** *adv.* —**wound´ing·ly** *adv.*

wraith *n.* an apparition of a person seen shortly before or after death; any specter

wran´gle *vi.* to argue noisily and angrily —*vt.* to argue, debate; to get by arguing stubbornly; to herd, as livestock —*n.* an angry dispute —**wran´gler** *n.*

wrap *vt.* to surround and cover, as with paper, a blanket, etc.; to fold or wind about something —*n.* an outer garment

wrap´per *n.* material enclosing something, as a gift, a stick of gum, etc.; a woman's dressing gown; one who wraps

wrap´ping *n.* a covering: material enclosing something

wrath *n.* violent rage or fury

wrath´ful *adj.* full of wrath;

extremely angry; expressing or resulting from rage —**wrath´ful·ly** *adv.* —**wrath´ful·ness** *n.*

wreak *vt.* to inflict or exact, as vengeance; to give free expression to, as passion

wreath *n.* a circular band of flowers, leaves, etc. as for a crown or decoration; a curling or spiral band, as of smoke

wreathe *vt.* to form into a wreath, as by twisting or twining; to adorn or encircle as with wreaths —*vi.* to take the form of a wreath; to twist, turn, or coil

wreck *vt.* to cause the destruction of; to bring ruin upon —*vi.* to suffer destruction; to engage in destroying, as for plunder or salvage —*n.* the act of destroying; that which has been ruined or destroyed; broken remnants or remains

wreck´age *n.* a broken remnant or fragments from a wreck

wreck´er *n.* one who causes destruction; one employed in tearing down and removing old buildings; a person or machine that clears away auto wrecks

wrench *n.* a violent twist; a sprain, twist, or pull of a part of the body; (*US*) a tool for turning, twisting, etc. —*vt.* to twist violently; to twist forcibly so as to cause injury —*vi.* to give a twist

wrest *vt.* to pull away by violent twisting; to seize forcibly; to gain by great effort

wres´tle *vi.* to engage in wrestling; to struggle or contend —*vt.* to contend in wrestling —*n.* a difficult struggle —**wres´tler** *n.*

wres´tling *n.* a sport in which unarmed contestants endeavor to force each other to the ground

wretch *n.* a vile person; a miserable or unhappy person

wretch´ed *adj.* profoundly unhappy;

marked by misery or poverty; despicable or contemptible: *it's a wretched approach to health care for the aged* —**wretch´ed·ly** *adv.* —**wretch´ed·ness** *n.*

wrig´gle *vi.* to twist in a sinuous manner; to make one's way by evasive or indirect means —*vt.* to cause to wriggle; to advance by evasive or sly means —*n.* the motion of one who or that wriggles —**wrig´gly** *adj.*

wrig´gler *n.* someone or something that wriggles; a mosquito larva

wring *vt.* to squeeze or compress by twisting; to force out, as water, by twisting; to acquire forcibly; to distress —*n.* a twisting or forcing —**wring´er** *n.*

wrin´kle *n.* a small fold or crease; a modification, as *a new wrinkle* —*vt.*, *vi.* to make or become creased —**wrin´kly** *adv.*

wrist *n.* the part of the arm between the forearm and hand; the part of a garment that covers the wrist

write *vt.* to inscribe on a surface with pen or pencil; to communicate by letter; to be the author or composer of; to leave evidence: *guilt is written all over his face* —*vi.* to inscribe on a surface; to communicate in writing; to be occupied as an author —**writ´er** *n.*

writhe *vi.* to twist or distort the body, as in pain; to suffer, as from embarrassment, sorrow, etc. —*vt.* to cause to be twisted or distorted —**with´er** *n.*

wrong *adj.* mistaken; inappropriate; not moral or legal; not working properly; unintentional —*adv.* in an incorrect direction or improper manner; erroneously —*n.* an injury or injustice; a violation of one's rights —*vt.* to violate the rights of; to impute evil unjustly; to treat dishonorably —**wrong´er** *n.* —**wrong´ly** *adv.* —**wrong´ness** *n.*

wrong´do·er *n.* one who does wrong; one who acts unlawfully —**wrong´do·ing** *n.*

wrong´ful *adj.* characterized by wrong or injustice; unlawful, illegal —**wrong´ful·ly** *adv.* —**wrong´ful·ness** *n.*

wrong´–head´ed *adj.* stubbornly clinging to a wrong judgement, opinion, etc. —**wrong´–head´ed·ly** *adv.* —**wrong´–head´ed·ness** *n.*

wroth *adj.* angry

wrought *adj.* hammered into shape; formed delicately or elaborately; made or fashioned

wrought up disturbed or excited

wry *adj.* bent to one side; contorted or askew; somewhat perverse or ironic: *wry humor* —**wry´ly** *adv.* —**wry´ness** *n.*

wurst *n.* sausage

x, X twenty–fourth letter of the English alphabet

xan´thous *adj.* yellow

X chromosome the sex chromosome that is paired in the female and coupled with a Y chromosome in the male

xen·o·pho´bi·a *n.* fear of strangers or foreigners —**xen´o·phobe** *n.* —**xen·o·pho´bic** *adj.*

xe·rog´ra·phy *n.* a system for copying documents —**xe·ro·graph´ic** *adj.* —**xe·ro·graph´i·cal·ly** *adv.*

x ray, x-ray *n.* radiation having a wavelength shorter than ultraviolet light and longer than that of a gamma ray; a photograph made with x-rays —*adj.* of, made by, or producing x-rays —*vt.* to examine, diagnose, or treat with x-rays

xy´lo·phone *n.* a percussion instrument of graduated wooden bars, played by striking with small mallets —**xy´lo·phon·ist** *n.*

y, Y twenty–fifth letter of the English alphabet

yacht *n.* a relatively small ship for pleasure or racing —**yacht´ing** *n.* —**yachts´man** *n.*

ya´hoo *n.* a crude or awkward person; a bumpkin

yak *n.* a large, shaggy wild ox; persistent chatter —*vi.* to talk a great deal

ya·ki·to´ri *n.* marinated and grilled chicken bits

ya´ku·za *n.* a Japanese gangster

yam *n.* a fleshy, edible tuberous root; a variety of sweet potato

yam´mer *vi.* to whine or complain — *vt.* to utter in a peevish manner — **yam´mer·er** *n.*

yank *vt., vi.* to jerk or pull suddenly —*n.* a sudden sharp jerk

yap *vi.* to talk or jabber; to yelp, as a dog —*n.* a yelp; worthless talk; the mouth —**yap´per** *n.*

yard *n.* a plot of ground enclosed or set apart for a special purpose; (*Brit.*) a paved area adjacent to a building, intended for vehicular traffic; (*US*) the grounds adjacent to a house, college, etc.; a long slender spar set crosswise to a ship's mast; (*US*) a unit of length equal to three feet

yard´age *n.* the length of something in yards; something dispensed in yards, as cloth

yard´stick *n.* a measuring stick one yard in length; any standard of comparison

yarn *n.* a spun fiber prepared for use in weaving, knitting, etc.; a tale of adventure

yaw *vi.* to move erratically or off course, as a ship in heavy seas — *vt.* to cause to yaw

yawl *n.* a small sailboat

yawn *vi.* to open the mouth wide with a full inhalation, as from boredom, drowsiness, etc.; to stand wide open —*vt.* to express with a yawn —*n.* a wide opening — **yawn´er** *n.*

yaws *n. pl.* a contagious tropical disease marked by skin lesions

yea *adv.* yes —*n.* an affirmative vote; one casting an affirmative vote

year *n.* the time Earth takes to complete one revolution around the sun; a period of 12 months; the time any planet takes to revolve around the sun; a part of the year devoted to a particular activity, as *the school year*

year´book *n.* a book documenting the events of the previous year

year´ly *adj.* of a year; occurring once a year; continuing for a year — *adv.* once a year; annually

yearn *vi.* to desire earnestly — **yearn´ing·ly** *adv.*

yearn´ing *n.* a strong emotional longing or desire

yeast *n.* a preparation used to leaven bread, make beer, etc.; froth or spume —*vi.* to foam

yeast·y *adj.* of or resembling yeast; causing fermentation; covered with froth or foam —**yeast´i·ness** *n.*

yell *vt., vi.* to shout, scream, or cheer —*n.* a sharp cry, as in terror, pain, etc.; a rhythmic cheer, as in support of a sports team

yel´low *adj.* of the color yellow; colored by age, sickness, etc.: *paper yellow with age*; having a light brown or yellowish complexion; offensively sensational: *yellow journalism*; cowardly —*n.* in the spectrum, the color between green and orange; the color of ripe lemons; the yolk of an egg —*vt., vi.* to make or become yellow —**yel´low·y** *adv.* —**yel´low·ness** *n.*

yelp *vi.* to utter a sharp or shrill cry —*vt.* to express with a yelp — **yelp´er** *n.*

yen *n.* the basic monetary unit of Japan; an ardent longing or desire —*vi.* to yearn

yen´ta *n.* a gossip or meddler

yeo´man *n.* a petty officer in the U.S.

508

Navy or Coast Guard; a yeoman of the guard; an attendant to nobility or royalty; a diligent worker

yeo´man·ly *adj.* pertaining to the attributes of a yeoman; brave or rugged —*adv.* like a yeoman; bravely

yes *n.* an affirmative response — *vt.* to give an affirmative response — *adv.* as you say; truly

yes man one who invariably agrees with his superiors

yes´ter·day *n.* the day before today; the near past —*adv.*

yes´ter·year *n.* last year; time past: *the songs of yesteryear* —*adv.*

yield *vt.* to produce by a natural process or by cultivation; to give in return, as for investment; to surrender or relinquish —*vi.* to provide a return; to give up or surrender; to give way; to comply —*n.* an amount produced; a result, as of cultivation, investment, etc. — **yield´er** *n.*

yield´ing *adj.* productive; flexible or pliant; obedient —**yield´ing·ly** *adv.* —**yield´ing·ness** *n.*

yip *n.* a yelp, as from a dog —*vi.* to yelp

yo´del *vt., vi.* to sing by alternating quickly between a low register and a falsetto —*n.* —**yo´del·er** *n.*

yo´ga *n.* a Hindu discipline directed to the attainment of spiritual illumination; exercises based on yoga techniques

yo´gi *n.* one who practices yoga

yo´gurt *n.* a soft food made from milk curdled with bacteria cultures

yoke *n.* a curved frame used for coupling draft animals; any similar contrivance; a pair of animals joined by a yoke; something that binds or connects; servitude —*vt.* to attach by means of a yoke; to join, as with a yoke —*vi.* to be joined or linked

yo´kel *n.* a country bumpkin

yon´der *adj.* at a distance —*adv.* in that place; there

yore *n.* time long past

young *adj.* pertaining to or being in the early period of life or growth; newly formed; fresh and vigorous; immature —*n.* young people as a group; the offspring of animals — **young´ish** *adj.* —**young´ster** *n.*

youth *n.* the condition of being young; the period when one is young; the early period of being or development; young people as a group

youth´ful *adj.* pertaining to youth; fresh or vigorous; having youth — **youth´ful·ly** *adv.* —**youth´ful·ness** *n.*

yowl *vi.* to howl —*n.* a prolonged wailing cry

z, Z twenty–sixth letter of the English alphabet

za´ny *adj.* absurdly funny; ludicrous —**za´ni·ly** *adv.* —**za´ni·ness** *n.*

zap *vt.* to strike or kill; to confront suddenly and forcefully

zeal *n.* ardor or enthusiasm, as for a cause

zeal´ot *n.* a fanatic —**zeal´ot·ry** *n.*

zeal´ous *adj.* filled with or showing exceptional enthusiasm —**zeal´ous·ly** *adv.* —**zeal´ous·ness** *n.*

ze´bra *n.* an African mammal allied to the horse, with alternating white and dark stripes

ze´nith *n.* the point of the celestial sphere that is exactly overhead; the highest or culminating point

zeph´yr *n.* a gentle wind; light weight woolen or worsted yarn

ze´ro *n.* the numeral or symbol *0*; nothing; the lowest or starting point —*vt.* to adjust, as instruments, to an arbitrary zero point

zero gravity a condition of apparent weightlessness

zero hour any critical moment

zero population growth a condition in which the number of deaths and live births in a population during a given period are closely matched

zero-sum a situation in which gains and losses offset each other, as of opposing sides, population segments, etc.

zest *n.* agreeable excitement; keen enjoyment; a quality that imparts emotion; piquant flavoring —**zest´ful, zest´y** *adj.* —**zest´ful·ly** *adv.* —**zest´ful·ness** *n.*

zig´zag *n.* a path or pattern characterized by sharp side–to–side turns or angles — *vt.*, *vi.* to move in zigzags —*adj.*, *adv.*

zilch *n.* nothing; zero

zil´lion *n.* a large, indeterminate number

zing *n.* a sharp buzzing or humming sound; energy, vitality; a sudden verbal attack —*vi.* to make a shrill humming sound —*vt.* to criticize sharply

zing´er *n.* a sharp, often witty, remark

zip *n.* a sharp, hissing sound, as of a bullet passing; energy, vitality —*vt.* to fasten with a zipper; to give speed and energy to —*vi.* to move with speed and energy

zip´py *adj.* brisk, energetic

zith´er *n.* a stringed instrument with 30 to 40 strings played by plucking —**zith´er·ist** *n.*

zi´ti *n.* a tubular pasta

zo´di·ac *n.* an imaginary belt divided into twelve parts, encircling the heavens —**zo·di´a·cal** *adj.*

zom´bie *n.* a snake diety in voodoo cults; a corpse believed to be re-animated by supernatural powers; a person who behaves mechanically

zone *n.* a region or area set off by some special characteristic —*vt.* to divide into zones, especially of a municipality where types of construction, activity, etc. are restricted by zones —**zon´al, zoned** *adj.* —**zon´al·ly** *adv.*

zoo *n.* a place where wild animals are kept on exhibit; a chaotic place or situation

zo·o·ge·og´ra·phy *n.* the study of the distribution of animals and their environment —**zo·o·ge·og´ra·pher** *n.* —**zo·o·ge·o·graph´ic** *adj.* —**zo·o·ge·o·graph´i·cal** *adv.*

zo·og´ra·phy *n.* the branch of zoology that deals with the description of animals —**zo·og´ra·pher** *n.* —**zo·o·graph´ic, zo·o·graph´i·cal** *adj.*

zo·ol´o·gy *n.* the study of animals and their structure, functions, development, etc.; the animal life of a particular area —**zo·o·log´i·cal** *adj.* **zo·o·log´i·cal·ly** *adv.* —**zo·ol´o·gist** *n.*

zo´o·phyte *n.* an invertebrate animal resembling a plant, as a coral or sponge —**zo·o·phyt´ic, zo·o·phyt´i·cal** *adj.*

zy·mol´o·gy *n.* the science of fermentation

zy´mur·gy *n.* the chemistry of fermentation as applied to brewing, the making of yeast, and the making of wine